This modern text is designed to prepare you for your future professional career. While theories, ideas, techniques, and data are dynamic, the information contained in this volume will provide you a quick and useful reference as well as a guide for future learning for many years to come. Your familiarity with the contents of this book will make it an important volume in your professional library.

EX LIBRIS

Accounting Principles

Accounting Principles

Roger H. Hermanson, Ph.D., C.P.A.
Research Professor of Accounting
Ernst & Whinney Alumni Professor
Georgia State University

James Don Edwards, Ph.D., C.P.A.
J. M. Tull Professor of Accounting
The University of Georgia

R. F. Salmonson, Ph.D., C.P.A.
Professor Emeritus of Accounting
Michigan State University

1986   Third edition

BUSINESS PUBLICATIONS, INC.
Plano, Texas   75075

ISBN 0-256-03415-X

Library of Congress Catalog Card No. 85–70562

Printed in the United States of America

1 2 3 4 5 6 7 8 9 0 K 3 2 1 0 9 8 7 6

Preface

This third edition of *Accounting Principles* is for use in introductory accounting courses, whether conducted in colleges and universities or in business settings. We recognize that people taking the first-year accounting course seek various careers. Some may choose accounting as a profession, while others will choose another area of business or possibly a nonbusiness career. All will find the ability to use and interpret accounting information valuable in both their work and their personal lives.

Accounting Principles covers both financial and managerial accounting topics, and serves as a foundation for subsequent courses in accounting and business. We assume that students using this text have a limited understanding of business concepts. Thus, when new terms and concepts are introduced they are defined, illustrated, and fully explained.

Two major reasons the previous edition of *Accounting Principles* had such "staying power" with adopters were that it was *readable* and *teachable*. These two attributes combined to make it easy for students to learn from the text. Early in the revision process we agreed to focus our work on improving readability and teachability even more. The result of our efforts is a text of which we are especially proud.

■ SPECIAL FEATURES THAT MAKE THIS EDITION MORE READABLE

□ Introductions have been written for all chapters. We worked hard to make the introductions both interesting to read and helpful as a preview to the chapter. Students discover in the first paragraph of each chapter what the chapter contains and how the contents fit into the accounting process covered up to that point. The introductions give continuity to the text and show students how accounting concepts relate to each other.

□ Summaries have been added to each chapter. The summary draws a complete picture of what the chapter covered. All topics presented are brought together in a logical review for the student. Every summary also gives the student a small "preview" of what the next chapter covers, giving continuity to the material.

□ Organization of material has been improved based on feedback from adopters, suggestions by reviewers, and a serious study of the learning process itself by the authors and editors. New material is introduced only when

the "proper stage has been set." These added transitional paragraphs between topic headings present students with the reasons for proceeding to
the new material. The transitions alert students to the "building process"
occurring within the chapter.

A lack of business experience among students sometimes prevents them
from having a frame of reference for relating to accounting concepts and business
transactions. In this edition we sought to involve the student more in real-
life business applications as we introduced and explained the material.

☐ In Chapter 1 students become owners of their own business entities (a
horse stable and a physical fitness center). References to "their" businesses
in certain later chapters makes learning about accounting principles more
personal and meaningful and also helps students learn and remember new
material.
☐ A "Business Situation for Discussion" is located at the end of each chapter.
These situations are taken from articles in current business periodicals (e.g.,
The Wall Street Journal, Business Week, Management Accounting) that
relate to material covered in that chapter. These real-world examples demonstrate the business relevance of accounting.
☐ We have kept and revised our popular "Business Decision Problems" at
the end of each chapter. These problems provide students with an opportunity to apply their newly learned accounting concepts to management situations in the business world.
☐ Numerous illustrations adapted from *Accounting Trends and Techniques*
have been added in this edition to show the frequency of use in business
of various accounting techniques. Scattered throughout the text, these illustrations give students real-world data to consider while learning about different accounting techniques.

Special attention was paid to improving the book's pedagogy in this edition.
Specifically,

☐ Key terms are set in a second color for emphasis.
☐ End-of-chapter glossaries now contain the page number where the new
term was first introduced and defined. Students can easily flip back to
the original discussion and study the term's significance in context with
the chapter material.
☐ A description of each exercise and problem is located beside each one in
the left-hand margin. These descriptions let students know what they are
expected to do in the problem.

Learning Aids for the Student—Supplementary Material

Study Guides.   Two comprehensive study guides are available, one for
each half of the book. The study guides were developed in cooperation with
Professor Gayle Rayburn, Memphis State University. The purpose of the study
guides is to review and reinforce the concepts the student has learned in studying
each chapter. Included for each chapter are learning objectives, reference outline, chapter review, a different demonstration problem and solution than is

shown in the text, matching and true-false questions, completion questions and exercises, multiple-choice questions, and solutions to all exercises and questions.

Working Papers.   Two sets of working papers (one for each half of the text) are available for completing assigned exercises, problems, and business decision problems. In many instances, the working papers are partially filled in to reduce the "pencil pushing" required to solve the problems. The format and spacing used in the working papers are identical to the Instructor's Solutions Manual and to the transparencies. This feature makes it easier for the grader to compare the students' solutions to the authors' solutions.

Check Figures.   A list of check figures gives key amounts for the A and B series problems and Business Decision Problems in the text. Check figures are available in bulk free to adopters. Students can determine whether they are "on the right track" when working a problem by comparing their solution with the key amount given for a particular problem.

Practice Sets.   Four practice sets are available. Practice Set I, developed by Professor Margaret Mills, Tidewater Community College, Virginia, illustrates special journals and includes a work sheet for a retailing company. Practice Set II illustrates the accounting system used by a manufacturing company and was developed by Herbert A. O'Keefe, Georgia Southern College. Practice Set III illustrates the use of business papers for a retailing company. Practice Set IV is a microcomputer practice set that can be used with the Apple and IBM personal microcomputers. Practice Sets I, III, and IV may be used any time after Chapter 8 has been covered. Practice Set II may be used any time after Chapter 21 has been covered.

■ SPECIAL FEATURES THAT MAKE THIS EDITION MORE TEACHABLE

□   We have included a vast amount of resource material *within* the text from which the instructor may draw: one of the largest selections of end-of-chapter exercises and problems available; two comprehensive review problems (after Chapters 4 and 6) that allow students to review all major concepts covered to that point; 28 Business Situations for Discussion to stimulate classroom discussion of accounting concepts; and financial statements of General Motors that can be used throughout the course to illustrate financial reporting.

□   All end-of-chapter problem material (exercises, problems, and business decision problems) has been thoroughly revised.

□   All end-of-chapter problem material has been traced back to the chapters to ensure that nothing is asked of a student that does not appear in the book. **This was a strength of the second edition,** ensuring that instructors could confidently assign problems without having to check for applicability.

□   Demonstration problems and solutions are included for each chapter. Because of the positive response to this feature in the previous edition, we have added more of these problems. The problems help students to assess their own progress by showing them how problems that focus on the topic(s) covered in the chapter are worked before students do assigned homework problems.

☐ In Chapter 5 we now present two variations of the closing process: merchandise-related expense accounts are treated first as closing entries and then as adjusting entries. Instructors can choose which method(s) to teach.

☐ Chapter 17 has been reorganized so that it now covers only bond issuances and bond investments. (In the previous edition both bond and stock investments were covered in this chapter.) All investments in capital stock of other companies are now covered in Chapter 18. This change makes Chapter 17 more teachable and gives Chapter 18 more substance. This reorganization was suggested by users, and we agree that the result is a more logical organization of material.

☐ In Chapter 19, the statement of changes in financial position material covers both the working capital and cash concepts of funds. While both of these concepts are used in business, many texts cover only the working capital concept. We have included both concepts because a 1983 survey of 600 companies revealed that the cash concept was used by more than half of the companies.

☐ An important topic in accounting today, international accounting, is covered in an appendix at the back of the text. We believe that this coverage is the most complete of any introductory text. This appendix will assist in meeting the accreditation standard of the American Assembly of Collegiate Schools of Business regarding internationalizing the curriculum.

Teaching Aids for the Instructor—Supplementary Material

A complete package of supplemental teaching aids contains all you need to efficiently and effectively teach the course. For universities where graduate students or part-time instructors teach accounting principles, we have an excellent instructor's resource guide and test bank that will assist them in preparing both lectures and examinations. The test bank has been substantially increased, providing more multiple-choice questions as well as three more problems per chapter.

Instructor's Resource Guide.   This supplement was developed for the previous edition, and we found it to be extremely helpful to both new instructors of accounting and new adopters of our text. Revised for this edition, each chapter contains (1) a summary of major concepts that can serve as a handy lecture organizer; (2) a basic outline of the chapter headings; (3) learning objectives from the text repeated for the instructor's convenience; and (4) detailed lecture notes that also refer to specific end-of-chapter problem materials illustrating the concepts. Any of these formats can serve as effective lecture notes depending on the instructor's personal preference. Also included are (5) teaching transparency masters for each chapter that may be used to emphasize important points. Each chapter concludes with (6) a summary of the estimated time, level of difficulty, and content of each exercise and problem that is useful in deciding which items to cover in class or to assign as homework.

Solutions Manual.   The instructor's solutions manual contains sample syllabi for both quarter- and semester-basis courses. Detailed answers to the exercises, questions (Series A and B), comprehensive review problems, and business decision problems are given for each chapter. Teaching notes are included at the bottom of many problems to explain questions commonly asked by students. The use of large type and paper identically lined to the students' Working Papers facilitates grading.

Transparencies.   Acetate transparencies of solutions to all exercises and problems are available free to adopters. These transparencies, while useful in many situations, are especially helpful when covering problems involving work sheets and in large classroom situations. The transparency solutions are formatted on the same lined working paper the students have in their supplemental Working Papers. The new large and bold type used facilitates projection, and the use of lines aids students' viewing.

Examination Material.   In this edition we have provided adopters with *four* different formats of examination material. Instructors need only to select the exam(s) that best fits their personal needs and resources, and then request a copy from their local BPI sales representative. Any and all are available free upon adoption and by request.

1. Pre-Printed Achievement Tests.   Three series of achievement tests—A, B, and C—have been prepared and printed, and are available in bulk to adopters. Each series consists of six one-hour exams and two two-hour final exams. In each series, three of the one-hour exams and a final exam cover Chapters 1–14, and the other three one-hour exams and a final exam cover Chapters 15–28. All questions are multiple choice for ease in grading.

2. Examination Book.   This test bank, **expanded in this edition,** contains over 1,500 questions and problems to choose from in preparing examinations. It contains true-false and multiple-choice questions and short problems for each chapter. The multiple-choice questions may also be used to freshen up the Achievement Tests, while the short problems may be used to supplement or replace them for those instructors who object to the sole use of multiple-choice questions.

3. COMPUTEST.   For instructors who have microcomputers, this form of exam preparation is convenient and effective. COMPUTEST is a microcomputer version of the Examination Book. It is available for use on the IBM PC, Apple II+, and Apple IIe. COMPUTEST can be used to prepare examinations by selecting questions and problems in a variety of ways. Instructors may even add their own exam material to the test bank. COMPUTEST is menu-driven and has a well-documented instruction manual.

4. TELETEST.   TELETEST is an in-house testing service that will prepare your exams. TELETEST has its own bank of examination questions and problems (taken from the Examination Book). To use TELETEST, all the instructor needs to do is call our 800 number, ask for TELETEST, and give the required information to BPI's TELETEST service representative. Or the instructor can mail in the required information. Either way, within 72 working hours of receiving the required information, the instructor will be mailed a copy of the exam and an answer key.

■ SPECIAL FEATURES OF THIS EDITION THAT HELP STUDENTS LEARN ACCOUNTING

Students often come into accounting principles courses feeling anxious about learning the material. Recognizing that apprehension, we studied ways to make learning easier and came up with some helpful ideas on how to make this edition work even better for students. Our "study of learning" resulted in the following improvements in *Accounting Principles,* third edition. Specifically, we:

☐ Organized ideas for improved flow of material. The newly written introductions preview the chapter material, letting students know exactly where they are and where they are going. Transitional paragraphs are used to improve the flow and continuity of material. Carefully worded and designed headings are strategically placed in the chapters as signposts. The summaries review the material covered and show its relationship to the overall accounting process. Every summary ends with a reference to what the next chapter covers and how it relates to the chapter just covered.

☐ Included examples to associate concepts with experiences. Throughout the text we used examples taken from everyday life to relate an accounting concept being introduced or discussed to students' experiences. For example, to help the student differentiate between the accounting process and an accounting system we ask them to think of the difference between going on a trip (the process) by the back roads (system) or by the highway (an alternative system). In the chapter on inventory, we have them recall the "pre-inventory sales" they all have seen advertisements for and possibly attended. It is much easier to learn a subject if you can associate it with something familiar.

☐ Used an informal style and the active voice. Our research showed that for an accounting principles text today, an informal writing style and the active voice are more effective for learning than the formal style and passive voice. In this edition we use the pronoun *you* more to involve students with the text material.

☐ Added several new graphics. Learning is enhanced when a picture reinforces a verbal understanding of new material. Wherever possible, we have added graphic illustrations to help explain accounting concepts to students. For example, in Chapter 7 we have illustrated cash flows in a business. In Chapter 19 we have a diagram showing the typical types of transactions that affect working capital. Graphics have been added to reinforce accounting concepts.

We are indebted to many individuals for reviewing the manuscript of the third edition. In addition to those listed on the acknowledgments page, we are especially indebted to colleagues and students at our respective universities for their helpful suggestions.

Roger H. Hermanson
James Don Edwards
R. F. Salmonson

Note to the Student

Professor Gayle Rayburn of Memphis State University has participated with the authors in revising the very comprehensive two-volume student Study Guide to assist you in understanding the material in this text. Students who used the study guide in the previous edition found it to be extremely helpful in maximizing their understanding and class performance. Each chapter of the Study Guide is keyed to a chapter of the text and provides learning objectives, a reference outline, a detailed chapter review, a demonstration problem and answer, matching questions concerning important new terms and concepts, completion questions and exercises, and true-false and multiple-choice questions. Answers to all exercises and questions are included in the Study Guide to provide you with immediate feedback on your responses. Explanations are also given for the answers to many of the true-false and multiple-choice questions. This student Study Guide, published by Business Publications, Inc., is available through your college bookstore. If it is not in stock, please ask your bookstore manager to order a copy for you.

R. H. H.
J. D. E.
R. F. S.

Acknowledgments

We are grateful to many individuals who have contributed to the development of this text. Special appreciation is due: Lane K. Anderson, Texas Tech University; Lloyd Badgett, University of Central Arkansas; Charles D. Bailey, Florida State University; Martin Batross, Franklin University; Atha Beard, Auburn University; Edgar T. Bitting, Elizabethtown College; Sallie Branscom, Virginia Western Community College; Robert M. Brown, Virginia Polytechnic Institute and State University; Bruce Caster, Valdosta State College; Trudy Chiaravalli, Lansing Community College; Charles Coleman, Bellvue Community College; G. Michael Crooch, Arthur Andersen & Co.; Lawrence Curbo, Memphis State University; Michael A. Dalton, Loyola University–New Orleans; Nita Dodson, University of Texas at Arlington; Linda Dykes, College of Charleston; George A. Fiebelkorn, Valdosta State College; Farrell G. Gean, Pepperdine University; Russell T. Gingras, Saginaw Valley State College; Daryl Gosse, Michigan State University; Raymond Green, Texas Tech University; Peter R. Grierson, University of Central Florida; Jean Gutman, University of Southern Maine; James O. Hicks, Jr., Virginia Polytechnic Institute and State University; George Holdren, University of Nebraska; James T. Hood, Northeast Louisiana University; the late Rita Huff, Sam Houston State University; Marty Jagers, University of South Carolina; Robert Kelley, Corning Community College; Dennis Knutson, Marquette University; Anthony T. Krzystofik, University of Massachusetts, Amherst; Tom Largay, Hudson College; Donald E. MacGilvera, Shoreline Community College; Alan P. Mayer-Sommer, Georgetown University; Thomas E. McLeod, University of Alabama, Birmingham; Katherine M. Means, University of Miami; Patricia H. Michel, Loyola College; Mary Middleton, Mercer University; Margaret Mills, Tidewater Community College; George S. Minmier, Memphis State University; John L. Nabholtz, Southern Methodist University; Herbert A. O'Keefe, Georgia Southern College; Philip R. Olds, Virginia Commonwealth University; Douglas Pfister, Lansing Community College; Thomas Phillips, Louisiana State University, Shreveport; Martin Premo, St. Bonaventure University; Cecily Raiborn, Loyola University–New Orleans; L. Gayle Rayburn, Memphis State University; Ruthie Reynolds, Tennessee State University; Arthur T. Roberts, University of Baltimore; David E. Rogers, Mesa College; Bonnie Stivers, Kennesaw College; Virgil E. Stone, Texas A & I University; James

Specht, North Dakota State University; G. A. Swanson, Tennessee Technological University; Mary J. Swanson, Mankato State University; Jean Tillery, Emory University; Deborah Turner, Georgia Institute of Technology; Joyce Valentine, Ernst & Whinney; James J. Wallace, Rochester Institute of Technology; Penny Wardlaw, University of Maryland; and Jackson A. White, University of Arkansas, Little Rock.

R. H. H.
J. D. E.
R. F. S.

Accounting Principles

P A R T

1

Accounting: The Language of Business

Introduction: The Accounting Environment

After studying this introduction, you should be able to:

1. Define accounting.
2. Describe the functions performed by accountants.
3. Describe employment opportunities in accounting.
4. Differentiate between managerial and financial accounting.
5. Identify the four organizations that have a role in the development of financial accounting standards.
6. Define and use correctly the new terms in the glossary.

Accounting is an interesting field of study that has many uses in society. In fact, accounting is useful in every profit-seeking business organization that has economic resources such as money, machinery, and buildings. While accounting has been called the language of business, it also serves as a language to provide financial information about not-for-profit organizations such as governments, churches, charities, fraternities, and hospitals. This text will concentrate on the use of accounting as it relates to the business firm.

The accounting system used by profit-seeking and not-for-profit organizations may be viewed as an information system designed to provide relevant financial information on the resources of a business and the effects of the use of these resources. This information is presented in financial statements.[1] In

---

[1] When first studying any discipline, new terms are encountered. Usually these terms are set in boldface color and defined at their first occurrence. However, sometimes it is more feasible not to define a term at its first occurrence. This is true with the term *financial statements*. It is defined later in the Introduction and set in boldface color. The boldface color terms are also listed and defined at the end of this Introduction, or in the case of the chapters, at the end of the chapter. After the definition of the term in the term list, a page number is given in parentheses indicating where the term is discussed in the chapter.

preparing these statements, accountants consider the types of users of the information, such as owners and creditors, and the kinds of decisions they make that require financial information.

As a background for studying accounting, this Introduction will define accounting and list the functions performed by accountants. You will learn about the employment opportunities in accounting and be able to differentiate between managerial and financial accounting. Accounting information must conform to certain standards. You will be introduced to the four prominent organizations contributing to these standards. As you continue your study of accounting in the chapters of this text, accounting as the language of business will also become your language as you realize you are constantly exposed to accounting information in your everyday life.

■ ACCOUNTING DEFINED

Accounting is defined by the American Accounting Association—one of the prominent accounting authorities discussed later in this Introduction—as **"the process of identifying, measuring, and communicating economic information to permit informed judgments and decisions by the users of the information."**[2] This information is primarily financial and generally stated in money terms. Accounting, then, is fundamentally a measurement and communication process used to report on the activity of profit-seeking business organizations and not-for-profit organizations.

Accounting is often confused with bookkeeping. Bookkeeping involves the routine recording of economic activities and is a mechanical process. Accounting includes bookkeeping but goes well beyond it in scope. Accountants analyze and interpret financial information, prepare financial statements, conduct audits, design accounting systems, prepare special business and financial studies, prepare forecasts and budgets, and provide tax services.

Specifically, the accounting process (also called the accounting cycle) consists of the following groups of functions (see Illustration 0.1):

1. Accountants **observe** many events and **identify** and **measure** in financial terms (dollars) those events considered evidence of economic activity. (These three functions are often collectively referred to as *analyze.*) The purchase and sale of goods and services are examples of economic activities.
2. Next, the economic events are **recorded, classified** into meaningful groups, and **summarized** for conciseness.
3. Accountants **report** on business activity by preparing financial statements and special reports. Accountants are often asked to **interpret** these statements and reports for various groups such as management and creditors. Interpretation may involve determining how the business is performing compared to prior years and other similar businesses.

---

[2] American Accounting Association, *A Statement of Basic Accounting Theory* (Evanston, Ill., 1966), p. 1.

Illustration 0.1

*Accounting
Functions Performed
by Accountants*

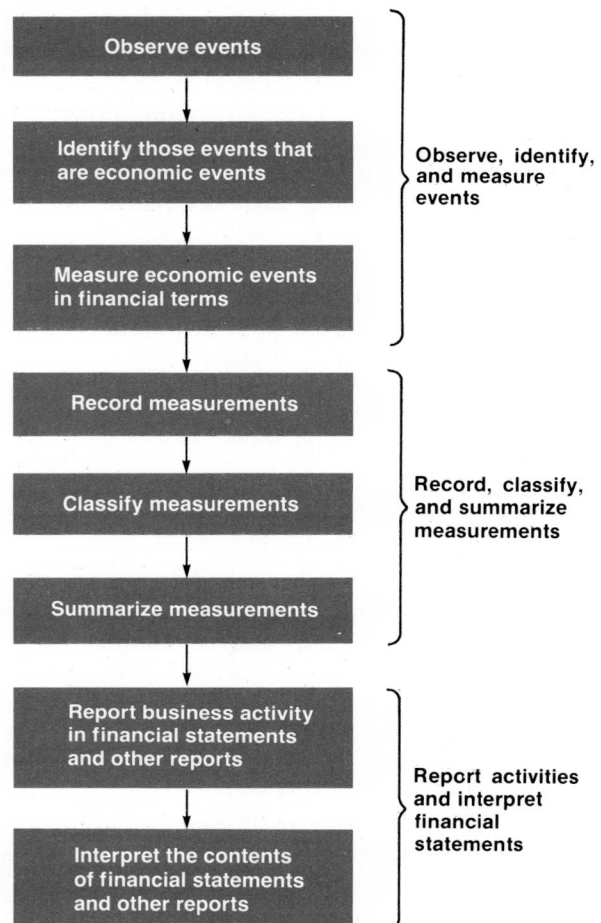

EMPLOYMENT OPPORTUNITIES IN ACCOUNTING

Accounting is an old profession. Records of business transactions have been prepared for centuries. However, it was only during the last half-century that accounting as a profession was accepted with the same importance as the medical and legal professions. Today, in the United States, well over a million people are employed as accountants, and several million are employed in accounting-related positions. Typically, accountants are employed in public accounting, private or industrial accounting, and governmental or other not-for-profit accounting.

Public Accounting

The **public accounting** profession offers accounting and related services for a fee to companies, other organizations, and the general public. An accountant may become a **certified public accountant (CPA).** A CPA is an accountant who has passed an examination prepared and graded by the American Institute of Certified Public Accountants (AICPA) and has met certain other requirements, including being licensed by the state. These requirements vary by state, but states typically require a CPA to have completed certain courses in accounting, worked a certain number of years in public accounting, and lived in that state a certain length of time before taking the examination. When all requirements are met, the accountant may be licensed by the state to practice as an independent professional. Generally, CPAs provide services in auditing, taxes, and management advising (or consulting).

Auditing.   When a business seeks a loan or attempts to have its securities traded on a stock exchange, it is usually required to provide statements concerning its financial affairs. Users of a company's statements are more assured that the statements are presented fairly when the company has been audited by a CPA. A CPA firm is hired by the company to conduct an examination (**independent audit**) of its accounting and related records. The independent auditor verifies some of these records by contacting external sources. For example, the accountant may contact a bank to verify cash balances of the client. **Independent auditors** of the CPA firm perform an audit of a business to enable them to give an **independent auditor's opinion or report** as to whether or not the financial statements fairly (equitably) report the economic performance of the business. As you will learn in the section "Private or Industrial Accounting," auditors **within** a business also conduct audits, but these audits are not independent audits.

Tax Services.   CPAs often provide expert advice on the preparation of federal, state, and local tax returns, as well as on tax planning. The objective in preparing tax returns is to use legal means to minimize the amount of taxes paid. Since almost every major business decision has a tax impact, clients also need tax planning so they know the tax effects of each financial decision.

Management Advisory (or Consulting) Services.   CPAs often are engaged to provide a wide range of advisory or consulting services. The audit services provided by CPAs often result in suggestions to clients on how to improve their operations. For example, CPAs might suggest improvements in the design and installation of an accounting system, the electronic processing of accounting data, inventory control, budgeting, or financial planning.

Private or Industrial Accounting

In contrast to public accountants, who provide services for many clients, **private or industrial accountants** provide services for a single business. Some companies employ only one private accountant, while other companies employ many. In a company with many accountants, the executive officer in charge of the accounting activity is often called a **controller.**

Private accountants may or may not be CPAs. If these accountants pass an examination prepared and graded by the National Association of Accountants (an organization of management accountants employed in private industry) and meet certain other requirements, they are awarded a **Certificate in Management Accounting (CMA).** An accountant may be either a CPA or a CMA, or both.

Private accountants may specialize in one particular job or task. For exam-

3. **Employees and their unions.** Does the company have the ability to pay increased wages? Is the company financially able to provide permanent employment?
4. **Customers.** Does the company offer useful products at fair prices? Will the company survive long enough to honor its product warranties?
5. **Governmental units.** Is the local public utility charging a fair rate for its services?
6. **General public.** Is the company providing useful products and gainful employment for citizens without causing serious environmental problems?

General-purpose financial statements provide most of the information needed by external users of financial accounting. These **financial statements** are formal reports providing information on a company's financial position (solvency), changes in this position, and the results of operations (profitability). Many companies publish these statements in an annual report. The **annual report** (see Appendix A at the end of the text) also contains the independent auditor's opinion as to the fairness of the financial statements, as well as information about the company's activities, products, and plans.

Financial accounting information is historical in nature, reporting on what has happened in the past. To facilitate comparisons between companies, this information must conform to certain standards or methods of presentation called **generally accepted accounting principles (GAAP).** These generally accepted accounting principles have been developed through accounting practice or have been established by an authoritative organization. You will learn about four of these authoritative organizations in the next section.

■ THE DEVELOPMENT OF FINANCIAL ACCOUNTING STANDARDS

The four organizations most influential in the establishment of generally accepted accounting principles (GAAP) are the American Institute of Certified Public Accountants, the Financial Accounting Standards Board, the Securities and Exchange Commission, and the American Accounting Association. Each of these organizations has contributed in a different way to the development of GAAP.

American Institute of Certified Public Accountants (AICPA)

The **American Institute of Certified Public Accountants (AICPA)** has been the dominant organization in the development of accounting standards over the past half-century. In a 20-year period ending in 1959, the AICPA Committee on Accounting Procedure issued 51 *Accounting Research Bulletins* recommending certain principles or practices. From 1959 through 1973, the committee's successor, the **Accounting Principles Board (APB),** issued 31 numbered *Opinions* that CPAs generally are required to follow. Through its monthly magazine, the *Journal of Accountancy,* its research division, and its other divisions and committees, the AICPA continues to influence the development of accounting standards and practices.

Financial Accounting Standards Board (FASB)

The **Accounting Principles Board (APB)** was replaced in 1973 by an independent, seven-member, full-time Financial Accounting Standards Board (FASB). The FASB has issued numerous *Statements of Financial Accounting Standards* and interpretations of those standards. The FASB is widely accepted as the major influence *in the private sector* in the development of new financial standards.

Securities and Exchange Commission (SEC)

Created under the Securities and Exchange Act of 1934, the Securities and Exchange Commission (SEC) administers a number of important acts dealing with the interstate sale of securities (stocks and bonds). The SEC has the power to prescribe accounting practices to be followed by companies under its jurisdiction. This includes virtually every major U.S. business corporation. But rather than exercise this power, the SEC has adopted a policy of working closely with the accounting profession, especially the FASB, in the development of accounting standards. The SEC indicates to the FASB the accounting topics it believes should be addressed.

American Accounting Association (AAA)

Consisting largely of accounting educators, the American Accounting Association (AAA) has sought to encourage research and study at a theoretical level into the concepts, standards, and principles of accounting. In recent years, its quarterly magazine, *The Accounting Review,* has carried many articles reporting on accounting research.

■ SUMMARY

Accounting is fundamentally a measurement and communication process used to report on the activity of profit-seeking and not-for-profit organizations. This process is performed by accountants who **observe** many events and **identify** and **measure** those events considered evidence of economic activity; **record, classify,** and **summarize** these events; **report** on business activity by preparing statements and special reports; and **interpret** these statements and reports for internal and external decision making.

An accountant may be employed in public, private, or governmental and not-for-profit accounting, including the academic segment of the accounting profession. Today, in the United States, well over a million people are employed as accountants, and several million are employed in accounting-related positions.

An accounting information system provides information to help the decision-making process of individuals inside the business as well as outside the business. Managerial accounting information is meant for internal use, while financial accounting information is primarily meant for external use.

Internal users of accounting information include various levels of management personnel. External users include actual and potential stockholders and creditors and their professional advisers, employees and their unions, customers, suppliers, governmental agencies, and the public at large.

Financial accounting information must conform to certain standards or principles called generally accepted accounting principles (GAAP). These principles have been developed through accounting practice or have been established or influenced by four accounting organizations: American Institute of Certified Public Accountants (AICPA), Financial Accounting Standards Board (FASB), Securities and Exchange Commission (SEC), and American Accounting Association (AAA).

NEW TERMS USED IN THIS INTRODUCTION

Accounting

"The process of identifying, measuring, and communicating economic information to permit informed judgments and decisions by the users of the information" (5).

Accounting Principles Board (APB)

An organization created in 1959 by the AICPA and empowered to speak for it on matters of accounting principle; replaced in 1973 by the Financial Accounting Standards Board (10).

American Accounting Association (AAA)

A professional organization of accountants, many of whom are college or university professors of accounting (11).

American Institute of Certified Public Accountants (AICPA)

A professional organization of certified public accountants, most of whom are in public accounting practice (10).

Annual report

A pamphlet or document of varying length containing audited financial statements and other information about a company, distributed annually to its owners (10).

Audit (independent)

Performed by independent auditors to determine whether the financial statements of a business fairly reflect the economic performance of the business (7).

Audit (internal)

Performed by accounting employees of a company to determine if company policies and procedures are being followed (8).

Certificate in Management Accounting (CMA)

Awarded to accountants who pass an examination prepared and graded by the National Association of Accountants and meet certain other requirements (7).

Certified internal auditor (CIA)

An accountant who has passed an examination prepared and graded by the Institute of Internal Auditors and who has met certain other requirements (8).

Certified public accountant (CPA)

An accountant who has passed an examination prepared and graded by the American Institute of Certified Public Accountants (AICPA) and has met certain other requirements, such as work experience in accounting and specified courses in accounting. The accountant is then awarded a CPA certificate and may be licensed by the state to practice as an independent professional (6).

Controller

The executive officer in charge of a company's accounting activity (7).

Financial accounting

Relates to the process of supplying financial information to parties external to the reporting entity (9).

Financial Accounting Standards Board (FASB)

The highest ranking nongovernmental authority on the development of accounting standards or principles (11).

Financial statements

Formal reports providing information on a company's financial position (solvency), changes in this position, and the results of operations (profitability) (10).

Generally accepted accounting principles (GAAP)

Accounting standards and principles that have been developed largely in accounting practice or have been established by an authoritative organization (10).

Governmental or other not-for-profit accounting

Governmental accountants are employed by government agencies at the federal, state, and local levels. Other not-for-profit accountants record and account for receipts and disbursements for churches, charities, fraternities, and universities. Accountants in the academic segment of the accounting profession teach accounting to students and conduct research on accounting issues (8).

Independent audit

See Audit (independent).

Independent auditors

Certified public accountants who perform audits to determine whether the financial statements of businesses fairly reflect the economic performance of these businesses (7).

Independent auditor's opinion or report

The formal written statement by a certified public accountant that states whether or not the client's financial statements fairly reflect the economic performance of the business (7).

Internal audit

See Audit (internal).

Internal auditors

Private accountants employed to see that the policies and procedures established by the business are followed in its divisions and departments (8).

Managerial accounting

Relates to the process of supplying financial information for internal management use (8).

Private or industrial accountants

Provide accounting services for a single business (7).

Public accounting

Relates to accounting and related services offered for a fee to companies, other organizations, and the general public (6).

Securities and Exchange Commission (SEC)

A governmental agency created by Congress to administer acts dealing with interstate sales of securities and having the authority to prescribe the accounting and reporting practices of firms under its jurisdiction (11).

QUESTIONS

---

1. Define accounting. What does the term *relevant* mean when speaking of accounting information? Give an example of relevant information.

2. What is the relationship between *(a)* accounting as an information system and *(b)* economic resources?

3. What is a CPA? What are some of the services usually provided by a CPA?

4. What is the role of the accountant in private industry? What are some of the services provided by the industrial accountant?

5. Name four organizations that have played or are playing an important role in the development of accounting standards. Describe each briefly.

Accounting and Its Use in Business Decisions

After studying this chapter, you should be able to:

1. Identify and describe the three basic forms of business organizations.
2. Distinguish between the three types of business activities performed by business organizations.
3. Describe the content and purposes of the balance sheet and income statement.
4. State the basic accounting equation and describe its relationship to the balance sheet.
5. Analyze business transactions and determine their effects on items in the financial statements.
6. Prepare a balance sheet and income statement.
7. Define and use correctly the new terms in the glossary.

The Introduction provided a background for your study of accounting. You now know how to define accounting and know the functions accountants perform. After reading about the employment opportunities in accounting, you may have already chosen a field of accounting employment to pursue as a career. Even if you do not become an accountant, you will use accounting information throughout your lifetime.

Now you are ready to learn about the forms of business organizations and the types of business activities they perform. Two of the financial statements used by these businesses are presented. Then you will learn about the accounting process (or accounting cycle) used to prepare those financial statements. In this accounting process, financial data—such as your daily personal purchases from businesses—are analyzed, recorded, classified, summarized, and finally reported in the financial statements of those businesses. Hopefully, as you study this chapter, you will recognize the unique, systematic nature of accounting—the language of business.

■ FORMS OF BUSINESS ORGANIZATIONS

Accountants frequently refer to a business organization as an **accounting entity** or a **business entity.** A business entity is any business organization, such as a hardware store or grocery store, that exists as an economic unit. For accounting purposes, each business organization has an existence separate from its owner(s), creditors, employees, customers, and other businesses. This separate existence of the business organization is known as the business entity concept. Thus, in the accounting records of the business entity, the activities of each business should be kept separate from other businesses and the personal financial activities of the owner(s).

If, for example, you own two businesses, a physical fitness center and a horse stable, each would be considered as an independent economic business unit. You would normally keep separate accounting records for each business. Your physical fitness center may be unprofitable because you are not charging enough for the use of your exercise equipment. You can best determine this fact if you treat your physical fitness center and horse stable as two separate business entities and keep separate accounting records for each business. In addition, the car you drive only for personal use does not enter into the business activities of your physical fitness center or your horse stable. However, the use of your truck to pick up feed for your horse stable is a business activity of your horse stable.

As you will see in the discussion that follows on the three forms of business organizations—single proprietorships, partnerships, and corporations—the business entity concept applies to all forms of businesses. For instance, all three forms are separate from other business entities and from their owners for accounting purposes. You will learn that corporations are also **legally** separate from their owners, while this is not true for single proprietorships and partnerships.

Single Proprietorship

A single proprietorship is a business owned by an individual and often managed by that same individual. Single proprietors include physicians, lawyers, electricians, and other people who are "in business for themselves." Many small service-type businesses and retail establishments are single proprietorships. There are no legal formalities in organizing such businesses, and usually only a limited investment is required to begin operations.

In a single proprietorship, the owner is held solely responsible for all debts of the business. For accounting purposes, however, the business is a separate entity. Thus, the financial activities of the business, such as the receipt of fees from selling services to the public, are kept separate from the personal financial activities of the owner. For example, the owner's personal house or car payment should not be entered in the financial records of the business.

Partnership

A partnership is a business owned by two or more persons associated as partners. The business is often managed by those same persons. Many small retail establishments and professional practices such as dentists, physicians, attorneys, and many CPA firms are organized as partnerships.

Partnerships are created by a verbal or written agreement. A written agreement is preferred; it provides a permanent record of the terms of the partnership. Included in the agreement are terms such as the initial investment of each partner, the duties of each partner, the means of dividing profits or losses between the partners each year, and the settlement to be made upon the death or withdrawal of a partner. Each partner may be held liable for all the debts of the partnership and for the actions of each partner within the scope of the business. However, as with the single proprietorship, for accounting purposes the partnership is a separate business entity.

Corporation

A corporation is a business that may be owned by a few persons or by thousands of persons and is incorporated under the laws of 1 of the 50 states. Almost all large businesses are corporations, and many small businesses also are incorporated.

The corporation is unique in that it is a legal business entity. The owners of the corporation are called stockholders or shareholders. They buy shares of stock, which are units of ownership, in the corporation. Should the corporation fail, the owners would lose only the amount they paid for their stock. The personal assets of the owners are protected from the creditors of the corporation.

The stockholders do not directly manage the corporation. They elect a board of directors to represent their interests. The board of directors selects the officers, such as the president and vice presidents, who manage the corporation for the stockholders.

Accounting is necessary for all three forms of business organizations, and generally accepted accounting principles (GAAP) are applicable to each. Since the single proprietorship is the simplest form of business, it will be used in the beginning chapters of this text to illustrate the basic accounting principles and concepts.

■ TYPES OF BUSINESS ACTIVITIES PERFORMED BY BUSINESS ORGANIZATIONS

The forms of business entities discussed in the previous section are classified according to the type of ownership of the business entity. Single proprietors have one owner, partnerships have two or more owners, and corporations usually have many owners. We can also group business entities by the type of business activities they perform—service companies, merchandising companies, and manufacturing companies.

1. **Service companies.** Service companies perform services for a fee. This group includes companies such as accounting firms, law firms, repair shops, dry cleaning establishments, and many others. Accounting for service companies is illustrated in the early chapters of this text.

2. **Merchandising companies.**   Merchandising companies purchase goods that are ready for sale and then sell them to customers. Merchandising companies include companies such as auto dealerships, clothing stores, and supermarkets. Accounting for merchandising companies is first illustrated in Chapter 5.

3. **Manufacturing companies.**   Manufacturing companies buy materials, convert them into products, and then sell the products to other companies or to final customers. Examples of manufacturing companies are steel mills, auto manufacturers, and clothing manufacturers. Manufacturing companies are discussed in the last part of the text, since these businesses are more complex and require more detailed accounting records.

All these companies produce financial statements as the final end product of their accounting process. As you learned in the Introduction, these financial statements provide relevant financial information both to those inside the company—management—and those outside the company—creditors, stockholders, and other interested parties. In the next section, you will learn about the two most common financial statements: the balance sheet and the income statement.

■ FINANCIAL STATEMENTS OF BUSINESS ORGANIZATIONS

Business entities may have many objectives and goals (for example, one of your objectives in owning a physical fitness center may be to get in shape yourself). However, the two primary objectives of every business are solvency and profitability. **Solvency** is the ability to pay debts as they become due. **Profitability** is the ability to generate income. Unless a business can produce satisfactory income and pay its debts as they become due, other objectives a business may have will never be realized simply because the business will not survive.

The financial statement that reflects a company's solvency is the **balance sheet;** the financial statement reflecting the company's profitability is the **income statement.** If you have seen balance sheets and income statements of actual companies, you will recall that they all contain the same main headings and elements as we describe in the next section.

The Balance Sheet

The **balance sheet,** sometimes called the statement of financial position, lists the company's assets, liabilities, and owner's equity (including dollar amounts) **as of a specific moment in time.** A balance sheet is like a still photograph; it captures the financial position of a company at a particular point in time. As you study about the assets, liabilities, and owner's equity contained in a balance sheet, you will understand why this financial statement provides information about the solvency of the business.

Assets are things of value owned by the business. They are also called the **resources** of the business. Assets have value because they can be used or exchanged to produce the services or products of the business. For example, in your horse stable, if you own the land and the stable (building) where horses are boarded, the land and stable are two assets of that business. Cash is also an asset because things such as the feed for your horses can be bought for cash and used in the business. Assets possess service potential or utility to their owner that can be measured and expressed in money terms.

Liabilities are the debts owed by a business. Typically, debts must be paid by certain dates. Many liabilities are incurred by purchasing an item on credit, such as the feed for your horses, and promising to pay for it later, or by going to the bank and borrowing money to pay for a new truck to pick up your horse feed. Purchasing horse feed on credit and borrowing from the bank to pay for your truck will result in liabilities on your company's balance sheet.

Owner's equity is the share of the business that the proprietor (owner) owns outright; that is, owner's equity is equal to assets minus liabilities. Owner's equity, then, consists of the owner's investment in the business plus profits made from the business (assuming the business is profitable) that are not withdrawn from the business by the owner.

To illustrate the relationship between assets, liabilities, and owner's equity, assume, for example, that you decided to purchase a new truck to pick up feed for your horse stable. The truck cost $10,000. You have $3,000 for a down payment. You borrow $7,000 from your banker. On your balance sheet, you now have an asset (truck) of $10,000, a liability (bank loan) of $7,000, and owner's equity of $3,000. In other words, your balance sheet shows that what you **own** minus what you **owe** is your **owner's equity.**

All financial statements have headings that include the (1) name of the organization, (2) title of the statement, and (3) date of, or period covered by, the statement. These three headings are shown in the balance sheet of Brent's Pool Service Company given in Illustration 1.1. The assets of Brent's Pool Service Company on December 31, 1987, amount to $38,700. These assets consist of cash, accounts receivable (amounts due from customers for services already provided), and various types of equipment. Brent's liabilities consist of accounts payable (amounts owed to suppliers for goods or services purchased on credit) and notes payable (amounts owed to parties who loan the company money after the owner signs a written agreement for the company to repay

Illustration 1.1 _Balance Sheet_

BRENT'S POOL SERVICE COMPANY
Balance Sheet
December 31, 1987

Assets		_Liabilities and Owner's Equity*_		
Cash	$15,500	Liabilities:		
Accounts receivable	700	Accounts payable	$ 600	
Truck	6,000	Notes payable	6,000	
Cleaning equipment	14,000	Total liabilities		$ 6,600
Office equipment	2,500	Owner's equity:		
		William Brent, capital		32,100
Total assets	$38,700	Total liabilities and owner's equity		$38,700

* The liabilities and owner's equity portion of the balance sheet may be shown directly beneath the assets instead of to the right of them as shown in the illustration. When liabilities and owner's equity are placed under the assets, it is called the _vertical format_ or _report form_. The vertical format is as acceptable as the _horizontal format_ (or account form) used above. For an example of the vertical format, see the solution to the demonstration problem, page 34.

each loan).[1] Brent's owner's equity is $32,100. On Brent's balance sheet, owner's equity is shown as "William Brent, capital" and can be calculated as the difference between assets of $38,700 and liabilities of $6,600.

The balance sheet of Brent's Pool Service Company shows the financial position of Brent's on December 31, 1987. However, the balance sheet does not show if Brent's is a profitable business. Profitability is shown by the income statement.

The Income Statement

The income statement, sometimes called an earnings statement, reports the profitability of a business organization for **a stated period of time.** In accounting, profitability is measured for a period of time, such as a month or year, by comparing the revenues generated with the expenses incurred to produce these revenues. Revenues are the inflows of assets (such as cash) resulting from the sale of products or the rendering of services to customers. Expenses are the costs incurred to produce revenues. Expenses are measured by the assets surrendered or consumed in servicing customers. If the revenues of a period exceed the expenses of the same period, net income results. Net income is often referred to as the earnings of the company. If expenses exceed revenues, the business has a net loss, and it has operated unprofitably.

Illustration 1.2 shows the income statement of Brent's Pool Service Company for the month of December 1987. Notice how the heading of the income statement differs from the heading of the balance sheet. This difference occurs because a balance sheet is for a specific **point** in time and an income statement is for a specified **period** of time. The company's balance sheet is as of the **end of the day,** December 31, 1987. The company's income statement is for the **month** ended December 31, 1987.

Brent's income statement for the month ended December 31, 1987, shows that the revenues generated by serving customers for December totaled $5,700. Expenses for the month amounted to $3,600. As a result of these business

Illustration 1.2

Income Statement

BRENT'S POOL SERVICE COMPANY Income Statement For the Month Ended December 31, 1987		
Revenues:		
Service revenues		$5,700
Expenses:		
Wages	$2,600	
Rent	400	
Gas and oil	600	
Total expenses		3,600
Net income		$2,100

---

[1] Most notes bear interest, but in this chapter we assume that all notes bear no interest. Interest is an amount paid by the borrower to the lender (in addition to the amount of the loan) for use of the money over time.

activities, Brent's net income for the month of December was $2,100. The **net income** amount is determined by subtracting the company's expenses of $3,600 from its revenues of $5,700.

The balance sheet and income statement of Brent's Pool Service Company are the end products of the accounting process, which is explained in the next section. These two financial statements give a picture of the solvency and profitability of the company. The accounting process details how this picture was made.

■ THE FINANCIAL ACCOUNTING PROCESS

In this section we explain first the accounting equation, which is the framework for the entire accounting process. Then you will learn how to recognize a business transaction and understand underlying assumptions accountants use to record business transactions. Next you will see how Brent's Pool Service Company records transactions affecting its balance sheet and income statement. Accounting—the language of business—is now also becoming your language.

The Accounting Equation

As explained in the discussion of the balance sheet earlier in the chapter, the balance sheet is made up of three essential elements—assets, liabilities, and owner's equity. The relationship between these three elements is shown in the basic **accounting equation** which is:

$$\text{Assets} = \text{Liabilities} + \text{Owner's Equity}$$

From the Brent's Pool Service Company's balance sheet in Illustration 1.1, we enter in the amounts of its assets, liabilities, and owner's equity:

$$
\begin{array}{ccccc}
A & = & L & + & OE \\
\$38,700 & = & \$6,600 & + & \$32,100
\end{array}
$$

The basic accounting equation must always be in balance. The left-hand side of the equation shows the assets, which are things of value owned by the business. The right-hand side of the equation shows who provided the funds to acquire the assets. These funds are provided by either **creditors** or **owners.** In this case, creditors provided $6,600 of the funds, and the owner provided $32,100. In accounting terminology, the right-hand side of the equation shows the equities, made up of the liabilities plus owner's equity. (Liabilities can be viewed as creditor's equity.) Equities are interests in, or claims upon, assets. The creditor's interest in the assets is $6,600, the amount of liabilities. The owner's interest is $32,100, the amount of owner's equity.

As a business engages in economic activity, the **dollar amounts** and the

composition of its assets, liabilities, and owner's equity **change. But the equality of the basic equation always holds.**

Analysis of Transactions

When you buy feed for the horses in your horse stable business, an economic exchange takes place. You may give cash and receive feed. Or, you may give a service—such as boarding horses—and receive cash. These exchanges of goods and services are called transactions.

Transactions provide much of the raw data used in the accounting process for two reasons. First, an exchange is an observable event providing evidence of business activity. For example, an exchange of cash for merchandise is a business event. Second, an exchange takes place at an agreed-upon price, and this price provides an objective measure of the economic activity that has occurred. For example, the objective measure of the exchange may be $5,000. These two factors—evidence and measurement—make possible the recording of a transaction.

The evidence of the transaction is usually backed by a source document. A source document is any written or printed evidence of a business transaction that describes the essential facts of that transaction. Examples of source documents are receipts for cash paid or received, checks written or received, bills sent to customers for services performed or bills received from suppliers for items purchased, cash register tapes, sales tickets, and notes given or received. The source document you received when you bought the feed for your horses was probably in the form of a sales invoice or receipt. We handle source documents constantly in our everyday life. Each source document initiates the process of recording a transaction.

Generally, in recording business transactions, accountants rely on four underlying assumptions or concepts. The business entity concept was introduced earlier in the chapter. It is mentioned again since it is basic to understanding the accounting process.

1. **Business entity concept.**   Data gathered in an accounting system are assumed to relate to a specific business unit or entity. The business entity concept assumes that each business has an existence separate from its owners, creditors, employees, customers, other interested parties, and other businesses.
2. **Money measurement concept.**   Economic activity is initially recorded and reported in terms of a **common monetary unit of measure**—the dollar in the United States. This form of measurement is referred to as money measurement.
3. **Cost concept.**   Most of the amounts entered in an accounting system are the objective money prices determined in the exchange process. The result is that most assets are recorded at their acquisition cost measured in terms of money paid. Cost is the sacrifice made or the resources given up, measured in money terms, to acquire some desired thing, such as a new truck (asset).
4. **Continuity or going-concern concept.**   Unless strong evidence exists to the contrary, the accountant assumes that the business entity will continue operations into the indefinite future. This assumption is referred to as the continuity or going-concern assumption. Assuming that the entity will con-

tinue indefinitely allows the accountant to value assets at cost on the balance sheet since they are to be used rather than sold. Market values of these assets would only be relevant if they were for sale.

Now that you understand what business transactions and the four basic accounting assumptions are, you are ready to follow step by step some actual business transactions. The transactions of Brent's Pool Service Company are used as examples. These transactions are grouped into the transactions affecting only the balance sheet and those affecting the income statement and/or the balance sheet. Then, a summary of the transactions is given, followed by a brief discussion of owner withdrawals.

Transactions Affecting Only the Balance Sheet.   The transactions that follow affect the assets, liabilities, and owner's equity on the balance sheet. The business transactions occurred during the month of November 1987.

1a. Owner Invested Cash.   When Brent's Pool Service Company was organized on November 1, 1987, the owner invested $30,000 cash in the business. This transaction increased assets (cash) of the company by $30,000 and increased owner's equity by $30,000. Consequently, the transaction yields the following basic accounting equation:

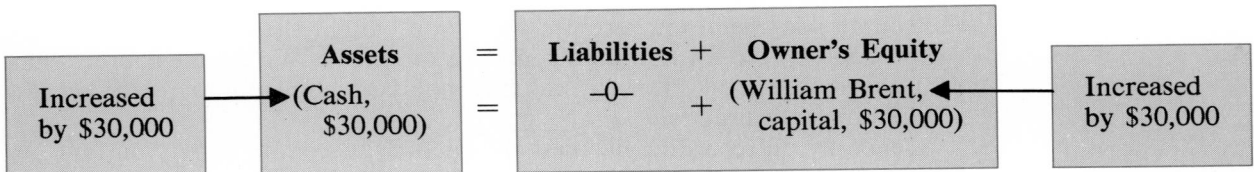

2a. Borrowed Money.   The company signed a note and borrowed $6,000 from Mrs. Brent's father. After including the effects of this second transaction, the basic equation is:

3a. Purchased Equipment for Cash.   Brent's Pool Service Company bought (by paying cash) a truck for $6,000, cleaning equipment for $14,000, and office equipment for $1,500. Equipment items are assets because they are used to earn revenues in the future. **Note that this transaction does not change the totals in the basic equation; it merely changes the composition of the assets.** Cash was decreased, and the truck, cleaning equipment, and office equipment (assets) were increased by the total amount of the cash decrease. Three assets were received, and one asset of equal value was given up. The accounting equation now is:

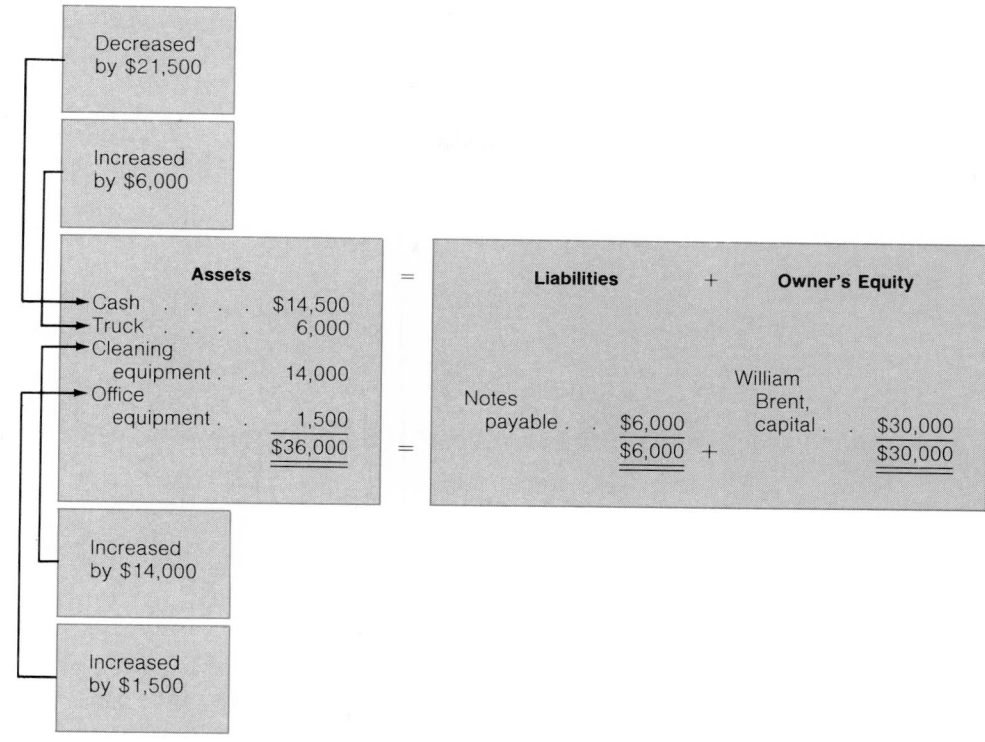

4a. Purchased Equipment on Account (for Credit).   Brent's Pool Service Company purchased $1,000 of office equipment on account, agreeing to pay within 10 days after receiving the bill. (To purchase an item "on account" means to buy it on credit.) This transaction increased assets in the form of office equipment and liabilities in the form of accounts payable by $1,000. As stated earlier, accounts payable are amounts owed to suppliers for items purchased on credit. The increase in the asset and the liabilities of $1,000 is shown as follows:

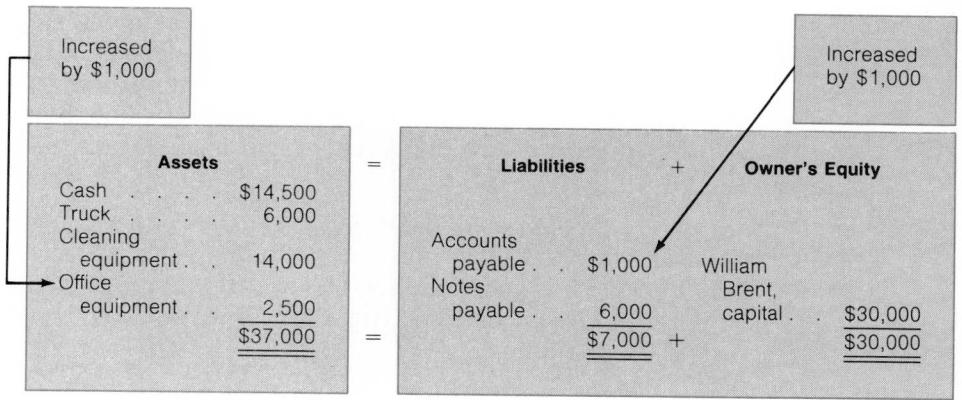

5a. Paid an Account Payable.   Eight days after receiving the bill, the company paid $1,000 for the office equipment purchased on account (transaction 4a). This transaction reduced cash by $1,000 and reduced the debt owed to the equipment supplier—shown as an account payable—by $1,000. Thus, the assets and liabilities both are reduced by $1,000, and the equation again balances as follows:

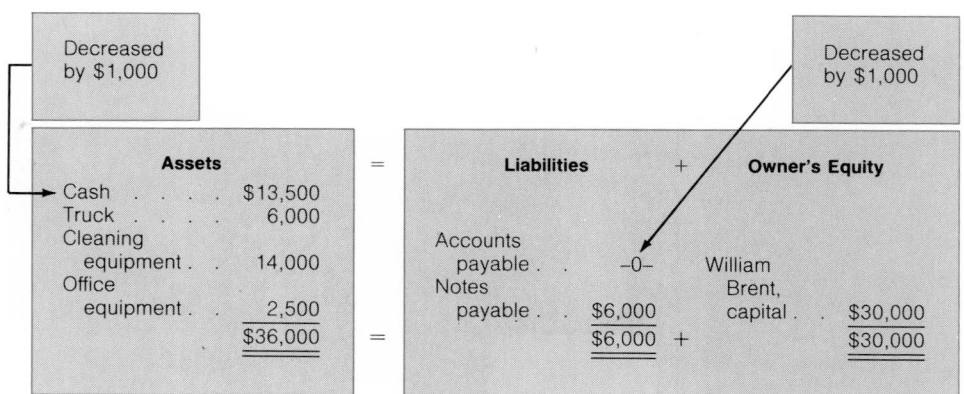

Illustration 1.3 shows a summary of transactions prepared in accounting equation form for the month of November. A **summary of transactions** is merely a teaching tool used to show the effects of transactions on the balance sheet. Note that the owner's equity has remained at $30,000. This amount will change as the business begins to earn revenues or incur expenses. You can see how the totals at the bottom of Illustration 1.3 tie into the balance sheet shown in Illustration 1.4. The balance sheet in Illustration 1.4 is dated November 30, 1987. These totals become the beginning balances for the month of December 1987.

Thus far, all transactions have consisted of exchanges or acquisitions of assets either by borrowing or by owner investment. This procedure was used so that you could focus on the accounting equation as it relates to the balance sheet. However, a business is not formed merely to **hold present assets.** Rather, a **business seeks to use its assets to generate greater amounts of assets.** A business increases its assets by providing goods or services to customers. The results of these activities are shown in the income statement. The section that follows carries on the transactions of Brent's Pool Service Company as it begins its business of earning revenues and incurring expenses.

Transactions Affecting the Income Statement and/or Balance Sheet. To survive, a business must be profitable. This means that the revenues earned by providing goods and services to customers must exceed the expenses incurred. In December 1987, Brent's Pool Service Company engaged in the transactions that follow.

1b. Earned Service Revenue and Received Cash. As its first transaction in December, Brent's performed cleaning services for a large motel chain and received $4,800 cash. This transaction increased the cash balance by $4,800.

Illustration 1.3   *Summary of Transactions*

BRENT'S POOL SERVICE COMPANY
Summary of Transactions
Month of November 1987

Trans-action	Explanation	Cash	Accounts receiv-able	Truck	Cleaning equip-ment	Office equip-ment		Accounts payable	Notes payable		William Brent, capital
				Assets			=	Liabilities		+	Owner's Equity
	Beginning balances	$ –0–	$–0–	$ –0–	$ –0–	$ –0–	=	$ –0–	$ –0–		$ –0–
1a	Owner invested cash	+ 30,000									+ 30,000
		$30,000					=				$30,000
2a	Borrowed money	+ 6,000							+ 6,000		
		$36,000					=		$6,000	+	$30,000
3a	Purchased equipment for cash	– 21,500		+ 6,000	+ 14,000	+ 1,500					
		$14,500		$6,000	$14,000	$1,500	=		$6,000	+	$30,000
4a	Purchased equipment on account					+ 1,000		+ 1,000			
		$14,500		$6,000	$14,000	$2,500	=	$1,000	$6,000	+	$30,000
5a	Paid an account payable	– 1,000						– 1,000			
	End of month balances	$13,500	$–0–	$6,000	$14,000	$2,500	=	$ –0–	$6,000	+	$30,000

Illustration 1.4   *Balance Sheet*

BRENT'S POOL SERVICE COMPANY
Balance Sheet
November 30, 1987

Assets		Liabilities and Owner's Equity	
Cash	$13,500	Liabilities:	
Truck	6,000	Notes payable	$6,000
Cleaning equipment	14,000	Total liabilities	$ 6,000
Office equipment	2,500	Owner's equity:	
		William Brent, capital	30,000
Total assets	$36,000	Total liabilities and owner's equity	$36,000

Owner's capital also increased by $4,800, and the accounting equation is again in balance.

The $4,800 is a revenue earned by the business and, as such, increases owner's equity because the owner prospers when the business earns profits. Likewise, the owner would sustain the losses if the business fails.

The effects of this $4,800 transaction on the financial status of Brent's Pool Service Company are:

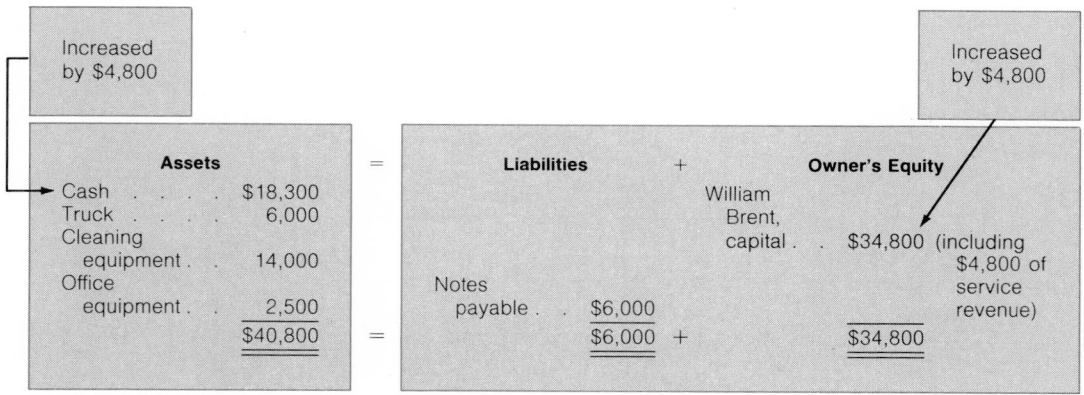

2b. Service Revenue Earned on Account (for Credit).   Brent's Pool Service Company performed services for a customer who agreed to pay $900 at a later date. The company granted credit rather than requiring the customer to pay cash immediately. This is called earning revenue "on account." The transaction consists of an exchange of services for a promise by the customer to pay later. This transaction is similar to the preceding transaction in that owner's equity is increased because revenues have been earned. But it differs because cash has not been received. Instead, another asset, called an account receivable, has been received. As noted earlier, an account receivable is the amount due from a customer for goods or services already provided. The company has a legal right to collect from the customer in the future. In accounting, such claims are recognized as assets. The accounting equation, including this $900 item, is as follows:

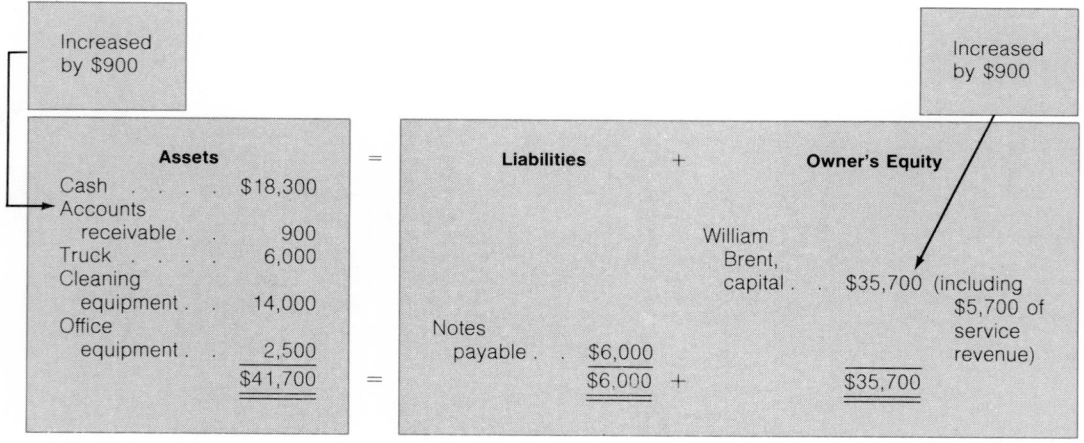

3b. Collected Cash on Accounts Receivable.   Brent's collected $200 "on account" from the customer in transaction 2b. The remaining $700 will be received later. This transaction affects only the balance sheet and consists of giving up a claim upon a customer in exchange for cash. The effects of the transaction are to increase cash by $200 and to decrease accounts receivable by $200. **Note that this transaction consists solely of a change in the composition of the assets.** The revenue was recorded when the services were performed.

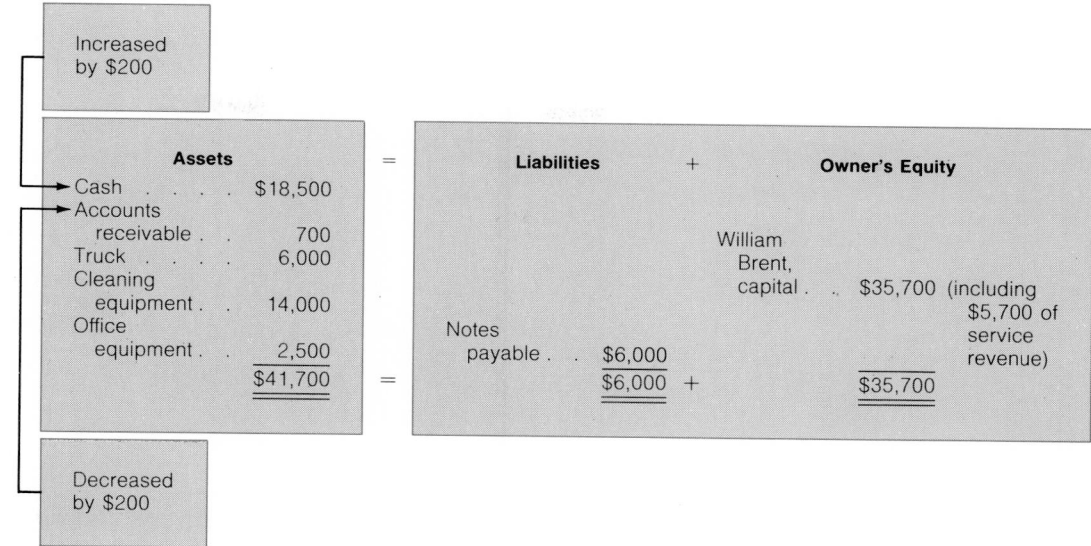

4b. Paid Wages.   Brent's paid employees $2,600 in wages, which is an exchange of cash for employee services. Typically, employees are paid for their services after their work is performed. Wages are costs incurred by the company to produce revenues and are considered an expense. Thus, the accountant treats the transaction as a decrease in an asset (cash) and a decrease in owner's equity because an expense has been incurred. Expense transactions reduce net income. Since net income becomes a part of the owner's capital balance, expense transactions reduce the owner's capital.

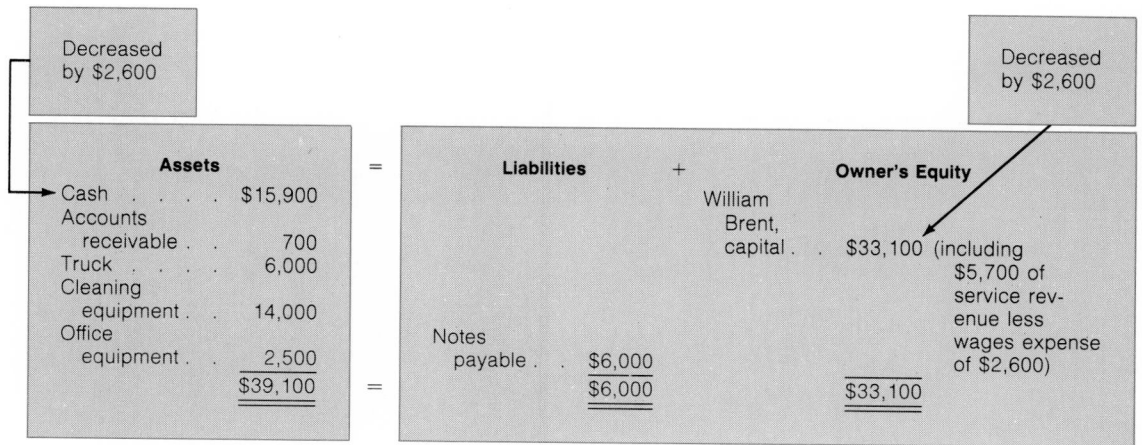

5b. Paid Rent.   In December, Brent's paid $400 cash for office space rental. This transaction causes a decrease in cash of $400 and a decrease in the owner's equity of $400 because of the incurrence of rent expense.

Transaction 5b has the following effects on the amounts in the accounting equation:

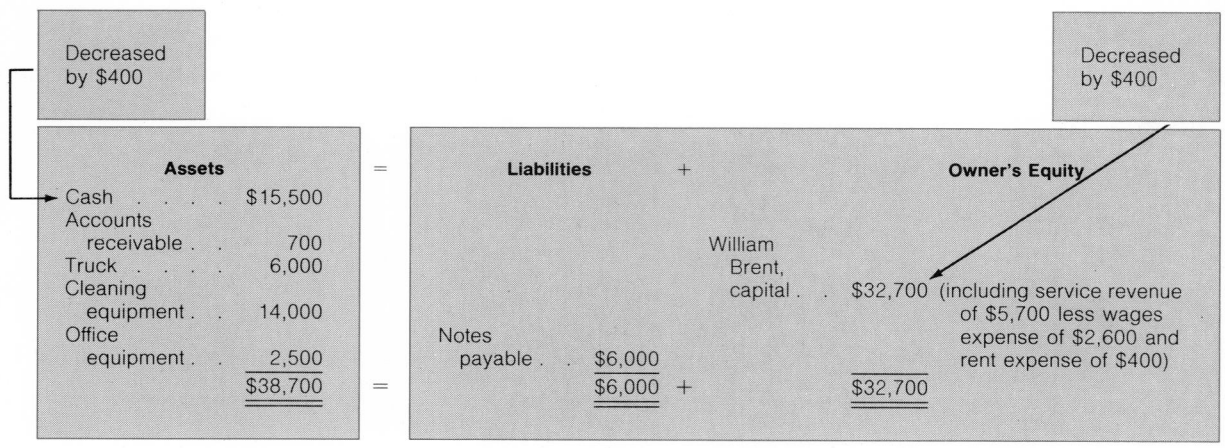

Paying cash for other expenses, such as advertising, gas and oil, and miscellaneous, would be recorded in the same way as transactions 4b and 5b.

6b. Received Bill for Gas and Oil Used.   At the end of the month, Brent's received a $600 bill for gasoline, oil, and other supplies consumed during the month. This transaction involves an increase in accounts payable (a liability) because the bill has not yet been paid and a decrease in owner's equity because an expense has been incurred. The accounting equation of Brent's Pool Service Company now reads:

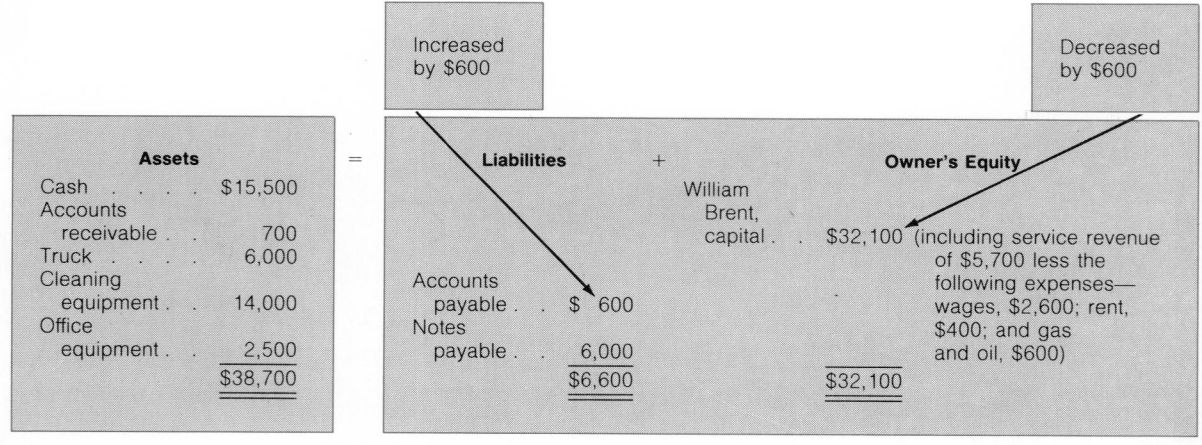

Summary of Balance Sheet and Income Statement Transactions.   The effects of all the preceding transactions upon the assets, liabilities, and owner's equity of Brent's Pool Service Company in its second month of operations are summarized in Illustration 1.5. The beginning balances are those shown as ending balances in Illustration 1.3. The summary shows subtotals after each transaction; these subtotals are optional and may be omitted. Note how the accounting equation remains in balance after each transaction and at the end of the month.

The totals shown at the bottom of Illustration 1.5 are the amounts reported in the balance sheet in Illustration 1.6. Illustration 1.7 shows the revenue and expense items listed in the owner's equity column of the transactions summary. Brent's capital account on the balance sheet consists of his $30,000 investment plus the $2,100 earned during the month of December.

Illustration 1.5 *Summary of Transactions*

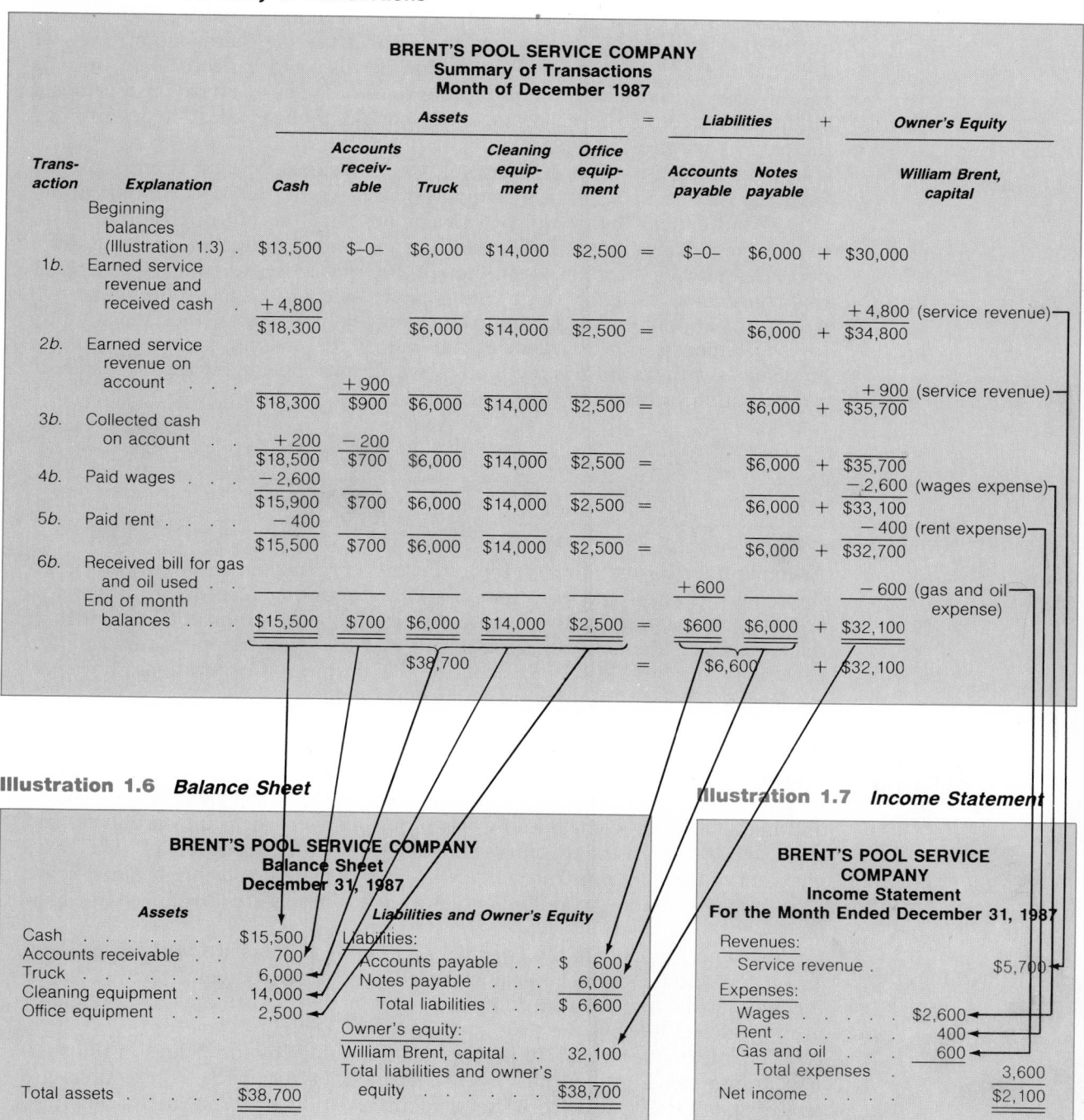

Illustration 1.6 *Balance Sheet*

BRENT'S POOL SERVICE COMPANY
Balance Sheet
December 31, 1987

Assets		Liabilities and Owner's Equity	
Cash	$15,500	Liabilities:	
Accounts receivable	700	Accounts payable	$ 600
Truck	6,000	Notes payable	6,000
Cleaning equipment	14,000	Total liabilities	$ 6,600
Office equipment	2,500	Owner's equity:	
		William Brent, capital	32,100
		Total liabilities and owner's	
Total assets	$38,700	equity	$38,700

Illustration 1.7 *Income Statement*

BRENT'S POOL SERVICE COMPANY
Income Statement
For the Month Ended December 31, 1987

Revenues:		
Service revenue		$5,700
Expenses:		
Wages	$2,600	
Rent	400	
Gas and oil	600	
Total expenses		3,600
Net income		$2,100

Remember that if the amount of revenues exceeds the amount of expenses, the business has net income. The net income is an addition to the owner's capital balance. Later chapters will show that revenues and expenses affect the owner's capital only at the end of an accounting period. The procedure shown above is a shortcut used to explain why the accounting equation remains in balance.

Withdrawals by Owner. A **withdrawal** is the taking of cash or other assets out of the business by the owner for personal use. Withdrawals of cash for personal use are recorded as a reduction in cash and a decrease in owner's equity. Also, withdrawals can occur as a result of the business paying a personal bill for the owner. However, personal bills should not be included in determining the entity's income for a period.

An example of such a withdrawal would occur if William Brent took $50 from the Brent's Pool Service Company's cash register to pay his home utility bill. Mr. Brent has every right to the money, but the bill does not relate to the business. This transaction would be recorded as a decrease in cash and a decrease in owner's capital. Even though the transaction summary would show this transaction reducing the owner's capital account balance, the withdrawl would not appear on the income statement of the business. (See the solution to the Demonstration Problem at the end of the chapter for an example of an owner's withdrawal transaction.) A withdrawal by the owner is considered a distribution of assets to the owners.

■ *SUMMARY*

Accountants recognize three forms of business organizations: single proprietorships, partnerships, and corporations. The accounting records of all business organizations should be kept separate from the personal financial activities of the owners. In the single proprietorship and the partnership, the owners are personally responsible for all debts of the business. Corporations, however, are legally separate from their owners (stockholders).

Business organizations are also classified by the types of business activities they perform: service companies, merchandising companies, and manufacturing companies. Service companies perform services for a fee; merchandising companies purchase goods that are ready for sale and then sell them to customers; and manufacturing companies buy materials, convert them into products, and then sell the products to other companies or to final customers. The early chapters of this text illustrate service businesses. Merchandising businesses are introduced in Chapter 5, and manufacturing businesses are introduced in Chapter 21.

Two end products of the financial accounting process are the balance sheet and income statement. The balance sheet reflects the company's solvency; the income statement reflects the company's profitability. Other financial statements are introduced later in the text.

The information reported in the financial statements originates in the business transactions entered into by the business entity. These transactions are **analyzed** and their effects **recorded** as increases or decreases in assets, liabilities, owner's equity, revenues, and expenses—the five basic elements of accounting. Assets, liabilities, and owner's equity are reported in the balance sheet. Revenues and expenses are subclassifications of owner's equity and are reported in the income statement. **The framework for analysis is the basic equation,** Assets = Equities, expanded to Assets = Liabilities + Owner's Equity. Revenues and expenses create income (or loss) that affects owner's equity.

Chapter 1 has introduced two important ingredients of the accounting process—the accounting equation and the business transaction. In Chapter 2, you will learn about debits and credits and how they are used in recording transactions.

NEW TERMS INTRODUCED IN CHAPTER 1

Accounting equation

Assets = Liabilities + Owner's Equity (20).

Accounts payable

Amounts owed to suppliers for goods or services purchased on credit (18).

Accounts receivable

Amounts due from customers for services already provided (18).

Assets

Things of value owned by the business. Examples include money, machines, and buildings. Assets possess service potential or utility to their owner that can be measured and expressed in money terms (17).

Balance sheet

Financial statement that list the company's assets, liabilities, and owner's equity (including dollar amounts) as of a specific moment in time. Also called a statement of financial position (17).

Business entity concept

Each business organization has an existence separate from its owners, creditors, employees, customers, and other businesses (15).

Continuity (going concern)

The assumption by the accountant that unless strong evidence exists to the contrary, a business entity will continue operations into the indefinite future (21).

Corporation

Business that may be owned by a few persons or by thousands of persons and is incorporated under the laws of 1 of the 50 states (16).

Cost

Sacrifice made or the resources given up, measured in money terms, to acquire some desired thing, such as a new truck—an asset (21).

Equities

Broadly speaking, all claims to or interests in assets; includes liabilities and owner's equity (20).

Expenses

Costs incurred to produce revenues (19).

Going concern

See continuity.

Income statement

Financial statement that shows the revenues and expenses and reports the profitability of a business organization for a stated period of time. Sometimes called an earnings statement (19).

Liabilities

Debts owed by a company—or creditor's equity. Examples include notes payable and accounts payable (18).

Manufacturing companies

Companies that buy materials, convert them into products, and then sell the products to other companies or to final customers (17).

Merchandising companies

Companies that purchase goods that are ready for sale and then sell them to customers (17).

Money measurement

Recording and reporting economic activity in terms of a common monetary unit of measure such as the dollar (21).

Net income

Amount by which the revenues of a period exceed the expenses of the same period (19).

Net loss

Amount by which the expenses of a period exceed the revenues of the same period (19).

Notes payable

Amounts owed to parties who loan the company money after the owner signs a written agreement (a note) for the company to repay each loan (18).

Owner's equity

That share of the business that the proprietor (owner) owns outright; it is equal to assets minus liabilities (18).

Partnership

Business owned by two or more persons associated as partners (15).

Profitability

Ability to generate income. The income statement reflects a company's profitability (17).

Revenues

Inflow of assets (such as cash) resulting from the sale of products or the rendering of services to customers (19).

Service companies

Companies that perform services (such as accounting firms, law firms, repair shops, or dry cleaning establishments) for a fee (16).

Single proprietorship

Business owned by an individual and often managed by that same individual (15).

Solvency

Ability to pay debts as they become due. The balance sheet reflects a company's solvency (17).

Source document

Any written or printed evidence of a business transaction that describes the essential facts of that transaction, such as receipts for cash paid or received (21).

Stockholders or shareholders

Owners of the corporation; they buy shares of stock, which are units of ownership in the corporation (16).

Summary of transactions

Teaching tool used in chapter to show effects of transactions on balance sheet items (24).

Transactions

Exchanges of goods and services. Transactions affect the assets, liabilities, owner's equity, revenues, and expenses of an entity (21).

Withdrawal

Cash or other assets taken out of the business by the owner for personal use (30).

DEMONSTRATION PROBLEM

On June 1, 1987, Joanna Willis formed the Briarcliff Riding Stable. The following transactions occurred during June:

Transactions:

June 1 The owner invested $10,000 cash in the business.
    4 A horse stable and riding equipment were rented (and paid for) for the month at a cost of $1,200.
    8 Horse feed for the month was purchased on credit, $800.
    20 Miscellaneous expenses of $600 for June were paid (to the supplier of various items and services).
    24 The owner withdrew $500 cash.
    29 Land was purchased for use in the business by borrowing $40,000 from a relative by signing a note. The note is due to be repaid in five years with no interest.
    30 Salaries of $700 for the month were paid.
    30 Riding and lesson fees were billed in the amount of $2,400 to a riding club, whose members used the stable facilities. (This bill is due on July 10.)
    30 Fees of $3,000 for the month were billed to the riding club, whose members were boarding their horses at the stable. (This amount is due on July 10.)

Required: a. Prepare a summary of the above transactions similar to Illustration 1.5. Use columns headed Cash, Accounts Receivable, Land, Accounts Payable, Notes Payable, and Joanna Willis, Capital. Determine balances after each transaction to show that the basic equation is in balance.

b. Prepare an income statement for the month of June 1987.

c. Prepare a balance sheet as of June 30, 1987.

Solution to demonstration problem

a.

BRIARCLIFF RIDING STABLE
Summary of Transactions
Month of June 1987

Date	Explanation	Cash	Accounts receivable	Land		Accounts payable	Notes payable	+	Joanna Willis, Capital
		Assets			**=**	**Liabilities**		**+**	**Owner's Equity**
June 1	Owner investment	$10,000			=				$10,000
4	Rent expense	− 1,200							− 1,200
		$ 8,800			=				$ 8,800
8	Feed expense					$+ 800			− 800
		$ 8,800			=	$ 800		+	$ 8,000
20	Miscellaneous expenses	− 600							− 600
		$ 8,200			=	$ 800		+	$ 7,400
24	Owner withdrawal	− 500							− 500
		$ 7,700			=	$ 800		+	$ 6,900
29	Purchased land by borrowing			$+ 40,000			$+ 40,000		
		$ 7,700		$ 40,000	=	$ 800	$ 40,000	+	$ 6,900
30	Salaries paid	− 700							− 700
		$ 7,000		$ 40,000	=	$ 800	$ 40,000	+	$ 6,200
30	Riding and lesson fees revenue billed		$+ 2,400						+ 2,400
		$ 7,000	$ 2,400	$ 40,000	=	$ 800	$ 40,000	+	$ 8,600
30	Boarding fees revenue		+ 3,000						+ 3,000
	End of month balances	$ 7,000	$ 5,400	$ 40,000	=	$ 800	$ 40,000	+	$11,600

b.

BRIARCLIFF RIDING STABLE
Income Statement
For the Month Ended June 30, 1987

Revenues:

Horse boarding fees	$3,000	
Riding and lesson fees	2,400	
Total revenues		$5,400

Expenses:

Rent	$1,200	
Feed	800	
Salaries	700	
Miscellaneous	600	
Total expenses		3,300
Net income		$2,100

c.

BRIARCLIFF RIDING STABLE
Balance Sheet
June 30, 1987

Assets

Cash	$ 7,000
Accounts receivable	5,400
Land	40,000
Total assets	$52,400

Liabilities and Owner's Equity

Liabilities:	
Accounts payable	$ 800
Notes payable	40,000
Total liabilities	$40,800
Owner's equity:	
Joanna Willis, capital	11,600
Total liabilities and owner's equity	$52,400

QUESTIONS

1. Identify and briefly describe the three forms of business organizations.

2. Identify and briefly describe the three types of businesses (according to functions performed).

3. What is a balance sheet? This statement provides information on what aspect of a business?

4. Define asset, liability, and owner's equity.

5. How do liabilities and owner's equity differ? In what respects are they similar?

6. What is an income statement? This statement provides information on what aspect of a business?

7. What are revenues?

8. Define expenses. How are expenses measured?

9. What is the basic accounting equation?

10. What is a transaction? What use does the accountant make of transactions? Why?

11. What is the accounting entity assumption?

EXERCISES

E–1

Analyze transactions

Crowley Company, engaged in a service business, completed the following selected transactions during the month of July 1987:

  a. Purchased office equipment on account.
  b. Paid an account payable.
  c. Earned service revenue on account.
  d. Borrowed money from a relative to use in the business by signing a note.
  e. Paid wages for month to employees.
  f. Received cash on account from a charge customer.
  g. Received gas and oil bill for month.
  h. Purchased truck for cash.

Using a tabular form similar to Illustration 1.5 of the chapter, indicate the effect of each transaction on the accounting equation using (+) for increase and (−) for decrease. Columns are needed for Cash, Accounts Receivable, Truck, Office Equipment, Accounts Payable, Notes Payable, and Crowley, Capital. No dollar amounts are needed, and you need not fill in the Explanation column.

E-2

Determine effect of transactions on owner's equity

Indicate the immediate amount of change (if any) in the owner's equity balance based on each of the following transactions:

a. The owner invested $30,000 cash in the business. *up*
b. Land costing $5,000 was purchased by paying cash. *no change*
c. The company performed services for a customer who agreed to pay $8,000 in one month. *inc acc Rec.*
d. Paid wages for the month, $7,200.
e. Paid $2,500 on an account payable.

E-3

Give examples of transactions

Give examples of transactions that would have the following effects upon the elements in a firm's accounting system:

a. Increase cash; decrease some other asset.
b. Decrease cash; increase some other asset.
c. Increase an asset; increase a liability.
d. Increase an expense; decrease an asset. *Rent Wage*
e. Increase an asset other than cash; increase revenue.
f. Decrease an asset; decrease a liability. *Pay off to get Rid of Liab*

E-4

Compute revenue

Assume that owner's capital increased because of net income by $64,000 from June 30, 1987, to June 30, 1988. Assume expenses for the year were $160,000. Compute the revenue for the year. *Revexp = 224.000*

E-5

Compute owner's equity

On December 31, 1987, P Company had assets of $460,000, liabilities of $260,000, and owner's equity of $200,000. During 1988, it earned revenues of $130,000 and incurred expenses of $102,000. Compute the owner's equity amount as of December 31, 1988.

E-6

Analyze transactions

For each of the following transactions present an analysis showing clearly its two-sided nature:

a. Purchased a truck for cash, $8,000. *-asset +?*
b. Purchased land for $40,000; payment to be made next month.
c. Paid $800 cash for the current month's utilities.
d. Paid for the land purchased in (b). *Decreas Cash Decreas Aatipa*

E-7

Identify transactions that increase expenses

Which of the following transactions result in an increase in an expense?

a. Cash of $42,000 was paid to employees for services received during the month.
b. Cash of $2,500 was paid to a supplier for some advertising supplies used during the month.
c. Paid $4,000 on a loan payable.
d. Paid $220 cash in payment of an account payable.
e. The owner withdrew $650 cash.

E-8

Determine total assets at beginning of year and owner's equity at end of year

At the start of the year, a company had liabilities of $108,000 and owner's equity of $360,000. Net income for the year was $150,000, and $45,000 cash was withdrawn by the owner. Compute total assets at the beginning of the year and owner's equity at the end of the year.

E-9

Compute net income

From the following selected data for the Baker Company compute net income for 1987:

Revenue from services rendered on account . .	$150,000
Revenue from services rendered for cash . . .	30,000
Cash collected from customers on account . .	84,000
Owner's equity, January 1, 1987	162,000
Expenses incurred on account	100,000
Expenses incurred for cash	40,000
Cash withdrawn by owner	12,000
Additional cash invested by owner	20,000
Owner's equity, December 31, 1987	210,000

Why would you not use all of the above items in your answer?

PROBLEMS, SERIES A

P1–1–A

Prepare income statement and balance sheet

Analysis of the summary of transactions for the Moonlight Drive-In Theater for the month of July 1987 disclosed the following ending balances:

Balances, July 31:

Cash	$ 40,000
Land	100,000
Accounts Payable	14,000
Notes Payable	20,000
Ron Mott, Capital	106,000

A breakdown of the owner's capital balance revealed the following revenues and expenses for the month:

Ticket revenue	$31,000
Equipment rent expense	5,000
Film rent expense	9,000
Advertising expense	700
Wages expense	4,200
Utilities expense	1,700
Commission revenue received from concessionaires (percentage of concessionaire sales is paid to Moonlight Drive-In)	5,400

Required: a.   Prepare an income statement for the month of July 1987.
b.   Prepare a balance sheet as of July 31, 1987.

P1–2–A

Prepare summary of transactions and balance sheet

The Vince Rossi Company began operations on March 1, 1987. During March, it engaged in the followng transactions:

Transactions:

1.   Vince Rossi invested $150,000 in the business.
2.   Vince's father loaned $75,000 to Vince to be used in the business. Vince signed a note bearing no interest.
3.   The following assets were purchased for cash: truck, $18,000; cleaning equipment, $30,000; and office equipment, $37,500.
4.   Office equipment was purchased on account, $22,500.
5.   The account payable in (4) was paid, $22,500.

Required: a.   Prepare a summary of transactions using a format similar to Illustration 1.3. Include money columns for Cash, Truck, Cleaning Equipment, Office Equipment, Accounts Payable, Notes Payable, and Vince Rossi, Capital. Determine new balances after each transaction.
b.   Prepare a balance sheet as of March 31, 1987.

P1–3–A

Prepare summary of transactions, income statement, and balance sheet

The Mark Taylor Company, which provides financial advisory services, engaged in the following transactions during the month of October 1987:

Transactions:

1.   Received $120,000 cash investment from the owner.
2.   The owner signed a note and borrowed $16,000 from a friend for use in the business.
3.   The company bought $100,000 of computer equipment for cash.
4.   Cash was received from a customer for services performed, $7,600.
5.   Services were performed for a customer who agreed to pay within a month, $6,000.
6.   Employee wages were paid, $6,600.
7.   A customer paid $1,600 of the amount owed the company.

Required: a.   Prepare a summary of the above transactions (Illustration 1.5). Use money columns headed Cash, Accounts Receivable, Equipment, Notes Payable, and Mark Taylor, Capital. Determine balances after each transaction.

b. Prepare an income statement for October 1987.

c. Prepare a balance sheet as of October 31, 1987.

P1–4–A

Prepare income statement and balance sheet

The following balances are for the Thomas Company. All revenues and expenses are for the month of September 1987. All asset and liability balances are as of September 30, 1987. The owner's equity balance is as of September 1, 1987.

Cash	$18,000
Service Revenue	12,000
Accounts Payable	2,160
Accounts Receivable	3,120
Cleaning Equipment	14,400
Office Equipment	3,600
Gas and Oil Expense	840
Advertising Expense	360
Wages Expense	5,760
Marcie Thomas, Capital, September 1, 1987	30,288
Truck	7,200
Notes Payable	9,600
Rent Expense	720
Miscellaneous Expense	48

Required:

a. Prepare an income statement for the month ended September 30, 1987.

b. Prepare a balance sheet as of September 30, 1987. You will need to calculate the September 30, 1987, balance in the owner's capital account.

P1–5–A

Prepare summary of transactions, income statement, and balance sheet

The transactions appearing below are those of the Russell Jacobs Company for the month of April 1987. This was the first month of operation of the business.

Transactions:

1. Owner invested capital, $100,000.
2. Purchased cleaning equipment on account, $30,000.
3. Earned service revenue on account, $24,000.
4. Collected cash on account, $8,000.
5. Paid wages, $6,000.
6. Paid rent, $4,000.
7. Received bill for advertising for April, $1,200.
8. Paid an account payable, $30,000.

Required:

a. Prepare a summary of transactions using a format similar to Illustration 1.5 in the chapter. Use money columns headed Cash, Accounts Receivable, Cleaning Equipment, Accounts Payable, and Russell Jacobs, Capital. Determine new balances after each transaction.

b. Prepare an income statement for April 1987.

c. Prepare a balance sheet as of April 30, 1987.

P1–6–A

Prepare summary of transactions, income statement, and balance sheet

Following are the transactions for August 1987 of the Twilite Theater, a theater owned by Robert Foster.

Transactions:

Aug. 2 Paid current month's rent of building, $8,400.

15 Cash withdrawal by owner was $800.

24 Received and paid month's advertising bill, $3,040.

27 Miscellaneous expenses were paid to the supplier of various items and services, $1,120.

31 Paid rental on films shown during month, $8,000.

31 Received $9,920 cash as concession revenue from the operator of various concessions who sold candy, popcorn, and similar items in the theater during August.

31 Cash ticket revenue for August was $18,640. (Actually cash would be received daily throughout the month, but we assume it was all received on August 31 to simplify the problem.)

31 Paid payroll for the month, $10,320.

Required: a.   Prepare a summary of transactions (see Illustration 1.5, except do not bother to include subtotals after each transaction). Include money columns for Cash and Robert Foster, Capital only. Beginning balances were Cash, $32,000, and Robert Foster, Capital, $32,000.
　　　　　b.   Prepare an income statement for August 1987.
　　　　　c.   Prepare a balance sheet as of August 31, 1987.

P1–7–A

Prepare summary of transactions, income statement, and balance sheet (beginning balances in the accounts)

The balance sheet of Tara Tucker Company as of April 30, 1987, was as follows:

TARA TUCKER COMPANY
Balance Sheet
April 30, 1987

Assets

Cash	$ 28,000
Accounts receivable	80,000
Land	300,000
Total assets	$408,000

Liabilities and Owner's Equity

Liabilities:

Accounts payable	$ 72,000

Owner's equity:

Marianne Mills, capital	336,000
Total liabilities and owner's equity . .	$408,000

Summarized, the transactions for the month of May 1987, were as follows:

Transactions:

1.   The owner invested an additional $100,000 cash in the business.
2.   Collected $60,000 on account receivable.
3.   Paid $52,000 on account payable.
4.   Sold land costing $100,000 for $100,000 cash.
5.   Decorating services were rendered to a major department store on account, $190,000.
6.   Paid payroll for the month, $110,000.
7.   The owner withdrew $12,000 cash.

Required: a.   Prepare a summary of transactions (Illustration 1.5) using column headings for items appearing in the above balance sheet. Enter the balances shown in the April 30, 1987, balance sheet as beginning balances in the summary of transactions. Determine balances after each transaction.
　　　　　b.   Prepare an income statement for the month of May 1987.
　　　　　c.   Prepare a balance sheet as of May 31, 1987.

PROBLEMS, SERIES B

P1–1–B

Prepare income statement and balance sheet

Analysis of the summary of transactions for the Ten-Pin Bowling Lanes for the month of January 1987 revealed the following ending balances:

Balances, January 31, 1987:

Cash	$ 35,000
Land	150,000
Accounts Payable	14,000
Notes Payable	30,000
John Lucia, Capital	141,000

A breakdown of the owner's capital balance showed the following revenues and expenses for the month:

Bowling revenue	$26,000
Rent expense for building and equipment .	11,000
Advertising expense	800
Wages expense	4,000
Utilities expense	1,100

Required:
  a. Prepare an income statement for the month of January 1987.
  b. Prepare a balance sheet as of January 31, 1987.

P1–2–B

Prepare summary of transactions and balance sheet

The Kelly Dillard Company engaged in the following transactions in January 1987, its first month of operations:

Transactions:

1. The owner, Kelly Dillard, invested cash of $100,000 in the business.
2. The owner borrowed $40,000 from his brother-in-law to use in the business after signing a note.
3. The following assets were purchased for cash: truck, $16,000; cleaning equipment, $8,000; and office equipment, $10,000.
4. Office equipment was purchased on account, $12,000.
5. The account payable in (4) was paid, $12,000.

Required:
  a. Prepare a summary of transactions using a format similar to Illustration 1.3 in the chapter. Include money columns for Cash, Truck, Cleaning Equipment, Office Equipment, Accounts Payable, Notes Payable, and Kelly Dillard, Capital. Determine new balances after each transaction.
  b. Prepare a balance sheet as of the end of January.

P1–3–B

Prepare summary of transactions, income statement, and balance sheet

The Drew Huff Company completed the following transactions in July 1987:

Transactions:

1. The company was organized and received $26,000 cash investment from the owner.
2. The company bought equipment for cash at a cost of $19,890.
3. The company performed services for a customer who agreed to pay $2,600 in one week.
4. The company received the $2,600 from transaction (3).
5. Equipment which cost $1,300 was acquired today; payment was postponed until August 28.
6. $780 was paid on the liability incurred in transaction (5).
7. Employee wages for the month were paid, $1,560.

Required:
  a. Prepare a summary of transactions (Illustration 1.5) for the company for the above transactions. Use money columns headed Cash, Accounts Receivable, Equipment, Accounts Payable, and Drew Huff, Capital. Determine balances after each transaction.
  b. Prepare an income statement for July 1987.
  c. Prepare a balance sheet as of July 31, 1987.

P1–4–B

Prepare income statement and balance sheet

The following is a list of balances for the Salem Company. The revenues and expenses are for the month of December 1987. The asset and liability balances are as of December 31, 1987. Edward Salem's equity balance on December 1, 1987, was $32,450.

Office Equipment . .	$ 6,000	Cash	$21,900
Wages Expense . .	5,800	Gas and Oil Expense .	850
Accounts Payable .	1,700	Notes Payable	6,200
Service Revenue . .	11,600	Accounts Receivable . .	4,800
Truck	11,800	Rent Expense	800

Required:
  a. Prepare an income statement for the month ended December 31, 1987.
  b. Prepare a balance sheet as of December 31, 1987. You will need to calculate the December 31, 1987, balance in the owner's capital account.

P1–5–B

Prepare summary of transactions, income statement, and balance sheet

The transactions shown below are for the Emily Gilmer Company for the month of June 1987. This was the first month of operation of the business.

Transactions:

1. Owner invested cash, $42,000.
2. Borrowed $7,000 from a relative to use in the business.
3. Purchased office equipment for cash, $8,400.
4. Performed services for a customer and received cash, $5,600.
5. Paid wages, $2,800.
6. Paid rent, $700.
7. Received bill for gas and oil used, $490.
8. Made a $3,500 payment on notes payable.

Required:

a. Prepare a summary of transactions using a format similar to Illustration 1.5 in the chapter. Use money columns headed Cash, Office Equipment, Accounts Payable, Notes Payable, and Emily Gilmore, Capital. Determine new balances after each transaction.
b. Prepare an income statement for June 1987.
c. Prepare a balance sheet as of June 30, 1987.

P1–6–B

Prepare summary of transactions, income statement, and balance sheet

The following selected transactions are data for the Sara Pattison Company, a parking ramp business, for the month of May 1987.

Transactions:

May 1 Paid May rent on the parking structure, $14,000.
   8 Cash was received for parking services, $34,300. (Actually, cash would be received daily throughout the month, but we assume it was all received on May 8 to simplify the problem.)
  17 Received cash from additional investment by owner, $7,000.
  19 Paid advertising expenses for May, $1,120.
  30 Purchased motorized sweeper to clean parking structure, $8,400. Payment will be made next month.
  31 Paid wages for May, $7,560.

Required:

a. Prepare a summary of transactions (see Illustration 1.5, except do not bother to include subtotals after each transaction). Include money columns for Cash, Equipment, Accounts Payable, and Sara Pattison, Capital. Beginning balances were Cash, $28,000, and Sara Pattison, Capital, $28,000.
b. Prepare an income statement for May 1987.
c. Prepare a balance sheet as of May 31, 1987.

P1–7–B

Prepare summary of transactions, income statement, and balance sheet (beginning balances in the accounts)

The following data are for the John Roebuck Company:

JOHN ROEBUCK COMPANY
Balance Sheet
September 30, 1987

Assets

Cash	$136,000
Accounts receivable	12,000
Total assets	$148,000

Liabilities and Owner's Equity

Liabilities:

Accounts payable	$ 36,000

Owner's equity:

John Roebuck, capital	112,000
Total liabilities and owner's equity	$148,000

Transactions:

Oct. 1   The account payable owed as of September 30 ($36,000) was paid.
2   The company paid rent for October, $12,800.
7   The company received cash from a customer for services performed, $2,800.
10   The company collected $10,000 on account receivable.
14   Cash received from a customer for services, $4,400.
15   Revenue earned but not yet collected from a customer was $2,000.
16   The company paid wages of $2,000 for the period October 1–15.
19   The company paid advertising expenses of $800 for October.
21   Cash received from a customer for services performed, $6,000.
24   The company incurred miscellaneous expenses of $560 for various items and services provided by a supplier. The bill will be paid November 10.
31   Cash received from a customer for services performed, $5,600.
31   The company paid wages of $2,000 for the period October 16–31.
31   A customer was sent a bill for $14,400 for services provided in October.

Required:

a.   Prepare a summary of transactions (Illustration 1.5) using column headings for items given in the above balance sheet. Enter the balances shown in the September 30, 1987, balance sheet as beginning balances in the summary of transactions. Determine balances after each transaction.
b.   Prepare an income statement for October 1987.
c.   Prepare a balance sheet as of October 31, 1987.

BUSINESS DECISION PROBLEM 1–1

Identify information needed to make decision

Upon graduation from high school, Jeff Nolan went to work for a builder of houses and small apartment buildings. During the next six years, Jeff earned a reputation as an excellent employee—hardworking, dedicated, and dependable—in the light construction industry. He could handle almost any job requiring carpentry, electrical, or plumbing skills.

Jeff then decided to go into business for himself under the name of Jeff's Fix-It Shop. He invested cash, some power tools, and a used truck in his business. He completed many repair and remodeling jobs for both homeowners and apartment owners. The demand for his services was so large that he had more than the could handle. He operated out of his garage, which he had converted into a shop, adding several new pieces of power woodworking equipment.

Now two years after going into business for himself, Jeff is faced with a decision of whether to continue in his own business or to accept a position as construction supervisor for a home builder. He has been offered an annual salary of $50,000 and a package of "fringe benefits'" (medical and hospitalization insurance, pension contribution, vacation and sick pay, and life insurance) worth approximately $10,000 per year. The offer is very attractive to Jeff. But he dislikes giving up his business since he has thoroughly enjoyed "being his own boss," even though it has led to an average workweek well in excess of the standard 40-hour week.

Required:

Suppose Jeff comes to you for assistance in gathering the information needed to help him make a decision. He brings along the accounting records that have been maintained for his business by an experienced accountant. Using logic and your own life experiences, indicate the nature of the information Jeff needs if he is to make an informed decision. Pay particular attention to the information likely to be found in the accounting records for his business that would be useful. Does the accounting information available enter directly into the decision? Explain.

BUSINESS DECISION PROBLEM 1–2

Prepare income statement and balance sheet; judge profitability of company

Analysis of the transactions of the Sunset Drive-In Theater, owned by Tom Summers, for the month of June 1987 discloses the following:

Ticket revenue	$71,000
Rent expense for premises and equipment	9,000
Film rental expense paid	17,800
Revenue received from operators of candy and popcorn concessions	10,000
Advertising expense	8,400
Wages and salaries expense	15,600
Utilities expense	5,000

Asset and liability amounts as of June 30 which the accountant has calculated include the following:

Cash	$100,000
Land	16,000
Accounts payable	20,800

The balance in the Tom Summers, Capital account on June 1 was $70,000.

Required:

a. Prepare an income statement for the month of June 1987.
b. Prepare a balance sheet as of June 30, 1987.
c. Did the month of June seem to be a profitable month for this company?

BUSINESS SITUATION FOR DISCUSSION

Goal: Ethical Standards for Accounting Practices*
Lee Berton

Los Angeles—It isn't often that accountants meet with theologians. But recently, the University of Southern California decided to put the two groups together.

One purpose of the conference, cosponsored by USC's schools of business and religion, was to give the two dozen top CPA partners attending some sort of ethical sextant by which to guide their moral viewpoint.

A lot of people think such a guide is needed. They believe that accounting ethics is an oxymoron, like the Long Island Expressway or government efficiency. And they worry that competition in the accounting profession is eroding ethics even more, making accountants increasingly wary of blowing the whistle on clients who are manipulating accounting rules. For example, critics have long charged that accountants, when asked by their

* Reprinted by permission of *The Wall Street Journal,* © Dow Jones & Company, May 24, 1984, p. 32. All rights reserved.

clients, "What does two plus two equal?" will respond: "What would you like it to be?"

The technical jargon of debt-equity ratios, audit sampling and internal controls isn't usual fare for philosophers.

Thus, it was a shock for the accountants when they were confronted by Norman Bowie, director of the University of Delaware's Center for Ethical Studies and an unstructured thinker by trade.

The accountants were particularly surprised that Mr. Bowie could so quickly grasp their perpetual ethics problem: how to balance their responsibility to the public against the fact that their corporate clients, whose annual reports they audit, pay their fees and can switch auditors at the blink of an eye.

Mr. Bowie suggested that accountants, like educators, be given tenure so that they couldn't be fired unless their clients proved incompetence or lack of morals. This tenure would be given only after a suitable trial period.

"Accountants, like teachers, are supposed to give their clients report cards," Mr. Bowie noted. "As teachers, we, too, judge students, but they don't directly pay our salaries and the stakes aren't so high."

Jack Farrell, a retired managing partner of Price Waterhouse, said that professional ethics can conflict with the growing pressures on accountants.

Citing a typical audit client, Mr. Farrell noted that the company's annual report had only three pages of financial data in 1970. "Today, that report has 12½ pages of such data," he noted. "Demand for good ac-

countants is growing much faster than supply, and with financial information exploding, it's tougher to meet burgeoning public expectations for accountability and precision."

To put it another way, Mr. Farrell noted that while professional ethics requires "technical competence," such competence sometimes takes a back seat to a partner's ability to churn out information.

*   *   *   *   *

PART 2

Processing Accounting Information

CHAPTER 2

Recording Business Transactions

LEARNING OBJECTIVES

After studying this chapter, you should be able to:

1. Use the account as the basic classifying and storage unit for information.
2. Express the effects of business transactions in terms of debits and credits to six different types of accounts.
3. Record the effects of business transactions in a journal.
4. Post journal entries to the accounts in the ledger.
5. Prepare a trial balance to test the equality of debits and credits in the journalizing and posting process.
6. Define and use correctly the new terms in the glossary.

As you learned in Chapter 1, there are three forms of business organizations—single proprietorships, partnerships, and corporations—performing three types of business activities—service, merchandising, and manufacturing. The two most common financial statements produced by these business organizations are the balance sheet (which indicates the solvency of the business) and the income statement (which indicates the profitability of the business). These statements are the end products of the financial accounting process (or cycle), which has as its foundation the accounting equation.

The raw data of accounting are the business transactions. In Chapter 1, transactions were recorded as increases or decreases in accounting equation items. However, as you probably noticed when working through the sample transactions given in Chapter 1, listing all business transactions under three categories would become most cumbersome in actual practice. Most businesses, even small ones, enter into many transactions every day. Chapter 2 teaches you how business transactions are actually recorded in the accounting process.

To understand the dual procedure of recording business transactions with debits and credits, you begin by using the T-account, which classifies and summarizes the measurements of business activity. Then you learn about the ledger—a collection of accounts. You will follow a company through its various business transactions using these new tools. The need for a journal is explained, and soon you will be "journalizing." The recording of transactions must be checked for the equality of debits and credits. The trial balance is useful in doing this.

■ THE ACCOUNT

A business may engage in thousands of transactions during a period of time. The data in these transactions must be classified and summarized before becoming useful information. Making the accountant's task somewhat easier is the fact that most business transactions are repetitive in nature and can be classified into groups having common characteristics. For example, there may be thousands of receipts or payments of cash. As a result, a part of every cash transaction can be recorded and summarized in a single place called an account.

An **account** is an element in an accounting system that is used to classify and summarize measurements of business activity. An account will be set up whenever it is necessary to provide useful information about a particular business item. Thus, every business will have a **Cash account** in its accounting system simply because knowledge of the amount of cash owned is useful information.

Accountants may differ on the account title (or name) they give for the same item. For example, one person might name an account Notes Payable and another might call it Loans Payable. Both account titles refer to the amounts borrowed by the company. The account title should be logical to facilitate the accountant grouping similar transactions into the same account. Once an account is given a title, that same title must be used throughout the accounting records.

Accounts may take on a variety of formats. Some accounts are printed and entries are written in by hand; others are on magnetic tape and "invisible" entries are encoded by a computer. Every account format must provide for increases and decreases in the item for which the account was established. Then the account balance (the difference between the increases and decreases) may be determined.

The number of accounts in a company's accounting system depends on what information is needed by those interested in the business. **The main requirement is that each account provide useful information.** Thus, one account may be set up for all cash rather than having a separate account for each form of cash (coins on hand, dollars on hand, and deposits in banks). The amount of cash is useful information; the form of cash is not.

The T-Account

To understand how the increases and decreases in an account are recorded, textbooks use the T-account; it derives its name from the fact that it looks like the letter *T*. The title (name) of the item accounted for, such as cash, is written across the top of the T. Increases are recorded on one side of the vertical line of the T and decreases on the other side, depending on the type of account. A T-account appears as follows:

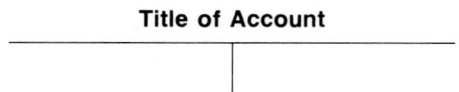

Title of Account

In Chapter 1, you saw that each business transaction affected at least two items. For example, if you—an owner—invest cash into your business, your assets would increase and your owner's equity would increase. This was illustrated in the summary of transactions schedule given in Illustration 1–3, Chapter 1. Using debits and credits and the double-entry procedure, in the next sections we explain how the increases and decreases caused by business transactions are actually recorded in accounting.

Debits and Credits

The accountant uses the term debit (or charge) in lieu of saying "place an entry on the left side of the T-account" and credit for "place an entry on the right side of the T-account." **Debit** (abbreviated Dr.) simply means left side; **credit** (abbreviated Cr.) means right side. A debit entry is an entry on the left side of an account, while a credit entry is an entry on the right side of an account. **Thus, for any account, the left side is the debit side and the right side is the credit side:**

Any Account

Left or debit side	Right or credit side

A synonym for **debit** an account is charge an account.

Double-Entry Procedure

Once a business event is recognized as a business transaction, it is analyzed to determine its increase or decrease effect on the assets, liabilities, owner's equity, revenues, or expenses of the business. These increase or decrease effects are then translated into debits and credits.

In each business transaction that is recorded, the total dollar amount of debits must equal the total dollar amount of credits. This means that when one account (or accounts) is debited for $100, another account (or accounts) must be credited for a total of $100. The requirement that each transaction must be recorded by an entry that has equal debits and credits is called the double-entry procedure, or duality. This double-entry procedure keeps the accounting equation in balance.

The dual recording process produces two sets of accounts—those with debit balances and those with credit balances. When the totals of these two groups of accounts are equal, the accountant has some assurance that the arithmetic part of the transaction recording process has been properly carried out. You are now ready to learn how to actually record business transactions in T-accounts using debits and credits.

Recording Changes in Assets, Liabilities, and Owner's Equity. In Chapter 1, you learned that the basic accounting equation is:

$$Assets = Liabilities + Owner's\ Equity$$

When you begin to record transactions into the T-accounts of the accounting equation, think first of the equal sign. Then you must remember that assets, to the left of the equal sign, are increased on the left side of the T-accounts. Liabilities and owner's equity, to the right of the equal sign, are increased on the right side of the T-accounts. You already know that the left side of the T-account is the debit side and the right side is the credit side. So you should be able to fill in the rest of the increases and decreases rules by deduction, such as:

Assets		=	Liabilities		+	Owner's Equity	
Debit for increases	Credit for decreases		Debit for decreases	Credit for increases		Debit for decreases	Credit for increases

To summarize:

1. Assets are **increased** by debits on the left side of the T-account and **decreased** by credits on the right side of the T-account.
2. Liabilities and owner's equity are **decreased** by debits on the left side of the T-account and **increased** by credits on the right side of the T-account.

Applying these two rules keeps the accounting equation in balance. And now we will apply these debit and credit rules for assets, liabilities, and owner's equity to actual business transactions.

Assume that John Stevens invested $10,000 in his company. The company records the receipt of $10,000 as follows:

(Dr.)	Cash	(Cr.)	(Dr.)	John Stevens, Capital	(Cr.)
(1)	10,000			(1)	10,000

The transaction involves an increase in the asset, cash, which is recorded on the left side of the Cash account, and an increase in owner's equity, which is recorded on the right side of the John Stevens, Capital account.

Assume John Stevens went to the bank and borrowed $5,000 on a note. As explained in Chapter 1, a **note** is a written promise to pay to another party (in this case the bank) the amount owed either when demanded or at a certain specified date. The transaction is recorded as follows:

(Dr.)	Cash	(Cr.)	(Dr.)	Notes Payable—Bank	(Cr.)
(2)	5,000			(2)	5,000

Note that liabilities, in this case Notes Payable—Bank, are increased by an entry on the right (credit) side of the account.

Recording Changes in Revenues and Expenses.   In Chapter 1, we recorded the revenues and expenses directly in the owner's capital account. However, in actual practice this is not recommended because of the volume of revenue and expense transactions. Since the amounts of revenues and expenses are needed to prepare the income statement, a separate account should be kept for each revenue and expense. Expense accounts are treated as if they were subclassifications of the debit side of the owner's capital account, and revenue accounts as if they were subclassifications of the credit side. The revenue and expense recording rules are:

1. Increases in revenues are recorded on the right (credit) side of the T-account and decreases on the left (debit) side. This is because revenues increase owner's equity and, as you learned earlier, increases in owner's equity are recorded on the right side.
2. Increases in expenses are recorded on the left (debit) side of the T-account and decreases on the right (credit) side. This is because expenses decrease owner's equity and, as you learned earlier, decreases in owner's equity are recorded on the left side.

To illustrate these rules, assume a company received $800 cash from a customer for services rendered. The Cash account, an asset, is increased on the left (debit) side of the T-account; and the Service Revenue account, an increase in owner's equity, is increased on the right (credit) side.

(Dr.)	**Cash**	(Cr.)	(Dr.)	**Service Revenue**	(Cr.)
(3)	800			(3)	800

Assume a company paid $600 wages to employees. The Cash account, an asset, is decreased on the right (credit) side of the T-account; and the Wages Expense account, a decrease in owner's equity, is increased on the left (debit) side.[1]

(Dr.)	**Cash**	(Cr.)	(Dr.)	**Wages Expense**	(Cr.)
	(4)	600	(4)	600	

Recording Withdrawals by the Owner. Owner withdrawals are a distribution of assets to the owner. Just as an owner investment increases owner's equity, owner withdrawals reduce it. Since owner withdrawals reduce the owner's equity in the business, they have the same effect on owner's equity as an expense.

Owner withdrawals could be shown directly as a reduction of the owner's capital account balance by entering the amount on the left (debit) side of that account. But a clearer record of withdrawals is available if a separate drawing account is used to record all amounts withdrawn. A drawing account acts like a subclassification of the owner's capital account, as are revenues and expenses. Withdrawals are shown as debits to the owner's drawing account. The drawing account is increased by debits and decreased by credits.

A withdrawal of $100 cash by John Stevens would be shown as follows:

(Dr.)	**Cash**	(Cr.)	(Dr.)	**John Stevens, Drawing**	(Cr.)
	(5)	100	(5)	100	

---

[1] Certain deductions are normally taken out of employees' pay for social security taxes, federal and state withholding, and so on. Those deductions will be ignored until the topic of payroll is covered in more detail (Chapter 12).

There comes a time when a business owner looks at the company accounts with all the debits and credits and asks, "Where am I financially—ahead or behind?" The only way the owner can determine this is to balance the accounts. The next section explains how to balance an account.

Determining the Balance of an Account

The balance of any T-account is obtained by totaling the debits to the account, totaling the credits to the account, and subtracting the smaller sum from the larger. If the sum of the debits exceeds the sum of the credits, the account has a **debit balance**. For example, the Cash account shown below uses the information from the preceding transactions. The account has a debit balance of $15,100, computed as total debits of $15,800 less total credits of $700.

(Dr.)		Cash		(Cr.)
(1)	10,000		(4)	600
(2)	5,000		(5)	100
(3)	800			
	15,800			700
Dr. bal.	15,100			

If, on the other hand, the sum of the credits exceeds the sum of the debits, the account will have a **credit balance**. For instance, assume that a company has an Accounts Payable account with a total of $10,000 in debits and $13,000 in credits. It will have a credit balance of $3,000 as shown in the following T-account:

(Dr.)	Accounts Payable	(Cr.)
10,000		7,000
		6,000
10,000		13,000
	Cr. Bal.	3,000

Normal Balances.   Since asset, expense, and drawing accounts are increased by debits, they **normally** have debit (or left side) balances. Conversely, liability, owner's equity, and revenue accounts are increased by credits and **normally** have credit (or right side) balances.

The normal balances of the six types of accounts we have used are given in the following diagram:

Accounts Normally Having a Debit Balance	Accounts Normally Having a Credit Balance
Assets	Liabilities
Expenses	Owner's equity
Owner's drawing	Revenues

Rules of Debit and Credit Summarized

It is important at this point to summarize the rules of debit and credit. You may find it necessary to memorize these rules at first. Later, as you proceed in your study of accounting, the rules will become automatic and you no longer will have to ask yourself, "Is this increase or decrease a debit or credit?"

As we stated earlier, asset accounts are increased on the debit side, while liabilities and owner's equity accounts are increased on the credit side. When the account balances are totaled, they will conform to the following two independent equations:

$$\text{Assets} = \text{Liabilities} + \text{Owner's equity}$$

$$\text{Debit} = \text{Credits}$$

The arrangement of these two formulas gives the first three rules of debit and credit:

1. Increases in asset accounts are debits; decreases are credits.
2. Decreases in liability accounts are debits; increases are credits.
3. Decreases in owner's equity accounts are debits; increases are credits.

The debit and credit rules for expense and revenue accounts follow if you remember that expenses are decreases in owner's equity and revenues are increases in owner's equity. Since owner's equity accounts decrease on the debit side, expense accounts increase on the debit side; and since owner's equity accounts increase on the credit side, revenue accounts increase on the credit side. Debit and credit rules 4 and 5 are:

4. Decreases in revenue accounts are debits; increases are credits.
5. Increases in expense accounts are debits; decreases are credits.

Illustration 2.1 *Rules of Debit and Credit*

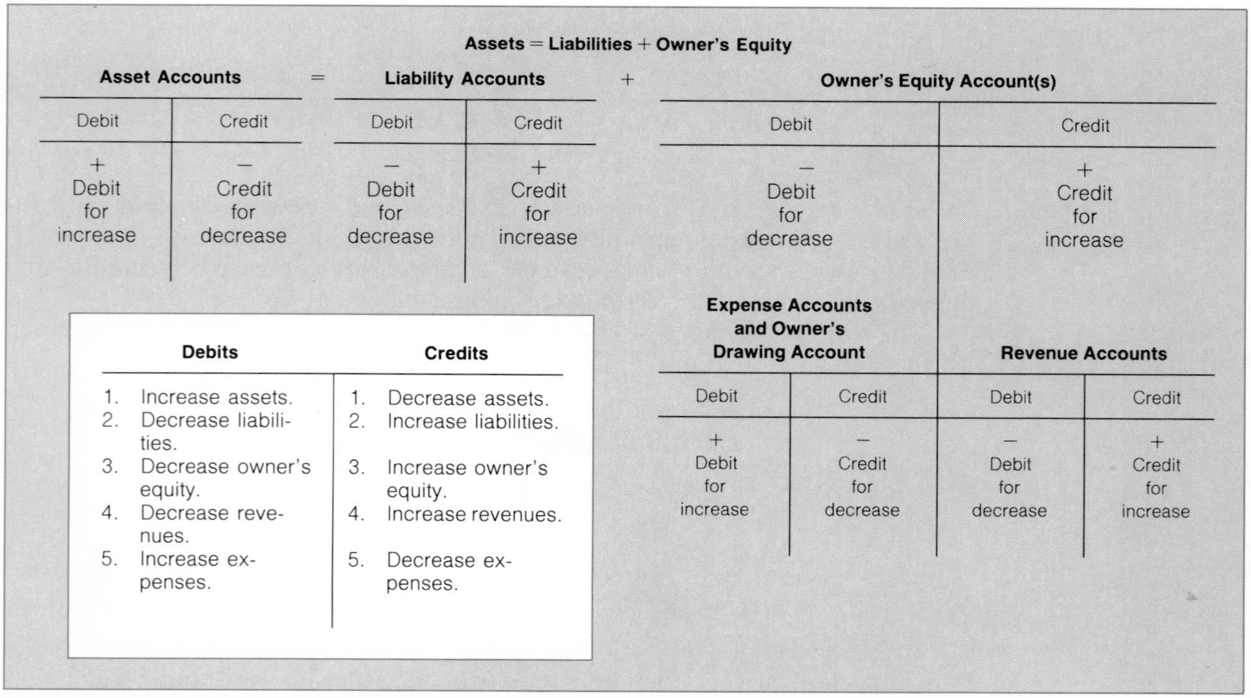

These five rules of debit and credit are shown in Illustration 2.1. Note the treatment of expense accounts as if they were merely subclassifications of the debit side of the owner's capital account and revenue accounts as if they were subclassifications of the credit side of the owner's capital account. Also note that assets, which are seemingly "good" things, and expenses, which are seemingly "bad" things, both increase on the debit side, and that liability and revenue accounts both increase on the credit side. This reinforces the fact that in accounting "debit" and "credit" are neutral terms and do not connote value judgments.

■ THE LEDGER

A ledger (general ledger) is the complete collection of all the accounts of a company. Accounts are classified into two general groups: (1) **balance sheet accounts** (assets, liabilities, and owner's equity) and (2) **income statement accounts** (revenues and expenses). Balance sheet accounts are also called real accounts because they are **not** subclassifications or subdivisions of any other account. Income statement accounts are also called nominal accounts because they are merely subclassifications of the owner's equity accounts. "Nominal" literally means, "in name only." Nominal accounts temporarily contain the revenue and expense information that eventually becomes part of the balance of a real account, owner's capital. The ledger may be in loose-leaf form, in a bound volume, or in a computer memory.

A complete listing of account titles and account numbers of all the accounts in the ledger is known as the chart of accounts. The chart of accounts is comparable to a table of contents. Each account typically has an identification number as well as a title to help locate accounts when recording data. For example, asset accounts might be numbered 100–199; liability accounts, 200–299; owner's equity accounts and drawing account, 300–399; revenue accounts, 400–499; and expense accounts, 500–599. Other numbering systems may be used. For instance, sometimes the accounts are numbered in sequence starting with 1, 2, and so on. **The important idea is that some numbering system typically is used.** The groups of accounts usually appear in the following order in the ledger—assets, liabilities, owner's equity, owner's drawing, revenues, and expenses. Individual accounts are arranged in numerical sequence in the ledger.

Now that you understand how to record debits and credits in an account and how all accounts together form a ledger, you are ready to study the accounting process in operation. To illustrate the accounting process, we use the Rapid Delivery Company, owned by John Turner, as our example.

■ THE ACCOUNTING PROCESS IN OPERATION

John Turner owns a small delivery service company, the Rapid Delivery Company. The accounting process used by John Turner is similar to that of any small company. The ledger accounts used in this chapter for the Rapid Delivery Company are as follows:

Account No.	Account title	Description
100	Cash	Bank deposits and cash on hand.
101	Accounts Receivable	Amounts owed to the company by customers.
102	Supplies on Hand	Items such as paper, envelopes, writing materials, rope, and other materials used in performing services for customers or in doing administrative and clerical office work.
103	Prepaid Insurance	Insurance policy premium paid in advance of the periods for which the insurance coverage applies.
104	Prepaid Rent	Rent paid in advance of the periods for which the rent payment applies.
110	Delivery Trucks	Trucks used to perform delivery services for customers.
200	Accounts Payable	Amounts owed to creditors for items purchased from them.
201	Unearned Delivery Fees	Amounts received from customers before the services have been performed for the customers.
300	John Turner, Capital	The owner's equity or interest in the business.
301	John Turner, Drawing	The amount of withdrawals made by the owner this accounting period.
400	Delivery Service Revenue	Amounts earned by performing delivery services for customers.
500	Advertising Expense	The cost of advertising incurred in the current period.
501	Gas and Oil Expense	The cost of gas and oil used in trucks in the current period.
502	Salaries Expense	The amount of salaries incurred in the current period.
503	Utilities Expense	The cost of utilities incurred in the current period.

Assets — 100–110
Liabilities — 200–201
Owner's equity — 300–301
Revenues — 400
Expenses — 500–503

Other accounts to be used for the Rapid Delivery Company will be introduced in the next chapter.

Transaction 1: **The Rapid Delivery Company was formed on November 28, 1987, when the owner, John Turner, invested $50,000 in the business. The accounts were affected as follows:**

(Dr.)	**Cash**	(Cr.)	(Dr.)	**John Turner, Capital**	(Cr.)
50,000					50,000

Cash is increased (debited) and John Turner, Capital is increased (credited) by $50,000. No other transactions occurred in November. The company prepares financial statements at the end of each month. The company's balance sheet at November 30, 1987, is shown in Illustration 2.2.

1. **Date column.** The first column on each general journal page is for the date. For the first journal entry on a page, the year, the month, and the day (number) are entered here. For all other journal entries on a page, only the day of the month is shown, until the month changes.

2. **Account Titles and Explanation column.** The first line of an entry shows the account debited. The second line shows the account credited. Notice that the account title for the credit is indented to the right. For instance, in Illustration 2.3 the debit to the Cash account is shown first and the credit to the John Turner, Capital account is shown next. Any necessary explanation of a transaction appears on the line(s) below the credit entry and is indented halfway between the debit and credit entries. A journal entry explanation should be complete enough to fully describe the transaction and prove the entry's accuracy, and yet should be concise. If a journal entry is self-explanatory, the explanation may be omitted.

3. **Posting Reference column.** This column shows the account number of the account that has been debited or credited. For instance, the number 100 in the first entry means that the Cash account number is 100. No number appears in this column until the information is posted to the appropriate ledger account. Posting is discussed later in the chapter.

4. **Debit column.** This column is where the amount of the debit is placed on the same line as the title of the account debited.

5. **Credit column.** The amount of credit is placed in this column on the same line as the title of the account credited.

Illustration 2.3 *General Journal*

	Date	Account Titles and Explanation	Post. Ref.	Debit	Credit
GENERAL JOURNAL					*Page 1*
1987 Nov.	28	Cash	100	5 0 0 0 0	
		John Turner, Capital	300		5 0 0 0 0
		The owner invested $50,000 cash in the			
		business.			

Illustration 2.4 shows how the December transactions of the Rapid Delivery Company presented on pages 55–60 would be journalized. As shown in Illustration 2.4, a line is skipped between each journal entry to show where one journal entry ends and another begins. This is standard practice among accountants. Note that dollar signs are not used in journals or ledgers. When amounts are in even dollar amounts, the cents column may be left blank, or zeros or a dash may be used. When lined accounting work papers are used, there is no need to use commas or a period in recording an amount. When using unlined paper, both commas and a period should be used.

Illustration 2.4 *General Journal—Extended Illustration*

RAPID DELIVERY COMPANY
GENERAL JOURNAL

Page 1

Date		Account Titles and Explanation	Post. Ref.	Debit	Credit
1987 Dec.	1.	Delivery Trucks	110	4 0 0 0 0	
		Cash	100		4 0 0 0 0
		To record the purchase of four delivery trucks.			
	1	Prepaid Insurance	103	2 4 0 0	
		Accounts Payable	200		2 4 0 0
		Purchased truck insurance to cover a one-year period.			
	1	Prepaid Rent	104	1 2 0 0	
		Cash	100		1 2 0 0
		Paid three months' rent on a building.			
	4	Supplies on Hand	102	1 4 0 0	
		Accounts Payable	200		1 4 0 0
		To record the purchase of supplies for future use.			
	7	Cash	100	4 5 0 0	
		Unearned Delivery Fees	201		4 5 0 0
		To record the receipt of cash from a customer in payment for future delivery services.			
	15	Cash	100	5 0 0 0	
		Delivery Service Revenue	400		5 0 0 0
		To record the receipt of cash for performing delivery services for a customer.			
	17	Accounts Payable	200	1 4 0 0	
		Cash	100		1 4 0 0
		Paid the account payable arising from the purchase of supplies on December 4.			
	20	Accounts Receivable	101	5 7 0 0	
		Delivery Service Revenue	400		5 7 0 0
		To record the performance of delivery services on account for which a customer was billed.			

Illustration 2.4 *(concluded)*

GENERAL JOURNAL   *Page 2*

Date	Account Titles and Explanation	Post. Ref.	Debit	Credit
24	Advertising Expense	500	5 0	
	Accounts Payable	200		5 0
	Received a bill for advertising for the month			
	of December.			
26	Cash	100	5 0 0	
	Accounts Receivable	101		5 0 0
	Received $500 from a customer			
	on accounts receivable.			
28	Salaries Expense	502	3 6 0 0	
	Cash	100		3 6 0 0
	Paid truck driver salaries for the first four			
	weeks of December.			
29	Utilities Expense	503	1 5 0	
	Cash	100		1 5 0
	Paid the utilities bill for December.			
30	Gas and Oil Expense	501	6 8 0	
	Accounts Payable	200		6 8 0
	Received a bill for gas and oil used in the			
	trucks in December.			
31	John Turner, Drawing	301	3 0 0 0	
	Cash	100		3 0 0 0
	The owner withdrew $3,000 to pay			
	personal expenses.			

Journalizing

Journalizing is the process of entering a transaction in a journal. Business information comes from a variety of source documents such as invoices, cash register tapes, timecards, and checks. The information appearing on these documents must be analyzed to determine the specific accounts affected and the dollar amounts of the changes. Then the proper journal entry must be recorded.

Posting

A journal entry is like a set of instructions. The carrying out of these instructions is known as posting. **Posting** is recording in the ledger the information contained in the journal. A journal entry directs the entry of a certain dollar amount as a debit in a specific ledger account and directs the entry of a certain dollar amount as a credit in a specific ledger account. First, let's use a new situation, the Sandra Jenks Company, to illustrate the posting process. In Illustration 2.5, the first journal entry directs that $10,000 be posted in the ledger as a debit to the Cash account and as a credit to the Sandra Jenks, Capital account. Later, you will be shown how the Rapid Delivery Company journal entries are posted.

The debit is posted in the general ledger Cash account by entering the date, a short explanation, the page number of the journal from which posted, and the $10,000 in the Debit column. Then the account number (100) to which the debit is posted is entered in the Posting Reference column of the general journal. The credit is posted in a similar manner but as a credit to Account No. 300. The arrows in the illustration show how these amounts have been posted to the correct accounts.

This illustration also shows the three-column balance type of account. In contrast to the two-sided T-account format shown so far, the three-column format has columns for debit, credit, and balance. One advantage of this form is that the balance of the account is shown after each item has been posted. In addition, in this chapter we indicate whether each balance is a debit or a credit. In subsequent chapters and in practice, the nature of the balance is not indicated since it is understood. Also, notice that an explanation is given for each item in the ledger accounts. Often these explanations are omitted because each item can be traced back to the general journal for the explanation.

Posting is always from the journal to the ledger accounts. Postings may be made (1) at the time the transaction is journalized; (2) at the end of the day, week, or month; or (3) as each journal page is filled.

Cross-Indexing

Since it is frequently necessary for accountants to check and trace the origin of their transactions, they provide for cross-indexing. **Cross-indexing** is the placing of (1) the account number of the ledger account in the general journal and (2) the general journal page number in the ledger account. As shown in Illustration 2.5, the account number of the ledger account to which the posting was made is placed in the Posting Reference column of the journal. Note the arrow from Account No. 100 in the ledger to the 100 in the Posting Reference column beside the first debit in the general journal. The number of the general journal page **from** which the entry was posted is placed in the Posting Reference column of the ledger account. Note the arrow from page 1 in the general journal to G1 in the Posting Reference column of the general ledger. The date of the transaction is also shown in the general ledger. Note the arrows from the date in the general journal to the dates in the general ledger.

Cross-indexing aids the tracing of any recorded transaction, either from general journal to ledger or from ledger to general journal. Cross-reference numbers normally are not placed in the Posting Reference column of the journal until the entry is posted. If this practice is followed, the cross-reference numbers indicate the entry has been posted.

An understanding of the posting and cross-indexing process can be obtained by tracing the entries from the general journal to the ledger. The ledger accounts

Illustration 2.5   *General Journal and General Ledger; Posting and Cross-Indexing*

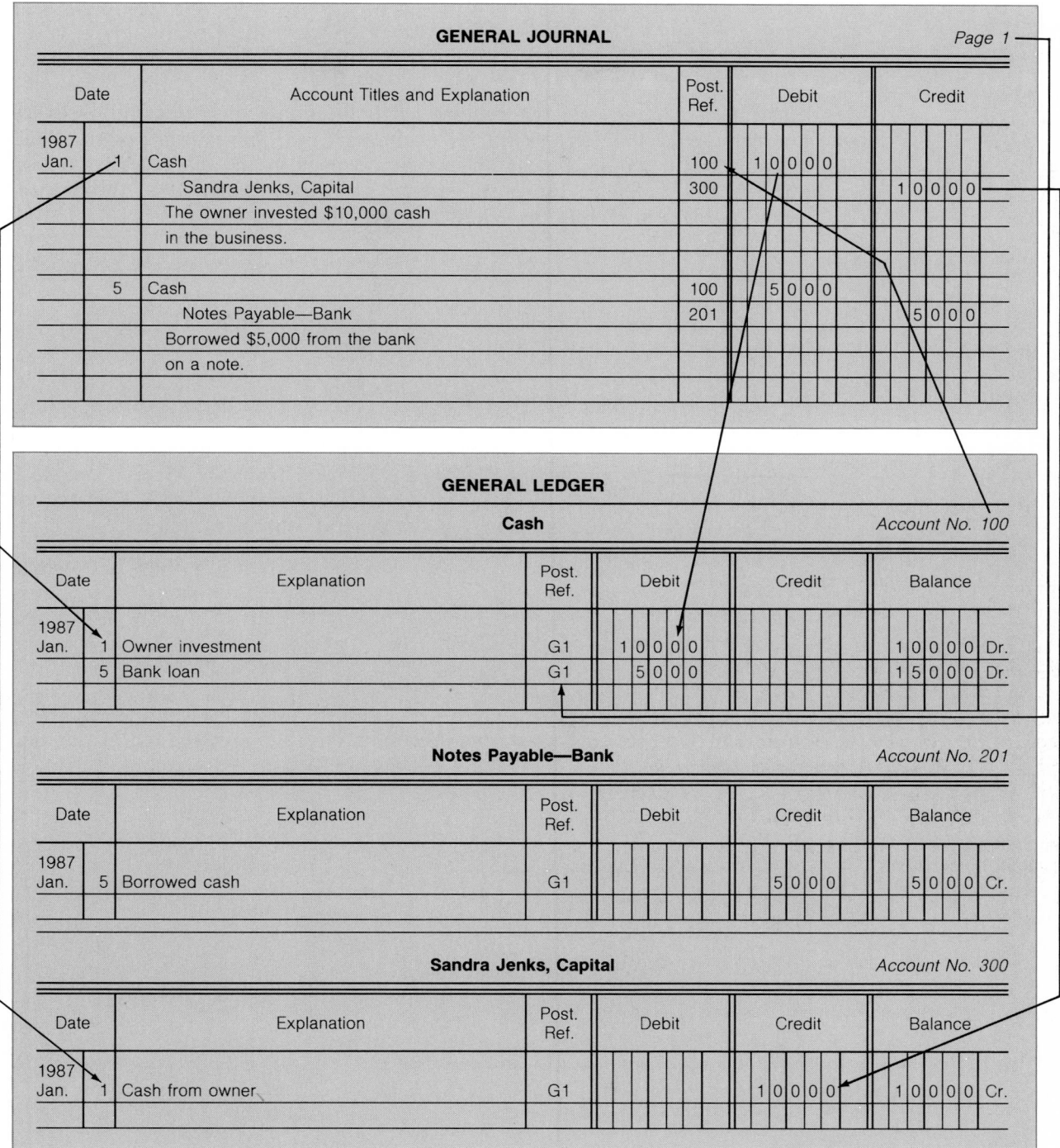

GENERAL JOURNAL   *Page 1*

Date		Account Titles and Explanation	Post. Ref.	Debit	Credit
1987 Jan.	1	Cash	100	1 0 0 0 0	
		Sandra Jenks, Capital	300		1 0 0 0 0
		The owner invested $10,000 cash			
		in the business.			
	5	Cash	100	5 0 0 0	
		Notes Payable—Bank	201		5 0 0 0
		Borrowed $5,000 from the bank			
		on a note.			

GENERAL LEDGER

Cash   *Account No. 100*

Date		Explanation	Post. Ref.	Debit	Credit	Balance
1987 Jan.	1	Owner investment	G1	1 0 0 0 0		1 0 0 0 0 Dr.
	5	Bank loan	G1	5 0 0 0		1 5 0 0 0 Dr.

Notes Payable—Bank   *Account No. 201*

Date		Explanation	Post. Ref.	Debit	Credit	Balance
1987 Jan.	5	Borrowed cash	G1		5 0 0 0	5 0 0 0 Cr.

Sandra Jenks, Capital   *Account No. 300*

Date		Explanation	Post. Ref.	Debit	Credit	Balance
1987 Jan.	1	Cash from owner	G1		1 0 0 0 0	1 0 0 0 0 Cr.

need not contain explanations of all the entries, since any needed explanations can be obtained from the journal.

Posting and Cross-Indexing—An Illustration

Illustration 2.6 presents the general ledger accounts of the Rapid Delivery Company after the journal entries on pages 62–63 have been posted. Each ledger account would appear on a separate page in the ledger. You should trace at least a few of the postings from the general journal to the general ledger to make sure you know how to post journal entries.

Compound Journal Entries

Many business transactions affect more than two accounts. The journal entry for these transactions will involve more than one debit and/or credit; such an entry is called a compound journal entry. An entry with one debit and one credit is a **simple journal entry.** All the journal entries illustrated so far have been simple journal entries.

As an illustration of a compound journal entry, assume that on July 1, 1988, John Turner purchased $8,000 of machinery from the Myers Company, paying $2,000 cash with the balance due on December 31, 1989. The journal entry for Turner would be shown in the general journal as follows:

		Debit	*Credit*
1988			
July 1	Machinery	8,000	
	Cash		2,000
	Accounts Payable		6,000
	Machinery purchased from Myers Company, Invoice No. 42.		

Note that two accounts, Cash and Accounts Payable, are credited in this one transaction.

Summary of Functions and Advantages of a Journal

The functions and advantages of using a journal are summarized below. The journal—

1. Records each transaction in chronological order.
2. Shows the analysis of each transaction in terms of debit and credit.
3. Supplies an explanation of each transaction when necessary.
4. Serves as a source for future reference to accounting transactions.
5. Removes lengthy explanations from the accounts.
6. Makes possible posting to the ledger at convenient times.
7. Assists in maintaining the ledger in balance.
8. Aids in tracing errors.

■ THE TRIAL BALANCE

Periodically accountants use a trial balance to test the equality of their debits and credits. A trial balance is a listing of the ledger accounts and their debit

Illustration 2.6   *General Ledger—Extended Illustration*

GENERAL LEDGER

Cash   Account No. 100

Date		Explanation	Post. Ref.	Debit	Credit	Balance	
1987 Dec.	1	Beginning balance*				5 0 0 0 0	Dr.
	1	Delivery trucks	G1		4 0 0 0 0	1 0 0 0 0	Dr.
	1	Prepaid rent	G1		1 2 0 0	8 8 0 0	Dr.
	7	Unearned delivery service revenue	G1	4 5 0 0		1 3 3 0 0	Dr.
	15	Delivery service revenue	G1	5 0 0 0		1 8 3 0 0	Dr.
	17	Paid account payable	G1		1 4 0 0	1 6 9 0 0	Dr.
	26	Collected account receivable	G2	5 0 0		1 7 4 0 0	Dr.
	28	Salaries	G2		3 6 0 0	1 3 8 0 0	Dr.
	29	Utilities	G2		1 5 0	1 3 6 5 0	Dr.
	31	Owner withdrawal	G2		3 0 0 0	1 0 6 5 0	Dr.

Accounts Receivable   Account No. 101

Date		Explanation	Post. Ref.	Debit	Credit	Balance	
1987 Dec.	20	Delivery service revenue	G1	5 7 0 0		5 7 0 0	Dr.
	26	Collections	G2		5 0 0	5 2 0 0	Dr.

Supplies on Hand   Account No. 102

Date		Explanation	Post. Ref.	Debit	Credit	Balance	
1987 Dec.	4	Purchased on account	G1	1 4 0 0		1 4 0 0	Dr.

Prepaid Insurance   Account No. 103

Date		Explanation	Post. Ref.	Debit	Credit	Balance	
1987 Dec.	1	One-year policy on trucks	G1	2 4 0 0		2 4 0 0	Dr.

* Beginning balances result from carrying forward a balance from a preceding page for this account. The Cash account, for example, is likely to use page after page over a period of time since so many transactions involve cash. This particular beginning balance came from John Turner's investment in November.

Illustration 2.6 *(continued)*

GENERAL LEDGER *(continued)*

Prepaid Rent
Account No. 104

Date		Explanation	Post. Ref.	Debit	Credit	Balance
1987 Dec.	1	Three-month payment	G1	1 2 0 0		1 2 0 0 Dr.

Delivery Trucks
Account No. 110

Date		Explanation	Post. Ref.	Debit	Credit	Balance
1987 Dec.	1	Paid cash	G1	4 0 0 0 0		4 0 0 0 0 Dr.

Accounts Payable
Account No. 200

Date		Explanation	Post. Ref.	Debit	Credit	Balance
1987 Dec.	1	Insurance	G1		2 4 0 0	2 4 0 0 Cr.
	4	Supplies	G1		1 4 0 0	3 8 0 0 Cr.
	17	Paid for supplies	G1	1 4 0 0		2 4 0 0 Cr.
	24	Advertising	G2		5 0	2 4 5 0 ·Cr.
	30	Gas and oil	G2		6 8 0	3 1 3 0 Cr.

Unearned Delivery Fees
Account No. 201

Date		Explanation	Post. Ref.	Debit	Credit	Balance
1987 Dec.	7	Received cash	G1		4 5 0 0	4 5 0 0 Cr.

John Turner, Capital
Account No. 300

Date		Explanation	Post. Ref.	Debit	Credit	Balance
1987 Dec.	1	Beginning balance				5 0 0 0 0 Cr.

Illustration 2.6 *(concluded)*

GENERAL LEDGER *(concluded)*

John Turner, Drawing   *Account No. 301*

Date		Explanation	Post. Ref.	Debit	Credit	Balance
1987 Dec.	31	Cash	G2	3000		3000 Dr.

Delivery Service Revenue   *Account No. 400*

Date		Explanation	Post. Ref.	Debit	Credit	Balance
1987 Dec.	15	Cash	G1		5000	5000 Cr.
	20	On account	G1		5700	10700 Cr.

Advertising Expense   *Account No. 500*

Date		Explanation	Post. Ref.	Debit	Credit	Balance
1987 Dec.	24	On account	G2	50		50 Dr.

Gas and Oil Expense   *Account No. 501*

Date		Explanation	Post. Ref.	Debit	Credit	Balance
1987 Dec.	30	On account	G2	680		680 Dr.

Salaries Expense   *Account No. 502*

Date		Explanation	Post. Ref.	Debit	Credit	Balance
1987 Dec.	28	Cash paid	G2	3600		3600 Dr.

Utilities Expense   *Account No. 503*

Date		Explanation	Post. Ref.	Debit	Credit	Balance
1987 Dec.	29	Cash paid	G2	150		150 Dr.

Illustration 2.7

Trial Balance

RAPID DELIVERY COMPANY
Trial Balance
December 31, 1987

	Debits	Credits
Cash	$10,650	
Accounts Receivable	5,200	
Supplies on Hand	1,400	
Prepaid Insurance	2,400	
Prepaid Rent	1,200	
Delivery Trucks	40,000	
Accounts Payable		$ 3,130
Unearned Delivery Fees		4,500
John Turner, Capital		50,000
John Turner, Drawing	3,000	
Delivery Service Revenue		10,700
Advertising Expense	50	
Gas and Oil Expense	680	
Salaries Expense	3,600	
Utilities Expense	150	
	$68,330	$68,330

or credit balances to determine that debits equal credits in the recording process. The trial balance for the Rapid Delivery Company is shown in Illustration 2.7. Note the listing of the account titles on the left (account numbers could be included if desired), the column for debit balances, the column for credit balances, and the equality of the two totals.

An inequality in the totals of the debits and credits would automatically signal the presence of an error. Errors that would cause the trial balance to be out of balance include:

1. Failing to post part of a journal entry.
2. Posting a debit as a credit, or vice versa.
3. Incorrectly determining the balance of an account.
4. Recording the balance of an account incorrectly in the trial balance.
5. Omitting an account from the trial balance.
6. Incorrectly determining the totals of the two columns of the trial balance.

To find the cause of such an error, the accountant should work backwards through the steps in the accounting process (e.g., start by re-adding the trial balance columns, then compare the trial balance figures with the account balances, verify the balance of each ledger account, verify postings to the ledger, verify journal entries, and then review the transactions). The equality of the two totals does not necessarily mean that the accounting has been error-free. Serious errors may have been made, such as failure to record a transaction, or posting a debit or credit to the wrong account. For instance, if a transaction involving payment of a $100 account payable is never recorded, the trial balance totals will still balance, but at an amount which is $100 too high. Both cash and accounts payable would be overstated by $100.

A trial balance may be prepared at any time—at the end of a day, a week, a month, a quarter, or a year. Typically, one is prepared prior to the preparation of financial statements. Dollar signs may be used but are not required.

■ SUMMARY

The basic component of the accounting process is the account. Based on the accounting equation, the equation of debits equals credits, and the use of double-entry procedure, the account is used to classify and summarize all business transactions.

To record transactions affecting assets, liabilities, and owner's equity, you must remember that assets are increased on the left (debit) side of the T-account and decreased on the right (credit) side of the T-account. However, liabilities and owner's equity are increased on the right (credit) side of the T-account and decreased on the left (debit) side of the T-account.

Revenues increase owner's equity, and expenses decrease owner's equity. Thus, increases in revenues are recorded on the right (credit) side of the T-account and decreases in revenues on the left (debit) side. Increases in expenses are recorded on the left (debit) side of the T-account and decreases on the right (credit) side.

Each account must be totaled (balanced) to determine its debit or credit balance. Assets, expenses, and owner's drawings accounts normally have a debit balance. Liabilities, owner's equity, and revenues normally have a credit balance.

The general ledger contains all of the accounts of a business, classified into balance sheet accounts (assets, liabilities, and owner's equity) and income statement accounts (revenues and expenses). Balance sheet accounts are also called real accounts; income statement accounts are also called nominal accounts. All the accounts in a ledger are listed in the chart of accounts.

Since the ledger only shows the increases and decreases in an account, a journal is needed to have a permanent record of the entire transaction. A journal is a chronological record of business transactions analyzed in terms of debits and credits. Business activity is analyzed, and certain transactions are recorded in the journal by a process known as journalizing. The amounts journalized are then posted to the accounts. To check the equality of debits and credits in journalizing and posting transactions, a trial balance is prepared. A trial balance is a listing of all of the accounts in the ledger together with their debit or credit balances, which, in total, must be equal.

What you have learned in this chapter is basic to your study of accounting. The entire process of accounting is based on the double-entry principle. In Chapter 3, you will learn that not all business transactions are "cut and dried." Sometimes adjustments are needed.

NEW TERMS INTRODUCED IN CHAPTER 2

Account

An element in an accounting system that is used to classify and summarize measurements of business activity. The three-column account is normally used. It contains columns for debit, credit, and balance (47).

Charge

Means the same as the word *debit* (48).

Chart of accounts

The complete listing of the titles and account numbers of all of the accounts in the ledger; somewhat comparable to a table of contents (53).

Compound journal entry

A journal entry with more than one debit and/or credit (66).

Credit

The right side of any account; when used as a verb, to enter a dollar amount on the right side of an account; credits increase liability, owner's equity, and revenue accounts and decrease asset, expense, and owner's drawing accounts (48).

Credit balance

The balance in an account when the sum of the credits to the account exceeds the sum of the debits to that account (51).

Cross-indexing

The placing of the account number in the journal and the placing of the journal page number in the ledger account (64).

Debit

The left side of any account; when used as a verb, to enter a dollar amount on the left side of an account; debits increase asset, expense, and owner's drawing accounts and decrease liability, owner's equity, and revenue accounts (48).

Debit balance

The balance in an account when the sum of the debits to the account exceeds the sum of the credits to that account (51).

Double-entry procedure

The accounting requirement that every transaction be recorded in an entry that has equal debits and credits (48).

Journal

A chronological (arranged in order of time) record of business transactions; the simplest form of journal is the two-column general journal (60).

Journal entry

Shows all of the effects of a business transaction as expressed in terms of debit and credit and may include an explanation of the transaction (60).

Journalizing

A step in the accounting recording process that consists of entering a transaction in a journal (63).

Ledger

The complete collection of all of the accounts of a company; often referred to as the general ledger (53).

Nominal accounts

Income statement accounts—revenues and expenses (53).

Note

A written promise to pay to another party the amount owed either when demanded or at a certain specified date (49).

Posting

Recording in the ledger the information contained in the journal (63).

Real accounts

Balance sheet accounts (assets, liabilities, and owner's equity) (53).

T-account

An account resembling the letter *T*, which is used for illustrative purposes only. Debits are entered on the left side of the account and credits are entered on the right side of the account (47).

Trial balance

A listing of the ledger accounts and their debit or credit balances to determine that debits equal credits in the recording process (66).

DEMONSTRATION PROBLEM

The Briarcliff Riding Stable, owned by Joanna Willis, had the following balance sheet on June 30, 1987:

BRIARCLIFF RIDING STABLE
Balance Sheet
June 30, 1987

Assets

Cash	$ 7,000
Accounts receivable	5,400
Land	40,000
Total assets	$52,400

Liabilities and Owner's Equity

Liabilities:

Accounts payable	$ 800
Loan payable	40,000
Total liabilities	$40,800

Owner's equity:

Joanna Willis, capital	11,600
Total liabilities and owner's equity	$52,400

Transactions for the month of July 1987 were as follows:

Transactions:

July 1 The owner invested additional cash of $25,000.
 1 Paid for a prefabricated building constructed on the land at a cost of $24,000.
 8 Paid an account payable of $800.
 10 Collected an account receivable of $5,400.
 12 Horse feed to be used in July purchased on credit for $1,100.
 24 A miscellaneous expense of $800 for July was paid.
 28 The owner withdrew $700 cash.
 31 Salaries of $1,600 for the month were paid.
 31 Riding and lesson fees for July were billed to a riding club in the amount of $3,600. Payment is due on August 10.
 31 Boarding fees for July were billed to the riding club in the amount of $4,500. This amount is due August 10.

Required: a. Prepare the journal entries to record the transactions for July 1987.
 b. Post the journal entries to the ledger accounts after entering the beginning balances in those accounts. Insert cross-indexing references in the journal and ledger. Use the following chart of accounts:

Account No.	*Account title*
100	Cash
101	Accounts Receivable
112	Land
114	Building
200	Accounts Payable
205	Loan Payable
300	Joanna Willis, Capital
301	Joanna Willis, Drawing
400	Horse Boarding Fees Revenue
401	Riding and Lesson Fees Revenue
501	Feed Expense
502	Salaries Expense
510	Miscellaneous Expense

 c. Prepare a trial balance

Solution to demonstration problem

a.

		GENERAL JOURNAL								Page 1				
Date		Account Titles and Explanation	Post. Ref.	Debit					Credit					
1987 July	1	Cash	100	2	5	0	0	0						
		Joanna Willis, Capital	300						2	5	0	0	0	
		Additional cash was invested by owner.												
	1	Building	114	2	4	0	0	0						
		Cash	100						2	4	0	0	0	
		Paid for a building.												
	8	Accounts Payable	200			8	0	0						
		Cash	100								8	0	0	
		Paid an account payable.												
	10	Cash	100			5	4	0	0					
		Accounts Receivable	101								5	4	0	0
		Collected an account receivable.												
	12	Feed Expense	501		1	1	0	0						
		Accounts Payable	200							1	1	0	0	
		Purchased feed on credit.												
	24	Miscellaneous Expense	510			8	0	0						
		Cash	100								8	0	0	
		Paid a miscellaneous expense.												
	28	Joanna Willis, Drawing	301			7	0	0						
		Cash	100								7	0	0	
		Owner withdrew cash.												
	31	Salaries Expense	502		1	6	0	0						
		Cash	100							1	6	0	0	
		Paid salaries for July.												
	31	Accounts Receivable	101		3	6	0	0						
		Riding and Lesson Fees Revenue	401							3	6	0	0	
		Billed riding and lesson fees for July.												
	31	Accounts Receivable	101		4	5	0	0						
		Horse Boarding Fees Revenue	400							4	5	0	0	
		Billed boarding fees for July.												

b.

GENERAL LEDGER

Cash

Account No. 100

Date		Explanation	Post. Ref.	Debit	Credit	Balance
1987 June	30	Balance				7 0 0 0 Dr.
July	1	Owner investment	G1	2 5 0 0 0		3 2 0 0 0 Dr.
	1	Building	G1		2 4 0 0 0	8 0 0 0 Dr.
	8	Accounts payable	G1		8 0 0	7 2 0 0 Dr.
	10	Accounts receivable	G1	5 4 0 0		1 2 6 0 0 Dr.
	24	Miscellaneous expense	G1		8 0 0	1 1 8 0 0 Dr.
	28	Owner withdrawal	G1		7 0 0	1 1 1 0 0 Dr.
	31	Salaries expense	G1		1 6 0 0	9 5 0 0 Dr.

Accounts Receivable

Account No. 101

Date		Explanation	Post. Ref.	Debit	Credit	Balance
1987 June	30	Balance				5 4 0 0 Dr.
July	10	Cash	G1		5 4 0 0	– 0 –
	31	Riding and lesson fees	G1	3 6 0 0		3 6 0 0 Dr.
	31	Horse boarding fees	G1	4 5 0 0		8 1 0 0 Dr.

Land

Account No. 112

Date		Explanation	Post. Ref.	Debit	Credit	Balance
1987 June	30	Balance				4 0 0 0 0 Dr.

Building

Account No. 114

Date		Explanation	Post. Ref.	Debit	Credit	Balance
1987 July	1	Cash	G1	2 4 0 0 0		2 4 0 0 0 Dr.

GENERAL LEDGER *(continued)*

Accounts Payable
Account No. 200

Date		Explanation	Post. Ref.	Debit	Credit	Balance
1987 June	30	Balance				8 0 0 Cr.
July	8	Cash	G1	8 0 0		– 0 –
	12	Feed expense	G1		1 1 0 0	1 1 0 0 Cr.

Loan Payable
Account No. 205

Date		Explanation	Post. Ref.	Debit	Credit	Balance
1987 June	30	Balance				4 0 0 0 0 Cr.

Joanna Willis, Capital
Account No. 300

Date		Explanation	Post. Ref.	Debit	Credit	Balance
1987 June	30	Balance				1 1 6 0 0 Cr.
July	1	Cash	G1		2 5 0 0 0	3 6 6 0 0 Cr.

Joanna Willis, Drawing
Account No. 301

Date		Explanation	Post. Ref.	Debit	Credit	Balance
1987 July	28	Cash	G1	7 0 0		7 0 0 Dr.

Horse Boarding Fees Revenue
Account No. 400

Date		Explanation	Post. Ref.	Debit	Credit	Balance
1987 July	31	Accounts receivable	G1		4 5 0 0	4 5 0 0 Cr.

Riding and Lesson Fees Revenue
Account No. 401

Date		Explanation	Post. Ref.	Debit	Credit	Balance
1987 July	31	Accounts receivable	G1		3 6 0 0	3 6 0 0 Cr.

Skip Putnam, Drawing . . .	$ 6,600	Skip Putnam, Capital . . .	$31,130
Accounts Payable	11,000	Rent Expense	3,960
Supplies Expense	1,320	Delivery Equipment	35,200
Office Equipment	9,900	Delivery Service Revenue . .	40,700
Notes Payable	16,940	Salaries Expense	17,600
Accounts Receivable . . .	16,390	Prepaid Insurance	1,980
Utilities Expense	2,640	Unearned Delivery Fees . .	3,300
Cash	7,480		

Required: Prepare a trial balance as of December 31, 1987. Arrange the accounts in the order in which they normally would appear in the ledger.

P2–4–A

Record transactions in T-accounts, determine ending balances, and prepare trial balance

The transactions listed below are those of the Kathy Green Company for the month of April 1987.

Transactions:

Apr. 1 The owner invested $90,000 cash in the business.
      3 Rent was paid for April, $600.
      6 Delivery equipment was purchased and paid for, $10,500.
      7 Office equipment was purchased on account from the Benton Company for $7,200.
     14 Wages were paid, $2,100.
     15 $4,350 was received from a customer for services performed.
     18 An invoice was received from Bill's Gas Station for $75 for gas and oil used.
     23 Borrowed $7,500 from the bank on a note.
     29 Purchased delivery equipment for $13,800 on account.
     30 Wages of $2,700 were paid.

Required: a. Mentally analyze each transaction in terms of debit and credit. Then enter them directly in suitable T-accounts. To identify each part of each transaction, also enter the date of the transaction in the accounts. Determine the ending balance in each T-account where more than one dollar amount has been entered.
             b. Prepare a trial balance as of April 30, 1987.

P2–5–A

Record transactions in T-accounts, determine ending balances, and prepare trial balance

The transactions given below are for the Slim & Trim Company.

Transactions:

Apr. 1 The owner invested $100,000 cash in the business.
      5 The company borrowed $50,000 from its bank and issued its note payable to the bank.
      9 Paid $40,000 cash for land and $95,000 cash for a building located on the land.
     14 Purchased $16,000 of exercise equipment on account.
     17 Paid $1,200 cash for supplies to be used in April.
     25 Sales of services to a customer on account were $10,000.
     30 Sales of services to a customer for cash were $2,000.
     30 Paid salaries for April, $2,000.

Required: a. Set up the following T-accounts: Cash; Accounts Receivable; Land; Building; Exercise Equipment; Accounts Payable; Notes Payable, Bank; Betty Allen, Capital; Service Revenue; Salaries Expense; and Supplies Expense. Enter the transactions in the T-accounts. Date each transaction entry as indicated. Determine the ending balance in each T-account where more than one dollar amount has been entered.
             b. Prepare a trial balance after entering the last transaction.

P2-6-A

Open ledger accounts, journalize transactions, post journal entries, and prepare trial balance; ledger accounts have beginning balances

The trial balance of the Tennis Court at the end of the first 11 months of its fiscal year is given below.

TENNIS COURT
Trial Balance
May 31, 1987

Account No.	Account title	Debit	Credits
100	Cash	$ 64,944	
102	Accounts Receivable	65,400	
121	Land	24,000	
210	Accounts Payable		$ 15,000
220	Notes Payable		12,000
310	Debra Lewis, Capital		85,440
320	Debra Lewis, Drawing	13,200	
400	Tennis Lesson Revenue		162,000
510	Tennis Professionals' Salaries Expense	39,600	
520	Advertising Expense	16,800	
530	Lesson Supplies Expense	1,800	
540	Equipment Repairs Expense	1,200	
550	Office Salaries Expense	13,200	
560	Building Rent Expense	26,400	
570	Utilities Expense	1,680	
580	Entertainment Expense	696	
590	Equipment Rent Expense	5,280	
600	Miscellaneous Expense	240	
		$274,440	$274,440

Transactions:

June	1	Paid building rent for June, $2,400.
	2	Paid an accounts payable, $4,580.
	5	Purchased a small tract of land for cash, $1,800.
	7	Gave tennis lessons to members of a large tennis organization on account, $2,600.
	10	Paid the note payable of $12,000.
	13	Received cash from a customer on account, $2,800.
	19	Received a bill for equipment repairs, $180.
	24	Paid the June telephone bill, $66, and the June electric bill, $78.
	28	Received a bill for June advertising, $1,320.
	30	Gave tennis lessons to members of a tennis club for cash, $3,600.
	30	Paid office salaries, $1,200, and tennis professionals' salaries, $3,600.
	30	Gave tennis lessons to members of a tennis club on account, $4,400.
	30	Costs paid in entertaining persons who subsequently became members, $204.
	30	Paid equipment rent expense for June, $480.
	30	The owner withdrew $1,200 cash.

Required:

a. Open three-column ledger accounts for each of the accounts in the trial balance. Place the word *Balance* in the explanation space, enter the date June 1, 1987, on the same line, and enter the proper beginning balance in each account.
b. Prepare general journal entries for the transactions given below for June 1987.
c. Post the journal entries to the general ledger accounts.
d. Prepare a trial balance as of June 30, 1987.

P2-7-A

Prepare corrected trial balance

Charlie Perdomo prepared the following trial balance from the ledger of the Spra-Rite Sprinkler Company. It did not balance.

SPRA-RITE SPRINKLER COMPANY
Trial Balance
December 31, 1987

	Debits	Credits
Cash	$ 14,800	
Accounts Receivable	10,200	
Furniture and Equipment	30,000	
Office Fixtures	12,000	
Accounts Payable		$ 5,600
Charlie Perdomo, Capital		60,000
Charlie Perdomo, Drawing	7,200	
Service Revenue		90,000
Salaries Expense	70,000	
Rent Expense	10,000	
Miscellaneous Expense	1,800	
	$156,000	$155,600

This fact caused Charlie to examine the accounting records very carefully. In searching back through the accounting records, Charlie found that the following errors had been made:

1. One entire entry was never posted. It included a debit to Cash and a credit to Accounts Receivable for $1,200.
2. In computing the balance of the Accounts Payable account, a credit of $800 was omitted from the computation.
3. In preparing the trial balance, the Charlie Perdomo, Capital account balance was shown as $60,000. The ledger account has the balance at its correct amount of $60,800.
4. One debit of $600 to the Charlie Perdomo, Drawing account was posted as a credit to that account.
5. Office fixtures of $2,000 were debited to Furniture and Equipment when purchased.

Required: Prepare a corrected trial balance for the Spra-Rite Sprinklers Company as of December 31, 1987. Hint: Some errors may not cause the trial balance to be out of balance.

PROBLEMS, SERIES B

P2-1-B

Record transactions in T-accounts

The Carlton Company engaged in the following transactions in the month of May 1987:

Transactions:

May 1 The owner invested $40,000 cash in the business.
  2 Purchased cleaning equipment on account, $10,000.
  3 Paid cash for a building, $25,000.
  5 Paid $450 to rent a truck for a three-month period.
  10 Performed cleaning services for a customer on account, $4,500.
  15 Paid for the cleaning equipment purchased on May 2.
  22 Performed cleaning services for a customer for cash, $2,200.
  27 Received bill and paid for cleaning supplies used this month, $1,600.
  31 Paid salaries for the month, $800.
  31 The owner, Rex Carlton, withdrew $400 for personal living expenses.

Required: Record the transactions directly into T-accounts.

P2–2–B

Prepare journal entries

Presented below are the transactions (partially summarized for the sake of brevity) of the Boyd Realty Company, owned by Donna Boyd, for the month of March 1987.

Transactions:

1. The owner invested $40,000 cash.
2. Paid $3,600 as the rent for March on an office building.
3. Billed a client for commissions revenue for March, $32,000.
4. Paid $400 for office supplies received and used in March.
5. Borrowed $10,000 from the bank on a note.
6. Collected $24,000 cash on an account receivable.
7. Received a bill for $1,200 for advertising appearing in the local newspaper in March.
8. Paid cash for gas and oil consumed in March, $850.
9. Paid $32,000 to employees for wages earned in March.
10. The owner withdrew $1,000 cash.

Required: Prepare the general journal entries that would be required to record the above transactions in the records of the Boyd Realty Company.

P2–3–B

Prepare trial balance

The following is a list of accounts and their balances for the Woodard Company as of December 31, 1987:

Jack Woodard, Drawing	$ 1,400	Cash	$5,600
Accounts Payable	1,680	Rent Expense	2,800
Salaries Expense	21,000	Miscellaneous Expense	1,050
Furniture and Equipment	8,400	Supplies on Hand	1,750
Accounts Receivable	3,220	Prepaid Insurance	2,660
Jack Woodard, Capital	9,590	Unearned Service Fees	4,410
Service Revenue	32,200		

Required: Prepare a trial balance as of December 31, 1987. Arrange the accounts in the order in which they would normally appear in the ledger.

P2–4–B

Record transactions in T-accounts, determine ending balances, and prepare trial balance

The transactions for October 1987 for the Fast Freight Company are given below. The owner of the business is Randy Hall.

Transactions:

Oct. 1   The owner invested cash, $20,800.
     3   Borrowed $6,500 from the bank on a note.
     4   Purchased a truck for $12,090 cash.
     6   Delivery services were performed for a customer who promised to pay later, $4,680.
     7   Employee services received and paid for, $1,820.
    10   Collection was made for the services performed on October 6, $1,040.
    14   Office supplies were purchased for $650 on account. They will be paid for and used next month.
    17   A bill for $700 was received for gas and oil used to date.
    25   Delivery services were performed for a customer who paid immediately, $5,850.
    31   Wages paid were $1,950.
    31   The owner withdrew $520 for personal use.

Required: a.   Open T-accounts and record the transactions. Place the date of each transaction in the accounts. Determine the ending balance of each T-account where more than one dollar amount has been entered.
   b.   Prepare a trial balance as of October 31, 1987.

P2–5–B

Record transactions in T-accounts, determine ending balances, and prepare trial balance

The transactions appearing below are those of the Mayflower Appliance Repair Service Company for the month of July 1987. The company is owned by Bob Sears.

Transactions:

July 2   The owner invested $20,000 cash in the business.
     3   The company paid rent for July, $1,000.
     5   A truck was purchased for $6,000 cash.

July 9 A bill for $1,000 for advertising for July was received and paid.
      14 Cash of $2,800 was received for appliance repair services performed for a condominium complex.
      15 Wages of $800 for the first half of July were paid.
      20 The company performed appliance repair services on account for a company, $800.
      22 Office furniture was acquired for $1,600 on account.
      25 The owner withdrew $600 cash for personal use.
      30 Cash of $4,500 was received for appliance repair service performed for a company.
      31 Wages of $800 for the second half of July were paid.

Required: *a.* Open T-accounts and record the transactions. Place the date of each transaction in the accounts. Determine the ending balance of each T-account where more than one dollar amount has been entered.

b. Prepare a trial balance as of July 31, 1987.

P2–6–B

Open ledger accounts, journalize transactions, post journal entries, and prepare trial balance; ledger accounts have beginning balances

The Summer Lawn Care Company, owned by Gene Harper, was formed several years ago. The company's trial balance at the end of the first 11 months of its current fiscal year is presented below.

SUMMER LAWN CARE COMPANY
Trial Balance
June 30, 1987

Account No.	Account title	Debits	Credits
101	Cash	$ 98,320	
102	Accounts Receivable	104,800	
110	Land	127,060	
201	Accounts Payable		$ 44,800
301	Gene Harper, Capital		171,380
302	Gene Harper, Drawing	44,000	
400	Lawn Care Revenue		360,000
410	Shrubbery Care Revenue		134,680
510	Salaries Expense	87,800	
520	Chemical Supplies Expense	99,200	
530	Advertising Expense	24,400	
540	Truck Operating Expense	29,200	
550	Office Rent Expense	44,000	
560	Office Supplies Expense	1,600	
570	Telephone and Utilities Expense	3,080	
580	Customer Entertainment Expense	3,400	
590	Truck Rent Expense	44,000	
		$710,860	$710,860

Transactions:

July 2 Paid office rent for July, $4,000.
      5 Paid an account payable of $44,800.
      8 Paid advertising for the month of July, $1,600.
      10 Purchased a small tract of land for cash, $1,400.
      13 Purchased on account $320 of office supplies for use in July.
      15 Collected cash from a large homeowners' association on account, $102,400.
      20 Paid for customer entertainment in July, $100.
      26 Paid for gasoline used in the trucks in July, $360.
      28 Billed homeowners' association for services performed in July; lawn care, $63,000; and shubbery care, $43,000.
      30 Paid for July chemical supplies, $26,400.
      31 Paid truck rent expense for July, $4,000.
      31 Paid July salaries, $20,400.
      31 The owner withdrew $4,000 cash.

Required: a. Open three-column ledger accounts for each of the accounts in the trial balance. Place the word *balance* in the explanation space, enter the date July 1, 1987, on the same line, and enter the proper beginning balance in each account.
b. Prepare general journal entries for the transactions given below for July 1987.
c. Post the journal entries to the general ledger accounts.
d. Prepare a trial balance as of July 31, 1987.

P2–7–B

Prepare corrected trial balance

Casey Jones prepared a trial balance for the Adams Company that did not balance. The trial balance she prepared was as follows:

ADAMS COMPANY
Trial Balance
December 31, 1987

	Debits	Credits
Cash	$ 16,000	
Accounts Receivable	10,200	
Equipment	40,000	
Accounts Payable		$ 6,000
J. Adams, Capital		40,000
J. Adams, Drawing	4,000	
Service Revenue		108,000
Advertising Expense	300	
Salaries Expense	44,000	
Rent Expense	16,000	
Utilities Expense	11,200	
	$141,700	$154,000

In trying to find out why the trial balance did not balance, Joan discovered the following errors:

1. Cash was understated (too low) by $2,000 because of an error in addition in determining the balance of that account in the ledger.
2. A credit of $1,200 to Accounts Receivable in the journal was not posted to the ledger at all.
3. A debit of $4,000 for a withdrawal by the owner was posted as a credit to the owner's capital account.
4. The balance of $3,000 in the Advertising Expense account was entered as $300 in the trial balance.
5. Miscellaneous Expense, with a balance of $800, was omitted from the trial balance.

Required: Prepare a correct trial balance as of December 31, 1987.

BUSINESS DECISION PROBLEM

Prepare journal entries, post to T-accounts, and judge profitability

Phillip Gunnells lost his job as a carpenter with a contractor when a recession hit the construction industry. Phillip had been making $50,000 per year. He decided to form his own company and do home repairs.

The following is a summary of the transactions of the business during the first three months of operations in 1987:

Transactions:

Jan. 15 Phillip invested $20,000 in the business.
Feb. 10 Owner withdrew $2,000 for living expenses.
25 Received payment of $4,400 for remodeling a basement into a recreation room. The homeowner purchased all of the building materials.

Adjusting entries bring the accounts to their proper balances before financial statements are prepared. That is, **adjusting entries convert the amounts that are actually in the accounts to the amounts that should be in the accounts for proper financial reporting.** Accountants make this conversion by analyzing the accounts and determining which ones need adjustment. For example, assume a three-year insurance policy costing $600 was purchased at the beginning of the year and debited to Prepaid Insurance. At year-end it is obvious that $200 of the cost should be removed from the asset and recorded as an expense. Failure to do so misstates assets and net income on the financial statements.

Events such as the using up of insurance coverage that has been prepaid are known as **continuous events.** Most adjusting entries are the result of continuous events. The need for adjusting entries is based on the matching principle. The matching principle requires that expenses incurred in producing revenues be deducted from the revenues they generated during the accounting period. This matching of expenses and revenues is necessary for the income statement to present an accurate picture of the profitability of a business.

Benefits from many assets such as prepaid expenses (e.g., prepaid insurance and prepaid rent) are being received **continuously** by a company. Thus, the expense relating to these items could also be recognized **continuously** as time elapses. An entry could be made frequently, even daily, to record the expense incurred. But typically, the entry is not made until financial statements are to be prepared. Therefore, if monthly financial statements are prepared, monthly adjusting entries are required. By custom, and in some instances by law, businesses report to their owners at least annually. Accordingly, adjusting entries will be required at least once a year. Remember, however, that the entry transferring an amount from an asset account to an expense account should transfer only the cost of the portion of the asset that has expired.

Cash versus Accrual Basis Accounting

Some relatively small business firms and professional persons, such as physicians, lawyers, and accountants, may account for their revenues and expenses on a cash basis. The cash basis of accounting recognizes revenues when cash is received and recognizes expenses when cash is paid out. For example, under the cash basis, services rendered to clients in 1987 for which cash was collected in 1988 would be treated as 1988 revenues. Similarly, under the cash basis, expenses incurred in 1987 for which cash was disbursed in 1988 would be treated as 1988 expenses. Because of these improper assignments of revenues and expenses, the cash basis of accounting is generally considered unacceptable. Companies using the cash basis may not have to prepare any adjusting entries. The cash basis is acceptable only under those circumstances in which the results approximate those obtained under the accrual basis of accounting; it may also be used for income tax purposes under certain circumstances.

Throughout the text we use the accrual basis of accounting. The accrual basis of accounting recognizes revenues when sales are made or services are performed, regardless of when cash is received. Expenses are recognized as incurred, whether or not cash has been paid out. For instance, when services are performed for a customer on account, the revenue is recorded at that time even though cash has not been received. Later, when the cash is received, no revenue is recorded because it has already been recorded. Under the accrual basis, adjusting entries are used to bring the accounts up-to-date for economic activity that has taken place but has not yet been recorded. Accurate financial statements can then be prepared.

An example of economic activity that would require an adjusting entry is the purchase and gradual use of office supplies. When office supplies are purchased, they are recorded in an asset account, Office Supplies on Hand. Even though office supplies are used during the accounting period, the accountant usually waits until the end of the accounting period to record their consumption. The cost and nuisance of making an entry every time a small amount of office supplies is used outweighs the benefits of having precisely accurate account balances during the period. Instead, an adjusting entry is made at the end of the period to bring the accounts to their proper balances before financial statements are prepared.

■ CLASSES AND TYPES OF ADJUSTING ENTRIES

Adjusting entries can be grouped into two broad classes: deferred (meaning to postpone or delay) items and accrued (meaning to grow or accumulate) items. **Deferred items** consist of adjusting entries involving data previously recorded in accounts. These entries involve the transfer of data already recorded in asset and liability accounts to expense and revenue accounts. **Accrued items** consist of adjusting entries relating to activity on which no data have been previously recorded in the accounts. These entries involve the initial, or first, recording of assets and liabilities and the related revenues and expenses (see Illustration 3.2).

Deferred items require two types of adjusting entries: asset/expense adjustments and liability/revenue adjustments. For example, prepaid insurance and prepaid rent are shown as assets until they are used up; then they become expenses. And, if a company receives cash for a service it has not yet rendered, this is recorded as an unearned revenue (liability); however, as the company renders the service, the unearned revenue becomes earned revenue.

Accrued items also require two types of adjusting entries: asset/revenue adjustments and liability/expense adjustments. For example, if a company performs a service for a customer but has not yet billed the customer, this is recorded as an asset in the form of a receivable and as revenue because the company expects to be paid. And, if a company owes its employees wages that have not yet been paid, this is recorded as a liability and expense because the company has incurred an expense that must soon be paid.

Each of the four types of adjusting entries—asset/expense, liability/revenue, asset/revenue, and liability/expense—are illustrated in this chapter using the Rapid Delivery Company example from Chapter 2. The trial balance of the Rapid Delivery Company at December 31, 1987, is shown in Illustration 3.3; it is the same trial balance shown in Illustration 2.7, Chapter 2. As you can see by looking at the trial balance, several accounts must be adjusted before the financial statements can be prepared. These accounts are mentioned in Chapter 2, and the adjustments involve data that have already been recorded in the company's accounts.

Illustration 3.2

Two Classes and Four Types of Adjusting Entries

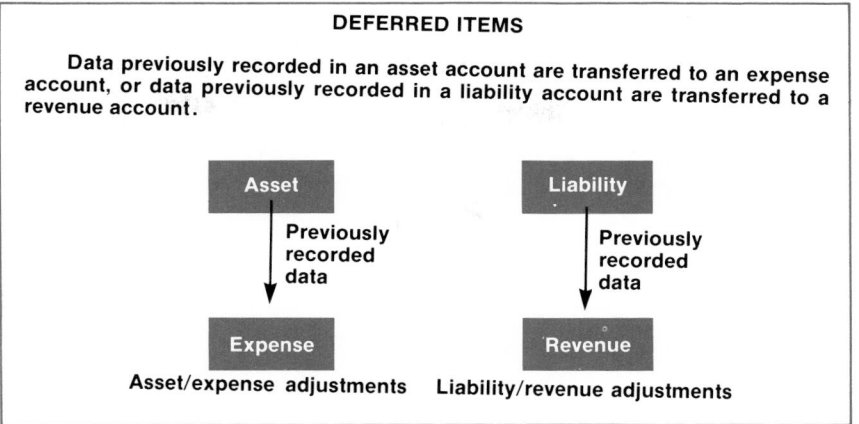

DEFERRED ITEMS

Data previously recorded in an asset account are transferred to an expense account, or data previously recorded in a liability account are transferred to a revenue account.

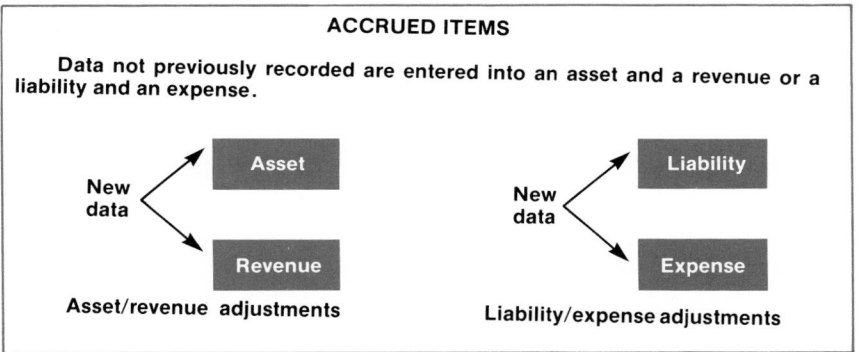

ACCRUED ITEMS

Data not previously recorded are entered into an asset and a revenue or a liability and an expense.

Illustration 3.3

Trial Balance

RAPID DELIVERY COMPANY
Trial Balance
December 31, 1987

	Debits	Credits
Cash	$10,650	
Accounts Receivable	5,200	
Supplies on Hand	1,400	
Prepaid Insurance	2,400	
Prepaid Rent	1,200	
Delivery Trucks	40,000	
Accounts Payable		$ 3,130
Unearned Delivery Fees		4,500
John Turner, Capital		50,000
John Turner, Drawing	3,000	
Delivery Service Revenue		10,700
Advertising Expense	50	
Gas and Oil Expense	680	
Salaries Expense	3,600	
Utilities Expense	150	
	$68,330	$68,330

In making adjustments for the Rapid Delivery Company, we will need to add several additional accounts to the company's chart of accounts shown in Chapter 2. These are:

Type of account	Account no.	Account title	Description
Contra asset*	110A	Accumulated Deprecia-tion—Delivery Equipment	The total depreciation cost taken on delivery equipment. The balance of this account is deducted from Delivery Equipment on the balance sheet.
Liability	202	Accrued Salaries Payable	The amount of salaries earned by employees but not yet paid by the company.
Expenses	504	Insurance Expense	The cost of insurance incurred in the current period.
	505	Rent Expense	The cost of rent incurred in the current period.
	506	Supplies Expense	The cost of supplies used in the current period.
	507	Depreciation Expense—Delivery Trucks	The cost of the portion of delivery equipment used up during the current period.

* A contra asset is deducted from an asset account on the balance sheet.

You are now ready to make the actual adjustments for deferred items. Should you find the process confusing, go back and restudy the beginning of this chapter so you clearly understand the purpose of adjusting entries.

■ ADJUSTMENTS FOR DEFERRED ITEMS

This section discusses the two types of adjustments for deferred items: asset/expense adjustments and liability/revenue adjustments. In the asset/expense group, you will learn how to prepare adjusting entries for prepaid expenses and depreciation; in the liability/revenue group, you will learn how to prepare adjusting entries for unearned revenues.

Asset/Expense Adjustments—Prepaid Expenses and Depreciation

Rapid Delivery Company must make several asset/expense adjustments for prepaid expenses. A prepaid expense is an asset awaiting assignment to expense, such as prepaid insurance, prepaid rent, and supplies on hand. As you will see, the nature of these three adjustments is the same.

Prepaid Insurance.   When an insurance policy premium is paid in advance, the purchase creates the asset, **prepaid insurance.** For accounting purposes, this advance payment is an asset because insurance coverage will be received in the future. With the passage of time, however, the asset gradually expires, and the portion that has expired becomes an expense. To illustrate this point, recall that in Chapter 2 the Rapid Delivery Company purchased on account an insurance policy on its delivery trucks for the period December 1, 1987, to December 1, 1988. The journal entry made on December 1, 1987, to record the purchase of the policy was:

```
1987
Dec.  1   Prepaid Insurance   . . . . . . . . . . .    2,400
              Accounts Payable  . . . . . . . . . . .          2,400
          Purchased truck insurance to cover a one-year
          period.
```

The two accounts that relate to insurance are Prepaid Insurance (an asset) and Insurance Expense (an expense). After posting the above entry, the Prepaid Insurance account has a $2,400 debit balance on December 1, 1987, the day the 12-month policy goes into effect. The Insurance Expense account has a zero balance on December 1, 1987, because no time has elapsed to use any of the policy's benefits.

(Dr.)	**Prepaid Insurance**	(Cr.)		(Dr.)	**Insurance Expense**	(Cr.)
1987 Dec. 1 Bal.	2,400			1987 Dec. 1 Bal.	–0–	

By December 31, part of the period covered by the policy has expired. Therefore, part of the **service potential** (or benefits that can be obtained from the asset) has expired. The asset now will provide fewer future benefits than when it was acquired. The future services that an asset can render make the asset a "thing of value" to a business. This reduction of the asset's ability to provide services must be recognized. The cost of the services received from the asset is treated as an expense. In this case. the service received was one month of insurance coverage. Since the policy provides the same services for every month of its one-year life, we assign an equal amount ($200) of cost to each month. Thus, $\frac{1}{12}$ of the annual premium is charged to Insurance Expense on December 31. The adjusting journal entry is as follows:

Adjustment 1— Insurance	

```
1987
Dec. 31   Insurance Expense  . . . . . . . . . . .    200
              Prepaid Insurance  . . . . . . . . . . .          200
          To record insurance expense for December.
```

In T-account format, the accounts appear as follows after posting the two journal entries above:

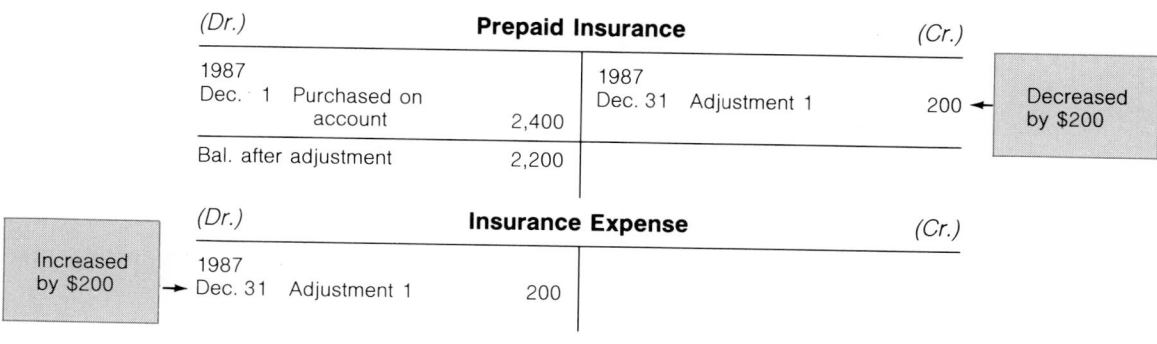

(Dr.)	**Prepaid Insurance**			(Cr.)
1987 Dec. 1 Purchased on account	2,400	1987 Dec. 31 Adjustment 1	200	Decreased by $200
Bal. after adjustment	2,200			

	(Dr.)	**Insurance Expense**		(Cr.)
Increased by $200	1987 Dec. 31 Adjustment 1	200		

In actual practice, accountants do not use T-accounts. Instead they use three-column ledger forms that have the advantage of showing a balance after each transaction. After posting the two entries above, the three-column ledger accounts appear as follows:

Prepaid Insurance   *Account No. 103*

Date		Explanation	Post. Ref.	Debit	Credit	Balance
1987 Dec.	1	Purchased on account	G1*	2400		2400 Dr.
	31	Adjustment	G3*		200	2200 Dr.

Insurance Expense   *Account No. 504*

Date		Explanation	Post. Ref.	Debit	Credit	Balance
1987 Dec.	31	Adjustment	G3*	200		200 Dr.

* Note: These posting references are assumed.

Before the above adjusting entry was made, the entire $2,400 insurance payment made on December 1, 1987, was a prepaid expense for 12 months of insurance protection. As explained earlier, a prepaid expense is an asset awaiting assignment to expense. So on December 31, 1987, one month of protection had passed, and an adjusting entry transferred $200 of the $2,400 ($2,400/ 12 = $200) to insurance expense. On the income statement for year ended December 31, 1987, one month of insurance expense, $200, is reported as one of the expenses incurred in generating that year's revenues. The remaining amount of the prepaid expense, $2,200, is reported on the balance sheet as an asset. The $2,200 prepaid expense represents the cost of 11 months of insurance protection that remains as a future benefit.

Prepaid Rent. Prepaid rent is another example of the gradual using up of a previously recorded asset. When rent is paid in advance to cover more than one accounting period, on the date it is paid the prepayment is debited to the Prepaid Rent account (an asset account). Benefits resulting from this expenditure are yet to be received. Thus, the expenditure creates an asset.

The measurement of rent expense usually is quite simple; it is similar to insurance expense. Generally, the rental contract specifies the amount of rent per unit of time. If the prepayment covers a three-month rental, one third of this rental is charged to each month. The same amount is charged to each month even though there are varying numbers of days in some months.

For example, in Chapter 2, the Rapid Delivery Company paid $1,200 rent in advance on December 1, 1987, to cover a three-month period beginning on that date. The journal entry made at that time was:

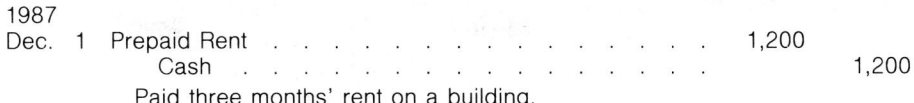

```
1987
Dec.  1  Prepaid Rent  .   .   .   .   .   .   .   .   .   .   .   .   .   .   1,200
             Cash   .   .   .   .   .   .   .   .   .   .   .   .   .   .   .           1,200
             Paid three months' rent on a building.
```

The two accounts relating to rent are Prepaid Rent (an asset) and Rent Expense. After this entry has been posted, the Prepaid Rent account has a $1,200 balance, and the Rent Expense account has a zero balance because no part of the rent period has yet elapsed.

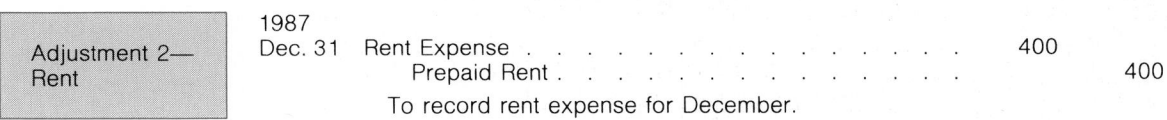

(Dr.)	**Prepaid Rent**	(Cr.)	(Dr.)	**Rent Expense**	(Cr.)
1987			1987		
Dec. 1			Dec. 1		
Bal. Cash paid 1,200			Bal. –0–		

On December 31, 1987, an adjusting entry must be prepared. Since one third of the period covered by the prepaid rent (one of three months) has elapsed, one third of the $1,200 of prepaid rent is charged to expense. The required adjusting entry is as follows:

Adjustment 2— Rent

```
1987
Dec. 31  Rent Expense  .   .   .   .   .   .   .   .   .   .   .   .   .   400
              Prepaid Rent  .   .   .   .   .   .   .   .   .   .   .   .          400
              To record rent expense for December.
```

The T-accounts appear as follows after posting this adjusting entry:

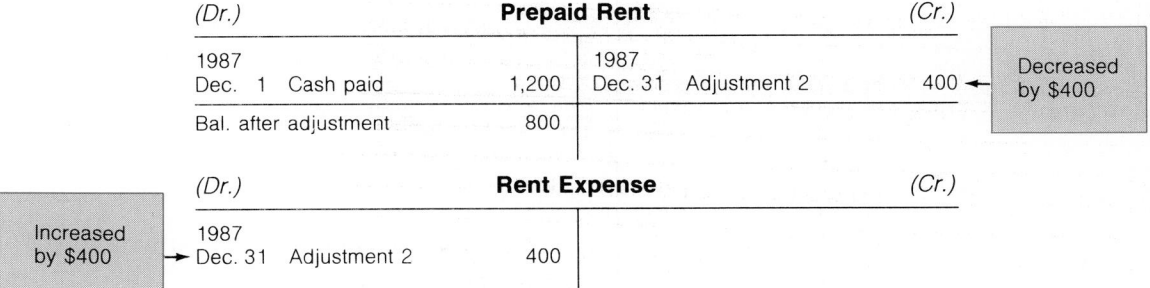

(Dr.)	**Prepaid Rent**		(Cr.)	
1987		1987		
Dec. 1 Cash paid	1,200	Dec. 31 Adjustment 2	400	Decreased by $400
Bal. after adjustment	800			

(Dr.)	**Rent Expense**		(Cr.)
	1987		
Increased by $400	Dec. 31 Adjustment 2	400	

The $400 rent expense appears in the income statement for the year ended December 31, 1987. The remaining $800 of prepaid rent is reported as an asset in the balance sheet for December 31, 1987. Thus, the adjusting entries have accomplished their purpose of maintaining the accuracy of the financial statements.

Supplies on Hand.   Every business uses supplies in its operations. Supplies may be classified simply as supplies (to include all types of supplies), or more specifically as office supplies (paper, stationery, carbon paper, pencils), selling supplies (gummed tape, string, paper bags or cartons, wrapping paper), or, possibly, cleaning supplies (soap, disinfectants). Supplies are frequently bought in bulk and are an asset until they are used. This asset may be called **supplies on hand** or **supplies inventory.** Even though this item is a prepaid expense, it does not use "prepaid" in its title.

On December 4, 1987, the Rapid Delivery Company purchased supplies and recorded the transaction as follows:

```
1987
Dec.  4  Supplies on Hand  . . . . . . . . . . . . . .   1,400
              Cash  . . . . . . . . . . . . . . . . .            1,400
             To record the purchase of supplies for future use.
```

The two accounts relating to supplies are Supplies on Hand (an asset) and Supplies Expense. After this entry has been posted, the Supplies on Hand account shows a debit balance of $1,400, and the Supplies Expense account has a zero balance as shown:

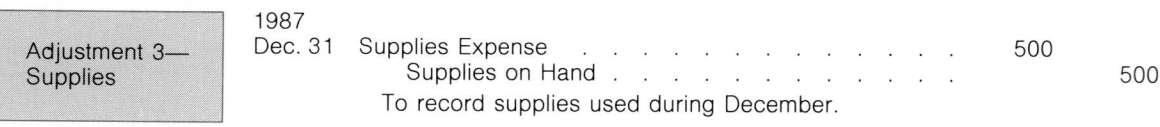

(Dr.)	Supplies on Hand	(Cr.)	(Dr.)	Supplies Expense	(Cr.)
1987 Dec. 4 Bal. Cash paid 1,400			1987 Dec. 4 Bal. –0–		

An actual physical inventory (a count of the supplies on hand) at the end of the month showed that only $900 of supplies were on hand at that time. Thus, $500 of supplies must have been used in December. An adjusting journal entry is required to bring the two accounts pertaining to supplies to their proper balances. The adjusting entry recognizes the reduction in the asset (Supplies on Hand) and the recording of an expense (Supplies Expense) by transferring $500 from the asset to the expense. From the information given, the asset balance should be $900 and the expense balance, $500. So the following adjusting entry is made:

Adjustment 3— Supplies

```
1987
Dec. 31  Supplies Expense  . . . . . . . . . . . . .    500
              Supplies on Hand  . . . . . . . . . . .            500
             To record supplies used during December.
```

The T-accounts, after posting this adjusting entry, appear as follows:

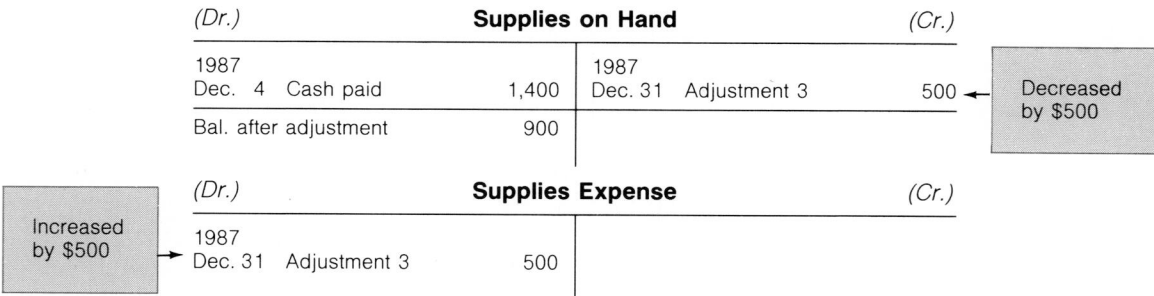

(Dr.)	Supplies on Hand	(Cr.)	
1987 Dec. 4 Cash paid 1,400	1987 Dec. 31 Adjustment 3 500		**Decreased by $500**
Bal. after adjustment 900			

	(Dr.)	Supplies Expense	(Cr.)
Increased by $500	1987 Dec. 31 Adjustment 3 500		

The entry to record the use of supplies could be made when the supplies are issued from the storeroom. But accounting carefully for small items each time they are issued is usually too costly a procedure to use.

Adjusting entries for supplies on hand, like for any other prepaid expense, are made before financial statements are prepared. Supplies expense appears in the income statement. Supplies on hand is reported as an asset in the balance sheet.

Sometimes prepaid expenses such as insurance, rent, and supplies are bought and will be fully used up within one accounting period (usually one month or one year). If so, accountants usually debit an expense rather than an asset at the time of purchase. This procedure avoids having to make an adjusting entry at the end of the accounting period. Sometimes an expense is debited even though the asset will benefit more than the current period. If so, the adjusting entry must transfer some of the cost from the expense to the asset. For instance, assume that on January 1, rent of $1,200 is paid to cover a three-year period and is debited to Rent Expense. At the end of the year $800 must be transferred from Rent Expense to Prepaid Rent. This situation will not be illustrated further in this text in an attempt to simplify the discussion.

Depreciation.   Just as prepaid insurance and prepaid rent indicate a gradual using up of a previously recorded asset, so does depreciation. However, the overall period of time involved in using up a depreciable asset such as a building, for example, is much longer and less definite than for prepaid expenses. A prepaid expense generally involves a fairly small amount of money; depreciable assets usually involve larger sums of money.

A depreciable asset is a man-made asset such as a building, machine, vehicle, or piece of equipment that provides service to a business. Since these assets are gradually used up over time, depreciation expense is recorded on them. Depreciation expense is the amount of asset cost assigned as an expense to a particular time period. The process of recording depreciation expense is called depreciation accounting.

The three factors involved in computing depreciation expense are:

1. **Asset cost.**   The asset cost is the amount a company paid to purchase the depreciable asset.
2. **Estimated salvage value.**   The estimated salvage value is the amount that the asset can probably be sold for at the end of its estimated useful life.
3. **Estimated useful life.**   The estimated useful life of an asset is the estimated number of time periods that a company can make use of the asset. Useful life is an estimate, not an exact measurement, that must be made in advance. Unfortunately, individuals are unable to see 10 to 15 years into the future with precise accuracy.

The equation for determining the amount of depreciation expense for each time period is:

$$\frac{\text{Asset cost} - \text{Estimated salvage value}}{\text{Estimated number of time periods in asset's useful life}} = \begin{array}{l}\text{Depreciation expense for}\\\text{each time period}\end{array}$$

Accountants use different methods for recording depreciation. The method illustrated here is known as the **straight-line method.** Other depreciation methods are discussed in Chapter 10. Straight-line depreciation assigns the same amount of depreciation expense to each accounting period over the life of the asset. The depreciation formula to compute straight-line depreciation for a one-year period is:

$$\frac{\text{Asset cost} - \text{Estimated salvage value}}{\text{Estimated number of years of useful life}} = \text{Annual depreciation}$$

To illustrate the use of this formula, recall that on December 1, Rapid Delivery Company purchased four trucks at a cost of $40,000. The journal entry made at that time was:

```
1987
Dec. 1  Delivery Trucks  . . . . . . . . . . . . .  40,000
              Cash  . . . . . . . . . . . . . .            40,000
            To record the purchase of four delivery trucks.
```

The estimated salvage value for each truck was $1,000, so total salvage value for all four trucks was estimated at $4,000. The useful life of each truck was estimated to be four years. Annual depreciation on the trucks is calculated using the straight-line depreciation formula:

$$\text{Annual depreciation} = \frac{\$40{,}000 - \$4{,}000}{4 \text{ years}} = \$9{,}000$$

The amount of depreciation expense for one month would be $\frac{1}{12}$ of the annual amount. Thus, depreciation expense for December is $9,000 ÷ 12 = $750.

The difference between an asset's cost and its estimated salvage value is sometimes referred to as an asset's **depreciable amount.** The depreciable amount must be allocated as an expense to the various periods in the asset's useful life to satisfy the matching principle.

The amount of depreciation for a period is debited to a depreciation expense account and credited to an accumulated depreciation account. The depreciation on the delivery trucks for December is $750 and is recorded as follows:

Adjustment 4— Depreciation

```
1987
Dec. 31  Depreciation Expense—Delivery Trucks  . . . . . .  750
               Accumulated Depreciation—Delivery Trucks  . . .        750
             To record depreciation expense for December.
```

The T-accounts appear as follows after posting the adjusting entry:

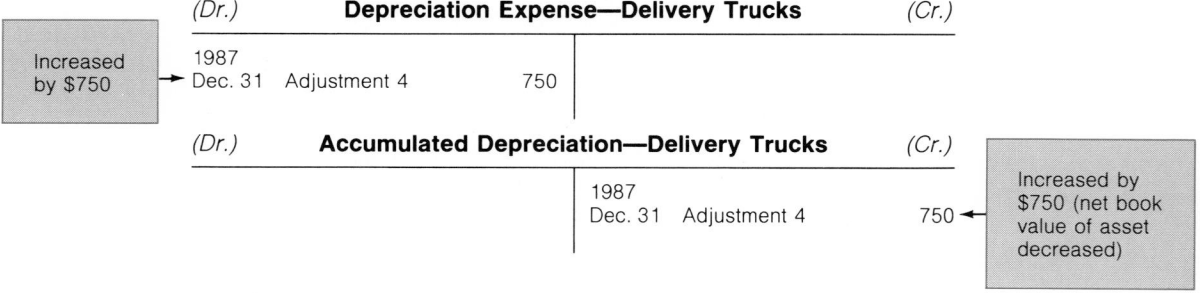

Depreciation expense is reported in the income statement. Accumulated depreciation is reported in the balance sheet as a deduction from the related asset.

The **accumulated depreciation account** is a contra asset account that shows the total of all depreciation recorded on the asset up through the balance sheet date. A **contra asset account** is a deduction from the asset to which it relates in the balance sheet. The purpose of a contra asset account is to reduce the original cost of the asset down to its undepreciated cost or book value.

The debit balance in the asset account (original cost) minus the credit balance in the accumulated depreciation contra account equals the **undepreciated cost of the asset.** An asset's cost less accumulated depreciation is called book value (or net book value). Book value is the cost not yet allocated to an expense. In the above example, the book value of the delivery equipment after the first month is:

Cost	$40,000
Less: Accumulated depreciation	750
Book value (or cost not yet allocated as an expense)	$39,250

Depreciation is credited to an accumulated depreciation account instead of directly to the asset because recorded amounts of depreciation are estimates. No one is sure that the estimates are correct. To provide more complete balance sheet information to users of the financial statements, both original acquisition cost and accumulated depreciation are shown. For example, on the December 31, 1987, balance sheet, the accumulated depreciation is shown as a deduction from the asset delivery trucks:

Assets

Delivery trucks	$40,000
Less: Accumulated depreciation—delivery trucks . .	750
	$39,250

The accumulated depreciation account balance increases each period by the amount of depreciation expense recorded until it finally reaches an amount equal to the original cost of the asset less estimated salvage value.

Liability/Revenue Adjustments—Unearned Revenues

A liability/revenue adjustment involving unearned revenues covers those situations in which the customer has transferred assets, usually cash, to the selling company prior to the receipt of merchandise or services. When assets are received before being earned, a liability called unearned revenue is created. Such receipts are debited to the asset account, Cash, and credited to a liability account. The liability account credited may be called Unearned Fees, Revenue Received in Advance, Advances by Customers, or some similar title. The seller is obligated either to provide the services or return the customer's money. By performing the services, revenue is earned and the liability is canceled.

Advance payments are received for many items such as delivery services, tickets, and magazine or newspaper subscriptions. While only advance receipt of delivery fees will be illustrated and discussed, the other items are treated similarly.

Unearned Delivery Fees.   On December 7, the Rapid Delivery Company received $4,500 from a customer in payment for future delivery services. The journal entry was recorded as follows:

```
1987
Dec. 7  Cash  . . . . . . . . . . . . . . . . . . .   4,500
              Unearned Delivery Fees  . . . . . . . . .          4,500
        To record the receipt of cash from a customer in
        payment for future delivery services.
```

The two T-accounts relating to delivery fees are Unearned Delivery Fees (a liability) and Delivery Service Revenue. These accounts appear as follows on December 31, 1987 (before adjustment):

(Dr.)	**Unearned Delivery Fees**	(Cr.)
	1987 Dec. 7 Cash received in advance	4,500

(Dr.)	**Delivery Service Revenue**	(Cr.)
	1987 Dec. 15 Cash 20 On account	5,000 5,700
	Bal. before adjustment	10,700*

* The $10,700 balance came from transactions discussed in Chapter 2.

The Unearned Delivery Fees liability account established when the cash was received by the company will be converted into revenue as the delivery services are performed. Before the financial statements are prepared, it will be necessary to make an adjusting entry to transfer the amount of the services performed by the company from a liability account to revenue account. If we assume that one third of the $4,500 in the Unearned Delivery Fees account has been earned by December 31, then $1,500 will be transferred to the Delivery Service Revenue account as follows:

Adjustment 5— Previously unearned revenue

```
1987
Dec. 31  Unearned Delivery Fees  . . . . . . . . . . .   1,500
              Delivery Service Revenue  . . . . . . . . .          1,500
         To transfer a portion of delivery fees from the liability
         account to the revenue account.
```

The T-accounts would appear as follows after the adjusting entry has been posted:

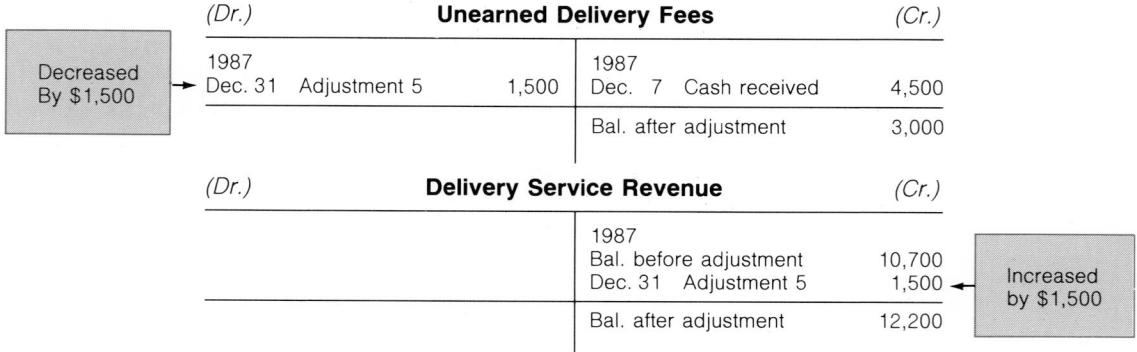

(Dr.)	**Unearned Delivery Fees**		(Cr.)
Decreased By $1,500 →	1987 Dec. 31 Adjustment 5	1,500	1987 Dec. 7 Cash received	4,500
			Bal. after adjustment	3,000

(Dr.)	**Delivery Service Revenue**	(Cr.)	
	1987 Bal. before adjustment Dec. 31 Adjustment 5	10,700 1,500 ←	**Increased by $1,500**
	Bal. after adjustment	12,200	

The delivery service revenue is reported in the income statement for 1987. The $3,000 balance in the Unearned Delivery Fees account is reported as a liability in the balance sheet. In 1988, the $3,000 will be earned and transferred to a revenue account.

The adjusting entries for deferred items are made on data already recorded in a company's asset and liability accounts. Adjusting entries on accrued items, which you will learn about in the next section, are made for business data not yet recorded in the accounting records. We will continue using the Rapid Delivery Company for our example transactions.

■ ADJUSTMENTS FOR ACCRUED ITEMS

Accrued items require two types of adjusting entries: asset/revenue adjustments and liability/expense adjustments. The first group—asset/revenue adjustments—involves accrued assets; the second group—liability/expense adjustments—involves accrued liabilities.

Asset/Revenue Adjustments—Accrued Assets

Accrued assets are assets that exist at the end of an accounting period but have not yet been recorded. These assets represent rights to receive future payments that are not legally due at the balance sheet date. To present an accurate picture of the affairs of the business on the balance sheet, these rights must be recognized at the end of an accounting period by preparing an adjusting entry to correct the account balances. An example of this type of adjustment would be revenues earned that have not been billed or collected. To indicate the dual nature of these adjustments, in addition to the asset recorded, a related revenue must also be recorded. Because the revenues must also be recorded, these adjustments may also be called **accrued revenues.**

Unbilled Delivery Fees.   Services may be performed for customers in one accounting period while the billing for those services takes place in a different accounting period.

The Rapid Delivery Company performed $1,000 of delivery services on account for a client in the last few days of December. Because it takes time to do the paper work, the client will be billed for the services in January. The necessary adjusting journal entry at December 31, 1987, is:

Adjustment 6— Unbilled revenues	1987 Dec. 31	Accounts Receivable (or Accrued Delivery Fees Receivable)	1,000	
		Delivery Service Revenue		1,000
		To record unbilled delivery services performed in December.		

After posting the adjusting entry the T-accounts will appear as follows:

(Dr.)   **Accounts Receivable**   (Cr.)

	1987	
Increased by $1,000	Previous bal.	5,200*
	Dec. 31 Adjustment 6	1,000
	Bal. after adjustment	6,200

* This previous balance came from transactions discussed in Chapter 2.

(Dr.)   **Delivery Service Revenue**   (Cr.)

1987		
Bal. before adjustment	10,700	
Dec. 31 Adjustment 5— previously unearned revenue	1,500	Increased by $1,000
Dec. 31 Adjustment 6	1,000	
Bal. after both adjustments	13,200	

The delivery service revenue appears in the income statement, and the asset, accounts receivable, appears in the balance sheet.

Liability/Expense Adjustments—Accrued Liabilities

Accrued liabilities are liabilities that exist at the end of an accounting period but have not yet been recorded. They represent obligations to make payments not legally due at the balance sheet date, such as employee salaries. At the end of the accounting period, these obligations are recognized by preparing an adjusting entry including both a liability and an expense. For this reason, they may also be called **accrued expenses.**

Salaries.   The recording of the payment of employee salaries usually involves a debit to an expense account and a credit to cash. Unless salaries are paid on the last day of the accounting period for a pay period ending on that date, an adjusting entry is required to record any salaries incurred but not yet paid.

The Rapid Delivery Company paid $3,600 of salaries on Friday, December 28, 1987, to cover the first four weeks of December. The entry made at that time was:

1987			
Dec. 28	Salaries Expense	3,600	
	Cash		3,600
	Paid truck driver salaries for the first four weeks of December.		

Assuming the last day of December 1987 falls on a Monday, the above expense account does not show salaries earned by employees for the last day of the month. Nor does the account show the employer's obligation to pay these salaries. The accounts pertaining to salaries appear as follows before adjustment:

(Dr.)	**Salaries Expense**	(Cr.)	(Dr.)	**Accrued Salaries Payable**	(Cr.)
1987 Dec. 28	3,600			1987 Dec. 28 Bal.	–0–

If salaries are $3,600 for four weeks, they are $900 per week. For a five-day workweek, daily salaries are $180. The following adjusting entry is needed on December 31:

Adjustment 7—Accrued salaries

Dec. 31   Salaries Expense   180
                Accrued Salaries Payable   180
                To accrue one day's salaries which were earned
                but are unpaid.

The two T-accounts involved appear as follows after adjustment:

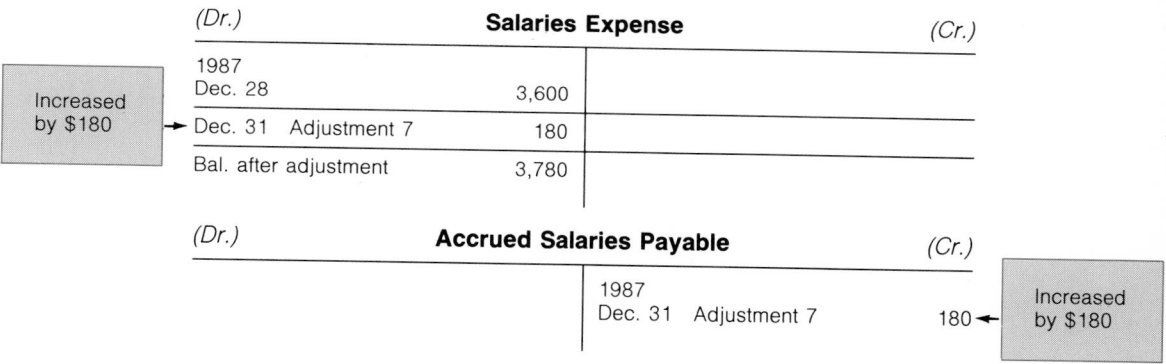

(Dr.)	**Salaries Expense**	(Cr.)
1987 Dec. 28	3,600	
Dec. 31 Adjustment 7	180	
Bal. after adjustment	3,780	

Increased by $180

(Dr.)	**Accrued Salaries Payable**	(Cr.)
	1987 Dec. 31 Adjustment 7	180

Increased by $180

The debit in the adjusting journal entry brings the month's salaries expense up to its correct $3,780 amount for income statement purposes. The credit to Accrued Salaries Payable records the $180 salary liability to employees. The accrued salaries payable is shown as a liability in the balance sheet.

■ EFFECTS OF FAILING TO PREPARE ADJUSTING ENTRIES

Failure to prepare proper adjusting entries causes net income and the balance sheet to be in error. The following diagram shows the effect on net income and balance sheet items of failing to record each of the major types of adjusting entries:

Failure to recognize	Effect on net income	Effect on balance sheet items
1. Consumption of the benefits of an asset (prepaid expense)	Overstates net income	Overstates assets Overstates owner's capital
2. Earning of previously unearned revenues	Understates net income	Overstates liabilities Understates owner's capital
3. Accrual of assets	Understates net income	Understates assets Understates owner's capital
4. Accrual of liabilities	Overstates net income	Understates liabilities Overstates owner's capital

Using the Rapid Delivery Company as an example, this chapter has discussed and illustrated many of the typical adjusting entries that companies must make at the end of an accounting period. Other types of adjusting entries such as those involving interest expense and interest revenue were not discussed in this chapter, but will be covered in later chapters.

■ SUMMARY

Accountants make adjusting entries to include in the accounts information on economic activity that has occurred but has not yet been recorded. The entries have not been made because either (1) it is more convenient and economical to wait until the end of the period to record the activities, or (2) source documents concerning the activities have not yet come to the accountant's attention.

Adjusting entries can be grouped into two broad classes: deferred items and accrued items. Deferred items consist of adjusting entries involving data previously recorded in the accounts. Accrued items consist of adjusting entries relating to activity on which no data have been previously recorded in the accounts.

Deferred items require two types of adjusting entries: asset/expense adjustments and liability/revenue adjustments. Asset/expense adjustments involve recognizing an expense as a result of the using up of a previously recorded asset; examples include insurance, rent, supplies, and depreciation. Liability/revenue adjustments involve recognizing the earning of revenue and the cancellation of a liability by providing services for which customers have paid in advance; examples include delivery services, tickets, and subscriptions.

Accrued items also require two types of adjusting entries: asset/revenue adjustments and liability/expense adjustments. Asset/revenue adjustments involve recognizing the growth of an asset and a revenue as a result of the rendering of services to customers; an example is unbilled delivery fees. Liability/expense adjustments involve recognizing an expense and the corresponding obligation to pay as a result of the receipt of services; an example is salaries.

In all cases, adjusting entries involve changing account balances at the end of the period from what they presently contain to what they should contain for proper financial reporting. Without adjusting entries, financial statements could not correctly show the solvency of the company in the balance sheet and the profitability of the company in the income statement.

In the first three chapters of this text, you have learned several of the steps of the accounting process. To help you understand them, some of these steps have been presented out of the actual order an accountant would use. These steps as a group are usually referred to as the accounting process (or cycle). Chapter 4 will organize these steps as actually performed by accountants and will complete the accounting cycle.

NEW TERMS INTRODUCED IN CHAPTER 3

Accounting period

A time period normally of one month, one quarter, or one year into which an entity's life is arbitrarily divided for financial reporting purposes (90).

Accounting year (fiscal year)

An accounting period of one year. The accounting year may or may not coincide with the calendar year (90).

Accrual basis of accounting

Recognizes revenues when sales are made or services are performed, regardless of when cash is received. Recognizes expenses as incurred whether or not cash has been paid out (91).

Accrued assets and liabilities

Assets and liabilities that exist at the end of an accounting period but have not yet been recorded; they represent rights to receive, or obligations to make, payments that are not legally due at the balance sheet date. Examples are accrued fees receivable and salaries payable (103–4).

Accrued items

See accrued assets and liabilities.

Accrued revenues and expenses

Other names for accrued assets and liabilities.

Accumulated depreciation account

A contra asset account that shows the total of all depreciation on the asset up to the balance sheet date (100).

Adjusting entries

Journal entries made at the end of an accounting period to change the balance of certain accounts; they reflect economic activity that has taken place but has not yet been recorded. Adjusting entries are made to bring the accounts to their proper balances before financial statements are prepared (90).

Book value

For depreciable assets, book value equals cost less accumulated depreciation (101).

Calendar year

The normal year ending on December 31 (90).

Cash basis of accounting

Recognizes revenues when cash is received and recognizes expenses when cash is paid out (91).

Contra asset account

An account shown as a deduction from the asset to which it relates in the balance sheet; used to give interested parties more complete financial information (100).

Deferred items

Those items involving data previously recorded in the accounts. Data are transferred from asset and liability accounts to expense and revenue accounts. Examples are prepaid expenses, depreciation, and unearned revenues (92).

Depreciable amount

The difference between an asset's cost and its estimated salvage value (100).

Depreciable asset

A building, machine, vehicle, or equipment on which depreciation expense is recorded (99).

Depreciation accounting

The process of recording depreciation expense (99).

Depreciation expense

The amount of asset cost assigned as an expense to a particular time period (99).

Depreciation formula (straight-line)

$$\frac{\text{Asset cost} - \text{Estimated salvage value}}{\text{Estimated number of years of useful life}} = \text{Annual depreciation (99).}$$

Fiscal year

An accounting year of 12 consecutive months that may or may not coincide with the calendar year. For example,

a company may have an accounting or fiscal year that runs from April 1 of one year to March 31 of the next (90).

Matching principle

An accounting principle requiring that expenses incurred in producing revenues be deducted from the revenues they generated during the accounting period (91).

Prepaid expense

An asset that is awaiting assignment to expense. An example is prepaid insurance. Assets such as cash and accounts receivable are not prepaid expenses (94).

Salvage value (scrap value)

The amount for which an asset can probably be sold at the end of its estimated useful life (99).

Service potential

The benefits that can be obtained from assets. The future services that assets can render make assets "things of value" to a business (95).

Unearned revenue

Assets received from customers before services are performed for them. Since the revenue has not been earned, it is a liability, often called *revenue received in advance,* or *advances by customers* (101).

Useful life

The estimated number of periods that a company can make use of an asset (99).

DEMONSTRATION PROBLEM

The trial balance of the Korman Company for December 31 of the current year includes, among other items, the following account balances:

	Debits	Credits
Office Supplies on Hand	$ 6,000	
Prepaid Rent	25,200	
Buildings	200,000	
Accumulated Depreciation—Buildings		$33,250
Salaries Expense	124,000	
Unearned Delivery Fees		4,000

Additional data:

1. Part of the supplies represented by the $6,000 balance of the Office Supplies on Hand account have been consumed. An inventory count of the supplies actually on hand at December 31 totaled to $2,400.
2. On May 1 of the current year, a rental payment of $25,200 was made for 12 months of rent; it was debited to Prepaid Rent.

3. The annual depreciation for the buildings is based on the cost shown in the Buildings account less an estimated salvage value of $10,000. The estimated useful lives of the buildings are 40 years each.
4. The salaries expense of $124,000 does not include $6,000 of unpaid salaries earned since the last payday.
5. One fourth of the unearned delivery fees have been earned by December 31.
6. Delivery services of $600 were performed for a customer, but a bill has not yet been sent.

Required: *a.* Prepare the adjusting journal entries for December 31, assuming adjusting entries are prepared only at year-end.

b. Based on the adjusted balance shown in the Accumulated Depreciation—Building account, how many years has the Korman Company owned the building?

Solution to demonstration problem

a.

KORMAN COMPANY
GENERAL JOURNAL

Date		Account Titles and Explanation	Post. Ref.	Debit	Credit
19— Dec.	31	Office Supplies Expense		3 6 0 0	
		Office Supplies on Hand			3 6 0 0
		To record office supplies expense			
		($6,000 − $2,400).			
	31	Rent Expense		1 6 8 0 0	
		Prepaid Rent			1 6 8 0 0
		To record rent expense ($25,200 × 8/12).			
	31	Depreciation Expense—Buildings		4 7 5 0	
		Accumulated Depreciation—Buildings			4 7 5 0
		To record depreciation			
		[($200,000 − 10,000) ÷ 40 years]			
	31	Salaries Expense		6 0 0 0	
		Accrued Salaries Payable			6 0 0 0
		To record accrued salaries.			
	31	Unearned Delivery Fees		1 0 0 0	
		Delivery Service Revenue			1 0 0 0
		To record delivery fees earned.			
	31	Accounts Receivable		6 0 0	
		Delivery Service Revenue			6 0 0
		To record delivery fees earned.			

b. Eight years; computed as:

$$\frac{\text{Total accumulated depreciation}}{\text{Annual depreciation expense}} = \frac{\$33,250 + \$4,750}{\$4,750} = 8$$

QUESTIONS

1. Why are adjusting entries necessary? Why not treat every cash disbursement as an expense and every cash receipt as revenue when the cash changes hands?

2. "Adjusting entries would not be necessary if the cash basis of accounting were followed (assuming no mistakes were made in recording cash transactions as they occurred). Under the cash basis, receipts that are of a revenue nature are considered revenue when received and expenditures that are of an expense nature are considered expenses when paid. It is the use of the accrual basis of accounting, where an effort is made to match expenses incurred against the revenues they create, that makes adjusting entries necessary." Do you agree with this statement? Why?

3. Why don't accountants keep all the accounts at their proper balances continuously throughout the period so that adjusting entries would not have to be made before financial statements are prepared?

4. Identify the two major classes of adjusting entries and the types of adjusting entries that are included in each.

5. Give an example of an adjusting journal entry for each of the following:

a. Increase an expense and decrease an asset.
b. Increase a revenue and decrease a liability.
c. Increase both an asset and a revenue.
d. Increase both an expense and a liability.

6. You notice that the Supplies on Hand account has a debit balance of $7,400 at the end of the accounting period. How would you determine the extent to which this account needs adjustment?

7. Some assets are converted into expenses as they expire, and some liabilities become revenues as they are earned. Give examples of asset and liability accounts for which the statement is true. Give examples of asset and liability accounts for which the statement does not apply.

8. Give the depreciation formula for straight-line depreciation.

9. What does the term *accrued liability* mean?

10. What is meant by the term *service potential?*

11. When assets are received before they are earned, what type of an account is credited? As the amounts are earned where must the data be transferred?

EXERCISES

E–1

Prepare and post adjusting entry for insurance

a. A one-year insurance policy was purchased on, and provided coverage from, October 1, 1987, for $7,200. The following entry was made at that time:

```
1987
  Oct.  1  Prepaid Insurance . . . . . . . . . . . .   7,200
              Cash . . . . . . . . . . . . . . . .            7,200
           To record the purchase of insurance to cover
           a one-year period.
```

The company prepares financial statements once a year at year-end. What adjusting entry is necessary on December 31?

b. Show how the T-accounts for Prepaid Insurance and Insurance Expense would appear after the two entries are posted.

E–2

Prepare adjusting entry for rent

Assume that rent of $14,400 was paid on September 1, 1987, to cover a one-year period from that date. Prepaid Rent was debited. If financial statements are prepared only on December 31 of each year, what adjusting entry is necessary on December 31, 1987, to bring the accounts involved to their proper balances?

E–3

Prepare entries for purchase of supplies and adjustment at year-end

Office supplies were purchased for cash on December 2, 1987, for $1,920. The supplies were to be used over the next several months. A physical inventory showed that $480 of the supplies were on hand on December 31, 1987. Show the entry for the purchase. What adjusting entry would be necessary at December 31 assuming that financial statements are prepared at that time?

E–4

Prepare adjusting entry for depreciation

Assume that a company acquires a building on January 1, 1987, at a cost of $500,000. The building has an estimated useful life of 40 years and an estimated salvage value of $100,000. What adjusting entry is needed on December 31, 1987, to record the depreciation for the entire year 1987?

E–5

Determine salvage value of building

A building is being depreciated by an amount of $36,400 per year. You know it had an original cost of $403,000 and was expected to last 10 years. What is the estimated salvage value?

E–6

Prepare entries for receipt of subscription fees and adjustment at year-end

On September 1, 1987, the Beardon Company received a total of $120,000 as payment in advance for a number of one-year subscriptions to a monthly magazine. By the end of the year, one third of the magazines paid for in advance had been delivered. Give the entries to record the receipt of the subscription fees and to adjust the accounts on December 31, assuming annual financial statements are prepared at year-end.

E–7

Prepare adjusting entry for accrued legal services

Johnson and Wells, a law firm, performed legal services in late December 1987 for clients. The $17,000 of services will be billed to the clients in January 1988. Give the adjusting entry that is necessary on December 31, 1987, if financial statements are prepared at the end of each month.

E–8

Prepare adjusting entry for accrued salaries

Bailey Company incurs salaries at the rate of $1,000 per day. The last payday in January is Friday, January 27. Salaries for Monday and Tuesday of the next week have not been recorded or paid as of January 31. Financial statements are prepared monthly. Give the necessary adjusting entry on January 31.

E–9

Determine effect on net income from failing to record adjusting entries

State the income statement and balance sheet effects that each of the following would have for 1987.

a. No adjustment was made for accrued salaries of $3,600 as of December 31, 1987.
b. The collection of $3,200 for services not yet performed as of December 31, 1987, was credited to a revenue account and not adjusted. The services are performed in 1988.

PROBLEMS, SERIES A

P3–1–A

Prepare adjusting entries

The trial balance of the Billy Reeves Company as of December 31, 1987, includes, among other items, the following account balances:

	Debits	Credits
Prepaid Rent	$ 24,000	
Prepaid Insurance	12,000	
Buildings	200,000	
Accumulated Depreciation—Buildings . .		$64,000
Salaries Expense	110,000	

Additional data:

1. The debit balance in the Prepaid Insurance account is the advance premium for one year from September 1 of the current year.
2. The buildings have an estimated useful life of 25 years and an estimated salvage value of $40,000.
3. Salaries incurred but not paid at December 31 are $8,800.
4. The debit balance in Prepaid Rent is for a one-year period that started March 1 of the current year.

Required: Prepare the annual adjusting journal entries for December 31, 1987.

P3–2–A

Prepare and post adjusting entries

The Pettigrew Company bought a new machine on January 1, 1987, at a cost of $14,000. The machine had an estimated life of three years and an estimated salvage value of $1,400.

Required:
a. Prepare annual adjusting journal entries for the end of 1987, 1988, and 1989 to record depreciation on the machine.
b. Using T-accounts, show how the entries made in *(a)* would appear.

P3–3–A

Prepare and post adjusting entries; show balance sheet and income statement data

The following data are for the Shaw Company:

	Account title	Trial balance	Information for adjustments
Case 1:	Equipment	$180,000	Depreciation is based on a five-year
	Accumulated Depreciation—Equipment	64,000	life and a $20,000 estimated salvage value. The amount shown for Accumulated Depreciation—Equipment resulted from credits to that account made in adjusting entries for previous years.
Case 2:	Salaries Expense	88,000	Unpaid salaries incurred amount to $4,000. The $4,000 is not included in the amount shown in the trial balance.
Case 3:	Prepaid Insurance	35,800	Of the prepaid insurance in the trial balance, only $10,800 is for additional protection after December 31.

Required: For each of the above cases:

a. Prepare the annual adjusting journal entry, dating it December 31, 1987.
b. Set up T-accounts for each of the accounts adjusted, enter balances before adjustment, post the adjusting entries made in part *(a)*, and determine balances after adjustment.
c. Show the data that would appear in the balance sheet.
d. Show the data for the year that would appear in the income statement.

P3–4–A

Prepare and post adjusting entries

Among the account balances shown in the trial balance of the Denson Company for December 31, 1987, are the following:

	Debits	Credits
Supplies on Hand	$ 6,960	
Prepaid Insurance	9,600	
Buildings	168,000	
Accumulated Depreciation—Buildings . .		$39,000

Additional data:

1. The amount of supplies on hand on December 31 is $1,200.
2. The balance in the Prepaid Insurance account is for a two-year policy, beginning June 1 of the current year.
3. Depreciation for the buildings is based on an estimated salvage value of $18,000 and an estimated useful life of 50 years.

Required:
a. Prepare the annual adjusting journal entries for December 31.
b. Open three-column ledger accounts for each of the accounts involved, enter the balances as shown in the trial balance, post the adjusting entries, and show balances.

P3–5–A

Prepare and post adjusting entries

The Walton Laundry Company has the following account balances included in its trial balance for December 31, 1987:

	Debits	Credits
Accounts Receivable	$26,000	
Prepaid Rent	1,200	
Equipment	15,000	
Unearned Laundry Fees		$ 3,000
Laundry Service Revenue		48,000
Salaries Expense		21,000

Additional data:

1. The balance in the Prepaid Rent account is for a one-year period beginning July 1, 1987.
2. The equipment was purchased on July 1, 1987, and is expected to have a useful life of six years, with a salvage value of $3,000.
3. Of the $3,000 unearned laundry service fees in the trial balance, $2,000 have been earned by December 31.
4. Laundry services of $48 were performed on account for a customer on December 30. No bill has been sent to the customer, and no journal entry has been made.
5. Salaries incurred but not paid at year-end are $500.

Required:
a. Prepare the annual adjusting entries for December 31.
b. Open three-column ledger accounts for each of the accounts involved, enter the balances as shown in the trial balance, post adjusting journal entries, and show balances.

P3–6–A

Prepare adjusting entries

The Delta Tank Company occupies rented quarters on the main street of the city. In order to get this location, it was necessary for the company to rent a store larger than needed, so a portion of the area is subleased (rented) to Dudley's Restaurant.

The following partial trial balance was taken from the company's ledger as of the close of business on December 31, 1987. You should study the partial trial balance to determine how certain transactions were originally recorded. Then you will be able to determine the necessary annual adjusting entries.

DELTA TANK COMPANY
Partial Trial Balance
December 31, 1987

	Debits	Credits
Cash	$60,000	
Prepaid Rent	2,000	
Prepaid Insurance	5,400	
Supplies on Hand	1,000	
Store Equipment	70,000	
Accumulated Depreciation—Store Equipment		$ 6,000
Service Revenue		450,000
Store Salaries Expense	73,500	
Rent Revenue		11,000

Additional data:

1. The salaries of the store clerks amount to $270 per day and were paid through Thursday, December 27. December 31 is a Monday. Saturday is a workday, and the store is closed on Sundays.
2. The equipment had a cost of $70,000, an estimated useful life of 20 years, and an estimated salvage value of $10,000.
3. The store carries one combined annual insurance policy that was taken out on August 1. The policy was new this year and costs $5,400 per year.
4. Supplies on hand on December 31, 1987, amount to $460.
5. The prepaid rent applies to December 1987 and January 1988.
6. Services of $8,000 were performed in December and will be billed to customers in January.

Required: Prepare the adjusting entries required by the data presented above. Show your calculations.

PROBLEMS, SERIES B

P3–1–B

Prepare adjusting entries

The trial balance of the Space Company at December 31, 1987, includes, among other items, the following account balances:

	Debits
Prepaid Insurance	$45,000
Prepaid Rent	51,840
Supplies on Hand	11,880

Examination of the records shows that annual adjustments should be made for the following items:

1. Of the prepaid insurance in the trial balance, $18,000 is for coverage during the months after December 31 of the current year.
2. The balance in the Prepaid Rent account is for a 12-month period that started October 1 of the current year.
3. Supplies on hand at the end of the year are $6,480.

Required: Prepare the annual adjusting journal entries at December 31.

P3–2–B

Prepare and post adjusting entries

The Tanner Company acquired a new truck on January 1, 1987. The truck has a cost of $16,000, an estimated useful life of three years, and an estimated salvage value of $1,000.

Required:
a. Prepare annual adjusting journal entires as of the end of 1987, 1988, and 1989 to record depreciation on the truck.
b. Using T-accounts, show how the entries made in *(a)* would appear.

P3–3–B

Prepare and post adjusting entries; show balance sheet and income statement data

The following data for the Ward Company are:

	Account title	Trial balance	Information for adjustments
Case 1:	Office Building	$935,000	The useful life is 50 years. Salvage value is esti-
	Accumulated Depreciation		mated at $55,000. The amount shown for Accu-
	—Office Building	176,000	mulated Depreciation—Office Building resulted from credits to that account made in adjusting entries for previous years
Case 2:	Salaries Expense	112,200	Salaries earned by employees since the last pay-day are $3,256. These have not been recorded.
Case 3:	Office Supplies on Hand . .	6,600	At the end of the period, office supplies on hand are $2,200.

Required: For each of the above cases:

  a. Prepare the annual adjusting journal entry, dating it December 31, 1987.
  b. Set up T-accounts for each of the accounts adjusted, enter balances before adjustment, post the adjusting entries made in part *(a),* and determine balances after adjustment.
  c. Show the data that would appear in the balance sheet.
  d. Show the data for the year that would appear in the income statement.

P3–4–B

Prepare and post adjusting entries

Watkins Company has the following account balances included in its trial balance for December 31, 1987:

	Debits	Credits
Accounts Receivable	$50,000	
Supplies on Hand	2,580	
Prepaid Rent	4,800	
Service Revenue		$174,000
Salaries Expense	82,000	

Additional data:

  1. The amount of supplies on hand on December 31 is $180.
  2. The balance in the Prepaid Rent account is for a one-year period, starting October 1 of the current year.
  3. Since the last payday, the employees of the company have earned additional salaries of $4,060.
  4. Services performed in December which will not be billed until January amount to $12,000.

Required: a. Prepare the annual adjusting journal entries for December 31.
  b. Open three-column ledger accounts for each of the accounts involved, enter the balances as shown in the trial balance, post the adjusting journal entries, and show balances.

P3–5–B

Prepare and post adjusting entries

The Driston Delivery Company has the following account balances included in its trial balance for December 31, 1987:

	Debits	Credits
Accounts Receivable	$ 22,000	
Prepaid Insurance	4,800	
Supplies on Hand	2,600	
Building	100,000	
Accumulated Depreciation—Building . .		$ 8,000
Unearned Delivery Fees		2,000
Delivery Service Revenue		64,000

Additional data:

  1. The balance in the Prepaid Insurance account is for a four-year period beginning January 1, 1987.
  2. At December 31, 1987, supplies on hand totaled $800.
  3. The building was acquired on January 1, 1985, and had an expected useful life of 20 years, with a salvage value of $20,000.
  4. $1,500 of the unearned delivery fees in the trial balance have now been earned.
  5. Delivery services were performed on account for a customer on December 31, $1,200. No bill has been sent to the customer, and no journal entry has been made.

Required: a. Prepare the annual adjusting entries for December 31.
  b. Open three-column ledger accounts for each of the accounts involved, enter the balances as shown in the trial balance, post the adjusting entries, and show balances.

P3–6–B

Prepare adjusting entries

The Dorothy Price Company adjusts and closes its books each December 31. Given below are a number of the company's account balances prior to adjustment on December 31, 1987:

	Debits	Credits
Prepaid Insurance	$ 10,000	
Supplies on Hand	4,300	
Building	170,000	
Accumulated Depreciation—Building . .		$ 68,000
Unearned Delivery Fees		3,600
Service Revenue		185,000
Salaries Expense	46,000	

Additional data (number your entries to match these items):

1. The Prepaid Insurance account balance represents the remaining cost of a four-year insurance policy dated June 30, 1985, having a total premium of $16,000.
2. The physical inventory of the supply stockroom indicates that the supplies on hand on December 31 total $1,500.
3. The building was originally acquired on January 1, 1970, with an estimated useful life of 40 years and a salvage value of $10,000.
4. Salaries earned since the last payday, but unpaid as of December 31, amount to $5,000.
5. Of the delivery fees received in advance, $900 have been earned by year-end.

Required: Prepare the adjusting entries indicated by the additional data. Show your calculations.

BUSINESS DECISION PROBLEM

Prepare report giving appraisal of offer to sell a business, correct computation of net income, determine book value of assets

A friend of yours, Daisy Glover, is quite excited over the opportunity she has to purchase the land, building, equipment, and several other assets of the Jackson Bowling Lanes for $375,000. Daisy tells you that the owner (who is moving because of poor health) reports that the business had net income of $75,000 in 1987 (last year). Daisy believes that annual net income of $75,000 on an investment of $375,000 is a really good deal. But, before completing the deal, she asks you to look it over. You agree to look it over and discover the following:

1. The owner has computed his annual income for 1987 as the sum of his cash withdrawals plus the increase in the Cash account: Withdrawals of $45,000 + Increase in Cash account of $30,000 = $75,000 income.
2. As buyer of the business, Daisy will take over responsibility for repayment of a $300,000 loan owed to a relative of the previous owner. The land, building, and equipment were acquired seven years ago at a cost of $30,000, $800,000, and $320,000, respectively. The building has a useful life of 40 years and an estimated salvage value of $80,000. The equipment has an estimated useful life of eight years and an estimated salvage value of $32,000.
3. An analysis of the Cash account shows the following for 1987:

Revenues received		$420,000
Cash paid out in 1987 for:		
Wages paid to employees in 1987 . . .	$258,000	
Utilities paid for 1987	18,000	
Advertising expenses paid	15,000	
Supplies purchased and used in 1987 . .	24,000	
Payment on loan	30,000	
Owner withdrawals	45,000	390,000
Increase in cash balance for the year . . .		$ 30,000

4. You also find that the December utility bill of $3,000 and an advertising bill for December of $4,500 have not been paid.

Required: a.   Prepare a written report for Daisy giving your appraisal of the offer to sell the Jackson Bowling Lanes. Comment on the owner's method of computing the annual net income of the business.

b. Determine the book value of the land, buildings, and equipment employed in the business and an approximate income statement for 1987.

BUSINESS SITUATION FOR DISCUSSION

Merger Issue Is Dividing CPA Firms*
Lee Berton

NEW YORK—The prospect of mergers among some of the nation's largest accounting firms is far from generally acceptable to many of their smaller competitors.

"These mergers violate antitrust law and should be stopped by the appropriate government agencies," says Edward J. McGowen, executive director of the National CPA Group, an organization of 40 local and medium-sized accounting firms.

The subjects of these and similar charges are two sets of megamerger talks. Price Waterhouse & Co., the fifth largest U.S. accounting firm based on 1983 revenue, is discussing merger with seventh-ranked Deloitte Haskins & Sells;[1] together they would be the biggest U.S. CPA firm. Meanwhile, Alexander Grant & Co., the 11th largest accounting firm, is talking merger with Fox & Co., the 13th largest.

Big CPA firms say mergers like those under discussion wouldn't violate antitrust laws, and might even increase competition. Joseph E. Connor, chairman of Price Waterhouse, says a merger of his firm with Deloitte "would benefit not only our clients and the two firms, but the business community at large and the accounting profession as well."

John Thompson, chairman and chief executive officer of KMG Main Hurdman, the ninth biggest CPA firm, agrees. "Every other firm such as mine would react positively to such competition by rolling our sleeves up and doing a better job," he says.

But many small and medium-sized firms are worried. Over the past five years, they have been battered as the biggest firms—particularly the so-called Big Eight—expanded their practices by aggressively courting small business clients. Now they fear that even bigger accounting firms will need still smaller clients for continued growth—and will have the clout to go after them.

Among those who say a Price Waterhouse-Deloitte merger may violate antitrust law is Stanford L. Levin,

an associate professor of economics at Southern Illinois University in Edwardsville and a former consultant to the Federal Trade Commission. Mr. Levin and Wayne A. Label, an accounting professor at the University of San Diego, recently completed a study that they say shows that mergers among the Big Eight pose competitive problems.

The study says a combined Price Waterhouse-Deloitte firm would audit public companies with more than 33% of the sales of all public companies. "Their next competitor, Arthur Andersen & Co., would audit companies with only close to 15% of the sales of all public companies," Mr. Levin says. The share drops down to near 6% for Touche Ross & Co., the eighth biggest firm, and falls to below 1% for all others.

Mr. Label also says that there are 52 major U.S. cities where Price Waterhouse and Deloitte both have offices, and he estimates that "in the majority of them" the newly combined firm would be "the biggest CPA firm in town."

That kind of dominance scares smaller firms. "The bigger the Big Eight get, the more they're going to take our business away," says Arthur H. Metcalf, managing partner of Metcalf, Frix & Co., an Atlanta CPA firm.

Mr. Metcalf says that two months ago, Deloitte's Atlanta office took on a former client of Metcalf Frix—Appalachian Oil & Gas Co.—"at less than half the fees we were charging."

John Capito, president of Appalachian, says he switched to Deloitte, even though he'd been a Metcalf Frix client for a decade, because the local firm "wasn't competitive price-wise" and "doesn't have the expertise of the big firm."

At Deloitte, James Copeland, managing partner of the Atlanta Office, says, "Our fee (for Appalachian) is very reasonable by our standards."

Some smaller CPA firms have accused big firms of "low-balling," charging an extraordinarily low fee to win business and then raising the fee substantially after absorbing a loss.

The possibility that mergers among big accounting firms might lessen competition has also caused concern in Congress. Rep. John D. Dingell, chairman of the House Committee on Energy and Commerce's subcommittee that oversees the accounting profession, has urged the FTC and the Justice Department to examine the implications of a Price Waterhouse-Deloitte merger.

---

* *The Wall Street Journal,* October 16, 1984, p. 31. Reprinted by permission of *The Wall Street Journal,* © Dow Jones & Company, Inc., 1984. All rights reserved.

[1] Authors' note: This merger is no longer being considered by the parties.

Such a combination "could have the unintended and untoward result of setting off a merger wave among the Big Eight firms, resulting in the creation of the Big Four," Mr. Dingell said in a letter to the FTC's chairman, James Miller. "This kind of concentration would be unacceptable and inimical to the normally competitive nature of the accounting industry."

Government officials and lawyers say, however, that proving antitrust violations among professional firms is harder than for manufacturing companies. They call the area of antitrust violations among big professional organizations a black hole that current legal case law hasn't really explored.

In addition, "private partnerships isn't an area where public information is readily available as with public companies, so it makes an antitrust case even tougher to establish," says Charles Corddry, deputy assistant director of the FTC's bureau of competition.

Illustration 4.5 *Partially Completed Work Sheet—Income Statement Columns*

RAPID DELIVERY COMPANY
Work Sheet
For the Month Ended December 31, 1987

Acct. No.	Account Titles	Trial Balance Debit	Trial Balance Credit	Adjustments Debit	Adjustments Credit	Adjusted Trial Balance Debit	Adjusted Trial Balance Credit	Income Statement Debit	Income Statement Credit
100	Cash	10,650				10,650			
101	Accounts Receivable	5,200		(6) 1,000		6,200			
102	Supplies on Hand	1,400			(3) 500	900			
103	Prepaid Insurance	2,400			(1) 200	2,200			
104	Prepaid Rent	1,200			(2) 400	800			
110	Delivery Trucks	40,000				40,000			
200	Accounts Payable		3,130				3,130		
201	Unearned Delivery Fees		4,500	(5) 1,500			3,000		
300	John Turner, Capital, 12/1/87		50,000				50,000		
301	John Turner, Drawing	3,000				3,000			
400	Delivery Service Revenue		10,700		(5) 1,500 (6) 1,000		13,200		13,200
500	Advertising Expense	50				50		50	
501	Gas and Oil Expense	680				680		680	
502	Salaries Expense	3,600		(7) 180		3,780		3,780	
503	Utilities Expense	150				150		150	
		68,330	68,330						
504	Insurance Expense			(1) 200		200		200	
505	Rent Expense			(2) 400		400		400	
506	Supplies Expense			(3) 500		500		500	
507	Depreciation Expense— Delivery Trucks			(4) 750		750		750	
110A	Accumulated Depreciation— Delivery Trucks				(4) 750		750		
202	Accrued Salaries Payable				(7) 180		180		
				4,530	4,530	70,260	70,260	6,510	13,200
	Net Income							6,690	
								13,200	13,200

The Balance Sheet Columns

Assets, liabilities, and owner's equity accounts listed in the Adjusted Trial Balance columns are extended to the Balance Sheet columns—assets as debits and liabilities and owner's equity amounts as credits (see Illustration 4.6).[1]

---

[1] In actual practice, accountants often work straight down from the first account appearing on the work sheet and continue down, sorting each item to the appropriate column of the work sheet. This procedure typically results in sorting the balance sheet accounts before the income statement accounts.

Illustration 4.6 *Completed Work Sheet—Balance Sheet Columns*

RAPID DELIVERY COMPANY
Work Sheet
For the Month Ended December 31, 1987

Acct. No.	Account Titles	Trial Balance Debit	Trial Balance Credit	Adjustments Debit	Adjustments Credit	Adjusted Trial Balance Debit	Adjusted Trial Balance Credit	Income Statement Debit	Income Statement Credit	Balance Sheet Debit	Balance Sheet Credit
100	Cash	10,650				10,650				10,650	
101	Accounts Receivable	5,200		*(6)* 1,000		6,200				6,200	
102	Supplies on Hand	1,400			*(3)* 500	900				900	
103	Prepaid Insurance	2,400			*(1)* 200	2,200				2,200	
104	Prepaid Rent	1,200			*(2)* 400	800				800	
110	Delivery Trucks	40,000				40,000				40,000	
200	Accounts Payable		3,130				3,130				3,130
201	Unearned Delivery Fees		4,500	*(5)* 1,500			3,000				3,000
300	John Turner, Capital, 12/1/87		50,000				50,000				50,000
301	John Turner, Drawing	3,000				3,000				3,000	
400	Delivery Service Revenue		10,700		*(5)* 1,500 / *(6)* 1,000		13,200		13,200		
500	Advertising Expense	50				50		50			
501	Gas and Oil Expense	680				680		680			
502	Salaries Expense	3,600		*(7)* 180		3,780		3,780			
503	Utilities Expense	150				150		150			
		68,330	68,330								
504	Insurance Expense			*(1)* 200		200		200			
505	Rent Expense			*(2)* 400		400		400			
506	Supplies Expense			*(3)* 500		500		500			
507	Depreciation Expense— Delivery Trucks			*(4)* 750		750		750			
110A	Accumulated Depreciation— Delivery Trucks				*(4)* 750		750				750
202	Accrued Salaries Payable				*(7)* 180		180				180
				4,530	4,530	70,260	70,260	6,510	13,200		
	Net Income							6,690			6,690
								13,200	13,200	63,750	63,750

Note that the beginning, rather than the ending, balance of John Turner's capital account is carried into the credit column because closing entries have not yet been prepared and posted.

Note also that the net income that was determined in the Income Statement columns appears again in the Balance Sheet columns. The net income amount was shown as a debit in the Income Statement columns in order to force balance those columns. Net income is shown as a credit in the Balance Sheet columns because it increases owner's equity or capital, and increases in owner's equity are accounted for as credits. With the inclusion of the net income amount, the Balance Sheet columns balance.

If the Balance Sheet column totals do not agree on the first attempt, work backwards through the process used in preparing the work sheet. Specifically, the following steps should be taken until the error is discovered:

1. Retotal the two Balance Sheet columns to see if an error in addition was made. If the column totals do not agree, check to see if some balance sheet item was not extended or was extended incorrectly from the Adjusted Trial Balance columns.
2. Retotal the Income Statement columns and determine whether the correct amount of net income or net loss for the period was entered in the appropriate columns in the Income Statement and Balance Sheet columns.
3. Retotal the Adjusted Trial Balance columns. If the totals agree, check to see that each item was transferred to the correct Income Statement or Balance Sheet column. If the totals do not agree, make sure that each adjustment was properly added to or subtracted from the related amount in the Trial Balance column.
4. Retotal the Adjustments columns.
5. Retotal the Trial Balance columns. If the totals do not agree, the ledger accounts must be reviewed to find the error.

■ PREPARING FINANCIAL STATEMENTS FROM THE WORK SHEET

When the work sheet has been completed, all the information needed to prepare the income statement, statement of owner's equity, and balance sheet is readily available. Now the information only needs to be recast into the appropriate financial statement format.

Income Statement

Information needed to prepare the income statement can be taken from the Income Statement columns in the work sheet. The income statement in Illustration 4.7 is based on the information in the Income Statement columns in Illustration 4.6.

Illustration 4.7

Income Statement

RAPID DELIVERY COMPANY
Income Statement
For the Month Ended December 31, 1987

Revenue:

Delivery service revenue . . .		$13,200

Expenses:

Advertising	$ 50	
Gas and oil	680	
Salaries	3,780	
Utilities	150	
Insurance	200	
Rent	400	
Supplies	500	
Depreciation—delivery trucks . .	750	
Total expenses		6,510
Net income		$ 6,690

Statement of Owner's Equity

The **statement of owner's equity** (also called statement of owner's capital) is a financial statement that summarizes the transactions affecting the owner's capital account balance. Information needed to prepare this financial statement is taken from the Balance Sheet columns in the work sheet (Illustration 4.6). Such a statement (Illustration 4.8) is prepared by showing the beginning capital account balance (Account No. 300), adding net income (or deducting net loss), and then subtracting the owner's withdrawals (Account No. 301). The ending capital balance is then carried forward to the balance sheet. **The statement of owner's equity helps to relate income statement information to balance sheet information;** it indicates how net income, shown on the income statement, relates to the amount of owner's capital, shown on the balance sheet under owner's equity.

Illustration 4.8

Statement of Owner's Equity

RAPID DELIVERY COMPANY
Statement of Owner's Equity
For the Month Ended December 31, 1987

John Turner, Capital, December 1, 1987 . .	$50,000
Net income for December	6,690
Total	$56,690
Less: Drawings	3,000
John Turner, Capital, December 31, 1987 .	$53,690

Balance Sheet

The balance sheet is completed from the information in the Balance Sheet columns of the work sheet (Illustration 4.6). The beginning balance shown for owner's capital must be revised to include net income less owner's withdraw-

Illustration 4.9

Balance Sheet

RAPID DELIVERY COMPANY
Balance Sheet
December 31, 1987

Assets

Cash		$10,650
Accounts receivable		6,200
Supplies on hand		900
Prepaid insurance		2,200
Prepaid rent		800
Delivery trucks	$40,000	
Less: Accumulated depreciation . .	750	39,250
Total assets		$60,000

Liabilities and Owner's Equity

Liabilities:

Accounts payable	$ 3,130
Unearned delivery fees	3,000
Accrued salaries payable	180
Total liabilities	$ 6,310

Owner's equity:

John Turner, capital	53,690
Total liabilities and owner's equity . .	$60,000

als for December. The correct amount for ending owner's equity is shown on the statement of owner's equity. The balance sheet for Rapid Delivery Company is shown in Illustration 4.9.

JOURNALIZING ADJUSTING ENTRIES

Now that the financial statements have been completed from the work sheet, the adjusting entries entered in the Adjustments columns must be entered in the general journal and posted to the appropriate ledger accounts. The process of preparing these adjusting entries is the same as we used in Chapter 3, except the work sheet is now the source for making the entries. **The preparation of a work sheet does not eliminate the need to prepare and post adjusting entries because the work sheet is only an accounting tool and is not part of the formal accounting records.**

Each adjusting entry can be identified through the numerical notations in the Adjustments columns and the adjustments explanations at the bottom of the work sheet, and each entry is shown with its appropriate debit(s) and credit(s). The adjusting entries for the Rapid Delivery Company as they would appear in the general journal are:

		GENERAL JOURNAL					*Page 3*		
Date		Account Titles and Explanation	Post. Ref.		Debit			Credit	
1987		**Adjusting Entries**							
Dec.	31	Insurance Expense	504		2 0 0				
		Prepaid Insurance	103					2 0 0	
		To record insurance expense for December.							
	31	Rent Expense	505		4 0 0				
		Prepaid Rent	104					4 0 0	
		To record rent expense for December.							
	31	Supplies Expense	506		5 0 0				
		Supplies on Hand	102					5 0 0	
		To record supplies used during December.							
	31	Depreciation Expense—Delivery Trucks	507		7 5 0				
		Accumulated Depreciation—Delivery Trucks	110A					7 5 0	
		To record depreciation expense for December.							
	31	Unearned Delivery Fees	201	1 5 0 0					
		Delivery Service Revenue	400				1 5 0 0		
		To transfer a portion of delivery fees from							
		the liability account to the revenue account.							
	31	Accounts Receivable	101	1 0 0 0					
		Delivery Service Revenue	400				1 0 0 0		
		To record unbilled delivery services							
		performed in December.							
	31	Salaries Expense	502		1 8 0				
		Accrued Salaries Payable	202					1 8 0	
		To accrue one day's salaries that							
		were earned but are unpaid.							

■ THE CLOSING PROCESS

From Chapter 3, you learned that (1) revenue and expense accounts are **nominal (temporary) accounts** since they are merely subclassifications of a **real (permanent) account,** Owner's Equity; and (2) financial statements are prepared for certain accounting periods. The closing process is (1) the act of transferring the balances in the revenue and expense accounts to a clearing account called Income Summary and then to owner's capital, and (2) the act of transferring the balance in the owner's drawing account to the owner's capital account. The closing process reduces revenue, expense, and owner's drawing account balances to zero so they will be ready to receive data for the next accounting period.

The **Income Summary account** is a clearing account used only at the end of an accounting period to summarize revenues and expenses for the period. After all revenue and expense account balances have been transferred to Income Summary, the balance in the Income Summary account represents the net income or net loss for the period. The balance in the Income Summary account is then closed, or transferred, to the owner's capital account, resulting in a zero balance in Income Summary.

The owner's drawing account is also closed at the end of the period. The owner's drawing account shows how many dollars of cash or goods the owner took out of the business during the current period. This drawing account is closed directly to the capital account; it is not closed to Income Summary because drawings have no effect on income or loss for the period.

The process of closing is often referred to as "closing the books." Remember, though, that only revenue, expense, and drawing accounts are closed—not asset, liability, or owner's equity accounts.

There are four basic steps in the closing process:

1. **Closing the revenue account(s)**—the balances in the revenue accounts are transferred to a clearing account called Income Summary.
2. **Closing the expense accounts**—the balances in the expense accounts are transferred to a clearing account called Income Summary.
3. **Closing the Income Summary account**—the balance of the Income Summary account is transferred to the owner's capital account.
4. **Closing the owner's drawing account**—the balance of the owner's drawing account is transferred to the owner's capital account.

An explanation of each of these steps follows, using the closing process for the Rapid Delivery Service as an example.

Step 1: Closing the Revenue Account(s)

Revenues appear in the Income Statement credit column of the work sheet. The only revenue appearing in the Income Statement credit column for Rapid Delivery Company is delivery service revenue of $13,200 (Illustration 4.6). Since revenue accounts have credit balances, they must be debited for an equal amount to bring them to a zero balance. When Delivery Service Revenue is debited, Income Summary (Account No. 600) is credited. This entry is made in the general journal to close the Delivery Service Revenue account. The account numbers in the Posting Reference column are entered when the journal entry has been posted to the ledger. This same statement is true for the other closing journal entries illustrated.

		GENERAL JOURNAL				Page 4
Date		Account Titles and Explanation	Post. Ref.	Debit	Credit	
1987		**Closing Entries**				
Dec.	31	Delivery Service Revenue	400	1 3 2 0 0		
		Income Summary	600		1 3 2 0 0	
		To close the revenue account in				
		the Income Statement credit				
		column to Income Summary.				

After closing, the Delivery Service Revenue account (in T-account format) appears as shown below. Note that the account now has a zero balance.

Delivery Service Revenue   *Account No. 400*

Decreased by $13,200	1987 Dec. 31 To close to Income Summary 13,200	Bal. before closing 13,200
		Bal. after closing –0–

The Income Summary account was credited for $13,200 as a result of the above entry. The Income Summary account will be shown later.

Step 2: Closing the Expense Accounts

Expenses appear in the Income Statement debit column of the work sheet. There are eight expenses for Rapid Delivery Company appearing in the Income Statement debit column (Illustration 4.6). As shown by the column subtotal, they add up to $6,510. Since expense accounts have debit balances, **each one** must be credited to bring it to a zero balance. The debit in the closing entry is made to the Income Summary account for $6,510. The following entry is made to close the expense accounts:

	GENERAL JOURNAL																Page 4

GENERAL JOURNAL   *Page 4*

Date		Account Titles and Explanation	Post. Ref.	Debit	Credit
1987 Dec.	31	Income Summary	600	6 5 1 0	
		Advertising Expense	500		5 0
		Gas and Oil Expense	501		6 8 0
		Salaries Expense	502		3 7 8 0
		Utilities Expense	503		1 5 0
		Insurance Expense	504		2 0 0
		Rent Expense	505		4 0 0
		Supplies Expense	506		5 0 0
		Depreciation Expense—Delivery Trucks	507		7 5 0
		To close the expense accounts			
		appearing in the Income Statement			
		debit column to Income Summary.			

The debit of $6,510 to the Income Summary account agrees with the Income Statement debit column subtotal in the work sheet. The comparison with the work sheet can serve as a check to make certain that all revenue and expense items are listed and have been closed; had the debit in the above entry been for a different amount than the column subtotal, there would be an error in the closing entry for expenses.

The expense accounts appear as shown below after they have been closed. Note that each account has a zero balance after closing.

Advertising Expense   *Account No. 500*

Bal. before closing	50	1987 Dec. 31 To close to Income Summary	50	Decreased by $50
Bal. after closing	–0–			

Gas and Oil Expense   *Account No. 501*

Bal. before closing	680	1987 Dec. 31 To close to Income Summary	680	Decreased by $680
Bal. after closing	–0–			

Salaries Expense   *Account No. 502*

Bal. before closing	3,780	1987 Dec. 31 To close to Income Summary	3,780	Decreased by $3,780
Bal. after closing	–0–			

Utilities Expense   *Account No. 503*

Bal. before closing	150	1987	
		Dec. 31 To close to Income Summary	150
Bal. after closing	–0–		

Decreased by $150

Insurance Expense   *Account No. 504*

Bal. before closing	200	1987	
		Dec. 31 To close to Income Summary	200
Bal. after closing	–0–		

Decreased by $200

Rent Expense   *Account No. 505*

Bal. before closing	400	1987	
		Dec. 31 To close to Income Summary	400
Bal. after closing	–0–		

Decreased by $400

Supplies Expense   *Account No. 506*

Bal. before closing	500	1987	
		Dec. 31 To close to Income Summary	500
Bal. after closing	–0–		

Decreased by $500

Depreciation Expense—Delivery Trucks   *Account No. 507*

Bal. before closing	750	1987	
		Dec. 31 To close to Income Summary	750
Bal. after closing	–0–		

Decreased by $750

The expense accounts could be closed before closing the revenue accounts. The end result is the same either way.

Step 3: Closing the Income Summary Account

After the revenues and expenses have been closed, the total amounts that formerly were carried in those accounts now are carried in the Income Summary account.

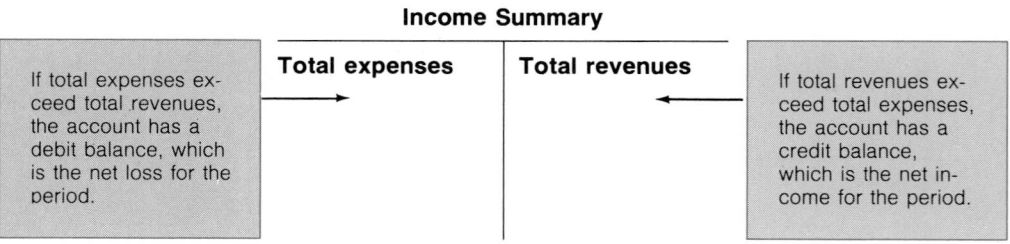

Income Summary

Total expenses	**Total revenues**
If total expenses exceed total revenues, the account has a debit balance, which is the net loss for the period.	If total revenues exceed total expenses, the account has a credit balance, which is the net income for the period.

For the Rapid Delivery Company, the Income Summary account appears as follows:

Income Summary   *Account No. 600*

1987		1987	
Dec. 31 From closing the		Dec. 31 From closing the	
expense accounts	6,510	revenue account	13,200
		Bal. before closing this	
		account (net income)	6,690

The credit balance of $6,690 is the net income for December.

Now the Income Summary account needs to be closed to the owner's capital account. The journal entry to do this is:

GENERAL JOURNAL   *Page 4*

Date		Account Titles and Explanation	Post. Ref.	Debit	Credit
1987 Dec.	31	Income Summary	600	6 6 9 0	
		John Turner, Capital	300		6 6 9 0
		To close the Income Summary			
		account to the owner's capital			
		account.			

The Income Summary and John Turner, Capital accounts will appear as follows after the Income Summary account is closed:

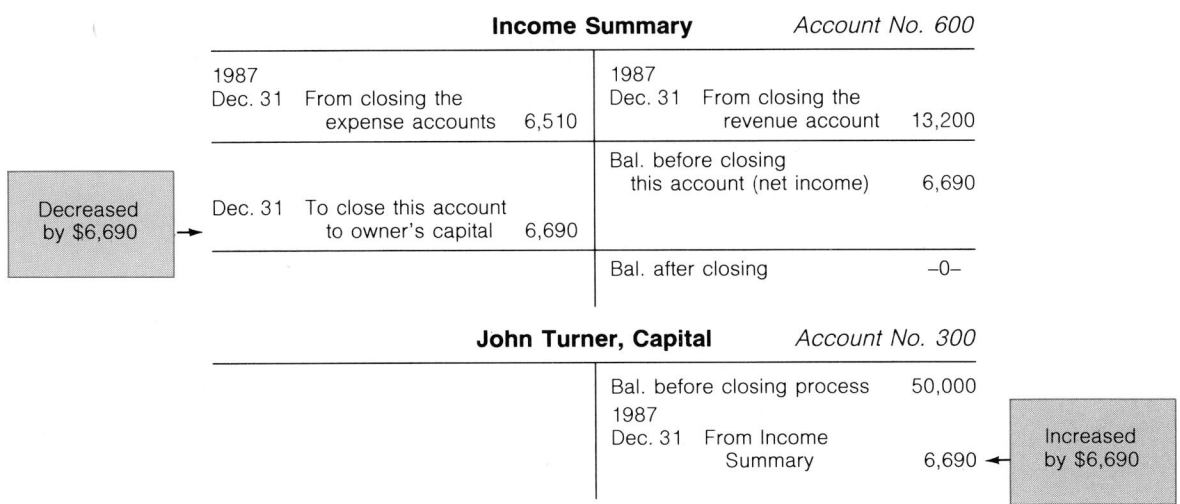

Income Summary   *Account No. 600*

	1987			1987		
	Dec. 31 From closing the			Dec. 31 From closing the		
	expense accounts	6,510		revenue account	13,200	
				Bal. before closing		
Decreased by $6,690	Dec. 31 To close this account			this account (net income)	6,690	
	to owner's capital	6,690				
				Bal. after closing	–0–	

John Turner, Capital   *Account No. 300*

Bal. before closing process	50,000	
1987		
Dec. 31 From Income		Increased
Summary	6,690	by $6,690

Step 4: Closing the Owner's Drawing Account

The last closing entry that needs to be made is to close the owner's drawing account. This account has a debit balance before closing. To close the account, the owner's drawing account is credited and the owner's capital account is debited. Notice that the drawing account is not closed to Income Summary. The drawing account is not an expense and does not enter into income determination.

For the Rapid Delivery Company, the journal entry to close the owner's drawing account is:

	Date		Account Titles and Explanation	Post. Ref.	Debit	Credit
			GENERAL JOURNAL			*Page 4*
1987 Dec.	31		John Turner, Capital	300	3 0 0 0	
			John Turner, Drawing	301		3 0 0 0
			To close the owner's drawing			
			account to the owner's capital			
			account.			

The owner's drawing and owner's capital accounts as they appear after this closing entry has been posted are:

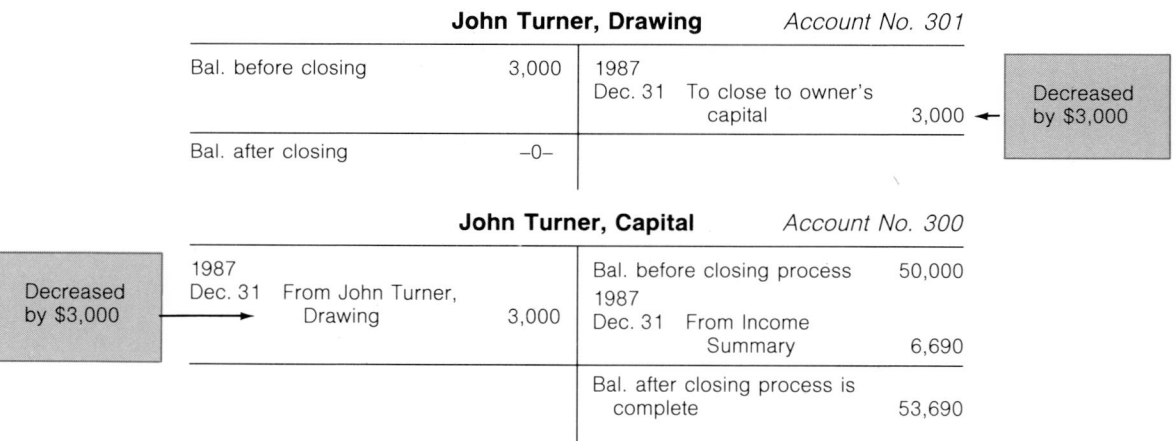

John Turner, Drawing   *Account No. 301*

| Bal. before closing | 3,000 | 1987 Dec. 31   To close to owner's capital | 3,000 | Decreased by $3,000 |

| Bal. after closing | –0– |

John Turner, Capital   *Account No. 300*

Decreased by $3,000	1987 Dec. 31 From John Turner, Drawing	3,000	Bal. before closing process	50,000
			1987 Dec. 31 From Income Summary	6,690
			Bal. after closing process is complete	53,690

Closing Process Summarized

The closing process is the transferring of revenue and expense account balances to a clearing account called Income Summary and then transferring from Income Summary to Owner's Capital the amount of net income or net loss for the period. Closing also includes the elimination of the balance in the owner's drawing account by transferring that amount to owner's capital. A summary of the process used to close the Rapid Delivery Company accounts shown on the work sheet in Illustration 4.6 is as follows:

1. The only revenue account appearing in the Income Statement credit column (revenues) was debited, and the Income Summary account was credited for the amount of revenue earned for the period, $13,200. Note that the credit to Income Summary is equal to the subtotal of the Income Statement credit column of the work sheet. This will be true no matter how many revenue accounts are closed.

2. Each expense account appearing in the Income Statement debit column (expenses) was credited for its balance, and the Income Summary account was debited for the total amount of expenses incurred for the period, $6,510. Note that the debit to Income Summary is equal to the subtotal of the Income Statement debit column of the work sheet.

3. The balance of the Income Summary account, $6,690 was closed to the owner's capital account. The Income Summary account balance was a credit (net income), so to close it the Income Summary account was debited and owner's capital was credited. If a net loss had occurred, Income Summary would have had a debit balance and closing would have been through a credit to Income Summary and a debit to owner's capital.

4. The balance in the owner's drawing account was closed to the owner's capital account by debiting the capital account and crediting the drawing account. The balance in the drawing account is found in the Balance Sheet debit column of the work sheet.

In our explanation of the closing process, we have used the T-account format to illustrate the adjusting and closing entries for the Rapid Delivery Company. In Appendix 4–B at the end of this chapter, these same adjusting and closing entries are shown in three-column ledger accounts.

Post-Closing Trial Balance

After closing has been completed, the only accounts in the ledger that have not been closed are the balance sheet accounts (the permanent, or real, accounts). Since these accounts contain the opening balances for the coming accounting period, they must, of course, be in balance. The preparation of a post-closing trial balance serves as a means of checking the accuracy of the closing process and ensures that the books are in balance at the start of the new accounting period.

A **post-closing trial balance** is a trial balance taken after the closing entries have been posted. The only accounts that should be open are assets, liabilities, and owner's capital. Account balances are listed in debit and credit columns and totaled to make sure debits and credits are equal.

A post-closing trial balance for the Rapid Delivery Company as of December 31, 1987, is shown in Illustration 4.10.

The amounts appearing in the post-closing trial balance are taken from the ledger after the closing entries have been posted. You can verify this by comparing the amounts below with those appearing in the ledger accounts for the Rapid Delivery Company shown in chapter Appendix 4–B. (This concludes the Rapid Delivery Company illustration, which has been used in Chapters 2, 3, and 4.)

Illustration 4.10

*Post-Closing Trial
Balance*

	RAPID DELIVERY COMPANY Post-Closing Trial Balance December 31, 1987		
Account No.		**Debits**	**Credits**
100	Cash	$10,650	
101	Accounts Receivable	6,200	
102	Supplies on Hand	900	
103	Prepaid Insurance	2,200	
104	Prepaid Rent	800	
110	Delivery Trucks	40,000	
110A	Accumulated Depreciation—Delivery Trucks . .		$ 750
200	Accounts Payable		3,130
201	Unearned Delivery Fees		3,000
202	Accrued Salaries Payable		180
300	John Turner, Capital		53,690
		$60,750	$60,750

THE CLASSIFIED BALANCE SHEET

All of the balance sheets presented so far in this text have been unclassified balance sheets. An **unclassified balance sheet** has three major categories: assets, liabilities, and owner's equity. Illustration 4.9 shows an unclassified balance sheet. A **classified balance sheet** subdivides some of the three major categories in order to provide more specific information for the users of financial statements. For example, assets may be subdivided into many different categories. At this point in the text we will divide assets into (1) current assets and (2) property, plant, and equipment. Liabilities may be classified as either current or long term. Owner's equity for a single proprietorship cannot be subdivided into classifications.

An example of a classified balance sheet for the Jamestown Sports Arena is shown in Illustration 4.11. This new example is used in order to include accounts that were not used in the illustration involving the Rapid Delivery Company. Jamestown Sports Arena rents its facilities for sporting events, concerts, and other activities. This balance sheet is presented in a vertical format (assets appearing above liabilities and owner's equity) rather than the horizontal format (assets on the left and liabilities and owner's equity on the right) which has been used previously in the text. The two formats are equally acceptable.

In this section, the following major categories of a classified balance sheet are discussed: current assets; property, plant, and equipment; current liabilities; and long-term liabilities. Owner's equity is no different in a classified balance sheet than it is in an unclassified one.

Current Assets

Current assets are cash and other assets that will be converted into cash or used up by the business in a relatively short period of time, usually a year or less. Current assets commonly found in a service-type business include cash,

GENERAL LEDGER (*continued*)

John Turner, Drawing

Account No. 301

Date		Explanation	Post. Ref.	Debit	Credit	Balance
1987 Dec.	31	Balance				3 0 0 0 Dr.
	31	To close	G4		3 0 0 0	– 0 –

Delivery Service Revenue

Account No. 400

Date		Explanation	Post. Ref.	Debit	Credit	Balance
1987 Dec.	31	Balance				1 0 7 0 0 Cr.
	31	Adjustment	G3		1 5 0 0	1 2 2 0 0 Cr.
	31	Adjustment	G3		1 0 0 0	1 3 2 0 0 Cr.
	31	To close	G4	1 3 2 0 0		– 0 –

Advertising Expense

Account No. 500

Date		Explanation	Post. Ref.	Debit	Credit	Balance
1987 Dec.	31	Balance				5 0 Dr.
	31	To close	G4		5 0	– 0 –

Gas and Oil Expense

Account No. 501

Date		Explanation	Post. Ref.	Debit	Credit	Balance
1987 Dec.	31	Balance				6 8 0 Dr.
	31	To close	G4		6 8 0	– 0 –

Salaries Expense

Account No. 502

Date		Explanation	Post. Ref.	Debit	Credit	Balance
1987 Dec.	31	Balance				3 6 0 0 Dr.
	31	Adjustment	G3	1 8 0		3 7 8 0 Dr.
	31	To close	G4		3 7 8 0	– 0 –

GENERAL LEDGER (*continued*)

Utilities Expense
Account No. 503

Date		Explanation	Post. Ref.	Debit	Credit	Balance
1987 Dec.	31	Balance				1 5 0 Dr.
	31	To close	G4		1 5 0	– 0 –

Insurance Expense
Account No. 504

Date		Explanation	Post. Ref.	Debit	Credit	Balance
1987 Dec.	31	Balance				– 0 –
	31	Adjustment	G3	2 0 0		2 0 0 Dr.
	31	To close	G4		2 0 0	– 0 –

Rent Expense
Account No. 505

Date		Explanation	Post. Ref.	Debit	Credit	Balance
1987 Dec.	31	Balance				– 0 –
	31	Adjustment	G3	4 0 0		4 0 0 Dr.
	31	To close	G4		4 0 0	– 0 –

Supplies Expense
Account No. 506

Date		Explanation	Post. Ref.	Debit	Credit	Balance
1987 Dec.	31	Balance				– 0 –
	31	Adjustment	G3	5 0 0		5 0 0 Dr.
	31	To close	G4		5 0 0	– 0 –

Depreciation Expense—Delivery Trucks
Account No. 507

Date		Explanation	Post. Ref.	Debit	Credit	Balance
1987 Dec.	31	Balance				– 0 –
	31	Adjustment	G3	7 5 0		7 5 0 Dr.
	31	To close	G4		7 5 0	– 0 –

P4–2–A

Prepare work sheet, adjusting entries, and closing entries

The trial balance of the Robison Auto Repair Company for December 31, 1987, appears below:

ROBISON AUTO REPAIR COMPANY
Trial Balance
December 31, 1987

	Debits	Credits
Cash	$ 33,000	
Accounts Receivable	5,600	
Prepaid Rent	9,600	
Equipment	38,600	
Accumulated Depreciation—Equipment		$ 4,400
Accounts Payable		9,000
T. E. Robison, Capital		41,000
T. E. Robison, Drawing	9,600	
Auto Repair Service Revenue		134,000
Salaries Expense	72,100	
Supplies Expense	16,000	
Insurance Expense	3,900	
	$188,400	$188,400

Additional data:

1. The prepaid rent is for the period of July 1, 1987, to June 30, 1988.
2. The depreciation on the equipment is $2,660.
3. Salaries incurred but unpaid as of December 31 are $6,000.

Required:

a. Prepare a 10-column work sheet for the year ended December 31, 1987.
b. Prepare adjusting journal entries.
c. Prepare closing journal entries.

P4–3–A

Prepare and post closing entries and prepare income statement

The account balances below are for Chuck Rogers, Architect, as they appeared in the work sheet for the month ended December 31, 1987.

	Income Statement	
	Debit	Credit
Architect Service Revenue		20,000
Salaries Expense	4,000	
Advertising Expense	800	
Insurance Expense	100	
Supplies Expense	340	
Depreciation Expense—Building	500	
Miscellaneous Expense	400	
	6,140	20,000
Net income	13,860	
	20,000	20,000

Required:

a. Prepare the closing journal entries. Assume that on December 31, 1987, the Chuck Rogers, Drawing account has a debit balance of $8,000 and the Chuck Rogers, Capital account has a credit balance of $100,000 before the closing process begins.
b. Using T-accounts, show how the accounts would appear after all of the closing entries have been posted.
c. Prepare an income statement for the month of December 1987.

P4-4-A

Prepare and post closing entries

Given below are the amounts appearing in the Adjusted Trial Balance columns of the December 31, 1987, work sheet for the Sutton Advertising Agency.

	Adjusted Trial Balance	
	Debit	Credit
Cash .	42,000	
Accounts Receivable	20,400	
Office Equipment	120,000	
Accumulated Depreciation—Office Equipment . .		72,000
Accounts Payable		12,960
G. Sutton, Capital		145,800
G. Sutton, Drawing .	33,600	
Advertising Service Revenue		132,000
Rent Expense	14,400	
Travel Expense .	6,000	
Salaries Expense	108,000	
Supplies Expense	1,800	
Insurance Expense .	1,440	
Depreciation Expense—Office Equipment	14,400	
Miscellaneous Expense	720	
	362,760	362,760

Required:

a. Based on the above data, prepare closing entries. (You may want to mentally determine which of the above items would appear in the Income Statement columns of the work sheet.) In preparing the third closing entry, you will need to determine whether the agency had a net income or a net loss for the period.

b. Using T-accounts show how the accounts appear after all of the closing entries have been posted.

P4-5-A

Prepare work sheet, income statement, statement of owner's equity, classified balance sheet, and closing entries.

The trial balance for December 31, 1987, of the Sherrill Photography Company is given below:

SHERRILL PHOTOGRAPHY COMPANY
Trial Balance
December 31, 1987

	Debits	Credits
Cash	$ 91,325	
Accounts Receivable .	11,050	
Prepaid Insurance .	2,145	
Land	46,475	
Building	71,500	
Accumulated Depreciation— Building		$ 21,450
Photography Equipment .	36,140	
Accumulated Depreciation— Photography Equipment .		7,228
Accounts Payable .		3,835
Sherrill, Capital .		182,637
Sherrill, Drawing	13,000	
Photography Service Revenue .		155,285
Salaries Expense	91,000	
Advertising Expense	7,800	
	$370,435	$370,435

Additional data:

1. Depreciation on the building is $1,430 for the year.
2. Depreciation on the photography equipment is $3,614 for the year.
3. Salaries incurred but unpaid are $910.
4. Prepaid insurance at year-end is $260.

Required:
   a. A 10-column work sheet for the year ended December 31, 1987.
   b. An income statement.
   c. A statement of owner's equity.
   d. A classified balance sheet.
   e. The required closing entries.

P4–6–A

Prepare work sheet, income statement, statement of owner's equity, classified balance sheet, adjusting entries, and closing entries

The trial balance for the Powell Printing Company as of December 31, 1987, contains the following account balances:

POWELL PRINTING COMPANY
Trial Balance
December 31, 1987

	Debits	Credits
Cash	$ 61,200	
Accounts Receivable	13,500	
Prepaid Insurance	3,000	
Supplies on Hand	2,000	
Building	80,000	
Accumulated Depreciation—		
Building		$ 40,000
Printing Equipment	40,000	
Accumulated Depreciation—		
Printing Equipment		20,000
Accounts Payable		10,000
J. Powell, Capital		56,400
J. Powell, Drawing	18,000	
Printing Service Revenue		160,000
Salaries Expense	60,000	
Advertising Expense	1,800	
Utilities Expense	6,200	
Miscellaneous Expense	700	
	$286,400	$286,400

Additional data:

1. Insurance expense for the year is $2,400.
2. A physical inventory shows that supplies costing $400 are on hand at December 31, 1987.
3. Depreciation expense on the building is $8,000.
4. Depreciation expense on the equipment is $2,500.
5. Salaries incurred but unpaid are $6,000.

Required:
   a. A 10-column work sheet for the year ended December 31, 1987.
   b. An income statement.
   c. A statement of owner's equity.
   d. A classified balance sheet.
   e. Adjusting journal entries.
   f. Closing journal entries.

P4-7-A

Prepare work sheet, income statement, statement of owner's equity, classified balance sheet, adjusting and closing entries, and post-closing trial balance

Piedmont Realty had the following trial balance for December 31, 1987:

PIEDMONT REALTY
Trial Balance
December 31, 1987

	Debits	Credits
Cash	$ 40,000	
Prepaid Rent	7,200	
Prepaid Insurance on Automobile	1,920	
Supplies on Hand	600	
Office Equipment	6,000	
Accumulated Depreciation— Office Equipment		$ 1,440
Automobile	16,000	
Accumulated Depreciation— Automobile		4,000
Accounts Payable		720
Unearned Management Fees		3,120
R. Goff, Capital		89,160
R. Goff, Drawing	47,000	
Sales Commissions Revenue		60,000
Management Service Revenue		4,800
Salaries Expense	39,960	
Advertising Expense	600	
Automobile Expense	3,560	
Miscellaneous Expense	400	
	$163,240	$163,240

Additional data:

1. Insurance expense on the automobile for the year is $960.
2. Rent expense for the year is $4,800.
3. Depreciation expense is: office equipment, $720; and automobile, $3,200.
4. Salaries incurred but unpaid as of December 31 are $6,660.
5. Supplies on hand on December 31, $200.
6. The unearned management fees were received and recorded on October 1, 1987. The advance payment covered six month's management of an apartment building.

Required:
   a. A 10-column work sheet for the year ended December 31, 1987.
   b. An income statement.
   c. A statement of owner's equity.
   d. A classified balance sheet.
   e. Adjusting and closing entries.
   f. A post-closing trial balance. Normally the post-closing trial balance would be prepared from the ledger accounts, but use the information in the Balance Sheet columns of the work sheet to prepare it. You will have to determine the ending balance in the owner's capital account to prepare the post-closing trial balance.

PROBLEMS, SERIES B

P4-1-B

Prepare work sheet

The trial balance of the Fletcher Plumbing Company as of December 31, 1987, is as follows:

FLETCHER PLUMBING COMPANY
Trial Balance
December 31, 1987

	Debits	Credits
Cash	$ 90,000	
Accounts Receivable	27,200	
Supplies on Hand	4,000	
Prepaid Insurance	3,600	
Building	140,000	
Accumulated Depreciation—Building		$ 25,000
Plumbing Tools and Equipment	36,000	
Accumulated Depreciation—Plumbing Tools and		
Equipment		9,000
Accounts Payable		22,000
D. Fletcher, Capital		104,200
D. Fletcher, Drawing	40,000	
Plumbing Service Revenue		280,000
Salaries Expense	96,000	
Utilities Expense	3,400	
	$440,200	$440,200

Additional data:

1. Supplies on hand at December 31, 1987, have a cost of $1,200.
2. The balance in the Prepaid Insurance account represents the cost of a two-year insurance policy covering the period from January 1, 1987, through December 31, 1988.
3. Depreciation expense is $2,500 on the building and $1,800 on the equipment.

Required: Prepare a work sheet for the Fletcher Plumbing Company for the year ended December 31, 1987.

P4-2-B

Prepare work sheet, adjusting entries, and closing entries

The following trial balance of Gooch Equipment Rental Company, as of December 31, 1987, contains the following account balances:

GOOCH EQUIPMENT RENTAL COMPANY
Trial Balance
December 31, 1987

	Debits	Credits
Cash	$ 70,400	
Accounts Receivable	48,400	
Prepaid Rent	7,920	
Prepaid Insurance	3,960	
Equipment	132,000	
Accumulated Depreciation—Equipment . .		$ 44,000
Accounts Payable		34,100
Pamela Gooch, Capital		153,120
Pamela Gooch, Drawing	26,400	
Rental Service Revenue		385,000
Salaries Expense	275,000	
Travel Expense	38,940	
Miscellaneous Expense	13,200	
	$616,220	$616,220

Additional data:

1. The prepaid rent was for the period January 1, 1987, to December 31, 1988.
2. The depreciation on the equipment is $8,800 per year.
3. The prepaid insurance was for the period April 1, 1987, to March 31, 1988.
4. Salaries incurred but unpaid total $3,300 at December 31.

Required:

a. Prepare a 10-column work sheet for the year ended December 31, 1987.
b. Prepare the adjusting journal entries.
c. Prepare the closing journal entries.

P4–3–B

Prepare and post closing entries and prepare income statement

The following account balances appeared in the Income Statement columns of the work sheet prepared for the Dependable TV Repair Company for the year ended December 31, 1987.

	Income Statement	
	Debit	Credit
TV Repair Service Revenue		598,400
Advertising Expense	2,550	
Salaries Expense	187,000	
Utilities Expense	3,400	
Insurance Expense	1,700	
Rent Expense	10,200	
Supplies Expense	3,400	
Depreciation Expense—Equipment	7,650	
	215,900	598,400
Net income	382,500	
	598,400	598,400

Required:

a. Prepare the closing journal entries. Assume that on December 31, 1987, the J. M. Thompson, Drawing account had a debit balance of $42,500 and the J. M. Thompson, Capital account had a credit balance of $119,000 before the closing process began.
b. Using T-accounts show how the accounts appear after all of the closing entries have been posted.
c. Prepare an income statement.

P4–4–B

Prepare and post closing entries

Given below are the amounts appearing on the Adjusted Trial Balance columns of the June 30, 1987, work sheet for the Boyd Real Estate Company.

	Adjusted Trial Balance	
	Debit	Credit
Cash .	160,000	
Accounts Receivable	19,500	
Office Equipment	70,000	
Accumulated Depreciation—Office Equipment . .		28,000
Automobiles	110,000	
Accumulated Depreciation—Automobiles		40,000
Accounts Payable		6,000
Donna Boyd, Capital		310,800
Donna Boyd, Drawing .	10,000	
Sales Commissions Revenue		260,000
Office Salaries Expense	50,000	
Salespersons' Commissions Expense	180,000	
Automobile Operating Expense .	8,000	
Rent Expense	8,500	
Supplies Expense	1,800	
Utilities Expense .	4,000	
Depreciation Expense—Office Equipment	7,000	
Depreciation Expense—Automobiles .	16,000	
	644,800	644,800

Required:

a. Based on the above data, prepare closing entries. (You may want to mentally determine which of the above items would appear in the Income Statement columns of the work sheet.) In preparing the third closing entry, you will also need to determine whether the company had a net income or a net loss for the period.

b. Using T-accounts show how the accounts appear after all of the closing entries have been posted.

P4–5–B

Prepare work sheet, income statement, statement of owner's equity, classified balance sheet, and closing entries

Preston Electric Contracting Company has the following trial balance as of December 31, 1987:

PRESTON ELECTRICAL CONTRACTING COMPANY
Trial Balance
December 31, 1987

	Debits	Credits
Cash	$ 272,000	
Accounts Receivable .	31,520	
Prepaid Insurance .	4,800	
Prepaid Rent—Building	57,600	
Supplies on Hand .	5,360	
Equipment	168,000	
Accumulated Depreciation—Equipment . .		$ 17,600
Accounts Payable .		3,800
Preston, Capital .		552,000
Preston, Drawing	30,000	
Electrician Service Revenue		477,360
Salaries Expense	380,200	
Rent Expense—Truck .	78,000	
Advertising Expense	9,880	
Legal and Accounting Expense	9,000	
Miscellaneous Expense	4,400	
	$1,050,760	$1,050,760

Additional data:

1. Insurance expense is $3,400.
2. Supplies on hand are $1,700.
3. Rent expense on the building is $50,600.
4. Depreciation expense on the equipment is $8,800.
5. Salaries incurred but unpaid are $7,000.

Required:
a. A 10-column work sheet for the year ended December 31, 1987.
b. An income statement.
c. A statement of owner's equity.
d. A classified balance sheet.
e. The December 31, 1987, closing entries.

P4–6–B

Prepare work sheet, income statement, statement of owner's equity, classified balance sheet, adjusting entries, and closing entries

The trial balance for the Fendley Cleaning Service Company as of December 31, 1987, is as follows:

FENDLEY CLEANING SERVICE COMPANY
Trial Balance
December 31, 1987

	Debits	Credits
Cash	$ 58,000	
Accounts Receivable	43,600	
Prepaid Insurance	9,600	
Prepaid Rent	18,000	
Supplies on Hand	23,000	
Office Equipment	20,000	
Accumulated Depreciation— Office Equipment		$ 7,000
Cleaning Equipment	60,000	
Accumulated Depreciation— Cleaning Equipment		17,500
Service Trucks	150,000	
Accumulated Depreciation— Service Trucks		46,876
Accounts Payable		14,000
M. Fendley, Capital		118,324
M. Fendley, Drawing	60,000	
Cleaning Service Revenue		480,000
Salaries Expense	228,500	
Gas and Oil Expense	7,000	
Utilities Expense	6,000	
	$683,700	$683,700

Additional data:

1. The balance in the Prepaid Insurance account represents the remaining cost of a five-year insurance policy purchased on January 2, 1986. The account was last adjusted on December 31, 1986.
2. The balance in the Prepaid Rent account represents the amount paid on January 2, 1987, to cover rent for the period from January 2, 1987, through June 30, 1988.
3. Depreciation on the plant assets is: office equipment, $2,000; cleaning equipment, $5,000; and service trucks, $18,750.
4. Salaries incurred but unpaid as of December 31, 1987, are $6,200.
5. A physical inventory shows that $4,000 of the supplies are on hand at December 31, 1987.

Required:
a. A 10-column work sheet for the year ended December 31, 1987.
b. An income statement.
c. A statement of owner's equity.
d. A classified balance sheet.
e. Adjusting journal entries.
f. Closing journal entries.

P4–7–B

Prepare work sheet, income statement, statement of owner's equity, classified balance sheet, adjusting and closing entries, and post-closing trial balance

K. Holding, CPA, has prepared the following trial balance for December 1987:

K. HOLDING, CPA
Trial Balance
December 31, 1987

	Debits	Credits
Cash	$ 96,000	
Accounts Receivable	19,200	
Supplies on Hand	4,000	
Prepaid Rent	12,240	
Prepaid Insurance	7,280	
Office Equipment	7,600	
Accumulated Depreciation—		
Office Equipment		$ 2,760
Furniture and Fixtures	29,200	
Accumulated Depreciation—		
Furniture and Fixtures		8,280
Accounts Payable		1,200
K. Holding, Capital		128,600
K. Holding, Drawing	42,520	
Accounting Service Revenue		200,000
Salaries Expense	98,800	
Utilities Expense	6,000	
Travel Expense	14,000	
Miscellaneous Expense	4,000	
	$340,840	$340,840

Additional data:

1. Supplies on hand December 31, 1987, are $1,000.
2. $9,200 of the prepaid rent was consumed in 1987.
3. $2,400 of the prepaid insurance expired in 1987.
4. Depreciation expense is: office equipment $800; and furniture and fixtures, $3,000.
5. Salaries incurred but unpaid are $4,350.

Required:

a. A 10-column work sheet for the year ended December 31, 1987.
b. An income statement.
c. A statement of owner's equity.
d. A classified balance sheet.
e. Adjusting and closing entries.
f. A post-closing trial balance. Normally the post-closing trial balance would be prepared from the ledger accounts, but use the information in the Balance Sheet columns of the work sheet to prepare it. You will have to determine the ending balance in the owner's capital account to prepare the post-closing trial balance.

BUSINESS DECISION PROBLEM 4–1

Prepare report on profitability of business

Sandy and Robbie Barron met while both were employed in the interior trim and upholstery department of an auto manufacturer. After their marriage, they decided to earn some extra income by doing small jobs involving canvas, vinyl, and upholstered products. Their work was considered excellent. At the urging of their customers, they decided to go into business for themselves, operating out of the basement of the house they owned. To do this, they invested $20,000 cash in their business. They spend $14,000 for a sewing machine (expected life is 10 years) and $2,000 for other miscellaneous tools and equipment (expected life is

5 years). They undertook only custom work, with the customer purchasing the required materials other than miscellaneous supplies. An advance deposit was generally required on all jobs.

The business seemed to be successful from the start, but they felt something was wrong. They worked hard and charged competitive prices. Yet there seemed to be barely enough cash available for withdrawal from the business to cover immediate personal needs. Summarized, the checkbook of the business for 1987, their second year of operation, shows:

Balance, January 1, 1987		$ 3,200
Cash received from customers:		
For work done in 1986	$ 6,000	
For work done in 1987	96,000	
For work to be done in 1988	8,000	110,000
		$113,200
Cash paid out:		
Two-year insurance policy dated January 1, 1987 . . .	$ 3,200	
Utilities	8,000	
Supplies	24,000	
Taxes	4,400	
Miscellaneous	12,000	
Owner withdrawals	58,000	109,600
Balance, December 31, 1987		$ 3,600

The Barrons feel, considering how much they have worked, that they should have earned more than the $58,000 of cash flow they withdrew from their business. This is $10,000 less than their combined income when they were employed by the auto manufacturer. They are seriously considering giving up their business and going back to work for the auto manufacturer. They turn to you for advice. You discover the following:

1. Of the supplies purchased in 1987, $4,000 were used on jobs billed to customers in 1987; no supplies were used for any other work.
2. Work completed in 1987 and billed to customers for which cash had not yet been received by year-end amounted to $18,000 (which is considered fully collectible).

Required: Prepare a written report for the Barrons, responding to their belief that their business is not sufficiently profitable. (Hint: Prepare an income statement for 1987 and include it in your report.)

BUSINESS DECISION PROBLEM 4–2

Prepare income statement and statement of owner's equity; determine effect of closing entries on income statement and balance sheet accounts; complete closing process

On December 31, 1987, Eddie Brown's bookkeeper quit his job without even notifying Mr. Brown of his net income for 1987. The bookkeeper had taken Mr. Brown's accounting records home with him the previous night and failed to bring them to work on December 31, 1987. But Mr. Brown found the following closing entries on a pad in the bookkeeper's desk:

1987				
Dec. 31	Service Revenue	90,000	
	Income Summary		90,000
	To close the revenue account appearing in the Income Statement credit column of the work sheet to Income Summary.		
31	Income Summary	37,600	
	Rent Expense		4,000
	Salaries Expense		24,000
	Advertising Expense		2,000
	Utilities Expense		2,400

Depreciation—Automobiles	2,000
Depreciation—Office Equipment	500
Insurance Expense	2,520
Miscellaneous Expense	180

To close the expense accounts appearing in the
Income Statement debit column of the work sheet to
Income Summary.

Mr. Brown knows that his capital account balance was $40,000 on January 1, 1987, and that he withdrew $20,000 for personal use during 1987.

Required:

a. Using the information given above, prepare an income statement and a statement of owner's equity for the year ended December 31, 1987.
b. What effect do the closing journal entries have on the income statement accounts?
c. What effect do the closing journal entries have on the balance sheet accounts?
d. Did the bookkeeper make all of the necessary closing entries? If not, what other entries should be made?

COMPREHENSIVE REVIEW PROBLEM

Problem covers all steps in the accounting cycle covered in Chapters 1–4. Open ledger accounts and enter beginning balances. Journalize transactions and post to ledger accounts. Prepare work sheet, income statement, statement of owner's equity, classified balance sheet, adjusting and closing entries, and post-closing trial balance.

The Moore Delivery Service Company has the following chart of accounts:

Account No.	Account title	Account No.	Account title
100	Cash	301	M. Moore, Drawing
101	Accounts Receivable	400	Delivery Service Revenue
102	Supplies on Hand	500	Supplies Expense
103	Prepaid Insurance	501	Insurance Expense
104	Prepaid Rent	502	Rent Expense
110	Building	503	Depreciation Expense—Building
110A	Accumulated Depreciation—Building	504	Depreciation Expense—Trucks
111	Trucks	505	Salaries Expense
111A	Accumulated Depreciation—Trucks	506	Utilities Expense
200	Accounts Payable	507	Miscellaneous Expense
201	Accrued Salaries Payable	600	Income Summary
300	M. Moore, Capital		

The post-closing trial balance as of May 31, 1987, was as follows:

MOORE DELIVERY SERVICE COMPANY
Post-Closing Trial Balance
May 31, 1987

	Debits	Credits
Cash	$ 20,000	
Accounts Receivable	30,000	
Supplies on Hand	14,000	
Prepaid Insurance	4,800	
Prepaid Rent	12,000	
Building	320,000	
Accumulated Depreciation—Building . .		$ 36,000
Trucks	80,000	
Accumulated Depreciation—Trucks . .		30,000
Accounts Payable		24,000
M. Moore, Capital		390,800
	$480,800	$480,800

The transactions for June 1987 were as follows:

Transactions:

June 1 Performed delivery services for customers on account, $40,000.
3 M. Moore withdrew $10,000 to pay some personal bills.
4 Purchased a $20,000 truck on account.
7 Collected $22,000 of the accounts receivable.
8 Paid $16,000 of the accounts payable.
11 Purchased $4,000 of supplies on account. The asset account for supplies was debited.
17 Performed delivery services for cash, $32,000.
20 Paid the utilities bills for June, $1,200.
23 Paid miscellaneous expenses for June, $600.
28 Paid salaries of $28,000.

Supplemental data needed to prepare adjusting entries:

1. Depreciation expense on the building for June is $800.
2. Depreciation expense on the trucks for June is $400.
3. Salaries incurred but unpaid as of June 30 are $2,000.
4. A physical count showed that there are $12,000 of supplies on hand as of June 30.
5. The prepaid insurance balance of $4,800 applies to a two-year period beginning June 1, 1987.
6. The prepaid rent of $12,000 applies to a one-year period beginning on June 1, 1987.
7. The company performed $12,000 of delivery services for customers as of June 30 that will not be billed to those customers until July.

Required: a. Open three-column ledger accounts for the accounts listed in the chart of accounts.
b. Enter the May 31, 1987, account balances in the accounts.
c. Journalize the transactions for June 1987.
d. Post the June journal entries and include cross-references (assume all journal entries appear on page 10 of the journal).
e. Prepare a 10-column work sheet as of June 30, 1987.
f. Prepare an income statement, a statement of owner's equity, and a classified balance sheet.
g. Prepare and post the adjusting entries (assume they appear on page 11 of the general journal).
h. Prepare and post the closing entries (assume they appear on page 12 of the general journal).
i. Prepare a post-closing trial balance.

BUSINESS SITUATION FOR DISCUSSION

Financial Strategies for Strengthening the Balance Sheet*

Robert F. Reilly, CPA, Editor

* * * * *

The Balance Sheet: Guideline of Planning Strategies

☐ The balance sheet provides an excellent guideline for some important long-term strategies. This contrasts with the income statement, which reports only the operating results of one year. Furthermore, the cumulative nature of the balance sheet allows us to see today

* Adapted from *The Ohio CPA Journal,* a publication of The Ohio Society of CPAs, Winter 1984, pp. 43–44. Used with permission.

the results of transactions that occurred over a period of many years.

The assumed data in Exhibit I for X [Co.] and Y [Co.] illustrate this point. First, observe X Co. Its total short-term liabilities are less than one-half of current assets. (The general norm is that current assets should be twice current liabilities.) The ratio of current assets to current liabilities is 2.08, and working capital of $36,200 (excess of current assets over current liabilities) suggests that cash flow is strong. Also, nonoperating short-term debt is low. Furthermore, X has no long-term debt . . . This indicates that there are no fixed charges and no pressure to restructure long-term debt. Finally, X has a significantly positive balance in . . . [owner's capital], indicating cumulative retention of profits. Its total equity is a strong 82.4 percent of total capitalization.

Exhibit I

X CO. AND Y CO.
Comparative Balance Sheets
June 30, 1983

Assets	X (Healthy)	Y (Troubled)
Current:		
Cash	$ 10,400	$ 2,060
Accounts receivable	24,600	27,920
Inventories	34,800	41,220
Total current assets	$ 69,800	$ 71,200
Plant and equipment (net)	140,200	144,784
Total assets	$210,000	$215,984
Liabilities and Owner's Equity		
Current Liabilities:		
Accounts payable and other	$ 29,600	$ 32,024
Banks loans, short-term paper and maturing long-term debt	4,000	64,000
Total current liabilities	$ 33,600	$ 96,024
Long-term debt	–0–	64,000
Owner's Equity:		
Owner's capital	176,400	55,960
Total liabilities and owner's equity	$210,000	$215,984

Now notice that Y's situation contrasts sharply with that of X. Current liabilities significantly in excess of current assets signal trouble with liquidity and cash flow. Bank loans, short-term paper and maturing long-term debt comprise a staggering two-thirds of current liabilities. Long-term debt is significant. . . . [Owner's equity] is a scant 13.0 percent of capitalization.

It should be emphasized that there is no universally desirable balance sheet. X [Co.'s] statement in Exhibit I could be used as a general model, since it meets general financial norms. But financial norms vary company by company and industry by industry. For a particular company, the desirable capital structure depends on: (1) the expected stability of earnings; (2) the amount of debt service risk it is willing to bear; (3) its goals; (4) industry norms; and (5) the cost and availability of different types of capital.

*   *   *   *   *

CHAPTER 5

Merchandising Transactions, Introduction to Inventories, and Classified Income Statement

LEARNING OBJECTIVES

After studying this chapter, you should be able to:

1. Record journal entries for sales and purchase transactions using periodic inventory procedure.
2. Describe the terms under which merchandise is sold, including freight terms, and distinguish cash discounts from trade discounts.
3. Prepare a classified income statement.
4. Prepare a work sheet and closing entries for a merchandising company.
5. Define and use correctly the new terms in the glossary.

In the first four chapters, you learned about the accounting process and how it begins with recording business transactions and results in the preparation of financial statements. As you studied the accounting process, you followed step-by-step the business transactions of a service company—the Rapid Delivery Company. This company provided a delivery service to customers in return for a fee. Because service companies are the least complicated type of business, they are shown first as examples in the study of accounting. You are now ready to apply the accounting process to a more complex type of business—a merchandising company. The fundamental accounting concepts for service-type businesses also apply to merchandising businesses, but some additional accounts and techniques are needed to account for purchases and sales.

The normal flow of goods from manufacturer to final customer is as follows:

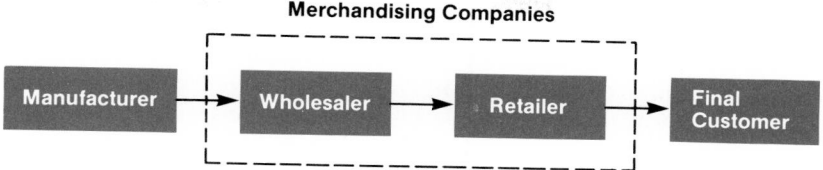

Merchandising Companies

Manufacturer → Wholesaler → Retailer → Final Customer

Manufacturers produce goods from raw materials and normally sell them to wholesalers. After performing certain functions, such as packaging or labeling, wholesalers normally sell the goods to retailers. Retailers sell the goods to final customers. The two middle boxes in the diagram above represent merchandising companies. These companies buy goods in finished form for resale.

In this chapter you will see a comparison of the income statements of a service company and a merchandising company. Then you will learn how to record merchandise-related transactions. Finally, a work sheet and the closing process for a merchandising company are described.

■ TWO INCOME STATEMENTS COMPARED—SERVICE COMPANY AND MERCHANDISING COMPANY

Illustration 5.1 compares the main divisions of an income statement of a service company with those of a merchandising company. To determine profitability or net income for a service company, total expenses incurred are deducted from revenues earned. A merchandising company is a more complex type of business and, therefore, has a more complex income statement.

As shown in Illustration 5.1, merchandising companies first must deduct from revenues the cost of the goods they sell to customers. Then they deduct other expenses. The income statement of a merchandising company has three main divisions: (1) sales revenues, (2) cost of goods sold, and (3) expenses. Sales revenues result from the sale of goods by the company; cost of goods sold indicates how much the goods that were sold cost the company; and the expenses are the company's expenses in running the business.

Illustration 5.1

Condensed Income Statement of a Service Company Compared with a Merchandising Company

SERVICE COMPANY Income Statement For the Year Ended December 31, 1987		MERCHANDISING COMPANY Income Statement For the Year Ended December 31, 1987	
Service revenues	$13,200	Sales revenues	$262,000
		Cost of goods sold	159,000
		Gross margin	$103,000
Expenses	6,510	Expenses	74,900
Net income	$ 6,690	Net income	$ 28,100

The next two sections of the chapter discuss the first two main divisions of the income statement of a merchandising company. The third division (expenses) is similar to expenses for a service company and has been illustrated in preceding chapters. As you study these chapter sections, keep in mind how the divisions of the merchandising income statement are related to each other, producing the final figure—net income or net loss—which indicates the profitability of the company.

■ SALES REVENUES

The sale of goods occurs between two parties. The seller of the goods gives them to the buyer in exchange for cash or a promise to pay at a later date. If all goes well, this exchange is a relatively simple business transaction.

From the seller's point of view, sales are made to create revenue. As you recall, revenue is the inflow of assets resulting from the rendering of services or the sale of goods to customers. Illustration 5.1 showed a condensed income statement so that major divisions could be emphasized. Now the more complete income statement actually prepared by accountants is described. The merchandising company we will use to illustrate the income statement is called the Hanlon Retail Food Store. This section explains first how to record sales revenues, including the effect of trade discounts. Next you will learn how to record the two deductions from sales revenues—sales discounts and sales returns and allowances (see Illustration 5.2). The amount that remains is **net sales.** The formula, then, for determining net sales is:

$$\text{Net sales} = \text{Gross sales} - (\text{Sales discounts} + \text{Sales returns and allowances})$$

Illustration 5.2

Partial Income Statement of Merchandising Company

HANLON RETAIL FOOD STORE Partial Income Statement For the Year Ended December 31, 1987		
Operating revenues:		
Gross sales		$282,000
Less: Sales discounts	$ 5,000	
Sales returns and allowances	15,000	20,000
Net sales		$262,000

Recording Gross Sales

In a sales transaction, the legal ownership (title) of goods is transferred from the seller to the buyer. The sale is usually accompanied by the physical delivery of goods, and the recording of the sale is based on a business document called an invoice (usually called a sales invoice by the seller and a purchase invoice by the buyer).

An **invoice** is a document, prepared by the seller of merchandise and sent to the buyer, that contains the details of a sale, such as the number of units, unit price, total price billed, terms of sale, and manner of shipment. In a retail company, the invoice is prepared at the point of sale. In a wholesale company, which supplies goods to retailers, the invoice is prepared after the accounting department receives notification from the shipping department that the goods have been shipped to the retailer. Illustration 5.3 shows an invoice prepared by a wholesale company for goods sold to a retail company.

Illustration 5.3

Invoice

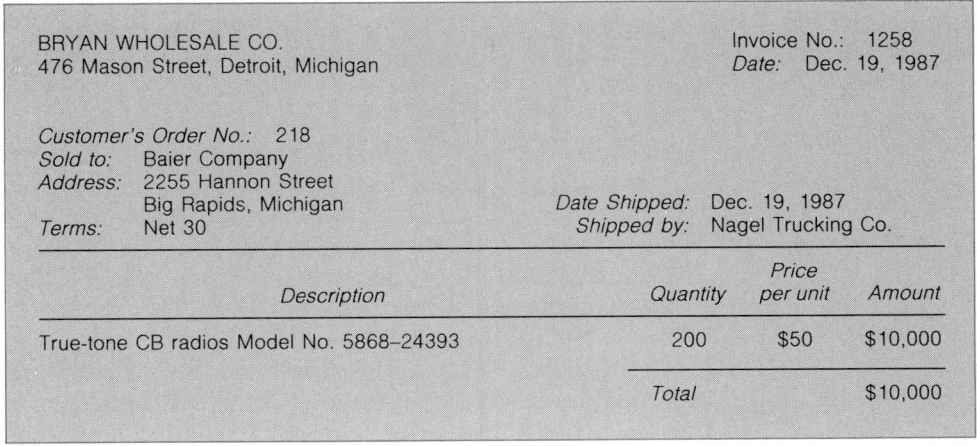

		Price	
Description	Quantity	per unit	Amount
True-tone CB radios Model No. 5868–24393	200	$50	$10,000
	Total		$10,000

Using the invoice as the source document, the revenue from the sale is recorded at the time of the sale for the following reasons:

1. **Legal title** to the goods has passed, and the goods are now the responsibility and property of the buyer.
2. The selling price of the goods has been established.
3. The seller's obligation has been completed.
4. The goods have been exchanged for another asset, such as cash or accounts receivable.
5. The costs incurred can be determined.

Each time a sale is made, revenue is produced for the company. This revenue increases a revenue account called Sales. As you learned in Chapter 2, revenues are increased by credits. So the Sales account is credited for the amount of the sale.

Usually sales are for cash or on account. When a sale is for cash, the credit to the Sales account is accompanied by a debit to Cash; when a sale is on account, the Sales account credit is accompanied by a debit to Accounts Receivable. For example, a $10,000 sale for cash is recorded as follows:

Cash	10,000	
Sales		10,000
To record the sale of merchandise for cash.		

A $10,000 sale on account is recorded as follows:

Accounts Receivable	10,000	
Sales		10,000
To record the sale of merchandise on account.		

Usually a seller will quote the gross invoice price of goods to the buyer. But sometimes a seller instead quotes a list price of goods along with trade discounts that are available. In this latter situation, the buyer must calculate the gross invoice price. The list price less all trade discounts is the **gross selling price.** The gross selling price is used by the merchandising company to determine the actual selling price to the customer.

Determining Gross Sales Price When There Are Trade Discounts. Unlike cash discounts (discussed later), which are related to the prompt payment of an invoice, a **trade discount** is a percentage deduction, or discount, from the specified list price or catalog price of merchandise. Trade discounts are used to:

1. Reduce the cost of catalog publication. If list prices are printed in the catalog and separate discount sheets are given to the salespersons whenever prices change, a catalog may be used for a longer period of time.
2. Grant quantity discounts.
3. Allow quotation of different prices to different types of customers, such as retailers and wholesalers.

Trade discounts may be shown on the seller's invoice, but they are not recorded in the seller's accounting records because they are only used to calculate the gross selling price. Nor are trade discounts recorded on the books of the purchaser. To illustrate, assume an invoice contains the following data:

List price, 200 swimsuits at $6 . . .	$1,200
Less: Trade discount, 30%	360
Gross invoice price	$ 840

The seller records a sale of $840. The purchaser records a purchase of $840. In other words, list prices and their trade discounts are not entered on the books of either the seller or the purchaser.

Sometimes the list price of a product is subject to several trade discounts; this is called a **chain discount.** Chain discounts exist, for example, when a wholesaler receives two trade discounts because of certain services performed, such as packaging and distributing. When more than one discount is given, each discount is applied to the declining balance successively. If a product has a list price of $100 and is subject to trade discounts of 20% and 10%, the actual price paid by the purchaser would be: $100 - 0.2($100) = $80; $80 - 0.1($80) = $72. The same results can be obtained by multiplying the list price by the complements of the trade discounts allowed. The complement of 20% is 80% (100% - 20% = 80%). The complement of 10% is 90% (100% - 10% = 90%). Thus, the gross invoice price is $100 × 0.8 × 0.9 = $72.

Recording Deductions from Gross Sales

Two common deductions from gross sales are (1) sales discounts and (2) sales returns and allowances. These deductions are recorded in contra accounts to the Sales account. Contra accounts have normal balances that are opposite the balance of the account they reduce. For example, since the Sales account normally has a credit balance, the Sales Discounts account and Sales Returns and Allowances account will have debit balances. The methods accountants use to record these contra accounts are explained below.

Sales Discounts.   Whenever goods are sold on account, terms of payment are clearly specified on the invoice. For example, in Illustration 5.3, the terms of payment are stated as "net 30," which really means "gross 30." "Net 30" is sometimes written as "n/30." This means that the $10,000 gross amount of the invoice must be paid on or before 30 days after December 19, 1987—in other words, on or before January 18, 1988. If the terms read "n/10/EOM" (EOM means end of month), the invoice would be due on the 10th day of the month following the month of sale—or January 10, 1988, in the case of the invoice in Illustration 5.3. Credit terms vary from industry to industry.

Credit terms in some industries include a cash discount to induce the early payment of an account. A **cash discount** is a deduction from the gross invoice price that can be taken only if the invoice is paid within a specified period of time. A cash discount is called a **sales discount** by the seller and a **purchase discount** by the buyer.

Cash discount terms are often stated as follows:

2/10, n/30—means a discount of 2% of the gross invoice price of the merchandise may be taken if payment is made within 10 days following the invoice date. The **gross** invoice price is due 30 days from the invoice date.

2/EOM, n/60—means a 2% discount may be deducted if the invoice is paid by the end of the month. The gross invoice amount is due 60 days from the date of the invoice.

2/10/EOM, n/60—means a 2% discount may be deducted if the invoice is paid by the 10th day of the month following the date of sale. The gross invoice amount is due 60 days from the date of the invoice.

Since a cash discount taken by the buyer reduces the amount of cash the seller actually collects from the sale of goods, the seller must indicate this in the accounting records of the company. The following illustration shows how this is done.

Assume that on July 12 a business sold merchandise for $2,000 on account; terms are 2/10, n/30. A check in payment of the account was received on July 21 (nine days after invoice date) in the amount $1,960. The required journal entries for the seller are:

July 12	Accounts Receivable	2,000	
	Sales		2,000
	To record sale on account; terms 2/10, n/30.		
21	Cash	1,960	
	Sales Discounts	40	
	Accounts Receivable		2,000
	To record collection on account, less discount.		

The **Sales Discounts account** is a contra revenue account to the Sales account. In the income statement, this contra account is deducted from gross sales. The Sales Discounts account is used (rather than directly reducing the Sales account) so that the owners can use the sales discounts figure to evaluate the company's sales discount policy. Note that the Sales Discounts account is not an expense incurred in generating revenue. Rather, the purpose of the account is to reduce recorded revenue to the amount actually realized from the sale, which is the net invoice price when the discount is taken.

Sales Returns and Allowances. Merchandising companies usually allow a customer to return goods that are defective or unsatisfactory for a variety of reasons, such as wrong color, wrong size, wrong style, wrong amounts, or inferior quality. In fact, when the seller's policy is "satisfaction guaranteed," some companies allow customers to return goods simply because the customer does not like the merchandise. A **sales return** is merchandise returned by a buyer and is considered a cancellation of a sale. Sometimes the customer keeps the unsatisfactory goods and is given an allowance off the original price. A **sales allowance** is a deduction from the original invoiced sales price granted to a customer when the customer keeps the merchandise but is dissatisfied.

Both sales returns and sales allowances could, in theory, be recorded as debits to the Sales account because they cancel part of the recorded selling price. However, the amount of sales returns and sales allowances is useful information to owners. The amount of returns and allowances in relation to goods sold can be an indication of the quality of the goods (high-return percentage, low quality) or of pressure applied by salespersons (high-pressure sales, high returns). Thus, sales returns and sales allowances are recorded in a separate Sales Returns and Allowances account. **Sales Returns and Allowances** is a contra revenue account (to Sales) used to record the selling price of merchandise returned by buyers or reductions in selling prices granted. (Some companies use separate accounts for sales returns and for sales allowances, but this text does not.)

Following are two examples illustrating the recording of sales returns in the Sales Returns and Allowances account:

1. Assume that $300 of goods sold on account are returned by a customer. If payment has not yet been received, the required entry is:

Sales Returns and Allowances	300	
Accounts Receivable		300
To record a sales return from a customer.		

2. Assume the customer has already paid the account and the seller gives the customer a refund, the credit is to Cash rather than Accounts Receivable. The customer either receives a cash (or check) refund or the customer's account is credited for the amount of the original sale. If a 2% discount was taken by the customer when the account was paid, only the sales price less the sales discount amount would be returned to the customer. For example, if a customer returns a $300 sale on which a 2% discount was taken, the following entry would be made:

Sales Returns and Allowances	300	
Cash		294
Sales Discounts		6
To record a sales return from a customer who had taken a		
discount and was sent a cash refund.		

The debit to the Sales Returns and Allowances account is for the full selling price of the purchase. The credit to Sales Discounts reduces the balance of that account.

Now we will illustrate the recording of a sales allowance in the Sales Returns and Allowances account. Assume that a $400 allowance is granted to a customer for damage resulting from improperly packed merchandise. If the customer has not yet paid the account, the required entry would read:

Sales Returns and Allowances	400	
Accounts Receivable		400
To record sales allowance granted for damaged merchandise.		

If the customer has already paid the account, the credit is to Cash instead of Accounts Receivable. If the customer took a 2% discount when paying the account, only the net amount ($392) would be refunded, and Sales Discounts would be credited for $8.

Reporting Net Sales in the Income Statement

Illustration 5.4 contains a partial income statement showing how sales, sales discounts, and sales returns and allowances would be reported. Many times the income statement published in the annual report will begin with "Net sales" because the details of this computation are not important to financial statement users outside the company.

Illustration 5.4

Partial Income Statement*

HANLON RETAIL FOOD STORE
Partial Income Statement
For the Year Ended December 31, 1987

Operating revenues:		
Gross sales		$282,000
Less: Sales discounts	$ 5,000	
Sales returns and allowances . .	15,000	20,000
Net sales		$262,000

* This is the same as Illustration 5.2, repeated here for your convenience.

■ COST OF GOODS SOLD

The second main division of an income statement for a merchandising business is cost of goods sold. Cost of goods sold is the cost to the seller of the goods sold to customers. For a merchandising company, the cost of goods sold can be very large. Since all merchandising companies usually have goods on hand to sell to customers, they have what is called merchandise inventory. Merchandise inventory (or inventory) is the quantity of goods on hand and available for sale at any given time. Cost of goods sold is determined by computing the cost of (1) the beginning inventory, (2) the net cost of goods purchased, and (3) the ending inventory.

Illustration 5.5 gives the cost of goods sold section of the Hanlon Retail Food Store's income statement. The merchandise inventory on December 31, 1986, was $24,000. The net cost of purchases for the year was $166,000. Thus, Hanlon had $190,000 of merchandise available for sale during 1987. On December 31, 1987, the merchandise inventory was $31,000, meaning that this amount was left unsold. Subtracting the unsold amount of inventory, $31,000, from

Illustration 5.5

*Determination of
Cost of Goods Sold
for Hanlon Retail
Food Store*

Cost of goods sold:			
Merchandise inventory, December 31, 1986			$ 24,000
Purchases		$167,000	
Less: Purchase discounts	$3,000		
Purchase returns and allowances	8,000	11,000	
Net purchases		$156,000	
Add: Transportation-in		10,000	
Net cost of purchases			166,000
Cost of goods available for sale			$190,000
Less: Merchandise inventory, December 31, 1987			31,000
Cost of goods sold			$159,000

the amount Hanlon had for sale during the year, $190,000, gives the cost of goods sold for the year of $159,000. Understanding this relationship, as shown on the Hanlon Retail Food Store partial income statement in Illustration 5.5, gives you the necessary background to study the steps taken by accountants to determine the cost of goods sold as presented in this section. This illustration is repeated at the end of the discussion.

Two Procedures for Accounting for Inventories

To determine the cost of goods sold, accountants must have accurate merchandise inventory figures. Accountants use two basic methods in determining the amount of merchandise inventory—perpetual inventory procedure and periodic inventory procedure. Perpetual inventory procedure is only mentioned briefly in this chapter. Periodic inventory procedure is used extensively in this chapter.

Perpetual Inventory Procedure.   Perpetual inventory procedure is usually used by companies that sell merchandise with a high individual unit value, such as automobiles, furniture, and appliances. For retail companies selling goods such as these items, it is a relatively easy task to maintain records of the cost of each unit of purchased merchandise and, in turn, the cost of each unit sold. Since the advent of computerized cash registers, some retail stores find it economical to use perpetual inventory procedure even for goods of low unit value.

When perpetual inventory procedure is used, inventory records are designed and maintained to provide close control over the actual goods on hand by showing exactly which goods are supposed to be on hand at any particular point in time. The Merchandise Inventory account is debited for each purchase and credited for each sale so that the current balance is shown in the account at all times. At the end of the accounting period, a physical inventory is taken by actually counting the number of units of inventory on hand. This physical count can be compared with the records showing the number of units that should be on hand. Perpetual procedures will be described in more detail in Chapter 9.

Periodic Inventory Procedure.   Merchandising companies that sell merchandise with a low value per unit (such as nuts and bolts, nails, Christmas cards, pencils, etc.) often find that the extra costs of record-keeping under perpetual procedure more than outweigh the benefits. Close control of such items is not necessary nor is it economically wise. These merchandising companies use periodic inventory procedure.

Under **periodic inventory procedure,** the inventory account is not used to record each purchase and sale of merchandise as it is under perpetual inventory procedure. Instead, adjustments are made to the Merchandise Inventory account only at the end of the accounting period to bring it to its proper balance. Also, the company usually does not maintain other records that show the exact number of units that should be on hand. Record-keeping is reduced considerably, but so is the control over inventory items.

No entries are made to the Merchandise Inventory account during the accounting period. Thus, there is no up-to-date account balance against which to check the physical count at the end of the accounting period. Under periodic inventory procedure, no attempt is made to determine the cost of the goods sold at the time of each sale. Instead, the cost of all the goods sold during the accounting period is determined at the **end** of the period. To do this requires the knowledge of these three items:

1. Beginning inventory (cost of goods on hand at the beginning of the period).
2. Net cost of purchases during the period.
3. Ending inventory (cost of unsold goods on hand at the end of the period).

This information would be shown as follows:

Beginning inventory	$ 24,000
Add: Net cost of purchases during the period	140,000
Cost of goods available for sale during the period	$164,000
Deduct: Ending inventory	20,000
Cost of goods sold during the period	$144,000

From the above schedule you see that the company began the accounting period with $24,000 of merchandise and purchased an additional $140,000, making a total of $164,000 of goods that could have been sold during the period. Then, a physical inventory showed that $20,000 remained unsold at the end of the period, which implies that $144,000 was the cost of goods sold during the period. Of course, the $144,000 is not necessarily the precise amount of goods sold during the period because no actual record was made of the dollar amount of goods sold. Periodic inventory procedure basically assumes that everything that is not on hand at the end of the period has been sold. This method disregards problems such as theft or breakage because there is not an up-to-date balance in the Merchandise Inventory account at the end of the accounting period against which the physical count can be compared.

The main emphasis of this text will be on periodic inventory procedure since it is the most widely used method. You are now ready for an in-depth discussion of the accounts and journal entries accountants use under periodic inventory procedure.

Purchases of Merchandise

Under periodic inventory procedure, a merchandising company uses the **Purchases account** to record cost of goods or merchandise bought for resale during the current accounting period. The Purchases account is increased by debits and is listed with the income statement accounts in the chart of accounts.

To illustrate entries affecting the Purchases account, assume that Hanlon Retail Food Store made two purchases of merchandise from Smith Wholesale Company. Hanlon purchased $30,000 of merchandise on credit (on account) on May 4, and on May 21 purchased $20,000 of merchandise for cash. The required journal entries for Hanlon are:

May 4	Purchases	30,000	
	Accounts Payable		30,000
	To record purchase of merchandise on account.		
21	Purchases	20,000	
	Cash		20,000
	To record purchase of merchandise for cash.		

Deductions from Purchases

On the buyer's books, purchase discounts and purchase returns and allowances are deducted from purchases to arrive at net purchases. These items are recorded in contra accounts to the Purchases account.

Purchase Discounts.   Merchandise is often purchased under credit terms that permit the buyer to deduct a stated discount if the invoice is paid within a specified period of time. Assume credit terms for Hanlon's May 4 purchase are 2/10, n/30. If the merchandise is paid for by May 14, a 2% discount may be taken. Thus, only $29,400 must be paid to pay the $30,000 account payable. The entry to record the payment of the invoice on May 14 is:

May 14	Accounts Payable	30,000	
	Cash		29,400
	Purchase Discounts		600
	To record payment on account within discount period.		

The purchase discount is recorded only when the invoice is paid within the discount period and the discount is taken. The **Purchase Discounts account** is a contra account to Purchases that reduces the recorded gross invoice cost of the purchase to the price actually paid. Purchase discounts are reported in the income statement as a deduction from purchases.

Note that the May 4 purchase was recorded at gross invoice price. This method is called the gross invoice price method. An alternative is to record purchases at net invoice price. This latter alternative is described in Chapter 7.

Purchase discounts are based on the invoice price of goods. If there are purchase returns or allowances, they must be deducted from the invoice price before calculating purchase discounts. For example, in the transaction above, the invoice price of goods purchased was $30,000. If $2,000 of the goods were returned, the purchase discount would be calculated on $28,000.

Purchase Returns and Allowances.   A purchase return occurs when a buyer returns merchandise to a seller. When a buyer receives an allowance (or reduction in the price of goods shipped), a purchase allowance results. Both returns and allowances serve to reduce the buyer's debt to the seller and to reduce the cost of the goods purchased. The buyer may be interested in knowing the amount of returns and allowances as the first step in controlling the costs incurred in returning unsatisfactory merchandise or negotiating purchase allowances. For this reason, purchase returns and allowances are recorded in a separate **Purchase Returns and Allowances account.** If Hanlon returned $350 of merchandise to Smith Wholesale before paying for the goods, the following journal entry would be made:

```
Accounts Payable . . . . . . . . . . . . . . . . .        350
     Purchase Returns and Allowances . . . . . . . . .          350
     To record return of damaged merchandise to supplier.
```

The entry would have been the same to record a $350 allowance. Only the explanation would change.

If the company had already paid the account, the debit would be to Cash instead of Accounts Payable, since a refund of cash would be received. If the company took a discount at the time it paid the account, then only the net amount would be refunded. For instance, if a 2% discount had been taken, the buyer's journal entry for the return would be:

```
Cash . . . . . . . . . . . . . . . . . . . . . .        343
Purchase Discounts . . . . . . . . . . . . . . . .          7
     Purchase Returns and Allowances . . . . . . . . .          350
     To record return of damaged merchandise to supplier and
     record receipt of cash.
```

Purchase Returns and Allowances is a contra account to the Purchases account and is shown on the income statement as a deduction from purchases. When both purchase discounts and purchase returns and allowances are deducted from purchases, the result is called **net purchases.**

Transportation Costs

Transportation costs are an important part of cost of goods sold. To understand how to account for transportation costs you need to know the meaning of the following terms:

☐ **FOB shipping point:** The term FOB shipping point means free on board at shipping point; that is, the buyer incurs all transportation costs after the merchandise is loaded on a railroad car or truck at the point of shipment. Thus, the buyer is responsible for paying the freight charges.

☐ **FOB destination:** The term FOB destination means free on board at destination; that is, goods are shipped to their destination without charge to the buyer. Thus, the seller is responsible for paying the freight charges.

☐ **Passage of title:** Passage of title is a legal term used to indicate transfer of legal ownership of goods. Title to the goods passes from seller to buyer at the FOB point. Thus, when goods are shipped FOB shipping point, title passes to the buyer at the shipping point. When goods are shipped FOB destination, title passes at destination.

☐ **Freight prepaid:** When the **seller** pays the freight at the time of shipment, the term freight prepaid is used.

□ **Freight collect:** When the **buyer** pays the freight bill upon the arrival of the goods, the term **freight collect** is used.

To illustrate the use of these terms, assume that certain goods are shipped FOB shipping point, freight collect. Title passes at the shipping point. The buyer is responsible for paying the $100 freight costs and does so. There is no entry for freight charges on the seller's books. The entry on the buyer's books is:

```
Transportation-In (or Freight-In)  . . . . . . . . . . . .     100
    Cash . . . . . . . . . . . . . . . . . . . . . . . . . .         100
    To record payment of freight bill on goods purchased.
```

The Transportation-In account is used to record freight costs incurred in the acquisition of merchandise. Transportation-In is an adjunct account in that it is added to net purchases to arrive at **net cost of purchases.** An **adjunct account** is closely related to another account (Purchases in this instance), and its balance is added to the balance of the related account in the financial statements.

If goods are shipped FOB destination, freight prepaid, the seller pays the freight bill and is responsible for it. No separate freight cost is billed to the buyer. No entry is required on the buyer's books. The freight cost undoubtedly was taken into consideration by the seller in setting selling prices. The following entry is required on the seller's books:

```
Delivery Expense (or Transportation-Out Expense) . . . . . . .    100
    Cash . . . . . . . . . . . . . . . . . . . . . . . . . .          100
    To record freight cost on goods sold.
```

Delivery expense is a selling expense recorded by the seller for freight costs incurred when terms are FOB destination; it is shown on the income statement with other selling expenses.

FOB terms are especially important at the end of an accounting period. Goods that are in transit at the end of an accounting period belong to either the seller or the buyer and must be included in ending inventory by one of the parties. Goods shipped FOB destination belong to the seller while in transit and should be included in the seller's ending inventory. Goods shipped FOB shipping point belong to the buyer while in transit and should be recorded as a purchase and included in the buyer's ending inventory. For example, assume that goods are shipped by a seller on December 30, 1986, and arrive at their destination on January 5, 1987. If terms are FOB destination, the seller includes the goods in its December 31, 1986, inventory, and neither the seller nor buyer records the exchange transaction until January 5, 1987. If terms are FOB shipping point, the buyer includes the goods in its December 31, 1986, inventory, and the exchange transaction is recorded by both parties as of December 30, 1986.

Sometimes the seller prepays the freight as a convenience to the buyer even though the buyer is responsible for paying it. In such cases, the buyer merely reimburses the seller for the amount of freight paid.

Purchase discounts may only be taken on the purchase price of goods. Therefore, if a buyer owes the seller for freight charges, no discount can be taken on the freight charges owed, even if payment is made within the discount period.

Merchandise Inventories

As stated earlier, **merchandise inventory** is the cost of goods on hand and available for sale at any given time. For a company to determine the cost of goods sold in any accounting period, inventory information is needed. Cost of goods on hand at the start of the period (beginning inventory), purchases made during the period, and the cost of goods on hand at the close of the period (ending inventory) must be known. Since the ending inventory of the preceding period is the beginning inventory for the current period, the cost of the beginning inventory is already known. Purchases are recorded throughout the period. Therefore, only the cost of the ending inventory need be determined at the end of the period.

Taking a Physical Inventory.   Under periodic inventory procedure, ending inventory cost is determined by taking a physical inventory. Taking a **physical inventory** consists of counting physical units of each type of merchandise on hand. To calculate inventory cost, it is necessary to multiply the number of units of each kind of merchandise by its unit cost. Total costs of the various kinds of merchandise are then totaled to provide the total ending inventory cost.

In taking a physical inventory, care must be exercised to ensure that all goods owned, regardless of where they are located, are counted and included in the inventory. Thus, goods shipped to a potential customer "on approval" should not be recorded as sold. They should be included in the owner's inventory. Similarly, **consigned goods,** which are goods delivered to another party who will attempt to sell the goods for the owner at a commission, should not be recorded as sold. In such a case, the goods remain the property of the owner (consignor) until sold by the consignee. Such goods must be included in the owner's inventory.

Merchandise in transit is merchandise in the hands of a freight company on the date of a physical inventory. Merchandise in transit at the end of the accounting period must be recorded as a purchase and included in the buyer's inventory if passage of title to the buyer has occurred. In general, the goods belong to the party who must bear the transportation charges.

Determining Cost of Goods Sold

When beginning and ending inventories and the various items making up the net cost of purchases are known, cost of goods sold can be determined.

To illustrate, assume the following account balances for Hanlon Retail Food Store as of December 31, 1987:

Merchandise inventory, December 31, 1986	$ 24,000 Dr.
Purchases	167,000 Dr.
Purchase discounts	3,000 Cr.
Purchase returns and allowances	8,000 Cr.
Transportation-in	10,000 Dr.

By taking a physical inventory, merchandise inventory on December 31, 1987, was determined to be $31,000. Cost of goods sold would be calculated as shown in Illustration 5.6. This computation appears in a section of the income statement directly below the calculation of net sales.

In Illustration 5.6, beginning inventory ($24,000) plus net cost of purchases

Illustration 5.6

Determination of
Cost of Goods Sold
for Hanlon Retail
Food Store*

Cost of goods sold:			
Merchandise inventory, December 31, 1986			$ 24,000
Purchases		$167,000	
Less: Purchase discounts	$3,000		
Purchase returns and allowances	8,000	11,000	
Net purchases		$156,000	
Add: Transportation-in		10,000	
Net cost of purchases			166,000
Cost of goods available for sale			$190,000
Less: Merchandise inventory, December 31, 1987 . .			31,000
Cost of goods sold			$159,000

* This is the same illustration as Illustration 5.5, repeated for your convenience.

($166,000) is equal to **cost of goods available for sale** ($190,000). Ending inventory cost ($31,000) is deducted from cost of goods available for sale to arrive at cost of goods sold ($159,000). The relationship between these items is shown in the diagram below:

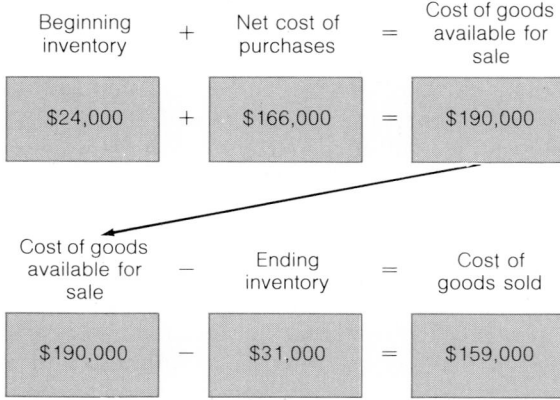

Net cost of purchases ($166,000) is equal to purchases ($167,000), **less** purchase discounts ($3,000) and purchase returns and allowances ($8,000), **plus** transportation-in ($10,000). The calculation also appears in Illustration 5.6.

As shown above, ending inventory cost appears in the income statement as a deduction from cost of goods available for sale to compute cost of goods sold. Ending inventory cost (merchandise inventory) is also reported as a current asset in the end-of-period balance sheet.

Lack of Control under Periodic Inventory Procedure

The periodic inventory method is used because of its simplicity and relatively low cost, but, as mentioned earlier, it provides for little control over inventory. Any items not included in the physical count of inventory at the end of the period are assumed to have been sold. Thus, even if items have been stolen, the accountant would assume they had been sold and their cost would be included in cost of goods sold.

To illustrate, assume the cost of goods available for sale was $200,000 and ending inventory is $60,000. These figures suggest that the cost of goods sold was $140,000. But assume that $2,000 of goods were actually shoplifted during the year. If such goods had not been stolen, the ending inventory would have been $62,000 and the cost of goods sold only $138,000. Thus, the $140,000 cost of goods sold calculated under periodic inventory procedure includes both the cost of the merchandise delivered to customers and the cost of merchandise stolen.

■ CLASSIFIED INCOME STATEMENT

In preceding chapters, we illustrated only an unclassified income statement. An **unclassified income statement** has only two categories of items—revenues and expenses. In contrast, a **classified income statement** divides both revenues and expenses into operating and nonoperating items. The statement also separates operating expenses into selling and administrative expenses. A classified income statement, also called a multiple-step income statement, is introduced in this section.

A classified income statement for the Hanlon Retail Food Store is presented in Illustration 5.7. This statement uses the previously presented data on sales (Illustration 5.4) and cost of goods sold (Illustration 5.6), together with additional assumed data on operating expenses and other expenses and revenues. Note in Illustration 5.7 that a classified income statement has the following four major sections:

1. Operating revenues.
2. Cost of goods sold.
3. Operating expenses.
4. Nonoperating revenues and expenses (other revenues and other expenses).

The classified income statement shows important relationships that help in analyzing how well the company is performing. For example, by deducting cost of goods sold from operating revenues one can determine by how much sales revenues exceed the cost of items being sold. If this margin is inadequate, selling prices may need to be increased or the prices paid for the goods being sold may need to be decreased. Operating expenses are subdivided into selling and administrative expenses so the statement user can see how much expense is being incurred in selling the product and how much in administering the business. Comparisons can be made with other years for the same business and with other businesses. Nonoperating revenues and expenses appear at the bottom of the income statement because they are less significant in assessing the profitability of the business.

The major headings of the classified income statement shown in Illustration 5.7 are explained in the paragraphs that follow. The terms in some of these headings are already familiar to you.

1. **Operating revenues** are the revenues generated by the major activities of the business—usually the sale of products or services or both.

2. **Cost of goods sold** is the major expense in merchandising companies. The cost of goods sold section of the classified income statement was shown

Illustration 5.7

Classified Income Statement for a Merchandising Company

HANLON RETAIL FOOD STORE
Income Statement
For the Year Ended December 31, 1987

Operating revenues:			
Gross sales			$282,000
Less: Sales discounts		$ 5,000	
Sales returns and allowances		15,000	20,000
Net sales			$262,000
Cost of goods sold:			
Merchandise inventory, January 1, 1987		$ 24,000	
Purchases	$167,000		
Less: Purchase discounts	$3,000		
Purchase returns and allowances	8,000	11,000	
Net purchases		$156,000	
Add: Transportation-in		10,000	
Net cost of purchases		166,000	
Cost of goods available for sale		$190,000	
Less: Merchandise inventory,			
December 31, 1987		31,000	
Cost of goods sold			159,000
Gross margin			$103,000
Operating expenses:			
Selling expenses:			
Sales salaries and commissions		$ 26,000	
Salespersons' travel		3,000	
Delivery		2,000	
Advertising		4,000	
Rent—store building		2,500	
Supplies used		1,000	
Utilities		1,800	
Depreciation—store equipment		700	
Other selling expense		400	$ 41,400
Administrative expenses:			
Salaries, executive		$ 29,000	
Rent—administrative building		1,600	
Insurance		1,500	
Supplies used		800	
Depreciation—office equipment		1,100	
Other administrative expense		300	34,300
Total operating expenses			75,700
Net income from operations			$ 27,300
Nonoperating revenues and expenses:			
Nonoperating revenues:			
Interest revenue			1,400
			$ 28,700
Nonoperating expenses:			
Interest expense			600
Net income			$ 28,100

in Illustration 5.6, and the items used in calculating cost of goods sold have already been discussed in this chapter. It is common to highlight the amount by which sales revenues exceed the cost of goods sold in the top part of the income statement. The excess of net sales over cost of goods sold is called **gross margin** or **gross profit.** Gross margin may also be expressed as a percentage rate, computed by dividing gross margin by net sales. In Illustration 5.7, the gross margin rate is approximately 39.3% ($103,000/$262,000). The gross margin rate indicates that out of each sales dollar, approximately 39 cents is available to cover other expenses and produce income. The gross margin rate is watched closely by the owner since a small percentage fluctuation can cause a large dollar change in net income.

3. **Operating expenses** for a merchandising company are those expenses other than cost of goods sold incurred in the normal business functions of a company. Operating expenses are usually classified as either selling expenses or administrative expenses. **Selling expenses** are expenses incurred in selling and marketing efforts. Examples include salaries and commissions of salespersons, expenses for salespersons' travel, delivery, advertising, rent and utilities on sales building, sales supplies used, and depreciation on equipment used in sales. **Administrative expenses** are expenses incurred in the overall management of a business. Examples include administrative salaries, rent and utilities on administrative building, insurance expense, administrative supplies used, and depreciation on office equipment.

Certain operating expenses may be related partly to the selling function and partly to the administrative function. For example, rent, taxes, and insurance on a building might be incurred for both sales and administrative purposes. Expenses covering both the selling and administrative functions are analyzed and prorated between the two functions in the income statement. For instance, if $1,000 of depreciation expense relates 60% to selling and 40% to administrative, $600 would be shown as a selling expense and $400 as an administrative expense.

4. **Nonoperating revenues (other revenues)** are revenues not related to the sale of products or services regularly offered for sale by a business. An example of a nonoperating revenue is interest that a business earns on notes receivable. **Nonoperating expenses (other expenses)** are expenses not related to the acquisition and sale of the products or services regularly offered for sale. An example of a nonoperating expense is interest incurred on money borrowed by the company.

Important Relationships in the Income Statement

The more important relationships in the income statement of a merchandising firm can be summarized in equation form, as follows:

1. **Net sales** = Gross sales − (Sales discounts + Sales returns and allowances).
2. **Net purchases** = Purchases − (Purchase discounts + Purchase returns and allowances).
3. **Net cost of purchases** = Net purchases + Transportation-in.
4. **Cost of goods sold** = Beginning inventory + Net cost of purchases − Ending inventory.
5. **Gross margin** = Net sales − Cost of goods sold.
6. **Net income from operations** = Gross margin − Operating (selling and administrative) expenses.
7. **Net income** = Net income from operations + Nonoperating revenues − Nonoperating expenses.

Each of these relationships is important because of the way it relates to an overall measure of business profitability. For example, a company may produce a high gross margin on sales. However, because of large sales commissions and delivery expenses, only a very small percentage of the gross margin may ever be realized by the owner as profit. The classifications in the income statement allow a user to focus on the whole picture (net income) as well as on how it was derived (statement relationships).

Future illustrations may vary somewhat in form, but the basic organization of the classified income statement described above will be retained.

■ THE WORK SHEET FOR A MERCHANDISING COMPANY

Illustration 5.8 shows a work sheet for a merchandising company. To keep the illustration simple, a different retail company will be introduced. The Lyons Company is a small sporting goods firm. The illustration for the Lyons Company focuses on the merchandise-related accounts. For this reason, selling and administrative expenses have been grouped into two accounts rather than including all actual expense accounts. Except for the merchandise-related accounts, the work sheet for a merchandising company is the same as for a service company. Recall that use of a work sheet assists in the preparation of the adjusting and closing entries. The work sheet also contains all of the information needed for the preparation of the financial statements.

To further simplify this illustration, assume no adjusting entries are necessary at month-end. The trial balance is taken from the ledger accounts at December 31, 1987. The $7,000 merchandise inventory in the trial balance is the beginning inventory. The sales and sales-related accounts and the purchases and purchases-related accounts summarize the merchandising activity for December 1987.

Completing the Work Sheet

Any revenue accounts (Sales) and contra purchases accounts (Purchase Discounts, Purchase Returns and Allowances) that appear in the Adjusted Trial Balance credit columns of the work sheet are carried to the Income Statement credit column. Beginning inventory, contra revenue accounts (Sales Discounts, Sales Returns and Allowances), Purchases, Transportation-In, and expense accounts (Selling Expenses, Administrative Expenses) shown in the Adjusted Trial Balance debit column are carried to the Income Statement debit column.

Note that the amount of ending merchandise inventory, $8,000, is entered in the Income Statement credit column to reduce cost of goods sold and in the Balance Sheet debit column to establish the proper balance in the Merchandise Inventory account. The reason both beginning and ending inventories are brought to the Income Statement columns is because both are used to calculate cost of goods sold in the income statement. Net income or net loss for the period will balance the Income Statement columns as it did in previous work sheets. Net income/loss is carried to the Balance Sheet credit/debit column. For the Lyons Company, the net income is $5,843 for the month of December.

All other assets (Cash and Accounts Receivable) and the owner's drawing account balance are carried to the Balance Sheet debit column. The liability (Accounts Payable) and owner's capital are carried to the Balance Sheet credit column.

Illustration 5.8 Work Sheet for a Merchandising Company

LYONS COMPANY
Work Sheet
For the Month Ended December 31, 1987

Acct. No.	Account Titles	Trial Balance Debit	Trial Balance Credit	Adjustments Debit	Adjustments Credit	Adjusted Trial Balance Debit	Adjusted Trial Balance Credit	Income Statement Debit	Income Statement Credit	Balance Sheet Debit	Balance Sheet Credit
1	Cash	19,663				19,663				19,663	
2	Accounts Receivable	1,880				1,880				1,880	
3	Merchandise Inventory, December 1	7,000				7,000		7,000	8,000	8,000	
4	Accounts Payable		700				700				700
5	Lyons, Capital, December 1		25,000				25,000				25,000
6	Lyons, Drawing	2,000				2,000				2,000	
7	Sales		14,600				14,600		14,600		
8	Sales Discounts	44				44		44			
9	Sales Returns and Allowances	20				20		20			
10	Purchases	6,000				6,000		6,000			
11	Purchase Discounts		82				82		82		
12	Purchase Returns and Allowances		100				100		100		
13	Transportation-In	75				75		75			
14	Selling Expenses	2,650				2,650		2,650			
15	Administrative Expenses	1,150				1,150		1,150			
		40,482	40,482			40,482	40,482	16,939	22,782	31,543	5,843
	Net Income							5,843			5,843
								22,782	22,782	31,543	31,543

Financial Statements for a Merchandising Company

Once the work sheet has been completed, the financial statements are prepared. Next, any adjusting and closing entries are entered in the journal and posted to the ledger. This process clears the accounting records for the next accounting period.

Income Statement. The income statement in Illustration 5.9 is prepared from the work sheet in Illustration 5.8. The focus in this income statement is on the determination of the cost of goods sold. That is why other expenses are shown in summary form.

Statement of Owner's Equity. The statement of owner's equity, as you recall, is a financial statement that summarizes the transactions affecting the owner's capital account balance. In Illustration 5.10, the statement of owner's equity shows the increase in equity resulting from net income and the decrease in equity resulting from the owner's withdrawals.

Balance Sheet. The balance sheet, Illustration 5.11, contains the assets, liabilities, and owner's equity items taken from the work sheet. Note the $8,000 ending inventory is shown as a current asset. The Lyons capital account balance comes from the statement of owner's equity.

Illustration 5.9

Income Statement for a Merchandising Company

LYONS COMPANY
Income Statement
For the Month Ended December 31, 1987

Operating revenues:				
Gross sales				$14,600
Less: Sales discounts		$ 44		
Sales returns and allowances		20		64
Net sales				$14,536
Cost of goods sold:				
Merchandise inventory, December 1, 1987			$ 7,000	
Purchases	$6,000			
Less: Purchase discounts	$ 82			
Purchase returns and allowances	100	182		
Net purchases	$5,818			
Add: Transportation-in	75			
Net cost of purchases		5,893		
Cost of goods available for sale		$12,893		
Merchandise inventory, December 31, 1987		8,000		
Cost of goods sold			4,893	
Gross margin			$ 9,643	
Operating expenses:				
Selling expenses (summary)		$ 2,650		
Administrative expenses (summary)		1,150		
Total operating expenses			3,800	
Net income			$ 5,843	

Illustration 5.10

Statement of Owner's Equity

LYONS COMPANY
Statement of Owner's Equity
For the Month Ended December 31, 1987

Lyons, capital, December 1, 1987 . . .	$25,000
Net income for the month	5,843
Total	$30,843
Lyons, drawing	2,000
Lyons, capital, December 31, 1987 . . .	$28,843

Illustration 5.11

Balance Sheet for a Merchandising Company

LYONS COMPANY
Balance Sheet
December 31, 1987

Assets

Current assets:

Cash	$19,663
Accounts receivable	1,880
Merchandise inventory	8,000
Total assets	$29,543

Liabilities and Owner's Equity

Current liabilities:

Accounts payable	$ 700

Owner's equity:

Lyons, capital	28,843
Total liabilities and owner's equity . .	$29,543

Closing Entries

Recall from Chapter 4 that the closing process normally takes place after the financial statements for the period have been prepared. The closing process closes revenue and expense accounts by transferring their balances to a clearing account called Income Summary and then to Owner's Capital. The closing process reduces the revenue and expense account balances to zero so that information for each accounting period may be accumulated separately from any previous period.

Closing entries may be prepared directly from the work sheet in Illustration 5.8 using the same procedure as presented in Chapter 4. The journal entries to perform the closing process for the Lyons Company are:

1st entry	Merchandise Inventory	8,000	
	Sales	14,600	
	Purchase Discounts	82	
	Purchase Returns and Allowances	100	
	Income Summary		22,782
	To close accounts with a credit balance in the Income Statement columns and to establish ending merchandise inventory.		

The first journal entry **debits** all items appearing in the Income Statement credit column of the work sheet and **credits** Income Summary for the total of that column, $22,782.

2d entry	Income Summary	16,939	
	Merchandise Inventory		7,000
	Sales Discounts		44
	Sales Returns and Allowances		20
	Purchases		6,000
	Transportation-In		75
	Selling Expenses		2,650
	Administrative Expenses		1,150
	To close accounts with a debit balance in the Income Statement columns.		

The second entry **credits** all items appearing in the Income Statement debit column and **debits** Income Summary for the total of that column, $16,939.[1]

3d entry	Income Summary	5,843	
	Lyons, Capital		5,843
	To close the Income Summary account to the owner's capital account.		

In the third entry, the credit balance in the Income Summary account of $5,843 is closed to the owner's capital account.

4th entry	Lyons, Capital	2,000	
	Lyons, Drawing		2,000
	To close the owner's drawing account to the owner's capital account.		

In the fourth entry, the owner's drawing account balance of $2,000 is closed to the owner's capital account by debiting Lyons, Capital and crediting Lyons, Drawing.

Note how the first three closing entries tie into the totals shown in the Income Statement columns of the work sheet in Illustration 5.8. In the first closing journal entry, the credit to the Income Summary account is equal to the total of the Income Statement credit column. In the second entry, the debit to the Income Summary account is equal to the subtotal of the Income Statement debit column. The difference between the totals of the two Income Statement columns ($5,843) represents net income and is the amount of the third closing entry.

The effects of these closing entries are shown in the following T-accounts:

Merchandise Inventory

			1987		
Bal. before closing		7,000	Dec. 31	To close to Income Summary	7,000
1987					
Dec. 31	To establish actual ending inventory balance	8,000			

---

[1] You may close debit balanced accounts (in the Income Statement) before credit balanced accounts. This practice does not affect the balance of the Income Summary account or the amount of net income.

Sales

1987			Bal. before closing	14,600
Dec. 31	To close to Income Summary	14,600	Bal. after closing	–0–

Sales Discounts

Bal. before closing	44	1987		
Bal. after closing	–0–	Dec. 31	To close to Income Summary	44

Sales Returns and Allowances

Bal. before closing	20	1987		
Bal. after closing	–0–	Dec. 31	To close to Income Summary	20

Purchases

Bal. before closing	6,000	1987		
Bal. after closing	–0–	Dec. 31	To close to Income Summary	6,000

Purchase Discounts

1987			Bal. before closing	82
Dec. 31	To close to Income Summary	82	Bal. after closing	–0–

Purchase Returns and Allowances

1987			Bal. before closing	100
Dec. 31	To close to Income Summary	100	Bal. after closing	–0–

Transportation-In

Bal. before closing	75	1987		
Bal. after closing	–0–	Dec. 31	To close to Income Summary	75

Selling Expenses

Bal. before closing	2,650	1987		
Bal. after closing	–0–	Dec. 31	To close to Income Summary	2,650

Administrative Expenses

Bal. before closing	1,150	1987		
Bal. after closing	–0–	Dec. 31	To close to Income Summary	1,150

Income Summary

1987 Dec. 31	From closing accounts appearing in Income State-ment debit column of work sheet	16,939	1987 Dec. 31	From closing accounts appearing in Income State-ment credit column of work sheet	22,782
1987 Dec. 31	To close to owner's capital account	5,843		Bal. (net income) before closing this account	5,843
				Bal. after closing	–0–

Lyons, Capital

1987 Dec. 31	From closing owner's drawing account	2,000	1987 Dec. 31	Beg. bal. From closing Income Summary account	25,000 5,843
				End. bal.	28,843

Lyons, Drawing

Bal. before closing	2,000	1987 Dec. 31	To close to owner's capital account	2,000
Bal. after closing	–0–			

After the entries have been posted to the ledger, only the balance sheet accounts have balances. The revenue, expense, and drawing accounts have zero balances.

■ SUMMARY

At the beginning of this chapter the income statements of a service company and a merchandising company are compared. This comparison establishes a framework for the study of the merchandising company—a framework that is developed as the chapter progresses.

The three basic divisions of a merchandising company's income statement are: (1) sales revenues, (2) cost of goods sold, and (3) expenses. Sales revenues result from the sales of goods by the company; cost of goods sold shows what the merchandising company paid for the goods sold; and the expenses are the company's expenses in running the business.

From sales revenues, or gross sales, accountants deduct (1) sales discounts and (2) sales returns and allowances to find net sales. Then, to determine the cost of goods sold, accountants need accurate merchandise inventory amounts. Two procedures are used in determining the balance in the inventory account— perpetual inventory procedure and periodic inventory procedure. Companies selling merchandise with a high individual unit value, such as automobiles, usually use perpetual inventory procedure. Companies selling merchandise with a low individual unit value, such as nuts and bolts, usually use periodic inventory procedure. This chapter illustrates periodic inventory procedure. In determining the cost of goods sold under periodic inventory procedure, accountants use accounts such as Purchases, Purchase Discounts, Purchase Returns and Allowances, and Transportation-In. Cost of goods sold is equal to beginning inventory, plus net cost of purchases, less ending inventory. When cost of goods sold is deducted from net sales, the result is gross margin. Finally, expenses are subtracted from the gross margin figure to arrive at a net income figure.

This chapter introduces a more detailed income statement—the classified income statement. A classified income statement has four major divisions: (1) operating revenues, (2) cost of goods sold, (3) operating expenses, and (4) nonoperating revenues and expenses. Each of these divisions is discussed in the chapter.

A work sheet for a merchandising company is illustrated. Then the financial statements of this merchandising company are presented. The chapter concludes by showing the company's closing entries.

You should now understand the distinction between accounting for a service company and a merchandising company. The next chapter takes you back to the accounting process (or cycle) and builds on the knowledge you have already acquired as you study accounting systems and special journals.

APPENDIX: ALTERNATIVE CLOSING PROCEDURE

Many of the users of this text prefer the closing process just illustrated in the chapter because it is easy to perform. If you are in this group, you need not read this appendix. But some users prefer an alternative procedure because it seems to them to better communicate an understanding of the purposes behind the closing process. Since the end result of both methods is the same, both are correct. The one used depends on personal preference.

This appendix illustrates the alternative closing procedure. Under this alternative procedure, the beginning inventory balance and balances in all purchase-related accounts are transferred into the Cost of Goods Sold account in an **adjusting entry.** In a separate **adjusting entry,** the ending inventory is established by debiting Merchandise Inventory and crediting Cost of Goods Sold.

Using the same data from Illustration 5.8, the required adjusting entries for inventory and cost of goods sold under this alternative procedure are as follows:

1987			
Dec. 31	Cost of Goods Sold	12,893	
	Purchase Discounts	82	
	Purchase Returns and Allowances	100	
	Merchandise Inventory		7,000
	Purchases		6,000
	Transportation-In		75
	To transfer the beginning inventory and the accounts comprising net purchases to the Cost of Goods Sold account.		
31	Merchandise Inventory	8,000	
	Cost of Goods Sold		8,000
	To set up ending inventory and reduce Cost of Goods Sold by the cost of goods not sold.		

The first adjusting entry transfers into the Cost of Goods Sold account the net cost of all the goods available for sale during the year. The second adjusting entry then removes from the Cost of Goods Sold account the cost of goods unsold at year-end and establishes this amount as the ending inventory. The result of these two entries is that the Cost of Goods Sold account contains the amount of expense incurred during the year for merchandise delivered to customers. The Cost of Goods Sold account is closed as follows:

```
1987
Dec. 31   Income Summary .  .  .  .  .  .  .  .  .  .  .  .  .  .  .     4,893
              Cost of Goods Sold   .  .  .  .  .  .  .  .  .  .  .               4,893
          To close Cost of Goods Sold to Income Summary.
```

This final entry would generally be included in the compound closing entry for all expenses closed at the end of the period rather than being journalized separately. A difference between the two alternatives is that the method in the chapter does not set up a ledger account for Cost of Goods Sold, while this method does.

The example in Illustration 5.12 shows how a work sheet is prepared using this alternative procedure and focuses on the merchandise-related accounts.

Trial Balance Columns.   The Trial Balance columns have the same data as shown in Illustration 5.8 in this chapter.

Adjusted Trial Balance Columns.   Note that under this method the net balance in Cost of Goods Sold ($4,893) is shown in the Adjusted Trial Balance debit column. Also, the $8,000 ending inventory appears in this same column.

Income Statement Columns.   The only purchase-related item that appears in the Income Statement columns is the cost of goods sold ($4,893).

Balance Sheet Columns.   The Balance Sheet columns have the same data as shown in Illustration 5.8 in the chapter.

Closing Entries.   The closing entries under this alternative procedure are as follows:

```
1st entry   Sales    .  .  .  .  .  .  .  .  .  .  .  .  .  .  .  .  .   14,600
                Income Summary .  .  .  .  .  .  .  .  .  .  .  .               14,600
            To close accounts with a credit balance in the Income
            Statement columns.

2d entry    Income Summary    .  .  .  .  .  .  .  .  .  .  .  .  .     8,757
                Sales Discounts    .  .  .  .  .  .  .  .  .  .  .  .                44
                Sales Returns and Allowances    .  .  .  .  .  .                 20
                Selling Expenses .  .  .  .  .  .  .  .  .  .  .  .             2,650
                Administrative Expenses    .  .  .  .  .  .  .  .            1,150
                Cost of Goods Sold .  .  .  .  .  .  .  .  .  .            4,893
            To close accounts with a debit balance in the Income
            Statement debit columns.

3d entry    Income Summary    .  .  .  .  .  .  .  .  .  .  .  .  .     5,843
                Lyons, Capital .  .  .  .  .  .  .  .  .  .  .  .  .                5,843
            To close the Income Summary account to the owner's
            capital account.

4th entry   Lyons, Capital    .  .  .  .  .  .  .  .  .  .  .  .  .  .     2,000
                Lyons, Drawing   .  .  .  .  .  .  .  .  .  .  .  .                2,000
            To close the owner's drawing account to the owner's
            capital account.
```

Illustration 5.12 Work Sheet Using Alternative Procedure

LYONS COMPANY
Work Sheet
For the Month Ended December 31, 1987

Acct. No.	Account Titles	Trial Balance Debit	Trial Balance Credit	Adjustments Debit	Adjustments Credit	Adjusted Trial Balance Debit	Adjusted Trial Balance Credit	Income Statement Debit	Income Statement Credit	Balance Sheet Debit	Balance Sheet Credit
1	Cash	19,663				19,663				19,663	
2	Accounts Receivable	1,880				1,880				1,880	
3	Merchandise Inventory, December 1	7,000			(1) 7,000						
4	Accounts Payable		700				700				700
5	Lyons, Capital, December 1		25,000				25,000				25,000
6	Lyons, Drawing	2,000				2,000				2,000	
7	Sales		14,600				14,600		14,600		
8	Sales Discounts	44				44		44			
9	Sales Returns and Allowances	20				20		20			
10	Purchases	6,000			(1) 6,000						
11	Purchase Discounts		82	(1) 82							
12	Purchase Returns and Allowances		100	(1) 100							
13	Transportation-In	75			(1) 75						
14	Selling Expenses	2,650				2,650		2,650			
15	Administrative Expenses	1,150				1,150		1,150			
		40,482	40,482								
	Cost of Goods Sold			(1) 12,893	(2) 8,000	4,893		4,893			
	Merchandise Inventory, December 31*			(2) 8,000		8,000				8,000	
				21,075	21,075	40,300	40,300	8,757	14,600	31,543	5,843
	Net Income							5,843			5,843
								14,600	14,600	31,543	31,543

Adjustments:

(1) To transfer the beginning inventory and the accounts comprising net purchases to the Cost of Goods Sold account.

(2) To set up ending inventory and reduce Cost of Goods Sold by the cost of goods not sold.

* If desired, the $8,000 in the Adjustments column and in the Balance Sheet columns may be placed on the same line as the $7,000 beginning inventory figure.

NEW TERMS INTRODUCED IN CHAPTER 5

Adjunct account

Its balance is shown as an addition to another item to which it closely relates (184).

Administrative expenses

Expenses incurred in the overall management of a business (189).

Cash discount

A deduction from the gross invoice price that can be taken only if the invoice is paid within a specified period of time: to the seller, it is a sales discount; to the buyer, it is a purchase discount (177).

Chain discount

Occurs when a list price of a product is subject to several trade discounts (176).

Classified income statement

Divides both revenues and expenses into operating and nonoperating items. The statement also separates operating expenses into selling and administrative expenses (187).

Consigned goods

Goods delivered to another party who will attempt to sell the goods for the owner at a commission (185).

Cost of goods available for sale

Equal to beginning inventory plus net purchases (186).

Cost of goods sold

Shows the cost to the seller of the goods sold to customers; under periodic procedure cost of goods sold is computed as Beginning inventory + Net cost of purchases − Ending inventory (179, 189).

Delivery expense

A selling expense recorded by the seller for freight costs incurred when terms are FOB destination (184).

FOB destination

Means free on board at destination; goods are shipped to their destination without charge to the buyer; the seller is responsible for paying the freight charges (183).

FOB shipping point

Means free on board at shipping point; buyer incurs all transportation costs after the merchandise is loaded on a railroad car or truck at the point of shipment (183).

Freight collect

Terms that require the buyer to pay the freight bill upon the arrival of the goods (184).

Freight prepaid

Terms that indicate the seller has paid the freight bill at the time of shipment (183).

Gross profit

Net sales − Cost of goods sold (188).

Gross margin

Net sales − Cost of goods sold; identifies the number of dollars available to cover expenses; may be expressed as a percentage rate (188, 189).

Gross selling price

The list price less all trade discounts (176).

Inventory

See Merchandise inventory.

Invoice

A document, prepared by the seller of merchandise and sent to the buyer, that contains the details of a sale, such as the number of units, unit price, total price billed, terms of sale, and manner of shipment; a purchase invoice from the buyer's point of view and a sales invoice from the seller's point of view (174).

Manufacturers

Companies that produce goods from raw materials and normally sell them to wholesalers (173).

Merchandise in transit

Merchandise in the hands of a freight company on the date of a physical inventory (185).

Merchandise inventory

The quantity of goods on hand and available for sale at any given time (179).

Net cost of purchases

Net purchases + Transportation-in (184, 189).

Net income

Net income from operations + Nonoperating revenues − Nonoperating expenses (189).

Net income from operations

Gross margin − Operating (selling and administrative) expenses (189).

Net purchases

Purchases − (Purchase discounts + Purchase returns and allowances) (183, 189).

Net sales

Gross sales − (Sales discounts + Sales returns and allowances) (174, 189).

Nonoperating expenses (other expenses)

Expenses incurred by a business that are not related to the acquisition and sale of the products or services regularly offered for sale (189).

Nonoperating revenues (other revenues)

Revenues not related to the sale of products or services regularly offered for sale by a business (189).

Operating expenses

Those expenses other than cost of goods sold incurred in the normal business functions of a company (189).

Operating revenues

Those revenues generated by the major activities of the business (187).

Passage of title

A legal term used to indicate transfer of legal ownership of goods (183).

Periodic inventory procedure

A method of accounting for merchandise acquired for sale to customers wherein the cost of merchandise sold and the cost of merchandise on hand are determined only at the end of the accounting period by taking a physical inventory (181).

Perpetual inventory procedure

A method of accounting for merchandise acquired for sale to customers wherein the Merchandise Inventory account is debited for each purchase and credited for each sale so that the current balance is shown in the account at all times (180).

Physical inventory

Consists of counting physical units of each type of merchandise on hand (185).

Purchase discount

See Cash discount.

Purchase Discounts account

A contra account to Purchases that reduces the recorded gross invoice cost of the purchase to the price actually paid (182).

Purchase Returns and Allowances account

An account used under periodic inventory procedure to record the cost of merchandise returned to a seller and to record reductions in selling prices granted by a seller because merchandise was not satisfactory to a buyer; viewed as a reduction in the recorded cost of purchases (183).

Purchases account

An account used under periodic inventory procedure to record the cost of goods or merchandise bought for resale during the current accounting period (181).

Retailers

Companies that sell goods to final consumers (173).

Sales allowance

A deduction from original invoice sales price granted to a customer when the customer keeps the merchandise but is dissatisfied for any of a number of reasons, including inferior quality or damage or deterioration in transit (178).

Sales discount

See Cash discount.

Sales Discounts account

A contra revenue account to Sales and is shown as a deduction from gross sales in the income statement (177).

Sales return

From the seller's point of view, merchandise returned by a buyer for any of a variety of reasons; to the buyer, a purchase return (178).

Sales Returns and Allowances account

A contra revenue account to Sales used to record the selling price of merchandise returned by buyers or reductions in selling prices granted (178).

Selling expenses

Expenses incurred in the selling and marketing efforts (189).

Trade discount

A percentage deduction, or discount, from the specified list price or catalog price of merchandise to arrive at the gross invoice price; granted to particular categories of customers (e.g., retailers and wholesalers). Also see Chain discount (176).

Transportation-In account

An account used under periodic inventory procedure to record transportation costs incurred in the acquisition of merchandise; a part of cost of goods sold (184).

Unclassified income statement

Shows only major categories for revenues and expenses (187).

Wholesalers

Companies that sell goods to other companies for resale (173).

DEMONSTRATION PROBLEM 5–1

The following transactions occurred between Companies A and B.

Transactions:

June 10 Company A purchased merchandise from Company B, $40,000; terms 2/10/EOM, n/60, FOB destination.
 11 Company B paid freight of $600.
 14 Company A received an allowance of $2,000 from the gross invoice price because of damaged goods.
 23 Company A returned $4,000 of goods purchased because they were not the quality ordered.
 30 Company B received payment in full from Company A.

Required: a. Journalize the transactions for Company A.
 b. Journalize the transactions for Company B.

Solution to demonstration problem 5–1

GENERAL JOURNAL

Date		Account Titles and Explanation	Post. Ref.	Debit	Credit
a.		**Company A**			
1987 June	10	Purchases		4 0 0 0 0	
		Accounts Payable			4 0 0 0 0
		Purchased merchandise from Company B,			
		terms 2/10/EOM, n/60.			
	14	Accounts Payable		2 0 0 0	
		Purchase Returns and Allowances			2 0 0 0
		Received an allowance from Company B			
		for damaged goods.			
	23	Accounts Payable		4 0 0 0	
		Purchase Returns and Allowances			4 0 0 0
		Returned merchandise to Company B			
		because of improper quality.			
	30	Accounts Payable ($40,000 − $2,000 − $4,000)		3 4 0 0 0	
		Purchase Discounts ($34,000 × 0.02)			6 8 0
		Cash ($34,000 − $680)			3 3 3 2 0
		Paid the amount due to Company B.			

Solution to demonstration problem 5–1 (concluded)

GENERAL JOURNAL

Date		Account Titles and Explanation	Post. Ref.	Debit	Credit
b.		**Company B**			
1987 June	10	Accounts Receivable		4 0 0 0 0	
		Sales			4 0 0 0 0
		Sold merchandise to Company A,			
		terms 2/10/EOM, n/60.			
	11	Delivery Expense		6 0 0	
		Cash			6 0 0
		Paid freight on sale of merchandise			
		shipped FOB destination.			
	14	Sales Returns and Allowances		2 0 0 0	
		Accounts Receivable			2 0 0 0
		Granted an allowance to Company A			
		for damaged goods.			
	23	Sales Returns and Allowances		4 0 0 0	
		Accounts Receivable			4 0 0 0
		Merchandise returned from Company A			
		due to improper quality.			
	30	Cash ($34,000 − $680)		3 3 3 2 0	
		Sales Discounts ($34,000 × 0.02)		6 8 0	
		Accounts Receivable ($40,000 − $2,000 − $4,000)			3 4 0 0 0
		Received the amount due from Company A.			

DEMONSTRATION PROBLEM 5–2

CAMP'S MUSIC STORE
Trial Balance
July 31, 1987

	Debits	Credits
Cash .	$ 34,780	
Accounts Receivable	4,600	
Merchandise Inventory, 8/1/86	31,400	
Prepaid Fire Insurance	720	
Prepaid Rent .	4,800	
Office Equipment	12,000	
Accumulated Depreciation—Office Equipment . .		$ 4,500
Accounts Payable		8,000
Clay Camp, Capital .		22,000
Clay Camp, Drawing	20,000	
Sales		300,000
Sales Returns and Allowances .	1,000	
Purchases .	194,000	
Purchase Returns and Allowances		1,400
Transportation-In .	5,200	
Advertising Expense	1,000	
Supplies Expense	1,800	
Salaries Expense	23,200	
Utilities Expense .	1,400	
	$335,900	$335,900

Clay Camp has prepared the above trial balance for Camp's Music Store. The following information will be used to prepare the work sheet.

1. A 12-month fire insurance policy was purchased for $720 on April 1, 1987, the date on which insurance coverage began.
2. On February 1, 1987, Camp paid $4,800 for the next 12 months' rent. The payment was recorded in the Prepaid Rent account.
3. Depreciation expense on the office equipment is $1,500.
4. Merchandise Inventory at July 31, 1987, was $26,400.

Required:
a. Prepare a 10-column work sheet for Camp's Music Store for the fiscal year ended July 31, 1987.
b. Prepare a classified income statement for the fiscal year ended July 31, 1987. Do not separate operating expenses into selling and administrative categories.
c. Prepare a statement of owner's equity for the fiscal year ended July 31, 1987.
d. Prepare a classified balance sheet for July 31, 1987.
e. Prepare closing entries.

Solution to demonstration problem 5–2

a. See work sheet on following page.

CAMP'S MUSIC STORE
Work Sheet
For the Year Ended July 31, 1987

Account Titles	Trial Balance Debit	Trial Balance Credit	Adjustments Debit	Adjustments Credit	Adjusted Trial Balance Debit	Adjusted Trial Balance Credit	Income Statement Debit	Income Statement Credit	Balance Sheet Debit	Balance Sheet Credit
Cash	34,780				34,780				34,780	
Accounts Receivable	4,600				4,600				4,600	
Merchandise Inventory	31,400				31,400		31,400	26,400	26,400	
Prepaid Fire Insurance	720			(1) 240	480				480	
Prepaid Rent	4,800			(2) 2,400	2,400				2,400	
Office Equipment	12,000				12,000				12,000	
Accumulated Depreciation—Office Equipment		4,500		(3) 1,500		6,000				6,000
Accounts Payable		8,000				8,000				8,000
Clay Camp, Capital		22,000				22,000				22,000
Clay Camp, Drawing	20,000				20,000				20,000	
Sales		300,000				300,000		300,000		
Sales Returns and Allowances	1,000				1,000		1,000			
Purchases	194,000				194,000		194,000			
Purchase Returns and Allowances		1,400				1,400		1,400		
Transportation-In	5,200				5,200		5,200			
Advertising Expense	1,000				1,000		1,000			
Supplies Expense	1,800				1,800		1,800			
Salaries Expense	23,200				23,200		23,200			
Utilities Expense	1,400				1,400		1,400			
	335,900	335,900								
Fire Insurance Expense			(1) 240		240		240			
Rent Expense			(2) 2,400		2,400		2,400			
Depreciation Expense—Office Equipment			(3) 1,500		1,500		1,500			
			4,140	4,140	337,400	337,400	263,140	327,800	100,660	64,660
Net income							64,660			64,660
							327,800	327,800	100,660	100,660

Adjustments:

(1) Expiration of prepaid fire insurance ($720 × 4/12).

(2) Expiration of prepaid rent ($4,800 × 6/12).

(3) Depreciation expense on office equipment for the fiscal year ended July 31, 1987.

b.

CAMP'S MUSIC STORE
Income Statement
For the Year Ended July 31, 1987

Operating revenues:

Gross sales			$300,000
Less: Sales returns and allowances			1,000
Net sales			$299,000

Cost of goods sold:

Merchandise inventory, August 1, 1986		$ 31,400	
Purchases	$194,000		
Less: Purchase returns and allowances	1,400		
Net purchases	$192,600		
Add: Transportation-in	5,200		
Net cost of purchases		197,800	
Cost of goods available for sale		$229,200	
Merchandise inventory, July 31, 1987		26,400	
Cost of goods sold			202,800
Gross margin			$ 96,200

Operating expenses:

Advertising	$ 1,000	
Supplies	1,800	
Salaries	23,200	
Utilities	1,400	
Fire insurance	240	
Rent	2,400	
Depreciation—office equipment	1,500	
Total operating expenses		31,540
Net income		$ 64,660

c.

CAMP'S MUSIC STORE
Statement of Owner's Equity
For the Year Ended July 31, 1987

Clay Camp, capital, August 1, 1986	$22,000
Net income for the year	64,660
Total	$86,660
Less: Drawings	20,000
Clay Camp, capital, July 31, 1987	$66,660

d.

CAMP'S MUSIC STORE
Balance Sheet
July 31, 1987
Assets

Current assets:

Cash	$34,780	
Accounts receivable	4,600	
Merchandise inventory	26,400	
Prepaid fire insurance	480	
Prepaid rent	2,400	
Total current assets		$68,660

Property, plant, and equipment:

Office equipment	$12,000	
Less: Accumulated depreciation	6,000	
Total property, plant, and equipment		6,000
Total assets		$74,660

Liabilities and Owner's Equity

Liabilities:

Accounts payable	$ 8,000

Owner's equity:

Clay Camp, capital	66,660
Total liabilities and owner's equity	$74,660

e. Closing entries:

1987

July 31	Merchandise Inventory		26,400	
	Sales		300,000	
	Purchase Returns and Allowances		1,400	
	Income Summary			327,800
	To close accounts with credit balances in the Income Statement columns and to set up the ending merchandise inventory.			
31	Income Summary		263,140	
	Merchandise Inventory			31,400
	Sales Returns and Allowances			1,000
	Purchases			194,000
	Transportation-In			5,200
	Advertising Expense			1,000
	Supplies Expense			1,800
	Salaries Expense			23,200
	Utilities Expense			1,400
	Fire Insurance Expense			240
	Rent Expense			2,400
	Depreciation Expense—Office Equipment			1,500
	To close accounts with debit balances in the Income Statement columns.			
31	Income Summary		64,660	
	Clay Camp, Capital			64,660
	To close the Income Summary account to the owner's capital account.			
31	Clay Camp, Capital		20,000	
	Clay Camp, Drawing			20,000
	To close drawing account.			

QUESTIONS

1. What account titles are likely to appear in the ledger of a merchandising company that do not appear in the ledger of a service enterprise?

2. What entry is made to record a sale of merchandise on account?

3. Describe trade discounts and chain discounts.

4. Sales discounts and sales returns and allowances are deducted from sales on the income statement to arrive at net sales. Why not deduct these directly from the Sales account by debiting sales each time a sales discount, return, or allowance occurs?

5. What are the two basic procedures for accounting for inventory? How do these two procedures differ?

6. What useful purpose does the Purchases account serve?

7. What do the letters FOB stand for? When terms are *FOB destination,* who incurs the cost of freight?

8. What type of an expense is delivery expense? Where is it reported in the income statement?

9. Periodic inventory is said to afford little control over inventory. Explain why.

10. How does the accountant arrive at the total dollar amount of the inventory after taking a physical inventory?

11. How is cost of goods sold determined under periodic inventory procedure?

12. If the cost of goods available for sale and the cost of the ending inventory are known, what other amount appearing on the income statement can be calculated?

13. What are the major sections in a classified income statement for a merchandising company, and in what order do they appear?

14. What is gross margin? Why might management be interested in the percentage of gross margin to sales?

EXERCISES

E-1

Apply rules of debit and credit for merchandise-related accounts

In the following table, indicate how each account shown is increased and decreased (debit or credit), and indicate the normal balance (debit or credit).

Title of Account	Increased by (debit or credit)	Decreased by (debit or credit)	Normal balance (debit or credit)
Merchandise Inventory			
Sales			
Sales Returns and Allowances			
Sales Discounts			
Accounts Receivable			
Purchases			
Purchase Returns and Allowances			
Purchase Discounts			
Accounts Payable			
Transportation-In			

E-2

Prepare entries for merchandise purchase/sale, return, and allowance on both buyer's and seller's books

a. The Duncan Company purchased $15,000 of merchandise from the Short Company on account. Before paying its account, the Duncan Company returned damaged merchandise with an invoice price of $3,200. Assuming use of periodic inventory procedure, prepare entries on both companies' books to record both the purchase/sale and the return.

b. Show how any of the required entries would change assuming that the Short Company granted an allowance of $1,200 on the damaged goods instead of giving permission to return the merchandise.

E–3

Determine end of discount period and prepare entry to record payment

What is the last payment date on which the cash discount can be taken on goods sold on March 5 for $32,000; terms 3/10/EOM, n/60? Assume that the bill is paid on this date, and prepare the correct entry on both the buyer's and seller's books to record the payment.

E–4

Calculate effect of trade and cash discounts on payment

You have purchased merchandise with a list price of $8,000. Because you are a wholesaler, you are granted trade discounts of 30%, 20%, and 10%. The cash discount terms are 2/EOM, n/60. How much will you remit if you pay the invoice by the end of the month of purchase? How much will you remit if you do not pay the invoice until the following month?

E–5

Determine cost of goods sold

The A Company uses periodic inventory procedure. Determine the cost of goods sold for the company assuming purchases during the period were $12,000, transportation-in was $90, purchase returns and allowances were $300, beginning inventory was $7,500, purchase discounts were $600, and ending inventory was $3,900.

E–6

Prepare entries for purchase, transportation-in, purchase discounts, and payment

The Franco Company purchased goods for $9,200 on June 14 under the following terms: 3/10, n/30; FOB shipping point, freight collect. The bill for the freight amounted to $300.

a. Assume that the invoice was paid within the discount period, and prepare all entries required on Franco Company's books.

b. Assume that the invoice was paid on July 11. Prepare the entry to record the payment made on that date.

E–7

Prepare partial work sheet using merchandise-related accounts

Given the balances shown in the partial trial balance, indicate how the balances would be treated in the work sheet. The ending inventory is $32. (The amounts are unusually small for ease in rewriting the numbers.)

Account Title	Trial Balance		Adjustments		Adjusted Trial Balance		Income Statement		Balance Sheet	
	Debit	Credit	Debit	Credit	Debit	Credit	Debit	Credit	Debit	Credit
Merchandise Inventory	40									
Sales		280								
Sales Discounts	6									
Sales Returns and Allowances	16									
Purchases	200									
Purchase Discounts		4								
Purchase Returns and Allowances		8								
Transportation-In	12									

E–8

Prepare and post closing entries using T-accounts

Using the data in Exercise E–7:

a. Prepare closing entries for the accounts shown above. Do not close the Income Summary account.

b. Show in T-account format how the accounts would appear after this portion of the closing process has been completed.

E-9

Supply missing terms in formulas showing income statement relationships

In each of the following equations supply the missing term(s):

a.   Net sales = Gross sales − (_____ _____ + Sales returns and allowances).

b.   Cost of goods sold = Beginning inventory + Net cost of purchases − _____ _____.

c.   Gross margin = _____ _____ − Cost of goods sold.

d.   Net income from operations = _____ _____ − Operating expenses.

e.   Net income = Net income from operations + _____ _____ − _____ _____.

E-10

Supply missing amounts in the income statement

In each case below use the information provided to calculate the missing information:

	Case 1	Case 2	Case 3
Gross sales	200,000	?	?
Sales discounts	?	8,000	6,000
Sales returns and allowances	6,000	14,000	10,000
Net sales	190,000	378,000	?
Merchandise inventory, January 1	80,000	?	120,000
Purchases	120,000	240,000	?
Purchase discounts	2,400	4,200	4,000
Purchase returns and allowances	7,600	9.800	10,000
Net purchases	110,000	?	210,000
Transportation-in	8,000	12,000	10,000
Net cost of purchases	118,000	238,000	?
Cost of goods available for sale	?	338,000	340,000
Merchandise inventory, December 31	?	120,000	140,000
Cost of goods sold	100,000	?	200,000
Gross margin	?	160,000	100,000

PROBLEMS, SERIES A

P5-1-A

Journalize merchandise transactions for two different companies

a.   The following transactions were entered into by the Kemp Carpet Company in August 1987:

Transactions:

Aug. 2   Sold merchandise on account for $30,000; terms 2/10, n/30, FOB destination.
     18   Received payment for the sale of August 2.
     20   A total of $1,000 of the merchandise sold on August 2 was returned, and a full refund was made because it was the wrong merchandise.
     28   An allowance of $1,600 was granted on the sale of August 2 because some merchandise was found to be damaged. $1,600 cash was returned to the customer.

b.   The Evans Furniture Company engaged in the following transactions in August 1987:

Transactions:

Aug. 4   Purchased merchandise on account at a cost of $14,000; terms 2/10, n/30, FOB shipping point.
      6   Paid freight of $200 on the purchase of August 4.
     10   Sold goods for $10,000; terms 2/10, n/30.
     12   Returned $2,400 of the merchandise purchased on August 4.
     14   Paid the amount due on the purchase of August 4.

Required: Prepare journal entries for the transactions.

P5–2–A

Journalize merchandise transactions on both buyer's and seller's books

The Abbott Auto Parts Company purchased merchandise with a list price of $40,000, FOB destination, freight prepaid, from Cooper Company, on August 15, 1987. Trade discounts of 20% and 10% were allowed, and credit terms were 2/10, n/30. Cooper Company paid the freight charges of $500 on August 16. On August 17, Abbott Company requested a purchase allowance of $940 because some of the merchandise had been damaged in transit. On August 20, the Cooper Company granted the allowance. Payment was made on the last day of the discount period.

Required: Record all the entries required on the books of both the buyer and the seller.

P5–3–A

Journalize merchandise transactions on both buyer's and seller's books

On August 1, 1987, the Kelley Hardware Store bought merchandise from the Pittman Company, $18,000 list price, FOB destination. The seller prepaid the freight of $120 on August 1, 1987. Terms included trade discounts of 30% and 10% and a cash discount of 2/10/ EOM, n/60. On August 8, 1987, the Kelley Hardware Store returned $1,500 (at list price) of the merchandise. The balance due was paid on September 10, 1987.

Required: Journalize all entries required on the books of both the buyer and the seller.

P5–4–A

Prepare and post journal entries, and prepare trial balance and classified income statement

The Maddox Company engaged in the following transactions in the month of June 1987:

Transactions:

June	1	The owner, Paul Maddox, invested $40,000 cash and $15,000 of inventory in the business.
	3	Merchandise was purchased on account, $20,000; terms 2/10, n/30, FOB shipping point.
	4	Paid freight on the June 3d purchase, $550.
	7	Merchandise was purchased on account, $10,000; terms 2/10, n/30, FOB destination.
	10	Sold merchandise on account, $24,000; terms 2/10, n/30, FOB shipping point.
	11	Returned $3,000 of the merchandise purchased on June 3.
	12	Paid the amount due on the purchase of June 3.
	13	Sold merchandise on account, $25,000; terms 2/10, n/30, FOB destination.
	14	Paid freight on sale of June 13, $1,500.
	20	Paid the amount due on the purchase of June 7.
	21	$5,000 of the goods sold on June 13 were returned for credit.
	22	Received the amount due on sale of June 13.
	25	Received the amount due on sale of June 10.
	29	Paid rent for the administration building for June, $2,000.
	30	Paid sales salaries of $6,000 for June.
	30	Purchased merchandise on account, $5,000; terms 2/10, n/30, FOB shipping point.

Additional data:

The inventory on hand on June 30 was $30,000.

Required: a.   Prepare journal entries for the transactions.
b.   Post the journal entries to the proper ledger accounts.
c.   Prepare a trial balance as of June 30, 1987.
d.   Prepare a classified income statement.

P5–5–A

Prepare work sheet, classified income statement and balance sheet, and closing entries

The following data are for the Oakes Lamp Company:

OAKES LAMP COMPANY
Trial Balance
December 31, 1987

	Debits	Credits
Cash	$ 57,200	
Accounts Receivable	48,300	
Prepaid Insurance	2,900	
Merchandise Inventory, 1/1/87	41,600	
Land	60,000	
Store Building	110,000	
Accumulated Depreciation—Store Building		$ 33,000
Store fixtures	55,600	
Accumulated Depreciation—Store Fixtures		11,120
Accounts Payable		37,900
Oakes, Capital		220,180
Sales		551,500
Sales Discounts	3,700	
Sales Returns and Allowances	2,000	
Purchases	312,900	
Purchase Discounts		2,600
Purchase Returns and Allowances		1,400
Transportation-In	7,300	
Sales Salaries Expense	64,000	
Advertising Expense	12,000	
Delivery Expense	4,600	
Office Salaries Expense	74,000	
Interest Revenue		400
Interest Expense	2,000	
	$858,100	$858,100

Additional data:

1. Depreciation expense on the store building is $2,200.
2. Depreciation expense on the store fixtures is $5,560.
3. Accrued sales salaries are $1,400.
4. Insurance expired in 1987 is $2,500. Insurance is an administrative expense.
5. Cost of merchandise inventory on hand December 31, 1987, is $55,500.

Required: Prepare:

a. A work sheet for the year ended December 31, 1987.
b. A classified income statement. The only administrative expenses are office salaries and insurance.
c. A classified balance sheet.
d. The required closing entries.

P5–6–A

Prepare and post journal entries; prepare work sheet, classified income statement, classified balance sheet, and closing entries

The Connors Cabinet Company was organized May 1, 1987, and engaged in the following transactions:

Transactions:

May 1 Ron Connors invested $300,000 in his new business.
1 Purchased merchandise on account from the Robertson Company, $15,600; terms n/60, FOB shipping point.
3 Sold merchandise for cash, $9,600.
6 Paid transportation charges on May 1 purchase, $480 cash.
7 Returned $1,200 of merchandise to the Robertson Company due to improper size.

May 10   Requested and received an allowance of $600 from the Robertson Company for improper quality of certain items.
14   Sold merchandise on account to Lewis Company, $6,000; terms 2/20, n/30.
16   Issued cash refund for return of merchandise relating to sale made on May 3, $60.
18   Purchased merchandise on account from White Company invoiced at $9,600; terms 2/15, n/30, FOB shipping point.
18   Received a bill for freight charges of $300 from the Ace Trucking Company on the purchase from White Company.
19   Lewis Company returned $120 of merchandise purchased on May 14.
24   Returned $960 of defective merchandise to White Company. Received full credit.
28   Lewis Company remitted balance due on sale of May 14.
31   Paid White Company for the purchase of May 18 after adjusting for transaction of May 24.
31   Paid miscellaneous selling expenses of $2,400.
31   Paid miscellaneous administrative expenses of $3,600.

Additional data:

The May 30 inventory is $19,200.

Required: From the information for the Connors Cabinet Company:

a.   Journalize the transactions. Round all amounts to the nearest dollar.
b.   Post the entries to the proper ledger accounts.
c.   Prepare a work sheet as of May 31. There were no adjusting entries.
d.   Prepare a classified income statement for May.
e.   Prepare and post the required closing entries.

PROBLEMS, SERIES B

P5–1–B

Journalize merchandise transactions for two different companies

a.   The Norris Sporting Goods Company engaged in the following transactions in April 1987:

Transactions:

Apr. 1   Sold merchandise on account for $32,000; terms 2/10, n/30, FOB destination.
5   $4,800 of the goods sold on account on April 1 were returned for full credit. Payment for these goods had not yet been received.
8   A sales allowance of $640 was granted on the merchandise sold on April 1 because the merchandise was damaged in shipment.
10   Payment was received for the net amount due from the sale of April 1.

b.   Classic Stereo Company engaged in the following transactions in July 1987:

Transactions:

July 2   Purchased stereo merchandise on account at a cost of $4,800; terms 2/10, n/30, FOB destination.
15   Sold $3,200 of the merchandise purchased on July 2 for $7,200; terms 2/10, n/30, FOB destination.
16   Paid freight costs on the merchandise sold, $240.
20   Classic Stereo Company was granted an allowance of $320 on the purchase of July 2 because of damaged merchandise.
31   Paid the amount due on the purchase of July 2.

Required: Prepare journal entries to record the transactions. Round all amounts to the nearest dollar.

P5–2–B

Journalize merchandise transactions on both buyer's and seller's books

On July 2, 1987, the Calvary Musical Instrument Company purchased merchandise with a list price of $8,000 from the Reynolds Company. The terms were 3/EOM, n/60, FOB shipping point, freight collect. Trade discounts of 15%, 10%, and 5% were granted by the Reynolds Company. The Calvary Musical Instrument Company paid the freight bill of $184 on July 5. On July 6, an employee discovered that merchandise with a list price of $640 had been seriously damaged in transit; these items were returned for full credit. Calvary Musical Instrument Company made payment on the last day of the discount period.

Required: Prepare all the necessary entries for the Calvary Musical Instrument Company.

P5–3–B

Journalize merchandise transactions on both buyer's and seller's books

The Saxon Ski Shop purchased merchandise on March 1, 1987, from the Locke Company at a list price of $12,000, FOB shipping point. Trade discounts of 30%, 25%, and 5% were granted. Cash discount terms were 2/EOM, n/60. The buyer paid the freight of $248 on March 4, 1987. The buyer notified the seller that a $1,200 credit should be granted against the amount due because of damaged merchandise. The seller granted the allowance on March 25, 1987.

Required: Assuming payment on March 31, record all entries on the books of both the buyer and seller.

P5–4–B

Prepare and post journal entries, and prepare trial balance and classified income statement

The data for the month of June 1987 given below are for the Tate Company:

Transactions:

June 1 The Tate Company was organized, and the owner, Sam Tate, invested $105,000 cash, $35,000 of merchandise, and a $30,000 plot of land.
  4 Merchandise was purchased for cash, $45,000; FOB shipping point.
  9 Cash of $1,050 was paid to a trucking company for delivery of the merchandise purchased June 4.
  13 The company sold merchandise on account, $30,000; terms 2/10, n/30.
  15 The company sold merchandise on account, $24,000; terms 2/10, n/30.
  16 Of the merchandise sold May 13, $3,300 was returned for credit.
  20 Salaries for services received were paid as follows: to office employees, $3,300; to salespersons, $8,700.
  22 The company collected the amount due on $26,700 of the accounts receivable arising from the sale of June 13.
  24 The company purchased merchandise on account at a cost of $36,000; terms 2/10, n/30, FOB shipping point.
  26 $6,000 of the merchandise purchased June 24 was returned to the vendor for credit.
  27 A trucking company was paid $750 for delivery to the Tate Company of the goods purchased June 24.
  29 The company sold merchandise on account, $40,000; terms 2/10, n/30.
  30 Sold merchandise for cash, $18,000.
  30 Payment was received for the sale of June 15.
  30 Paid store rent for June, $4,500.
  30 Paid the amount due on the purchase of June 24.

Additional data:

The inventory on hand at the close of business June 30 was $70,000 at cost.

Required:
a. Prepare journal entries for the transactions.
b. Post the journal entries to the proper ledger accounts.
c. Prepare a trial balance as of June 30, 1987.
d. Prepare a classified income statement for the month ended June 30, 1987.

P5–5–B

Prepare work sheet, classified income statement and balance sheet, and closing entries

The following data are for the Wilson Lumber Company:

WILSON LUMBER COMPANY
Trial Balance
December 31, 1987

	Debits	Credits
Cash	$ 21,192	
Accounts Receivable	47,856	
Merchandise Inventory	85,560	
Sales Supplies on Hand	1,608	
Prepaid Fire Insurance	1,440	
Prepaid Rent	17,280	
Store Equipment	26,400	
Accumulated Depreciation—Store Equipment		$ 5,280
Accounts Payable		30,840
Wilson, Capital		125,892
Sales		336,708
Sales Returns and Allowances	1,548	
Purchases	150,252	
Purchase Returns and Allowances		1,212
Transportation-In	2,352	
Sales Salaries Expense	41,520	
Advertising Expense	23,400	
General Office Expense	2,964	
Office Salaries Expense	24,240	
Officers' Salaries Expense	48,000	
Legal and Auditing Expense	3,000	
Telephone and Telegraph Expense	1,440	
Interest Revenue		300
Interest Expense	180	
	$500,232	$500,232

Additional data as of December 31, 1987:

1. Prepaid fire insurance expired, $1,020.
2. Sales supplies consumed, $1,098.
3. Prepaid rent expired during the year, $15,180.
4. Depreciation expense on store equipment, $2,640.
5. Accrued sales salaries, $1,200.
6. Accrued office salaries, $900.
7. Merchandise inventory on hand, $105,000.

Required: Prepare:

a. A work sheet for the year ended December 31, 1987.
b. A classified income statement. The only selling expenses are sales salaries, advertising, sales supplies, and depreciation—store equipment.
c. A classified balance sheet.
d. The December 31, 1987, closing entries.

P5–6–B

Prepare and post journal entries; prepare work sheet, classified income statement, classified balance sheet, and closing entries

The Hall Western Wear Company is a wholesaler of western wear clothing. The company sells its merchandise to retailers. The company entered into the following transactions in May 1987:

Transactions:

May 1 The Hall Western Wear Company was organized as a single proprietorship. Mark Hall invested the following assets in the business: $154,000 cash, $56,000 merchandise, and $35,000 land.

1 Paid rent on administrative offices for May, $8,400.

5 The company purchased merchandise from Andco Company on account, $63,000; terms 2/10, n/30. Freight terms were FOB shipping point.

May 8 Cash of $2,800 was paid to a trucking company for delivery of the merchandise purchased May 5.

14 The company sold merchandise on account, $105,000; terms 2/10, n/30.

15 Paid Andco Company the amount due on the purchase of May 5.

16 Of the merchandise sold May 14, $4,620 was returned for credit.

19 Salaries for services received were paid for the month of May as follows: office employees, $5,600; and salespersons, $11,200.

24 The company collected the amount due on $42,000 of the accounts receivable arising from the sale of May 14.

25 The company purchased merchandise on account from Hill Company, $50,400; terms 2/10, n/30. Freight terms were FOB shipping point.

27 Of the merchandise purchased May 25, $8,400 was returned to the vendor.

28 A trucking company was paid $700 for delivery to the Hall Western Wear Company of the goods purchased May 25.

29 The company sold merchandise on open account, $5,040; terms 2/10, n/30.

30 Cash sales were $24,696.

30 Cash of $33,600 was received from the sale of May 14.

31 Paid Hill Company for the merchandise purchased on May 25, taking into consideration the merchandise returned on May 27.

Additional data:

The inventory on hand at the close of business on May 31 is $99,680.

Required: From the data given for the Hall Western Wear Company:

a. Prepare journal entries for the transactions.
b. Post the journal entries to the proper ledger accounts.
c. Prepare a work sheet. (There were no adjusting journal entries.)
d. Prepare a classified income statement for the month ended May 31, 1987.
e. Prepare a classified balance sheet as of May 31, 1987.
f. Prepare and post the necessary closing entries.

BUSINESS DECISION PROBLEM

Prepare income statement and balance sheet for merchandising company

Tom Steele taught physical education classes at Brooke High School for 20 years. In 1986, Tom's uncle died and left Tom $100,000. Tom quit his teaching job in December of 1986 and opened a hardware store in January of 1987. On January 2, 1987, Tom deposited $60,000 in a checking account opened in the store's name, Steele's Hardware Store. During the first week of January, Tom rented a building and paid the first year's rent of $4,800 in advance. Also during that week, he purchased the following assets for cash:

Delivery truck	$10,000
Store equipment	5,000
Office equipment	3,000

During the remainder of the first six months of 1987, Tom received cash of $70,000 from customers and disbursed cash of $52,000 for merchandise purchases and $15,000 for operating expenses.

Tom never took an accounting course, but he was familiar with the term **net income.** He decided to compute his net income for the first six months of 1987 and prepared the following schedule:

Cash receipts		$ 70,000
Cash disbursements:		
Delivery truck	$10,000	
Store equipment	5,000	
Office equipment	3,000	
Prepaid rent	4,800	
Merchandise purchases . .	52,000	
Operating expenses . . .	15,000	89,800
Net loss		$(19,800)

Assume that the depreciation amounts for the six-month period are as follows:

Delivery truck $1,000
Store equipment 250
Office equipment 175

Also assume that you obtained the following information:

1. Steele owes $8,000 to creditors for merchandise purchases.
2. Customers owe Steele $10,000 on June 30, 1987 for goods purchased.
3. Merchandise costing $16,000 is on hand at the end of the six months.

Required:

a. Do you agree with Tom Steele's statement that his hardware store suffered a net loss of $19,800 for the six months ended June 30, 1987? If not, show how you would determine the net income (or net loss).

b. Is it possible to prepare a balance sheet on June 30, 1987, or does Mr. Steele have to wait until December 31, 1987, to prepare a balance sheet? If a balance sheet can be prepared on June 30, 1987, prepare one.

BUSINESS SITUATION FOR DISCUSSION

Retailers: Head Off Credit Cards with Cash Discounts?*

Michael Levy and Charles A. Ingene

Calls for a cashless society appeared regularly in the business press in the 1970s. Futurists predicted that plastic cards, both credit and debit, would replace green paper. Alas, polish for the crystal ball is in order. High interest rates and state usury laws have caused many retailers to examine their consumer credit policies for ways to wipe out red ink. Many retailers are experimenting with new strategies.

* * * * *

Exxon, Amoco, Sohio, and Mobil have been trying out various ways of offering discounts for cash in lieu of credit card sales. Mobil has lowered its wholesale price while adding a 3% processing fee for credit sales to induce station managers to favor cash sales. As a result, signs have sprouted at Mobil stations offering consumers gasoline at 4 cents a gallon less if they pay cash.

Retailers of other goods have jumped on the bandwagon too. Breuners, a furniture dealer in California, offers a 5% discount for cash, while 4 Day Tire Stores, also based in California, advertises 2%.

The idea received a boost in the summer of 1981 when Congress passed the Cash Discount Act, permitting businesses to give discounts exceeding 5% to consumers paying cash. Previously, a rebate of more than 5% was considered a finance charge levied against credit card users and was therefore illegal.

The retailer incurs two costs in each credit card transaction: the factoring fee to convert the charge to cash and the interest expense arising from the time lag between the sale and collection of funds. If, for example, his cost of capital is 20%, if an average six days elapse between the sale and collection of the proceeds, and if the factor's fee is 5%, then $10,000 in credit sales are equivalent to $9,472 in cash sales. The retailer could offer a cash discount of 5.3% and still be as well off as with a credit card sale.

Although many retailers might like to reject credit cards altogether because of their expense, up to now they have been ill-advised to take this step unless most of their competitors followed suit. Otherwise, they could suffer a differential disadvantage.

The retailer should consider four elements before adopting a discount-for-cash policy:

The reasons why his customers use credit cards. If it's just because they like the convenience of not carrying cash or consider it an advantage to buy now and pay later, they are candidates for a cash discount strategy. If, however, customers *need* the credit in order to make a purchase, a small cash reduction for cash payment probably would not deter their use of credit cards.

The proportion of his volume made up by cash sales. If the proportion is high, a discount-for-cash policy would give many customers who would have paid cash anyway a "free" deduction. Obviously, the effect on the retailer's earnings would not be healthy.

The cost of implementing the new policy. Computerized cash registers permit programming of a dis-

* Reprinted by permission of the *Harvard Business Review.* Excerpts from "Retailers: Head Off Credit Cards with Cash Discounts?" by Michael Levy and Charles A. Ingene (May/June 1983, pp. 18–21). Copyright © 1983 by the President and Fellows of Harvard College; all rights reserved.

count. Without electronic cash-handling technology, calculating the rebates could result in slower checkouts and clerical errors.

His customers' attitudes toward such an incentive—if he can ascertain them. If his competitors have a cash discount policy, the retailer could match this and wait for customer reaction. This "competitive parity" assumes, however, that rivals have determined an optimal discount policy that is applicable to others. This is a dangerous assumption that the retailer might regret making.

* * * * *

The broadest approach to establishing a discount-for-cash policy is of course to offer it to everybody. But the strategy is more profitable if the retailer extends the incentive only to those customers who are most apt to use credit cards. To differentiate these from regular cash customers and maximize the potential of the policy, the retailer can try one of these possibilities:

☐ Limit the discount to those products that have a high proportion of credit sales—if they can be identified. Presumably these are big-ticket items.

☐ Limit the discount to a specified high level of dollars spent by the customer on a visit, irrespective of the price of each item bought. Consumers are apt to pay for large dollar amounts by credit card.

☐ Vary the discount with the amount bought. For example, the retailer could offer a 1% discount on a sale of $25 to $100, 2% on a sale of $100.01 to $250, and 3% on a sale exceeding that.

☐ Sell customers cards entitling them to a discount or range of discounts. Presumably those who buy the card are ready to spend enough money to recoup the cost of the card. The retailer gets the card fee and the difference between the cost of credit and the discount. And he avoids extending the incentive to all cash buyers. He may also benefit from higher customer loyalty sometimes generated by such "membership" cards.

CHAPTER 6

Accounting Systems and Special Journals

LEARNING OBJECTIVES

After studying this chapter, you should be able to:

1. Describe the relationship between subsidiary accounts in subsidiary ledgers and control accounts in the general ledger.
2. Describe the relationship between special journals and the general journal.
3. Describe computer applications in business (covered in Appendix).
4. Define and use correctly the new terms in the glossary.

In Chapters 1–5, you learned how to process the raw data of business transactions through the steps of the accounting cycle to produce financial statements. This process of analyzing, recording, classifying, summarizing, and reporting business transactions is the same for all businesses. However, the speed and efficiency of the processing depends on which accounting system is used.

For example, assume you decide to drive home after your accounting class. You can either go home the "long way" by using the side roads or "make time" by using the superhighway. Whichever route you take, your destination is going to be the same—home. The process of going home is the same whether you take the side roads or the superhighway—you are driving your car. However, the system you use to get to your destination—the side roads or the superhighway—is different. You probably decide to take the superhighway because it is faster. The same is true of processing accounting information. The accounting process also can often be accomplished faster and more efficiently by using one particular accounting system rather than any other accounting system. This chapter identifies various accounting systems and describes their features.

So far in this text you have used the manual accounting system with one journal and one ledger. Now you will be introduced to two additions to that manual system—subsidiary ledgers and special journals. Then you will proceed to a discussion of other systems used in accounting, ending with the computerized accounting system. This chapter makes it possible for you to process business transactions in a more efficient and time-saving manner.

■ THE PROCESSING OF DATA—MANUAL SYSTEM

The masses of raw data generated by even a small business are not useful until processed. Businesses must routinely process these data in an orderly and efficient manner to accomplish the following:

1. Results of operations and financial position of the firm are determined and reported on a timely basis.
2. Bills are paid when due.
3. Proper quantities and items of inventory are sent to customers.
4. Other aspects of business, such as sending invoices to customers and ordering merchandise, are conducted in an orderly and purposeful manner.
5. Reports required by the government or regulatory agencies are prepared efficiently.

Businesses accomplish this orderly and efficient processing of accounting data by using the accounting system that best fits their needs. The basic accounting system is the manual system with one journal and one ledger. This basic system is generally used by very small businesses. Given an unlimited amount of time, all business transactions can be processed through this manual system. However, as a business grows, its number of business transactions also grows, and the company looks for ways to speed up the accounting process by streamlining its accounting system.

An accounting system can be defined as a set of records (journals, ledgers, work sheets, trial balances, and reports) plus the procedures and equipment regularly used to process business transactions. To be effective, accounting systems should:

1. Provide for the efficient processing of data at the least cost. The cost of the system should be equal to or less than the benefits received.
2. Ensure a high degree of accuracy.
3. Provide for internal control to prevent theft or fraud.
4. Provide for the growth of a business.

First, you will learn how a business begins to enlarge its accounting system by using control accounts in the general ledger and adding subsidiary ledgers that are periodically totaled to these control accounts. Then you will learn about other journals (called special journals) that can be used along with the general journal.

■ CONTROL ACCOUNTS AND SUBSIDIARY LEDGERS

To efficiently process information, a business must adapt its accounting system to the type and quantity of information it needs. When a business has only a few customers and suppliers, a separate account can be set up for each customer and supplier in the general ledger. However, when a business has many customers and suppliers, a control account for accounts receivable and a control account for accounts payable are established in the general ledger. Also, subsidiary ledgers for receivables and payables are added to the accounting system to show the balances for individual customers and suppliers.

A **control account** is an account in the general ledger that shows the total balance of all the subsidiary accounts related to it. An example of a control account is the general ledger **Accounts Receivable** control account, which summarizes all of the amounts owed to the company. Since this is a summary account, it would be impossible to send out customer statements based on the summary data provided in this account.

Subsidiary ledger accounts show the details supporting the related general ledger control account balance. The subsidiary accounts for **receivables** may be used to send out customer statements. The subsidiary accounts for **payables** may be used to determine the amount payable to each supplier. The accounts are normally alphabetized by the name of the customer or supplier. The sum of the subsidiary accounts in a subsidiary ledger should agree with the balance in the related general ledger control account when the financial statements are prepared.

A **subsidiary ledger,** then, is a group of related accounts showing the details of the balance of a general ledger control account. Subsidiary ledgers are separated from the general ledger in order to relieve the general ledger of a mass of detail and thereby shorten the general ledger trial balance. Also, having separate ledgers promotes a division of labor.

In T-account form, the relationship between a control account and subsidiary accounts is as follows:

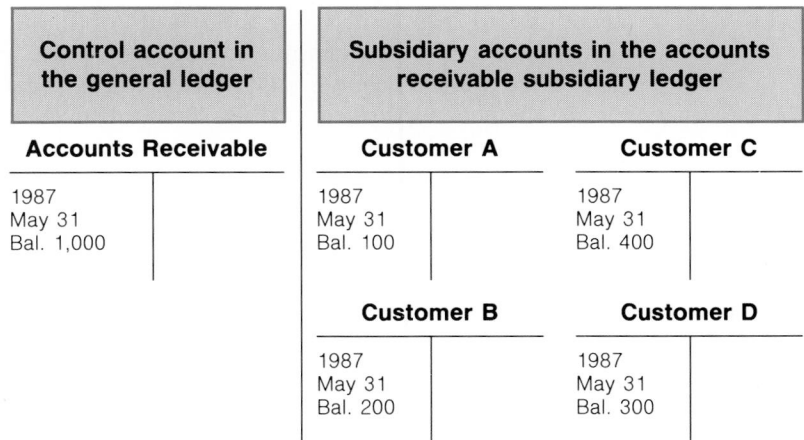

Note that the sum of all balances in the subsidiary accounts ($100 + $200 + $400 + $300) on May 31, 1987, is equal to the balance on that same date in the control account ($1,000).

When a transaction occurs that affects a control account, some account(s) in the subsidiary ledger will also be affected. Since a transaction is entered into the journal before it is entered in the ledger accounts, the journal entry will need to indicate which of the subsidiary ledger accounts is affected. Posting will be made to both the control account and the subsidiary ledger account (indicated by the √). For example, if a $400 sale is made on July 10 to Debbi Kahan on account, the journal entry would be:

July 10	Accounts Receivable—D. Kahan	111/✓	400	
	Sales	301		400
	To record sale of merchandise on account.			

The amount of the sale ($400) would be posted as a debit to both the Accounts Receivable control account (111) in the general ledger and D. Kahan's account in the subsidiary ledger (✓) and as a credit to the Sales account (301) in the general ledger.

The general ledger has backup subsidiary ledgers for accounts in addition to the Accounts Receivable account. Some examples of accounts that frequently have backup subsidiary ledgers are:

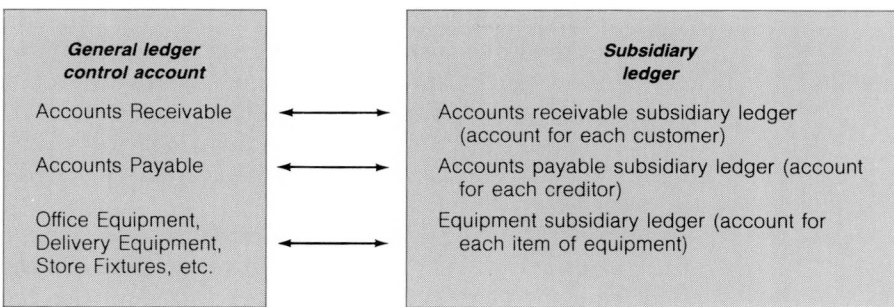

The number of subsidiary ledgers maintained by a company varies according to the company's information requirements. Control accounts and subsidiary ledgers are generally set up whenever there are many transactions in a given account and information on the details of these transactions is needed on a continuing basis. This chapter focuses on the use of accounts receivable subsidiary ledgers and accounts payable subsidiary ledgers.

In the next section you will learn about special journals. You should remember that control accounts and subsidiary ledgers may be used even if special journals are not used. Both subsidiary ledgers and special journals are likely to be used when there are numerous transactions that are similar.

■ SPECIAL JOURNALS

Until now, only one book of original entry, the general journal, has been used to record transactions. As the transactions of a company increase, the first step in altering the manual accounting system is usually to use special journals along with the original general journal. Each special journal records one particular type of transaction, such as sales on account, cash receipts, purchases on account, or cash disbursements.

The following advantages are obtained from the use of special journals:

1. **Time is saved in journalizing.** Only one line is used for each transaction; usually a full description is not necessary. The amount of writing is reduced because it is not necessary to repeat the account titles printed at the top of the special column or columns.
2. **Time is saved in posting.** Many amounts are posted as column totals rather than individually.

3. **Detail is eliminated from the general ledger.**   Column totals are posted to the general ledger, and the detail is left in the special journals.
4. **Division of labor is promoted.**   Several persons can work simultaneously on the accounting records. This specialization and division of labor pinpoints responsibility and allows for more rapid location of errors.
5. **Management analysis is aided.**   The journals themselves can be useful to management in analyzing classes of transactions, such as credit sales, because all similar transactions are in one place.

Special journals, then, are designed to systematize the original recording of major recurring types of transactions. The number and format of the special journals actually used in a company depend primarily on the nature of the company's business transactions. The special journals illustrated in this chapter are the sales, cash receipts, purchases, and cash disbursements journals:

☐   The **sales journal** is used to record all sales of merchandise on account (on credit).

☐   The **cash receipts journal** is used to record all inflows of cash into the business.

☐   The **purchases journal** is used to record all purchases of merchandise on account (on credit). Merchandise refers to items of inventory that are available for sale to customers.

☐   The **cash disbursements journal** is used to record all payments (or outflows) of cash by the business.

The **general journal** is not eliminated by the use of special journals; it is used to record all transactions that cannot be entered in one of the special journals. All five of these journals are books of original entry. If a transaction is recorded in a journal, it will be posted and is part of the accounting records. Therefore, if a transaction is recorded in a special journal, it should **not** be recorded in the general journal because this would record the transaction twice.

Since the journals are posted to ledger accounts, the Posting Reference column in the ledger should indicate the source of the posting. The following abbreviations are used for the five journals:

	Journal	Transaction	Abbreviation
Special journals	Sales journal	Merchandise sold on account	S
	Cash receipts journal	Cash receipts from all sources	CR
	Purchases journal	Merchandise purchased on account	P
	Cash disbursements journal .	Cash payments for all purposes	CD
	General journal	Any transactions that are not included in the special journals are recorded in the general journal	G

You will learn how to use each of the four special journals in the sections that follow. As you study these journals, you will realize how effective they are in accelerating the recording process.

Sales Journal

Sales are normally made either for cash or on credit. The sales journal is used only for sales on account; cash sales would be recorded in the cash receipts journal. The simplest form of sales journal has only one money column labeled Accounts Receivable Dr. and Sales Cr. because every sale on account is journalized by this same debit and credit. The headings in this form of sales journal might appear as follows:

Date	Customer	Invoice No.	Accounts Receivable Dr. Sales Cr.	
			Amount	✓

Variations in the sales journal can be made depending on the information needs of the business. For example, there could be a separate Sales Cr. column for each department in a company. If this is done, a separate column will be needed for Accounts Receivable Dr. because the debit will always be to Accounts Receivable regardless of which department sold the goods. The headings in a sales journal with separate columns for each department might appear as follows:

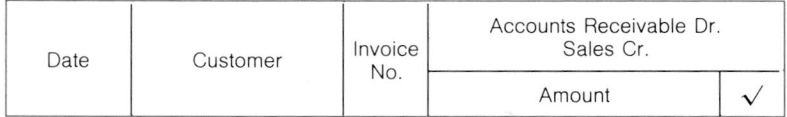

Accounts Receivable Dr.		Date	Customer	Invoice No.	Sales Cr.		
Amount	✓				Dept. A	Dept. B	Dept. C

In either format, the customer's name is necessary in order to know which subsidiary ledger account is affected by the sales transaction. The invoice number simply provides documentation that a sale actually occurred. The column with the check mark is similar to a posting reference column; a check mark is placed in that column when the amount of the sale is posted to the customer's subsidiary ledger account. No posting reference column is needed because the column heading indicates to which account and in what manner (debit or credit) the column total will be posted.

Illustration 6.1 shows a sales journal with only one money column for the John Mason Company, a retail clothing store. In Illustration 6.1, five credit sales transactions occurred in April.

Posting the Sales Journal. Individual amounts in the money column are posted daily to each individual customer's account in the subsidiary ledger. Posting is done daily to show the amount currently due from the customer. As each individual amount is posted, a check mark, ✓, is placed in the column headed ✓ opposite the amount to show that it has been posted. At the end of the month, the total of the money column, $290, is posted in the general ledger as a debit to the Accounts Receivable control account and as a credit to the Sales account. The posting reference of S1 (sales journal, p. 1) is entered in the Accounts Receivable control account and the Sales account. The account numbers, 111 for Accounts Receivable and 301 for Sales, are written in the sales journal under the total of the money column to show that $290 was posted to those accounts.

Illustration 6.1 *Sales Journal*

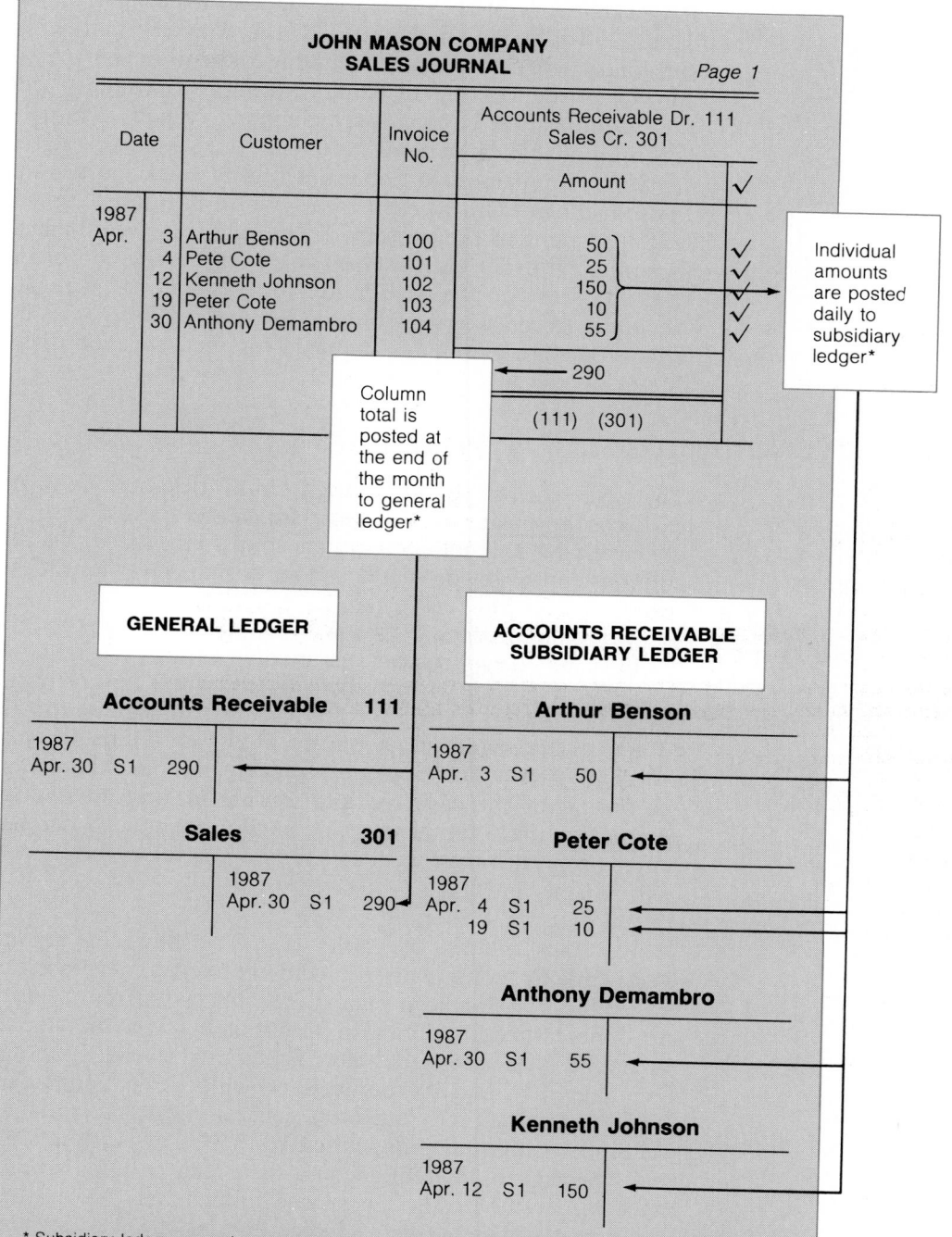

* Subsidiary ledger accounts are posted daily to keep up-to-date balances in the subsidiary ledger. The general ledger accounts will usually be posted at end-of-month or end-of-page (whichever comes first) because the balances in the control accounts are not really necessary until the end of the period for financial statement purposes.

When the posting of accounts receivable has been completed, the Accounts Receivable control account in the general ledger will show a balance of $290. This $290 is equal to the sum of the balances in the Accounts Receivable subsidiary ledger accounts, assuming there were no previous balances in the control account or the subsidiary accounts. Subsidiary ledger accounts, since their composition is constantly changing, usually are not numbered but are kept in alphabetical order.

Some companies do not use a formal sales journal for sales on account. Instead, the amount of each sales invoice is entered directly in the subsidiary ledger account of the customer. The sales invoices for a month are arranged in numerical order and fastened together. At the end of the month, all of the sales invoices for the month are totaled and an entry is made debiting the Accounts Receivable control account and crediting Sales for the total amount. This procedure eliminates the need for separate recording of each credit sale in a sales journal.

Cash Receipts Journal

The cash receipts journal is used for all transactions involving the receipt of cash by the business. The most frequent types of cash receipts transactions are cash sales and collections on accounts receivable. Therefore, separate credit columns appear for those items in the cash receipts journal shown in Illustration 6.2.

Many other types of transactions may result in the receipt of cash by the business, but these transactions involve various accounts as the credits. Since these **other accounts** (miscellaneous accounts) do not occur with enough frequency to warrant special columns, they appear in the **Other Accounts** Cr. column of the cash receipts journal. However, if after several months or periods, a certain transaction appears regularly in the Other Accounts Cr. column, the format of the cash receipts journal may be revised to provide a special column for that type of transaction. For example, a company that has several rental properties may wish to provide a column for Rent Revenue Cr. in the cash receipts journal.

Posting the Cash Receipts Journal.   Individual amounts in the Accounts Receivable Cr. column are posted daily to customers' accounts in the subsidiary ledger in order to keep customer balances current. The items in the Other Accounts Cr. column are also posted daily to the individual accounts indicated (Account Nos. 138 and 303). The totals of the Cash Dr., Sales Discounts Dr., Sales Cr., and Accounts Receivable Cr. columns are posted at the end of the month to their respective general ledger accounts.

Since the amounts appearing in the Other Accounts Cr. column will normally pertain to different accounts, the column total is not posted, and a check mark in parentheses ($\checkmark$) is placed immediately below the column total. This check mark in parentheses indicates that the amount shown as the column total is not posted to any account.

The ledger accounts in Illustration 6.2 show only the postings from the cash receipts journal of the John Mason Company.

The Accounts Receivable control account in the general ledger appears as follows after both the sales and cash receipts journals in Illustration 6.1 and 6.2 have been posted:

Accounts Receivable   *Account No. 111*

Date		Explanation	Post. Ref.	Debit	Credit	Balance
1987 Apr.	30		S1	2 9 0		2 9 0 Dr.
	30		CR5		2 2 5	6 5 Dr.

Illustration 6.3 shows the subsidiary accounts at the same point in time.

A **schedule of accounts receivable** is prepared at the end of the month to ensure that the total of the balances in the subsidiary ledger accounts agrees with the control account. This schedule is merely a listing of open account balances. An example of this schedule for the John Mason Company follows:

JOHN MASON COMPANY
Schedule of Accounts Receivable
As of April 30, 1987

Peter Cote	$10
Anthony Demambro	55
Balance in the control account . .	$65

Combined Sales and Cash Receipts Journal

The sales and cash receipts journals may be combined into one journal. A combined sales and cash receipts journal is illustrated in Demonstration Problem 6–1 at the end of the chapter. In considering whether or not to combine these journals, posting and journalizing convenience is only one consideration. Remember that having separate sales and cash receipts journals allows more people to work with the data in the journals at the same time.

The Purchases Journal

The purchases journal is used to record all purchases of merchandise made on account. There are a number of formats that can be used for the purchases journal. One common format has only one money column headed Purchases Dr. and Accounts Payable Cr. The headings in a purchases journal with one money column might be as follows:

Date	Creditor	Terms	Invoice No.	Purchases Dr. Accounts Payable Cr.	
				Amount	✓

Note that in the above purchases journal there is a Terms column. The sales journal discussed in the previous section did not have a Terms column

Illustration 6.2 Cash Receipts Journal

JOHN MASON COMPANY
CASH RECEIPTS JOURNAL
Page 5

Cash Dr. (101)	Sales Discounts Dr. (302)	Date	Description	Sales Cr. (310)	Accounts Receivable Cr. (111) Amount	Other Accounts Cr. Account Title	Acct No.	Amount
		1987 Apr.						
5,000		1	Cash sales	5,000				
49	1	6	Arthur Benson—Invoice No. 100		50			
8,000		7	Cash sales	8,000				
6,000		10	Sold land at cost to Wells Corporation			Land	138	6,000
7,000		14	Cash sales	7,000				
25		19	Peter Cote—Invoice No. 101		25			
147	3	20	Kenneth Johnson—Invoice No. 102		150			
9,000		25	Cash sales	9,000				
200		26	Cash received from sale of scrap			Miscellaneous Revenue	303	200
35,421	4			29,000	225			6,200
(101)	(302)			(301)	(111)			(✓)

Individual amounts in Accounts Receivable Cr. column are posted daily to subsidiary ledger accounts. Individual amounts in the Other Accounts Cr. column are posted daily to general ledger accounts

Total is not posted because it relates to more than one general ledger account

Totals are posted at the end of the month to general ledger accounts

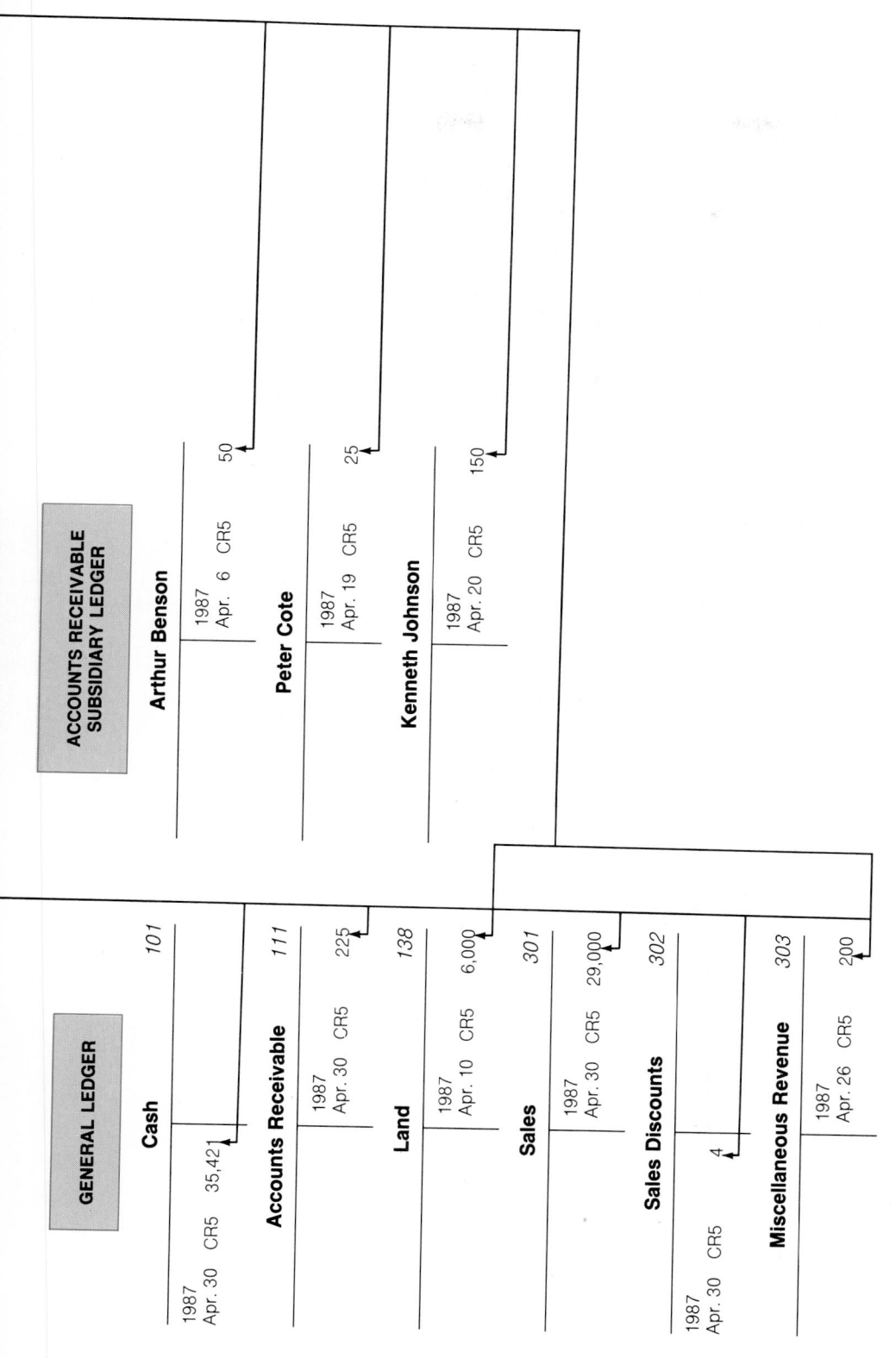

ACCOUNTS RECEIVABLE SUBSIDIARY LEDGER

Arthur Benson

1987		
Apr. 6	CR5	50

Peter Cote

1987		
Apr. 19	CR5	25

Kenneth Johnson

1987		
Apr. 20	CR5	150

GENERAL LEDGER

Cash   *101*

1987		
Apr. 30	CR5	35,421

Accounts Receivable   *111*

1987		
Apr. 30	CR5	225

Land   *138*

1987		
Apr. 10	CR5	6,000

Sales   *301*

1987		
Apr. 30	CR5	29,000

Sales Discounts   *302*

1987		
Apr. 30	CR5	4

Miscellaneous Revenue   *303*

1987		
Apr. 26	CR5	200

Illustration 6.3 *Accounts Receivable Subsidiary Ledger*

JOHN MASON COMPANY
SUBSIDIARY ACCOUNTS RECEIVABLE LEDGER
Arthur Benson

Date		Explanation	Post. Ref.	Debit	Credit	Balance
1987 Apr.	3		S1	50		50 Dr.
	6		CR5		50	– 0 –

Peter Cote

Date		Explanation	Post. Ref.	Debit	Credit	Balance
1987 Apr.	4		S1	25		25 Dr.
	19		S1	10		35 Dr.
	19		CR5		25	10 Dr.

Anthony Demambro

Date		Explanation	Post. Ref.	Debit	Credit	Balance
1987 Apr.	30		S1	55		55 Dr.

Kenneth Johnson

Date		Explanation	Post. Ref.	Debit	Credit	Balance
1987 Apr.	12		S1	150		150 Dr.
	20		CR5		150	– 0 –

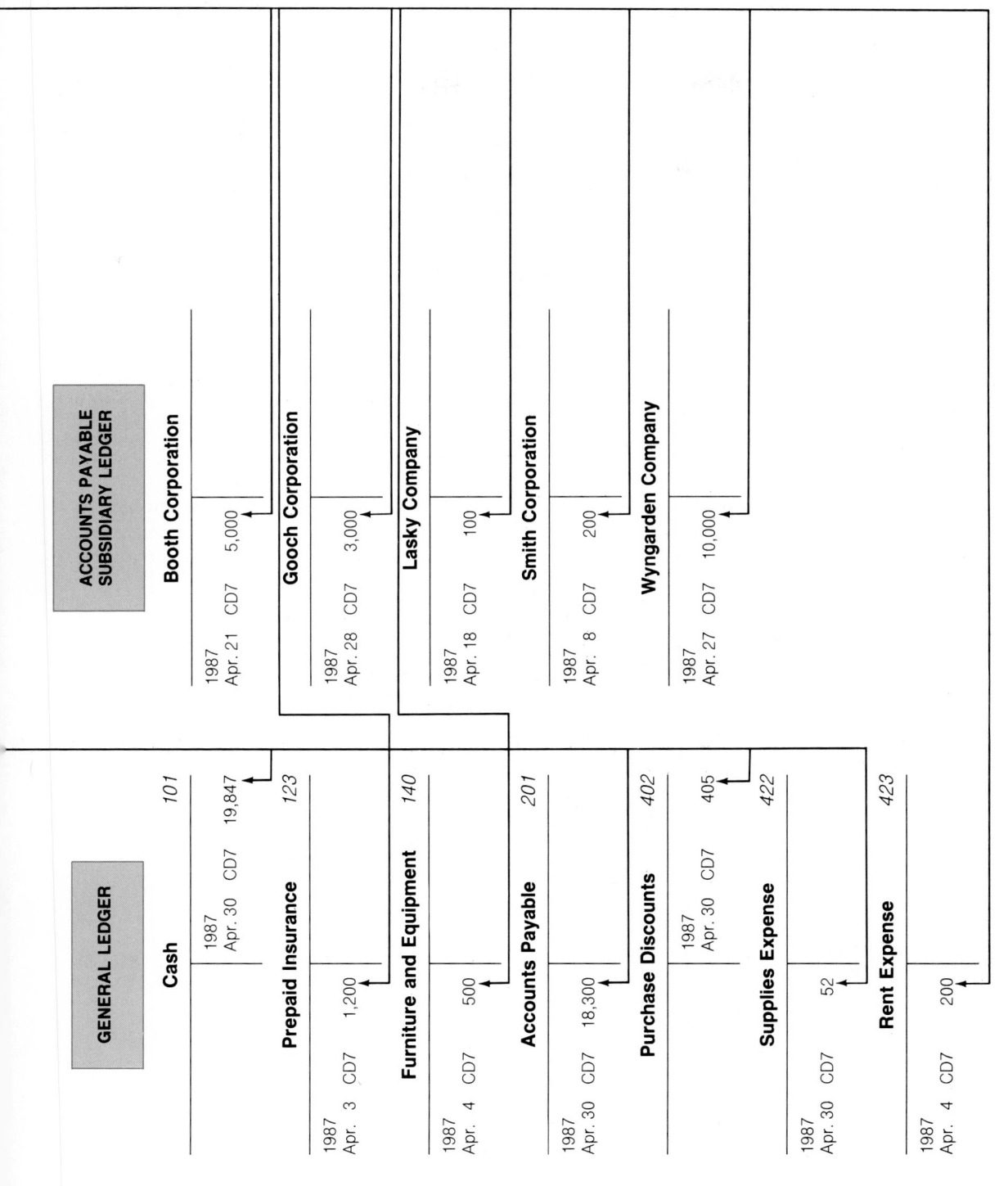

GENERAL LEDGER

Cash *101*

1987			
Apr. 30	CD7	19,847	

Prepaid Insurance *123*

1987			
Apr. 3	CD7	1,200	

Furniture and Equipment *140*

1987			
Apr. 4	CD7	500	

Accounts Payable *201*

1987			
Apr. 30	CD7	18,300	

Purchase Discounts *402*

1987			
Apr. 30	CD7		

Supplies Expense *422*

1987			
Apr. 30	CD7	52	

Rent Expense *423*

1987			
Apr. 4	CD7	200	

ACCOUNTS PAYABLE SUBSIDIARY LEDGER

Booth Corporation

1987			
Apr. 21	CD7	5,000	

Gooch Corporation

1987			
Apr. 28	CD7	3,000	

Lasky Company

1987			
Apr. 18	CD7	100	

Smith Corporation

1987			
Apr. 8	CD7	200	

Wyngarden Company

1987			
Apr. 27	CD7	10,000	

are those from the posting of the cash disbursements journal to make it easier to trace the postings.

The general ledger Accounts Payable control account appears as follows after both the purchases and cash disbursements journals have been posted:

	Accounts Payable				Account No. 201
Date	Explanation	Post. Ref.	Debit	Credit	Balance
1987 Apr. 30		P10		2 4 1 0 0	2 4 1 0 0 Cr.
30		CD7	1 8 3 0 0		5 8 0 0 Cr.

After both the purchases journal and the cash disbursements journal have been posted, the accounts payable subsidiary ledger appears as shown in Illustration 6.6.

A **schedule of accounts payable** is prepared at the end of the month to make certain that the total of the balances in the subsidiary ledger accounts agrees with the control account. The schedule for the John Mason Company appears below.

JOHN MASON COMPANY
Schedule of Accounts Payable
As of April 30, 1987

Booth Corporation	$1,500
Mertz Company	300
Nelson Company	4,000
Balance in the control account . . .	$5,800

Illustration 6.6 *Accounts Payable Subsidiary Ledger*

	JOHN MASON COMPANY ACCOUNTS PAYABLE SUBSIDIARY LEDGER Booth Corporation				
Date	Explanation	Post. Ref.	Debit	Credit	Balance
1987 Apr. 12		P10		5 0 0 0	5 0 0 0 Cr.
21		CD7	5 0 0 0		– 0 –
30		P10		1 5 0 0	1 5 0 0 Cr.

Gooch Corporation

Date		Explanation	Post. Ref.	Debit	Credit	Balance
1987 Apr.	15		P10		3 0 0 0	3 0 0 0 Cr.
	28		CD7	3 0 0 0		– 0 –

Lasky Company

Date		Explanation	Post. Ref.	Debit	Credit	Balance
1987 Apr.	7		P10		1 0 0	1 0 0 Cr.
	18		CD7	1 0 0		– 0 –

Mertz Company

Date		Explanation	Post. Ref.	Debit	Credit	Balance
1987 Apr.	26		P10		3 0 0	3 0 0 Cr.

Nelson Company

Date		Explanation	Post. Ref.	Debit	Credit	Balance
1987 Apr.	30		P10		4 0 0 0	4 0 0 0 Cr.

Smith Corporation

Date		Explanation	Post. Ref.	Debit	Credit	Balance
1987 Apr.	1		P10		2 0 0	2 0 0 Cr.
	8		CD7	2 0 0		– 0 –

Wyngarden Company

Date		Explanation	Post. Ref.	Debit	Credit	Balance
1987 Apr.	21		P10		1 0 0 0 0	1 0 0 0 0 Cr.
	27		CD7	1 0 0 0 0		– 0 –

A Combined Purchases and Cash Disbursements Journal

The purchases and the cash disbursements journals could be combined into one journal. A combined purchases and cash disbursements journal is illustrated in Demonstration Problem 6–2 at the end of the chapter. But use of a combined journal limits the number of persons who can work with the data in the journals at any one time.

General Ledger Illustrated

After all four special journals for the John Mason Company have been posted, the general ledger appears as shown in Illustration 6.7.

Illustration 6.7 *General Ledger*

JOHN MASON COMPANY
GENERAL LEDGER
Cash

Account No. 101

Date		Explanation	Post. Ref.	Debit	Credit	Balance
1987 Apr.	1	Beginning balance (assumed)				1 0 0 0 0 Dr.
	30		CR5	3 5 4 2 1		4 5 4 2 1 Dr.
	30		CD7		1 9 8 4 7	2 5 5 7 4 Dr.

Accounts Receivable

Account No. 111

Date		Explanation	Post. Ref.	Debit	Credit	Balance
1987 Apr.	30		S1	2 9 0		2 9 0 Dr.
	30		CR5		2 2 5	6 5 Dr.

Prepaid Insurance

Account No. 123

Date		Explanation	Post. Ref.	Debit	Credit	Balance
1987 Apr.	3		CD7	1 2 0 0		1 2 0 0 Dr.

Land
Account No. 138

Date		Explanation	Post. Ref.	Debit	Credit	Balance
1987 Apr.	1	Beginning balance (assumed)				1 8 0 0 0 Dr.
	10		CR5		6 0 0 0	1 2 0 0 0 Dr.

Furniture and Equipment
Account No. 140

Date		Explanation	Post. Ref.	Debit	Credit	Balance
1987 Apr.	4		CD7	5 0 0		5 0 0 Dr.

Accounts Payable
Account No. 201

Date		Explanation	Post. Ref.	Debit	Credit	Balance
1987 Apr.	30		P10		2 4 1 0 0	2 4 1 0 0 Cr.
	30		CD7	1 8 3 0 0		5 8 0 0 Cr.

John Mason, Capital
Account No. 250

Date		Explanation	Post. Ref.	Debit	Credit	Balance
1987 Apr.	1	Beginning balance (assumed)				2 8 0 0 0 Cr.

Sales
Account No. 301

Date		Explanation	Post. Ref.	Debit	Credit	Balance
1987 Apr.	30		S1		2 9 0	2 9 0 Cr.
	30		CR5		2 9 0 0 0	2 9 2 9 0 Cr.

Illustration 6.7 *(concluded)*

GENERAL LEDGER *(concluded)*

Sales Discounts
Account No. 302

Date		Explanation	Post. Ref.	Debit	Credit	Balance
1987 Apr.	30		CR5	4		4 Dr.

Miscellaneous Revenue
Account No. 303

Date		Explanation	Post. Ref.	Debit	Credit	Balance
1987 Apr.	26		CR5		2 0 0	2 0 0 Cr.

Purchases
Account No. 401

Date		Explanation	Post. Ref.	Debit	Credit	Balance
1987 Apr.	30		P10	2 4 1 0 0		2 4 1 0 0 Dr.

Purchase Discounts
Account No. 402

Date		Explanation	Post. Ref.	Debit	Credit	Balance
1987 Apr.	30		CD7		4 0 5	4 0 5 Cr.

Supplies Expense
Account No. 422

Date		Explanation	Post. Ref.	Debit	Credit	Balance
1987 Apr.	30		CD7	5 2		5 2 Dr.

Rent Expense
Account No. 423

Date		Explanation	Post. Ref.	Debit	Credit	Balance
1987 Apr.	4		CD7	2 0 0		2 0 0 Dr.

The **storage unit** (sometimes called core storage) of a computer is its internal memory system; it records and retains data until they are required by and transferred to other areas of the computer. This unit is the most expensive component of the computer. To determine the optimum size of the storage unit, speed and cost factors must be considered. Generally, the greater the speed and storage required, the greater the cost. Storage space can be added to the computer by utilizing peripheral devices such as disks, drums, or tape units for temporary external storage.

The **arithmetic unit** of a computer performs simple computations and comparisons. Mathematical operations such as addition, subtraction, multiplication, and division are handled through the arithmetic unit. This unit is also the logic unit of the computer.

The **control unit** of a computer is the unit that interprets the **program** (the set of **instructions** submitted to the computer that specifies the operations to be performed and the correct sequence), assigns storage space, and alters the sequence of operations if so instructed by the program. If the unit encounters a situation for which no explicit instructions are given, it will instruct the computer to halt operations. The computer operator can then find and correct the problem situation and restart the processing by means of a console. The **console** allows the operator to exercise control over the computer when necessary.

Peripheral equipment can be attached to the computer and used mainly to feed unprocessed information into the computer and receive the output of processed information. Examples of peripheral equipment are tape drives, card readers, and printers. The manner in which this peripheral equipment is connected and controlled varies from computer to computer.

Illustration 6.8 shows a schematic design of a simple computer system. The control unit controls operation of the system. The peripheral equipment is not part of the computer but is used to transmit data into and out of the computer as directed by the control unit. The control unit sends the data to the storage unit until there is time available to process the data. At that time, the data are recalled from storage and transferred to the arithmetic unit where the required arithmetic operations are performed. Upon completion, processed

Illustration 6.8 *Main Elements of a Computer*

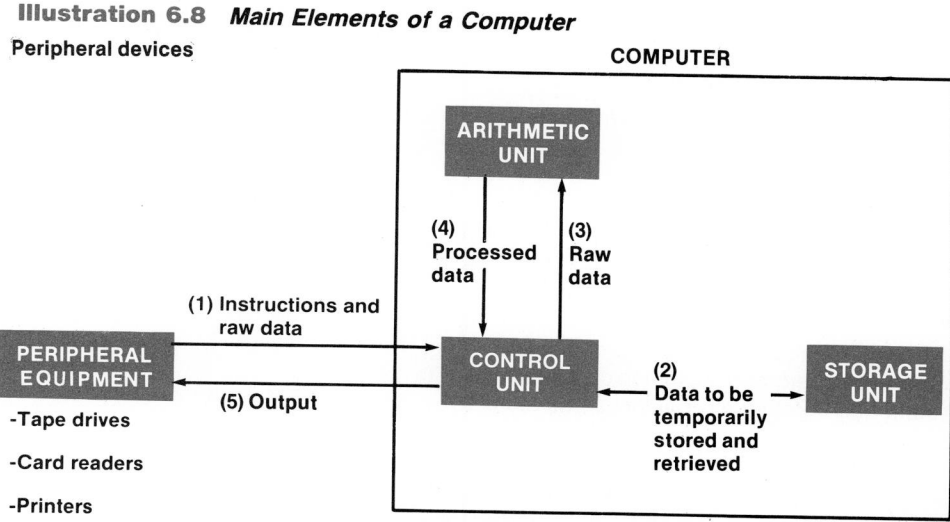

data are sent by the control unit either to the peripheral equipment or, if there is more processing to be done using the data, the data will be sent back to storage. The peripheral equipment will display the processed output in a predefined format.

■ APPLICATIONS OF ELECTRONIC DATA PROCESSING TO ACCOUNTING

Early electronic data processing applications to accounting were in the areas of payroll, accounts receivable, accounts payable, and inventory. Now programs exist for all phases of accounting, including manufacturing operations and total integration of other accounting programs with the general ledger. Nearly all applications of data processing, and particularly those that involve the accounting process, have made considerable use of files.

A file is a grouping of similar data arranged in an identifiable order. For example, the accounts receivable ledger is a file. The data of this file are the individual account balances, invoices, and payments received. These data may be stored by customer number. As transactions with customers occur, processing is undertaken to update this file; the end result is a new, updated accounts receivable file created by the computer.

Files also exist for accounts payable and inventory. Recently, an effort has been made to create one large data base for a company that would include all of the data in these files in addition to other information regarding company operations and the current status of resources. The data base can be used for many purposes, including accounting functions. Developments in the hardware and software areas will have a significant impact on how accounting tasks will be performed in the future.

NEW TERMS INTRODUCED IN CHAPTER 6

Arithmetic unit

A central component of a computer; it performs simple computations and comparisons (245).

Cash disbursements journal

A special journal used for all payments (or outflows) of cash by the business (223).

Cash receipts journal

A special journal used for all transactions involving the inflows of cash into the business (223).

Console

The component of an electronic computer system that enables an operator to communicate manually with the system and start, stop, or alter operations (245).

Control account

An account in the general ledger that shows the total balance of all the subsidiary accounts related to it (221).

Control unit

The unit of a computer that interprets the program, assigns storage space, and alters the sequence of operations if so instructed by the program (245).

File

A grouping of similar data arranged in an identifiable order. This may be a group of cards or a reel of magnetic tape (246).

General journal

A general-purpose journal used to record all transactions that cannot be entered in one of the special journals (223).

Instructions

Coded information that causes the computer's control unit to perform specified operations (245).

Microcomputers

Small computers that can be used to maintain the accounting records for a small business; designed for use by one person (242).

Minicomputers

Medium-size computers that can be used to maintain the accounting records for a small or medium-size business; designed for use by several persons (242).

Other accounts

Miscellaneous accounts (226).

Peripheral equipment

Can be attached to a computer and used mainly to feed unprocessed information into the computer and receive the output of processed information (245).

Program

The set of instructions submitted to the computer that specifies the operations to be performed and the correct sequence (245).

Purchases journal

A special journal used to record all purchases of merchandise on account (on credit) (223).

Sales journal

A special journal used to record all sales of merchandise on account (on credit) (223).

Schedule of accounts payable

Prepared at the end of the period to make certain that the total of the balances in the subsidiary ledger accounts agrees with the control account (236).

Schedule of accounts receivable

Prepared at the end of the period to ensure that the total of the balances in the subsidiary ledger accounts agrees with the control account (227).

Service bureau

A large computer facility that takes data from a client, enters the data into its computer, produces required statements or reports, and returns this output to the client (242).

Special journal

Used to record one particular type of transaction, such as sales on account, cash receipts, purchases on account, or cash disbursements (222).

Storage unit

A computer's internal memory system; it serves to record and retain data until they are required by and transferred to other areas of the computer (245).

Subsidiary ledger

A group of related accounts showing the details of the balance of a general ledger control account (221).

Subsidiary ledger accounts

Accounts in a subsidiary ledger that show the details supporting the related general ledger control account balance (221).

Time sharing

A system whereby several users utilize the same computer to process data (243).

DEMONSTRATION PROBLEM 6–1

The chapter mentioned, but did not illustrate, that the sales journal and cash receipts journal could be combined.

Required: Using the data in Illustrations 6.1 and 6.2, prepare a combined sales and cash receipts journal for the John Mason Company. Show all the posting marks as they would be made.

DEMONSTRATION PROBLEM 6–2

The chapter mentioned, but did not illustrate, that the purchases journal and the cash disbursements journal could be combined.

Required: Using the data in Illustrations 6.4 and 6.5, prepare a combined purchases and cash disbursements journal for the John Mason Company. Show all the posting marks as they would be made.

Solution to demonstration problem 6–1

COMBINED SALES AND CASH RECEIPTS JOURNAL

101 Cash Dr.	302 Sales Discounts Dr.	111 Accounts Receivable Dr. Amount	✓	Date	Description	Invoice No.	301 Sales Cr.	111 Accounts Receivable Cr. Amount	✓	Other Accounts Cr. Account Title	Acct. No.	Amount	✓
				1987 Apr.									
5,000				1	Cash sales		5,000						
		50	✓	3	Arthur Benson	100	50						
		25	✓	4	Peter Cote	101	25						
49	1			6	Arthur Benson	100		50	✓				
8,000				7	Cash sales		8,000						
6,000				10	Sold land at cost to Wells Corporation					Land	138	6,000	✓
		150	✓	12	Kenneth Johnson	102	150						
7,000				14	Cash sales		7,000						
		10	✓	19	Peter Cote	103	10						
25				19	Peter Cote	101		25	✓				
147	3			20	Kenneth Johnson	102		150	✓				
9,000				25	Cash sales		9,000						
200				26	Cash received from sale of scrap					Miscellaneous Revenue	303	200	✓
		55	✓	30	Anthony Demambro	104	55						
35,421	4	290					29,290	225				6,200	
(101)	(302)	(111)					(301)	(111)				(✓)	

Solution to demonstration problem 6-2

COMBINED PURCHASES AND CASH DISBURSEMENTS JOURNAL

401 Purchases Dr.	201 Accounts Payable Dr. Amount	✓	422 Supplies Expense Dr.	Other Accounts Dr. Account Title	Acct. No.	Amount	✓	Date	Terms	Invoice No.	Description	Check No.	101 Cash Cr.	402 Purchase Discounts Cr.	201 Accounts Payable Cr. Amount	✓
								1987								
200								Apr. 1	2/10,n/30	862	Smith Corporation				200	✓
								2			Brooklyn Square					
			42								Paint Company	524	42			
								3			Insurance policy to					
											cover May 1, 1987—					
				Prepaid Insurance	123	1,200	✓				April 30, 1988	525	1,200			
				Furniture and Equipment	140	500	✓	4			Furniture—office	526	500			
				Rent Expense	423	200	✓	4			Rent for April 1987	527	200			
100								7	1/15,n/60	121	Lasky Company				100	✓
	200	✓						8			Smith Corporation—					
											Invoice No. 862	528	196	4		
5,000								12	2/10,n/60	561	Booth Corporation				5,000	✓
			10					14			Allan Park Sta-					
											tionery Company	529	10			
3,000								15	2/10,n/30	1042	Gooch Corporation				3,000	✓
	100	✓						18			Lasky Company—					
											Invoice No. 121	530	99	1		
10,000								21	3/15,n/60	633	Wyngarden Company				10,000	✓
	5,000	✓						21			Booth Corporation—					
											Invoice No. 561	531	4,900	100		
300								26	2/10,n/30	734	Mertz Company				300	✓
	10,000	✓						27			Wyngarden Company—					
											Invoice No. 633	532	9,700	300		
	3,000							28			Gooch Corporation—					
											Invoice No. 1042	533	3,000			
4,000								30	2/10,n/30	287	Nelson Company				4,000	✓
1,500								30	2/20,n/60	568	Booth Company				1,500	✓
24,100	18,300		52			1,900							19,847	405	24,100	
(401)	(201)		(422)			(✓)							(101)	(402)	(201)	

QUESTIONS

1. The processing of data is usually very costly. Why bother with this task?

2. Is the balance of a control account equal to the total of its subsidiary accounts at all times? Explain.

3. In a manual system, the subsidiary accounts receivable and accounts payable accounts usually do not have account numbers. Why?

4. What is the definition of a special journal?

5. Describe the purpose of each of the following journals by giving the types of entries that would be recorded in each: sales, purchases, cash receipts, cash disbursements, and general.

6. Why might a sales journal or a purchases journal have more than one money column?

7. Why are some column totals in special journals posted while others are not?

8. Why does the purchases journal have a Terms column while the sales journal does not?

9. How can you tell whether a special journal has been completely posted? Describe the posting marks.

10. What is the purpose in preparing a schedule of accounts receivable and a schedule of accounts payable?

11. Of what use is the general journal when special journals are used?

12. Identify the alternative methods of processing data. What factors should a company consider in deciding which alternative to select?

EXERCISES

E–1

Prepare T-accounts to show Accounts Receivable and subsidiary accounts

The correct accounts receivable subsidiary ledger account balances for a company are as follows at the end of an accounting period:

Langley . . . . $ 600
Gibson 800
Golden 1,200
Martin 1,000

Using T-accounts, show how these accounts would appear and what the balance on this same date would be in the control account in the general ledger. If the balance in the control account is $4,000, what should be done?

E–2

Design sales journal for company with three selling departments

You are employed by a company that has three selling departments. You are asked to design a sales journal that will provide a departmental breakdown of credit sales. Give the column headings that you would use, and describe how postings would be made.

E–3

Post data from cash receipts journal to T-accounts

The column totals of a cash receipts journal are as follows:

Cash Dr. $19,700
Sales Discounts Dr. 100
Sales Cr. 10,000
Accounts Receivable Cr. 5,000
Other accounts Cr. (sold land at cost
   for $4,500 and sold scrap for $300) . . 4,800

Using T-acounts, post the amounts that appear in the cash receipts journal. How would the individual amounts in the Accounts Receivable Cr. column be posted? How would the information in the Other Accounts Cr. column be posted?

E-4

Match transactions with journals in which they would be recorded

Match each transaction in column A with the appropriate journal in column B in which it would be recorded. Assume each of the journals listed is used as a book of original entry and is designed as illustrated in the chapter.

Column A	Column B
1. Purchased merchandise on account.	a. Sales journal.
2. Recorded depreciation expense.	b. Cash receipts journal.
3. Sold merchandise on account.	c. Purchases journal.
4. Sold merchandise for cash.	d. Cash disbursements journal.
5. Collected cash on account.	e. General journal.
6. Gave a note to a trade creditor.	
7. Received cash for services performed.	
8. Granted a sales allowance to a customer.	
9. Paid rent for the month.	
10. Received notice of a purchase allowance from a trade creditor.	
11. Paid a trade creditor.	
12. Recorded closing entries at the end of the period.	

E-5

Determine postings to general ledger

Which of the following amounts would be posted to the general ledger?

a. The Cash Cr. column total in the cash disbursements journal.
b. The Other Accounts Dr. column total in the cash disbursements journal.
c. The individual items in the purchases journal.
d. The individual items in the sales journal.
e. The column total in the sales journal.

E-6

Answer multiple-choice questions

For each of the following questions select the one best answer.

1. Select the **true** statement regarding control accounts and subsidiary accounts.
   a. A control account must equal the total of the related subsidiary accounts at all times during the accounting period.
   b. The only subsidiary accounts are those for accounts receivable and accounts payable.
   c. Both control and subsidiary accounts appear in the general ledger.
   d. In a given company there are fewer control accounts than there are subsidiary accounts.
2. The sales journal is:
   a. Used to record only sales on credit.
   b. Used to record all sales.
   c. Used only to record cash sales.
   d. None of the above.
3. The cash receipts journal:
   a. Cannot be used to record cash sales.
   b. Is used to record amounts received on accounts receivable.
   c. Cannot be used to record the sales of a plant asset for cash.
   d. Usually only has one money column.
4. The cash disbursements journal:
   a. Cannot be used to record purchases on account.
   b. Is used only to record the payment of accounts payable.
   c. Cannot be used to record the purchase of a plant asset for cash.
   d. Usually has only one money column.
5. Which of the following statements is **true?**
   a. The end result (financial statements) is different depending on which method of processing is used.
   b. One method of processing data is the best for all companies.
   c. Microcomputers can be used to maintain the accounting records of a small company.
   d. The purchase of a mainframe in-house computer is almost never justified.

E–7

Answer matching question regarding computer terminology

(Based on the Appendix)   Match each description in column A with the appropriate term in column B.

Column A	Column B
1. A computer's internal memory system.	a. Program.
2. Equipment that is attached to the computer.	b. Arithmetic unit.
3. A part of the computer that interprets the program.	c. Service bureau.
	d. Peripheral equipment.
4. Any grouping of similar items of data arranged in some identifiable order.	e. Minicomputer.
	f. File.
5. A part of a computer that does the computing.	g. Storage unit.
	h. Control unit.
6. A set of instructions submitted to a computer that specifies the operations to be performed and their correct sequence.	
7. A large computer facility that rents out time for data processing.	
8. A small computer that can be used to maintain the accounting records for a small company.	

PROBLEMS, SERIES A

P6–1–A

Record transactions in sales and purchases journals; post to T-accounts in general and subsidiary ledgers

a.   The Abbey Stereo Store sold merchandise on account to the following customers on the dates indicated:

Date	Customer	Invoice no.	Amount
1987			
Dec. 2	Susan Moore	300	$ 200
8	Margarett Allen	301	2,400
14	Barbara Malloy	302	1,800
21	Janet Gibson	303	1,200
31	Susan Miller	304	900

Required: Record the transactions on page 5 of a sales journal. Using T-accounts, then post the data to accounts in the general ledger and accounts receivable subsidiary ledger. The general ledger account numbers are:

Accounts Receivable   101
Sales   300

b.   The Dana Appliance Store purchased merchandise from the following companies on the dates indicated:

Date	Creditor	Terms	Invoice no.	Amount
1987				
Sept. 2	Baker Company	2/20, n/60	642	$30,000
7	Dexter Company	2/10, n/30	441	36,000
15	Hanley Corporation	2/EOM	543	12,000
23	Stanton Company	1/15, n/30	286	27,000
28	Welker Corporation	2/10, n/30	324	45,000

Required: Record the transactions on page 20 of a purchases journal. Using T-accounts, post the data to accounts in the general ledger and accounts payable subsidiary ledger. The general ledger account numbers are:

Accounts Payable 201
Purchases   410

P6–2–A

Journalize transactions in appropriate journal; post to accounts in general and subsidiary ledgers; prepare schedule of accounts receivable

On June 30, 1987, the Accounts Receivable control account balance on the books of the Gray Wholesale Shoe Company was equal to the total balances of the accounts in the accounts receivable subsidiary ledger. The balances were as follows: Accounts Receivable control account (Account No. 131), $34,360; Billings, Inc., $13,200; Haygood Products, Inc., $6,160; and Johnson Company, $15,000.

Transactions (ignore the fact that usually the terms to all customers are the same):

July 1   Sales of merchandise on account to Johnson Company, $2,400; Invoice No. 306; terms n/30.
      3   Cash sales, $6,900.
      5   Received cash for land sold at its original cost of $10,000.
      5   Received $9,000 cash as partial collection of amount due today from Billings, Inc. No discount was allowed.
      9   Sold merchandise on account to the Glasco Company, $1,800; Invoice No. 307; terms 3/10, n/30.
     11   Received $6,036.80 from Haygood Products, Inc. A discount of 2% of the account balance was granted.
     16   Sold merchandise on account to the Wilson Company, $2,000; Invoice No. 308; terms n/30.
     18   Sold merchandise on account to Haygood Products, Inc., $3,600; Invoice No. 309; terms n/30.
     20   Allowed Haygood Products, Inc., credit for $500 on goods returned to Gray on Invoice No. 309.
     22   Sold $2,400 of merchandise to Billings, Inc.; Invoice No. 310; terms n/10.
     23   Received $8,000 cash on balance due today from Johnson Company. No discount was taken.
     25   Sold $3,000 of merchandise on account to Billings, Inc.; Invoice No. 311; terms n/10.
     27   Allowed Billings, Inc., credit of $200 on goods sold July 25 and damaged in transit due to faulty packing by Gray Company.
     31   Sold $2,600 of merchandise on account to the May Company; Invoice No. 312; terms 2/10, n/30.
     31   Cash sales, $41,200.

Required: Prepare a sales journal (Illustration 6.1) and cash receipts journal (Illustration 6.2). Also set up a general journal. Then using the above information:

a.   Completely journalize each of the transactions in the appropriate journal.
b.   Post only the amounts pertaining to accounts receivable to the subsidiary accounts and to the control account. You will have to set up some additional subsidiary accounts. Keep all subsidiary accounts in alphabetical order. You will need additional accounts for the Glasco Company, May Company, and Wilson Company.
c.   Prepare a schedule of accounts receivable at July 31, 1987, and compare it with the balance of the control account at the same date.

P6–3–A

Journalize transactions in appropriate journal; post to general and subsidiary ledger accounts; prepare schedule of accounts payable

On June 30, 1987, the Accounts Payable control account on the books of the Gray Wholesale Shoe Company was equal to the total of the accounts in the accounts payable subsidiary ledger. The balances were as follows: Accounts Payable control account (Account No. 201), $7,750; Gate Company, $3,525; Jones Corporation, $1,225; and White Company, $3,000.

Transactions:

July 1   Purchased merchandise on account costing $2,500 from the Hall Company; Invoice No. 562; terms 2/10, n/30.
      2   Paid the Gate Company $2,500 on account with Check No. 101. No discount was available when the purchase was originally made.

July 3 Paid rent for the month of July with Check No. 102, $300.
5 Gave the Jones Corporation a 60-day, 12% note for the amount owed.
6 Purchased merchandise on account costing $1,250 from the Gate Company; Invoice No. 261; terms 2/10, n/30.
9 Paid $2,450 to the Hall Company on the July 1 purchase with Check No. 103.
11 Paid $1,000 for a life insurance policy on top executives to cover the period from August 1, 1987, to July 31, 1988. Used Check No. 104.
17 Purchased merchandise on account costing $2,000 from the Hall Company; Invoice No. 581; terms 2/10, n/30.
21 Received credit from the White Company for $500 on merchandise returned to it. No discount was available as of the date of purchase.
23 Purchased merchandise on account costing $750 from the Andrews Corporation; Invoice No. 1031; terms n/30.
25 Paid $1,500 to White Company with Check No. 105. No discount was allowed as of the date of purchase.
27 Purchased merchandise on account costing $1,750 from the Sand Corporation; Invoice No. 328; terms 2/10, n/30.
29 Paid the Hall Company $1,000 on the purchase of July 17, Check No. 106.
31 Purchased merchandise on account costing $2,000 from the Dodge Company; Invoice No. 168; terms 2/20, n/60.

Required: Prepare a purchases journal (Illustration 6.4) and a cash disbursements journal (Illustration 6.5). Also set up a general journal. Then using the above information:

a. Completely journalize each of the transactions in the appropriate journal.
b. Post only the amounts pertaining to accounts payable to the subsidiary accounts and to the control account. You should arrange all subsidiary accounts in alphabetical order. You will need additional accounts for Andrews Corporation, Hall Company, Dodge Company, and Sand Corporation.
c. Prepare a schedule of accounts payable at July 31, 1987, and compare it with the balance of the control account at the same date.

P6-4-A

Post data from journals to ledger accounts after entering beginning balances in the accounts; prepare trial balance

The Pierce Department Store uses five journals as records of original entry. They are as follows: sales journal, cash receipts journal, purchases journal, cash disbursements journal, and general journal. At December 31, 1987, the column totals in the sales journal were as follows:

Accounts Receivable Dr.	Sales Cr.					
	Men's Clothing	Women's Clothing	Appliances	Furniture	Bargain Basement	Other Departments
56,375	10,000	11,250	8,750	15,000	7,500	3,875

The column totals of the cash receipts journal columns were as follows:

Cash Dr.	Sales Discounts Dr.	Sales Cr.						Accounts Receivable Cr.	Other Accounts Cr.
		Men's Clothing	Women's Clothing	Appliances	Furniture	Bargain Basement	Other Departments		
83,250	769	5,625	6,250	5,000	8,125	3,000	3,375	48,206	4,438

The entries in the Other Accounts Cr. column resulted from the collection of $3,250 of rental revenue (December 8) and $1,188 of miscellaneous revenue from the sale of scrap (December 14).

The column totals in the purchases journal were as follows:

Purchases Dr.						Accounts Payable Cr.
Men's Clothing	Women's Clothing	Appliances	Furniture	Bargain Basement	Other Departments	
13,125	13,500	6,875	12,750	9,375	5,437	61,062

The column totals of the cash disbursements journal columns were:

Accounts Payable Dr.	Supplies Expense Dr.	Other Accounts Dr.	Cash Cr.	Purchase Discounts Cr.
48,250	6,875	5,694	60,444	375

The entries in the Other Accounts Dr. column result from the payment of $319 for ordinary repairs to the buildings (December 15) and $5,375 for the purchase of a small warehouse building (December 22).

The general journal includes the following entry at the date indicated:

Dec. 18 Office Equipment 1,000
            Notes Payable 1,000

An abbreviated trial balance of the general ledger immediately prior to posting the above journals for the year was as follows:

PIERCE DEPARTMENT STORE
Trial Balance
December 31, 1987

	Debits	Credits
Cash	$ 8,750	
Accounts Receivable	6,875	
Notes Receivable	625	
Inventory—Men's Clothing	1,875	
Inventory—Women's Clothing	2,250	
Inventory—Appliances	1,500	
Inventory—Furniture	3,500	
Inventory—Bargain Basement	875	
Inventory—Other Departments	625	
Office Equipment	2,500	
Accumulated Depreciation—Office Equipment . .		$ 1,000
Buildings	35,000	
Accumulated Depreciation—Buildings		6,875
Accounts Payable		5,438
L. Pierce, Capital		51,062
	$64,375	$64,375

Required: Present the general ledger of the Pierce Department Store including the balances in the above trial balance and postings based on the other data given in the problem. After posting, prepare a trial balance.

P6–5–A

Journalize transactions; post to general ledger accounts; prepare trial balance

The Harris Wholesale Food Company uses special journals for sales, cash receipts, purchases, and cash disbursements, as well as a general journal. These journals follow the same general design as those illustrated in this chapter.

Transactions:

Dec. 1 Purchased merchandise on account from Dixon Company, $11,200; Invoice No. C1109; terms 2/10, n/30.

2 Purchased merchandise on account from Bailey Company, $6,400; Invoice No. 1888Z; terms n/10.

3 Bought office equipment from Harrell Company, $15,520; Invoice No. 854. Gave a 30-day, 12% note in payment.

5 Purchased merchandise on account from Abel Company, $8,800; Invoice No. X9784; terms 2/10, n/30.

6 Cash sales, $11,360.

7 Collected rent revenue for December, $15,200.

8 Sold $8,000 of merchandise on account to David, Inc.; Invoice No. 3345; terms 2/10, n/30.

9 Collected $12,000 on an overdue account receivable form R. Ray.

10 Sold $11,200 of merchandise on account to Potts Company; Invoice No. 3346; terms 2/10, n/30.

11 Sold $12,800 of merchandise on account to Zap Company; Invoice No. 3347; terms 2/10, n/30.

12 Paid Dixon Company for purchase of December 1 with Check No. 201.

12 Paid Bailey Company for purchase of December 2 with Check No. 202.

14 Paid Abel Company for purchase of December 5 with Check No. 203.

16 Cash sales, $31,520.

18 Collected amount due on sale of December 8 to David, Inc.

20 Collected amount due on sale of December 10 to Potts Company.

21 Collected amount due on sale of December 11 to Zap Company.

23 Cash sales, $20,000.

24 Paid *The Newton News* for advertising expense, $1,200 (Check No. 204).

26 Sold $9,600 of merchandise on account to Zap Company; Invoice No. 3348; terms 2/10, n/30.

26 Sold $22,400 of merchandise on account to Dee Company; Invoice No. 3349; terms 2/10, n/30.

27 Sold $47,520 of merchandise on account to Kote Company; Invoice No. 3350; terms 2/10, n/30.

Required:

a. Enter the transactions for December 1987 in the proper journals. All journals are to be numbered page 40.

b. Post the entries to the general ledger accounts. The Cash account and the Harris, Capital account each have a beginning balance of $40,000.

c. Prepare a trial balance as of the end of the period. General ledger accounts are:

1. Cash.	7. Sales.
2. Accounts Receivable.	8. Sales Discounts.
3. Office Equipment.	9. Purchases.
4. Accounts Payable.	10. Purchase Discounts.
5. Notes Payable.	11. Advertising Expense.
6. Harris, Capital.	12. Rental Revenue.

PROBLEMS, SERIES B

P6-1-B

Record transactions in sales and purchases journals; post to T-accounts in general and subsidiary ledgers

a. The Norman Clothing Store sold goods on account to the following persons on the dates indicated:

Date		Customer	Invoice no.	Amount
1987				
June	1	John James	200	$ 900
	4	David Jones	201	600
	12	Joseph Branch	202	1,200
	18	Bob Blake	203	1,800
	29	Craig Jacobi	204	1,500

Required: Record the transactions on page 1 of a sales journal. Then, using T-accounts, post the data to accounts in the general ledger and accounts receivable subsidiary ledger. The general ledger account numbers are:

Accounts Receivable 101
Sales 300

b. The Hawkins Book Store purchased merchandise from the following companies on the dates indicated:

Date		Customer	Terms	Invoice no.	Amount
1987					
July	3	Able Company	2/10, n/30	240	$ 6,000
	5	Crane Company	1/15, n/30	360	3,000
	14	Greer Company	2/20, n/30	142	12,000
	22	Rextex Corporation	2/20, n/60	58	15,000
	30	Zeetex Corporation	2/10, n/30	410	21,000

Required: Record the transactions on page 10 of a purchases journal. Then, using T-accounts, post the data to accounts in the general ledger and accounts payable subsidiary ledger. The general ledger account numbers are:

Accounts Payable 201
Purchases 410

P6-2-B

Journalize transactions in appropriate journals; post to accounts in general ledger and subsidiary ledger; prepare schedule of accounts receivable

On August 31, 1987, the Accounts Receivable control account on the books of the Wholesale Furniture Store was equal to the total of the accounts in the accounts receivable subsidiary ledger. The balances were as follows: Accounts Receivable control account (Account No. 120), $180,000; Battle Corporation, $72,000; Ferguson Company, $60,000; and East Corporation, $48,000.

Transactions (ignore the fact that normally the terms to all customers are the same):

Sept. 1 Received $27,440 from the Ferguson Company. A discount of $560 had been taken.
2 On this date, merchandise was sold on account for $44,000 to the Oliva Company; Invoice No. 501; terms 2/20, n/30.
4 Cash sales, $100,000.
7 Received $36,000 on account from the Battle Corporation. No discount was taken.
8 Received $80,000 cash for land sold at cost.
12 Sold merchandise on account to the Ferguson Company, $36,000; Invoice No. 502; terms n/30.

Sept. 15 Received payment for $20,000 of the merchandise purchased on September 2 by the Oliva Company. The discount was taken on this payment.

18 Sold merchandise on account to the Miles Corporation, $136,000; Invoice No. 503; terms n/30.

21 Cash sales, $228,000.

23 Allowed $4,000 credit to Miles Corporation for goods returned.

26 Sold merchandise on account to the Newton Company, $40,000; Invoice No. 504; terms 2/20, n/30.

29 Recevied $40,000 cash from the Miles Corporation to apply against the amount due on Invoice No. 503.

30 Cash sales were $156,000.

Required: Prepare a sales journal (Illustration 6.1) and cash receipts journal (Illustration 6.2). Also set up a general journal. Then using the above information:

a. Completely journalize the transactions in the appropriate journals.

b. Post only the amounts pertaining to accounts receivable to the subsidiary accounts and to the control account. You will have to prepare additional subsidiary accounts and should keep them all in alphabetical order. You will need additional accounts for Miles Corporation, Newton Company, and Oliva Company.

c. Prepare a schedule of accounts receivable at September 30, 1987, and compare it with the balance of the control account at the same date.

P6–3–B

Journalize transactions in appropriate journal; post to general ledger and subsidiary ledger accounts; prepare schedule of accounts payable

On August 31, 1987, the Accounts Payable control account on the books of the Wholesale Furniture Store was equal to the total of the accounts in the accounts payable subsidiary ledger. The balances were as follows: Accounts Payable control account (Account No. 220), $144,000; Helzburg Company, $64,000; Zales Corporation, $48,000; and Bond Corporation, $32,000.

Transactions:

Sept. 1 Purchased merchandise on account costing $60,000 from the Werling company; Invoice No. 542; terms 2/10, n/30.

3 Paid the Bond Corporation $32,000 with Check No. 451. The original discount of 2% was not taken because the discount period had expired.

4 Paid rent for the month of September, $2,000, with Check No. 452.

5 Paid the Helzburg Company $36,000 on account with Check No. 453. No discount was offered.

6 Gave the Helzburg Company a $28,000, 30-day, 12% note for the balance due.

7 Purchased merchandise on account costing $32,000, from the York Corporation; Invoice No. 982; terms 2/10, n/30.

8 Purchased merchandise on account costing $36,000, from the Bond Corporation; Invoice No. 1522; terms 2/10, n/30.

9 Received credit from the York Corporation for returning $4,000 of the $32,000 of merchandise purchased.

12 Paid the Werling Company the amount due on the purchase of September 1 with Check No. 454.

15 Purchased merchandise on account costing $48,000 from the New Point Corporation; Invoice No. 841; terms n/30.

17 Paid Bond Corporation the amount due on the purchase of September 8 with Check No. 455.

20 Purchased merchandise on account costing $52,000 from the Bond Corporation; Invoice No. 1566; terms 2/10, n/30.

22 Purchased merchandise on account costing $28,000 from the Quarter Company; Invoice No. 1910; terms n/30.

25 Paid $32,000 on account to the New Point Corporation on the purchase of September 15 with Check No. 456.

29 Received $12,000 credit from the Bond Corporation for returning part of the merchandise purchased on September 20.

30 Purchased merchandise on account having a cost of $20,000 from the Jane Company; Invoice No. 2125; terms n/60.

Required: Prepare a purchases journal (Illustration 6.4) and cash disbursements journal (Illustration 6.5). Also set up a general journal. Then using the above information:

a. Completely journalize each of the transactions in the appropriate journals.
b. Post only the amounts pertaining to accounts payable to the subsidiary accounts and to the control account. You will have to create some additional subsidiary accounts. You should arrange all subsidiary accounts in alphabetical order. You will need additional accounts for Jane Company, New Point Corporation, Quarter Company, Werling Company, and York Corporation.
c. Prepare a schedule of accounts payable at September 30, 1987, and compare it with the balance of the control account at the same date.

P6–4–B

Post data from journals to ledger accounts after entering beginning balances in the accounts; prepare trial balance

The King Department Store uses five journals as records of original entry—sales journal, cash receipts journal, purchases journal, cash disbursements journal, and general journal. At December 31, 1987, the column totals in the sales journal were as follows:

Accounts Receivable Dr.	Sales Cr.					
	Men's Clothing	Women's Clothing	Shoes	Cosmetics and Jewelry	Sporting Goods	Miscellaneous
40,500	10,000	12,500	4,200	4,000	7,800	2,000

The totals of the cash receipts journal columns were as follows:

Cash Dr.	Sales Discounts Dr.	Sales Cr.						Accounts Receivable Cr.	Other Accounts Cr.
		Men's Clothing	Women's Clothing	Shoes	Cosmetics and Jewelry	Sporting Goods	Miscel-laneous		
70,100	560	6,000	8,000	3,300	6,000	3,200	4,000	36,000	4,160

The entries in the Other Accounts Cr. column resulted from the sale of land at cost of $3,160 (December 4) and $1,000 of revenue from the operation of a delivery service for other companies (December 31).

The column totals in the purchases journal were as follows:

Purchases Dr.						Accounts Payable Cr.
Men's Clothing	Women's Clothing	Shoes	Cosmetics and Jewelry	Sporting Goods	Miscellaneous	
14,000	19,000	6,000	7,500	13,900	4,000	64,400

The column totals of the cash disbursements journal columns were as follows:

Accounts Payable Dr.	Supplies Expense Dr.	Other Accounts Dr.	Cash Cr.	Purchase Discounts Cr.
58,500	9,700	7,900	74,700	1,400

The entries in the Other Accounts Dr. column resulted from the payment of $960 for a delivery truck (December 7) and $6,940 for the purchase of a garage (December 15).
The two-column general journal includes the following entry during the month:

Dec. 21 Buildings 8,700
Notes payable 8,700

An abbreviated trial balance of the general ledger immediately prior to posting the above journals for the year follows:

KING DEPARTMENT STORE
Trial Balance
December 31, 1987

	Debits	Credits
Cash	$ 17,500	
Accounts Receivable	12,000	
Inventory—Men's Clothing	6,000	
Inventory—Women's Clothing	10,000	
Inventory—Shoes	1,000	
Inventory—Cosmetics and Jewelry	4,000	
Inventory—Sporting Goods	5,500	
Inventory—Miscellaneous	1,300	
Office Equipment	5,000	
Accumulated Depreciation—Office Equipment . .		$ 1,700
Land	3,160	
Buildings	40,000	
Accumulated Depreciation—Buildings		9,700
Accounts Payable		10,100
Notes Payable		1,000
A. King, Capital		82,960
	$105,460	$105,460

Required: Present the general ledger of the King Department Store, including the balances in the above trial balance and postings based on the other data given in the problem. Use three-column format. After posting, prepare a trial balance.

P6–5–B

Journalize transactions; post to general ledger accounts; prepare trial balance

The Dillard Microcomputer Store uses special journals for sales, cash receipts, purchases, and cash disbursements, as well as a general journal. These journals follow the same general design as those illustrated in this chapter.

Transactions:

Aug. 1 Sold Cod, Inc., a $12,000 computer on account; terms 2/10, n/30; Invoice No. WI-A1.
3 Bought computer merchandise on account from the Brad Company; Invoice No. 33-NP; terms n/10, $8,400.
5 Cash sales, $38,000.
9 Rent revenue received, $1,600.
11 Received amount due from Cod, Inc., for sale of August 1. The discount was taken.
11 Paid for office equipment received today, $4,800 (Check No. 132). The equipment was for the company's own use.
12 Paid Brad Company for purchase of August 3 (Check No. 133).
14 Sold a $8,000 computer on account to McGuinn, Inc.; Invoice No. WI-A2; terms 2/10, n/30.
15 Sold a $2,800 computer on account to Franks Company; Invoice No. WI-A3; terms 2/10, n/30.
15 Bought computer merchandise on account from Brad Company, $3,960; Invoice No. 34-NP; terms n/10.
17 Bought computer merchandise on account from Brown Company, $6,000; Invoice No. 98-VX; terms 2/10, n/30.
18 Bought office equipment today for $3,800 and gave a 30-day, 12% note in payment. The equipment was for the company's own use.
19 Received a 90-day, 12% note receivable for an account receivable (Paul McAllister) in the amount of $1,400.
19 Cash sales of computer software, $7,200.
20 Collected $3,080 on account from Charles Barfield.
21 Cash sales of computer software, $4,480.

mented, especially those policies that require compliance with federal law. Personnel must perform their assigned duties to promote efficiency of operations. Correct accounting records must be maintained so that accurate and reliable information is presented in the accounting reports. In this chapter you will learn how internal control is established through control of cash receipts and cash disbursements, proper use of the bank checking account, preparation of the bank reconciliation statement, protection of petty cash funds, and usage of the net price method and the voucher system. The establishment of internal control is enhanced by hiring competent and trustworthy employees, a fact you will appreciate if you ever become a business owner.

■ INTERNAL CONTROL

An internal control system is defined as the plan of organization and all the procedures and actions taken by an entity to:

1. Protect its assets against theft and waste.
2. Ensure compliance with company policies and federal law.
3. Evaluate the performance of all personnel in the company so as to promote efficiency of operations.
4. Ensure accurate and reliable operating data and accounting reports.

As you study the basic procedures and actions comprising an internal control system, you will realize that even the small, one-owner businesses can benefit from the use of some internal control measures. Preventing theft and waste is only a part of internal control. In general terms, the purpose of internal control is to ensure the efficient operations of a business, thus making it possible for the business to effectively reach its goals.

Protection of Assets

Assets can be protected by (1) segregation of employee duties, (2) separation of employee functions, (3) rotation of employee job assignments, and (4) use of mechanical devices.

Segregation of Employee Duties.   The segregation of duties is accomplished by having the person responsible for safeguarding an asset someone other than the person who maintains the accounting records for that asset. Responsibility for related transactions should be divided among individuals so that the work of one person serves as a check on the work of others.

When the work of one person is such that it serves as a check on the work of others, then collusion between at least two persons would be necessary to steal assets and cover up the theft in the accounting records. For example, a person could not steal cash from a company and have it go undetected unless the cash records can be changed to cover the shortage. Changing the records can only be accomplished if the person stealing the cash maintains the cash records or is in collusion with the person who maintains the cash records.

Separate Employee Functions.   When the responsibility for a particular work function is assigned to a specific person, that person is accountable for specific tasks. Then, in the event of a problem, the person responsible can be quickly identified.

It is relatively easy to trace lost documents or determine how a particular transaction is recorded when employees are given specific duties. The person responsible for a given task is the person best able to provide information about that task. With this division of responsibilities also goes a sense of pride and importance that tends to make people want to perform to the best of their ability.

Rotating Employee's Job Assignments.   When it is the company policy to rotate job assignments, this often discourages employees from engaging in long-term schemes to steal from the company. Employees realize that if they steal from the company, the theft may be discovered by the next employee assigned to that position.

Frequently, companies have the policy that all employees must take an annual vacation. This also discourages theft because many dishonest schemes collapse when the employee does not attend to the job on a daily basis.

Mechanical Devices.   Companies can use mechanical devices to help protect their assets. Devices such as check protectors (machines that perforate the check amount into the check), cash registers, and time clocks make it impossible for employees to alter certain company documents and records.

Compliance with Company Policies and Federal Law

To be effective, internal control policies must be followed by employees. To ensure that a company's internal control policies are carried out, the company must hire competent and trustworthy employees. The execution of effective internal control begins with the time and effort a company expends in hiring employees. Once the employees are hired, the company must train those employees and clearly communicate to them company policies, such as proper authorization before making a cash disbursement. Frequently, written job descriptions are effective in establishing the responsibilities and duties of employees. The initial training of employees should be such that they know exactly what they are expected to do, as well as how to do it.

In publicly held corporations, the company's internal control system must satisfy the requirements of federal law. In December 1977, the Foreign Corrupt Practices Act (FCPA) was enacted by Congress. Under this law, publicly held corporations are **required** to devise and maintain an effective system of internal control and to keep accurate accounting records. The passage of this law came about partly because of the cover-ups in company accounting records of bribes and kickbacks made to foreign governments or government officials. The FCPA made this specific type of bribery illegal.

Evaluation of Personnel Performance

To evaluate how well company employees are doing their jobs, many companies employ internal auditing. Internal auditing consists of investigating and evaluating employees' compliance with the company's policies and procedures. Companies hire internal auditors to perform internal audits; these individuals are trained regarding internal auditing, company policies, and their duties as internal auditors.

Internal auditors should encourage operating efficiency throughout the company and be constantly alert for breakdowns in the company's system of internal control. In addition, internal auditors make recommendations for the improvement of the company's internal control system when necessary. All companies can benefit from internal auditing; however, internal auditing is especially necessary in large organizations because the owner(s) cannot be personally involved with all aspects of the business.

Accuracy of Accounting Reports

Companies should maintain complete and accurate accounting records. The best method to ensure that this is done is to hire and train competent individuals. Periodically, supervisors should evaluate an employee's performance to make sure the employee is following company policies. Accounting records that are inaccurate or inadequate serve as an invitation to theft by dishonest employees because the theft can be easily concealed.

Almost all accounting transactions are supported by one or more business documents. These source documents are an integral part of the internal control system. For optimal control, source documents should be serially numbered. (Transaction documentation and related aspects of internal control will be presented throughout the text.)

Since source documents serve as documentation of business transactions, from time to time the validity of these documents should be checked. For example, to review a merchandise transaction, the documents used to record the transaction should be checked against the proper accounting records. When the accounting department records a merchandise transaction, it should receive copies of the following four documents:

1. **Purchase requisition.** A purchase requisition is a written request from an employee inside the company to the purchasing department to purchase certain items.
2. **Purchase order.** A purchase order is a document sent from the purchasing department to a supplier requesting that merchandise or other items be shipped to the purchaser.
3. **Invoice.** An invoice is the bill sent from the supplier to the purchaser requesting payment for the merchandise shipped.
4. **Receiving report.** A receiving report is a document prepared by the receiving department showing the descriptions and quantities of all items received from a supplier in a particular shipment.

These four documents together serve as authorization to pay for merchandise and should be checked against the accounting records. In the absence of these documents, a company might fail to pay a legitimate invoice, pay fictitious invoices, or pay an invoice more than once. Proper internal control can be accomplished only by periodically checking the source documents of business transactions with the accounting records of those transactions. Illustration 7.1 shows the flow of documents and goods in a merchandising transaction.

Illustration 7.1

Flow of Documents and Goods in a Merchandising Transaction

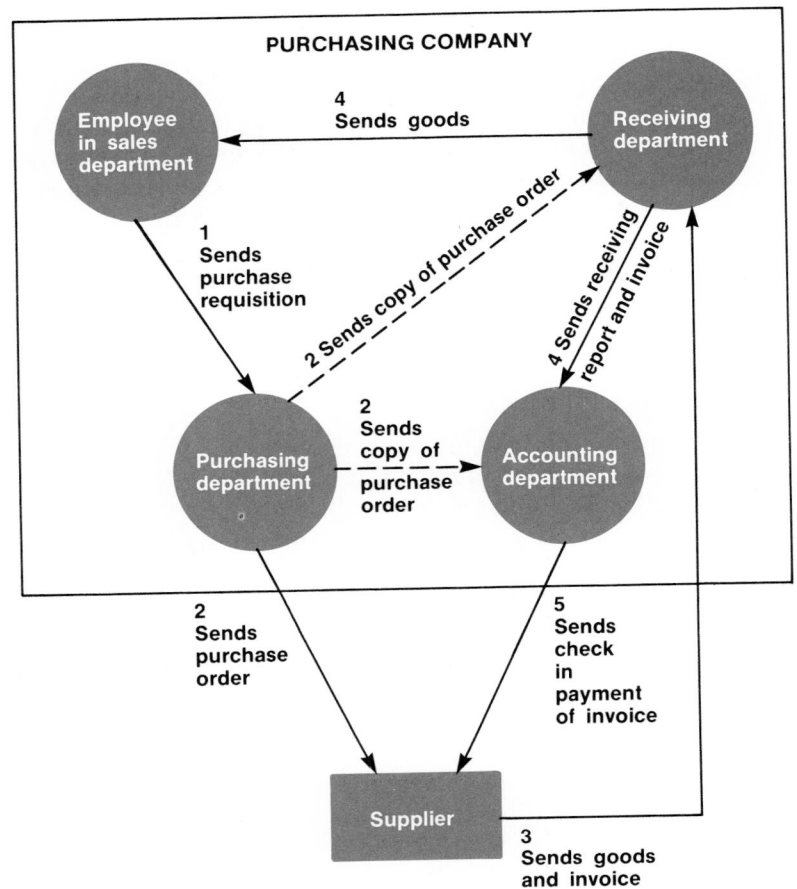

PURCHASING COMPANY

Employee in sales department

4 Sends goods

Receiving department

1 Sends purchase requisition

2 Sends copy of purchase order

4 Sends receiving report and invoice

Purchasing department

2 Sends copy of purchase order

Accounting department

2 Sends purchase order

5 Sends check in payment of invoice

Supplier

3 Sends goods and invoice

Steps:

1. Employee in sales department sends purchase requisition to purchasing department.
2. Purchasing department sends purchase order to supplier, with copies going to the receiving department and the accounting department.
3. Supplier sends goods and invoice to receiving department, which checks goods against purchase order and invoice.
4. Receiving department sends goods to sales department and sends receiving report and invoice to accounting department.
5. Accounting department sends check in payment of invoice to the supplier.

Unfortunately, even if a company implements all of the above features in its internal control system, theft may occur. If employees are dishonest, they can usually figure out a way to steal from a company, thus circumventing even the most effective internal control system. Therefore, it is advisable to carry adequate casualty insurance on assets. This insurance will reimburse the company for loss of a nonmonetary asset such as specialized equipment. Companies should also have **fidelity bonds** on employees handling cash and other negotiable instruments. These bonds will ensure that the company is reimbursed for losses due to theft of cash and other monetary assets. With both casualty insurance on assets and fidelity bonds on employees, a company can recover at least a portion of any loss that occurs.

■ CONTROLLING CASH

In the preceding section you learned about some of the general principles of internal control. This section focuses specifically on the control of cash. Since cash is the most liquid of all assets, a business cannot survive and prosper if it does not have adequate control over its cash.

In accounting, cash includes coins; paper money; certain undeposited negotiable instruments such as checks, bank drafts, and money orders; amounts in checking and savings accounts; and demand certificates of deposit. A certificate of deposit is an interest-bearing deposit in a bank that can be withdrawn at will (demand CD) or at a fixed maturity date (time CD). Cash does not include postage stamps, IOUs, or notes receivable.

In the general ledger, usually two cash accounts are maintained—Cash (bank checking account balance) and Petty Cash. The balances of these two accounts are combined into one amount and reported as "Cash" on the company's balance sheet.

Since many business transactions involve cash, it is a vital factor in the operation of a business. Of all the company's assets, cash is the most easily mishandled either through theft or carelessness. To protect its cash, companies should:

1. Account for all cash transactions accurately so that correct information will be available regarding cash flows and balances.
2. Make certain there is enough cash available to pay bills as they come due.
3. Avoid holding too much idle cash, because excess cash could be invested to generate income such as interest.
4. Prevent loss of cash due to theft or fraud.

The need to control cash is clearly evident. Although you might think first about how to protect cash from the greedy hands of a dishonest employee, as you can see from the list above there is more to controlling cash. Without the proper timing of cash flows and the protection of idle cash, a business cannot survive. This section discusses cash receipts and cash disbursements. Later in the chapter you will learn about the importance of preparing a bank reconciliation statement for each bank checking account, as well as controlling the petty cash fund. The net price method and voucher system are also described.

Controlling Cash Receipts

When a merchandising company sells its merchandise, it may receive cash immediately or several days or weeks later. The cash that is received immediately "over the counter" usually is recorded and placed in a cash register. The presence of the customer as the sale is "rung up" usually ensures that the correct amount of the sale is entered in the cash register. At the end of each day, the cash in each cash register is reconciled with the cash register tape or computer printout for that register. When cash is received later, it is almost always in the form of checks. A record of the checks received should be prepared as soon as they are received. Some merchandising companies receive all their cash receipts on a delayed basis in the form of payments on accounts receivable (see the cash receipts cycle for merchandise transactions in Illustration 7.2).

Illustration 7.2

Cash Receipts Cycle for Merchandise Transactions

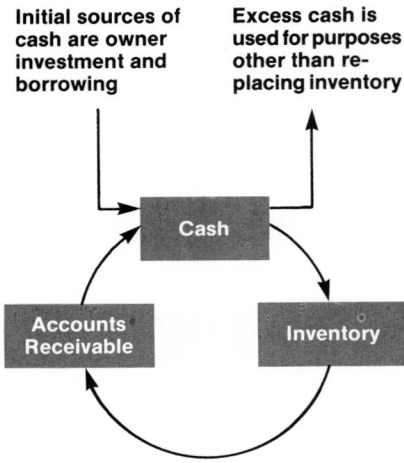

Initial sources of cash are owner investment and borrowing

Excess cash is used for purposes other than replacing inventory

Cash initially comes into the business from owner investment and borrowing. Cash is invested in inventory and other assets. When inventory is sold, cash may be received immediately, or receipt may be delayed and involve accounts receivable. The inventory generally is sold at more than cost so the company can make a profit. Each time the cycle is completed, the amount of cash grows and may be used for purposes other than replacing inventory.

Although the specific procedures for controlling cash receipts vary with each business, there are several basic principles:

1. A record of all cash receipts should be prepared as soon as cash is received. Most thefts of cash occur before a record is made of the receipt. Once a record is made, it is easier to trace a theft.
2. All cash receipts should be deposited on the day they are received or on the next business day. Undeposited cash is more susceptible to misappropriation.
3. The person who handles cash receipts should not also be the person who records the receipts in the accounting records. This control feature follows the general principle of "segregation of duties" given earlier in the chapter, as does item 4 below.
4. If possible, the person who receives the cash should not also be the person to disburse the cash. This control measure is possible in all but the smallest companies.

Controlling Cash Disbursements

Controls are also needed over cash disbursements. Since most of a firm's cash is spent by check, many of the internal controls for cash disbursements deal with checks and authorizations for cash payments. The basic principle of segregation of duties is also applied in controlling cash disbursements. Following are some basic control procedures for cash disbursements:

1. All disbursements should be made by check or from petty cash. Proper approval for all disbursements should be obtained, and a permanent record of each disbursement should be created. In many retail stores, refunds for returned merchandise are made from the cash register. If this practice is followed, refund tickets should be prepared and approved by a supervisor before cash is refunded.
2. All checks should be serially numbered, and access to checks should be limited to employees authorized to write checks.
3. Preferably, two signatures should be required on each check so that one person alone cannot withdraw funds from the bank account.
4. If possible, the person who authorizes payment of a bill should not be allowed to sign checks. Otherwise, the checks could be written to "friends" in payment of fictitious invoices.
5. Approved documents should be required to support all checks issued.
6. The person authorizing cash disbursements should be certain that payment is for a legitimate purpose and is made out for the exact amount and to the proper party.
7. When liabilities are paid, the supporting documents should be stamped "paid," and the date and number of the check issued should be indicated. These procedures lessen the chance of paying the same debt more than once.
8. The person(s) who signs checks should not have access to canceled checks and should not prepare the bank reconciliation. This feature makes it more difficult to conceal a theft.
9. The bank reconciliation should be prepared each month, preferably by a person who has no other cash duties, so that errors and shortages will be quickly discovered.
10. All checks that are prepared incorrectly should be voided. Such checks should be physically marked "void" and retained to prevent their unauthorized use.
11. A voucher system (described later) may be needed in large firms for close control of cash.
12. Use of the net price method of recording purchases (described later in this chapter) helps avoid loss of purchase discounts through planned timing of cash payments.

Illustration 7.3 shows an overview of some of the internal control considerations relating to cash.

Almost without exception, companies use checking accounts to handle their cash transactions. The company deposits its cash receipts in a bank checking account and writes checks to pay its bills. The bank sends the company a statement each month. The company checks this statement against its records to determine if any corrections or adjustments are needed in either the company's balance or the bank's balance. You will learn how to do this later in the chapter when the bank reconciliation statement is discussed. In the next section you will learn about the bank checking account. If you have a personal checking account, some of this information will be familiar to you.

Illustration 7.3

*Some Internal
Control
Considerations
Regarding Cash*

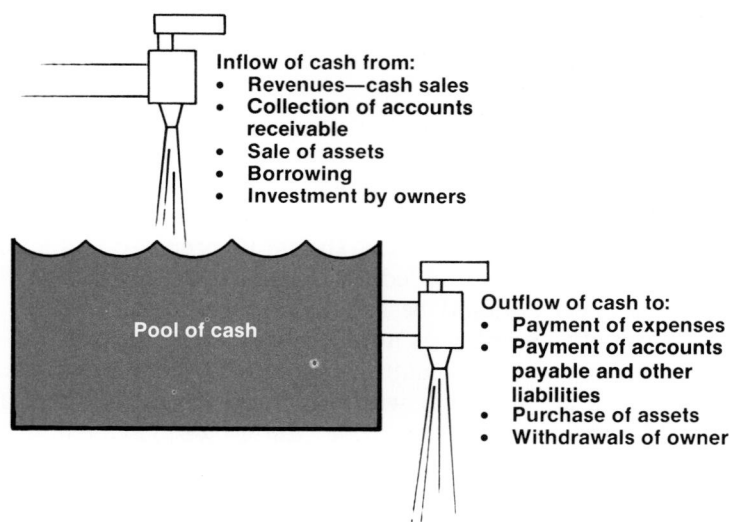

Inflow of cash from:
- **Revenues—cash sales**
- **Collection of accounts receivable**
- **Sale of assets**
- **Borrowing**
- **Investment by owners**

Pool of cash

Outflow of cash to:
- **Payment of expenses**
- **Payment of accounts payable and other liabilities**
- **Purchase of assets**
- **Withdrawals of owner**

Internal Control Considerations

☐ Are all cash receipts being properly recorded and actually going into the company's pool of cash, or are individuals siphoning off some of these receipts for their own use?

☐ Is the pool of cash protected from theft? Is the cash on hand managed so as to produce income for the company and yet be available when needed to make legitimate disbursements?

☐ Is there close control over cash disbursements to ensure that only legitimate disbursements are made in the proper amounts and on a timely basis?

■ THE BANK CHECKING ACCOUNT

Banks seek to earn income by providing a variety of services to individuals, businesses, and other entities such as churches, libraries, and so on. One of these services is the checking account. A **checking account** is a money balance maintained in the bank that is subject to withdrawal by the depositor, or owner of the money, on demand. To provide depositors with an accurate record of depositor funds received and disbursed, a bank uses the business documents discussed in this section.[1]

The Signature Card

A bank requires a new depositor to complete a **signature card,** which provides the signatures of persons authorized to sign checks drawn upon an account. The card is retained at the bank to identify signatures on checks paid by the bank. The bank does not compare every check with this signature card; it usually makes the comparison only when the depositor disputes the validity of a check paid by the bank.

---

[1] Due to relaxed federal regulations, institutions other than banks—such as savings and loan associations and credit unions—now offer checking account services. All of these institutions function somewhat similarly, but for simplicity's sake only banks will be discussed here.

Deposit Ticket

When a bank deposit is made, the depositor prepares a deposit ticket or slip. A **deposit ticket** is a form that shows the date and the items that make up the deposit (see Illustration 7.4). The ticket is often preprinted to show the depositor's name, address, and account number for the account into which the deposit is made. Items comprising the deposit—cash and a list of checks— are entered on the ticket when the deposit is made. Upon making the deposit, the depositor is given a receipt showing the date and amount deposited.

Illustration 7.4

Deposit Ticket

CHECKING ACCOUNT DEPOSIT		DOLLARS	CENTS
NAME R. L. LEE COMPANY	CURRENCY	140	—
	COINS	15	50
ADDRESS 1021 Roy Lane, East Lansing, Mich. 48823	CHECKS AS FOLLOWS PROPERLY ENDORSED		
ACCOUNT NUMBER 0936 162 01	DATE May 3 19 87	Adams	200	50
		Baker	170	—
East Lansing State Bank East Lansing, Michigan			
CHECKS AND OTHER ITEMS ARE RECEIVED FOR DEPOSIT SUBJECT TO TERMS AND CONDITIONS OF THIS BANK'S COLLECTION AGREEMENT.	TOTAL DEPOSITS	526	00

⑆072409927⑈   093061621⑈01

Check

A **check** is a written order on a bank to pay a specific sum of money to the party designated as the payee by the party issuing the check. Thus, there are three parties to every check transaction: the **bank**, the **payee** (party to whom the check is made payable), and the **drawer** (depositor). Most checks are serially

Illustration 7.5

Check with Attached Remittance Advice

					No. 9531
R.L. LEE COMPANY 1021 Roy Lane East Lansing, Mich. 48823			May 4 19 87		74-992 / 724
PAY TO THE ORDER OF K.F. Frazer Co. ----------------------				$ 1,250.00	

One thousand two hundred fifty and no/100 ---------------------- DOLLARS

Brookfield Plaza Branch
East Lansing State Bank
WITH TRUST SERVICES
East Lansing, Michigan 48823

R. L. Lee

⑆072409927⑈   093061621⑈01   9531

Remittance advice (detach before depositing)

Date	P.O. No.	Description	Amount
5/4/87	R204	Payment in full of your invoice #4556	$1,250.00

numbered and preprinted with information about the depositor, such as name, address, and telephone number. Often a business check will have an attached remittance advice. A **remittance advice** informs the payee why the drawer (or maker) of the check is making this payment; it is detached from the check before the check is cashed or deposited (see Illustration 7.5).

Bank Statement

A **bank statement** is a statement issued (usually monthly) by a bank describing the activities in a depositor's checking account during the period. Illustration 7.6 shows a bank statement that includes the following data:

1. Deposits made to the checking account during the period.
2. Checks paid out of the depositor's checking account by the bank during the period. These checks have "cleared" the bank and are "canceled."
3. Other deductions from the checking account for items such as service

Illustration 7.6

Bank Statement

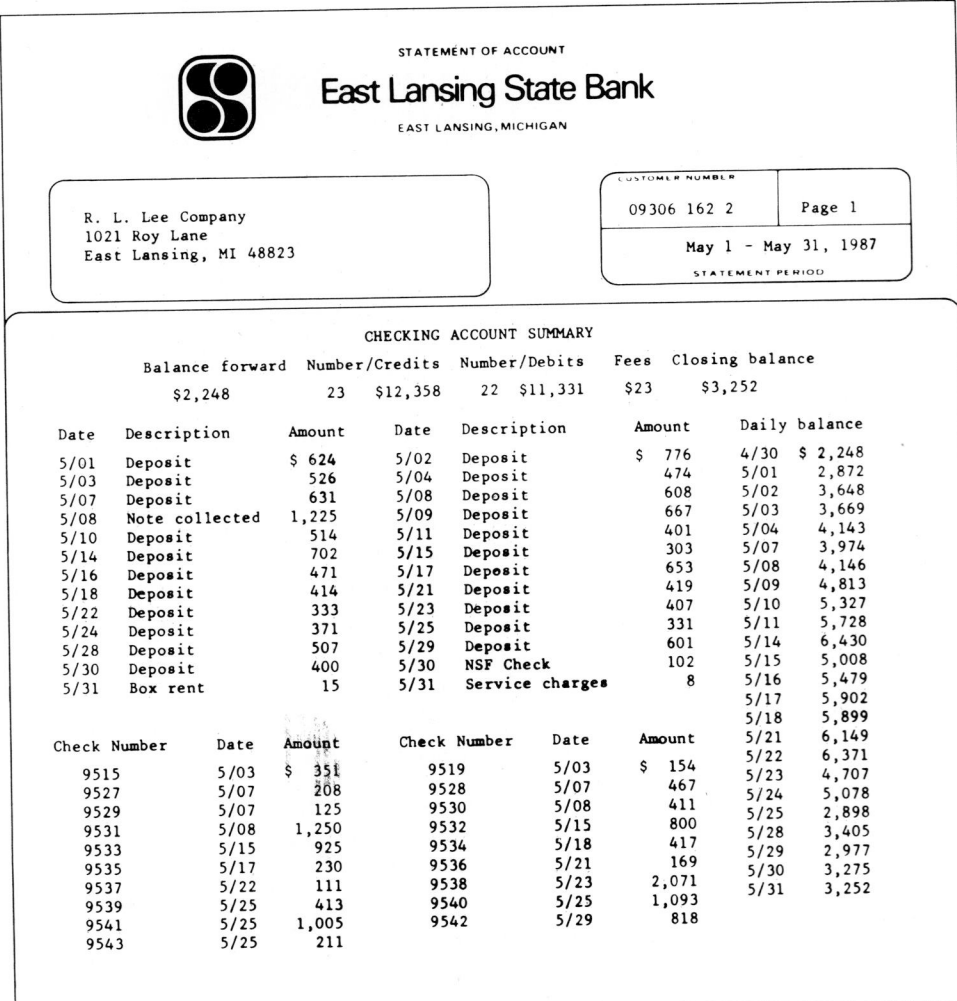

STATEMENT OF ACCOUNT

East Lansing State Bank

EAST LANSING, MICHIGAN

R. L. Lee Company
1021 Roy Lane
East Lansing, MI 48823

CUSTOMER NUMBER	
09306 162 2	Page 1
May 1 - May 31, 1987	
STATEMENT PERIOD	

CHECKING ACCOUNT SUMMARY

Balance forward	Number/Credits		Number/Debits		Fees	Closing balance
$2,248	23	$12,358	22	$11,331	$23	$3,252

Date	Description	Amount	Date	Description	Amount		Daily balance
5/01	Deposit	$ 624	5/02	Deposit	$ 776	4/30	$ 2,248
5/03	Deposit	526	5/04	Deposit	474	5/01	2,872
5/07	Deposit	631	5/08	Deposit	608	5/02	3,648
5/08	Note collected	1,225	5/09	Deposit	667	5/03	3,669
5/10	Deposit	514	5/11	Deposit	401	5/04	4,143
5/14	Deposit	702	5/15	Deposit	303	5/07	3,974
5/16	Deposit	471	5/17	Deposit	653	5/08	4,146
5/18	Deposit	414	5/21	Deposit	419	5/09	4,813
5/22	Deposit	333	5/23	Deposit	407	5/10	5,327
5/24	Deposit	371	5/25	Deposit	331	5/11	5,728
5/28	Deposit	507	5/29	Deposit	601	5/14	6,430
5/30	Deposit	400	5/30	NSF Check	102	5/15	5,008
5/31	Box rent	15	5/31	Service charges	8	5/16	5,479
						5/17	5,902
						5/18	5,899
						5/21	6,149
						5/22	6,371

Check Number	Date	Amount	Check Number	Date	Amount	Daily balance	
9515	5/03	$ 351	9519	5/03	$ 154	5/23	4,707
9527	5/07	208	9528	5/07	467	5/24	5,078
9529	5/07	125	9530	5/08	411	5/25	2,898
9531	5/08	1,250	9532	5/15	800	5/28	3,405
9533	5/15	925	9534	5/18	417	5/29	2,977
9535	5/17	230	9536	5/21	169	5/30	3,275
9537	5/22	111	9538	5/23	2,071	5/31	3,252
9539	5/25	413	9540	5/25	1,093		
9541	5/25	1,005	9542	5/29	818		
9543	5/25	211					

charges, NSF (nonsufficient funds) checks, safe-deposit box rent, and check printing fees. **Service charges** are assessed by the bank on the depositor to cover the cost of handling the checking account, such as check clearing charges. An **NSF check** is a customer's check returned from the customer's bank because the customer's checking account balance was insufficient to cover the check. As a result, the check is returned to the depositor's bank, and the depositor's bank deducts the amount of the check from the depositor's checking account. Since the customer still owes the depositor money, the depositor will restore the amount of the NSF check to the account receivable for that customer in the company's books.

4. Other additions to the checking account for items such as proceeds of a note collected by the bank for the depositor and interest earned on the account.[2]

In addition to the data shown in the bank statement in Illustration 7.6, bank statements also can show nonroutine deposits made to the depositor's checking account. Such deposits are not made directly by the depositor but, rather, by a third party. For example, the bank may have received a wire transfer of funds for the depositor.

A **wire transfer of funds** is an interbank transfer of funds by telephone. An interbank transfer of funds is often used by companies that operate in many widely scattered locations and therefore have checking accounts with several different local banks. These companies may set up special procedures to avoid accumulating too much idle cash in local bank accounts. One such procedure involves the use of special-instruction bank accounts. For example, **transfer bank accounts** may be set up so that local banks automatically transfer to a central bank (by wire or bank draft) all amounts on deposit in excess of a stated amount. In this way, funds not needed for local operations are sent quickly to company headquarters, where the funds can be used or invested as the company deems necessary.

Frequently, the bank returns canceled checks and original deposit tickets with the bank statement. Since it is expensive to sort, handle, and mail these items, banks are beginning to discontinue returning them. These documents are usually stored on microfilm at the bank, with photocopies available if needed. Most depositors need only a detailed bank statement, as shown in Illustration 7.6, and not the original documents to show what transactions occurred during a given period.

When banks debit or credit a depositor's checking account, they prepare debit and credit memos. These memos may also be returned with the bank statement. A **debit memo** is a form used by a bank to explain a deduction from the depositor's account; a **credit memo** explains an addition to the account. The terms *debit memo* and *credit memo* may seem reversed, but remember that the depositor's checking account is a liability—an account payable—of the bank. So, when the bank seeks to reduce a depositor's balance, a debit memo is prepared. To increase the balance, a credit memo is prepared. Examples of debit and credit memos are shown in Illustration 7.7. Banks are also trying to eliminate the mailing of these documents to the depositor and to rely instead on explanations on the bank statement.

---

[2] Effective January 1, 1982, revised federal regulations permit banks to pay interest on a depositor's checking account balance.

Illustration 7.7

Debit Memorandum (top) and Credit Memorandum (bottom)

Debit memo

EAST LANSING STATE BANK
EAST LANSING, MICHIGAN

DATE May 31, 1987

WE CHARGE YOUR ACCOUNT

DESCRIPTION	AMOUNT
Safe-deposit box rental	15 00

ACCOUNT NUMBER 09306 162 2

Brookfield Plaza
DEPARTMENT OR BRANCH

R. Waters
MANAGER

MAIL TO →

R. L. Lee Company
1021 Roy Lane
East Lansing, Mich. 48823

Credit memo

EAST LANSING STATE BANK
EAST LANSING, MICHIGAN

DATE 5/8/87

	AMOUNT
Collection of note for the Lee Company from X Company	1,225 00

WE CREDIT YOUR ACCOUNT SUBJECT TO TERMS AND CONDITIONS ON REVERSE SIDE OF STATEMENT OF ACCOUNT

CREDIT ADVICE - MAIL TO

R. L. Lee Company
1021 Roy Lane
East Lansing, Mich. 48823

APPROVED R. M. H.

09306 162 2 ACCOUNT NO.

Information the depositor did not know prior to receiving the bank statement (items 3 and 4 on pages 278–79) requires new journal entries. After the entries have been made to record the new information, the balance in the Cash account is the actual cash available to the company. When the depositor has already received notice of NSF checks and other bank charges or credits, the needed journal entries may have been made earlier. In this chapter we assume no entries have been made for these items unless stated otherwise.

When a company receives its bank statement, the company must check the bank record of company cash with its own record. If you have a personal checking account, you also should check your bank statement with your checkbook. You can use the form on the back of the bank statement to record your checks that have not yet been paid by the bank and your deposits not yet shown on the bank statement. Some small businesses may also use this form. However, in addition they may prepare a bank reconciliation statement, which you will learn how to prepare in the next section.

■ BANK RECONCILIATION STATEMENT

A **bank reconciliation statement,** often called a **bank reconciliation,** is a statement the company prepares to "reconcile," or explain, the difference between

Illustration 7.8 *Bank Reconciliation Statement*

R. L. LEE COMPANY
Bank Reconciliation Statement
May 31, 1987

Balance per bank statement, May 31, 1987		$3,252	Balance per ledger, May 31, 1987		$1,891
Add: Deposit in transit		452	Add: Note collected		1,225
		$3,704			$3,116
Less: Outstanding checks:					
No. 9544	$322		Less: NSF check	$102	
No. 9545	168		Safe-deposit box rent	15	
No. 9546	223	713	Service charges	8	125
Adjusted balance, May 31, 1987		$2,991	Adjusted balance, May 31, 1987		$2,991

the cash balance shown on the bank statement and the cash balance on the company's books. The bank reconciliation is prepared to determine the company's actual cash balance. An example of a bank reconciliation statement is shown in Illustration 7.8.

The bank reconciliation statement is divided into two main sections. One section, on the left in Illustration 7.8, begins with the balance shown on the bank statement. The second section, on the right in Illustration 7.8, begins with the company's balance as shown on the company's books. Adjustments are made to both the "bank" and "book" balances; after these adjustments, both adjusted balances should be the same.

The following steps are used in preparing the bank reconciliation statement:

1. **Deposits.** The deposits listed on the bank statement are compared with the deposits on the company's books. This can be done by placing check marks in the bank statement and in the company's books by the deposits that agree. Then the deposits in transit are determined. A **deposit in transit** is typically a day's cash receipts recorded in the depositor's books in one period but recorded as a deposit by the bank in the succeeding period. The most common deposit in transit is the deposit of the cash receipts of the last business day of the month. Normally, deposits in transit occur only near the end of the period covered by the bank statement. For example, a deposit made in a bank's night depository on May 31 would be recorded by the company on May 31 and by the bank on June 1. Thus, the deposit will not appear on a bank statement for the month ended May 31. The deposits in transit listed in last month's bank reconciliation should also be checked against the bank statement. Any missing deposit that does not involve a deposit made at the end of the period should be investigated immediately.

2. **Paid checks.** If canceled checks are returned with the bank statement, first compare them to the bank statement to be sure the amounts on the statement agree with the checks. Then sort the checks in numerical order. Next determine which checks are outstanding. **Outstanding checks** are checks issued by a depositor that have not yet been paid by the bank upon which they are drawn. The party receiving the check may not deposit it immediately. As a result, sometimes it takes several days or even weeks for checks written to clear the banking system. The outstanding checks are determined by a process of elimination. The check numbers that have cleared the bank are compared with a list of the check numbers issued by the company. Check marks are used in the

company's record of checks issued to identify those checks returned by the bank. Checks issued that have not yet been returned by the bank are the outstanding checks. If the bank does not return checks but provides only a listing of the cleared checks on the bank statement, the outstanding checks are determined by comparing this list with the company's record of checks issued.

Sometimes checks written long ago will still be outstanding. Checks outstanding as of the beginning of the month will appear on the prior month's bank reconciliation. Most of these will have cleared during the current month; those that have not cleared should be listed as still outstanding on the current month's reconciliation.

3. **Bank debit and credit memos.**   Verify all debt and credit memos on the bank's statement. These are memos for such items as service charges, NSF checks, safe-deposit box rent, notes collected for the depositor by the bank, and so on. The bank debits and credits should be checked with the depositor's books to see if they have already been recorded. The accountant should make journal entries for any such items not in the company's books.

4. **Errors.**   List any errors that have been found. A common error that occurs is when the depositor records a check in the accounting records at an amount that differs from the actual amount on the check. For example, a $47 check may be recorded at $74. The check will clear the bank at the amount written on the check ($47), but the depositor frequently does not catch the error until the bank statement or canceled checks are reviewed. Any error in the depositor's books will require an adjustment on the depositor's books.

Deposits in transit, outstanding checks, and bank service charges usually account for the difference between the company's Cash account and the bank balances. (This is also true in your personal checkbook record and the bank balance shown on your bank statement.) Remember that **all items shown on the bank reconciliation as adjustments of the book (ledger) balance will require journal entries to adjust the cash account; items appearing on the bank side do not require entries by the depositor.** Any bank errors, of course, should be called to the bank's attention.

To illustrate the preparation of the bank reconciliation shown in Illustration 7.8, assume the following:

1. On May 31, 1987, R. L. Lee Company showed a balance in its Cash account of $1,891. On June 2, Lee received its bank statement for the month ended May 31, which showed an ending balance of $3,252.
2. A matching of debits to the Cash account on the books with deposits on the bank statement showed that the $452 receipts of May 31 are included in Cash but not included as a deposit on the bank statement.
3. An examination of checks issued and checks cleared showed three checks outstanding:

No. 9544	$322
No. 9545	168
No. 9546	223
Total	$713

4. Included with the bank statement was a credit memo for $1,225 for collection of a note owed to Lee by Shipley Company. Lee did not earn interest on the note.[3] Such a note is called a noninterest-bearing note.

---

[3] Normally, interest is earned on notes, but this topic is not covered until the next chapter.

5. Included with the bank statement is a $102 debit memo for an NSF check written by R. Johnson and deposited by Lee.
6. Charges made to Lee's account include $15 for safe-deposit box rent and $8 for service charges.

After reconciling the book and bank balances, Lee Company finds that its actual cash balance is $2,991. The following entries are needed to record information from the bank reconciliation:

Cash	1,225	
Notes Receivable—Shipley Company		1,225
To record note collected from Shipley Company.		
Bank Service Charges Expense	23	
Cash		23
To record bank service charges.		
Accounts Receivable—R. Johnson*	102	
Cash		102
To charge NSF check back to customer, R. Johnson.		

* This debit would be posted to the Accounts Receivable control account in the general ledger and to R. Johnson's account in the accounts receivable subsidiary ledger.

The income statement for the period ending May 31, 1987, would include the $23 bank service charges as an expense. The May 31 balance sheet will show $2,991 cash, the actual cash balance.

The deposit in transit and the outstanding checks are already recorded in the depositor's books and will be handled routinely when they reach the bank. Since these items appear on the bank side of the reconciliation, they require no entry in the company's books. These items will be processed by the bank in the subsequent period.

When more than one checking account is maintained by a company, each account must be reconciled separately with the balance on the bank statement for that account. The depositor should then also check carefully to see that the bank did not make an error in keeping separate the transactions of the two accounts.

Certified and Cashier's Checks

To make sure a check will not "bounce" and become an NSF check, a payee may demand that the maker's check be a certified or cashier's check. Both certified checks and cashier's checks are liabilities of the bank rather than the depositor. As a result, these checks usually are accepted without question.

☐ A **certified check** is a check written, or drawn, by a **depositor** and taken to the depositor's bank for certification. The bank will stamp "certified" across the face of the check and insert the name of the bank and the date; the certification will be signed by a bank official. A check is certified only when the depositor's balance is large enough to cover the check. The amount of the check is deducted from the depositor's account at the time it is certified by the bank.

☐ A **cashier's check** is a check drawn by a **bank** made out to either the depositor or a third party after deducting the amount of the check from the depositor's account or receiving cash from the depositor.

In this section you learned that all cash receipts should be deposited in the bank and all cash disbursements should be made by check. However, the next section explains that it is sometimes convenient to have small amounts of cash (petty cash) available for minor expenditures.

■ PETTY CASH FUNDS

At times, every business finds it convenient to have small amounts of cash available for immediate payment of items such as delivery charges, postage stamps, taxi fares, supper money for employees working overtime, and other small items. To permit these disbursements to be made in cash and still maintain adequate control over the cash, companies frequently establish a **petty cash fund** of a round figure such as $100 or $500.

Usually one individual, called the petty cash custodian or cashier, is responsible for the operation of the fund, which includes the control of the petty cash and documenting the disbursements made from the fund. By assigning the responsibility for the fund to one individual, the company has internal control over the cash in the fund. In this section you will learn how to both establish and operate a petty cash fund.

Establishing the Fund

The petty cash fund is established by writing a check for, say, $100. The amount of a petty cash fund should be large enough to make disbursements for a reasonable period, such as a month.

For example, assume a $100 petty cash fund is to be established. A check in that amount is drawn, payable to cash or the petty cash custodian. The following entry is required:

Petty Cash	100	
Cash		100
To establish a petty cash fund.		

The check is cashed, and the money is turned over to the petty cash custodian, who normally places the money in a small box that can be locked. The fund is now ready to be disbursed as needed.

Operating the Fund

One of the conveniences of the petty cash fund is that no journal entries are required when payments are made from the fund. Thus, using a petty cash fund avoids the need for making many entries for small amounts. Only when the fund is reimbursed will an entry be made in the journal.

When there is a need to disburse cash from the fund, a petty cash voucher is prepared by the petty cash custodian and should be signed by the person receiving the funds. A **petty cash voucher** (see Illustration 7.9) is a document or form that shows the amount of and reason for a petty cash disbursement. A voucher should be prepared for each disbursement from the fund. If an invoice for the expenditure is provided, the invoice should be stapled to the

Illustration 7.9

Petty Cash Voucher

```
┌─────────────────────────────────────────────────────────┐
│           PETTY CASH VOUCHER NO.  359                     │
│                                                           │
│  To   Local Cartage, Inc.            Date June 29,  1987  │
│  ┌──────────────────┬──────────────┬─────────────────┐   │
│  │   EXPLANATION     │   ACCT. NO.  │     AMOUNT       │   │
│  ├──────────────────┼──────────────┼─────────────────┤   │
│  │  Freight on parts │      27      │    2 27          │   │
│  │                   │              │                  │   │
│  │                   │              │                  │   │
│  │                   │              │                  │   │
│  ├──────────────────┼──────────────┴─────────────────┤   │
│   APPROVED                  RECEIVED                       │
│   BY  a E S                 PAYMENT Ken Black             │
└─────────────────────────────────────────────────────────┘
```

petty cash voucher. The person responsible for petty cash is at all times accountable for having cash and petty cash vouchers equal to the total amount of the fund.

Replenishing the Fund

When the petty cash fund becomes low, it should be replenished. The petty cash vouchers are presented to the person having authority to order that the fund be reimbursed. The vouchers are examined by that person, and, if all is in order, a check is drawn to restore the fund to its original amount.

To determine which accounts to debit, the petty cash vouchers are summarized according to the reasons for expenditure. The petty cash vouchers are then stamped or defaced to prevent reuse. The journal entry to record replenishing the fund would debit the various accounts indicated by the summary and credit Cash.

For example, assume the $100 petty cash fund currently has a money balance of $7.40. A summary of the vouchers shows payments of $22.75 for transportation-in, $50.80 for stamps, and $19.05 for an advance to an employee; these payments total $92.60. After the vouchers have been examined and approved, a check is drawn for $92.60 which, when cashed, restores the cash in the fund to its $100 balance. The journal entry to record replenishment is:

Transportation-In	22.75	
Postage Expense	50.80	
Advances to Employees	19.05	
Cash		92.60
To replenish petty cash fund.		

At the end of an accounting period, any petty cash disbursements for which the fund has not yet been replenished must be recorded. Since the fund has not been replenished, the credit would be to Petty Cash rather than Cash. Failure to make an entry at the end of an accounting period would cause errors in both the income statement and balance sheet. The easiest way to record these disbursements is to replenish the fund. Replenishing the fund at the end of an accounting period is handled exactly as at any other time.

If, after some experience, a petty cash fund is found to be larger than needed, the excess petty cash should be deposited in the company's checking account. The required entry debits Cash and credits Petty Cash for the amount returned and deposited. On the other hand, a petty cash fund may be too small, requiring replenishment every few days. The entry to record an increase in the size of the fund debits Petty Cash and credits Cash for the amount of the increase.

Cash Short and Over

Errors can be made in making change from the petty cash fund. In such cases, the amount of cash in the fund will be more or less than the amount of the fund less the total vouchers. When the fund is restored to its original amount, the credit to Cash is for the difference between the established amount and the actual cash in the fund. Debits are made for all vouchered items. Any discrepancy should be debited or credited to an account called Cash Short and Over. The Cash Short and Over account is an expense or a revenue, depending upon whether it has a debit or credit balance.

To illustrate, assume in the preceding example that the balance in the fund was only $6.10 instead of $7.40. To restore the fund to $100, a check for $93.90 is needed. Since the petty cash vouchers total only $92.60, the fund is short $1.30. In this case, the entry for replenishment is:

Transportation-In	22.75	
Postage Expense	50.80	
Advances to Employees	19.05	
Cash Short and Over	1.30	
Cash		93.90
To replenish petty cash fund.		

Entries in the Cash Over and Short account may be entered from other change-making activities. For example, assume that a clerk accidentally short-changes a customer $1 and that total cash sales for the day are $740.50. At the end of the day, actual cash will be $1 over the sum of the sales tickets or the total of the cash register tape. The journal entry to record the day's cash sales is:

Cash	741.50	
Sales		740.50
Cash Short and Over		1.00
To record cash sales for the day.		

In Chapter 5, you learned how to record the purchases of the Hanlon Retail Food Store using the gross invoice price method. In the section that follows, an alternative method—the net price method—is explained. As you will see, the net price method has two advantages over the gross invoice price method.

■ NET PRICE METHOD

Most well-managed companies take advantage of all the discounts made available to them by their suppliers. Effective internal control over cash disbursements makes certain that these discounts are taken. Even with today's high interest rates, a company may find it advisable to borrow cash to pay invoices within the discount period.

For example, assume goods are purchased for $10,000 under terms 2/10, n/30. The buyer is unable to pay at the end of 10 days but expects to be able to pay at the end of 30 days. To take the $200 discount offered, the buyer needs a $9,800 loan for 20 days, beginning on the last day of the 10-

day discount period. The buyer would benefit if the interest cost of such a loan was less than $200. (Short-term loans and interest computations are discussed in Chapter 8.)

In Chapter 5, purchase discounts were recorded under the gross price method. However, some companies prefer to use the net price method because (1) the accounting theory behind the method is superior and (2) the method strengthens internal control.

In the **net price method,** a purchase is recorded in Purchases and Accounts Payable "net" of the discount. Thus, the discount is **deducted** from the gross invoice price **before** entering the transaction in the accounts. To illustrate, assume a $1,500 purchase was made on May 14 under terms 2/10, n/30. The invoice was paid on May 24, and the discount taken. The entries comparing the net price method and gross price method are:

		Net		*Gross*	
May 14	Purchases	1,470		1,500	
	Accounts Payable		1,470		1,500
	Purchased goods under terms 2/10, n/30.				
24	Accounts Payable	1,470		1,500	
	Cash		1,470		1,470
	Purchase Discounts*				30
	Paid account within discount period.				

* This account would not appear in the net price entry.

Theoretically, the net price method is preferred over the gross price method because the goods are recorded at their actual cost. Thus, the cost principle of accounting is applied, goods are recorded at the total amount of resources given up to acquire them. Also, the liability is shown in the Accounts Payable account at the amount for which it could be settled.

Note that in the above net price example, discounts taken are not shown. If the invoice had not been paid within 10 days, there would have been an entry to Discounts Lost. For example, assume that the invoice in the above example was paid on May 28 instead of May 24. Then the entries for the payment comparing the net price and gross price methods are:

		Net		*Gross*	
May 28	Accounts Payable	1,470		1,500	
	Discounts Lost*	30			
	Cash		1,500		1,500
	Paid account after discount had expired.				

* This account would not appear in the gross price entry.

Under the net price method, the only time discounts appear is when they are lost. When discounts of 2% or more are available, good cash management calls for internal control procedures ensuring that all invoices are paid within the discount period. The failure to take a discount highlights a deviation from company policy and directs management's attention to this deviation. The Discounts Lost account actually contains losses resulting from inefficiency, and it is reported among nonoperating expenses near the bottom of the income statement. Many companies prefer the net price method because it strengthens internal control over cash disbursements.

Companies also use the voucher system to strengthen internal control over cash disbursements. As shown in the next section, the nature of the voucher system is such that it provides a high level of internal control.

■ THE VOUCHER SYSTEM

Companies often suffer substantial losses from the embezzlement of cash. Frequently, the embezzlement results from the paying of fictitious invoices. Thus, every business must make sure that its cash payments are proper and timely. In small companies this is often not a problem because the owner usually has personal knowledge of all transactions and personally signs all checks. However, in larger companies the owners and high-level officers may have no direct part in the payment process. These companies can effectively control cash disbursements by using the voucher system.

The **voucher system** is a set of procedures, special journals, and authorization forms designed to provide control over cash payments. The special journals

Illustration 7.10

A Voucher

ATWELL   SUPPLY   COMPANY
Atwell Plaza
Atwell, Texas 78712

VOUCHER

VOUCHER NO.   141
OUR P.O. NO.   2514
VENDOR'S INVOICE   416
PAID BY CHECK NO.   587
DATE PAID   7/18/87

Payable To: Gregory Corporation
48 Cadillac Square
Detroit, Michigan 48226

DATE		ACCT. NO.	DESCRIPTION	QUANTITY	UNIT PRICE	TOTAL
July	14	126	X-16 Transistors	100	$2.00	$200.00
			TOTAL			$200.00
			DISCOUNT	2%		4.00
			NET PAYABLE			$196.00

TERMS 2/10, n/30
EXPLANATIONS: *Due date is August 13, 1987*

AUDITED AS TO CORRECTNESS *a.T.*	APPROVED FOR PAYMENT *L.J.W.*	ENTERED IN VOUCHER REGISTER *R.E.L*	DATE ENTERED 7/14/87

used are the voucher register and the check register. These journals are defined later in this section.

When a company uses the voucher system, each transaction that involves a cash payment is entered on a voucher (see Illustration 7.10) and recorded in the voucher register prior to payment. A **voucher** is a form with spaces provided for data about a liability that must be paid. The data include items such as creditor's name and address, description of the goods or services received, invoice number, terms of payment, due date, and amount due. The voucher also has spaces for signatures of those approving the liability for payment.

An invoice or other business document is the basis for making a journal entry in the voucher register. The voucher usually forms a "jacket" for the invoice and supporting documents, such as the receiving department's report. Each voucher should undergo careful examination and receive either approval or disapproval for payment. By the time a voucher is approved for payment, several persons have confirmed that the claim being paid is proper and accurate, thus reducing the chances of embezzlement.

Procedures for Preparing a Voucher

The preparation of a voucher begins with the receipt of an invoice from a creditor or with approved evidence that a liability has been incurred and cash should be disbursed. Then the procedures are as follows:

1. Basic data are entered on the voucher from the invoice.
2. The invoice, voucher, and receiving report are sent to the persons responsible for verifying the correctness of the description of the goods as to quantity and quality, dollar amounts, and other details. Each person initials the voucher when satisfied as to its correctness.
3. When the voucher and accompanying documents are received by the accounting department, a notation is made on the voucher as to the proper accounts to be debited and credited.
4. After a final review by an authorized person, the proper entry is made in the voucher register, and the voucher is filed in the unpaid voucher file.

The name **voucher system** comes from the fact that **every check issued is authorized by a voucher.** A voucher really can be any written form that serves as a receipt or evidence of authority to act. However, as applied to the voucher system, a voucher is a form that confirms a liability and, as such, serves as the basis for an accounting entry.

In some businesses the discount and payment terms run from the invoice date. Then, a voucher should be prepared for each invoice (see Illustration 7.10). The voucher should be filed according to the date on which the discount period terminates or payment is due. However, when the discount and payment terms are computed from the end of the month, it is possible to modify the voucher, reducing the number of vouchers prepared and the entries made in the voucher register. Then, all invoices received from a particular creditor are accumulated and listed on one voucher at the end of the month. One check is written on the due date to pay for all invoices listed on the voucher. These vouchers are filed according to due dates.

Special Journals Used

The special journals used in the voucher system are the voucher register and the check register. Illustration 7.11 shows a voucher register, and Illustration 7.12 shows a check register for the Jackson Company.

Voucher Register. A voucher register is a multicolumn special journal; it contains a record of all vouchers prepared, listed in order by date and voucher number. A brief explanation of each transaction also may be included. Since each entry in the voucher register includes a credit to a new account, called the Vouchers Payable account, a column titled "Vouchers Payable Cr." is included in the voucher register (see Illustration 7.11). In addition to this credit column, the voucher register has debit columns for the accounts the company most frequently debits when a liability is incurred, as well as a column to enter the other accounts (Other Accounts Dr. column).

At the end of each month, the Vouchers Payable Cr. column total is posted to the general ledger control account, Vouchers Payable. In Illustration 7.11, a voucher is prepared for each invoice. Note that the vouchers are recorded

Illustration 7.11 *A Voucher Register*

JACKSON COMPANY
VOUCHER REGISTER

Line No.	Voucher Date 1987		Voucher No.	Payee	Explanation	Terms	Date Paid		Check No.	Vouchers Payable Cr. 101
1	May	2	223	Hanley Company	Ring binders	2/10,n/30	May	12	1350	980.00
2		4	224	Moore Transport	Transportation, binders			5	1347	13.00
3		6	225	White Stationery Company	Office supplies	2/10,n/30		12	1351	102.00
4		8	226	Specialty Advertisers	Advertising			8	1348	1,200.00
5		10	227	Blanch Company	Office equipment and supplies			10	1349	1,010.00
6										
7		14	228	Swanson Company	Filler paper	2/10,n/30		26	1356	3,920.00
8		16	229	Rizzo Company	Office desk	n/30		25	1355	640.00
9		18	230	Warren Company	Spiral binders	2/10,n/30		28	1357	4,900.00
10		20	231	First National Bank	Mortgage payment			20	1353	154.00
11		22	232	Falconer Company	Books	n/30				10,000.00
12		24	233	Petty cash	Reimbursement			24	1354	132.00
13		26	234	Swanson Company	Discount lost (No. 228)			26	1356	80.00
14		28	235	Celoron Company	Drawing sets	2/20,n/30				9,800.00
15		31	236	Payroll account	Salaries and wages			31	1358	24,000.00
16										56,931.00

net of purchase discounts allowed. If a discount is missed, another voucher is prepared for the discount lost (see line 13 of Illustration 7.11). (As described below, the voucher system can also be used when purchases are recorded at the gross amount.) The total of each of the specifically titled columns is posted to the account named. The debits in the Other Accounts Dr. column are posted individually to the accounts named, usually on a daily basis. The total of the Other Accounts column is not posted because it includes amounts affecting more than one account.

Check Register.   A **check register** is a special journal showing all checks issued, listed by date and check number. One line is allotted to each check. No check may be issued unless authorized by an approved voucher.

The check register in Illustration 7.12 shows the entry and procedure when a check is issued in payment of a voucher. Note that Check No. 1352 is marked "void." This notation usually means that a mistake was made in writing the check, and another check had to be prepared.

Page No. *15*
Month *May 1987*

Dis-counts Lost Dr. 122	Mer-chandise Purchases Dr. 131	Transpor-tation-In Dr. 144	Salaries and Wages Dr. 158	Office Expense Dr. 175	Advertising Expense Dr. 262	Other Accounts Dr.			
						Account Name	Acct. No.	Amount Dr.	✓
	980.00								
		13.00							
				102.00					
					1,200.00				
						Office Equipment	42	1,000.00	
						Office Supplies	33	10.00	
	3,920.00								
						Office Equipment	42	640.00	
	4,860.00	40.00							
						Mortgage Note Payable	151	154.00	
	10,000.00								
		31.88		60.12	40.00				
80.00									
	9,800.00								
			24,000.00						
80.00	29,560.00	84.88	24,000.00	162.12	1,240.00			1,804.00	

Illustration 7.12

Check Register

			JACKSON COMPANY CHECK REGISTER		Page No. *24* Month *May, 1987*	
Line No.	Date 1987		Payee	Voucher No.	Check No.	Vouchers Payable Dr., Cash Cr.
1	May	5	Moore Transport	224	1347	13.00
2		8	Specialty Advertisers	226	1348	1,200.00
3		10	Blanch Company	227	1349	1,010.00
4		12	Hanley Company	223	1350	980.00
5		12	White Stationery Company	225	1351	102.00
6		20	VOID		1352	
7		20	First National Bank	231	1353	154.00
8		24	Petty Cash	233	1354	132.00
9		25	Rizzo Company	229	1355	640.00
10		26	Swanson Company	228} 234}	1356	4,000.00
11		28	Warren Company	230	1357	4,900.00
12		31	Payroll account	236	1358	24,000.00
						37,131.00

The net price method was used in Illustration 7.12, so the check register has only one money column. The column total is posted in the general ledger as a debit to Vouchers Payable and a credit to Cash. If the gross price method is used, invoices are entered gross (before discount deductions) in the voucher register, and a Purchase Discounts Cr. column should be included in the check register. Separate columns would be needed for the debit to Vouchers Payable and the credit to Cash, since the dollar amounts posted to these two accounts would differ by the amount of the discount taken.

In a voucher system, the voucher register and the check register are the two primary journals from which postings are made to the Vouchers Payable control account in the general ledger. When a company uses a voucher system, these two journals replace the traditional purchases and cash disbursements journals.

Procedures for Paying a Voucher

When a voucher is due for payment, it is removed from the unpaid voucher file in the accounting department. A check is prepared for the amount payable. The check, voucher, and supporting documents are then typically sent to the person authorized to sign checks, usually the treasurer (the top financial officer in the company). The treasurer examines the documents. If they are in order, the treasurer initials the voucher to show that final approval has been given and signs the check. The check is mailed to the creditor, usually with a remittance advice attached. The voucher is then returned to the accounting department.

On receipt of the paid voucher, the accounting department makes an entry in the check register showing the date paid, check number, voucher number,

Either cash or inventory is being stolen or given away in the ice cream parlor. It may be that cash is being pocketed by the employees or outsiders. Or the employees may be giving very liberal cones to friends or eating the ice cream themselves. There are several things which could be done to improve the sales control procedures:

1. The manager could hire an investigator to come in and watch the employees in action. If cash is being pocketed, the employees could be fired.
2. The prices of cones could be changed to odd amounts so that employees would not be as able to make change without going to the cash register. Also, the "No Sale" lever could be removed from the cash register.
3. The customers could be encouraged to ask for their cash register receipts by having a monthly drawing (for some prize) by cash register receipt number.
4. The cash register should be placed in a very prominent position so that each customer could see the amount recorded for each sale. The customer is not going to be willing to pay 65 cents when the employee rings up 50 cents.
5. The cash register tapes should be inaccessible to the employees. The manager (and possibly assistant manager) should have the only keys to the cash registers.
6. Mention to the employees the fact that you have a control system. They don't have to know what it is.
7. Pay the employees a competitive wage.
8. Require that all sales be rung up immediately after the sale.
9. The manager or assistant manager should reconcile the cash register tapes at the end of each day.

DEMONSTRATION PROBLEM 7–2

The following data pertain to the Nunn Company:

1. Balance per bank statement, dated March 31, 1987, is $8,900.
2. Balance of the Cash account on the company's books as of March 31, 1987, is $8,918.
3. The $2,600 deposit of March 31 was not shown on the bank statement.
4. Of the checks recorded as cash disbursements in March, some checks, totaling $2,100, have not yet cleared the bank.
5. Service and collection charges for the month were $20.
6. The bank erroneously charged the Nunn Company account for the $400 check of another company. The check was included with the canceled checks returned with the bank statement.
7. The bank credited the company's account with the $2,000 proceeds of a noninterest-bearing note that it collected for the company.
8. A customer's $150 check marked NSF was returned with the bank statement.
9. As directed, the bank paid and charged to the company's account a $1,015 noninterest-bearing note of the Nunn Company. This payment has not been recorded by the company.
10. An examination of the cash receipts and the deposit tickets revealed that the bookkeeper erroneously recorded a customer's check of $263 as $236.
11. The bank credited the company for $40 of interest earned on the company's checking account.

Required: a. Prepare a bank reconciliation statement as of March 31, 1987.
             b. Prepare the necessary journal entries to adjust the Cash account.

Solution to demonstration problem 7–2

a.

NUNN COMPANY
Bank Reconciliation Statement
March 31, 1987

Balance per bank statement, March 31, 1987		$ 8,900
Add: Deposit in transit	$2,600	
Check charged in error	400	3,000
		$11,900
Less: Outstanding checks		2,100
Adjusted balance, March 31, 1987		$ 9,800
Balance per ledger, March 31, 1987		$ 8,918
Add: Note collected	$2,000	
Interest earned on checking account	40	
Error in recording customer's check	27	2,067
		$10,985
Less: Service and collection charges	$ 20	
NSF check	150	
Nunn Company note charged against account	1,015	1,185
Adjusted balance, March 31, 1987		$ 9,800

b.

Cash	882	
Accounts Receivable	150	
Notes Payable	1,015	
Bank Service Charge Expense	20	
Notes Receivable		2,000
Interest Revenue		40
Accounts Receivable		27

To record adjustments to Cash account.

Alternatively:

Cash	2,067	
Accounts Receivable		27
Notes Receivable		2,000
Interest Revenue		40

To record additions to Cash account.

Notes Payable	1,015	
Accounts Receivable	150	
Bank Service Charge Expense	20	
Cash		1,185

To record deductions from Cash account.

DEMONSTRATION PROBLEM 7–3

The Blankenship Company uses a voucher system to control cash disbursements. Purchases are recorded at gross invoice prices. As of April 30, 1987, two vouchers are unpaid: Voucher No. 404 payable to Akers Company for $850 and Voucher No. 405 payable to Hanson Company for $50.

The Blankenship Company engaged in the following transactions affecting vouchers payable:

Transactions:

May 1 Prepared Voucher No. 406 payable to Carol Company for merchandise purchased; price on invoice dated April 30 is $400. Terms are 2/10, n/30, FOB destination.

2 Issued Check No. 385 in payment of Voucher No. 405; no discount was offered on this purchase.

4 Received a credit memo for $100 for merchandise returned to Akers Company. Purchase was originally recorded in Voucher No. 404. (Record in general journal with notation of return on Voucher No. 404.)

5 Prepared Voucher No. 407 payable to Allen Brothers for merchandise with an invoice price of $950 on invoice dated May 3; terms are 2/10, n/30, FOB shipping point, freight prepaid. Supplier paid $50 freight bill and added $50 to the invoice for a total billing of $1,000.

6 Prepared Voucher No. 408 payable to API, Inc., for cost incurred to deliver merchandise sold, $120; terms n/10.

8 Issued Check No. 386 to pay Voucher No. 404, less return and less a 2% discount.

9 Issued Check No. 387 to pay Voucher No. 406.

12 Prepared Voucher No. 409 payable to Ames Insurance Company for $300, the three-year premium on an insurance policy. Issued Check No. 388 to pay Voucher No. 409.

13 Issued Check No. 389 to pay Voucher No. 407.

15 Prepared Voucher No. 410 payable to Cash for $2,000 salaries for the first half of May. Issued Check No. 390 in payment of Voucher No. 410. Cashed the check and paid employees in cash.

16 Issued Check No. 391 to pay Voucher No. 408.

23 Prepared Voucher No. 411 payable to Manders Company for merchandise with an invoice price of $300 on invoice dated May 22; terms are 2/10, n/30, FOB shipping point, freight collect.

24 Prepare Voucher No. 412 payable to Short Lines, Inc., for $50 freight on merchandise purchased on May 23.

26 Prepared Voucher No. 413 payable to Bell Telephone Company for $125 for monthly telephone service.

28 Prepared Voucher No. 414 payable to We-Deliver, Inc., for costs incurred to deliver merchandise sold, $80; terms n/30.

31 Prepared Voucher No. 415 payable to Cash for salaries for the last half of May, $2,200. Issued Check No. 392 in payment of Voucher No. 415. Cashed the check and paid employees in cash.

Required: a. Record the transactions above, using a voucher register, check register, and a general journal.

b. Prepare a Vouchers Payable account, and post the portions of the entries that affect this account.

c. Prepare a schedule (list) of unpaid vouchers to prove the accuracy of the balance in the Vouchers Payable account.

Solution to demonstration problem 7–3

a.

					VOUCHER REGISTER*								*Page 12*

Date 1987	Vouch-er No.	Payee	Paid		Vouchers Payable Cr.	Pur-chases Dr.	Freight-In Dr.	Delivery Expense Dr.	Salaries Expense Dr.	Other Accounts Dr.		
			Date	Ck. No.						Account Name	Post. Ref.	Amount Dr.
May 1	406	Carol Company	5/9	387	400	400						
5	407	Allen Brothers	5/13	389	1,000	950	50					
6	408	API, Inc.	5/16	391	120			120				
12	409	Ames Insurance Company	5/12	388	300					Unexpired Insurance		300
15	410	Cash	5/15	390	2,000				2,000			
23	411	Manders Company			300	300						
24	412	Short-Lines, Inc.			50		50					
26	413	Bell Telephone Company			125					Telephone Expense		125
28	414	We-Deliver, Inc.			80			80				
31	415	Cash	5/31	392	2,200				2,200			
					6,575	1,650	100	200	4,200			425

* A column for terms could have been included.

		CHECK REGISTER					*Page 5*

Date 1987	Payee	Voucher No.	Check No.	Vouchers Payable Dr.	Purchase Discounts Cr.	Cash Cr.
May 2	Hanson Company	405	385	50		50
8	Akers Company	404	386	750	15	735
9	Carol Company	406	387	400	8	392
12	Ames Insurance Company	409	388	300		300
13	Allen Brothers	407	389	1,000	19	981
15	Cash	410	390	2,000		2,000
16	API, Inc.	408	391	120		120
31	Cash	415	392	2,200		2,200
				6,820	42	6,778

GENERAL JOURNAL   *Page 17*

Date		Account Titles and Explanation	Post. Ref.	Debit	Credit
1987 May	4	Vouchers Payable		1 0 0	
		Purchase Returns and Allowances			1 0 0
		To record receipt of credit memo for merchandise			
		returned. Voucher No. 404.			

b.

GENERAL LEDGER

Vouchers Payable   *Account No. 201*

Date		Explanation	Post. Ref.	Debit	Credit	Balance
1987 Apr.	30	Beginning balance				9 0 0 Cr.
May	4	Credit memo; Voucher No. 404	J17	1 0 0		8 0 0 Cr.
	31		VR12		6 5 7 5	7 3 7 5 Cr.
	31		CR5	6 8 2 0		5 5 5 Cr.

c.   SCHEDULE OF
          UNPAID VOUCHERS

Voucher No.	Amount
411 . . .	$300
412 . . .	50
413 . . .	125
414 . . .	80
Total . .	$555

QUESTIONS

1. Why should a system of internal control be established?

2. Identify some features that, if present, would strengthen an internal control system.

3. Name some control documents that are used in merchandise transactions.

4. What are the four objectives sought in effective cash management?

5. List four essential features of a system of internal control over cash receipts.

6. The bookkeeper of a given company was stealing cash received from customers in payment of their accounts. To conceal the theft, the bookkeeper made out false credit memos indicating returns and allowances made by or granted to customers. What feature of internal control would have prevented the thefts?

7. List six essential features of a system of internal control over cash disbursements.

8. "The difference between a company's Cash account balance and the balance on its bank statement is usually a matter of timing." Do you agree or disagree? Why?

9. Explain how transfer bank accounts can help bring about effective cash management.

10. Describe the operation of a petty cash fund, and cite the advantages from its use. Indicate how control is maintained over petty cash transactions.

11. Explain how the net price method of accounting for purchases can improve internal control.

12. What can be accomplished with a voucher system that is not accomplished through use of a purchases journal and a cash disbursements journal?

13. What should be the relationship between the balance in the Vouchers Payable account, the "open" items in the voucher register, and the total of all vouchers in the unpaid vouchers file?

14. You are the chief accountant of the Magnuson Company. An invoice has just been received from the Arnott Company in the amount of $2,000, with credit terms of 2/10, n/30. List the procedures you would follow in processing this invoice through the point of filing it in the unpaid vouchers file.

15. Refer to the situation described in Question 14. Assume that the time for payment of the voucher has arrived and the payment is to be made within the discount period. List the actions that would be taken if the company uses the net price method.

16. What would the procedures be if the discount period had elapsed before payment was made in Question 15?

17. List the posting steps that would be used to post the data shown in Illustration 7.11. How many amounts would actually be posted?

EXERCISES

E–1

Answer true-false questions about internal control

State whether each of the following statements about internal control is true or false:

a. Those persons responsible for safeguarding an asset should maintain the accounting records for that asset.

b. Complete, accurate, and up-to-date accounting records should be maintained.

c. Whenever possible, responsibilities should be assigned and duties subdivided in such a way that only one person is responsible for a given function.

d. Employees should be assigned to one job and should remain in that job so that skill levels will be as high as possible.

e. The use of check protectors, check registers, and time clocks is recommended.

f. An internal auditing function should not be implemented because it leads the employees to believe that management does not trust them.

g. One of the best protections against theft is to hire honest, competent employees.

h. A foolproof system of internal control can be devised if management puts forth the effort.

E–2

Answer multiple-choice question about internal control

Concerning internal control, which one of the following statements is correct? Explain.

a. Broadly speaking, internal control is only necessary in very large organizations.

b. The purposes of internal control are to check the accuracy of accounting data, safeguard assets against theft, promote efficiency of operations, and ensure that management's policies are being followed.

c. Once an internal control system has been established, it should be effective as long as the formal organization remains unchanged.

d. An example of internal control is having one individual count the day's cash receipts and compare the total with the total of the cash register tapes.

E–3

Determine available cash balance from bank statement and Cash account data

The bank statement for the Davis Company at the end of August showed a balance of $34,300. Checks outstanding totaled $10,500, and deposits in transit were $15,975. If these are the only pertinent data available to you, what was the adjusted balance of cash at the end of August?

E–4

Prepare bank reconciliation statement and specify cash available

From the following data, prepare a bank reconciliation statement, and determine the correct available cash balance for ACE, Inc., as of October 31, 1987.

Balance per bank statement, October 31, 1987 . .	$9,316
Ledger account balance, October 31, 1987	5,392
Note collected by bank not yet entered in ledger . .	4,000
Bank charges not yet entered by Ace, Inc	12
Deposits in transit	1,120
Outstanding checks:	
No. 327	436
No. 328	192
No. 329	260
No. 331	168

E–5

Record necessary journal entries

The following is a bank reconciliation statement for the Carraway Company as of August 31, 1987:

Balance per bank, August 31, 1987 . .		$1,245
Add: Deposit in transit		946
		$2,191
Less: Outstanding checks		1,004
Adjusted balance, August 31, 1987 . .		$1,187
Balance per books, August 31, 1987 . .		$1,208
Add: Error correction		9*
		$1,217
Less: NSF check	$25	
Service charges	5	30
Adjusted balance, August 31, 1987 . .		$1,187

* The error occurred when the bookkeeper debited Accounts Payable and credited Cash for $32, instead of the correct amount, $23.

Prepare the journal entry needed to adjust or correct the Cash account.

E–6

Determine checks outstanding

On March 1 of the current year, the Jarman Company had outstanding checks of $30,000. During March, the company issued an additional $114,000 of checks. As of March 31, the bank statement showed $96,000 of checks had cleared the bank during the month. What is the amount of outstanding checks on March 31?

E–7

Determine deposits in transit

The Long Company's bank statement as of August 31, 1987, shows total deposits into the company's account of $12,835 and a total of 14 separate deposits. On July 31, deposits of $675 and $525 were in transit. The total cash receipts for August were $16,460, and the company's records show 13 deposits made in August. What is the amount of deposits in transit at August 31?

E–8

Prepare bank reconciliation statement and necessary journal entry

Smith Company deposits all cash receipts intact each day and makes all payments by check. On October 31, after all posting was completed, its Cash account had a debit balance of $3,460. The bank statement for the month ended on October 31 showed a balance of $3,190. Other data are:

1. Outstanding checks total $340.
2. October 31 cash receipts of $670 were placed in the bank's night depository and do not appear on the bank statement.

3. Bank service charges for October are $12.
4. Check No. 772 for store supplies was entered at $324, but paid by the bank at its actual amount of $252.

Prepare a bank reconciliation statement for Smith as of October 31. Also prepare any needed journal entries.

E–9

Record reimbursement of petty cash fund

On August 31, 1987, the Silver Company's petty cash fund contained coins and currency of $82.40, an IOU from an employee of $10, and vouchers showing expenditures of $40 for postage, $17 for taxi fare, and $46 to entertain a customer. The Petty Cash account shows a balance of $200. The fund is replenished on August 31 because financial statements are to be prepared. What journal entry is required on August 31?

E–10

Record reimbursement of petty cash fund

Use the data in Exercise E–9. What entry would have been required if the amount of coin and currency had been $87? Which of the accounts debited would not appear in the income statement?

E–11

Prepare journal entries regarding petty cash

Austin Company has a $600 petty cash fund. The following occurred in December:

Transactions:

Dec. 2   The petty cash fund was increased to $900.
      8   Petty Cash Voucher No. 318 for $16.14 of delivery expense was prepared and paid. The fund was not replenished at this time.
     20   The company decided that the fund was too large and reduced it to $750.

Prepare any necessary journal entries for the above transactions.

E–12

Record purchases using net price method

Elkins Company uses the net price method for handling purchase discounts.

Prepare the journal entries necessary to record the following 1987 transactions:

Transactions:

Oct. 6   Purchased $300 of merchandise; terms 2/10, n/30.
      7   Purchased $1,000 of merchandise; terms 2/10, n/30.
     17   Paid the invoice for the October 7 purchase.
     31   Paid the invoice for the October 6 purchase.

E–13

Determine vouchers payable balance; compute current month's vouchers paid

Refer to Illustration 7.11.

a.   Assuming that all vouchers written before May 1, 1987, have been paid, what is the balance in the Vouchers Payable account on May 31, 1987?
b.   All checks written in May were in payment of May vouchers. What is the total dollar amount of vouchers paid in May?
c.   Explain how it is possible to determine the cash paid out in May to pay May's vouchers without looking at the check register.

E–14

Prepare general journal entries to record selected transactions and indicate whether recorded in voucher or check register

Lime Company uses a voucher system. Recently the company: *(a)* prepared Voucher No. 801 for purchase of merchandise from Balke Company, $250; *(b)* issued Check No. 723 to pay Voucher No. 801; *(c)* prepared Voucher No. 802 to set up a petty cash fund, $75; *(d)* issued Check No. 724 to pay Voucher No. 802; *(e)* prepared Voucher No. 804 for $10 freight on merchandise in Voucher No. 801; *(f)* prepared Voucher No. 805 to replenish petty cash when it contained cash of $14 and receipts for postage, $33, supplies, $17, and miscellaneous expense, $10; and *(g)* issued Check No. 725 to pay Voucher No. 805.

Prepare entries in general journal form to record the above transactions. Identify the journal or book of original entry in which each transaction would normally appear.

E-15

Describe what amounts and information would appear in a voucher system to record payment for purchase under net price procedure when discount is lost

Assume that Sellars Company uses a voucher register and a check register exactly like Illustration 7.11 and Illustration 7.12. On May 1, Sellars Company purchased merchandise from Baird Company, $1,000; terms 2/10, n/30. Sellars prepared Voucher No. 567 for $980. On May 29, Sellars paid for the merchandise purchased from Baird Company and missed the discount (Check No. 489).

State what information should be entered in the voucher register and the check register to record the payment of May 29. Assume that the last voucher used was 598.

PROBLEMS, SERIES A

P7-1-A

Prepare bank reconciliation statement with necessary journal entries

The following information pertains to the Ulrich Company:

Balance per bank statement, September 30, 1987	$48,900
Ledger account balance for cash on September 30, 1987 . .	42,450
Note collected by bank	3,000
Bank charges	30
Deposits in transit	2,772
NSF check deposited and returned	252
Outstanding checks	5,154
Bank error—deducted $150 from Ulrich account for check actually written for $1,500.	

Required: a. Prepare a bank reconciliation statement as of September 30, 1987.
b. Give the necessary journal entries to correct the accounts.

P7-2-A

Prepare journal entries to record establishment and reimbursement of petty cash fund

Transactions involving the petty cash fund of the Gordon Company during 1987 are as follows:

Transactions:

Mar. 1   Established a petty cash fund of $250, which will be under the control of the assistant office manager.

Apr. 3   Fund was replenished on this date. Prior to replenishment, the fund consisted of the following:

Coins and currency	$163.85
Petty cash vouchers indicating disbursements for—	
Postage stamps	27.00
Supper money for office employees working overtime . .	12.00
Office supplies	10.90
Window washing service	20.00
Flowers for wedding of employee	5.00
Flowers for hospitalized employee	5.00
Employee IOU	5.00

The employee's IOU is to be deducted from the employee's next paycheck.

Required: Present journal entries for the above transactions. Use the Cash Short and Over account for any shortage or overage in the fund.

P7–3–A

Prepare journal entries to record establishment, reimbursement, and increase of a petty cash fund

The Baste Company has decided to use a petty cash fund. Listed below are transactions involving this fund in 1987:

Transactions:

June 4   Set up a petty cash fund of $75.
    22   When the fund had a cash amount of $10.45, the custodian of the fund was reimbursed for expenditures made, including:

Transportation-in . .	$27.50
Postage	9.00
Office supplies . .	27.25

    30   The fund was reimbursed so as to include petty cash items in the financial statements prepared for the fiscal year ending on this date. The fund had the following before reimbursement:

Coins and currency . . .		$58.00
Petty cash vouchers for:		
Employee IOU	$5.00	
Postage	9.00	
Office supplies	3.70	17.70
		$75.70

July 1   The fund balance was raised to $100.

Required: Prepare journal entries for all of the above.

P7–4–A

Prepare bank reconciliation statement with necessary journal entries

The following data pertain to the Cloy Company:

1.   Balance per the bank statement dated June 30, 1987, is $20,380.
2.   Balance of the Cash in Bank account on the company books as of June 30, 1987, is $5,990.
3.   Outstanding checks as of June 30, 1987, total $9,977.
4.   Bank deposit of June 30 for $1,570 was not included in the deposits per the bank statement.
5.   The bank had collected a $15,075 note that it credited to the Cloy Company account. The bank charged the company a collection fee of $10 on the above note.
6.   The bank erroneously charged the Cloy Company account for a $7,000 check of another company that has a similar account number.
7.   Bank service charges for June, exclusive of the collection fee, amounted to $50.
8.   Among the canceled checks was one for $345 given in payment of an account. The bookkeeper had recorded the check at $480 in the company records.
9.   A check of Crosley, a customer, for $2,077, deposited on June 20, was returned by the bank marked NSF. No entry has been made to reflect the returned check on the company records.
10.   A check for $890 of Moran, a customer, which had been deposited in the bank, was erroneously recorded by the bookkeeper as $980.

Required: Prepare a bank reconciliation statement as of June 30, 1987. Also prepare any necessary journal entries.

P7–5–A

Prepare bank reconciliation statement with necessary journal entries

The bank statement of the Yorke Company's checking account with the First National Bank shows:

Balance, June 30, 1987 . .		$ 73,830
Deposits		109,200
		$183,030
Less: Checks deducted . .	$108,000	
Service charges . .	30	108,030
Balance, July 31, 1987 . .		$ 75,000

The following additional data are available:

1.   A credit memorandum included with the bank statement indicated the collection of a note by the bank for the Yorke Company, $6,000.
2.   An NSF check in the amount of $2,760 was returned by the bank and included in the total of checks deducted on the bank statement.

3. Deposits in transit as of July 31 totaled $15,000, and as of June 30, $7,200.
4. Checks outstanding as of June 30, all of which cleared the bank in July, amounted to $10,200; checks outstanding as of July 31 were $24,600.
5. Balance per ledger account as of July 31 was $56,982.
6. The bank added the $12,900 deposit of another company to Yorke's account in error.
7. The bank deducted one of Yorke's checks as $9,000 instead of the correct amount of $900.
8. Deposit of July 21 was recorded by the company as $1,911 and by the bank at the actual amount of $2,019. The receipts for the day were from collections on account.
9. The deposits amount shown on the bank statement includes $300 of interest earned by Yorke on its checking account with the bank.

Required: *a.* Prepare a bank reconciliation statement as of July 31, 1987, for the Yorke Company.
b. Prepare any journal entries needed at July 31, 1987.

P7–6–A

Prepare entries in voucher and check registers, using net price method for purchase discounts

The Wilson Company was organized January 1 of the current year. The company uses a voucher register and a check register with the same column headings as in Illustrations 7.11 and 7.12, except that there are only four voucher register debit columns—headed Merchandise Purchases, Transportation-In, Discounts Lost, and Other Accounts. Vouchers are prepared for the net amount of the invoice. For discounts lost, a new voucher is prepared for the amount of the discount.

Transactions:

Jan. 1 Received an invoice from the Modern Company in the amount of $1,200 for office equipment. Terms were 2/10, n/30, FOB shipping point.
   3 Received an invoice from the Bailey Company for merchandise in the amount of $2,100. Terms were 2/10, n/30.
   5 Received an invoice from the Simpson Company for merchandise in the amount of $1,550. Terms were 2/10, n/30.
   7 Paid $180 to the Lund Advertising Service for services received in January.
  10 Paid $135 of freight charges to the James Company. Of this, $30 was applicable to the office equipment received on January 1 and the rest to merchandise received from the Bailey Company.
  14 Paid the Simpson Company the amount due.
  20 Paid the Bailey Company the correct amount due.
  31 Paid the Thomas Company the net amount of $12,105 for merchandise received today. (Hint: Has the voucher authorizing this payment been prepared?)
  31 The Modern Company voucher of January 1 was misfiled and had not been paid as of the end of the month. A voucher was prepared for the discount missed.

Required: Enter the above approved transactions for the month of January in these registers. Total and rule the registers. Start with Voucher No. 1 and Check No. 1.

P7–7–A

Prepare entries in voucher and check registers, using net price method for purchase discounts; confirm balance in Vouchers Payable

The Bock Company uses a voucher register and a check register with the same column headings as in Illustrations 7.11 and 7.12, except that there are only four voucher register debit columns—headed Merchandise Purchases, Transportation-In, Discounts Lost, and Other Accounts. The last voucher number used was 9743, and the last check issued was No. 2096. As of August 31, 1987, there were three vouchers in the unpaid voucher file:

Voucher No. 9696 . . $1,320
Voucher No. 9741 . .   2,660
Voucher No. 9742 . .   1,140
                      $5,120

The total of the unpaid voucher file agreed with the credit balance in the Vouchers Payable control account.

The following transactions occurred during September 1987. Vouchers are prepared for the net amount of the invoice. For any discounts lost, a new voucher is prepared for the amount of the discount.

Transactions:

Sept. 3 Paid Citizens Bank $1,220 for a noninterest-bearing note that matured on this date.
5 Received an invoice for $1,700 from the Reese Company for merchandise. Terms were 2/10, n/30.
6 Paid Voucher No. 9696 to the Tims Company, $1,320.
10 Received an invoice for $588 from the Zink Company for merchandise. Terms were 2/10, n/30.
15 Paid the Reese Company the amount owed on its invoice of September 5.
17 Paid $260 to the Jacklin Company for advertising in September.
30 Paid $17,800 to the Arlin Company. This amount included $356 chargeable to the Transportation-In account. The balance paid was the net cost of merchandise received today. Terms were 2/10, n/30.
30 Paid the Zink Company the amount due on the purchase of September 10.

Required: Enter these transactions in the voucher register and the check register. You need not show unpaid vouchers from preceding months in the voucher register. Total and rule the registers as of September 30. List the unpaid vouchers at September 30, and compare the total with the balance in the Vouchers Payable control account (Account No. 250) at that date after posting has been completed.

PROBLEMS, SERIES B

P7–1–B

Prepare bank reconciliation statement with necessary journal entries

The bank statement for Polk, Inc., showed a balance of $11,701.90 on July 31, 1987. On the same date, the company's Cash account balance was $8,259.30. Returned with the bank statement was a credit memorandum for $2,050 for a note that was collected by the bank for the company. There were two debit memoranda—one for service charges of $19 and one for an NSF Check of Greer Company for $70. By comparing the canceled checks with the check register, it was found that $4,861.60 of checks were outstanding. The deposit made after banking hours on July 31 of $3,380 was not listed on the bank statement.

Required: a. Prepare a bank reconciliation statement for July 31, 1987.
b. Prepare any necessary journal entries.

P7–2–B

Prepare journal entries to record establishment and reimbursement of petty cash fund

The following data pertain to the petty cash fund of the Benson Company during 1987:

Transactions:

Nov. 2 A $600 check is drawn, cashed, and the cash placed in the care of the assistant office manager to be used as a petty cash fund.
Dec. 17 The fund is replenished. An analysis of the fund shows:

Coins and currency	$196.54
Petty cash vouchers for—	
Delivery expenses	231.30
Transportation-in	148.16
Postage stamps purchased	20.00

31 The end of the accounting period falls on this date. The fund was replenished. The fund's contents on this date consist of—

Coins and currency	$469.40
Petty cash vouchers for—	
Delivery expenses	42.20
Postage stamps purchased	48.40
Employee's IOU	40.00

Required: Present journal entries to record the above transactions. Use the Cash Short and Over account for any shortage or overage in the fund.

P7–3–B

*Prepare journal
entries to record
establishment,
reimbursement, and
increase of petty
cash fund*

The following data relate to the petty cash fund of the Boone Wrecking Company in 1987:

Transactions:

Apr. 1 The petty cash fund is set up with a $150 cash balance.

19 Because the money in the fund is down to $31.20, the fund is replenished. Petty cash vouchers are as follows:

Flowers for hospitalized employee (miscellaneous expense)	$37.50
Postage stamps	60.00
Office supplies	20.76

30 The cash in the fund is $80.25. The fund is replenished to include petty cash payments in this period's financial statements. The petty cash vouchers are for the following:

Transportation-in	$28.50
Office supplies	41.25

May 1 The petty cash fund balance is increased to $225.

Required: Prepare the journal entries to record the above transactions.

P7–4–B

*Prepare bank
reconciliation
statement with
necessary journal
entries*

The following information pertains to the Megee Company. The June 30 bank reconciliation statement follows:

	Cash account	Bank statement
Balance on June 30	$12,762.24	$12,429.54
Add: Deposit not credited by bank. .		628.40
Total		$13,057.94
Deduct: Outstanding checks:		
No. 724 . . . . $ 12.30		
No. 886 . . . . 10.00		
No. 896 . . . . 95.70		
No. 897 . . . . 125.10		
No. 898 . . . . 52.60		295.70
Adjusted cash balance, June 30 . . .	$12,762.24	$12,762.24

The July bank statement appears below:

Balance on July 1		$12,429.54	
Deposits during July		3,627.96	$16,057.50
Canceled checks returned:			
No. 724	$ 12.30		
No. 896	95.70		
No. 897	125.10		
No. 898	52.60		
No. 899	12.57		
No. 900	899.70		
No. 902	631.28		
No. 904	29.34	$ 1,858.59	
NSF check of Manley Company . . .		93.32	1,951.91
Bank statement balance, July 31 . . .			$14,105.59

The cash receipts deposited in July, including receipts of July 31, amounted to $3,452.20. Checks written in July are listed below:

No. 899 . .	$ 12.57
No. 900 . .	899.70
No. 901 . .	18.50
No. 902 . .	631.28
No. 903 . .	39.80
No. 904 . .	29.34
No. 905 . .	729.00
No. 906 . .	10.00

The cash balance per the ledger on July 31 was $13,844.25.

Required: Prepare a bank reconciliation statement and any necessary journal entries.

P7–5–B

Prepare bank reconciliation statement with necessary journal entries

The following information pertains to the Boyer Company as of May 31, 1987:

1. Balance per bank statement as of May 31, 1987, was $21,960.
2. Balance per the Boyer Company's Cash account at May 31, 1987, was $22,624.
3. A late deposit on May 31 did not appear on the bank statement, $1,900.
4. Outstanding checks as of May 31 totaled $3,384.
5. During May, the bank credited Boyer Company with the proceeds, $3,020, of a noninterest-bearing note which it had collected for the company.
6. Service and collection charges for the month amounted to $8.
7. Comparison of the canceled checks with copies of these checks revealed that one check in the amount of $648 had been recorded in the books at $684. The check had been issued in payment of an account payable.
8. A review of the deposit slips with the bank statement showed that a deposit for $1,000 of a company with a similar account number had been credited to the Boyer Company account in error.
9. A $120 check received from a customer, R. Perry, was returned with the bank statement marked NSF.
10. During May, the bank paid a $6,060 noninterest-bearing note of the Boyer Company and charged it to the company's account per instructions received. Boyer Company had not recorded the payment of this note.
11. An examination of the cash receipts and the deposit tickets revealed that the bookkeeper erroneously recorded a check from a customer, C. Smith, of $648 as $864.
12. The bank statement showed a credit to the company's account for interest earned on the account balance in May of $200.

Required: a. Prepare a bank reconciliation statement as of May 31, 1987.
b. Prepare the journal entries necessary to adjust the accounts as of May 31, 1987.

P7–6–B

Prepare entries in voucher and check registers, using net price method for purchase discounts

The Eckart Company was organized January 1 of the current year, 1987. It uses a voucher register and a check register with the same column headings as in Illustrations 7.11 and 7.12, except that there are only four voucher register debit columns—headed Merchandise Purchases, Transportation-In, Discounts Lost, and Other Accounts.

Vouchers are prepared for the net amount of the invoice. For discounts lost, a new voucher is prepared for the amount of the discount.

Transactions:

Jan. 2   Received merchandise from the Lind Company, with terms of 2/10, n/30. The invoice received was in the amount of $5,200.
3   Paid transportation charges to Moyer Trucking Company on purchase of January 2, $87.
6   Paid Wilson Display Company $3,300 for billboard advertising for a three-month period beginning February 1, 1987.
15   Paid the Lind Company for the purchase of January 2.
17   Received merchandise from Bradly Company, with terms of 2/10, n/30. The invoice received was for $4,200.
18   Received merchandise from Casp Company, with terms of 2/10, n/30. The invoice received was for $17,750. Paid net amount today to establish a good credit rating.
23   Received invoice for $1,800 from Office Equipment, Inc., for office equipment recently received. Terms are 2/10, n/30.

Required: Enter the above approved transactions for the month of January in these registers, and total and rule the registers. Start with Voucher No. 1 and Check No. 1.

To adhere to the matching principle, the bad debts operating expense must be matched against the revenues it generates. Thus, a bad debt arising from a sale made in 1987 must be treated as a 1987 expense even though to do so requires the use of estimates. Estimates are necessary because the company cannot determine until 1988 or later which customer accounts existing at year-end 1987 will become uncollectible.

Recording the Bad Debts Adjustment.   When bad debts are estimated, the company makes an adjusting entry at the end of each accounting period. Bad Debts Expense is debited, thus recording the operating expense in the proper period. The credit is to an account called Allowance for Doubtful Accounts (also called Allowance for Bad Debts or Allowance for Uncollectible Accounts).

The **Allowance for Doubtful Accounts** is a contra-asset account to the Accounts Receivable account; it reduces accounts receivable to their net realizable value. **Net realizable value** is the amount expected to be collected from accounts receivable. The allowance lets the company show, without crediting the Accounts Receivable control account, that a certain amount of the accounts receivable will not be collected. When the bad debts adjusting entry is made, the company does not know which specific accounts will be uncollectible. If the specific uncollectible accounts and their amounts were known, they would be written off immediately. However, since the specific uncollectible accounts are not known, credits cannot be entered in either the Accounts Receivable control account or the customers' subsidiary ledger accounts. If only one or the other was credited, the Accounts Receivable control account balance would not agree with the total of the balances in the accounts receivable subsidiary ledger.

To illustrate the adjusting entry for bad debts, assume that a company has $100,000 of accounts receivable and estimates its bad debts expense for a given year at $4,000. The required year-end adjusting entry is:

```
Dec. 31   Bad Debts Expense .   .   .   .   .   .   .   .   .   .   .   .   4,000
               Allowance for Doubtful Accounts .   .   .   .   .   .   .           4,000
          To record estimated bad debts
```

The debit to Bad Debts Expense brings about the desired matching of expenses and revenues; bad debts expense is matched against the revenues of the accounting period. The credit to Allowance for Doubtful Accounts reduces accounts receivable to their net realizable value. Bad Debts Expense is closed to Income Summary when the books are closed. The allowance is reported on the balance sheet as a deduction from accounts receivable as follows:

```
Accounts receivable .   .   .   .   .   .   .   .   .   $100,000
   Less: Allowance for doubtful accounts .   .      4,000    $96,000
```

Recording the estimated amount of bad debts accomplishes two goals: (1) bad debts expense is matched against revenues in the year of sale, and (2) accounts receivable are shown on the balance sheet at their net realizable value. Now the question is: How is the estimate of bad debts determined? The next section answers this question.

Estimating Bad Debts.   There are two basic methods for estimating bad debts for a period. The first method—percentage-of-sales method—focuses attention on the income statement and the relationship of bad debts to sales.

The second method—percentage-of-receivables method—focuses attention on the balance sheet and the relationship of the allowance for doubtful accounts to accounts receivable. Either of these two estimation methods is acceptable, and over time the results obtained under both methods are likely to be quite similar. However, some accountants prefer the percentage-of-sales method because it does a better job of matching expenses with revenues.

Percentage-of-Sales Method.   The **percentage-of-sales method** estimates uncollectible accounts from a given period's sales. In theory, the method is based on a percentage of prior years' actual bad debt losses to prior years' credit sales. **If cash sales are small or make up a fairly constant percentage of total sales, the calculation can be based on total net sales.** Since at least one of these conditions is usually met, total net sales rather than credit sales are commonly used.

The percentage of uncollectible bad debts to last year's sales is reviewed annually to see if it is still valid; if not, the percentage is increased or decreased to reflect the changed condition. For example, in periods of inflation and high interest rates, the percentage rate may have to be increased to reflect decreased customer ability to pay. Alternatively, if the company adopts a more stringent credit policy, the percentage rate may have to be decreased because fewer uncollectible accounts are expected.

To illustrate, assume that the Rankin Company's uncollectible accounts from 1985 sales were 1.1% of total net sales. It does not matter when the accounts were found to be uncollectible; the important point is that they arose from 1985 sales. A similar calculation for 1986 showed a bad debt percentage of 0.9%. The average for the two years is 1% [(1.1 + 0.9) ÷ 2]. The Rankin Company does not expect 1987 to differ from the average of the previous two years. Total net sales for 1987 were $600,000; receivables at year-end are $100,000; and the Allowance for Doubtful Accounts has a zero balance. Rankin would make the following adjusting entry for 1987:

```
Dec. 31   Bad Debts Expense .  .  .  .  .  .  .  .  .  .  .  .  .  .  . 6,000
                Allowance for Doubtful Accounts .  .  .  .  .  .  .  .           6,000
              To record estimated bad debts ($600,000 × 0.01).
```

Bad Debts Expense is closed to Income Summary. The accounts receivable less the allowance is reported among current assets in the balance sheet as follows:

```
Accounts receivable .  .  .  .  .  .  .  .  . $100,000
   Less: Allowance for doubtful accounts .  .     6,000   $94,000
```

This information could also be presented in a published balance sheet as:

```
Accounts receivable (less estimated
   uncollectible accounts, $6,000)  .  .  .  .  .  .  .  .  $94,000
```

The Allowance for Doubtful Accounts account usually has a balance prior to the year-end adjustment. **Under the percentage-of-sales method, any existing balance in the allowance generally is ignored in calculating the amount of the year-end adjustment.** The expense and addition to the allowance are based on the past average relationship of actual bad debts to either credit sales or total net sales. Any given year can be expected to vary from the average. Hence, minor balances in the allowance account are ignored.

Assume that in the example above, Rankin's allowance had a $300 credit balance prior to adjustment. The adjusting entry would be the same. But the balance sheet would show $100,000 accounts receivable less a $6,300 allowance for net receivables of $93,700. Bad Debts Expense would still appear on the income statement as 1% of credit sales, or $6,000.

Percentage-of-Receivables Method.   The **percentage-of-receivables method** estimates bad debts by determining the desired size of the allowance for doubtful accounts. The ending balance in Accounts Receivable is multiplied by a rate (or rates) based on past experience regarding uncollectible accounts. In the percentage-of-receivables method, either an overall rate may be used or a different rate may be used for each age category of receivables.

The overall rate of the percentage-of-receivables method is calculated as follows. Using the same information as before, Rankin will make an estimate of bad debts at the end of the 1987. The balance of accounts receivable is $100,000, and the allowance account has no balance. If Rankin estimates that 6% of the receivables will be uncollectible, the adjusting entry is the same as before:

```
Dec. 31   Bad Debts Expense .  .   .   .   .   .   .   .   .   .   .   .   6,000
               Allowance for Doubtful Accounts .   .   .   .   .   .   .       6,000
          To record estimated bad debts ($100,000 × 0.06).
```

If there was a $300 credit balance in the allowance, the entry would be the same as the one just given, except that the amount would be for $5,700. The difference in amounts arises because the firm wants the allowance to contain a balance equal to 6% of the outstanding receivables when the two accounts are presented on the balance sheet. **Thus, under the percentage-of-receivables method, any balance in the allowance must be considered when adjusting for bad debts.**

As another example, suppose that Rankin had a $300 **debit** balance in the allowance prior to adjustment. In this case, a credit of $6,300 would be necessary to get the balance to the required $6,000 credit balance. T-accounts would show:

Bad Debts Expense		**Allowance for Doubtful Accounts**	
Dec. 31 Adjustment 6,300		Bal. before adjustment 300	Dec. 31 Adjustment 6,300
			Bal. after adjustment 6,000

No matter what the preadjustment allowance balance is, using the percentage-of-receivables method Rankin Company will adjust the Allowance for Doubtful Accounts so that it has a credit balance of $6,000—which is equal to 6% of its $100,000 in Accounts Receivable.

When the percentage-of-receivables method is calculated by using a **different rate** for each age category of receivables, an aging schedule is used. An **aging schedule** classifies accounts receivable according to their age (how long they have been outstanding) and uses a different uncollectibility percentage rate for each age category. The percentages used are based on past experience. An aging schedule is presented in Illustration 8.1. This schedule shows that the older a receivable is, the more likely it will not be collected.

Illustration 8.1

*Accounts
Receivable Aging
Schedule*

| Customer | Debit Balance | Not Yet Due | Number of Days Past Due | | | |
			1–30	31–60	61–90	Over 90
X	$ 5,000					$ 5,000
Y	14,000		$ 12,000	$2,000		
Z	400				$200	200
All others	808,600	$560,000	240,000	2,000	600	6,000
	$828,000	$560,000	$252,000	$4,000	$800	$11,200
Estimated uncollectible percentage		1%	5%	10%	25%	50%
Estimated amount uncollectible	$ 24,400	$ 5,600	$ 12,600	$ 400	$200	$ 5,600

DARCY COMPANY
Accounts Receivable Aging Schedule
December 31, 1987

Classifying accounts receivable according to age gives the company a basis for estimating the total amount of uncollectible accounts. For example, only 1% of the accounts not yet due (sales made less than 30 days prior to the end of the accounting period) are expected to be uncollectible. At the other extreme, 50% of all accounts over 90 days past due are expected to be uncollectible. For each age category, the accounts receivable are multiplied by the estimated uncollectible percentage to find the estimated amount uncollectible. The sum of the estimated amounts uncollectible for all categories yields the total estimated amount uncollectible and is the desired credit balance in the Allowance for Doubtful Accounts.

Since the aging schedule is used under the percentage-of-receivables method, the journal entry to record bad debts is affected by the balance in the allowance prior to adjustment. For example, Illustration 8.1 shows that $24,400 is needed in the allowance. If the allowance currently has a $5,000 credit balance, the adjustment will be for $19,400.

The information contained in an aging schedule may be useful to management for purposes other than estimating bad debts. Visible information on collection patterns of accounts receivable may suggest the need for changes in credit policies or for added financing. For example, if the age of many customer balances has increased to the 61–90 days past-due category, collection efforts may have to be strengthened, or the company may have to find other sources of cash to pay its debts.

The process of estimating the amount of a company's uncollectible accounts establishes the Allowance for Doubtful Accounts, which is a contra account to the Accounts Receivable account. As time passes and it becomes evident that certain customer accounts will not be collected, these accounts must be written off. In the next section you will learn how accountants write off uncollectible accounts.

Write-Off of Receivables. When a specific customer's account is considered uncollectible, a portion of the allowance account, as well as the specific customer's account, is written off. The Allowance for Doubtful Accounts is debited. The credit is to the Accounts Receivable control account in the general ledger and to the customer's subsidiary ledger account in the accounts receivable subsidiary ledger. For example, assume Smith's $750 account has been determined to be uncollectible. The entry to write off this account is:

Allowance for Doubtful Accounts	750	
Accounts Receivable—Smith		750
To write Smith's account off as uncollectible.		

The credit balance that existed in Allowance for Doubtful Accounts before the above entry was made represented potential bad debts that had not yet been specifically identified. Debiting the allowance account shows that the particular account of Smith has now been **identified** as uncollectible. Notice that this debit entry in the write-off of receivables **does not involve recording an expense.** The bad debts expense was recognized in the year of the sale. If Smith's $750 uncollectible account is recorded in Bad Debts Expense again, it would be "double counted" as an expense.

The net realizable value of accounts receivable is not affected by a write-off. For example, suppose that Amos Company has total accounts receivable of $50,000 and an allowance of $3,000 before the above entry; the net realizable value of the accounts receivable is $47,000, as shown below. After posting the above entry, accounts receivable are $49,250, and the allowance is $2,250; net realizable value is still $47,000.

	Before write-off	After write-off
Accounts receivable	$50,000	$49,250
Allowance for doubtful accounts . .	3,000	2,250
Net realizable value	$47,000	$47,000

If the Allowance for Doubtful Accounts is adjusted only at year-end, it may have a debit balance before adjustment. One reason for this debit balance is that companies do not often carry accounts receivable in their records that are more than one year old. Consequently, by the end of 1987, all accounts from 1986 sales will have either been collected or written off. If the estimates were exact, the allowance resulting from 1986 would have a zero balance. But it may develop a debit balance if estimates were less than actual write-offs. Also, some accounts from 1987 sales probably have been charged off in 1987. Yet no bad debts adjusting entry has been made for 1987. The result is very likely to be a debit balance in the allowance account before the annual adjustment.

After a company has used the allowance method for several years, the balance in the allowance consists of the net amount of inadequate or excessive estimates of bad debts of prior years. Errors in estimating preceding years' uncollectibles are corrected by increasing or decreasing the current year's estimate.

Bad Debts Recovered.   Sometimes accounts considered to be uncollectible are collected after the account has already been written off. A company usually learns that an account has been written off erroneously when payment, by cash or check, is received. When the payment is received, the original write-off is reversed. The account is reinstated by debiting the Accounts Receivable and crediting Allowance for Doubtful Accounts for the amount received. The debit is posted to both the general ledger account and to the customer's subsidiary ledger account. The amount received is also recorded as a debit to Cash and a credit to Accounts Receivable. The credit is posted to both the general ledger account and to the customer's subsidiary ledger account.

To illustrate, assume that on May 17 a $750 check is received from Smith in payment of the account that was previously written off. The two required journal entries are:

May 17	Accounts Receivable—Smith	750	
	Allowance for Doubtful Accounts		750
	To reverse original write-off of Smith's account.		
17	Cash	750	
	Accounts Receivable—Smith		750
	To record collection of account.		

If only part of a previously written off account is collected, the usual procedure is to reinstate only that portion of the account actually collected unless there is evidence that the entire account will be collected.

The Direct Write-Off Method for Recording Bad Debts

In contrast to the allowance method of writing off bad debts, the **direct write-off method** directly charges the identified uncollectible accounts receivable to an expense account, Bad Debts Expense. No adjusting entry is made to record estimated bad debts. This method is used by some companies with accounts receivable and bad debts so small that they are immaterial.

To illustrate this method, assume that a $200 account for Robert Hill is considered uncollectible. Under the direct write-off method, the journal entry to write off the account is:

Bad Debts Expense	200	
Accounts Receivable—Robert Hill		200
To write off an uncollectible account.		

Assume that several months later, $125 is received on Robert Hill's account. The required journal entries are:

Accounts Receivable—Robert Hill	125	
Bad Debts Expense		125
To reinstate portion of account written off.		
Cash	125	
Accounts Receivable—Robert Hill		125
To record collection on account.		

Although acceptable for income tax purposes, the direct write-off method is not acceptable for financial accounting in most cases because (1) it does not properly match expenses and revenues, and (2) it overstates accounts receivable in the balance sheet because the allowance for doubtful accounts is not used.

Because of the bad debts that may arise when a company offers customers its credit, many companies now allow customers to use bank or external credit cards. As you will see, this relieves the company of the headaches involved in trying to collect overdue accounts.

Credit Cards

Credit cards are charge cards such as American Express, Diners Club, VISA, and MasterCard that are used by customers to charge purchases of goods and services. Businesses that find bad debt losses and other costs of extending credit a burden pass these costs on to banks and other credit agencies issuing national credit cards. These businesses must pay a service charge of from 2% to 8% of the sales price to the credit agency. Credit card agencies then absorb the bad debts and costs of extending credit and maintaining records previously borne by the company.

Credit card agencies issue credit cards, often at an annual fee, to approved credit applicants. When a business agrees to honor these credit cards, it also agrees to pay the percentage fee charged by the credit card agency. Upon making a credit card sale, the seller checks the customer's card against a list of canceled cards and calls the credit agency for approval if the sale exceeds a prescribed amount, such as $50. This procedure allows the seller to avoid accepting a lost, stolen, or canceled card. Also, the credit agency is protected from the sale causing the customer to exceed an established credit limit. The accounting procedures of the seller differ depending on whether the business accepted a nonbank or a bank credit card.

To illustrate the entries for the use of **nonbank** credit cards (such as American Express or Diners Club), assume that a restaurant has Diners Club invoices amounting to $1,400 at the end of a day. The restaurant makes the following entry:

Accounts Receivable—Diners Club	1,400	
Sales		1,400
To record credit card sales.		

The invoices are mailed to Diners Club. Payment is received from Diners Club some time later with a 5% service charge deducted. Then the following entry is made:

Cash	1,330	
Credit Card Expense	70	
Accounts Receivable—Diners Club		1,400
To record remittance from Diners Club.		

Credit card expense is the credit card agency's service charge for services rendered in processing credit card sales.

To illustrate the accounting entries for the use of **bank** credit cards (such as VISA or MasterCard), assume that a retailer has made sales of $1,000 for which VISA cards were accepted and the VISA service charge is $50 (or 5 percent of sales). VISA sales are treated as cash sales because the receipt of cash is certain. The sales invoices are deposited in a checking account maintained in a bank just as checks are deposited in a regular checking account. The entry to record this deposit is:

Cash	950	
Credit Card Expense	50	
Sales		1,000
To record VISA credit card sales.		

Credit card companies bill the customer for all sales charges made during the month. If the customer fails to pay, the credit card company, not the retailer, suffers the loss.

So far in this chapter, we have discussed recording revenue from accounts receivable using the accrual basis of accounting and adhering to the matching principle of accounting. Accounts receivable refer to the credit sales that are made through the seller extending credit or the buyer using a credit card. No formal written promises to pay are required. However, many companies have transactions in which written promises to pay (notes) are used to account for sales, purchases, or loans. The remainder of this chapter discusses notes receivable and notes payable.

■ NOTES RECEIVABLE AND NOTES PAYABLE

In Chapter 4, you learned that a note (also called a **promissory note**) is an unconditional written promise by a borrower **(maker)** to pay a definite sum of money to the lender **(payee)** on demand or on a specific date. A note is a receivable on the balance sheet of the lender (payee); it is a payable on the balance sheet of the borrower (maker). Since the note is usually negotiable, the payee may transfer it to another party, who then receives payment from the maker. An example of a promissory note is shown in Illustration 8.2.

Illustration 8.2

Promissory Note

$ 2,000.00	June 1 , 19 87

Sixty days- -AFTER DATE We PROMISE TO PAY TO

THE ORDER OF **MOTOR WHEEL CORPORATION**

Two Thousand and no/100- -DOLLARS

AT Motor Wheel Corporation, Lansing, Michigan

FOR VALUE RECEIVED WITH INTEREST AT THE RATE OF 10% PER ANNUM FROM June 1, 1987

This note is one of a series of 1 notes of even date herewith, numbered 487 to -- inclusive, and all of said notes shall become immediately due and payable at the option of the holder hereof on default being made in the payment of any one at maturity.

NO. 487 DUE July 31, 1987 THE PETERSON COMPANY

John J. Lucia, Treasurer

A customer may give a note to a business for an amount due on an account receivable or for the sale of a large item such as a refrigerator. Also, a business may give a note to a supplier in exchange for merchandise to sell or to a bank or an individual for a loan. Thus, a company may have notes receivable or payable arising from transactions with customers, suppliers, banks, or individuals.

Interest Calculation

Most promissory notes have an explicit interest charge. **Interest** is the fee charged for use of money through time. To the maker of the note, or borrower, interest is an expense; to the payee of the note, or lender, interest is a revenue. A borrower incurs interest expense; a lender earns interest revenue. For convenience, interest is commonly calculated on the basis of a 360-day year.

The basic formula for computing interest is:

$$\text{Interest} = \text{Principal} \times \text{Rate} \times \text{Time, or } I = P \times R \times T$$

Principal is the face value of the note. The **rate** is the stated interest rate on the note; interest rates are generally stated on an annual basis. **Time** is the amount of time the note is to run; it can be expressed in either days or months.

To show how interest is calculated, assume a company borrowed $20,000 from a bank. The note has a principal (face value) of $20,000, an interest rate of 15%, and a life of 90 days. The interest calculation is:

$$\text{Interest} = \$20,000 \times 0.15 \times 90/360$$
$$\text{Interest} = \$750$$

Note that in this calculation the time period is expressed as a fraction of a 360-day "year" because the interest rate is expressed on an annual basis.

Determination of Maturity Date

The maturity date is the date on which a note becomes due and payment must be made. The wording used in the note expresses the maturity date and determines when the note is to be paid. Examples of the maturity date wording are:

1. *On demand.* "On demand, I promise to pay. . . ." In this case, the maturity date is at the option of the holder and cannot be computed. The holder is the payee or another person who legally acquired the note from the payee.
2. *On a stated date.* "On July 18, 1986, I promise to pay. . . ." The maturity date is designated, and a computation is not necessary to determine it.
3. *At the end of a stated period.*
   a. "One year after date, I promise to pay. . . ." If the maturity is expressed in years, the note matures on the same day of the same month as the date of the note in the year of maturity.
   b. "Four months after date, I promise to pay. . . ." If the maturity is expressed in months, the note will mature on the same date in the month of maturity. For example, one month from July 18, 1986, is August 18, 1986, and two months from July 18, 1986, is September 18, 1986. If a note is issued on the last day of a month and the month of maturity has fewer days than the month of issuance, the note matures on the last day of the month of maturity. A one-month note dated January 30, 1986, matures on February 28, 1986.
   c. "Ninety days after date, I promise to pay. . . ." If the maturity is expressed in days, the exact number of days must be counted. The first day (date of origin) is omitted and the last day (maturity date) is included in the count. For example, a 90-day note dated October 19, 1986, matures on January 17, 1987, as shown below:

Life of note (days) . . . .   90 days
Days remaining in October not counting date of origin of note:
   Days to count in October (31–19)   12
Total days in November   30
Total days in December   31   73
Maturity date in January   17

A note falling due on a Sunday or a holiday is due on the next business day.

Accounting for Notes in Normal Business Transactions

Sometimes a note is received when high-priced merchandise is sold, but often a note results from the conversion of an overdue open account. When a customer does not pay an account receivable when due, the company (creditor) may insist that the customer (debtor) give a note in place of the account. This action allows the customer more time to pay the balance of the account, and the company earns interest on the balance until paid. Also, the company may be able to sell the note to a bank or other financial institution, as you will learn later.

To illustrate the conversion of an open account to a note, assume that Price Company (maker) had purchased $18,000 of merchandise on August 1 from Cooper Company (payee) on open account. The normal credit period has elapsed, and Price Company cannot pay the bill. Cooper Company agrees to accept Price Company's $18,000, 15%, 90-day note dated September 1 to settle Price Company's open account. Assuming Price Company paid the note at maturity and both Price Company and Cooper Company have a December 31 year-end, the entries on the books of the maker and the books of the payee are:

	Price Company, maker		
Aug. 1	Purchases	18,000	
	Accounts Payable—Cooper Company		18,000
	To record purchase of merchandise on account.		
Sept. 1	Accounts Payable—Cooper Company	18,000	
	Notes Payable—Cooper Company		18,000
	To record exchange of note for open account.		
Nov. 30	Notes Payable—Cooper Company	18,000	
	Interest Expense	675	
	Cash		18,675
	To record payment of note and interest.		

	Cooper Company, payee		
Aug. 1	Accounts Receivable—Price Company	18,000	
	Sales		18,000
	To record sale of merchandise on account.		
Sept. 1	Notes Receivable—Price Company	18,000	
	Accounts Receivable—Price Company		18,000
	To record exchange of note for open account.		
Nov. 30	Cash	18,675	
	Notes Receivable—Price Company		18,000
	Interest Revenue		675
	To record receipt of note principal and interest.		

The $18,675 paid by Price Company to Cooper Company is called the maturity value of the note. **Maturity value** is the amount that the maker must pay on a note on its maturity date; typically, it includes principal and accrued interest, if any.

The journal entry Clark Company would make to record this transaction is:

May 14	Cash	10,009.03	
	Notes Receivable Discounted		10,000.00
	Interest Revenue		9.03
	To record sale of notes receivable.		

Notes Receivable Discounted is a contra account to Notes Receivable and is used to show the contingent liability for customers' notes that have been discounted. Note that the contingent liability is shown by recording the discounted note in the Notes Receivable Discounted account **at face value,** even though the contingent liability also includes the interest.

When a note is discounted, the proceeds received rarely, if ever, equal the amount at which the note is carried in the accounts—usually face value. The difference between the proceeds and face value of the note is recorded as interest expense or interest revenue. If the proceeds are less than the face value, interest expense is recorded; if the proceeds are greater than the face value, interest revenue is recorded.

Balance Sheet Presentation of Notes Receivable Discounted.   In the Clark Company example above (assume a June 30 accounting year-end), the Clark Company should show a contingent liability of $10,000 for notes receivable discounted in its June 30, 1987, balance sheet. If we assume that the total of all Clark Company's notes receivable is $70,000, an acceptable method of presenting this information in the balance sheet is:

Notes receivable	$70,000	
Less: Notes receivable discounted	10,000	$60,000

An alternative balance sheet presentation of the above data is:

Assets

Current assets:
Cash	$xx,xxx
Accounts receivable	xx,xxx
Notes receivable (Note 1)	60,000

Notes to Financial Statements:
Note 1: At June 30, 1987, the company is contingently liable for $10,000 of customers' notes receivable that it has endorsed and discounted at the local bank.

Discounted Notes Receivable Paid by Maker.   When a discounted note receivable matures, it is usually the duty of the holder (the bank in the above illustration) to present the note to the maker for payment. If the maker pays the holder at maturity, the endorser (the company that discounted the note) is thereby relieved of its contingent liability.

Assume that in the above example, Kent Company pays the $10,000 note plus interest of $150 to the Michigan National Bank on July 3, 1987, the note's maturity date. Clark Company, which discounted the note at the bank, is no longer liable for the note and therefore makes the following entry:

```
July  3  Notes Receivable Discounted  . . . . . . . . .   10,000
             Notes Receivable—Kent Company  . . . . . .            10,000
         To remove the note and the contingent liability from
         the accounts.
```

This entry completely removes the Kent Company note from the accounts.

Discounted Notes Receivable Not Paid by Maker.   In the above illustration, the maker paid the bank when the note matured. However, if the note is not paid at maturity and is written with recourse, the holder can collect from the endorser who, in turn, can try to collect from the maker. Now that the endorser possesses the note again, the accounting records of the endorser must be changed.

Assume that Kent Company dishonors its note. The Michigan National Bank will collect the principal ($10,000) and interest ($150) from Clark Company (the bank usually charges a small protest fee but for illustration purposes we are ignoring this fee). Clark Company must make the following two entries:

```
July  3  Notes Receivable Discounted . . . . . . . . . .   10,000
             Notes Receivable—Kent Company  . . . . .             10,000
         To remove note and contingent liability from the
         accounts.

      3  Accounts Receivable—Kent Company . . . . . . .   10,150
             Cash  . . . . . . . . . . . . . . . . . .             10,150
         To record cash paid to bank for Kent Company's
         dishonored note.
```

Clark Company, of course, will now try to collect $10,150 from Kent Company. However, if this is unsuccessful, the $10,150 will be removed from Accounts Receivable and treated as a loss from bad debts.

Short-Term Financing through Notes Payable

Businesses sometimes need short-term financing. This may occur when (1) the company's cash receipts are delayed because of lenient credit terms granted customers, or (2) the company needs cash to finance the buildup of seasonal inventories, such as before Christmas. Short-term financing may be secured by issuing interest-bearing notes or by issuing noninterest-bearing notes.

Interest-Bearing Notes.   To receive short-term financing from a bank, a company may issue an interest-bearing note to the bank. An interest-bearing note specifies the interest rate that will be charged on the principal borrowed. The company receives from the bank the principal borrowed and, when the note matures, pays the bank the principal plus the interest.

Accounting for an interest-bearing note is simple. For example, assume that Needham Company issued a $10,000, 90-day, 18% note on August 18. The following entries would be made to record the loan and its payment on November 16:

```
Aug. 18  Cash  . . . . . . . . . . . . . . . . . . . . .   10,000
             Notes Payable  . . . . . . . . . . . . . .            10,000
         To record 90-day bank loan.
```

```
Nov. 16  Notes Payable . . . . . . . . . . . . . . . .     10,000
         Interest Expense . . . . . . . . . . . . . .         450
             Cash . . . . . . . . . . . . . . . . . . .              10,450
         To record principal and interest paid on bank loan.
```

If the term of the note extended beyond a balance sheet date, an adjusting entry would be needed on that date to record the accrued interest payable.

Noninterest-Bearing Notes. A company may also issue a noninterest-bearing note to receive short-term financing from a bank. A noninterest-bearing note does not have a stated interest rate applied to the face value of the note. Instead, the note is drawn for a maturity amount from which a bank discount is deducted, and the proceeds are given to the borrower. **Bank discount** is the difference between the maturity value of the note and the actual amount—the note's proceeds—given to the borrower. The **cash proceeds,** as defined earlier, are equal to the maturity amount of a note less the bank discount. This entire process is referred to as **discounting a note payable.** The purpose of this process is to introduce interest into what appears to be a noninterest-bearing note. The meaning of "discounting" here is to deduct interest in advance.

Because interest is related to time, the bank discount is not interest on the date the loan is made; however, it becomes interest expense to the company and interest revenue to the bank as time passes. To illustrate, assume that on December 1, 1987, Needham Company presented its $10,000, 90-day, noninterest-bearing note to the bank, which discounted the note at 18%. The discount is $450 ($10,000 × 0.18 × 90/360), and the proceeds to Needham are $9,550. The entry required on the date of the note's issue is:

```
Dec.  1  Cash . . . . . . . . . . . . . . . . . . . . .      9,550
         Discount on Notes Payable . . . . . . . . .           450
             Notes Payable . . . . . . . . . . . . . .              10,000
         Issued 90-day note to bank.
```

Notes Payable are recorded at face value. **Discount on Notes Payable** is a contra account used to reduce Notes Payable from face value to the net amount shown on the balance sheet. The account is reported on the balance sheet as a deduction from the Notes Payable account.

Over time, the discount becomes interest expense. If the note in the example above was paid before the end of the fiscal year, the entire $450 of discount would be charged to Interest Expense and credited to Discount on Notes Payable when the note was paid. However, if Needham's fiscal year ended on December 31, an adjusting entry would be required as follows:

```
Dec. 31  Interest Expense . . . . . . . . . . . . . .        150
             Discount on Notes Payable . . . . . . . .             150
         To record interest on a note payable.
```

This entry records the interest expense incurred by Needham for the 30 days the note has been outstanding. The expense can be calculated as $10,000 × 0.18 × 30/360, or 30/90 × $450. Notice that, for entries involving discounted notes payable, no separate Interest Payable account is needed. The Notes Payable account already contains the total liability that will be paid at **maturity,** $10,000. From the date the proceeds are given to the borrower to the maturity date, the liability grows by reducing the balance in the Discount on Notes

Payable contra account. Thus, the current liability section of the December 31, 1987, balance sheet would show:

```
Notes Payable  . . . . . . . .  $10,000
Less: Discount on notes payable . .    300   $9,700
```

The $9,700 is the amount that would have to be paid to the bank if the company wished to repay the loan on December 31 rather than at maturity date (if the interest rate has not changed). The original amount borrowed, $9,550, plus the accrued interest for 30 days, $150, equals $9,700.

When the note is paid at maturity, the entry is:

```
Mar.  1   Notes Payable . . . . . . . . . . . . . . . . . .  10,000
          Interest Expense . . . . . . . . . . . . . . . .      300
              Cash  . . . . . . . . . . . . . . . . . . . .          10,000
              Discount on Notes Payable . . . . . . . . .              300
          To record note payment and interest expense.
```

This entry removes the above note from the Notes Payable account and records the remaining discount as interest expense of the current period.

Long-Term Mortgage Notes Payable

When purchasing plant assets, companies sometimes give notes to finance the purchase rather than paying cash. These notes are usually long-term liabilities secured by a mortgage on the property acquired. A **mortgage** is a legal document that gives a lender possession of pledged property if the borrower does not pay the obligation as required in the terms of the agreement. Most family homes are purchased this way.

Assume that a company acquired a building by giving a $100,000, 16%, 20-year mortgage note payable. The note calls for equal monthly payments, exclusive of real estate taxes and insurance. In the early years of the monthly payments, a very large portion of the payment is for interest and only a limited amount for reducing principal. Mortgage payment schedule books are used that indicate how much of the monthly payment is for interest and how much for principle. On $100,000, the monthly payment for principal and interest is $1,391.26. The interest and principal for the first two months and for the last month are as follows:

	Monthly payment	Interest	Principal	Principal balance
Date of purchase				$100,000.00
First month	$1,391.26	$1,333.33	$ 57.93	99,942.07
Second month	1,391.26	1,332.56	58.70	99,883.37
240th month	1,391.26	18.31	1,372.95	–0–

Note that interest is calculated on the latest principal balance. For example when the first $1,391.26 payment is made, interest for the month is calculated as follows:

$$\$100,000 \times 0.16 \times \tfrac{1}{12} = \$1,333.33$$

The entry to record the first month's mortgage payment is:

Interest Expense	1,333.33	
Mortgage Note Payable	57.93	
Cash		1,391.26

To record interest expense and reduction of mortgage
principal resulting from mortgage payment.

In the first payment, the $1,333.33 interest is subtracted from the total payment ($1,391.26), and the excess is applied against the principal ($57.93). Thus, the principal balance decreases slowly (but more rapidly each month), so that the last payment at the end of 20 years pays interest of $18.31 on the remaining principal balance of $1,372.95 and reduces the principal balance to zero.

■ SUMMARY

Chapter 8 is divided into two main sections—receivables and payables. Receivables are any sums of money due to be received from any party for any reason. Payables are amounts due to be paid to any party for any reason.

Two methods are used to record bad debts—the allowance method and the direct write-off method. The allowance method provides in advance for uncollectible accounts by crediting an Allowance for Doubtful Accounts account, which is a contra account to accounts receivable, and debiting a Bad Debts Expense account. The direct write-off method directly charges the identified uncollectible accounts receivable to the Bad Debts Expense account.

Bad debts are estimated by the percentage-of-sales method or the percentage-of-receivables method. The percentage-of-sales method is based on the percentage of prior years' actual bad debt losses to prior years' credit sales or total net sales. The percentage-of-receivables method estimates bad debts by determining the desired size of the Allowance for Doubtful Accounts; the ending balance in Accounts Receivable is multiplied by a rate (or rates) based on past experience regarding uncollectible accounts.

To avoid the burden of bad debt losses and other costs of extending credit, businesses may accept credit cards by paying credit agencies a percentage of the sales price. The accounting procedures of the seller differ depending on whether the business accepts a nonbank or bank credit card.

Notes receivable and notes payable may arise from the company's normal business transactions with customers or suppliers or from the need of the company to borrow for short-term business operations or long-term facilities such as plant assets. Promissory notes are written promises to pay; they are assets to their holders and liabilities to their makers.

Notes receivable may be discounted (sold). Three parties are involved in the transaction: the party that wrote the note, the company that accepted it and sold it to the bank, and the bank that bought it. A company is contingently liable (it will pay only if the maker does not) for paying a discounted note receivable.

When a company borrows for short-term financing or long-term plant acquisitions, there are only two parties involved in the transaction—the company and the bank. Companies are directly liable for paying their own notes.

From the study of receivables and payables, you go to the study of measuring and reporting inventories in Chapter 9. Inventories can be the largest asset of a company, and cost of goods sold can be a company's largest expense. For this reason, accurate accounting for inventories is most important.

NEW TERMS INTRODUCED IN CHAPTER 8

Aging schedule

A means of classifying accounts receivable according to their age, used to determine the necessary balance in an Allowance for Doubtful Accounts. A different uncollectibility rate is used for each age category (319).

Allowance for Doubtful Accounts

A contra-asset account to the Accounts Receivable account; it reduces accounts receivable to their net realizable value. Also called Allowance for Bad Debts or Allowance for Uncollectible Accounts (317).

Bad debts expense

An operating (usually a selling) expense a business incurs when it sells on credit (316).

Bank discount

The difference between maturity value of a note and its proceeds (333).

Cash proceeds

The maturity amount of a note less the bank discount (329).

Contingent liability

A condition that may become an actual liability if a specific action does or does not occur (329).

Credit card expense

The credit agency's service charge for services rendered in processing credit card sales (323).

Credit cards

Charge cards such as American Express, Diners Club, VISA, and MasterCard which are used by customers to charge their purchases of goods and services (323).

Direct write-off method

A way of accounting for uncollectible accounts receiva-

ble in which identified uncollectible amounts are charged directly to an expense account (322).

Discount on Notes Payable

A contra account used to reduce notes payable from face value to the net amount shown in the balance sheet (333).

Discounting a note receivable

The act of selling a note receivable with recourse to a bank. With recourse means that the bank can collect from the company that sold the note to the bank if the maker does not pay at maturity (329).

Dishonored note

A note that the maker failed to pay at maturity (327).

Interest

The fee charged for use of money through time (324).

Interest Payable account

An account showing the liabilty for interest expense incurred but not yet paid (328).

Interest Receivable account

An account showing the asset for interest earned but not yet collected (328).

Maker (of a note)

The party who prepares a note and is responsible for paying the note at maturity (324).

Maturity date

The date on which a note becomes due and must be paid (325).

Maturity value

The amount that the maker must pay on the note on its maturity date (326).

Mortgage

A legal document that gives a lender possession of pledged property if the borrower does not pay the obligation as required in the terms of the agreement (334).

Net realizable value

The amount expected to be collected from accounts receivable (317).

Notes Receivable Discounted

A contra account to Notes Receivable used to show the contingent liability for customers' notes that have been discounted (331).

Payable

Any sum of money due to be paid by a company to any party for any reason (315).

Payee (of a note)

The party who receives a note and will be paid cash at maturity (324).

Percentage-of-receivables method

A method for determining the desired size of the Allowance for Doubtful Accounts by basing the calculation on the Accounts Receivable balance at the end of the period (319).

Percentage-of-sales method

A method of estimating uncollectible accounts from a given period's credit sales (318).

Principal (of a note)

The face value of a note (325).

Promissory note

An unconditional written promise by a borrower (maker) to pay a definite sum of money to the lender (payee) on demand or at a specific date (324).

Receivable

Any sum of money due to be paid to a company from any party for any reason (315).

Trade receivables

Amounts due from customers for goods sold or services rendered on open account. Also called accounts receivable or trade accounts receivable (316).

With recourse

A legal term meaning that if the maker does not pay the bank at maturity, the bank can collect the amount due from the company that sold the note to the bank (329).

DEMONSTRATION PROBLEM

Part a: The Best Company estimates its bad debts expense to be 1% of sales. Sales in 1987 were $750,000.

Required: Prepare the journal entries for the following transactions:

Transactions:
1. The company prepared the adjusting entry for bad debts for the year 1987.
2. On January 15, 1988, the company decided that the account for James Ryan in the amount of $500 was uncollectible.
3. On February 12, 1988, James Ryan's check for $500 arrived.

Part b: A $15,000, 90-day, 12% note dated June 15, 1987, was received by the Long Company from the Short Company in payment of its account.

Required: Prepare the journal entries in the records of the Long Company for each of the following:
1. The Long Company received the note on June 15, 1987.
2. The Long Company discounted the note on July 15, 1987, at 10% at the Citizens' National Bank.
3. The Short Company paid the note at maturity.
4. Assume that the Short Company did not pay the note at maturity. The Citizen's National Bank charged the note to the Long Company. The Long Company decided that the note was uncollectible.

Solution to demonstration problem

Part a:

1. 1987
   Dec. 31 Bad Debts Expense 7,500
       Allowance for Doubtful Accounts . . .   7,500
       To record estimated bad debts for the
       year.

2. 1988
   Jan. 15 Allowance for Doubtful Accounts   500
       Accounts Receivable—James Ryan . .   500
       To write off the account of James Ryan
       as uncollectible.

3. 1988
   Feb. 12 Accounts Receivable—James Ryan . . .   500
       Allowance for Doubtful Accounts . . .   500
       To correct the write-off of James Ryan's
       account on January 15.

     12 Cash   500
       Accounts Receivable—James Ryan . .   500
       To record the collection of James Ryan's
       account receivable.

Part b:

1. 1987
   June 15 Notes Receivable—Short Company . . .   15,000.00
       Accounts Receivable—Short
        Company 15,000.00
       To record receipt of a note from Short
       Company.

2. July 15 Cash 15,192.50
       Notes Receivable Discounted 15,000.00
       Interest Revenue 192.50
       To record the discounting of the Short
       Company note.

   > Computation of cash proceeds:
   > Maturity value (Days until
   >   maturity = 60) $15,450.00
   > Discount = $15,450 × 10% × 60/360 . .   257.50
   > $15,192.50

3. Sept. 13 Notes Receivable Discounted 15,000.00
       Notes Receivable—Short Company . .   15,000.00
       To remove the note and contingent
       liability.

4. Sept. 13 Notes Receivable Discounted 15,000.00
       Notes Receivable—Short Company . .   15,000.00
       To remove the note and contingent
       liability.

Sept. 13   Accounts Receivable—Short Company   .   .   15,450.00
     Cash 15,450.00
     To record the charge made against our
     account for the Short Company note of
     $15,000 and interest of $450.

    13   Allowance for Doubtful Accounts* 15,450.00
     Accounts Receivable—Short
     Company 15,450.00
     To write off the Short Company note as
     uncollectible.

* This debit assumes that notes receivable were taken into consideration when an allowance was established. If not, the debit should be either to Bad Debts Expense or Loss from Dishonored Notes Receivable.

QUESTIONS

1. In view of the difficulty in estimating future events, would you recommend that accountants wait until collections are made from customers before recording sales revenue? Should they wait until known accounts prove to be uncollectible before charging an expense account?

2. The credit manager of a company has established a policy of seeking to completely eliminate all losses from uncollectible accounts. Is this a desirable objective for a company? Explain.

3. What are the two major purposes to be accomplished in establishing an allowance for uncollectible accounts?

4. In view of the fact that it is impossible to estimate the exact amount of uncollectible accounts receivable for any one year in advance, what exactly does the Allowance for Doubtful Accounts account contain after a number of years?

5. How might information in an aging schedule prove useful to management for purposes other than estimating the size of the required allowance for doubtful accounts?

6. For a company using the allowance method of accounting for uncollectible accounts, which of the following affects its reported net income: (1) the establishment of the allowance, (2) the writing off of a specific account, or (3) the recovery of an account previously written off as uncollectible?

7. Explain why the direct write-off method of accounting for uncollectible accounts is generally unacceptable.

8. Why might a retailer agree to sell by credit card when such a substantial discount is taken by the credit card agency in paying the retailer?

9. How do a dishonored note receivable and a discounted note receivable differ? How is each reported in the balance sheet?

10. Under what circumstances does the account Discount on Notes Payable arise? How is it reported in the financial statements? Explain why.

11. For what purpose might a company issue a mortgage note payable?

EXERCISES

E–1

Prepare journal entries to record bad debts expense

The accounts of the Blue Bird Company as of December 31, 1986, show Accounts Receivable, $55,000; Allowance for Doubtful Accounts, $350 (credit balance); Sales, $362,500; and Sales Returns and Allowances, $6,500. Prepare journal entries to adjust for possible uncollectible accounts under each of the following assumptions:

a.   Uncollectible accounts are estimated at 1% of net sales.
b.   The allowance is to be increased to 3% of accounts receivable.

E–2

Record write-off and subsequent recovery of account

On April 1, 1987, Oliver Company, which uses the allowance method of accounting for uncollectible accounts, wrote off Bill Combs' $132 account. On December 14, 1987, the company received a check in that amount from Combs marked "in full payment of account." Prepare the necessary entries for all of the above.

E–3

Use aging schedule to estimate Allowance for Doubtful Accounts

Compute the required balance of the Allowance for Doubtful Accounts for the following receivables:

Accounts receivable	Age (months)	Probability of collection
$220,000	Less than 1	0.95
110,000	1–3	0.85
52,000	3–6	0.75
14,000	6–9	0.35
3,000	9–12	0.10

E–4

Prepare journal entries for write-off and subsequent collection of account under direct write-off method

Because its credit sales are immaterial in amount, the Shady Tree Company accounts for its uncollectible accounts using the direct write-off method. During 1987, the following accounts were written off as uncollectible:

Apr. 10	J. Jones	. . . .	$250
July 17	B. Smith	. . . .	480
Oct. 11	L. Jackson .	. . .	340

On December 10, payment in full is received from J. Jones. Prepare journal entries for the above.

E–5

Record use of nonbank credit card

Andersons Inc. sold $22,000 of goods in May to customers who used their Carte Blanche credit cards. Such sales are subject to a 3% discount by Carte Blanche. Prepare journal entries to record the sales and the subsequent receipt of cash from the credit card company.

E–6

Determine maturity dates on several notes

Determine the maturity date for each of the following notes:

Issue date	Life
January 13, 1987 . . .	30 days
January 31, 1987 . . .	90 days
June 4, 1987	1 year
December 2, 1987 . . .	1 month

E–7

Prepare entries for a note

James gave a $60,000, 120-day, 12% note to Burt in exchange for merchandise. James uses periodic inventory procedure. Prepare journal entries needed to record the issuance of the note and the entries needed at maturity for both parties, assuming payment is made.

E–8

Prepare entries when maker defaults

Prepare the entries that James and Burt (Exercise E–7) would make at maturity date, assuming James defaults.

E–9

Prepare entries at date of discounting of note

On May 7, 1987, Able Company gave a 180-day, $15,000, 14% note to Ready Company. On August 20, Ready Company discounted the note at 14%. Prepare the entries each company would make on the discounting date.

E-10

Prepare entries at maturity date

In Exercise E–9 prepare the entries that would be recorded on the books of each company assuming Able Company *(a)* fails to pay the note at maturity and *(b)* pays the note at maturity.

E-11

Prepare entries for noninterest-bearing note and interest-bearing note

Day Kreuzburg is negotiating a bank loan of $5,000 for 90 days. The bank's current interest rate is 16%. Prepare Kreuzburg's entries to record the loan under each of the following assumptions:

a. Kreuzburg signs a note for $5,000. Interest is deducted in calculating the proceeds turned over to him.

b. Kreuzburg signs a note for $5,000 and receives that amount. Interest is to be paid at maturity.

E-12

Prepare entries at maturity date

Prepare the entry or entries that would be made at maturity date for each of the alternatives in Exercise E–11 assuming the loan is paid before the end of the accounting period.

E-13

Prepare entry to record mortgage payment

Assume a company acquired a building by giving a $200,000, 12%, 20-year mortgage note payable. Prepare the journal entry to record the first month's mortgage payment assuming the payment is $2,086.89.

PROBLEMS, SERIES A

P8-1-A

Write-off bad debt and record expense under alternative methods of estimation

Presented below are selected accounts of the Salem Company as of December 31, 1987. Prior to closing the books, the $2,000 account of the Park Company (originating from credit sales on February 12, 1987) is to be written off.

Accounts receivable . . . . $ 105,000
Allowance for doubtful accounts (credit balance) . . 1,500
Sales 1,050,000
Sales returns and allowances 25,000

Required:

a. Present the journal entries to record the above transaction and to record bad debts expense for the year, assuming the estimated expense is 1% of net sales.

b. Give the entry to record the estimated expense if the allowance is to be adjusted to 7% of outstanding receivables instead of as in *(a)* above.

P8-2-A

Record expense (two methods) and write-offs, record expense under direct write-off method

The following data pertain to the Easy Credit Company:

	1986	1987	1988
Total net sales	$270,000	$300,000	$440,000
Accounts receivable balance, December 31	90,000	48,000	60,000
Actual accounts written off during the year:			
From 1985 sales	2,000		
From 1986 sales	3,200	3,600	
From 1987 sales		1,200	2,400
From 1988 sales			2,600

For parts *(a)* and *(b)* below assume that the Allowance for Doubtful Accounts had a credit balance of $2,200 when properly adjusted on December 31, 1985. Use the following format:

Account Titles	1986		1987		1988	
	Dr.	Cr.	Dr.	Cr.	Dr.	Cr.

Required:

a. Prepare the actual entries that were made to record the accounts written off in each year. Then prepare journal entries for 1986, 1987, and 1988 to record bad debts expense for the year using the percentage-of-sales method with bad debts estimated at 2% of total net sales.

b. Repeat part *(a)* using the percentage-of-receivables method with the allowance adjusted to 5% of year-end receivables.

c. Prepare journal entries to record bad debts expense for 1986, 1987, and 1988 using the direct write-off method.

P8–3–A

Record use of bank and nonbank credit cards

The cash register at Becky's Place at the close of business on a certain date showed cash sales of $3,600 and credit card sales of $4,400 ($2,400 VISA and $2,000 American Express). The VISA invoices were discounted 5% when they were deposited. The American Express charges were mailed to the company. A few days later, a check was received for the amount of the charges, less a discount of 5%.

Required: Prepare journal entries to record all of the above transactions.

P8–4–A

Account for discounted note receivable

The Nelson Company received a note from the Hill Company on July 24, 1987. The company discounted the note at the bank on August 23, 1987. A summary of the facts concerning the note follows:

Face amount	$120,000
Life of note	120 days
Date of note	7/24/87
Interest rate on note	12%
Date of discounting note at the bank . .	8/23/87
Discount rate charged by the bank . . .	15%

Required: Determine:

a. The maturity date of the note.
b. The maturity value of the note.
c. The number of days from the discount date to the maturity date.
d. The dollar amount of the discount.
e. The cash proceeds received by the company.
f. The entry to record the receipt of the proceeds at the date of discount.
g. The entry needed on the maturity date assuming Hill paid its notes.

P8–5–A

Account for discounted note payable

On November 1, 1987, the Rogers Company discounted its own $90,000, 180-day, noninterest-bearing note at its bank at 18%. The note was paid on its maturity date. Rogers Company uses a calendar-year accounting period.

Required: Prepare dated journal entries to record *(a)* the discounting of the note, *(b)* the year-end adjustment, and *(c)* the payment of the note.

P8–6–A

Prepare entries to record a number of note transactions, discounting of a note (customer's and own), adjusting entries for interest, and payment of notes

The Leary Company engaged in the following transactions in 1987:

Transactions:

May 31 Discounted its own 30-day, $12,000, noninterest-bearing note at the First National Bank at 12%.

June 8 Received an $8,000, 90-day, 9% note from the Second Company in settlement of its account balance. The note is dated June 8.

15 Issued an $8,400, 120-day, 10% note, dated today, to purchase merchandise. Leary Company uses periodic inventory procedure.

20 Discounted the Second Company note at 12% at the First National Bank.

30 The bank notified Leary Company that it had charged the note of May 31 against the company's checking account balance.

All notes falling due after June 30 were paid in full on their due dates by their respective makers.

Required: Prepare dated journal entries for the Leary Company for all of the above transactions (including the payment of the notes after June 30) and all necessary adjusting entries for accrued interest, assuming that the fiscal year ends on June 30.

P8–7–A

Prepare entries to record a number of note transactions, discounting of a note (customer's and own), adjusting entries for interest, and payment of notes

The Baker Company has a fiscal year ending on July 31. On July 1, 1987, the balances of certain ledger accounts are Notes Receivable, $49,600; Notes Receivable Discounted, $36,000; and Notes Payable, $120,000. The balance in Notes Receivable consists of the following:

Face amount	Maker	Date of note	Life	Interest rate	Date discounted	Discount rate
$36,000	Good Co.	5/15/87	60 days	14%	6/1/87	12%
4,000	Bad Co.	6/1/87	60 days	14	—	—
9,600	Rugly Co.	6/15/87	30 days	12	—	—
$49,600						

The note payable is a 60-day bank loan dated May 20, 1987. Discount on Notes Payable was debited for the discount of $1,200.

Required: Prepare dated journal entries for the following transactions and the necessary July 31 adjustments for accrued interest:

Transactions:

July 1   The Baker Company discounted its own $44,000, 90-day, noninterest-bearing note at the State Bank. The discount rate was 12%, and the note was dated today.

3   Received a 20-day, 12% note, dated today, from the Jones Company in settlement of an account receivable of $7,200.

6   Purchased merchandise from the Hood Company, $43,800, and issued a 30-day, 12% note, dated today, for the purchase. Baker Company uses periodic inventory procedure.

8   Sold merchandise to the Brass Company, $12,000. A 45-day, 8% note, dated today, was received to cover the sale.

14   The $36,000 note discounted on June 1, 1987, was paid by the Good Company directly to the holder.

15   The Rugly Company sent a $6,000, 30-day, 12% note, dated today, and a check to cover its note of June 15, 1987, and interest in full to this date.

18   The Brass Company note of July 8 was discounted at the State Bank for the remaining life of the note. The discount rate was 14%.

19   The note payable dated May 20, 1987, was paid in full.

23   The Jones Company dishonored its note of July 3, due today.

26   The Jones Company sent a check for the interest on the dishonored note and a new 30-day, 12% note dated July 23, 1987.

30   The Bad Company note dated June 1, 1987, was paid with interest in full.

PROBLEMS, SERIES B

P8–1–B

Write off bad debt, record expense under alternative methods of estimation

As of December 31, 1986, Kirby Company's accounts prior to adjustment showed:

Accounts receivable . . . . $ 92,000
Allowance for doubtful accounts (credit balance) . .   3,500
Net sales   750,000

Kirby Company follows a practice of estimating uncollectible accounts at 3% of net sales.

On February 23, 1987, the account of Don Cole in the amount of $1,150 was considered uncollectible and was written off. On August 12, 1987, Cole remitted $400 and indicated that he intends to pay the balance owed as soon as possible. By December 31, 1987, no further remittance had been received from Cole.

Required:
a. Prepare journal entries to record bad debts expense for 1986 and to record the above transactions.
b. Prepare the bad debts adjusting entry as of December 31, 1986, assuming Kirby estimated its uncollectible accounts at 11% of outstanding accounts receivable rather than 3% of net sales.

P8-2-B

Record expense (two methods) and write-offs, record expense under direct write-off method

The following data pertain to the Donlow Company which began operations in 1986:

	1986	1987	1988
Total net sales	$40,000	$35,000	$55,000
Accounts receivable balance			
December 31	17,500	20,000	30,000
Actual accounts written off during the year:			
From 1986 sales	500	350	150
From 1987 sales		300	400
From 1988 sales			600

For parts *(a)* and *(b)* below, assume that the write-offs were made during the year and that the company expected to use the allowance method and make a year-end adjustment for bad debts. Use the following format:

Account Titles	1986		1987		1988	
	Dr.	Cr.	Dr.	Cr.	Dr.	Cr.

Required:
a. Prepare the entries that were made to record the actual accounts written off in each year. Then prepare journal entries for 1986, 1987, and 1988 to record the bad debts expense for the year using the percentage-of-sales method with bad debts estimated at 2% of total net sales.
b. Repeat part *(a)* using the precentage-of-receivables method with the allowance adjusted to 5% of year-end receivables.
c. Prepare journal entries to record bad debts expense for 1986, 1987, and 1988 using the direct write-off method.

P8-3-B

Record use of bank and nonbank credit cards

At the close of business on a certain date, David's Restaurant had credit card sales of $4,800. Of this amount, $3,200 were VISA sales invoices which can be deposited in a bank for immediate credit, less a discount of 3%. The balance of $1,600 consisted of American Express charges. These invoices were mailed to American Express. Shortly thereafter, a check was received for $1,552.

Required: Prepare journal entries for all of the above.

P8-4-B

Account for discounted note receivable

On June 1, 1987, the Dobbs Company received a $54,000, 90-day, 16% note from the Thomas Company dated June 1, 1987. On August 15, 1987, the note was discounted at the bank. The bank discount rate was 18%.

Required: Determine:

a. The maturity value of the note.
b. The number of days from the discount date to the maturity date.
c. The dollar amount of the discount.

d. The cash proceeds received by the company.
e. The entry to record the receipt of proceeds at the date of discount.
f. The entry on Dobbs' books when Thomas paid the note at maturity.

P8–5–B

Account for discounted note payable

The Oliver Company discounted its own $30,000, noninterest-bearing, 60-day note on November 16, 1987, at the Chautauqua County Bank at a discount rate of 12%.

Required: Prepare dated journal entries for the following:

a. The original discounting on November 16.
b. The adjustment required at the end of the company's calendar-year accounting period.
c. Payment at maturity.

P8–6–B

Prepare entries to record a number of note transactions, discounting of a note (customer's and own), adjusting entries for interest, and entries for payment of notes

Following are selected transactions of the Blue Thumb Company for 1987:

Transactions:

Oct. 31 Discounted its own 30-day, $6,000, noninterest-bearing note at the First State Bank at 12%.
Nov. 8 Received a $4,000, 90-day, 9% note from the Worst Company in settlement of an account receivable. The note is dated November 8.
    15 Purchased merchandise by issuing its own 120-day note for $4,200. The note is dated November 15 and bears interest at 10%. Blue Thumb Company uses periodic inventory procedure.
    20 Discounted the Worst Company note at 12% at the First State Bank.
    30 The First State Bank notified the Blue Thumb Company that it had charged the note of October 31 against the company's checking account.

All notes falling due after November 30 were paid in full on their due dates by the respective makers. (Remember that 1988 is a leap year; February has 29 days.)

Required: Prepare dated journal entries for the Blue Thumb Company for all of the above transactions (including the payment of the notes after November 30) and all necessary adjusting entries, assuming that the fiscal year ends on November 30.

P8–7–B

Prepare entries to record a number of note transactions, discounting of a note (customer's and own), adjusting entries for interest, and entries for payment of notes

The Pleasant Company is in the chain saw manufacturing business. As of September 1, the balance in its Notes Receivable account was $177,000. The balance in the Notes Receivable Discounted account was $72,000, and the balance in Accounts Receivable included $45,450 for Yahoo's dishonored note. A schedule of the notes (including the dishonored note) is as follows:

Face amount	Maker	Date	Life	Interest rate	Comments
$ 60,000	A. Box Co.	6/1/87	150 days	12%	
45,000	C. Davis Co.	6/15/87	90 days	8	
72,000	Chase Co.	7/1/87	90 days	10	Discounted 8/16/84 at 9%
45,000	Yahoo Co.	7/1/87	60 days	6	Dishonored, interest $450
$222,000					

Required: Prepare dated journal entries for the following 1987 transactions:

Transactions:

Sept. 5 The A. Box Company note was discounted at the Fulton County Bank. The discount rate was 10%.
    10 Received $21,450 from the Yahoo Company as full settlement of the amount due from it. The company charges losses on notes to the Allowance for Doubtful Accounts account.
   ? The C. Davis Company note was collected when due.
   ? Chase Company paid its note at maturity.

? The A. Box Company note was not paid at maturity. The bank deducted the balance from the Pleasant Company's bank balance.

Oct. 30 Received a new 60-day, 12% note from the A. Box Company for the total balance due on the dishonored note. The note was dated as of the maturity date of the dishonored note. The Pleasant Company accepted the note in good faith.

BUSINESS DECISION PROBLEM 8–1

Compare costs of maintaining own accounts receivable with costs of allowing credit cards; identify other factors to consider

Larry Johnson runs an appliance store, selling items for cash and on account. During 1986, which seemed to be a typical year, some of his operating and other data were as follows:

Sales:	
For cash	$500,000
On credit	700,000
Cost of obtaining credit reports on customers	1,500
Cost incurred in paying a part-time bookkeeper to keep the accounts receivable subsidiary ledger up to date	5,000
Cost associated with preparing and mailing invoices to customers and other collection activities	8,000
Bad debts arising from uncollectible accounts	22,000
The average outstanding accounts receivable balance (on which Larry estimates he could have earned 10% if it had been invested in other assets)	54,000

A national credit card agency has approached Larry and tried to convince him that instead of carrying his own accounts receivable he should only accept its credit card for sales on credit. The agency would pay Larry within two days after he submits sales charges. It would deduct 4% from the amount and pay him 96%.

Required:
  a. Using the data given, prepare an analysis showing whether or not it would pay Larry to switch to the credit card method of selling on credit.
  b. What other factors should be taken into consideration?

BUSINESS DECISION PROBLEM 8–2

Evaluate alternative means of making sales

Ken Blake operates a large garden supplies store on the outskirts of a city. In a typical year he sells $1,000,000 of goods to regular customers. His sales are 35% for cash and 65% on credit. He carries all of the credit himself. Only after a customer has a total unpaid balance of $100 on which no payments have been made for two months does he refuse that customer credit for future purchases. His income before taxes is approximately $325,000. The total of uncollectible accounts for a given year is about 10% of credit sales, or $65,000.

You are one of Ken's regular customers. He knows that you are taking a course in accounting and has asked you to tell him your opinion of several alternatives that have been recommended to him to reduce or eliminate $65,000 per year bad debt loss. The recommended alternatives are as follows:

1. Do not sell on credit.
2. Sell on credit by national credit card only.
3. Allow customers to charge only until their account balance reaches $50.
4. Allow a bill collector to "go after" bad debts. He would keep half of what he collects.
5. Require all credit customers to sign a note so that Ken can discount these at the local bank.

Required: Using your own logic and experiences plus the information in this chapter, give your opinion on these alternatives. Which alternative do you recommend he follow?

BUSINESS SITUATION FOR DISCUSSION

IU International Sees Loss in Quarter from Write-Down*

By a WALL STREET JOURNAL *Staff Reporter*

Philadelphia—IU International Corp. said it expects a loss for the third quarter, resulting from a $4.7 million write-down.

The write-down stems from problems in combining IU's expanded trucking operations. The company also said it will restate previously reported first-half results.

IU declined to forecast the third-quarter loss. For the 1983 third quarter, the company had net income of $16.4 million on sales of $547.7 million.

The company said restated first-half earnings will total $12.5 million . . . compared with the previously released figure of $19.5 million. . . . Revenue will total $1.18 billion, compared with the previously announced $1.2 billion.

IU said the write-down resulted primarily from errors in recording revenue from shipments the company shared with other carriers. "Due to a computer glitch, revenues were overstated for that kind of shipment," said and IU spokesman. The problem didn't affect payments to connecting carriers.

The difficulty arose from changes in the computer system of IU's largest subsidiary, Ryder/P-I-E, during

the integration of Ryder Truck Lines and Pacific Intermountain Express into a single carrier in July 1983 and the further integration of Helms/Byrns Express into Ryder/P-I-E in May 1983.

In addition, in the months following the truck carrier mergers, normal billing and collection procedures were disrupted. This resulted in bills being mailed "far later" than normal, IU said. The company said it plans to increase its reserve for "uncollectibles" amid concern that it may have trouble recovering all its receivables, or amounts owed to it.

John Gilray Christy, IU's chairman and president said: "We always knew the task of two major trucking integrations was formidable, but we thought we would get our costs under control much sooner than has proved the case."

Earlier this month, IU warned that it didn't expect earnings to improve progressively each quarter this year, because of problems in integrating its trucking operations and price discounting in the industry.

But some outsiders weren't prepared for the extent of the problem. Said Louis A. Marckesano, senior transportation analyst at Janney Montgomery Scott Inc. in Philadelphia: "This comes as quite a shock. We knew there were inefficiencies involved in the mergers, but we didn't know it would go this deep."

IU's trucking divisions represent about 59% of the company's revenue. IU also distributes paper and food products and grows sugar cane.

---

* *The Wall Street Journal,* September 26, 1984, p. 12. Reprinted by permission of *The Wall Street Journal,* © Dow Jones & Company, Inc., 1984. All rights reserved.

CHAPTER 9

Measuring and Reporting Inventories

LEARNING OBJECTIVES

After studying this chapter, you should be able to:

1. Indicate what costs are properly included in inventory.
2. Calculate the effects of inventory errors on certain financial statement items.
3. Calculate cost of ending inventory, cost of goods sold, and effects on net income under the four major inventory cost methods.
4. Indicate the advantages and disadvantages of the four major inventory cost methods.
5. Apply the lower-of-cost-or-market method to inventory.
6. Estimate cost of ending inventory using the gross margin and retail inventory methods.
7. Record merchandise transactions under perpetual inventory procedure.
8. Define and use correctly the new terms in the glossary.

You may have been to a "pre-inventory sale" at your favorite retail store and witnessed the bargain prices that were designed to reduce the merchandise inventory on hand so as to minimize the time and expense of "taking the inventory." A smaller inventory enhances the probability of taking an accurate inventory since there is less merchandise to count. As you learned in Chapter 5, inventory amounts are used in determining the cost of the goods sold, which is a major expense of a merchandising company and affects the company's net income. In this chapter you will learn how important inventories are in preparing an accurate income statement, statement of owner's equity, and balance sheet.

This chapter discusses merchandise inventory carried by merchandising companies—retailers and wholesalers. Other types of inventory carried by manufacturers are discussed in a later chapter. Merchandise inventory is defined as the quantity of goods on hand or held by a merchandising company for resale to customers.

The merchandise inventory figure used by accountants depends on the quantity of inventory items and the cost of the items. The quantity of inventory items is determined by a physical count. Four accepted methods of costing the items are discussed in the chapter: (1) specific identification; (2) weighted-average; (3) first-in, first-out (Fifo); and (4) last-in, first-out (Lifo). Each of these methods has its advantages and disadvantages.

In studying this chapter, you should be impressed by the importance of having accurate inventory figures and the serious consequences of using inaccurate inventory figures. Then when you read or hear that a store is closing early to "take inventory" or that employees are working late to "take inventory," you will connect this taking of inventory with the cost of goods sold figure on the store's income statement, the owner's capital account shown on the statement of owner's equity, and the inventory figure and the owner's capital amount on the store's balance sheet.

■ INVENTORIES AND COST OF GOODS SOLD

Often inventory is the largest and most important asset owned by a merchandising business. The inventory of some companies, like car dealerships or jewelry stores, may cost several times more than any other asset the company owns. As an asset, the inventory figure has a direct impact on reporting the solvency of the company in the balance sheet. As a factor in determining cost of goods sold, the inventory figure has a direct impact on reported profitability of the company's operations as shown in the income statement. Thus, the importance of the inventory figure should not be underestimated.

To arrive at a current inventory figure, accountants must begin with an accurate physical count of inventory items. This section first discusses taking a physical inventory. Then you will learn why it is important to correctly cost this physical inventory. The remainder of the chapter discusses the methods of costing the physical inventory, departures from the cost basis of inventory measurement, and perpetual inventory procedure.

Taking a Physical Inventory

To take a physical inventory, the physical quantities of the goods on hand must be counted, weighed, measured, or estimated. For example, the suits in a clothing store may be counted; items such as bolts, washers, and nails may be weighed; items such as wire, cloth, and gasoline in storage tanks may be measured; and quantities of lumber, coal, or other bulky materials may be estimated by experts. Throughout the taking of a physical inventory, the goal should be accuracy.

Taking a physical inventory may disrupt the normal operations of a business. Thus, it is desirable that the count be administered as efficiently as possible. The actual taking of the inventory is not considered an accounting function; however, accountants often plan and coordinate the count. Proper forms are required to record accurate counts and determine totals. Identification names or symbols must be chosen, and those who count, weigh, or measure the inventory items must know these symbols.

Several inventory-taking methods involve the use of inventory tags. These tags are consecutively numbered for control purposes. A tag usually consists of a stub and a duplicate detachable section. The duplicate section facilitates checking in case of discrepancies. The format of tags can vary, but space is usually provided for (1) a detailed description and identification of inventory items by product, class, and model; (2) location of items; (3) quantity of items on hand; and (4) initials of the counters and checkers.

After the descriptive information is entered on the tags, they may be attached to the bins, shelves, or racks that contain the goods. The counters usually work in pairs and record their counts on the detachable sections of the tags and turn them in. Discrepancies between counts of the same items by different teams are reconciled by supervisors, and the correct counts are assembled on intermediate inventory sheets. When the inventory counts are completed and checked, the final sheets are sent to the accounting department for pricing and extensions. The tabulated result is the dollar amount of the physical inventory. Later in the chapter you will learn the different methods accountants use to cost an inventory.

Importance of Proper Inventory Valuation

A merchandising company can prepare accurate income statements, statements of owner's equity, and balance sheets only if the company has correctly valued its inventory. On the income statement, inventory is used to determine the cost of goods sold. Since the cost of goods sold figure affects the company's net income, it also affects the owner's capital account balance, which is shown in the statement of owner's equity. On the balance sheet, incorrect inventory amounts affect both the reported ending inventory and owner's capital. Inventories appear under the heading "Current assets." Current assets are reported in descending order of liquidity. Inventories follow cash and receivables in order of liquidity because they will be consumed or converted into cash within a year or one operating cycle, whichever is longer.

The cost of goods sold figure, as you will recall from Chapter 5, is determined by computing the cost of the (1) beginning inventory, (2) net cost of goods purchased, and (3) ending inventory. In each accounting period, the appropriate costs must be matched with the revenues of that period to determine the net income. As applied to inventory, matching involves determining how much of the cost of goods available for sale during the period should be deducted from current revenues and how much should be allocated to goods on hand and thus carried forward in the balance sheet to be matched against future revenues. Cost of goods sold is determined by deducting the ending inventory from the cost of goods available for sale. As a result, a highly significant relationship exists: **net income for an accounting period depends directly on the valuation of ending inventory.** Because of this relationship, note the following.

First, it is essential that the ending inventory be properly valued. If the ending inventory is overstated, cost of goods sold will be understated, resulting in an overstatement of gross margin, net income, and owner's equity. Also, overstatement of ending inventory will cause current and total assets to be overstated as well as owner's capital. Thus, any change in the calculation of ending inventory will be reflected, dollar for dollar (ignoring any income tax effects), in net income, current and total assets, and in owner's capital.

Second, when ending inventory is misstated in the current year, that misstatement is carried forward into the next year. This misstatement occurs because the ending inventory amount of the current year is the beginning inventory amount for the next year.

Third, an error in one period's ending inventory automatically causes an error in the opposite direction in the next period. After two years, however, the error will "wash out," and assets and owner's equity will be properly stated.

Illustrations 9.1 and 9.2 prove that net income for an accounting period depends directly on the valuation of the ending inventory. This is shown in both the income statements and statements of owner's equity of the Taylor Company for the years 1987 and 1988.

In Illustration 9.1, the correctly stated ending inventory for the year 1987 is $70,000. As a result, the company has a gross margin of $270,000 and net income after expenses of $100,000. The statement of owner's equity shows a beginning owner's equity of $240,000 and an ending owner's equity of $340,000. When the ending inventory is overstated by $10,000, as shown on the right, the gross margin is $280,000 and net income after expenses is $110,000. The statement of owner's equity then has an ending owner's equity of $350,000. The ending inventory overstatement of $10,000 is carried down to a $10,000 overstatement of net income, as well as a $10,000 overstatement of owner's equity. The balance sheet would show both an overstated inventory and owner's capital. Both management of the business and creditors of the business may overestimate the profitability of the business.

Illustration 9.1

Effects of an Overstated Ending Inventory

		Ending inventory correctly stated	Ending inventory overstated by $10,000
TAYLOR COMPANY			
For year ended December 31, 1987			
Income Statement			
Sales		$800,000	$800,000
Cost of goods available for sale	$600,000		$600,000
Ending inventory	70,000		80,000
Cost of goods sold		530,000	520,000
Gross margin		$270,000	$280,000
Other expenses		170,000	170,000
Net income		$100,000	$110,000
Statement of Owner's Equity			
Beginning owner's equity		$240,000	$240,000
Net income		100,000	110,000
Ending owner's equity		$340,000	$350,000

Illustration 9.2 is a continuation of Illustration 9.1 and gives the Taylor Company's operations for the year ended December 31, 1988. Note that the ending inventory in Illustration 9.1 now becomes the beginning inventory of Illustration 9.2. However, the company's inventory at December 31, 1988, is

now an accurate inventory of $90,000. As a result, the gross margin in the income statement with the beginning inventory correctly stated is $290,000, and the company has net income after expenses of $183,000 and an ending owner's equity of $523,000. In the income statement at the right, in which the beginning inventory is overstated by $10,000, the gross margin is $280,000, and net income after expenses is $173,000, with the ending owner's equity also at $523,000.

Illustration 9.2

Effects of an Overstated Beginning Inventory

	TAYLOR COMPANY	
	For year ended December 31, 1988	
	Beginning inventory correctly stated	**Beginning inventory overstated by $10,000**
Income Statement		
Sales	$850,000	$850,000
Beginning inventory . . . . $ 70,000		$ 80,000
Purchases 580,000		580,000
Cost of goods available for sale $650,000		$660,000
Ending inventory 90,000		90,000
Cost of goods sold	560,000	570,000
Gross margin	$290,000	$280,000
Other expenses	107,000	107,000
Net income	$183,000	$173,000
Statement of Owner's Equity		
Beginning owner's equity	$340,000	$350,000
Net income	183,000	173,000
Ending owner's equity	$523,000	$523,000

Thus, in contrast to an overstated ending inventory, which results in an overstatement of net income, an overstated beginning inventory results in an understatement of net income. If the cost of goods available for sale is overstated, then cost of goods sold will also be overstated. Consequently, gross margin and net income will be understated. Note, however, that when net income in the second year is closed to owner's equity, the owner's equity account will be stated at its proper amount. The overstatement of net income in the first year is offset by the understatement of net income in the second year. For the two years combined, then, the net income is correct. At the end of the second year, the balance sheet contains the correct amount for both inventory and owner's capital.

■ DETERMINING INVENTORY COST

To place the proper valuation on inventory, a business must answer the question: What costs should be included in inventory cost? Then when identical goods are purchased at different costs, a business must answer the question: Which cost should be assigned to the items sold? In this section you will learn how accountants answer these questions.

Costs Included in Inventory Cost

Generally, inventory cost includes all necessary outlays to obtain the goods, get the goods ready to sell, and have the goods in the desired location for sale to customers. Thus, inventory cost includes:

1. Seller's invoice price less purchase discount.
2. Cost of insurance on the goods while in transit.
3. Transportation charges when borne by the buyer.
4. Handling costs, such as the cost of pressing clothes wrinkled during shipment.

In theory, the cost of **each** unit of inventory should include its net invoice price plus its share of other costs incurred in shipment. However, practical difficulties arise in applying this rule.

Assume, for example, that the freight bill on a shipment of clothes does not state separately the cost of shipping one shirt. If the freight cost is to be included as part of the inventory cost of the shirt, it would have to be **allocated** in some manner to each unit because it cannot be measured directly. As a practical matter, allocations of freight, insurance, and handling costs to the individual units of inventory purchased are often not worth the additional cost incurred to perform the allocations. Consequently, in many companies, these costs of freight, insurance, and handling are not assigned to inventory but are expensed as incurred. The effect on net income of expensing these costs is minimized when the costs are omitted from both beginning and ending inventories.

Even if a cost is derived for each unit in inventory, the inventory valuation problem is not solved. Still to be resolved are these two problems:

1. If goods were purchased at varying unit costs, how should cost of goods available for sale be allocated between the units sold and those that remain in inventory? For example, assume Storey Company purchased two identical VCRs for resale. One was purchased for $450 and the other for $400. If one recorder was sold during the period, should Storey Company assign it a cost of $450, $400, or an average cost of $425?
2. Does the fact that current market prices are less than the cost of some units in inventory have any bearing on the amount at which inventory should be carried? Using the same example as above, if Storey Company can currently buy all VCRs at a price of $400, is it reasonable to carry some units in inventory at $450 rather than $400?

These questions are answered in the next section.

Inventory Valuation under Changing Prices

Inventories generally should be accounted for at historical cost, which is the cost at which the items were purchased. But this rule does not indicate how to assign costs to the ending inventory and to cost of goods sold when the goods have been purchased at different unit costs. For example, suppose a retailer has three units of a given product on hand. One unit was bought for $20, another for $22, and the third for $24. If the retailer sells two of the units for $30 each, what is the cost of the two units sold?

Methods of Determining Inventory Cost

Four inventory costing methods have been developed to solve this type of problem. They are: (1) specific identification; (2) first-in, first-out (Fifo); (3) last-in, first-out (Lifo); and (4) weighted-average. These costing methods are explained below. The frequency of use of these methods in a sample of 600 companies for the years 1980–83 is given in Illustration 9.3. Obviously, some companies use one method for certain inventory items and another method for other inventory items.

Illustration 9.3

Frequency of Use of Inventory Methods

	Number of Companies			
Methods	*1983*	*1982*	*1981*	*1980*
Last-in, first-out (Lifo) . .	408	407	408	396
First-in, first-out (Fifo) . .	366	373	371	382
Weighted-average . . .	235	238	241	238
Other	52	53	52	57

Source: Based on American Institute of Certified Public Accountants, *Accounting Trends & Techniques* (New York: AICPA, 1984), p. 123.

The data for purchases, sales, and beginning inventory given in Illustration 9.4 will be used to illustrate each of these four methods, and the use of periodic inventory procedure is assumed. Total goods available for sale consist of 80 units with a total cost of $690. A physical inventory determined that 20 units are on hand at the end of the period. Sales revenue for the 60 units sold was $780. The questions to be answered are: What is the cost of the 20 units in inventory? What is the cost of the 60 units sold?

Illustration 9.4   *Beginning Inventory, Purchases, and Sales*

Beginning inventory and purchases				Sales			
Date	*Units*	*Unit cost*	*Total cost*	*Date*	*Units*	*Price*	*Total*
Beginning inventory . .	10	$8.00	$ 80	March 10	10	$12.00	$120
March 2	10	8.50	85	July 14	20	12.00	240
May 28	20	8.40	168	September 7	10	14.00	140
August 12	10	9.00	90	November 22	20	14.00	280
October 12	20	8.80	176				
December 21	10	9.10	91				
	80		$690		60		$780

Ending inventory = 20 units, determined by taking a physical inventory.

Specific Identification.   The specific identification pricing method attaches the actual cost to an identifiable unit of product. This method is easily applied when large inventory items such as autos are purchased and sold. Under the specific identification method, each unit in inventory, unless it is unique, must be identified with a serial number plate or identification tag.

To illustrate, assume that in Illustration 9.4 the 20 units on hand at year-end can be identified as 10 units from the August 12 purchase and 10 units from the December 21 purchase. The ending inventory is computed as shown in Illustration 9.5, where the **$181 ending inventory cost is subtracted from the $690 cost of goods available for sale to get the $509 cost of goods sold.** Note that it is also possible to determine the cost of goods sold for the year by recording the cost of each unit sold. The $509 cost of goods sold is reported as an expense on the income statement, and the $181 ending inventory is a current asset on the balance sheet.

Illustration 9.5

Determining Ending Inventory under Specific Identification

	Units	Unit cost	Total cost
Ending inventory comprised of purchases made on:			
August 12	10	$9.00	$ 90
December 21	10	9.10	91
Ending inventory	20		$181
Cost of goods available for sale			$690
Ending inventory			181
Cost of goods sold			$509

Advantages and Disadvantages of Specific Identification.   When using the specific identification method of inventory pricing, cost of goods sold and ending inventory are stated at the actual cost of specific units sold and on hand. Some accountants argue that this method provides the most precise matching of costs and revenues and is, therefore, the most theoretically sound method. This statement is true for some one-of-a-kind items such as autos or real estate, and use of any other method for these items would seem completely illogical.

Accountants criticize the specific identification method, however, because with some items it results in identical units being included in inventory at different costs. For example, when the same television sets, differing only in their serial numbers, are purchased at different prices, they will be included in inventory at different costs.

Another disadvantage of the specific identification method is that it permits the manipulation of income. For example, assume a company has three identical units of a given product that were bought at different prices. One unit cost $2,000, the second cost $2,100, and the third cost $2,200. One unit is sold for $2,800. The units are alike, so the customer does not care which of the identical units is shipped. However, the gross margin on the sale could be either $800, $700, or $600 depending upon which unit is shipped.

Fifo (First-In, First-Out).   The Fifo method of inventory pricing assumes that the costs of the first goods purchased are the first costs charged to cost of goods sold when the goods are actually sold. In other words, the company assumes that the first goods purchased are the first goods sold. In some companies, the first units "in" (bought) must be the first units "out" (sold) to avoid large losses from spoilage. Such items as fresh dairy products, fruits, and vegetables should be sold on a Fifo basis. In these cases, an assumed first-in, first-out flow corresponds with the actual physical flow of goods.

Since the older units are assumed to be the first units sold and the newer units are assumed to be still on hand, the ending inventory consists of the most recent purchases. Thus, to determine the cost of the ending inventory under the Fifo method, begin by listing the cost of the most recent purchase. If the ending inventory contains more units than acquired in the most recent purchase, it will also include units from the next-to-the-latest purchase at the unit cost incurred, and so on. These units from the latest purchases must be listed until the number of units agrees with the number of units in the inventory.

Illustration 9.6 shows how the cost of ending inventory is determined under the Fifo method. The 20 units in inventory are assumed to consist of 10 units purchased December 21 and 10 units purchased October 12. The total cost of the inventory is $179. Subtracting $179 from the $690 cost of goods available for sale gives $511 as the cost of goods sold to be reported on the income statement. The $179 ending inventory is reported as a current asset on the balance sheet.

Illustration 9.6

Determining Fifo Cost of Ending Inventory under Periodic Procedure

	Units	Unit cost	Total cost
Ending inventory comprised of purchases made on:			
December 21	10	$9.10	$ 91
October 12	10	8.80	88
Ending inventory	20		$179
Cost of goods available for sale			$690
Ending inventory			179
Cost of goods sold			$511

Advantages and Disadvantages of Fifo. The Fifo method has several major advantages: (1) it is easy to apply, (2) the assumed flow of costs corresponds with the normal physical flow of goods, (3) no manipulation of income is possible, and (4) the balance sheet amount for inventory is likely to approximate the current market value. All the advantages of Fifo stem from the fact that the oldest unit costs are the first costs removed from inventory when goods are sold. Income cannot be manipulated by choosing which unit to ship because the cost of a unit sold is not determined by a serial number. Instead, the cost attached to the unit sold is always the oldest cost. Thus, purchases made at the end of the period have no effect on cost of goods sold or income under Fifo.

The disadvantages of Fifo include (1) the recognition of "paper" profits and (2) a heavier tax burden if used for tax purposes. These disadvantages are discussed later as advantages of Lifo.

Lifo (Last-In, First-Out). The Lifo method of inventory pricing assumes that the costs of the most recent purchases are the first costs charged to cost of goods sold when goods are actually sold. Since the latest costs are charged to cost of goods sold, the ending inventory consists of the oldest costs. Therefore, when determining the cost of inventory under the Lifo method, the oldest

Illustration 9.12

Inventory Estimation Using Retail Method

	Cost	Retail
Beginning inventory, January 1, 1987	$ 22,000	$ 40,000
Purchases, net	182,000	300,000
Goods available for sale	$204,000	$340,000
Cost/retail price ratio:		
$204,000/$340,000 = 60%		
Sales		280,000
Ending inventory at retail prices		$ 60,000
Times cost/retail price ratio		×60%
Ending inventory at cost, December 31, 1987 . .	36,000	
Cost of goods sold	$168,000	

of the cost/retail price ratio. In the example, the cost/retail price ratio is 60%, which means that on the average, 60 cents of each sales dollar is cost of goods sold. Ending inventory at retail ($60,000) is multiplied by 60% to find inventory at cost ($36,000). Once ending inventory has been estimated at cost ($36,000), the cost of ending inventory can be deducted from cost of goods available for sale ($204,000) to determine cost of goods sold ($168,000).

In 1988, the $36,000 and $60,000 amounts will appear on the schedule as beginning inventory at cost and retail, respectively. Purchases at cost and at retail will be added to determine goods available for sale at cost and at retail, and from these amounts a new cost/retail price ratio for 1988 will be computed.

At the end of each year a physical inventory usually is taken at retail prices. Since the retail prices are marked on the individual items (while the cost is not), taking an inventory at retail prices is more convenient than taking the inventory at cost. The results of the physical inventory can then be compared to the calculation of inventory at retail under the retail inventory method to determine whether a shortage exists.

Both the gross margin and the retail methods can be used to detect inventory shortages. To illustrate using the example given above, assume a physical inventory taken on December 31, 1987, shows only $56,000 of retail-priced goods in the store. Comparing this to the $60,000 of goods that should be on hand, shown in Illustration 9.12, indicates a $4,000 inventory shortage at retail. The $4,000 will be converted to $2,400 of cost ($4,000 × 0.60) and reported as a "Loss from inventory shortage" in the income statement. Knowledge of such shortages may lead to management action to reduce or prevent them, such as increasing security or improving the training of employees.

■ PERPETUAL INVENTORY PROCEDURE

Emphasis thus far in this chapter has been on periodic inventory procedure. Under periodic procedure, the Purchases account is debited when goods are acquired; other accounts are used for purchase-related items, and cost of goods sold is determined only at the end of the period as the difference between cost of goods available for sale and ending inventory. No records are kept of the cost of items as they are sold, and no information is provided on possible inventory shortages. Any goods not in ending inventory are assumed to have been sold.

Under perpetual inventory procedure, there are no purchases and purchase-related accounts. All entries involving merchandise purchased for sale to customers are entered directly in the Merchandise Inventory account. An entry is also made to reduce inventory for the cost of each item sold. Therefore, Merchandise Inventory at the end of the period will show the cost of the goods that should be on hand. Comparison of this amount with the cost obtained by taking and pricing a physical inventory will reveal inventory shortages. Thus, perpetual inventory procedure is an important element in providing internal control over goods with a high unit cost, such as automobiles, television sets, jewelry, and cameras.

Perpetual Inventory Records

Perpetual inventory procedure can be applied manually or by use of computers. In either procedure, a record will be maintained for each item in inventory. An example of an inventory record is given in Illustration 9.13 for Entertainment World, a firm that sells many different brands of television sets. Illustration 9.13 shows the information on one particular brand and model of television set carried in inventory. Other information given on the record includes the maximum and minimum number of units the company wishes to stock at any time, when and how many units were acquired and at what cost, and when and how many units were sold and what cost was assigned to cost of goods sold. The number of units on hand and their cost are readily available also.

Entertainment World is using the Fifo method of inventory costing on the record shown in Illustration 9.13. The method being used can be determined from the calculation of the cost of the eight units sold on July 22. Prior to this sale, there were 16 units on hand—6 with a unit cost of $300 and 10 with a unit cost of $315. Cost assigned to the units sold on July 22 consists

Illustration 9.13

Perpetual Inventory Record (Fifo Method)

Item	TV-96874				Maximum		26			
Location					Minimum		6			

	Purchased				Sold			Balance		
1987 Date	*Units*	*Unit cost*	*Total*	*Units*	*Unit cost*	*Total*	*Units*	*Unit cost*	*Total*
July 1							8	$300	$2,400
5	10	$300	$3,000				18	300	5,400
7				12	$300	$3,600	6	300	1,800
12	10	315	3,150				6	300	1,800
							10	315	3,150
22				6	300	1,800			
				2	315	630	8	315	2,520
24	8	320	2,560				8	315	2,520
							8	320	2,560

Illustration 9.14

Perpetual Inventory Record (Weighted-Average Method)

1987 Date	Purchased			Sold			Balance		
	Units	Unit cost	Total	Units	Unit cost	Total	Units	Unit cost	Total
July 1							8	$300.000	$2,400
5	10	$300	$3,000				18	$300.000	$5,400
7				12	$300	$3,600	6	$300.000	$1,800
12	10	315	3,150				10	315.000	3,150
							16	309.375*	$4,950
22				8	309.375	2,475	8	$309.375	$2,475
24	8	320	2,560				8	320.000	2,560
							16	$314.6875†	$5,035

* $4,950/16 = $309.375.
† $5,035/16 = $314.6875.

of the cost of the six oldest units and two of the more recently purchased units. Thus, costs are being removed from inventory on a Fifo basis.

Perpetual inventory procedure can also be used with the weighted-average method. Illustration 9.14 shows the same information as in Illustration 9.13 except that the weighted-average method is used rather than Fifo. Note that a new weighted-average unit cost is computed after **each purchase** by dividing total cost of goods available for sale by total units available for sale. Thus, the unit cost after the purchase of July 12 is $309.375 ($4,950/16). The cost of the eight units sold on July 22 is $2,475 (8 × $309.375). A new weighted-average unit cost is computed after the purchase of July 24. Under perpetual inventory procedures, the unit cost is referred to as a moving weighted-average because it changes after each purchase.

Because the advantages of Lifo are maximized when it is applied on an annual basis, Lifo is not likely to be applied on a perpetual basis. If Lifo is applied on a perpetual basis, special adjustments that are beyond the scope of this text must be made. For this reason, this text does not illustrate the application of Lifo under perpetual procedure.

Journal Entries under Perpetual Procedure

Some of the data in Illustration 9.14 are used to show the entries required under perpetual procedure. The purchase of 10 units on July 5 would be recorded as follows:

```
July 5   Merchandise Inventory  . . . . . . . . . . . .   3,000
              Accounts Payable   . . . . . . . . . . .            3,000
         To record purchase on account.
```

The 10 sets purchased must also be recorded on the perpetual inventory record, as shown in Illustration 9.14. Merchandise acquisitions are best recorded at net invoice prices to avoid having to adjust the gross invoice prices on all the inventory records when purchase discounts are subsequently taken.

Assuming the 12 sets sold on July 7 had a retail price of $450, the following entries are required:

July 7	Accounts Receivable	5,400	
	Sales		5,400
	To record 12 sets sold on account.		
7	Cost of Goods Sold	3,600	
	Merchandise Inventory		3,600
	To record cost of 12 sets sold.		

Perpetual procedure requires an entry to merchandise inventory whenever goods are purchased, returned, sold, or otherwise adjusted, so that inventory records reflect actual units on hand at all times. Thus, an entry is required to record cost of goods sold for each sale. Also, transportation costs incurred on goods purchased are debited to Merchandise Inventory.

At year-end, a physical inventory is taken and compared with perpetual records. If a shortage is discovered, an adjusting entry is required. The entry, assuming a $2,000 shortage is discovered, is:

Loss from Inventory Shortage	2,000	
Merchandise Inventory		2,000
To record inventory shortage.		

At the end of the period, the Cost of Goods Sold account is closed to Income Summary. There are no other purchase-related accounts to be closed.

■ SUMMARY

This chapter discusses merchandise inventory, which is the inventory merchandising companies own and hold for sale in the normal course of business. The inventory of manufacturers is discussed in a later chapter.

A company must place an accurate value on its ending inventory because this figure affects the company's income statement, statement of owner's equity, and balance sheet. To arrive at an accurate ending inventory figure, companies begin by taking an accurate physical count of inventory items. Then a correct monetary value must be placed on the physical inventory.

To correctly value an inventory, accountants first determine what costs should be included in the inventory cost and then decide how to value identical goods purchased at different costs. This chapter discusses the costs to be included in inventory cost as well as the four methods of inventory valuation: (1) specific identification; (2) first-in, first-out (Fifo); (3) last-in, first-out (Lifo): and (4) weighted-average. All four methods of inventory valuation are acceptable, and no one method can be considered the only correct method. Each method possesses attributes that make it attractive in certain circumstances.

Two departures from the cost basis of inventory measurement are discussed: (1) net realizable value and (2) lower-of-cost-or-market (LCM) method. The net realizable value is the estimated selling price, less any costs of preparing the goods for sale and selling them. Goods should not be carried in inventory at more than their net realizable value. The lower-of-cost-or-market (LCM) method is an inventory pricing method that values inventory at the lower of its historical cost or its current market (replacement) cost. In the accounting records, the LCM method may be applied to each item of inventory, to each class of inventory, or to the total inventory.

There are two recognized methods of estimating the cost of ending inventory: (1) the gross margin method and (2) the retail inventory method. The gross margin method estimates inventory cost by deducting estimated cost of goods sold from cost of goods available for sale. The retail inventory method estimates the cost of the ending inventory by applying a cost/retail price ratio to ending inventory stated at retail prices. Some companies estimate their inventory to (1) obtain an inventory cost figure to use for monthly or quarterly financial statements, (2) decide whether inventory shortages exist, or (3) determine the amount recoverable when an inventory is destroyed by fire or stolen.

You should now understand the importance of taking an accurate ending inventory, as well as how to value this inventory. In Chapter 10, accounting for another important group of assets is discussed—property, plant, and equipment.

NEW TERMS INTRODUCED IN CHAPTER

Fifo (first-in, first-out)

A method of pricing inventory under which the costs of the first goods purchased are the first costs charged to cost of goods sold when goods are actually sold (355).

Gross margin method

A procedure for estimating inventory cost in which estimated cost of goods sold (determined using an estimated gross margin) is deducted from the cost of goods available for sale to determine estimated ending inventory. The estimated gross margin is calculated using gross margin rates (in relation to net sales) of prior periods (363).

Inventory, or "paper," profits

Equal to the current replacement cost to purchase a unit of inventory at time of sale minus the unit's historical cost (357).

Lifo (last-in, first-out)

A method of pricing inventory under which the costs of the most recent purchases are the first costs charged to cost of goods sold when goods are actually sold (356).

Lower-of-cost-or-market (LCM) method

An inventory pricing method that values inventory at the lower of its historical cost or its current market (replacement) cost (362).

Merchandise inventory

The quantity of goods on hand and available for sale at any given time (348).

Net realizable value

Estimated selling price of an item less the estimated costs that will be incurred in preparing the item for sale and selling it (361).

Retail inventory method

A procedure for estimating the cost of the ending inventory by applying a cost/price ratio to ending inventory stated at retail prices (364).

Specific identification

An inventory pricing method that attaches the actual cost to an identifiable unit of product (354).

Weighted-average method

A method of pricing ending inventory using a weighted-average unit cost, determined by dividing the total number of units purchased plus those in beginning inventory into total cost of goods available for sale. Units in the ending inventory are carried at this per unit cost (359).

DEMONSTRATION PROBLEM 9–1

Following are data related to the beginning inventory and purchases of a product of the Van Company for the year 1987:

Inventory, January 1	5,000 @ $2.00
March 15	4,000 @ $2.10
May 10	7,000 @ $2.25
August 12	5,000 @ $2.40
November 20	3,000 @ $2.60
	24,000

During the year, 20,000 units were sold. Periodic inventory procedure is used.

Required: Compute (1) the ending inventory and (2) the cost of goods sold under each of the following methods:

a. Fifo.
b. Lifo.
c. Weighted-average.

Solution to demonstration problem 9–1

1. The ending inventory consists of 4,000 units (24,000 − 20,000).

a. Ending inventory under Fifo:

Purchased	Units	Unit cost	Total cost
November 20	3,000	$2.60	$ 7,800
August 12	1,000	2.40	2,400
	4,000		$10,200

b. Ending inventory under Lifo:

	Units	Unit cost	Total cost
Inventory, January 1	4,000	$2.00	$ 8,000

c. Ending inventory under weighted-average:

Purchased	Units	Unit cost	Total cost
Inventory, January 1	5,000	$2.00	$10,000
March 15	4,000	2.10	8,400
May 10	7,000	2.25	15,750
August 12	5,000	2.40	12,000
November 20	3,000	2.60	7,800
	24,000		$53,950

Weighted-average unit cost is $53,950 ÷ 24,000, or $2.248.
Ending inventory cost is $2.248 × 4,000 = $8,992.

2. Cost of goods sold under each method is:

    a. Cost of goods available for sale . . $53,950
           Ending inventory   10,200
                Cost of goods sold $43,750

    b. Cost of goods available for sale . . $53,950
           Ending inventory   8,000
                Cost of goods sold $45,950

    c. Cost of goods available for sale . . $53,950
           Ending inventory   8,992
                Cost of goods sold $44,958

DEMONSTRATION PROBLEM 9–2

a. The Meaders Company reported annual net income as follows:

1985 . . . . $68,000
1986   71,000
1987   60,000

Analysis of the inventories shows that certain clerical errors were made with the following results:

	Incorrect inventory amount	Correct inventory amount
December 31, 1985	$12,000	$14,200
December 31, 1986	14,000	11,700

What is the corrected net income for 1985, 1986, and 1987?

b. The records of Munch Corporation show the following account balances on the day a fire destroyed the company's inventory:

Inventory, January 1 . . . . $100,000
Purchases (to date) 500,000
Sales (to date) 750,000
Average rate of gross margin for
  the past five years . . . .   30% of net sales

Compute an estimated value of the ending inventory using the gross margin method.

c. The records of Turner Company show the following account balances at year-end:

	Cost	Retail
Beginning inventory, January 1 . .	$ 44,000	$ 62,500
Purchases	170,000	250,000
Transportation-in	4,750	
Sales		252,500

Compute the estimated ending inventory at cost using the retail inventory method.

Solution to demonstration problem 9–2

a.

	1985	1986	1987	Total
Net income as reported . .	$68,000	$71,000	$60,000	$199,000
Adjustments:				
(1)	2,200			
(2)		(2,200)		
		(2,300)		
(3)			2,300	
Adjusted net income . . .	$70,200	$66,500	$62,300	$199,000

(1) Ending inventory understated ($14,200 − $12,000 = $2,200).
(2) Beginning inventory understated ($14,200 − $12,000 = $2,200).
  Ending inventory overstated ($14,000 − $11,700 = $2,300).
(3) Beginning inventory overstated ($14,000 − $11,700 = $2,300).

b. Computation of inventory:

Inventory, January 1	$100,000
Purchases	500,000
Cost of goods available for sale . . .	$600,000
Less: Estimated cost of goods sold	
Net sales $750,000	
Gross margin ($750,000 × 0.30) . . 225,000	
Estimated cost of goods sold . . .	525,000
Inventory at cost, estimated by gross margin method	$ 75,000

c.

	Cost	Retail
Beginning inventory January 1	$ 44,000	$ 62,500
Purchases	170,000	250,000
Transportation	4,750	—
Goods available for sale	$218,750	$312,500
Cost/retail price ratio:		
$218,750/$312,500 = 70%		
Sales		252,500
Ending inventory at retail price		$ 60,000
Times cost/retail price ratio		× 70%
Ending inventory at cost, December 31 . .	42,000	
Cost of goods sold	$176,750	

QUESTIONS

1. Why is proper inventory valuation so important?

2. Why does an understated ending inventory understate net income for the period by the same amount?

3. Why does an error in ending inventory affect two accounting periods?

4. What cost elements are included in inventory? What practical problems are faced in including the costs of such elements?

5. What is the meaning of "to take a physical inventory?"

6. What is the accountant's responsibility regarding the taking of a physical inventory?

7. What are cost flows? What is meant by the physical flow of goods? Is there or should there be a relationship between cost flows and the physical flow of goods?

8. Indicate how a company can manipulate its net income if it uses Lifo. Is the same opportunity available under Fifo? Why or why not?

9. What are the main advantages of using Fifo and Lifo?

10. Which inventory method is the "correct" one? Can a company change inventory methods?

11. What is net realizable value, and how is it used?

12. Why is it considered acceptable accounting practice to recognize a loss by writing down an item of merchandise in inventory to market, but unacceptable to recognize a gain by writing up an inventory item?

13. Under what conditions will the gross margin method of computing an estimated inventory yield approximately correct amounts?

14. What are the main reasons for estimating ending inventory?

15. How can the retail method be used to estimate inventory?

16. When is it advisable to use perpetual inventory procedure? What problem is faced in accounting for purchase discounts under perpetual procedure? How is this problem best resolved?

EXERCISES

E-1

Determine effect of inventory errors

The Shane Company reported annual net income as follows:

1986 . . . . $75,700
1987   76,200
1988   64,060

Analysis of its inventories shows that the following incorrect inventory amounts were used (the correct amounts are also shown):

	Incorrect inventory amount	Correct inventory amount
December 31, 1986	$12,000	$14,000
December 31, 1987	13,500	11,500

Compute the annual net income for each of the three years assuming the correct inventories had been used.

E-2

Compute ending inventory under Fifo, Lifo, and weighted-average methods

The Parker Company inventory records show:

	Units	Unit Cost	Total Cost
Beginning inventory . .	3,000	$9.00	$27,000
February 14	900	8.40	7,560
March 18	2,400	8.25	19,800
July 21	1,800	8.70	15,660
September 27 . . .	1,800	8.40	15,120
November 27	600	8.85	5,310

The December 31 inventory was 4,200 units. Present a short schedule showing the measurement of the ending inventory using:

a. The Fifo method.
b. The Lifo method.
c. The weighted-average method.

E-3

Compute cost of goods sold under Fifo and Lifo and compare the results

The Wood Company's inventory of a certain product was 12,000 units with a cost of $32 each on January 1, 1987. During 1987, numerous units of this product were purchased and sold. Also during 1987, the purchase price of this product fell steadily until at year-end it was $24. The inventory at year-end was 18,000 units. State which of the two methods of inventory measurement, Lifo or Fifo, would have resulted in the higher reported net income, and explain briefly.

E–4

Prepare journal entries affecting inventory using periodic procedure

Following are inventory data for 1987 for the Franks Company:

1. January 1 inventory on hand, 400 units @ $6.
2. January sales were 80 units.
3. February sales totaled 120 units.
4. March 1, purchased 200 units @ $6.30.
5. Sales for March through August were 160 units.
6. September 1, purchased 40 units @ $6.90.
7. September through December sales were 180 units.

Prepare only the journal entries affecting inventory assuming use of periodic procedure. A physical inventory on December 31, 1987, showed 100 units on hand. Price the ending inventory at its weighted-average cost.

E–5

Compute cost of ending inventory using Fifo, Lifo, and weighted-average

Listed below are the purchases of Product A made by the Red Company in its first year of operations:

January 2	700 @ $2.96
March 31	600 @ $2.80
July 5	1,200 @ $3.04
November 1 . . .	900 @ $3.20

The ending inventory for the year consisted of 1,200 units.

a. Compute the cost of the ending inventory using each of the following methods: (1) Fifo, (2) Lifo, and (3) weighted-average.
b. Which method would yield the highest amount of gross margin? Explain why it does.

E–6

Compute inventory profit under Fifo

A company purchased 1,000 units of a product at $20 and 2,000 units at $22. It sold all of these units at $30 each at a time when the current cost to replace the units sold was $23. Compute the amount of gross margin under Fifo that Lifo supporters would call inventory, or "paper," profits.

E–7

Compute value of ending inventory using LCM applied on an item-by-item basis

Your assistant has compiled the following data to assist you in determining the decline in inventory from cost to the lower-of-cost-or-market method applied on an item-by-item basis:

Item	Quantity (units)	Unit cost	Unit market	Total cost	Total market
A	300	$48	$46	$14,400	$13,800
B	300	24	28	7,200	8,400
C	900	18	18	16,200	16,200
D	500	10	11	5,000	5,500

Determine the dollar amount of the ending inventory using the lower-of-cost-or-market method, determined on an item-by-item basis, and the amount of the decline from cost to lower-of-cost-or-market.

E–8

Compute value of total inventory using LCM

Use the data in Exercise E–7 above to compute the cost of the ending inventory using the lower-of-cost-or-market method applied to the total inventory.

E–9

Compute carrying cost of inventory items

Kelley Motor Company owns an automobile that it has used as a demonstrator for eight months. The auto has a list or sticker price of $20,000 and cost Kelley $17,000. The auto is on hand at the end of the fiscal year, at which time it has an expected selling price of $18,000. Costs expected to be incurred to sell the auto include tune-up and maintenance costs of $400, advertising of $100, and a commission to the employee selling the auto of 5% of selling price. Compute the amount at which the auto should be carried in inventory.

E-10

Estimate ending inventory using gross margin method

Westside Company takes a physical inventory at the end of each calendar-year accounting period to establish the ending inventory amount for financial statement purposes. Its financial statements for the past few years indicate an average gross margin on net sales of 25%. On July 18, a fire destroyed the entire store building and its contents. The records were in a fireproof vault and are intact. These records, through July 17, show:

Merchandise inventory, January 1	$ 420,000
Merchandise purchases	5,880,000
Purchase returns	84,000
Transportation-in	315,000
Sales	8,960,000
Sales returns	420,000

The company was fully covered by insurance and asks you to determine the amount of its claim for loss of merchandise.

E-11

Estimate ending inventory using gross margin method

Kobs Company takes a physical inventory at the end of each calendar-year accounting period. Its financial statements for the past few years indicate an average gross margin on net sales of 30%.

On June 12, a fire destroyed the entire store building and the inventory. The records were in a fireproof vault and are intact. These records, through June 11, show:

Merchandise inventory, January 1	$ 25,000
Merchandise purchases	625,000
Purchase returns	7,500
Transportation-in	42,500
Sales	775,000

The company was fully covered by insurance and asks you to determine the amount of its claim for loss of merchandise.

E-12

Estimate ending inventory using retail inventory method

The Michaels Company, Inc., records show the following account balances for the year ending December 31, 1986:

	Cost	Retail
Purchases	$10,000	$15,000
Beginning inventory	16,400	23,000
Transportation-in	200	
Sales		21,000

Using the above data, compute the estimated cost of ending inventory using the retail method of inventory valuation.

E-13

Prepare journal entries for inventory under perpetual Fifo procedure

The following are selected transactions and other data of the Bonner Company:

1. Purchased 20 units @ $75/unit on account on September 18, 1986.
2. Sold 6 units on account for $120/unit on September 20, 1986 (assume Fifo).
3. At year-end a physical inventory was taken, and a shortage of $550 was discovered.

Prepare journal entries for the above transactions using perpetual inventory procedure. Assume the beginning inventory consists of 20 units @ $70/unit.

E-14

Prepare journal entries under perpetual Fifo procedure

Following are selected transactions of the Nash Company:

Transactions:

1. Purchased 100 units of merchandise at $200 each, terms 2/10, n/30.
2. Paid the invoice in No. 1 within the discount period.
3. Sold 80 units at $320 each for cash.
4. Purchased 100 units at $300, terms 2/10, n/30.
5. Paid the invoice in No. 4 within the discount period.
6. Sold 60 units at $460 each for cash.

Prepare journal entries for the six numbered items above. Assume goods acquired are recorded at net invoice prices, accounted for under perpetual procedure, and the Fifo inventory method is used.

E-15

Compute the cost of goods sold assuming perpetual moving weighted-average procedure

Compute the cost of the goods sold in Exercise E–14 above, item No. 6, assuming perpetual procedure is used, with unit costs calculated under the weighted-average method. Round decimals to three places.

PROBLEMS, SERIES A

P9-1-A

Determine effects of inventory errors

Nix Company reported net income of $130,000 for 1987, $135,000 for 1988, and $145,000 for 1989, using the incorrect inventory amounts shown for December 31, 1987, and 1988. The correct inventory amounts are also shown for those dates. The correct December 31, 1989, inventory amount was used in calculating 1989 net income.

	Incorrect	*Correct*
December 31, 1987	$40,000	$45,000
December 31, 1988	38,000	35,000

Required: Prepare a schedule that shows: (1) the reported net income for each year in one column, (2) the amount of correction needed for each year in a second column, and (3) the correct net income for each year in a third column.

P9-2-A

Determine effects of inventory errors

An examination of the records of the Bond Company on December 31, 1987, disclosed the following with regard to merchandise inventory for 1987 and prior years:

1. December 31, 1983, inventory was correct.
2. December 31, 1984, inventory was understated $30,000.
3. December 31, 1985, inventory was overstated $21,000.
4. December 31, 1986, inventory was understated $18,000.
5. December 31, 1987, inventory was correct.

The reported net income for each year was as follows:

1984	$175,500
1985	213,000
1986	229,500
1987	210,000

Required: (Assume that the errors were not discovered until the end of 1987, so that no correcting entries have been made.)

a. What is the correct net income for each of the four years—1984–87?
b. What errors would have been included in each December 31 balance sheet? Assume each year's error is independent of the other years' errors.
c. Comment on the implications of the corrected net income as contrasted with reported net income.

P9–3–A

Maximize and minimize gross margin and net income using various cost-flow methods

Sea-Surf Company sells the Ultra-Light model wind surfer. All of the Ultra-Lights are identical except for identifying serial numbers. Sea-Surf Company had three Ultra-Lights in its inventory on August 1, 1987, that cost $5,600 each. During the month, the company purchased five Ultra-Lights from a dealer going out of business at $5,200 each. On August 17, six units were purchased at $5,800 each, and on August 28, six units were purchased at $6,000 each.

Sea-Surf Company sold 13 Ultra-Lights in August at $8,000 each. The company uses the specific identification method of accounting for its sales and purchases of Ultra-Lights.

Required:

a. Compute the gross margin earned by the company in August if it shipped the units that would maximize gross margin and net income.

b. Repeat part *(a)* assuming the company shipped the units that would minimize gross margin and net income.

c. Do you think Sea-Surf Company should be permitted to use the specific identification method of accounting for Ultra-Lights in view of the manipulation possible as shown by your calculations in *(a)* and *(b)*?

P9–4–A

Compute gross margin using Fifo and Lifo illustrating effects of end-of-year purchases

Wright Company accounts for its inventory using the Lifo method under periodic procedure. Data on purchases, sales, and inventory for the year ended December 31, 1987, are:

Inventory, January 1 .   .   4,000 units @ $7.50

Purchases:

January 7	. . . .	10,000 units @ $ 9.00
July 7 .	. . . .	20,000 units @ $10.50
December 21	. . .	12,000 units @ $12.00

During 1987, 32,000 units were sold for $480,000, leaving an inventory on December 31, 1987, of 14,000 units.

Required:

a. Compute the gross margin earned on sales during 1987.

b. Compute the change in gross margin that would have resulted if the purchase of December 21 had been delayed until January 6, 1988.

c. Recompute the gross margin that would have resulted if 18,000 units rather than 12,000 units had been purchased on December 21.

d. Solve parts *(a), (b),* and *(c)* using the Fifo method.

P9–5–A

Compute ending inventory under Fifo, Lifo, and weighted-average

Following are data for the Maddox Company for the year 1987:

Inventory, January 1 .   .   700 @ $5.20

Purchases:

February 2	. . . .	500 @ $5.00
April 5 .	. . . .	1,000 @ $4.00
June 15	. . . .	600 @ $3.50
September 30	. . .	700 @ $3.40
November 28	. . .	900 @ $4.50

During the year, 3,300 units were sold. Periodic inventory procedure is used.

Required:

a. Compute the ending inventory as of December 31, 1987, under each of the following methods: (1) Fifo, (2) Lifo, and (3) weighted-average.

b. Give the journal entries to record the purchases for the year and necessary year-end entries to charge Income Summary with the cost of goods sold for the year under Fifo.

P9–6–A

Compute cost of goods sold and gross margin under Fifo and Lifo

The Oglesby Company was organized on January 1, 1985. Selected data for 1985–87 are as follows:

Year ended December 31	Inventory		Annual data	
	Fifo	Lifo	Purchases	Sales
1985 .	. . .	$3,840	$2,880	$17,280	$19,440
1986 .	. . .	4,800	3,360	14,400	22,800
1987 .	. . .	7,920	4,800	17,760	19,680

Required: a. Compute the cost of goods sold and gross margin for each of the three years 1985–87, using the Fifo method of inventory measurement.
b. Repeat part *(a)* using Lifo.

P9–7–A

Compute difference in net income between Lifo and Fifo

The Kerns Company determined its net income for the years 1986, 1987, and 1988 as $408,000, $392,400, and $403,800, respectively, using the Fifo method of inventory measurement. Given below are ending inventories based on both the Fifo and Lifo methods:

December 31	Fifo	Lifo
1985	$ 90,000	$ 84,000
1986	103,200	94,800
1987	100,800	93,600
1988	109,800	100,200

Required: Compute the net income that would have been reported in 1986, 1987, and 1988 by the Kerns Company had it used the Lifo method of inventory measurement.

P9–8–A

Compute ending inventory using LCM

Data on the ending inventory of the Butler Company on December 31, 1987, are:

Item	Quantity	Unit cost	Unit market
1	4,200	$2.00	$1.95
2	8,400	1.80	1.90
3	2,800	1.75	1.80
4	7,000	2.40	2.25
5	5,600	2.25	2.30
6	1,400	1.90	1.80

Required: a. Compute the ending inventory applying the lower-of-cost-or-market method to the total inventory.
b. What would be the ending inventory applying the lower-of-cost-or-market method on an item-by-item basis?

P9–9–A

Estimate inventory using gross margin method

The sales and cost of goods sold for the Chapman Company for the past five years were as follows:

Year	Sales (net)	Cost of goods sold
1982	$2,080,200	$1,300,125
1983	2,248,800	1,405,500
1984 . . . :	2,572,200	1,607,625
1985	2,484,600	1,515,000
1986	2,655,800	1,650,000

For the seven months ended July 31, 1987, the following information is available from the accounting records of the company:

Sales	$1,614,200
Purchases	956,000
Purchase returns	6,000
Sales returns	36,200
Inventory, January 1, 1987 . .	197,500

In order to secure a loan, the Chapman Company has been asked to present current financial statements. But the company does not wish to take a complete physical inventory as of July 31, 1987.

Required: a. Indicate how financial statements can be prepared without taking a complete physical inventory.
b. From the data given, compute the estimated inventory as of July 31, 1987.

P9–10–A

Estimate ending inventory using retail inventory method

The Moore Company records disclosed the following inventory information for 1986:

	Cost	Retail
Sales	—	$700,000
Purchases	$660,000	970,000
Purchase returns . . .	14,000	20,000
Transportation-in . . .	18,000	
Inventory, January 1 . .	36,000	50,000

Required: Compute the estimated year-end inventory balance at cost using the retail method of inventory valuation.

P9–11–A

Compute cost of goods sold using Fifo for both perpetual and periodic inventory procedure

The inventory records of Tally Company show the following:

Jan. 1 Beginning inventory consists of 12 units costing $10/unit.
  5 Purchased 15 units @ $10.40/unit.
  10 Sold 9 units @ $22.50/unit.
  12 Sold 7 units @ $22.50/unit.
  20 Purchased 20 units @ $10.45/unit.
  22 Purchased 5 units @ $10.00/unit.
  30 Sold 20 units @ $23.00/unit.

Assume all purchases and sales are made on account.

Required:
a. Using perpetual Fifo inventory procedure, compute cost of goods sold for January.
b. Using perpetual Fifo inventory procedure, prepare the journal entries for the month of January.
c. Compute the cost of goods sold under periodic Fifo inventory procedure. Is there a difference between the amount computed using the two different methods?

PROBLEMS, SERIES B

P9–1–B

Determine effects of inventory errors

Thornton Company reported net income of $476,800 for 1987, $495,200 for 1988, and $434,400 for 1989, using the incorrect inventory amounts shown for December 31, 1987, and 1988. The correct inventory amounts for those dates are also given. The correct December 31, 1989, inventory amount was used in calculating 1989 net income.

	Incorrect	Correct
December 31, 1987	$ 96,800	$113,600
December 31, 1988	112,000	93,600

Required: Prepare a schedule that shows: (1) the reported net income for each year in one column, (2) the amount of correction needed for each year in a second column, and (3) the correct net income for each year in a third column.

P9–2–B

Determine effects of inventory errors

As of December 31, 1987, the financial records of the Parsons Company were examined for the years ended December 31, 1984, 1985, 1986, and 1987. With regard to the inventory, the examination disclosed the following:

1. December 31, 1983, inventory was correct.
2. December 31, 1984, inventory was overstated $45,000.
3. December 31, 1985, inventory was overstated $22,500.
4. December 31, 1986, inventory was understated $49,500.
5. December 31, 1987, inventory was correct.

The reported net income for each year was:

1984	$ 86,400
1985	122,400
1986	150,750
1987	190,350

Required: (Assume that the errors were not discovered until the end of 1987, so no correcting entries have been made.)

a. What is the correct net income for each of the four years—1984–87?
b. What error(s) would have been included in each December 31 balance sheet? Assume each year's error is independent of the other years' errors.
c. Comment on the implications of your corrected net income as contrasted with reported net income.

P9–3–B

Maximize and minimize gross margin and net income using various cost-flow methods

The Chip Company sells home computers. It uses the specific identification method to account for its inventory. As of November 30, 1987, the company has 23 Orange III model home computers on hand which were acquired on the following dates and at the stated costs:

July 3	5 @ $3,200
September 10 . .	10 @ $3,000
November 29 . .	8 @ $3,500

Chip sold 18 Orange III computers at $4,600 each in December. There were no purchases of this model in December.

Required:
a. Calculate gross margin on December sales of Orange III computers assuming the company shipped those units that would maximize reported gross margin.
b. Repeat part *(a)* assuming the company shipped those units that would minimize reported gross margin for December.
c. In view of your answers to parts *(a)* and *(b),* what would be your reaction to an assertion that the specific identification method should not be considered an acceptable method for costing inventory?

P9–4–B

Compute gross margin using Lifo and Fifo illustrating effects of end-of-year purchases

The Salter Company accounts for a certain product that it handles using periodic Lifo inventory procedure. Data relative to this product for the year ended December 31, 1987, are:

Inventory January 1, 3,000 units @ $12

Purchases			Sales		
January 5 . . .	6,000 @ $15		January 10 . .	4,000 @ $24	
March 31 . . .	18,000 @ $18		April 2	15,000 @ $27	
August 12 . . .	12,000 @ $22.50		August 22 . . .	16,000 @ $30	
December 26 . .	6,000 @ $24		December 24 . .	3,000 @ $33	

Required:
a. Compute the gross margin earned on sales of this product for 1987.
b. Repeat part *(a)* assuming that the December 26 purchase was made in January of 1988.
c. Recompute the gross margin assuming that 10,000 rather than 6,000 units were purchased on December 26.
d. Solve parts *(a), (b)* and *(c)* using the Fifo method.

P9–5–B

Compute ending inventory under Fifo, Lifo, and weighted-average

The purchases and sales of a certain product for the Cutter Company for April 1987 are shown below. There was no inventory on April 1.

Purchases			Sales		
April 3	2,000 units @ $7.00		April 4	1,200 units	
April 10	1,600 units @ $7.20		April 11	1,000	
April 22	3,200 units @ $6.60		April 16	1,000	
April 28	1,800 units @ $6.80		April 26	800	
			April 30	1,200	

Required: a.   Using periodic procedure, compute the ending inventory of the above product as of April 30 under each of the following methods: (1) Fifo, (2) Lifo, and (3) weighted-average.

b.   Give the journal entries to record the purchases and the necessary year-end entries to charge Income Summary with the cost of goods sold for the month under both Fifo and Lifo.

P9–6–B

Compute ending inventory and cost of goods sold using Fifo and Lifo

Listed below are the purchases and sales of a certain product made by the Fairfield Company during 1987 and 1988. The company had 30,000 units of this product on hand at January 1, 1987, with a cost of $2.50 per unit.

Purchases			*Sales*		
1987			**1987**		
February 20	. .	6,000 @ $2.50	February 2 .	. .	9,000 @ $3.50
April 18 .	. . .	15,000 @ $2.45	April 23 .	. . .	12,000 @ $3.00
August 28 .	. .	15,000 @ $2.40	September 3 .	.	12,000 @ $2.90
December 22 .	.	12,000 @ $2.42	December 24 .	.	10,500 @ $2.95
1988			**1988**		
January 26	. .	9,000 @ $2.50	January 7 .	. .	7,500 @ $3.00
March 6	. . .	15,000 @ $2.50	March 21 .	. .	12,000 @ $3.10
August 12 .	. .	9,000 @ $2.60	September 8 .	.	7,500 @ $3.10
November 15 .	.	12,000 @ $2.70	December 2 .	.	13,500 @ $3.25

The company uses periodic inventory procedure.

Required: a.   Compute the cost of the ending inventory and the cost of goods sold for both years assuming the use of the Fifo method of inventory measurement.

b.   Repeat (a) above using the Lifo method.

P9–7–B

Compute difference in net income between Lifo and Fifo

Given below are the inventory amounts under Fifo and Lifo for the Bibb Company:

December 31		*Fifo*	*Lifo*
1986 .	. . .	$240,000	$196,000
1987 .	. . .	248,000	232,000
1988 .	. . .	276,000	272,000

The Bibb Company has used the Fifo method of inventory measurement and reported net income of $660,000 in 1987 and $680,000 in 1988.

Required: State the amount of net income that the company would have reported in 1987 and 1988 if it had used the Lifo method rather than Fifo.

P9–8–B

Compute ending inventory using LCM

The accountant for the Goldberg Company prepared the following schedule of the company's inventory at December 31, 1987, and used the lower of the total cost or total market value in determining cost of goods sold.

Item	*Quantity*	*Unit cost*	*Unit market*	*Total cost*	*Total market*
Q	4,200	$3.00	$3.00		
R	2,400	2.50	2.40		
S	5,400	2.00	1.90		
T	4,800	1.75	1.80		

Required: a.   State whether this is an acceptable method of inventory measurement, and determine the amounts computed.

b.   Compute the amount of the ending inventory using the lower-of-cost-or-market method on an item-by-item basis.

c.   State the effect on net income in 1987 if the method in (b) was used rather than the method in (a).

P9-9-B

Estimate inventory using gross margin method

As part of a loan agreement with a local bank, the Hudson Company must present quarterly and cumulative income statements for the year 1987. The company uses periodic inventory procedure and marks its merchandise to sell at a price that will yield a gross margin of 30%. Selected data for the first six months of 1987 are as follows:

	First quarter	Second quarter
Sales	$310,000	$320,000
Purchases	200,000	230,000
Purchase returns and allowances	12,000	14,000
Purchase discounts	4,000	4,400
Sales returns and allowances	10,000	6,000
Transportation-in	10,000	10,400
Selling expenses	32,000	30,000
Administrative expenses	12,000	10,000

The cost of the physical inventory taken December 31, 1986, was $38,000.

Required:
a. Indicate how income statements may be prepared without taking a physical inventory at the end of each of the first two quarters of 1987.
b. Prepare income statements for the first quarter, the second quarter, and the first six months of 1987.

P9-10-B

Estimate ending inventory using retail inventory method

The Roberts Company records show the following information:

	Cost	Retail
Sales	—	$584,000
Purchases	$450,000	700,000
Transportation-in	43,800	—
Inventory, January 1	20,000	29,000
Purchase returns	25,200	31,000

Required: Compute the year-end inventory balance at cost using the retail method of estimating inventory.

P9-11-B

Prepare journal entries for purchases and sales using perpetual Fifo procedure

The inventory records of Monroe Company show the following:

Mar. 1 Beginning inventory consists of 12 units costing $10/unit.
     3 Sold 6 units at $23.50/unit.
    10 Purchased 20 units at $12.00/unit.
    12 Sold 10 units at $24.00/unit.
    20 Sold 9 units at $24.00/unit.
    25 Purchased 20 units at $12.50/unit.
    31 Sold 10 units at $24.00/unit.

Assume all sales and purchases are made on credit.

Required: Using perpetual Fifo inventory procedure, prepare the appropriate journal entries for the month of March.

BUSINESS DECISION PROBLEM 9–1

9–1

Determine tax effects of Fifo, Lifo, and weighted-average

The Jackson Company, which began operations on January 2, 1987, sells a single product, product X. Purchases for the year were:

January 2	1,500 at $4.00
February 15	2,400 at $4.00
April 8	3,000 at $4.15
June 6	1,200 at $4.25
August 19	2,400 at $4.30
October 5	1,800 at $4.50
November 22	1,200 at $4.80

Periodic inventory procedure is used. On December 31, a physical inventory shows 2,400 units on hand.

Mr. Jackson is trying to decide which of the following inventory costing methods he should adopt for tax purposes: Fifo, Lifo, or weighted-average. Since Mr. Jackson is short of cash, he wants to minimize the amount of income taxes payable.

Required: What will be the cost of goods sold and the cost of the ending inventory under this method? Which of the three inventory costing methods will minimize Mr. Jackson's net income (and income taxes)?

BUSINESS DECISION PROBLEM 9–2

9–2

Determine insurance settlement using gross margin method

Anne Ferrell owns and operates a sporting goods store. On February 2, 1987, the store suffered extensive fire damage, and all of the inventory was destroyed. Ms. Ferrell uses periodic inventory procedure and has the following information in her accounting records, which were undamaged:

Inventory, January 1 . .	$ 60,000
Purchases:	
January 8	24,000
January 20	36,000
January 30	48,000
Net sales:	
During January . . .	180,000
February 1 and 2 . .	12,000

Ms. Ferrell also knows that her gross margin rate on net sales has been 40% for the past three years. Ms. Ferrell's insurance company has offered to pay $42,000 to settle her inventory loss unless she can show that she suffered a greater loss.

Required: Should Ms. Ferrell settle for $42,000? If not, how can she show that she suffered a greater loss? What is the estimated loss?

BUSINESS SITUATION FOR DISCUSSION

Is LIFO Dead?*
Excerpt from Digest *(Anchin Block & Anchin) April 1984.*

Back during inflation's rampage through the 1970s, many companies adopted the LIFO method (last-in, first-out) for pegging their inventory cost. A radical change from FIFO costing (first-in, first-out), LIFO was made necessary because sharply rising prices created a false sense of profit growth. Earnings statements were inflated—self-deceiving because of how expensive it had become to replace that inventory.

By adopting LIFO accounting, inflationary "inventory profits" were effectively eliminated, and reported earnings were lower and more realistic for tax and financial statement purposes.

But don't assume that LIFO will always be a more conservative approach than FIFO. Today, with sharply reduced inflation—and even deflation—in commodity prices, some companies may again be experiencing an artificial rise in earnings. For example, the wholesale cost of petroleum-based products, various agricultural goods, and imports actually dropped during 1983, making it cheaper to replace the sold inventory.

In the hypothetical situation shown in the table comparing LIFO to FIFO, note that purchases and sales are identical. The only difference is how we valued the opening and closing inventories.

As you can see in a falling price market the LIFO method did not present the results on a more conservative basis than FIFO—and there are inventory profits which are not "real." In fact, if business conditions also lead to a reduction in inventory *quantities,* reported earnings could be affected to an even greater extent.

Reduced inflation and even some falling costs are not likely to bring about a swing back to FIFO. But one message is clear; it takes a little extra work and savvy to read and understand a financial statement in changing times.

	Units	Price	FIFO	LIFO
Sales	150,000	$10	$1,500,000	$1,500,000
Cost of Sales:				
Opening Inventory	50,000			
FIFO		$ 8	$ 400,000	
LIFO		$ 5		250,000
Purchases:				
First Lot	75,000	$ 8	600,000	600,000
Second Lot	75,000	$ 6	450,000	450,000
Available for Sale	200,000		1,450,000	1,300,000
Closing Inventory	50,000			
FIFO		$ 6	300,000	
LIFO		$ 5		250,000
Cost of Sales	150,000			
FIFO		$ 7.67	1,150,000	
LIFO		$ 7		1,050,000
Gross Profit			$ 350,000	$ 450,000

---

* *The CPA Journal,* September 1984, p. 8. Used with permission.

Property, Plant, and Equipment

After studying this chapter, you should be able to:

1. State the characteristics of plant assets.
2. Determine the "cost" of plant assets.
3. Show how accounting records are used to account for and help control plant assets.
4. Compute plant asset depreciation under various methods and circumstances.
5. Cite and discuss the theoretical and practical advantages of the major depreciation methods.
6. Illustrate the reporting of plant assets and their related depreciation.
7. Distinguish between capital and revenue expenditures on plant assets.
8. Define and use correctly the new terms in the glossary.

In Chapter 4, you learned about the classified balance sheet. The asset section of that balance sheet was divided into (1) current assets and (2) property, plant, and equipment. Current assets were discussed in Chapters 7–9. This chapter discusses property, plant, and equipment, which are often referred to as **plant and equipment** or simply **plant assets.** Plant assets consist of land and manufactured or constructed assets, such as buildings, machinery, vehicles, and furniture.

In accounting for plant assets, accountants must:

1. Identify the original (acquisition) cost of the asset.
2. Distinguish between:
   a. Routine maintenance.
   b. Repair expenditures and expenditures that increase the asset's service capacity or extend its useful life.

3. Allocate the asset's cost to periods of its useful life through the process of depreciation.
4. Recognize the gain or loss, if any, upon the retirement or disposal of the asset.

These tasks must be done so that there is a proper matching of costs with the revenues generated by the asset. Since the measurement of periodic expense associated with plant assets affects net income, accounting for property, plant, and equipment is important to financial statement readers.

There is a difference between the economic life and the physical life of a plant asset. For example, on TV you may have seen a demolition crew setting off explosives in a huge building and wondered why a decision was made to destroy what looked like a perfectly good building. The reason was that the building had "lived" its economic life. The land on which the building stood could be put to better use, possibly by constructing a new building.

■ NATURE OF PLANT ASSETS

To be classified as a plant asset, an asset must (1) be tangible, that is, capable of being seen and touched; (2) have a useful service life of more than one year; and (3) be used in business operations rather than held for resale to a customer. Plant assets include buildings, machines, tools, office equipment, and so on. On the balance sheet, these assets are included under the heading "Property, plant, and equipment."

Plant assets can be viewed as a collection of **service potentials** that are used up or consumed over a long period of time. For example, a delivery truck may provide 100,000 miles of delivery service over several years. A new building may provide 40 years of shelter, while a machine may perform a certain operation on 400,000 parts. In each instance, purchase of the plant asset actually consists of the advance payment or prepayment for expected services. Plant asset costs are an **extreme form of prepaid expense.** As was the case with short-term prepayments, the accountant must allocate the cost of these services to the accounting periods benefited.

Plant assets include all long-lived tangible assets that are used to generate the principal revenues of the firm. Inventory is a tangible asset but not a plant asset, because it is held for sale rather than use. A delivery truck may be classified by one business (a dealership) as inventory because it is held for sale and by another business (a retail appliance store) as a plant asset because it is being used rather than offered for sale. Land held for speculation or not yet put into service is a long-term investment rather than a plant asset because it is not being used by the business. Standby equipment that is used only in peak or emergency periods is classified as a plant asset because it is used in the operations of the business.

■ INITIAL RECORDING OF PLANT ASSETS

When plant assets are acquired, they are recorded in an asset account at the cost of acquisition (historical cost) because this cost is objective, verifiable, and the best measure of an asset's fair value. Even if the market value of the asset changes over time, the acquisition cost continues to be the amount reported in the asset account in subsequent accounting periods.

Cost is the amount of cash and/or cash equivalent given up to acquire a plant asset and place it in operating condition at its proper location. Thus, cost includes all normal, reasonable, and necessary expenditures to obtain the asset and get it ready for use. Cost also includes the repair and reconditioning costs for assets that were acquired in used or damaged condition.

Cost does not include losses, such as the cost of waste or inefficiency. For example, cost does not include fines or penalties from traffic violations for failure to secure necessary permits to move heavy machinery on city streets. Nor does cost include expenditures incurred to repair damages resulting from vandalism or improper handling of an asset suffered after purchase. Interest charges incurred on a debt arising from the purchase of a plant asset are also not normally included in the cost of a plant asset; these charges are treated as expenses of the accounting period. However, there is an exception to this general rule. When interest charges are incurred on funds borrowed to finance the construction of a major asset, they must be added to the asset's cost if the construction period extends over one year.[1] Thus, interest paid must be included as plant asset cost for construction projects such as dams, buildings, ships, and similar major assets.

Sometimes a company receives compensation from the temporary use of an asset by outside parties during its construction period. These amounts should be credited to the asset account rather than to a revenue account. The cost of the asset is thereby reduced. The following section discusses which costs are capitalized for specific plant assets.

Land and Land Improvements

Cost of land includes the purchase price of the land and other costs such as option cost, if any; real estate commissions; title search and title transfer fees; title insurance premiums; existing mortgage note assumed; unpaid taxes (back taxes) assumed by the purchaser; cost of surveying, clearing, grading, and landscaping; and local assessments for sidewalks, streets, sewers, and water mains. When land purchased as a building site contains an old unusable building that must be removed, the entire purchase price should be debited to Land, including the cost of removing the old building less any cash received from the sale of salvaged materials. The Land account should be credited for the sales price of salvaged items, such as crops or fruit on the land, that occur while the land is being readied for use.

Land usually does not deteriorate gradually with use, except agricultural land which may lose its fertility or be subject to erosion. When land is purchased as a building site or location, it generally retains its ability to render services indefinitely and is not subject to depreciation. However, certain improvements made to land are depreciable. Land improvements are attachments to land, such as driveways, parking lots, fences, lighting systems, and sprinkler systems, that have limited lives and therefore are depreciable. These depreciable land improvements should be recorded in a separate account from the Land account, such as a Land Improvements account.

---

[1] FASB, "Capitalization of Interest Cost," *Statement of Financial Accounting Standards No. 34* (Stamford, Conn., 1979).

Buildings

When an existing building is purchased, its cost includes purchase price, repair and remodeling costs, unpaid taxes assumed by the purchaser, legal costs, and real estate commissions paid. The cost of a newly constructed building, however, is often more difficult to determine.

The cost of constructing a building usually includes architect's fees; building permits; payments to contractors; labor and materials; salaries of officers supervising construction; and insurance, taxes, and interest during the construction period. Any miscellaneous amounts earned from the building during construction reduce the cost of the building. For example, if a small completed portion of the building is rented out during construction of the remainder of the building, the rental proceeds are credited to the Buildings account.

Land and Buildings Purchased Jointly

When land and buildings are purchased together, the total cost should be divided to show the cost of the land and the cost of the buildings. Then separate accounts must be established for land and for buildings so that proper depreciation charges on the buildings can be recorded.

To illustrate, assume that Bonner Company purchased a farm for $180,000 on the outskirts of Lima, Ohio, as a factory site. The farm consisted of land and one building, which is to be remodeled for use. The purchase price, $180,000, must be allocated to the land and the building. A common method of allocating this cost is to use appraised values by having the land and buildings appraised separately.

The total of the appraised values of the assets often differs from the total price paid. An example of this difference is when assets are priced below appraised values for a "quick sale." The relative appraised values are used to determine the apportionment of total cost of the individual assets. For example, if the land was appraised at $160,000 and the building at $40,000, the $180,000 purchase price would be allocated 80% to land and 20% to the building as follows:

	Appraised value	Percent of total appraised value	Allocated cost
Land	$160,000	80%	$144,000 (80% × $180,000)
Building	40,000	20	36,000 (20% × $180,000)
Total	$200,000	100%	$180,000

The journal entry to record the purchase of the farm by Bonner would be:

Land	144,000	
Building	36,000	
Cash		180,000
To record purchase of land and building.		

Instead of the above situation, assume Bonner Company purchased the $180,000 farm and intended to tear down (raze) the building and construct

c.   Sum-of-the-years'-digits.
d.   Double-declining-balance.

E–7

Compute DDB depreciation

Mann Company purchased a machine for $800 and incurred installation costs of $200. The estimated salvage value of the machine is $50. The machine has an estimated useful life of four years.

Compute the annual depreciation charges for this machine under the double-declining-balance method.

E–8

Compute depreciation before and after revision of expected life

The Spurling Company acquired a delivery truck on January 2, 1987, for $16,750. The truck had an estimated salvage value of $750 and an estimated useful life of eight years. At the beginning of 1990, a revised estimate shows that the truck has a remaining useful life of six years. The estimated salvage value changed to $250.

Compute the depreciation charge for 1987 and the revised depreciation charge for 1990 using the straight-line method.

E–9

Allocate periodic depreciation to building and to expense

Assume that the truck described in Exercise E–8 was used 40% of the time in 1988 to haul materials used in the construction of a building by the Spurling Company for its own use. (Remember that 1988 is before the revision was made on estimated life.) In the remaining time, the truck was used to deliver merchandise sold by Spurling to its customers.

Prepare the journal entry to record straight-line depreciation on the truck for 1988.

E–10

Compute depreciation under SYD and DDB methods

Brim Company purchased a machine on April 1, 1987, for $15,000. The machine has an estimated useful life of five years with no expected salvage value. The company's accounting year ends on December 31.

Compute the depreciation expense for 1988 under *(a)* the sum-of-the years'-digits method and *(b)* the double-declining-balance method.

E–11

Compute straight-line depreciation after major overhaul

On January 2, 1987, a company purchased and placed in operation a new machine at a total cost of $24,000. Depreciation was recorded on the machine for 1987 and 1988 under the straight-line method using an estimated useful life of four years and no expected salvage value. Early in 1989, the machine was overhauled at a cost of $8,000. The total useful life of the machine was revised upward to a total of seven years.

Compute the depreciation on the machine for 1989.

E–12

Compute straight-line depreciation given reduced estimated life and salvage value

Nix Company purchased a computer for $12,500 and placed it in operation on January 2, 1986. Depreciation was recorded for 1986 and 1987 using the straight-line method, a six-year life, and an of expected salvage value of $500. The introduction of a new model of this computer caused the company in 1988 to revise its estimate of useful life to a total of four years and to reduce the estimated salvage value to zero.

Compute the revised depreciation for 1988.

E–13

Compute error in net income when installation and freight costs are expensed

Rich Company purchased a machine on January 3, 1987, at a cost of $60,000. Freight and installation charges of $12,000 were incurred and debited to Repairs Expense. Straight-line depreciation was recorded on the machine in 1987 and 1988 using an estimated life of 10 years and no expected salvage value.

Compute the amount of the error in net income for 1987 and 1988, and state whether net income is understated or overstated.

PROBLEMS, SERIES A

P10-1-A

Determine cost of land

Jacob Company paid a local realtor $2,000 to find a suitable site for its new factory. When found, Jacob agreed to pay the owner of the site $30,000 cash, to assume responsibility for a $10,000 mortgage note on the property and $200 of accrued interest on the note, and to pay back taxes on the property of $500. Jacob also paid legal fees of $250 and a $300 title insurance premium in acquiring the property. A local lumber yard paid Jacob $400 for some walnut trees that it removed from the property. Jacob also paid the city $3,500 to widen the street in front of the property and received $1,000 for a narrow strip of land deeded to the city in order to widen the street. Grading and leveling costs of $1,500 were also incurred by Jacob.

Required: Prepare a schedule showing the amount to be recorded as the cost of the land.

P10-2-A

Determine cost of machine

Street Company purchased a machine for use in its operations that had a gross invoice price of $40,000 excluding sales tax. A 4% sales tax was levied on the sale. The company paid freight costs of $1,000. Special electrical connections were run to the machine at a cost of $1,400, and a special reinforced base for the machine was built at a cost of $1,800. The machine was dropped and damaged while being mounted on this base. Repairs cost $400. Raw materials with a cost of $100 were consumed in testing the machine. Safety guards were installed on the machine at a cost of $140, and the machine was placed in operation.

Required: Prepare a schedule showing the amount at which the machine should be recorded in the Street Company's accounts.

P10-3-A

Determine cost of land

The Evans Company purchased two square miles of farmland under the following terms: $302,500 cash; liability assumed on mortgage note of $100,000 and interest accrued on mortgage note assumed, $4,000. The company paid $21,000 of legal and brokerage fees and also paid $1,000 for a title search on the property.

The company planned to use the land as a site for a new office building and a new factory. Clearing and leveling costs of $9,000 were paid. Crops on the land were sold for $2,300, and one of the houses on the property was sold for $6,000. The other buildings were torn down at a cost of $4,500; sale of salvaged materials yielded cash proceeds of $4,250. Approximately 1% of the land acquired was deeded to the county for roads. The cost of excavating a basement for the office building amounted to $2,850.

Required: Prepare a schedule showing the amount at which the land should be carried on Evans Company's books.

P10-4-A

Determine cost of truck; prepare entry for depreciation under DDB and for straight-line depreciation assuming change in estimated life

Austin Company purchased a used panel truck for $18,000 cash. The next day the company's name and business were painted on the truck at a total cost of $930. The truck was then given a minor overhaul at a cost of $120, and new tires were mounted on the truck at a cost of $1,200, less a trade-in allowance of $150 for the old tires. The truck was placed in service on April 5, 1987, at which time it had an estimated useful life of five years and a salvage value of $2,100.

Required: a. Prepare a schedule showing the cost to be recorded for the truck.
b. Prepare the journal entry needed to record depreciation at the end of the calendar-year accounting period, December 31, 1987. Use the double-declining-balance method.

c. Now assume that the straight-line depreciation method is being used and that at the beginning of 1990 it is estimated the truck will last another four years. Prepare the entry to record depreciation for 1990. The estimated salvage value changed to $1,200.

P10–5–A

Compute cost of land, land improvements, building, and machinery; prepare entry to correct the accounts

You are the new controller for Rainbow Company, which began operations on October 1, 1987, after a "start-up" period that ran from the middle of 1986. While reviewing the accounts, you find an account entitled "Fixed Assets," which contains the following items:

Cash paid to previous owner of land and old building	$ 40,000
Treasury bills given to construction company as partial payment	15,000
Legal and title search fees	500
Real estate commission	3,000
Cost of demolishing old building	3,500
Cost of leveling and grading	2,000
Architect's fee (90% building and 10% improvements)	7,500
Cost of excavating basement for new building	4,500
Cash paid to construction company for new building	60,000
Repair damage done by vandals	1,500
Sprinkler system for lawn	6,500
Lighting system for parking lot	8,500
Paving of parking lot	12,500
New invoice price of machinery	240,000
Freight cost incurred on machinery	10,500
Installation and testing of machinery	4,000
Medical bill paid for employee injured in installing machinery	750
Landscaping	8,000
Repair damage to building in installation of machinery	1,000
Special assessment paid to city for water mains and sewer line	9,500
Account balance	$438,750

In addition to the above, you discover that cash receipts of $250 from selling materials salvaged from the old building were credited to Miscellaneous Revenues in 1987. Digging deeper, you find that the plant manager spent all of his time for the *first nine months* of 1987 supervising installation of land improvements (10%), building construction (40%), and installation of machinery (50%). The plant manager's nine-month salary of $22,500 was debited to Officers' Salaries Expense.

Required:

a. List the above items on a form containing columns for Land, Land Improvements, Building, and Machinery. Sort the items into the appropriate columns, omitting those items not properly included as an element of asset cost. Show negative amounts in parentheses. Total your columns.

b. Prepare one compound journal entry to reclassify and adjust the accounts and to eliminate the Fixed Assets account. Do not attempt to record depreciation for the partial year.

P10–6–A

Compute depreciation for first year under each of four different methods

Corbin Company acquired and put into use a machine on January 1, 1987, at a cash cost of $48,000 and immediately spent $2,000 to install it. The machine was estimated to have a useful life of eight years and a scrap value of $10,000 at the end of this time. It was further estimated that the machine would produce 500,000 units of product during its life. In the first year, the machine produced 100,000 units.

Required: Prepare journal entries to record depreciation for 1988, using:

a. The straight-line method.
b. The units-of-production method.
c. The sum-of-the-years'-digits method.
d. The double-declining-balance method.

P10-7-A

Compute depreciation for two years using three methods; partial-year depreciation used first year

The Brooke Company paid $12,000 for a machine on April 1, 1987, and placed it in use on that same date. The machine has an estimated life of 10 years and an estimated salvage value of $2,000.

Required: Compute the amount of depreciation to the nearest dollar the company should record on this asset for the years ending December 31, 1987, and 1988, under each of the following methods:

a. Straight-line.
b. Sum-of-the-years'-digits.
c. Double-declining-balance.

PROBLEMS, SERIES B

P10-1-B

Determine cost of land

In seeking a site for its new home office building, Tall Company paid a local realtor $6,000 to find the appropriate location. Tall agreed to pay the owner of the site $100,000 cash, to assume responsibility for a $40,000 mortgage note on the property and $600 of accrued interest on the note, and to pay back taxes on the property of $1,600. Tall also paid legal fees of $800 and a $1,000 title insurance premium in acquiring the property. A local salvage company paid Tall $18,000 for a building that it moved from the property. Tall also paid the city $16,000 to extend water mains and sewer lines to the property.

Required: Prepare a schedule showing the amount to be recorded as the cost of the land.

P10-2-B

Determine cost of machine

Drexel Company purchased a machine for use in its operations that had a gross invoice price of $5,000 excluding sales tax. A 4% sales tax was levied on the sale. The company estimated the total cost of hauling the machine from the dealer's warehouse to the company's plant at $350, which did not include a fine of $100 for failure to secure the necessary permits to use city streets in transporting the machine. In delivering the machine to its plant, a Drexel employee damaged the truck used; repairs cost $225. The machine was also slightly damaged with repair costs amounting to $100.

Drexel incurred installation costs of $2,000 that included the $250 cost of shoring up the floor under the machine. Testing costs amounted to $150. Safety guards were installed on the machine at a cost of $40, and the machine was placed in operation.

Required: Prepare a schedule showing the amount at which the machine should be recorded in Drexel's accounts.

P10-3-B

Determine cost of land and building

Blue Company planned to erect a new factory building and a new office building in Atlanta, Georgia. A report on a suitable site showed an appraised value of $150,000 for land and orchard and $100,000 for a building.

After considerable negotiation, the company and the owner reached the following agreement. Blue Company was to pay $180,000 in cash, assume a $75,000 mortgage note on the property, assume the interest accrued on the mortgage note of $1,600, and assume unpaid property taxes of $11,000. Blue Company paid $15,000 cash for brokerage and legal services in acquiring the property.

Shortly after acquisition of the property, Blue Company sold the fruit on the trees for $2,200, remodeled the building into an office building at a cost of $32,000, and removed the trees from the land at a cost of $7,500. Construction of the factory building was to begin in a week.

Required: Prepare schedules showing the proper valuation of the assets acquired by the Blue Company.

P10–4–B

Prepare entry for acquisition of machine, for depreciation under DDB and for straight-line depreciation assuming change in estimated life

Cone Company acquired and placed into use a heavy factory machine on October 1, 1987. The machine had an invoice price of $144,000, but the company received a 3% cash discount by paying the bill on the date of acquisition. An employee of Cone Company hauled the machine down a city street without a permit. As a result, the company had to pay a $600 fine. Installation and testing costs totaled $14,320. The machine is estimated to have a $14,000 salvage value and a seven-year useful life.

Required:

a. Prepare the journal entry to record the acquisition of the machine.
b. Prepare the journal entry to record depreciation for 1987 under the double-declining-balance method.
c. Now assume that the straight-line depreciation method is being used and that at the beginning of 1990 it is estimated the machine will last another six years. Prepare the journal entry to record depreciation for 1990. The estimated salvage value will not change.

P10–5–B

Compute cost of land, land improvements, building, and machinery; prepare entry to correct the accounts

Medley Company has the following entries in its Building account:

Debits

1987			
May	5	Cost of land and building purchased	$250,000
	5	Broker fees incident to purchase of land and building	15,000
1988			
Jan.	3	Contract price of new wing added to south end of building . .	105,000
	15	Cost of new machinery, estimated life 10 years	200,000
June	10	Real estate taxes for six months ended 6/30/88	4,500
Aug.	10	Cost of building parking lot for employees	
		in back of building	6,200
Sept.	6	Replacement of windows broken in August	200
Oct.	10	Repairs due to regular usage	2,800

Credits

1987			
Dec.	31	Transfer to Land account, per allocation of purchase	
		cost authorized in minutes of board of directors	40,000
1988			
Jan.	5	Proceeds from lease of second floor for	
		six months ended 12/31/87	10,000

The original property was acquired on May 5, 1987. Medley Company immediately engaged a contractor to construct a new wing on the south end of the building. While the new wing was being constructed, the company leased the second floor as temporary warehouse space to Charles Company. During this period (July 1 to December 31, 1987), the company installed new machinery costing $200,000 on the first floor of the building. Regular operations began on January 2, 1988.

Required:

a. Compute the correct balance for the Building account as of December 31, 1988. The company employs a calendar-year accounting period.
b. Prepare the necessary journal entries to correct the records of Medley Company at December 31, 1988. No depreciation entries are required.

P10–6–B

Compute depreciation for first year under each of four different methods

Redding Company acquired and placed into use equipment on January 2, 1987, at a cash cost of $374,000. Transportation charges amounted to $3,000, and installation and testing costs totaled $22,000. The equipment was damaged while being installed, and the cost of repairing the damage was $1,800.

The equipment was estimated to have a useful life of nine years and a salvage value of $15,000 at the end of its life. It was further estimated that the equipment would be used in the production of 1,920,000 units of product during its life. During 1987, 426,000 units of product were produced.

Required: Compute the depreciation for the year ended December 31, 1987, using:

a. The straight-line method.
b. The units-of-production method.
c. The sum-of-the-years'-digits method.
d. The double-declining-balance method.

P10–7–B

Compute depreciation for two years using three methods; partial-year depreciation used first year

The Clarke Company purchased a machine on October 1, 1987, for $20,000. The machine has an estimated salvage value of $6,000 and an estimated useful life of eight years.

Required: Compute the amount of depreciation to the nearest dollar Clarke should record on the machine for the years ending December 31, 1987, and 1988, under each of the following methods:

a. Straight-line.
b. Sum-of-the-years'-digits.
c. Double-declining-balance.

BUSINESS DECISION PROBLEM 10–1

Compute correct cost of land, building, and land improvements; compute depreciation; prepare entry to correct the accounts last quarter

Rolland Company has the following entries in its Building account:

Debits

1987			
Jan.	2	Cost of land and old buildings purchased	$ 900,000
	2	Legal fees incident to purchase	12,000
	2	Fee for title search	1,500
	12	Cost of demolishing old buildings on land	24,000
June	16	Cost of insurance during construction of new building . . .	6,000
July	30	Payment to contractor upon completion of new building . .	1,350,000
Aug.	5	Architect's fees for design of new building	60,000
Sept.	15	City assessment for sewers and sidewalks	21,000
Oct.	6	Cost of landscaping	12,000
Nov.	1	Cost of driveways and parking lots	75,000

Credit

Jan.	15	Proceeds received upon sale of salvaged materials from old buildings	6,000

You are in charge of auditing the Rolland Company's Building account. In addition to the entries in the account, you are given the following information:

1. The company began using the new building on September 1, 1987. The building is estimated to have a 40-year useful life and no salvage value.
2. The company began using the driveways and parking lots on November 1, 1987. The driveways and parking lots are estimated to have a 10-year useful life and no salvage value.
3. The straight-line depreciation method is used to depreciate all of the company's plant assets.

Required:
a. Prepare a schedule that shows separately the cost of land, buildings, and land improvements.
b. Compute the amount of depreciation expense for 1987.
c. What journal entries are required to correct the accounts at December 31, 1987? (Assume that Depreciation Expense, Buildings was debited for the entire amount of depreciation credited to the Buildings account. Also assume that closing entries have not been made.)

BUSINESS DECISION PROBLEM 10–2

Compute partial-year depreciation under each of four different methods; cite circumstances in which each of the different methods seems most appropriate

On October 1, 1988, Melton Company acquired and placed into use new equipment costing $105,000. The equipment has a useful life of five years and an estimated salvage value of $5,000. It is estimated that the equipment will produce 2,000,000 units of product during its life. In the last quarter of 1988, the equipment produced 120,000 units of product.

Required:
a. Compute the depreciation for the last quarter of 1988 using each of the following methods:
  1. Straight-line.
  2. Units-of-production.
  3. Sum-of-the-years'-digits.
  4. Double-declining-balance.
b. Describe the conditions in which each of the above four methods would be most appropriate.

BUSINESS SITUATION FOR DISCUSSION

General Fixed Asset Accounting*
Barry E. Vallee, CPA

Fixed asset accounting for a commercial organization plays an important part in determining the net income of the entity. However, . . . [even though] a municipality does not consider the determination of net income as critical as a commercial unit, fixed asset accounting is every bit as important. Municipalities must account for fixed assets to uphold the stewardship commitment.

General fixed assets are those fixed assets of a governmental unit which are not accounted for in an enterprise, working capital, or trust fund. To be classified as a fixed asset in this category, the property must possess three attributes: (1) tangible nature; (2) a life longer than the current fiscal year; and (3) a significant value. There are several classes of assets that a municipality will possess that will meet criteria (1) and (2). That tends to make criteria (3) as perhaps the single most important "test" to determine the placement of a fixed asset into the general fixed assets group of accounts. However, what constitutes significant value may vary from one governmental unit to another. The "judgment factor" will still remain prevalent.

For those fixed assets which are determined to have significant value, the importance of having a complete and accurate accounting cannot be emphasized too

* *The Michigan CPA,* September–October, 1980, pp. 13–14. Used with permission.

strongly. Adequate accounting procedures and records for fixed assets are essential to the protective custody of governmental property. The responsibilities of stewardship involved in accounting for the usually large public investment is of the utmost importance to sound financial administration, and this responsibility can be effectively discharged only through adequate fixed asset accounting.

* * * * *

Proper accounting for general fixed assets requires proper classification of the individual assets within the recommended asset classes, and the capitalization of appropriate costs and charges within each class. The recommended classes for accounting and statement presentation purposes are: Land; Buildings; Improvements Other Than Buildings; Equipment; and Construction in Progress. Land cost should include legal fees, title fees, surveying fees, appraisal fees, damage payments, cleaning, filling, leveling, and any demolition of unwanted structures. Costs of buildings include purchase price, professional fees, damage claims, cost of fixtures attached to the building, related costs during construction, and any other costs necessary to put the structure into its intended state of operation. Equipment should be valued at the total purchase price before trade in allowance and minus any trade discounts. Other costs that should be included in capitalized value are transportation charges, installation costs, taxes, or any other cost necessary to get the equipment into use.

* * * * *

The general fixed assets of a municipality should be accounted for in a group of accounts separate and distinct from the accounts of any fund. The value of general fixed assets is not available to meet fund obligations. For that reason the general fixed assets, except as previously mentioned, those of utility funds or other business type funds, should not be reflected in any fund. The records kept for these assets make it possible to hold the proper officials accountable for the assets assigned to them or under their control, since they show the acquisition, sale, retirement, and present location of each asset.

Physical inventories of general fixed assets should be taken at least annually. Assets that are carried in the accounts but not reflected in the inventory count should be made the subject of an investigation to determine why the assets are missing. The accounts should be adjusted by eliminating fixed assets found to be missing and adding assets not carried in the accounts but found to be on hand.

* * * * *

Plant Asset Disposals, Natural Resources, and Intangible Assets

LEARNING OBJECTIVES

After studying this chapter, you should be able to:

1. Prepare entries to record the disposal of a plant asset.
2. Explain and illustrate how to account for trade-ins of plant assets for accounting purposes and for income tax purposes.
3. Determine the cost of natural resources, record depletion on such resources, and determine the cost of resources sold.
4. Prepare entries to account for the acquisition, amortization, and disposition of intangible assets.
5. Define and use correctly the new terms in the glossary.

The study of long-term assets, which includes plant assets, natural resources, and intangible assets, began in Chapter 10. Discussion in that chapter focused on determining plant asset cost, computing depreciation, and distinguishing between capital and revenue expenditures. This chapter begins by discussing the disposal of plant assets. The next topic is accounting for natural resources such as ores, minerals, oil and gas, and timber. The final topic is accounting for intangible assets, such as patents, copyrights, franchises, trademarks and trade names, and leases.

Although several different long-term assets are discussed in this chapter, you will see that accounting for all long-term assets is basically the same. When a company purchases a long-term asset, the asset is recorded at cost. As the company receives benefits from the asset and the future service potential is reduced, the cost is transferred from an asset account to an expense account. Since the lives of long-term assets can extend for many years, the methods accountants use in reporting them can have a dramatic effect on the financial statements of many accounting periods.

■ DISPOSAL OF PLANT ASSETS

All plant assets except land eventually wear out or become inadequate or obsolete and must be sold, retired, or traded in on new assets. When a plant asset is disposed of, both the asset's cost and accumulated depreciation must be removed from the accounts. In this section you will learn how to account for the (1) sale of plant assets, (2) retirement of plant assets without sale, (3) destruction of plant assets, (4) exchanges of dissimilar and similar plant assets, and (5) costs of dismantling and removing an asset.

Sale of Plant Assets

Companies frequently dispose of plant assets by selling them. By comparing an asset's book value (cost less accumulated depreciation) with its sales price (or net amount realized if there are selling expenses), the company will show either a gain or loss. If the sales price is greater than the asset's book value, the company will show a gain. If the sales price is less than the asset's book value, the company will show a loss. Of course, if the sales price is equal to the asset's book value, there is no gain or loss.

To illustrate accounting for the sale of a plant asset, assume equipment costing $30,000 with accumulated depreciation of $12,000 is sold for $20,000. A gain of $2,000 is realized as computed below:

Equipment cost	$30,000
Accumulated depreciation . .	12,000
Book value	$18,000
Sales price	20,000
Gain realized	$ 2,000

The journal entry to record the sale is:

Cash	20,000	
Accumulated Depreciation—Equipment	12,000	
Equipment		30,000
Gain on Disposal of Plant Assets		2,000
To record sale of equipment at a price greater than book value.		

If, on the other hand, the equipment is sold for $16,500, a loss of $1,500 ($18,000 book value − $16,500 sales price) is realized, and the journal entry to record the sale is:

Cash	16,500	
Accumulated Depreciation—Equipment	12,000	
Loss on Disposal of Plant Assets	1,500	
Equipment		30,000
To record sale of equipment at a price less than book value.		

If the equipment is sold for $18,000, there is no gain or loss, and the journal entry to record the sale is:

Cash	18,000	
Accumulated Depreciation—Equipment	12,000	
Equipment		30,000
To record sale of equipment at a price equal to book value.		

Accounting for Depreciation to Date of Disposition.   When a plant asset is sold or otherwise disposed of, it is important to record the depreciation up to the date of sale or disposition. For example, if an asset is sold on April 1 and depreciation was last recorded on December 31, depreciation for three months (January 1–April 1) should be recorded. If depreciation is not recorded for the three months, operating expenses for that period will be understated, and the gain on the sale of the asset will be understated or the loss overstated.

To illustrate, assume that on August 1, 1988, Ray Company sold a machine for $1,500. The machine cost $12,000 and was being depreciated at the straight-line rate of 10% per year. As of December 31, 1987, after closing entries were made, the machine's accumulated depreciation account had a balance of $9,600. Before a gain or loss can be determined and before an entry can be made to record the sale, the following entry must be made to record depreciation for the seven months ended July 31, 1988:

July 31	Depreciation Expense—Machinery	700	
	Accumulated Depreciation—Machinery		700
	To record depreciation for seven months ($12,000 × 0.10 × $\frac{7}{12}$).		

The $200 loss on the sale is computed as shown below:

Machine cost	$12,000
Accumulated depreciation ($9,600 + $700)	10,300
Book value	$ 1,700
Sales price	1,500
Loss realized	$ 200

The journal entry to record the sale is:

Cash	1,500	
Accumulated Depreciation—Machinery	10,300	
Loss on Disposal of Plant Assets	200	
Machinery		12,000
To record sale of machinery at a price less than book value.		

Retirement of Plant Assets without Sale

When a plant asset is retired from productive service, the asset's cost and accumulated depreciation must be removed from the plant asset accounts. For example, Hayes Company would make the following journal entry when a fully depreciated machine that cost $15,000 and had no salvage value is retired:

Accumulated Depreciation—Machinery	15,000	
Machinery		15,000
To record the retirement of a fully depreciated machine.		

Occasionally, a plant asset is continued in use after it has been fully depreciated. In such a case, the asset's cost and accumulated depreciation should **not** be removed from the accounts until the asset is sold, traded, or retired from service. Of course, no more depreciation can be recorded on a fully depreciated asset because total depreciation expense taken on an asset may never exceed the asset's cost.

Sometimes a plant asset is retired from service or discarded before it is fully depreciated. If the asset is to be sold as scrap (even if not immediately), its cost and accumulated depreciation should be removed from the asset and accumulated depreciation accounts. In addition, its estimated scrap value should be recorded in a Salvaged Materials account, and a gain or loss on disposal should be recognized. To illustrate, assume a machine with a $7,000 original cost and $6,200 of accumulated depreciation is retired. If the machine's estimated scrap value is $375, the following entry is required:

Salvaged Materials	375	
Accumulated Depreciation—Machinery	6,200	
Loss on Disposal of Plant Assets	425	
Machinery		7,000
To record retirement of machinery, which will be sold for scrap at a later time.		

Destruction of Plant Assets

Plant assets are sometimes wrecked in accidents or destroyed by fire, flood, storm, or other causes. Losses are normally incurred in such situations. For example, assume that an **uninsured** building costing $40,000 with accumulated depreciation of $12,000 was completely destroyed by a fire. The journal entry is:

Fire Loss	28,000	
Accumulated Depreciation—Building	12,000	
Building		40,000
To record fire loss.		

If the building was **insured,** only the amount of the fire loss exceeding the amount to be recovered from the insurance company would be debited to the Fire Loss account. To illustrate, assume that in the example above, the building was partially insured and that $22,000 is recoverable from the insurance company. The journal entry is:

Receivable from Insurance Company	22,000	
Fire Loss	6,000	
Accumulated Depreciation—Building	12,000	
Building		40,000
To record fire loss and amount recovered from insurance company.		

Exchanges of Dissimilar Plant Assets

Sometimes a machine is traded for a dissimilar plant asset such as a truck. Exchanges of dissimilar plant assets are accounted for by recording the new asset at the fair market value of the asset received or the asset(s) given up, whichever is more clearly evident.[1] The cash price of the new asset may be stated; if so, the cash price should be used to record the new asset. If the cash price is not stated, the fair market value of the old asset plus any cash paid is used to record the new asset. Thus, the asset received would normally be recorded at either (1) a stated cash price of the new asset or (2) a known fair value of the asset given up plus any cash paid.

The book value of the old asset is removed from the accounts by debiting accumulated depreciation and crediting the old asset. The Cash account is

---

[1]APB, "Accounting for Nonmonetary Transactions," *APB Opinion No. 29* (New York: AICPA, May 1973), par. 16.

credited for any amount paid. If the amount at which the new asset is recorded exceeds the book value of the old asset plus any cash paid, a gain is recorded to balance the journal entry. If the situation is vice versa, a loss is recorded to balance the journal entry.

To illustrate such an exchange, assume that an old factory machine is exchanged for a new delivery truck. The machine cost $40,000 and had an accumulated depreciation balance of $33,000. The truck had a $50,000 cash price and was acquired by trading in a machine with a fair value of $3,000 and paying $47,000 cash. The journal entry to record the exchange is:

Delivery Truck	50,000	
Accumulated Depreciation—Factory Machinery	33,000	
Loss on Disposal of Plant Assets	4,000	
Factory Machinery		40,000
Cash		47,000
To record loss on exchange of dissimilar plant assets.		

The $4,000 loss on the exchange can also be computed as the book value of the old asset less the fair market value of the old asset. The calculation is as follows:

Machine cost	$40,000
Accumulated depreciation	33,000
Book value	$ 7,000
Fair market value of old asset (trade-in allowance)	3,000
Loss realized	$ 4,000

To illustrate the recognition of a gain from an exchange of dissimilar plant assets, assume that the fair market value of the above machine was $8,000 instead of $3,000, and that $42,000 was paid in cash. The gain would be $1,000 ($8,000 fair market value less $7,000 book value). The journal entry to record the exchange would be:

Delivery Truck	50,000	
Accumulated Depreciation—Factory Machinery	33,000	
Factory Machinery		40,000
Cash		42,000
Gain on Disposal of Plant Assets		1,000
To record gain on exchange of dissimilar plant assets.		

Exchanges of Similar Plant Assets

Plant assets such as automobiles, trucks, and office equipment are often exchanged by trading the old asset for a similar new one. In such cases, the company usually receives a trade-in allowance for the old asset,[2] and the balance is paid in cash. The cash price of the new asset is often stated. If not, the cash price is assumed to be the fair market value of the old asset plus the cash paid.

When similar assets are exchanged, the general rule that new assets are recorded at the fair market value of what is given up or received is modified

---

[2] Trade-in allowance is sometimes expressed as the difference between *list* price and cash paid, but we choose to define it as the difference between *cash* price and cash paid because this latter definition seems to agree with current practice for exchange transactions.

slightly. The new asset is recorded at (1) the book value of the old asset plus the cash paid or (2) the cash price of the asset received, whichever is lower. When this rule is applied to exchanges of similar assets, **losses are recognized (or recorded), but gains are not.**

To illustrate the accounting for exchanges of similar plant assets, assume $47,000 cash and delivery truck No. 1, which cost $40,000 and had $33,000 accumulated depreciation, were exchanged for delivery truck No. 2. The new truck has a cash price (fair market value) of $50,000. A loss of $4,000 is realized on the exchange.

Cost of delivery truck No. 1	$40,000
Accumulated depreciation	33,000
Book value	$ 7,000
Fair market value of old asset (trade-in allowance)	3,000
Loss on exchange of plant assets	$ 4,000

The journal entry to record the exchange is:

Delivery Trucks (cost of No. 2)	50,000	
Accumulated Depreciation—Delivery Trucks	33,000	
Loss on Disposal of Plant Assets	4,000	
Delivery Trucks (cost of No. 1)		40,000
Cash		47,000
To record loss on exchange of similar plant assets.		

Note that exchanges of similar plant assets are recorded just like exchanges of dissimilar plant assets when a *loss* occurs from the exchange.

Accounting for any gain resulting from exchanges of similar assets is handled differently than a gain resulting from exchanges of dissimilar plant assets. To illustrate, assume that in the preceding example, delivery truck No. 1 and $42,000 cash were given in exchange for delivery truck No. 2. A gain of $1,000 is indicated on the exchange:

Cost of delivery truck No. 1	$40,000
Accumulated depreciation	33,000
Book value	$ 7,000
Fair market value of old asset (trade-in allowance)	8,000
Gain indicated	$ 1,000

The journal entry to record the exchange is:

Delivery Trucks (cost of No. 2)	49,000	
Accumulated Depreciation—Delivery Trucks	33,000	
Delivery Trucks (cost of No. 1)		40,000
Cash		42,000
To record exchange of similar plant assets.		

When similar assets are exchanged, a gain is **not** recognized. The new asset is recorded at book value of the old asset ($7,000) plus cash paid ($42,000). The gain is deducted from the cost of the new asset ($50,000). Thus, the cost basis of the new delivery truck is equal to $50,000 less the $1,000 gain, or $49,000. This cost basis is used in recording depreciation on the truck and determining any gain or loss on its disposal.

Since the life of the mine (10 years or 1,000,000 tons) is shorter than the life of the building (20 years), the building should be depreciated over the life of the mine. In this case, the depreciation charge should be based on tons of ore rather than years because the mine's "life" could be longer or shorter than 10 years depending on how rapidly the ore is removed from the mine.

Suppose that during the first year of operations, 150,000 tons of ore are extracted. Building depreciation for the first year is $45,000, computed as follows:

$$\text{Depreciation per unit} = \frac{\text{Cost} - \text{Estimated salvage value}}{\text{Total tons of ore in mine}}$$

$$\text{Depreciation per unit} = \frac{\$310,000 - \$10,000}{1,000,000 \text{ tons}} = \$0.30 \text{ per ton}$$

$$\text{Depreciation for year} = \text{Depreciation per unit} \times \text{Units extracted}$$

$$\text{Depreciation for year} = \$0.30 \text{ per ton} \times 150,000 \text{ tons} = \$45,000$$

Depreciation on the building would be included on the income statement as part of the cost of ore that was sold and would be carried as part of inventory cost for those tons of ore that were not sold during the period. Accumulated depreciation on the building would be reported on the balance sheet with the related asset account.

Plant assets and natural resources are tangible assets used by a company to produce revenues. A company may also acquire intangible assets to assist in producing revenues.

■ INTANGIBLE ASSETS

Intangible assets have no physical characteristics but are of value because of the advantages or exclusive privileges and rights they provide to a business. Intangible assets generally arise from two sources: (1) exclusive privileges granted by governmental authority or by legal contract, such as patents, copyrights, franchises, trademarks and trade names, and leases; and (2) superior entrepreneurial capacity or management know-how and customer loyalty, which is called goodwill.

All intangible assets are nonphysical, but not all nonphysical assets are classified as intangibles. For example, accounts receivable and prepaid expenses are nonphysical, but they are classified as current assets. Intangible assets are generally both nonphysical and noncurrent.

Acquisition of Intangible Assets

Like most other assets, intangible assets are recorded initially at cost. However, computing an intangible asset acquisition cost is different from computing a plant asset acquisition cost. **Only outright purchase costs are included in the acquisition cost of an intangible asset;** the acquisition cost does **not** include cost of internal development or self-creation of the asset. If an intangible asset is internally generated in its entirety, none of its costs will be capitalized. Therefore, some companies have extremely valuable assets that may not even be recorded in their asset accounts. The reasons for this practice can be understood by studying the history of accounting for research and development costs.

Research and development (R&D) costs are costs incurred in a planned search for new knowledge and in translating such knowledge into a new product or process. Prior to 1975, research and development costs were often capitalized as intangible assets when future benefits were expected from their incurrence. Since it was often difficult to determine the costs applicable to future benefits, many companies expensed all such costs as they were incurred. Other companies capitalized those costs that related to proven products and expensed the rest as incurred.

As a result of these varied accounting practices, the Financial Accounting Standards Board in *Statement No. 2* in 1974 ruled that all research and development costs, other than those directly reimbursable by government agencies and others, must be expensed when incurred. Immediate expensing is justified on the grounds that (1) the amount of costs applicable to the future cannot be measured with any high degree of precision; (2) doubt exists as to whether any future benefits will be received; and (3) even if benefits are expected, they cannot be measured. Thus, research and development costs no longer appear as intangible assets on the balance sheet. The same line of reasoning is applied to other costs associated with internally generated intangible assets to prevent them from being capitalized and reported as intangible assets.

Amortization of Intangible Assets

Amortization is the systematic write-off of the cost of an intangible asset to expense. A portion of intangible asset cost is allocated to each accounting period in the economic (useful) life of the asset. All intangible assets are subject to amortization, which is similar to plant asset depreciation. Generally, amortization is recorded by debiting Amortization Expense and crediting the intangible asset account. An accumulated amortization account could be used to record amortization. However, usually the information gained from such accounting would not be significant because intangibles do not normally account for as significant an amount of total asset dollars as do plant assets.

Intangibles should be amortized over the shorter of (1) their economic life, (2) their legal life, or (3) 40 years. The 40-year limitation was established by the Accounting Principals Board. *APB Opinion No. 17* requires that an intangible asset acquired after October 1, 1970, be amortized over a period not to exceed 40 years. Straight-line amortization must be used unless another method of amortization (such as units-of-production) can be shown to be superior. Straight-line amortization is calculated in the same way as straight-line depreciation for plant assets.

Patents

A **patent** is a right granted by the federal government giving the owner the exclusive right to manufacture, sell, lease, or otherwise benefit from an invention. The real value of a patent lies in its ability to produce revenue. Patents have a legal life of 17 years. Protection for the patent owner begins at the time of patent application and lasts for 17 years from the date the patent is granted.

The purchase of a patent should be recorded in the Patents account at cost. The Patents account should also be debited for the cost of successfully

The $75,000 is the amount of goodwill to be recorded as an intangible asset on the books of Foster Company; all of the other assets will be recorded at fair market value, and the liability will be recorded at the amount due. Specific reasons for the existence of goodwill in a company might include good reputation, customer loyalty, product design, and superior human resources. Since these are not individually quantifiable, they are all grouped together and referred to as goodwill. The journal entry to record the above purchase is:

Accounts Receivable	100,000	
Inventories	90,000	
Land	150,000	
Buildings	250,000	
Equipment	200,000	
Patents	35,000	
Goodwill	75,000	
Cash		600,000
Mortgage Note Payable		300,000

To record the purchase of Hiser Company's assets and assumption of mortgage note payable.

Goodwill, like all other intangibles, must be amortized. There is no legal life for goodwill, and the useful life of goodwill cannot be reasonably estimated. If, for example, the new owner made substantial changes in the method of doing business, goodwill that existed at the purchase date could rapidly disappear. Therefore, current accounting practice requires the amortization of goodwill over a period not to exceed 40 years. This requirement is due to the fact that the value of purchased goodwill will eventually disappear. Other goodwill may be generated in its place, but the organization cannot record its internally created goodwill any more than it can record other internally generated intangible assets.

The entry to amortize the $75,000 goodwill over a 40-year period is:

Goodwill Amortization Expense	1,875	
Goodwill		1,875

To amortize goodwill ($75,000/40 years).

Reporting Amortization

Illustration 11.2 shows the frequencies of intangible assets being amortized by a sample of 600 companies for the years 1980–83.

Illustration 11.2

Intangible Assets Held by Sample of 600 Companies

	Number of companies			
	1983	*1982*	*1981*	*1980*
Goodwill	270	267	277	266
Patents	50	50	52	56
Trademarks, brand names, copyrights	21	20	20	22
Licenses, franchises, memberships	23	24	20	21
Other	11	13	16	18
Intangible assets (not otherwise described)	24	33	26	24

Source: American Institute of Certified Public Accountants, *Accounting Trends & Techniques* (New York: AICPA, 1984), p. 158.

Amortization expense for most intangible assets discussed in this chapter appears among the operating expenses on the income statement. The account titles used are all of this type: "Amortization of Goodwill (or Patents, Copyrights, Franchises, Leaseholds) Expense." Periodic amortization of leaseholds and leasehold improvements is often reported as rent expense. The amortization of goodwill is an expense in determining accounting income, but is not a deductible item in determining taxable income.

■ SUMMARY

When plant assets are sold, retired from service, traded in, destroyed, or otherwise disposed of, the company must remove the assets' cost and accumulated depreciation from the accounts. On the sales of plant assets, both gains or losses may be recognized. Losses may also occur when assets that have not been fully depreciated are retired. When insured plant assets are destroyed, a company's losses are reduced by the amounts recoverable from insurance.

When plant assets are exchanged for dissimilar plant assets, both losses and gains are recognized for both accounting and income tax purposes. When similar assets are exchanged, losses are recorded, but gains are not recorded for accounting purposes. Income tax rules do not allow recognition of either gains or losses on exchanges of similar assets.

Natural resources are usually recorded at the cost of acquisition and development. The gradual exhaustion of a natural resource resulting from its physical removal from its natural setting is called depletion. Charges for depletion are usually based on the number of physical units (pounds, tons, or barrels) involved. The depletion costs and removal costs are totaled and then assigned to either the cost of natural resources sold or the inventory of the natural resource still on hand. Plant assets located at a natural resource site are depreciated over their useful lives or the life of the resource, whichever is shorter.

All intangible assets are recorded at cost, but the cost of acquisition does not include cost of internal development or self-creation of the asset. Research and development costs are not assets and must be expensed as incurred unless directly reimbursable by government agencies or others. Intangible assets have limited lives and are subject to amortization.

Individually identifiable intangible assets grant exclusive privileges to the owner. Purchased intangible assets should be recorded at cost. All intangible assets should be amortized over the shorter of (1) their useful life, (2) their legal life, or (3) 40 years. Patents are usually amortized over their legal life of 17 years because their useful life would normally be longer than 17 years if protection were to continue. Copyright costs are usually amortized over their useful life because their useful life is normally less than 40 years. Franchises and trademarks purchased for a lump sum are often amortized over 40 years, since their useful life is often longer than 40 years.

Although leases are intangible assets, they are often listed with plant assets on the balance sheet. Under certain conditions, a lease may transfer virtually all risks and rewards of property ownership. These leases are known as capital leases and are capitalized as if the asset were purchased. Leases that do not transfer rewards and risks of ownership are operating leases and are not capitalized. Leasehold improvements are betterments made to a leased asset; they revert to the owner of the leased property at the end of the lease and are amortized over the life of the lease or the life of the improvement, whichever is shorter.

Goodwill is the intangible value of an entity resulting from favorable reputation, customer loyalty, product design, or the capacity of its human resources to produce an above-average rate of return on investment. Goodwill is not an individually identifiable asset and is recorded only if purchased; it must be amortized over a period not to exceed 40 years.

Having concluded your study of accounting for long-term assets, in Chapter 12 you will learn about payroll accounting. Federal and state income tax deductions, as well as other deductions, make careful accounting for payrolls mandatory.

NEW TERMS INTRODUCED IN CHAPTER 11

Amortization

The term used to describe the systematic write-off of the cost of an intangible asset to expense (428).

Boot

The additional cash outlay made when one asset is traded for a similar asset (423).

Capital lease

A lease that transfers to the lessee virtually all of the rewards and the risks that accompany ownership of property (430).

Copyright

An exclusive right granted by the federal government giving the owner protection against the illegal reproduction by others of the owner's written works, designs, and literary productions (429).

Depletion

The exhaustion of a natural resource; an estimate of the cost of the resource that was removed during the period (425).

Franchise

A contract between two parties granting the franchisee (the purchaser of the franchise) certain rights and privileges ranging from name identification to complete monopoly of service (429).

Goodwill

An intangible value attached to a company resulting mainly from the company's management skill or know-how and a favorable reputation with customers. Evi-

denced by the ability to generate an above-average rate of income on each dollar invested in the business (432).

Intangible assets

Items that have no physical characteristics but are of value because of the advantages or exclusive privileges and rights they provide to a business (427).

Lease

A contract to rent property. Grantor of the lease is the **lessor;** the party obtaining the rights to possess and use property is the **lessee** (430).

Leasehold

The rights granted under a lease (430).

Leasehold improvement

Any physical alteration to leased property in which benefits are expected beyond the current accounting period (431).

"Material" gains or losses

Gains or losses large enough to affect the decisions of an informed user of the financial statements (423).

Materiality concept

Allows the accountant to deal with immaterial (unimportant) items in a theoretically incorrect manner (423).

Natural resources

Ore deposits, mineral deposits, oil reserves, gas deposits, and timber stands supplied by nature (424).

Operating lease

A lease that does not qualify as a capital lease (430).

Patent

A right granted by a government giving the owner the exclusive right to manufacturer, sell, lease, or otherwise benefit from an invention (428).

Research and development (R&D) costs

Costs incurred in a planned search for new knowledge and in translating such knowledge into a new product or process (428).

Trademark

A symbol, design, or logo that is used in conjunction with a particular product or company (429).

Trade name

A brand name under which a product is sold or a company does business (429).

Wasting assets

See Natural resources.

DEMONSTRATION PROBLEM 11–1

On January 2, 1984, the Hopper Company purchased a machine for $60,000 cash. The machine has an estimated useful life of six years and an estimated salvage value of $3,000. The straight-line method of depreciation is being used.

Required: *a.* Compute the book value of the machine as of July 1, 1987.
   b. Assume the machine was disposed of on July 1, 1987. Prepare the journal entries to record the disposition of the machine under each of the following unrelated assumptions:

1. The machine was sold for $20,000 cash.
2. The machine was sold for $30,000 cash.
3. The machine and $40,000 cash were exchanged for a new machine that had a cash price of $65,000. Use the accounting method rather than the income tax method.
4. The machine was completely destroyed by fire. Cash of $18,000 is expected to be recovered from the insurance company.

Solution to demonstration problem 11–1

a.

HOPPER COMPANY
Schedule to Compute Book Value
July 1, 1987

Cost	$60,000
Less accumulated depreciation:	
$\dfrac{\$60{,}000 - \$3{,}000}{6 \text{ years}} = \$9{,}500 \text{ per year}$	
$9,500 × 3½ years = $33,250	33,250
Book value	$26,750

b.

1.
Cash	20,000	
Accumulated Depreciation—Machinery	33,250	
Loss on Disposal of Plant Assets	6,750	
Machinery		60,000

To record sale of machinery at a loss.

2. Cash   30,000
      Accumulated Depreciation—Machinery   33,250
        Machinery   60,000
        Gain on Disposal of Plant Assets   3,250
        To record sale of machinery at a gain.

3. Machinery (New)   65,000
      Accumulated Depreciation—Machinery   33,250
      Loss on Disposal of Plant Assets   1,750
        Machinery (Old)   60,000
        Cash   40,000
        To record exchange of machines.

4. Receivable from Insurance Company   18,000
      Accumulated Depreciation—Machinery   33,250
      Fire Loss   8,750
        Machinery   60,000
        To record loss of machinery.

DEMONSTRATION PROBLEM 11–2

The Kim Company acquired on January 1, 1987, a tract of property containing timber at a cost of $5,000,000. After the timber is removed, the land will be worth about $2,000,000 and will be sold to another party. Costs of developing the site were $500,000. A building was erected at a cost of $100,000. The building had an estimated physical life of 20 years and will have an estimated salvage value of $50,000 when the timber is gone. It was expected that 25,000,000 board feet of timber can be economically cut. During the first year, 8,000,000 board feet were cut. The units-of-production basis is used to depreciate the building.

Required: Prepare the entries to record:

a. The acquisition of the property.
b. The development costs.
c. Depletion cost for the first year.
d. Depreciation on the building for the first year.

Solution to demonstration problem 11–2

a.

Land   2,000,000
Timber Stands   3,000,000
  Cash   5,000,000
  To record purchase of land and timber.

b.

Timber Stands   500,000
  Cash   500,000
  To record costs of development of the site.

c.

Depletion of Timber Stands   1,120,000
  Accumulated Depletion—Timber Stands   1,120,000
  To record depletion for 1987:
    ($3,000,000 + $500,000)/25,000,000 = $0.14 per
    board foot. $0.14 × 8,000,000 = $1,120,000.

d.

Depreciation Expense—Building	16,000	
Accumulated Depreciation—Building		16,000

To record depreciation expense:

$$\frac{\$100,000 - \$50,000}{25,000,000 \text{ board feet}} = \$0.002 \text{ per board foot.}$$

$$\$0.002 \times 8,000,000 = \$16,000.$$

QUESTIONS

1. When depreciable plant assets are sold for cash, how is the gain or loss measured?

2. A plant asset that cost $15,000 and has a related accumulated depreciation account balance of $15,000 is still being used in business operations. Would it be appropriate to continue recording depreciation on this asset? Explain. When should the asset's cost and accumulated depreciation be removed from the accounting records?

3. A machine and $10,000 cash were exchanged for a delivery truck. How should the cost basis of the delivery truck be measured?

4. A plant asset was exchanged for a new asset of a similar type. How is the cost of the new asset determined for *(a)* accounting purposes and *(b)* income tax purposes?

5. *a.* Distinguish between depreciation, depletion, and amortization. Name two assets that are subject to depreciation, to depletion, and to amortization.

   b. Distinguish between tangible and intangible assets, and classify the above-named assets in part *(a)* accordingly.

6. A building with an estimated physical life of 40 years was constructed at the site of a coal mine. The coal mine is expected to be completely exhausted within 20 years. Over what length of time should the building be depreciated, assuming the building will be abandoned after all the coal has been extracted?

7. What are the characteristics of intangible assets? Give an example of an asset that has no physical existence but is not classified as an intangible asset.

8. What reasons justify the immediate expensing of most research and development costs?

9. Over what length of time should intangible assets be amortized?

10. Should intangible assets be amortized over their economic life or their legal life?

11. Describe the typical accounting for a patent.

12. What is a capital lease? What features may characterize a capital lease?

13. What is the difference between a leasehold (under an operating lease contract) and a leasehold improvement? Is there any difference in the accounting procedures applicable to each?

14. Brush Company leased a tract of land for 40 years at an agreed annual rental fee of $10,000. The effective date of the lease was July 1, 1987. During the last six months of 1987, Brush constructed a building on the land at a cost of $250,000. The building was placed in operation on January 2, 1988, at which time it was estimated to have a physical life of 50 years. Over what period of time should the building be depreciated? Why?

15. You note that a certain store seems to have a steady stream of regular customers, a favorable location, courteous employees, high-quality merchandise, and a reputation for fairness in dealing with customers, employees, and suppliers. Does it follow automatically that this business should have goodwill recorded as an asset? Explain.

EXERCISES

E–1

Record sale of equipment; account for removal costs

Plant equipment originally costing $18,000, on which $12,000 of depreciation has been accumulated, was sold for $4,500.

a. Prepare the journal entry to record the sale.
b. Prepare the entry to record the sale of the equipment if $50 of removal costs were incurred to allow the equipment to be moved.

E–2

Record destruction of machinery by fire—uninsured and insured asset

A machine costing $16,000, on which $12,000 of depreciation has been accumulated, was completely destroyed by fire. What journal entry should be made to record the machine's destruction and the resulting fire loss under each of the following unrelated assumptions?

a. The machine was *not* insured.
b. The machine was insured, and it is estimated that $3,000 will be recovered from the insurance company.

E–3

Record exchange of autos

Britt Company owned an automobile acquired on January 1, 1985, at a cash cost of $9,360; at that time, it was estimated to have a life of four years and a $720 salvage value. Depreciation has been recorded through December 31, 1987, on a straight-line basis. On January 1, 1988, the auto was traded for a new auto. The old auto had a fair market value (trade-in allowance) of $1,800. Cash of $8,280 was paid.
  Prepare the journal entry to record the trade-in under generally accepted accounting principles.

E–4

Record variety of cases involving sale, retirement, or exchange of equipment

Equipment costing $44,000, on which $30,000 of accumulated depreciation had been recorded, was disposed of on January 2, 1987. What journal entries are required to record the equipment's disposition under each of the following unrelated assumptions?

a. The equipment was sold for $18,000 cash.
b. The equipment was sold for $11,600 cash.
c. The equipment was retired from service and hauled to the junkyard. No material was salvaged.
d. The equipment was exchanged for similar equipment having a cash price of $60,000. A trade-in allowance of $20,000 from the cash price was received, and the balance was paid in cash.
e. The equipment was exchanged for similar equipment having a cash price of $60,000. A trade-in allowance of $10,000 was received, and the balance was paid in cash. (Record this transaction twice—first for tax purposes, and second for financial reporting purposes.)

E–5

Update depreciation and record sale of truck

On August 31, 1987, Shaw Company sold a truck for $4,600 cash. The truck was acquired on January 1, 1984, at a cost of $11,600. Depreciation of $7,200 on the truck has been recorded through December 31, 1986, using the straight-line method, a four-year expected life, and an expected salvage value of $2,000.
  Prepare the journal entries to update the depreciation on the truck on August 31, 1987, and to record the sale of the truck.

E–6

Determine depletion cost and expense

Pan Company paid $2,000,000 for the right to extract all of the mineral-bearing ore, estimated at 5,000,000 tons, that can be economically extracted from a certain tract of land. During the first year, Pan Company extracted 500,000 tons of the ore and sold 400,000 tons. What part of the $2,000,000 should be charged to expense during the first year?

E–7

Determine patent cost and periodic amortization

Jackson Company purchased a patent on January 1, 1971, at a total cost of $34,000. In January 1982, the company successfully defended the patent in a lawsuit. The legal fees amounted to $7,500. What will be the amount of patent cost amortized in 1985? (The useful life of the patent is the same as its legal life—17 years.)

E-8

Record leasehold; record rent accrued and leasehold amortization

Staton Company leased the first three floors in a building under an operating lease contract for a 10-year period beginning January 1, 1987. The company paid $64,000 in cash (not representing a specific period's rent) and agreed to make annual payments equal to 1% of the first $400,000 of sales and 0.5% of all sales over $400,000. Sales for 1987 amounted to $1,200,000. Payment of the annual amount will be made in January 1988.

Prepare journal entries to record the cash payment of January 1, 1987, and the proper expense to be recognized for the use of the space in the leased building for 1987.

E-9

Record franchise; record accrued franchise fees and franchise amortization

Joe Young paid Hungry Hank's Hamburgers $60,000 for the right to operate a fast-food restaurant in Gordonville under the Hungry Hank's name. Joe also agreed to pay an operating fee of 0.5% of sales for advertising and other services rendered by Hungry Hank's. Joe began operations on January 2, 1987. Sales for 1987 amounted to $600,000.

Give the entries needed to record the payment of the $60,000 and to record expenses incurred relating to the right to use the Hungry Hank's name.

E-10

Determine amount of goodwill

The Husek Company purchased all of the assets of Burke Company for $500,000. Husek Company also agreed to assume responsibility for Burke Company's liabilities of $50,000. The fair market value of the assets acquired was $450,000. How much goodwill should be recorded in this transaction?

PROBLEMS, SERIES A

P11-1-A

Update depreciation and record sale of typewriter

On January 1, 1985, Prewitt Company purchased an electronic typewriter for $14,100 cash. The typewriter has a useful life of five years and an expected salvage value of $600; it is being depreciated annually under the straight-line method. The company spent $360 to clean and adjust the typewriter on February 2, 1988, and sold the typewriter on August 1, 1988, for $3,000.

Required: Prepare journal entries to record the above data for 1988, assuming Prewett Company has a calendar-year accounting period.

P11-2-A

Update depreciation and record exchange of autos under GAAP

Lear, Inc., purchased a new 1988 model automobile on December 31, 1988. The cash price of the new auto was $15,600, from which Lear received a trade-in allowance of $2,400 for a 1986 model traded in. The 1986 model had been acquired on January 1, 1986, at a cost of $11,500. Depreciation has been recorded on the 1986 model through December 31, 1987, using the straight-line method, an expected four-year useful life, and an expected salvage value of $1,500.

Required:
a. Record depreciation expense for 1988.
b. Prepare the journal entries needed to record the exchange of autos using the method required under generally accepted accounting principles.

P11-3-A

Update depreciation and record six cases of asset disposal

On January 1, 1985, the Alex Company purchased a truck for $12,000 cash. The truck has an estimated useful life of six years and an expected salvage value of $1,500. Depreciation on the truck was computed using the straight-line method.

Required:
a. Prepare a schedule showing the computation of the book value of the truck on December 31, 1987.
b. Prepare the journal entry to record depreciation for the six months ended June 30, 1988.

c. Prepare journal entries to record the disposal of the truck on June 30, 1988, under each of the following unrelated assumptions:

1. The truck was sold for $1,000 cash
2. The truck was sold for $7,000 cash.
3. The truck was scrapped. Used parts valued at $1,850 were salvaged.
4. The truck (which has a fair value of $3,000) and $9,000 of cash were exchanged for a used back hoe that did not have a known market value.
5. The truck and $8,250 cash were exchanged for another truck that had a cash price of $14,250.
6. The truck was stolen on July 1, and insurance proceeds of $2,100 were expected.

P11–4–A

Update depreciation and record exchange of plant asset for similar asset

Sanchez Company purchased a new Model II computer on October 1, 1987. The cash price of the new computer was $33,280, and Sanchez received a trade-in allowance of $12,400 from the cash price for a model I computer. The old computer was acquired on January 1, 1985, at a cost of $30,720. Depreciation has been recorded through December 31, 1986, on a straight-line basis, with an estimated useful life of four years and $5,120 expected salvage value.

Required: a. Prepare the entries needed to record the exchange using the income tax method.
              b. Repeat part *(a)* applying generally accepted accounting principles.

P11–5–A

Record leasehold amortization; record depreciation and trade-in

On July 1, 1987, Ashe Company had the following balances in its plant asset and accumulated depreciation accounts:

	Asset	Accumulated depreciation
Land	$ 280,000	
Leasehold	105,000	
Buildings	1,313,200	$180,950
Equipment	571,200	182,000
Trucks	99,400	29,855

Additional data:

1. The leasehold covers a plot of ground leased on July 1, 1982, for a period of 25 years under an operating lease.
2. The office building is on the leased land and was completed on July 1, 1983, at a cost of $403,200; its physical life is set at 40 years. The factory building is on the owned land and was completed on July 1, 1982, at a cost of $910,000; its life is also set at 40 years with no expected salvage value.
3. The equipment has a 15-year useful life with no expected salvage value.
4. The company owns three trucks—A, B, and C. Truck A, purchased on July 1, 1985, at a cost of $22,400, had an expected life of three years and a scrap value of $1,400. Truck B, purchased on January 2, 1986, at a cost of $35,000, had an expected life of four years and a scrap value of $2,800. Truck C, purchased on January 2, 1987, at a cost of $42,000, had an expected life of five years and a scrap value of $4,200.

The following events occurred in the fiscal year ended June 30, 1988:

Transactions:

1987
July 1   Rent for July 1, 1987, through June 30, 1988, on leased land was paid, $13,300.
Oct. 1   Truck A was traded in on Truck D. Cash price of the new truck was $44,800. Cash of $37,800 was paid. Truck D has an expected life of four years and a scrap value of $2,450.

1988
Feb. 2   Truck B was sold for $19,600 cash.
June 1   Truck C was completely demolished in an accident. The truck was not insured.

Required: Prepare journal entries to record the above transactions and the necessary June 30, 1988, adjusting entries. Use the straight-line depreciation method.

P11-6-A

Determine depletion for period and depreciation on mining equipment; compute average cost per ton of ore mined

Craddock Company acquired a mine for $2,250,000. The mine contained an estimated five million tons of ore. It was also estimated that the land would have a value of $200,000 when the mine was exhausted and that only four million tons of ore could be economically extracted. A building was erected on the property at a cost of $300,000. The building had an estimated useful life of 35 years and no scrap value. Specialized mining equipment was installed at a cost of $412,500. This equipment had an estimated useful life of seven years and an estimated $27,500 salvage value. The company began operating on January 1, 1987 and put all of its assets into use on that date. During the year ended December 31, 1987, 400,000 tons of ore were extracted. The company decided to use the units-of-production method to record depreciation on the building and the straight-line method to record depreciation on the equipment.

Required: Prepare journal entries to record the depletion and depreciation charges for the year ended December 31, 1988. Show calculations.

P11-7-A

Record cost and amortization of patent

Woodrow Company purchased a patent for $180,000 on Jaunary 2, 1987. The patent was estimated to have a useful life of 10 years. The $180,000 cost was properly charged to an asset account and amortized in 1987. On July 1, 1988, the company incurred legal and court costs of $54,000 in a successful defense of the patent in a lawsuit.

Required:
a. Compute the patent amortization expense for 1987, and give the entry to record it.
b. Compute the patent amortization expense for 1988, and give the entry to record it.

P11-8-A

Record amortization expense for a vareity of intangible assets

Given below are selected transactions and other data for Gray Company:

a. The company purchased a patent in early January 1984 for $60,000 and began amortizing it over 10 years. In 1986, the company defended the patent in an infringement suit at a cost of $16,000.
b. Research and development costs incurred in 1986 of $18,000 were expected to provide benefits over the three succeeding years.
c. On January 2, 1987, the company rented space in a warehouse for five years at an annual fee of $4,000. Rent for the first and last years was paid in advance.
d. A total of $40,000 was spent uniformly throughout 1987 by the company in promoting its lesser known trademark, which is expected to have an indefinite life.
e. In January 1985, the company purchased all of the assets and assumed all of the liabilities of another company, paying $80,000 more than the fair market value of all identifiable assets acquired, less the liabilities assumed. The company expects the benefits for which it paid the $80,000 to last 10 years.

Required: For each of the unrelated transactions given above, prepare journal entries to record only those entries required for 1987. If any of the items do not require an entry in 1987, state so.

PROBLEMS, SERIES B

P11-1-B

Update depreciation and record sale of truck

On July 31, 1987, Cohen Company sold a truck for $7,840 cash. The truck was acquired on January 1, 1984, at a cost of $37,120; depreciation has been recorded on the truck through December 31, 1986, using the straight-line method, a four-year useful life, and $6,400 expected salvage value.

Required: Prepare all entries needed to record the above information for the year 1987.

P11–2–B

Record exchange of autos

Thurmond Company traded-in an auto that cost $9,000 and on which $7,500 of depreciation has been recorded for a new auto with a cash price of $17,250. The company received a trade-in allowance (its fair value) for the old auto of $1,050 and paid the balance in cash.

Required: a.   Record the exchange of the autos applying generally accepted accounting principles.
b.   Record the exchange of the autos applying federal income tax regulations.

P11–3–B

Update depreciation and record six cases of asset disposal

On January 2, 1985, the Mosley Company purchased a delivery truck for $52,500 cash. The truck has an estimated useful life of six years and an estimated salvage value of $4,500. The straight-line method of depreciation is being used.

Required: a.   Prepare a schedule that shows how the truck's book value on January 1, 1988, would be computed.
b.   Assume the truck is to be disposed of on July 1, 1988. What journal entry is required to record depreciation for the six months ended June 30, 1988?
c.   Prepare the journal entries to record the disposition of the truck on July 1, 1988, under each of the following unrelated assumptions:

1.   The truck was sold for $17,500 cash.
2.   The truck was sold for $32,000 cash.
3.   The truck was retired from service, and it is expected that $13,750 will be received from the sale of salvaged materials.
4.   The truck and $40,000 cash were exchanged for office equipment that had a cash price of $70,000.
5.   The truck and $45,000 cash were exchanged for a new delivery truck that had a cash price of $75,000.
6.   The truck was completely destroyed in an accident. Cash of $17,000 is expected to be recovered from the insurance company.

P11–4–B

Update depreciation and record exchange of plant asset for similar asset

Lowe Moving Company purchased a new moving van on October 1, 1987. The cash price of the new van was $54,000, and the company received a trade-in allowance from the cash price of $8,000 for a 1985 model. The balance was paid in cash. The 1985 model had been acquired on January 1, 1985, at a cost of $36,000. Depreciation had been recorded through December 31, 1986, on a straight-line basis, with three years of useful life expected and no expected salvage value.

Required: Present journal entries to record the exchange of the moving vans using the method required by generally accepted accounting principles.

P11–5–B

Record leasehold amortization; record depreciation and trade-in

On January 1, 1987, Paulk Company had the following balances in its plant asset and accumulated depreciation accounts:

	Asset	Accumulated depreciation
Land.	$104,000	
Leasehold	130,000	
Buildings	570,960	$ 47,775
Equipment. . . .	499,200	231,660
Trucks	74,880	36,465

Additional data:

1.   The leasehold covers a plot of ground leased on January 1, 1983, for a period of 20 years.
2.   Building No. 1 is on the owned land and was completed on July 1, 1986, at a cost of $327,600; its life is set at 40 years. Building No. 2 is on leased land and was completed on July 1, 1983, at a cost of $243,360; its life is also set at 40 years with no expected salvage value.

3. The equipment had an expected useful life of eight years with no estimated salvage value.
4. Truck A, purchased on January 1, 1985, at a cost of $24,960, had an expected life of 2½ years and a scrap value of $1,560. Truck B, purchased on July 1, 1985, at a cost of $21,840, had an expected life of two years and a scrap value of $3,640. Truck C, purchased on July 1, 1986, at a cost of $28,080, had an expected life of three years and a scrap value of $3,510.

The following events occurred in 1987:

Transactions:

Jan. 2 Rent for 1987 on leased land was paid, $14,560.
Apr. 1 Truck B was traded-in for Truck D. The cash price of the new truck was $24,960. A trade-in allowance of $4,680 was granted from the cash price. The balance was paid in cash. Truck D has an expected life of 2½ years and a scrap value of $1,560. (Use GAAP method.)
   1 Truck A was sold for $4,680 cash.

Required: Prepare journal entries to record the 1987 transactions and the necessary December 31, 1987, adjusting entries, assuming a calendar-year accounting period. Use the straight-line depreciation method.

P11-6-B

Determine depletion for period and depreciation on mining equipment; compute average cost per ton of ore mined

On January 2, 1987, Manning Mining Company acquired land with ore deposits at a cash cost of $992,500. Exploration and development costs amounted to $100,000. The residual value of the land is expected to be $200,000. The ore deposits contain an estimated three million tons. Present technology will allow the economical extraction of only 85% of the total deposit. Machinery, equipment, and temporary sheds were installed at a cost of $153,000. The assets will have no further value to the company when the ore body is exhausted; they have a physical life of 12 years. In 1987, 175,000 tons of ore were extracted. The company expects the mine to be exhausted in 10 years, with sharp variations in annual production.

Required:
a. Compute the depletion charge for 1987.
b. Compute the depreciation charge for 1987 under the units-of-production method.
c. If all other mining costs, except depletion, amounted to $700,000, what was the average cost per ton mined in 1987?

P11-7-B

Record cost and amortization of patent

Anderson Company spent $266,560 to purchase a patent on January 2, 1987. It is assumed that the patent will be useful during its full legal life. In January 1988, the company successfully defended the patent in a lawsuit at a cost of $51,200. Also in January 1988, the company paid $76,800 to obtain patents that could, if used by competitors, make the earlier Anderson patent useless. The purchased patents will never be used.

Required: Give the entries for 1987 and 1988 to record the information relating to the patents.

P11-8-B

Record amortization expense for a variety of intangible assets

Following are selected transactions and other data relating to the Willow Company for the year ended December 31, 1987:

a. The company rented the second floor of a building for five years on January 2, 1987, and paid the annual rent of $10,000 for the first and fifth years in advance.
b. In 1986, the company incurred legal fees of $30,000 in applying for a patent and paid a bonus of $10,000 to an employee who conceived of a device that substantially reduced the cost of manufacturing one of the company's products. The patent on the device has a market value of $300,000 and is expected to be useful for 10 years.
c. In 1986, the company entered into a 10-year operating lease on several floors of a building, paying $20,000 in cash immediately and agreeing to pay $10,000 at the end of each of the 10 years of life in the lease. It then incurred costs of $40,000 to install partitions, shelving, and fixtures. These items would normally last 25 years.
d. The company spent $12,000 promoting a trademark in a manner that it believed enhanced its value considerably. The trademark has an indefinite life.
e. Incurred costs amounting to $100,000 in 1986 and $130,000 in 1987 for research and development of new products that are expected to enhance the company's revenues for at least five years.

f. The company paid $100,000 to the author of a book that the company published on July 2, 1987. Sales of the book are expected to be made over a two-year period from that date.

Required: For each of the situations described above, prepare only the journal entries to record the expense applicable to 1987.

BUSINESS DECISION PROBLEM 11–1

Record exchange of similar assets; adjust accounts for errors in accounting for depreciable assets

Johnston Company acquired machine A for $100,000 on January 2, 1985. Machine A had an estimated useful life of four years and no salvage value. The machine was depreciated on the straight-line basis. On January 2, 1987, machine A was exchanged for machine B. Machine B had a cash price of $120,000. In addition to machine A, cash of $100,000 was given up in the exchange. The company recorded the exchange in accordance with income tax regulations instead of in accordance with generally accepted accounting principles. Machine B has an estimated useful life of five years and no salvage value. The machine is being depreciated using the straight-line method.

Required:
a. What journal entry did the Johnston Company make when it recorded the exchange of machines? (Show computations.)
b. What journal entry should the Johnston Company have made to record the exchange of machines in accordance with generally accepted accounting principles?
c. Assume the error is discovered on December 31, 1988, before adjusting journal entries have been made. What journal entries should be made to correct the accounting records? What adjusting journal entry should be made to record depreciation for 1988? (Ignore income taxes.)
d. What effect did the error have on reported net income for 1987? (Ignore income taxes.)
e. How should machine B be reported on the December 31, 1988, balance sheet?

BUSINESS DECISION PROBLEM 11–2

Record purchase of two businesses and explain differences between the two; advise client as to which company should be purchased

Will Rawley is trying to decide whether to buy Company A or Company B. Both Company A and Company B have assets with the following book values and fair market values:

	Book value	Fair market value
Accounts receivable . .	$240,000	$ 240,000
Inventories	720,000	1,200,000
Land	600,000	1,080,000
Buildings	720,000	1,680,000
Equipment	288,000	480,000
Patents	192,000	240,000

Liabilties that would be assumed on the purchase of either company include accounts payable, $480,000, and notes payable, $120,000.

The only difference between Company A and Company B is that Company A has net income that is about average for the industry, while Company B has net income that is greatly above average for the industry.

Required:
a. Assume Rawley can buy Company A for $4,320,000 or Company B for $5,520,000. Prepare the journal entry to record the acquisition of (1) Company A and (2) Company B. What accounts for the difference between the purchase price of the two companies?
b. Assume Rawley can buy either company for $4,320,000. Which company would you advise Rawley to buy? Why?

BUSINESS SITUATION FOR DISCUSSION

Schering-Plough's Prescription for Success: Pumping Profits into R&D ∗

In 1980 nearly half of Schering-Plough Corp.'s profits and 25% of its sales came from one prized antibiotic, Garamycin; that, however, was the year its patent expired (BW—Aug. 18, 1980). Schering researchers had sought for a decade to find a substitute for the company's keystone product and failed, so President Robert P. Luciano began to push development of new drugs. He also bought 15% of the Swiss-based genetic research company Biogen to start a long-range biotechnology thrust. But first he planned to defend Garamycin's market share with price cuts. "We will not have a down year— or even a down quarter," he predicted.

☐ Luciano was wrong. The next year, with profits battered when competitors slashed antibiotic prices, Schering's earnings fell 24%. Since then, Luciano, named chairman last January, has managed to hold sales at the $1.8 billion level and increased earnings a slight 6% while implementing strategies that were loosely defined in 1980.

To replace Garamycin, Luciano chose to expand Schering's investment in biotechnology and genetic engineering. In 1982, the company paid $29 million for DNAX Ltd., a biotech think tank in Palo Alto, Calif., and has focused its work on the study of allergies, infections, and inflammatory diseases such as arthritis. Those three plus cardiovascular ills, are the basic areas in which Schering now concentrates its research.

Stress on Research

The strategy calls for spending 30%—or about $50 million this year—of the research and development budget on biotech and the rest on traditional chemical synthesis and clinical testing of new drugs. Since 1980, total R&D spending has risen 89%, to $170 million this year, and the staff has grown 30%, to 1,400, while the company's total employment fell by 3,000.

The effort is beginning to pay off. Normodyne, a drug that controls high blood pressure, was approved for sale in early August by the Food & Drug Administration. Schering says its tests demonstrate that the drug works better than any other antihypertensive on blacks, who are especially susceptible to the disease, and on asthmatics who have trouble tolerating some of the substances in existing hypertension drugs. Normodyne, however, was co-developed by Glaxo Holdings Ltd., the British inventor of the basic compound, and that company's sales force will compete to market the drug.

Patent and license disputes cloud the prognosis for new biotech drugs, including one called alpha-2 interferon—a protein molecule created through recombinant DNA technology by Biogen and produced in commercial quantities by Schering. The company holds the worldwide marketing license for the product and is seeking production patents. It expects to be first to get FDA approval to market it, initially for treatment of two types of cancer and—at the other end of the medical spectrum—as a nasal spray to prevent the common cold.

Biogen has been promised a broad-ranging European patent for interferon by mid-August. But that is sure to be fought by competitiors, including Genentech Inc. and Hoffmann-LaRoche Inc. Meanwhile, Schering will start making the drug next spring in Ireland at a $54 million plant, the size and cost of which was halved last fall when researchers achieved a fortyfold jump in yield.

Conversions

Schering's strategy also calls for a steady but undramatic expansion of all of its consumer businesses. The company has rushed to convert prescription drugs to over-the-counter sales. "That opens a much larger market," says Luciano. He notes the prescription decongestant Drixoral, which racked up sales of $30 million in 1982. Switched to an over-the-counter drug, sales hit $41 million last year, while a new prescription drug, Trinalin, broke in with $6 million, boosting combined sales by 57%.

As Garamycin faded, Luciano expected Schering's business balance to move from 62% pharmaceuticals to close to a 50-50 split with the numerous toiletry and cosmetics lines sold by the Plough side of the enterprise. But last year, ethical and related over-the-counter drugs accounted for 55% of sales, and that is as close to parity as the consumer business is likely to come. "My preference and drive is for a heavier weighting in pharmaceuticals," says Luciano.

With the sale of the DAP Inc. home products business, which makes caulking compounds, and 12 radio stations, for $93 million, Schering has concentrated consumer operations in health and beauty products. The model for growth will be Maybelline, a line Schering built from a few mascara products to become the largest-selling cosmetics brand—with a 21% market share, to Revlon Inc.'s 17%. "We took Maybelline step by step from eye shadow to lips, to nails, the face, and finally fragrances, always with a consistent distribution pattern and price point," says Executive Vice-President Hugh A. D'Andrade.

Toiletries and proprietary drugs such as St. Joseph

∗ Reprinted from the April 20, 1984, issue of *Business Week* (p. 122) by special permission. © 1984 by McGraw-Hill, Inc.

aspirin have not been expanded as aggressively as cosmetics, and Luciano has been willing to let some product shares decline in exchange for higher profits—needed to support R&D. He says: "We will milk selected product lines, but we won't milk the business."

Hurt by a drop of nearly 15% in the past two years in sales of Dr. Scholl foot-care products, consumer sales volume has been flat. But operating profits have risen about 50% since 1980, to $121.3 million. The earnings have helped give Luciano cash to build Schering's research effort. "We will invest in health and beauty aids," Luciano says. "But we are first and foremost a research-based, ethical pharmaceutical company."

CHAPTER 12 Payroll Accounting

LEARNING OBJECTIVES

After studying this chapter, you should be able to:

1. Describe the essential internal control features for payrolls.
2. Prepare and record a payroll.
3. Illustrate the use of a payroll checking account.
4. Prepare an employee's earnings record.
5. Prepare entries to record employer's payroll taxes and vacation pay.
6. Define and use correctly the new terms in the glossary.

Most of you have had either a part-time or full-time job and have been paid weekly or semimonthly. You probably were disappointed when you received your first paycheck because the deductions were greater than expected. Payroll accounting includes the record-keeping necessary to account for employees' paychecks and deductions. Since a company's payroll costs are one of the largest expenses the company incurs, payroll accounting is an important function.

This chapter discusses the objectives of payroll accounting and the methods of achieving these objectives. Computations of gross and net earnings and the major documents and forms used in payroll accounting are explained. Even though many businesses today use computerized payroll systems, the objectives and methods used to compute amounts and deductions are the same as for manual systems.

■ OBJECTIVES OF PAYROLL ACCOUNTING

In general, the objectives of payroll accounting are to process data such as hours worked, pay rates, and payroll deductions so that the firm can:

1. Provide accurate and timely paychecks to employees.
2. Provide an explanation of payroll data for employees.
3. Produce necessary employee and employer records, withholding statements, and reports to governmental agencies.
4. Protect against fraud in payroll transactions.
5. Control salary and wage expense.

■ INTERNAL CONTROL OVER PAYROLL

In small companies, adequate internal control over payroll transactions may be provided by the owner-manager, who may actually compute and prepare the payroll. In larger companies, internal control is obtained through application of the general principles of internal control and the more specific guides to control over cash disbursements provided in Chapters 6 and 7. Separation of duties is a crucial aspect of payroll internal control. Ideally, timekeeping, payroll preparation, payroll record-keeping, and payroll distribution functions should be performed by different persons.

If compensation is based on hours worked, an accurate method must be used to record the time each employee works. In small companies, the owner may simply make notations in a notebook when employees report to and leave work. In larger companies, a time clock is often used for hourly employees. Each day when employees report to work, every employee inserts a **timecard** into the time clock. The time clock prints the date and the time on the card. The same procedure is used when employees leave work. Safeguards must be set up to ensure that no employee punches in or out for another employee. For example, an employee may be stationed at the time clock to supervise the check-in and check-out procedures.

In small companies, the owner usually knows the amount of hours each employee works. The owner, or a bookkeeper, may keep the payroll records and compute the employees' earnings and deductions, as well as prepare, sign, and distribute the paychecks.

Most large companies use the following procedure to prepare paychecks. At a regular interval before payday, timecards are collected by the payroll department. The payroll department then verifies each employee's pay rate and hours worked to compute total (gross) pay. At this point all legally required and authorized deductions are subtracted from the total (gross) pay, individual payroll records are updated, and payroll checks are prepared. Checks are then sent to the treasurer's office for signature. Supporting documents, such as employees' earnings statements showing earnings and deductions to date, may accompany the checks. Each check should be delivered to the employee in person or deposited directly by the employer into the employee's bank account.

Payroll Fraud

Whenever cash is disbursed, the potential for fraud exists. Some payroll fraud schemes used successfully in the past are listed below:

1. A payroll department employee pays another employee more than that employee has actually earned, and then the payroll employee receives a kickback of part of the overpayment from that employee .
2. A payroll department employee makes out a payroll check payable to a former or fictitious employee and then cashes the check.
3. A payroll department employee prepares and cashes duplicate payroll checks.

Because of these and other schemes, great care must be exercised to ensure payroll accuracy. Separation of duties is one way to help ensure accuracy. It is difficult to arrange and cover up fraudulent transactions when one employee's work serves as a check on another's. For example, if a payroll department employee falsifies the hours worked by a plant employee in an attempt to overpay that employee, the changed hours on the payroll record will not agree with the timecard record. Collusion by two payroll department employees would be required to commit such a fraud unless the same employee has access to timecards, other payroll records, and payroll checks.

Maintenance of accurate employment and payroll records is also crucial. The payroll department must be informed of any hirings and terminations as soon as possible so that the payroll department knows which employees currently work for the company. This information will help prevent fictitious checks from being written. Current copies of documents authorizing payroll deductions should be on hand. Payroll fraud can be reduced by keeping accurate, detailed records for each employee. Companies must be alert to the possibility of payroll fraud and take steps to prevent it.

■ GROSS EARNINGS OF EMPLOYEES

Although the terms often are used interchangeably, wages differ from salaries. The term *wages* generally refers to gross earnings of employees who are paid by the hour for only the actual hours worked. The term *salaries* on the other hand, usually refers to gross earnings of employees who are paid a flat amount per week or month regardless of the number of hours worked in a period.

Computing Gross Earnings

The first step in preparing a payroll is to compute the gross earnings of each employee. Gross earnings is total pay or compensation of an employee, including regular pay and overtime premium. Computation of gross earnings for wages usually consists of simply multiplying the number of hours the employee worked by the employee's hourly wage rate. For example, 40 hours times $10 per hour gives gross earnings of $400 for the week. The computation of gross earnings for salaried workers is specified per period; for example, an annual salary of $36,000 is divided by 12 months to determine monthly gross earnings of $3,000. In some instances, however, the calculation of gross earnings is a little more detailed due to legal or contractual requirements.

The federal Wages and Hours Law (also called the Fair Labor Standards

Act) requires that most employees who are paid by the hour be paid a minimum of 1½ times their normal rate for hours worked in excess of 40 per week. This law also requires that at least the minimum wage be paid to employees. The minimum wage rate is set by the federal government and changes frequently. In addition to this federal law, some union contracts also call for premium pay rates for certain hours worked, such as double time for work on Sunday. Detailed time records must be maintained by the payroll department to ensure that legal and contractual requirements are being met. In the absence of valid records, assessments for overtime pay may later be made against the employer. Executive, administrative, and some professional employees are salaried and are exempt from both the minimum wage and overtime pay provisions. Lower-level, non-professional, salaried employees generally are subject to the minimum wage and overtime pay provisions.

Following are three situations that illustrate how to make computations under the above conditions for gross pay, including overtime premiums:

1. Mary Kennedy's basic wage rate is $6 per hour. Her overtime premium, then, is one half of $6, or $3 per hour. Mary's gross pay for a week in which she worked 48 hours is $312. The $312 is computed as (48 × $6) + (8 × $3), or ($288 + $24) = $312.

2. Grace Early's $13,000 annual salary is paid over 52 weeks at a guaranteed weekly minimum of $250 (40 × $6.25 per hour), even though she often works only 37.5 hours a week. She is entitled to time and a half overtime pay for hours worked in excess of 40 per week. Her gross earnings for working 42 hours in a week are $268.75, computed as $250 + (2 × 1.5 × $6.25).

3. Dan Brown is paid $0.50 for each unit of product he makes. In the current week, he worked 44 hours and made 924 units. His gross pay before overtime premium is $462 (924 × $0.50). The $462 is divided by 44 hours to get $10.50 as his regular hourly rate for the week. Therefore, Dan's overtime premium is $5.25 per hour, and his total overtime pay is $21 (4 × $5.25). His gross earnings for the week are $462 + $21, or $483.

■ PAYROLL TAXES AND DEDUCTIONS

Required deductions from gross earnings include withholdings for federal income taxes, state income taxes, and FICA (social security) taxes. There are also various other deductions that employees may choose to have taken from their checks.

Federal and State Income Tax

Wage earners in the United States are under a pay-as-you-go federal income tax system. This means that most employees must pay federal income taxes on wages as they are earned during the year. Employers withhold federal income tax when the employee's earnings are paid, and the amount withheld is noted on the employee's check stub. These federal taxes are remitted (sent) periodically by the employer to federally specified banks or to the Internal Revenue Service (IRS). Employers in states with state income taxes also must withhold **state income taxes** from employees' paychecks and remit these amounts to the revenue authority in those states.

The amount of income tax withheld from each employee's pay depends on the (1) amount of earnings, (2) frequency of the payroll period, and (3) the number of **withholding allowances** claimed by the employee. Withholding allowances are claimed by the employee on an **Employee's Withholding Allowance Certificate (Form W-4)** filed with the employer, usually the first day on the job. Illustration 12.1 shows the W-4 form of Ronald Kyle who claims four withholding allowances, which usually means that he will claim four exemptions on his federal income tax return—one for himself, one for his wife, and one each for his two children. An **exemption** is a fixed amount of income ($1,040 in 1985) that is not subject to taxation.

Illustration 12.1

Employee's Withholding Allowance Certificate (Form W-4)

If wages and withholding allowances claimed are known for each employee for each payroll period, the amount of federal income tax withheld can be found in a **wage bracket withholding table** provided by the IRS. Such a table for a recent year is shown in Illustration 12.2. If Kyle's gross pay for a week is $400, the amount of income tax withheld from his wages will be $39. This amount is found by following the line labeled "at least $400—but less than $410" across to the column headed "4."

The withholding table used to determine the amount of tax withheld from Kyle's wages is specifically for married employees who are paid weekly. Different tables are used for biweekly or monthly payroll periods and for single taxpayers. Note that the amount of income taxes withheld changes with the number of withholding allowances claimed. The table amounts are updated periodically by the IRS to reflect changes in federal income tax laws.

On or before January 31, after the end of each calendar year, an employer is required to prepare for each employee a four-copy **Wage and Tax Statement (Form W-2)** for the previous calendar-year earnings. An example of a W-2 is shown in Illustration 12.3. This form provides wage and tax data needed to prepare the employee's personal federal and state income tax returns. One copy is sent by the employer to the Social Security Administration, which then transmits data contained on the form to the Internal Revenue Service. The other three copies of the W-2 are given to the employee. Of these three, one copy is filed with the employee's federal income tax return, one is filed

Illustration 12.2

Federal Wage Bracket Withholding Table

MARRIED Persons—WEEKLY Payroll Period
(For Wages Paid After December 1984)

At least	But less than	0	1	2	3	4	5	6	7	8	9	10
And the wages are—		And the number of withholding allowances claimed is—										
		The amount of income tax to be withheld shall be—										
$0	$52	$0	$0	$0	$0	$0	$0	$0	$0	$0	$0	$0
52	54	1	0	0	0	0	0	0	0	0	0	0
54	56	1	0	0	0	0	0	0	0	0	0	0
56	58	1	0	0	0	0	0	0	0	0	0	0
58	60	1	0	0	0	0	0	0	0	0	0	0
60	62	1	0	0	0	0	0	0	0	0	0	0
62	64	2	0	0	0	0	0	0	0	0	0	0
64	66	2	0	0	0	0	0	0	0	0	0	0
66	68	2	0	0	0	0	0	0	0	0	0	0
68	70	2	0	0	0	0	0	0	0	0	0	0
70	72	3	0	0	0	0	0	0	0	0	0	0
72	74	3	1	0	0	0	0	0	0	0	0	0
74	76	3	1	0	0	0	0	0	0	0	0	0
76	78	3	1	0	0	0	0	0	0	0	0	0
78	80	3	1	0	0	0	0	0	0	0	0	0
80	82	4	1	0	0	0	0	0	0	0	0	0
82	84	4	2	0	0	0	0	0	0	0	0	0
84	86	4	2	0	0	0	0	0	0	0	0	0
86	88	4	2	0	0	0	0	0	0	0	0	0
88	90	5	2	0	0	0	0	0	0	0	0	0
90	92	5	3	0	0	0	0	0	0	0	0	0
92	94	5	3	1	0	0	0	0	0	0	0	0
94	96	5	3	1	0	0	0	0	0	0	0	0
96	98	5	3	1	0	0	0	0	0	0	0	0
98	100	6	3	1	0	0	0	0	0	0	0	0
100	105	6	4	2	0	0	0	0	0	0	0	0
105	110	7	4	2	0	0	0	0	0	0	0	0
110	115	7	5	3	0	0	0	0	0	0	0	0
115	120	8	6	3	1	0	0	0	0	0	0	0
120	125	9	6	4	2	0	0	0	0	0	0	0
125	130	9	7	4	2	0	0	0	0	0	0	0
130	135	10	7	5	3	0	0	0	0	0	0	0
135	140	10	8	6	3	1	0	0	0	0	0	0
140	145	11	9	6	4	2	0	0	0	0	0	0
145	150	12	9	7	4	·2	0	0	0	0	0	0
150	160	13	10	8	5	3	1	0	0	0	0	0
160	170	14	11	9	6	4	2	0	0	0	0	0
170	180	16	13	10	8	5	3	1	0	0	0	0
180	190	17	14	11	9	6	4	2	0	0	0	0
190	200	18	16	13	10	8	5	3	1	0	0	0
200	210	20	17	14	11	9	6	4	2	0	0	0
210	220	21	18	16	13	10	8	5	3	1	0	0
220	230	23	20	17	14	11	9	6	4	2	0	0
230	240	24	21	18	16	13	10	8	5	3	1	0
240	250	26	23	20	17	14	11	9	6	4	2	0
250	260	28	24	21	18	16	13	10	8	5	3	1
260	270	29	26	23	20	17	14	11	9	6	4	2
270	280	31	28	24	21	18	16	13	10	8	5	3
280	290	32	29	26	23	20	17	14	11	9	6	4
290	300	34	31	28	24	21	18	16	13	10	8	5
300	310	36	32	29	26	23	20	17	14	11	9	6
310	320	38	34	31	28	24	21	18	16	13	10	8
320	330	39	36	32	29	26	23	20	17	14	11	9
330	340	41	38	34	31	28	24	21	18	16	13	10
340	350	43	39	36	32	29	26	23	20	17	14	11
350	360	45	41	38	34	31	28	24	21	18	16	13
360	370	47	43	39	36	32	29	26	23	20	17	14
370	380	48	45	41	38	34	31	28	24	21	18	16
380	390	50	47	43	39	36	32	29	26	23	20	17
390	400	52	48	45	41	38	34	31	28	24	21	18
400	410	55	50	47	43	39	36	32	29	26	23	20
410	420	57	52	48	45	41	38	34	31	28	24	21
420	430	59	55	50	47	43	39	36	32	29	26	23
430	440	61	57	52	48	45	41	38	34	31	28	24
440	450	63	59	55	50	47	43	39	36	32	29	26
450	460	66	61	57	52	48	45	41	38	34	31	28
460	470	68	63	59	55	50	47	43	39	36	32	29
470	480	70	66	61	57	52	48	45	41	38	34	31
480	490	73	68	63	59	55	50	47	43	39	36	32

Illustration 12.2

(concluded)

MARRIED Persons–**WEEKLY** Payroll Period
(For Wages Paid After December 1984)

And the wages are–		And the number of withholding allowances claimed is–										
At least	But less than	0	1	2	3	4	5	6	7	8	9	10
		The amount of income tax to be withheld shall be–										
$490	$500	$75	$70	$66	$61	$57	$52	$48	$45	$41	$38	$34
500	510	78	73	68	63	59	55	50	47	43	39	36
510	520	80	75	70	66	61	57	52	48	45	41	38
520	530	83	78	73	68	63	59	55	50	47	43	39
530	540	85	80	75	70	66	61	57	52	48	45	41
540	550	88	83	78	73	68	63	59	55	50	47	43
550	560	90	85	80	75	70	66	61	57	52	48	45
560	570	93	88	83	78	73	68	63	59	55	50	47
570	580	95	90	85	80	75	70	66	61	57	52	48
580	590	98	93	88	83	78	73	68	63	59	55	50
590	600	101	95	90	85	80	75	70	66	61	57	52
600	610	103	98	93	88	83	78	73	68	63	59	55
610	620	106	101	95	90	85	80	75	70	66	61	57
620	630	109	103	98	93	88	83	78	73	68	63	59
630	640	112	106	101	95	90	85	80	75	70	66	61
640	650	115	109	103	98	93	88	83	78	73	68	63
650	660	117	112	106	101	95	90	85	80	75	70	66
660	670	120	115	109	103	98	93	88	83	78	73	68
670	680	123	117	112	106	101	95	90	85	80	75	70
680	690	126	120	115	109	103	98	93	88	83	78	73
690	700	129	123	117	112	106	101	95	90	85	80	75
700	710	132	126	120	115	109	103	98	93	88	83	78
710	720	136	129	123	117	112	106	101	95	90	85	80
720	730	139	132	126	120	115	109	103	98	93	88	83
730	740	142	136	129	123	117	112	106	101	95	90	85
740	750	146	139	132	126	120	115	109	103	98	93	88
750	760	149	142	136	129	123	117	112	106	101	95	90
760	770	152	146	139	132	126	120	115	109	103	98	93
770	780	155	149	142	136	129	123	117	112	106	101	95
780	790	159	152	146	139	132	126	120	115	109	103	98
790	800	162	155	149	142	136	129	123	117	112	106	101
800	810	165	159	152	146	139	132	126	120	115	109	103
810	820	169	162	155	149	142	136	129	123	117	112	106
820	830	172	165	159	152	146	139	132	126	120	115	109
830	840	175	169	162	155	149	142	136	129	123	117	112
840	850	179	172	165	159	152	146	139	132	126	120	115
850	860	182	175	169	162	155	149	142	136	129	123	117
860	870	185	179	172	165	159	152	146	139	132	126	120
870	880	188	182	175	169	162	155	149	142	136	129	123
880	890	192	185	179	172	165	159	152	146	139	132	126
890	900	195	188	182	175	169	162	155	149	142	136	129
900	910	199	192	185	179	172	165	159	152	146	139	132
910	920	202	195	188	182	175	169	162	155	149	142	136
920	930	206	199	192	185	179	172	165	159	152	146	139
930	940	210	202	195	188	182	175	169	162	155	149	142
940	950	213	206	199	192	185	179	172	165	159	152	146
950	960	217	210	202	195	188	182	175	169	162	155	149
960	970	221	213	206	199	192	185	179	172	165	159	152
970	980	225	217	210	202	195	188	182	175	169	162	155
980	990	228	221	213	206	199	192	185	179	172	165	159
990	1,000	232	225	217	210	202	195	188	182	175	169	162
1,000	1,010	236	228	221	213	206	199	192	185	179	172	165
1,010	1,020	239	232	225	217	210	202	195	188	182	175	169
1,020	1,030	243	236	228	221	213	206	199	192	185	179	172
1,030	1,040	247	239	232	225	217	210	202	195	188	182	175
1,040	1,050	250	243	236	228	221	213	206	199	192	185	179
1,050	1,060	254	247	239	232	225	217	210	202	195	188	182
1,060	1,070	258	250	243	236	228	221	213	206	199	192	185
1,070	1,080	262	254	247	239	232	225	217	210	202	195	188
1,080	1,090	265	258	250	243	236	228	221	213	206	199	192
1,090	1,100	269	262	254	247	239	232	225	217	210	202	195
1,100	1,110	273	265	258	250	243	236	228	221	213	206	199
1,110	1,120	276	269	262	254	247	239	232	225	217	210	202
1,120	1,130	280	273	265	258	250	243	236	228	221	213	206
1,130	1,140	284	276	269	262	254	247	239	232	225	217	210
		37 percent of the excess over $1,140 plus–										
$1,140 and over		286	278	271	263	256	249	241	234	226	219	212

with the state income tax return (if the employee lives in a state that has a state income tax), and one is retained by the employee as a personal record. The IRS uses data from the form to determine whether the employee has claimed the proper amount of earned income and taxes withheld on the tax return.

The use of a payroll account has several advantages:

1. A distinctive payroll check form may be used, with spaces provided on an attachment for gross earnings, various payroll deductions, and net cash paid. See Illustration 12.7.
2. Payroll checks, identifiable as such, are easily cashed by employees.
3. The work of reconciling the bank balances can be divided among employees. Only one check is drawn on the general bank account. The hundreds or thousands of payroll checks issued each payday are drawn on the payroll bank account. Occasionally, payroll checks will be negotiated many times or lost before clearing the bank. Including these items in the payroll reconciliation simplifies the reconciliation of the general Cash account.
4. Only one authorization is prepared, calling for one check drawn on the general bank account; therefore, payroll checks are issued without separately prepared and signed authorizations.
5. Individual payroll checks need not be entered in the regular cash disbursements record; payroll check numbers are inserted in the payroll journal, and repetition of the entering of checks is avoided.

Illustration 12.7

Payroll Check and Supporting Employee's Earnings Statement

Employee	Hours Worked	Rate per Hour	Regular Earnings	Extra for Overtime	Gross Earnings	Fed. Inc. Tax W/H	Soc. Sec. Tax	State Inc. Tax W/H	Hosp. Ins.	Net Pay
Ronald Mark Kyle	40	10.00	400.00		400.00	39.00	28.20	10.40	20.00	302.40

Retain this stub for your records – Detach before cashing check

ACE HARDWARE

BEACHAM-MOORHEAD ACE HARDWARE
7360 ROSWELL RD.
ATLANTA, GEORGIA 30328

335

64-1240 / 611

March 30   19 85

PAY TO THE ORDER OF   Ronald Mark Kyle $ 302.40

Three hundred two and 40/100 --- DOLLARS

The CITIZENS and SOUTHERN BANK
NORTH SPRINGS OFFICE
ATLANTA, GEORGIA

George C. Beacham

FOR_____

⑈000335⑈ ⑆0611⑈1240⑆ 038 82 131⑈

■ EMPLOYER PAYROLL TAXES

An employer is generally obligated to pay three taxes levied upon payrolls: FICA (social security) taxes and federal and state unemployment taxes.

FICA (Social Security) Taxes

An employer is required to match the amount of FICA tax withheld from each employee's pay. For example, total FICA tax in 1985 amounted to 14.1%

of the first $39,600 of each employee's earnings; 7.05% was paid by the employee, and 7.05% by the employer.

Federal Unemployment Tax

The Federal Unemployment Tax Act (FUTA) requires that employers pay a federal unemployment tax based on employee salaries and wages. This tax helps finance a cooperative federal-state system of unemployment compensation. Unemployment benefits are paid to qualified unemployed persons by each of the states and territorial governments. State unemployment laws vary only in minor respects; the Federal Unemployment Tax Act sets forth certain minimum standards that must be met by each state.

The federal unemployment tax rate generally has varied between 3% and 3.5%. The rate at this writing (1985) is 3.5% of the first $7,000 of gross wages paid to each employee. This rate will be used for illustrative purposes. The Federal Unemployment Tax Act also allows employers to apply a maximum credit of 2.7% against their federal unemployment tax for amounts paid to the state for state unemployment tax. This provision, in effect, makes the federal unemployment tax rate 0.8% (3.5% − 2.7%) of the first $7,000 of individual employee wages.

State Unemployment Tax

The state unemployment tax generally is 2.7% of the first $7,000 of gross earnings per employee. This rate and base will be used for illustrative purposes in the text. A merit rate can be gained by employers to reduce the state rate to as little as 0.5% in some states and even to zero in other states. A reduced rate is earned by employers with low turnover and few layoffs. Employers with lower merit rates can still deduct a credit of 2.7% against its federal unemployment tax rate.

Employer payroll taxes are usually recorded at the same time as the payroll to which they relate. For example, the employer's payroll taxes (at 1985 rates) on the March 27 payroll in Illustration 12.6 are recorded as follows:

Mar. 27	Payroll Taxes Expense	253.20
	FICA Taxes Payable	169.20
	State Unemployment Taxes Payable	64.80
	Federal Unemployment Taxes Payable . . .	19.20
	To record employer's payroll taxes.	

Remember that these amounts are in **addition to** amounts withheld from employees. This journal entry debits Payroll Taxes Expense for the total of the employer's three payroll taxes. The credit to FICA Taxes Payable is equal to the amount deducted from the employees' gross pay. Both the employer's and employees' FICA taxes can be credited to the same liability account, since both are payable at the same time to the same agency. The credits to the state and federal unemployment accounts are for 2.7% and 0.8%, respectively, of the $2,400 of gross pay for this payroll period. It was assumed that no employee had been paid more than $7,000 in the current year. Any earnings in excess of $7,000 would have been excluded from the computation, since unemployment taxes are levied only on the first $7,000 of annual income per employee.

■ REMITTING WITHHOLDING, TAXES, AND DEDUCTIONS

Generally, within one month after the end of each calendar quarter, an employer must file an **Employer's Quarterly Federal Tax Return (Form 941)** with the Internal Revenue Service. This form reports the amount of FICA and income taxes withheld for each quarter. The employer reports (1) total wages subject to withholding, (2) federal income taxes withheld, (3) total wages subject to FICA tax, (4) amount of FICA taxes due (from both employer and employees), and (5) combined amount of income tax withheld and FICA taxes due. A similar form is required by states with state income tax laws.

Taxes Withheld

For remittance purposes, federal income taxes withheld and both the employees' and employer's FICA taxes are combined. Generally, employers are required to deposit such taxes in a Federal Reserve Bank or an authorized commercial bank called a **federal depository bank.** When deposited, these amounts are credited by the bank to an Internal Revenue Service account. Deposit requirements are quite detailed and depend upon the amount of taxes collected relative to the time elapsed since the last deposit. The more dollars of taxes that are collected, the more rapidly deposits must be made. Taxes properly deposited are considered paid.

The journal entry to record a deposit of $1,150 of federal income taxes withheld and $925 of FICA taxes is:

```
Employees' Federal Income Taxes Payable . . . . . . . .   1,150
FICA Taxes Payable . . . . . . . . . . . . . . . . . . .     925
    Cash   . . . . . . . . . . . . . . . . . . . . . . .           2,075
    To record deposit of taxes withheld and employer FICA
    taxes.
```

State and city income taxes must be withheld by employers in most states and in many cities. The procedures for withholding and the required remittances are usually modeled after federal income tax regulations. The entry for employers to record payment of these taxes debits Employees' State (City) Income Taxes Payable and credits Cash.

Unemployment Taxes

The amount of federal unemployment taxes to be deposited is determined quarterly. Upon reaching a certain amount, these taxes must be deposited in a federal depository bank. The entry to record a $125 deposit of federal unemployment taxes is:

```
Federal Unemployment Taxes Payable   . . . . . . . . . .    125
    Cash   . . . . . . . . . . . . . . . . . . . . . . .            125
    To record deposit of federal unemployment taxes.
```

Remittance requirements for state unemployment taxes vary from state to state. Quarterly reports and payments are usually required by the end of the month following the quarter's end. The entry to record the payment is a debit to State Unemployment Taxes Payable and a credit to Cash.

Other Payroll Deductions

The remittance of other types of payroll deductions varies based on the agency or organization to which payment is to be made. Monthly payment is likely for union dues, medical insurance premiums, charitable contributions, and pension contributions.

A summary of the various payroll taxes appears in Illustration 12.8.

Illustration 12.8

Summary of Payroll Taxes

Tax	Paid by	Rate
FICA (social security)	Both employer and employee at current rate	7.05% of first $39,600 each employee earns annually*
Federal and state income tax	Employee	Varies with earnings and exemptions
State unemployment	Employer (usually)	2.7% of first $7,000 each employee earns annually†
Federal unemployment	Employer	0.8% of first $7,000 each employee earns annually‡

* This rate and base are for 1985. The base is expected to be $46,200 in 1986.
† Some states have a higher rate and/or base than this. Also, most states allow a reduction from the basic rate to firms with low labor turnover.
‡ The federal rate varies, but in this text it is assumed to be 3.5%. An allowance of 2.7% is granted for amounts paid to the state, thus reducing the effective rate to 0.8%.

■ END-OF-PERIOD ACCRUALS

Adjusting entries are usually needed at year-end to accrue wages and employer's payroll taxes and vacation pay.

Wages and Payroll Taxes

The matching principle requires that accrued wages and employer payroll taxes on these wages be recorded at the end of every period. To illustrate, assume that Kelly Appliance Company accrues the following salaries and payroll taxes on December 31, 1986: sales salaries, $850; delivery salaries, $150; office salaries, $200; and payroll tax expense, $84.60. The required entries are:

Dec. 31	Sales Salaries Expense	850.00	
	Delivery Salaries Expense	150.00	
	Office Salaries Expense	200.00	
	Salaries Payable		1,200.00
	To accrue salaries.		
31	Payroll Taxes Expense	84.60	
	FICA Taxes Payable		84.60
	To accrue payroll taxes.		

Note in the first entry that credits are not entered in separate liability accounts for payroll deductions. These deductions will be recorded when the payroll is paid since they are not actually withheld from the employees until then. The second entry recorded the employer's FICA taxes on $1,200 of salaries. The assumption was made that no employee had reached the maximum FICA limit; therefore, all accrued salaries would be subject to FICA taxation. Accrued federal and state unemployment taxes were not included in this example because by year-end all employees' earnings should have surpassed the $7,000 maximum amount subject to taxation.

Some companies do not accrue employer's payroll taxes at year-end. The following reasons are given for this violation of the matching principle: (1) there is no legal liability for such taxes until the wages are paid, (2) such taxes do not vary much in amount from year to year, and (3) the amounts of such taxes are likely to be immaterial. A policy of not accruing payroll taxes is acceptable under these circumstances.

Vacation Pay

Most employees in this country are entitled to annual vacations of from one to four weeks at full regular pay. The compensation received while on vacation is called vacation pay. Thus, the employer annually pays an employee for 52 weeks, but receives services for a lesser number of weeks.

How to account for vacation pay brings up an important question: Should vacation pay be expensed when paid, or should it be accrued over the period in which the employee works to earn the vacation? *FASB Statement No. 43*, "Accounting for Compensated Absences," requires the accrual of a liability for vacation pay if the following conditions are met:

1. The employer is obligated to pay as a result of services already received.
2. The employee's right to vacation pay does not depend upon continued performance of services.
3. It is probable the vacation pay will be paid.
4. The amount of vacation pay can be reasonably estimated.

Assume the Sun Company estimates that out of every 20 workdays employees will earn one day of vacation pay. As a result, vacation pay is to be accrued at a rate of 5% (1 day/20 days) of gross pay. The entry to accrue vacation pay on a $2,400 payroll is:

Vacation Pay Expense ($2,400 × 0.05)	120.00	
Estimated Vacation Pay Payable		120.00
To accrue vacation pay.		

Accruing vacation pay in this manner records the expense over the period in which it was earned rather than when it was paid, which results in better matching of expenses and revenues. A liability is also recorded for the vacation pay currently owed by the employer to the employees. Often employees must forfeit vacation pay earned if they leave the company before some minimum length of time, such as one year. If turnover of these employees is expected, the amount of the entry to accrue vacation pay should be reduced accordingly.

When vacation pay is paid, the estimated liability account is debited and various accounts are credited for taxes, other deductions, and cash payment. To illustrate, assume an employee like Ronald Kyle, the man discussed earlier who is earning $400 per week, is paid for three weeks' vacation. A payroll check is drawn for the net pay due and is entered in the payroll journal. Using the deductions computed earlier, the entry in general journal form would be:

Estimated Vacation Pay Payable	1,200.00	
Employees' Federal Income Taxes Payable		117.00
Employees' State Income Taxes Payable		31.20
FICA Taxes Payable		84.60
Employees' Medical Insurance Premiums Payable . . .		60.00
Cash		907.20
To record payment of vacation pay.		

■ MORE EFFICIENT METHODS OF PAYROLL ACCOUNTING

The payroll procedures described in this chapter are used effectively by many small businesses. In larger companies where there are many employees, a more efficient method is desirable.

Many businesses use what is called a **pegboard system of payroll accounting** to increase efficiency. Such a system aligns the payroll check, the individual earnings record, and the payroll journal in such a way that all three are completed with one writing. Instead of having to record gross pay, deductions, and net pay three different times for each employee, it is done only once by using a pegboard system of payroll accounting. Of course, the forms must be designed so that they are compatible. Use of such a system can reduce clerical time dramatically.

Other methods of increasing efficiency include using a payroll machine to serve the same function as the pegboard system, or using a computer. As payrolls grow, the speed and efficiency of the computer make its use a virtual necessity. Many banks offer computerized payroll processing services to their customers.

■ *SUMMARY*

The costs associated with payroll are often the largest expense many companies incur. Thus, payroll expense receives special attention.

The objectives of payroll accounting are to process data so that a company can (1) provide accurate paychecks on time, (2) provide an explanation of payroll data for each employee, (3) produce necessary employee earnings records, and (4) protect against fraud in payroll transactions. Where the owner cannot personally handle the payroll transactions, there should be a separation of duties to enhance internal control over these transactions and reduce chances of payroll fraud. Internal control over payroll must ensure that only current, legitimate employees of the company are being paid, and that each employee receives the proper amount of wages for time worked.

One of the first steps in preparing a payroll is to compute the gross earnings of each employee. Gross earnings is total pay (or total compensation) of an employee, including regular pay and overtime. Legal or contractual requirements must be considered in computing gross earnings. Employees must be paid at least 1½ times their normal rate for hours worked in excess of 40 per week. Unions often state in their contracts that special premium pay rates be paid for certain hours worked, such as holidays or Sundays. Federal law requires that the employer pay at least the minimum wage to most employees.

Deductions commonly made from gross earnings include amounts withheld for federal income tax, FICA tax, and state income tax. Other items for which an employer may make deductions include union dues, hospital and life insurance premiums, repayments on loans from or savings in an employees' credit union, pledges to charities, payments for pension or retirement plans, payments on merchandise purchased from the company, and payments on purchases of U.S. Savings Bonds. Most individuals must pay their federal income taxes as wages are received throughout the year. The amount of tax to be withheld each period can be found on the Wage Bracket Withholding Table provided by the IRS. The amount of federal tax withheld depends on (1) the amount of the employee's earnings, (2) the frequency of the payroll period, and (3) the number of withholding allowances claimed. On or before January 31, an employer must furnish each employee with a wage and tax statement. This form provides information on total wages paid and taxes withheld to use in preparing the employee's personal federal income tax return.

FICA (social security) taxes are paid by both the employer and the employee on the employee's wages. In 1985, each was taxed at a rate of 7.05% that was applied to a base of the first $39,600 of employee wages earned. Both the employer's and the employee's portions of the tax are recorded in the FICA Taxes Payable account in the general ledger.

Unemployment taxes are always levied only against the employer. The federal unemployment tax rate and base in 1985 were 3.5% on the first $7,000 of wages paid. A credit of up to 2.7% may be applied against this rate for amounts paid to the state for state unemployment taxes, thus lowering the effective federal unemployment tax rate to 0.8%.

Recording payroll information is an important task. An earnings record is maintained for each employee to show that various federal laws relating to payroll are being observed. A formal payroll journal may be used to record payroll data. Some companies also maintain a separate payroll checking account.

At the end of an accounting period, it is necessary to accrue wages that have been earned but not paid. The payroll taxes on these wages may or may not be accrued. Vacation pay must be accrued over the portion of the year during which the employee works to earn the vacation.

Several methods have been developed for increasing the efficiency of payroll accounting. Some businesses use a pegboard system of payroll accounting; others have turned to computerized payroll processing.

You should now know the accounting process behind the various deductions in your paychecks. Chapter 13 discusses the accounting theory you were first introduced to in Chapter 1 and explains the effect inflation has on financial reporting.

NEW TERMS USED IN CHAPTER 12

Deductions from gross earnings

Required payroll deductions, such as federal and state income taxes withheld, FICA taxes withheld, and other deductions, such as medical insurance premiums and union dues (451).

Employee earnings record

A record maintained by an employer for each employee showing details such as hours worked, pay rate, gross earnings, payroll deductions, net pay, and personal biographical data (456).

Employee Withholding Allowance Certificate (Form W-4)

The form on which an employee indicates the number of withholding allowances to be used in calculating federal (and state) income taxes to be withheld (452).

Employer's Quarterly Federal Tax Return (Form 941)

A form used to report income and FICA taxes withheld and deposits of such taxes, if any (461).

Exemption

A fixed amount of income ($1,040 in 1985) not subject to federal income taxation. The amount will change in the future because of indexing based on the rate of inflation or new legislation (452).

Federal depository bank

A bank authorized to accept deposits of taxes by employers for credit to the Internal Revenue Service (461).

Federal (state) income taxes withheld

The amount of federal (state) income taxes deducted from employee earnings by the employer and remitted to the appropriate governmental agency under the pay-as-you-go system of government financing (451–52).

Federal unemployment tax

A tax of 3.5% levied upon the first $7,000 of wages paid per employee to help finance the joint federal-state system of unemployment compensation. A credit of up to 2.7% may be taken for amounts paid to a state unemployment fund, thus reducing the rate to 0.8% (460).

FICA (social security) tax

The amount deducted from an employee's wages and paid into a special fund used to pay retirement and other benefits. In 1985, the tax rate was 7.05% of the first $39,600 of wages paid each employee. The employer matches this amount (455).

Gross earnings

Total pay or compensation of an employee, including regular pay and overtime premium (450).

Merit rate

A reduction in the state unemployment tax rate below 2.7% as a reward for low turnover and few layoffs (460).

Minimum wage

Lowest hourly compensation an employer can pay an employee as required by the Wages and Hours Law (451).

Payroll checking account

A separate checking account used only for payroll checks. Each payday funds are transferred from the general Cash account to cover the amount of the payroll checks. One of the purposes is to keep the "clutter" of outstanding payroll checks from making more complex the reconciliation of the general Cash account (458).

Payroll journal

A formal record showing the details of each payroll including gross pay, deductions, net pay, and check number for each employee. It may be used as a book of original entry (in which case postings to accounts would be made from it), or it may be only a memorandum record (457).

Pegboard system of payroll accounting

A system that aligns the payroll check, the individual earnings record, and the payroll journal in such a way that all three are completed simultaneously with one writing (464).

Social security tax

See FICA tax.

State unemployment tax

A tax of 2.7% (typically) on the first $7,000 of earnings per employee per year to finance unemployment benefits. A **merit rate** for low labor turnover may reduce the rate to less than 2.7% (460).

Timecard

A form used to show the time an employee reports to and leaves work (449).

Vacation pay

Compensation paid to employees while on vacation; it is actually earned by employees in the periods worked prior to the vacation (463).

Wage and Tax Statement (Form W-2)

A form that the employer must furnish to each employee after the end of the year showing gross wages, amounts withheld, and net pay. It is used by the employee in preparing the personal federal income tax return (452).

Wage bracket withholding table

A table supplied by the IRS that shows the amount of income tax to be withheld given the wage and number of withholding allowances claimed (452).

Wages and Hours Law (Fair Labor Standards Act)

Requires that employees engaged in interstate commerce be paid at least 1½ times their normal rate for hours worked in excess of 40 hours per week. It also requires that at least the minimum wage be paid to employees (450).

Withholding allowances

A means of adjusting income taxes withheld from employee periodic earnings for exemptions that will be claimed on the income tax return (452).

DEMONSTRATION PROBLEM

The Fargo Company employs four persons (all are married) and pays them weekly salaries as shown below. The number of exemptions and weekly deductions for medical insurance for each employee are also given.

	Weekly salary	Withholding allowances	Medical insurance	Position
Robbin Lucia	$375	3	$15	Salesperson
Jo Ann Morgan	400	2	15	Salesperson
Robert Pearson	390	4	20	Salesperson
John Travis	310	2	15	Office manager

Each employee has 5% withheld for state income tax and 8% withheld for the retirement plan. Use the wage bracket withholding table in Illustration 12.2 to determine the federal income taxes to be withheld.

Required:

a. Prepare the payroll journal for the week ending January 8, 1985, including only those headings that are necessary. (The check numbers used are 604–7.) Use a 7% rate for FICA taxes.

b. Assuming that the payroll journal is a memorandum record only, prepare the general journal entry to record the payroll.

c. Prepare the entry to transfer funds from general cash to the special payroll checking account.

d. Prepare the entry to record the employer's payroll taxes using 7% for FICA taxes and other rates given in this chapter. (In actual practice, this entry often is made only at the end of the month.)

e. Prepare the entry to record payment on January 14 of the federal income taxes and FICA taxes owed to the federal government. (In actual practice, payment often is made at various times, depending on the amounts involved.)

Solution to demonstration problem

a.

PAYROLL JOURNAL

Date Week Ended	Employee	Office Salaries Expense	Sales Salaries Expense	Federal Income Taxes Payable	FICA Taxes Payable	State Income Taxes Payable	Medical Insurance Premiums Payable	Retirement Plan	Salaries Payable (Net Pay)	Check No.
1985 Jan. 8	Robbin Lucia		375.00	38.00	26.25	18.75	15.00	30.00	247.00	604
	Jo Ann Morgan		400.00	47.00	28.00	20.00	15.00	32.00	258.00	605
	Robert Pearson		390.00	38.00	27.30	19.50	20.00	31.20	254.00	606
	John Travis	310.00		31.00	21.70	15.50	15.00	24.80	202.00	607
		310.00	1,165.00	154.00	103.25	73.75	65.00	118.00	961.00	

b.

```
1985
Jan.  8  Office Salaries Expense  . . . . . . . . . .     310.00
         Sales Salaries Expense  . . . . . . . . . .   1,165.00
              Employees' Federal Income Taxes Payable . .          154.00
              FICA Taxes Payable . . . . . . . . . .               103.25
              Employees' State Income Taxes Payable . . .           73.75
              Employees' Medical Insurance Premiums
                Payable  . . . . . . . . . . . . . .                65.00
              Employees' Retirement Plan Premiums
                Payable  . . . . . . . . . . . . . .               118.00
              Salaries Payable  . . . . . . . . . .               961.00
         To record the payroll for the week ending January 8.
```

c.

```
1985
Jan.  8  Salaries Payable . . . . . . . . . . . . .     961.00
              Cash  . . . . . . . . . . . . . . . .               961.00
         To record the transfer of funds to cover the
         January 8 payroll.
```

d.

```
1985
Jan.  8  Payroll Taxes Expense  . . . . . . . . . .     154.88
              FICA Taxes Payable . . . . . . . . . .               103.25
              State Unemployment Taxes Payable  . . . .            39.83
              Federal Unemployment Taxes Payable  . . .            11.80
         To record payroll taxes on the January 8 payroll.
```

e.

```
1985
Jan. 14  Employees' Federal Income Taxes Payable  . . .    154.00
         FICA Taxes Payable  . . . . . . . . . . . .       206.50
              Cash  . . . . . . . . . . . . . . . .               360.50
         To record payment of federal income tax withheld
         and FICA taxes payable from the January 8
         payroll.
```

QUESTIONS

1. Describe some of the purposes of a payroll accounting system.

2. List the various steps involved in the preparation of a payroll, and suggest methods of establishing internal control over each of these steps.

3. What requirements does the Wages and Hours Law place on employers? Why should accurate records be maintained of the hours worked by employees?

4. List the most common deductions from gross pay.

5. What is the purpose of the Employee's Withholding Allowance Certificate (Form W-4)?

6. What purposes does the Wage and Tax Statement (Form W-2) serve?

7. Against what parties are FICA taxes levied and in what amounts?

8. What is the purpose of the Employer's Quarterly Federal Tax Return (Form 941)?

9. What are the federal and state rates for unemployment tax? What is a merit rate and what effect does it have on the credit granted by the federal government for amounts paid to the state?

10. Why should an employer maintain an earnings record for each employee?

11. Under what conditions would the use of a special payroll checking account be desirable? How does such an account operate?

12. What are the arguments for and against accruing employer's payroll taxes at the end of the accounting period?

13. Under what conditions should an employer accrue a liability for future vacation pay earned by employees in the current accounting period?

EXERCISES

E–1

Determine withholding amounts for employees

The Hernandez Company employs four persons, all married, whose weekly wages and withholding allowances are:

	Wages	Withholding allowances
David John	$370	5
Robert Thomas	550	3
Pascual Villa	325	4
Nancy Jones	430	2

Using Illustration 12.2, determine the correct amount of federal income taxes to be withheld per week for each employee.

E–2

Compute employer's unemployment taxes

Using the data in Exercise E–1, calculate in which one of the weekly payroll periods the Hernandez Company can stop recording state and federal unemployment taxes for each one of the employees. Also, compute the annual amount of these taxes that the company will incur on the wages paid to these employees assuming the same weekly wages are earned by each employee throughout the year.

E–3

Compute FICA taxes

Using the data in Exercise E–1 and the rate and base for 1985, compute the amount of FICA taxes the employer will withhold from each employee for the entire year, assuming the same weekly wage is paid each week. Also, calculate the employer's FICA tax expense for the year.

E–4

Prepare journal entry to record payroll

The gross payroll for salaries of the Weston Corporation is $1,600. Federal income taxes withheld amount to $325. The employees' FICA taxes withheld amount to $112. Give the entry to record the payroll at the time of payment, assuming no prior recording of salaries.

E–5

Compute difference in unemployment taxes under two alternatives

Osborne Company is trying to decide whether to hire four workers at $40,000 each per year, or 16 workers on a part-time basis at $10,000 each per year. Using the rates given in the chapter for 1985, calculate the difference in the employer's payroll tax expense for a year under the two alternatives.

E–6

Prepare journal entry to record unemployment taxes

The H. Davis Company operates in a state that has a 2.7% unemployment tax rate. Due to a record of stable employment, the company has earned a merit rate of 2.1%. Total wages on which it incurred federal and state unemployment taxes for March were $12,000. Prepare the entry to record federal and state unemployment taxes for the month.

E–7

Prepare journal entries to record accrued wages and payroll taxes

At the end of December 1985, the B. George Company had accrued wages of $1,000 ($500 for sales salaries, $300 for office salaries, and $200 for maintenance wages). The company accrues payroll taxes on accrued salaries and wages. Assume that no employee has earnings over $30,000 (including the above accrued wages) and that unemployment taxes accrue only on the maintenance wages. Prepare the necessary adjusting entries to accrue wages and payroll taxes.

E–8

Compute gross pay, payroll deductions, and net pay

Frank Myers worked 44 hours last week, 4 of which are considered overtime hours. His pay rate for regular hours is $8 per hour. His weekly pay is subject to federal income tax withholding and to FICA tax withholding at a rate of 7.05%. Frank is married and claims three withholding allowances. Calculate Frank's gross pay, payroll deductions, and net pay, using Illustration 12.2 to compute federal income taxes withheld.

E–9

Prepare journal entries to accrue and pay vacation pay to employee

Baker Company estimated its accrued vacation pay liability at the end of the year at $3,500. Frank Myers (Exercise E–8) took one week of vacation in the following year for which he was paid one week's regular earnings of 40 hours at $8 per hour. Give the entry for the vacation pay accrual. Also, give the entry to record the payment of a week's vacation pay to Frank Myers.

PROBLEMS, SERIES A

P12–1–A

Compute gross earnings, deductions, and net pay; prepare journal entry to record payroll and employer's payroll taxes

The payroll of a company for a recent week includes gross earnings for the following three employees:

1. Lucie is guaranteed a weekly salary of $600 plus overtime for hours worked in excess of 40 per week. She is married, but claims no withholding allowances. She worked 48 hours during the week.
2. Angie is paid $7.50 per hour. She is married and claims three withholding allowances. She worked 48 hours this week, including 8 hours of overtime.
3. Mary is paid $0.10 per unit completed. She is married and claims two withholding allowances. She worked 43 hours this week and completed 4,386 units.

Required:
a. Compute the regular pay, the overtime premium, and the net pay for each of the above employees.
b. Prepare the journal entry to record the payroll, including the withholdings for federal income taxes (Illustration 12.2), FICA taxes at a rate of 7.05%, $20 contributed by Angie to United Way, and $40 to repay a payroll advance given to Mary and recorded in Loans to Employees. Also prepare the journal entry to record the employer's state and federal unemployment taxes at the typical rates of 2.7% and 0.8%.

P12–2–A

Compute FICA taxes, unemployment taxes, and total employer tax expense

The Avalon Health Spa has 63 employees and a payroll of $630,000; 9 employees earned $40,000 each, and 54 employees each earned an equal share of the rest.

Required:
a. What is the 1985 FICA tax for (1) the employees and (2) the employer? (Use a 7.05% rate and a $39,600 maximum base.)
b. What is the amount of the federal and state unemployment tax per year assuming a federal rate of 0.8% and a state rate of 2.7% for this employer?
c. Which of the preceding items would constitute expenses on the records of the Avalon Health Spa?

ing process helps you make decisions in unusual accounting situations. Accounting theory provides a logical framework for accounting practice.

The second half of this chapter is devoted to inflation accounting. The higher the rate of inflation, the less relevant are financial statements prepared solely on a historical cost basis.

■ UNDERLYING ASSUMPTIONS

The major underlying assumptions of accounting are (1) entity, (2) going concern (continuity), (3) money measurement, and (4) periodicity. In this section the effects of these assumptions on the accounting process are discussed.

Entity

Data gathered in an accounting system are assumed to relate to a specific business unit or entity. The business **entity** concept assumes that each business has an existence separate from its owners, creditors, employees, customers, other interested parties, and other businesses. For each business (such as a horse stable or a fitness center), the business, not the business owner, is the accounting entity. Financial statements are prepared for a particular business entity that must be identified on the statements. The content of the financial statements must be limited to reporting the activities, resources, and obligations of that entity.

A business entity may be made up of several different *legal* entities. For instance, a large business, such as General Motors Corporation, may consist of several separate corporations, each of which is a separate legal entity. But, because the corporations have a common ownership, they may be considered one business entity for reporting purposes. This concept is illustrated in Chapter 18.

Going Concern (Continuity)

Accountants record business transactions for an entity assuming the entity will continue to be a "going concern." The **going-concern (continuity)** assumption states that an entity will continue to operate indefinitely unless there is strong evidence that the entity will terminate. An entity is terminated by ceasing business operations and selling off its assets. The process of termination is called **liquidation.** If liquidation appears likely, the going-concern assumption can no longer be used.

The going-concern assumption is often cited to justify the use of historical costs, rather than market values, in measuring assets. Market values are thought to be of little or no significance to an entity that intends to use, rather than sell, its assets. On the other hand, if an entity is to be liquidated, market values should be used to report assets.

The going-concern assumption permits the accountant to record certain items as assets. For example, printed advertising matter may be on hand to promote a special sale next month. This advertising material may have little, if any, value to anyone but its owner. But, because its owner is expected to continue operating long enough to benefit from it, the accountant classifies the expenditure as an asset, prepaid advertising, rather than as an expense.

Money Measurement

The economic activity of a business is normally recorded and reported in money terms. Money measurement is the use of a monetary unit of measurement, such as the dollar, instead of physical or other units of measurement. The use of a particular monetary unit provides accountants with a common unit of measurement to report economic activity. Without a monetary unit, it would be impossible to add such items as buildings, equipment, and inventory on a balance sheet.

The unit of measure (the dollar in the United States) is identified in the financial statements so the statement user can make valid comparisons of values. For example, it would be difficult to compare relative asset values or profitability of a company reporting in U.S. dollars with a company reporting in Japanese yen.

Stable Dollar. In the United States, accountants make another assumption regarding money measurement—the stable dollar assumption. Under the stable dollar assumption, the dollar is accepted as a **reasonably stable** unit of measurement. Thus, no adjustments are made in the primary financial statements for the changing value of the dollar.

One of the difficulties that has developed as a result of following the stable dollar assumption occurs in depreciation accounting. Assume, for example, that a company acquired a building in 1957 and the 30-year depreciation on the building is computed without adjusting for any changes in the value of the dollar. Thus, the depreciation deducted in 1987 is the same as the depreciation deducted in 1957, and no adjustments are made for the difference in the values of the 1957 dollar and the 1987 dollar. Both dollars are treated as **equal monetary units** of measurement even though substantial price inflation has occurred over the 30-year period. Accountants and business executives have expressed concern over this inflation problem, especially since 1970. Today there is great interest in reflecting the effects of inflation on the financial statements. Inflation accounting is discussed in more detail later in this chapter.

Periodicity (Time Periods)

According to the periodicity (time periods) assumption, an entity's life can be subdivided into time periods (such as months or years) for purposes of reporting its economic activities. After subdividing an entity's life into time periods, accountants attempt to prepare accurate reports on the entity's activities for these periods—reports that will provide useful and timely financial information to investors and creditors. In fact, however, the financial reports may be inaccurate for certain of these time periods because accountants use estimates, such as depreciation expense and certain other adjusting entries.

Accounting reports cover relatively short periods of time. The time periods are usually of equal length so that valid comparisons can be made of a company's performance from period to period. The length of the accounting period must be stated in the financial statements.

Accrual Basis and Periodicity.   In Chapter 3, you learned that financial statements more accurately reflect the financial status and operations of a company when prepared under the accrual basis of accounting rather than the cash basis. Under the cash basis of accounting, revenues are recorded when cash is received, and expenses are recorded when cash is paid. Under the accrual basis, however, revenues are recorded when services are rendered or products are sold and delivered, and expenses are recorded when incurred.

The periodicity assumption makes necessary the adjusting entries prepared under the accrual basis. Without the periodicity assumption, there would only be one time period running from the inception of the business to its termination. Then the concepts of cash basis and accrual basis accounting would be irrelevant because all revenues and all expenses would be recorded in that one time period and would not have to be assigned to artificially short time periods of one year or less.

Approximation and Judgment because of Periodicity.   To provide periodic financial information, estimates must often be made of such things as expected uncollectible accounts and useful lives of depreciable assets. Uncertainty about future events prevents precise measurement and makes estimates necessary in accounting. Estimates are often reasonably accurate when they are made by an informed accountant. A qualified accountant is able to exercise judgment rather than adhering to a set of inflexible rules, such as "depreciate all trucks over three years regardless of their actual useful lives."

■ OTHER BASIC CONCEPTS

Other basic accounting concepts that affect the accounting for entities are (1) general-purpose financial statements, (2) substance over form, (3) consistency, (4) double-entry, and (5) articulation. These basic accounting concepts are discussed in the sections that follow.

General-Purpose Financial Statements

As you know, results of the financial accounting process are presented in financial statements. These are general-purpose financial statements that are prepared at regular intervals to meet many of the general information needs of external parties and top-level internal managers. In contrast, special-purpose financial information can be gathered for a specific decision, usually on a one-time basis. For example, management may need specific information to decide whether or not to purchase a new computer. Because special-purpose financial information must be specific, that information is best obtained from the detailed accounting records rather than from the financial statements.

Substance over Form

In some business transactions, the economic substance of the transaction may conflict with its legal form. For example, a contract that is legally a lease may, in fact, be equivalent to a purchase. A company may have a three-year contract to lease (rent) an auto at a stated monthly rental fee. At the end of the lease period, the company will receive title to the auto after paying a nominal sum (say, $1). The economic substance of this transaction is a purchase rather than a lease of the auto. Thus, under the substance-over-form concept, the auto should be carried as an asset on the balance sheet and should be depreciated rather than only reporting the lease fee as rent expense on the income statement. Accountants should record the **economic substance** of a transaction rather than be guided by the **legal form** of the transaction.

Consistency

When discussing inventories in Chapter 9, we introduced the consistency concept. Consistency generally requires a company to use the same accounting principles and reporting practices through time. This concept prohibits indiscriminate switching of principles or methods, such as changing inventory methods every year. However, consistency does not prohibit a change in principles if the information needs of financial statement users are better served by the change. When a change in principle is made, the following disclosures are required—nature of the change, reasons for the change, and effect of the change on net income, if significant.

Double Entry

Chapter 2 introduced the basic accounting principle of the double-entry method of recording transactions. Under the double-entry approach, every transaction has a two-sided effect on **each** company or party engaging in the transaction. Thus, to record each transaction, each company or party debits at least one account and credits at least one account. The total debits equal the total credits in each journal entry.

Articulation

When you learned how to prepare work sheets in Chapter 4, you also learned that financial statements are fundamentally related and **articulate** (interact) with each other. For example, the amount of net income is carried from the income statement to the statement of owner's equity. The ending balance on the statement of owner's equity is carried to the balance sheet to bring total assets and total equities into balance.

■ MEASUREMENT IN ACCOUNTING

In the Introduction of this text, accounting was defined as "the process of identifying, measuring, and communicating economic information to permit informed judgments and decisions by the users of the information."[2] In this section we focus on the **measurement** process of accounting.

---

[2] American Accounting Association, *A Statement of Basic Accounting Theory* (Evanston, Ill., 1966), p. 1.

The accountant seeks to measure the assets, liabilities, and owner's equity of a business entity and any changes that occur in them. The effects of these changes are assigned to particular time periods (periodicity) to find net income or net loss of the accounting entity.

Measuring Assets and Liabilities

Assets may be measured in different ways in accounting. Cash is measured at its specified amount. Claims to cash, such as notes and accounts receivable, are measured at their expected cash inflows, taking into consideration possible uncollectibles. Inventories, prepaid expenses, plant assets, and intangibles initially are measured at their historical costs. Some items, such as inventory, are later carried at the lower of cost or market value. Plant assets and intangibles are later carried at original cost less accumulated depreciation or amortization. Liabilities are measured in terms of the cash that will be paid or the value of services that will be performed to satisfy the liabilities.

Measuring Changes in Assets and Liabilities

From the previous chapters, you have learned that some changes in assets and liabilities are easily measured by the accountant, such as the exchange of one asset for another of equal value, acquisition of an asset on credit, and payment of a liability. Other changes in assets and liabilities, such as those recorded in adjusting entries, are more difficult to measure because they often involve estimates and/or calculations. The accountant must determine when a change has taken place and the amount of the change. These decisions involve matching revenues and expenses and are guided by the principles discussed below.

■ THE MAJOR PRINCIPLES

As was mentioned in the Introduction of this text, generally accepted accounting principles (GAAP) set forth standards or methods for presenting financial accounting information. By having a standardized presentation format, it is easier for users to compare the financial information of different companies. Generally accepted accounting principles have been developed largely through accounting practice or have been established by authoritative organizations. Four major authoritative organizations that have contributed to the development of the principles are the American Institute of Certified Public Accountants (AICPA), Financial Accounting Standards Board (FASB), Securities and Exchange Commission (SEC), and the American Accounting Association (AAA).

In this section you will study the following principles:

1. Exchange-price (or cost) principle.
2. Matching principle.
3. Revenue recognition principle.
4. Expense and loss recognition principle.
5. Full disclosure principle.

Exchange-Price (or Cost) Principle

When a transfer of resources takes place between two parties, such as buying merchandise on account, the accountant must follow the exchange-price (or cost) principle when presenting that information. The **exchange-price (or cost) principle** requires that transfers of resources be recorded at prices agreed upon by the parties to the exchange at the time of exchange. This principle sets forth (1) what goes into the accounting system—transaction data; (2) when it is recorded—at the time of exchange; and (3) the amounts—exchange prices—at which assets, liabilities, owner's equity, revenues, and expenses are recorded.

As applied to most assets, this principle is often called the **cost principle,** meaning that purchased or self-constructed assets are initially recorded at historical cost. **Historical cost** is the amount paid, or the fair value of the liability incurred or other resources surrendered, to acquire an asset. The term *exchange-price principle* is preferred to *cost principle* because it seems inappropriate to refer to liabilities, owner's equity, and assets such as cash and accounts receivable as being measured in terms of cost.

Matching Principle

Using the **matching principle,** net income of a period is determined by associating or relating revenues earned in a period with expenses incurred to generate those revenues. The logic underlying this principle is that whenever economic resources are used, someone will want to know what was accomplished and at what cost. Every evaluation of economic activity will involve matching benefit with sacrifice. The application of the matching principle is discussed and illustrated below.

Revenue Recognition Principle

Revenue is not difficult to define or measure; it is the inflow of assets from the sale of goods and services to customers, measured by the amount of cash expected to be received from the customer. But **when** revenue should be recorded (credited to a revenue account) is a crucial question for the accountant. The general answer provided under the **revenue recognition principle** is that the revenue should be **earned** and **realized** before it is recognized (recorded).

The Earning of Revenue.   All economic activities undertaken by a company to create revenues are part of the earning process. The actual receipt of cash from a customer may have been preceded by many activities, including (1) placing advertisements, (2) calling on the customer several times, (3) submitting samples, (4) acquiring or manufacturing goods, and (5) delivering goods. Costs are incurred by the company for these activities. Although revenue was actually being earned by these activities, in most instances accountants do not recognize revenue until the time of sale because of the requirement that revenue be **substantially** earned before it is recognized (recorded). This requirement is referred to as the **earning principle.**

The Realization of Revenue.   Under the **realization principle,** the accountant does not recognize (record) revenue until the seller acquires the right to receive payment from the buyer. The seller acquires the right to receive payment from the buyer at the time of sale for merchandise transactions, or when services

to recording accounting data been severely criticized. During times of inflation, the historical cost approach often reports a positive net income when the economic value of the owner's investment has not even been maintained.

There are two widely recommended accounting approaches to the problem of inflation. One approach is current cost accounting. The current cost accounting approach shows the current cost or value of items in the financial statements. The other approach is constant dollar accounting, also known as general price-level adjusted accounting. The constant dollar accounting approach shows financial statement historical cost figures as adjusted for changes in the general price level.

The Nature and Measurement of Inflation

In a period of inflation, the "real value" of the dollar—its ability to purchase goods and services—falls. In a period of deflation, the real value of the dollar rises.

Changes in the general level of prices are measured by means of a general price index such as the consumer price index (CPI). A **price index** is a weighted average of prices for various goods and services. A base year is chosen and assigned a value of 100 for comparative purposes. If the index stands at 108 a year later, this means that prices in general rose 8% during the year. An index of 200 would mean that prices on the average doubled. Because the index is an average, prices of individual types of items may change at different rates and may, in some cases, actually decline. For example, the CPI shows that prices for a "basket" of selected consumer goods doubled in the decade of the 1970s. But during that same decade, gasoline prices quadrupled, while the price of electronic handheld calculators declined very sharply.

The real value or purchasing power of the dollar relative to that of the base year is shown by the reciprocal of the price index; the ratio is simply inverted. For example, if the index for 1987 is 200 and for 1977 is 100, the price index is 200/100, meaning that prices have doubled since 1977. Alternatively, the reciprocal of the price index is 100/200, meaning that the value of the dollar in 1987 has dropped to one half, or 50%, of its purchasing power in 1977.

Because accounting measurements consist largely of dollars of historical cost, financial reports are inadequate in periods of inflation. **Historical cost accounting** measures accounting transactions in terms of the actual dollars expended or received. Such a measurement system has worked well in periods of stable prices. But the system does not work well when the dollar, in terms of its purchasing power, is a sharply changing unit of measure.

To illustrate, assume that a tract of land was purchased for $2,000 and held several years before being sold for $2,500. While the land was held, a general price index rose from 100 to 140. Historical cost accounting would report recovery of the $2,000 cost and income of $500 as a gain on sale of the land. But if we measure this transaction in terms of dollars of constant purchasing power, a far different result is obtained. To get back the purchasing power originally invested in the land, the land would have to be sold for $2,800 ($2,000 × 140/100). Since only $2,500 was received, no real income has been earned because the cost has not been recovered. In fact, a loss of $300 of current purchasing power was incurred.

Consequences of Ignoring Effects of Inflation

As shown in the example above, transactions and, therefore, financial statements that have not been adjusted for the effects of inflation may yield misleading information. Such information may make comparisons between companies difficult. Suppose Company A acquired a tract of land for $100,000 several years ago. Now Company B acquires a virtually identical tract of land for $150,000, paying the higher price because prices in general have risen 50% since Company A bought its land. Immediately, both companies sell their land for $150,000 each. Company A would appear to have the more efficient management because it was able to earn $50,000 on the sale of the land, while Company B earned nothing. In reality, the two companies are in the same position relative to the sale of the land because they have the same number of dollars of current purchasing power. The financial statement difference is caused by recording and continuing to carry the land at its historical cost.

As another example of the consequences of ignoring the effects of inflation, assume the above land was instead a depreciable asset, such as a building. Company A and Company B earn exactly the same number of dollars of revenues and incur, except for depreciation, exactly the same number of dollars of expenses. If both companies had assumed a 10-year useful life on the asset and apply straight-line depreciation to the building, Company A will have a larger net income than Company B simply due to the fact that the historical cost of its asset and, therefore, its recorded depreciation expense is lower than for Company B.

Failure to adjust for the impact of inflation may lead to conclusions that are not valid. A five-year summary of sales may show that sales dollars have increased 50% over the period. If sales prices have increased 60% over the five years, physical sales volume has actually declined.

There are many other consequences that flow from a failure to adjust financial reports for the effects of inflation. Companies are paying taxes on "income" when in reality, costs may not have been covered. Also, financial reports that fail to reflect the impact of inflation may be misleading to individual decision makers, causing them to make decisions that are not in their best interest.

Accounting Responses to Changing Prices

Specific price-level changes relate to changes in the price of a particular good or service, such as calculators or computers. General price-level changes relate to the changes in the economy as a whole, such as those reflected by the Consumer Price Index. A specific price-level change may change in the same, or opposite, direction as the general price-level, and at the same or a different rate. Because of this, there are two types of price changes (specific and general) and two recommended approaches to accounting for changing prices. These recommended approaches are:

1. Change the basis of measurement from historical cost to current cost or value; this approach is called **current cost accounting.**
2. Change the basis of measurement from the actual historical (nominal) dollar to a dollar of constant purchasing power; this approach is referred to as **constant dollar accounting.**

An example of these two approaches is necessary before turning to a more detailed illustration. Assume the following facts regarding the purchase and resale of 1,000 units of a product:

Date	Transaction	Amount	Price-level index
January 1, 1987	Purchased 1,000 units	$3,000	100
December 31, 1987	Sold 1,000 units	5,000	120

The current cost of the units on December 31, 1987, was $3,900. The company incurred $800 of expenses to sell the units.

Under conventional (historical cost) accounting, net income from operations for 1987 would be:

Sales		$5,000
Cost of goods sold	$3,000	
Other expenses	800	3,800
Income from continuing operations*		$1,200

* Income from continuing operations in most cases is the same as income from operations. The technical difference between these terms is covered in intermediate accounting.

The $1,200 of income results from deducting the historical cost of the goods sold as well as the other expenses from sales revenue. The company appears to be better off after the transactions because it has not only recovered the original dollar investment in the goods, together with the expenses incurred, but also has an additional $1,200. The fact that current replacement cost of the goods sold exceeds their historical cost by $900 ($3,900 − $3,000) is ignored. Also, no attention is paid to the fact that the dollars recovered do not have the same purchasing power as those originally invested.

Using the preceding example, Illustration 13.2 compares net income from continuing operations under historical cost and each of the two inflation accounting methods.

Illustration 13.2

Alternative Reporting Approaches— Statement of Net Income from Continuing Operations

Statement of Net Income from Continuing Operations

	Historical cost accounting		Current cost accounting		Constant dollar accounting	
Sales		$5,000		$5,000		$5,000
Cost of goods sold	$3,000		$3,900		$3,600	
Other expenses	800		800		800	
Total expenses		$3,800		$4,700		$4,400
Income from continuing operations		$1,200		$ 300		$ 600

The second set of columns in Illustration 13.2 shows the income from continuing operations using the current cost method. The **current cost** of an asset is the amount that would have to be paid currently to acquire the asset. In the column headed "Current cost accounting," net income from continuing operations is computed by deducting the current cost of replacing the goods sold and the other expenses from current revenues. No adjustments are made for **general** price-level changes. Calculating net income from continuing operations in this manner is supported on the grounds that the sale of an inventory item leads directly to a further action—replenishment of the inventory—if the company is to remain a going concern. A better picture of a company's ability to compete in its markets may also be provided by comparing current revenues with current costs rather than with outdated historical costs. In addition, we can say that only the $300 represents "disposable" income. Only $300 or less can be distributed to owners without reducing the scale of operations since the remainder of the funds is necessary to replace inventory sold and to maintain productive facilities at their present level.

In Illustration 13.2, in the column headed "Constant dollar accounting," cost of goods sold is restated in end-of-1987 dollars by use of a ratio of the current price index to the old price index: $3,000 \times 120/100 = \$3,600$. The $3,600 is the amount of purchasing power invested in the goods expressed in the end-of-1987 dollars. Thus, the $3,600 is restated into the same dollars in which the sales revenue is expressed. The $800 of other expenses is assumed to be selling expenses incurred at point of sale (such as sales commissions), which are already stated in end-of-1987 dollars. All dollar amounts are now expressed in comparable terms—end-of-1987 dollars. The company is better off because it has increased its purchasing power by $600. Under constant dollar accounting, net income is a measurement of increased purchasing power—the entity's increased ability to acquire goods and services.

The next two sections illustrate the current cost and constant dollar accounting methods applied to the income statement of a hypothetical company—the Carol Company.

■ CURRENT COST ACCOUNTING

In the past, inflation adjusted statements generally have been recommended, not required, as supplementary information to conventional financial statements. In 1979, the FASB issued a standard that **requires** certain large, publicly held corporations to present certain supplementary information about the effects of inflation.[3]

To illustrate a statement from continuing operations prepared on a current cost basis, we use the data from the historical cost income statement of the Carol Company in Illustration 13.3.

---

[3] FASB, "Financial Reporting and Changing Prices," *Statement of Financial Accounting Standards No. 33* (Stamford, Conn., 1979). Copyright © by Financial Accounting Standards Board, High Ridge Park, Stamford, Connecticut 06905, U.S.A. Quoted (or excerpted) with permission. Copies of the complete document are available from the FASB.

Illustration 13.3

*Statement of
Income from
Continuing
Operations—
Historical Cost Basis*

**CAROL COMPANY
Statement of Income from Continuing Operations
For the Year Ended December 31, 1987**

Sales		$200,000
Cost of goods sold:		
Inventory, January 1, 1987	$ 20,000	
Purchases	160,000	
Goods available for sale	$180,000	
Inventory, December 31, 1987	40,000	
Cost of goods sold		140,000
Gross margin		$ 60,000
Depreciation	$ 4,000	
Other expenses	46,000	50,000
Income from continuing operations		$ 10,000

Management has determined that the cost of goods sold in terms of current cost is $146,000, and the current cost of the plant assets was $160,000 on December 31, 1986, and $180,000 on December 31, 1987. There were no additions or retirements of plant assets in 1987. Carol Company depreciates its plant assets over a 20-year life, or an annual rate of 5% on a straight-line basis.

Current cost depreciation for 1987 can be computed by multiplying the average current cost of the plant assets for the year by the annual depreciation rate of 5%. The amount is:

$$\frac{\$160,000 + \$180,000}{2} \times 5\% = \$8,500$$

The $146,000 current cost of goods sold and $8,500 current cost depreciation are shown in an income statement prepared under current cost accounting. There is no need to adjust sales or other expenses since they are already expressed at current cost for the year.

Illustration 13.4 shows the amounts that would be reported in the historical cost and current cost income statements shown for the Carol Company.

Illustration 13.4

*Comparison of
Historical Cost
and Current Cost
Income Statements*

**CAROL COMPANY
Statements of Income from Continuing Operations
For the Year Ended December 31, 1987**

	Historical cost	Current cost
Sales	$200,000	$200,000
Cost of goods sold	$140,000	$146,000
Depreciation expense	4,000	8,500
Other expenses	46,000	46,000
Total	$190,000	$200,500
Income (loss) from continuing operations	$ 10,000	$ (500)

Current Cost Accounting—Pro and Con

The advantages of current cost accounting include:

1. Specific current costs incurred by a company are shown.
2. Current costs, rather than historical costs, are deducted from current revenues to calculate net income; this provides for a more meaningful matching of effort and accomplishment.
3. If owner withdrawals are limited to an amount equal to or less than current cost income from continuing operations, the economic capital of the company is maintained.

The disadvantages of current cost include:

1. Current costs may be subjective.
2. Current costs may be difficult and costly to determine.

■ CONSTANT DOLLAR ACCOUNTING

As already discussed briefly, historical dollar amounts in an income statement may be converted or restated into a number of constant dollars that have an equivalent amount of purchasing power. When adjusted for inflation, conventional financial statements are called constant dollar or general price-level adjusted financial statements.

To illustrate an income statement prepared on a constant dollar basis, we again refer to Illustration 13.3 for the Carol Company.

To convert historical dollars into constant end-of-year dollars, the formula is:

$$\text{Historical dollars} \times \frac{\substack{\text{Price index at} \\ \text{end of current period}}}{\substack{\text{Price index at date} \\ \text{of historical transaction}}} = \text{Constant dollars}$$

In order to convert the income statement of the Carol Company, certain assumptions must be made or information provided. These data follow:

1. The general price-level index stood at 100 on December 31, 1986, and at 108 on December 31, 1987.
2. Sales, purchases, other expenses, and taxes were incurred uniformly throughout the year. This means that, on the average, these items were incurred when the price index was 104.
3. Inventories are costed on a Fifo basis. The beginning inventory was acquired when the price index was 98, and the ending inventory was acquired when the index stood at 106.
4. The price index was 54 when the plant assets were acquired.

The procedure for converting the Carol Company income statement in Illustration 13.3 to constant dollars is as follows. First, all revenues, purchases, and expenses were assumed to occur uniformly throughout the year; therefore, these items are converted by multiplying their historical amounts by a ratio of 108/104. Beginning inventory is converted using a ratio of 108/98, while ending inventory is converted using a 108/106 ratio. Since depreciation is calculated on the historical costs of the related assets that were acquired when the index stood at 54, depreciation expense is converted using a ratio of 108/54. Illustration 13.5 shows the restated income statement for the Carol Company. Purchasing power gains and losses are discussed in the next section.

Illustration 13.5

Income Statement—Constant Dollar Basis (end-of-year dollars)

CAROL COMPANY
Restated Income for the Year Ended December 31, 1987
(in constant end-of-year 1987 dollars)

	Historical dollars	Conversion ratio	Constant dollars
Sales	$200,000 ×	108/104	= $207,692
Cost of goods sold:			
Inventory, January 1, 1987	$ 20,000 ×	108/98	= $ 22,041
Purchases	160,000 ×	108/104	= 166,154
Goods available for sale	$180,000		$188,195
Inventory, December 31, 1987	40,000 ×	108/106	= 40,755
Cost of goods sold	$140,000		$147,440
Gross margin	$ 60,000		$ 60,252
Expenses:			
Depreciation	$ 4,000 ×	108/54	= $ 8,000
Other expenses	46,000 ×	108/104	= 47,769
Total expenses	$ 50,000		$ 55,769
Income from continuing operations	$ 10,000		$ 4,483
Purchasing power gain on monetary items			2,625
Net income	$ 10,000		$ 7,108

Purchasing Power Gains and Losses.   Purchasing power gains and losses result from holding monetary assets and liabilities during inflation or deflation. Monetary items are cash and other assets and liabilities that represent fixed claims to cash, such as accounts and notes receivable and payable. Nonmonetary items include all items on the balance sheet other than monetary items. A purchasing power gain results from holding monetary liabilities during inflation or monetary assets during deflation. A purchasing power loss results from holding monetary assets during inflation or monetary liabilities during deflation.

Assume that Bill Allen holds $1,000 of cash during a year in which prices in general rose 25%. Even though Bill still has his $1,000 at year-end, he has less purchasing power than he did at the beginning of the year. Bill needs to have $1,250 ($1,000 × 125/100) at year-end to be as well off as he was at the start of the year. Therefore, during the year, Bill has sustained a purchasing power loss of $250.

Conversely, a gain results from being in debt during inflation. Assume that Kathy Rice owes $600 during a year in which prices rise 40%. The original debt has a year-end purchasing power equivalent of $840 ($600 × 140/100). Kathy can satisfy the debt by paying $600 currently. Thus, she has experienced a purchasing power gain of $240.

Assume that the Carol Company, in Illustration 13.5, experienced a purchasing power gain of $2,625 during 1987. This amount would be added to net income from continuing operations on the restated income statement. Carol company has net income on a constant dollar basis of $7,108, which is nearly 30% less than the net income shown on the conventional (historical cost) income statement.

Constant Dollar Accounting—Pro and Con

The advantages of constant dollar accounting include the following:

1. Measurement of the impact of inflation on a company is objective because adjustments made to convert the statements to a constant dollar basis are based on historical cost.
2. Comparability of the financial statements between companies is improved because of the use of the same procedures and the same index numbers for each firm.
3. There is greater comparability of the financial statements of a single company through time since effects of price-level changes are removed by stating all amounts in dollars of the same purchasing power.

The disadvantages of constant dollar accounting include:

1. Benefits resulting from the use of such statements have not been shown to be in excess of the cost of preparing these statements.
2. The assumption that the impact of inflation affects all companies equally is not true.
3. Only one deficiency—the changing value of the measuring unit—is corrected; the effects of specific price changes are ignored. This is undoubtedly the most significant limitation of constant dollar accounting.

Illustration 13.6 shows a comparison of all three income statements for the Carol Company.

Which method of adjusting for inflation is correct? There is no simple answer. Each method is correct if one accepts the definitions of cost and income assumed under the method. A much more important question is: Which method

Illustration 13.6

Inflation Impact Disclosures

CAROL COMPANY
Statement of Income Adjusted for Changing Prices
For the Year Ended December 31, 1987

	Historical cost	Current cost	Constant dollar (end-of-year dollars)
Sales	$200,000	$200,000	$207,692
Cost of goods sold	$140,000	$146,000	$147,440
Expenses:			
Depreciation expense	4,000	8,500	8,000
Other expenses	46,000	46,000	47,769
Total	$190,000	$200,500	$203,209
Income (loss) from continuing operations	$ 10,000	$ (500)	$ 4,483
Purchasing power gain on monetary items			$ 2,625
Net income	$ 10,000	$ (500)	$ 7,108

is more useful to users of the financial reports? The answer to this question has been of considerable concern to many people, including members of the FASB and the staff of the SEC.

■ THE FASB REQUIREMENTS

FASB Statement No. 33 initially called for disclosure by companies in their annual reports of both the impact of specific price changes and of general inflation on earnings and other selected items. The *Statement* does not require full, completely adjusted financial statements, nor does it affect the way in which the basic (primary) financial statements are prepared, since all required disclosures appear as supplementary information. The *Statement* applies only to publicly held companies (1) with total assets in excess of $1 billion (after deducting accumulated depreciation) or (2) having $125 million (before deducting accumulated depreciation) of inventories and property, plant, and equipment. Thus, about 1,200 to 1,400 large, publicly held companies are directly affected. The FASB also encourages all companies to report the effects of inflation by applying the methods described in *FASB Statement No. 33.*

For fiscal years ended on or after December 25, 1979, affected companies initially had to report as supplementary information:

a. Net income on a current cost basis.
b. Net income on a constant dollar basis (historical cost adjusted for the effects of general inflation).
c. Purchasing power gain or loss on monetary items.[4]

Other disclosure requirements, including a five-year summary of selected financial data, are discussed in more advanced texts on accounting. An example of how an actual company reports inflation data can be seen in the General Motors annual report in Appendix B at the end of the text.

Uncertainty over whether constant dollar information or current cost information is preferable caused the FASB to initially require both types. This uncertainty was shown in responses sent to the FASB by various users when the proposed statement was circulated. Some knowledgeable persons preferred current cost information, while others preferred constant dollar information.

Since *FASB Statement No. 33* was released in 1979, companies and financial statement users have had several years of experience with both approaches. In 1984, the FASB indicated its preference for current cost information over constant dollar information. In *FASB Statement No. 82,* the FASB eliminated the requirement for reporting constant dollar information in supplemental financial statements to reduce the cost incurred in preparing financial statements.[5] The reporting of current cost information is still required. However, a company may substitute constant dollar information for current cost information if there is no material difference between the amount of income that would be disclosed by the two methods.

---

[4] *FASB Statement No. 33,* pars. 29–35.

[5] FASB, "Financial Reporting and Changing Prices: Elimination of Certain Disclosures," *Statement of Financial Accounting Standards No. 82* (Stamford, Conn., 1984). Copyright © by Financial Accounting Standards Board, High Ridge Park, Stamford, Connecticut, 06905, USA.

■ *SUMMARY*

Accounting theory is a set of basic assumptions, concepts, and related principles. This theory explains and guides the accountant's actions in identifying, measuring, and communicating economic information. The underlying assumptions and concepts include entity, going concern, money measurement, and periodicity. Other basic concepts include general-purpose financial statements, substance over form, consistency, double entry, and articulation.

The accountant seeks to measure the assets, liabilities, and owner's equity of an accounting entity. Changes in these items are also measured and assigned to particular time periods to determine net income.

The major principles used in accounting include the exchange-price (cost), matching, revenue recognition, expense and loss recognition, and full disclosure principles. Exceptions are sometimes made in following these principles. For instance, in recognizing revenue sometimes the cash basis, installment basis, percentage-of-completion basis, or production basis is used.

Modifying conventions are customs emerging from accounting practice that alter results that would be obtained from a strict application of accounting principles. Three such modifying conventions are cost-benefit, materiality, and conservatism.

Inflation represents a serious reporting problem. In periods of high inflation, the use of historical cost in financial statements has been criticized. Accountants have developed two approaches to report the effects of inflation. One approach is the current cost approach, which shows the current cost of items in the financial statements. The other approach is constant dollar accounting, also called general price-level adjusted accounting. This approach shows historical cost amounts adjusted for changes in the general price level.

In 1979, the FASB issued *FASB Statement No. 33,* which required certain large, publicly held corporations to present certain supplementary information about the effects of inflation. These companies had to report both current cost and constant dollar information. However, in 1984, the FASB indicated its preference for current cost information over constant dollar information. As of 1985, these companies are no longer required to report constant dollar information. Current cost information must still be reported in supplemental financial statements.

So far, this text has discussed accounting for single proprietorships. The next chapter introduces partnership accounting. You will find that accounting for partnerships involves some new procedures, but the basic underlying accounting theory is the same as for single proprietorships.

APPENDIX: THE CONCEPTUAL FRAMEWORK PROJECT

The exact nature of the basic concepts and related principles comprising accounting theory has been debated for years. The debate continues today even though numerous references can be found to "generally accepted accounting principles" (GAAP). To date, all attempts to present a concise statement of GAAP have received only limited acceptance.

Due to this limited success, many accountants suggest that the starting point in reaching a concise statement of GAAP is to seek agreement on the objectives of financial accounting and reporting. The belief is that if one (1) carefully studies the environment, (2) knows what objectives are sought, (3) can identify certain qualitative traits of accounting information, and (4) can define the basic elements of financial statements, one can discover the principles and standards that will lead to the attainment of the stated objectives. The FASB has taken the first three steps in "Objectives of Financial Reporting by Business Enterprises" and in "Qualitative Characteristics of Accounting Information."[6] The fourth step is represented by "Elements of Financial Statements of Business Enterprises."[7]

■ OBJECTIVES OF FINANCIAL REPORTING

Financial reporting objectives are the broad overriding goals sought by accountants engaging in financial reporting. According to the FASB, the first objective of financial reporting is to:

> provide information that is useful to present and potential investors and creditors and other users in making rational investment, credit, and similar decisions. The information should be comprehensible to those who have a reasonable understanding of business and economic activities and are willing to study the information with reasonable diligence.[8]

The term *other users* is interpreted broadly and includes employees, security analysts, brokers, and lawyers. Financial reporting should provide information to all who are willing to learn to use it properly. Although the Board's objectives are stated in terms of the corporate form of business organization, they apply equally well to single proprietorships and partnerships.

The second objective of financial reporting is to:

> provide information to help present and potential investors and creditors and other users in assessing the amounts, timing, and uncertainty of prospective cash receipts from dividends [owner withdrawals] or interest and the proceeds from the sale, redemption, or maturity of securities or loans. Since investors' and creditors' cash flows are related to enterprise cash flows, financial reporting should provide information to help investors, creditors, and others assess the amounts, timing, and uncertainty of prospective net cash inflows to the related enterprise.[9]

This objective ties the cash flows of investors (owners) and creditors to the cash flows of the enterprise, a tie-in that appears entirely logical. Enterprise

---

[6] FASB, "Objectives of Financial Reporting by Business Enterprises," *Statement of Financial Accounting Concepts No. 1* (Stamford, Conn., 1978). FASB, "Qualitative Characteristics of Accounting Information," *Statement of Financial Accounting Concepts No. 2* (Stamford, Conn., 1980). Copyright © by the Financial Accounting Standards Board, High Ridge Park, Stamford, Connecticut 06905, U.S.A. Quoted (or excerpted) with permission. Copies of the complete document are available from the FASB.

[7] FASB, "Elements of Financial Statements of Business Enterprises," *Statement of Financial Accounting Concepts No. 3* (Stamford, Conn., 1980). Copyright © by the Financial Accounting Standards Board, High Ridge Park, Stamford, Connecticut 06905, U.S.A. Quoted (or excerpted) with permission. Copies of the complete document are available from the FASB.

[8] FASB, "Objectives of Financial Reporting by Business Enterprises," p. viii.

[9] Ibid.

cash inflows are the source of cash for dividends (owner withdrawals), interest, and redemption of maturing debt.

Third, financial reporting should:

> provide information about the economic resources of an enterprise, the claims to those resources (obligations of the enterprise to transfer resources to other entities and owners' equity), and the effects of transactions, events, and circumstances that change its resources and claims to those resources.[10]

A number of conclusions can be drawn from the three objectives and from a study of the environment in which financial reporting is carried out. Financial reporting should provide information about an enterprise's past performance because such information is used as a basis for prediction of future enterprise performance. Financial reporting should focus on earnings and its components, despite the emphasis in the objectives on cash flows. Earnings computed under the accrual basis provide a better indicator of ability to generate favorable cash flows than do statements prepared under the cash basis. Financial reporting does not seek to measure the value of a business, but to provide information that may be useful for doing so. Financial reporting does not seek to evaluate management's performance, predict earnings, assess risk, or estimate earning power, but should provide information to persons who wish to do so.

These conclusions are some of those reached in *Statement of Financial Accounting Concepts No. 1.* As the Board says, these statements "are intended to establish the objectives and concepts that the Financial Accounting Standards Board will use in developing standards of financial accounting and reporting."[11] How successful the Board will be in the approach adopted remains to be seen.

■ QUALITATIVE CHARACTERISTICS

Qualitative characteristics are those characteristics that accounting information should possess to be useful in decision making. This criterion is difficult to apply. The usefulness of accounting information in a given instance depends not only on information characteristics but also on the capabilities of the decision makers and their professional advisers, if any. Accountants cannot specify who the decision makers are, their characteristics, the decisions to be made, or the methods chosen to make the decisions; therefore, attention is directed to characteristics of accounting information. The FASB's graphic summarization of the problems faced is presented in Illustration 13.7.[12]

Relevance

For information to have **relevance,** it must be pertinent to or bear upon a decision. The information must "make a difference" to someone who does not already have the information. Relevant information is capable of making a difference in a decision either by affecting user predictions of outcomes of

---

[10] Ibid.

[11] Ibid., p. i.

[12] FASB, "Qualitative Characteristics of Accounting Information," p. 15.

Illustration 13.7 *A Hierarchy of Accounting Qualities*

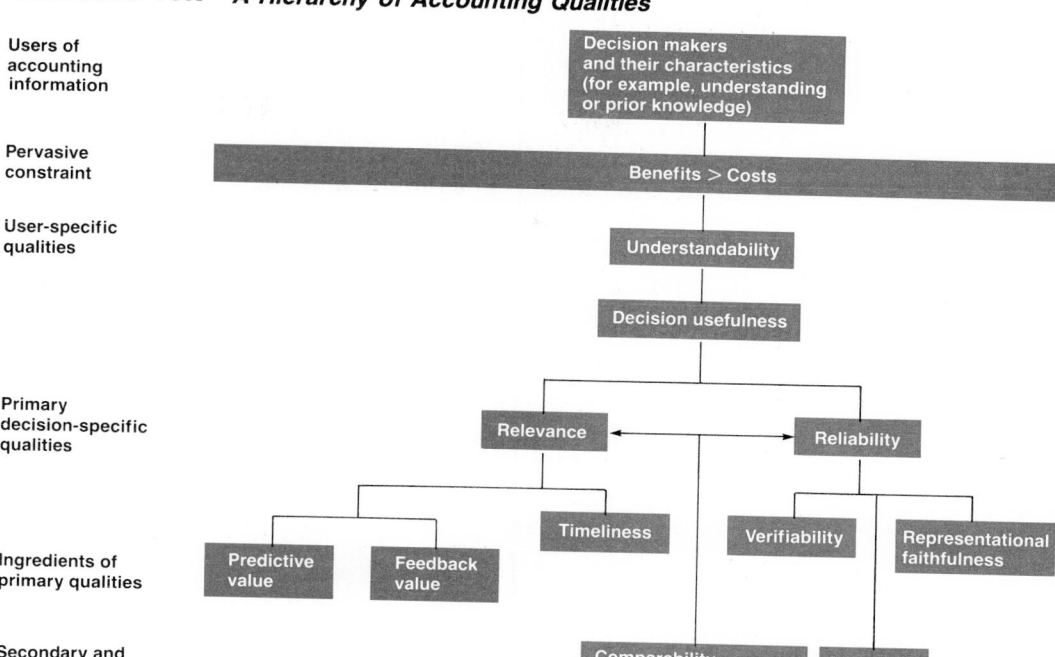

past, present, or future events or by confirming or correcting expectations. Note that information need not be a prediction to be useful in developing, confirming, or altering expectations. Expectations are commonly based on the present or past. For example, any attempt to predict future earnings of a firm would quite likely start with a review of present and past earnings. Also, information that merely confirms prior expectations may be less useful, but is still relevant since it reduces uncertainty.

Certain types of accounting information have been criticized because of an alleged lack of relevance. For example, some would argue that a cost of $1 million paid for a tract of land 40 years ago and reported in the current balance sheet at that amount is irrelevant (except for possible tax implications) to users for decision making today. Such criticism has encouraged research into the types of information that are relevant to users. Suggestions have also been made that a different valuation basis, such as current cost, be used in reporting such assets.

Predictive Value and Feedback Value. Because actions taken now can affect only future events, information is obviously relevant when it possesses **predictive value,** or improves users' abilities to predict outcomes of events. Information that reveals the relative success of users in predicting outcomes possesses **feedback value.** Because feedback reports on past activities, it can make a difference in decision making by (1) reducing uncertainty in a situation, (2) refuting or confirming prior expectations, and (3) providing a basis for further predictions. For example, a report on the first quarter's earnings of a company reduces the uncertainty surrounding the amount of such earnings, confirms or refutes the predicted amount of such earnings, and provides a possible basis on which to predict earnings for the full year. It is important to remember that although accounting information may possess predictive value, it does not consist of predictions. Making predictions is a function performed by the decision maker, not the accountant.

Timeliness. Timeliness requires that accounting information be provided at a time when it may be considered in reaching a decision. Utility of information decreases with age. It is much more useful to know what the net income for 1986 was in early 1987 than to receive this information a year later. If information is to be of any value in decision making, it must be available **before** the decision is made. If not, the information is useless. In determining what constitutes timely information, consideration must be given to the other qualitative characteristics and to the cost of gathering information. For example, a timely estimated amount for uncollectible accounts may be more valuable than a later, verified actual amount. Timeliness alone cannot make information relevant, but otherwise relevant information might be rendered irrelevant by a lack of timeliness.

Reliability

In addition to being relevant, information must be reliable to be useful. Information has **reliability** when it faithfully depicts for users what it purports to represent. Thus, accounting information is reliable if users can depend on it to reflect the underlying economic activities of the organization. The reliability of information depends upon its representational faithfulness, verifiability, and neutrality. The information must also be complete and free of bias.

Representational Faithfulness. Insight into this quality may be gained by considering a map. A map possesses representational faithfulness when it shows roads and bridges (among other things) where roads and bridges actually exist. There is correspondence between what is shown on the map and what is present physically. Similarly, there is **representational faithfulness** when accounting statements on economic activity correspond to the actual underlying activity. Where there is no correspondence, the cause may be bias or lack of completeness.

Effects of Bias. Accounting measurements are biased if they are consistently too high or too low. Bias in accounting measurements may exist due to the choice of measurement method or to bias introduced either deliberately or through lack of skill by the measurer. These two types of bias are discussed below.

Completeness. To be free from bias, information must be sufficiently complete to ensure that it validly represents underlying events and conditions. **Completeness** means that all significant information must be disclosed in a way that aids understanding and does not mislead. Relevance of information also may be reduced if information that would make a difference to a user is omitted. Currently, full disclosure generally requires presentation of a balance sheet, an income statement, a statement of changes in financial position, and necessary notes to the financial statements and supporting schedules. Such statements must be complete, with items properly classified and segregated (such as reporting sales revenue separately from other revenues). Required disclosures may be made in (1) the body of the financial statements, (2) the notes to such statements, (3) special communications, and (4) the president's letter or in other management reports in the annual report.

Another aspect of completeness is that full disclosure must be made of all changes in accounting principles and their effects.[13] Also disclosure should be made of unusual activities (loans to officers), changes in expectations (losses on inventory), depreciation expense for the period, long-term obligations entered into that are not recorded by the accountant (a 20-year lease on a building), new arrangements with certain groups (pension and profit-sharing plans for employees), significant events that occur after the date of the statements (loss of a major customer), and accounting policies (major principles and their manner of application) followed in preparing the financial statements.[14] Because of its emphasis upon disclosure, this aspect of reliability is often called the full-disclosure principle.

Verifiability.   Financial information has verifiability when it can be substantially duplicated by independent measurers using the same measurement methods. Verifiability is directed toward eliminating measurer bias, rather than measurement method bias. The requirement that financial information be based upon objective evidence is based upon demonstrated needs of users for reliable, unbiased financial information. Unbiased information is needed especially when parties with opposing interests (credit seekers and credit grantors) rely upon the same information. Reliability of information is enhanced if it is verifiable.

Financial information will never be free of subjective opinion and judgment; it will always possess varying degrees of verifiability. Some measurements can be supported by canceled checks and invoices. Others, such as periodic depreciation charges, can never be verified because of their very nature. Thus, financial information in many instances is verifiable only in that it represents a consensus as to what would be reported if the same procedures had been followed by other accountants.

Neutrality.   Neutrality in accounting information means that the information should be free of measurement method bias. The primary concern should be relevance and reliability of the information that results from application of the principle, not the effect that the principle may have on a particular interest. Nonneutral accounting information is designed to favor one set of interested parties over others. For example, a particular form of measurement might favor owners over creditors, or vice versa. "To be neutral, accounting information must report economic activity as faithfully as possible, without coloring the image it communicates for the purpose of influencing behavior in *some particular direction.*"[15] Accounting standards should not be developed and used like certain tax regulations which seek deliberately to foster or restrain certain types of activity. Verifiability seeks to eliminate measurer bias; neutrality seeks to eliminate measurement method bias.

---

[13] APB, "Accounting Changes," *APB Opinion No. 20* (New York: AICPA, July 1971).

[14] APB, "Disclosure of Accounting Policies," *APB Opinion No. 22* (New York: AICPA, April 1971).

[15] FASB, "Qualitative Characteristics of Accounting Information," par. 100.

Comparability (and Consistency)

When comparability in financial information exists, reported differences and similarities in information are real and are not the result of differing accounting treatments. Comparable information will reveal relative strengths and weaknesses in a single company through time and between two or more companies at the same point in time.

Consistency requires a company to use the same accounting principles and reporting practices through time. Consistency leads to comparability of financial information for a single company through time. Comparability between companies is more difficult to achieve because the same activities may be accounted for in different ways. For example, B may use one method of depreciation, while C accounts for an identical asset in similar circumstances using another method. A high degree of intercompany comparability in accounting information will not exist unless the same activities are required to be accounted for in the same manner across companies and through time.

Pervasive Constraints

As Illustration 13.7 shows, there are two pervasive constraints faced in providing useful information. First, benefits secured from the information must be greater than the cost of providing that information. Second, only material items need be disclosed and accounted for strictly in accordance with generally accepted accounting principles (GAAP).

Cost-Benefit Analysis. Accounting information is a commodity and, like all commodities, is desired only if it provides benefits greater than its cost. But, unlike most commodities, accounting information has no direct cost to users, since all costs are borne by the provider of the information. This fact has led users and authoritative organizations to demand ever greater amounts of financial information, which have often been answered with claims that the information desired costs more than it is worth. Such a contention was encountered frequently when the FASB proposed requiring disclosure of the impact of inflation upon financial statements. Complicating the issue is the fact that there is no agreed-upon method of measuring benefits of information and that even measurement of cost cannot be carried out without some disagreement. Yet, in the development of accounting standards, an attempt must be made to ensure that the benefits of required disclosures exceed the costs of providing the disclosures.

Materiality. As discussed earlier in the chapter, the basic idea inherent in materiality is that relatively large items must be accounted for in a theoretically correct way; relatively small, insignificant items need not be. Materiality has been defined by the FASB as "the magnitude of an omission or misstatement of accounting information that, in the light of surrounding circumstances, makes it probable that the judgment of a reasonable person relying on the information would have been changed or influenced by the omission or misstatement."[16] The term **magnitude** in this definition suggests that the materiality of an item may be assessed by looking at its **relative** size. A $10,000 error in an expense

---

[16] Ibid., p. xv.

in a company with earnings of $30,000 is material. The same error in a company earning $30,000,000 may not be material.

■ THE BASIC ELEMENTS OF FINANCIAL STATEMENTS

Thus far we have discussed objectives of financial reporting and qualitative characteristics of accounting information. A third important task in developing a conceptual framework for any discipline is that of identifying and defining its basic elements. The basic elements of financial statements have been identified and defined by the FASB. Most of the terms were defined earlier in this text in a less precise way to convey a general understanding of the terms. The more technical definitions follow (these items are not repeated in the glossary):

Assets are probable future economic benefits obtained or controlled by a particular entity as a result of past transactions or events affecting the enterprise.

Liabilities are probable future sacrifices of economic benefits arising from present obligations of a particular entity to transfer assets or provide services to other entities in the future as a result of past transactions or events.

Equity is the residual interest in the assets of an entity that remains after deducting its liabilities. In a business enterprise, the equity is the ownership interest.

Comprehensive income is the change in equity (net assets) of an entity during a period from transactions and other events and circumstances from nonowner sources. It includes all changes in equity during a period except those resulting from investments by owners and distributions to owners.

Revenues are inflows or other enhancements of assets of an entity or settlements of its liabilities (or a combination of both) during a period from delivering or producing goods, rendering services, or other activities that constitute the entity's ongoing major or central operations.

Expenses are outflows or other using up of assets or incurrences of liabilities (or a combination of both) during a period from delivering or producing goods, rendering services, or carrying out other activities that constitute the entity's ongoing major or central operations.

Gains are increases in equity (net assets) from peripheral or incidental transactions of an entity and from all other transactions and other events and circumstances affecting the entity during a period except those that result from revenues or investments by owners.

Losses are decreases in equity (net assets) from peripheral or incidental transactions of an entity and from all other transactions and other events and circumstances affecting the entity during a period except those that result from expenses or distributions to owners.

Investments by owners in the entity are increases in net assets of a particular enterprise resulting from transfers to it from other entities of something of value to obtain or increase ownership interests (or equity) in it. Assets are most commonly received as investments by owners, but that which is received may also include services or satisfaction or conversion of liabilities of the enterprise.

Distributions by the entity to owners are decreases in net assets of a particular enterprise resulting from transferring assets, rendering services, or incurring liabilities by the enterprise to owners. Distributions to owners decrease ownership interests (or equity) in an enterprise.[17]

Note that the requirement that assets and liabilities be based upon past transactions normally rules out the recording of contracts that are mutual promises to do something, such as entering into an employment contract with

---

[17] FASB, "Elements of Financial Statements of Business Enterprises."

an officer. On a similar basis, the accountant refuses to record an asset and a liability when a contract is signed whereby the entity agrees to purchase a certain number of units of a product over a coming period of time.

Recognition and Measurement in Financial Statements

In December 1984, the FASB issued *Statement of Financial Accounting Concepts No. 5,* "Recognition and Measurement in Financial Statements of Business Enterprises,"[18] describing recognition criteria and providing guidance as to the timing and nature of information to be included in financial statements. The recognition criteria established in the *Statement* are fairly consistent with those used in current practice. The *Statement* indicates, however, that when information that is more useful than currently reported information is available at a reasonable cost, it should be included in financial statements. A slightly modified income statement format is recommended. This new format is described in Chapter 16 of this text. The statement indicates that a balance sheet does not show the value of a business, but when used in combination with other information and other financial statements, the balance sheet is helpful in estimating the value of an entity. The importance of cash flow information (covered in Chapter 19 of this text) is also mentioned.

NEW TERMS INTRODUCED IN CHAPTER 13

Accounting theory

"A set of basic concepts and assumptions and related principles that explain and guide the accountant's actions in identifying, measuring, and communicating economic information" (478).

Comparability

A qualitative characteristic of accounting information; when information is comparable, it reveals differences and similarities that are real and are not the result of differing accounting treatments (506).

Completed-contract method

A method of recognizing revenue on long-term projects in which no revenue is recognized until the period in which the project is completed; similar to recognizing revenue upon the completion of a sale (486).

Completeness

A qualitative characteristic of accounting information; requires disclosure of all significant information in a way that aids understanding and does not mislead; sometimes called the full-disclosure principle (504).

Conservatism

Being cautious or prudent and making sure that any errors in estimates tend to understate rather than overstate net assets and net income (490).

Consistency

Requires a company to use the same accounting principles and reporting practices through time (482).

Constant dollar accounting

A recommended approach to deal with the problem of accounting for inflation by changing the unit of measure from the actual historical (nominal) dollar to a dollar of constant purchasing power (492).

Cost-benefit consideration

Determining whether benefits exceed costs (489).

---

[18] FASB, "Recognition and Measurement in Financial Statements of Business Enterprises," *Statement of Accounting Concepts No. 5* (Stamford, Conn., 1984). Copyright © by the Financial Accounting Standards Board, High Ridge Park, Stamford, Connecticut 06905, USA. Copies of the complete document are available from the FASB. (In case you are wondering why we do not mention *Statement of Financial Accounting Concepts No. 4,* it pertains to accounting for not-for-profit organizations and is, therefore, not relevant to this text.)

Cost principle

See Exchange-price principle.

Current cost

The amount that would have to be paid currently to acquire an asset (494).

Current cost accounting

A recommended approach to deal with the problem of accounting for inflation by showing current cost or value of items in the financial statements (492).

Deflation (period of)

Exists when prices in general are falling (490).

Earning principle

The requirement that revenue be substantially earned before it is recognized (recorded) (484).

Entity

The specific unit, such as a business, for which accounting information is gathered. Entities have a separate existence from owners, creditors, employees, customers, other interested parties, and other businesses (479).

Exchange-price (or cost) principle

Transfers of resources are recorded at prices agreed on by the parties to the exchange at the time of the exchange (484).

Feedback value

A qualitative characteristic that information has when it reveals the relative success of users in predicting outcomes (503).

Financial reporting objectives

The broad overriding goals sought by accountants engaging in financial reporting (501).

General price-level accounting

See Constant dollar accounting.

Going-concern (continuity) assumption

The assumption that an entity will continue to operate indefinitely unless there is strong evidence that the entity will terminate (479).

Historical cost

The amount paid, or the fair value of a liability incurred or other resource surrendered, to acquire an asset (484).

Historical cost accounting

Conventional accounting in which accounting measurements are in terms of the actual dollars expended or received (491).

Inflation (period of)

Exists when prices in general are rising (490).

Installment basis

A revenue recognition procedure in which the percentage of total gross margin recognized in a period on an installment sale is equal to the percentage of total cash from the sale that is received in that period (485).

Liquidation

Terminating a business by ceasing business operations and selling off the assets (479).

Losses

Asset expirations that are usually involuntary and do not create revenues (488).

Matching principle

The principle that net income of a period is determined by associating or relating revenues earned in a period with expenses incurred to generate the revenues (484).

Materiality

A modifying convention that allows the accountant to deal with immaterial (unimportant) items in a theoretically incorrect, expedient manner; also a qualitative characteristic specifying that financial accounting report only information significant enough to influence decisions or evaluations (489).

Modifying conventions

Customs emerging from accounting practice that alter the results that would obtained from a strict application of accounting principles; conservatism is an example (489).

Monetary items

Cash and other assets and liabilities that represent fixed claims to cash, such as accounts and notes receivable and payable (497).

Money measurement

Use of a monetary unit of measurement, such as the dollar, instead of physical or other units of measurement—feet, inches, grams, and so on (480).

Neutrality

A qualitative characteristic that requires accounting information to be free of measurement method bias (505).

Nonmonetary items

All items on the balance sheet other than monetary items; examples are inventories, plant assets, capital stock, and owner's equity (497).

Percentage-of-completion method

A method of recognizing revenue based on the estimated stage of completion of a long-term project. The stage of completion is measured by comparing actual costs incurred in a period with total estimated costs to be incurred in all periods (486).

Period costs

Costs that cannot be traced to specific revenue and are expensed in the period in which incurred (489).

Periodicity (time periods)

An assumption of the accountant that an entity's life can be subdivided into time periods for purposes of reporting its economic activities (480).

Predictive value

A qualitative characteristic that information has when it improves users' abilities to predict outcomes of events (503).

Price index

A weighted average of prices for various goods and services. A base year is chosen and assigned a value of 100 for comparative purposes (491).

Product costs

Costs incurred in the acquisition or manufacture of goods. Product costs are accounted for as if they were attached to the goods, with the result that they are charged to expense when the goods are sold (488).

Production basis

A method of revenue recognition used in limited circumstances which recognizes revenue at the time of completion of production or extraction (487).

Purchasing power gain

The gain that results from holding monetary liabilities during inflation or monetary assets during deflation (497).

Purchasing power loss

The loss that results from holding monetary assets during inflation or monetary liabilities during deflation (497).

Qualitative characteristics

Characteristics that accounting information should possess to be useful in decision making (502).

Realization principle

A principle that directs that revenue is recognized only after the seller acquires the right to receive payment from the buyer (484).

Relevance

A qualitative characteristic requiring that information be pertinent to or bear upon a decision (502).

Reliability

A qualitative characteristic requiring that information faithfully depict for users what it purports to represent (504).

Representational faithfulness

A qualitative characteristic requiring that accounting statements on economic activity correspond to the actual underlying activity (504).

Revenue recognition principle

The principle that revenue should be earned and realized before it is recognized (recorded) (484).

Stable dollar

An assumption that the dollar is a reasonably stable unit of measurement (480).

Timeliness

A qualitative characteristic requiring that accounting information be provided at a time when it may be considered in reaching a decision (504).

Verifiability

A qualitative characteristic of accounting information; information is verifiable when it can be substantially duplicated by independent measurers using the same measurement methods (505).

DEMONSTRATION PROBLEM 13–1

For each of the transactions or circumstances described below and the entries made, state which, if any, of the assumptions or concepts, principles, or modifying conventions of accounting have been violated. For the violations, give the entry to correct the improper accounting assuming the books have not been closed.

During the year, the Dorsey Company did the following:

1. Had its buildings appraised. They were found to have a market value of $410,000, although their book value was only $380,000. The accountant debited the Buildings and Accumulated Depreciation—Buildings accounts for $15,000 each and credited R. Dorsey, Capital. No separate mention was made of this action in the financial statements.
2. Purchased a number of new electric pencil sharpeners for its offices at a total cost of $60. These were recorded as assets and are being depreciated over five years.
3. Produced a number of agricultural products at a cost of $26,000. These costs were charged to expense when the products were harvested. The products were set up in inventory at their net market value of $35,000, and the Farm Revenues Earned account was credited for $35,000.

Solution to demonstration problem 13–1

1. The realization principle and the modifying convention of conservatism may have been violated. Such write-ups simply are not looked upon with favor in accounting. To correct the situation, the entry made needs to be reversed:

R. Dorsey, Capital	30,000	
Buildings		15,000
Accumulated Depreciation—Buildings		15,000

2. Theoretically, there were no violations unless there is one relating to the cost of compiling insignificant information. As a practical matter, the $60 could have been expensed on materiality grounds.
3. There were no violations. The procedures followed are considered acceptable for farm products that are interchangeable and readily marketable. No correcting entry is needed provided due allowance has been made for the costs to be incurred in delivering the products to the market.

DEMONSTRATION PROBLEM 13–2

Duncan Book Company's financial statements included the following partial income statement:

DUNCAN BOOK COMPANY
Partial Income Statement
For the Year Ended December 31, 1987

Sales		$250,000
Cost of goods sold	$180,000	
Depreciation	3,000	
Other expenses	15,000	198,000
Income from continuing operations . .		$ 52,000

Sales were made uniformly throughout the year. The cost of goods sold consisted of books acquired when the general price index stood at 105. This same index ended the year at 120 and averaged 110 for the year. The current cost of the goods sold was $200,000.

The $3,000 depreciation reported is on a delivery truck that cost $12,000 when the general price index stood at 100. The truck had a current cost of $14,000 at the beginning of 1987 and a current cost of $16,000 at the end of 1987. The other expenses were incurred uniformly throughout the year, were paid in cash, and are substantially equal to their current cost at time of incurrence.

Assume that Duncan Company experienced a purchasing power gain of $1,500 during 1987.

Required: a.   Prepare a statement showing current cost income from continuing operations for the year ended December 31, 1987.

b.   Prepare a statement showing constant dollar income in December 31, 1987, dollars for the year then ended.

Solution to Demonstration Problem 13–2

a.

DUNCAN BOOK COMPANY
Statement of Current Cost Income from Continuing Operations
For the Year Ended December 31, 1987

Sales		$250,000
Cost of goods sold	$200,000	
Depreciation ($14,000 + $16,000)/2 × 0.25 . .	3,750	
Other expenses	15,000	218,750
Income from continuing operations		$ 31,250

b.

DUNCAN BOOK COMPANY
Statement of Constant Dollar Income
In End-of-Year Dollars
For the Year Ended December 31, 1987

Sales ($250,000 × 120/110)		$272,727
Cost of goods sold ($180,000 × 120/105) . .	$205,714	
Depreciation ($3,000 × 120/100)	3,600	
Other expenses ($15,000 × 120/110)	16,364	225,678
Income from continuing operations		$ 47,049
Purchasing power gain on monetary items . .		1,500
Net income		$ 48,549

QUESTIONS

1. Name the assumptions underlying generally accepted accounting principles. Comment on the validity in recent years of the stable unit of measurement assumption.

2. Why does the accountant assume the existence of an entity?

3. When is the going-concern assumption not to be used?

4. What is meant by the term *accrual basis of accounting?* What is its alternative?

5. What does it mean to say that accountants record substance rather than form?

6. If a company changes an accounting principle because the change better meets the information needs of users, what disclosures must be made?

7. What is the exchange-price (or cost) principle? What is the significance of adhering to this principle?

8. What two requirements generally must be met before revenue will be recognized in a period?

9. Under what circumstances, if any, is the receipt of cash an acceptable time to recognize revenue?

10. What two methods may be used in recognizing revenues on long-term construction contracts?

11. Define expense. What principles guide the recognition of expense?

12. How does an expense differ from a loss?

13. What is the full-disclosure principle?

14. What role does cost-benefit play in financial reporting?

15. What is meant by the accounting term *conservatism*? How does it affect the amounts reported in the financial statements?

16. Does materiality relate only to the relative size of dollar amounts?

17. How might it be argued that a tax supposedly on income is really a tax on capital?

18. What are the two basic approaches that might be used to reveal the impact of inflation on financial statements?

19. When items in a set of financial statements are all converted into constant dollars, what do they have in common?

20. If an index of the general level of prices rose 15% in a period, what is the effect upon the value or real worth of the dollar?

21. How is the dollar amount for land adjusted under constant dollar accounting?

22. Explain the typical adjustment of sales and most expenses under constant dollar accounting.

23. Identify whether each of the following items is a monetary or nonmonetary item:

    a. Cash.
    b. Equipment.
    c. Notes receivable.
    d. Merchandise inventory.
    e. Accounts receivable.
    f. Patents.
    g. Common stock.
    h. Land.
    i. Accounts payable.
    j. Buildings.

24. What are purchasing power gains and losses? When do purchasing power gains occur? When do purchasing power losses occur?

25. In the supplementary disclosures required by the FASB, how are the effects of inflation shown?

26. What is the major deficiency in constant dollar accounting?

27. (Based on the Appendix)   Identify the three major parts of the conceptual framework project that are included in the text.

28. (Based on the Appendix)   What are the two primary qualitative characteristics?

EXERCISES

E–1

Match theory terms with definitions

Match the items in Column A with the proper descriptions in column B.

Column A

1. Going concern (continuity).
2. Consistency.
3. Disclosure.
4. Periodicity.
5. Conservatism.
6. Stable dollar.
7. Matching.
8. Materiality.
9. Exchange-price.
10. Entity.

Column B

a. An assumption relied on in the preparation of the primary financial statements that would be unreasonable when the inflation rate is high.
b. Concerned with relative dollar amounts.
c. The usual basis for the recording of assets.
d. Required if the accounting treatment differs from that previously used for a particular item.
e. An assumption that would be unreasonable to use in reporting on a firm that had become insolvent.
f. None of these.
g. Requires a company to use the same accounting procedures and practices through time.
h. An assumption that the life of an entity can be subdivided into time periods for reporting purposes.
i. Discourages undue optimism in measuring and reporting net assets and net income.
j. Requires separation of personal from business activity in the recording and reporting processes.

E–2

Compute income under accrual basis and installment method

Royce Company sells its products on an installment sales basis. Data for 1986 and 1987 follow:

	1986	1987
Installment sales	$50,000	$60,000
Cost of goods sold on installment . .	35,000	45,000
Other expenses	7,500	10,000
Cash collected from 1986 sales . .	30,000	15,000
Cash collected from 1987 sales . .		40,000

a. Compute the net income for 1987 assuming use of the accrual (sales) basis of revenue recognition.
b. Compute the net income for 1987 assuming use of the installment method of recognizing gross margin.

E–3

Recognize revenue under percentage-of-completion method

A company has a contract to build a ship at a price of $500 million and an estimated cost of $400 million. In 1987, costs of $100 million were incurred. Under the percentage-of-completion method how much revenue would be recognized in 1987?

E–4

Compute effect on financial statements of incorrectly expensing an asset

A company follows a practice of expensing the premium on its fire insurance policy when it is paid. In 1987, it charged to expense the $1,440 premium paid on a three-year policy covering the period July 1, 1987, to June 30, 1990. In 1984, a premium of $1,320 was charged to expense on the same policy for the period July 1, 1984, to June 30, 1987.

a. State the principle of accounting that was violated by this practice.
b. Compute the effects of this violation on the financial statements for the calendar year 1987.
c. State the basis upon which the company's practice might be justified.

E–5

Compute gross margin under GAAP and then by recognizing revenue as production is completed

Blair Company produces a product at a cost of $30 per unit that it sells for $45. The company has been very successful and is able to sell all of the units that it can produce. During 1987, the company manufactured 50,000 units, but because of a transportation strike, it was able to sell and deliver only 40,000 units.

a. Compute the gross margin for 1987 following generally accepted accounting principles. The cost of the units sold should be entitled "cost of goods sold" and treated as an expense.
b. Compute the gross margin for 1987 assuming that the realization principle is ignored and that revenue is recognized as production is completed.

E–6

Compute income under historical cost accounting, constant dollar accounting, and current cost accounting

Assume the following facts regarding the purchase and sale of 100 units of a product:

Date	Transaction	Amount	Price-level index
January 1, 1987 . . .	Purchased 100 units	$18,000	100
December 31. 1987 . .	Sold 100 units	30,000	110

The company incurred $3,600 of expenses to sell the units. The replacement cost of the units on December 31, 1987, was $21,000. Prepare a schedule showing net income from continuing operations under historical cost accounting, current cost accounting, and constant dollar accounting.

E–7

Convert cost of goods sold section of income statement to constant dollar amounts

The cost of goods sold section of the conventional (historical cost) income statement for the Howard Company appears below:

Cost of goods sold:	
Inventory, January 1, 1987	$ 36,000
Purchases	108,000
Goods available for sale	$144,000
Inventory, December 31, 1987 . .	18,000
Cost of goods sold	$126,000

The general price-level index was 100 on December 31, 1986, and 110 on December 31, 1987. The Fifo inventories were acquired when the index stood at 96 for the beginning inventory and 108 for the ending inventory. Purchases were incurred uniformly throughout the year. Convert the cost of goods sold section of the income statement to end-of-year constant dollar amounts.

E-8

Compute current cost depreciation

R Company's plant assets at December 31, 1986, had a historical cost of $50,000 and accumulated depreciation of $20,000 (10% annual depreciation rate). There were no additions or retirements in 1987. The current cost of the plant assets on December 31, 1986, was $65,000 and on December 31, 1987, was $75,000. Compute the current cost depreciation for 1987.

E-9

Determine purchasing power gain or loss

In each of the situations given, determine the amount of purchasing power gain or loss:

a. You hold cash of $10,000 during a year in which prices in general rose 10%.
b. You are in debt $5,000 during a year in which prices in general rose 8%.

PROBLEMS, SERIES A

P13-1-A

Compute income assuming revenues are recognized at time of sale and then assuming installment method is used

The Shapiro Real Estate Sales Company sells lots in its development in Flash Flood Canyon under terms calling for small cash down payments with monthly installment payments spread over a few years. Following are data on the company's operations for its first three years:

	1985	1986	1987
Gross margin rate	45%	48%	50%
Cash collected in 1987 from sales of lots made in . . .	$160,000	$200,000	$240,000

The total selling price of the lots sold in 1987 was $800,000, while general and administrative expenses (which are not included in the costs used to determine gross margin) were $200,000.

Required:

a. Compute net income for 1987 assuming revenue is recognized upon the sale of a lot.
b. Compute net income for 1987 assuming use of the installment method of accounting for sales and gross margin.

P13-2-A

Compute income under completed-contract and percentage-of-completion methods

Given below are the contract prices and costs relating to all of the Zimmerman Company's long-term construction contracts (in millions of dollars):

	Contract price	Costs incurred		Costs yet to be incurred
		Prior to 1987	In 1987	
On contracts completed in 1987 . .	$ 46.0	$ -0-	$42.0	$ -0-
On incomplete contracts	144.0	24.0	48.0	48.0

General and administrative expenses for 1987 amounted to $1,800,000.

Required: a. Compute net income for 1987 using the completed-contract method.

b. Compute net income for 1987 using the percentage-of-completion method. Assume that the general and administrative expenses are not to be treated as a part of the construction cost.

P13–3–A

Indicate agreement or disagreement with accounting practices followed and comment

In each of the circumstances described below, the accounting practices followed may be questioned. You are to indicate whether you agree or disagree with the accounting employed and to state the assumptions, concepts, or principles that justify your position.

1. The cost of certain improvements to leased property having a life of five years was charged to expense because the improvements would revert to the lessor when the lease expires in three years.
2. The salaries paid to the top officers of the company were charged to expense in the period in which they were incurred even though the officers spent over half of their time planning next year's activities.
3. A company spent over $4.8 million in developing a new product and then spent an additional $5.4 million promoting it. All of these costs were incurred and charged to expense this year even though future years would also benefit.
4. No entry was made to record the belief that the market value of the land owned (carried in the accounts at $69,600) had increased.
5. No entry was made to record the fact that costs of $60,000 were expected to be incurred in fulfilling warranty provisions on products sold this year. The revenue from products sold was recognized this year.
6. The acquisition of a tract of land was recorded at the price paid for it of $129,600, even though the company would have been willing to pay $150,000.
7. A truck acquired at the beginning of the year was reported at year-end at 80% of its acquisition price even though its market value then was only 65% of its original acquisition price.

P13–4–A

Compute income on both current cost and constant dollar basis

A partial income statement for the Knight Company for the year ended December 31, 1987, in terms of historical dollars is given below:

KNIGHT COMPANY Partial Income Statement For the Year Ended December 31, 1987		
Sales		$630,000
Cost of goods sold	$405,600	
Depreciation	24,000	
Other expenses	126,000	555,600
Income from continuing operations . .		$ 74,400

The sales were made rather uniformly throughout the year. Other expenses were also incurred rather uniformly throughout the year and largely on a cash basis. The depreciation reported relates to a machine acquired at a cost of $240,000 that is being depreciated over a 10-year life on a straight-line basis.

The current cost of the goods sold was $450,000 at the time of their sale. The current cost (gross) of the machine was $390,000 at the beginning of 1987 and $450,000 at the end of the year. An index of the general level of prices stood at 80 when the machine was acquired, at 100 at the beginning of 1987, averaged 105 for 1987, and ended the year at 110. This same index stood at 104 when the goods sold were acquired.

Required: a. Prepare a statement showing current cost net income from continuing operations for the year ended December 31, 1987.

b. Prepare a statement showing constant dollar net income from continuing operations in end-of-year dollars for the year ended December 31, 1987.

within the apparent scope of the partnership's business. For example, a partner could bind a partnership composed of physicians to a contract for medical supplies, but not to a contract to deliver an airplane. The individual partners must act in the best interests of the partnership and not their own personal interests when dealing in partnership matters.

Limited Life

A partnership can be terminated at any time since it is a voluntary association. The **termination (dissolution)** of a partnership may be caused by the withdrawal, retirement, insanity, death, or bankruptcy of any one of the partners. Thus, a partnership is said to have a limited life. If any of the events that may cause dissolution occur, the remaining partners may continue the business, but a new partnership entity is created. A partnership may also end because the period for which it was formed has expired or the specific purpose for which it was organized has been achieved.

Unlimited Liability

Each partner may be held liable for all debts of the partnership—a potential peril known as **unlimited liability** of each partner. If the partnership cannot pay its debts, creditors may satisfy their claims by attaching (seizing) the partners' personal assets. Each partner's personal creditors have first claim on that partner's personal assets, but any remaining personal assets may be used to satisfy partnership creditors. For example, assume partner A has $10,000 of personal assets and $8,000 of personal liabilities, and the partnership is now unable to pay its creditors. The partnership's creditors could require partner A to pay the $2,000 excess of personal assets over personal debts to satisfy their claims on the partnership. The partnership creditors do not have to divide the debts among all partners; the creditors could seize the assets of only **one** partner to satisfy their claims. A partner who pays all of the partnership's debts acquires the right to be reimbursed by the other partners for their shares of the debts. This unlimited liability feature must be carefully considered by persons thinking of entering into a partnership agreement.

■ ADVANTAGES OF A PARTNERSHIP

There are several advantages to forming a partnership. A partnership is sufficiently flexible to permit reasonable accumulations of capital and talent. It may be advantageous to form a partnership when (1) business capital requirements exceed the amount that may be raised by a single proprietor, or (2) it is possible to obtain a variety of talent or knowledge from other persons who are also willing to share the risks and rewards of ownership. Also, a partnership is easier and less expensive to organize than a corporation. A partnership is not required to observe as many laws and regulations as a corporation, nor is it subject to separate income taxation as is a corporation. Each partner reports his or her share of partnership income to the Internal Revenue Service and is taxed individually.

■ DISADVANTAGES OF A PARTNERSHIP

Perhaps the greatest disadvantage of a partnership lies in the unlimited liability feature, or the fact that each partner may be held liable for all partnership debts. In this respect, corporations have an advantage over partnerships. A corporation's stockholders are not liable for the corporation's debts, and stockholders' losses usually cannot exceed the amount invested.

Another disadvantage is the feature of mutual agency. Since one partner may bind the partnership to a contract, a partner who fails to exercise good judgment can cause the loss of partnership assets and, possibly, the loss of personal assets of the other partners.

As a functioning organization, the partnership generally becomes unwieldy when there are many partners. And by virtue of the limited life feature, a partnership is subject to possible termination due to many uncontrollable circumstances, such as the death of a partner.

Because partners are co-owners of a partnership's net assets, the transfer of ownership from one partner to another person may be difficult to accomplish. When a partner withdraws from the partnership, the remaining partners will either have to purchase the withdrawing partner's interest or approve of the person to whom that interest is sold. Since a partnership is a **voluntary** association of persons, the remaining partners do not have to accept the buyer of an interest in a partnership as a partner. If a buyer acceptable as a partner cannot be found, the partners may have to terminate the partnership.

■ UNIQUE FEATURES IN PARTNERSHIP ACCOUNTING

Because a division of interest exists in a partnership that does not exist in a single proprietorship, the accounting records for a partnership differ somewhat from those presented thus far. The unique accounting features in a partnership relate specifically to the partners' capital and drawing accounts, division of business income or loss, and changes in ownership of the partnership.

The Partners' Capital Accounts

A capital account is maintained for each partner. The total balance in the partner's capital account after year-end closing entries represents the partner's ownership equity in the business. Each partner's capital account is:

1. Credited with the original investment.
2. Credited with subsequent investments.
3. Credited with the agreed-upon share of net income.
4. Debited with the agreed-upon share of net loss.
5. Debited with permanent capital reductions.
6. Debited with the balance of the partner's drawing account at the end of each fiscal period.

To illustrate the use of the capital accounts, assume that James Law and Todd Hart, who have been in business as single proprietors, decide to form a partnership. The formation of the partnership creates a new accounting entity. Since assets of a business should be accounted for at fair market value when they are acquired, the assets contributed by each partner will be recorded at their current market values. These values may differ from the historical cost amounts shown on the separate accounting records of the individual proprietorships. Shown below are the assets contributed, liabilities assumed, and their fair market values:

Law		**Hart**	
Cash .	$ 5,600	Cash .	$ 6,600
Accounts receivable	6,800	Merchandise inventory .	3,400
Merchandise inventory .	12,000	Land .	8,000
Delivery equipment .	3,000	Building .	20,000
Accounts payable	(3,200)	Accounts payable	(2,200)

The journal entries on January 1, 1987, to record the investment of each partner are as follows:

Cash	5,600	
Accounts Receivable	6,800	
Merchandise Inventory	12,000	
Delivery Equipment	3,000	
Accounts Payable		3,200
James Law, Capital		24,200
To record the investment of Law in the partnership of Law and Hart.		

Cash	6,600	
Merchandise Inventory	3,400	
Land	8,000	
Building	20,000	
Accounts Payable		2,200
Todd Hart, Capital		35,800
To record the investment of Hart in the partnership of Law and Hart.		

On August 1, 1987, the partners made the following additional cash investments that were credited to their capital accounts. The required journal entry is:

Cash	5,800	
James Law, Capital		2,400
Todd Hart, Capital		3,400
To record additional cash investments.		

On December 31, 1987, before closing the books, the capital accounts of the partners would appear as follows:

James Law, Capital

Date		Explanation	Post. Ref.	Debit	Credit	Balance
1987						
Jan.	1	Original investment			24,200	24,200
Aug.	1	Additional cash investment			2,400	26,600

Todd Hart, Capital

Date		Explanation	Post. Ref.	Debit	Credit	Balance
1987						
Jan.	1	Original investment			35,800	35,800
Aug.	1	Additional cash investment			3,400	39,200

During the accounting period, partners sometimes withdraw cash or merchandise for personal use. A drawing account is maintained for each partner to record the partner's withdrawals. The next section discusses the withdrawals by partners.

Partners' Drawing Accounts

Partners may withdraw either cash or merchandise from the business. **Withdrawals of cash** are charged to the partner's drawing account and credited to Cash. The partnership agreement should specify whether **withdrawals of merchandise** are to be valued at **cost** or **selling price.** If merchandise is valued at cost, the withdrawal is debited to the partner's drawing account and credited to Purchases. If merchandise is valued at selling price, the withdrawal is debited to the partner's drawing account and credited to Sales.

To illustrate drawing accounts, assume that Hart and Law made withdrawals as indicated below:

James Law, Drawing

Date		Explanation	Post. Ref.	Debit	Credit	Balance
1987						
Feb.	7	Cash		1,600		1,600
Apr.	8	Merchandise (at cost)		1,700		3,300
July	31	Cash		1,750		5,050
Dec.	1	Cash		1,650		6,700

Todd Hart, Drawing

Date		Explanation	Post. Ref.	Debit	Credit	Balance
1987						
Mar.	1	Cash		1,900		1,900
June	7	Cash		1,700		3,600
Sept.	18	Cash		2,000		5,600
Dec.	4	Merchandise (at cost)		1,600		7,200

As a rule, partners cannot withdraw any part of their original investment without the consent of all partners. Whether partners may withdraw against any future investments to their capital accounts depends on the partnership agreement. **Withdrawals of investments** should be debited directly to the capital account rather than to the drawing account unless stated otherwise in the agreement. Withdrawals of investments are not considered normal withdrawals, so they are not entered in the drawing account.

End-of-Period Entries

At the end of the fiscal period, adjusting entries are made, and all expense and revenue accounts are closed to Income Summary in the same manner as was illustrated for a single proprietorship. The Income Summary account is closed to the partners' capital account (like it was to the owner's capital account in a single proprietorship). The amount of net income or loss assigned to each partner is based on methods outlined in the partnership agreement. Each partner's drawing account is then closed to that partner's capital account. The drawing account is not closed to the Income Summary account because it is not an expense of the business; it is merely a temporary owners' equity account used to accumulate total withdrawals during a period.

To illustrate, assume that the partnership of Law and Hart has net income of $30,000 for the year ended December 31, 1987, and that the partners decide to divide income equally. The journal entry to close net income to the capital accounts is:

Income Summary	30,000	
James Law, Capital		15,000
Todd Hart, Capital		15,000
To close net income to the capital accounts.		

The next step is to close the balances of the partners' drawing accounts (shown in the ledger accounts above) to their capital accounts by the following journal entries:

James Law, Capital	6,700	
James Law, Drawing		6,700
To close the December 31, 1987, drawing account balance.		

Todd Hart, Capital	7,200	
Todd Hart, Drawing		7,200
To close the December 31, 1987, drawing account balance.		

After the entries are posted, the drawing accounts and capital accounts of Law and Hart appear as follows:

James Law, Drawing

Date		Explanation	Post. Ref.	Debit	Credit	Balance
1987						
Feb.	7	Cash		1,600		1,600
Apr.	8	Merchandise (at cost)		1,700		3,300
July	31	Cash		1,750		5,050
Dec.	1	Cash		1,650		6,700
	31	To capital			6,700	–0–

James Law, Capital

Date		Explanation	Post. Ref.	Debit	Credit	Balance
1987						
Jan.	1	Original investment			24,200	24,200
Aug.	1	Additional cash investment			2,400	26,600
Dec.	31	Net income			15,000	41,600
	31	From drawing		6,700		34,900

Todd Hart, Drawing

Date		Explanation	Post. Ref.	Debit	Credit	Balance
1987						
Mar.	1	Cash		1,900		1,900
June	7	Cash		1,700		3,600
Sept.	18	Cash		2,000		5,600
Dec.	4	Merchandise (at cost)		1,600		7,200
	31	To capital			7,200	–0–

Todd Hart, Capital

Date		Explanation	Post. Ref.	Debit	Credit	Balance
1987						
Jan.	1	Original investment			35,800	35,800
Aug.	1	Additional cash investment			3,400	39,200
Dec.	31	Net income			15,000	54,200
	31	From drawing		7,200		47,000

■ DIVISION OF PARTNERSHIP INCOME OR LOSS

Partnership income and losses are divided in accordance with provisions in the partnership agreements. The agreed-upon way that a partnership's income or losses are to be shared is called the income and loss ratio (profit and loss ratio or earnings and loss ratio). If the agreement is silent with respect to the division of income, income is divided equally among the partners. If the agreement is silent as to loss distribution, losses are divided in the same manner as income. However, a partnership agreement will usually specify the means by which income and losses are to be distributed to the partners.

The method of distribution of income and losses may be based on many factors. If each of the partners invests an equal amount of assets, has approximately equal ability, devotes the same amount of time to the business, and has the same wealth at risk, then net income or net losses should probably be divided equally. If variations in the foregoing factors exist between partners, a method of income or loss distribution should be devised to reflect such differences. For example, a partner who manages the business all week may be allocated a salary out of net income prior to an equal distribution of the remainder to all partners. This "salary" is part of the income sharing agreement and is **not** an expense of the partnership in the determination of net income.

For example, A and B have a partnership in which Partner A manages the store during the week and both partners share the work load equally on the weekends. The partnership agreement states that in sharing income and loss, A is to be given credit for a "salary" of $10,000 and the remaining net income is to be shared equally by the two partners. Net income for the year is $50,000. When the Income Summary account is closed, A's capital account will be credited with $30,000, and B's capital account will be credited with $20,000, as shown:

	A	B	Total	Net income to be distributed
Net income				$50,000
Salary to A . . .	$10,000		$10,000	40,000
Remainder equally . .	20,000	$20,000	40,000	–0–
Total	$30,000	$20,000	$50,000	

In some partnerships, one partner invests a larger amount of capital than another. In this case, the partner with the larger capital investment may insist that interest be allowed on capital balances in the division of income, with the remainder to be divided equally between the partners. This **interest** would simply be a means of equitable compensation to the partner with the larger investment. As in the salary example, this interest factor is **not** an expense in income determination.

Common methods of dividing income are listed below. Illustrations of each method follow.

1. Net income divided in a set ratio such as:
   a. Equally.
   b. Agreed ratio other than equal.
   c. Ratio of partners' capital account balances at the beginning of fiscal period.
   d. Ratio of average capital investment.
2. Net income divided by allowing interest on the capital investments, or salaries, or both, with remaining net income divided in an agreed ratio.

Examples showing the division of net income (or net loss) are given in the next section.

Illustrations of Distributions of Partnership Income

The illustrations that follow are based on data about the partnership of Anders and Budd. Net income for the year ended December 31, 1987, was $60,000. During 1987, Anders' drawings were $14,000, and Budd's drawings were $22,000. The capital account balances of the partners on December 31, 1987, before closing were Anders, $85,000, and Budd, $134,000.

Case 1. Net Income Divided in a Set Ratio.   The division of income (or losses) may be based on only one factor as is shown in each of the following situations.

a.   **Net income divided equally.** In this instance, the income and loss ratio is 1:1, or 50% and 50%. The capital accounts of Anders and Budd would each be credited with $30,000 of net income ($60,000/2).

Income Summary	60,000	
Anders, Capital		30,000
Budd, Capital		30,000
To record distribution of net income to partners.		

b.   **Net income divided in an agreed ratio other than equal**—60% to Anders and 40% to Budd. Such an income and loss sharing ratio may reflect an attempt to take such factors as work load or special talent into consideration. In this case, Anders would be credited with $36,000 and Budd with $24,000 ($60,000 × 0.60 = $36,000; $60,000 × 0.40 = $24,000). The journal entry to close Income Summary would read:

Income Summary	60,000	
Anders, Capital		36,000
Budd, Capital		24,000
To record distribution of net income to partners.		

c.   **Net income divided in ratio of partners' capital account balances at the beginning of the fiscal period.** Assume that Anders' beginning capital balance on January 1, 1987, was $40,000, and Budd's was $80,000. Total capital of the partnership at the beginning of the year was $120,000. Anders had one third ($40,000/$120,000) of the total capital and Budd, two thirds ($80,000/$120,000). Net income is allocated $20,000 (one third of $60,000) to Anders and $40,000 (two thirds of $60,000) to Budd.

Income Summary	60,000	
Anders, Capital		20,000
Budd, Capital		40,000
To record distribution of net income to partners.		

d.   **Net income divided in ratio of average capital investment.** In this case, details must be provided showing the timing of the investment by each partner. Illustration 14.1 contains assumed data on Anders' and Budd's capital balances. The "month-dollars" amount in each case is found by multiplying the balance times the number of months for which this balance remained unchanged. The average capital is found by dividing the total month-dollars by 12.

The ratio of average capital investment is computed by dividing each partner's average capital by the total average capital of $140,000 ($50,000 for Anders and $90,000 for Budd). This ratio is then used to compute the distribution of net income. Thus, Anders is credited with $21,429 ($50,000/$140,000 × $60,000) of net income; Budd is credited with $38,571 ($90,000/$140,000 × $60,000).

Income Summary	60,000	
Anders, Capital		21,429
Budd, Capital		38,571
To record distribution of net income to partners.		

Case 2. Net Income Divided by Allowing Interest on Capital Investments, or Salaries, or Both, with Remaining Net Income Divided in an Agreed Ratio.   Interest and salary allocations may be specified in the partnership agree-

Illustration 14.1

Computation of Average Capital

Anders, capital

Date	Debits	Credits	Balance	Months unchanged	Month-dollars (weighted equivalent)
Jan. 1			$ 40,000	6	$ 240,000
July 1		$15,000	55,000	5	275,000
Dec. 1		30,000	85,000	1	85,000
				12	$ 600,000

Average capital of Anders: $600,000 ÷ 12 = $50,000.

Budd, capital

Date	Debits	Credits	Balance	Months unchanged	Month-dollars (weighted equivalent)
Jan. 1			$ 80,000	7	$ 560,000
Aug. 1		$ 4,000	84,000	3	252,000
Nov. 1		50,000	134,000	2	268,000
				12	$1,080,000

Average capital of Budd: $1,080,000 ÷ 12 = $90,000.

ment to compensate partners for differences in investment, time spent with the business, and other factors.

a. Continuing the example of Anders and Budd, assume that the partners are to be allowed 6% interest on their beginning capital balances. January 1 capital balances were: Anders, $40,000; and Budd, $80,000. Salaries allowed are: Anders, $16,000; and Budd, $10,000. The $60,000 income for the current year is distributed as follows:

	Anders	Budd	Total	Income to be distributed
Net income				$60,000
Interest (6% on beginning capital balance)	$ 2,400	$ 4,800	$ 7,200	52,800
Salary	16,000	10,000	26,000	26,800
Remainder	13,400	13,400	26,800	–0–
Distribution	$31,800	$28,200	$60,000	

The entry to divide net income is:

Income Summary	60,000	
Anders, Capital		31,800
Budd, Capital		28,200

To divide net income between the partners.

b. Even if the allowances for salaries or interest exceed net income, or if there is a net loss for the period, the partners still are given credit for their full amounts of interest and salary. For example, in the situation above, if there was a net loss of $20,000 instead of net income of $60,000 for the year, the division would be as follows:

	Anders	Budd	Total	Loss to be distributed
Net loss				$(20,000)
Interest (6% on beginning capital balance) . . .	$ 2,400	$ 4,800	$ 7,200	(27,200)
Salary	16,000	10,000	26,000	(53,200)
Remainder	(26,600)	(26,600)	(53,200)	–0–
Distribution	$ (8,200)	$(11,800)	$(20,000)	

To entry to divide the net loss would be:

```
Anders, Capital . . . . . . . . . . . . . . . . . . . .   8,200
Budd, Capital  . . . . . . . . . . . . . . . . . . . .  11,800
     Income Summary  . . . . . . . . . . . . . . . . . .        20,000
  To divide net loss between the partners.
```

c.   The sharing of income may result in a credit to one partner's capital account and a debit in another partner's capital account. As a final example, assume that Anders and Budd earned $3,200 of net income for a year. The $3,200 would be shared as follows:

	Anders	Budd	Total	Income to be distributed
Net income				$ 3,200
Interest (6% on beginning capital balance) . . .	$ 2,400	$ 4,800	$ 7,200	(4,000)
Salary	16,000	10,000	26,000	(30,000)
Remainder	(15,000)	(15,000)	(30,000)	–0–
Distribution	$ 3,400	$ (200)	$ 3,200	

The entry to close the Income Summary account would be:

```
Income Summary . . . . . . . . . . . . . . . . . . .   3,200
Budd, Capital  . . . . . . . . . . . . . . . . . . .     200
     Anders, Capital . . . . . . . . . . . . . . . . .          3,400
  To divide net income between partners.
```

Partnership Agreement Governs.   This section has illustrated some factors that partners might consider when drawing up the income or sharing provisions in the partnership agreement. However, income may be shared in **any** manner the partners decide. Once the partners agree on how income is to be shared, the accountant's task is simply to apply the agreed-upon provisions as literally as possible.

■ FINANCIAL STATEMENTS OF A PARTNERSHIP

Since a partnership is very similar to a single proprietorship, the accounting and financial reporting for these forms of organization are basically the same.

$100,000 and $60,000, respectively. They share income and losses in a 3:2 ratio. The partnership desperately needs cash, so the partners are willing to give Kirby a one-fourth equity interest in the partnership for an investment of only $40,000 cash. Kirby agrees, invests $40,000, and receives an equity interest computed as follows:

Equities of old partners ($100,000 + $60,000) . . .	$160,000
Investment of new partner	40,000
Total equities of new partnership	$200,000
Kirby's one-fourth interest ($200,000 × ¼)	$ 50,000

The entry to record Kirby's investment in the partnership is:

Cash	40,000	
Bentz, Capital (⅗ of $10,000)	6,000	
Hahn, Capital (⅖ of $10,000)	4,000	
Kirby, Capital		50,000
To record Kirby's investment in partnership.		

Notice that the $10,000 bonus is contributed by the old partners in their income and loss sharing ratio of 3:2. After Kirby is admitted to the partnership, the partners should agree on new income sharing provisions.

There are alternative methods that could be used to record the admission of a new partner, but these will be left for an advanced text. Considered next are changes in partnership ownership brought about by the retirement or withdrawal of a partner.

Retirement of a Partner

A partnership agreement should contain provisions that describe the procedures to be followed when a partner retires. Specifically, these procedures should indicate how to compute the price to be paid by the partnership for the retiring partner's equity interest.

To compute this price, the first step usually is to audit the accounts to ensure their accuracy. Also, the fair market values of the assets must be determined. If asset values are revalued at fair market values, gains and losses from this revaluation should be reflected in the partners' capital accounts. One reason for revaluation is that after the withdrawal by a partner, a new entity is created, which should record its assets at fair values at the time of formation. Second, the withdrawing partner will be credited or charged for a share of previously unrecorded gains or losses. Such unrecorded gains or losses must be considered in computing the retiring partner's share of the partnership's net assets at the time of withdrawal. The retiring partner typically is paid an amount equal to the new balance in that partner's capital account.

In some cases, however, asset revaluations are not recorded, and the retiring partner is paid an amount that differs from that partner's capital account balance. Such revaluations may not be reflected for several reasons. First, the partnership may not wish to change recorded book values because it would take "too much effort." Second, the partners may not wish to pay auditors for an audit of the books and records. Third, the partners may not realize that the recorded book values differ substantially from fair market values, and they underestimate the effects such differences would have on partners' capital balances. Three cases illustrating the accounting for the retirement of a partner are presented next.

Case 1. Retiring Partner Receives Adjusted Book Value of Equity.

As-sume that Green, South, and Rock are partners sharing income and losses in a 3:1:1 ratio. Rock decides to retire when the partnership books show the following recorded values:

Assets			Equities	
Cash		$ 30,000	Green, capital	$ 50,000
Accounts receivable		10,000	South, capital	30,000
Merchandise inventory		40,000	Rock, capital	20,000
Plant and equipment	$50,000			
Less: Accumulated depreciation	30,000	20,000		
Total assets		$100,000	Total equities	$100,000

The partnership books are audited. Certain accounts receivable, recorded at $500, are found to be uncollectible and are written off. Because of changes in replacement costs, merchandise inventory is revalued at $45,500, and plant and equipment are revalued at $54,000. Accumulated depreciation is increased to $32,000. The journal entries to record this information are:

Green, Capital	300	
South, Capital	100	
Rock, Capital	100	
Accounts Receivable		500
To write off uncollectible accounts receivable.		
Merchandise Inventory	5,500	
Green, Capital		3,300
South, Capital		1,100
Rock, Capital		1,100
To revalue inventory.		
Plant and Equipment	4,000	
Accumulated Depreciation—Plant and Equipment		2,000
Green, Capital		1,200
South, Capital		400
Rock, Capital		400
To revalue plant and equipment.		

It is assumed that the gains and losses computed from asset revaluations eventually would have been realized and reflected in net income. Thus, gains and losses should be shared by the partners in their income and loss ratio. After the above entries have been posted, the partnership's assets and equities with restated amounts are:

Assets			Equities	
Cash		$ 30,000	Green, capital	$ 54,200
Accounts receivable		9,500	South, capital	31,400
Merchandise inventory		45,500	Rock, capital	21,400
Plant and equipment	$54,000			
Less: Accumulated depreciation	32,000	22,000		
Total assets		$107,000	Total equities	$107,000

With assets revalued and capital accounts adjusted, Rock has a $21,400 interest in partnership net assets. Assuming Rock is paid cash, the entry to record Rock's retirement is:

Rock, Capital 21,400
    Cash 21,400
    To record Rock's withdrawal from the partnership.

Instead of cash, Rock could have received any combination of assets (such as some inventory and a car owned by the partnership) totaling $21,400 to which the partners agreed. Or Rock could have accepted a note payable by the new partnership of Green and South. In any case, Green and South must now agree on a new income and loss sharing provision because a new partnership entity exists.

Case 2.   Retiring Partner Receives More than the Book Value of Equity.

Sometimes the partners may not revalue assets or adjust the accounts when a partner withdraws. In such cases, the partners may agree that the assets are undervalued and that the withdrawing partner should receive assets worth **more** than the book value of that partner's equity. At other times, the remaining partners may be so anxious for the partner to withdraw that they are willing to give up assets worth **more** than the book value of that partner's equity. In both cases, the retiring partner, in effect, withdraws assets equal to the book value of that partner's own equity plus part of the book value of the remaining partners' equities.

To illustrate, assume that North, East, and West are partners who share income and losses in a 3:2:1 ratio. East withdraws from the partnership at a time when it has the following assets and equities:

Assets		Equities	
Cash	$30,000	North, capital	$50,000
Merchandise inventory	40,000	East, capital	25,000
Equipment, net	20,000	West, capital	15,000
Total assets	$90,000	Total equities	$90,000

The partners agree that the assets are undervalued by $3,000, but they do not wish to adjust the accounts to current market values. If the accounts had been revalued, East's capital account would have been increased by $1,000, or two sixths of the $3,000 adjustment. East is therefore allowed to withdraw $26,000 cash from the partnership for his equity interest. The entry to record East's withdrawal is:

East, Capital 25,000
North, Capital 750
West, Capital 250
    Cash 26,000
    To record East's withdrawal from partnership.

East withdrew $1,000 more than the book value of his equity. Instead of revaluing the assets and adjusting the accounts (as shown in Case 1), the excess amount of $1,000 is charged to North's and West's capital accounts on the basis of their income and loss ratio of 3:1 (¾ × $1,000 = $750 to North, and ¼ × $1,000 = $250 to West).

Case 3.   Retiring Partner Receives Less than the Book Value of Equity.

Sometimes the partners may agree that the assets are overvalued but do not want to adjust the accounts when one partner retires. In such cases, the partners may also agree that the withdrawing partner should receive assets worth **less** than the book value of that partner's equity. At other times, a partner who is very anxious to withdraw from a partnership may be willing to accept assets worth **less** than the book value of that partner's equity. The undrawn equity is divided between the remaining partners in their income and loss ratio and credited to their capital accounts.

To illustrate, assume that Alda, Fonda, and Moore are partners who share income and losses in an 8:7:5 (40%, 35%, 25%) ratio. The partnership's assets and equities follow:

Assets		**Equities**	
Cash	$21,000	Alda, capital	$25,000
Merchandise inventory	24,000	Fonda, capital	22,000
Plant and equipment, net	20,000	Moore, capital	18,000
Total assets	$65,000	Total equities	$65,000

Moore is very anxious to withdraw from the partnership and is willing to accept $16,000 in settlement of her equity. Alda and Fonda agree to the settlement. The entry to record Moore's withdrawal is:

Moore, Capital	18,000	
Cash		16,000
Alda, Capital		1,067
Fonda, Capital		933

To record Moore's withdrawal from partnership.

Moore withdrew $2,000 less than the book value of her equity. The undrawn $2,000 is credited to the capital accounts of Alda and Fonda in their income and loss sharing ratio of 8:7; that is, 8/15 × $2,000 and 7/15 × $2,000.

The illustrations above involved technical terminations or dissolutions of partnerships. One partnership was terminated but was succeeded immediately by another partnership which carried on substantially the same business operations. In the next section, attention is given to circumstances in which business operations cease and the partnership is legally terminated.

◼ LIQUIDATION OF A PARTNERSHIP

The **liquidation** of a partnership means that business operations have ended, assets have been sold for cash, cash has been paid to creditors and partners, and the partnership has been legally terminated.

Partnerships may be liquidated for a number of reasons. Some common reasons for liquidation include:

1.   The objective sought in forming the partnership has been achieved.
2.   The time period for which the partnership was formed has expired.
3.   Newly enacted legislation has made the partnership's activities illegal.
4.   The partnership or one of its partners is bankrupt.

Liquidation may take place rapidly or over an extended period. If liquidation is rapid, a single cash distribution may be made to the partners after all assets are sold and the liabilities paid. If liquidation is prolonged, more than one cash distribution may be made to the partners. Only those liquidations that involve a single payment to partners are discussed below.

Partnership Liquidation Illustrated

In the following illustrations it is assumed that all assets are sold, all liabilities paid, and that a single distribution is made to partners to liquidate their capital accounts.

The partnership of Ring, Scott, and Terry is liquidated on August 1, 1987. The income and loss ratio is Ring, 40%; Scott, 35%; and Terry, 25%. A condensed trial balance prepared just before liquidation is shown in Illustration 14.5. The three cases that follow are based on the Ring, Scott, and Terry partnership.

Illustration 14.5

Condensed Trial Balance

RING, SCOTT, AND TERRY
Trial Balance
August 1, 1987

	Debits	Credits
Cash	$ 10,000	
Other Assets	90,000	
Liabilities		$ 10,000
Ring, Capital		30,000
Scott, Capital		30,000
Terry, Capital		30,000
	$100,000	$100,000

Case 1.   Assets Sold at a Gain.   The noncash assets are sold for $95,000, and the $5,000 gain on the sale is distributed to the partners in their income and loss ratio. The liabilities are paid in full. The remaining cash is distributed to the partners in accordance with the balances of their capital accounts, **not** in the income and loss ratio.

The journal entries to record the foregoing facts and the liquidation of the partnership on August 1, 1987, follow:

Cash	95,000	
Other Assets		90,000
Gain on Sale of Assets		5,000
To record the sale of the assets.		

Gain on Sale of Assets	5,000	
Ring, Capital ($5,000 × 0.40)		2,000
Scott, Capital ($5,000 × 0.35)		1,750
Terry, Capital ($5,000 × 0.25)		1,250
To distribute the gain on the sale of the assets.		

Liabilities	10,000	
Cash		10,000
To record the settlement of partnership liabilities.		

After the above entries are posted, the partners' capital accounts show:

Ring, Capital		Scott, Capital		Terry, Capital	
Beg. bal.	30,000	Beg. bal.	30,000	Beg. bal.	30,000
Gain from		Gain from		Gain from	
sale of		sale of		sale of	
assets	2,000	assets	1,750	assets	1,250
End. bal.	32,000	End. bal.	31,750	End. bal.	31,250

The Cash account now shows a balance of $95,000 ($10,000 + $95,000 − $10,000). The entry to record the cash distributed to partners is:

Ring, Capital	32,000	
Scott, Capital	31,750	
Terry, Capital	31,250	
Cash		95,000

To distribute remaining cash to partners based on balances of their capital accounts.

Case 2.   Assets Sold at a Loss.   The noncash assets of Ring, Scott, and Terry are sold for $70,000, and the $20,000 loss on the sale is distributed to the partners in the income and loss ratio. The liabilities are paid in full. The remaining cash is distributed to the partners in accordance with the balances of their capital accounts.

The journal entries are:

Cash	70,000	
Loss on Sale of Assets	20,000	
Other Assets		90,000

To record the sale of the assets.

Ring, Capital (20,000 × 0.40)	8,000	
Scott, Capital (20,000 × 0.35)	7,000	
Terry, Capital (20,000 × 0.25)	5,000	
Loss on Sale of Assets		20,000

To distribute the loss on the sale of the assets.

Liabilities	10,000	
Cash		10,000

To record the settlement of partnership liabilities.

After the above entries have been posted, the accounts show Cash, $70,000; Ring, Capital, $22,000; Scott, Capital, $23,000; and Terry, Capital, $25,000. The entry to record the cash distributed to partners is:

Ring, Capital	22,000	
Scott, Capital	23,000	
Terry, Capital	25,000	
Cash		70,000

To distribute cash to partners.

Case 3.   Assets Sold at a Loss When One Partner's Share of the Loss Is Greater than the Balance of that Partner's Capital Account.   In Case 2, the loss charged to the capital account of each partner is smaller than that partner's capital account balance. But it is possible that a partner's portion of the loss may be greater than that partner's capital account balance. When a loss is charged to a partner and a debit balance is created in that partner's capital account, the debit balance represents an amount owed by that partner to the other partners. The cash available for distribution will be insufficient to pay the other partners in full until the partner with the debit balance pays in the amount owed. If the partner with the debit balance is unable to pay, the remaining partners must bear this loss in the income and loss ratio existing between them.

To illustrate, assume that the noncash assets of Ring, Scott, and Terry are sold for only $10,200. Entries to record the foregoing facts and the liquidation follow:

Cash	10,200	
Loss on Sale of Assets	79,800	
Other Assets		90,000
To record the sale of the assets.		
Ring, Capital (79,800 × 0.40)	31,920	
Scott, Capital (79,800 × 0.35)	27,930	
Terry, Capital (79,800 × 0.25)	19,950	
Loss on Sale of Assets		79,800
To distribute the loss on the sale of the assets.		
Liabilities	10,000	
Cash		10,000
To record the settlement of partnership liabilities.		

At this stage of the liquidation, the partner's capital accounts have the following balances:

Ring, Capital			Scott, Capital			Terry, Capital		
	Beg. bal.	30,000		Beg. bal.	30,000		Beg. bal.	30,000
Loss from sale of assets 31,920			Loss from sale of assets 27,930			Loss from sale of assets 19,950		
End. bal. 1,920				End. bal.	2,070		End. bal.	10,050

Only $10,200 ($10,000 + $10,200 − $10,000) of cash is available for distribution to Scott and Terry, while the combined balance of their capital accounts is $12,120. To pay Scott and Terry the amounts owed, the partnership needs $1,920 more cash, which is the amount owed the partnership by Ring and which Ring is unable to pay. The $1,920 is thus a loss that must be shared by Scott and Terry in their income and loss sharing ratio of 35:25. Thus, Scott's share of the loss is $1,120 (35/60 × $1,920), and Terry's share is $800 (25/60 × $1,920).

The debit balance in Ring's capital account is closed and the loss absorbed by Scott and Terry as shown in the following entry:

Scott, Capital	1,120	
Terry, Capital	800	
Ring, Capital		1,920
To charge Scott and Terry with Ring's capital deficiency.		

The only accounts left on the books now are the Cash account and Scott's and Terry's capital accounts. The remaining cash is distributed to Scott and Terry in the amounts now shown in their capital accounts:

Scott, Capital	950	
Terry, Capital	9,250	
Cash		10,200
To record final cash distribution to partners.		

With this entry, all accounts of the partnership now have a zero balance, and the partnership is ended. As individuals, Scott and Terry have the legal right to collect the $1,920 Ring owes them. But the partnership is now liquidated; no further entries will be made on its books.

Suppose that, in the example above, Ring was able to pay the $1,920 owed the partnership prior to closing the account. The following entries would be needed:

Cash	1,920	
Ring, Capital		1,920
To record payment of capital deficiency by Ring.		
Scott, Capital	2,070	
Terry, Capital	10,050	
Cash		12,120
To distribute cash to partners in liquidation.		

Notice that Ring does not receive any cash in the final settlement. He had to pay cash to the partnership to bring his capital account to a zero balance.

The analysis of the partnership liquidation, assuming Ring pays the amount owed to the partnership, may be aided by the preparation of a liquidation work sheet as shown in Illustration 14.6.

The liquidation work sheet brings together in one place all the necessary calculations and graphically illustrates the amounts involved in a partnership liquidation. This work sheet can be helpful for the accountant, the partners, and other interested parties.

Illustration 14.6

Liquidation Work Sheet

	Ring	Scott	Terry	Total
Income and loss ratio	40%	35%	25%	100%
Original capital account balance	$30,000	$30,000	$30,000	$90,000
Apportionment of loss on sale of assets	(31,920)	(27,930)	(19,950)	(79,800)
Capital balances after loss apportionment	$ (1,920)	$ 2,070	$10,050	$10,200
Ring's cash contribution	1,920			1,920
Ending capital account balances	$ –0–	$ 2,070	$10,050	$12,120
Liquidating distribution		(2,070)	(10,050)	(12,120)
Balance	$ –0–	$ –0–	$ –0–	$ –0–

Note: ( ) = debit.

■ *SUMMARY*

A partnership is defined in the Uniform Partnership Act as "an association of two or more persons to carry on as co-owners a business for profit." The formation, operation, and liquidation of a partnership are based on a contract, or partnership agreement, known as the articles of copartnership. Among the features that distinguish a partnership from a corporation are voluntary association of the partners, mutual agency of the partners, limited life of the partnership, and unlimited liability of partners for partnership debts.

The advantages of a partnership include: permits reasonable accumulations of capital and talent, is easier and less expensive than a corporation to organize, and is not required to observe as many laws and regulations nor pay a separate income tax as does a corporation. The disadvantages of a partnership include: mutual agency and unlimited liability of partners exist, ownership interests are difficult to transfer from one person to another, and operations may become unwieldy as the number of partners increases.

Most of the unique features of accounting for a partnership involve accounting for the ownership interests of the partners. A capital account and a drawing account are maintained for each partner. The capital account records the partner's initial and subsequent investments and the partner's share of partnership income or loss. Income and loss are distributed to partners according to the terms of the partnership agreement; if the partnership agreement is silent on the distribution of income and losses, then income and losses are shared equally among the partners. The drawing account records the partner's withdrawals of cash and merchandise for personal use. Since drawings are not expenses of the partnership, the drawing accounts are closed directly to the respective partners' capital accounts, not to the Income Summary account, at the end of each period.

The financial statements of a partnership differ only slightly from those of a proprietorship. The income statement contains a section showing the distribution of income or loss to the partners. The balance sheet shows the ending balance in each partner's capital account. The statement of partners' capital is presented to detail the changes in each partner's capital account.

When a new partner is admitted or an existing partner withdraws or retires, the partnership is legally terminated. However, in most cases the old partnership is immediately succeeded by a new partnership consisting of the new group of partners. A new partner may be admitted either by purchasing an interest from one or more existing partners or by investing assets in the partnership. If the new partner purchases a partnership interest from an existing partner, differences between the purchase price and the book value of the purchased interest are not reflected on the books of the partnership; only the portion of the book value of the equity transferred is shown in the affected partners' capital accounts. However, if a new partner invests assets and the value of the assets invested differs from the new partner's equity interest in the partnership, the difference is accounted for as a bonus, either to the old partners or to the new partner. If it is a bonus to the old partners it is shared among them in their income and loss sharing ratio.

When a partner retires, the accounts may be audited, and partnership assets may be adjusted to their current market values. If the assets are revalued, the gains and losses on revaluation are shared by the partners in their income and loss ratio, thereby adjusting the balances in the partners' capital accounts. A difference between the amount paid to the retiring partner and the book value of that partner's equity interest is accounted for as a bonus, either to the remaining partners or to the retiring partner. If the difference is a bonus to the remaining partners, it is shared among them in their income and loss sharing ratio.

When a partnership is liquidated, its assets are sold and the proceeds are first used to pay partnership creditors. Gains or losses on the sale of the assets are shared among the partners according to their income and loss sharing ratio. Any partner who has a capital account debit balance is required to pay assets into the partnership to cover the deficiency. If the partner is unable to repay that debt, the loss is shared among the remaining partners, and the unpaid debit balance becomes a personal debt of that partner to the other partners. Any remaining assets are then distributed to any partners having credit balances in their capital accounts.

In Chapter 15, you begin the study of corporations. Corporations are unique in that the owners are legally separate from the company. The corporate form of business makes it possible for individuals with small amounts of capital to become owners in large companies.

NEW TERMS INTRODUCED IN CHAPTER 14

Agent

One who has the authority to act for another (the partnership) or in the place of another. See Mutual agency (524).

Articles of copartnership

See Partnership agreement.

Income and loss ratio

The agreed-upon way that a partnership's income or losses are shared. Often called the **profit and loss ratio** or the **earnings and loss ratio** (530).

Interest (on capital invested)

A means often used in the sharing of income to give weight to the relative amounts of capital invested by the partners. The interest is sometimes based on the beginning-of-year balances in the capital accounts and sometimes on the average balances in the capital accounts. The interest is **not** an expense to be deducted in arriving at net income (531).

Liquidation (of a partnership)

Means that business operations have ended, assets have been sold for cash, cash has been paid to creditors and partners, and the partnership has been legally terminated (542).

Mutual agency

The power possessed by a partner to bind a partnership to any contract within the apparent scope of the partnership's business (524).

Partnership

"An association of two or more persons to carry on, as co-owners, a business for profit" (523).

Partnership agreement

Also known as articles of copartnership (when in written form); the conditions or provisions accepted by all of the partners to serve as the basis for the formation, operation, and liquidation of the partnership (524).

Salary (granted to partners)

A means often used in the sharing of income to reward certain partners for spending more time than other partners in running the affairs of the business. This kind of "salary" is **not** an expense of the partnership in determining net income (531).

Statement of partners' capital

A financial statement that summarizes the transactions affecting the capital balance of each partner and in total for all partners (535).

Termination (dissolution)

The legal dissolution of a partnership brought on by a change in partners (525).

Uniform Partnership Act

A written law adopted in many states that provides the general framework of law relating to the formation, operation, and termination of a partnership (524).

Unlimited liability

A characteristic of partnerships under which owners are liable for more than merely the amounts invested in the business, since their personal assets may also be taken to satisfy the claims of business creditors (525).

DEMONSTRATION PROBLEM

The Short and Long partnership had the following income and loss sharing agreement:

1. Short receives an annual salary of $12,000.
2. Short and Long each receive interest of 10% on their capital balances at the beginning of the year.
3. The remainder is divided by Short and Long in a 2:1 ratio.

On January 1, 1987, the partners' capital account balances were Short, $30,000, and Long, $40,000. On December 31, 1987, the partners' drawing account balances were Short, $10,000, and Long, $8,000. Net income for the year ended December 31, 1987, was $20,000.

Required:
a. Prepare a schedule showing the distribution of net income to the partners.
b. Prepare journal entries to close the Income Summary account and the drawing accounts.
c. Assume that on January 1, 1988, Short and Long admit Neil to a 25% interest in capital for an investment of $32,000 cash. Prepare the entry to admit Neil using the bonus method.

Solution to demonstration problem

a.

	Short	Long	Total	Amount to be distributed
Net income				$20,000
Salaries	$12,000	$ –0–	$12,000	8,000
Interest on beginning capital balances:				
Short (10% of $30,000)	3,000			
Long (10% of $40,000)		4,000	7,000	1,000
Remainder (2:1)	667	333	1,000	–0–
Distribution	$15,667	$4,333	$20,000	

b.

```
1987
Dec. 31  Income Summary . . . . . . . . . . . . . . . . .  20,000
             Short, Capital . . . . . . . . . . . . . .           15,667
             Long, Capital . . . . . . . . . . . . . .             4,333
         To distribute balance in Income Summary.

     31  Short, Capital . . . . . . . . . . . . . . . .  10,000
         Long, Capital . . . . . . . . . . . . . . . .    8,000
             Short, Drawing . . . . . . . . . . . . .            10,000
             Long, Drawing . . . . . . . . . . . . .              8,000
         To close drawing accounts.
```

c.

Cash		32,000
Neil, Capital	26,000	
Short, Capital	4,000	
Long, Capital	2,000	

To record admission of Neil to the partnership.

Computations are:

Capital on January 1, 1987 ($30,000 + $40,000) . .	$ 70,000
Net income for 1987	20,000
Drawings in 1987	(18,000)
Total capital, January 1, 1988	$ 72,000
Capital contributed by Neil	32,000
Total capital after admission of Neil	$104,000
Neil's share ($104,000 × 25%)	$ 26,000
Bohus to the old partners:	
$32,000 − $26,000 = ...	$ 6,000
Short: $6,000 × ⅔ = ...	$ 4,000
Long: $6,000 × ½ = ...	2,000

QUESTIONS

1. Jim Black currently is operating a small machine shop. He is considering forming a partnership with an employee, Fred Brown, whom he considers an excellent worker and supervisor and with whom he gets along well. Prepare a brief list of the advantages and disadvantages to Black of the potential partnership.

2. Many matters are covered in the typical partnership agreement. Some of them are of little significance to the accountant, while others are quite crucial. What are some of the crucial provisions as far as the accountant is concerned?

3. Jones and Smith are partners in a local grocery store. Both take home sufficient merchandise to feed their families. Would you suggest that the merchandise taken home be recorded at selling price or cost? Why?

4. Give an example of a set of circumstances in which you might be willing to enter into a partnership with another person, do all of the work needed to run the business, provide all of the capital, and yet be willing to allow the other person a substantial share of the net income.

5. Why should a partnership agreement be quite specific regarding the treatment of withdrawals by partners insofar as the sharing of income and losses is concerned?

6. What are three reasons for the formation of partnerships?

7. What is a statement of partners' capital?

8. Describe two different ways in which a new partner can be admitted to a partnership.

9. Why might a newly admitted partner's capital account balance differ from the amount actually invested?

10. Why might a withdrawing partner receive assets worth more or less than the book value of his or her equity?

11. What are three acts or conditions that will lead to the liquidation of a partnership?

12. What procedures are followed in liquidating a partnership?

EXERCISES

E-1

***Compute partners'
shares of income***

Bob, Doug, and Sue are partners. In 1987, net income of their partnership was $360,000. How much will be credited to each partner in the income distribution if:

a.   Nothing is stated in the partnership agreement concerning the division of income?
b.   The income and loss sharing ratio is 50:30:20, respectively?

a. The allowed monthly drawings were salaries and are used in determining the distribution of income.
b. The allowed monthly drawings were normal drawings (not salaries) and are not to be used in determining the distribution of income.

P14–5–A

Prepare schedule showing division of income for several years

Burt and Kent, as partners, have agreed to the following distribution of net income:

1. Salaries of $24,000 to Burt and $18,000 to Kent.
2. A bonus to Burt of 25% of net income in excess of salaries.
3. The remainder divided equally.

Net income for 1986 and 1987 was $90,000 and $30,000, respectively, and in 1988 there was a net loss of $15,000.

Required: Prepare schedules showing the distribution of the income and losses to the partners for each of the years 1986, 1987, and 1988.

P14–6–A

Prepare adjusting and closing entries, income statement, statement of partners' capital, and balance sheet

The following trial balance was taken for the Black and Gold partnership on December 31, 1987:

BLACK AND GOLD
Trial Balance
December 31, 1987

	Debits	Credits
Cash	$ 30,800	
Accounts Receivable	45,000	
Allowance for Doubtful Accounts		$ 750
Inventory	27,750	
Equipment	52,500	
Accumulated Depreciation—Equipment		12,750
Prepaid Insurance	682	
Accounts Payable		38,250
Black, Capital		27,750
Gold, Capital		54,750
Black, Drawing	700	
Gold, Drawing	9,000	
Sales		412,500
Purchases	330,000	
Selling Expenses	30,000	
Administrative Expenses	24,750	
Other Revenue		4,432
	$551,182	$551,182

The articles of copartnership for Black and Gold provide for the distribution of income and losses in the following manner:

1. Each partner is allowed 6% interest per year on his capital investment as of the beginning of the year.
2. Black is allowed a salary of $22,500 and Gold a salary of $27,000 per year as a distribution of income.
3. The remaining income and losses are to be divided equally.

Your analysis of the books and records discloses the following data that require consideration: the ending inventory is $23,250; 1% of sales is to be added to the allowance for doubtful accounts; and depreciation on the equipment should be recorded at 10% of cost. Black's capital account includes a credit for $3,000 invested on July 15 of the current year. Prepaid insurance at December 31, 1987, should be $60.

Required: You are to prepare the following for the partnership:

a. Adjusting and closing journal entries.
b. An income statement for the year.
c. A statement of partners' capital for the year.
d. A balance sheet for December 31, 1987.

P14–7–A

Record admission of new partner

Jim and Ray are partners who share income and losses in a 3:2 ratio. They decided to admit Kelly as a new partner at a time when their capital account balances were $480,000 for Jim and $240,000 for Ray.

Required: Prepare journal entries to record Kelly's admission to the partnership in each of the following unrelated situations:

a. Kelly acquired one half of Jim's interest for $250,000 cash paid to Jim personally.
b. Kelly acquired one fifth of Jim's equity for $100,000 cash and one fourth of Ray's equity for $62,000 cash. Both amounts were paid to the partners personally.
c. Kelly invested $180,000 for a 20% interest in capital.
d. Kelly invested $120,000 and was granted a 15% interest in capital because the old partnership was badly in need of cash to pay maturing debts.
e. Kelly invested $420,000 for a one-third interest in capital; her admission was recorded using the bonus method.

P14–8–A

Record admission of new partner

C and L are partners who have capital account balances of $60,000 and $30,000, respectively, and who share income and losses in a 3:2 ratio. They negotiated the admission of T to their partnership.

Required: Prepare journal entries to record T's admission to the partnership under each of the following unrelated situations:

a. T invested $54,000 cash and received a one-third interest in the capital of the new firm. The bonus method is used to record T's admission.
b. T invested $40,500 for a one-third interest in capital. T was granted a bonus upon joining the firm.
c. T invested sufficient cash to secure exactly a 40% interest in the new firm.

P14–9–A

Record withdrawal of partner

On July 31, 1987, Joe Howe, a member of the company of Howe and Orr, decided to retire. The partners have shared income and losses equally. On this date, their capital balances were Joe Howe, $160,000; Beth Howe, $200,000; and Mike Orr, $120,000.

Required: Prepare entries to record the withdrawal of Joe Howe under each of the following unrelated assumptions. All payments are made in cash, and the assets are not to be revalued.

a. Joe Howe was paid $160,000.
b. Joe Howe was paid $168,000.
c. Joe Howe was paid $148,000.

P14–10–A

Record withdrawal of partner

T, U, and V are partners who share income and losses in a 4:2:2 ratio. On December 31, 1987, T decided to retire. At that time, the partners' capital account balances were:

T, capital $60,000
U, capital 52,500
V, capital 90,000

Required: Prepare entries to record the retirement of T in each of the following unrelated situations:

a. The partners agreed that inventory was undervalued by $27,000 and that the books should be adjusted to reflect market values. After the books were adjusted, T received cash equal to the balance in his capital account.
b. The partners agreed that inventory was undervalued on the books by $27,000, but the books should *not* be adjusted to reflect market values. T was paid cash equal to the balance that would have been shown in his capital account if the increase to market value had been recorded.
c. The partners agreed that the amount shown for inventory was $18,000 more than its current market value, but the inventory was *not* to be adjusted to reflect market values. T was paid cash equal to the balance that would have been in his capital account if the books had been adjusted.

P14-11-A

Record partnership liquidation

The ABC partnership was liquidated on January 2, 1987. Before any of the company's $780,000 of assets (all noncash) were sold, the liabilities and capital account credit balances were:

Accounts Payable	$400,000
A, Capital	40,000
B, Capital	160,000
C, Capital	180,000

The assets were sold for $540,000. Income and losses are shared equally.

Required: Prepare the journal entries to record the sale of the assets (credit an Assets account) and the distribution of the cash to creditors and partners. Assume that none of the partners has other assets to cover a debit balance in his capital account.

P14-12-A

Record partnership liquidation

The partners of the MNO Company decided to liquidate because of their creditors' demands for payment of amounts owed. The March 31, 1987, balance sheet data for the partnership follows:

Cash	$ 45,000	Accounts payable	$247,500
Accounts receivable	97,500	Moore, capital	112,500
Merchandise inventory	135,000	Neal, capital	135,000
Plant and equipment	397,500	Oscar, capital	180,000
	$675,000		$675,000

The noncash assets were sold on April 1, 1987, for $270,000. The partners share income and losses in a 50:25:25 ratio, respectively.

Required: Prepare journal entries to record the sale of the assets and the distribution of cash to creditors and partners. Assume that partners developing debit balances in their capital accounts are not able to pay them from other assets.

PROBLEMS, SERIES B

P14-1-B

Record formation of partnership from two single proprietorships

Karen Fisher and Arthur Swain, who have been in business as single proprietors, decided to combine all of their business assets and liabilities in a new partnership in which they will share income and losses equally. Balance sheets of the two individuals on the date of the formation of the partnership are shown below:

KAREN FISHER
Balance Sheet
September 4, 1987

Assets

Cash	$ 8,000
Accounts receivable (net)	30,000
Inventory	18,000
Equipment (net)	40,000
Total assets	$96,000

Liabilities and Owner's Equity

Accounts payable	$46,000
Karen Fisher, capital	50,000
Total liabilities and owner's equity . .	$96,000

```
                    ARTHUR SWAIN
                     Balance Sheet
                   September 4, 1987
                        Assets
    Cash .  .  .  .  .  .  .  .  .  .  .  .   $ 28,000
    Accounts receivable (net)   .  .  .  .     34,000
    Inventory  .  .  .  .  .  .  .  .  .  .     40,000
    Total assets  .  .  .  .  .  .  .  .     $102,000

              Liabilities and Owner's Equity
    Accounts payable  .  .  .  .  .  .  .    $ 44,000
    Arthur Swain, capital  .  .  .  .  .  .     58,000
    Total liabilities and owner's equity .  .  $102,000
```

An appraisal of the assets showed market values for the assets of Fisher as follows: accounts receivable, $28,000; inventory, $24,000; and equipment, $30,000. A similar appraisal placed the following market values upon Swain's assets: accounts receivable, $34,000; and inventory, $26,000.

Required: Prepare journal entries to record the capital contributions of Fisher and Swain to their newly formed partnership.

P14-2-B

Determine and journalize division of income under alternative provisions; close drawing accounts

An analysis of the capital accounts for 1987 of Clark and Dixon, partners, showed:

		Clark	
Jan. 1	Balance	$135,000
June 1	Capital withdrawal . . .	22,500
Nov. 1	Additional investment . .	33,750
		Dixon	
Jan. 1	Balance	$ 22,500
July 1	Additional investment . .	45,000

The balance in the Income Summary account showed net income of $67,500 for 1987.

Required: Prepare a schedule showing the distribution of the net income under each of the following unrelated assumptions with regard to income distribution. Also prepare the entries to distribute the income and to close the drawing accounts. (Note: In each instance assume drawings were equal to salaries allowed for each partner.)

a. Clark and Dixon are allowed annual salaries of $18,000 and $22,500, respectively; 8% interest is allowed on average capital balances; and the balance of the income is shared equally.

b. Equal annual salaries of $27,000 are allowed to each partner; interest of 10% is allowed on capital balances at the beginning of the year; and the balance is shared in a 3:2 ratio between Clark and Dixon.

P14-3-B

Determine division of income; prepare entries to distribute income and close drawing accounts; prepare schedule of changes in partners' capital accounts

The S and C partnership has the following agreement for the sharing of income and losses: (1) S is to be allowed interest of 10% on her capital account balance as of the beginning of the year; (2) C is to be allowed a salary of $3,600 per month; and (3) any remaining balance of income or loss is to be shared equally. The net income for 1987 was $108,000.

Required: a. Assuming that S's and C's capital account balances on January 1, 1987, were $360,000 and $90,000, respectively, prepare a schedule showing the distribution of net income and the entry required to record it.

b. Prepare the entry needed to close the drawing accounts of the partners, which had the following balances (before closing) on December 31, 1987; S, zero; and C, $43,200.

c. Present a schedule showing the changes occurring in 1987 in the capital account of each partner.

P14–4–B

Prepare schedules showing division of income under alternative provisions

The capital account balances (unchanged during the year) on December 31, 1987, for T and G, partners, are $360,000 for T and $180,000 for G. T withdrew $36,000, and G withdrew $90,000 during the year, with all withdrawals charged to the respective drawing accounts. The net loss for the year was $36,000.

Required: Prepare schedules showing the distribution of income to each partner for the year 1987 under each of the following provisions:

a. Salaries are allowed of $27,000 to T and $67,500 to G; remaining income is divided according to capital account balances at the beginning of the year.

b. Salaries are allowed of $18,000 to T and $30,000 to G; interest of 10% is allowed on capital account balances at the beginning of the year; no further provisions relating to income sharing are included in the partnership agreement.

P14–5–B

Prepare schedules showing division of income at various amounts of income and loss

David and Scott are partners in a retail hardware store. Their partnership agreement calls for salaries to David and Scott of $24,000 and $48,000, respectively, and interest of 10% on average capital for the year. Any remaining balance is to be shared equally.

During 1987, each partner drew his allowed salary; there were no withdrawals in excess of allowed salaries. The capital accounts of the two partners remained unchanged during the year at $120,000 for David and $180,000 for Scott.

Required: Present schedules showing the distribution of net income assuming that the income statement for 1987 showed:

a. $144,000 of net income.

b. $60,000 of net income.

c. A net loss of $24,000.

P14–6–B

Prepare adjusting and closing entries, income statement, statement of partners' capital, and balance sheet

Bass and Carr are partners operating a retail store having a fiscal year ending on June 30. Their partnership agreement calls for annual salaries of $18,000 to Bass and $24,000 to Carr, interest of 8% on average capital account balances throughout the year, and the equal sharing of the balance of the income. Their June 30, 1987, trial balance follows:

BASS AND CARR
Trial Balance
June 30, 1987

	Debits	Credits
Cash	$ 60,600	
Accounts Receivable	96,000	
Inventory, July 1, 1986	43,200	
Accounts Payable		$ 61,200
Notes Payable		30,000
Bass, Capital		42,000
Carr, Capital		30,000
Bass, Drawing	12,000	
Carr, Drawing	15,000	
Sales		642,000
Purchases	408,000	
Purchase Returns		6,000
Employee Salaries and Wages	18,000	
Rent Expense	78,000	
Delivery Expense	25,200	
Store Expense	55,200	
	$811,200	$811,200

The $30,000 note payable is a 120-day note dated April 1, 1987, and calls for interest of 10% per year. The inventory at June 30, 1987, is $49,800. The only change in the capital accounts during the year was an additional $8,000 investment by Bass on January 1.

Required: You are to prepare the following for the partnership:

a. The necessary adjusting and closing entries.
b. An income statement for the year ended June 30, 1987.
c. A statement of partners' capital for the year ended June 30, 1987.
d. A balance sheet for June 30, 1987.

P14–7–B

Record admission of new partner

Ed, Bruce, and Jay are partners who share income and losses in a 3:2:1 ratio. They decided to admit Lee to the partnership at a time when their capital account balances were:

Ed, capital $120,000
Bruce, capital 60,000
Jay, capital 60,000

Required: Prepare journal entries to record Lee's admission to the partnership under each of the following unrelated conditions:

a. Lee acquired 40% of Bruce's interest for $36,000.
b. Lee acquired all of Jay's interest for $54,000 cash.
c. Lee invested $200,000 in the partnership for a one-half interest in capital.
d. Lee was admitted to a one-fifth interest in capital for an investment of $40,000 because the old partnership was badly in need of cash to pay a maturing debt.

P14–8–B

Record admission of new partner

P and Q are partners with capital account balances of $99,000 and $54,000, respectively. Income and losses are shared in a 3:2 ratio.

Required: Prepare the journal entries to record the admission of R to the partnership in each of the following independent situations:

a. R paid Q $30,000 for one half of Q's interest.
b. R invested sufficient cash in the firm to acquire a one-fourth interest in capital of the new partnership.
c. R invested $57,000 for a one-fifth interest in capital (use the bonus method).
d. R invested $39,000 for a one-fourth interest (use the bonus method).

P14–9–B

Record withdrawal of partner

On December 31, James Burns, a member of the company of Burns and Parks, decided to retire. The partners have shared income and losses equally. On this date their capital account credit balances were:

James Burns $180,000
Helen Burns 120,000
Bob Parks 120,000

Required: Prepare entries to record the withdrawal of James Burns under each of the following assumptions. All payments are to be in cash, and the assets are not to be revalued.

a. James Burns was paid $180,000.
b. James Burns was paid $192,000.
c. James Burns was paid $160,000.

P14–10–B

Record withdrawal of partner

Dan, Frank, and Gene are partners in the DFG Company. Ledger account balances on January 1, 1987, follow:

Cash	$10,500	
Accounts Receivable	18,000	
Allowance for Doubtful Accounts		$ 1,500
Merchandise Inventory	37,500	
Equipment	9,000	
Accumulated Depreciation—Equipment . .		3,000
Accounts Payable		12,000
Dan, Capital		30,000
Frank, Capital		22,500
Gene, Capital		6,000
	$75,000	$75,000

The partners share income and losses in a 3:2:1 ratio.

Required: Assume that Gene retires from the partnership and receives a check for $7,500. Prepare entries to record Gene's retirement assuming:

a.   The assets were not revalued.
b.   Inventory was revalued at $46,500, and equipment was revalued at $9,000 with accumulated depreciation of $4,500.

P14–11–B

Record partnership liquidation

Use the data in Problem 14–10–B above, but ignore the revaluation of assets in part (b). Assume that the partners decided to liquidate. All of the noncash assets were sold for $22,500. After the assets were sold, the liabilities were paid, the remaining cash was distributed to the partners, and the books were closed.

Required: Prepare journal entries to record liquidation of the partnership. Assume that none of the partners has other assets to cover possible debit balances in his capital account.

P14–12–B

Record partnership liquidation

Given below is the balance sheet of the FGH Partnership on April 30, 1987—the date the partners decided to liquidate their partnership.

FGH PARTNERSHIP
Balance sheet
April 30, 1987

Assets

Cash	$ 10,000
Accounts receivable	20,000
Merchandise inventory	50,000
Plant and equipment	100,000
Total assets	$180,000

Liabilities and Owners' Equity

Accounts payable	$ 95,000
F, capital	35,000
G, capital	25,000
H, capital	25,000
Total liabilities and owner's equity . .	$180,000

On May 1, the noncash assets were sold for $89,000. F, G, and H share income and losses in a 5:3:2 ratio.

Required: Prepare all necessary journal entries to record the sale of the assets and the distribution of cash to creditors and partners. Assume that any partners who had debit balances in their capital accounts after loss distributions immediately paid cash to the partnership equal to the debit balances.

BUSINESS DECISION PROBLEM 14-1

Analyze effects of proposed change in income and loss sharing provisions

Lewis Hull and Troy Davis have owned and operated a men's clothing store as a partnership. Their capital account balances as of December 31, 1987, were: Hull, $320,000; and Davis, $108,000. Income and losses are shared equally after allowing salaries of $32,000 to Hull and $28,000 to Davis. Applying these provisions to the net income of $120,000 in 1987 resulted in a distribution of $62,000 to Hull and $58,000 to Davis. Hull considers this sharing to be quite unfair. He notes that he devotes full time to the store, while Davis has other interests that occupy about half of his time. Hull also notes that his equity was substantially more than Davis' in the partnership because he has not drawn all of his income. He proposes that the partnership agreement be changed to call for salaries of $40,000 and $20,000 to himself and to Davis, that interest of 10% per year be allowed on beginning of the year capital account balances, and that any remaining income be shared equally.

Davis agrees that some modification seems necessary because of changed circumstances. But before agreeing to Hull's proposed changes, he wants to know the effects of such changes.

Required: Assume that the capital account balances as of January 1, 1987, were Hull, $280,000, and Davis, $100,000.

a. Prepare a schedule showing how the income for 1987 would have been shared if Hull's suggested provisions had been in effect for the year.
b. Prepare a schedule showing how much each partner's share of the 1987 income would have increased or decreased if Hull's proposed revisions of the partnership agreement had been in effect in 1987.
c. Is Davis more or less likely to accept Hull's proposals if future net income is substantially greater or less than $120,000 per year?

BUSINESS DECISION PROBLEM 14-2

Determine proper amount for partner to receive in liquidation settlement

Harry Fields and Fred Sims are partners sharing income and losses equally in a business that has been very successful for all 25 years of its existence. The partners have been studying what they consider a very tempting offer to buy their business, thus allowing the partners to retire. Shortly after receiving this offer, Fields was hospitalized as a result of an auto accident. The partners agreed that they should sell, and Sims was authorized to negotiate the sale of the business.

Some time later, Sims appeared at the hospital and gave Fields a check for $120,000 as his share of the cash available to the partners upon liquidation of the partnership. He also gave Fields a balance sheet for the partnership as of the day before the date of the sale. Summarized, this balance sheet showed:

Cash	$ 15,000
Other assets	195,000
Total	$210,000
Liabilities	$ 45,000
Fields, capital	90,000
Sims, capital	75,000
Total	$210,000

Sims explained that he had sold all of the other assets and the partnership name for $270,000—a price he considered excellent. Fields agreed the price was excellent, but was unsure about whether the check Sims gave him was in the correct amount.

Required: a. Show the computations Sims made to arrive at an $120,000 check for Fields.
b. Is $120,000 the correct amount? If not, compute the correct amount.

BUSINESS SITUATION FOR DISCUSSION 14–1

Making a Partnership Work*

Critical decisions must be reached before you go into business together.

David H. Bennet

Starting a new business is always an adventure into the unknown, and few of us want to go it alone. And so we are faced with the question: "Should I have a business partner?"

There are, of course, pros and cons. The wrong partner can become the albatross that drags your company down or stunts its growth. He or she can even send it to ruin. In one recent study of 170 small businesses started by partners, more than two thirds broke up, often because of the partners' changing interests or personal conflicts.

So why have a partner at all? Why not do it all yourself—borrow the money from investors, friends or a bank and thus keep the maximum amount of equity in your company?

My own experience as one of four partners in an engineering and management consulting firm, Dynamic Systems, Inc., has convinced me that there are good reasons for seriously considering partners—even though you pay a price in less equity and control.

The biggest advantages: You lower your own risk and required investment; you share the burden of decision making and benefit from the strengths of each other; and you add one or more cooperative, hard-charging members to your team—members as highly motivated as yourself.

Most people are not smart enough by themselves to make all the decisions in a company in a way that maximizes its health and financial strength. We all make mistakes and lose perspective from time to time. A partnership provides an open forum for proposing, analyzing and defending potential decisions, filtering out possible mistakes. This kind of debate is not easy to achieve in an organization where there is one owner and everyone else is an employee.

* * * * *

Having a partner can also reduce stress because each knows there is at least one other person who is equally concerned about the welfare of the company. So, if your partnership works well—that is, if trust, cooperation and competence are present—you can go on vacation secure in the knowledge that someone is looking after your interests.

When my partners and I first considered forming DSI, we went to a banker friend for advice. He identified what I believe to be the most critical factor in determining the success or failure of a new business.

"A partnership is very much like a marriage," he told us. "As you work with each other, you will get to know each other's strengths, limitations, idiosyncrasies, goals, values, skills, and behavior patterns. How well these human characteristics complement or conflict with one another and how much they help or harm a young company are the often-hidden forces that heavily influence long-term success."

* * * * *

Here are some guidelines, based on our experience, that I suggest to others who are thinking of going into a partnership:

☐ When choosing partners, do it with the long-term health of the company in mind.

* * * * *

☐ Take time to know each other well.

* * * * *

☐ Establish, ahead of time, the ground rules under which you will operate.

* * * * *

☐ Keep your spouses informed, and be aware of their expectations.

* * * * *

☐ When your business is off and running, you and your partners should continue to nourish your relationship.

---

* Excerpted by permission from *Nation's Business*, May 1984 (p. 66). Copyright 1984, U.S. Chamber of Commerce.

by a stockholder, giving another designated person the authority to vote the stockholder's shares at a stockholders' meeting.

Board of Directors.   The **board of directors** is elected by the stockholders and is primarily responsible for formulating broad policies for the corporation. The board appoints administrative officers and delegates to them the execution of the policies established by the board. The board also has more specific duties including (1) authorizing contracts, (2) declaring dividends, (3) establishing executive salaries, and (4) granting authorization to borrow money. The decisions of the board are recorded in the minutes of its meetings. These minutes are an important source of information to the independent auditor, since they may serve as notice to record transactions (such as a dividend declaration) or to recognize that certain transactions may be taking place in the near future (such as a large loan).

Corporate Officers.   Officers of a corporation usually are specified in the corporation's bylaws. The number of officers and their exact titles vary from corporation to corporation, but most have a president, several vice presidents, a secretary, and a treasurer.

The president is the chief executive officer of the corporation. He is empowered by the bylaws to hire all necessary employees except those appointed by the board of directors.

Most corporations have more than one vice president. Each vice president is usually responsible for one particular corporate operation, such as sales, engineering, or production. The corporate secretary is responsible for maintaining the official records of the company and records the proceedings of meetings of stockholders and directors. The treasurer is accountable for corporate funds and may be charged with the general supervision of the accounting function within the company. A controller is usually directly charged with carrying out the accounting function. The controller usually reports to the treasurer of the corporation.

■ DOCUMENTS, BOOKS, AND RECORDS RELATING TO CAPITAL STOCK

Capital stock consists of transferable units of ownership in a corporation. Each unit of ownership is called a share of stock. Millions of shares of corporate capital stock are traded every business day on organized stock exchanges such as the New York Stock Exchange, the American Stock Exchange, and on the over-the-counter market. These sales (or "trades") seldom involve the corporation issuing the stock as a party to the exchange, but rather are made by existing stockholders to other individual or institutional investors. These trades are followed by the physical transfer of the stock certificates.

A **stock certificate** is a printed or engraved document serving as evidence that the holder owns a certain number of shares of capital stock. When a stockholder sells shares of stock, the stockholder signs over the stock certificate to the new owner who presents it to the issuing corporation. When the old certificate arrives at the issuing corporation, the certificate is canceled and attached to its corresponding stub in the stock certificate book. A new certificate is prepared for the new owner. The number of shares of stock outstanding at any time can be determined by summing the shares shown on the open stubs (stubs without certificates attached) in the stock certificate book.

Stockholders' Ledger

Among the more important records maintained by a corporation is the stockholders' ledger. The stockholders' ledger contains a group of subsidiary accounts showing the number of shares of stock currently held by each stockholder. Because it contains an account for **each** stockholder, in a large corporation this ledger may have more than a million individual accounts. Each stockholder's account shows the number of shares owned, their certificate numbers, and the dates on which shares were acquired or sold. Entries are made in terms of the number of shares rather than in dollars.

The stockholders' ledger contains the same information as the stock certificate book but summarizes it alphabetically by stockholder since a stockholder may own a dozen or more certificates, each representing a number of shares. This summary enables a corporation to determine the number of shares a stockholder is entitled to vote at a stockholders' meeting and to prepare one dividend check per stockholder rather than one per stock certificate.

Many large corporations with actively traded shares turn the task of maintaining reliable stock records over to an outside stock-transfer agent and a stock registrar. The stock-transfer agent, usually a bank or trust company, is employed by a corporation to transfer stock between buyers and sellers. The stock-transfer agent cancels the certificates covering shares sold, issues new stock certificates, and makes appropriate entries in the stockholder's ledger. New certificates are then sent to the stock registrar, typically another bank, that maintains separate records of the shares outstanding. This control system makes it difficult for a corporate employee to issue stock certificates fraudulently and steal the proceeds.

The Minutes Book

The minutes book, kept by the secretary of the corporation, is a record book in which actions taken at stockholders' and board of directors' meetings are recorded. The minutes book is the written authorization for many actions taken by corporate officers. All actions taken by the board of directors and the stockholders must be in accordance with the provisions contained in the charter and in the bylaws. The minutes book contains a variety of data, including the following:

1. A copy of the corporate charter.
2. A copy of the bylaws.
3. Dividends declared by the board of directors.
4. Authorization for the acquisition of major assets.
5. Authorization for borrowing.
6. Authorization for increases or decreases in capital stock.

■ CAPITAL STOCK AUTHORIZED AND OUTSTANDING

The corporate charter states the number of shares and the par value, if any, per share of each class of stock that the corporation is permitted to issue.

Capital stock authorized is the number of shares of stock that a corporation is entitled to issue as designated in its charter. **Par value** is an arbitrary amount printed on each stock certificate that may be assigned to each share of a given class of stock, usually at the time of incorporation.

A corporation might not issue all of its authorized stock immediately; some stock might be held for future issuance when additional funds are needed. If all authorized stock has been issued and more funds are needed, the consent of the state of incorporation will be required to increase the number of authorized shares.

The authorization to issue stock is not a transaction that results in a journal entry with a debit and credit. Instead, the authorization is noted in the capital stock account in the ledger (and often in the general journal) as a reminder of the number of shares authorized.

Capital stock outstanding is the number of authorized shares of stock that have been issued and that are currently held by stockholders. The total owner-ship of a corporation rests with the holders of the capital stock outstanding. If, for example, a corporation is authorized to issue 10,000 shares of capital stock but has issued only 8,000 shares, the holders of the 8,000 shares own 100% of the corporation.

Each outstanding share of stock of a given class is identical to any other outstanding share of that class with respect to the rights and privileges possessed. Shares authorized but not yet issued are referred to as unissued shares (there are 2,000 unissued shares in the above example). No rights or privileges attach to these shares until they are issued; they are not, for example, entitled to dividends, nor can they be voted at stockholders' meetings.

There is a difference between outstanding stock and issued stock. Issued stock includes shares that have been issued at some point in time, while outstand-ing shares are those shares that are currently held by stockholders. All outstand-ing stock is issued stock, but the reverse is not necessarily true. The difference is due to shares, called treasury stock, that have been returned to the corporation by stockholders. Treasury stock will be discussed in Chapter 16.

■ PAR VALUE AND NO-PAR CAPITAL STOCK

Par Value Stock

Many times par value stock is issued. As noted earlier, **par value** is an arbitrary amount assigned to each share of a given class of stock and printed on the stock certificate. Par value per share is no indication of the amount for which the stock will sell; it is simply the amount per share that is credited to the capital stock account for each share issued. Also, the total par value of all issued stock constitutes the legal capital of the corporation. The concept of legal capital exists to help protect creditors from losses. Legal capital, or stated capital, is an amount prescribed by law below which a corporation may not reduce stockholders' equity through declaration of dividends or other payments to stockholders. Legal capital does not guarantee that a company will be able to pay its debts, but it does serve to keep a company from compensating owners to the detriment of creditors.

No-Par Stock

Laws permitting the issuance of **no-par stock** (stock without par value) were first enacted in New York in 1912. Similar, but not uniform, legislation has since been passed in many states.

A corporation might issue no-par stock for two reasons. One reason is to avoid confusion. The use of a par value may confuse some investors because the par value usually does not conform to market value. When there is no par value, this source of confusion is avoided.

A second reason is related to state laws regarding the original issue price per share. A **discount on capital stock** is the amount by which the par value of shares issued exceeds their issue price. Thus, if stock with a par value of $100 is issued at $80, the discount is $20. Most states will not permit the original issuance of stock at a discount. Only a few states (e.g., Maryland and California) allow its issuance. The original purchasers of the shares are contingently liable for the discount unless they have transferred (by contract) the discount liability to subsequent holders. If the contingent liability has been transferred, the present stockholders are contingently liable to creditors for the difference between par value and issue price. Although this liability is seldom paid, the issuance of no-par stock avoids such a possibility.

No-Par Stock with a Stated Value

The board of directors of a corporation issuing no-par stock may assign a stated value to each share of capital stock. **Stated value** is an arbitrary amount assigned by the board of directors to each share of a given class of no-par stock. This stated value, like par value, may be set at any amount by the board, although some state statutes specify a minimum amount such as $5 per share. Stated value may be established either before or after the shares are issued, if not specified by applicable state law.

■ OTHER VALUES COMMONLY ASSOCIATED WITH CAPITAL STOCK

Market Value

Market value is the price at which shares of capital stock are bought and sold by investors in the market; it is generally the value of greatest interest to investors. Market price is directly affected by (1) all the factors that influence general economic conditions, (2) investors' expectations concerning the corporation, and (3) the corporation's earnings.

Book Value

Book value per share is the amount per share that each stockholder would receive if the corporation were liquidated without incurring any further expenses and if assets were sold and liabilities liquidated at their recorded amounts. A later section discusses book value per share in greater detail.

Liquidation Value

Liquidation value is the amount a stockholder will receive if a corporation discontinues operations and liquidates by selling its assets, paying its liabilities, and distributing the remaining cash among the stockholders. Since the assets might be sold for more or less than the amounts at which they are recorded in the corporation's accounts, liquidation value may be more or less than book value. If only one class of capital stock is outstanding, each stockholder will receive, per share, the amount obtained by dividing the remaining cash by the number of shares of stock outstanding. If two or more classes of stock are outstanding, liquidation values depend on the rights of the various classes.

Redemption Value

Certain capital stock may be issued with the stipulation that the corporation has the right to redeem it. Redemption value is the price per share at which a corporation may call in (or redeem) its capital stock for retirement.

■ CLASSES OF CAPITAL STOCK

Two classes of capital stock—common and preferred—may be issued by a corporation. These classes are discussed in the following sections.

Common Stock

If only one class of stock is issued, it is known as common stock. The rights of the stockholder are enjoyed equally by all the holders of shares. Common stock is usually referred to as the **residual equity** in the corporation. This means that all other claims against the corporation rank ahead of the claims of the common stockholder.

Preferred Stock

A corporation may also issue preferred stock. Preferred stock is capital stock that carries certain features not carried by common stock. Different classes of preferred stock may exist, each with slightly different characteristics.

Preferred stock is issued by a company for the following reasons: (1) to avoid the use of bonds that have fixed interest charges that must be paid regardless of the amount of net income; (2) to avoid issuing so many additional shares of common stock that earnings per share will be less in the current year than in prior years; and (3) to avoid diluting the common stockholders' control of the corporation, since preferred stockholders generally have no voting rights.

Unlike common stock, which has no set maximum or minimum dividend, the dividend return on preferred stock is usually stated at an amount per share or as a percentage of par value. Therefore, the amount of the dividend per share is usually fixed.

Illustration 15.2 shows the various classes and combinations of capital stock outstanding for a sample of 600 companies.

Illustration 15.2

Capital Structures

	1983	1982	1981	1980
Common stock with:				
No preferred stock	381	378	386	387
One class of preferred stock	157	150	140	133
Two classes of preferred stock	47	55	54	57
Three or more classes of preferred stock	15	17	20	23
Total companies	600	600	600	600

Source: American Institute of Certified Public Accountants, *Accounting Trends & Techniques* (New York: AICPA, 1984), p. 213.

■ TYPES OF PREFERRED STOCK

When a corporation issues both preferred and common stock, the preferred stock may be:

1. Preferred as to dividends. If it is, it may be:
   a. Cumulative or noncumulative.
   b. Participating or nonparticipating.
2. Preferred as to assets in the event of liquidation.
3. Convertible or nonconvertible.
4. Callable.

Stock Preferred as to Dividends

A **dividend** is a distribution of assets (usually cash) that represents a withdrawal of earnings by the owners. Dividends are similar in nature to withdrawals by single proprietors and partners.

Stock preferred as to dividends means that the preferred stockholders are entitled to a specified dividend per share before any dividend on common stock is paid. A **dividend on preferred stock** is the amount paid to preferred stockholders as a return for the use of their money. For no-par preferred stock, the dividend is stated as a specific dollar amount per share per year, such as $4.40. For par value preferred stock, the dividend is usually stated as a percentage of the par value, such as 8% of par value, although the dividend can be stated as a specific dollar amount per share. Most preferred stock has a par value.

Dividends on preferred stock usually are paid quarterly. A dividend—in full or in part—can be paid on preferred stock only if it is declared by the board of directors. In some states, preferred stock dividends can be declared only if the corporation has retained earnings (income that has been retained in the business) at least equal in dollar amount to the dividend declared.

Noncumulative Preferred Stock. **Noncumulative preferred stock** is preferred stock on which the right to receive a dividend expires if the dividend is not declared. When noncumulative preferred stock is outstanding, a dividend omitted or not paid in any one year need not be paid in any future year. Because omitted dividends are usually lost forever, noncumulative preferred stocks hold little attraction for investors and rarely are issued.

are fully paid. The data are for the Lake Company, organized as a corporation with 100,000 authorized shares of stock, of which 20,000 shares are already outstanding. The number of shares authorized is noted in memorandum form in both the general journal and the Common Stock account.

Issuance at Par Value.   If the stock has a par value of $100 and subscriptions at par value are received for 5,000 shares of stock on June 20, 1987, the entry is:

```
1987
June 20   Subscriptions Receivable—Common (5,000 × $100) .   500,000
               Common Stock Subscribed .   .   .   .   .   .   .            500,000
          To record subscriptions to 5,000 shares at par.
```

On June 30, 1987, 80% of the subscription price is collected from each of the subscribers. The journal entry to record this collection is:

```
1987
June 30   Cash   .   .   .   .   .   .   .   .   .   .   .   .   .   .   .   .   .   400,000
               Subscriptions Receivable—Common .   .   .   .   .   .          400,000
          To record partial collection of the subscriptions.
```

If the subscription had originally been accompanied by an 80% partial payment, the two entries shown above would be combined as follows:

```
1987
June 20   Cash   .   .   .   .   .   .   .   .   .   .   .   .   .   .   .   .   .   400,000
          Subscriptions Receivable—Common   .   .   .   .   .   .   100,000
               Common Stock Subscribed .   .   .   .   .   .   .   .            500,000
          To record subscriptions to 5,000 shares at par and
          an 80% partial payment.
```

When subscriptions are collected in full on July 15, 1987, certificates are issued, and the following entries are prepared:

```
1987
July 15   Cash   .   .   .   .   .   .   .   .   .   .   .   .   .   .   .   .   .   100,000
               Subscriptions Receivable—Common .   .   .   .   .   .          100,000
          To record collection of the remaining subscriptions.

     15   Common Stock Subscribed   .   .   .   .   .   .   .   .   500,000
               Common Stock  .   .   .   .   .   .   .   .   .   .   .   .          500,000
          Certificates issued for 5,000 shares paid in full.
```

Issuance at an Amount in Excess of Par Value.   If the $100 par value stock had been subscribed at $600,000 (an amount $100,000 in excess of par value), the entry would be:

```
1987
June 20   Subscriptions Receivable—Common (5,000 × $120) .   600,000
               Common Stock Subscribed (5,000 × $100)   .   .            500,000
               Paid-In Capital in Excess of Par Value—
                   Common   .   .   .   .   .   .   .   .   .   .   .   .   .            100,000
          To record subscriptions to 5,000 shares of $100
          par value common stock at $120 per share.
```

The collection of 80% of each subscription on June 30, 1987, would be recorded as follows:

```
1987
June 30  Cash  .  .  .  .  .  .  .  .  .  .  .  .  .  .  .  .  .  .  480,000
              Subscriptions Receivable  .  .  .  .  .  .  .              480,000
              Received 80% on each of the subscriptions of
              June 20, 1987.
```

The entries to record the collection of the remaining 20% and issuance of the shares on July 15, 1987, would be:

```
1987
July 15  Cash  .  .  .  .  .  .  .  .  .  .  .  .  .  .  .  .  .  120,000
              Subscriptions Receivable—Common  .  .  .  .  .              120,000
              To record collection of the remaining subscriptions.

      15  Common Stock Subscribed  .  .  .  .  .  .  .  .  500,000
              Common Stock  .  .  .  .  .  .  .  .  .  .  .  .  .              500,000
              Certificates were issued for 5,000 shares paid in
              full.
```

When par value preferred stock instead of common stock is involved, the entries are the same except that the corresponding preferred stock account titles would be used.

Issuance by Subscription of No-Par Stock with a Stated Value

Assume the Lake Company shares above were no-par stock with a stated value of $100 per share. Assume that on June 20, 1987, subscriptions were received by the Lake Company for 5,000 shares at $120 per share; 80% of each of the subscriptions was collected on June 30, 1987. Certificates for these shares are to be issued on July 15 when the subscriptions are collected in full.

The journal entry needed to record the subscription on June 20 would be:

```
1987
June 20  Subscriptions Receivable—Common (5,000 × $120) .  600,000
              Common Stock Subscribed (5,000 × $100)  .  .              500,000
              Paid-In Capital in Excess of Stated Value—
              Common  .  .  .  .  .  .  .  .  .  .  .  .  .  .  .  .              100,000
              Subscriptions received for 5,000 shares of no-par
              stock at $120 per share. The stated value is $100
              per share.
```

The entries for June 30 and July 15 would be identical to those shown above for par value stock issued in excess of par value.

Issuance by Subscription of No-Par Stock without a Stated Value

Now the subscription of no-par stock that has no stated value will be considered. Assume the Lake Company no-par common stock had no stated value and was subscribed for at $120 per share. The journal entry on June 20 would be:

```
1987
June 20  Subscriptions Receivable—Common  .  .  .  .  .  .  600,000
              Common Stock Subscribed .  .  .  .  .  .  .  .  .              600,000
              To record subscriptions to 5,000 shares of no-par
              common stock without a stated value at
              $120 per share.
```

The entry for June 30 and the first entry on July 15 for the collection of the subscription would be the same as those shown for par value stock issued in excess of par value. The entry for the issuance of the shares on July 15 would be:

```
1987
July 15   Common Stock Subscribed  . . . . . . . . . .   600,000
                Common Stock  . . . . . . . . . . . . .             600,000
             Certificates were issued for 5,000 shares paid in
             full.
```

Balance Sheet Presentation of Subscriptions Receivable and Stock Subscribed

Illustration 15.3 presents the June 30, 1987, partial balance sheet for the Lake Company, assuming 5,000 shares of $100 par value stock were subscribed at $120 per share and that subscriptions receivable of $120,000 were still due as of June 30, 1987. Two accounts, Subscriptions Receivable—Common and Common Stock Subscribed, are included because the subscriptions of June 20 have not been collected in full.

Illustration 15.3

Partial Balance Sheet

THE LAKE COMPANY
Partial Balance Sheet
June 30, 1987

Assets

Current assets:
  Subscriptions receivable—common $120,000

Stockholders' Equity

Paid-in capital:
  Common stock, $100 par value per share;
    100,000 shares authorized:
    Issued and outstanding, 20,000 shares $2,000,000
    Subscribed but not issued, 5,000 shares (see
      subscriptions receivable) 500,000 $2,500,000
  Paid-in capital in excess of par value—common   100,000
      Total paid-in capital $2,600,000

The Common Stock Subscribed account is regarded as a temporary capital stock account. The $500,000 balance of this account represents the par value of shares subscribed but not yet issued. The balance of the Common Stock Subscribed account is presented immediately below the Common Stock account. The reference in Illustration 15.3 to subscriptions receivable (following the caption "Subscribed but not issued, 5,000 shares") informs the reader that $120,000 remains to be paid in before the 5,000 subscribed shares will be issued.

Subscriptions receivable normally will be collected within a matter of days or weeks. Subscriptions receivable are, therefore, properly classified as a current asset in the balance sheet. The account should be displayed separately and not included in the total of trade accounts receivable. In some instances, the subscriptions will not be collected within the coming operating cycle. The account, Subscriptions Receivable, is then properly classified as a noncurrent asset and preferably shown under the caption "Other assets" near the bottom of the assets section of the balance sheet.

Defaulted Subscriptions

A **defaulted subscription** occurs when a subscriber to a stock subscription contract fails to make a required installment payment. Since these contracts often call for an immediate initial cash payment, with the balance payable in periodic installments, the defaulting subscriber may have paid part of the total subscription price. State incorporation laws generally govern the disposition of the amount paid in and the balance of the contract. Three usual courses of action are: (1) the subscriber may receive as many shares as have been paid for in full, with the balance of the contract being canceled; (2) the amount paid in may be refunded (often after deducting any expenses and losses incurred in selling the shares to another party); or (3) the amount paid in may be declared forfeited to the corporation. In the third case, the amount retained should be credited to a Paid-In Capital from Defaulted Subscriptions account to indicate the source of the capital.

■ CAPITAL STOCK ISSUED FOR PROPERTY OR SERVICES

When capital stock is issued for property or services, the dollar amount of the exchange must be determined. Accountants generally record the transaction at the fair value of (1) the property or services received or (2) the stock issued, whichever is more clearly evident.

To illustrate, assume the owners of a tract of land deeded the land to a corporation in exchange for 1,000 shares of $12 par value common stock. The fair market value of the land can only be estimated. At the time of the exchange the stock has an established market value of $14,000. The required entry is:

Land .	14,000	
Common Stock		12,000
Paid-in Capital in Excess of Par Value—Common .		2,000
To record the receipt of land for capital stock.		

As another example, assume 100 shares of common stock with a par value of $40 per share are issued in exchange for legal services received in organizing a corporation. No shares had been recently traded, so they do not have an established market value. The attorney previously agreed to a price of $5,000 for these legal services but decided to accept stock in lieu of cash. In this example, the correct entry is:

Organization Costs .	5,000	
Common Stock		4,000
Paid-In Capital in Excess of Par Value—Common .		1,000
To record the receipt of legal services for capital stock.		

The services should be valued at the price previously agreed on since that value is more clearly evident than the market value of the shares. An asset account should be debited because these services will benefit the corporation indefinitely. The amount by which the value of the services received exceeds the par value of the shares issued is properly credited to a Paid-In Capital in Excess of Par Value—Common account.

■ BALANCE SHEET PRESENTATION OF PAID-IN CAPITAL IN EXCESS OF PAR (OR STATED) VALUE—COMMON OR PREFERRED

As already noted, amounts received in excess of the par or stated value of shares issued should be credited to an account called Paid-In Capital in Excess of Par (or Stated) Value—Common (or Preferred). The amounts received in excess of par or stated value should be carried in separate accounts for each class of stock issued. Using the following assumed data, the stockholders' equity section of the balance sheet of a company with both preferred and common stock outstanding would appear as follows:

Stockholders' equity:			
Paid-in capital:			
Preferred stock—$100 par value, 6% cumulative; 1,000 shares authorized, issued, and outstanding		$100,000	
Common stock—without par value, stated value $5; 100,000 shares authorized, 80,000 shares issued and outstanding		400,000	$500,000
Paid-in capital in excess of par or stated value:			
From preferred stock issuances		$ 5,000	
From common stock issuances		20,000	25,000
Total paid-in capital			$525,000
Retained earnings			200,000
Total stockholders' equity			$725,000

■ BOOK VALUE

The total book value of a corporation's outstanding shares is equal to the recorded net asset value of the corporation—that is, assets minus liabilities. Quite simply, **the amount of net assets is equal to stockholders' equity.** When **only** common stock is outstanding, **book value per share** is computed by dividing total stockholders' equity by the number of common shares outstanding plus common shares subscribed but not yet issued. In calculating book value, an assumption is made that (1) the corporation could be liquidated without incurring any further expenses, (2) the assets could be sold at their recorded amounts, and (3) the liabilities could be satisfied at their recorded amounts.

Assume the stockholders' equity of a corporation is as follows:

Stockholders' equity:		
Paid-in capital:		
Common stock without par value, stated value $10; authorized, 20,000 shares; issued and outstanding, 15,000 shares	$150,000	
Paid-in capital in excess of stated value	10,000	
Total paid-in capital		$160,000
Retained earnings		50,000
Total stockholders' equity		$210,000

The book value per share of the stock is determined as follows:

Total stockholders' equity	$210,000
Total shares outstanding	÷ 15,000
Book value per share	$ 14

When two or more classes of capital stock are outstanding, the computation of book value per share is more complex. The book value for each share of stock depends upon the rights of the preferred stockholders. Preferred stockholders typically are entitled to a specified liquidation value per share, plus cumulative dividends in arrears, if any, since most preferred stocks are preferred as to assets and are cumulative. In each case, the specific provisions in the preferred stock contract will govern.

To illustrate, the Celoron Corporation's stockholders' equity is as follows:

Stockholders' equity:
  Paid-in capital:
    Preferred stock, $100 par value, 5,000 shares . . $ 500,000
    Common stock, $10 par value, 200,000 shares . . 2,000,000
    Paid-in capital in excess of par value—preferred . . 200,000
    Retained earnings 400,000
        Total stockholders' equity $3,100,000

The preferred stock is 6%, cumulative, and nonparticipating. It is preferred as to dividends and as to assets in liquidation to the extent of the liquidation value of $100 per share, plus any cumulative dividends on the preferred stock Dividends for four years are unpaid. Book values of each class of stock ar· calculated as follows:

		Total	Per share
Total stockholders' equity		$3,100,000	
Book value of preferred stock (5,000 shares):			
Liquidation value (5,000 × $100)	$500,000		
Dividends (four years at $30,000)	120,000	620,000	$124.00
Book value of common stock (200,000 shares) . .		$2,480,000	12.40

Notice that the paid-in capital in excess of par value—preferred did not get assigned to the preferred stock in determining the book values. Only the liquidation value and cumulative dividends on the preferred stock are assigned to the preferred stock.

Assume now that the features attached to the preferred stock in the above example are the same except that the preferred stockholders have the right to receive $103 per share in liquidation. The book values of each class of stock would be:

		Total	Per share
Total stockholders' equity		$3,100,000	
Book value of preferred stock (5,000 shares):			
Liquidation value (5,000 × $103)	$515,000		
Dividends (four years at $30,000)	120,000	635,000	$127.00
Book value of common stock (200,000 shares) . .		$2,465,000	12.33

Book value rarely equals market value of a stock because many of the assets have increased in value due to inflation. Thus, the shares of many corporations are traded regularly at market prices different from their book values. The next chapter continues the discussion of stockholders' equity.

■ *SUMMARY*

A corporation is an association of individuals recognized by law as a separate legal entity. A corporation is granted legal existence when a proper application for incorporation is submitted to and approved by the appropriate state agency and a charter is granted. The board of directors selects officers to guide the corporation and carry out policies.

The corporate charter establishes a maximum number of shares that may be issued by the corporation; this is referred to as the total authorized stock. Stock that has been sold and is in the hands of stockholders is issued and outstanding.

Par value is an arbitrary dollar amount assigned to capital stock. No-par stock may be assigned a stated value by the board of directors. The legal capital of a corporation is generally computed as the number of issued shares times the par or stated value. If no-par stock has no stated value, the legal capital normally is equal to the amount received from stockholders for all issued shares.

The two classes of stock a corporation may issue are common and preferred stock. Common stock represents the residual equity in the corporation, and common stockholders are generally the only owners who are allowed to vote. Preferred stock has certain preference rights greater than common stock, such as preference in receiving dividends and/or in receiving assets in the event of liquidation of the corporation. Regarding dividends, preferred stock may be cumulative or noncumulative; it may also be participating or nonparticipating. As a special incentive to purchase preferred stock, such stock may be convertible into common shares of stock.

When a stock subscription is received, a subscriptions receivable account and a stock subscribed account will always be needed unless payment in full is received immediately and the stock is issued. Depending on the price agreed upon, an excess over par or stated value account may also be involved.

Capital stock issued for property or services is recorded at the fair market value of either the property or services received or the shares issued, whichever is more clearly evident. When shares are issued for an amount greater than their par or stated value, this excess should be credited to an account called Paid-In Capital in Excess of Par (or Stated) Value, with separate accounts established for each class of stock.

Since the stock market is frequently referred to as an economic indicator, the knowledge you now have on corporation stock issuances should help you relate to stocks traded in the market. Chapter 16 continues the discussion of paid-in capital and also discusses retained earnings, dividends, and treasury stock.

NEW TERMS INTRODUCED IN CHAPTER 15

Articles of incorporation

The application for the corporation's charter (575).

Board of directors

Elected by the stockholders and is primarily responsible for formulating broad policies for the corporation. The

board also authorizes contracts, declares dividends, establishes executive salaries, and grants authorization to borrow money (577).

Book value per share

Stockholders' equity per share; computed as the amount per share each stockholder would receive if the corporation were liquidated without incurring any further expenses and if assets were sold and liabilities liquidated at their recorded amounts (580).

Bylaws

A set of rules or regulations adopted by the board of directors of a corporation to govern the conduct of corporate affairs. The bylaws must be in agreement with the laws of the state and the policies and purposes in the corporate charter (575).

Call premium (on preferred stock)

The difference between the amount at which a corporation may call its preferred stock for redemption and the par value of the stock (585).

Callable preferred stock

If the stock is nonconvertible, it must be surrendered to the company when the holder is requested to do so. If the stock is convertible, it may be either surrendered or converted into common shares when called (585).

Capital stock

Transferable units of ownership in a corporation (577).

Capital stock authorized

The number of shares of stock that a corporation is entitled to issue as designated in its charter (579).

Capital stock outstanding

The number of shares of authorized stock that have been issued and that are currently held by stockholders (579).

Common stock

Shares of stock representing the residual equity in the corporation. If only one class of stock is issued, it is known as common stock. All other claims rank ahead of common stockholders' claims (581).

Convertible preferred stock

Preferred stock that is convertible into common stock of the issuing corporation (584).

Corporate charter

The contract between the state and the incorporators of a corporation, and their successors, granting the corporation its legal existence (575).

Corporation

An entity recognized by law as possessing an existence separate and distinct from its owners; that is, it is a separate legal entity. A corporation is granted many of the rights and placed under many of the obligations of a natural person. In any given state, all corporations

organized under the laws of that state are **domestic corporations;** all others are **foreign corporations** (573–74).

Cumulative preferred stock

Preferred stock for which the right to receive a basic dividend accumulates if not paid; dividends in arrears must be paid before any dividends can be paid on the common stock (583).

Defaulted subscription

Occurs when a subscriber to a stock subscription contract fails to make a required installment payment (592).

Discount on capital stock

The amount by which the par value of shares issued exceeds their issue price. The original issuance of shares at a discount is illegal in most states (580).

Dividend

A distribution of assets (usually cash) that represents a withdrawal of earnings by the owners. Dividends are similar in nature to withdrawals by sole proprietors and partners (582).

Dividend on preferred stock

The amount paid to preferred stockholders as a return for the use of their money; usually a fixed or stated amount expressed in dollars per share or as a percentage of par value per share (582).

Dividends in arrears

Cumulative unpaid dividends, including passed quarterly dividends for the current year (583).

Domestic corporation

See Corporation.

Foreign corporation

See Corporation.

Incorporators

Persons seeking to bring a corporation into existence (574).

Legal capital (stated capital)

An amount prescribed by law (often par value or stated value of shares outstanding) below which a corporation may not reduce stockholders' equity through the declaration of dividends or other payments to stockholders (579).

Liquidation value

The amount a stockholder will receive if a corporation discontinues operations and liquidates by selling its assets, paying its liabilities, and distributing the remaining cash among the stockholders (581).

Market value

The price at which shares of stock are bought and sold in the open market (580).

Minutes book

The record book in which actions taken at stockholders' and board of directors' meetings are recorded (578).

Noncumulative preferred stock

Preferred stock on which the right to receive a dividend expires if the dividend is not declared (582).

Nonparticipating preferred stock

Preferred stock that is entitled to its stated cumulative dividend only, regardless of the size of the dividend paid on common stock (584).

No-par stock

Capital stock without par value, to which a stated value may or may not be assigned (580).

Organization costs

Costs of organizing a corporation, such as incorporation fees and legal fees applicable to incorporation (575).

Paid-in capital

Amount of stockholders' equity that normally results from the cash or other assets invested by owners; it may also result from services provided for shares of stock and certain other transactions (585).

Paid-in capital in excess of par (or stated) value—common or preferred

Capital contributed to a corporation in addition to that assigned to the shares issued and recorded in capital stock accounts (587).

Participating preferred stock

Preferred stock that is entitled to receive dividends above the stated preference rate under certain conditions specified in the preferred stock contract (583).

Par value

An arbitrary amount printed on each stock certificate that may be assigned to each share of a given class of stock, usually at the time of incorporation (579).

Preemptive right

The right of stockholders to buy additional shares in a proportion equal to the percentage of shares already owned (576).

Preferred stock

Capital stock that carries certain features or rights not carried by common stock. Preferred stock may be pre-ferred as to dividends, preferred as to assets, or pre-ferred as to both dividends and assets. Preferred stock may be cumulative or noncumulative and participating or nonparticipating (581).

Proxy

A legal document signed by a stockholder, giving another person the authority to vote the stockholder's shares at a stockholders' meeting (576).

Redemption value

The price per share at which a corporation may call in (or redeem) its capital stock for retirement (581).

Retained earnings

The part of stockholders' equity resulting from net income; the account in which the results of corporate activity are reflected and to which dividends are charged (585).

Shares of stock

Units of ownership in a corporation (573).

Stated value

An arbitrary amount assigned by the board of directors to each share of a given class of no-par stock (580).

Stock certificate

A printed or engraved document serving as evidence that the holder owns a certain number of shares of capital stock (577).

Stock preferred as to assets

Means that in liquidation the preferred stockholders are entitled to receive the par value (or a larger stipulated liquidation value) per share before any assets may be distributed to common stockholders (584).

Stock preferred as to dividends

Means that the preferred stockholders are entitled to receive a specified dividend per share before any dividend on common stock is paid (582).

Stock registrar

Typically a bank that maintains records of the shares outstanding for a company (578).

Stock-transfer agent

Typically a bank or trust company employed by a corporation to transfer stock between buyers and sellers (578).

Stock without par value

See No-par stock.

Stockholders' ledger

Contains a group of subsidiary accounts showing the number of shares of stock currently held by each stockholder (578).

Subscribed stock

Stock for which subscriptions have been received but for which stock certificates have not been issued (588).

Subscribers

Persons who contract to acquire shares, usually in an original issuance of stock by a corporation (575).

Subscription

A contract to acquire a certain number of shares of stock, at a specified price, with payment to be made at a specified date or dates (588).

DEMONSTRATION PROBLEM 15–1

The Dey Company has paid all required preferred dividends through December 31, 1982. Its outstanding stock consists of 10,000 shares of $100 par value common stock and 4,000 shares of 6%, $100 par value preferred stock. During five successive years, the company's dividend declarations were as follows:

1983	$140,000
1984	84,000
1985	12,000
1986	24,000
1987	108,000

Required: Compute the amount of dividends that would have been paid to each class of stock in each of the last five years assuming the preferred stock is:

a. Cumulative and nonparticipating.
b. Noncumulative and nonparticipating.

Solution to demonstration problem 15–1

DEY COMPANY

		Assumptions	
Year	**Dividends to**	**(a)**	**(b)**
1983	Preferred . .	$ 24,000*	$ 24,000
	Common . .	116,000	116,000
1984	Preferred . .	24,000	24,000
	Common . .	60,000	60,000
1985	Preferred . .	12,000	12,000
	Common . .	–0–	–0–
1986	Preferred . .	24,000	24,000
	Common . .	–0–	–0–
1987	Preferred . .	36,000†	24,000‡
	Common . .	72,000	84,000

* (4,000 shares × $100 × 0.06).
† $24,000 + $12,000 preferred dividend missed in 1985.
‡ Only the basic $24,000 dividend is paid because the stock is noncumulative.

DEMONSTRATION PROBLEM 15–2

The Pinto Company has been authorized to issue 100,000 shares of $10 par value common stock and 1,000 shares of 14%, cumulative, nonparticipating preferred stock with a par value of $20.

Required: *a.*   Prepare the entries for the following transactions which all took place in June 1987:

1. 50,000 shares of common stock are subscribed at $40 per share, with a down payment of 25% of the issue price.
2. 750 shares of preferred stock are issued for cash at $30 per share.
3. 1,000 shares of common stock are issued in exchange for legal services received in the incorporation process. The fair market value of the legal services is $15,000.
4. The balance of the stock subscriptions is paid, and the stock is issued.

b.   Prepare the paid-in capital section of Pinto's balance sheet as of June 30, 1987.

Solution to demonstration problem 15–2

a.

1.	Cash	500,000	
	Subscriptions Receivable—Common	1,500,000	
	Common Stock Subscribed		500,000
	Paid-In Capital in Excess of Par Value—Common		1,500,000
	To record subscriptions to 50,000 shares at $40 per share, with 25% down payment.		
2.	Cash	22,500	
	Preferred Stock		15,000
	Paid-In Capital in Excess of Par Value—Preferred		7,500
	To record the issuance of 750 shares for cash, at $30 per share.		
3.	Organization Costs	15,000	
	Common Stock		10,000
	Paid-In Capital in Excess of Par Value—Common		5,000
	To record issuance of 1,000 shares in exchange for legal services.		
4.	Cash	1,500,000	
	Subscriptions Receivable—Common		1,500,000
	To record collection of balance due on subscriptions.		
	Common Stock Subscribed	500,000	
	Common Stock		500,000
	To record issuance of certificates for 50,000 shares, fully paid.		

b.

THE PINTO COMPANY
Partial Balance Sheet
June 30, 1987

Paid-in capital:			
Preferred stock, $20 par value per share; 1,000 shares authorized; issued and outstanding, 750 shares		$ 15,000	
Common stock, $10 par value per share; 100,000 shares authorized; issued and outstanding, 51,000 shares		510,000	$ 525,000
Paid-in capital in excess of par value:			
From preferred stock issuances		$ 7,500	
From common stock issuances		1,505,000	1,512,500
Total paid-in capital			$2,037,500

QUESTIONS

1. Cite the major advantages of the corporation form of business organization and indicate why each is considered an advantage.

2. What is meant by the statement that corporate income is subject to double taxation? Cite several other disadvantages of the corporation form of organization.

3. Why is Organization Expense not a good title for the account that records the costs of organizing a corporation? Could you justify leaving the balance of an Organization Costs account intact throughout the life of a corporation?

4. What are the basic rights associated with a share of capital stock if there is only one class of stock outstanding?

5. Explain the purpose or function of (a) the stockholders' ledger, (b) the minutes book, (c) the stock-transfer agent, and (d) the stock registrar.

6. What are the differences between par value stock and stock with no-par value?

7. Corporate capital stock is seldom issued for less than par value. Give two reasons why this is true.

8. Explain the terms *liquidation value* and *redemption value*.

9. What is the meaning of the terms *stock preferred as to dividends* and *stock preferred as to assets?*

10. What do the terms (a) *cumulative* and *noncumulative* and (b) *participating* and *nonparticipating* mean in regard to preferred stock?

11. A coporation has 1,000 shares of 8%, $100 par value, cumulative, preferred stock outstanding. Dividends on this stock have not been declared for three years. Is the corporation legally liable to its preferred stockholders for these dividends? How should this fact be shown in the balance sheet, if at all?

12. Explain why a corporation might issue a preferred stock that is both convertible into common stock and callable.

13. Explain the nature of the account entitled Paid-In Capital in Excess of Par Value. Under what circumstances is this account credited?

14. Explain the nature of the Subscriptions Receivable account. How should it be classified in the balance sheet? On what occasions is it debited or credited?

15. What is the general approach of the accountant in determining the dollar amount at which to record the issuance of capital stock for services or property other than cash?

16. Assuming there is no preferred stock outstanding, how can the book value per share of common stock be determined? Of what significance is it? What is its relationship to market value per share?

EXERCISES

E–1

Determine dividends for common and preferred stock

Welch Corporation has outstanding 1,000 shares of noncumulative, nonparticipating preferred stock and 2,000 shares of common stock. The preferred stock is entitled to an annual dividend of $10 per share before dividends are declared on common stock. What are the total dividends received by preferred stockholders and common stockholders if Welch Corporation distributes $28,000 in dividends in 1987?

E–2

Determine dividends for common and preferred stock

Burnett Corporation has 2,000 shares outstanding of cumulative, nonparticipating preferred stock and 6,000 shares of common stock. The preferred stock is entitled to an annual dividend of $6 per share before dividends are declared on common stock. No preferred dividends were paid for last year and the current year. What are the total dividends received by preferred stockholders if Burnett Corporation distributes $72,000 in dividends?

E–3

Determine dividends for common and preferred stock for five-year period

The preferred stock contract of Warwick Corporation specifies that the preferred shares will participate on an equal amount per share basis with the common shares after $2 has been distributed per share of preferred stock and common stock. There are 1,000 shares of preferred stock outstanding and 9,000 shares of common stock outstanding. Determine the dividends that will be paid to each class for the following years:

	Total dividend to be distributed
1987	$ 2,000
1988	10,000
1989	20,000
1990	25,000
1991	30,000

E–4

Journalize stock issuance

Doyle Company issued 10,000 shares of common stock for $105,000 cash. The common stock has a par value of $10 per share. Give the journal entry for the stock issuance.

E–5

Prepare entries for stock issuance

Green Company issued 20,000 shares of $20 par value common stock for $680,000. What is the journal entry for this transaction? What would the journal entry be if the common stock had no par or stated value?

E–6

Journalize stock subscriptions

Lewis Company has been authorized to issue 100,000 shares of $50 par value common stock, of which 20,000 shares are outstanding. On February 20, 1987, the company received subscriptions for 15,000 shares at $80 per share. What would be the journal entry on February 20, 1987?

E–7

Journalize stock issuance for property

One hundred shares of $50 par value common stock were issued to the incorporators of a corporation in exchange for land (which cost the incorporators $6,500 one year ago) needed by the corporation for use as a plant site. Experienced appraisers recently estimated the value of the land to be $7,500. What journal entry would be appropriate to record the acquisition of the land?

E–8

Journalize stock issuance to satisfy liability

Strickland Corporation owes a trade creditor $24,000 on open account which it does not have sufficient cash to pay. The trade creditor suggests that Strickland Corporation issue to him 750 shares of the company's $20 par value common stock, which is currently selling on the market at $32. Present the entry or entries that should be made on Strickland Corporation's books.

E–9

Journalize stock issuance for legal services

Why would a law firm ever consider accepting stock of a new corporation having a total par value of $30,000 as payment in full of a $45,000 bill for legal services rendered? If such a transaction occurred, give the journal entry the issuing company would make on its books.

E–10

Compute the book value and average price of common stock

The stockholders' equity section of the Hubert Company's balance sheet is as follows:

Stockholders' equity:
   Paid-in capital:
      Common stock without par value, $10 stated
      value; authorized 100,000 shares; issued
      and outstanding, 70,000 shares . . . . . . $ 700,000
      Paid-in capital in excess of stated value . . .   272,000
         Total paid-in capital . . . . $ 972,000
   Retained earnings   108,000
         Total stockholders' equity $1,080,000

Compute the average price at which the 70,000 issued shares of common stock were sold. Compute the book value per share of common stock.

PROBLEMS, SERIES A

P15-1-A

Prepare partial balance sheet involving par value stock

Certain post-closing account balances for the Webb Company as of December 31, 1987, were as follows:

WEBB COMPANY
Post-Closing Account Balances
December 31, 1987

Common Stock Subscribed, 4,000 shares	$100,000
Preferred Stock, 6%, $60 par; 2,000 shares authorized, issued, and outstanding	120,000
Common Stock, $25 par; 10,000 shares authorized, 6,000 shares issued and outstanding	150,000
Paid-In Capital in Excess of Par—Common	12,800
Subscriptions Receivable—Common	23,040
Paid-In Capital in Excess of Par—Preferred	6,000
Retained Earnings	18,840

Required: From the above list of accounts and balances, present in good form the stockholders' equity section of the December 31, 1987, balance sheet.

P15-2-A

Determine dividends for common stock and cumulative and noncumulative preferred stock

On January 1, 1983, the retained earnings of the Wilkins Company were $45,000. Net income for the succeeding five years was as follows:

1983	$30,000
1984	22,500
1985	500
1986	5,000
1987	27,500

The outstanding capital stock of the corporation consisted of 2,000 shares of preferred stock with a par value of $50 per share that pays a dividend of $2 per year and 8,000 shares of no-par common stock with a stated value of $25 per share. No dividends were in arrears as of January 1, 1983.

Required: Prepare schedules showing how the net income for the above five years was distributed to the two classes of stock if, in each of the years, the entire current net income was distributed as dividends and the preferred stock was:

a. Cumulative and nonparticipating.
b. Noncumulative and nonparticipating.

P15-3-A

Journalize stock subscriptions and issuances for cash and prepare resulting stockholders' equity section

The Blackmon Company had the following stockholders' equity and related accounts on January 1, 1987:

Subscriptions Receivable—Preferred Stock	$ 8,000
Preferred Stock, 8%, $10 par, 20,000 shares authorized, 10,000 shares issued	100,000
Preferred Stock Subscribed (2,500 shares)	25,000
Common Stock, $80 par, 10,000 shares authorized, 7,500 shares issued	600,000
Paid-In Capital in Excess of Par Value—Common . .	60,000
Retained Earnings	200,000

The following transactions occurred during 1987:

Transactions:

Jan. 10   Received the balance due on preferred stock subscribed; issued stock certificates.

Mar. 1   Received subscriptions for 5,000 shares of preferred stock at $14; 40% of the subscription price was paid in cash.

Aug. 3   Issued 2,000 shares of common stock for $92 cash per share.

Required: a.   Prepare journal entries for the transactions that occurred in 1987.

b.   Prepare the stockholders' equity section of the balance sheet as of August, 3, 1987.

P15-4-A

Post transactions; prepare balance sheets for par value stock, stated value stock, and no-par or stated value stock

On July 3, 1987, the American Company was authorized to issue 15,000 shares of common stock; 3,000 shares were issued immediately to the incorporators of the company for cash at $40 per share. On July 5, an additional 300 shares were issued to the incorporators for services rendered in organizing the company.

On July 6, 1987, legal and printing costs of $1,500 were paid. These costs related to securing the corporate charter and the stock certificates.

On July 10, subscriptions were received from the general public for 4,500 shares at $36 per share, with 25% of the subscription price paid in cash immediately. The balance is due August 10, 1987.

Required: a.   Set up T-accounts, and post the above transactions. Then prepare the balance sheet of the American Company as of the close of July 10, 1987, assuming the authorized stock has a $20 par value.

b.   Repeat *(a)* for the T-accounts involving stockholders' equity assuming the stock is no-par stock with a $30 stated value. Only prepare the stockholders' equity section of the balance sheet.

c.   Repeat *(a)* for the T-accounts involving stockholders' equity assuming the stock is no-par stock with no stated value. Only prepare the stockholders' equity section of the balance sheet.

P15-5-A

Journalize stock subscriptions and issuance of stock for cash

On July 1, 1987, the York Company was authorized to issue 20,000 shares of $30 par value common stock. On July 7, subscriptions for 1,500 shares at $36 per share were received. The subscription contract requires a 10% immediate payment, with the remainder due on July 31. No stock certificates are to be issued until the subscriptions are paid in full.

Required: a.   Prepare the entries to record all transactions during July 1987, assuming the subscriptions are collected when due.

b.   Prepare the July 1987 entries assuming the stock is no-par stock without a stated value.

c.   Prepare the entry for July 7, 1987, assuming the subscriptions for the no-par stock are accompanied by cash payment in full and the stock is issued.

P15-6-A

Journalize stock transactions, including conversions; prepare stockholders' equity section

The Ballard Company received its charter on April 1, 1987, authorizing it to issue 5,000 shares of $100 par value, $8 cumulative, convertible preferred stock; 10,000 shares of $3 cumulative no-par preferred stock having a stated value of $5 per share and a liquidation value of $25 per share; and 100,000 shares of no-par common stock without a stated value.

On April 2, incorporators of the corporation acquired 50,000 shares of the common stock for cash at $20 per share, and 200 shares were issued to an attorney for services rendered in organizing the corporation. On April 3, the company issued all of its authorized shares of $8 convertible preferred stock for land valued at $400,000 and a building valued at $1,200,000. The property was subject to a mortgage of $600,000.

On April 4, subscriptions for 5,000 shares of the $3 preferred stock were received at $52 per share, with one half of the subscription price paid in cash. On April 8, the remaining 5,000 shares of $3 preferred stock were issued to an inventor for a patent. A subscription for 1,000 shares of common stock at $20 per share was also received, with a cash payment of $2,000 accompanying the subscription.

On April 25, the balance due on the April 4 subscriptions was collected, and the shares were issued. By April 30, the subscriber to 1,000 shares of common stock had failed to pay the balance of her subscription, which she had agreed to pay in 10 days. Shares were issued for her down payment, and the balance of the contract was canceled.

Required: a.   Prepare general journal entries for the above transactions.

b.   Prepare the stockholders' equity section of the April 30, 1987, balance sheet. Assume retained earnings of $20,000.

c.   Assume that each share of the $8 convertible preferred stock is convertible into six shares of common stock and that all of the preferred is converted on September 1, 1990. Give the required journal entry.

P15–7–A

Prepare stockholders' equity section; determine book values of stock; and determine dividends for each class of stock

The Heath Company issued all of its 2,500 shares of authorized preferred stock on January 1, 1986, at $206 per share. The preferred stock is no-par stock, has a stated value of $10 per share, is entitled to a cumulative basic preference dividend of $12 per share, is callable at $210 beginning in 1991, and is entitled to $200 per share in liquidation plus cumulative dividends. On this same date, Heath also issued its 5,000 authorized shares of no-par common stock with a $20 stated value at $100 per share.

On December 31, 1987, the end of its second year of operations, the company's retained earnings amounted to $160,000. No dividends have been declared or paid on either class of stock since the date of issue.

Required: a.   Prepare the stockholders' equity section of the Heath Company's December 31, 1987, balance sheet.

b.   Compute the book value in total and per share of each class of stock as of December 31, 1987, assuming the preferred stock is nonparticipating.

c.   If $110,000 of dividends are to be declared as of December 31, 1987, compute the amount payable to each class of stock assuming the preferred stock is nonparticipating.

P15–8–A

Determine book value for each class of stock

The stockholders' equity sections from three different corporations' balance sheets follow:

1.   Stockholders' equity:
  Paid-in capital:
   Preferred stock, 7% cumulative and nonparticipating, $75 par
    value, 500 shares authorized and outstanding . . . . $ 37,500
   Common stock, $15 par value, 10,000 shares authorized
    and outstanding   150,000
     Total paid-in capital   . . . . $ 187,500
  Retained earnings   132,000
     Total stockholders' equity   . . . . $ 319,500

2.   Stockholders' equity:
  Paid-in capital:
   Preferred stock, 6% cumulative and nonparticipating, $25 par
    value, 10,000 shares authorized and outstanding . . . . $ 250,000
   Common stock, $75 par value, 30,000 shares authorized
    and outstanding   2,250,000
     Total paid-in capital $2,500,000
  Retained earnings   27,500
     Total stockholders' equity $2,527,500

  (The current year's dividends have not been paid.)

3.   Stockholders' equity:
  Paid-in capital:
   Preferred stock, 7% cumulative and nonparticipating, $150 par
    value, 10,000 shares authorized and outstanding $1,500,000
   Common stock, $75 par value, 50,000 shares authorized
    and outstanding   3,750,000
     Total paid-in capital $5,250,000
  Retained earnings (deficit) . . . .   (585,000)
     Total stockholders' equity $4,665,000

  (Dividends have not been paid for 2 previous years or the current year.)

Required: Compute the book values per share of the preferred and common stock of each corporation assuming that in a liquidation the preferred stock receives par value plus dividends in arrears.

P15–9–A

Compute book values of a stockholder's preferred and common stock

Larson, Inc., is a corporation in which all of the outstanding preferred and common stock is held by the four Larson brothers. The brothers have an agreement stating that the remaining brothers will, upon the death of a brother, purchase from the estate his holdings of stock in the company at book value.

The stockholders' equity section of the balance sheet for the company on December 31, 1987, the date of the death of Edward Larson, shows:

Stockholders' equity:
Paid-in capital:
Preferred stock, 6%; $200 par value; $200 liquidation value;	
4,000 shares authorized, issued, and outstanding	$ 800,000
Paid-in capital in excess of par—preferred	40,000
Common stock without par value, $10 stated value,	
60,000 shares authorized, issued, and outstanding	600,000
Paid-in capital in excess of par—common	600,000
Retained earnings	80,000
Total stockholders' equity	$2,120,000

No dividends have been paid for the last year on the preferred stock, which is cumulative and nonparticipating. At the time of his death, Edward Larson held 2,000 shares of preferred stock and 10,000 shares of common stock of the company.

Required:

a. Compute the book value of the preferred stock.
b. Compute the book value of the common stock.
c. Compute the amount the remaining brothers must pay to the estate of Edward Larson for the preferred and common stock that he held at the time of his death.

PROBLEMS, SERIES B

P15–1–B

Prepare partial balance sheet involving par value stock

Certain post-closing account balances for Rigdon, Inc., as of December 31, 1987, were as follows:

RIGDON, INC.
Partial List of Post-Closing Account Balances
December 31, 1987

Paid-In Capital in Excess of Par Value—Preferred	$ 15,000
Common Stock Subscribed, 2,000 shares	100,000
Subscriptions Receivable—Common	120,000
Preferred Stock, 8%, $100 par value; 3,000 shares	
authorized, issued, and outstanding	300,000
Paid-In Capital in Excess of Par Value—Common	36,000
Common Stock, $50 par value; 30,000 shares authorized;	
8,000 shares issued and outstanding	400,000
Retained Earnings	377,000

Required:

From the above list of account balances, prepare the stockholders' equity section of the December 31, 1987, balance sheet in good form.

P15–2–B

Determine dividends for common stock and cumulative and noncumulative preferred stock

The outstanding capital stock of the Precision Corporation consisted of 3,000 shares of 10% preferred stock, $100 par value, and 30,000 shares of no-par common stock with a stated value of $100. The preferred was issued at $164.80, the common at $192 per share. On January 1, 1983, the retained earnings of the company were $100,000. During the succeeding five years, net income was as follows:

1983	. . . . .	$307,000
1984	. . . . .	204,000
1985	. . . . .	19,200
1986	. . . . .	64,000
1987	. . . . .	265,000

No dividends were in arrears as of January 1, 1983, and during the five years 1983–87, the board of directors declared dividends in each year equal to net income of the year.

Required: Prepare a schedule showing the dividends declared each year on each class of stock assuming the preferred stock is:

a. Cumulative and nonparticipating.
b. Noncumulative and nonparticipating

P15–3–B

Journalize stock issuances for cash, services (organization costs), and property; prepare resulting balance sheet

On December 27, 1986, the Stoddard Company was authorized to issue 250,000 shares of $5 par value common stock. It then completed the following transactions:

Transactions:

1987
Jan. 14   Issued 45,000 shares of common stock at $6 per share for cash.
  29   Gave the promoters of the corporation 25,000 shares of common stock for their services in organizing the company. The board of directors valued these services at $155,000.
Feb. 19   Exchanged 50,000 shares of common stock for the following assets at fair market values:

Land	. . . . .	$ 45,000
Building	. . . .	110,000
Machinery	. . . .	150,000

Required: a. Prepare general journal entries to record the transactions.
  b. Prepare the balance sheet of the company as of March 1, 1987.

P15–4–B

Prepare balance sheets for par value stock, stated value stock, and no-par or stated value stock

In the corporate charter that it received on May 1, 1987, the Woodard Company was authorized to issue 15,000 shares of common stock. The company issued 500 shares immediately to each of two of the promoters for $54 per share, cash.

On July 2, the company issued 100 shares of stock to a lawyer to satisfy a $5,600 bill for legal services rendered in organizing the corporation.

On July 3, subscriptions, accompanied by a 10% down payment, were received from the general public for 6,000 shares at $56 per share.

On July 5, the company issued 1,000 shares to the principal promoter of the corporation in exchange for a patent. Another 200 shares were issued to this same person for costs incurred and services rendered in bringing the corporation into existence.

Required: a. Set up T-accounts, and post the above transactions. Then prepare a balance sheet for the Woodward Company as of July 5, 1987, assuming the authorized stock has a par value of $50 per share.
  b. Repeat part *(a)* for the stockholders' equity accounts, and prepare the stockholders' equity section of the July 5 balance sheet assuming the stock authorized has no par value but has a $20 per share stated value.
  c. Repeat part *(a)* for the stockholders' equity accounts assuming the stock authorized has neither par nor stated value. Only prepare the stockholders' equity section of the balance sheet.

P15–5–B

Journalize stock subscriptions and prepare resulting balance sheet

In the charter granted January 2, 1987, the Thomas Corporation was authorized to issue 2,000 shares of no-par common stock. The stock is to be issued under subscription agreements that call for immediate payment of one fourth of each subscription, with the remainder due on the first day of the following month.

On January 5, subscriptions for 600 shares at $25 per share were received, and on May 1 an additional 400 shares were subscribed at $30 per share. All subscriptions were collected in accordance with the agreements.

Required: a. Prepare the entries to record all the transactions of January through May 1987, assuming no stock was issued until the subscriptions were paid in full.

b. Prepare the May 31, 1987, balance sheet assuming there were no transactions other than those described above.

P15–6–B

Journalize stock issuances for cash, property, and services; journalize stock subscriptions; and prepare resulting stockholders' equity section

On May 1, 1987, Conrad Company received a charter that authorized it to issue:

1. 4,000 shares of no-par preferred stock to which a stated value of $6 per share is assigned. The stock is entitled to a cumulative dividend of $4.80, convertible into two shares of common stock, callable at $104, and entitled to $100 per share in liquidation.

2. 1,500 shares of $200 par value, $10 cumulative preferred stock which is callable at $210 and entitled to $206 in liquidation.

3. 60,000 shares of no-par common stock to which a stated value of $20 is assigned.

Transactions:

May 1   All of the $4.80 cummulative convertible preferred was subscribed and issued at $102 per share, cash.

2   All of the $10 cumulative preferred was exchanged for inventory, land, and buildings valued at $64,000, $80,000, and $170,000, respectively.

2   Subscriptions were received for 50,000 shares of common at $40 per share, with 10% of the subscription price paid immediately in cash.

3   Cash of $6,000 was paid to reimburse promoters for costs incurred for accounting, legal, and printing services. In addition, 1,000 shares of common stock were issued to the promoters for their services.

31   All of the subscriptions to the common stock were collected and the shares issued.

Required: a. Prepare journal entries for the above transactions.

b. Assume that retained earnings were $100,000. Prepare the stockholders' equity section of the May 31, 1987, balance sheet.

P15–7–B

Prepare stockholders' equity section; determine book values of stock; and determine dividends for each class of stock

On January 2, 1986, the date the Clark Company received its charter, it issued all of its authorized 3,000 shares of no-par preferred stock at $104 and all of its 12,000 authorized shares of no-par common stock at $40 per share. The preferred stock has a stated value of $50 per share, is entitled to a basic cumulative preference dividend of $6 per share, is callable at $106 beginning in 1988, and is entitled to $100 per share plus cumulative dividends in the event of liquidation. The common stock has a stated value of $10 per share.

On December 31, 1987, the end of the second year of operations, retained earnings were $90,000. No dividends have been declared or paid on either class of stock.

Required: a. Prepare the stockholders' equity section of the Clark Company's December 31, 1987, balance sheet.

b. Compute the book value of each class of stock assuming the preferred stock is nonparticipating.

c. If $42,000 of dividends were declared as of December 31, 1987, compute the amount paid to each class of stock assuming the preferred stock is nonparticipating.

P15–8–B

Compute total market value for common stock; compute book value of common and preferred stock

The common stock of Mattox Corporation is selling on a stock exchange for $75 per share. The stockholders' equity of the corporation at December 31, 1987, consists of:

Stockholders' Equity:

Paid-in capital:	
Preferred stock, 9% cumulative and nonparticipating, $100 par value, 3,000 shares authorized and outstanding	$ 300,000
Common stock, $60 par value, 30,000 shares authorized and outstanding	1,800,000
Total paid-in capital	$2,100,000
Retained earnings	295,500
Total stockholders' equity	$2,395,500

Assume that in liquidation the preferred stock is entitled to par value plus cumulative unpaid dividends.

Required:
a. What is the total market value of all of the corporation's common stock?
b. If all dividends have been paid on the preferred stock as of December 31, 1987, what are the book values of the preferred stock and the common stock?
c. If two years' dividends were due on the preferred stock as of December 31, 1987, what are the book values of the preferred stock and common stock?

P15-9-B

Compute book values of a stockholder's preferred and common stock

Goode Corporation has an agreement with each of its 15 preferred and 30 common stockholders that in the event of the death of a stockholder, it will purchase at book value from the stockholder's estate or heirs the shares of Goode Corporation stock held by the deceased at the time of death. The book value is to be computed in accordance with generally accepted accounting principles.

Following is the stockholders' equity section of the Goode Corporation's December 31, 1987, balance sheet.

Stockholders' equity:
  Paid-in capital:
    $6 no-par preferred stock, $20 stated value;
      3,000 shares authorized, issued, and outstanding . . . . $ 60,000
    Common stock, $25 par value, 60,000 shares authorized,
      issued, and outstanding 1,500,000
    Paid-in capital in excess of stated value—preferred 336,000
    Paid-in capital in excess of par value—common 12,000
  Retained earnings 720,000
        Total stockholders' equity $2,628,000

The preferred stock is cumulative and entitled to $120 per share plus cumulative dividends in liquidation. No dividends have been paid for 1½ years.

A stockholder who owned 100 shares of preferred stock and 1,000 shares of common stock died on December 31, 1987. You have been employed by the stockholder's widow to compute the book value of each class of stock and to determine the price to be paid for the stock held by her late husband.

Required: Prepare a schedule showing the computation of the amount to be paid for the deceased stockholder's preferred and common stock.

BUSINESS DECISION PROBLEM 15-1

Compute dividends on preferred stock and common stock and determine their relationship to stock prices

Eastern Company and Western Company are two companies that have extremely stable net income amounts of $3,000,000 and $2,000,000, respectively. Both companies distribute all their net income as dividends each year. Eastern Company has 100,000 shares of $50 par value, 6% preferred stock and 500,000 shares of $5 par value common stock outstanding. Western Company has 50,000 shares of $25 par value, 8% preferred stock and 400,000 shares of $5 par value common stock outstanding. Both preferred stocks are cumulative and nonparticipating.

Required:
a. Compute the annual dividend per share of preferred stock and per share of common stock for each company.
b. Based solely on the above information, which common stock would you predict to have the higher market price per share? Why?

BUSINESS DECISION PROBLEM 15–2

Determine book values and their relationship to investment decisions

Frank Clayborn recently inherited $96,000 cash that he wishes to invest in one of the following securities: common stock of the Durden Corporation or common stock of the Simmons Corporation. Both corporations manufacture the same types of products and have been in existence for five years. The stockholders' equity sections of the two corporations' latest balance sheets are shown below:

DURDEN CORPORATION

Stockholders' equity:
  Paid-in capital:
    Common stock, $25 par value, 30,000 shares authorized,

issued, and outstanding	$ 750,000
Retained earnings	690,000
Total stockholders' equity	$1,440,000

SIMMONS CORPORATION

Stockholders' equity:
  Paid-in capital:
    Preferred stock, 8%, $100 par value, cumulative and
    nonparticipating, 4,000 shares authorized, issued,

and outstanding	$ 400,000
Common stock, $25 par value, 40,000 shares authorized,	
issued, and outstanding	1,000,000
Retained earnings	112,000
Total stockholders' equity	$1,512,000

The Durden Corporation has paid a cash dividend of $1.20 per share each year since its creation; its common stock is currently selling for $118 per share. The Simmons Corporation's common stock is currently selling for $96 per share. The current year's dividend and three prior years' dividends on the preferred stock are in arrears. The preferred stock has a liquidation value of $120 per share.

Required: a. What is the book value per share of the Durden Corporation common stock and the Simmons Corporation common stock? Is book value the major determinant of market value of the stock?
       b. Based solely upon the above information, which investment would you recommend? Why?

BUSINESS SITUATION FOR DISCUSSION

It Can Pay Off Big to Turn Common Into Preferred*

☐   When Teledyne Inc. bought back some 18% of its common shares in 1980, the company's executives got more or less what they had hoped for: a 28% higher price in a year's time. But when Advanced Systems Inc.

swapped a new issue of preferred shares for 24% of its common in 1982, Chief Financial Officer Norman Walack got a lot more than he expected: a 100% jump in the common stock's price, from 11 a share to 22 a year later.

Shelling out cash to repurchase common shares has become an increasingly popular way for corporations to obtain, among other things, a more favorable balance between the market supply of their stock and the demand

* Reprinted from the March 5, 1984, issue of *Business Week,* (p. 76) by special permission. © 1984 by McGraw-Hill, Inc.

Swapping Preferred for Common: A Faster Track than Buy-backs—Average Price Gain in 12 Months after Transactions in 1980–83 Period

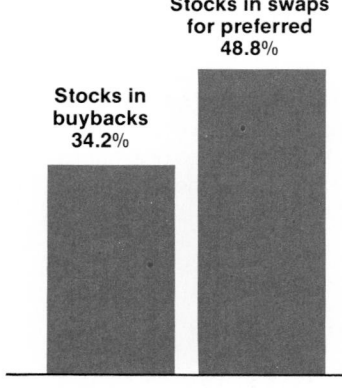

Stocks in buybacks 34.2%

Stocks in swaps for preferred 48.8%

Data: Mitchell & Co.

for it. But, according to a study by Mitchell & Co., a Boston management-consulting firm, creating new preferred shares and swapping them for common stock is often more rewarding (see chart).

"Reacquiring common shares through an exchange of preferred stock generally does not hurt the company in any way, and avoids all the negatives that have thrown the entire stock-buyback idea into a deep well of controversy," says Carol Bruckner Coles, Mitchell's president and chief operating officer. While analysts increasingly criticize the costs of stock repurchases (BW—June 25), companies keep on doing them, for a variety of reasons: to reduce dividend payments, to gain an almost automatic assurance of higher earnings per share, to make feared takeover plots or proxy fights more difficult, and to reinvest excess cash in the companies' own "undervalued assets."

Thinking Big

The still relatively undiscovered method of swapping preferred serves the same purposes but skirts most of the pitfalls; about the only drawback to a company is that it may have to jack up its preferred dividend to compete with any rise in interest rates. The swappers, notes Coles, do not have to divert cash from more productive purposes, nor do they have to take on extra debt. "For a company that borrows funds to reacquire shares, interest charges may offset any earnings benefits and increase as well its debt-to-equity ratio," notes a Standard & Poor's Corp. analyst.

The stocks of companies that have resorted to straight buybacks, according to Mitchell analysts' calcu-

lations, increased, on average, over the past five years by about 30% above where the stock would have been without the repurchase. But the stocks of companies that have swapped preferred shares or, in some cases, even convertible debentures [unsecured bonds], for their common stock have, on the same basis, jumped an average of 199%. Thinking big helps, strategists contend: For maximum impact, the conversion should involve no fewer than 20% of outstanding shares.

Thus, not all stocks involved in swaps enjoy a surge in price. Manufacturers Hanover Trust Co., for example, pulled in only 11.8% of its common for new preferred shares in May, 1982. Result: Its common stock rose a meager 2% after a year. And Ashland Oil Inc. reacquired 14% of its common in January, 1980, with a $2.50-a-share dividend, in return for preferred shares that will pay a dividend almost twice that on its common stock. Dividends on preferred stock typically run up to 60% above the yield on common stocks. Even so, the Ashland common rose a disappointing 5%.

Snowball?

A large-scale preferred swap, however, may have preserved Development Corp. of America as a public company. Officers of the Hollywood (Fla.) real estate company had considered taking the company private, recalls Pedro Diaz, its chief financial officer. Then they had thought of economizing by cutting the dividend on the common stock. "But on second thought, we just decided to issue subordinated 12% debentures in exchange for about 27% of our common stock," he says. The stock, trading at about 5½ before the swap, rose to about 16 a year later.

That may, in part, explain why Advanced Systems' exchange of preferred shares was so well received. "Investors would do well to scout for companies that are in the process of, or about to offer, such a preferred-for-common stock swap," says Coles. Such offers have yet to snowball on Wall Street, "but we expect to see many more companies in the later half of the 1980s use this kind of a stock swap," says Coles.

Companies whose stocks are trading below their year-earlier prices, and which have authorized-but-unissued preferred stock, are likely to resort to such swaps. A number of steel companies, suggests Coles, could find the swaps rewarding. Among other logical candidates, she adds, are Johnson & Johnson, Gulf & Western Industries, Bristol-Meyers, and Revlon.

CHAPTER 16 Corporations: Paid-In Capital, Retained Earnings, Dividends, and Treasury Stock

LEARNING OBJECTIVES

After studying this chapter, you should be able to:

1. Identify the different sources of paid-in capital and describe how they would be presented in a balance sheet.
2. Give journal entries for a cash dividend, a large or small stock dividend, a stock split, a retained earnings appropriation, and an acquisition and reissuance of treasury stock.
3. Define extraordinary items and prior period adjustments and show their proper presentation in the financial statements.
4. Describe the proper accounting treatment of changes in accounting principle.
5. Define and use correctly the new terms in the glossary.

As owners of a corporation, stockholders provide much of the capital for the operation of the corporation. On the balance sheet, this ownership is shown as paid-in capital under stockholders' equity. Also included in stockholders' equity is the capital accumulated through the retention of earnings of the corporation (retained earnings). Paid-in capital is a relatively permanent portion of stockholders' equity; retained earnings are a relatively temporary portion of corporate capital and are the source of stockholders' dividends.

The preceding chapter discussed the paid-in capital obtained by issuing shares of stock for cash, other property, or services. In this chapter you will learn about additional sources of paid-in capital and other matters affecting stockholders' equity.

■ PAID-IN (OR CONTRIBUTED) CAPITAL

As you learned in the preceding chapter, paid-in capital, or contributed capital, refers to all of the contributed capital of a corporation, including that carried in the capital stock accounts. In the general ledger, no single account titled "Paid-in Capital" is maintained. Instead, a separate account is established for each source of paid-in capital.

Illustration 16.1 summarizes several sources of stockholders' equity and gives examples of general ledger account titles used to record increases and decreases in capital from each of these sources. Some of these general ledger accounts were discussed in Chapter 15; the others will be discussed in this chapter.

Illustration 16.1

Sources of Stockholders' Equity

Sources of stockholders' equity	Illustrative general ledger account titles
I. Capital paid in (or contributed).	
A. For, or assigned to, shares:	
1. Issued to the extent of par or stated value or the amount received for shares without par or stated value.	Common Stock 5% Preferred Stock
2. Subscribed but not issued to the extent of par or stated value or the amount subscribed for shares without par or stated value.	Common (Preferred) Stock Subscribed
3. To be distributed as a stock dividend.	Stock Dividend Distributable—Common (Preferred)
4. In addition to par or stated value:	
a. In excess of par.	Paid-In Capital in Excess of Par Value—Common (Preferred)
b. In excess of stated value.	Paid-In Capital in Excess of Stated Value—Common (Preferred)
c. Resulting from declaration of stock dividends.	Paid-In Capital—Stock Dividends
d. Resulting from reissue of treasury stock at a price above its acquisition price.	Paid-In Capital—Common (Preferred) Treasury Stock Transactions
B. Other than for shares, whether from shareholders or from others.	Paid-In Capital—Donations
II. Capital accumulated by retention of earnings (retained earnings).	
A. Appropriated retained earnings.	Appropriation per Loan Agreement
B. Free and unappropriated retained earnings.	Retained Earnings (Unappropriated)

The stockholders' equity section of the balance sheet should show the different sources of the corporation's paid-in capital since this is important information. For example, assume a corporation has issued both preferred and common stock at various times and amounts. The total paid-in capital in excess of par value currently is $25,000 for preferred stock and $15,000 for common stock. If only one Paid-In Capital in Excess of Par Value account were established for all classes of stock, it would be impossible to determine whether the capital came from preferred stock or from common stock issuances.

Paid-In Capital—Stock Dividends

When a corporation declares a stock dividend, the corporation distributes additional shares of stock (instead of cash) to its present stockholders. In a later section, this chapter discusses and illustrates how the issuance of a stock dividend results in a credit to a Paid-In Capital—Stock Dividends account.

Paid-In Capital—Treasury Stock Transactions

Another source of capital is treasury stock transactions. Treasury stock is the corporation's own stock, either preferred or common, that has been issued and reacquired by the issuing corporation; it is legally available for reissuance. If a corporation reacquires shares of its own outstanding capital stock at one price and later reissues them at a higher price, corporate capital is increased by the difference between the two prices. If the reissue price is **less** than acquisition cost, corporate capital is decreased. Treasury stock transactions are treated at length later in this chapter.

Paid-In Capital—Donations

Occasionally, a corporation receives gifts of assets, such as a gift of a $500,000 building. These donated gifts increase stockholders' equity and are called donated capital. The entry to record the gift of a $500,000 building is a debit to Buildings and a credit to Paid-In Capital—Donations. The entry should be made in the amount of the $500,000 fair market value of the gift when received.

■ RETAINED EARNINGS

Retained earnings is that part of stockholders' equity resulting from earnings; it represents the source of certain assets received but not distributed to stockholders as dividends. Like paid-in capital, retained earnings is a source of assets received by a corporation. Paid-in capital is the actual investment by the stockholders; retained earnings is the investment by the stockholders through earnings not yet withdrawn.

The balance in the corporation's Retained Earnings account is the corporation's net income from the date the corporation began to the present, less the sum of dividends paid during this period. Net income increases Retained Earnings, while dividends decrease Retained Earnings in any given year. Thus, the balance in Retained Earnings represents the corporation's accumulated net income not distributed to stockholders.

When the Retained Earnings account has a debit balance, a deficit exists. A deficit is shown as retained earnings with a negative amount in the stockholders' equity section of the balance sheet. The title of the general ledger account need not be changed even though it contains a debit balance. The most common debits and credits made to Retained Earnings are for income (or losses) and dividends. Occasionally, other entries are made to the Retained Earnings account. Some of these entries are discussed later in the chapter.

■ PAID-IN CAPITAL AND RETAINED EARNINGS IN THE BALANCE SHEET

The following stockholders' equity section of a balance sheet presents the various sources of capital in proper form:

Stockholders' equity:
Paid-in capital:

Preferred stock, 6% $100 par value; authorized, issued, and outstanding, 4,000 shares	$ 400,000	
Common stock, no par value, $5 stated value; authorized, issued, and outstanding, 400,000 shares	2,000,000	$2,400,000
Paid-in capital—		
From preferred stock issuances*	$ 40,000	
From donations	10,000	50,000
Total paid-in capital		$2,450,000
Retained earnings		500,000
Total stockholders' equity		$2,950,000

* This label is not the exact account title but is representative of the descriptions used on balance sheets. The exact account title could be used, but shorter descriptions are often shown.

In highly condensed, published balance sheets, the details regarding the sources of the paid-in capital in excess of par or stated value are often omitted and replaced by a single item, such as:

Paid-in capital in excess of par or stated value . . $50,000

■ DIVIDENDS

Dividends are distributions of earnings by a corporation to its stockholders. Usually dividends are paid in cash, but additional shares of the corporation's own capital stock may also be distributed as dividends. Occasionally, dividends are paid in merchandise or other assets. Since dividends are the means whereby the owners of a corporation share in the earnings of the corporation, they usually are charged against retained earnings.

Before dividends can be paid, they must be declared by the board of directors and recorded in the minutes book. Three dividend dates are significant:

1. **Date of declaration.** This date indicates when the board of directors takes action in the form of a motion and declares that dividends should be paid. The board action creates the liability for dividends payable.
2. **Date of record.** This date is established by the board and means that the stockholders on the date of record will receive the dividends. The corporation's stockholders as of the date of record are determined from the corporation's records (the stockholders' ledger).
3. **Date of payment.** This date indicates when the dividend is actually paid to the stockholders.

To illustrate how these three dates relate to an actual situation, assume the board of directors of the Allen Corporation declared a cash dividend on May 5, 1987 (date of declaration). The cash dividend declared is $1.25 per share to stockholders of record on July 1, 1987 (date of record), payable on

Legality of Dividends

In the preceding chapter you learned that corporate laws differ as to their provisions on the legality of a dividend. The **legal** or **stated capital** of a corporation is established by state law as that portion of the stockholders' equity that must be maintained intact, unimpaired by dividend declarations or other distributions to stockholders. The legal capital is often established at an amount equal to the par or stated value of the shares issued or at an amount equal to a minimum price per share issued.

The objective of these state corporate laws is to protect the corporation's creditors whose claims are superior to the corporation's stockholders. To illustrate the significance of the legal capital concept, assume a corporation has severe financial difficulty and is about to go out of business. If there were no legal capital restriction on dividends, the stockholders of a corporation in financial difficulty might attempt to pay themselves a cash dividend leaving no funds available for the corporation's creditors.

The board of directors of a corporation possesses sole power to declare dividends. The legality of a dividend generally depends on the amount of retained earnings available for dividends—not on the net income of any one period or the size of the cash balance. Dividends may be paid in periods in which losses are incurred, provided retained earnings and the cash position justify the dividend. And in some states, dividends may be declared from current earnings even though there is an accumulated deficit. The financial advisability of declaring a dividend depends on the cash position of the corporation.

Liquidating Dividends

Normally, dividends are reductions of retained earnings since they are distributions of the corporation's net income. However, dividends may be distributions of contributed capital. These dividends are called liquidating dividends.

Liquidating dividends are debited to a paid-in capital account. Corporations should disclose to stockholders the source of any dividends that are not distributions of net income by indicating which paid-in capital account was debited as the result of the dividend. The legality of liquidating dividends depends on the precise source of the paid-in capital and the laws of the state of incorporation.

■ RETAINED EARNINGS APPROPRIATIONS

The amount of a corporation's retained earnings that may be paid as cash dividends may be less than total retained earnings for several reasons, contractual or voluntary. For example, a loan contract may state that part of a corporation's $100,000 of retained earnings is not available for cash dividends until the loan is paid, or a board of directors may decide that assets resulting from net income should be used for plant expansion rather than cash dividends. These contractual or voluntary restrictions or limitations on retained earnings are called retained earnings appropriations.

Retained earnings appropriations may be formally recorded by transferring amounts from Retained Earnings to accounts such as "Appropriation for Loan Agreement" or "Retained Earnings Appropriated for Plant Expansion." Retained earnings appropriations are sometimes referred to as retained earnings reserves.

Appropriations of retained earnings may also be made for pending litigation, for debt retirement, for contingencies in general, and for other purposes. Such appropriations do not reduce total retained earnings. Their purpose is merely to disclose to balance sheet readers that a portion of retained earnings is not available for cash dividends. Thus, the recording of these appropriations simply guarantees that the corporation will limit its outflow of cash dividends while repaying a loan, expanding a plant, or taking on some other costly endeavor. Recording retained earnings appropriations does not involve the setting aside of cash for the indicated purpose. The establishment of a separate fund would require a specific directive from the board of directors. Thus, the only entry required to record the appropriation of $25,000 of retained earnings to fulfill the provisions in a loan agreement is:

Retained Earnings	25,000	
Appropriation per Loan Agreement		25,000
To record restriction on retained earnings.		

When the retained earnings appropriation has served its purpose of restricting dividends and the loan has been repaid, the board of directors may decide to return the appropriation intact to Retained Earnings. The entry to do this is:

Appropriation per Loan Agreement	25,000	
Retained Earnings		25,000
To return balance in Appropriation per Loan Agreement account		
to Retained Earnings.		

Retained Earnings Appropriations in the Balance Sheet

In the balance sheet, retained earnings appropriations should be shown in the stockholders' equity section as follows:

Stockholders' equity:			
Paid-in capital:			
Preferred stock, $50 par value; 500 shares authorized, issued,			
and outstanding		$25,000	
Common stock, $5 par value; 10,000 shares authorized,			
issued, and outstanding		50,000	
Total paid-in capital			$ 75,000
Retained earnings:			
Appropriated:			
Per loan agreement		$25,000	
Unappropriated		20,000	
Total retained earnings			45,000
Total stockholders' equity			$120,000

Note that a retained earnings appropriation does not reduce stockholders' equity; it merely earmarks (restricts) a portion of that equity for a specific reason.

The formal practice of recording and reporting retained earnings appropriations is a practice that is decreasing and is being replaced by footnote explanations such as the following:

> Note 7. Retained earnings restrictions. According to provisions in the loan agreement, retained earnings available for dividends are limited to $20,000.

Such footnotes appear after the formal financial statements in a section called "Notes to Financial Statements." The Retained Earnings account in the balance sheet would be referenced as follows: "Retained Earnings (see note 7) . . . $45,000."

Changes in the composition of retained earnings reveal important information about a corporation to financial statement users. A separate formal financial statement is issued to disclose such changes. This statement is called the statement of retained earnings.

■ THE STATEMENT OF RETAINED EARNINGS

Most corporations include four financial statements in their annual reports to stockholders: a balance sheet, an income statement, a statement of retained earnings, and a statement of changes in financial position (to be discussed in Chapter 19). A statement of retained earnings is a formal statement showing the items causing changes in unappropriated and appropriated retained earnings during a stated period of time. Changes in unappropriated retained earnings usually consist of the addition of net income (or deduction of net loss) and the deduction of dividends and appropriations. Changes in appropriated retained earnings consist of increases or decreases in appropriations.

A typical statement of retained earnings is shown in Illustration 16.3. The only new appropriation during 1987 was an additional $35,000 for plant expansion. This new $35,000 is added to the $25,000 beginning balance in that account and subtracted from unappropriated retained earnings.

Illustration 16.3

Statement of Retained Earnings

WARD CORPORATION Statement of Retained Earnings For Year Ended December 31, 1987		
Unappropriated retained earnings:		
January 1, 1987, balance		$180,000
Add: Net income		80,000
		$260,000
Less: Dividends	$15,000	
Appropriation for plant expansion	35,000	50,000
Unappropriated retained earnings, December 31, 1987		$210,000
Appropriated retained earnings:		
Appropriation for plant expansion, January 1, 1987, balance	$25,000	
Add: Increase in 1987	35,000	$ 60,000
Appropriation for contract obligation, January 1, 1987, balance		20,000
Appropriated retained earnings, December 31, 1987		$ 80,000
Total retained earnings, December 31, 1987		$290,000

■ TREASURY STOCK

Treasury stock is the corporation's own capital stock that has been issued and then reacquired by the corporation; it has not been canceled and is legally available for later reissuance. Thus, treasury stock is not classified as **unissued stock** because unissued stock is stock that has never been issued.

As you may recall, if a corporation has additional **authorized** but **unissued** shares of stock that are to be issued after the date of original issue, the preemptive right requires that additional authorized and unissued shares must, in most states, be offered first to existing stockholders on a prorata basis. However, treasury stock may be reissued without violating the preemptive right provisions of state laws; that is, treasury stock does not have to be offered to current stockholders on a prorata basis.

A corporation may reacquire its own capital stock as treasury stock to (1) cancel and retire the stock, (2) reissue the stock later at a higher price, (3) reduce the number of shares outstanding and thereby increase earnings per share, or (4) use the stock for issuance to employees. If the intent of reacquisition is cancellation and retirement, the treasury shares exist only until they are retired and canceled by formal reduction of the authorized capital.

Most state corporate laws consider treasury stock as issued but not outstanding for dividend or voting purposes, since the shares are no longer in the possession of stockholders. But treasury shares usually are considered to be outstanding for purposes of determining legal capital. Thus, the legal capital would include outstanding shares plus those held in the corporation's treasury. In states that consider treasury stock part of legal capital, the cost of treasury stock may not exceed the amount of retained earnings at the date the shares are reacquired. The purpose of this regulation is to protect creditors by preventing the corporation from using funds to purchase stock instead of paying its debts when the corporation is in financial difficulty. Thus, if a corporation is subject to such a law (as is assumed in this text), the retained earnings available for dividends are limited to the amount in excess of the cost of the treasury shares on hand.

Acquisition and Reissuance of Treasury Stock

When treasury stock is acquired, the stock is recorded at cost in a debit-balanced stockholders' equity account called Treasury Stock.[3] Reissuances are credited to the Treasury Stock account at the cost of acquisition. Any excess of the reissue price over cost is credited to Paid-In Capital—Treasury Stock Transactions because it represents additional paid-in capital.

To illustrate, assume that on February 18, 1987, the Hillside Corporation reacquired 100 shares of its outstanding common stock for $55 each. (The company's stockholders' equity consisted solely of common stock and retained earnings.) On April 18, 1987, the company reissued 30 shares for $58 each. The entries are:

---

[3] Another acceptable method of accounting for treasury stock transactions is called the par value method. Further discussion of the par value method is left to intermediate accounting texts.

```
1987
Feb. 18   Treasury Stock—Common (100 shares × $55) . . .      5,500
              Cash. .   .   .   .   .   .   .   .   .   .   .   .              5,500
          Acquired 100 shares of treasury stock at $55.

Apr. 18   Cash (30 shares × $58) .   .   .   .   .   .   .   .   .      1,740
              Treasury Stock—Common (30 shares × $55) .   .           1,650
              Paid-In Capital—Common Treasury Stock
                  Transactions   .   .   .   .   .   .   .   .   .   .             90
          Reissued 30 shares of treasury stock at $58; cost
          $55 per share.
```

When the reissue price of subsequent shares is **less** than the acquisition price, the difference between cost and reissue price is debited to Paid-In Capital— Common Treasury Stock Transactions. But this account is not permitted to develop a debit balance. By definition, no paid-in capital account can have a debit balance. If the Hillside Corporation reissued an additional 20 shares at $52 per share on June 12, 1987, the entry is:

```
1987
June 12   Cash (20 shares × $52)   .   .   .   .   .   .   .   .      1,040
          Paid-In Capital—Common Treasury Stock
              Transactions .   .   .   .   .   .   .   .   .   .              60
              Treasury Stock—Common (20 shares × $55).   .           1,100
          Reissued 20 shares of treasury stock at $52; cost
          $55 per share.
```

At this point, the credit balance in the Paid-In Capital—Common Treasury Stock Transactions account is $30. If the remaining 50 shares are reissued on July 16, 1987, for $53 per share, the entry is:

```
1987
July 16   Cash (50 shares × $53) .   .   .   .   .   .   .   .   .      2,650
          Paid-In Capital—Common Treasury Stock
              Transactions .   .   .   .   .   .   .   .   .   .              30
          Retained Earnings .   .   .   .   .   .   .   .   .   .              70
              Treasury Stock—Common (50 shares × $55) .   .           2,750
          Reissued 50 shares of treasury stock at $53; cost
          $55 per share.
```

Note that the Paid-In Capital—Common Treasury Stock Transactions account credit balance has been exhausted. If more than $30 is debited to that account, it would develop a debit balance. Thus, the remaining $70 of the excess of cost over reissue price is regarded as a special distribution to the stockholders involved and is debited to the Retained Earnings account.

When stockholders **donate** stock to a corporation, the treatment is slightly different. Since donated treasury shares have no cost, only a memo entry is made when they are received.[4] The only formal entry required is to debit Cash and credit the Paid-In Capital—Donations account when the stock is reissued. For example, if donated treasury stock is sold for $5,000, the entry is:

```
Cash   .   .   .   .   .   .   .   .   .   .   .   .   .   .   .   .   .   .      5,000
    Paid-In Capital—Donations   .   .   .   .   .   .   .   .   .           5,000
    To record the sale of donated treasury stock.
```

---

[4] The method illustrated here is called the *memo* method. Other acceptable methods of accounting for donated stock are the *cost* method and *par value* method. These latter two methods are discussed in intermediate accounting texts.

Treasury Stock in the Balance Sheet

When treasury stock is held on a balance sheet date, it customarily is shown in that statement at cost, as a deduction from the sum of total paid-in capital and retained earnings, as follows:

Stockholders' equity:
  Paid-in capital:
    Common stock, authorized and issued, 20,000 shares, of which 2,000 shares
      are in the treasury $200,000
  Retained earnings (including $22,000 restricted by acquisition of treasury stock) . .   80,000
    Total paid-in capital and retained earnings $280,000
  Less: Treasury stock at cost, 2,000 shares   22,000
    Total stockholders' equity $258,000

Stockholders' Equity in the Balance Sheet

Much of what has been discussed so far in Chapters 15 and 16 can be summarized through presentation of the stockholders' equity section of the balance sheet of a hypothetical corporation (Illustration 16.4). This partial balance sheet shows (1) the amount of capital assigned to shares outstanding; (2) the capital contributed for outstanding shares in addition to that assigned to the shares; (3) other forms of paid-in capital; and (4) retained earnings, appropriated and unappropriated.

Illustration 16.4

Stockholders' Equity Section of the Balance Sheet

HYPOTHETICAL CORPORATION
Partial Balance Sheet
December 31, 1987

Stockholders' Equity:
  Paid-in capital:
    Preferred stock, 8%, $100 par value; 2,000 shares authorized,
      issued, and outstanding . . . . $ 200,000
    Common stock, $10 par value; authorized, 100,000 shares,
      issued, 80,000 shares of which 1,000 are held in the
      treasury $800,000
    Stock dividend distributable on common stock on January 15,
      1988, 7,900 shares   79,000   879,000
    Paid-in capital—
      From common stock issuances . . . . $ 40,000
      From stock dividends   60,000
      From treasury stock transactions   30,000
      From donations   50,000   180,000
      Total paid-in capital $1,259,000
  Retained earnings:
    Appropriated:
      Per loan agreement $250,000
    Unappropriated (restricted to the extent of $20,000, the cost of
      treasury shares held)   150,000
      Total retained earnings   400,000
    Total paid-in capital and retained earnings $1,659,000
  Less: Treasury stock, common, 1,000 shares at cost   20,000
    Total stockholders' equity $1,639,000

■ NET INCOME INCLUSIONS AND EXCLUSIONS

Accounting has long faced the problem of what to include in the net income reported for a period. Should net income include only the revenues and expenses related to normal operations? Or should it include unusual, nonrecurring gains and losses? And further, should the determination of net income for 1987, for example, include an item that can be clearly associated with a prior year, such as additional federal income taxes for 1986? Or should such items, including corrections of errors, be carried directly to retained earnings? How are the effects of making a change in accounting principle (like a change in depreciation methods) to be reported?

APB Opinion No. 9 (December 1966) sought to provide answers to some of these questions. The *Opinion* directed that unusual and nonrecurring items that have an earnings or loss effect be classified as extraordinary items (reported in the income statement) or as prior period adjustments (reported in the statement of retained earnings). Extraordinary items were to be reported separately after net income from regular continuing activities.

The reporting of extraordinary items, changes in accounting principle, and prior period adjustments is shown in Illustrations 16.5 (p. 626) and 16.7 (p. 629). For these illustrations, assume the following facts:

1. Anson Company had a taxable gain in 1987 of $40,000 from voluntary early retirement of debt (extraordinary item).
2. The company changed depreciation methods in 1987 (change in accounting principle), and the cumulative effect of the change was a $6,000 decrease in prior years' depreciation expense.
3. In 1987, it was discovered that the $200,000 cost of land acquired in 1986 had been expensed for both financial accounting and tax purposes. A prior period adjustment was made in 1987.
4. Anson Company has 1,000,000 shares of common stock outstanding.
5. The current tax rate is 40%. As a separate legal entity, corporations are required to pay federal income taxes.

Extraordinary Items

Prior to 1973, there was a tendency for companies to report a gain or loss as an extraordinary item if it was **either** unusual in nature or occurred infrequently. As a result, companies were inconsistent in the financial reporting of certain gains and losses. This inconsistency led to the issuance of *APB Opinion No. 30* (September 1973). *Opinion No. 30* redefined extraordinary items as those that are unusual in nature **and** that occur infrequently. Note that both conditions must be met—unusual nature and infrequent occurrence. Whether an item is unusual and infrequent is to be determined in light of the environment in which the company operates. Examples include gains or losses that are the direct result of a major casualty (a flood), a confiscation of property by a foreign government, or a prohibition under a newly enacted law. *FASB Statement No. 4* further directs that gains and losses from the voluntary early **extinguishment** (retirement) of debt are extraordinary items.

Extraordinary items are to be included in the determination of periodic

Illustration 16.5   Income Statement

ANSON COMPANY
Income Statement
For the Year Ended December 31, 1987

Net sales		$41,000,000
Other revenues		2,250,000
Total revenue		$43,250,000
Cost of goods sold	$22,000,000	
Administrative, selling, and general expenses	12,000,000	34,000,000
Net income before income taxes		$ 9,250,000
Federal income taxes (40%)		3,700,000
Net income before extraordinary item and the cumulative effect of a change in accounting principle (net income from regular operations)		$ 5,550,000
Extraordinary item:		
Gain on voluntary early retirement of debt	$ 40,000	
Less: Tax effect (40%)	16,000	24,000
Net income after extraordinary item		$ 5,574,000
Change in accounting principle:		
Cumulative positive effect on prior years' income of changing to a different depreciation method (net of 40% tax effect of $2,400)		3,600
Net income		$ 5,577,600
Earnings per share of common stock:		
Net income before extraordinary item and the cumulative effect of a change in accounting principle		$5.550
Extraordinary item		0.024
Cumulative effect on prior years' income of changing to a different depreciation method		0.004
Net income		$5.578

Callouts: Income before extraordinary item · Income after extraordinary item · Earnings per share · Extraordinary item · Change in accounting principle net income, but disclosed separately (net of their tax effects, if any) in the income statement. As shown in the income statement presented in Illustration 16.5, income before extraordinary items must be reported and then income after extraordinary items is reported. **Income before extraordinary items** is income from operations less applicable income taxes.

Gains or losses related to ordinary business activities are not extraordinary items regardless of their size. For example, material write-downs of uncollectible receivables, obsolete inventories, and intangible assets are not extraordinary items. But such items may be separately disclosed as part of net income from regular operations.

Illustration 16.6 shows that in a sample of 600 companies for the years 1980–83, the number reporting extraordinary items has increased each year. Also, the total number of extraordinary items reported has increased each year.

Illustration 16.6

Extraordinary Items

	1983	1982	1981	1980
Number of companies:				
Presenting extraordinary items . . .	84	69	53	47
Not presenting extraordinary items . .	516	531	547	553
Total companies	600	600	600	600
Total extraordinary items	95	79	57	48

Source: Based on American Institute of Certified Public Accountants, *Accounting Trends & Techniques* (New York: AICPA, 1984), p. 303.

Changes in Accounting Principle

A company's reported net income and financial position can be altered materially by changes in accounting principle. **Changes in accounting principle** are changes in accounting methods pertaining to such items as inventory and depreciation. Examples of changes in accounting principle are a change in inventory valuation method from Fifo to Lifo or a change in depreciation method from accelerated to straight line. According to *APB Opinion No. 20,* a company should consistently apply the same accounting methods from one period to another. But a change may be made if the newly adopted method is preferable and if the change is adequately disclosed in the financial statements. In the period in which a change in principle is made, the nature of the change, its justification, and its effect on net income must be disclosed in the financial statements. Also, the cumulative effect of the change on prior years' income (net of tax) must be shown in the income statement for the year of change (see Illustration 16.5).

As an example of a change in accounting principle, assume that Anson Company purchased a machine on January 2, 1985, for $30,000. The machine has a useful life of five years with no scrap value expected. Anson Company decided to depreciate the machine for financial reporting purposes using the sum-of-the-years'-digits method. At the beginning of 1987, the company decided to change to the straight-line method of depreciation. The cumulative effect of the change in accounting principle is computed as follows:

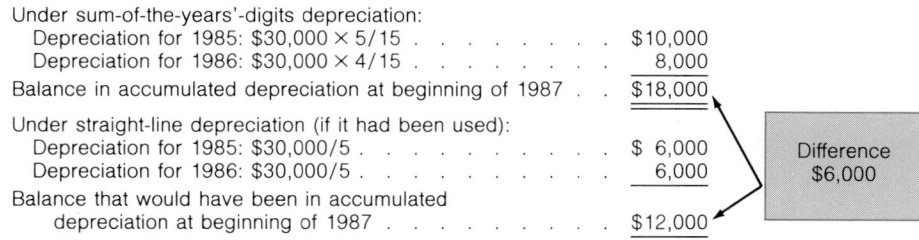

Under sum-of-the-years'-digits depreciation:
Depreciation for 1985: $30,000 × 5/15 . . . . $10,000
Depreciation for 1986: $30,000 × 4/15   8,000
Balance in accumulated depreciation at beginning of 1987 . . $18,000

Under straight-line depreciation (if it had been used):
Depreciation for 1985: $30,000/5 . . . . $ 6,000
Depreciation for 1986: $30,000/5   6,000
Balance that would have been in accumulated
    depreciation at beginning of 1987 . . . . $12,000

Difference
$6,000

The accumulated depreciation account balance would have been $6,000 less under the straight-line method. Also, depreciation expense over the two years would have been $6,000 less. Assume that federal income tax would have been $2,400 more ($6,000 × 0.4). The net effect of the change is $6,000 − $2,400 = $3,600. Therefore, Anson Company corrects the appropriate account balances by reducing (debiting) the accumulated depreciation account balance by $6,000, crediting an account entitled Cumulative Effect of Change in Accounting Principle for $3,600 (which will be closed to Retained Earnings during the normal closing process), and crediting Federal Income Taxes Payable for $2,400. The journal entry would be:

Accumulated Depreciation—Machinery   6,000
    Cumulative Effect of Change in Accounting Principle . . .   3,600
    Federal Income Taxes Payable   2,400
    To record the effect of changing from sum-of-the-years'-digits
    depreciation to straight-line depreciation on machinery.

The cumulative effect of changing to the straight-line depreciation method is reported in Illustration 16.5 at the after-tax amount of $3,600.

Prior Period Adjustments

According to *FASB Statement No 16,* **prior period adjustments** consist almost entirely of corrections of errors in previously published financial statements. Corrections of abnormal, nonrecurring errors that may have been caused by the improper use of an accounting principle or by mathematical mistakes are considered to be prior period adjustments. Normal, recurring corrections and adjustments, which follow inevitably from the use of estimates in accounting practice, are not treated as prior period adjustments. Also, mistakes corrected in the same year they occur are not prior period adjustments. To illustrate a prior period adjustment, suppose that land purchased in 1986 by the Anson Company at a total cost of $200,000 was recorded in an expense account instead of in the Land account. Discovery of the error on May 1, 1987, after publication of the 1986 financial statements, would require a prior period adjustment. The adjustment would be recorded directly in the Retained Earnings account. Assuming the error had resulted in an $80,000 underpayment of taxes in 1986, the entry to correct the error would be:

1987
May 1 Land 200,000
            Federal Income Taxes Payable   80,000
            Retained Earnings (or Prior Period Adjustment—
            Land)   120,000
        To correct an accounting error expensing land.

Prior period adjustments are not reported in the income statement but are shown in the financial statements as adjustments to the opening balance of retained earnings in the statement of retained earnings (Illustration 16.7).

Illustration 16.7   *Statement of Retained Earnings*

Prior period adjustment

ANSON COMPANY
Statement of Retained Earnings
For the Year Ended December 31, 1987

Retained earnings, January 1, 1987	$ 5,000,000
Prior period adjustment:	
Correction of error of expensing land (net of tax effect of $80,000)	120,000
Adjusted retained earnings, January 1, 1987	$ 5,120,000
Add: Net income	5,577,600
	$10,697,600
Less: Dividends	500,000
Retained earnings, December 31, 1987	$10,197,600

Accounting for Tax Effects

Most extraordinary items, changes in accounting principle, and prior period adjustments will affect the amount of income taxes required to be paid by a corporation. A question arises as to how to report the income tax effect of these items. *APB Opinion No. 9* recommends that all of these items be reported **net of their tax effects,** as shown in Illustration 16.5 and 16.7. Net-of-tax effect means that items are shown at the dollar amounts remaining after deducting the income tax effects. Thus, the total effect of an extraordinary item, change in accounting principle, or prior period adjustment is shown in one place. Net income before extraordinary items represents the results of transactions (including income taxes) that are normal for the business and may be expected to recur. The tax effect of an item may be shown separately, as it is for the gain on voluntary early retirement of debt in Illustration 16.5. Alternatively, the tax effect may be mentioned parenthetically with only the net amount shown (see change in accounting principle in Illustration 16.5 and correction of error illustrated in 16.7).

■ EARNINGS PER SHARE

A major item of interest to investors and potential investors is how much a company earned during the current year, both in total and for each share of stock outstanding. The earnings per share amount is calculated only for the common shares of ownership. Earnings per share (EPS) is computed as net income available to common stockholders divided by the number of common shares outstanding. Income available to common stockholders is net income less any dividends on preferred stock.

EPS is usually calculated and presented for each major category on the face of the income statement. In other words, an EPS calculation is made for ordinary income after taxes, extraordinary items, and changes in accounting principle. Note in Illustration 16.5 that the EPS amounts are reported at the bottom of the income statement.

Stockholders can compare the EPS of two companies more easily than total dollars of earnings. EPS is useful in making decisions about the price to pay for stock and the return on that investment. Also, EPS is related to market price per share of stock in that if EPS increases, generally market price per share also increases. EPS is covered in more detail in Chapter 20.

Summary of Illustrative Financial Statements

Note especially the following facts in Illustrations 16.5 and 16.7:

1. Net income of $5,550,000 before the extraordinary item and the cumulative effect of an accounting change is more representative of the continuing earning power of the company than is the final net income figure of $5,577,600.
2. The gain on retirement of debt is reported at its actual impact upon the company—that is, net of its tax effect.
3. EPS is reported both before ($5.550) and after ($5.578) the extraordinary item and the cumulative effect of a change in accounting principle.
4. The correction of the $200,000 error adds only $120,000 to retained earnings. This is because the mistake was included in the 1986 tax return and taxes were therefore underpaid by $80,000. In the 1987 return, the $80,000 of taxes would have to be paid.

■ POSSIBLE FUTURE CHANGE IN INCOME STATEMENT FORMAT

In December 1984, the FASB published *Concepts Statement No. 5, "Recognition and Measurement in Financial Statements of Business Enterprise."*[5] Rather than suggesting radical changes in present accounting practice, the Concepts Statement endorses present practice while allowing for gradual evolutionary changes. One such future change may be in the format of the income statement. The statement may become a statement of earnings and comprehensive income. "Earnings" would generally be computed like income after extraordinary items is presently calculated. Then cumulative account adjustments (such as changes in accounting principle) and other nonowner changes in equity would be added or deducted in arriving at "comprehensive income." The lower part of the statement would appear as follows:

Earnings	xx
+or− Cumulative account adjustments (e.g., cumulative effect of changes in accounting principle)	xx
+or− Other nonowner changes in equity (e.g., gains or losses on market changes in noncurrent marketable equity securities*) . .	xx
Comprehensive income	xx

* This item is discussed in Chapter 18.

---

[5] FASB, "Recognition and Measurement in Financial Statements of Business Enterprises," *Statement of Financial Accounting Concepts No. 5* (Stamford, Conn., 1984). Copyright © by the Financial Accounting Standards Board, High Ridge Park, Stamford, Connecticut 06905, U.S.A. Copies of the complete document are available from the FASB.

Concepts statements are part of the conceptual framework. This framework serves as a guide for the FASB in establishing accounting standards that resolve future accounting and reporting questions. Therefore, we are not certain that this change in format will be required in the future but wanted you to be aware of the possible change.

■ *SUMMARY*

The term *paid-in-capital* is applied to all of the contributed capital of a corporation, including that part carried in the capital stock accounts. The stockholders' equity section of the balance sheet should show the different sources of paid-in capital.

Retained earnings is that part of stockholders' equity resulting from net income. The balance in Retained Earnings consists of net income (or loss) of the corporation from the date business began to the present, less total dividends declared and certain other deductions during the same period.

The typical dividend is a cash distribution of corporate income to stockholders. A corporation may also distribute additional shares of its own capital stock (a stock dividend) as a dividend.

Stock dividends of less than 20% to 25% are recorded at current market value. Stock dividends greater than 20% to 25% are recorded at par or stated value. The amount transferred to the capital stock account is equal to the par or stated value of the shares issued. For stocks without par or stated value, the amount is established by law or by the board of directors.

A stock split is a distribution of additional shares of the issuing company's stock for which the corporation receives no assets. The par value per share is usually reduced (e.g., in a two-for-one split, the par value per share is usually halved) so that the total dollar amount credited to Common Stock remains the same. Retained earnings appropriations are restrictions on the declaration of cash dividends. Retained earnings appropriations are reported as a part of total retained earnings in the balance sheet.

Changes in retained earnings reveal important information about a company to interested parties. Thus, a statement of retained earnings is prepared, which shows the items that caused increases or decreases in retained earnings during a specified period of time.

Shares of capital stock that have been issued and are then reacquired by the issuing corporation are called treasury stock. Such stock is considered issued but not outstanding. The cost of treasury stock is reported as a deduction from total stockholders' equity. If treasury stock is reissued at more than cost, the difference between cost and reissue price is recorded in a Paid-In Capital—Common (Preferred) Treasury Stock Transactions account. If treasury stock is reissued at less than cost, the Paid-in Capital—Common (Preferred) Treasury Stock Transactions account is debited for the difference between cost and reissue price until its credit balance is exhausted. Any remaining debit needed to balance the journal entry is to Retained Earnings.

Donated treasury shares have no cost. The only formal entry made for them is to credit the entire amount received upon reissue to a Paid-In Capital—Donations account.

Extraordinary items are gains or losses that are both unusual in nature and infrequent in occurrence. They are reported on the income statement, net of their tax effects, separately from the results of ordinary operations. Changes in accounting principle also must be separately disclosed (net of their tax effect) in the income statement. Prior period adjustments are material adjustments primarily resulting from current corrections of accounting errors that occurred in prior years. They are treated as adjustments (net of their tax effect) to the opening balance of retained earnings in the statement of retained earnings.

This chapter completes the study of stockholders' equity. In Chapter 17, you will learn about bonds—another source of capital for companies and a vehicle for investment by investors. Perhaps someday you will buy bonds issued by a company.

NEW TERMS INTRODUCED IN CHAPTER 16

Cash dividends

Cash distributions of net income by a corporation to its stockholders (615).

Changes in accounting principle

Changes in accounting methods pertaining to such items as inventory and depreciation (627).

Contributed capital

All capital paid into a corporation, including that carried in capital stock accounts (612).

Date of declaration (of dividends)

The date the board of directors takes action in the form of a motion that dividends be paid (614).

Date of payment (of dividends)

The date of actual payment of a dividend, or issuance of additional shares in the case of a stock dividend (614).

Date of record (of dividends)

The date established by the board to determine who will receive a dividend (614).

Deficit

A debit balance in the Retained Earnings account (613).

Dividends

Distribution of earnings by a corporation to its stockholders (614).

Dividends (cash)

See Cash dividends.

Dividends (stock)

See Stock dividends.

Donated capital

Results from donation of assets to the corporation, which increases stockholders' equity (613).

Earnings per share (EPS)

Earnings to the common stockholders on a per share basis, computed as net income available to common stockholders divided by the number of common shares outstanding (629).

Extraordinary items

Items that are unusual in nature and that occur infrequently; reported in the income statement net of their tax effects, if any (625).

Income available to common stockholders

Net income less any dividends on preferred stock (629).

Income before extraordinary items

Income from operations less applicable income taxes, if any (627).

Liquidating dividends

Dividends that are a return of contributed capital, not a distribution chargeable to retained earnings (619).

Net-of-tax effect

Used for extraordinary items, prior period adjustments, and changes in accounting principle, whereby items are shown at the dollar amounts remaining after deducting the effects of such items on income taxes, if any, payable currently (629).

Paid-in capital

All of the contributed capital of a corporation, including that carried in capital stock accounts. When the words *paid-in capital* are included in the account title, the account contains capital contributed in addition to that assigned to the shares issued and recorded in the capital stock accounts (612).

Paid-In Capital—Treasury Stock Transactions

The account credited when treasury stock is reissued for more than its cost; this account is debited to the extent of its credit balance when such shares are reissued at less than cost (622).

Prior period adjustments

Consist almost entirely of corrections of errors in previously published financial statements. Prior period adjustments are reported in the statement of retained earnings net of their tax effects, if any (628).

Retained earnings

That part of stockholders' equity resulting from earnings; the account to which the results of corporate activity, including prior period adjustments, are carried and to which dividends and certain items resulting from capital transactions are charged (613).

Retained earnings appropriations

Contractual or voluntary restrictions or limitations on retained earnings that reduce the amount of dividends that may be declared (619).

Statement of retained earnings

A formal statement showing the items causing changes in unappropriated and appropriated retained earnings during a stated period of time (621).

Stock dividends

Dividends that are payable in additional shares of the declaring corporation's capital stock (616).

Stock Dividend Distributable—Common account

The stockholders' equity account that is credited for the par or stated value of the shares distributable when recording the declaration of a stock dividend (617).

Stock split

A distribution of additional shares of the issuing corporation's stock for which the corporation receives no assets. The purpose of a stock split is to cause a large reduction in the market price per share of the outstanding stock (618).

Treasury stock

Shares of capital stock issued and reacquired by the issuing corporation; they have not been formally canceled and are available for reissuance (613, 622).

DEMONSTRATION PROBLEM 16–1

The Benston Corporation has outstanding 10,000 shares of $100 par value common stock.

Required: Prepare the entries to record:

a.   The declaration of a cash dividend of $1 per share.
b.   The declaration of a stock dividend of 10% at a time when the market value per share is $125.
c.   The declaration of a stock dividend of 40% at a time when the market value per share is $130.

Solution to demonstration problem 16–1

a.   Retained earnings (or Dividends)   10,000
       Dividends Payable   10,000
    To record declaration of a cash dividend.

b.   Retained Earnings (or Stock Dividends) (1,000 × $125). .   125,000
       Stock Dividend Distributable—Common (1,000 × $100)   100,000
       Paid-In Capital—Stock Dividends   25,000
    To record declaration of a small stock dividend (10%).

c.   Retained Earnings (4,000 × $100)   400,000
       Stock Dividend Distributable—Common   400,000
    To record declaration of a large stock dividend (40%).

DEMONSTRATION PROBLEM 16–2

Following are selected transactions of the Morgan Company:

Transactions:

1. The company acquired 200 shares of its own $100 par value common stock, previously issued at a premium of 5%, for $20,600 cash.
2. Fifty of the treasury shares were reissued at $110 per share, cash.
3. Seventy of the treasury shares were reissued at $95 per share, cash.
4. Stockholders of the corporation donated 100 shares of their common stock to the company.
5. The 100 shares of treasury stock received by donation were reissued for $9,000.

Required: Prepare the necessary journal entries to record the above transactions.

Solution to demonstration problem 16–2

1. Treasury Stock 20,600
    Cash 20,600
    Acquired 200 shares at $20,600 ($103 per share).

2. Cash (50 × $110 per share) 5,500
    Treasury Stock (50 × $103 per share) 5,150
    Paid-In Capital—Treasury Stock Transactions 350
    Reissued 50 shares at $110 per share; cost is $5,150.

3. Cash (70 × $95 per share) 6,650
    Paid-In Capital—Treasury Stock Transactions 350
    Retained Earnings 210
    Treasury Stock (70 × $103 per share) 7,210
    Reissued 70 shares at $95 per share; cost is $7,210.

4. Stockholders donated 100 shares of common stock to the company.

5. Cash 9,000
    Paid-In Capital—Donations (100 × $90 per share) . . . 9,000
    Reissued donated shares at $90 per share.

DEMONSTRATION PROBLEM 16–3

Selected account balances of the Clark Company at December 31, 1987, are:

Common stock—no par value; 100,000 shares authorized, issued, and outstanding; stated value of $20 per share	2,000,000
Retained earnings	570,000
Dividends payable (in cash, declared December 15 on preferred stock)	16,000
Preferred stock—8%, par value, $200; 1,000 shares authorized, issued, and outstanding	200,000
Paid-in capital from donation of plant site	100,000
Paid-in capital in excess of par value—preferred	8,000

Required: Present in good form the stockholders' equity section of the balance sheet.

Solution to demonstration problem 16-3

CLARK CORPORATION
Partial Balance Sheet
December 31, 1987

Stockholders' Equity:
Paid-in capital:
Preferred stock, 8%, par value, $200; 1,000 shares authorized,
issued, and outstanding . . . . $ 200,000
Common stock, no par value, stated value of $20 per share;
100,000 shares authorized, issued, and outstanding   2,000,000
Paid-in capital from donation of plant site   100,000
Paid-in capital in excess of par value—preferred   8,000
Total paid-in capital $2,308,000
Retained earnings   570,000
Total stockholders' equity $2,878,000

QUESTIONS

1. What are the two main elements of stockholders' equity in a corporation? Explain the difference between them.

2. Name several sources of paid-in capital. Would it suffice to maintain one account called Paid-In Capital for all sources of paid-in capital? Why or why not?

3. What is the effect of each of the following on the total stockholders' equity of a corporation: *(a)* declaration of a cash dividend, *(b)* payment of a cash dividend already declared, *(c)* declaration of a stock dividend, and *(d)* issuance of a stock dividend already declared?

4. The following dates are associated with a cash dividend of $50,000: July 15, July 31, and August 15. Identify each of the three dates, and give the journal entry required on each date, if any.

5. How should a declared but unpaid cash dividend be shown on the balance sheet? How should a declared but unissued stock dividend be shown?

6. On May 8, the board of directors of the Tanner Corporation declared a dividend, payable on June 5 to stockholders of record on May 17. On May 10, Power sold his capital stock in the Tanner Corporation directly to Bright for $10,000, endorsing his stock certificate and giving it to Bright. Bright placed the stock

certificate in her safe. On May 30, Bright sent the certificate to the transfer agent of the Tanner Corporation for transfer. Who received the dividend? Why?

7. What are liquidating dividends?

8. What is the purpose of a retained earnings appropriation?

9. Does accounting for treasury stock resemble accounting for an asset? Is treasury stock an asset? If not, where is it properly shown in a balance sheet?

10. What are some possible reasons for a corporation to acquire its own capital stock as treasury stock?

11. What are extraordinary items? Where and how are they reported?

12. Give an example of a change in accounting principle. How are the effects of changes in accounting principle reported?

13. What are prior period adjustments? Where and how are they reported?

14. Why are stockholders and potential investors interested in the amount of a corporation's EPS? What does the EPS amount reveal that total earnings do not?

EXERCISES

E-1

Prepare stockholders' equity section of balance sheet

The trial balance of the Cane Corporation at December 31, 1987, had the following account balances:

Common Stock, no par value; 200,000 shares authorized, issued, and outstanding; stated value of $5 per share	$1,000,000
Notes Payable, 12% due May 1, 1988	125,000
Retained Earnings, Unappropriated	625,000
Dividends Payable in Cash, declared December 15, on preferred stock	3,000
Appropriation per Loan Agreement	120,000
Preferred Stock, 6%, par value $50; 2,000 shares authorized, issued, and outstanding	100,000
Paid-In Capital in Excess of Stated Value—Common Stock . . .	75,000
Paid-In Capital in Excess of Par Value—Preferred Stock	10,000

Present in good form the stockholders' equity section of the balance sheet.

E-2

Prepare journal entries for cash dividends

Leonard Company has issued all of its authorized 5,000 shares of $50 par value common stock. On February 1, 1987, the board of directors declared a dividend of $1.50 per share payable on March 15, 1987, to stockholders of record on March 1, 1987. Give the necessary journal entries.

E-3

Prepare journal entries for stock split and small stock dividend

May Corporation's stockholders' equity consisted of 30,000 authorized shares of $20 par value common stock, of which 15,000 shares had been issued at par, and retained earnings of $750,000. The company then split its stock, two for one, by changing the par value of the old shares and issuing new $10 par shares.

a. Give the required journal entry to record the stock split.
b. Suppose instead that the company declared and later issued a 10% stock dividend. Give the required journal entries, assuming that the market value on the date of declaration is $25 per share.

E-4

Prepare journal entries for cash dividend when treasury stock is held

The stockholders' equity section of Howard Company's balance sheet on December 31, 1987, shows 100,000 shares of authorized and issued $20 stated value common stock, of which 9,000 shares are held in the treasury. On this date, the board of directors declared a cash dividend of $2 per share payable on January 21, 1988, to stockholders of record on January 10. Give dated journal entries for the above.

E-5

Prepare journal entry for small stock dividend and discuss large stock dividend

Swanson Company has outstanding 75,000 shares of common stock without par or stated value, which were issued at an average price of $18 per share, and retained earnings of $720,000. The current market price of the common stock is $27 per share. Total authorized stock consists of 500,000 shares.

a. Give the required entry to record the declaration of a 10% stock dividend.
b. If, alternatively, the company declared a 30% stock dividend, what additional information would you need before making a journal entry to record the dividend?

E-6

Prepare journal entry for appropriation of retained earnings and explain

The balance sheet of Echols Company contains the following:

Appropriation per loan agreement $750,000

a. Give the journal entry made to create this account.
b. Explain the reason for the appropriation's existence and its manner of presentation in the balance sheet.

E-7

Prepare journal entries for acquisition and reissuance of treasury stock

Trestle Company had outstanding 50,000 shares of $30 stated value common stock, all issued at $36 per share, and had retained earnings of $1,200,000. The company reacquired 2,000 shares of its stock for cash at book value from the widow of a deceased stockholder.

a. Give the entry to record the reacquisition of the stock.
b. Give the entry to record the subsequent reissuance of this stock at $75 per share.
c. Give the entry required if the stock is instead reissued at $45 per share and there have been no prior treasury stock transactions.

E-8

Prepare journal entry(ies) for reissuance of donated stock

Merlin Company received 200 shares of its $25 stated value common stock on December 1, 1987, as a donation from a stockholder. On December 15, 1987, it reissued the stock for $7,800 cash. Give the journal entry or entries necessary for these transactions.

E-9

Prepare income statement and statement of retained earnings

April Company has revenues of $20 million, expenses of $16 million, a tax-deductible earthquake loss (its first such loss) of $1 million, and a tax-deductible loss of $1.5 million resulting from the voluntary early extinguishment (retirement) of debt. The income tax rate is 40%. The company's beginning-of-the-year retained earnings were $7.5 million, and a dividend of $500,000 was declared.

a. Prepare an income statement for the year.
b. Prepare a statement of retained earnings for the year.

E-10

Prepare statement of retained earnings

The Sherwin Company had retained earnings of $21,000 as of January 1, 1987. In 1987, Sherwin Company had sales of $60,000, cost of goods sold of $36,000, and other operating expenses, excluding taxes, of $12,000. In 1987, Sherwin Company discovered that it had, in error, depreciated land over the last three years resulting in a balance in the accumulated depreciation account of $12,000. The tax rate for Sherwin Company is 40%. Present in proper form a statement of retained earnings for the year ended December 31, 1987.

E-11

Calculate EPS; present information in income statement format

The following information relates to the L. M. Stevens Corporation for the year ended December 31, 1987:

Common stock outstanding	75,000 shares
Net income before extraordinary items	$952,000
Extraordinary gain	$ 90,000

Calculate EPS for the year ended December 31, 1987. Present the information in the same format as would be used in the corporation's income statement.

E-12

Calculate EPS; comment on resulting amount

The Metro Company had common stock outstanding of 200,000 and 215,000 shares at December 31, 1987 and 1988, respectively. Net income for these two years was as follows:

December 31, 1987	$1,840,000
December 31, 1988	1,920,000

a. Calculate EPS for the years ended December 31, 1987, and 1988.
b. What might the resulting figures tell a potential investor or stockholder?

PROBLEMS, SERIES A

P16–1–A

Present stockholders' equity section of balance sheet

The trial balance of the Nail Corporation as of December 31, 1987, contains the following selected balances:

Notes Payable, 17%, due May 1, 1989	$1,000,000
Allowance for Doubtful Accounts	15,000
Common Stock without par value, $5 stated value; 300,000 shares authorized, issued, and outstanding	1,500,000
Retained Earnings, Unappropriated	125,000
Dividends Payable in cash declared December 15 on preferred stock	3,500
Appropriation for Pending Litigation	150,000
Preferred Stock, 6%, $50 par value; 3,000 shares authorized issued, and outstanding	150,000
Paid-In Capital—Donations	100,000
Paid-In Capital in Excess of Par Value—Preferred	2,500

Required: Present in good form the stockholders' equity section of the balance sheet.

P16–2–A

Prepare journal entries for cash dividend and small stock dividend

The stockholders' equity section of the Justin Company's December 31, 1986, balance sheet follows:

Stockholders' equity:

Paid-In capital:	
Capital stock—common, $60 par value; authorized, 2,000 shares; issued and outstanding, 1,000 shares	$60,000
Paid-in capital in excess of par value	3,000
Total paid-in capital	$63,000
Retained earnings	24,000
Total stockholders' equity	$87,000

On July 15, 1987, the board of directors declared a cash dividend of $6 per share, which was paid on August 1, 1987. On December 1, 1987, the board declared a stock dividend of 10%, and the shares were issued on December 15, 1987. Market value of the stock was $72 on December 1 and $84 on December 15.

Required: Prepare journal entries for the above dividend transactions.

P16–3–A

Prepare journal entries for appropriations of retained earnings

The ledger of the Mooreberry Company includes the following account balances on September 30, 1987:

Appropriation for Contingencies	$ 84,000
Appropriation for Plant Expansion	156,800
Retained Earnings, Unappropriated	280,000

During the month of October 1987, the company took action to:

1. Increase the appropriation for contingencies by $25,200.
2. Decrease the appropriation for plant expansion by $65,800.
3. Establish an appropriation per loan agreement, with an annual increase of $21,000.
4. Declare a cash dividend of $63,000.

Required: Prepare the general journal entries to record the transactions of the Mooreberry Company.

P16-4-A

Present statement of retained earnings

Using the information given in Problem 16-3-A, prepare a statement of retained earnings for the Mooreberry Company for the period ended October 31, 1987.

P16-5-A

Prepare journal entries for retained earnings appropriation and small stock dividend

Following are selected transactions of the Allana Corporation:

Transactions:

1982

Dec. 31   By action of the board of directors, $90,000 of retained earnings was appropriated to provide for future expansion of the company's main building. (On the last day of each of the four succeeding years, the same action was taken. You need not make entries for these years.)

1987

Jan. 3   Obtained, at a cost of $900, a building permit to construct a new wing on the main plant building.

July 30   Paid $360,000 to the Able Construction Company for completion of the new wing.

Aug. 4   The board of directors authorized the release of the sum appropriated for expansion of the plant building.

      4   The board of directors declared a 10% common stock dividend on the 25,000 shares of $100 par value common stock outstanding. The market price on this date was $132 per share.

Required: Prepare journal entries to record all of the above transactions.

P16-6-A

Present statement of retained earnings

The following information relates to the Summers Corporation for the year 1987:

Net income for the year	$ 700,000
Dividends declared on common stock	98,000
Dividends declared on preferred stock	56,000
Retained earnings, January 1, unappropriated	2,100,000
Appropriation for retirement of bonds	280,000
Balance in "Appropriation for possible loss of a lawsuit," no longer needed on December 31 because of favorable court decision, is (at directors' orders) returned to unappropriated retained earnings	350,000

Required: Prepare a statement of retained earnings for the year ended December 31, 1987.

P16-7-A

Prepare journal entries for treasury stock transactions and for cash dividends; present stockholders' equity section

The stockholders' equity of the Joyner Company as of December 31, 1986, consisted of 20,000 shares of authorized and outstanding $10 par value common stock, paid-in capital in excess of par of $48,000, and retained earnings of $80,000. Following are selected transactions for 1987:

Transactions:

May 1   Acquired 3,000 shares of its own common stock at $20 per share.

June 1   Reissued 500 shares at $24.

    30   Reissued 700 shares at $18.

Oct. 1   Declared a cash dividend of $1 per share.

    31   Paid the cash dividend declared on October 1.

Net income for the year was $16,000. No other transactions affecting retained earnings occurred during the year.

Required:
a.   Prepare general journal entries for the above transactions.
b.   Prepare the stockholders' equity section of the December 31, 1987, balance sheet.

P16-8-A

Prepare journal entries for stock transactions, cash dividend, small stock dividend, and retained earnings appropriation; prepare statement of retained earnings and stockholders' equity section of balance sheet

The stockholders' equity section of Todd Company's December 31, 1986, balance sheet appears below:

Stockholders' equity:
Paid-in capital:
Preferred stock: $50 par value, 5%; authorized, 5,000 shares; issued and outstanding, 2,500 shares $125,000
Common stock without par or stated value; authorized, 50,000 shares; issued, 25,000 shares of which 500 are held in treasury 187,500
Paid-in capital in excess of par—preferred 2,500
Total paid-in capital $315,000

Retained earnings:
Appropriated:
For plant expansion . . . . $ 12,500
Unappropriated (restricted as to dividends to the extent of $5,000, the cost of the treasury stock held) 105,000
Total retained earnings 117,500
Total $432,500
Less: Treasury stock, common at cost (500 shares) 5,000
Total stockholders' equity $427,500

Following are selected transactions which occurred in 1987:

Transactions:

Jan. 13 Subscriptions were received for 550 shares of previously unissued common stock at $11.
Feb. 4 A plot of land was accepted as payment in full for 500 shares of common, and the stock was issued. Closing market price of the common stock on this date was $10 per share.
Mar. 24 All of the treasury stock was reissued at $12 per share.
June 22 All stock subscriptions were collected in full, and the shares were issued.
   23 The regular semiannual dividend on the preferred stock was declared.
   30 The preferred dividend was paid.
July 3 A 10% stock dividend was declared on the common stock. Market price on this date was $14.
   18 The stock dividend shares were issued.
Oct. 4 The company reacquired 105 shares of its common stock at $12.
Dec. 18 The regular semiannual dividend on the preferred stock and a $0.20 per share dividend on the common stock were declared.
   31 Both dividends were paid.
   31 An additional appropriation of retained earnings of $2,500 for plant expansion was authorized.

Required:

a. Prepare journal entries to record the 1987 transactions.
b. Prepare a statement of retained earnings for the year 1987, assuming net income for the year was $21,562.
c. Prepare the stockholders' equity section of the December 31, 1987, balance sheet.

P16-9-A

Present income statement and statement of retained earnings

Selected data of the Pate Company for the year ended December 31, 1987, are:

Sales, net $800,000
Interest expense 72,000
Cash dividends on common stock 120,000
Selling and administrative expense 196,000
Cash dividends on preferred stock 56,000
Rent revenue 320,000
Cost of goods sold 520,000
Flood loss (has never occurred before) 160,000
Interest revenue 72,000
Other revenue 120,000
Depreciation and maintenance on rental equipment . . 216,000
Stock dividend on common stock 240,000
Litigation loss 320,000
Cumulative positive effect on prior years' income of changing to a different depreciation method . . . 64,000

The applicable federal income tax rate is 40%. All above items of expense, revenue, and loss are included in the computation of taxable income. The litigation loss resulted from a court award of damages for patent infringement on a product that the company produced and sold in 1983 and 1984, but was discontinued in 1984. Retained earnings as of January 1, 1987, were $4,480,000. Assume there were 10,000 shares of common stock outstanding for the entire year.

Required: Prepare an income statement and a statement of retained earnings for 1987.

PROBLEMS, SERIES B

P16–1–B

Present stockholders' equity section of balance sheet

Following are selected data and accounts of Leather, Inc., as of May 31, 1987:

Paid-In Capital in Excess of Par Value—Preferred	$ 4,200
Retained Earnings, Unappropriated	72,000
Allowance for Doubtful Accounts	24,000
Common Stock without par value, stated value $30; 20,000 shares authorized, issued, and outstanding	600,000
Appropriation for Retirement of Bonds	90,000
Dividends Payable (cash)	3,600
Paid-In Capital in Excess of Stated Value—Common	24,000
Notes Payable, 17%, due April 1, 1993	360,000
Preferred Stock: 7%, par value $60; 2,000 shares authorized, issued, and outstanding	120,000
Paid-In Capital—Donations	18,000

Required: Present the stockholders' equity section of the company's balance sheet as of May 31, 1987.

P16–2–B

Prepare journal entries for cash dividend and small stock dividend

The only stockholders' equity items of the Health Company at June 30, 1987, are:

Stockholders' equity:	
Paid-in capital:	
Common stock, $100 par value, 5,000 shares authorized, 3,000 shares issued and outstanding	$300,000
Paid-in capital in excess of par value	120,000
Retained earnings	120,000
Total stockholders' equity	$540,000

On August 4, a 4% cash dividend was declared, payable on September 3. On November 16, a 10% stock dividend was declared. The shares were issued on December 1. The market value of the common stock was $180 per share on November 16 and $177 per share on December 1.

Required: Prepare journal entries for the above transactions.

P16–3–B

Prepare stockholders' equity section of balance sheet

The bookkeeper of C. J. Simpson Company has prepared the following incorrect statement of stockholders' equity for the year ended December 31, 1987:

Stockholders' equity:	
Paid-in capital:	
Preferred stock, 6%, cumulative (8,000 shares) . .	$ 418,000
Common stock (50,000 shares)	1,190,000
Retained earnings	682,000
Total stockholders' equity	$2,290,000

The authorized stock consists of 12,000 shares of preferred stock with a $50 par value and 75,000 shares of common stock, $20 par value. The preferred stock was issued on two occasions; first, 5,000 shares at par; and second, 3,000 shares at $56 per share. The 50,000 shares of common stock were issued at $26 per share. Five thousand shares of treasury common stock were reacquired for $110,000; the bookkeeper deducted the cost of the treasury stock from the Common Stock account.

Required: Prepare the correct stockholders' equity section of the balance sheet at December 31, 1987.

P16-4-B

Prepare journal entries for stock dividend, treasury stock transactions, and retained earnings appropriation

The stockholders' equity of the Wayne A. Rutledge Company at January 1, 1987, is as follows:

Common stock, stated value of $5, 100,000 shares
  authorized, 60,000 shares issued $300,000
Paid-in capital in excess of stated value 50,000
Appropriation per loan agreement 18,800
Unappropriated retained earnings 106,000
Treasury stock (3,000 shares at cost) . . . . . (18,000)

During 1987, the following transactions occurred in the order listed:

Transactions:

1. Issued 10,000 shares of stock for $92,000.
2. Declared a 4% stock dividend when the market price was $12 per share.
3. Sold 1,000 shares of treasury stock for $10,800.
4. Issued stock certificates for the stock dividend declared in transaction (2).
5. Bought 2,000 shares of treasury stock for $16,800.
6. Increased the appropriation by $10,800 per loan agreement.

Required: Prepare journal entries as necessary for the above transactions.

P16-5-B

Prepare journal entries for retained earnings appropriation, asset acquisition, and stock dividend

Following are selected transactions of the Salter Corporation:

Transactions:

1980
Dec. 31 The board of directors authorized the appropriation of $50,000 of retained earnings to provide for the future acquisition of a new plant site and the construction of a new building. (On the last day of the six succeeding years, the same action was taken. You need not make entries for these six years.)

1985
Jan. 2 Purchased a new plant site for cash, $100,000.
Mar. 29 Entered into a contract for construction of a new building, payment to be made within 30 days following completion.

1987
Feb. 10 Following final inspection and approval of the new building, the Dome Construction Company was paid in full, $500,000.
Mar. 10 The board of directors authorized release of the retained earnings appropriated for the plant site and building.
Apr. 2 A 5% stock dividend on the 100,000 shares of $50 par value common stock outstanding was declared. The market price on this date was $55 per share.

Required: Prepare journal entries for all of the above transactions.

P16–6–B

Present statement of retained earnings

Following are selected data of the Sailsbury Corporation at December 31, 1987:

Net income for the year	$384,000
Dividends declared on preferred stock	54,000
Retained earnings appropriated for future plant	
expansion during the year	180,000
Dividends declared on common stock	48,000
Retained earnings, January 1, unappropriated	540,000
Directors ordered that the balance in the "Appropriation	
per loan agreement," related to a loan repaid	
on March 31, 1987, be returned to unappropriated	
retained earnings	360,000

Required: Prepare a statement of retained earnings for the year ended December 31, 1987.

P16–7–B

Prepare journal entries for treasury stock transactions and for cash dividend; present stockholders' equity section of balance sheet

The stockholders' equity of the Ryerson Company on December 31, 1986, consisted of 1,000 authorized and outstanding shares of $9 cumulative preferred stock, stated value $30 per share, which were originally issued at $149 per share; 100,000 shares authorized and outstanding of $20 stated value common stock, which were originally issued at $20; and retained earnings of $140,000. Following are selected transactions and other data relating to 1987:

Transactions:

1. The company reacquired 2,000 shares of its common stock at $42.
2. One thousand of the treasury shares were reissued at $36.
3. Stockholders donated 1,000 shares of common stock to the company. These shares were immediately reissued at $32 to provide working capital.
4. The first quarter's dividend of $2.25 per share was declared and paid on the preferred stock. No other dividends were declared or paid during 1987.

The company suffered a net loss of $28,000 for the year 1987.

Required: a. Prepare journal entries for the numbered transactions above.
  b. Prepare the stockholders' equity section of the December 31, 1987, balance sheet.

P16–8–B

Prepare journal entries to close retained earnings appropriation and for treasury stock transactions and cash dividends; present statement of retained earnings and stockholders' equity section of balance sheet

The stockholders' equity section of the Hodges Company's October 31, 1986, balance sheet appears below:

Stockholders' equity:
  Paid-in capital:

Preferred stock: $50 par value, 6%; 1,000 shares		
authorized, 350 shares issued and outstanding . . .		$ 17,500
Common stock: $5 par value; 100,000 shares		
authorized, 40,000 shares issued and outstanding . .		200,000
Paid-in capital from donation of plant site		12,500
Total paid-in capital		$230,000
Retained earnings:		
Appropriated:		
Appropriation for contingencies	$10,000	
Unappropriated	27,750	
Total retained earnings		37,750
Total stockholders' equity		$267,750

During the ensuing fiscal year, the following transactions were entered into by the Hodges Company:

Transactions:

1. The appropriation of $10,000 of retained earnings had been authorized in October 1986 because of the likelihood of an unfavorable court decision in a pending lawsuit. The suit was brought by a

customer seeking damages for the company's alleged breach of a contract to supply the customer with certain products at stated prices in 1985. The suit was concluded on March 6, 1987, with a court order directing the company to pay $8,750 in damages. These damages were not deductible in determining income tax liability. The board ordered the damages paid and the appropriation closed. The loss does not qualify as an extraordinary item.

2. The company acquired 1,000 shares of its own common stock at $7.50 in May 1987. On June 30, it reissued 500 of these shares at $6.

3. Dividends declared and paid during the year were 6% on preferred stock, and 15 cents per share on common stock. Both dividends were declared on September 1 and paid on September 30, 1987.

For the fiscal year, the company had net income after income taxes of $9,500, excluding the loss of the lawsuit.

Required:
a. Prepare general journal entries for the numbered transactions above.
b. Prepare a statement of retained earnings for the year ended October 31, 1987.
c. Prepare the stockholders' equity section of the October 31, 1987, balance sheet.

P16–9–B

Present income statement and statement of retained earnings

Selected data for the Shafer Company for 1987 are given below:

Common stock—$10 par value	$1,000,000
Sales, net	870,000
Selling and administrative expenses	160,000
Cash dividends declared and paid	60,000
Cost of goods sold	400,000
Depreciation expense	60,000
Interest revenue	10,000
Loss on write-down of obsolete inventory	20,000
Retained earnings (as of 12/31/86)	1,000,000
Earthquake loss	48,000
Cumulative negative effect on prior years' income of changing from straight-line to an accelerated method of computing depreciation	32,000

The applicable federal income tax rate is 40%. All of the items of expense, revenue, and loss are included in the computation of taxable income. The earthquake loss resulted from the first earthquake experienced at the company's location. In addition, the company discovered that in 1986 it had erroneously charged to expense the $80,000 cost of a tract of land purchased that year and had made the same error on its tax return for 1986.

Required:
a. Prepare an income statement for the year ended December 31, 1987.
b. Prepare a statement of retained earnings for the year ended December 31, 1987.

BUSINESS DECISION PROBLEM 16–1

Determine amount of dividends received and effects on stock prices

The stockholders' equity section of the Seeley Corporation's balance sheet for June 30, 1987, is shown below:

Stockholders' equity:
Paid-in capital:

Common stock—$5 par value; authorized 200,000 shares, issued and outstanding 80,000 shares	$ 400,000
Paid-in capital in excess of par value	240,000
Total paid-in capital	$ 640,000
Retained earnings	380,000
Total stockholders' equity	$1,020,000

On July 1, 1987, the corporation's directors declared a 10% stock dividend distributable on August 2 to stockholders of record on July 16. On November 1, 1987, the directors voted a $0.60 per share annual cash dividend payable on December 2 to stockholders of record on November 16. For four years prior to 1987, the corporation had paid an annual cash dividend of $0.63.

Bill Hale owns 8,000 shares of Seeley Corporation's common stock, which he purchased five years ago. The market value of his stock was $12 per share on July 1, 1987, and $10.91 per share on July 16, 1987.

Required: a.   What amount of cash dividends will Hale receive in 1987? How does this amount differ from the amount of cash dividends Hale received in the previous four years?

b.   For what logical reason did the price of the stock drop from $12 to $10.91 on July 16, 1987?

c.   Is Hale better off as a result of the stock dividend and the $0.60 cash dividend than he would have been if he had just received the $0.63 dividend? Why?

BUSINESS DECISION PROBLEM 16–2

Analyze journal entries for impropriety and make subsequent corrections

Shown below are some journal entries made by the bookkeeper for the Royal Corporation:

1.   Retained Earnings   3,000
         Reserve for Doubtful Accounts   3,000
     To record bad debts expense.

2.   Retained Earnings   12,000
         Reserve for Depreciation   12,000
     To record depreciation expense.

3.   Retained Earnings   30,000
         Reserve for Plant Expansion . . . . :   30,000
     To record retained earnings appropriation.

4.   Retained Earnings   2,000
         Stock Dividend Distributable   2,000
     To record 10% stock dividend declaration (100 shares to be distributed—$20 par value, $30 market value).

5.   Stock Dividend Distributable   2,000
         Common Stock   2,000
     To record distribution of stock dividend.

6.   Treasury Stock   8,000
         Cash   8,000
     To record acquisition of 200 shares of $20 par value common stock at $40 per share.

7.   Cash   4,400
         Treasury Stock   4,400
     To record sale of 100 treasury shares at $44 per share.

8.   Cash   1,700
         Treasury Stock   1,700
     To record sale of 50 treasury shares at $34 per share.

9.   Common Stock   4,000
         Dividends Payable   4,000
     To record declaration of cash dividend.

	10.	Dividends Payable	4,000	
		Cash		4,000

To record payment of cash dividend.

Required: Analyze the above journal entries in connection with their explanations and decide whether each is correct or incorrect. The explanations are all correct. If a journal entry is incorrect, prepare the journal entry that should have been made.

BUSINESS SITUATION FOR DISCUSSION

The Troubles that Led to ITT's Dividend Shocker*

☐   Giant ITT [International Telephone and Telegraph] Corp., which has been scrabbling to gain a toehold in the newly competitive U.S. telecommunications market, stunned Wall Street by slashing its dividend nearly two-thirds, to $1 per share annually from $2.76. After the brief announcement of the cut came from Chairman Rand V. Araskog late July 10, trading in ITT's stock was delayed on the New York Stock Exchange for more than an hour on July 11, and by the end of the day ITT's stock had lost nearly a third of its value, closing at $21.

The dividend cut will save ITT about $262 million a year, but that amount is unlikely to solve the company's problems. Less than a third of its revenues come from telecommunications, but other key businesses—notably its Hartford Insurance Group and forest-products operations—have not been performing up to expectations. ITT declined to discuss the dividend cut beyond its brief announcement, but consultants and analysts who deal with the company say its main weakness is a lack of strategic planning.

Big-Ticket Sales

In telecommunications, ITT has concentrated in Europe, while competitors such as Northern Telecom, Rolm, and NEC have been selling big-ticket telecommunications equipment in the U.S. in competition with AT&T for nearly a decade. ITT's only major U.S. products are conventional telephones, a small private branch exchange (PBX) system for offices, and an aging switch for telephone company central offices. It is still adapting its state-of-the-art European central office switch, which cost $1 billion to develop, to the U.S. market. Doing so will cost as much as $250 million more by 1989, says William W. Ambrose, an industry analyst with Northern Business Information Inc.

ITT has also shown scant ability to develop integrated office and communications products. For example, it recognized a need to market a personal computer, but the first ones it began to ship in June were stand-alone models that do not communicate with its PBX—or any other ITT product. And the company is only now establishing a task force to decide the direction it should take in communications services in the U.S.

One reason for the lack of focus, consultants say, is that there is little continuity in management. "It seems like every three weeks people change jobs," says one. More damaging, perhaps, is the sense that internal politics are occupying management. "It's devastating to see how far their eye has shifted from the external world to what's most important inside ITT," says Robin Williamson, a consultant with Logica Inc. in New York.

Success in the new telecommunications fields may be the key to ITT's future, but it will have to pay for it from its past. Yet its cash cow, Hartford insurance, has been having severe problems. Last year Hartford's commercial lines suffered an operating loss of $109 million, even after investment income. Although prices have firmed recently following a disastrous couple of years for the entire industry, an insurance executive notes that it takes "about 15 months for price increases to work their way through the income statement." That means ITT may yet have to contribute to Hartford instead of harvesting cash from it.

Takeover Target?

ITT's forest-products business has not provided much help. The company has had it on the block for several years, but, says an industry executive, nobody is interested in timberland these days.

Most of these problems have been kept secret. One analyst notes that as late as July 5, ITT was reassuring investors that the dividend was safe. Now Araskog seems to have damaged his credibility on Wall Street, and with its book value at $39 per share, the company seems vulnerable to takeover.

---

* Reprinted from the July 23, 1984, issue of *Business Week* (p. 77) by special permission. © 1984 by McGraw-Hill, Inc.

CHAPTER 17

Bonds Payable and Bond Investments

LEARNING OBJECTIVES

After studying this chapter, you should be able to:

1. Describe the features of bonds and tell how bonds differ from shares of stock.
2. List the advantages and disadvantages of financing with long-term debt and prepare examples showing how financial leverage is employed.
3. Explain how interest rates affect bond prices and what causes a bond to sell at a premium or discount.
4. Apply the concept of present value to compute the price of a bond.
5. Prepare journal entries to account for bonds payable.
6. Prepare journal entries to account for bond investments.
7. Define and use correctly the new terms in the glossary.

In previous chapters you learned that corporations obtain cash for recurring business operations from stock issuances, profitable operations, and short-term borrowing (current liabilities). However, when situations arise that require large amounts of cash, such as the purchase of a building, corporations also raise cash from long-term borrowing, that is, by issuing bonds. The issuing of bonds results in a Bonds Payable account. The first part of this chapter discusses the issuing of bonds and accounting for bonds payable.

Since corporations are legal entities, they, like individuals, can invest in stocks and bonds issued by other corporations that are regularly traded on national exchanges. These types of investments can offer a rate of return substantially greater than a savings account. The second part of this chapter discusses bond investments. Stock investments are discussed in Chapter 18.

■ BONDS PAYABLE

A **bond** is a long-term debt, or liability, owed by its issuer. Physical evidence of the debt lies in a negotiable bond certificate. Long-term notes usually mature in 10 years or less, while bond maturities often run for 20 years or more. A bond derives its value primarily from two promises made by the borrower to the lender, or bondholder. The borrower promises to pay (1) the **face value** or **principal amount** of the bond on a specific maturity date in the future, and (2) periodic interest at a specified rate on face value at stated dates, usually semiannually, until the maturity date.

A bond issue generally consists of a large number of $1,000 bonds, rather than one very large bond. For example, a company seeking to borrow $100,000 would issue one hundred $1,000 bonds, rather than one $100,000 bond. In this way, investors with less cash to invest are able to purchase some of the bonds.

Comparison with Stock

A bond differs from a share of stock in several ways:

1. A bond is a debt or liability of the issuer, while a share of stock is a unit of ownership.
2. A bond has a maturity date when it must be paid. A share of stock does not mature; stock remains outstanding indefinitely unless the company decides to retire it.
3. Most bonds require stated periodic interest payments by the company. In contrast, dividends to stockholders are payable only when declared; even preferred dividends may be passed in a particular period if the board of directors so decides.
4. Bond interest is deductible by the issuer in computing both net income and taxable income, while dividends are not deductible in either computation.

Selling (Issuing) Bonds

A company seeking to borrow millions of dollars generally will not be able to borrow from a single lender. In such an instance, the company will sell (issue) bonds to the public to secure the funds needed. Usually a bond issue is sold through an investment company or banker, called an **underwriter.** The underwriter performs many tasks for the issuer, such as advertising, selling, and delivering the bonds to the purchasers. The underwriter often guarantees the issuer a fixed price for the bonds, expecting to earn a profit by selling the bonds for more than the fixed price.

When bonds are sold to the public, many purchasers are involved. Rather than deal with each purchaser individually, the issuing corporation appoints a trustee to represent the bondholders. The **trustee** usually is a bank or trust company. The main duty of the trustee is to see that the borrower fulfills the provisions of the bond indenture. A **bond indenture** is the contract or loan agreement under which the bonds are issued. The indenture deals with matters such as the interest rate, maturity date and maturity amount, possible restrictions on dividends, repayment plans, and other provisions relating to the debt. If bond indenture provisions are not adhered to, the issuer is said to be in default. The trustee is expected to take action to force the issuer to comply with the indenture.

Characteristics of Bonds

All bonds have two common characteristics: (1) they promise to pay cash or other assets; and (2) they come due, or mature. In other respects, bonds may differ; they may be secured or unsecured bonds, registered or unregistered (bearer) bonds, and term or serial bonds. These differences and others are discussed below. Certain bond features are matters of legal necessity, such as the way interest is paid and ownership is transferred. Such differences usually do not affect the issue price of the bonds. Other features, such as convertibility into common stock, are designed to make the bonds more attractive to potential purchasers. These added features, called "sweeteners," may increase the issue price of a bond.

Secured Bonds. A secured bond is a bond for which specific property has been pledged to ensure its payment. Mortgage bonds are the most common type of secured bonds. A mortgage is a legal claim (lien) on a specific property which gives the bondholder the right to sell the pledged property if the company fails to make required payments.

Unsecured Bonds. An unsecured bond is called a debenture bond, or simply a debenture. A debenture is a bond backed only by the general creditworthiness of the issuer, not by a lien on any specific property. A financially sound company will be able to issue debentures more easily than a company experiencing financial difficulty.

Registered Bonds. A registered bond is a bond in which the owner's name appears on both the bond certificate and in the record of bond owners kept by the bond issuer or its agent, the registrar. Bonds may be registered as to principal (or face value of the bond) or as to both principal and interest. If a bond is registered as to both, interest on the bond is paid by check. Most bonds in our economy are registered as to principal only. Ownership of registered bonds is transferred by endorsing the bond and registering it in the new owner's name. Registered bonds are easily replaced if lost or stolen.

Unregistered (Bearer) Bonds. An unregistered (bearer) bond is assumed to be the property of its holder or bearer, since the owner's name does not appear on the bond certificate or in a separate record. Ownership is transferred by physical delivery of the bond.

Coupon Bonds. A coupon bond is a bond not registered as to interest. A coupon bond carries detachable coupons for the interest it pays. At the end of each interest period, the coupon for the period is clipped and presented to a stated party, usually a bank, for collection.

Term Bonds and Serial Bonds. A term bond is a bond that matures on the same date as all other bonds in a given bond issue. Serial bonds are bonds in a given bond issue with maturities spread over several dates. For instance, one fourth of the bonds may mature on December 31, 1988, another one fourth on December 31, 1989, and so on.

Callable Bonds.   A **callable bond** contains a provision that gives the issuer the right to call (buy back) the bond before its maturity date. The provision is similar to the call provision in some preferred stocks. A company might exercise this call right if outstanding bonds bear interest at a much higher rate than the company would have to pay if it issued new but similar bonds now. The exercise of the call provision normally requires the company to pay the bondholder a call premium of about $30 to $70 per $1,000 bond. A **call premium** is the price paid in excess of face value that the issuer of bonds is required to pay to redeem (call) bonds before their maturity date.

Convertible Bonds.   A **convertible bond** is a bond that may be exchanged, at the bondholder's option, for shares of stock of the issuing corporation. A convertible bond has a stipulated conversion rate of some number of shares for each $1,000 bond. Any type of bond may be convertible, but this feature usually is added to rather risky debenture bonds to make them more attractive to investors.

Bonds with Stock Warrants.   A **stock warrant** allows the bondholder to purchase shares of common stock at a fixed price for a stated period of time. Warrants issued with long-term debt may be detachable or nondetachable. A bond with **nondetachable warrants** is virtually the same as a convertible bond; the holder must surrender the bond in order to acquire the common stock. **Detachable warrants** allow bondholders to keep their bonds and still purchase shares of stock through exercise of the warrants.

Advantages of Issuing Debt

Several advantages come from raising cash by issuing bonds rather than stock. First, the current stockholders of a corporation do not have to dilute or surrender their control of the company if needed funds can be obtained by borrowing rather than issuing more shares of stock. It may also be less expensive to issue debt rather than additional stock because the interest payments made to bondholders are tax deductible while dividends are not. But probably the most important reason is that the use of debt may increase the earnings of stockholders through favorable financial leverage.

Favorable Financial Leverage.   A company has **favorable financial leverage** when borrowed funds are used to increase earnings per share (EPS) of common stock. Increased EPS usually result from earning a higher rate of return than the rate of interest paid for the borrowed money. For example, suppose a company borrowed money at 10% and earned a 15% rate of return. The 5% difference increases earnings.

A more complex example of favorable financial leverage is provided in Illustration 17.1. The two companies in the illustration are identical in every respect except in the way they are financed. Company A issued only capital stock, while Company B issued equal amounts of 10% bonds and capital stock. Both companies have $20,000,000 of assets, and both earned $4,000,000 of

Illustration 17.1

Favorable Financial Leverage

COMPANIES A AND B CONDENSED STATEMENTS Balance Sheets January 1, 1987		
	Company A	*Company B*
Total assets	$20,000,000	$20,000,000
Bonds payable, 10%		$10,000,000
Stockholders' equity (capital stock)	$20,000,000	10,000,000
Total equities	$20,000,000	$20,000,000

Income Statements For the Year Ended December 31, 1987		
Net income from operations	$ 4,000,000	$ 4,000,000
Interest expense		1,000,000
Net income before income taxes	$ 4,000,000	$ 3,000,000
Income taxes (40%)	1,600,000	1,200,000
Net income	$ 2,400,000	$ 1,800,000
Number of common shares outstanding	2,000,000	1,000,000
Earnings per share (EPS)	$1.20	$1.80
Rate of return on assets employed (both companies $4,000,000/$20,000,000)	20%	20%
Rate of return on stockholders' equity: Company A ($2,400,000/$20,000,000)	12%	
Company B ($1,800,000/$10,000,000)		18%

income from operations. If we divide income from operations by assets ($4,000,000 ÷ $20,000,000), we see that both companies earned 20% on assets employed. Yet B's stockholders fared far better than A's. The ratio of net income to stockholders' equity is 18% for B, while it is only 12% for A.

The 6% difference can be explained as follows:

Operating income earned on $10,000,000 debt (20%) . .	$2,000,000
Interest paid on the debt (10%)	1,000,000
Net increase in income before taxes due to debt	$1,000,000
Less income taxes (40%)	400,000
Net increase in income due to debt financing	$ 600,000

Net increase in income due to debt financing as a percentage of stockholders' equity, $600,000/$10,000,000 = 6%.

Assume that both companies issued their stock at the beginning of 1987 at $10 per share. B's $1.80 EPS are 50% greater than A's $1.20 EPS. This EPS difference probably would cause B's shares to sell at a substantially higher market price than A's shares. B's larger EPS would also allow a larger dividend on B's shares.

Company B, in the above illustration, is employing financial leverage, or is said to be **trading on the equity.** The company is using its stockholders' equity as a basis for securing funds on which a fixed return is paid. Company B expects to earn more from the use of such funds than their fixed after-tax cost, and as a result, Company B increases its rate of return on stockholders' equity and EPS.[1]

---

[1] Issuing bonds is only one method of using leverage. Other methods of using financial leverage include issuing preferred stock or long-term notes.

Disadvantages of Issuing Debt

Several disadvantages accompany the use of debt financing. First, the borrower has a fixed interest payment that must be met each period to avoid default. Use of debt also reduces a company's ability to sustain a major loss. For example, suppose that both Company A and Company B mentioned above sustain losses for 1987 of $11,000,000. At the end of 1987, Company A will still have $9,000,000 of stockholders' equity and can continue operations with a chance of recovery, as shown below. Company B, on the other hand, would have negative stockholders' equity of $1,000,000, and the bondholders could force the company to liquidate if B could not make interest payments as they came due.

	Partial Balance Sheets **December 31, 1987**	
	Company A	**Company B**
Stockholders' equity:		
Paid-in capital:		
Common stock	$ 20,000,000	$ 10,000,000
Retained earnings	(11,000,000)	(11,000,000)
Total stockholders' equity	$ 9,000,000	$ (1,000,000)

Debt financing also causes a company to experience unfavorable financial leverage when income from operations falls below a certain level. **Unfavorable financial leverage** results when the cost of borrowed funds exceeds the revenue they generate; it is the opposite of favorable financial leverage. In the above example, if income from operations fell to $1,000,000, the rates of return on stockholders' equity would be 3% for A and zero for B, as shown in the schedule below:

	Income Statements **For the Year End December 31, 1987**	
	Company A	**Company B**
Net income from operations	$1,000,000	$1,000,000
Interest expense		1,000,000
Net income before income taxes	$1,000,000	$ –0–
Income taxes (40%)	400,000	–0–
Net income	$ 600,000	$ –0–
Rate of return on stockholders' equity:		
Company A ($600,000/$20,000,000)	3%	
Company B ($0/$10,000,000)		0%

Another disadvantage of issuing debt is that loan agreements often require the maintenance of a certain amount of working capital (Current assets − Current liabilities) and place limitations on dividends and additional borrowings.

Accounting for Bonds

When a company issues bonds, it incurs a long-term liability on which periodic interest payments must be made, usually twice a year. If interest dates fall on other than balance sheet dates, interest will need to be accrued in the proper periods. The following example illustrates the accounting for bonds issued at face value on an interest date.

Bonds Issued at Face Value on an Interest Date.   Valley Company has an accounting year ending on December 31. On December 31, 1987, the company issued 10-year, 12% bonds with a $100,000 face value of cash for $100,000. The bonds are dated December 31, 1987, call for semiannual interest payments on June 30 and December 31, and mature on December 31, 1997. Valley Company made all required cash payments when due. The entries for the 10 years are summarized below.

On December 31, 1987, the date of issuance, the entry is:

```
1987
Dec. 31   Cash  . . . . . . . . . . . . . . . . .   100,000
              Bonds Payable  . . . . . . . . . . . .            100,000
          To record bonds issued at face value.
```

On each June 30 and December 31 for 10 years, beginning June 30, 1988 (ending June 30, 1997), the entry would be:

```
Each year
June 30
and
Dec. 31   Bond Interest Expense ($100,000 × 0.12 × ½)  . .   6,000
              Cash  . . . . . . . . . . . . . . . . .            6,000
          To record periodic interest payment.
```

On December 31, 1997, the maturity date, the entry would be:

```
1997
Dec. 31   Bond Interest Expense  . . . . . . . . . . .    6,000
          Bonds Payable .  . . . . . . . . . . . . .    100,000
              Cash  . . . . . . . . . . . . . . . . .            106,000
          To record bond redemption and final interest
          payment.
```

Note that no adjusting entries are needed when an interest payment date falls on the last day of the accounting period. The income statement for each of the 10 years 1988–97 would show Bond Interest Expense of $12,000 ($6,000 × 2); the balance sheet at the end of each of the years 1987–95 would report bonds payable of $100,000 in long-term liabilities. At the end of 1996, the bonds would be reclassified as a current liability because they will be paid within the next year.

But the real world is seldom so uncomplicated. For example, assume the Valley Company bonds were dated October 31, 1987, issued on that same date, and pay interest each April 30 and October 31. In this case, an adjusting entry is needed on December 31 to accrue interest for two months, November and December. That entry would read:

```
1987
Dec. 31   Bond Interest Expense ($100,000 × 0.12 × ²⁄₁₂)  . .   2,000
              Bond Interest Payable .  . . . . . . . . .            2,000
          To accrue two months' interest expense.
```

The April 30, 1988, entry would be:

```
1988
Apr. 30   Bond Interest Expense ($100,000 × 0.12 × 4/12)  . .    4,000
          Bond Interest Payable  . . . . . . . . . . .           2,000
              Cash .  . . . . . . . . . . . . . . . . .                   6,000
          To record semiannual interest payment.
```

The October 31, 1988, entry would be:

```
1988
Oct. 31   Bond Interest Expense  . . . . . . . . . . .           6,000
              Cash .  . . . . . . . . . . . . . . . . .                   6,000
          To record semiannual interest payment.
```

Each year similar entries would be made for the semiannual payments and the year-end accrual. The $2,000 Bond Interest Payable would be reported as a current liability on the December 31 balance sheet for each year.

    Bonds Issued at Face Value between Interest Dates.   Bonds are not always issued on the date they start to bear interest. Regardless of when the bonds are physically issued, interest starts to accrue from the **most recent** interest date. Investors purchasing such bonds after they begin to accrue interest are required to pay for the interest accrued since the preceding interest date. The issuer of the bonds is required to pay holders of the bonds a full six months' interest at each interest date. Thus, the bondholders will be reimbursed for this accrued interest when they receive their first six-month interest check. The bonds are reported to be selling at a stated price "plus accrued interest."

    Using the facts for the Valley Company bonds dated December 31, 1987, suppose Valley Company issued its bonds on May 31, 1988, instead of on December 31, 1987. The entry required is:

```
1988
May 31   Cash  . . . . . . . . . . . . . . . . . . .  105,000
             Bonds Payable  . . . . . . . . . . . . .            100,000
             Bond Interest Payable ($100,000 × 0.12 × 5/12) .      5,000
         To record bonds issued at face value plus accrued
         interest.
```

This entry records the amount of cash received for the accrued interest as a liability.

    The entry required on June 30, 1988, when the full six months' interest is paid, is:

```
1988
June 30   Bond Interest Expense ($100,000 × 0.12 × 1/12)  . .    1,000
          Bond Interest Payable  . . . . . . . . . . .           5,000
              Cash  . . . . . . . . . . . . . . . . . .                   6,000
          To record bond interest payment.
```

This entry records $1,000 interest expense on the $100,000 of bonds that were outstanding for one month. The $5,000 is the amount previously collected from the bondholders on May 31 as accrued interest and is now being returned to them.

Bond Prices and Interest Rates

The price of a bond issue sold to investors often differs from its face value. A difference between face value and issue price will exist whenever the contract rate of interest on the bonds differs from the market rate of interest for similar bonds. The **contract rate of interest** (also called the **stated, coupon,** or **nominal rate**) is stated in the bond indenture and printed on the face of each bond. The contract rate is used to determine the actual amount of cash that will be paid each interest period. The **market interest rate,** also called the **effective interest** or **yield rate,** is the minimum rate of interest investors are willing to accept on bonds of a particular risk category. The market rate fluctuates from day to day, responding to the supply of, and demand for, money.

Contract and market rates of interest are likely to differ. The contract rate must be set before the bonds are actually sold to allow time for such activities as printing the bonds. By the time the bonds are sold and the market rate becomes known, the contract rate could be higher or lower than the market rate. **If the contract rate is higher than the market rate, the bonds will sell for more than face value.** Investors will be attracted to bonds offering a contract rate greater than the market rate for such bonds and will bid up their price. **If the contract rate is lower than the market rate, the bonds will sell for less than face value.** Investors will not be interested in bonds bearing a contract rate less than the market rate until their price falls. The amount a bond sells for above face value is called a **premium;** if bonds are sold for less than face value, the reduction is called a **discount.**

The effect of selling a bond at a premium or discount is to change the **contract** rate of interest on the bond to the **market** rate. To illustrate this concept, consider the following short-term note. Assume that you loaned the McNeil Company $9,800 on its $10,000, 10% note which matures in one year. The contract interest rate is 10%. But, if McNeil pays the note at maturity, the effective (actual) rate of interest is about 12.2%. At the end of the year, the McNeil Company must pay the principal of the note ($10,000) plus interest for one year at 10% ($10,000 × 0.10 = $1,000) or a total of $11,000. Your actual interest earned is $1,200—the difference between the amount collected, $11,000, and the amount loaned, $9,800. The effective rate of interest is 12.2% ($1,200/$9,800) per annum, simple interest. This is a simple example of how a discount on a loan can adjust the contract rate of interest to the market rate.

Computing Bond Prices

Computing long-term bond prices is a more complex process than finding the effective rate of interest on a one-year note at simple interest. The process involves finding **present values** using compound interest. The concepts of future value and present value are explained in the Appendix to this chapter. If you do not understand the present value concept, you should read the Appendix before continuing.

Buyers and sellers negotiate a price that will yield the going rate of interest for bonds of a particular risk class. The price investors will pay for a given bond issue is equal to the present value of the bonds. Present value is computed by discounting the promised cash flows from the bonds—principal and interest—using the market, or effective, rate. Market rate is used because the bonds must yield at least this rate or investors will be attracted to alternative investments. The life of the bonds is stated in terms of interest (compounding) periods. The interest rate used is the effective rate **per interest period,** which often is found by dividing the annual rate by the number of times interest is paid per year. For example, if the annual rate is 12%, the semiannual rate is 6%.

Bond prices usually are quoted as percentages of face value—100 means 100% of face value, 97 means 97% of face value, and 103 means 103% of face value. For example, a $100,000 face value bond issued at 103 has a price of $103,000.

Bonds Issued at Face Value. The specific steps involved in computing the price of a bond are illustrated by the following example. Assume 12% bonds with a $100,000 face value are issued by Carr Company to yield 12%. The bonds are dated and issued on June 30, 1987, call for semiannual interest payments on June 30 and December 31, and mature on June 30, 1990.[2] The bonds will sell at face value because they offer 12% and investors seek 12%. There is no reason for potential purchasers to offer a premium or demand a discount. One way to prove the bonds would be sold at face value is by showing that their present value is $100,000:

	Cash flow	×	Present value factor	=	Present value
Principal of $100,000 due in six interest periods multiplied by present value factor for 6% from Table 3, Appendix C (end of text)	$100,000	×	0.70496	=	$ 70,496
Interest of $6,000 due at end of each of six interest periods multiplied by present value factor for 6% from Table 4, Appendix C (end of text)	$6,000	×	4.91732	=	29,504
Total price (present value)					$100,000

This schedule shows that if investors seek an effective rate of 6% per six-month period, they should pay $100,000 for these bonds. **Notice that the same number of interest periods and semiannual interest rates are used in discounting both the principal and interest payments to their present values.** The entry to record the sale of these bonds on June 30, 1987, debits Cash and credits Bonds Payable for $100,000.

Bonds Issued at a Discount. Assume the $100,000, 12% Carr Company bonds are sold to yield a current market rate of 14% annual interest, or 7% per semiannual period. The present value (selling price) of the bonds is computed as follows:

	Cash flow	×	Present value factor	=	Present value
Principal of $100,000 due in six interest periods multiplied by present value factor for 7% from Table 3, Appendix C (end of text)	$100,000	×	0.66634	=	$66,634
Interest of $6,000 due at end of each of six interest periods multiplied by present value factor for 7% from Table 4, Appendix C (end of text)	$6,000	×	4.76654	=	28,599
Total price (present value)					$95,233

---

[2] Bonds do not normally mature in such a short time; we use a three-year life for illustrative purposes only.

Note that in computing the present value of the bonds, the actual $6,000 cash interest payment that will be made each period is still used. **The amount of cash paid by the company as interest does not change with changes in the market interest rate.** But the market rate per semiannual period—7%—does change, and this new rate is used to find interest factors in the tables.

The journal entry to record issuance of the bonds is:

```
1987
June 30  Cash . . . . . . . . . . . . . . . . .  95,233
              Discount on Bonds Payable . . . . . . . .   4,767
                  Bonds Payable . . . . . . . . . . .            100,000
                  To record bonds issued at a discount.
```

In recording the bond issue, Bonds Payable is credited for the face value of the debt. The difference between face value and price received is debited to Discount on Bonds Payable, a contra account to Bonds Payable. Bonds payable and the discount on bonds payable are reported in the balance sheet as follows:

```
Long-term liabilities:
    Bonds payable, 12%, due July 1, 1990 . . . . .  $100,000
        Less: Discount on bonds payable . . . . .      4,767   $95,233
```

The $95,233 is called the carrying value, or net liability, of the bonds. Carrying value is the face value of the bonds minus any unamortized discount or plus any unamortized premium. Unamortized premium on bonds payable is discussed in the next section.

Bonds Issued at a Premium.   Assume that Carr Company issued the $100,000 face value of 12% bonds to yield a current market rate of 10%. The bonds would sell at a premium calculated as follows:

	Cash flow	×	Present value factor	=	Present value
Principal of $100,000 due in six interest periods multiplied by present value factor for 5% from Table 3, Appendix C (end of text)	$100,000	×	0.74622	=	$ 74,622
Interest of $6,000 due at end of each of six interest periods multiplied by present value factor for 5% from Table 4, Appendix C (end of text)	$6,000	×	5.07569	=	30,454
Total price (present value)					$105,076

The journal entry to record the issuance of the bonds is:

```
1987
June 30  Cash . . . . . . . . . . . . . . . . . .  105,076
              Bonds Payable . . . . . . . . . . . .            100,000
              Premium on Bonds Payable . . . . . . . .          5,076
                  To record bonds issued at a premium.
```

The carrying value of these bonds at issuance is $105,076, consisting of face value of $100,000 and premium of $5,076. The premium is shown on the balance sheet as an addition to bonds payable.

Discount/Premium Amortization

When bonds are issued at a premium or discount, bond interest expense recorded each period differs from bond interest actually paid in cash. A discount **increases** and a premium **decreases** the amount of interest expense. For example, if the Carr Company bonds with a face value of $100,000 were issued for $95,233, the total interest cost of borrowing would be $40,767: $36,000 (six payments of $6,000) plus the discount of $4,767. If the bonds had been issued at $105,076, the total interest cost of borrowing would be $30,924: $36,000 less the premium of $5,076. The $4,767 discount or $5,076 premium must be allocated or charged to the six periods that benefit from the use of borrowed money. Two methods are available for amortizing a discount or premium on bonds—the straight-line method and the effective interest rate method.

Interest expense is recorded at a **constant amount** under the straight-line method and at a **constant rate** under the interest method. *APB Opinion No. 21* states that the straight-line method may be used **only when it does not differ materially from the second method to be discussed, the effective interest rate method.** In many cases, the differences will not be material.

The Straight-Line Method. The straight-line method of amortization is a procedure that allocates an equal amount of discount or premium to each month the bonds are outstanding. The amount is calculated by dividing the discount or premium by the total number of months from the **date of issuance** to the maturity date. For example, if the Carr Company bonds with a face value of $100,000 were sold for $95,233, the $4,767 discount would be charged to interest expense at a rate of $132.42 ($4,767/36) per month. Total discount amortization for six months would be $794.52 ($132.42 × 6). Interest expense for each six-month period then would be $6,794.52 [$6,000 + ($132.42 × 6)]. The entry to record the expense on December 31, 1987, would be:

```
1987
Dec. 31   Bond Interest Expense  . . . . . . . . . . .    6,794.52
              Cash . . . . . . . . . . . . . . . . . . .               6,000.00
              Discount on Bonds Payable (132.42 × 6)  . .                 794.52
          To record interest payment and discount
          amortization.
```

To illustrate the straight-line method applied to a premium, recall that the $100,000 face value Carr Company bonds sold for $105,076. The $5,076 premium on these bonds would be amortized at a rate of $141 ($5,076/36) per month. The entry for the first period's semiannual interest expense on bonds sold at a premium is:

```
1987
Dec. 31   Bond Interest Expense . . . . . . . . . . .      5,154
          Premium on Bonds Payable ($141 × 6) . . . . .      846
              Cash . . . . . . . . . . . . . . . . . . .                6,000
          To record interest payment and premium
          amortization.
```

The Effective Interest Rate Method.   *APB Opinion No. 21* recommends an amortization procedure called the effective interest rate method, or simply the interest method. Under the interest method, **interest expense for any interest period is equal to the effective (market) rate of interest at the date of issuance times the carrying value of the bonds at the beginning of that interest period.** Using the Carr Company example of 12% bonds with a face value of $100,000 sold to yield 14%, the carrying value at the beginning of the first interest period is the selling price of $95,233. The interest expense for the first semiannual period would be recorded as follows:

```
1987
Dec. 31   Bond Interest Expense ($95,233 × 0.14 × ½) . . .    6,666
              Cash ($100,000 × 0.12 × ½) . . . . . . . .              6,000
              Discount on Bonds Payable . . . . . . . .               666
          To record discount amortization and interest
          payment.
```

Note that interest expense is calculated using the **effective** interest rate. The cash payment is calculated using the **contract** rate. The discount amortized for the period is the difference between the two amounts.

   After the above entry, the carrying value of the bonds is $95,899 ($95,233 + $666). The balance in the discount account was reduced by $666 to $4,101 ($4,767 − $666). Assuming the accounting year ends on December 31, the entry to record the payment of interest for the second semiannual period on June 30, 1988, is:

```
1988
June 30   Bond Interest Expense ($95,899 × 0.14 × ½) . . .    6,713
              Cash ($100,000 × 0.12 × ½) . . . . . . . .              6,000
              Discount on Bonds Payable . . . . . . . .               713
          To record payment of six months' interest and to
          show discount amortization.
```

   The effective interest rate method can also be applied to premium amortization. If the Carr Company bonds had been issued at $105,076 to yield 10%, the premium would be $5,076. Interest expense would be calculated in the same manner as for bonds sold at a discount. But the entry would differ somewhat, showing a debit to the premium account. The entry for the first interest period is:

```
1987
Dec. 31   Bond Interest Expense ($105,076 × 0.10 × ½)  . .    5,254
          Premium on Bonds Payable . . . . . . . . .            746
              Cash ($100,000 × 0.12 × ½) . . . . . . . .              6,000
          To record interest payment and premium
          amortization.
```

After the first entry, the carrying value of the bonds is $104,330 ($105,076 − $746). The premium account now carries a balance of $4,330 ($5,076 − $746). The entry for the second interest period is:

```
1988
June 30   Bond Interest Expense ($104,330 × 0.10 × ½)  . .    5,216
          Premium on Bonds Payable . . . . . . . . .            784
              Cash ($100,000 × 0.12 × ½) . . . . . . . .              6,000
          To record payment of six months' interest and to
          show premium amortization.
```

Discount and Premium Amortization Schedules. A discount amortization schedule (Illustration 17.2) and a premium amortization schedule (Illustration 17.3) can be used to aid in preparing entries for interest expense. Companies usually prepare such schedules when bonds are first issued, often using standard computer programs. The schedules are then referred to whenever journal entries for interest are to be made. Note that in each period the amount of interest expense changes; interest expense gets larger when a discount is involved and smaller when a premium is involved. This fluctuation occurs because the carrying value to which a constant interest rate is applied changes each interest payment date. With a discount, carrying value increases; with a premium, it decreases. But the actual cash paid as interest is always a constant amount determined by multiplying face value by the contract rate per interest period.

Illustration 17.2

Discount Amortization Schedule

(A)	(B)	(C)	(D)	(E)
Interest payment date	Interest Expense debit (E × 0.14 × ½)	Cash credit ($100,000 × 0.12 × ½)	Discount on Bonds Payable credit (B − C)	Carrying value of Bonds Payable (previous balance in E + D)
Issue price				$ 95,233
12/31/87	$ 6,666	$ 6,000	$ 666	95,899
6/30/88	6,713	6,000	713	96,612
12/31/88	6,763	6,000	763	97,375
6/30/89	6,816	6,000	816	98,191
12/31/89	6,873	6,000	873	99,064
6/30/90	6,936*	6,000	936	100,000
	$40,767	$36,000	$4,767	

* Includes rounding difference.

Note that total interest expense for the discount situation in Illustration 17.2 of $40,767 agrees with the earlier computation of total interest expense. In Illustration 17.3, total interest expense in the premium situation is shown as $30,924, which is equal to $36,000 (six $6,000 payments) **less** the $5,076 premium. In both illustrations, the carrying value of the bonds is equal to face value at the maturity date because the discount or premium has been fully amortized.

Adjusting Entry for Partial Period. Illustrations 17.2 and 17.3 can be

Illustration 17.3

Premium Amortization Schedule

(A)	(B)	(C)	(D)	(E)
Interest payment date	Interest Expense debit (E × 0.10 × ½)	Cash credit ($100,000 × 0.12 × ½)	Premium on Bonds Payable debit (C − B)	Carrying value of Bonds Payable (previous balance in E − D)
Issue price				$105,076
12/31/87	$ 5,254	$ 6,000	$ 746	104,330
6/30/88	5,216	6,000	784	103,546
12/31/88	5,177	6,000	823	102,723
6/30/89	5,136	6,000	864	101,859
12/31/89	5,093	6,000	907	100,952
6/30/90	5,048	6,000	952	100,000
	$30,924	$36,000	$5,076	

used to obtain amounts needed if interest must be accrued for a partial period. Instead of a calendar-year accounting period, assume the fiscal year of the bond issuer ends on August 31. Using the information provided in the premium amortization schedule (Illustration 17.3), the adjusting entry needed on August 31, 1987, is:

```
1987
Aug. 31   Bond Interest Expense ($5,254 × ²⁄₆) . . . . . .    1,751
          Premium on Bonds Payable ($746 × ²⁄₆) . . . . .      249
              Bond Interest Payable ($6,000 × ²⁄₆) . . . . .          2,000
          To record two months' accrued interest.
```

This entry records interest for two months, July and August, of the six-month interest period ending on January 1, 1988. The first line of Illustration 17.3 shows the interest expense and premium amortization for the six months. The above entry thus records two sixths (or one third) of the amounts for this six-month period. The remaining four months' interest is recorded when the first payment is made on December 31, 1987. That entry reads:

```
1987
Dec. 31   Bond Interest Payable . . . . . . . . . . . .    2,000
          Bond Interest Expense ($5,254 × ⁴⁄₆) . . . . . .    3,503
          Premium on Bonds Payable ($746 × ⁴⁄₆) . . . . .      497
              Cash  . . . . . . . . . . . . . . . . .          6,000
          To record interest expense and interest payment.
```

Similar entries for August 31 and December 31 will be made in the remaining years in the life of the bonds. But the amounts will differ because the interest method of accounting for bond interest is being used. The entry for each June 30 would be as indicated in Illustration 17.3.

Redeeming Bonds Payable

Bonds may be (1) paid at maturity, (2) called, or (3) purchased in the market and retired. Each of these actions is referred to as redemption of bonds or the extinguishment of debt. If bonds are paid at maturity, any related discount or premium would have been amortized already. The only entry required at maturity would debit Bonds Payable and credit Cash for the face amount of the bonds.

An issuer may redeem some or all of its outstanding bonds before maturity date by calling them. Or bonds may be purchased in the market and retired. In either case, the accounting is the same. Assume that on January 1, 1989, bonds totaling $10,000 of the $100,000 face value bonds in Illustration 17.3 are called (or else purchased in the market) at 103, or $10,300. Accrued interest, if any, will be added to the price. But in this example, assume that the interest due on this date has been paid. A look at the last column on the line dated 12/31/88 in Illustration 17.3 reveals that the carrying value of the bonds is $102,723, which consists of Bonds Payable of $100,000 and Premium on Bonds Payable of $2,723. Since 10% of the bond issue is being redeemed, 10% must be removed from each of these two accounts. A loss is incurred for the excess of the price paid for the bonds, $10,300, over their carrying value, $10,272. The required entry reads:

```
1989
Jan. 1  Bonds Payable  . . . . . . . . . . . . . . . . . . .      10,000
        Premium on Bonds Payable ($2,723 ÷ 10)  . . . .            272
        Loss on Bond Redemption ($10,272 − $10,300)  . .            28
            Cash  . . . . . . . . . . . . . . . . . .                        10,300
            To record bonds redeemed.
```

According to *FASB Statement No. 4,* gains and losses from **voluntary early** retirement of bonds are extraordinary items, if material. Such gains and losses are reported in the income statement, net of their tax effects, as described in Chapter 16.

Serial Bonds

To avoid the burden of redeeming an entire bond issue at one time, **serial bonds** may be issued that mature over several dates. Assume that on June 30, 1982, Jasper Company issued $100,000 face value of 12% serial bonds at 100. Interest is payable each year on June 30 and December 31. A total of $20,000 of the bonds mature each year starting on June 30, 1987. Jasper Company has a calendar accounting year. Entries required for 1987 for interest expense and maturing debt are:

```
1987
June 30  Bond Interest Expense ($100,000 × 0.12 × ½)  . .      6,000
             Cash  . . . . . . . . . . . . . . . . . . . .                6,000
             To record interest payment.

     30  Serial Bonds Payable  . . . . . . . . . . . . .      20,000
             Cash  . . . . . . . . . . . . . . . . . . . .               20,000
             To record retirement of serial debt.

Dec. 31  Bond Interest Expense ($80,000 × 0.12 × ½)  . . .     4,800
             Cash  . . . . . . . . . . . . . . . . . . . .                4,800
             To record payment of semiannual interest expense.
```

Note that interest expense for the last six months of 1987 is calculated only on the remaining outstanding debt ($100,000 original issue less the $20,000 that matured on June 30, 1987). Each year after the amount of bonds maturing that year is retired, interest expense decreases proportionately. The $20,000 amount maturing the next year is reported as a current liability in each year-end balance sheet. The remaining debt is a long-term liability.

Bond Redemption or Sinking Funds

Investors in bonds typically are concerned about the safety of their investments. To reduce risk of default at maturity date, provisions in modern bond indentures often require that periodic payments be made to a bond redemption fund, often called a sinking fund. Such payments are to be used by the fund trustee (usually a bank) to redeem a stated amount of bonds annually and to pay accrued interest on those bonds. The trustee determines which bonds are to be called. The cash deposited with the trustee can be used **only** to redeem issuer's bonds and pay accrued interest on bonds redeemed.

To illustrate, assume Hand Company has 12% coupon bonds outstanding

Illustration 17.8 shows that to find the present value of the three $100 cash flows, multiply the $100 by a present value of an annuity factor, 2.67301.

Suppose you won a prize in a lottery that awarded you your choice of $10,000 at the end of each of the next five years or $35,000 cash immediately. You believe you can earn interest on invested cash at 15% per year. Which option should you choose? To answer the question you should compute the present value of an annuity of $10,000 per period for five years at 15%. The present value is $33,521.60, ($10,000 × 3.35216). You should accept the immediate payment of $35,000 since it has the larger present value.

NEW TERMS INTRODUCED IN CHAPTER 17

Annuity

A series of equal cash flows spaced equally in time (672).

Bearer bond

See unregistered bond.

Bond

A long-term debt owed by its issuer. A **bond certificate** is a negotiable instrument and is the formal, physical evidence of the debt owed (648).

Bond indenture

The contract or loan agreement under which bonds are issued (648).

Bond redemption (or sinking) fund

A fund used to bring about gradual redemption of a bond issue (622).

Call premium

The price paid in excess of face value that the issuer of bonds may be required to pay to redeem (call) bonds before their maturity date (650).

Callable bond

A bond that gives the issuer the right to call (buy back) the bond before its maturity date (650).

Carrying value (of bonds)

The face value of bonds minus any unamortized discount or plus any unamortized premium. Sometimes referred to as **net liability** on the bonds when used for bonds payable (657).

Compound interest

Interest calculated on the principal and on interest of prior periods (669).

Contract rate of interest

The interest rate printed on the bond certificates and specified on the bond indenture; also called the **stated, coupon,** or **nominal rate** (655).

Convertible bond

A bond that may be exchanged, at the bondholder's option, for shares of stock of the issuing corporation (650).

Coupon bond

A bond not registered as to interest; it carries detachable coupons that are to be clipped and presented for payment of interest due (649).

Debenture bond

An unsecured bond backed only by the general credit worthiness of its issuer (649).

Discount (on bonds)

Excess of face value over issue or selling price (655).

Effective interest rate method (interest method)

A procedure for calculating periodic interest expense (or revenue) in which the first period's interest is computed by multiplying the carrying value of bonds payable (bond investments) by the market rate at the issue date. The difference between computed interest expense (revenue) and the interest paid (received), based on nominal rate times face value, is the discount or premium amortized for the period. Computations for subsequent periods are based on carrying value at the beginning of the period (659).

Face value

Principal amount, or maturity amount or value, of a bond (648).

Favorable financial leverage

An increase in EPS and rate of return on owners' equity resulting from earning a higher rate of return on borrowed funds than the fixed cost of such funds. **Unfavorable financial leverage** results when the cost of borrowed funds exceeds the income they generate, resulting in decreased income to owners (650).

Future value or worth

The amount to which a sum of money invested today will grow in a stated time period at a specified interest rate (669)

Interest method

See Effective interest rate method.

Market interest rate

The interest rate that an investor will earn on a bond investment by paying a specified price for it and the rate of interest expense a borrower will incur by issuing bonds at that price. Also called **effective interest** or **yield rate** (655).

Mortgage

A legal claim (lien) on a specific property that gives the bondholder the right to sell the pledged property if the company fails to make required payments. A bond secured by a mortgage is called a **mortgage bond** (649).

Premium (on bonds)

Excess of selling or issue price over face value (655).

Present value

The current worth of a future cash receipt(s); computed by discounting future receipts at a stipulated interest rate (671).

Registered bond

A bond for which the owner's name appears on both the bond certificate and in the record of bond owners kept by the bond issuer or its agent, the registrar (649).

Secured bond

A bond for which specific property has been pledged to ensure its payment (649).

Serial bonds

Bonds in a given bond issue with maturities spread over several dates (649).

Simple interest

Interest on principal only (669).

Sinking fund

See Bond redemption fund.

Stock warrant

A right that allows the bondholder to purchase shares of common stock at a fixed price for a stated period of time. Warrants may be detachable or nondetachable (650).

Straight-line method of amortization

A procedure that, when applied to bond discount or premium, allocates an equal amount of discount or premium to each period in the life of a bond (658).

Term bond

A bond that matures on the same date as all other bonds in a given bond issue (649).

Trading on the equity

See Favorable financial leverage.

Trustee

Usually a bank or trust company appointed to represent the bondholders in a bond issue and to enforce the provisions of the bond indenture against the issuer (648).

Underwriter

An investment company that performs many tasks for the bond issuer in issuing bonds; may also guarantee the issuer a fixed price for the bonds (648).

Unfavorable financial leverage

Results when the cost of borrowed funds exceeds the revenue they generate; it is the reverse of **favorable financial leverage** (652).

Unregistered (bearer) bond

Ownership transfers by physical delivery (649).

Unsecured bond

A **debenture bond,** or simply a **debenture** (649).

DEMONSTRATION PROBLEM 17–1

Jackson Company issued $100,000 face value of 15%, 20-year bonds on April 30, 1987. The bonds are dated April 30, 1987, call for semiannual interest payments on April 30 and October 31, and are issued to yield 16% (8% per period).

Required: *a.* Compute the amount received for the bonds.

b. Prepare an amortization schedule. Enter data in the schedule for only the first two interest periods. Use the interest method.

c. Prepare journal entries to record issuance of the bonds, the first six months' interest expense on the bonds, the adjustment needed on December 31, 1987 (assuming Jackson's accounting year ends on that date), and the second six months' interest expense on April 30, 1988.

Solution to demonstration problem 17–1

a.   Price received:

Present value of principal: $100,000 × .04603 . . . $ 4,603
Present value of interest: $7,500 × 11.92461 89,435
Total $94,038

b.

(A) Interest payment date	(B) Bond Interest Expense debit (E × 0.16 × ½)	(C) Cash credit ($100,000 × 0.15 × ½)	(D) Discount on Bonds Payable credit (B − C)	(E) Carrying Value of Bonds Payable (previous balance in E + D)
Issue price				$94,038
10/31/87	$7,523	$7,500	$23	94,061
4/30/88	7,525	7,500	25	94,086

c.

JACKSON COMPANY
GENERAL JOURNAL

1987				
Apr. 30	Cash	94,038	
	Discount on Bonds Payable	5,962	
	Bonds Payable		100,000
	Issued $100,000 face value of 20-year, 15% bonds to yield 16%.		
Oct. 31	Bond Interest Expense	7,523	
	Discount on Bonds Payable		23
	Cash		7,500
	Paid semiannual bond interest expense.		
Dec. 31	Bond Interest Expense ($7,525 × ⅓)	2,508	
	Discount on Bonds Payable		8
	Bond Interest Payable ($7,500 × ⅓)		2,500
	To record accrual of two months' interest expense.		
1988				
Apr. 30	Bond Interest Payable	2,500	
	Bond Interest Expense ($7,525 × ⅔)	5,017	
	Discount on Bonds Payable		17
	Cash		7,500
	To record semiannual bond interest expense.		

DEMONSTRATION PROBLEM 17–2

On May 31, 1987, Martin Company purchased $10,000 face value of 8%, 10-year bonds issued by Shane Company. The bonds mature on May 31, 1997, call for semiannual interest payments on May 31 and November 30, and were issued for cash of $8,754, a price that yields an effective rate of 10%. The bonds are considered a long-term investment by Martin Company, which has a December 31 accounting year-end.

Required Prepare journal entries to record the investment in the Shane bonds, to record the interest collected on November 30, 1987, and to adjust the accounts on December 31, 1987. Use the effective interest rate method.

Solution to demonstration problem 17–2

MARTIN COMPANY
GENERAL JOURNAL

1987

May 31   Bond Investments 8,754
             Cash 8,754
          To record purchase of $10,000 face value of bonds.

Nov. 30   Cash ($10,000 × 0.08 × ½) 400
         Bond Investments 38
             Bond Interest Revenue ($8,754 × 0.10 × ½) 438
         To record semiannual interest revenue.

Dec. 31   Bond Interest Receivable ($10,000 × 0.08 × $\frac{1}{12}$) 67
         Bond Investments 6
             Bond Interest Revenue [($8,754 + $38) × 0.10 × $\frac{1}{12}$] 73
         To accrue one month's interest revenue.

QUESTIONS

1. What are the advantages of obtaining long-term funds by the issuance of bonds rather than additional shares of capital stock? What are the disadvantages?

2. What is a bond indenture? What parties are usually associated with it? Explain why.

3. Explain what is meant by the terms *coupon, callable, convertible,* and *debenture.*

4. What is meant by the term *trading on the equity?*

5. When bonds are issued between interest dates, why is it appropriate that the issuing corporation should receive cash equal to the amount of accrued interest in addition to the issue price of the bonds?

6. Why might it be more accurate to describe a sinking fund as a bond redemption fund?

7. Indicate how each of the following items should be classified in a balance sheet on December 31, 1987.

   a. Cash balance in a sinking fund.
   b. Accrued interest on bonds payable.

   c. Debenture bonds payable due in 1997.
   d. Premium on bonds payable.
   e. First-mortgage bonds payable, due July 1, 1988.
   f. Discount on bonds payable.
   g. First National Bank—Interest account.
   h. Convertible bonds payable due in 1990.

8. Why is the effective interest rate method of computing periodic interest expense considered theoretically preferable to the straight-line method?

9. Why would an investor whose intent is to hold bonds to maturity pay more for the bonds than their face value?

10. Describe the amortization of a premium or discount on a short-term bond investment.

11. Describe the amortization of a premium or discount on a long-term bond investment.

12. Under what circumstances should bond investments be written down below their carrying value?

BUSINESS SITUATION FOR DISCUSSION

Street Smart
Jeffrey M. Laderman

Managers Who Outguess the Bond Market*

The $100 million in fixed-income accounts at Century Capital Associates is now entirely in commercial paper and other cash equivalents—a situation that often gives rise to grumbling from clients who are paying for supervision of a portfolio of bonds. Managers James W. Harpel, 46, and Paul A. Zoschke, 44, find their position frustrating but defend it vigorously. "We expect higher interest rates, so we're in very short maturities," says Harpel. "Your judgment on whether to be short or long makes all the difference in this business."

Harpel's judgment has made the critical difference since he started managing fixed-income accounts in 1977. This year, a disaster for most bond managers, Harpel and Zoschke—who joined the firm in January—are up about 7.7% on a total-return basis, compared with 4.67% for the Shearson Lehman Government/Corporate Index. From 1977 through 1983, Century Capital's fixed-income portfolio was up 112.2%, compared with 66.9% for the Shearson Lehman index.

Turning Bearish

Furthermore, Harpel's firm—which is known for equity management—has provided above-average returns without resorting to the higher-yielding "junk" bonds (BW—June 4). While Harpel, a senior partner, focuses on macroeconomics and interest-rate forecasting, Zoschke, as director of fixed-income research, helps out with "sectoral" analysis, finding the mix of securities and maturities that will provide optimal returns.

With a bias toward the short maturities, Century Capital trailed the 1982–83 bull market in bonds. "I was late in buying bonds," admits Harpel. But he made a smart move by turning bearish in June of 1983—just a few weeks after the low in interest rates and the peak in bond prices—and shifting into cash. Expecting a period of gradually rising short-term rates in early 1984, Harpel and Zoschke bought floating-rate notes, which are typically issues of bank holding companies that pay interest in line with short-term rates.

But by the end of the first quarter of this year, the managers were becoming edgy about the exposure of money-center banks to shaky Third World debtors. So they sold off the floaters and fled to cash in time to avoid the disastrous sinking of the floater market in May (BW—July 9).

Right now, Harpel and Zoschke have the funds parked in top-rated commercial paper and short-term investment funds, what could be called bank-managed money market mutual funds for institutions. They are not impressed by the recent bond market rally. "It's too soon in the business cycle to be the real thing," says Harpel. "Credit demands are still likely to increase." Thus, the duo do not expect to buy long-term Treasury bonds again until the onset of a recession, which, because of the economy's strength, they think is 12 to 18 months away.

Faster Payback

When it appears that a recession will force interest rates downward, Zoschke says the best play is deep-discount, mortgage-backed securities such as the Government National Mortgage Assn. (GNMA) pass-through certificate with an 8% coupon. When interest rates are declining, says Zoschke, an investor gets additional price appreciation because the yield spread between mortgages and government bonds typically narrows. But there is another kicker: When mortgage rates decline, homes sales pick up, increasing the number of older, lower-rate mortgages that are paid off.

So, says Zoschke, an investor with a Ginnie Mae bought for 70¢ on the dollar finds an increasing number of mortgage prepayments paid back at par. In addition, when the rate of prepayments increases, the GNMA typically rises in price to anticipate the faster payback. Such extra dollars can kick in an additional 2% return—and in fixed-income investing, that is a lot of money.

Stock Investments— Cost, Equity, and Consolidations

After studying this chapter, you should be able to:

1. Prepare journal entries to account for stock investments.
2. Distinguish between the cost and equity methods of accounting for stock investments.
3. Describe the nature of parent and subsidiary corporations.
4. Prepare consolidated financial statements through the use of a consolidated statement work sheet.
5. Identify the differences between purchase accounting and pooling of interests accounting.
6. Describe the uses and limitations fo consolidated financial statements.
7. Define and use correctly the new terms in the glossary.

You may have read about a large company attempting to "take over" a smaller company by acquiring a controlling interest (more than 50% of the outstanding shares) in that "target" company. Some of these takeover attempts are "friendly" (not resisted by the target company) and some are "unfriendly" (resisted by the target company). If the attempt is successful, the two companies become one business entity for accounting purposes, and consolidated financial statements are prepared. The company that takes over another company is called the parent company; the company acquired is called the subsidiary company. This chapter discusses accounting for parent and subsidiary companies.

When a corporation purchases the stock of another corporation, the method of accounting for the stock investment depends on the corporation's **motivation** for making the investment and the **relative size** of the investment. A corporation's motivation for purchasing the stock of another company may be as (1) a temporary investment of excess cash; (2) a long-term investment in a substan-

Illustration 18.2

Consolidation Policies

	1983	1982	1981	1980
Nature of subsidiaries not consolidated:				
Finance related:				
Credit	97	102	94	97
Insurance	60	60	53	49
Leasing	18	21	24	22
Banks	5	4	6	5
Real estate	31	33	29	27
Foreign	17	20	19	28
	228	240	225	228
Number of companies:				
Consolidating all significant subsidiaries	419	414	423	422
Consolidating certain significant subsidiaries	172	180	168	170
Not presenting consolidated financial statements	9	6	9	8
Total companies	600	600	600	600

Source: American Institute of Certified Public Accountants, *Accounting Trends & Techniques* (New York: AICPA, 1984), p. 42.

solidated financial statements, the effects of intercompany transactions must be eliminated by making **elimination entries.** Elimination entries allow the presentation of all account balances as if the parent and its subsidiaries were a single economic enterprise. **Elimination entries are made only on a consolidated statement work sheet, not in the accounting records of the parent or subsidiaries.** After elimination entries are prepared, the amounts remaining for each account on the work sheet are totaled and used to prepare the consolidated financial statements.

To illustrate the need for elimination entries, assume Y Company organized the Z Company, receiving all of Z Company's $100,000 par value common stock for $100,000 cash. The parent records the following entry on its books:

Investment in Z Company	100,000	
Cash		100,000
To record an investment in Z Company. Purchased 100% of Z Company stock.		

Z Company, the subsidiary, records the following on its books:

Cash	100,000	
Common Stock		100,000
To record issuance of all of the common stock to Y Company.		

An elimination entry is needed to offset the parent company's subsidiary investment account against the stockholders' equity accounts of the subsidiary. When the consolidated balance sheet is prepared, the required elimination on the work sheet is:

Common Stock—Z Company	100,000	
Investment in Z Company		100,000

This elimination is required because the parent company's investment in the stock of the subsidiary actually represents an equity in the net assets of the subsidiary. Unless the investment is eliminated, the same resources will appear twice on the consolidated balance sheet—first as the investment account of the parent and second as the assets of the subsidiary. The elimination of Z Company's common stock is necessary to avoid double counting stockholders' equity. Viewing the two companies as if they were one, the Z Company common stock is really not outstanding; it is held within the consolidated group.

Consolidated financial statements present financial data as though the companies were a single entity. Since no entity can owe an amount to itself or be due an amount from itself, intercompany receivables and payables (amounts owed to and due from companies within the consolidated group) are items that must be eliminated during the preparation of consolidated financial statements. For example, assume a subsidiary company owes its parent company $5,000, as evidenced by a $5,000 note receivable on the parent's books and a $5,000 note payable on the subsidiary's books. In this case, no debt is owed to or due from any entity outside the consolidated enterprise, so those balances would be eliminated by an entry like the following that offsets the note receivable against the note payable:

Note Payable (subsidiary company)	5,000	
Note Receivable (parent company)		5,000
To eliminate intercompany receivables and payables.		

Other intercompany balances would be similarly eliminated when consolidated statements are prepared.

■ CONSOLIDATED BALANCE SHEET AT TIME OF ACQUISITION

Acquisition of Subsidiary at Book Value

To combine assets and liabilities of a parent company and its subsidiaries, a consolidated statement work sheet similar to the one shown in Illustration 18.3 is prepared. A consolidated statement work sheet is an informal record on which elimination entries are made for the purpose of showing account balances as if the parent and its subsidiaries were a single economic enterprise. The first two columns of the work sheet show assets, liabilities, and stockholders' equity of the parent and subsidiary as they appear on each corporation's individual balance sheet. The pair of columns labeled Eliminations allows intercompany items to be offset and consequently eliminated from the consolidated statement. The final column shows the amounts that will appear on the consolidated balance sheet.

The work sheet shown in Illustration 18.3 consolidates the accounts of P Company and its subsidiary, S Company, on January 1, 1987. P Company acquired S Company on January 1, 1987, by purchasing all of its outstanding voting common stock for $106,000 cash, which was the **book value** of the stock. Book value is equal to stockholders' equity, or net assets. Thus, common stock ($100,000) plus retained earnings ($6,000) equals $106,000. When P Company acquired the S Company stock, P Company made the following entry:

Investment in S Company	106,000	
Cash		106,000
To record investment in S Company.		

The investment appears as an asset on P Company's balance sheet. By buying the subsidiary's stock, the parent acquired a 100% equity, or ownership, interest in the subsidiary's net assets. Thus, if both the investment account

Illustration 18.6

Consolidated Balance Sheet Work Sheet

P COMPANY AND SUBSIDIARY S COMPANY
Work Sheet for Consolidated Balance Sheet
January 1, 1987 (date of acquisition)

	P Company	S Company	Eliminations Debit	Eliminations Credit	Consolidated Amounts
Assets					
Cash	42,000	12,000			54,000
Notes receivable	5,000			(2) 5,000	
Accounts receivable, net	24,000	15,000			39,000
Inventory	35,000	30,000			65,000
Investment in S Company	90,000			(1) 90,000	
Equipment, net	41,000	15,000			56,000
Buildings, net	65,000	35,000			100,000
Land	20,000	10,000			30,000
Goodwill			(1) 5,200		5,200
	322,000	117,000			349,200
Liabilities and Stockholders' Equity					
Accounts payable	18,000	6,000			24,000
Notes payable		5,000	(2) 5,000		
Common stock	250,000	100,000	(1) 100,000		250,000
Retained earnings	54,000	6,000	(1) 6,000		54,000
Minority interest				(1) 21,200	21,200
	322,000	117,000	116,200	116,200	349,200

Illustration 18.7

Consolidated Balance Sheet

P COMPANY AND SUBSIDIARY S COMPANY
Consolidated Balance Sheet
January 1, 1987

Assets

Current assets:
Cash	$ 54,000	
Accounts receivable, net	39,000	
Inventory	65,000	
Total current assets		$158,000

Property, plant, and equipment:
Equipment, net	$ 56,000	
Buildings, net	100,000	
Land	30,000	
Total property, plant, and equipment		186,000
Goodwill		5,200
Total assets		$349,200

Liabilities and Stockholders' Equity

Liabilities:
Accounts payable		$ 24,000
Minority interest		21,200

Stockholders' equity:
Common stock	$250,000	
Retained earnings	54,000	
Total stockholders' equity		304,000
Total liabilities and stockholders' equity		$349,200

■ ACCOUNTING FOR INCOME, LOSSES, AND DIVIDENDS OF A SUBSIDIARY

If a subsidiary is operating profitably, its net assets and retained earnings increase. When the subsidiary pays dividends, both the parent company and minority stockholders share in the distribution. All transactions of the subsidiary are recorded in the accounting records of the subsidiary in a normal manner.

As noted earlier, two different methods used by an investor to account for investments in common stock are the **cost** and **equity methods.** The general rules for determining the appropriate method of accounting are again summarized below.

Percent of outstanding voting common stock of investee owned by investor	Method of accounting required by Accounting Principles Board in most cases
Less than 20%	Cost
20%–50%	Equity
More than 50%:	
Consolidated subsidiary	Cost or equity
Nonconsolidated subsidiary . . .	Equity

According to the table, a parent company can use either the cost or equity method of accounting for its investment in a consolidated subsidiary. This choice is allowed because the investment account is eliminated during the consolidation process; therefore, the results are identical after consolidation.

Cost Method for Investments in Subsidiaries

Under the cost method, the parent (investor) company records its investment in a subsidiary at cost (price paid at acquisition) and does not adjust the investment account balance subsequently. Dividends received from the subsidiary (investee) are recorded by debiting Cash and crediting Dividend Revenue. Thus, the investment account balance normally does not change under the cost method.

Equity Method for Investments in Subsidiaries

The equity method for investments in subsidiaries works just as we described earlier when applied to investments of 20% to 50% in nonconsolidated subsidiaries.

Under the equity method, as with the cost method, the parent company initially records its investment at cost. The major difference between the two methods is that the equity method calls for the investment account to be adjusted periodically for the parent company's share of the subsidiary's income, losses, and dividends as they are reported by the subsidiary. The parent company's share of the subsidiary's income is debited to the investment account and credited to an account labeled Income of S (subsidiary) Company.

For example, assume the subsidiary S Company, mentioned in the preceding illustrations, earned $20,000 during 1987. P Company owns 80% of S Company. P Company would record its share of S Company's income in the following manner:

```
Investment in S Company   . . .  .  .   . .   .  .   .  .      16,000
    Income of S Company ($20,000 × 0.80) . . .  .  .  .  .           16,000
    To record 80% of subsidiary's income.
```

The $16,000 debit to the investment account **increases the parent's equity in the subsidiary company.** The Income of S Company account will be closed at the end of the period to Income Summary, which then is closed to P Company's Retained Earnings.

If a subsidiary incurs a loss, the parent company debits a loss account and credits the investment account for the parent's share of the loss. For example, assume S Company incurs a loss of $10,000 in 1988. Since P Company still owns 80% of S Company, P Company records its share of the loss as follows:

```
Loss of S Company ($10,000 × 0.80)   .  .  .  .  .  .  .  .      8,000
    Investment in S Company .  .   .  .  .  .  .  .  .  .  .           8,000
    To record 80% of subsidiary's loss.
```

The $8,000 debit is closed first to Income Summary, which then is closed to Retained Earnings; the $8,000 **credit reduces P Company's equity in the subsidiary.**

When a subsidiary declares and pays a dividend, the assets and retained earnings of the subsidiary are reduced by the dividend payment amount. When the parent company receives its share of the dividends, it debits the asset received (Cash, in this case) and credits the investment account. For instance, assume S Company declares a cash dividend of $8,000 in 1987. P Company's share of the dividend amounts to $6,400 ($8,000 × 0.80) and is recorded as follows:

```
Cash   .  .   .  .  .  .   .  .   .  .  .  .  .  .  .  .  .  .      6,400
    Investment in S Company .  .   .  .  .  .  .  .  .  .           6,400
    To record dividend received from subsidiary.
```

The receipt of the dividend **reduces the parent's equity in the subsidiary** as shown by the credit to the investment account.

As noted earlier, a company may purchase all or part of another firm at more than book value and create goodwill on the consolidated balance sheet. The Accounting Principles Board in *APB Opinion No. 17* requires that all goodwill be amortized over a period not to exceed 40 years. This amortization is necessary under the equity method, but will be left to a more advanced text.

CONSOLIDATED FINANCIAL STATEMENTS AT A DATE AFTER ACQUISITION

As you have just seen, under the equity method the investment account on the parent company's books increases and decreases as the parent records its share of the income, losses, and dividends reported by the subsidiary. Thus, the balance in the investment account differs after acquisition from its balance on the date of acquisition. Consequently, the amounts eliminated on the consolidated statement work sheet will differ from year to year. As an illustration, assume the following facts:

1. P Company acquired 100% of the outstanding voting common stock of S Company on January 1, 1987. P Company paid $121,000 for stockholders' equity totaling $106,000. The excess of cost over book value is attributable to (a) an undervaluation of land amounting to $4,000 and (b) the remainder to S Company's above-average earnings prospects.
2. During 1987, S Company earned $20,000 from operations.
3. On December 31, 1987, S Company paid a cash dividend of $8,000.
4. S Company owes P Company $5,000 on a note at December 31.
5. Including its share (100%) of S Company's income, P Company earned $31,000 during 1987.
6. P Company paid a cash dividend of $10,000 during December 1987.
7. P Company uses the equity method of accounting for its investment in S Company.

The financial statements for the two companies as of December 31, 1987, are given in the first two columns of Illustration 18.8.

The type of work sheet shown in Illustration 18.8 will be used to prepare a consolidated income statement, statement of retained earnings, and balance sheet. Notice that in Illustration 18.8, P Company has a balance of $20,000 in its Income of S Company account and a balance of $133,000 in its Investment in S Company account. These balances are the result of the following journal entries actually made by P Company in 1987:

```
1987
Jan.  1  Investment in S Company . . . . . . . . . . .  121,000
            Cash     . . . . . . . . . . . . . . . .              121,000
         To record 100% investment in subsidiary.

Dec. 31  Investment in S Company . . . . . . . . . . .   20,000
            Income of S Company   . . . . . . . . . .               20,000
         To record income of subsidiary.

Dec. 31  Cash . . . . . . . . . . . . . . . . . . . .    8,000
            Investment in S Company   . . . . . . . . .              8,000
         To record dividends received from subsidiary.
```

The elimination entries on the work sheet in Illustration 18.8 are explained below.

Entry (1): During the year, S Company earned $20,000. P Company increased its investment account balance by $20,000. The first entry (1) on the work sheet eliminates the subsidiary's income from the investment account and Income of S Company ($20,000). This entry reverses the entries made on the books of P Company to recognize the parent's share of the subsidiary's income (December 31 entry above).

Entry (2): When S Company paid its cash dividend, P Company debited Cash and credited the investment account for $8,000 (December

Illustration 18.8

*Consolidated Work
Sheet One Year after
Acquisition*

P COMPANY AND SUBSIDIARY S COMPANY
Work Sheet for Consolidated Financial Statements
December 31, 1987

	P Company	S Company	Eliminations Debit	Eliminations Credit	Consolidated Amounts
Income Statement					
Revenue from sales	397,000	303,000			700,000
Income of S Company	20,000		*(1)* 20,000		
Cost of goods sold	(250,000)	(180,000)			(430,000)
Expenses (excluding depreciation and taxes)	(100,000)	(80,000)			(180,000)
Depreciation expense	(7,400)	(5,000)			(12,400)
Income tax expense	(28,600)	(18,000)			(46,600)
Net income—carried forward	31,000	20,000			31,000
Statement of Retained Earnings					
Retained earnings— January 1:					
P Company	54,000				54,000
S Company		6,000	*(3)* 6,000		
Net income— brought forward	31,000	20,000			31,000
	85,000	26,000			85,000
Dividends:					
P Company	(10,000)				(10,000)
S Company		(8,000)		*(2)* 8,000	
Retained earnings— December 31— carried forward	75,000	18,000			75,000
Balance Sheet Assets					
Cash	38,000	16,000			54,000
Notes receivable	5,000			*(4)* 5,000	
Accounts receivable, net	25,000	18,000			43,000
Inventory	40,000	36,000			76,000
Investment in S Company	133,000		*(2)* 8,000	*(3)* 121,000	
				(1) 20,000	
Equipment, net	36,900	12,000			48,900
Buildings, net	61,700	33,000			94,700
Land	20,000	10,000	*(3)* 4,000		34,000
Goodwill			*(3)* 11,000		11,000
	359,600	125,000			361,600
Liabilities and Stockholders' Equity					
Accounts payable	19,600	2,000			21,600
Notes payable	15,000	5,000	*(4)* 5,000		15,000
Common stock	250,000	100,000	*(3)* 100,000		250,000
Retained earnings— brought forward	75,000	18,000			75,000
	359,600	125,000	154,000	154,000	361,600

31 entry above). The second entry *(2)* restores the investment account to its balance before the dividends from S Company were deducted. That is, P Company's investment account is debited and S Company's dividends account is credited for $8,000. On a consolidated basis, a company cannot pay a dividend to itself.

Entry *(3):*   This entry eliminates the original investment account balance ($121,000) and the subsidiary's stockholders' equity accounts as of the date of acquisition (retained earnings of $6,000 and common stock of $100,000). The entry also establishes goodwill of $11,000 and increases land by $4,000 to account for the excess of acquisition cost over book value.

After the first three entries have been made, the investment account contains a zero balance from the viewpoint of the consolidated entity.

Entry *(4):*   This entry eliminates the intercompany debt of $5,000.

After the eliminations have been made, the corresponding amounts are added together and placed in the Consolidated Amounts column. The net income row in the Income Statement section is carried forward to the net income row in the Statement of Retained Earnings section. Likewise, the ending retained earnings row in the Statement of Retained Earnings section is carried forward to the retained earnings row in the Balance Sheet section. The final work sheet column is then used to prepare the consolidated income statement (Illustration 18.9), consolidated statement of retained earnings (Illustration 18.10), and consolidated balance sheet (Illustration 18.11).[5] As stated earlier, amortization of goodwill is ignored in the illustration.

■ PURCHASE VERSUS POOLING OF INTERESTS

In the illustrations in this chapter, it has been assumed that the parent company acquired the subsidiary's common stock in exchange for cash. The acquiring company could also have used assets other than cash in the exchange. This kind of transaction—the exchange of cash or other assets for the common stock of another company—is called a purchase. When assets other than cash are used, the cost of the acquired company's stock is the fair market value of the assets given up or of the stock received, whichever can be more clearly and objectively determined.

Another way a company can acquire the common stock of another company is to issue common stock of its own in exchange for the other company's common stock. In such cases, the stockholders of both companies maintain a joint ownership interest in the combined company. Such a business combination involving the issuance of common stock in exchange for common stock is

---

[5] Appendix A at the back of the text shows consolidated financial statements for an actual corporation.

Required: a. Prepare general journal entries to record the investment and the effect of the subsidiary's income, losses, and dividends on Hadley Company's accounts.

b. Compute the investment account balance on December 31, 1988.

P18–5–A

Prepare work sheet for consolidated balance sheet at acquisition

Ivory Company acquired all of the outstanding voting common stock of Jade Company on January 3, 1987, for $201,600. On the date of acquisition, the balance sheets for the two companies were as follows:

	Ivory Company	Jade Company
Assets		
Cash	$ 33,600	$ 28,800
Accounts receivable	64,800	60,000
Notes receivable	36,000	9,600
Inventory	93,600	43,200
Investment in Jade Company	201,600	
Equipment, net	172,800	79,200
Total assets	$602,400	$220,800
Liabilities and Stockholders' Equity		
Accounts payable	$ 62,400	$ 19,200
Common stock—$15 par value	288,000	139,200
Retained earnings	252,000	62,400
Total liabilities and stockholders' equity	$602,400	$220,800

Required: Prepare a work sheet for a consolidated balance sheet on the date of acquisition.

P18–6–A

Prepare work sheet and consolidated balance sheet at acquisition

Dark Company acquired all of the outstanding voting common stock of Dawn Company on January 2, 1987, for $360,000. On the date of acquisition, the balance sheets for the two companies were as follows:

	Dark Company	Dawn Company
Assets		
Cash	$ 75,000	$ 22,500
Accounts receivable	36,000	30,000
Notes receivable	15,000	9,000
Inventory	114,000	72,000
Investment in Dawn Company	360,000	
Equipment, net	102,000	61,500
Buildings, net	277,500	138,000
Land	117,000	37,500
Total assets	$1,096,500	$370,500
Liabilities and Stockholders' Equity		
Accounts payable	$ 66,000	$ 30,000
Notes payable	18,000	21,000
Common stock—$30 par value	795,000	297,000
Retained earnings	217,500	22,500
Total liabilities and stockholders' equity	$1,096,500	$370,500

The management of Dark Company thinks that the Dawn Company's land is undervalued by $13,500. The remainder of the excess of cost over book value is due to superior earnings potential.

On the date of acquisition, Dawn Company borrowed $15,000 from Dark Company by giving a note.

Required: a. Prepare a work sheet for a consolidated balance sheet on the date of acquisition.

b. Prepare a consolidated balance sheet for January 2, 1987.

P18-7-A

Prepare work sheet for consolidated financial statements

Refer back to Problem 18–6–A. Dark Company uses the equity method. Assume the following are taken from the adjusted trial balances of Dark Company and Dawn Company on December 31, 1987:

	Dark Company	Dawn Company
Cash	$ 72,000	$ 30,358
Accounts receivable	46,128	34,500
Notes receivable	28,500	7,500
Inventory, December 31	127,500	84,000
Investment in Dawn Company	376,613	
Equipment, net	95,625	57,655
Buildings, net	263,625	131,100
Land	117,000	37,500
Cost of goods sold	672,000	180,000
Expenses (excluding depreciation and taxes) . .	180,000	67,500
Depreciation expense	20,250	10,745
Income tax expense	47,472	10,292
Dividends	39,750	14,850
Total of the accounts with debit balances . . .	$2,086,463	$666,000
Accounts payable	$ 60,000	$ 31,500
Notes payable	22,500	15,000
Common stock—$30 par value	795,000	297,000
Retained earnings	217,500	22,500
Revenue from sales	960,000	300,000
Income of Dawn Company	31,463	
Total of the accounts with credit balances . . .	$2,086,463	$666,000

There is no intercompany debt at the end of the year.

Required: Prepare a work sheet for consolidated financial statements on December 31, 1987. Ignore the amortization of goodwill.

P18-8-A

Prepare consolidated income statement, statement of retained earnings, and balance sheet

Using the work sheet from Problem 18–7–A, prepare the following items:

a. Consolidated income statement for the year ended December 31, 1987.
b. Consolidated statement of retained earnings for the year ended December 31, 1987.
c. Consolidated balance sheet for December 31, 1987.

PROBLEMS, SERIES B

P18-1-B

Prepare entries for temporary investments in marketable equity securities

The Evans Company acquired on July 15, 1987, 200 shares of Tom Company $120 par value capital stock at $116.40 per share plus a broker's commission of $144. On August 1, 1987, Evans Company received a cash dividend of 72 cents per share. On November 3, 1987, it sold 100 of these shares at $126 per share less a broker's commission of $96. On December 1, 1987, the Tom Company issued shares comprising a 100% stock dividend declared on its capital stock on November 18.

On December 31, 1987, the end of the calendar-year accounting period, the market quotation for Tom's common stock was $55.20 per share. The decline was considered to be temporary.

Required: a. Prepare journal entries to record all of the above data assuming the securities are considered temporary investments and are to be valued at LCM.

b. Assume Tom Company has become a major customer. If the shares are held for affiliation purposes, indicate how they should be shown in the balance sheet.

P18-2-B

Prepare entries for temporary investments in marketable equity securities; compare entries to those for long-term investments

On October 17, 1986, Pitcher Company purchased the following common stocks at the indicated per share prices that included commissions:

300 shares of Cee Company common stock @ $72 . .	$21,600
500 shares of Dee Company common stock @ $48 . .	$24,000
800 shares of Fey Company common stock @ $24 . .	$19,200
	$64,800

On December 31, 1986, the market prices per share of the above common stocks were Cee, $74.40, Dee, $45.60, and Fey, $18.

Summarized, the cash dividends per share received in 1987 were Cee, $2.40; Dee, $1.20; and Fey, $0.90. Also, a 100% stock dividend (300 shares) was received on the Cee Company common stock after the cash dividend was paid.

On December 31, 1987, the per share market prices were Cee, $40.80; Dee, $38.40; and Fey, $24.

All of the changes in market prices given above are considered temporary.

Required: a. Prepare journal entries for all of the above, including calendar year-end adjusting entries, assuming the shares of common stock acquired are considered short-term investments.

b. If the securities acquired are considered long-term investments, how would the entries made in (a) differ?

c. For both parts (a) and (b), give the descriptions (titles) and the dollar amounts of the items that would appear in the income statements for 1986 and 1987.

P18-3-B

Prepare equity method entries for an investment and eliminating entries for consolidated work sheet

On January 1, 1987, Raven Company acquired 80% of the outstanding voting common stock of the Dalton Company for $336,000 cash. Raven Company uses the equity method. During 1987, Dalton reported $56,000 of net income and paid $24,000 in dividends. The stockholders' equity section of the December 31, 1986, balance sheet for Dalton follows:

Stockholders' equity:	
Common stock—$7 par . . .	$350,000
Retained earnings	70,000
Total stockholders' equity . .	$420,000

Required: a. Prepare the general journal entry to record the investment and the effect on Dalton's income and dividends on Raven Company's accounts.

b. Prepare the elimination entry that would be made on the work sheet for a consolidated balance sheet as of the date of acquisition.

P18-4-B

Prepare entries for investment, compute year-end balance in investment account

Technix Company acquired 75% of the outstanding voting common stock of Harmon Company for $481,600 cash on January 1, 1986. The investment is accounted for under the equity method. During 1986, 1987, and 1988, Harmon Company reported the following:

	Net income (loss)	Dividends paid
1986 . .	$119,280	$96,880
1987 . .	(15,120)	–0–
1988 . .	36,120	24,080

Required: a. Prepare general journal entries to record the investment and the effect of the subsidiary's income, losses, and dividends on Technix company's accounts.

b. Compute the balance in the investment account on December 31, 1988.

P18–5–B

Prepare a work sheet for consolidated balance sheet at acquisition

Tide Company acquired 100% of the outstanding voting common stock of Houston Company on January 2, 1987, for $121,600 cash. On the date of acquisition, the balance sheets for the two companies were as follows:

	Tide Company	Houston Company
Assets		
Cash	$ 9,600	$ 22,400
Accounts receivable	22,400	28,800
Notes receivable	16,000	9,600
Inventory	40,000	24,000
Investment in Houston Company	121,600	
Equipment, net	35,200	44,800
Total assets	$244,800	$129,600
Liabilities and Stockholders' Equity		
Accounts payable	$ 25,600	$ 8,000
Notes payable	19,200	
Common stock—$32 par value	160,000	96,000
Retained earnings	40,000	25,600
Total liabilities and stockholders' equity	$244,800	$129,600

Also on January 2, 1987, Tide Company borrowed $9,600 from Houston Company by giving a note.

Required: Prepare a work sheet for a consolidated balance sheet as of the date of acquisition.

P18–6–B

Prepare work sheet and consolidated balance sheet; prepare consolidated balance sheet

Outland Company acquired 100% of the outstanding voting common stock of Paul Company on January 2, 1987, for $450,000. On the date of acquisition, the balance sheets for the two companies were as follows:

	Outland Company	Paul Company
Assets		
Cash	$ 52,500	$ 30,000
Accounts receivable	39,000	24,000
Notes receivable	60,000	15,000
Inventory	82,500	39,000
Investment in Paul Company	450,000	
Equipment, net	108,000	75,000
Buildings, net	315,000	165,000
Land	127,500	67,500
Total assets	$1,234,500	$415,500
Liabilities and Stockholders Equity		
Accounts payable	$ 19,500	$ 22,500
Notes payable	15,000	18,000
Common stock—$15 par value	900,000	300,000
Retained earnings	300,000	75,000
Total liabilities and stockholders' equity	$1,234,500	$415,500

The excess of cost over book value is attributable to the above-average earnings prospects of Paul Company. On the date of acquisition, Paul Company borrowed $12,000 from Outland Company by giving a note.

Required: a.   Prepare a work sheet for a consolidated balance sheet as of the date of acquisition.
b.   Prepare a consolidated balance sheet for January 2, 1987.

alternative concepts or formats—working capital basis and cash basis. In this chapter you learn about these two concepts of funds and the procedures used to prepare the statement of changes in financial position under each concept.

■ USES OF THE STATEMENT OF CHANGES IN FINANCIAL POSITION

The **statement of changes in financial position** summarizes the financing and investing activities of a company for a period; it reports on past management decisions on such matters as issuance of capital stock or sale of long-term bonds. The statement reports on the flow of working capital or cash in the business. This information is available only in bits and pieces from the other financial statements. Because working capital and cash flows are vital to a company's financial health, the statement of changes in financial position provides useful information to management and other interested parties, especially creditors and investors.

Management Uses

Since the statement of changes in financial position presents all significant financing and investing activities, management can see the effects of its past major policy decisions in quantitative form by reviewing the statement. The statement may show a flow of funds from operations large enough to finance all projected capital needs internally rather than having to issue long-term debt or additional stock. Or, if the company has been experiencing working capital or cash shortages, management can use the statement to determine why such shortages are ocurring. After reviewing the statement, management may decide to reduce dividends in order to conserve funds and reduce cash shortages.

Creditor and Investor Uses

Information on the statement of changes in financial position may provide creditors and investors with valuable clues to:

1. The extent to which internally generated funds cover projected capital needs.
2. The likelihood of the company's paying or increasing future dividends.
3. Management's preferences toward financing and investing.
4. The company's ability to make principal and interest payments on its debt.
5. The feasibility of a planned expansion in the light of available resources.

■ THE CONCEPT OF FUNDS

The term *funds,* in a broad sense, means all financial resources of a company. But the definition of funds in reference to the statement of changes in financial position has a much more precise meaning. **Funds** are often defined as **working capital** or as **cash.** Either definition is an acceptable basis on which to prepare a statement of changes in financial position.

Funds Defined as Working Capital

Funds have typically been defined as working capital for purposes of preparing the statement of changes in financial position. **Working capital** is equal to current assets minus current liabilities. **Using the working capital definition of funds, the effects of any transaction that increases or decreases working capital are included in the statement of changes in financial position.** The borrowing of cash by the use of long-term bonds would be included because the transaction increases total current assets, thus **increasing** working capital. The purchase of a plant asset on a short-term credit basis would be included because it **reduces** working capital by increasing total current liabilities. Defining funds as working capital also permits the exclusion of many routine transactions. Examples of transactions that may be excluded are collection of an account receivable or payment of an account payable. The first transaction merely substitutes one current asset (cash) for another (accounts receivable). The second transaction reduces a current asset (cash) and reduces a current liability (accounts payable). Both transactions change the **composition** of working capital, but not the **amount** of working capital.

Illustration 19.1 diagrams the transactions that affect working capital. Four basic transaction types are identified that affect sources and uses of working capital.

Illustration 19.1

*Typical Transactions
that Affect
Working Capital*

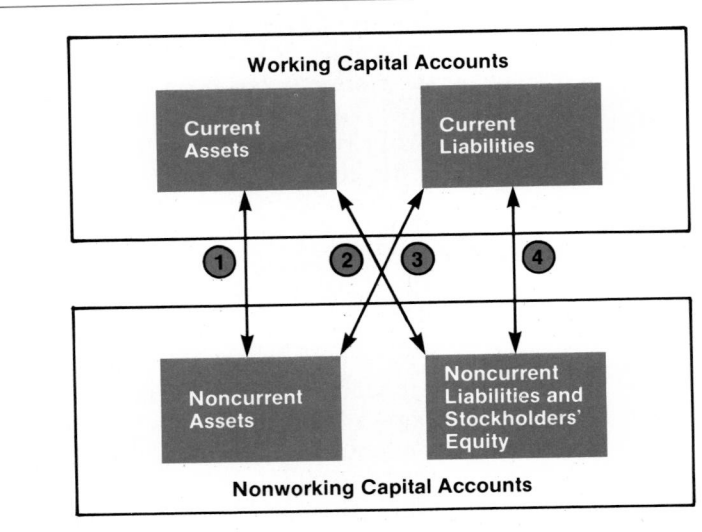

Transaction type	Sources	Transaction type	Uses
1	Sold a plant asset for cash	1	Purchased a plant asset for cash
2	Issued bonds and received cash	2	Retired bonds by paying cash
3	Returned a defective truck to an auto dealership and took back the 90-day note signed at date of purchase	3	Purchased a truck and gave a 90-day note
4	Signed a two-year note payable to settle an outstanding account payable	4	Declared a cash dividend

Illustration 19.7

Statement of Income and Retained Earnings

UNITED STATES CORPORATION Statement of Income and Retained Earnings For the Year Ended December 31, 1987		
Net sales		$1,464,200
Cost of goods sold		871,150
Gross margin		$ 593,050
Operating expenses:		
Salaries	$215,000	
Depreciation ($3,250, buildings; $31,050, equipment)	34,300	
Supplies	7,320	
Advertising	90,000	
Taxes, payroll and other	26,000	
General administrative expenses	123,780	
Total operating expenses		496,400
Net income from operations		$ 96,650
Other revenue:		
Interest revenue	$ 1,950	
Gain on sale of long-term investments	1,700	3,650
		$ 100,300
Other expenses:		
Interest expense	$ 3,800	
Loss on sale of equipment	900	4,700
Net income before federal income taxes		$ 95,600
Deduct: Federal income taxes		45,250
Net income to retained earnings		$ 50,350
Retained earnings, January 1		84,100
		$ 134,450
Deduct: Dividends declared and paid		18,000
Retained earnings, December 31		$ 116,450

financial position. The discussion that follows will describe the items and trace their effects in the entries made on the working paper.

The steps in preparing the working paper are described below:

1. Enter the account balances of all balance sheet accounts at the beginning of the period in the first column and at the end of the period in the fourth column. Notice that the debit items are listed first, followed by the credit items.
2. Total the debits and the credits in the first and fourth columns to make sure that debits equal credits in each column.
3. Write "Financial resources provided" immediately below the total of the credit items. Skip sufficient lines on which to record all sources of funds; then write "Financial resources applied."
4. Entries for analyzing transactions are entered in the second and third columns. The entries, which may be made in any order, serve two functions: (a) they explain the change in each account, and (b) they record the sources and uses of funds. These entries will be discussed individually.
5. Total the debits and credits in the second and third columns; they should be equal. There will be one pair of totals for the balance sheet items and another pair for the sources and uses of funds. The bottom portion of the working paper is used to prepare the formal statement of changes in financial position.

Illustration 19.8

*Comparative
Balance Sheet*

	UNITED STATES CORPORATION **Comparative Balance Sheet** **December 31, 1986, and 1987**		
	1987	**1986**	***Increase/*** ***decrease****
Assets			
Current assets:			
Cash	$ 46,300	$ 40,900	$ 5,400
Accounts receivable net	112,160	101,000	11,160
Inventories	130,600	115,300	15,300
Prepaid expenses	3,100	4,700	1,600*
Total current assets	$292,160	$261,900	$30,260
Investments	$ 17,000	$ 25,000	$ 8,000*
Property, plant, and equipment			
Land	$100,000	$ 80,000	$20,000
Buildings	175,000	130,000	45,000
Accumulated depreciation—buildings	(29,750)	(26,500)	(3,250)
Equipment	198,000	175,000	23,000
Accumulated depreciation—equipment	(57,650)	(43,100)	(14,550)
Total property, plant, and equipment	$385,600	$315,400	$70,200
Total assets	$694,760	$602,300	$92,460
Liabilities and Stockholders' Equity			
Current liabilities:			
Accounts payable	$ 91,420	$ 86,870	$ 4,550
Accrued liabilities	9,890	12,230	2,340*
Estimated federal income tax liability	12,000	14,100	2,100*
Total current liabilities	$113,310	$113,200	$ 110
Long-term liabilities:			
Mortgage note payable, 10% (on land and buildings)	$ 35,000	$ –0–	$35,000
Bonds payable, 8%, due 1991	40,000	40,000	–0–
Total long-term liabilities	$ 75,000	$ 40,000	$35,000
Total liabilities	$188,310	$153,200	$35,110
Stockholders' equity			
Common stock, stated value, $50 per share	$390,000	$365,000	$25,000
Retained earnings	116,450	84,100	32,350
Total stockholders' equity	$506,450	$449,100	$57,350
Total liabilities and stockholders' equity	$694,760	$602,300	$92,460

Completing the Working Paper

The working paper in Illustration 19.9 is completed by analyzing the change in each noncash balance sheet account. Although this procedure may seem odd at first, remember that the focus of this working paper is on cash and that every change in cash is accompanied by a change in a noncash balance sheet account. After entries have been properly made to analyze all changes in noncash balance sheet accounts, the working paper will show all sources and uses of cash. The explanations below are keyed by numbers to the entries on the working paper.

Entry (1). The beginning and ending cash balances are compared to determine the change for the year, which is a $5,400 increase. An entry is made on the working paper debiting Cash for $5,400 and crediting Increase in Cash for the Year under "Financial resources applied." This entry indicates that of the cash flowing into the company during the year, $5,400 was used to increase the Cash balance. The entry also sets out the change in cash that the statement seeks to explain. No further attention need be paid to cash in completing the working paper.

Attention is now directed toward changes in other balance sheet accounts. These accounts can be dealt with in any order. But, in order to group certain items, the noncurrent accounts are analyzed first.

Entry (2). Investments is the first noncurrent account. The additional information discloses that investments were sold at a gain, which was recorded in the following manner:

Cash	9,700	
Investments		8,000
Gain on Sale of Investments		1,700

Illustration 19.9

Working Paper for Statement of Changes in Financial Position—Cash Basis

UNITED STATES CORPORATION
Working Paper for Statement of Changes in Financial Position—Cash Basis for the Year Ended, December 31, 1987

	Account Balances 12/31/86	Analysis of Transactions for 1987		Account Balances 12/31/87
		Debit	Credit	
Debits				
Cash	40,900	(1) 5,400		46,300
Accounts Receivable	101,000	(10) 11,160		112,160
Inventories	115,300	(11) 15,300		130,600
Prepaid Expenses	4,700		(12) 1,600	3,100
Investments	25,000		(2) 8,000	17,000
Land	80,000	(3) 20,000		100,000
Buildings	130,000	(3) 45,000		175,000
Equipment	175,000	(5) 43,000	(4) 20,000	198,000
Totals	671,900			782,160
Credits				
Accumulated Depreciation— Buildings	26,500		(6) 3,250	29,750
Accumulated Depreciation— Equipment	43,100	(4) 16,500	(6) 31,050	57,650
Accounts Payable	86,870		(13) 4,550	91,420
Accrued Liabilities	12,230	(14) 2,340		9,890
Federal Income Tax Liability	14,100	(15) 2,100		12,000
Mortgage Note Payable	–0–		(3) 35,000	35,000
Bonds Payable	40,000			40,000
Common Stock	365,000		(7) 25,000	390,000
Retained Earnings	84,100	(9) 18,000	(8) 50,350	116,450
Totals	671,900	178,800	178,800	782,160

Illustration 19.9

(concluded)

	Account Balances 12/31/86	Analysis of Transactions for 1987		Account Balances 12/31/87
		Debit	**Credit**	
Financial Resources Provided:				
By Operations:				
Net Income		(8) 50,350		
Depreciation—Buildings		(6) 3,250		
Depreciation—Equipment		(6) 31,050		
Loss on Sale of Equipment		(4) 900		
Gain on Sale of Investments			(2) 1,700	
Increase in Accounts Receivable			(10) 11,160	
Increase in Inventories			(11) 15,300	
Decrease in Prepaid Expenses		(12) 1,600		
Increase in Accounts Payable		(13) 4,550		
Decrease in Accrued Liabilities			(14) 2,340	
Decrease in Federal Income Tax				
Liability			(15) 2,100	
Other Sources:				
Sale of Investments		(2) 9,700		
Assumption of Mortgage Note		(3) 35,000		
Sale of Equipment		(4) 2,600		
Issuance of Common Stock		(7) 25,000		
Financial Resources Applied:				
Acquisition of Land and Buildings			(3) 65,000	
Acquisition of Equipment			(5) 43,000	
Payment of Cash Dividends			(9) 18,000	
Increase in Cash for Year			(1) 5,400	
Totals		164,000	164,000	

Since cash changes and their causes are the focus of the working paper, the following entry is made on the working paper to show the source of cash.

```
Sale of Investments . . . . . . . . . . . . . . . . . . . . . . . . . .   9,700
    Investments . . . . . . . . . . . . . . . . . . . . . . . . .          8,000
    Gain on sale of investments  . . . . . . . . . . . . . . . .          1,700
```

The working paper now shows that $9,700 cash was provided by the sale of investments. The entry also removes the $1,700 gain on sale of investments from cash provided by operations because this amount is already included as part of the cash provided by sale of investments. If the $9,700 cash received from the sale is reported and the gain is not removed from cash provided by operations, the $1,700 gain is shown or counted twice. Note that the working paper entry is identical to the original journal entry for the sale, except for the $9,700 debit. Instead of debiting Cash, a properly described source of cash is debited. The sources and uses of cash are shown in the lower section of the working paper. The $8,000 credit accounts fully for the change (decrease) in the Investments account balance; if it had not fully accounted for the change, there would have to be other transactions involving the Investments account to analyze and report.

Entry *(3).* The changes in the Land and Buildings accounts resulted from the following entry:

Land	20,000	
Buildings	45,000	
Cash		30,000
Mortgage Note Payable		35,000

This transaction requires two entries on the working paper. First, Land and Buildings are debited for $20,000 and $45,000, respectively, and a cash applied item described as "Acquisition of Land and Buildings" is credited for $65,000. Second, a source of cash called "Assumption of Mortgage Note" is debited and Mortgage Note Payable is credited for $35,000. In other words, the transaction is treated as if the mortgage note was issued for cash, and then $65,000 cash had been spent to acquire land and buildings. This transaction is an example of a significant financing and investing activity that must be included on the statement even though part of it did not affect funds.

Entry *(4).* The Equipment account shows a net increase of $23,000 resulting from two transactions: a $43,000 purchase and a $20,000 retirement. The net change in the account must be analyzed to show both cash applied and cash provided.

Data relating to the $20,000 retirement were included in the additional information given. The computation of the loss on sale can be summarized as follows using data provided in the additional information:

Cost of equipment sold (given)	$20,000
Less: Accumulated depreciation (given)	16,500
Book value of equipment sold	$ 3,500
Less: Cash received (given)	2,600
Loss on sale (as shown in Income statement)	$ 900

The complete working paper entry for the sale of equipment is:

Sale of Equipment	2,600	
Accumulated Depreciation—Equipment	16,500	
Loss on Sale of Equipment	900	
Equipment		20,000

This entry records the cash provided by sale of equipment under the "Other sources" section on the working paper and explains part of the changes in the Equipment and the Accumulated Depreciation—Equipment accounts. The loss is added back to net income because it is a noncash item that was deducted in arriving at net income. The loss has exactly the same effect as depreciation expense.

Entry *(5).* This entry debits the Equipment account and credits Acquisition of Equipment for the $43,000 cash spent to acquire new equipment. The $43,000 debit to Equipment along with the $20,000 credit to Equipment in entry *(4)* fully accounts for the $23,000 increase in the account.

Entry *(6).* This entry adds $3,250 building depreciation and $31,050 equipment depreciation back to net income and credits the respective accumulated depreciation accounts. The $31,050 credit to the accumulated depreciation account for equipment less the $16,500 debit to this account in entry *(4)* explains fully the increase in this account from $43,100 to $57,650.

Entry *(7)*. This entry shows the $25,000 cash received from sale of common stock as an "Other source" of cash. The entry also explains completely the change in the Common Stock account. If stock had been sold for more than its stated value of $50 per share, the excess would be recorded in a separate Paid-In Capital in Excess of Stated Value account. But only the total amount of cash received from the issuance would have been reported on the statement of changes in financial position as a single figure because only the total amount received is significant.

Entry *(8)*. The statement of income and retained earnings reveals that net income for 1987 was $50,350. Entry *(8)* records the $50,350 as the starting point in measuring cash from operations and credits Retained Earnings as a partial explanation of the change in that account.

Entry *(9)*. This entry debits Retained Earnings and credits Payment of Cash Dividends for the $18,000 of dividends declared and paid. The entry also completes the explanation of the change in Retained Earnings ($84,100 + $50,350 − $18,000 = $116,450). Notice that on the cash basis statement the dividends must be **paid** to be included as funds applied. Under the working capital basis they only had to be declared because the declaration increases dividends payable (thereby reducing working capital).

If Retained Earnings had changed for reasons other than net income or cash dividends, the causes of the changes must be determined in order to decide whether they should be reported in the statement of changes in financial position. Transactions such as stock dividends and stock splits would **not** be reported on the statement of changes in financial position because they lack significance from an analytical viewpoint and because these items never affect cash or working capital. But an entry must be made on the working paper to explain the changes caused by a stock dividend or split, even if cash was not affected. All changes in all noncash accounts must be explained to show that a change affecting cash was not overlooked.

The next task is to analyze changes in current accounts other than Cash. All the current accounts of the United States Corporation are closely related to operations, and their changes are included in converting net income to cash from operations. The changes in the current accounts are analyzed in the manner previously discussed (see pages 733–35).

Entry *(10)*. The $11,160 increase in accounts receivable must be deducted from net income when converting it to cash from operations. If accounts receivable increased, sales to customers exceeded cash received from customers. Accrual basis on a cash basis. To convert net income to a cash basis, the $11,160 must be deducted.

The working paper technique used makes the recording of these effects almost mechanical. Accounts Receivable must be debited for $11,160 to increase it from $101,000 to $112,160. If Accounts Receivable is debited, a credit must be entered for an item that can be entitled "Increase in Accounts Receivable." The increase is deducted from net income in converting it to cash from operations.

Entry *(11)* is virtually a duplicate of entry *(10)*, except that it involves inventories rather than receivables.

Entry *(12)* is similar to the above two entries, except that it has the opposite effect because prepaid expenses decreased.

Entry *(13)* records the effect of an increase in accounts payable on net income in converting it to cash from operations.

Entries *(14)* and *(15)* record the effects of decreases in two other current liability accounts in converting net income to cash from operations.

The analysis of the noncash accounts is now complete. To be sure that a change has not been overlooked, the debits and credits in the middle two columns opposite the 1986 balances are added to or subtracted from those balances, line by line. If the working paper has been properly prepared, the results will be the 1987 balances listed in the fourth column. For example, the $43,000 debit is added to the beginning balance for Equipment, and the $20,000 credit deducted to get an ending balance of $198,000.

Next, the debits and credits for the balance sheet account entries and for the statement of changes in financial position items are added to make sure that they are equal in both sections. Note that entries made in the working paper are used only to derive cash flows into and out of the company. These entries are not entered in the company's accounting system because the transactions that caused the fund flows have already been recorded.

The Formal Statement

The data in the lower section of the working paper are now used to prepare the formal statement of changes in financial position—cash basis shown in Illustration 19.10. A standard format has not been prescribed for this statement. Both the APB and the FASB have recommended experimentation using alternative forms.

Two features of Illustration 19.10 should be noted. First, the two sections are headed "Financial resources provided" and "Financial resources applied" reflecting the reporting of all significant financing and investing activities as required by *Opinion No. 19.* The headings are appropriate since an exchange involving assumption of liability on a mortgage note for land and buildings is reported. Also note that the statement reports both working capital and cash provided by operations.

Working Paper for Statement of Changes in Financial Position— Working Capital Basis

Entries *(2)* through *(9)* shown above for a statement of changes of financial position prepared under the cash basis analyze noncurrent account changes that had a cash effect. Since cash is an element of working capital, the same entries would be made in preparing a statement of changes of financial position focusing on working capital.

The first line of a working paper for a statement of changes of financial position—working capital basis for the United States Corporation would show $148,700 of working capital at the end of 1986 and $178,850 at the end of 1987. Entry *(1)* would debit Working Capital for $30,150 and credit Increase in Working Capital on the last line of the working paper. This single working capital amount would be substituted for the six current asset and current liability accounts listed on the working paper for a statement of changes of financial position—cash basis.

Also, note in the United States Corporation illustration that entries for net income and nonworking capital charges and credits are grouped to make it easy to compute working capital from operations. This amount is $83,850,

Illustration 19.10

Statement of Changes in Financial Position—Cash Basis

UNITED STATES CORPORATION
Statement of Changes in Financial Position—Cash Basis
For the Year Ended December 31, 1987

Financial resources provided:			
By operations:			
Net income			$ 50,350
Add: Charges not requiring outlay of funds:			
Depreciation—building		$ 3,250	
Depreciation—equipment		31,050	
Loss on sale of equipment		900	35,200
			$ 85,550
Deduct: Credits not providing funds:			
Gain on sale of investments			1,700
Working capital provided by operations			$ 83,850
Effect of change in components of operating			
working capital on cash:			
Increase in accounts receivable		$(11,160)	
Increase in inventories		(15,300)	
Decrease in prepaid expenses		1,600	
Increase in accounts payable		4,550	
Decrease in accrued liabilities		(2,340)	
Decrease in federal income tax liability		(2,100)	(24,750)
Cash provided from operations			$ 59,100
Other resources provided:			
Sale of investments		$ 9,700	
Assumption of mortgage note		35,000	
Sale of equipment		2,600	
Issuance of common stock		25,000	72,300
Total financial resources provided			$131,400
Financial resources applied:			
Acquisition of land and building		$ 65,000	
Acquisition of equipment		43,000	
Payment of cash dividends		18,000	
Total financial resources applied			126,000
Increase in cash for the year			$ 5,400

computed by adding the first four items shown in the lower section of the working paper in Illustration 19.9 and deducting the $1,700 gain (see page 740).

Losses on the Working Paper

If a company incurs a net loss for a period, the entry on the working paper debits Retained Earnings and credits Net Loss under Financial Resources Provided by Operations. Then the net loss is adjusted for the nonfund items. For instance, depreciation and other nonfund expenses are added back and may more than offset the net loss. If so, the company will have funds provided by operations even though it had a net loss. If these nonfund adjustments do not offset the entire loss, then the company will have funds applied to operations. If the adjustments for the nonfund items result in funds provided by operations, all data relative to the net loss and its adjustments are shown in the "Resources provided" section of the statement of changes in financial position. If funds were applied to operations, all data relative to the net loss and its adjustments will be shown in the "Resources applied" section.

■ WORKING CAPITAL OR CASH FLOWS

In the past, statements of changes in financial position have generally focused on working capital flows. Such statements were prepared for several reasons. Accurate information was needed about the flows of liquid assets (working capital) through a company because such flows are the lifeblood of a business. Yet constant changes in accounting principles yielded net income amounts that often were not good measures of such liquid assets flows from operations. In addition, attention focused on working capital rather than cash because little significance was attached to the composition of working capital. In general, working capital turned over in a business quickly enough so that if not now in cash form, it would be shortly.

The Shift toward Cash Flows

Recent events suggest that in the future, statements of changes in financial position will focus increasingly on cash flows. Many companies experience severe cash flow, not working capital, problems. The FASB noted the importance of cash flows in the Conceptual Framework Project, stating "that the reporting of meaningful components of cash flows is generally more useful than reporting changes in working capital."[4] Shortly after the publication of this statement, the Financial Executives Institute (FEI) recommended that its members adopt the cash basis in preparing a statement of changes in financial position.[5] The FEI represents approximately 95% of the companies with securities traded on the New York Stock Exchange and the American Stock Exchange.

Illustration 19.11 shows that for a sample of 600 companies the emphasis has shifted steadily from working capital to cash. In 1980, only 59 of the companies emphasized cash flows, while in 1983 more than half did so.

Illustration 19.11

Definitions of "Funds" in Statement of Changes in Financial Position

	1983	1982	1981	1980
Changes in working capital	286	346	466	541
Changes in cash	314	254	134	59
Total	600	600	600	600

Source: Based on American Institute of Certified Public Accountants, *Accounting Trends & Techniques* (New York: AICPA, 1984), p. 366.

The shifting of attention from working capital flows to cash flows also is supported by developments in modern finance. The investment decision is seen more clearly as one in which cash outlays are compared with expected cash returns, appropriately discounted for time and risk. Management, investors, and creditors are all alike in that each "invests" cash to get future cash returns. Thus, information is needed to enable users to make predictions of the amounts,

---

[4] FASB, "Reporting Income, Cash Flows, and Financial Position of Business Enterprises," *Proposed Statement of Financial Accounting Concepts,* Exposure Draft (Stamford, Conn., 1981), p. xi.

[5] Financial Executives Institute, *Alert,* December 14, 1981.

timing, and uncertainty surrounding expected cash receipts. Information also is needed to provide feedback on prior assessments of cash flow.

Information on prior **cash** flows provides a better basis for making predictions of cash flows than does information on prior **working capital** flows. Cash flows often differ sharply from working capital flows. For example, a rapidly expanding business that increases its working capital by expanding inventories and accounts receivable may not have enough cash to meet current bills. Cash flow analysis, rather than working capital analysis, is required to reveal such problems.

■ SUMMARY

The statement of changes in financial position is one of the four major financial statements prepared by companies. The purpose of the statement of changes in financial position is analytical in that it attempts to explain how financial resources were acquired during a period, how financial resources were used, and what the net effect was on a company's working capital or cash position. Being an analytical tool, the statement of changes in financial position is an excellent means for assessing the quality of an organization's management.

Financial resources or funds are commonly defined as either working capital or cash. In the past, statements of changes in financial position have generally focused on working capital flows. Recent events suggest, however, that the emphasis in coming years will increasingly be on cash flows. Whichever definition of funds is used, the statement must report the effects of **all significant financing** and **investing activities,** even those that do not directly affect funds. This is known as the all financial resources concept.

In preparing a statement of changes in financial position—working capital basis, the first step is to prepare a schedule of changes in working capital. Then each noncurrent balance sheet account is analyzed to see what effect changes in it had on working capital during the period. These changes in noncurrent account balances are organized in terms of representing either financial resources provided or financial resources applied during the period. Finally, the statement is prepared using the analyses of the noncurrent accounts.

The statement of changes in financial position—cash basis focuses on cash flows into and out of an organization. A key element in the preparation of the cash basis statement is the adjustment of the income statement from an accrual basis to a cash basis. Changes in noncurrent balance sheet accounts are analyzed for their effects on working capital just as is done when the working capital basis is used. Then, all current accounts other than Cash are analyzed for changes in order to adjust working capital from operations to cash from operations. Finally, the resulting cash inflows and cash outflows are organized into a formal statement of changes in financial position—cash basis.

This chapter illustrated the use of a working paper to help in preparing a statement of changes in financial position. The working paper may be used with either a working capital or cash basis statement of changes in financial position; it helps to analyze changes in accounts and helps to format the final presentation of the statement of changes in financial position.

Now that you have studied the statement of changes of financial statement, you should realize its importance in presenting a more complete picture of the business operations of a company. In Chapter 20, you will learn how to analyze and interpret a company's financial statements so that you can better judge its solvency and profitability.

NEW TERMS INTRODUCED IN CHAPTER 19

All financial resources concept

This concept requires that a business report all significant financing and investing activities, regardless of whether the cash or working capital definition of funds is used (727).

Cash flow from operations

The net amount of cash received or disbursed for a given period on items that normally appear on the income statement. Usually obtained by converting accrual basis net income to a cash basis amount (733).

Cash flow statement

Another title for a statement of changes in financial position prepared on a cash basis; sometimes used as a title for a statement or schedule showing cash flows into and out of a business together with beginning and ending cash balances (733).

Financial resources applied

An all-inclusive title used to describe the uses made of a company's resources in a period. In certain instances, the more restrictive titles of working capital applied or cash applied may be substituted (731).

Financial resources provided

The most all-inclusive title used to describe the sources of the resources flowing into a company in a period. In certain instances, the more restrictive titles such as "sources of working capital" or "sources of cash" may be appropriate (732).

Funds

Broadly speaking, the financial resources of a company; often defined as working capital or as cash (725).

Indirect method

A way of determining cash or working capital from operations that starts with net income and adjusts for expenses and revenues that do not affect cash or working capital. Also called the **addback** method (728).

Nonworking capital (or nonfund) charges or expenses

Expenses and losses that are added back to net income because they do not actually use funds of the company.

The items added back include amounts of depletion that were expensed, amortization of intangible assets such as patents and goodwill, amortization of discount on bonds payable, and losses from disposals of noncurrent assets (728).

Nonworking capital (or nonfund) credits or revenues

Revenues and gains included in arriving at net income that do not provide working capital; an example is a gain on the sale of a noncurrent asset (729).

Source of funds

A transaction that brings funds (working capital or cash) into the business (727).

Statement of changes in financial position

A statement that reports the flows of cash or working capital into and out of a business in a given time period; it also shows significant financing and investing activities that do not involve cash or working capital flows (725).

Statement of changes in working capital

A statement listing all current assets and current liabilities, their beginning and ending balances, and the changes in these balances summarized into a single amount—the net change in working capital. The **schedule of changes in working capital components** shows only the change in each working capital item summarized into a single amount (729).

Use of funds

A transaction that removes funds (working capital or cash) from the business (727).

Working capital

A possible definition of funds; equal to current assets minus current liabilities (726).

Working capital from operations

Working capital generated by the regular operations of a business; usually computed as net income plus nonworking capital expenses deducted in arriving at net income, minus nonworking capital revenues included, and less certain gains which are included in the total proceeds received from sale of a noncash or nonworking capital asset (731).

DEMONSTRATION PROBLEM

Given below are comparative balance sheets of the Dells Corporation as of June 30, 1986, and June 30, 1987. Also given are the income statement for the year ended June 30, 1987, and certain additional data.

DELLS CORPORATION
Comparative Balance Sheet
June 30, 1986, and 1987

	1987	1986	Increase decrease*
Assets			
Current assets:			
Cash	$ 30,000	$ 80,000	$ 50,000*
Accounts receivable	160,000	100,000	60,000
Inventory	100,000	70,000	30,000
Prepaid rent	20,000	10,000	10,000
Total current assets	$310,000	$260,000	$ 50,000
Property, plant, and equipment:			
Equipment	$400,000	$200,000	$200,000
Accumulated depreciation	(60,000)	(50,000)	(10,000)
Total property, plant, and equipment . . .	$340,000	$150,000	$190,000
Total assets	$650,000	$410,000	$240,000
Liabilities and Stockholders' Equity			
Current liabilities:			
Accounts payable	$ 50,000	$ 40,000	$ 10,000
Notes payable—bank	–0–	50,000	50,000*
Accrued salaries	10,000	20,000	10,000*
Federal income tax payable	30,000	20,000	10,000
Total current liabilities	$ 90,000	$130,000	$ 40,000*
Stockholders' equity:			
Common stock, $10 par	$300,000	$100,000	$200,000
Paid-in capital in excess of par	50,000	–0–	50,000
Retained earnings	210,000	180,000	30,000
Total stockholders' equity	$560,000	$280,000	$280,000
Total liabilities and stockholders' equity	$650,000	$410,000	$240,000

DELLS CORPORATION
Statement of Income and Retained Earnings
For the Year Ended June 30, 1987

Sales		$1,000,000
Cost of goods sold	$600,000	
Salaries and wages	200,000	
Rent	40,000	
Depreciation	20,000	
Interest	3,000	
Loss on sale of equipment	7,000	870,000
Net income before federal income taxes . .		$ 130,000
Federal income taxes		60,000
Net income		$ 70,000
Retained earnings, July 1, 1986		180,000
		$ 250,000
Dividends		40,000
Retained earnings, June 30, 1987		$ 210,000

Additional data

1. Equipment with a cost of $20,000, on which $10,000 of depreciation had been recorded, was sold for cash. Additional equipment was purchased.
2. Stock was issued for cash.

Required: Using the data given for the Dells Corporation, prepare a statement of changes in financial position—working capital basis. Prepare a working paper by examining Illustration 19.9 and reading the description given on page 743 for preparing a working paper on the working capital basis.

Solution to demonstration problem

DELLS CORPORATION
Working Paper for Statement of Changes in Financial Position—Working Capital Basis
For the Year Ended June 30, 1987

	Account Balances 6/30/86	Analysis of Transactions for Fiscal Year		Account Balances 6/30/87
		Debit	Credit	
Debits				
Working Capital	130,000	(1) 90,000		220,000
Equipment	200,000	(5) 220,000	(4) 20,000	400,000
Totals	330,000			620,000
Credits				
Accumulated Depreciation	50,000	(4) 10,000	(3) 20,000	60,000
Common Stock	100,000		(6) 200,000	300,000
Capital in Excess of Par	–0–		(6) 50,000	50,000
Retained Earnings	180,000	(7) 40,000	(2) 70,000	210,000
Totals	330,000	360,000	360,000	620,000
Financial resources provided:				
By operations:				
Net income		(2) 70,000		
Add: Depreciation		(3) 20,000		
Loss on sale of equipment		(4) 7,000		
Other sources:				
Sale of equipment		(4) 3,000		
Sale of common stock		(6) 250,000		
Financial resources applied:				
Purchase of equipment			(5) 220,000	
Declaration of cash dividends			(7) 40,000	
Increase in working capital				
during year			(1) 90,000	
Totals		350,000	350,000	

DELLS CORPORATION
Statement of Changes in Financial Position—Working Capital Basis
For the Year Ended June 30, 1987

Financial resources provided:

By operations.			
Net income			$ 70,000
Add: Depreciation	$20,000		
Loss on sale of equipment	7,000	27,000	
Working capital provided by operations			$ 97,000
Other sources of working capital:			
Sale of equipment			3,000
Sale of common stock			250,000
Total working capital provided			$350,000

Financial resources applied:

Purchase of equipment		$220,000	
Declaration of cash dividends		40,000	
Total working capital applied			260,000
Increase in working capital			$ 90,000

Schedule of changes in working capital components:

Increases (decreases) in current assets:		
Cash	$(50,000)	
Accounts receivable	60,000	
Inventory	30,000	
Prepaid rent	10,000	$ 50,000
Increase (decrease) in liabilities:		
Accounts payable	$ 10,000	
Notes payable—bank	(50,000)	
Accrued salaries	(10,000)	
Federal income tax payable	10,000	(40,000)
Increase in working capital		$ 90,000

QUESTIONS

1. What are the concepts of funds used in a statement of changes in financial position?

2. When funds are defined as working capital, what are the major sources of funds in a business? What are the major uses of funds?

3. Explain the difference between the direct and indirect methods for computing working capital from operations.

4. What are nonfund (nonworking capital or noncash) expenses? How are they treated in computing working capital from operations?

5. Describe the treatment of a gain on the sale of equipment in preparing a statement of changes in financial position.

6. In the preparation of a statement of changes in financial position—working capital basis, why are the noncurrent accounts analyzed rather than the current accounts?

7. Does the declaration or payment of dividends affect working capital? Why?

8. Depreciation is often referred to as a source of funds. Is it a source of funds? Explain.

9. In what respects does cash flow analysis differ from working capital flow analysis?

10. Why is it unlikely that cash flow from operations will be equal to net income for the same period?

11. If the net income for a given period is $25,000, does this mean that there is an increase of cash of the same amount? Why or why not?

12. Why might a company have a positive inflow of cash from operations even though operating at a net loss?

13. Why might an analysis of working capital flows be unsuitable for short-run planning?

14. Give two reasons why analysts seem to prefer cash flow statements to statements that report working capital flows.

EXERCISES

E-1

Report specific items on statement of changes in financial position

Indicate how the following data should be reported in a statement of changes in financial position—working capital basis. A company purchased land valued at $24,000 and a building valued at $48,000 by payment of $12,000 by check, signing a $18,000 interest-bearing note due in six months, and assuming a $42,000 mortgage on the property.

E-2

Report specific items on statement of changes in financial position

A company sold equipment having an original cost of $8,400, on which $4,800 of depreciation had been recorded, for $6,000. The gain was included in net income. How should these data be shown in the statement of changes in financial position? Why?

E-3

Report specific items on statement of changes in financial position

The following data are from the Automobile and Accumulated Depreciation—Automobile accounts of a certain company:

Automobile

Date			Debit	Credit	Balance
1987					
Jan.	1	Balance brought forward			4,800
July	1	Traded for new auto		4,800	–0–
		New auto	5,280		5,280

Accumulated Depreciation—Automobile

Jan.	1	Balance brought forward			3,600
July	1	One-half year's depreciation		600	4,200
		Auto traded	4,200		–0–
Dec. 31		One-half year's depreciation		660	660

The old auto was traded for a new one and cash was paid in the exchange. The income statement for the year shows a loss on the exchange of autos of $360.

For all amounts involved, indicate the descriptions of these amounts and their exact locations in a statement of changes in financial position—working capital basis.

E-4

Compute change in working capital

Following are balance sheet data for the Badger Corporation:

	December 31, 1987	December 31, 1986
Cash	$ 65,800	$ 36,400
Accounts receivable	197,400	187,600
Inventory	116,200	142,800
Prepaid expenses	12,600	15,400
Plant assets (net of accumulated depreciation)	329,000	322,000
Accounts payable	170,800	177,800
Accrued liabilities	56,000	57,400
Capital stock	420,000	420,000
Retained earnings	74,200	49,000

Calculate the change in working capital for the year 1987.

E-5

Compute cash used to purchase plant assets

Refer to the information in Exercise E–4. Assume that the depreciation recorded in 1987 was $21,000. Compute the cash used to purchase plant assets assuming no assets were sold or scrapped in 1987.

E-6

Prepare statement of changes in financial position—working capital basis

Use the data in Exercise E–4. Assume that net income for 1987 was $33,600, that depreciation was $21,000, and that dividends declared and paid were $8,400. Prepare a statement of changes in financial position—working capital basis.

E-7

Compute working capital provided by operations

Assume that a company's net income for the year was $28,000, patent amortization was $700, loss on sale of patents was $1,400, depreciation was $2,800, gain on sale of equipment was $840, and accumulated depreciation on equipment was $14,000. Compute working capital from operations.

E-8

Compute sales on a cash basis and its effect on cash provided by operations

A company's financial statements for a given year show sales of $800,000, net income of $80,000, and accounts receivable on January 1 of $70,400 and $75,200 on December 31. (a) Compute sales on a cash basis (cash collections). (b) Compute the effect of the above information on net income as a measure of cash from operations.

E-9

Compute cost of goods sold on a cash basis and its effect on cash provided by operations

The income statement of a company shows net income of $80,000. Inventory on January 1 was $81,600 and on December 31 was $100,800, and accounts payable for merchandise purchases were $60,800 on January 1 and $67,200 on December 31. Compute the effects of the above information on net income as a measure of cash from operations.

E-10

Compute cash provided by operations

The operating expenses (including $16,000 of depreciation) of a company for a given year were $160,000. Net income was $80,000. Prepaid Insurance decreased from $4,800 to $3,200 during the year, while Accrued Wages increased from $6,400 to $9,600 during the year. Compute the effects of the above on net income as a measure of cash from operations.

E-11

Prepare partial statement of changes in financial position

Assume that the data in Exercises E–8, E–9, and E–10 above are for the same company. Prepare the section of the statement of changes in financial position showing conversion of net income to cash from operations. Show both working capital and cash from operations.

E-12

Indicate treatment of dividend

Dividends payable increased by $4,800 during the year in which total dividends declared were $96,000. What amount of dividends would appear in the statement of changes in financial position—working capital basis? What amount would appear in the same statement prepared under the cash basis?

E-13

Prepare a statement of changes in financial position— cash basis

Refer to the data in Exercises E–4 and E–6. Prepare a statement of changes in financial position—cash basis.

PROBLEMS, SERIES A

P19-1-A

Prepare statement of changes in financial position—working capital basis

Following are comparative ledger balance data and a statement of retained earnings for the year ended May 31, 1987, for Scott Company (in thousands of dollars):

	May 31	
	1987	**1986**
Debits		
Cash	$ 126	$ 112
Accounts receivable, net	252	288
Inventories	300	248
Investment in subsidiary	190	160
Land	140	100
Buildings and equipment	866	760
Patents	22	32
Total	$1,896	$1,700
Credits		
Accumulated depreciation . . .	$ 156	$ 120
Accounts payable	180	128
Taxes payable	32	24
Bonds payable	400	400
Common stock, $100 par	800	800
Retained earnings	328	228
Total	$1,896	$1,700
Statement of Retained Earnings		
Balance, May 31, 1986	$ 228	
Net income	200	
	$ 428	
Dividends declared	100	
Balance, May 31, 1987	$ 328	

Additional data:

1. Additional shares of stock of the subsidiary company were acquired for cash as an investment.
2. A tract of land adjacent to land owned was purchased during the year.
3. Depreciation of $60,000 and patent amortization of $10,000 were charged to expense during the year.
4. New equipment with a cost of $130,000 was purchased during the year, while fully depreciated equipment with a cost of $24,000 was scrapped and discarded.

Required: Prepare a statement of changes in financial position—working capital basis and include a comparative schedule of changes in working capital components. Try to do so without preparing a working paper so that your conceptual understanding of the statement may be strengthened.

P19-2-A

Prepare statement of changes in financial position—cash basis

Use the data for Problem P19-1-A. Prepare a statement of changes in financial position—cash basis.

P19–3–A

Prepare working paper and statement of changes in financial position— working capital basis

The income statement for the Bartley Company for the year ended December 31, 1987, shows:

Net sales		$768,000
Cost of goods sold	$450,000	
Operating expenses	120,000	
Major repairs	60,000	
Interest expense	18,000	
Loss on sale of equipment . .	9,600	657,600
Net income before taxes . . .		$110,400
Federal income taxes . . .		57,600
Net income		$ 52,800

Comparative balance sheets for the company follow:

BARTLEY COMPANY
Comparative Balance Sheets
December 31, 1986, and 1987

	December 31	
	1987	**1986**
Assets		
Current assets:		
Cash	$ 57,600	$ 48,000
Accounts receivable, net	116,400	91,200
Inventories	252,000	216,000
Prepaid expenses	19,200	7,200
Total current assets	$445,200	$362,400
Property, plant, and equipment:		
Buildings	$120,000	$120,000
Accumulated depreciation—buildings	(66,000)	(60,000)
Equipment	222,000	156,000
Accumulated depreciation—equipment . . .	(75,600)	(72,000)
Total property, plant, and equipment . . .	$200,400	$144,000
Total assets	$645,600	$506,400
Liabilities and Stockholders' Equity		
Current liabilities:		
Accounts payable	$ 56,400	$ 90,000
Accrued liabilities	19,800	17,400
Federal income taxes payable	57,600	54,000
Wages payable	11,400	9,000
Total current liabilities	$145,200	$170,400
Long-term liabilities:		
Bonds payable (15%)	120,000	120,000
Total liabilities	$265,200	$290,400
Stockholders' equity:		
Paid-in capital:		
Capital stock—par $140	$300,000	$180,000
Paid-in capital in excess of par value . . .	30,000	–0–
Retained earnings	50,400	36,000
Total stockholders' equity	$380,400	$216,000
Total liabilities and stockholders' equity	$645,600	$506,400

Additional data:

1. Capital stock was issued for cash.
2. Accrued liabilities relate solely to operating expenses.
3. The depreciation on equipment for the year amounted to $18,000. The equipment sold had an original cost of $36,000.

4. Dividends declared and paid during the year totaled $38,400.
5. Accounts payable arose solely from purchases of merchandise.

Required: *a.* Prepare a working paper for a statement of changes in financial position—working capital basis. (See the solution to the demonstration problem.)
b. Prepare a statement of changes in financial position—working capital basis.

P19–4–A

Prepare working paper and statement of changes in financial position— cash basis

Use the data for problem P19–3–A.

Required: *a.* Prepare a working paper for a statement of changes in financial position—cash basis.
b. Prepare a statement of changes in financial position—cash basis.

P19–5–A

Prepare working paper and statement of changes in financial position— working capital basis

Given below are comparative balance sheet account balances and other data of the West Corporation:

	June 30	
	1987	**1986**
Debit balances		
Cash	$173,600	$ 95,200
Accounts receivable	539,000	310,800
Inventories	588,000	610,400
Prepaid insurance	2,800	4,200
Land	224,000	252,000
Buildings	1,568,000	868,000
Machinery and tools	616,000	336,000
Patent	5,600	7,000
Total	$3,717,000	$2,483,600
Credit balances		
Accumulated depreciation	$ 581,000	$ 366,800
Accounts payable	91,000	126,000
Accrued liabilities	61,600	8,400
Bank loans (90-day)	40,600	47,600
Mortgage bonds payable	280,000	140,000
Common stock, $100 par	1,260,000	420,000
Paid-in capital in excess of par value	42,000	–0–
Retained earnings	1,360,800	1,374,800
Total	$3,717,000	$2,483,600

Additional data:

1. Net income for the year was $56,000.
2. Patent amortization expense was $1,400.
3. Depreciation for the year was $256,200.
4. Dividends declared and paid were $70,000.
5. Additional common stock was issued at $105 per share.
6. The mortgage bonds were issued at face value as partial payment for a building valued at $700,000. Machinery and tools were purchased for $322,000.
7. There was a gain of $5,600 on the sale of land.
8. Fully depreciated machinery with a cost of $42,000 was scrapped and written off.

Required: *a.* Prepare a working paper for a statement of changes in financial position—working capital basis. (See the solution to the demonstration problem.)
b. Prepare the formal statement of changes in financial position—working capital basis.

P19–6–A

Prepare working paper and statement of changes in financial position—cash basis

Use the data in Problem P19–5–A.

a. Prepare a working paper for a statement of changes in financial position—cash basis.

b. Prepare a statement of changes in financial position—cash basis.

PROBLEMS, SERIES B

P19–1–B

Prepare statement of changes in financial position—working capital basis including a schedule of changes in working capital components

CAIN CORPORATION
Comparative Balance Sheets
December 31, 1986, and 1987

	December 31	
	1987	1986
Assets		
Cash	$ 36,000	$ 48,000
Accounts receivable, net	134,400	96,000
Inventory	240,000	192,000
Equipment	660,000	504,000
Accumulated depreciation	(192,000)	(168,000)
Investments	120,000	24,000
Total assets	$998,400	$696,000
Liabilities and Stockholders' Equity		
Accounts payable	$ 34,800	$ 30,000
Accrued liabilites	3,600	6,000
Capital stock—common—$12 par value	600,000	480,000
Paid-in capital in excess of par value	240,000	120,000
Retained earnings	120,000	60,000
Total liabilities and stockholders' equity	$998,400	$696,000

Additional data:
1. Net income was $108,000 for the year.
2. Fully depreciated equipment costing $24,000 was sold for $6,000, and equipment costing $180,000 was purchased for cash.
3. Depreciation expense for the year was $48,000.
4. Investments were purchased for $96,000.
5. An additional 10,000 shares of common stock were issued for cash at $24 per share.
6. Cash dividends of $48,000 were declared.

Required: Prepare a statement of changes in financial position—working capital basis including a schedule of changes in working capital components.

P19–2–B

Prepare statement of changes in financial position—cash basis

Refer to the information in Problem P19–1–B. Prepare another statement of changes in financial position, this time using the cash basis.

P19–3–B

Prepare statement of changes in financial position—cash basis

GATLIN CORPORATION
Comparative Balance Sheets
June 30, 1986, and 1987

	June 30	
	1987	**1986**
Assets		
Current assets	$ 427,000	$ 329,000
Investment in stock of affiliated company	252,000	210,000
Buildings	532,000	392,000
Accumulated depreciation—buildings	(84,000)	(70,000)
Equipment	686,000	560,000
Accumulated depreciation—equipment	(210,000)	(168,000)
Total assets	$1,603,000	$1,253,000
Liabilities and Stockholders' Equity		
Current liabilities	$ 224,000	$ 168,000
Five-year note payable	140,000	–0–
Capital stock, par $140	1,120,000	980,000
Retained earnings	119,000	105,000
Total liabilities and stockholders' equity	$1,603,000	$1,253,000

Additional data:

1. Net income for year ended June 30, 1987, was $70,000.
2. Dividends declared amounted to $56,000.
3. Stock was issued at par for cash.
4. No equipment or building retirements occurred during the year.
5. The five-year note was issued to pay for a building erected on land leased by the company.
6. Additional shares of stock of the affiliated company were acquired for cash.
7. Equipment was also purchased for cash.

Required: Prepare a statement of changes in financial position—working capital basis. Try to do so without preparing a working paper so that your conceptual understanding of the statement might be strengthened.

P19–4–B

Prepare statement of changes in financial position—cash basis

Assume that the current assets and current liabilities in Problem P19–3–B consisted of the following:

	June 30, 1987	June 30, 1986
Current assets:		
Cash	$ 70,000	$ 56,000
Accounts receivable	224,000	112,000
Inventory	112,000	126,000
Prepaid expenses	21,000	35,000
Total current assets	$427,000	$329,000
Current liabilities:		
Accounts payable	$196,000	$126,000
Accrued liabilities	28,000	42,000
Total current liabilities	$224,000	$168,000

Required: a. Use the data in Problem P19–3–B along with the above data and prepare a working paper for a statement of changes in financial position—cash basis.
b. Prepare a statement of changes in financial position—cash basis for Gatlin Corporation for the year ended June 30, 1987.

P19–5–B

Prepare working paper and statement of changes in financial position— working capital basis

---

LARSON CORPORATION
Comparative Balance Sheets
December 31, 1986, and 1987

	December 31	
	1987	**1986**
Assets		
Current assets:		
Cash	$ 30,000	$ 40,000
Accounts receivable	254,000	196,000
Inventories	244,000	224,000
Prepaid insurance	6,000	8,000
Total current assets	$ 534,000	$468,000
Property, plant, and equipment:		
Land	$ 100,000	$ 60,000
Buildings	400,000	200,000
Accumulated depreciations—buildings . . .	(50,000)	(40,000)
Equipment	460,000	430,000
Accumulated depreciation—equipment . .	(250,000)	(200,000)
Total property, plant, and equipment . .	$ 660,000	$450,000
Total assets	$1,194,000	$918,000
Liabilities and Stockholders' Equity		
Current liabilities:		
Accounts payable	$ 164,000	$160,000
Federal income taxes payable	72,000	60,000
Accrued salaries and wages payable . . .	8,000	6,000
Accrued liabilities	36,000	28,000
Total current liabilities	$ 280,000	$254,000
Long-term liabilities:		
Bonds payable—9%	200,000	200,000
Total liabilities	$ 480,000	$454,000
Stockholders' equity:		
Paid-in capital:		
Capital stock—common	$ 600,000	$400,000
Paid-in capital in excess of par	30,000	–0–
Retained earnings	84,000	64,000
Total stockholders' equity	$ 714,000	$464,000
Total liabilities and stockholders' equity . . .	$1,194,000	$918,000

LARSON CORPORATION
Statement of Income and Retained Earnings
For Year Ended December 31, 1987

Sales, net		$1,800,000
Cost of goods sold		1,200,000
Gross margin		$ 600,000
Salaries and wages	$300,000	
Depreciation	74,000	
Insurance	4,000	
Other expenses	100,000	
Loss on sale of equipment	2,000	480,000
Net income before federal income taxes . . .		$ 120,000
Federal income taxes		52,000
Net income		$ 68,000
Retained earnings, January 1, 1987		64,000
		$ 132,000
Less: Dividends declared and paid		48,000
Retained earnings, December 31, 1987		$ 84,000

CHAPTER 20

Analysis and Interpretation of Financial Statements

LEARNING OBJECTIVES

After studying this chapter, you should be able to:

1. Explain how comparative financial statements may be used to analyze and appraise the financial position of a company and the results of its operations.
2. Calculate the amount of change in financial statement items for successive periods in dollars and percentages (horizontal and trend analysis).
3. Prepare common-size financial statements (vertical analysis).
4. Perform ratio analysis using the widely applied financial ratios and explain what each ratio seeks to show or measure.
5. Define and use correctly the new terms in the glossary.

As you will recall, the two primary objectives of every business are solvency and profitability. Solvency is the ability of a company to pay debts as they become due; it is reflected in the company's balance sheet. Profitability is the ability of a company to generate income; it is reflected in the company's income statement. Generally, all those interested in the affairs of a company are especially interested in a company's solvency and profitability.

This chapter discusses several common methods used to analyze and relate to one another the data in financial statements and, as a result, gain a clear picture of the solvency and profitability of a company. A company's financial statements are analyzed internally by management and externally by investors and creditors.

Management's analysis of financial statements primarily relates to **parts** of the company. Management conducts its analysis to plan, evaluate, and control operations within the company. The analysis by investors and creditors generally focuses on the company as a **whole.** Investors and creditors analyze financial statements to decide whether to invest in or extend credit to the company. In this chapter we discuss financial statement analysis as conducted by outside parties, such as investors and creditors, who rely primarily on a company's financial statements for their information.

■ OBJECTIVES OF FINANCIAL STATEMENT ANALYSIS

Financial statement analysis consists of applying analytical tools and techniques to financial statements and other relevant data to obtain useful information. This information is shown as significant relationships between data and trends in those data assessing the company's **past performance** and **current financial position.** The information shows the results or consequences of prior management decisions. In addition, the information is used to **make predictions** that may have a direct effect on decisions made by many users of financial statements.

Present company investors and potential company investors are both interested in the future ability of a company to earn profits—its profitability. These investors wish to predict future dividends and changes in the market price of the company's common stock. Since both dividends and price changes are likely to be influenced by earnings, investors may seek to predict earnings. The company's past earnings record is the logical starting point in predicting future earnings.

Sometimes outside parties are interested in predicting a company's solvency rather than its profitability. Short-term solvency is affected by the liquidity of the company. Liquidity is the state of possessing liquid assets, such as cash and other assets that will soon be converted into cash. Short-term debts must be paid soon, so liquid assets must be available for their payment. A bank that is asked to extend a 90-day loan to a company would be interested in that company's projected short-term liquidity. The company's predicted ability to repay the loan is likely to be based, at least partially, on proven past ability to pay off debts.

Long-term creditors are interested in a company's long-term solvency. A company is generally considered to be solvent when its assets exceed its liabilities so that it has a positive stockholders' equity. The larger the assets are in relation to the liabilities, the greater the long-term solvency of the company. The company's assets could shrink significantly before its liabilities would exceed its assets.

■ FINANCIAL STATEMENT ANALYSIS

Several types of analysis can be performed on a company's financial statements. All these analyses rely on comparisons or relationships of data because comparisons enhance the utility, or practical value, of accounting information. For example, knowing that a company's net income last year was $100,000 is not, by itself, very useful information. Some usefulness is added when it is known that the prior year's net income was $25,000. And even more useful information is gained if the amounts of sales and assets of the company are known. Such comparisons or relationships may be expressed as:

1. Absolute increases and decreases for an item from one period to the next.
2. Percentage increases and decreases for an item from one period to the next.

3. Trend percentages.
4. Percentages of single items to an aggregate total.
5. Ratios.

Items 1 and 2 make use of comparative financial statements. **Comparative financial statements** present the same company's financial statements for two or more successive periods in side-by-side columns. The calculation of dollar changes (see column 3 of Illustration 20.1 and column 9 of Illustration 20.2) or percentage changes (see column 4 of Illustration 20.1 and column 10 of Illustration 20.2) in the statement items or totals is known as horizontal analysis.

Illustration 20.1 *Comparative Balance Sheets*

THE KNIGHT CORPORATION
Comparative Balance Sheets
December 31, 1987, and 1988

Exhibit A

	(1) 1988	(2) 1987	(3) Dollars	(4) Percent	(5) 1988	(6) 1987
	December 31		Increase or decrease* 1988 over 1987		Percent of total assets December 31	
Assets						
Current assets:						
Cash	$ 80,200	$ 55,000	$25,200	45.8	12.6	10.0
Accounts receivable, net	124,200	132,600	8,400*	6.3*	19.6	24.1
Notes receivable	55,000	50,000	5,000	10.0	8.7	9.1
Inventories	110,800	94,500	16,300	17.2	17.4	17.1
Prepaid expenses	3,600	4,700	1,100*	23.4*	0.6	0.9
Total current assets	$373,800	$336,800	$37,000	11.0	58.8R	61.1R
Property, plant, and equipment:						
Land	$ 21,000	$ 21,000	$ –0–	–0–	3.3	3.8
Building	205,000	160,000	45,000	28.1	32.3	29.0
Less: Accumulated depreciation	(27,000)	(22,400)	(4,600)	21.0	(4.3)	(4.1)
Furniture and fixtures	83,200	69,800	13,400	19.2	13.1	12.7
Less: Accumulated depreciation	(20,800)	(14,100)	(6,700)	47.5	(3.3)	(2.6)
Total property, plant, and equipment	$261,400	$214,300	$47,100	22.0	41.2R	38.9R
Total assets	$635,200	$551,100	$84,100	15.3	100.0	100.0
Liabilities and Stockholders' Equity						
Current liabilities:						
Accounts payable	$ 70,300	$ 64,600	$ 5,700	8.8	11.1	11.7
Notes payable	20,000	15,100	4,900	32.5	3.1	2.7
Taxes accrued	36,800	30,200	6,600	21.9	5.8	5.5
Total current liabilities	$127,100	$109,900	$17,200	15.7	20.0	20.0R
Long-term liabilities:						
Mortgage notes payable, land and building, 12%, 1990	43,600	60,800	17,200*	28.3*	6.9	11.0
Total liabilities	$170,700	$170,700	$ –0–	0.0	26.9	31.0
Stockholders' equity:						
Common stock, par value $10 per share	$240,000	$200,000	$40,000	20.0	37.8	36.3
Retained earnings	224,500	180,400	44,100	24.4	35.3	32.7
Total stockholders' equity	$464,500	$380,400	$84,100	22.1	73.1	69.0
Total liabilities and stockholders' equity	$635,200	$551,100	$84,100	15.3	100.0	100.0

R Rounding difference.

Illustration 20.2 *Comparative Statements of Income and Retained Earnings*

	Year ended December 31		Increase or decrease* 1988 over 1987		Percent of net sales	
	(7) 1988	(8) 1987	(9) Dollars	(10) Percent	(11) 1988	(12) 1987

THE KNIGHT CORPORATION
Comparative Statements of Income and Retained Earnings
For the Years Ended December 31, 1987, and 1988   **Exhibit B**

	(7) 1988	(8) 1987	(9) Dollars	(10) Percent	(11) 1988	(12) 1987
Net sales	$986,400	$765,500	$220,900	28.9	100.0	100.0
Cost of goods sold	623,200	500,900	122,300	24.4	63.2	65.4
Gross margin	$363,200	$264,600	$ 98,600	37.3	36.8	34.6
Operating expenses:						
Selling	$132,500	$ 84,900	$ 47,600	56.1	13.4	11.1
Administrative	120,300	98,600	21,700	22.0	12.2	12.9
Total operating expenses	$252,800	$183,500	$ 69,300	37.8	25.6	24.0
Net operating income	$110,400	$ 81,100	$ 29,300	36.0	11.2	10.6
Other expenses	3,000	2,800	200	7.1	0.3	0.4
Net income before federal income taxes	$107,400	$ 78,300	$ 29,100	37.2	10.9	10.2
Federal income taxes	48,300	31,700	16,600	52.4	4.9	4.1
Net income	$ 59,100	$ 46,600	$ 12,500	26.8	6.0	6.1
Retained earnings, January 1	180,400	146,300	34,100	23.3		
	$239,500	$192,900	$ 46,600	24.2		
Dividends declared	15,000	12,500	2,500	20.0		
Retained earnings, December 31	$224,500	$180,400	$ 44,100	24.4		

This type of analysis helps detect changes in a company's performance and highlights trends.

Trend percentages (item 3) are similar to horizontal analysis except that a base year is selected and comparisons are made to the base year. Trend percentages are useful for comparing financial statements over **several years** because they disclose changes and trends occurring through time.

Information about a company can also be gained by the vertical analysis of the composition of a single financial statement, such as an income statement. Vertical analysis (item 4) consists of the study of a single financial statement in which each item is expressed as a **percentage of a significant total.** The use of vertical analysis is especially helpful in analyzing income statement data such as the percentage of cost of goods sold to sales or the gross margin on sales. For example, columns 11 and 12 of Illustration 20.2 show that in 1987, cost of goods sold was 65.4% of sales and decreased to 63.2% of sales in 1988.

Financial statements that show only percentages and no absolute dollar amounts are called common-size statements. All percentage figures in a common-size balance sheet are expressed as percentages of total assets (see columns 5 and 6 of Illustration 20.1), while all the items in a common-size income statement are expressed as percentages of net sales (see columns 11 and 12 of Illustration 20.2). The use of common-size statements facilitates vertical analysis of a company's financial statements. For instance, looking at columns 11 and 12 of Illustration 20.2 gives you a better idea of the relationship of each item to sales than looking at columns 7 and 8.

Ratios (item 5) are expressions of logical relationships between certain items in the financial statements. The financial statements of a single period are generally used. Many ratios can be computed from the same set of financial statements. A ratio can show a relationship between two items on the same financial statement or between two items on different financial statements (e.g., balance sheet and income statement). The choice of ratios to be prepared is limited only by the requirement that the items used to construct a ratio have a logical relationship to one another.

■ HORIZONTAL AND VERTICAL ANALYSIS: AN ILLUSTRATION

Illustrations 20.1 and 20.2 show comparative financial statements of the Knight Corporation for the years ended December 31, 1987, and 1988. These statements will serve as a basis for a more complete illustration of horizontal and vertical analysis of a balance sheet and a statement of income and retained earnings.

Analysis of Balance Sheet

Imagine that you are a prospective investor of the Knight Corporation and have acquired the comparative balance sheets shown in Illustrations 20.1 and 20.2. Columns 1, 2, and 3 in Illustration 20.1 show the absolute dollar amounts for each item for December 31, 1987, and December 31, 1988, and the change for the year. If the change between the two dates is an increase from 1987 to 1988, the change is shown as a positive figure. If the change is a decrease, it is followed by an asterisk (*). A few of the observations you could make from your horizontal analysis of Illustration 20.1 are:

1. Total current assets have increased $37,000, consisting largely of a $25,200 increase in cash, while total current liabilities have increased only $17,200.
2. Total assets have increased $84,100, while total liabilities have remained unchanged.
3. The increase in total assets has been financed by the sale of common stock, $40,000, and by the retention of earnings, $44,100.

Next, you study column 4 in Illustration 20.1, which expresses as a percentage the dollar change in column 3. Frequently, these percentage increases and decreases are more informative than absolute amounts, as is illustrated by the current asset and current liability changes. Although the absolute amount of current assets has increased more than twice the amount of current liabilities, the percentages reveal that current assets increased 11%, while current liabilities increased 15.7%. Thus, current liabilities are increasing at a rate faster than the current assets that will be used to pay them. But, in view of the substantial amount of cash possessed, the company is not likely to fail to pay its debts as they come due.

The percentages in column 4 lead you, the analyst, to several other observations. For one thing, the 28.3% decrease in mortgage notes payable indicates that interest charges will be lower; thus, this will tend to increase net income in the future. The 24.4% increase in retained earnings and the 45.8% increase in cash may indicate that higher dividends can be paid in the future.

Your vertical analysis of the Knight Corporation's balance sheet discloses each account's significance relative to total assets or equities. This comparison aids in assessing the importance of changes in each account. Columns 5 and 6 in Illustration 20.1 express the dollar amounts of each item in columns 1 and 2 as a percentage of total assets or equities. For example, although prepaid expenses declined $1,100 in 1988, a decrease of 23.4%, the account represents less than 1% of total assets and, therefore, probably does not have great significance. The vertical analysis also shows that total debt financing decreased by 4.1 percentage points, from 31% of total equities to 26.9% in 1988. At the same time, the percentage of stockholder financing to total assets of the company increased from 69.0% to 73.1%.

Analysis of Statement of Income and Retained Earnings

Illustration 20.2 provides you with the information to analyze the comparative statements of income and retained earnings of the Knight Corporation. Such a statement merely combines the income statement and the statement of retained earnings. Columns 7 and 8 in Illustration 20.2 show the dollar amounts for the years 1988 and 1987, respectively. Columns 9 and 10 show the absolute and percentage increase and decrease in each item from 1987 to 1988. The amounts and percentages in columns 11 and 12 are computed by dividing each item by net sales. Examination of the comparative statements of net income and retained earnings shows the following:

1. Sales increased 28.9% in 1988.
2. Gross margin increased 37.3% in 1988.
3. Selling expenses increased 56.1% in 1988.
4. Federal income taxes rose by 52.4% in 1988.
5. Net income increased 26.8%, while dividends increased 20.0%.
6. Net income per dollar of sales remained virtually constant over the two years (6.1% in 1987 and 6.0% in 1988).

Considering both horizontal and vertical analysis information, the analyst would conclude that an increase in the gross margin rate from 34.6% to 36.8%, coupled with a 28.9% increase in sales, resulted in a 37.3% increase in gross margin in 1988. The increase in net income was held to 26.8% because selling expenses increased 56.1% and income taxes increased 52.4%. Predicting net income for 1989 would be aided if you, the analyst, knew whether this increase in selling expenses is expected to recur. Other expenses remained basically the same, on a percentage-of-sales basis, over the two-year period.

Having completed the horizontal and vertical analysis of the balance sheet and statement of income and retained earnings of the Knight Corporation, you are ready to study trend percentages and ratio analysis. The last section in this chapter discusses some final considerations in financial statement analysis. Professional financial statement analysts use several tools and techniques to determine the solvency and profitability of companies.

■ TREND PERCENTAGES

Trend percentages are also referred to as index numbers and are used for the comparison of financial information over time to a base year. Trend percentages are calculated by:

the separate amounts of cash sales and credit sales are not reported on the income statement.

Accounts receivable turnover for the Knight Corporation is shown below. Since beginning-of-year data for 1987 are not provided in Illustration 20.1, assume net accounts receivable on January 1, 1987, totaled $121,200.

	1988	1987	Amount of increase or decrease*
Net sales (a)	$986,400	$765,500	$220,900
Accounts receivable:			
January 1	$132,600	$121,200	$ 11,400
December 31	124,200	132,600	8,400*
Total (b)	$256,800	$253,800	$ 3,000
Average accounts receivable (c) (b ÷ 2 = c) . .	$128,400	$126,900	
Turnover of accounts receivable (a ÷ c) . . .	7.68	6.03	

The turnover ratio provides an indication of how quickly the receivables are being collected. For the Knight Corporation in 1988, the turnover ratio indicates that accounts receivable are collected, or "turned over," slightly more than seven times per year. This ratio may be better understood and more easily compared with a company's credit terms if it is converted into a number of days, as is illustrated the next ratio.

Number of Days' Sales in Accounts Receivable. The **number of days' sales in accounts receivable** ratio, which also is called the **average collection period for accounts receivable,** is calculated as follows:

$$\text{Number of days' sales in accounts receivable (average collection period of accounts receivable)} = \frac{\text{Number of days in year (365)}}{\text{Accounts receivable turnover}}$$

The turnover ratios for the Knight Corporation given above can be used to show that the number of days' sales in accounts receivable decreased from about 61 days (365/6.03) in 1987 to 48 days (365/7.68) in 1988. The change means that the average collection period of the corporation's accounts receivable decreased from 61 to 48 days. Thus, the ratio measures the average liquidity of accounts receivable and gives an indication of their quality. Generally, the more rapid the collection period, the higher the quality of receivables. However, the average collection period will vary by industry; for example, they will be very rapid in utility companies and much slower in some retailing companies. A comparison of the average collection period with the credit terms extended customers by the company will provide further insight into the quality of the accounts receivable. For example, receivables arising under terms of 2/10, n/30 that have an average collection period of 75 days need to be investigated further. It is important to determine why customers are paying their accounts much later than expected.

Inventory Turnover. A company's inventory turnover ratio shows the number of times its average inventory is sold during a period. **Inventory turnover** is calculated as follows:

$$\text{Inventory turnover} = \frac{\text{Cost of goods sold}}{\text{Average inventory}}$$

Inventory turnover relates a measure of sales volume to the average amount of goods on hand to produce this sales volume.

Assume the inventory on January 1, 1987, for the Knight Corporation was $85,100. The following schedule shows that the inventory turnover increased slightly from 5.58 times per year in 1987 to 6.07 times per year in 1988. These turnover ratios can be converted to the number of days it takes a company to sell its entire stock of inventory; this is done by dividing 365 by the inventory turnover. For the Knight Corporation, the average inventory was sold in about 60 days (365/6.07) in 1988 as contrasted to about 65 days (365/5.58) in 1987.

	1988	1987	Amount of increase
Cost of goods sold (a)	$623,200	$500,900	$122,300
Inventories:			
January 1	$ 94,500	$ 85,100	$ 9,400
December 31	110,800	94,500	16,300
Total (b)	$205,300	$179,600	$ 25,700
Average inventory (c) (b ÷ 2 = c)	$102,650	$ 89,800	
Turnover of inventory (a ÷ c)	6.07	5.58	

Other things being equal, the management that is able to maintain the highest inventory turnover ratio is considered most efficient. Yet, other things are not always equal. For example, a company that achieves a high inventory ratio by keeping extremely small inventories on hand may incur larger ordering costs, lose quantity discounts, and lose sales due to lack of adequate inventory. In attempting to earn satisfactory income, management must balance the costs of inventory storage and obsolescence and the cost of tying up funds in inventory against possible losses of sales and other costs associated with keeping too little inventory on hand.

Total Assets Turnover. **Total assets turnover** shows the relationship between dollar volume of sales and average total assets used in the business and is calculated as follows:

$$\text{Total assets turnover} = \frac{\text{Net sales}}{\text{Average total assets}}$$

This ratio measures the efficiency with which a company uses its assets to generate sales. The larger the total assets turnover, the larger will be the income on each dollar invested in the assets of the business.

For the Knight Corporation, the total assets turnover ratios for 1988 and 1987 are shown below. Assume total assets as of January 1, 1987, were $510,200.

	1988	1987	Amount of increase
Net sales (a)	$ 986,400	$ 765,500	$220,900
Total assets:			
January 1	$ 551,100	$ 510,200	$ 40,900
December 31	635,200	551,100	84,100
Total (b)	$1,186,300	$1,061,300	$125,000
Average total assets (c) (b ÷ 2 = c)	$ 593,150	$ 530,650	
Turnover of total assets (a ÷ c)	1.66:1	1.44:1	

In 1987, each dollar of total assets produced $1.44 of sales; and in 1988, each dollar of assets produced $1.66 of sales. In other words, between 1987 and 1988, the Knight Corporation had an increase of $0.22 of sales per dollar of investment in assets.

Equity, or Long-Term Solvency, Ratios

Equity, or long-term solvency ratios show the relationship of debt and equity financing in a company.

Equity (or Stockholders Equity) Ratio.   The two basic sources of assets in a business are owners (stockholders) and creditors, and the interests of both groups are referred to as total equities. But in ratio analysis, the term *equity* generally refers only to stockholders' equity. Thus, the equity ratio indicates the proportion of total assets (or total equities) that is provided by stockholders (owners) on any given date. The formula for the equity ratio is:

$$\text{Equity ratio} = \frac{\text{Stockholders' equity}}{\text{Total assets (or total equities)}}$$

The Knight Corporation's liabilities and stockholders' equity, taken from Illustration 20.1, are given below. The Knight Corporation's equity ratio increased from 69.0% in 1987 to 73.1% in 1988. The schedule below shows that the company's stockholders increased their proportionate equity in the company's assets by additional investment in the company's common stock and by retention of income earned during the year.

	December 31, 1988 Amount	Percent	December 31, 1987 Amount	Percent
Current liabilities	$127,100	20.0	$109,900	20.0
Long-term liabilities	43,600	6.9	60,800	11.0
Total liabilities	$170,700	26.9	$170,700	31.0
Common stock	$240,000	37.8	$200,000	36.3
Retained earnings	224,500	35.3	180,400	32.7
Total stockholders' equity	$464,500	73.1	$380,400	69.0
Total equity (equal to total assets)	$635,200	100.0	$551,100	100.0

The equity ratio must be interpreted carefully. From a creditor's point of view, a high proportion of stockholders' equity is desirable. A high equity ratio indicates the existence of a large protective buffer for creditors in the event a company suffers a loss. But from an owner's point of view, a high proportion of stockholders' equity may or may not be desirable. If borrowed funds can be used by the business to generate income in excess of the net after-tax cost of the interest on such borrowed funds, a lower percentage of stockholders' equity may be desirable.

To illustrate the effect of higher leveraging (i.e., a larger proportion of debt), assume that Knight Corporation could have financed its present operations with $40,000 of 12% bonds instead of 4,000 shares of common stock. The effect on income for 1988 would be as follows, assuming a federal income tax rate of 50%:

Net income as presently stated (Illustration 20.2)	$59,100
Deduct additional interest on debt (0.12 × $40,000)	4,800
	$54,300
Add reduced tax due to interest deduction (0.5 × $4,800) . .	2,400
Adjusted net income	$56,700

As shown, net income is reduced when leverage is increased by issuing bonds instead of common stock. But there are also fewer shares outstanding, so earnings per share (EPS) increase from $2.46 ($59,100/24,000 shares) to $2.84 ($56,700/20,000 shares). Since investors place heavy emphasis on EPS amounts, many companies in recent years have introduced large portions of debt into their capital structures in order to increase EPS.

It should be pointed out, though, that too low a percentage of owners' equity (too much debt) has its dangers. Financial leverage magnifies losses per share as well as EPS since there are fewer shares of stock over which to spread the losses. A period of business recession may result in operating losses and shrinkage in the value of assets, such as receivables and inventory, which in turn may lead to an inability to meet fixed payments for interest and principal on the debt. The result could be that the company may be forced into liquidation and the stockholders would lose their investments.

Stockholders' Equity to Debt Ratio. The relative equities of owners and creditors may be expressed in several ways. To say that creditors hold a 26.9% interest in the assets of the Knight Corporation on December 31, 1988, is equivalent to saying stockholders hold a 73.1% interest. In many cases, this relationship is expressed as a ratio—**stockholders' equity to debt ratio.**

$$\text{Stockholders' equity to debt ratio} = \frac{\text{Stockholders' equity}}{\text{Total debt}}$$

Such a ratio for the Knight Corporation would be 2.23:1 ($380,400/$170,700) on December 31, 1987, and 2.72:1 ($464,500/$170,700) on December 31, 1988. This ratio is sometimes inverted and called the **debt to equity ratio.** Some analysts use only long-term debt rather than total debt in calculating these ratios. These analysts do not consider short-term debt to be part of the capital structure since it will be paid within one year.

Profitability Tests

Profitability is a very important measure of a company's operating success. Generally, there are two areas of concern when judging profitability: (1) relationships on the income statement that indicate a company's ability to recover costs and expenses, and (2) relationships of income to various balance sheet measures that indicate the company's relative ability to earn income on assets employed.

Rate of Return on Operating Assets.

The best measure of earnings performance without regard to the sources of assets is the relationship of net operating income to operating assets, which is known as the **rate of return on operating assets.** This ratio is designed to show the earning power of the company as a bundle of assets. By disregarding both nonoperating assets and nonoperating income elements, the rate of return on operating assets measures the profitability of the company in carrying out its primary business functions. The ratio can be broken down into two elements—the operating margin and the turnover of operating assets.

Operating margin reflects the percentage of each dollar of net sales that becomes net operating income. Net operating income excludes **nonoperating income elements.** These elements include extraordinary items; nonoperating revenues, such as interest revenue; and nonoperating expenses, such as interest expense and income taxes. The formula for operating margin is:

$$\text{Operating margin} = \frac{\text{Net operating income}}{\text{Net sales}}$$

Turnover of operating assets shows the amount of sales dollars generated for each dollar invested in operating assets. Year-end operating assets typically are used, even though in theory an average would be better. **Operating assets** are all assets actively used in producing operating revenues. **Nonoperating assets** are assets owned but not used in producing operating revenues; they include items such as land held for future use, a factory building rented to another company, and long-term bond investments. Total assets should not be used in evaluating earnings performance because they include nonoperating assets that do not contribute to the generation of sales. The formula for the turnover of operating assets is:

$$\text{Turnover of operating assets} = \frac{\text{Net sales}}{\text{Operating assets}}$$

The rate of return on operating assets of a company is equal to operating margin multiplied by turnover of operating assets. The more a company earns per dollar of sales and the more sales it makes per dollar invested in operating assets, the higher will be the return per dollar invested. Rate of return on operating assets is expressed by the following formulas:

$$\text{Rate of return on operating assets} = \text{Operating margin} \times \text{Turnover of operating assets}$$

or

$$\text{Rate of return on operating assets} = \frac{\text{Net operating income}}{\text{Net sales}} \times \frac{\text{Net sales}}{\text{Operating assets}}$$

Since net sales appears in both ratios (once as a numerator and once as a denominator), it can be canceled out, and the formula for rate of return on operating assets becomes:

$$\text{Rate of return on operating assets} = \frac{\text{Net operating income}}{\text{Operating assets}}$$

It is, however, more useful for analytical purposes to leave the formula in the form that shows margin and turnover separately since it provides more information to analysts.

The rates of return on operating assets for the Knight Corporation for 1988 and 1987 are calculated below.

	1988	1987	Amount of increase
Net operating income (a)	$110,400	$ 81,100	$ 29,300
Net sales (b)	$986,400	$765,500	$220,900
Operating assets* (c)	$635,200	$551,100	$ 84,100
Operating margin (a ÷ b)	11.19%	10.59%	
Turnover of operating assets (b ÷ c)	1.55:1	1.39:1	
Rate of return on operating assets (a ÷ c) . .	17.34%	14.72%	

* For the Knight Corporation there were no nonoperating assets, so total assets are used in the calculation.

Securing Desired Rate of Return on Operating Assets.   Companies that are to survive in the economy must attain some minimum rate of return on operating assets. But this minimum can be attained in many different ways. To illustrate, consider a grocery store and a jewelry store, each with a rate of return of 8% on operating assets. The grocery store normally would attain this rate of return with a low margin and a high turnover, while the jewelry store would have a high margin and a low turnover as shown below:

	Margin	×	Turnover	=	Rate of return on operating assets
Grocery store . .	1%	×	8.0 times		8%
Jewelry store . .	20%	×	0.4 times		8%

Net Income to Net Sales.   Another measure of a company's profitability is the **net income to net sales** ratio, calculated as follows:

$$\text{Net income to net sales} = \frac{\text{Net income}}{\text{Net sales}}$$

This ratio measures the proportion of the sales dollar that remains after the deduction of all expenses. The computations for the Knight Company are:

	1988	1987	Amount of increase
Net income (a)	$ 59,100	$ 46,600	$ 12,500
Net sales (b)	$986,400	$765,500	$220,900
Ratio of net income to net sales (a ÷ b) . .	5.99%	6.09%	

Although the ratio of net income to net sales indicates the net amount of profit on each sales dollar, a great deal of care must be exercised in the use and interpretation of this ratio. The amount of net income includes all types of nonoperating items that may occur in a particular period; therefore, net income includes the effects of such things as extraordinary items and interest charges. Thus, a period that contains the effects of an extraordinary item will not be comparable to a period that contains no extraordinary items. Also, since interest expense is deductible in the determination of net income while dividends are not, net income is affected by the methods used to finance the firm's assets.

Net Income to Average Stockholders' Equity.   From the stockholders' point of view, an important measure of the income-producing ability of a company is the relationship of **net income to average stockholders' equity,** also called the **rate of return on average stockholders' equity,** or simply the **return on equity (ROE).** Stockholders are interested in the ratio of operating income to operating assets as a measure of the efficient use of assets by management. But stockholders are even more interested in knowing what return is earned by the company on each dollar of stockholders' equity invested. The formula for net income to average stockholders' equity is:

$$\text{Net income to average stockholders' equity} = \frac{\text{Net income}}{\text{Average stockholders' equity}}$$

The ratios for the Knight Company are shown below. Assume that total stockholders' equity on January 1, 1987, was $321,500.

	1988	1987	Amount of increase
Net income (a)	$ 59,100	$ 46,600	$ 12,500
Total stockholders' equity:			
January 1	$380,400	$321,500	$ 58,900
December 31	464,500	380,400	84,100
Total (b)	$844,900	$701,900	$143,000
Average stockholders' equity (c) (b ÷ 2 = c)	$422,450	$350,950	
Ratio of net income to stockholders' equity (a ÷ c) . .	13.99%	13.28%	

The increase in the ratio from 13.28% to 13.99% would be regarded favorably by stockholders. This ratio indicates that for each average dollar of capital invested by a stockholder, the company earned nearly 14 cents in 1988.

Earnings per Share.   Probably the measure used most widely to appraise a company's operations is **earnings per share (EPS)** of common stock. EPS is equal to earnings available to common stockholders divided by the weighted-average number of shares of common stock outstanding. The financial press regularly publishes actual and forecasted EPS amounts for many corporations, together with period-to-period comparisons. The Accounting Principles Board noted the significance attached to EPS by requiring that such amounts be reported on the face of the income statement.[2]

The calculation of EPS may be fairly simple or highly complex, depending on the corporation's capital structure. A company has a simple capital structure if it has no outstanding securities (e.g., convertible bonds, convertible preferred stocks, warrants, or options) that can be exchanged for common stock. If a company has such securities outstanding, it has a complex capital structure.

A company with a simple capital structure reports a single EPS amount calculated as follows:

$$\text{EPS of common stock} = \frac{\text{Net income available to common stockholders}}{\text{Weighted-average number of common shares outstanding}}$$

Earnings available to common stockholders is equal to net income minus the current year's preferred dividends, whether such dividends have been declared or not.

Determining the Weighted-Average Number of Shares.   The denominator in the EPS fraction is the weighted-average number of common shares outstanding for the period. If the number of shares outstanding did not change during the period, the weighted-average number of shares outstanding would, of course, be the number of shares outstanding at the end of the period. The balance in the common stock account of Knight Corporation (Illustration 20.1) was $200,000 on December 31, 1987, and the common stock has a $10 par value. Assuming that no shares were issued or redeemed during 1987, the weighted-average number of shares outstanding was 20,000 ($200,000/$10 per share).

If the number of shares changed during the period, such a change increases or decreases the capital invested in the company and should affect earnings available to shareholders. To compute the weighted-average number of shares outstanding, the change in the number of shares is weighted by the fractional portion of the year that those shares were outstanding. Shares are only considered outstanding during those periods that the related capital investment is available to produce income.

To illustrate, note that Knight Corporation's common stock balance increased by $40,000 (4,000 shares) during 1988. Assume that 3,000 of these shares were issued on April 1 and the other 1,000 shares were issued October 1. The computation of weighted-average shares outstanding would be as follows:

20,000 shares × 1 year	20,000
3,000 shares × ¾ year (April–December)	2,250
1,000 shares × ¼ year (October–December)	250
Weighted-average number of shares outstanding	22,500

---

[2] Accounting Principles Board, "Reporting Earnings per Share," *Opinion No. 15* (New York: AICPA, 1969), par. 12.

Total assets turnover

Net sales divided by average total assets (774).

Trend percentages

Similar to horizontal analysis except that a base year is selected and comparisons are made to the base year (766).

Turnover

The relationship between the amount of an asset and some measure of its use. See accounts receivable turnover, inventory turnover, and total assets turnover (772).

Turnover of operating assets

Net sales divided by operating assets (777).

Vertical analysis

The study of a single financial statement in which each item is expressed as a percentage of a significant total; for example, percentages of sales calculations (766).

Working capital ratio

Same as current ratio.

Yield (on stock)

The yield on a stock investment refers to either an earnings yield or a dividend yield (782). Also see Earnings yield on common stock and Dividend yield on common stock and preferred stock.

DEMONSTRATION PROBLEM 20–1

Comparative financial statements of the Roscoe Company for 1987 and 1988 follow:

ROSCOE COMPANY
Comparative Income Statements
For the Years Ended December 31, 1987, and 1988
(in thousands)

	1988	1987
Net sales	$800	$700
Cost of goods sold	497	427
Gross margin	$303	$273
Operating expenses	220	198
Net income before income taxes	$ 83	$ 75
Income taxes	33	30
Net income	$ 50	45

ROSCOE COMPANY
Comparative Balance Sheets
December 31, 1987, and 1988
(in thousands)

	1988	1987
Assets		
Cash	$ 23	$ 24
Accounts receivable	51	58
Inventory	85	63
Plant assets, net	177	178
Total assets	$336	$323
Liabilities and Stockholders' Equity		
Current liabilities	$ 60	$ 52
Long-term liabilities	70	70
Common stock	180	180
Retained earnings	26	21
Total liabilities and stockholders' equity	$336	$323

Required: a.   Prepare comparative common-size income statements for 1987 and 1988.
       b.   Perform a horizontal analysis of the comparative balance sheets.
       c.   Comment on the results of *(a)* and *(b)*.

Solution to demonstration problem 20–1

a.

ROSCOE COMPANY
Common-Size Comparative Income Statements
For the Years Ended December 31, 1987, and 1988

	1988	*1987*
Net sales	100.00	100.00
Cost of goods sold	62.13	61.00
Gross margin	37.87	39.00
Operating expenses	27.50	28.29
Net income before income taxes . .	10.37	10.71
Income taxes	4.12	4.28
Net income	6.25	6.43

b.

ROSCOE COMPANY
Comparative Balance Sheets
December 31, 1987, and 1988
(in thousands)

	1988	*1987*	*Increase or decrease* 1988 over 1987* Amount	Percent
Assets				
Cash	$ 23	$ 24	$ 1*	4.17*
Accounts receivable	51	58	7*	12.07*
Inventory	85	63	22	34.92
Plant assets, net	177	178	1*	0.56*
Total assets	$336	$323	$13	4.02
Liabilities and Stockholders' Equity				
Current liabilities	$ 60	$ 52	$ 8	15.38
Long-term liabilities	70	70	–0–	–0–
Common stock	180	180	–0–	–0–
Retained earnings	26	21	5	23.81
Total liabilities and stockholders' equity . .	$336	$323	$13	4.02

c.   The $100,000 increase in sales yielded only a $30,000 increase in gross margin because the gross margin rate decreased from 39% to 37.87%. Although operating expenses increased from $198,000 to $220,000, they declined relatively from 28.29% to 27.50% of sales. This change together with the change in gross margin combined to hold net income to an increase of $5,000, which represents a decline of 0.18% in the rate of net income to sales. The significant change in the balance sheet was the 35% increase in inventory that was financed by decreases in cash and accounts receivable and by increases in current liabilities and in retained earnings. The company is in a less liquid position at the end of 1988 than at the end of 1987.

DEMONSTRATION PROBLEM 20–2

The balance sheet and supplementary data for the Turner Corporation are shown below:

TURNER CORPORATION
Balance Sheet
December 31, 1987

Assets

Cash		$ 50,000
Marketable securities		30,000
Accounts receivable, net		70,000
Inventory		150,000
Building	$400,000	
Less: Accumulated depreciation	100,000	300,000
Total assets		$600,000

Liabilities and Stockholders' Equity

Accounts payable	$ 30,000
Bank loans payable	10,000
Mortgage notes payable, due in 1990	40,000
Bonds payable, 10%, due December 31, 1992	100,000
Common stock, $100 par value	300,000
Retained earnings	120,000
Total liabilities and stockholders' equity	$600,000

Supplementary data:

1. 1987 net income: $60,000.
2. 1987 cost of goods sold: $540,000.
3. 1987 sales: $900,000.
4. Inventory, January 1, 1987: $100,000.
5. Interest expense: $15,000.
6. 1987 net income before interest and taxes: $130,000.
7. Net accounts receivable on January 1, 1987: $50,000.
8. Total assets on January 1, 1987: $540,000.

Required: Compute the following ratios:

a. Current ratio.
b. Acid-test ratio.
c. Accounts receivable turnover.
d. Inventory turnover.
e. Total assets turnover.
f. Equity ratio.
g. EPS of common stock.
h. Times interest earned ratio.

Solution to demonstration problem 20–2

a. Current ratio:

$$\frac{\text{Current assets}}{\text{Current liabilities}} = \frac{\$300,000}{\$40,000} = 7.5 : 1$$

b. Acid-test ratio:

$$\frac{\text{Quick assets}}{\text{Current liabilities}} = \frac{\$150,000}{\$40,000} = 3.75 : 1$$

c. Accounts receivable turnover:

$$\frac{\text{Net sales}}{\text{Average net accounts receivable}} = \frac{\$900,000}{\$60,000} = 15 \text{ times}$$

d. Inventory turnover:

$$\frac{\text{Cost of goods sold}}{\text{Average inventory}} = \frac{\$540,000}{\$125,000} = 4.32 \text{ times}$$

e. Total assets turnover:

$$\frac{\text{Net sales}}{\text{Average total assets}} = \frac{\$900,000}{\$570,000} = 1.58 \text{ times}$$

f. Equity ratio:

$$\frac{\text{Stockholders' equity}}{\text{Total assets}} = \frac{\$420,000}{\$600,000} = 70\%$$

g. EPS of common stock:

$$\frac{\begin{array}{c}\text{Net income available} \\ \text{to common stockholders}\end{array}}{\begin{array}{c}\text{Weighted-average number of} \\ \text{common shares outstanding}\end{array}} = \frac{\$60,000}{3,000} = \$20$$

h. Times interest earned ratio:

$$\frac{\text{Income before interest and taxes}}{\text{Interest expense}} = \frac{\$130,000}{\$15,000} = 8.67 \text{ to } 1, \text{ or } 8.67 \text{ times}$$

QUESTIONS

1. Distinguish between horizontal and vertical analysis of financial statements.

2. What are common-size financial statements? What item is assigned a value of 100% in the common-size income statement, and what item is assigned a value of 100% in the common-size balance sheet?

3. How do trend percentages differ from comparative financial statements?

4. What are the changes, absolute and percentage, if net income of $40,000 earned in 1988 is compared to a net loss sustained in 1987 of $10,000? What are the changes if the net loss was sustained in 1988 after earning net income in 1987?

5. Explain the meaning of this statement: "With 1979 equal to 100, net sales increased from 225 in 1987 to 260 in 1988."

6. Think of a situation where the current ratio is misleading as an indicator of short-term debt-paying ability. Does the acid-test ratio offer a remedy to the situation you have described? Describe a situation where the acid-test ratio will not suffice either.

7. A provision in a bond indenture requires the borrower to maintain positive working capital. Explain what this means and why such a provision is included in an indenture.

8. The higher the accounts receivable turnover rate, the better off is the company. Do you agree? Why?

9. Through the use of turnover ratios, explain why a company might seek to increase the volume of its sales even though such an increase can be secured only at reduced prices.

10. Of what significance is the equity ratio? What are the alternative ways of conveying the same information?

11. Before the John Company issued $10,000 of long-term notes (due more than a year from the date of issue) in exchange for a like amount of accounts payable, its acid-test ratio was 2 : 1. Will this transaction increase, decrease, or have no effect on (a) the current ratio and (b) the equity ratio?

12. How is rate of return on operating assets determined? Is it possible for two companies with "operating margins" of 5% and 1%, respectively, both to have rates of return of 20% on operating assets? How?

13. Indicate which of the relationships illustrated in this chapter would be used to judge:
   a. The short-term debt-paying ability of the company.
   b. The overall efficiency of the company without regard to the sources of assets.
   c. The return to owners of a corporation.
   d. The safety of bondholders' interest.
   e. The safety of preferred stockholders' dividends.

14. Indicate how each of the following ratios or measures is calculated:
   a. Payout ratio.
   b. EPS of common stock.
   c. Price-earnings ratio.
   d. Earnings yield on common stock.
   e. Dividend yield on preferred stock.
   f. Times interest earned ratio.
   g. Times preferred dividends earned ratio.
   h. Return on stockholders' equity.

15. Explain why the EPS for 1986 must be adjusted in a three-year summary of earnings data (presented in 1988) for a 20% stock dividend distributed in June 1988.

16. Cite some deficiencies in accounting information that would limit its usefulness for analyzing a particular company over a 10-year period.

EXERCISES

E–1

Perform horizontal and vertical analysis

Income statement data for Black Company for 1987 and 1988 are given below:

	1988	1987
Net sales	$870,000	$645,600
Cost of goods sold	609,600	418,800
Selling expenses	132,000	116,400
Administrative expenses	78,000	66,000
Income taxes	19,200	18,000

   Prepare a horizontal and vertical analysis of the above income data in a form similar to that in Illustration 20.2. Comment on the results of this analysis.

E–2

Determine effects of various transactions on current ratio

A company engaged in the following three independent transactions:

1. Merchandise purchased on account, $200,000.
2. Machinery purchased for cash, $200,000.
3. Issued capital stock for cash, $200,000.

   a. Compute the current ratio after each of these transactions assuming current assets were $400,000 and the current ratio was 1:1 before the transactions occurred.
   b. Repeat part (a) assuming current assets were $400,000 and the current ratio was 2:1.
   c. Repeat part (a) assuming current assets were $400,000 and the current ratio was 1:2.

E–3

Compute average number of days receivables are outstanding; determine effect of increase in turnover

A company has sales of $360,000 per year. Its average net accounts receivable balance is $120,000.

   a. What is the average number of days accounts receivable are outstanding?
   b. By how much would the capital invested in accounts receivable be reduced if the turnover could be increased to 6 without a loss of sales?

E–4

Compute inventory turnover

From the following partial income statement, calculate the inventory turnover for the period.

Net sales		$845,000
Cost of goods sold:		
Beginning inventory	$ 97,500	
Purchases	552,500	
Cost of goods available for sale . .	$650,000	
Less: Ending inventory	110,500	
Cost of goods sold		539,500
Gross margin		$305,500
Operating expenses		136,500
Net operating income		$169,000

E–5

Compute rate of return on operating assets

Picken, Inc. had net sales of $330,000, gross margin of $140,000, and operating expenses of $85,000. Total assets (all operating) were $275,000. Compute Picken's rate of return on operating assets.

E–6

Compute rate of return on stockholders' equity

Omega Company started 1987 with total stockholders' equity of $225,000. Its net income for 1987 was $60,000, and $10,000 of dividends were declared. Compute the rate of return on average stockholders' equity for 1987.

E–7

Compute EPS

The Cone Company had 60,000 shares of common stock outstanding on January 1, 1987. On April 1, 1987, it issued 20,000 additional shares for cash. The earnings available for common stockholders for 1987 were $200,000. What amount of EPS should the company report?

E–8

Compute weighted-average number of shares outstanding

Sapp Company started 1988 with 100,000 shares of common stock outstanding. On March 31 it issued 16,000 shares for cash, and on September 30 it purchased 8,000 shares for cash. Compute the weighted-average number of common shares outstanding for the year.

E–9

Compute EPS for current and prior year

A company reported EPS of $2 ($200,000/100,000 shares) for 1986, ending the year with 100,000 shares outstanding. In 1987, the company earned net income of $660,000, issued 40,000 shares of common stock for cash on September 30, and distributed a 100% stock dividend on December 31, 1987. Compute EPS for 1987, and compute the adjusted EPS for 1986 that would be shown in the 1987 annual report.

E–10

Compute times interest earned

A company paid interest of $12,000, incurred federal income taxes of $34,000, and had net income (after taxes) of $50,000. How many times was interest earned?

E–11

Compute times dividends earned and dividend yield

The Nash Company had 8,000 shares of $75 par value, 6%, preferred stock outstanding. Net income after taxes was $504,000. The market price per share was $90.

a. How many times were the preferred dividends earned?
b. What was the yield on the preferred stock assuming the regular preferred dividends were declared and paid?

E–12

Compute price-earnings ratio

A company had 9,000 shares of $100 par value common stock outstanding. Net income was $90,000. Current market price per share is $150. Compute the price-earnings ratio.

PROBLEMS, SERIES A

P20–1–A

Perform horizontal and vertical analysis

Neal Company's comparative statements of income and retained earnings for the years ended December 31, 1987, and 1988, and its comparative balance sheets as of the end of each of these years follow:

NEAL COMPANY
Comparative Statements of Income
and Retained Earnings
For the Years Ended December 31, 1987, and 1988
(in thousands)

	1988	1987
Net sales	$906,950	$864,270
Cost of goods sold	575,410	551,210
Gross margin	$331,540	$313,060
Operating expenses:		
Selling	$133,210	$141,350
Administrative	123,420	114,290
Total operating expenses . . .	$256,630	$255,640
Net operating income	$ 74,910	$ 57,420
Interest expense	20,240	13,200
Income before income taxes . . .	$ 54,670	$ 44,220
Income taxes	22,000	17,600
Net income	$ 32,670	$ 26,620
Retained earnings, January 1 . . .	82,500	66,880
	$115,170	$ 93,500
Dividends	11,770	11,000
Retained earnings, December 31 . .	$103,400	$ 82,500

NEAL COMPANY
Comparative Balance Sheets
December 31, 1987, and 1988
(in thousands)

	1988	1987
Assets		
Current assets:		
Cash	$ 26,520	$ 14,430
Accounts receivable, net	75,530	73,450
Inventory	187,850	195,130
Total current assets	$289,900	$283,010
Plant asssets, net	244,400	232,700
Total assets	$534,300	$515,710
Liabilities and Stockholders' Equity		
Current liabilities:		
Accounts payable and accrued liabilities . .	$ 74,100	$158,210
Notes payable	52,000	130,000
Total current liabilities	$126,100	$288,210
Long-term liabilities:		
Bonds payable (due 1995)	156,000	–0–
Total liabilities	$282,100	$288,210
Stockholders' equity:		
Common stock	$130,000	$130,000
Retained earnings	122,200	97,500
Total stockholders' equity	$252,200	$227,500
Total liabilities and stockholders' equity . . .	$534,300	$515,710

Required: a. Perform a horizontal and vertical analysis of the above financial statements in a manner similar to that shown in Illustrations 20.1 and 20.2.

b. Comment on the results obtained.

P20–2–A

Perform trend analysis

You are given the following data for Myra Corporation:

	1987	1988	1989	1990
Sales	$225,000	$257,500	$300,000	$425,000
Cost of goods sold . .	150,000	162,500	225,000	325,000
Gross margin	$ 75,000	$ 95,000	$ 75,000	$100,000
Operating expenses . .	60,000	64,000	73,500	88,000
Net operating income . .	$ 15,000	$ 31,000	$ 1,500	$ 12,000

Required:

a. Prepare a statement showing the trend percentages for each of the above items, using 1987 as the base year.

b. Comment on the trends noted.

P20–3–A

Compute working capital, current ratio, and acid-test ratio

The following data are for the Stoke Company:

	December 31, 1988	December 31, 1987
Notes payable (due in 90 days) . .	$ 47,000	$ 37,500
Merchandise inventory	150,000	130,000
Cash	62,500	80,000
Marketable securities	31,000	18,750
Accrued liabilities	12,000	13,750
Accounts receivable	117,500	115,000
Accounts payable	70,000	45,000
Allowance for doubtful accounts . .	15,000	9,500
Bonds payable, due 1992	97,500	100,000
Prepaid expenses	4,000	4,600

Required:

a. Compute the amount of working capital at both year-end dates.

b. Compute the current ratio at both year-end dates.

c. Compute the acid-test ratio at both year-end dates.

e. Comment briefly on the company's short-term financial position.

P20–4–A

Determine effects of various transactions on working capital and current ratio

Stevens Products, Inc. has a current ratio on December 31, 1987, of 2:1 before the following transactions were completed.

Transactions:

1. Sold a building for cash.
2. Exchanged old equipment for new equipment. (No cash was involved.)
3. Declared a cash dividend on preferred stock.
4. Sold merchandise on account (at a profit).
5. Retired mortgage notes that would have matured in 1995.
6. Issued a stock dividend to common stockholders.
7. Paid cash for a patent.
8. Temporarily invested cash in government bonds.
9. Purchased inventory for cash.
10. Wrote off an account receivable as uncollectible. Uncollectible amount is less than balance of the Allowance for Doubtful Accounts.
11. Paid the cash dividend on preferred stock that was declared earlier.
12. Purchased a computer and gave a two-year promissory note.
13. Collected accounts receivable.
14. Borrowed from the bank on a 120-day promissory note.
15. Discounted a customer's note. Interest expense was involved.

Required:

a. Indicate whether the amount of working capital will increase, decrease, or be unaffected by each of the transactions.

b. Indicate whether the current ratio will increase, decrease, or be unaffected by each of the transactions.

Consider each transaction independently of all the others.

BUSINESS DECISION PROBLEM 20–1

Compute net income, identify reason for cash increase, state main sources of financing, and indicate further analyses needed

Shown below are the comparative balance sheets of the Dell Corporation for December 31, 1988 and 1987.

DELL CORPORATION
Comparative Balance Sheets
December 31, 1987, and 1988

	December 31, 1988	December 31, 1987
Assets		
Cash	$200,000	$ 40,000
Accounts receivable, net	36,000	48,000
Inventory	160,000	168,000
Plant and equipment	112,000	120,000
Total assets	$508,000	$376,000
Liabilities and Stockholders' Equity		
Accounts payable	$ 40,000	$ 40,000
Common stock	280,000	280,000
Retained earnings	188,000	56,000
Total liabilities and stockholders' equity . .	$508,000	$376,000

Required:
a. What was the net income for 1988 assuming there were no dividend payments?
b. What was the primary source of the large increase in the cash balance from 1987 to 1988?
c. What are the two main sources of assets for the Dell Corporation?
d. What other comparisons and procedures would you use to complete the analysis of the balance sheet begun above?

BUSINESS DECISION PROBLEM 20–2

Compute turnover ratios for four years and number of days sales in accounts receivable; evaluate effectiveness of company's credit policy

The information below was obtained from the annual reports of the Lyle Manufacturing Company:

	1985	1986	1987	1988
Net accounts receivable . .	$ 150,000	$ 300,000	$ 375,000	$ 500,000
Net sales	1,500,000	1,937,500	2,375,000	2,750,000

Required:
a. If cash sales account for 30% of all sales and credit terms are always 1/10, n/60, determine all turnover ratios possible and the number of days' sales in accounts receivable at all possible dates. (The number of days' sales in accounts receivable should be based on year-end accounts receivable and net credit sales.)
b. How effective is the company's credit policy?

BUSINESS DECISION PROBLEM 20–3

Analyze investment alternatives

Brenda Freeman is interested in investing in one of three companies (A, B, or C) by buying its common stock. The companies' shares are selling at about the same price. The long-term capital structures of the companies are as follows:

	Company A	Company B	Company C
Bonds with a 10% interest rate			$ 500,000
Preferred stock with an 8% dividend rate		$ 500,000	
Common stock, $10 par value	$1,000,000	500,000	500,000
Retained earnings	80,000	80,000	80,000
Total long-term equity	$1,080,000	$1,080,000	$1,080,000
Number of common shares outstanding . .	100,000	50,000	50,000

Ms. Freeman has consulted two investment advisers. One adviser believes that each of the companies will earn $62,500 per year before interest and taxes. The other adviser believes that each company will earn about $200,000 per year before interest and taxes.

Required:

a. Compute each of the following, using the estimate made by the first adviser and then the one made by the second adviser:

1. Earnings available for common stockholders assuming a 40% tax rate.
2. EPS of common stock.
3. Rate of return on total stockholders' equity.

b. Which stock should Ms. Freeman select if she believes the first adviser?
c. Are the stockholders as a group (common and preferred) better off with or without the use of long-term debt in the above companies?

BUSINESS SITUATION FOR DISCUSSION

Financial Statement Analysis—A Two-Minute Drill*

William L. Stone

) * * * * *

☐ Commercial loan officers often face the situation where they would like to make a quick appraisal of a financial statement. Some loan requests, for example, can be declined in short order because the financial statements reflect a weak condition. However, loan officers must have the skill to focus on those factors that would reveal that further discussion is fruitless. More important, they should be able to develop several pertinent questions regarding the problem areas of a company's operation as revealed by a brief analysis of the financial statements.

It is not uncommon for a loan applicant to present a loan officer with two or three years of financial statements in support of an application being presented orally. The loan officer does not have the luxury of analyzing the statements thoroughly while the applicant patiently sits in silence.

* * * * *

Within that two-minute period, the loan officer should be able to make an analysis that is thorough enough to reveal the company's problem areas on which the

subsequent questioning should focus. This article will explain how those two minutes can be spent most efficiently so that the loan officer will have a clear picture of the company's financial strengths and weaknesses.

* * * * *

Three ratios—current, debt to worth, and net profit margin—and three turnovers—receivables, inventory, and payables—form the basis of the two minute drill. These six relationships (turnovers are often referred to as ratios, but in the strictest sense, they are not ratios) were selected for several reasons. First, they are important indicators of a specific aspect of a company's financial condition. Second, taken together, they are indicative of the three important areas for credit purposes: liquidity, leverage, and profitability. Third, we can establish a standard that is easy to compute and understand against which a company's performance can be measured.

* * * * *

The writer suggests that loan officers have a simple worksheet available that looks like . . . [the table below].

Sample Worksheet

	1980	1981	1982
CR			2.1
D/W			0.9
NPM			5%
AR T/O			70
INV T/O			40
AP T/O			45

```
1987
Dec. 31  Finished Goods Inventory (ending)  . . . . .     60,000
         Sales .  . . . . . . . . . . . . . . . .      1,800,000
              Income Summary . . . . . . . . . .                   1,860,000
              To set up the ending Finished Goods Inventory
              and close Sales to the Income Summary account.
```

At this point in the closing process the Income Summary account has a credit balance of $114,500, which is the amount of net income on the work sheet. The fifth (and last) closing entry closes the Income Summary account by debiting Income Summary and crediting Retained Earnings:

```
1987
Dec. 31  Income Summary  . . . . . . . . . . .    114,500
              Retained Earnings  . . . . . . . . . .                114,500
              To close the Income Summary account to
              Retained Earnings.
```

■ FINANCIAL REPORTING BY MANUFACTURING COMPANIES

The major difference between a merchandiser and a manufacturer is in the types of inventories carried. Because inventories are reported on the balance sheet and also affect income (through cost of goods sold) on the income statement, the balance sheet and income statement of a merchandiser will differ from the balance sheet and income statement of a manufacturer.

The Statement of Cost of Goods Manufactured

The **statement of cost of goods manufactured** is used to support the cost of goods sold figure on the income statement. The two most important calculations on this statement are (1) the cost to manufacture and (2) the cost of goods manufactured. Careful attention should be given so that the terms **cost to manufacture** and **cost of goods manufactured** are not confused with one another or with cost of goods sold. The relationship between these terms is shown in Illustration 21.7. **Cost to manufacture** includes the costs of all **resources** put into production during the period. **Cost of goods manufactured** consists of the cost of all **goods completed** during the period; it includes "cost to manufacture" plus the beginning work in process inventory minus the ending work in process inventory. Cost of goods sold includes the cost of goods manufactured plus the beginning finished goods inventory minus the ending finished goods inventory.

Illustration 21.8 is the statement of cost of goods manufactured for the Jernigan Manufacturing Company for 1987. Note how the statement shows the costs incurred for materials, direct labor, and manufacturing overhead; it describes the total of these three costs as **cost to manufacture** during the period. When beginning work in process inventory is added and ending work in process is deducted, we obtain cost of goods manufactured (completed). Cost of goods sold does not appear on the cost of goods manufactured statement but is shown on the income statement.

In this illustration, all materials (both direct and indirect) are included in

Illustration 21.7

Relationship of Cost to Manufacture, Cost of Goods Manufactured, and Cost of Goods Sold

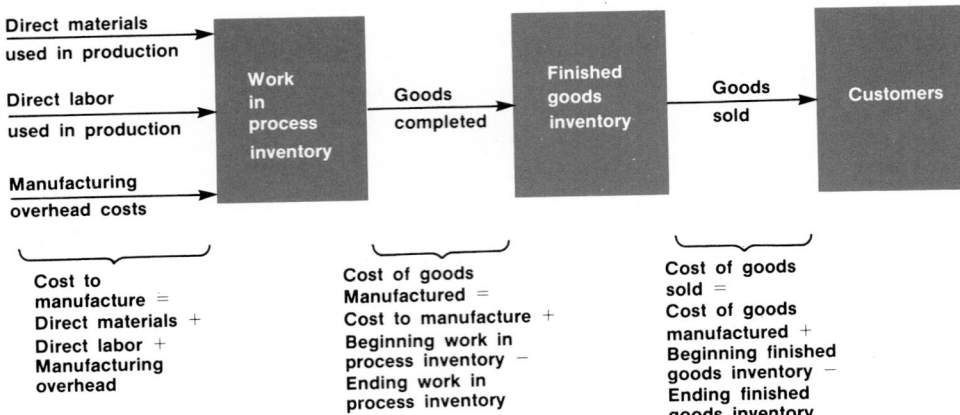

Cost to manufacture = Direct materials + Direct labor + Manufacturing overhead

Cost of goods Manufactured = Cost to manufacture + Beginning work in process inventory − Ending work in process inventory

Cost of goods sold = Cost of goods manufactured + Beginning finished goods inventory − Ending finished goods inventory

Illustration 21.8

Statement of Cost of Goods Manufactured

JERNIGAN MANUFACTURING COMPANY
Statement of Cost of Goods Manufactured
For the Year Ended December 31, 1987

Materials:

Materials inventory, January 1	$ 40,000	
Materials purchases	480,000	
Transportation-in	6,000	
Materials available for use	$526,000	
Less: Materials inventory, December 31	38,000	
Materials used		$ 488,000
Direct labor		380,000
Manufacturing overhead:		
Indirect labor	$ 65,000	
Supervisors' salaries	130,000	
Maintenance and repairs	17,000	
Utilities expense	5,000	
Factory taxes	15,000	
Depreciation expense—factory building	20,000	
Depreciation expense—factory equipment	46,000	
Insurance expense—factory	6,000	
Total manufacturing overhead		304,000
Cost to manufacture		$1,172,000
Add: Work in process inventory, January 1		84,000
		$1,256,000
Less: Work in process inventory, December 31		80,000
Cost of goods manufactured		$1,176,000

the Materials Inventory account. Therefore, materials used consists of both direct materials and indirect materials. These amounts could have been separated and the amount of indirect materials could have been shown as a line item included under manufacturing overhead.

The Income Statement

Income statement preparation for a manufacturer may be considerably more complex than for a merchandiser. This is because a manufacturer incurs more types of costs than a merchandiser who buys goods that are ready for sale. In order to make the income statement more understandable to the readers of the financial statements, only the cost of goods manufactured is shown on the income statement. A statement of cost of goods manufactured has already been prepared to support this amount. The income statement for the Jernigan Manufacturing Company is shown in Illustration 21.9. The data are taken directly from the work sheet in Illustration 21.6. Notice in Illustration 21.9 the relationship of the statement of cost of goods manufactured to the income statement. The cost of goods manufactured appears in the cost of goods sold section as an addition to the beginning inventory of finished goods to derive the cost of goods available for sale. Cost of goods manufactured is shown in the same place that purchases would be presented on a merchandiser's income statement. When financial statements are released to the public, it is common practice to include previous years' income statements alongside the current year's for comparison.

Illustration 21.9

Income Statement of a Manufacturer

JERNIGAN MANUFACTURING COMPANY
Income Statement
For the Year Ended December 31, 1987

Operating revenues:		
Sales		$1,800,000
Cost of goods sold:		
Finished goods inventory, January 1	$ 56,000	
Cost of goods manufactured (see statement of cost of goods manufactured)	1,176,000	
Cost of goods available for sale	$1,232,000	
Less: Finished goods inventory, December 31, 1987	60,000	
Cost of goods sold		1,172,000
Gross margin		$ 628,000
Operating expenses:		
Selling	$ 200,000	
Administrative	185,000	
Other operating expenses	1,500	
Total operating expenses		386,500
Net income from operations		$ 241,500
Nonoperating revenues and expenses:		
Interest expense		20,000
Net income before income taxes		$ 221,500
Less: Income tax expense		107,000
Net income		$ 114,500

The Balance Sheet

Unlike the balance sheet for a merchandiser, which reports a single inventory amount, the balance sheet for a manufacturer typically shows materials, work in process, and finished goods inventories separately. Illustration 21.10 shows the balance sheet for the Jernigan Manufacturing Company, using data taken from the work sheet in Illustration 21.6. A manufacturer's balance sheet may also show greater detail in the property, plant, and equipment section because of the significant investment in plant assets.

Illustration 21.10

Balance Sheet of a Manufacturer

JERNIGAN MANUFACTURING COMPANY
Balance Sheet
December 31, 1987

Assets

Current assets:		
Cash		$ 62,000
Accounts receivable	$160,000	
Less: Allowance for doubtful accounts	2,000	158,000
Prepaid insurance		1,000
Inventories:		
Materials	$ 38,000	
Work in process	80,000	
Finished goods	60,000	178,000
Total current assets		$ 399,000
Property, plant, and equipment:		
Land		$ 32,000
Factory building	$400,000	
Less: Accumulated depreciation	60,000	340,000
Factory equipment	$460,000	
Less: Accumulated depreciation	138,000	322,000
Total property, plant, and equipment		$ 694,000
Total assets		$1,093,000

Liabilities and Stockholders' Equity

Current liabilities:		
Accrued payroll payable	$ 15,000	
Accounts payable	60,000	$ 75,000
Long-term liabilities		
Mortgage payable		200,000
Total liabilities		$ 275,000
Stockholders' equity:		
Common stock—$5 par value, 120,000 shares authorized,		
issued, and outstanding		$ 600,000
Retained earnings		218,000
Total stockholders' equity		$ 818,000
Total liabilities and stockholders' equity		$1,093,000

■ PERPETUAL INVENTORY PROCEDURE—THE GENERAL COST ACCUMULATION MODEL

Periodic inventory systems are designed to determine the **total** cost of goods manufactured and the **total** cost of goods sold at the end of the accounting period so that financial statements can be prepared. But in many manufacturing companies, a primary accounting objective is to measure the cost of manufacturing a product line on a **per unit** basis **during** the period so that timely cost control and product pricing decisions can be made. Under perpetual procedure, unit product costs are determined during the period, rather than estimated at the end of the period, by transferring the cost of direct materials, direct labor, and manufacturing overhead to work in process and then to finished goods inventory accounts as goods are processed. Unit costs are available throughout the period because they can be obtained quickly without having to take a physical inventory. Before proceeding with an illustration of perpetual inventory procedure, it is important to first understand the basic pattern of cost accumulation under perpetual inventory procedure in a manufacturing environment.

Product and Cost Flows

Under perpetual procedure, accounting records are usually set up so that the flow of costs through the records will match the physical flow of products through the production process, as shown in Illustration 21.11.

Illustration 21.11 *Product and Cost Flows*

The physical flow of the manufacturing process begins when materials are received from suppliers and placed in the materials storeroom. When needed for processing, the materials are moved from the materials storeroom to the production departments. During production, the materials are processed by laborers and machines and become partially manufactured products. At any time during production, these partially manufactured products are collectively known as **work in process.** Eventually the products are completed, at which time they are known as **finished goods.** The completed products are then moved to the finished goods storeroom for later sale and delivery to customers.

The accounting flow of costs under perpetual procedure follows the physical flow of the manufacturing process. The accounting records show the flow of direct material costs from Materials Inventory into Work in Process Inventory. Here, the costs of direct labor and other factory services are added. When the products are completed and transferred to the finished goods storeroom, their costs are removed from Work in Process Inventory and assigned to Finished Goods Inventory. As the goods are sold, the related costs are transferred from Finished Goods Inventory to Cost of Goods Sold.

Illustration 21.12 shows the manufacturing cost flows along with the selling, administrative, and financing costs of a company. These three expense categories plus the cost of goods sold are the total expenses of the company and are deducted from sales to arrive at net income.

Manufacturing Cost Flows under Perpetual Inventory Procedure Illustrated

Illustration 21.13 uses T-accounts to trace the flow of materials, labor, and overhead costs through the production process to finished goods inventory.

Illustration 21.12 *A Manufacturing Company's Total Operations*

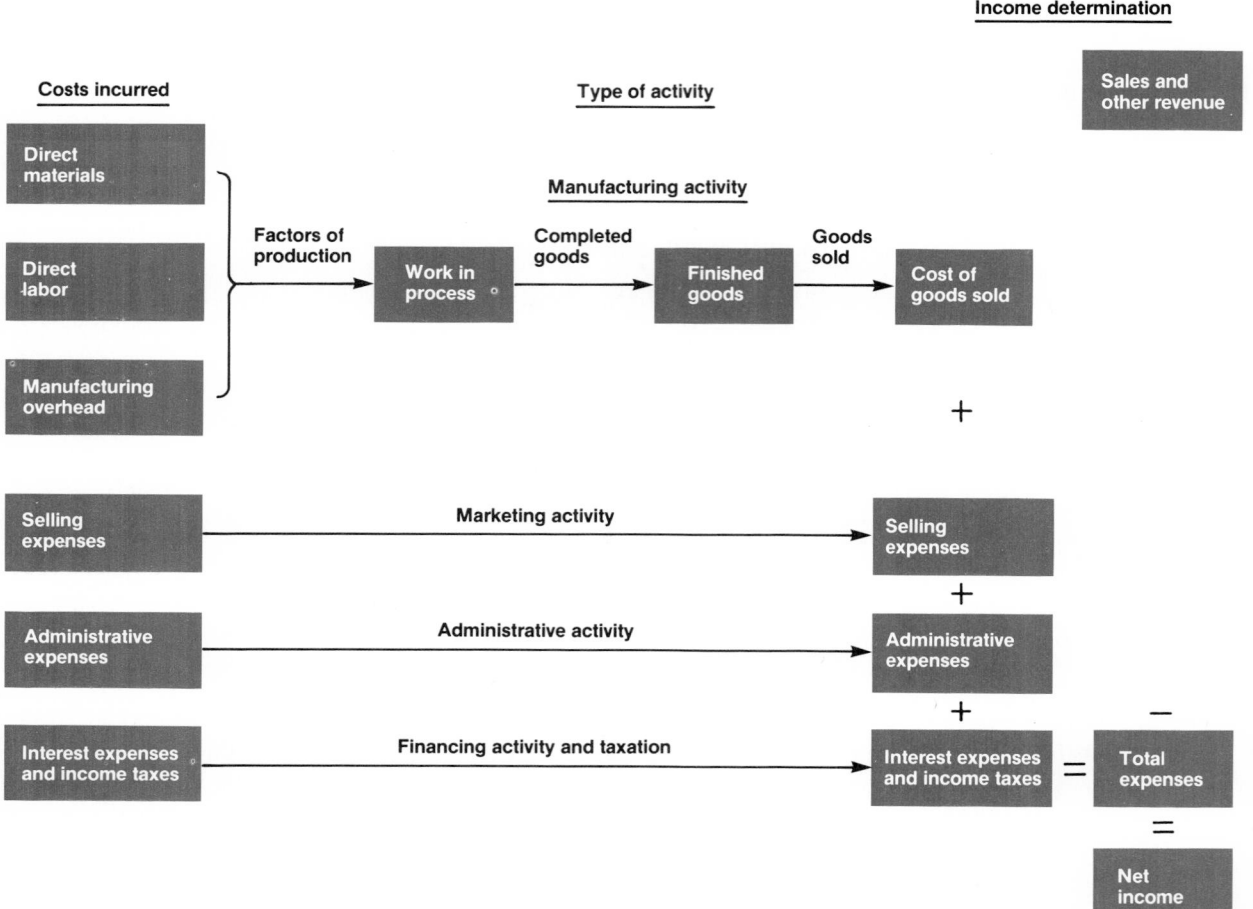

The sale of finished goods inventory to customers and the closing of the revenue and expense accounts for the year are then illustrated. Then the procedures followed in Illustration 21.13 are explained step by step, including examples of the journal entries necessary to record the transactions.

Flow of Direct and Indirect Materials Cost. During July, $40,000 of materials and supplies were purchased on account; $28,000 of direct materials and $2,000 of indirect materials (supplies) were issued to production from the storeroom. The required entries (keyed numerically to the entries in the T-accounts in Illustration 21.13 are:

(1) Materials Inventory 40,000
　　　Accounts Payable 40,000
　　To record purchases of materials and supplies on
　　account.

(2) Work in Process Inventory 28,000
　　Manufacturing Overhead 2,000
　　　Materials Inventory 30,000
　　To record direct and indirect materials issued to
　　production.

Note that purchases of both direct and indirect materials (supplies) are debited to Materials Inventory. But when materials are issued to production, direct materials are debited to Work in Process Inventory, while indirect materials are recorded in Manufacturing Overhead because they are not easily traceable to specific products.

Flow of Labor Costs. Two kinds of labor costs must be accounted for in this procedure. **Payroll accounting** involves determining the total wages earned, the various deductions, and the net pay of each employee. **Labor cost accounting** involves determining which accounts are to be charged with what amount of labor costs. Under such a procedure, an account common to both groups is needed to tie together the separate accounting activities. This account is called Payroll Summary. The Payroll Summary account is a temporarily established (clearing) account that is debited when payrolls are prepared by the payroll department and credited when labor costs are distributed by the factory accounting department. Normally, the Payroll Summary account has a zero balance at the end of any accounting period. During the period, the account has a balance only because of the time lag between preparation of the payroll and classification of the payroll costs as direct or indirect labor.

The factory payrolls for July amounted to $75,000—direct labor of $60,000 and indirect labor of $15,000. Payroll withholdings amounted to $3,500 social security taxes, $8,000 federal income taxes, and $500 union dues. The entries required are:

(3)	Payroll Summary		75,000	
	FICA Taxes Payable			3,500
	Employees' Federal Income Taxes Payable . . .			8,000
	Employees' Union Dues Payable			500
	Accrued Payroll Payable			63,000
	To record factory payroll and various withholdings.			

(4)	Work in Process Inventory		60,000	
	Manufacturing Overhead		15,000	
	Payroll Summary			75,000
	To distribute labor costs for July.			

Accrued payroll shown in entry *(3)* will be paid in cash to the employees, while the amounts withheld will be paid at a later date on the employees' behalf to the federal government (social security taxes and federal income taxes) and the labor union (union dues). Entry *(4)* adds to Work in Process Inventory all labor cost traceable to the products being manufactured (direct labor), while nontraceable labor costs (indirect labor) are transferred to Manufacturing Overhead.[1]

Flow of Overhead Costs. Indirect costs of operating the factory during the period included repairs of $1,000 paid in cash, property taxes of $1,500, expiration of prepaid equipment rent of $2,500, and insurance of $2,000, payroll

---

[1] Selling and administrative salaries are ignored since this chapter concentrates on aspects that are unique to a manufacturer.

Illustration 21.13 *Cost and Revenue Flowchart (Perpetual Inventory System)*

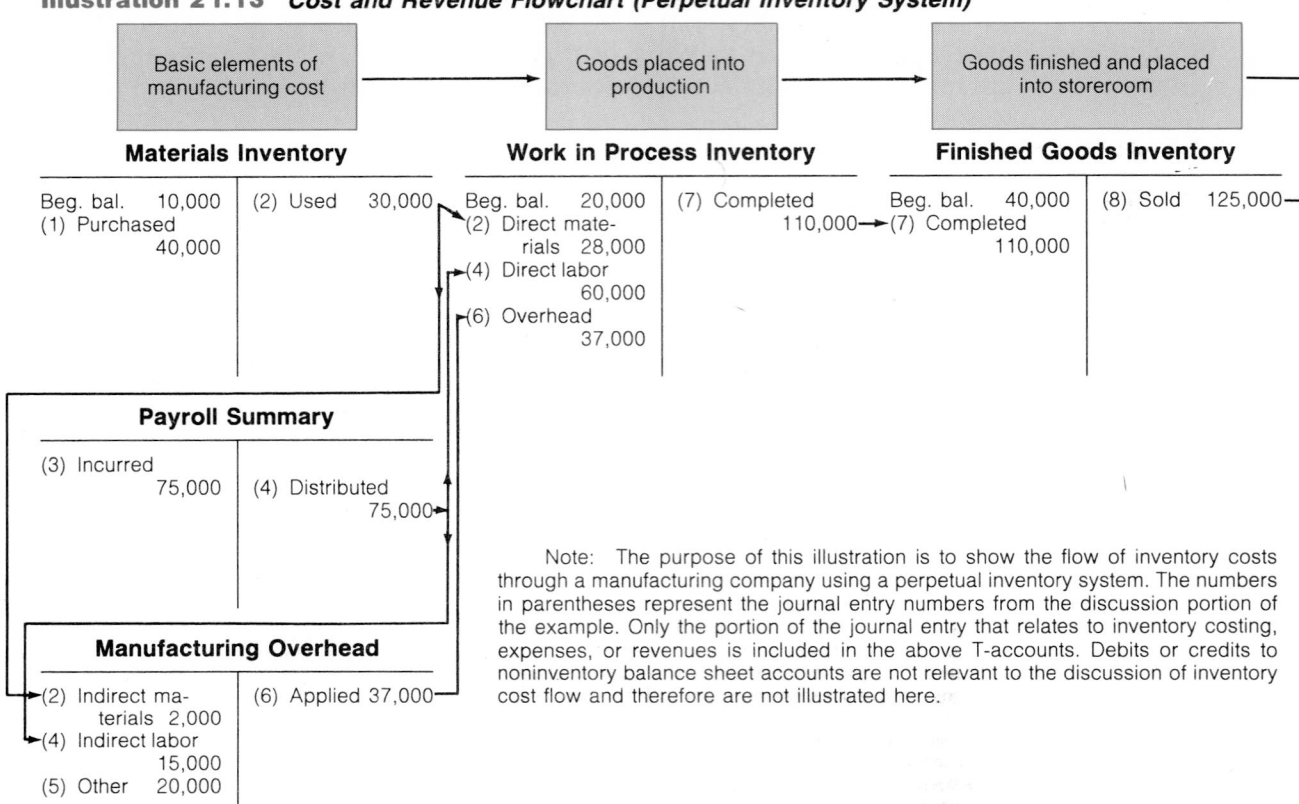

Note: The purpose of this illustration is to show the flow of inventory costs through a manufacturing company using a perpetual inventory system. The numbers in parentheses represent the journal entry numbers from the discussion portion of the example. Only the portion of the journal entry that relates to inventory costing, expenses, or revenues is included in the above T-accounts. Debits or credits to noninventory balance sheet accounts are not relevant to the discussion of inventory cost flow and therefore are not illustrated here.

taxes accrued of $3,500, utilities accrued of $4,000, and factory building depreciation of $5,500. Entry *(5)* below shows the recording of these indirect costs.

(5)	Manufacturing Overhead	20,000	
	Cash		1,000
	Accrued Property Taxes Payable		1,500
	Prepaid Rent		2,500
	Prepaid Insurance		2,000
	Accrued Payroll Taxes Payable		3,500
	Accounts Payable		4,000
	Accumulated Depreciation—Factory Building . .		5,500
	To record factory indirect costs for July.		

Manufacturing overhead costs are as much a part of a period's production cost as are the costs of direct materials and direct labor. Manufacturing overhead costs must, therefore, be added to the Work in Process Inventory account; this is done in entry *(6)* below:

(6)	Work in Process Inventory	37,000	
	Manufacturing Overhead		37,000
	To assign overhead to work in process.		

Manufacturing overhead costs are generally assigned to production using overhead rates. For purposes of this illustration however, it is assumed that **all** overhead incurred during July is assigned to production.

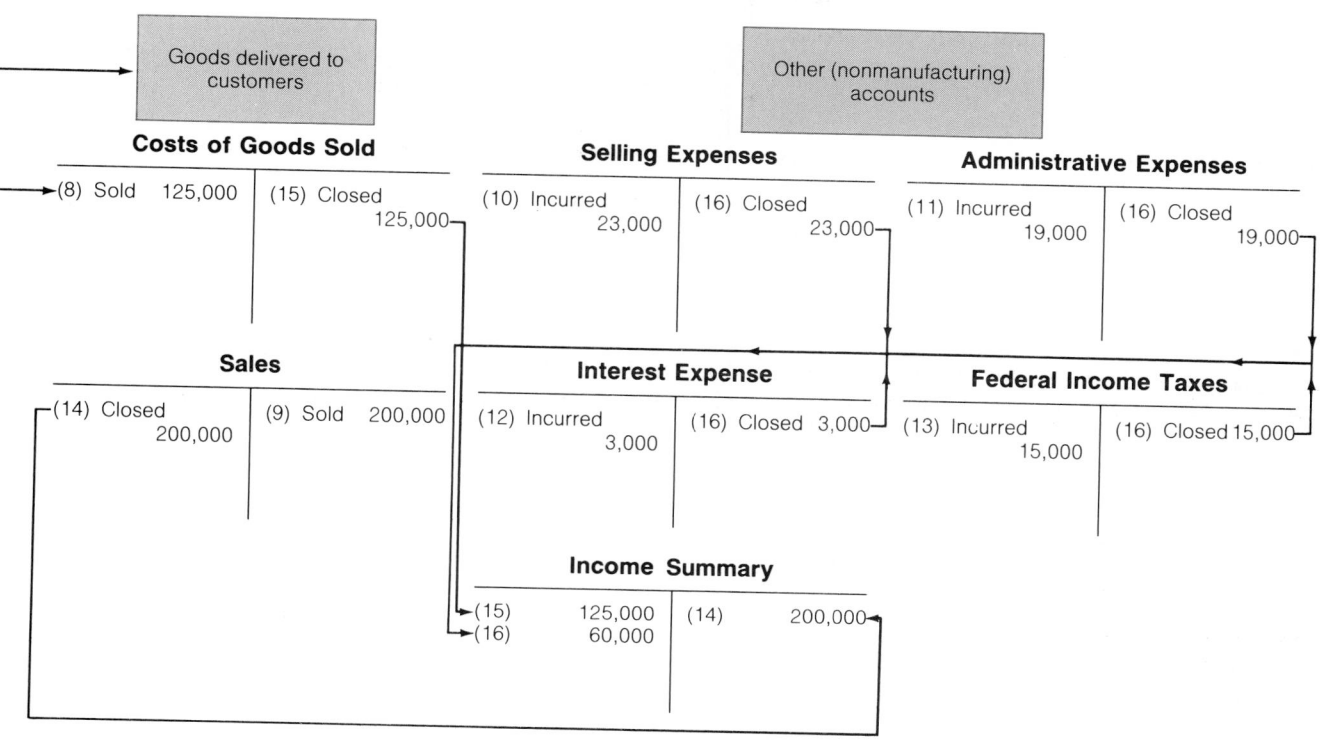

Flow of Finished Goods. As shown in Illustration 21.13, for product cost purposes Work in Process Inventory is charged with materials, labor, and overhead costs. When the goods are completed and transferred out of production, an entry is made to transfer their cost from Work in Process Inventory to Finished Goods Inventory. Assuming goods costing $110,000 were completed and transferred, the entry needed is:

(7) Finished Goods Inventory 110,000
         Work in Process Inventory   110,000
     To record transfer of completed goods.

Now assume that goods costing $125,000 were sold on account for $200,000. Entries are required to transfer the cost of the inventory out of finished goods to cost of goods sold and to record the sale. The required entries are:

(8) Costs of Goods Sold 125,000
         Finished Goods Inventory   125,000
     To record cost of goods sold.

(9) Accounts Receivable 200,000
         Sales   200,000
     To record sales on account.

To complete the explanation of the entries in Illustration 21.13, assume that selling expenses of $23,000, administrative expenses of $19,000, interest expense of $3,000, and federal income taxes of $15,000 were incurred in July. The required entries are:

(10)	Selling Expenses	23,000	
	Various asset and liability accounts		23,000
	To record selling expenses incurred in July.		

(11)	Administrative Expenses	19,000	
	Various asset and liability accounts		19,000
	To record administrative expenses incurred in July.		

(12)	Interest Expense	3,000	
	Accrued Interest Payable		3,000
	To record interest expense incurred in July.		

(13)	Federal Income Taxes	15,000	
	Federal Income Taxes Payable		15,000
	To record estimated income taxes for July.		

Subsidiary records or accounts would be kept for the various types of selling and administrative expenses incurred. The credits in entries *(10)* and *(11)* would be to accounts such as Cash, Accounts Payable, Salaries Payable, and Accumulated Depreciation.

Although the accounts are usually closed only at the end of the accounting year, entry *(14)* records the closing of the Sales revenue account for the month of July as an illustration of the annual entry:

(14)	Sales	200,000	
	Income Summary		200,000
	To close Sales revenue account.		

Entries *(15)* and *(16)* are required to close the expense accounts:

(15)	Income Summary	125,000	
	Cost of Goods Sold		125,000
	To close Cost of Goods Sold account.		

(16)	Income Summary	60,000	
	Selling Expenses		23,000
	Administrative Expenses		19,000
	Interest Expense		3,000
	Federal Income Taxes		15,000
	To close other expense accounts.		

Entries (15) and (16) could be combined into one entry. Although it is not shown in Illustration 21.13, the closing process would be completed by transferring net income to the Retained Earnings account.

Income Summary	15,000	
Retained Earnings		15,000
To close Income Summary.		

Use of a Work Sheet under Perpetual Procedure

A manufacturing company using perpetual procedure can use the same work sheet as illustrated in Chapter 5. The work sheet has columns labeled Trial Balance, Adjustments, Adjusted Trial Balance, Income Statement, and Balance Sheet. The amounts shown in the trial balance for materials inventory, work in process inventory, and finished goods inventory will be the end of period balances. The amounts would be carried to the Balance Sheet debit column. The cost of goods sold amount will be included with the other expenses in the trial balance. All other steps in preparing the work sheet are as described in Chapter 5 and will not be illustrated here.

■ *SUMMARY*

This chapter focused on accounting for inventory and cost of goods sold for a manufacturer. Unlike a merchandiser (retailer or wholesaler), who purchases and resells goods that are already in their finished state, a manufacturer purchases raw materials and uses equipment and labor to process those materials into products for sale. While the merchandiser has only one inventory—merchandise available for sale—a manufacturer has three inventories—unprocessed materials, partially complete work in process, and ready-for-sale finished goods.

Manufacturing costs can be divided into direct materials, direct labor, and manufacturing overhead. Direct materials are materials that are (1) included in the finished product, (2) used only in the manufacture of the product, and (3) clearly and easily traceable to the product. Direct labor is the cost of labor by employees actually working on materials to convert them into finished goods. Manufacturing overhead includes all other manufacturing costs, except those that are accounted for as direct material or direct labor. Prime cost is a term used to refer to the sum of direct materials cost and direct labor cost, and conversion cost refers to the sum of direct labor cost and manufacturing overhead cost.

Product costs are costs incurred in the manufacture of products. They are associated with products rather than with periods of time. Product costs are considered to be the costs of manufacturing inventory, and they are expensed only when the related inventory is sold. Period costs, on the other hand, are more closely related to periods of time than to products produced. Period costs are expensed in the period in which they are incurred. All selling and nonmanufacturing administrative costs are treated as period costs.

Costs that remain constant in total amount over a wide range of variations in the level of manufacturing activity are considered to be fixed costs. Variable costs, on the other hand, vary in total amount directly with changes in the level of manufacturing activity.

Like merchandisers, manufacturers can use either periodic or perpetual inventory procedure to account for inventory costs. When a manufacturer uses periodic inventory procedure, the Materials Purchases, Transportation-In, Materials Purchase Returns and Allowances, and Materials Inventory accounts are used in the same manner as they are by a merchandiser. In addition, the manufacturer has to account for work in process and finished goods inventories. Use of a work sheet aids in the preparation of the necessary adjusting and closing entries to compute ending inventories and cost of goods sold.

When a periodic inventory system is in use, inventory quantities are determined at year-end by making a physical count of the materials, work in process, and finished goods on hand. After the quantity of these inventories has been established, their cost must be determined. Cost of the raw materials inventory may be determined by multiplying purchase cost per unit of material by the amount of material on hand. To obtain the cost of the work in process and finished goods inventories, the manufacturer must estimate the per unit cost of direct materials used, direct labor used, and manufacturing overhead incurred in producing each unit. The amounts of materials may differ, while the amounts of labor and overhead will differ, for units in work in process inventory and units in finished goods inventory. Direct materials cost per unit can be established by referring to a materials specification list for the product and knowing when materials are added in the production process. Direct labor cost per unit is normally based on observations made by management to determine the normal amount of time it takes workers to complete the product. Manufacturing overhead costs must be allocated to the product based on a manufacturing overhead rate, which expresses overhead costs in relation to some measure of manufacturing activity.

Under perpetual inventory procedure, accounting records are set up so that the flow of costs through the records matches the physical flow of products through the production process. All materials purchases are debited to the Materials Inventory account. Materials issued to production are credited to Materials Inventory; direct materials are debited to the Work in Process Inventory account, and indirect materials are debited to the Manufacturing Overhead account. All labor costs are recorded in a Payroll Summary account. Direct labor costs are credited to Payroll Summary and debited to Work in Process Inventory, while indirect labor costs are credited to Payroll Summary and debited to Manufacturing Overhead. Other factory overhead costs are also debited to Manufacturing Overhead. Overhead applied to production is credited to Manufacturing Overhead and debited to Work in Process Inventory. The cost of goods completed is transferred from the Work in Process Inventory account to the Finished Goods Inventory account, and the cost of goods sold is transferred from Finished Goods Inventory to Cost of Goods Sold.

Perpetual inventory systems are superior to periodic inventory systems in their ability to provide information about manufacturing costs during the accounting period so that timely cost control and pricing decisions can be made. Under a periodic inventory system, total cost of goods manufactured and total cost of goods sold are determined only at the end of the accounting period, and the per unit production costs can only be estimated. A perpetual inventory system, by contrast, provides per unit production cost information throughout the period. A perpetual inventory system involves considerably more detailed accounting records.

The balance sheet and income statement of a manufacturer differ from those of a merchandiser. The statement of cost of goods manufactured is a statement used by a manufacturer to show cost to manufacture and cost of goods manufactured for the period. Only cost of goods manufactured is shown in the income statement in order to make the income statement more understandable to readers of the financial statements. The balance sheet for a manufacturer typically shows materials, work in process, and finished goods inventories separately. A manufacturer's balance sheet may also show greater detail in property, plant, and equipment because of the significant investment in plant assets.

In Chapter 22, you continue your study of manufacturing costs. Without efficient cost systems for accumulating manufacturing costs, manufacturing companies cannot evaluate past performance and adequately plan for the future.

NEW TERMS INTRODUCED IN CHAPTER 21

Administrative costs

Nonmanufacturing costs that include the costs of top administrative functions and various staff departments such as accounting, data processing, and personnel (814).

Conversion cost

The sum of direct labor and manufacturing overhead costs (813).

Cost

A financial measure of the resources used or given up to achieve a stated purpose (811).

Cost of goods manufactured

Consists of the costs of all goods completed during the period; total manufacturing cost plus beginning work in process inventory minus ending work in process inventory (823, 825).

Cost to manufacture

Includes the costs of all resources put into production during the period (823, 825).

Direct labor

Labor costs of all employees actually working on materials to convert them into finished goods (812).

Direct materials

Materials that are (1) included in the finished product, (2) used only in the manufacture of the product, and (3) clearly and easily traceable to the product (812).

Factory cost

See Manufacturing cost.

Finished goods

Completed manufactured products ready to be sold; also, Finished Goods Inventory is the title of an inventory account maintained for such products (811).

Fixed costs

Costs that remain constant in total amount over wide variations in the level of manufacturing activity (815).

Indirect labor

The services of factory employees that cannot or will not, for practical reasons, be traced to the products being manufactured (812).

Indirect materials

Materials used in the manufacture of a product that cannot or will not, for practical reasons, be traced directly to the products being manufactured (812).

Manufacturing cost

The cost incurred to produce or create a product. It includes direct materials, direct labor, and manufacturing overhead costs (812).

Manufacturing overhead

All manufacturing costs except for those costs accounted for as direct materials and direct labor (812).

Manufacturing overhead rate

Expresses manufacturing overhead costs in relation to some measure of manufacturing activity (818).

Materials

Unprocessed items that will be used in the manufacturing process (811).

Period costs

Costs related more closely to periods of time than to products produced. Period costs cannot be traced directly to the manufacture of a specific product; they are expensed in the period in which they are incurred (814).

Prime cost

The sum of the direct materials costs and direct labor costs incurred to manufacture a product (813).

Product costs

(See also Manufacturing cost.) Costs incurred in the manufacture of products and assigned to units of the product produced by the manufacturing company. These costs include costs of direct materials, direct labor, and manufacturing overhead (814).

Selling costs

Costs incurred to obtain customer orders and get the finished product into the customer's possession (813).

Statement of cost of goods manufactured

An accounting report showing the cost to manufacture and the cost of goods manufactured (825).

Variable costs

Costs that directly vary in total amount with changes in the volume of production activity or output (816).

Work in process

Partially manufactured products; also, Work in Process Inventory is the title of an inventory account maintained for such products (811).

DEMONSTRATION PROBLEM

Data needed to prepare the work sheet of the Douglas Manufacturing Company are given below. The company uses a periodic inventory system.

1. The December 31, 1988, trial balance was taken from the general ledger of the company. (The inventories in the trial balance are those of January 1, 1988.)
2. The only entry in the Retained Earnings account during the year ended December 31, 1988, was a debit of $18,000 for the declaration of cash dividends.
3. The inventories at December 31, 1988, were as follows:

    a. Materials inventory $24,000
    b. Work in process inventory . . 44,000
    c. Finished goods inventory . . 34,000

    Adjustments are as follows:

1. The allowance for doubtful accounts is to be adjusted to 5% of the accounts receivable.
2. Accrued wages and salaries are:

    Accrued direct labor $2,400
    Accrued sales salaries 4,000
    Accrued office and officers' salaries . . 6,000

3. Interest on the mortgage bonds was last paid on July 1.
4. Factory supplies used, $2,200.
5. Factory insurance expired during the period, $1,200.
6. Accrued factory taxes, $1,400.
7. Depreciation of factory building, $4,000.
8. Depreciation of machinery and equipment, $23,000.
9. Depreciation of office equipment, $1,000.

The Trial Balance columns of the work sheet and the proper totals of other columns on the work sheet have already been completed (see pages 840–41).

Required: Prepare the necessary adjusting entries for the work sheet, and extend the amounts in the work sheet Trial Balance columns (plus or minus any adjustments) to their proper columns.

Solution to demonstration problem

The adjusting entries for the Douglas Manufacturing Company for the year ended December 31, 1988, are shown below:

(1) Bad Debts Expense 3,800
          Allowance for Doubtful Accounts 3,800
       To increase allowance to 5% of outstanding accounts receivable:
          $0.05 \times \$80,000 = \$4,000; \$4,000 - \$200 = \$3,800$.

(2) Direct Labor 2,400
     Sales Salaries 4,000
     Office and Officers' Salaries 6,000
          Accrued Wages and Salaries Payable 12,400
       To record accrual of salaries and wages.

(3)   Mortgage Bond Interest Expense   1,500
        Bond Interest Payable   1,500
      To record accrual of 6 months' interest on bonds ($100,000
      × 0.03 × ½).

(4)   Factory Supplies Expense   2,200
        Factory Supplies on Hand   2,200
      To record factory supplies used.

(5)   Factory Insurance Expense   1,200
        Prepaid Factory Insurance   1,200
      To record expired factory insurance.

(6)   Factory Taxes Expense   1,400
        Accrued Taxes Payable   1,400
      To record the accrual of $1,400 of factory taxes.

(7)   Depreciation Expense—Factory Building   4,000
        Accumulated Depreciation—Factory Building   4,000
      To record depreciation on factory building.

(8)   Depreciation Expense—Machinery and Equipment   23,000
        Accumulated Depreciation—Machinery and Equipment .   23,000
      To record depreciation on machinery and equipment.

(9)   Depreciation Expense—Office Equipment   1,000
        Accumulated Depreciation—Office Equipment   1,000
      To record depreciation on office equipment.

The completed work sheet for the Douglas Manufacturing Company for the year ended December 31, 1988, is shown on pages 842–43.

THE DOUGLAS MANUFACTURING COMPANY
Work Sheet for the Year Ended December 31, 1988

Account Titles	Trial Balance		Adjustments		Manufacturing Statement		Income Statement		Balance Sheet	
	Debit	Credit	Debit	Credit	Debit	Credit	Debit	Credit	Debit	Credit
Cash	31,000									
Accounts Receivable	80,000									
Allowance for Doubtful Accounts		200								
Prepaid Factory Insurance	1,800									
Materials Inventory	20,000									
Work in Process Inventory	42,000									
Finished Goods Inventory	28,000									
Factory Supplies on Hand	2,800									
Land	16,000									
Factory Building	200,000									
Accumulated Depreciation— Factory Building		20,000								
Machinery and Equipment	230,000									
Accumulated Depreciation— Machinery and Equipment		46,000								
Small Tools	700									
Office Equipment	18,000									
Accumulated Depreciation— Office Equipment		2,600								
Accounts Payable		29,400								
Income and FICA Taxes Withheld		2,600								
Mortgage Bonds Payable, 3%		100,000								
Common Stock		300,000								
Retained Earnings		103,600								
Sales		800,000								
Sales Discounts	4,000									
Materials Purchases	240,000									
Purchase Returns		2,000								
Transportation-In	3,000									
Direct Labor	184,000									
Supervisors' Salaries	64,000									
Indirect Labor	16,000									

Building Maintenance and Repairs	2,200						
Maintenance of Machinery and							
Equipment	6,400						
Heat, Light, Power	2,400						
Factory Taxes Expense	9,800						
Small Tools Expense	3,100						
General Factory Expense	5,600						
Advertising and Sales Promotion	21,600						
Sales Salaries	60,000						
Sales Travel Expense	3,400						
Sales Office Expense	7,300						
Office and Officers' Salaries	90,000						
Stationery and Supplies Expense	2,200						
Office Taxes, Property and Payroll	4,800						
General Office Operating Expense	8,400						
Mortgage Bond Interest Expense	1,500						
Gain on Sale of Plant Assets		3,600					
	1,410,000	1,410,000					
Bad Debts Expense							
Factory Insurance Expense							
Accrued Wages and Salaries Payable							
Bond Interest Payable							
Factory Supplies Used							
Accrued Taxes Payable							
Depreciation Expense—Factory Building							
Depreciation Expense— Machinery and Equipment							
Depreciation Expense— Office Equipment				50,500	50,500		
Manufacturing Summary							
(Cost of Goods Manufactured)						632,700	632,700
Net Income							
						837,600	837,600	678,900	678,900

Account Titles	Trial Balance		Adjustments		Manufacturing Statement		Income Statement		Balance Sheet	
	Debit	Credit	Debit	Credit	Debit	Credit	Debit	Credit	Debit	Credit
Cash	31,000								31,000	
Accounts Receivable	80,000								80,000	
Allowance for Doubtful Accounts		200		(1) 3,800						4,000
Prepaid Factory Insurance	1,800			(5) 1,200					600	
Materials Inventory	20,000				20,000	24,000			24,000	
Work in Process Inventory	42,000				42,000	44,000			44,000	
Finished Goods Inventory	28,000						28,000	34,000	34,000	
Factory Supplies on Hand	2,800			(4) 2,200					600	
Land	16,000								16,000	
Factory Building	200,000								200,000	
Accumulated Depreciation—Factory Building		20,000		(7) 4,000						24,000
Machinery and Equipment	230,000								230,000	
Accumulated Depreciation—Machinery and Equipment		46,000		(8) 23,000						69,000
Small Tools	700								700	
Office Equipment	18,000								18,000	
Accumulated Depreciation—Office Equipment		2,600		(9) 1,000						3,600
Accounts Payable		29,400								29,400
Income and FICA Taxes Withheld		2,600								2,600
Mortgage Bonds Payable, 3%		100,000								100,000
Common Stock		300,000								300,000
Retained Earnings		103,600								103,600
Sales		800,000						800,000		
Sales Discounts	4,000						4,000			
Materials Purchases	240,000				240,000					
Purchase Returns		2,000				2,000				
Transportation-In	3,000				3,000					
Direct Labor	184,000		(2) 2,400		186,400					
Supervisors' Salaries	64,000				64,000					
Indirect Labor	16,000				16,000					

Account	Trial Balance Dr	Trial Balance Cr	Adjustments Dr	Adjustments Cr	Manufacturing Dr	Manufacturing Cr	Income Statement Dr	Income Statement Cr	Balance Sheet Dr	Balance Sheet Cr
Building Maintenance and Repairs	2,200				2,200					
Maintenance of Machinery and Equipment	6,400				6,400					
Heat, Light, Power	2,400				2,400					
Factory Taxes Expense	9,800		(6) 1,400		11,200					
Small Tools Expense	3,100				3,100					
General Factory Expense	5,600				5,600					
Advertising and Sales Promotion	21,600						21,600			
Sales Salaries	60,000		(2) 4,000				64,000			
Sales Travel Expense	3,400						3,400			
Sales Office Expense	7,300						7,300			
Office and Officers' Salaries	90,000		(2) 6,000				96,000			
Stationery and Supplies Expense	2,200						2,200			
Office Taxes, Property, and Payroll	4,800						4,800			
General Office Operating Expense	8,400						8,400			
Mortgage Bond Interest Expense	1,500		(3) 1,500				3,000			
Gain on Sale of Plant Assets		3,600						3,600		
	1,410,000	1,410,000								
Bad Debts Expense			(1) 3,800				3,800			
Factory Insurance Expense			(5) 1,200		1,200					
Accrued Wages and Salaries Payable				(2) 12,400						
Bond Interest Payable				(3) 1,500						
Factory Supplies Used			(4) 2,200		2,200					
Accrued Taxes Payable				(6) 1,400						
Depreciation Expense—Factory Building			(7) 4,000		4,000					
Depreciation Expense—Machinery and Equipment			(8) 23,000		23,000					
Depreciation Expense—Office Equipment			(9) 1,000				1,000			
			50,500	50,500						
Manufacturing Summary (Cost of Goods Manufactured)						562,700	562,700			
					632,700	632,700	810,200	837,600		
Net Income							27,400			27,400
							837,600	837,600	678,900	678,900

QUESTIONS

1. Identify the three elements of cost incurred in manufacturing a product, and indicate the distinguishing characteristics of each.

2. Why might a company claim that the total cost of employing a person is $10.30 per hour even though the employee's wage rate is $6.50 per hour? How should this difference be classified and why?

3. What is the typical accounting for the overtime wage premium paid to a direct laborer? Why?

4. Identify the two broad classifications of costs incurred by manufacturing companies and what is included in each. Indicate why it is important that costs be correctly classified.

5. Why are certain costs referred to as period costs? What are the major types of period costs incurred by a manufacturer?

6. Explain the differences between fixed costs and variable costs.

7. Explain how the income statement of a manufacturing company differs from the income statement of a merchandising company.

8. What is the general content of a statement of cost of goods manufactured? What is its relationship to the income statement?

9. Under perpetual inventory procedure what is the relationship between cost flows in the accounts and the flow of physical products through a factory?

EXERCISES

E–1

Classify various items according to types of costs

Given below are some costs incurred by an electrical appliance manufacturer. Classify these costs as direct materials, direct labor, manufacturing overhead, selling, or administrative.

a. President's salary.
b. Cost of electrical wire.
c. Cost of janitorial supplies.
d. Wages of assembly-line workers.
e. Cost of promotional displays.
f. Plant supervisor's salary.
g. Cost accountant's salary.
h. Research and development costs.
i. Cost of aluminum used for toasters.
j. Cost of market research survey.

E–2

Classify items as product or period costs

Classify the costs listed in Exercise E–1 as either product costs or period costs.

E–3

Identify variable cost items and prime cost items

Which of the items in Exercise E–1 would most likely vary directly with the number of appliances produced? Which would be considered prime costs?

E–4

Compute cost of goods manufactured

The following data pertain to the Thomas Company for the year ended December 31, 1987:

Materials inventory, January 1, 1987	$ 37,500
Materials inventory, December 31, 1987	50,000
Materials purchases	137,500
Direct labor	175,000
Work in process inventory, January 1, 1987	25,000

Work in process inventory, December 31, 1987 . .	37,500
Manufacturing overhead	100,000
Finished goods inventory, January 1, 1987 . . .	62,500
Finished goods inventory, December 31, 1987 . .	110,000

Compute the cost of goods manufactured and the cost of goods sold.

E–5

Prepare journal entries for labor costs

Bill Cash was paid $588 for 46 hours as an assembly-line worker at a manufacturing plant. This sum consisted of 40 hours regular time at $12 per hour and 6 hours overtime at time and a half.

a.   Prepare the entry to distribute this labor cost to the accounts.
b.   Prepare the entry to distribute the labor cost to the accounts assuming Bill is a salesman.
c.   Prepare the entry assuming Bill is a factory supervisor.

E–6

Compute manufacturing overhead rate

Compute the manufacturing overhead rate for the Maddox Manufacturing Company based on direct labor costs, given the following information:

Estimated direct labor costs	$750,000
Estimated manufacturing overhead costs . .	450,000

E–7

Calculate estimated ending inventory costs

The following data pertain to the TKR Company for the year ended December 31, 1987:

Estimated direct materials cost per unit included in work in process inventory for product D	$22
Estimated direct materials cost per unit included in finished goods inventory for product D	22
Estimated direct labor cost per unit included in work in process inventory for product D	20
Estimated direct labor cost per unit included in finished goods inventory for product D	32
Manufacturing overhead rate	75% of direct labor cost
Units of product D included in work in process inventory . .	300 units
Units of product D included in finished goods inventory . . .	150 units

Compute the ending work in process inventory and finished goods inventory for product D.

E–8

Prepare cost and revenue flowchart under perpetual inventory procedure

The Flair Company uses perpetual inventory procedure. The following data are for the month of June:

1.   Materials purchased on account, $78,000.
2.   Direct materials issued, $90,000.
3.   Repairs and maintenance on factory buildings, $9,000.
4.   Factory depreciation, taxes, and utilities, $75,000.
5.   Factory payroll for June, $54,000, including $4,800 of indirect labor. (Assume no withholdings.)
6.   Manufacturing overhead is assigned in full to production.
7.   Cost of goods completed and transferred, $247,500.
8.   Cost of goods sold, $240.000.
9.   Sales for the month on account, $450,000.

The June 1 inventory account balances were:

Materials	$24,000
Work in process	60,000
Finished goods	18,000

Prepare a cost and revenue flowchart similar to the one in Illustration 21.13, incorporating the above data.

E–9

Prepare journal entries under perpetual inventory procedure

Prepare journal entries to record the transactions in Exercise E–8.

PROBLEMS—SERIES A

P21-1-A

Prepare statement of cost of goods manufactured and closing entries

The Manufacturing Statement columns of a work sheet prepared by Benton Manufacturing, Inc. at June 30, 1987, contain the following adjusted amounts:

Account Titles	Manufacturing Statement	
	Debit	Credit
Inventories:		
Materials	15,750	27,000
Work in Process	25,000	13,000
Materials Purchases	168,500	
Materials Purchase Returns		1,500
Transportation-In	17,500	
Direct Labor	112,500	
Indirect Labor	35,000	
Supervisors' Salaries	22,500	
Factory Building Rent	6,000	
Factory Utilities	18,000	
Factory Supplies Used	9,750	
Depreciation Expense—Machinery . .	25,000	
Other Factory Overhead	37,500	
	493,000	41,500
Manufacturing Summary		
(Cost of goods manufactured) . .		451,500
	493,000	493,000

Required:
a. Prepare a statement of cost of goods manufactured for Benton Manufacturing, Inc., for the year ended June 30, 1987.
b. Prepare all necessary closing entries, including the entry to establish the ending inventory balances and the entry to close the Manufacturing Summary account.

P21-2-A

Prepare statement of cost of goods manufactured and income statement

The information given below was taken from a work sheet prepared by the Davis Company on December 31, 1987:

Account Titles	Manufacturing Statement		Income Statement	
	Debit	Credit	Debit	Credit
Sales				925,000
Materials Purchases	118,750			
Materials Purchase Returns		6,250		
Transportation-In	1,250			
Inventories:				
Materials	15,000	12,500		
Work in Process	32,500	27,000		
Finished Goods			45,000	37,500
Direct Labor	140,000			
Indirect Materials	4,000			
Overtime Wages	8,000			
Payroll Taxes—Factory	42,500			
Utilities Expense	4,250			
Maintenance and Repairs	1,500			
Selling Expenses			150,000	
Administrative Expenses			225,000	
Property Taxes—Factory	1,100			
Income Tax Expense			50,000	
Insurance Expense—Factory	1,500			
Depreciation Expense—Factory Building	7,500			
Depreciation Expense—Factory Equipment	10,000			
	387,850	45,750		
Manufacturing Summary (Cost of goods manufactured)		342,100	342,100	
	387,850	387,850	812,100	962,500
Net income			150,400	
			962,500	962,500

Required:

a. Prepare a statement of cost of goods manufactured for the Davis Company for the year ended December 31, 1987.

b. Prepare an income statement for the Davis Company for the year ended December 31, 1987.

P21-3-A

Prepare closing entries

Refer to the information given for the Davis Company in Problem 21-2-A. Prepare all necessary entries to set up the ending inventory balances and to close the books for 1987.

P21-4-A

Prepare statement of cost of goods manufactured, income statement, and closing entries

The following data were taken from the completed work sheet of Logo's Corner Manufacturing Company at December 31, 1987:

Direct labor	$300,000	Materials purchases		$ 180,000
Indirect labor	37,500	Transportation-in		9,000
Factory supervision	66,000	Insurance expense (70%		
Selling and administrative		applicable to factory)		15,000
salaries	150,000	Repairs and maintenance		
Factory supplies used	9,000	expense		2,250
Inventories, January 1:		Utilities expense (70%		
Materials	12,000	applicable to factory)		4,500
Work in process	30,000	Payroll taxes (factory)		45,000
Finished goods	27,000	Depreciation expense (80%		
Inventories, December 31:		applicable to factory)		60,000
Materials	18,000	Delivery expense		24,000
Work in process	37,500	Sales		1,110,000
Finished goods	33,000	Other selling and		
		administrative expenses		30,000

Required: a. Prepare a statement of cost of goods manufactured for 1987.
b. Prepare an income statement for the year ended December 31, 1987 (ignore income taxes).
c. Prepare all necessary closing entries.

P21-5-A

Prepare work sheet, financial statements, and closing entries

Wand Products, Inc. prepared the following trial balance and supplementary information on December 31, 1987, the end of its first year of operations:

	Debits	Credits
Cash	$ 45,070	
Accounts Receivable	153,000	
Prepaid Factory Insurance	9,492	
Factory Supplies on Hand	14,916	
Office Supplies on Hand	6,430	
Factory Machinery	362,000	
Factory Equipment	66,800	
Office Equipment	23,800	
Accounts Payable		$ 35,030
Mortgage Notes Payable		80,000
Common Stock		500,000
Sales		644,470
Sales Returns	3,000	
Sales Discounts	6,170	
Materials Purchases	122,300	
Direct Labor	175,160	
Factory Supervision	32,500	
Indirect Labor	17,000	
Heat, Light, Power—Factory	33,564	
Machine Maintenance	9,200	
Rent of Factory	24,000	
Property Taxes—Factory	3,200	
General Factory Expense	11,520	
Sales Office Salaries	54,240	
Advertising Expense	8,400	
Rent of Sales Office	4,800	
Officers' Salaries	41,594	
Office Salaries	22,034	
Miscellaneous Office Expense	5,310	
Rent of Administrative Office	2,200	
Interest Expense	1,800	
	$1,259,500	$1,259,500

Supplementary information:

Inventories at December 31, 1987:

Materials	$17,800
Work in process	6,400
Finished goods	23,200

Information needed for adjustments:

1. Estimated bad debts expense for the year: 1% of net sales.
2. Factory insurance expired . . . . $ 2,292
3. Factory supplies used 13,066
4. Office supplies used 5,510

Depreciation rates:

5. Factory machinery 10%
6. Factory equipment 15%
7. Office equipment 7%
8. Accrued factory payroll at December 31, 1987:

Direct labor	$ 7,100
Factory supervision	950
	$ 8,050

9. Accrued salaries of December 31, 1987:

Sales office salaries	$ 2,000
Office salaries	1,140
	$ 3,140

10. Accrued rent of office (administrative) . . . . . $ 200
11. Accrued interest on mortgage note 600

Required: Using the information given, prepare the following for the year ended December 31, 1987:

a.   Work sheet.
b.   Statement of cost of goods manufactured.
c.   Income statement (ignore income taxes).
d.   Balance sheet.
e.   Entries to set up the ending inventories and to close the accounts.

P21-6-A

Calculate manufacturing overhead rate, cost of ending work in process and finished goods inventories, cost of goods manufactured, and cost of goods sold

The Ideal Company incurred the following manufacturing costs for the first quarter of 1987:

Materials used	$384,600
Direct labor	620,000
Manufacturing overhead . .	496,000

The work in process and finished goods inventories were $64,800 and $268,000, respectively, on January 1, 1987. The production department provided the following information relating to the cost of the work in process and finished goods inventories on March 31, 1987:

		Estimated cost per unit	
	Units in inventory	*Direct materials*	*Direct labor*
Work in process:			
Product A	500	$ 8.00	$20.00
Product B	1,000	12.00	10.00
Finished goods:			
Product A	2,000	18.00	30.00
Product B	2,610	16.80	24.00

Required: a.   Compute the manufacturing overhead rate, based on direct labor cost.
b.   Using the rate computed in *(a)*, determine the cost of the inventories of work in process and finished goods at March 31, 1987.
c.   Compute the cost of goods manufactured and the cost of goods sold during the first quarter of 1987.

P21-7-A

Prepare cost and revenue flowchart for perpetual inventory procedure

The McArthur Company uses perpetual inventory procedure. The following data are for the month of June:

1.   Materials purchased on account, $67,200.
2.   Direct materials issued, $78,400.
3.   Repairs and maintenance on factory buildings, $8,400.
4.   Factory depreciation, taxes, and utilities, $58,240.
5.   Factory payroll for June, $50,400, including $4,480 of indirect labor.
6.   Actual manufacturing overhead is assigned to production.
7.   Cost of goods completed and transferred, $218,400.
8.   Cost of goods sold, $224,000.
9.   Sales for the month on account, $420,000.

The June 1 inventory account balances were:

Materials	$22,400
Work in process	56,000
Finished goods	16,800

Required: Using T-accounts, prepare a cost and revenue flowchart similar to the one shown in Illustration 21.13. Key your entries using the numbers given.

P21-8-A

Prepare journal entries and ending inventory balances under perpetual inventory procedure

The Penrod Company uses perpetual inventory procedure. Assume the inventories at August 1, 1987, were as follows:

Materials inventory	$30,800
Work in process inventory	44,800
Finished goods inventory	63,000

Transactions:

1. During August, $112,000 of raw materials were purchased on account and $91,000 were issued to production.
2. The factory payrolls (gross) for August were $133,000. Direct labor was $98,000, and indirect labor was $35,000. Payroll withholdings included $8,400 of FICA taxes, $25,200 of federal income taxes, and $2,100 of union dues.
3. The indirect costs of production included machinery repairs of $2,100, equipment rental of $4,200, utilities of $14,000, payroll taxes of $8,400, amortization of prepaid insurance of $5,600, and factory building depreciation of $4,480.
4. Overhead was assigned in full to production.
5. Goods costing $196,000 were completed and transferred to finished goods inventory.
6. Goods costing $210,000 were sold on account for $308,000.

Required: *a.* Give the journal entries for the above transactions.
b. Using T-accounts, compute the balance in each of the three inventory accounts at August 31, 1987.

P21–9–A

Prepare journal entries, income statement, and closing entries under perpetual inventory procedures

The Bailey Manufacturing Company, which uses perpetual inventory procedure, had the following transactions for the month of May 1987:

Transactions:

1. Materials and supplies purchased on account, $36,000.
2. Materials issued to production, $42,000; indirect materials issued, $3,000.
3. Repairs and maintenance on factory equipment, $2,250.
4. Recorded factory depreciation, $15,000; property taxes, $6,000; and utilities, $10,200.
5. Administrative salaries paid, $18,000.
6. Depreciation on administration building, $7,500.
7. Factory payroll (gross), $27,000; withholdings FICA taxes, $1,650; federal income taxes, $4,800.
8. Factory payroll distribution: direct labor, $24,600; indirect labor, $2,400.
9. Paid advertising expense, $750, and delivery expense, $525.
10. Sales salaries and commissions paid, $6,750.
11. Actual manufacturing overhead cost was assigned to production.
12. Cost of goods completed and transferred, $117,000.
13. Sales on account, $225,000; cost of goods sold, $120,000.
14. Other selling expenses, $420; other administrative expenses, $750; and interest expense, $60, were paid in cash.
15. Federal income taxes were accrued at 40% of net income from operations.

Required: *a.* Prepare journal entries to record the May transactions.
b. Prepare an income statement for the Bailey Manufacturing Company for the month of May 1987.
c. Prepare closing entries at May 31, 1987.

PROBLEMS—SERIES B

P21-1-B

Prepare statement of cost of goods manufactured and closing entries

The following data are from a work sheet prepared by the Coleman Manufacturing Company at December 31, 1987:

Account Titles	Manufacturing Statement	
	Debit	Credit
Inventories:		
Materials	17,500	30,000
Work in Process	27,500	7,500
Materials Purchases (net)	187,500	
Transportation-In	25,000	
Direct Labor	125,000	
Indirect Labor	50,000	
Supervisors' Salaries	25,000	
Factory Utilities	20,000	
Factory Supplies Used	15,000	
Depreciation Expense—Factory Building . .	40,000	
Depreciation Expense—Equipment	30,000	
Other Manufacturing Overhead	75,000	
	637,500	37,500
Manufacturing Summary		
(Cost of goods manufactured)		600,000
	637,500	637,500

Required:

a. Using this information, prepare a statement of cost of goods manufactured for Coleman Manufacturing Company for the year ended December 31, 1987.

b. Prepare all necessary closing entries, including the entry to set up the new balances in the inventory accounts and the entry to close the Manufacturing Summary account.

P21-2-B

Prepare statement of cost of goods manufactured and income statement

The following account balances were taken from the December 31, 1987, work sheet for the Hollis Company:

Account Titles	Manufacturing Statement		Income Statement	
	Debit	Credit	Debit	Credit
Sales				450,000
Materials Purchases	120,000			
Transportation-In	1,000			
Inventories:				
Materials	10,000	9,500		
Work in Process	21,000	20,000		
Finished Goods			14,000	10,000
Direct Labor	95,000			
Utilities Expense	1,250			
Maintenance and Repairs	4,250			
Selling Expenses			50,000	
Administrative Expenses			46,250	
Income Tax Expense			25,000	
Insurance Expense—Factory	3,000			
Depreciation Expense—Factory Building	5,000			
Depreciation Expense—Factory Equipment	11,500			
	272,000	29,500		
Manufacturing Summary (Cost of goods manufactured)		242,500	242,500	
	272,000	272,000	377,750	460,000
Net income			82,250	
			460,000	460,000

Required:

a. Prepare a statement of cost of goods manufactured for the Hollis Company for the year ended December 31, 1987.

b. Prepare an income statement for the Hollis Company for the year ended December 31, 1987.

P21-3-B

Prepare closing entries

Refer to the information given in Problem P21-2-B. Give all necessary entries to set up the ending inventory balances and to close the books of the Hollis Company on December 31, 1987.

P21-4-B

Prepare statement of cost of goods manufactured, income statement, and closing entries

The following account balances were taken in alphabetical order from the completed work sheet of Gerald Manufacturing, Inc. at December 31, 1987:

Administrative Salaries Expense*	$30,000	Inventories, December 31:	
Advertising and Promotion Expense	36,000	Materials	$ 18,000
		Work in Process	24,000
Depreciation Expense—Factory Equipment	21,000	Finished Goods	39,000
		Materials Purchases	90,000
Depreciation Expense—Office Equipment*	15,000	Materials Purchase Returns	3,000
		Rent—Factory	12,000
Depreciation Expense—Sales Fixtures	12,000	Rent—Selling and Administrative*	45,000
Direct Labor	195,000	Repairs and Maintenance— Factory	9,000
Factory Supervision and Inspection	18,000	Sales	660,000
Factory Supplies Used	18,000	Sales Salaries	30,000
Indirect Labor	15,000	Transportation-In	12,000
		Other Factory Overhead	27,000
Inventories, January 1:		Other Selling Expenses	15,000
Materials	6,000		
Work in Process	9,000		
Finished Goods	54,000		

* These amounts are to be allocated 40% to general (nonfactory) administration and 60% to the sales department.

Required: a.   Prepare a statement of cost of goods manufactured for Gerald Manufacturing, Inc. for 1987.
b.   Prepare an income statement for the year ended December 31, 1987 (ignore taxes).
c.   Prepare all necessary closing entries.

P21-5-B

Prepare work sheet, all financial statements, and closing entries

The following trial balance and supplementary information pertain to the Allgood Manufacturing Company for the year ended June 30, 1987:

	Debits	Credits
Cash	$ 17,250	
Accounts Receivable	81,900	
Allowance for Doubtful Accounts		$ 300
Factory Supplies on Hand	17,550	
Office Supplies on Hand	1,275	
Materials Inventory	28,500	
Work in Process Inventory	6,300	
Finished Goods Inventory	18,000	
Prepaid Insurance—Factory	10,125	
Factory Machinery	67,500	
Accumulated Depreciation—Machinery . .		27,000
Factory Building	525,000	
Accumulated Depreciation—Building . .		31,500
Office Equipment	22,500	
Accumulated Depreciation—Office		
Equipment		6,750
Accounts Payable		60,800
Mortgage Note Payable (10%)		75,000
Common Stock ($10 par value)		435,000
Retained Earnings		18,600
Sales		745,900
Materials Purchases (net)	112,500	
Direct Labor	124,500	
Factory Supervision	21,300	
Indirect Labor	15,450	
Utilities—Factory	34,650	
Machine Maintenance	7,125	
Rent on Factory Equipment	3,000	
Property Taxes—Factory	4,200	
General Factory Costs	12,600	
Sales Office Salaries	60,750	
Selling Expenses	58,800	
Officers Salaries	75,000	
Administrative Expenses	40,500	
Interest Expense	3,750	
Income Taxes	30,825	
	$1,400,850	$1,400,850

Supplementary information:

Inventories, June 30, 1987:
    Materials $15,000
    Work in process   12,000
    Finished goods   22,500

Information needed for adjustments:

1.   Estimated bad debts expense for the year: 1% of sales.
2.   Factory insurance expired   . . . . $ 8,325
3.   Factory supplies used   16,762
4.   Office supplies used   863

Depreciation rates per year are:

5. Factory building 2%
6. Factory machinery 20%
7. Office equipment 15%
8. Accrued factory payroll at June 30, 1987:
    Direct labor . . . . $ 2,925
    Factory supervision 900
    Indirect labor 450
    _____
    $ 4,275
    ═══════
9. Accrued salaries at June 30, 1987:
    Officers' salaries . . . . $ 1,950
    Sales office salaries 1,275
    _____
    $ 3,225
    ═══════

Required: Prepare the following for the year ended June 30, 1987:

a. Work sheet.
b. Statement of cost of goods manufactured.
c. Income statement.
d. Balance sheet.
e. Entries to set up the ending inventories and to close the accounts.

P21-6-B

Calculate manufacturing overhead rate and ending inventory amounts under periodic inventory procedure

The following information was taken from the December 31, 1987, statement of cost of goods manufactured of the Dean Corporation:

Direct materials used (100,000 units) . . $150,000
Direct labor (100,000 hours) 450,000
Manufacturing overhead 396,000

All materials are issued to production at the beginning of the manufacturing process. Factory supervisors estimate that products still in production have received 1½ hours of direct labor per unit, while finished products have received 2 hours of direct labor per unit.

Required:

a. Compute the overhead rate for 1987 as a percentage of direct labor costs.
b. Estimate the per unit and total cost of the work in process and finished goods inventories. The year-end physical count showed 10,000 units still in production and 5,000 units in the finished goods storeroom.

P21-7-B

Prepare cost and revenue flowchart

The Gary Company uses perpetual inventory procedure. The operations for the quarter ended March 31, 1986, are summarized as follows:

1. Materials purchased on account . . . . $ 67,500
2. Direct materials issued to production 82,500
3. Indirect materials used (from materials inventory) 2,250
4. Gross payroll costs incurred 102,000
5. Payroll costs distributed:
    Direct labor 75,000
    Indirect labor 27,000
6. Other overhead costs incurred:
    Depreciation of equipment 72,000
    Repairs and maintenance 11,250
    Utilities 18,750
    Other 9,750
7. Selling expenses 52,500
8. Administrative expenses 60,000
9. Overhead costs actually incurred are assigned to production
    (determine from above data).
10. Cost of goods completed and transferred to finished goods inventory . . 300,000
11. Cost of goods sold 270,000
12. Sales on account 405,000

Inventory balances on January 1 were as follows:

Materials $23,250
Work in process 28,500
Finished goods 67,500

Required: Using T-accounts, prepare a cost and revenue flowchart similar to Illustration 21.13. Key your entries using the numbers given.

P21–8–B

Prepare journal entries under perpetual inventory procedure

Assume each of the companies in this problem uses perpetual inventory procedure.

a. In June, Company L purchased on account $225,000 of direct materials and $60,000 of supplies. Also in June, $150,000 of direct materials and $30,000 of indirect materials (supplies) were issued by the storeroom to the production department.

Required: Prepare the necessary journal entries.

b. Company M's payroll department records indicate that the week's payroll amounted to $75,000 (gross pay) with the following amounts withheld:

FICA taxes	$ 2,700
Union dues	1,125
Federal income taxes	13,500

Further analysis reveals that of the $75,000, $52,500 was for direct labor. The indirect labor consists of the following wages and salaries:

Inspectors	$5,250
Supervisors	6,750
Janitors	1,500
Timekeepers	3,000
Toolroom personnel	4,500
Storeroom personnel	1,500

Required: Record the incurrence of the above labor costs and their distribution to the proper accounts.

c. In August, Company N incurred the following factory related costs: prepaid insurance expired, $1,500; depreciation of factory building, $3,750; prepaid rent expired, $2,250; payroll taxes, $5,700; utilities, $1,350; repairs, $675 (cash). The company assigns actual overhead costs to production at the end of each month.

Required: Prepare journal entries to record and assign overhead costs.

d. In September, Company O completed the production of goods costing $285,000 and transferred them to the finished goods storeroom. Also in September, Company O sold goods costing $262,500 to customers for $380,625, on account.

Required: Prepare journal entries to record these transactions.

P21–9–B

Prepare journal entries under perpetual inventory procedure; compute inventory balances; prepare income statement and closing entries

The following data relate to the Howell Company for the month of October 1987. The company uses perpetual inventory procedure.

1. Purchased materials on account, $105,000.
2. Materials issued to production, $120,000 (including $3,000 of indirect materials).
3. Factory payroll (gross) for the month, $138,000. Withholdings were $8,250 for FICA taxes and $24,000 for federal income taxes.
4. Payroll costs distributed: direct labor, $120,000; indirect labor, $18,000.
5. Other overhead costs incurred: factory depreciation, $105,000; property taxes, $24,000; repairs, $15,000; utilities, $12,000; and other, $9,000.
6. Selling expenses incurred, $90,000; administrative expenses incurred, $82,500.
7. Actual overhead costs were assigned to production.
8. Costs of goods completed and transferred, $390,000.
9. Sales on account, $600,000; cost of goods sold, $375,000.
10. Interest expense incurred, $450; federal income taxes payable, $26,250.

October 1 inventory balances were:

Materials	$27,000
Work in process	33,000
Finished goods	63,000

Required: a. Prepare journal entries to record the above transactions.
                   b. Using T-accounts, compute the balance in each of the inventory accounts at the end of October.
                   c. Prepare an income statement for the Howell Company for the month of October, 1987.
                   d. Prepare the closing entries for October 31, 1987.

BUSINESS DECISION PROBLEM

Classify costs by behavior and type of production cost

A number of costs that would affect business decisions in manufacturing companies are listed below. These costs may be fixed or variable with respect to some measure of volume or output and may be classified as direct materials (DM), direct labor (DL), or manufacturing overhead (MO).

1. Glue used to attach labels to bottles containing a patented medicine.
2. Compressed air used in operating machines turning out products.
3. Insurance on factory building and equipment.
4. A production department supervisor's salary.
5. Rent on factory machinery.
6. Iron ore in a steel mill.
7. Oil, gasoline, and grease for forklift trucks.
8. Services of painters in building construction.
9. Cutting oils used in machining operations.
10. Cost of food in a factory employees' cafeteria.
11. Payroll taxes and fringe benefits related to direct labor.
12. The plant electricians' salaries.
13. Sand in a glass manufacturer.
14. Copy editor's salary in a book publisher.

Required: a. List the numbers 1 through 14 down the left side of a sheet of paper. After each number write the letters V (for variable) or F (for fixed) and either DM (for direct materials), DL (for direct labor), or MO (for manufacturing overhead) to show how you would classify the similarly numbered cost item given above.
                   b. Which of your own answers given for part *(a)* could you challenge? Discuss.

BUSINESS SITUATION FOR DISCUSSION

Why We Should Account for the 4th Cost of Manufacturing*

Henry R. Schwarzbach and Richard G. Vangermeersch

Cost accounting may be 200 years behind the times. It continues to stress the same three types of product costs—raw materials, direct labor, and overhead, but ignores "machine labor."

Recent cost accounting texts note the growing mechanization of production but do not propose adding this fourth cost component, machine labor. The major reason for this neglect is that cost accounting practice has not been updated to reflect current manufacturing technol-

ogy. Texts tend to follow practice. For example, one major text states "in practice, however, machine time is rarely used (for allocating overhead) because of the added clerical cost and the difficulty of computing machine time on individual jobs." . . . Low-cost micro processers, digital clocks, and counters, however, now make it much less costly and difficult to track machine time.

We suggest here a revised approach to this old problem. The revised approach with the fourth class of product costs provides management with an improved picture of product costs and cost flows. Our concept is similar to the ideas espoused by accountant/engineer A. Hamilton Church in the early 1900s; however, data collection techniques of the early 1900s made this system costly to maintain. . . .

    * Reprinted from the July 1984 issue of *Management Accounting*, (pp. 24–25). Copyright by the National Association of Accountants.

Accounting for the Cost of Key Machines

The first step in developing a cost system for the machine-intensive firm is to design cost and information collection systems for certain key machines and types of overhead. An analysis of a firm's production process may show that the costs of many machines will be best monitored and allocated as overhead items and not be managed as key machines. The first facet of the planning and control system for key machines is that of acquisition.

The acquisition of a key machine usually is a much more important decision than the hiring of a direct labor employee, even though personnel terminations have become a more difficult and serious matter in recent years. In contrast with the hiring decision for an employee, errors on the acquisition of a key machine are much more costly to the firm. For instance, the shop floor layout may have to be adjusted to accommodate the machine, employees may have to be laid off or retrained, and a large commitment of funds may have to follow the acquisition. Should the machine not operate up to standard however, termination is not an option.

A plan for placing the machine in operation (installation, personnel to operate, maintenance schedule, back up, and so on) is a necessity and should be fully developed before the acquisition transaction is completed. Management's job does not end after a machine is placed in operation. It must still be managed so that it operates efficiently and effectively from both a technical and cost perspective. We suggest that machine cost cards be developed for each key machine to aid in evaluating its cost effectiveness and in charging its cost to the products it helps produce.

Job Order and Process Cost Systems

After studying this chapter, you should be able to:

1. Describe and distinguish between the two major types of cost accumulation systems employed by manufacturing companies under perpetual inventory procedure.

2. Describe the documents used to accumulate product costs in a job order system and a process cost system.

3. Show how a predetermined overhead rate is computed and how it is used to assign overhead to production.

4. Discuss the determination of unit costs in a process cost system.

5. Prepare a production cost report for a process cost system and discuss its relationship to the Work in Process Inventory account.

6. Define and use correctly the new terms in the glossary.

This chapter continues the discussion of perpetual inventory procedure begun in Chapter 21. Perpetual inventory procedure is used when a manufacturing company wants to determine the costs of its product units **before** taking a physical inventory at year-end.

A product unit cost figure depends on many factors, such as which inventory costing method (Fifo, Lifo, or weighted-average) is chosen and how indirect costs (manufacturing overhead) are allocated to products. For some decisions, information about future costs is more relevant than product unit cost information based on past costs. The determination of product unit cost is always dependent on the type of cost accumulation system used by a company.

This chapter discusses the two major types of cost accumulation systems under perpetual procedure, the job order cost system and the process cost system. In each system, the goal is to **determine before year-end the unit costs of the products being manufactured.** These unit costs provide important data for management; they are used throughout the period to compute (1) cost of goods sold, (2) cost of work in process and finished goods ending inventories, (3) payments to be received under contracts based on "full" costs,[1] and (4) selling prices.

■ JOB ORDER COST SYSTEMS

A job order cost system is a cost accounting system in which the costs incurred to produce a product are accumulated for each individual job. For example, a job may consist of 1,000 chairs, 5 miles of highway, a single machine, a dam, or a building. A job cost system is generally used when the products being manufactured can be separately identified or when goods are produced to meet a customer's particular needs. Job costing is commonly used in construction, motion pictures, printing, and other industries where many heterogeneous (dissimilar) products are produced.

Under job order costing, an up-to-date record of the costs incurred on a job is kept in order to provide management with timely cost data. Reports to management can be revised as often as desired, even daily, on such matters as materials used, labor costs incurred, manufacturing overhead assigned, goods completed, total production costs incurred, and budgeted and actual cost comparisons.

Up-to-date information for each job is made available by maintaining a job order cost sheet for each job. A job order cost sheet is a form used to summarize the costs of direct materials, direct labor, and manufacturing overhead incurred for a job. It is the **key document** in the system. The file of job order cost sheets for jobs not yet completed represents the subsidiary ledger for the Work in Process Inventory account.

Illustration 22.1 depicts the cost flows in a job order cost system.

Illustration 22.1   *Cost Flows in a Job Order Cost System*

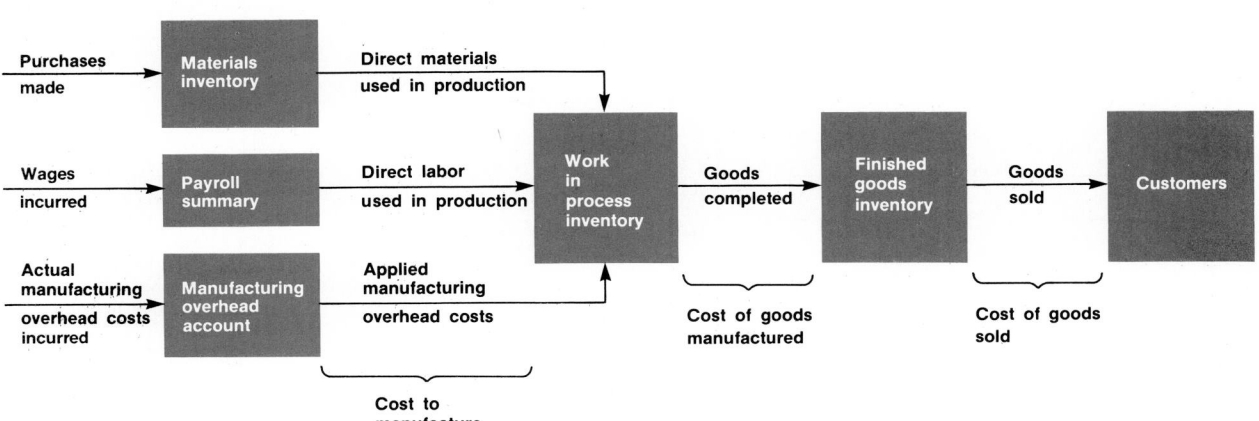

---

[1] A "full" cost contract basically guarantees the manufacturer total recovery of the costs incurred in producing the product and, usually, a specified profit margin.

Basic Records Used in Job Order Systems

Illustration 22.2 shows the basic records or source documents used in a job order cost system:

1. The job order cost sheet summarizes all costs—direct materials, direct labor, and applied manufacturing overhead—of producing a given job or batch of products. One sheet is maintained for each job order. When goods are completed and transferred, the job order cost sheets are transferred to a completed jobs file. The number of units and their unit costs are recorded on inventory cards supporting the Finished Goods Inventory account. An example of a job order cost sheet is shown in Illustration 22.2.

2. A stores (or materials) card is kept for each type of direct and indirect material maintained in inventory. The stores card shows the quantities (and costs) of each type of material received, issued, and on hand for which the storekeeper is responsible. When a job is started, direct materials are ordered from the storeroom on a materials requisition, which shows the types and quantities of the materials ordered.

3. The work ticket shows who worked on what job for how many hours and at what wage rate. All of each employee's daily hours must be accounted for on one or more work tickets.

Illustration 22.2   *Basic Records in a Job Order Cost System*

STORES CARD		
Material A		
Received	Issued	Balance
PI	MR	

JOB ORDER COST SHEET			
Job no. _____			
Date	Direct material	Direct labor	Manufacturing overhead
	MR	WT	Applied by overhead rate

Summary:
Direct material   xx
Direct labor   xx
Overhead   xx
Total   xxx

FINISHED GOODS CARD		
Product DG		
Received	Issued	Balance
JOCS	ST	

WORK TICKET
Employee no. _____ Date _____ Job no. _____
Operation _____ Dept .no. _____
Stop _____ Rate _____
Start _____ Amount _____
WT

cost

PI   = Purchase invoice
MR   = Materials requisition
WT   = Work ticket
JOCS = Job cost sheet
ST   = Sales ticket
V   = Voucher
GJ   = General journal

MANUFACTURING OVERHEAD COST SHEET						
Depreciation	Indirect labor	Indirect materials	Power	Payroll taxes	Insurance	Other
GJ	WT	MR	V	V	V	V

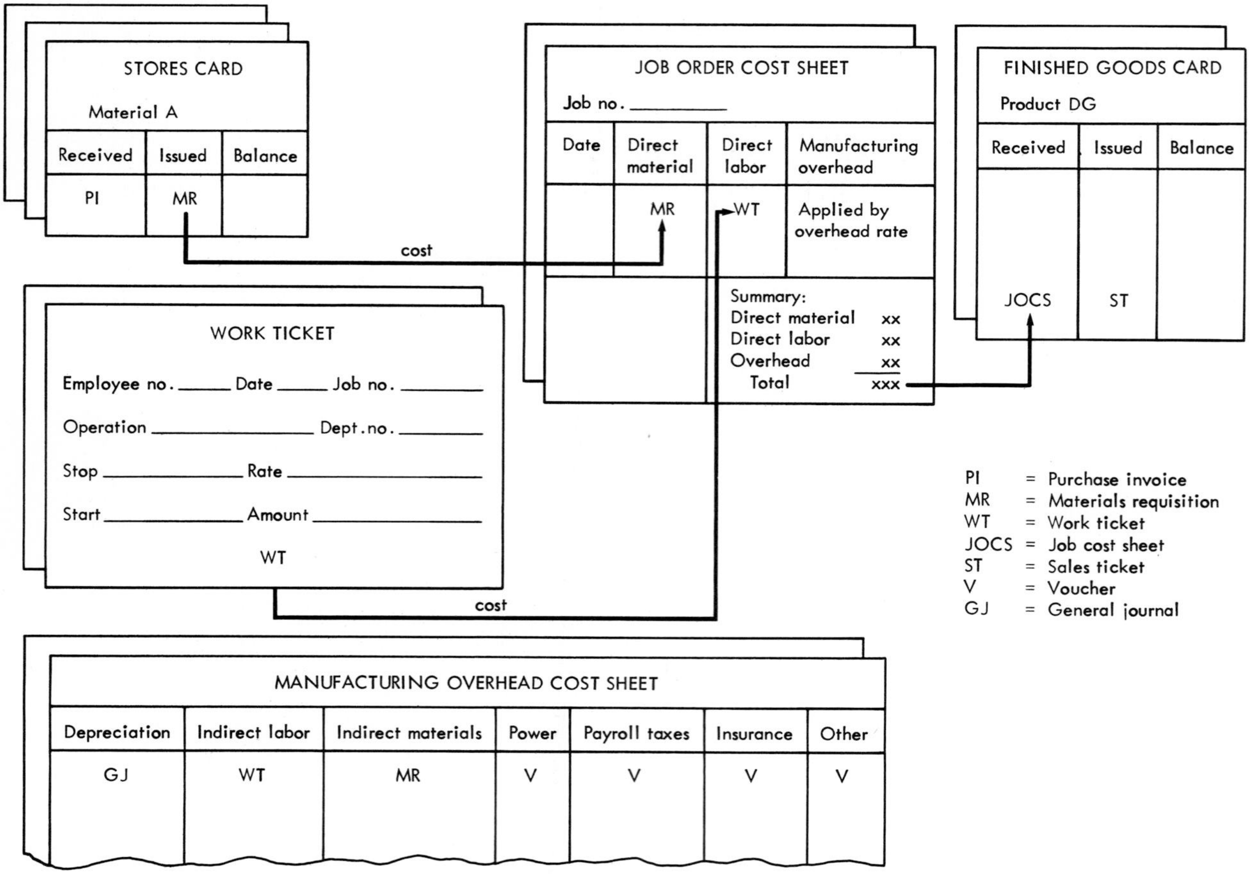

4. The manufacturing overhead cost sheet summarizes the various factory indirect costs incurred. One sheet is maintained for each production center.

5. A **finished goods card** is a running record of units and costs of products completed, sold, and on hand. A card is maintained for each type of product manufactured and sold.

The flow of manufacturing costs through the accounting system of a company using a job order cost system is shown in Illustration 22.3. To gain a full understanding of a job order cost system, this illustration should be studied carefully and related to the documents shown in Illustration 22.2 and to the journal entries in the following example.

Illustration 22.3   *Cost Flows in a Job Order Cost System*

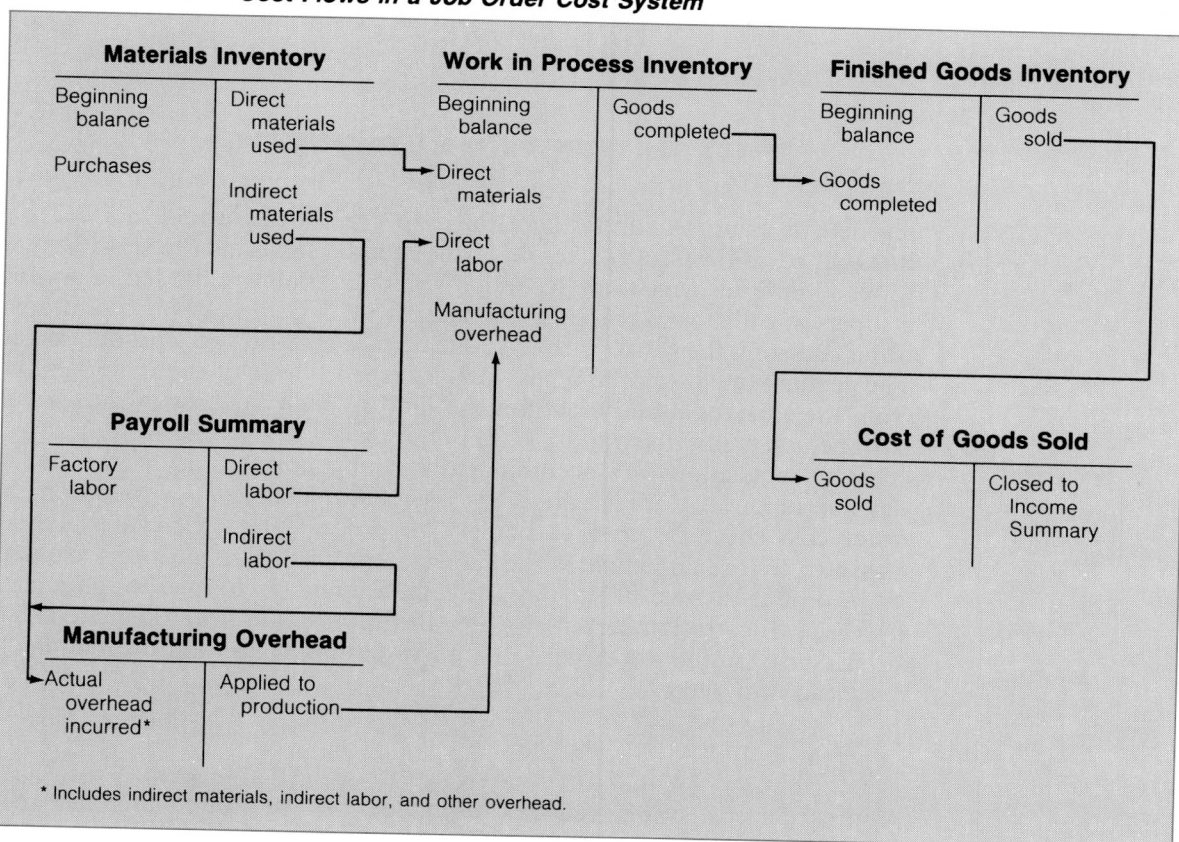

The following section will explain the specific procedure followed in accounting for materials, labor, and manufacturing overhead costs in a job order cost system.

Accounting for Materials

As materials are received from vendors, they are placed in the materials storeroom. A **stores (or materials) card** is a perpetual inventory record that shows the quantities and costs of each type of material received, issued to a job,

Illustration 22.4

Materials Requisition

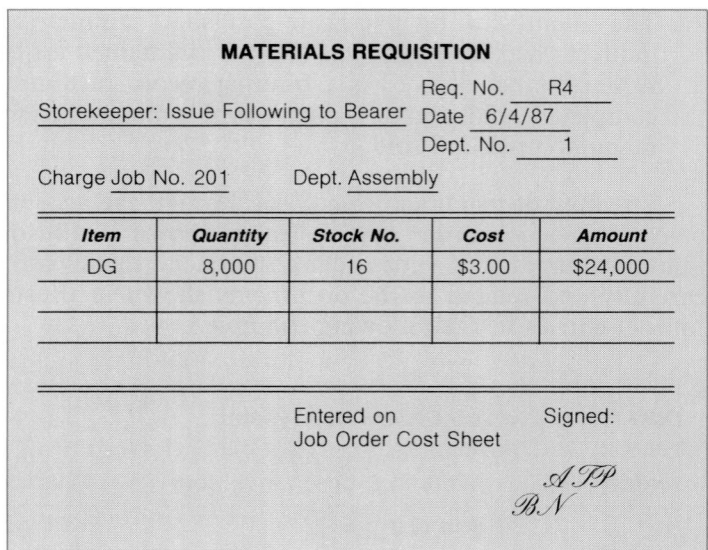

MATERIALS REQUISITION

Storekeeper: Issue Following to Bearer

Req. No.   R4
Date   6/4/87
Dept. No.   1

Charge Job No. 201   Dept. Assembly

Item	Quantity	Stock No.	Cost	Amount
DG	8,000	16	$3.00	$24,000

Entered on   Signed:
Job Order Cost Sheet

A FP
B N

and left on hand. A card is kept for each type of direct and indirect material maintained in inventory. The file of these cards serves as the subsidiary ledger for the Materials Inventory account. When materials are needed in production, a supervisor fills out a materials requisition. A **materials requisition** is a written order directing the store's clerk to issue certain materials to a production center. The requisition shows the types, quantities, and costs of the materials ordered from the storeroom and identifies the job to which the cost of those materials is to be assigned (Illustration 22.4).

The requisitions are accumulated by job number, and at the end of the day the amount of direct materials issued for each job is entered on the job order cost sheet for that particular job order. When the material issued is classified by the company as indirect material, those requisitions are accumulated, and at the end of the day the total amount is charged to manufacturing overhead. Illustration 22.2 shows how the information from the materials requisition is used in the store's card, the job order cost sheet, and the manufacturing overhead cost sheet.

Accounting for Labor

A job order cost system requires that labor costs be accumulated and recorded for each job. As each employee works on a particular job assignment, that employee fills out a **work (labor time) ticket,** which is a form used to record labor costs. Information recorded on the work ticket includes employee number, job number, number of hours worked, and any other important information. At the end of the day work tickets for each job are accumulated, and the total direct labor costs for each job are entered on the job order. A work ticket is shown in Illustration 22.2.

Work tickets are also used to accumulate and record indirect labor costs. When an employee is assigned work that is not directly related to any job (such as general maintenance work), this work is also recorded on a work ticket. Work not directly related to any job is indirect labor and is accounted for as part of manufacturing overhead. At the end of the day these tickets are accumulated, and the total indirect labor cost is recorded on the manufacturing overhead cost sheet.

The use of work tickets not only permits the accumulation and recording of direct labor costs for each job and indirect labor costs each day; it also provides control over the labor cost for each employee. Since each employee fills out a work ticket for each task performed, all of that employee's hours should be accounted for on one or more work tickets.

Accounting for Manufacturing Overhead

In order to exert some control over manufacturing overhead costs incurred, each production center or department must summarize its factory indirect costs. A **manufacturing overhead cost sheet** is the record used to summarize the various manufacturing overhead costs incurred. The file of manufacturing overhead cost sheets serves as the subsidiary ledger for the Manufacturing Overhead account. An example of a manufacturing overhead cost sheet was shown in Illustration 22.2.

Predetermined Overhead Rates.   In most manufacturing operations, unit costs are computed at the time a job is completed. The costs of direct materials and direct labor have already been entered on the job order cost sheet as a result of posting information from materials requisitions and work tickets. Each job must then be assigned its share of the manufacturing overhead costs.

In the last chapter, the manufacturing overhead rate was computed using actual overhead costs for the period. But most manufacturing companies prefer the use of a **predetermined** overhead rate rather than waiting to accumulate all overhead costs during a period and developing an actual manufacturing overhead rate. A **predetermined overhead rate** is calculated by dividing **estimated** total overhead costs for a period by an **expected level** of activity, such as total estimated direct labor-hours or direct labor cost for the period. Predetermined overhead rates are set at the **beginning** of the year in which they will be used.

Reasons for Using Predetermined Rates.   In addition to the need for current information on unit costs, other reasons for using a predetermined overhead rate in manufacturing operations include:

1. Overhead costs are seldom incurred uniformly throughout the year. For example, heating costs are larger during winter. No useful purpose is served by allocating less cost to a unit produced in the summer than to one produced in the winter. Use of a predetermined rate results in applying overhead based on direct labor cost, hours incurred, or some other measure of activity rather than on actual overhead incurred in a particular month.
2. Some overhead costs, like factory building depreciation, are fixed costs. Thus, if the volume of goods produced varies from month to month, there will be sharp fluctuations in average unit cost unless a predetermined rate is used.
3. Total unit costs of production are known sooner. Using a predetermined rate, overhead costs can be assigned to production when direct materials and direct labor costs are assigned. Without use of a predetermined rate,

unit costs would not be known until the end of the month or even later if bills for costs had not arrived by then. For example, the electric bill for the month of July will probably not arrive until August. If actual overhead were used to compute unit cost, products purchased in July could not be costed until August.

Computing Predetermined Overhead Rates.   Predetermined overhead rates are computed in the same basic manner as actual rates except that **estimated** rather than **actual** levels of activity and cost are used. As part of the budgeting process (discussed in Chapter 25), management estimates the level of manufacturing activity for the next year. This activity level is expressed in terms of some specified base, such as direct labor-hours or machine-hours. Next, expected overhead costs for the year are estimated, based on the expected level of activity. The overhead rate can then be calculated using the following formula:

$$\frac{\text{Estimated manufacturing overhead costs}}{\text{Expected level of activity (such as direct labor-hours)}} = \frac{\text{Predetermined}}{\text{overhead rate}}$$

This process of estimating the expected level of activity and the expected overhead costs and then calculating the predetermined overhead rate may be done for the company as a whole (if the company desires a single, company-wide overhead rate), or it may be done separately for each production center (department) within the company.[2] To illustrate the calculation of a predetermined overhead rate for a single production center, assume that the expected level of activity in a certain production center is 60,000 direct labor-hours. Assume also that, at that level of activity, the estimated overhead costs are $540,000.

The predetermined overhead rate would be:

$$\frac{\$540,000}{60,000 \text{ hours}} = \$9 \text{ per direct labor-hour}$$

Since Work in Process Inventory must contain amounts for direct materials, direct labor, and manufacturing overhead, the predetermined overhead rate is used to apply overhead to Work in Process Inventory. Actual amounts for direct materials and direct labor will already be posted to the Work in Process Inventory account from the materials requisitions and the work tickets. In the above situation, overhead would be applied to Work in Process Inventory at the rate of $9 of overhead for each **actual** direct labor-hour worked on a job. If 2,000 direct labor-hours have been worked, the journal entry to apply overhead is:

Work in Process Inventory	18,000	
Manufacturing Overhead		18,000
To apply overhead to Work in Process Inventory using a predetermined overhead rate of $9 per direct labor-hour.		

Note that the credit in the above entry is to the Manufacturing Overhead account. Actual manufacturing overhead is accumulated in the Manufacturing

---

[2] Sometimes separate rates are computed for variable overhead and fixed overhead. Later chapters illustrate how these separate rates may be useful.

Overhead account on the debit side. When overhead is applied to Work in Process Inventory, the Manufacturing Overhead account is credited. If the estimates used for overhead costs and expected level of activity are **exactly** the same as the actual amounts incurred for overhead and direct labor-hours worked, the Manufacturing Overhead account will have a zero balance at the end of the period.

Underapplied or Overapplied Overhead. Because it is highly unlikely that the estimates used in computing the predetermined overhead rate will be exactly equal to the actual overhead cost or direct labor-hours worked, the Manufacturing Overhead account will normally have a debit or credit balance at the end of the period. A **debit** balance will remain if actual overhead exceeds the applied overhead for the period; in this case we say that the overhead is underapplied (underabsorbed). Underapplied overhead is the amount by which actual overhead costs incurred in a period exceed the overhead applied to production in that period. In contrast, a **credit** balance will remain if applied overhead exceeds actual overhead; in this case we say that overhead is overapplied or overabsorbed. Overapplied overhead is the amount by which the overhead applied to production exceeds the actual overhead costs incurred in that same period. Remember that overhead is applied to Work in Process Inventory (production) using the **predetermined** overhead rate times the **actual** level of activity (such as direct labor-hours) incurred during the period.

To illustrate the use of a predetermined overhead rate during a period, consider the following facts:

Estimated manufacturing overhead for year	$48,000
Estimated level of activity for year	80,000 direct labor-hours
Predetermined overhead rate ($48,000 ÷ 80,000 hours)	$0.60 per direct labor-hour
Actual overhead costs incurred during year	$45,000
Actual direct labor-hours worked	70,000 hours

The following journal entries are necessary to record the above information:

Manufacturing Overhead	45,000	
Various Accounts		45,000
To record actual manufacturing overhead costs incurred during period, machinery repair, indirect materials, etc.		

Work in Process Inventory	42,000	
Manufacturing Overhead		42,000
To apply manufacturing overhead to Work in Process Inventory at predetermined rate of $0.60 per direct labor-hour for 70,000 hours worked.		

It is essential to point out that in reality these entries are not made at a single point in time for these total amounts. The accountant will record actual manufacturing overhead (the first entry above) continuously during the period as indirect materials are issued to production, as work tickets are accumulated for indirect labor, and as other circumstances require entries (machinery repair, utility bills, etc.). The second entry above, to record applied manufacturing overhead, will be recorded each time a job is completed (in order to properly compute the total cost of the job) or at the end of each period (so that financial statements containing proper balances can be prepared).

Based on these two entries, the Manufacturing Overhead account will appear as follows:

Manufacturing Overhead

Actual costs	45,000	Applied to production	42,000
Balance	3,000		

The $3,000 debit balance is the amount of **underapplied** overhead during the period.

Reasons for Underapplied or Overapplied Manufacturing Overhead. Two different factors determine whether overhead will be underapplied or overapplied for the period. The first factor has to do with the difference between the amount of indirect manufacturing cost actually incurred and the amount management estimated for the period. The second factor relates to the difference between the estimated level of manufacturing activity (expected activity) used to set the predetermined overhead rate and the actual level of activity on which overhead is applied.

A difference between actual and estimated overhead costs can arise because unanticipated events cause overhead costs to be more or less than the budgeted amount. High heating bills caused by a severe winter, excess repairs to factory machinery, and increases in prices of supplies are all examples of events that cause actual overhead costs to exceed expected costs and tend to result in underapplied overhead. Unanticipated cost savings, on the other hand, tend to cause overapplied overhead.

Unanticipated events can also cause the estimated and actual levels of activity to differ. For example, a company could find itself without essential raw materials and have to cut back production, or, alternatively, a company could produce a product that becomes a "fad" and have to increase production in order to meet demand. Recall that in every manufacturing business some overhead costs are fixed costs that do not change with the level of manufacturing activity. As a result, **total actual** overhead costs do not vary in direct proportion to the actual level of activity. However, applied overhead costs do vary in direct proportion to the actual level of activity because applied overhead is being applied to Work in Process Inventory at a constant amount per actual unit of activity (such as direct labor-hours). Therefore, if actual operations are at a higher level of activity than that used to set the predetermined overhead rate, more overhead will be applied to Work in Process Inventory than originally anticipated and will tend to cause overapplied overhead. Operating at a lower level than originally estimated will tend to cause underapplied overhead.

Disposition of Underapplied or Overapplied Manufacturing Overhead. An underapplied or overapplied manufacturing overhead balance can be carried forward in monthly or quarterly (interim) financial statements if the probability exists that it will be reduced or offset by operations for the remainder of the year. If a balance in overhead remains at year-end, it can be allocated (or disposed of) to Work in Process Inventory, Finished Goods Inventory, and Cost of Goods Sold. This disposition is done by recomputing the cost of production for the year using actual overhead rates and adjusting the three account balances to their appropriate actual amounts. As an alternative, underapplied overhead can be charged off as a loss of the period, particularly if it resulted from idle production capacity or from unusual circumstances.

As a practical matter, however, **underapplied or overapplied overhead is usually transferred to Cost of Goods Sold.** Little distortion of net income or of assets results from this treatment if the amount transferred is small or if most of the goods produced during the year were sold. Thus, if the $3,000 of underapplied overhead in the previous example is a year-end balance, the journal entry to dispose of it will read:

```
Cost of Goods Sold  . . . . . . . . . . . . . . . . . . . . . .   3,000
     Manufacturing Overhead   . . . . . . . . . . . . . . . . .            3,000
     To dispose of underapplied overhead.
```

Job Order Costing—an Example

To illustrate a job order costing system in use, the following example includes nine transactions of the Casting Company for the month of July. On July 1, the Casting Company had beginning inventories as follows:

```
Materials inventory (material A, $10,000; material B, $6,000;
   various indirect materials, $4,000)  . . . . . . . . . . . .   $20,000
Work in process inventory (Job No. 106: direct materials, $4,200;
   direct labor, $5,000; and overhead, $4,000)   . . . . . . . .    13,200
Finished goods inventory (500 units of product AB at a cost
   of $11 per unit)   . . . . . . . . . . . . . . . . . . . . .      5,500
```

Job No. 106, which was in process at the beginning of July, was completed in July. Of the two jobs started in July (Nos. 107 and 108), only Job No. 107 was completed by the end of July.

The transactions and the journal entries to record these transactions are given below. You may want to refer back to Illustration 22.3 to follow the cost flows in a job order cost system.

1. Purchased $10,000 of material A and $15,000 of material B on account.

```
Materials Inventory   . . . . . . . . . . . . . . . . . . . .   25,000
     Accounts Payable   . . . . . . . . . . . . . . . . . . .           25,000
     To record purchase of direct materials.
```

2. Issued direct materials: material A to Job No. 106, $1,000; to Job No. 107, $8,000; to Job No. 108, $2,000; material B to Job No. 106, $2,000; to Job No. 107, $6,000; to Job No. 108, $4,000. Indirect materials issued to all jobs, $1,000.

```
Work in Process Inventory . . . . . . . . . . . . . . . . . .   23,000
Manufacturing Overhead  . . . . . . . . . . . . . . . . . . .    1,000
     Materials Inventory . . . . . . . . . . . . . . . . . . .           24,000
     To record direct and indirect materials issued.
```

3. Factory payroll for the month, $25,000; FICA and income taxes withheld, $4,000.

```
Payroll Summary  . . . . . . . . . . . . . . . . . . . . . .   25,000
     Various liability accounts for taxes withheld   . . . . .            4,000
     Accrued Wages Payable  . . . . . . . . . . . . . . . . .           21,000
     To record factory payroll for July.
```

4. Factory payroll paid, $21,000.

Accrued Wages Payable	21,000	
Cash		21,000
To record cash paid to factory employees in July.		

5. Payroll costs distributed: direct labor, $20,000 (Job No. 106, $5,000; Job No. 107, $12,000; and Job No. 108, $3,000); and indirect labor, $5,000.

Work in Process Inventory	20,000	
Manufacturing Overhead	5,000	
Payroll Summary		25,000
To distribute factory labor costs incurred.		

6. Other indirect manufacturing costs incurred:

Payroll taxes accrued	$ 3,000
Repairs (on account)	1,000
Property taxes accrued	4,000
Heat, light, and power (on account)	2,000
Depreciation	5,000
	$15,000

Manufacturing Overhead	15,000	
Accounts Payable		3,000
Accrued Payroll Taxes Payable		3,000
Accrued Property Taxes Payable		4,000
Accumulated Depreciation		5,000
To record manufacturing overhead costs incurred.		

7. Manufacturing overhead applied to production (assume a predetermined rate of 80% of direct labor cost):

Job No. 106, Product DG (0.80 × $5,000)	$ 4,000
Job No. 107, Product XY (0.80 × $12,000)	9,600
Job No. 108, Product OR (0.80 × $3,000)	2,400
	$16,000

Work in Process Inventory	16,000	
Manufacturing Overhead		16,000
To record application of overhead to production.		

8. Jobs completed and transferred to finished goods storeroom (see Illustration 22.5 for details):

Job No. 106 (4,000 units of product DG @ $6.30)	$25,200
Job No. 107 (10,000 units of product XY @ $3.56)	35,600
	$60,800

Finished Goods Inventory	60,800	
Work in Process Inventory		60,800
To record completed production for July.		

9. Sales on account for the month: 500 units of product AB for $8,000, cost, $5,500; and 10,000 units of product XY for $62,000, cost, $35,600 (Job No. 107).

Accounts Receivable	70,000	
Sales		70,000
To record sales on account for July.		

Cost of Goods Sold	41,100	
Finished Goods Inventory		41,100
To record cost of goods sold in July.		

After the above entries have been posted, the Work in Process Inventory and Finished Goods Inventory accounts appear (in T-account form) as follows:

Work in Process Inventory

July 1 balance	13,200	Completed	60,800
Direct materials used	23,000		
Direct labor cost incurred	20,000		
Overhead applied	16,000		
July 31 balance	11,400		

Finished Goods Inventory

July 1 balance	5,500	Sold	41,100
Completed	60,800		
July 31 balance	25,200		

On July 31, the Work in Process Inventory account has a balance of $11,400, which agrees with the total costs charged thus far to Job No. 108, as shown in Illustration 22.5. The balance consists of direct materials, $6,000; direct labor, $3,000; and manufacturing overhead, $2,400. Finished Goods Inventory has a balance on July 31 of $25,200, supported by the finished goods inventory card for Job No. 106 (Illustration 22.5), which shows that the 4,000 units of product DG on hand have a total cost of $25,200.

Ledger account entries like the ones given above, are often made from summaries of cost, and thus are recorded only at the end of the month. If, on the other hand, management wants to be informed more frequently as to costs incurred, details of the various costs can be recorded more often, even daily.

The main advantage of using a predetermined overhead rate is shown in this example. Three jobs were worked on during the month. Job No. 106 was started last month and completed in July. Job No. 107 was started and completed in July. And Job No. 108 was started but not finished in July. Each required different amounts of direct materials and direct labor. Under these conditions, there is simply no timely way to apply overhead to products without the use of a predetermined rate based on some common level of activity. Note that the use of a predetermined overhead rate permits the computation of unit costs to be made for Job Nos. 106 and 107 at the time of their completion rather than waiting until the end of the month. But this advantage is secured only at the expense of keeping more detailed records of the costs incurred. As discussed below, the other major cost accumulation system—process cost—requires far less record keeping, but the computation of unit costs is more complex.

Illustration 22.5 *Supporting Inventory Cards and Job Order Cost Sheets*

STORES CARD
Material A

Received	Issued	Balance
$10,000		$10,000
		20,000
	$1,000	19,000
	8,000	11,000
	2,000	9,000

STORES CARD
Material B

Received	Issued	Balance
$15,000		$ 6,000
		21,000
	$2,000	19,000
	6,000	13,000
	4,000	9,000

JOB ORDER COST SHEET (Product DG)   Job No. 106

Date	Direct Materials	Direct Labor	Manufacturing Overhead
July 1	$ 4,200	$ 5,000	$4,000
July	A: 1,000	5,000	4,000
	B: 2,000	$10,000	$8,000
	$7,200		

Job completed (4,000 units of product DG @ $6.30). Total cost, $25,200.

JOB ORDER COST SHEET (Product XY)   Job No. 107

Date	Direct Materials	Direct Labor	Manufacturing Overhead
July	A: $ 8,000	$12,000	$9,600
	B: 6,000		
	$14,000		

Job completed (10,000 units of product XY @ $3.56). Total cost, $35,600.

JOB ORDER COST SHEET (Product OR)   Job No. 108

Date	Direct Materials	Direct Labor	Manufacturing Overhead
July	A: $ 2,000	$3,000	$2,400
	B: 4,000		

Job incomplete (1,000 units of product OR). Cost to date, $11,400.

FINISHED GOODS CARD
Product AB

Received	Issued	Balance
		$5,500
	$5,500	–0–

FINISHED GOODS CARD
Product DG

Received	Issued	Balance
$25,200		$25,200

FINISHED GOODS CARD
Product XY

Received	Issued	Balance
$35,600		$35,600
	$35,600	–0–

■ PROCESS COST SYSTEMS

Many businesses manufacture huge quantities of a single product or similar products (paint, paper, chemicals, gasoline, rubber, and plastics) on a continuous basis over long periods of time. For these kinds of products, there is no separate job order; rather, production is ongoing over the year or even several years. In these types of operations, costs must be accumulated for **each process** that a product undergoes on its way to completion. The processes or departments serve as "cost centers" where costs are accumulated for the entire period (usually a month). These costs are divided by the number of units produced (tons, pounds, gallons, or feet) to get an average unit cost. The cost system used in these circumstances is called a process cost system. A process cost system (process costing) is a manufacturing cost system in which costs incurred to produce a product are accumulated according to the processes or departments a product goes through on its way to completion.

Basic System Design

As shown in Illustration 22.6, process cost systems have the same cost flows as found in a job order system. Costs of the factors of production are first recorded in separate accounts for materials inventory, labor, and overhead. Costs are then transferred to Work in Process Inventory. A process cost system usually has more than one Work in Process Inventory account. An account is kept for each processing center in order to determine the unit cost of each process.

The system depicted in Illustration 22.6 is one in which products are processed in a specified **sequential** order; that is, the products are started and processed in Department A, transferred to Department B and processed further, and then transferred to Finished Goods Inventory. For the purposes of illustration in this chapter, we will assume that all the process cost systems are sequential.

Process Costing Illustration

Assume that Ajax Company sells a chemical product that is processed in two departments. In Department A, basic materials are crushed, powdered, and blended. In Department B, the product is packaged and transferred to finished goods. This manufacturing process is shown in Illustration 22.7. Production and cost data for Ajax Company for the month of June are as follows:

	Department A	Department B
Units started, completed, and transferred	11,000	9,000
Units on hand at June 30, partially completed	–0–	2,000
Beginning inventory	$ –0–	$ –0–
Direct materials	16,500	1,100
Direct labor	5,500	5,880
Actual manufacturing overhead	4,500	5,600
Applied manufacturing overhead	4,400	5,880

Illustration 22.6 *Cost Flows in a Process Cost System*

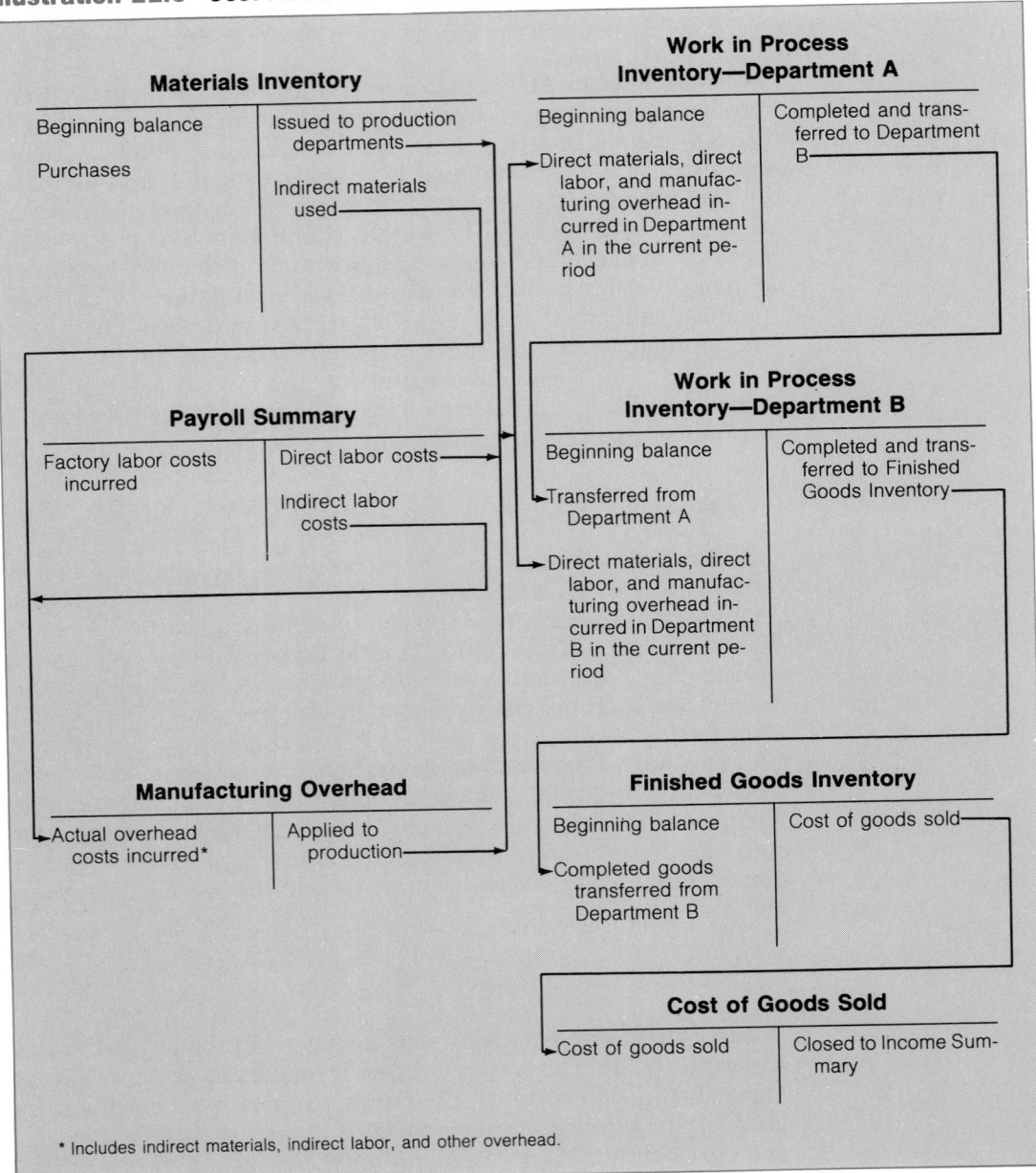

In Department A, manufacturing overhead is applied on the basis of a predetermined rate of 80% of direct labor cost. In Department B, manufacturing overhead is applied at the rate of 100% of direct labor cost.

From these data, the Work in Process Inventory—Department A account can be constructed and summarized as follows:

Work in Process Inventory—Department A

Direct materials	16,500	Transferred to Department B—	
Direct labor	5,500	11,000 units @ $2.40	26,400
Applied overhead (80% of direct labor cost)	4,400		
Total	26,400		

Since all units started in June in Department A were completed and transferred to Department B, it follows that all costs assigned to those goods should also be transferred. The unit cost in Department A is computed by dividing $26,400 of total costs by the 11,000 units completed and transferred to get an average unit cost of $2.40.

Computations are seldom this simple. One complication is faced whenever partially completed inventories are present, as is true for Department B. Department B's Work in Process Inventory account for June is as follows before the cost of completed units is transferred out:

Work in Process Inventory—Department B

Transferred in from Department A	26,400
Direct material	1,100
Direct labor	5,880
Overhead (100% of direct labor)	5,880
Total	39,260

Recall that direct materials, direct labor, and manufacturing overhead are product costs, that is, they "attach" to the product. Thus the "Transferred in from Department A" line in the T-accounts above represents the material, labor, and overhead costs assigned to products in Department A. These costs have "followed" the physical units to Department B.

The task now faced is to divide the $39,260 total costs charged to the department in June between the units transferred out and those remaining on hand in the department. The $39,260 cannot be divided by 11,000 to get an average unit cost because the 11,000 units are not alike; 9,000 are finished, and 2,000 are only partially finished. The problem is solved by using the concept of equivalent units of production.

Illustration 22.7

Product Flows in a Process Cost System (Ajax Company example)

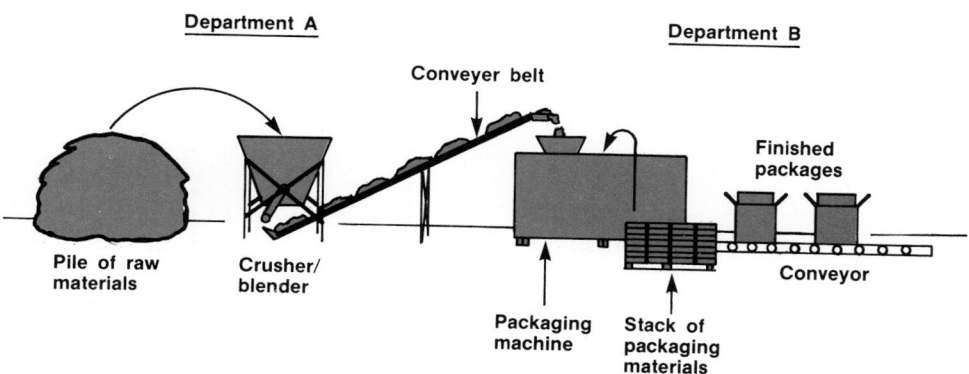

Equivalent Units. Essentially, the concept of equivalent units involves expressing a given number of partially completed units as a smaller number of fully completed units. For example, 1,000 units brought to a 40% state of completion are equivalent to 400 units that are 100% complete. This concept is based on the fact that approximately the same amount of costs must be incurred to bring 1,000 units to a 40% level of completion as would be required to complete 400 units.

The first step in computing equivalent units produced in Department B for the example above is to determine the stage of completion of the unfinished units. These units are 100% complete as to transferred-in costs or they would not have been transferred out of Department A. But the units may have different stages of completion as to materials, labor, and overhead costs added in Department B. Assume that all materials are added at the beginning of the production process in Department B. Thus, both ending inventory and units transferred out are 100% complete as to materials, and equivalent production for materials is 11,000 units. Units are usually assumed to be at the same stage of completion regarding labor and overhead. This assumption is made because overhead is often applied to work in process on a direct labor basis (recall that direct labor and overhead together are termed *conversion costs*). Next, assume that the 2,000 units in ending inventory are, on the average, 40% complete as to conversion. Equivalent production for labor and overhead is 9,800 units—9,000 units transferred out fully complete and 2,000 brought to a 40% completion state, which is the equivalent of 800 fully completed units.

Once the equivalent units of production are known, unit costs of processing in Department B can be computed as follows:

	Transferred in	Materials	Conversion	Total
Costs to be accounted for:				
Charged to Department B	$26,400	$ 1,100	$11,760*	$39,260
Equivalent units	11,000	11,000	9,800†	
Unit costs	$2.40	$0.10	$1.20	$3.70

* Conversion costs consist of direct labor + overhead ($5,880 + $5,880).
† Units transferred out (9,000) + equivalent units in ending inventory (800).

Using the computed unit costs, the $39,260 of costs charged to Department B in June is divided between costs associated with units completed and transferred out and costs of units remaining in the department's ending inventory:

	Transferred in (@ $2.40)	Materials (@ $0.10)	Conversion (@ $1.20)	Total
Costs accounted for:				
Units completed and transferred out (9,000 units)	$21,600	$ 900	$10,800	$33,300
Units remaining in ending inventory (2,000 units)	4,800	200	960*	5,960
Costs accounted for	$26,400	$1,100	$11,760	$39,260

* Equivalent units = 800 units.

The $33,300 total costs transferred out consists of $21,600 of Department A's cost (9,000 × $2.40), $900 of materials costs (9,000 × $0.10), and $10,800 of conversion costs (9,000 × $1.20) or $3.70 per unit. The 2,000 units of ending inventory in Department B are fully complete as to materials and 40% complete as to conversion. Ending inventory cost, then, consists of the following:

Costs from Department A (2,000 × $2.40) . . .		$4,800
Costs added by Department B:		
Materials (2,000 × $0.10)	$200	
Conversion (800 equivalent units × $1.20) . .	960	1,160
Total cost of ending inventory		$5,960

The units transferred out of Department B will be carried in finished goods inventory at a cost of $3.70 each until they are sold, at which time the costs will be charged to Cost of Goods Sold.

The June journal entries for the above activities follow:

(1)   Work in Process Inventory—Department A   16,500
      Work in Process Inventory—Department B   1,100
         Materials Inventory 17,600
      To record materials placed in production in June.

(2)   Payroll Summary 11,380
         Various withholding accounts and accrued wages
           payable 11,380
      To record factory payroll for June.

(3)   Work in Process Inventory—Department A   5,500
      Work in Process Inventory—Department B   5,880
         Payroll Summary 11,380
      To distribute factory labor costs (assuming that all such costs are chargeable directly to production departments).

(4)   Manufacturing Overhead 10,100
         Various accounts—cash, accounts payable, accruals,
           and accumulated depreciation 10,100
      To record actual overhead costs incurred in June.

(5)   Work in Process Inventory—Department A   4,400
      Work in Process Inventory—Department B   5,880
         Manufacturing Overhead 10,280
      To apply overhead to production using predetermined rates based on direct labor cost: Department A, 80%; and Department B, 100%.

(6)   Work in Process Inventory—Department B   26,400
         Work in Process Inventory—Department A 26,400
      To record transfer of goods from Department A to Department B.

(7)   Finished Goods Inventory 33,300
         Work in Process Inventory—Department B 33,300
      To record transfer of completed goods from Department B to finished goods.

Assuming that 6,000 completed units were sold in June at a price of $10 per unit on account, the following entries would be required:

(8) Accounts Receivable 60,000
      Sales 60,000
    To record sales on account.

(9) Cost of Goods Sold 22,200
      Finished Goods Inventory 22,200
    To record cost of goods sold in June, 6,000 units
    @ $3.70.

Production Cost Report. The key document in a process costing system is the production cost report. A production cost report shows both the flow of units and the flow of costs through a processing center. It also shows how these costs are divided between the cost of units completed and transferred out and the cost of units still in the processing center's ending inventory. This report is designed to make equivalent unit and unit cost computations easier.

To illustrate the preparation of a production cost report where there are partially completed beginning and ending inventories, assume the following data for Department 3 of the Storey Company, for the month of June 1987:

Units

Units in beginning inventory, complete as to materials, 60% complete as to conversion	6,000
Units transferred in from Department 2	18,000
Units completed and transferred out	16,000
Units in ending inventory, complete as to materials, 50% complete as to conversion	8,000

Costs

Cost of beginning inventory:		
Cost transferred in from preceding department in May	$12,000	
Materials added in May in Department 3	6,000	
Conversion costs (equal amounts of labor and overhead)	3,000	$21,000
Costs transferred in from preceding department in June		37,200
Costs added in Department 3 in June:		
Materials	$18,480	
Conversion (equal amounts of labor and overhead)	18,000	36,480
Total costs in beginning inventory and placed in production in Department 3 in June		$94,680

The production cost report for Department 3, shown in Illustration 22.8, is developed using the above data. There are four steps in the preparation of the production cost report:

1. Tracing the physical flow of the units through the production department.
2. Converting actual units to equivalent units.
3. Computing unit costs for each cost element.
4. Distributing the total cost between the units completed and transferred and the units remaining in the ending inventory.

These are the same four steps that were followed in the Ajax Company illustration of the process cost system.

The first step in the preparation of a production cost report is to trace the physical flow of actual units into and out of the department. The section entitled "UNITS" in Illustration 22.8 shows that 6,000 units were in the June beginning inventory and that 18,000 units were transferred in from the previous department, making a total of 24,000 units that must be accounted for. Of

Illustration 22.8   *Production Cost Report*

STOREY COMPANY
Production Cost Report—Department 3
For the Month of June 1987

	Actual units	Transferred in	Materials	Conversion	
		Equivalent units			
UNITS:					
Units in beginning inventory	6,000				
Units transferred in from Department 2	18,000				
Units to be accounted for	24,000				
Units completed and transferred	16,000	16,000	16,000	16,000	
Units in ending inventory*	8,000	8,000	8,000	4,000	
Units accounted for	24,000	24,000	24,000	20,000	

* Inventory is complete as to materials added, 50% complete as to conversion.

	Transferred in	Materials	Conversion	Total
COSTS:				
Costs to be accounted for:				
Costs in beginning inventory	$12,000	$ 6,000	$ 3,000	$21,000
Costs transferred in from Department 2	37,200			37,200
Costs added in Department 3		18,480	18,000	36,480
Costs to be accounted for	$49,200	$24,480	$21,000	$94,680
Equivalent units (as above)	24,000	24,000	20,000	
Unit costs (per equivalent unit)	$2.05	$1.02	$1.05	$4.12
Costs accounted for:				
Costs completed and transferred out	$32,800	$16,320	$16,800	$65,920
Costs remaining in ending inventory	16,400	8,160	4,200	28,760
Costs accounted for	$49,200	$24,480	$21,000	$94,680

these 24,000 units, 16,000 units were completed and transferred out (either to the next processing department or to finished goods), and 8,000 remained partially completed in Department 3 at the end of the month.

The next step is to convert actual units to equivalent units of production. The cost of production report illustrated uses an **average cost** procedure.[3] **Under an average cost procedure, the number of equivalent units for each cost element equals the number of units transferred out plus the number of equivalent units of that cost element in the ending inventory.** The number of units in beginning inventory and the degree of completion of the beginning inventory are not considered under the average cost method. In this example, since the units in the ending inventory are fully complete as to cost transferred in and as to materials, the number of equivalent units for each of these cost elements is 24,000 (16,000 units completed and transferred + 8,000 units in the ending inventory × 100% complete for transferred-in cost and for materials). But the units in ending inventory were only 50% complete as to conversion; therefore, equivalent units for conversion cost purposes are 20,000 (16,000 units completed and transferred + 8,000 units in the ending inventory × 50% complete for conversion).

---

[3] Discussion of Fifo and Lifo procedures in a process cost system is reserved for an advanced cost accounting text.

Now that equivalent units have been computed, the next step is to calculate unit costs. Costs are accumulated for each cost element of production—costs transferred in, materials, and conversion. Notice that the costs of beginning inventory and costs of the current month are totaled for each cost element. The summation of all costs charged to the department is referred to as "costs to be accounted for." These costs will either be transferred out or will appear in ending inventory of Department 3. Total cost assignable to each cost element is divided by the appropriate number of equivalent units of production related to that cost element to determine the cost per equivalent unit for that cost element. Since all costs for each cost element are totaled before the division, the unit costs computed are averages across the current and the prior period. As shown in Illustration 22.8, average per unit costs for June are as follows: transferred-in cost, $2.05; materials, $1.02; and conversion, $1.05. These costs are monitored closely by management for cost control purposes in the event that there are extreme fluctuations from one month to the next.

The last step is to distribute costs between the units completed and transferred out and those remaining in ending inventory. The units that were transferred out were fully complete as to all elements of production. Therefore, the 16,000 units can be multiplied by $4.12, the total cost per unit. The result is $65,920, the amount to be assigned to the next department as "cost transferred in" or to finished goods as the cost of current period production. The cost of ending inventory is computed as follows:

8,000 equivalent units transferred in @ $2.05	$16,400
8,000 equivalent units of materials costs @ $1.02 . .	8,160
4,000 equivalent units of conversion costs @ $1.05 . .	4,200
Total cost of ending inventory	$28,760

The sum of the ending inventory cost and the cost of the units transferred out must equal the total costs for which the department is accountable. Thus, a built-in check is provided to determine whether the procedures of cost allocation have been properly followed. Note that cost transferred out of $65,920 is added to ending inventory cost of $28,760, and the total equals costs accountable for of $94,680 as shown in the production cost report.

■ SUMMARY

Two major types of cost accumulation systems under perpetual inventory cost procedure are found in practice—the job order cost system and the process cost system. In each system, the goal is to determine before year-end the unit costs of the products being manufactured. Unit costs may be used throughout the period to compute (1) cost of goods sold, (2) cost of work in process and finished goods inventories, (3) payments to be received under contracts based on "full" cost, and (4) selling prices.

A job order cost system is a cost accounting system in which the costs incurred to produce a product are accumulated according to the individual job. A job order cost system is generally used when the products being manufactured can be grouped into separately identifiable jobs.

The key document in a job order cost system is the job order cost sheet, which summarizes the costs of direct materials, direct labor, and manufacturing overhead incurred for a job. The file of job order cost sheets for the incomplete jobs constitutes a subsidiary ledger for the Work in Process Inventory account. The actual costs of direct materials issued to a job and direct labor used on a job are recorded on the job order cost sheet. However, overhead cost is generally applied to the job through the use of a predetermined overhead rate.

A predetermined overhead rate is computed by dividing estimated overhead costs by the expected level of manufacturing activity. Overhead costs applied to production are debited to Work in Process Inventory and credited to the Manufacturing Overhead account. Actual overhead costs incurred are debited to Manufacturing Overhead and credited to Cash, various accounts payable, or similar accounts. Since overhead is applied via a predetermined, estimated overhead rate, it is unlikely that the actual costs debited to Manufacturing Overhead will equal the applied overhead that was credited to Manufacturing Overhead during the period. The debit balance (underapplied overhead) or credit balance (overapplied overhead) in the Manufacturing Overhead account can be allocated to Work in Process Inventory, Finished Goods Inventory, and Cost of Goods Sold, or it can simply be closed directly to Cost of Goods Sold.

A process cost system is a manufacturing cost system in which costs incurred to produce a product are accumulated according to the processes or departments a product goes through on its way to completion. A process cost system is generally used where huge quantities of a single product or similar products are manufactured on a continuous basis over long periods of time.

Computing per unit costs of products in a process cost system requires first computing the number of equivalent units completed during the period. Equivalent units must be determined for (1) units transferred-in (if this department receives products from a previous processing department), (2) materials, and (3) conversion. The costs of transferred-in units (if any), materials, and conversion are then divided by their respective numbers of equivalent units to obtain costs per equivalent unit. Finally, the numbers of equivalent units (for transferred-in units, materials, and conversion) in the units completed and transferred and in the ending work in process inventory are multiplied by their respective costs per equivalent unit to determine the total cost of the units completed and transferred and of the ending work in process inventory. This cost computation is performed on a production cost report, which is a key document in a process costing system.

The importance of accurate accounting for product unit costs should be evident to you. Without accurate cost accounting information, a manufacturing company cannot determine its selling prices, prepare accurate financial statements, or determine the cost of its ending inventory. Chapter 23 discusses how costs can be used to assess the efficiency of a manufacturing process.

NEW TERMS INTRODUCED IN CHAPTER 22

Equivalent units

A method of expressing a given number of partially completed units as a smaller number of fully completed units; for example, bringing 1,000 units to a 75% level of completion is the equivalent of bringing 750 units to a 100% level of completion (874).

Finished goods card

A running record of units and costs of products completed, sold, and on hand (861).

Job order cost sheet

A form used to summarize the costs of direct materials, direct labor, and manufacturing overhead incurred for a job. The job order cost sheets for all partially completed jobs form the subsidiary ledger for the Work in Process Inventory account (859).

Job order cost system (job costing)

A cost accounting system in which the costs incurred to produce a product are accumulated according to the individual job, such as a building, dam, 1,000 chairs, or 10 desks (859).

Manufacturing overhead cost sheet

A record that summarizes the various manufacturing overhead costs incurred (863).

Materials requisition

A written order directing the stores clerk to issue certain materials to a production center (862).

Overapplied (overabsorbed) overhead

The amount by which the overhead applied to production exceeds the actual overhead costs incurred in that same period (865).

Predetermined overhead rate

Calculated by dividing estimated total overhead costs for a period by the expected level of activity, such as direct labor-hours or direct labor costs for the period.

The use of a predetermined rate is a means of applying manufacturing overhead to production such that unit costs can be determined immediately after production has been completed (863).

Process cost system (process costing)

A manufacturing cost system in which costs incurred to produce a product are accumulated according to the processes or departments a product goes through on its way to completion (871).

Production cost report

A report that shows both the flow of units and the flow of costs through a processing center; it also shows how those costs are divided between the cost of units transferred out and the cost of units still in the processing center's ending inventory (876).

Stores (or materials) card

A record that shows the quantities and costs of each type of material received, issued to a job, and left on hand (861).

Underapplied (underabsorbed) overhead

The amount by which actual overhead costs incurred in a period exceeds the overhead applied to production in that period (865).

Work (labor time) ticket

A form used to record labor costs. Information recorded on the work ticket includes employee number, job number, number of hours worked, and any other important information; may be prepared for both direct and indirect labor (862).

DEMONSTRATION PROBLEM 22–1

Heille Company employs a job order cost system. As of January 1, 1987, its records showed:

Materials and supplies	$ 80,000
Work in process	172,000
Finished goods (50,000 units at $4)	200,000

The work in process inventory consisted of two jobs:

No.	Materials	Labor	Manufacturing overhead	Total
212	$30,000	$40,000	$20,000	$ 90,000
213	34,000	32,000	16,000	82,000
	$64,000	$72,000	$36,000	$172,000

Summarized below are manufacturing data for the company for 1987:

1. Materials and supplies purchased on account, $330,000.
2. Factory payrolls accrued, $680,000; FICA taxes withheld, $34,000; and federal income taxes withheld, $60,000.

3. Manufacturing overhead costs incurred: depreciation, $20,000; heat, light, and power, $8,000; and miscellaneous, $12,000.
4. Direct materials and supplies requisitioned: Job No. 212, $52,000; Job No. 213, $96,000; Job No. 214, $160,000; and indirect supplies requisitioned, $8,000.
5. Payrolls distributed: direct labor—Job No. 212, $80,000; Job No. 213, $160,000; Job No. 214, $240,000; factory supervision, $80,000; and other indirect labor, $120,000.
6. Overhead is assigned to work in process at 50% of direct labor costs.
7. Job Nos. 212 and 213 were completed.
8. Goods with a cost of $688,000 were sold for $900,000.

Required: Prepare general journal entries to record the above summarized data, as well as all closing entries for which you have sufficient information.

Solution to demonstration problem 22–1

HEILLE COMPANY
General Journal

(1)	Materials Inventory	330,000	
	Accounts Payable		330,000
	To record materials purchased on account.		
(2)	Payroll Summary	680,000	
	FICA Taxes Withheld		34,000
	Federal Income Taxes Withheld		60,000
	Accrued Wages Payable		586,000
	To record accrued factory payrolls.		
(3)	Manufacturing Overhead	40,000	
	Accumulated Depreciation		20,000
	Accounts Payable (Accrued Liabilities, Cash, etc.)		20,000
	To record various manufacturing overhead costs.		
(4)	Work in Process Inventory	308,000	
	Manufacturing Overhead	8,000	
	Materials inventory		316,000
	To record requisitions of materials and supplies:		

Job No. 212	$ 52,000
213	96,000
214	160,000
Indirect supplies	8,000
	$316,000

(5)	Work in Process Inventory	480,000	
	Manufacturing Overhead	200,000	
	Payroll Summary		680,000
	To distribute labor costs:		

Direct labor to Work in Process Inventory:

Job No. 212	$ 80,000	
213	160,000	
214	240,000	$480,000

Manufacturing overhead:

Factory supervision	$ 80,000	
Other indirect labor	120,000	200,000
		$680,000

(6)	Work in Process Inventory	240,000	
	Manufacturing Overhead		240,000
	Overhead assigned: Job No. 212, $40,000; Job No. 213, $80,000; and Job No. 214, $120,000.		

```
(7) Finished Goods Inventory . . . . . . . . . . . . . . . .   680,000
        Work in Process Inventory . . . . . . . . . . . . .             680,000
    Completed and transferred jobs:
        No. 212 . . . . . . . . . . . . . . . . . . .  $262,000
        No. 213 . . . . . . . . . . . . . . . . . . .   418,000
                                                       $680,000


(8) Accounts Receivable . . . . . . . . . . . . . . . .   900,000
        Sales . . . . . . . . . . . . . . . . . . . .             900,000
    To record sales on account.

    Cost of Goods Sold . . . . . . . . . . . . . . . .   688,000
        Finished Goods Inventory . . . . . . . . . . .             688,000
    To record cost of goods sold.

    Cost of Goods Sold . . . . . . . . . . . . . . . .     8,000
        Manufacturing Overhead . . . . . . . . . . . .               8,000
    To close underapplied manufacturing overhead.

    Sales . . . . . . . . . . . . . . . . . . . . . .   900,000
        Income Summary . . . . . . . . . . . . . . . .             900,000
    To close Sales account.

    Income Summary . . . . . . . . . . . . . . . . .   696,000
        Cost of Goods Sold . . . . . . . . . . . . . .             696,000
    To close Cost of Goods Sold expense account.
```

DEMONSTRATION PROBLEM 22–2

AFA, Inc. uses a process cost system to accumulate the costs it incurs to produce aluminum awning stabilizers. The May 1 inventory consisted of 30,000 units, fully complete as to materials, 80% complete as to conversion. The beginning inventory cost of $240,000 consisted of $180,000 of costs transferred in from the molding department, $25,000 of finishing department material costs, and $35,000 of finishing department conversion costs. The costs incurred in the finishing department for the month of May appear below:

Costs from molding department (excluding costs in beginning inventory)		$600,000
Costs added in finishing department in May (excluding costs in beginning inventory):		
Materials	$ 53,000	
Conversion	109,480	162,480
		$762,480

The finishing department received 100,000 units from the molding department in May. During the month, 106,000 units were completed by the finishing department and transferred out. As of May 31, 24,000 units, complete as to materials and 60% complete as to conversion, were left in inventory of the finishing department.

Required:
a. Prepare a production cost report for the finishing department for the month of May.
b. Compute the average unit cost for conversion in the finishing department in April.

Solution to demonstration problem 22–2

a.

AFA, INC.
Finishing Department
Production Cost Report
For the Month Ending May 31

	Actual units	*Equivalent units* — *Transferred in*	*Materials*	*Conversion*
UNITS:				
Units in May 1 inventory	30,000			
Units transferred in	100,000			
Units to be accounted for	130,000			
Units completed and transferred	106,000	106,000	106,000	106,000
Units in May 31 inventory*	24,000	24,000	24,000	14,400†
Units accounted for	130,000	130,000	130,000	120,400

* Inventory is complete as to materials, 60% complete as to conversion.
† (24,000 × 60% = 14,400).

	Transferred in	*Materials*	*Conversion*	*Total*
COSTS:				
Costs to be accounted for:				
Costs in May 1 inventory	$180,000	$ 25,000	$ 35,000	$ 240,000
Costs transferred in	600,000			600,000
Costs added in department		53,000	109,480	162,480
Costs to be accounted for	$780,000	$ 78,000	$144,480	$1,002,480
Equivalent units (as above)	130,000	130,000	120,400	
Unit costs	$6.00	$0.60	$1.20	$7.80
Costs accounted for:				
Units completed and transferred out	$636,000	$ 63,600	$127,200	$ 826,800
Units remaining in May 31 inventory	144,000	14,400	17,280	175,680
Costs accounted for	$780,000	$ 78,000	$144,480	$1,002,480

b. The unit cost of conversion in the finishing department in April was $1.46 [$35,000 ÷ (0.8 × 30,000)].

QUESTIONS

1. What is the basic purpose of any costing system?
2. What is a job order cost sheet? Explain how it is used.
3. How is a predetermined overhead rate calculated? Why is the use of a predetermined rate necessary in a perpetual inventory cost system?
4. Under what circumstances is the assignment of overhead to production by applying a predetermined rate definitely preferable to assigning actual overhead incurred?
5. What is a reason, other than errors in estimating costs, for overapplied overhead?
6. How does a process cost system differ from a job order cost system? What factors should be taken into consideration in determining which type of system should be employed?
7. What is meant by the term *equivalent units?* Of what use is the computation of the number of equivalent units of production?
8. Distinguish between the number of units completed and transferred during a period and the equivalent units for the same period.
9. Under what circumstances would the number of equivalent units of materials differ from the equivalent units of labor and overhead in the same department

in the same period? Under what circumstances would they be the same?

10. What is the basic information reported in a production cost report?

11. Less effort is required to operate a job cost system than a process cost system. Do you agree or disagree? Explain.

EXERCISES

E-1

Compute job costs; prepare journal entries related to production activities

In September, Hays Company worked only on Job No. 714, completing it on September 30. During the month, the company purchased and used $5,000 of direct materials and incurred $7,500 of direct labor costs. Assuming manufacturing overhead is applied at the rate of 120% of direct labor costs, what is the total cost of Job No. 714? Prepare journal entries to assign the materials, labor, and manufacturing overhead costs to production and to record the transfer of Job No. 714 to finished goods inventory.

E-2

Compute job cost per unit; prepare journal entries to record transfer and sale

As of August 1, Job. No. 210 had already accumulated $7,500 in total costs. During August, Job No. 210 required $10,500 of direct materials and $21,000 of direct labor. Manufacturing overhead is applied to production at the rate of 80% of direct labor costs. Assuming completed Job No. 210 consisted of 800 units, what is the total cost per unit? Give the journal entries necessary to record the transfer of Job No. 210 to finished goods inventory and the ultimate sale of all 800 units at 150% of cost.

E-3

Prepare journal entries related to production; calculate unit cost (job order)

The Gable Company builds desks to fit customers' specifications. It engaged in the following transactions during June:

Transactions:

1. Purchased precut wood for desk tops, $15,000.
2. Wood and other direct materials were issued to production, $10,500.
3. Direct labor costs were $7,500.
4. Manufacturing overhead was assigned to production, $9,000.
5. Job No. 312 was completed and transferred.

Job No. 312 was the only order worked on in June, and it consisted of 5,000 desks. The total cost assigned to Job. No. 312 in May amounted to $6,750.

a. Journalize the transactions listed above.
b. Compute the cost per unit of Job No. 312.

E-4

Compute costs of three jobs

The Flower Company, which uses a job order cost system, engaged in the following activities during December:

1. Three jobs were started: Nos. 122,123, and 124.
2. Direct materials issued:

To Job 122 . . $2,500
Job 123 . . 3,500
Job 124 . . 2,000

3. Direct labor costs incurred:

For Job 122 . . . 250 hours @ $7/hour
Job 123 . . . 375 hours @ $6/hour
Job 124 . . . 100 hours @ $8.50/hour

4. Assume manufacturing overhead is applied at the rate of $4 per direct labor-hour.

Compute the cost of each job, and give the necessary journal entry to record the transfer of Job No. 123 to Finished Goods Inventory.

E-5

Prepare journal entry for disposition of overhead

S Company estimated its manufacturing overhead for 1987 at $400,000. At the end of 1987, manufacturing overhead was overapplied by $1,500. Give the journal entry required to reflect a practical disposition of the manufacturing overhead balance.

E-6

Prepare journal entries for allocation of overhead

Using the data in Exercise E-5, assume the balance in Manufacturing Overhead is to be allocated to the following accounts in the amounts indicated: Work in Process Inventory, $200; Finished Goods Inventory, $300; and Cost of Goods Sold, $1,000. Give the journal entry to allocate the manufacturing overhead balance to these accounts.

E-7

Calculate equivalent units

In Department C, materials are added at the beginning of the process. The ending inventory in Department C in April, was 20% complete as to conversion costs. There were 600 units in beginning inventory, 7,200 units were started during the month, and 4,800 units were completed and transferred to finished goods inventory. Under the average method, what are the equivalent units of production for materials and conversion costs?

E-8

Calculate cost per equivalent unit; determine costs of units transferred and those reamining in ending inventory

The following cost data relate to Exercise E-7:

	Materials	Conversion	Total
Costs in beginning inventory . . .	$ 8,400	$ 4,200	$12,600
Costs incurred during month . . .	26,700	25,500	52,200
Total costs to be accounted for . .	$35,100	$29,700	$64,800

Compute the cost of goods completed and transferred to finished goods inventory and the cost of the ending work in process inventory.

PROBLEMS, SERIES A

P22-1-A

Compute predetermined overhead rate and total overhead cost of a job

a.   The Lawrence Company has established the following budget for 1987:

	Assembly	Packaging
Manufacturing overhead . .	$500,000	$ 700,000
Direct labor cost	$900,000	$1,100,000
Direct labor-hours	75,000	110,000
Machine-hours	37,500	100,000

Lawrence Company uses predetermined rates to apply manufacturing overhead. These rates are based on machine-hours in assembly and on direct labor costs in packaging.

Required: Compute the predetermined manufacturing overhead rate for each department.

b.   During June, the job cost sheet for Job No. 104 showed the following:

	Assembly	Packaging
Direct materials used . .	$12,000	$12,000
Direct labor cost . . .	$ 9,000	$ 3,750
Direct labor-hours . . .	750	375
Machine-hours	375	250

Required: Using the overhead rates computed in (a), compute the total manufacturing overhead cost of Job No. 104.

P22-2-A

*Compute
predetermined
overhead rate and
overhead cost of
one job*

Stockwell Company uses a job order cost system, applying manufacturing overhead at predetermined rates based on direct labor-hours in Department A and machine-hours in Department B. Budgeted estimates for 1987 are:

	Department A	Department B
Manufacturing overhead . .	$144,000	$192,000
Direct labor cost	$120,000	$132,000
Direct labor-hours	24,000	32,000
Machine-hours	16,000	48,000

Detailed cost records show the following for Job No. 105 which was completed in 1987:

	Department A	Department B
Materials used	$10,000	$500
Direct labor cost . . .	$ 8,000	$600
Direct labor-hours . .	200	100
Machine-hours	50	80

Required: a.   Compute the predetermined overhead rates for 1987 for Departments A and B.
             b.   Compute the amount of manufacturing overhead applied to Job No. 105 in each department.

P22-3-A

*Compute
predetermined
overhead rate and
under- or
overapplied
overhead*

Ballard Company applies overhead to production using a predetermined overhead rate based on machine-hours. Budgeted data for 1987 are:

Budgeted machine-hours   50,000
Budgeted manufacturing overhead . . $290,000

Required: a.   Compute the predetermined overhead rate.
             b.   Assume that in 1987, actual manufacturing overhead amounted to $332,500, and that 61,000 machine-hours were used. Compute the amount of underapplied or overapplied manufacturing overhead for 1987.

P22-4-A

*Compute total and
per unit costs of
three jobs; calculate
ending work in
process inventory
amount*

Timothy Corporation employs a job order cost system. Its manufacturing activities in June 1987, its first month of operations, are summarized below:

	Job number		
	101	102	103
Direct materials cost	$18,000	$12,000	$27,000
Direct labor cost	$15,000	$13,500	$18,000
Direct labor-hours	1,500	1,600	2,000
Units produced	300	150	1,500

Manufacturing overhead is applied at a rate of $10.50 per direct labor-hour.
Job Nos. 101 and 102 were completed in June.

Required: a.   Compute the amount of manufacturing overhead charged to each job.
             b.   Compute the total and unit cost of each completed job.
             c.   Prepare the entry, in general journal form, to record the transfer of completed jobs to finished goods inventory.
             d.   Compute the balance in the June 30, 1987, Work in Process Inventory account and provide a schedule of the costs charged to each incomplete job to support this balance.

P22–5–A

Compute cost of ending inventories of materials, work in process, and finished goods

The Apollo Company engaged in the following activities during 1987:

Materials purchased	$195,000
Factory payroll incurred (all direct, all employees paid $5 per hour)	157,500

The following jobs were worked on during 1987:

	Job No. 1	Job No. 2	Job No. 3
Direct materials	$51,000	$39,000	$60,000
Direct labor	75,000	60,000	22,500
Manufacturing overhead (applied at $3.50 per direct labor-hour)	?	?	?

Job No. 1 was completed and sold (at 150% of cost), Job No. 2 was completed but not sold, and Job No. 3 was not completed.

Required: Compute the balance in each inventory account (Materials, Work in Process, and Finished Goods) at December 31, 1987.

P22–6–A

Prepare journal entries in job order system and T-accounts

Judson Company employs a job order cost system. As of January 1, 1987, its records showed the following inventory balances:

Materials	$22,500
Work in process	43,000
Finished goods (25,000 units @ $2) . .	50,000

The work in process inventory consisted of two jobs:

Job No.	Materials	Direct labor	Manufacturing overhead	Total
212 . .	$ 7,500	$10,000	$5,000	$22,500
213 . .	8,500	8,000	4,000	20,500
	$16,000	$18,000	$9,000	$43,000

Summarized below are production and sales data for the company for 1987:

1. Materials purchased, $80,000.
2. Factory payroll costs incurred, $170,000.
3. Factory indirect costs incurred (other than indirect labor and indirect materials): depreciation, $5,000; heat, light, and power, $2,000; and miscellaneous, $3,000.
4. Materials requisitioned: direct materials for Job No. 212, $13,000; for Job No. 213, $24,000; and for Job No. 214, $40,000; supplies (indirect materials) requisitioned, $2,000.
5. Factory payroll distributed: direct labor to Job No. 212, $20,000; to Job No. 213, $40,000; and to Job No. 214, $60,000; indirect labor, $50,000.
6. Manufacturing overhead is assigned to work in process at the same rate per dollar of direct labor cost as in 1986.
7. Job Nos. 212 and 213 were completed.
8. Sales for the year amounted to $300,000; cost of goods sold, $172,000.

Required: a. Prepare journal entries to record the above transactions.
b. Prepare all closing entries for which you have information.
c. Set up T-accounts for Materials Inventory, Payroll Summary, Manufacturing Overhead, Work in Process Inventory, Finished Goods Inventory, and Cost of Goods Sold. Post the parts of the entries made in (a) and (b) that affect these accounts.
d. Show that the total cost charged to incomplete jobs agrees with the balance in the Work in Process Inventory account.

P22-7-A

Prepare production cost report

The following information relates to the Cohn Company:

Units in beginning inventory	2,250
Cost of units in beginning inventory:	
Materials	$22,500
Conversion	$10,500
Units placed in production	60,000
Costs incurred during current period:	
Materials	$133,125
Conversion	$119,910
Units remaining in ending inventory (100% complete as to materials, 50% complete as to conversion) . .	3,750

Required: Prepare a production cost report using the average method.

P 22-8-A

Prepare production cost report

Health Company uses a process cost system to account for the costs incurred in making its single product, a health food called Vita-Myte. This product is processed first in Department A and then in Department B. Materials are added in both departments. Production for May was as follows:

	Department A	Department B
Units started or transferred in	150,000	112,500
Units completed and transferred out	112,500	90,000
Stage of completion of May 31 inventory:		
Materials	100%	80%
Conversion	50%	40%
Direct materials costs	$ 90,000	$ 16,200
Conversion costs	$262,500	$178,200

There was no May 1 inventory in either department.

Required:
a. Prepare a production cost report for Department A for May.
b. Prepare a production cost report for Department B for May.

PROBLEMS, SERIES B

P22-1-B

Compute predetermined overhead rate and total cost of a job

a. The John Company has established the following budget for 1987:

	Assembling	Welding
Manufacturing overhead . .	$350,000	$450,000
Direct labor cost	$600,000	$750,000
Direct labor-hours	50,000	75,000
Machine-hours	26,000	75,000

John Company uses predetermined rates to apply manufacturing overhead. These rates are based on machine-hours in assembling and on direct labor costs in welding.

Required: Compute the predetermined overhead rate for each department.

b. During May, the job cost sheet for Job No. 195 showed the following:

	Assembling	Welding
Direct materials used . .	$2,000	$8,000
Direct labor cost	$6,000	$2,500
Direct labor-hours . . .	500	250
Machine-hours	240	150

Required: Using the overhead rates computed in part *(a)*, compute the total cost of Job No. 195.

P22-2-B

Compute three different overhead rates and under- or overapplied manufacturing overhead using each rate; discuss disposition of over- or underapplied overhead

Manning Company intends to start a policy of using a predetermined rate to charge manufacturing overhead to production. Selected actual and budgeted production data and costs for 1987 follow:

	Budgeted	Actual
Manufacturing overhead . .	$300,000	$303,500
Direct labor-hours	37,500	38,000
Machine-hours	30,000	29,500
Units of production	100,000	97,500

Required:

a. Compute three possible rates by which the manufacturing overhead can be applied to production. Also compute the underapplied or overapplied manufacturing overhead for 1987 under each rate.

b. Theoretically, what disposition should be made for financial reporting of the underapplied or overapplied manufacturing overhead in part *(a)?*

P22-3-B

Compute total and per unit costs of four jobs; calculate ending work in process inventory

Carrington Corporation employs a job order cost system. Its manufacturing activities in July 1987, its first month of operation, are summarized below:

	Job number			
	201	202	203	204
Direct materials . .	$12,000	$8,700	$18,900	$9,000
Direct labor cost . .	$ 9,900	$9,000	$12,600	$3,600
Direct labor-hours . .	1,100	1,000	1,400	400
Units produced . .	200	100	1,000	300

Manufacturing overhead is applied at a rate of $3 per direct labor-hour for variable overhead and $4.50 per direct labor-hour for fixed overhead, for a total rate of $7.50 per direct labor-hour.

Job Nos. 201, 202, and 203 were completed in July.

Required:

a. Compute the amount of manufacturing overhead charged to each job.
b. Compute the total and unit cost of each completed job.
c. Prepare the entry, in general journal form, to record the transfer of completed jobs to finished goods inventory.
d. Compute the balance in the July 31, 1987, Work in Process Inventory account and provide a schedule of the costs charged to each incomplete job to support this balance.

P22-4-B

Prepare journal entries for a job order system; calculate cost of work in process inventory

The Newby Company's general ledger showed the following balances as of January 1, 1987:

Materials inventory	$ 75,000
Work in process inventory . .	33,750
Finished goods inventory . .	123,000

The work in process inventory consisted of the following:

Job No. 1858:

Material	$24,750
Labor	3,000
Manufacturing overhead . .	6,000
	$33,750

The following transactions took place in January:

Transactions:

1. Materials purchased on account, $210,000.
2. Materials issued during the month: direct, $150,000; indirect, $25,500. Of the direct materials issued,

$21,000 were assigned to Job No. 1858, with the balance going equally to Job Nos. 1859 and 1860.

3. Gross payroll for January was $112,500; FICA taxes withheld amounted to $6,000; federal income taxes withheld totaled $12,750.
4. The $112,500 payroll consisted of $90,000 of direct labor (one third charged to each job) and $22,500 of indirect labor.
5. Manufacturing overhead is applied at 200% of direct labor cost.
6. Job No. 1858 was completed.

Required: a.   Prepare journal entries for the above transactions.
         b.   Compute the ending balance in Work in Process Inventory.

P22–5–B

Calculate equivalent units, costs per equivalent unit, cost of goods completed, and cost of ending inventory

The following data pertain to a production center of the Rockdale Company:

Work in process inventory, February 1, 5,000 units.
Direct materials	$ 5,250
Direct labor	2,500
Manufacturing overhead (150% of direct labor cost)	3,750
	$11,500

Units started in February	15,000

Costs incurred in February:
Direct materials	$15,150
Direct labor	23,000
Manufacturing overhead applied	?

The ending inventory consisted of 7,500 units (100% complete as to materials, 60% complete as to conversion).

Required: Compute the following:

a. Number of units completed and transferred to finished goods inventory.
b. The equivalent units of production for materials and conversion costs using the average method.
c. Cost per equivalent unit.
d. Cost of units completed and transferred.
e. Cost of ending inventory.

P22–6–B

Prepare production cost report

Vedder Company manufactures a product called Savem and determines product costs using a process cost system. Following are cost and production data for the handle department for the month of June:

	Units	Materials costs	Conversion costs
Inventory, June 1	30,000	$2,685	$ 3,300
Placed in production in June	90,000	8,115	14,340
Inventory, June 30	45,000	?	?

The June 30 inventory was 100% complete as to materials and 20% complete as to conversion.

Required: Prepare a production cost report using the average method.

P22–7–B

Prepare production cost report

Holcomb Company manufactures a product called DOG and determines product costs using a process cost system. Materials costing $11,000 were introduced at the start of processing, and $9,700 of conversion costs were incurred. During the period, 20,000 units of product were started, and 19,000 were completed. At the end of the period, 1,000 units were still in process and were 40% complete as to conversion.

Required: Prepare a production cost report using the average method.

P22–8–B

Prepare production cost report

Lee Drug Company manufactures an ointment for relieving sore muscles. The product is moved through two departments, mixing and bottling. Production and cost data for the bottling department in December follow:

Work in process, December 1 (30,000 pints):
   Costs transferred in $15,000
   Materials costs   6,000
   Conversion costs   4,000

Costs incurred in December:
   Transferred in (90,000 pints) . . $46,200
   Materials costs   19,200
   Conversion costs   18,365

All materials are added at the beginning of the bottling process. Ending inventory consists of 22,500 pints, 100% complete as to materials and 40% complete as to conversion.

Required: Prepare a production cost report for December using the average method.

BUSINESS DECISION PROBLEM

Determine how overhead should be applied; give advantages of predetermined rate; justify use of applied overhead

The Ball Manufacturing Company produces one product, an orange industrial dye. The demand for this dye is highly seasonal, and because of this, Ball adjusts its production schedule so that it is in line with demand (the dye is susceptible to spoilage). The president of Ball, Mona LeAnn, has received complaints from the sales department that it is having difficulty in setting a stable price for the dye. The sales department is under orders from Mrs. LeAnn to set prices on the basis of "cost plus 30% of cost." It complains that the cost figures it receives from the production manager vary widely from quarter to quarter, which in turn cause the selling price to fluctuate.

In an attempt to settle the dispute, Mrs. LeAnn calls the production manager, Charlie Serners, into her office for a conference. Mr. Serners reports that he has no choice but to change the cost every quarter, as to do otherwise would mean that a loss would result during periods of low demand. He tells Mrs. LeAnn that she has the numbers to back up this statement and reminds Mrs. LeAnn that figures don't lie. As proof, he offers the following information:

	First quarter	Second quarter	Third quarter	Fourth quarter
Direct materials	$ 90,000	$ 36,000	$ 18,000	$ 72,000
Direct labor	112,500	45,000	22,500	90,000
Variable manufacturing overhead . .	22,500	9,000	4,500	18,000
Fixed manufacturing overhead . . .	150,000	150,000	150,000	150,000
Total	$375,000	$240,000	$195,000	$330,000
Number of gallons to be produced . .	75,000	30,000	15,000	60,000
Cost per gallon	$5.00	$8.00	$13.00	$5.50

Mrs. LeAnn realizes that the root of the problem is manufacturing overhead. Manufacturing overhead costs cannot be reduced enough to make a difference during the periods of low demand. She asks Mr. Serners to find a better way to allocate the manufacturing overhead costs to each gallon of dye produced in order to arrive at a more uniform cost figure per gallon.

Required:　a.　How would you recommend to Mr. Serners that manufacturing overhead costs be assigned to production? How would this differ from his present method?

b.　What benefits would be gained by using your recommended solution?

c.　To justify your recommendation made in *(a)* above, recalculate the per gallon cost of the dye using your recommendation.

BUSINESS SITUATION FOR DISCUSSION

A Look at Accounting for Small Manufacturers*

George F. Hanks and Pamela L. Murphy

A company's profitability depends on its ability to control costs, as well as its ability to generate revenues, a fact that is overlooked by many small companies. Small manufacturing firms face many of the same accounting and control problems as large firms. The smaller the company, however, the less likely it is to possess the in-house expertise and other resources required to deal with those problems and the greater the probability is that the company is losing hard-earned dollars because of a lack of control.

We undertook a study in an effort to provide information that might be helpful to small manufacturing firms by identifying the most serious problem areas and by providing possible measures for correction. Efforts to improve accounting and related controls seem to be especially worthwhile in view of the country's existing economic situation and the resulting cash squeeze for firms of all sizes.

We studied 29 small manufacturing firms with the following specific objectives before us:

1. To evaluate the quality of four particular aspects of the accounting and control system;
2. To determine if any demographic factors, such as size or type of ownership, were related to the quality of the accounting and control systems; and
3. To make specific recommendations to correct areas that we observed to be particularly weak or common to many of the firms.

* Reprinted from the April 1984 issue of *Management Accounting* (pp. 40–44). Copyright by the National Association of Accountants.

Targets for Change

Over the past five years, information was gathered on the accounting systems of approximately 75 small manufacturing firms in eastern Indiana. These data were collected by graduate students who conducted on-site studies. From the total, 29 of the firms were selected for this study based on the completeness of the information received by the researchers.

We decided to center our investigation on four key aspects of control that we felt represented the essential features of an adequate manufacturing accounting system. The four were:

1. Cash control,
2. Materials control,
3. Cost accounting, and
4. Performance evaluation

*　　*　　*　　*　　*

The findings generally indicate that the accounting systems of the small manufacturers in this study are weak in each of the areas investigated. . . . Over half (51.7%) of the firms had very weak or somewhat weak material control systems. Fifty-five percent had weak cash control, while 69% had less than adequate cost accounting systems. Finally, a very large number of the firms (86%) made little or no attempt at measuring the performance of their operations beyond the use of the income statement. We found these overall findings surprisingly dismal.

*　　*　　*　　*　　*

Cost accounting was another general area in which the companies in the study were deficient. Almost 70% were judged to have inadequate cost accounting systems. A good cost accounting system serves two main purposes for a manufacturing firm: it allows the identification of cost which is necessary for control, and it allows the firm to compare actual costs incurred on work done to costs that were expected to be incurred. Cost accounting systems also are used for valuing work-in-process and finished-goods inventories and the computation of cost-of-goods sold for financial statements, but, from a management point of view, these benefits are secondary.

All of the companies studied were job shops but not all had job cost systems in use. In fact, several made no attempt to keep track of actually incurred cost at all. Undoubtedly, managers of small manufacturing firms often feel that their operations cannot justify the expense of a job cost system. However, an effective job cost system can be very simple using off-the-shelf time tickets and job cost sheets duplicated in-house. Even if only direct materials and direct labor are assigned to jobs, the effort will probably be worthwhile. With this information, management can determine where costs are being incurred, and make comparisons to original estimates (on the bid). This will determine how well the operation was performed and yield feedback information that may be useful in preparing future bids. While this comparison step seems so obvious, few firms actually took that step.

PART

8

Planning, Control, and Decision Making

Control through Standard Costs

LEARNING OBJECTIVES

After studying this chapter, you should be able to:

1. Discuss the concept of a standard cost system, specifically addressing how standards are set and the advantages achieved through their use.

2. Calculate the six variances from standard and prepare journal entries based on that information.

3. Discuss possible reasons for the existence of variances and how the isolation of these variances can support a management by exception philosophy.

4. Discuss theoretical and practical methods for disposing of variances from standard.

5. Discuss standard costs in relation to job order or process cost systems (covered in Appendix).

6. Define and use correctly the new terms in the glossary.

You will recall that the job order and process cost systems discussed in Chapter 22 are based on actual historical cost data. Because these data say little about how efficiently operations were conducted, many companies find it helpful to introduce standard costs into their cost systems. Standard costs can be used in both job order and process cost systems as shown in the Appendix to this chapter.

Standard and actual cost systems differ in that an actual cost system collects **actual** costs for materials, labor, and manufacturing overhead, while a standard cost system gathers both actual costs and **standard** costs for these elements of production. The standard costs flow through the accounting system to determine a standard, or "normal," cost for finished goods inventory. Actual costs incurred during the period are then compared with standard costs to assist management in decision making and to determine whether proper control is being maintained over production costs.

This chapter discusses the nature of standard costs and how to compute the difference between an actual cost and a standard cost, which is called a variance. The variances discussed are: materials variances, labor variances, and overhead variances. As you work with variances you will become aware of how important variances are in controlling costs.

■ STANDARD COSTS

Possibly you have set goals in your own life that you have sought to achieve. These goals could well have been called standards. Periodically, you might measure your actual performance against these standards and analyze the differences. Similarly, management sets goals, such as standard costs, and compares actual costs with these goals to identify possible problems.

Nature of standard costs

A standard cost is a carefully predetermined measure of what a cost **should be** under stated conditions. A standard cost is not merely an estimate of what a cost will be; it represents a goal. If a standard is properly set, achieving it represents a reasonably efficient level of performance.

Standards are set in many ways, but to be of any real value they should be more than mere estimates found by extending historical trends into the future. Usually, engineering studies and time and motion studies are undertaken to determine the amounts of materials, labor, and other services required to produce a product. General economic conditions should also be considered in setting standards because economic conditions affect the cost of materials and other services that must be purchased by a manufacturing company. A standard cost is found for each manufactured unit of product by determining the standard costs of direct materials, direct labor, and manufacturing overhead needed to produce that unit.

Standard direct materials cost per unit is made up of the standard amount of material required to produce that unit multiplied by the standard price of the material. It is extremely important to distinguish between the terms *standard price* and *standard cost*. Standard price usually refers to the price per unit of inputs into the production process. For example, the price per pound of raw materials is a standard price. Standard cost, on the other hand, is the product of the standard quantity of an input required per unit of output times the standard price per unit of that input. For example, if the standard price of cloth is $3 per yard and the standard quantity of material required to produce a dress is 3 yards, then the standard direct materials cost of the dress is $9 (3 yards × $3 per yard). Similarly, the standard direct labor cost per unit for a product is computed as the standard number of hours needed to produce one unit multiplied times the standard labor or wage rate.

The standard manufacturing overhead cost of a unit is determined as follows. First, the expected level of output is determined for the year. This level of output is called the standard level of output. Next, the total budgeted manufacturing overhead cost at the standard level of output is determined. The total budgeted overhead cost includes both fixed and variable components. Total fixed cost is the same at every level of output. Variable overhead varies in direct proportion to the number of units produced. Finally, the standard manufacturing overhead cost per unit is computed by dividing the budgeted manufacturing overhead cost by the standard level of output. The result is an overhead cost (or rate) per unit of output. Sometimes accountants find the standard overhead cost (or rate) per direct labor-hour instead of per unit. To find the cost per unit, merely multiply the direct labor-hours per unit times the standard overhead cost per direct labor-hour. For instance, if the standard overhead cost per direct labor-hour is $5 and the standard number of direct labor-hours is two hours per unit, the standard overhead cost per unit is $10 ($5 × 2 hours).

■ COMPUTING VARIANCES

As stated earlier, standard costs represent **goals.** Standard cost is the amount that a cost should be under a given set of circumstances. The accounting records, however, contain information regarding **actual** costs. The amount by which actual cost differs from standard cost is called a **variance.** A variance is designated as favorable when actual costs are less than standard, and unfavorable when actual costs exceed standard. But it does not automatically follow that favorable and unfavorable variances should be equated with good and bad. As you will see, such an appraisal should only be made after the causes of the variance are known.

The following section explains how to compute the dollar amount of variances, a process called **isolating variances,** using data for the Beta Company. Beta Company manufactures and sells a single product, each unit of which has the following standard costs:

Materials—5 sheets at $6 . . . . $30
Direct labor—2 hours at $10 20
Manufacturing overhead—2 direct labor-hours at $5 . . 10
Total standard cost per unit $60

Additional data regarding the production activities of the company will be presented as needed.

Materials Variances

The standard materials cost of any product is simply the standard **quantity** of materials that should be used multiplied by the **standard price** that should be paid for those materials. Actual costs may differ from standard costs for materials because the **price** paid for the materials and/or the **quantity** of materials used varied from the standard amounts management had set. These two factors are accounted for by isolating two variances for materials—a **price variance** and a **usage variance.**

There are several reasons for isolating two materials variances. First, different individuals may be responsible for each—a purchasing agent for the price variance and a production manager for the usage variance. Second, materials might not be purchased and used in the same period. The variance associated with the purchase should be isolated in the period of purchase, and the variance associated with usage should be isolated in the period of use. As a general rule, the sooner a variance can be isolated, the greater its value in cost control. Finally, it is unlikely that a single materials variance—the difference between the standard cost and the actual cost of the materials used—would be of any real value to management for effective cost control. A single variance would not show management what **caused** the difference, or one variance might simply offset another and make the total difference appear immaterial.

Materials Price Variance.   In a manufacturing company, the standard price for materials meeting certain engineering specifications is usually set by the purchasing and accounting departments. Consideration is given to factors such as market conditions, vendors' quoted prices, and the optimum size of a purchase order when setting a standard price. The materials price variance (MPV) is caused by paying a higher or lower price than the standard price set for materials. Materials price variance (MPV) is the difference between actual price paid (AP) and standard price allowed (SP) multiplied by the actual quantity of materials purchased (AQ). In equation form, the materials price variance is:

$$MPV = (AP - SP) \times AQ \text{ purchased}$$

To illustrate, assume that a new foreign supplier entered the market and the Beta Company was able to purchase 60,000 sheets of material from this supplier at a price of $5.90 each. Since the standard price set by management is $6 per sheet, the materials price variance is computed as:

$$MPV = (AP - SP) \times AQ \text{ purchased}$$
$$MPV = (\$5.90 - \$6.00) \times 60,000$$
$$MPV = \$-0.10 \times 60,000$$
$$MPV = \$-6,000 \text{ (favorable)}$$

The materials price variance of $6,000 is considered favorable since the materials were acquired for a price less than standard. (Why it is expressed as a negative amount will be explained later.) If the actual price had exceeded the standard price, the variance would be unfavorable because more costs would have been incurred than allowed by the standard.

In T-account form, the entry to record the purchase of the materials is:

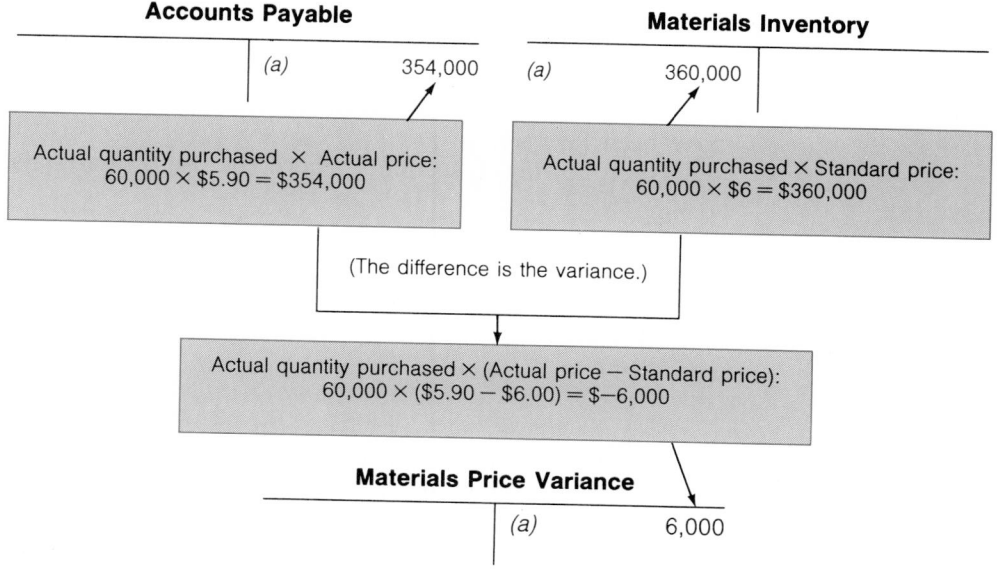

The general journal entry to record the purchase of materials is:

a. Materials Inventory 360,000
        Materials Price Variance   6,000
        Accounts Payable   354,000
    To record the purchase of materials at less than
    standard cost.

Note that the Accounts Payable account shows the actual debt owed to suppliers, while the Materials Inventory account shows the **standard** price of the actual quantity of materials **purchased.** The Materials Price Variance account shows the difference between actual price and standard price multiplied by the actual quantity purchased.

Materials Usage Variance.   Since the standard **quantity** of materials to be used in making a product is largely a matter of physical requirements or product specifications, it is usually set by the engineering department. But if the **quality** of materials used varies with price, the accounting and purchasing departments may take part in special studies to find the "right" quality.

The materials usage variance (MUV) is caused by using more or less than the standard amount of materials to produce a product or complete a process. **The variance shows only differences from standard caused by the quantity of materials used; it does not include any effect of variances in price.** Thus, the materials usage variance (MUV) is equal to actual quantity used (AQ) minus standard quantity allowed (SQ) multiplied by standard price (SP):

$$MUV = (AQ \text{ used} - SQ) \times SP$$

To illustrate, assume that the Beta Company used 55,500 sheets of materials to produce 11,000 units of a product for which the standard quantity allowed is 55,000 sheets (5 × 11,000). Since the standard price of the material is $6 per sheet, the materials usage variance of $3,000 would be computed as follows:

$$MUV = (AQ \text{ used} - SQ) \times SP$$
$$MUV = (55,500 - 55,000) \times \$6$$
$$MUV = 500 \times \$6$$
$$MUV = \$3,000 \text{ (unfavorable)}$$

The variance is unfavorable because more materials were used than the standard amount allowed to complete the job. If the standard quantity allowed had exceeded the quantity actually used, the materials usage variance would have been favorable.

The following T-accounts record the use of materials:

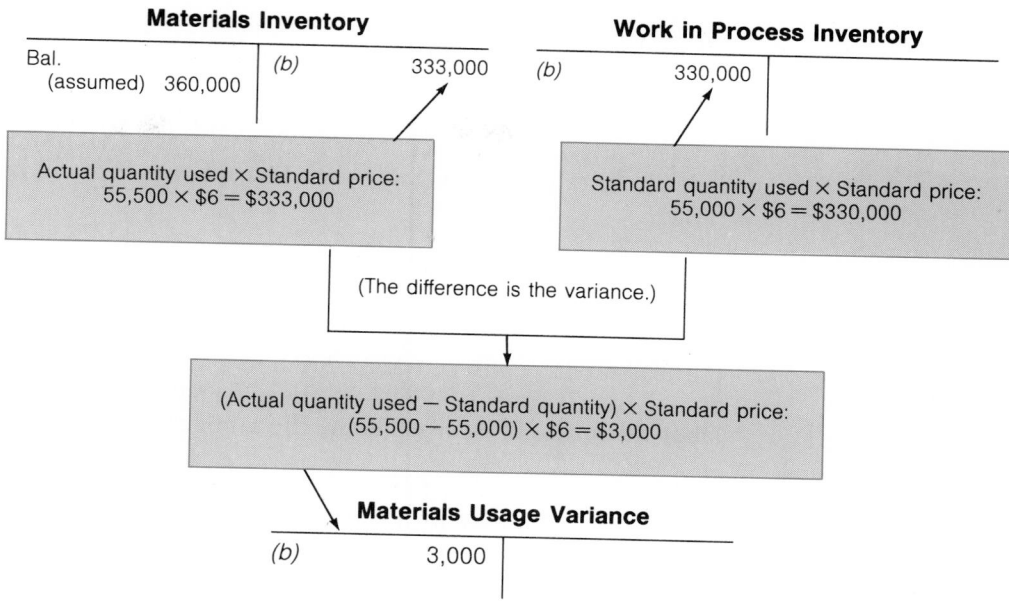

The general journal entry to record the use of materials is:

b. Work in Process Inventory 330,000
    Materials Usage Variance 3,000
        Materials Inventory 333,000
    To record the use of materials and to establish the
    materials usage variance.

The Materials Usage Variance shows the standard cost of the excess materials **used.** Note also that the Work in Process Inventory account contains both standard quantities and standard prices.

The equations for both of the above materials variances were expressed so that positive amounts were unfavorable variances and negative amounts were favorable variances. Unfavorable variances are debits in variance accounts because they add to the costs incurred, which are recorded as debits. Similarly, favorable variances are shown as negative amounts because they are reductions in costs. Thus, favorable variances are recorded in variance accounts as credits. This format will be used in this text, but a word of caution is in order. Far greater understanding is achieved if a variance is determined to be favorable or unfavorable by reliance upon reason or logic. If more materials were used than standard, or if a price greater than standard was paid, the variance is unfavorable. If the reverse is true, the variance is favorable.

Labor Variances

The standard labor cost of any product is equal to the standard quantity of labor time allowed multiplied by the wage rate that should be paid for this time. Here again it follows that the actual labor cost may differ from standard labor cost because of the **wages** paid for **labor,** the **quantity** of labor used, or both. Thus, there are two variances—a rate variance and an efficiency variance.

Labor Rate Variance.   The **labor rate variance (LRV)** is caused by paying a higher or lower rate of pay than standard to produce a product or complete a process. The labor rate variance is similar to the materials price variance.

The labor rate variance (LRV) is computed by multiplying the difference between the actual direct labor-hour rate paid (AR) and the standard direct labor-hour rate allowed (SR) by the actual hours of direct labor services required (AH):

$$LRV = (AR - SR) \times AH$$

To continue the Beta Company example, assume that the direct labor payroll of the company consisted of 22,200 hours at a total cost of $233,100 (an average actual hourly rate of $10.50). Since management has set a standard direct labor-hour rate of $10 per hour, the labor rate variance is:

$$
\begin{aligned}
LRV &= (AR - SR) \times AH \\
LRV &= (\$10.50 - \$10.00) \times 22,200 \\
LRV &= \$0.50 \times 22,200 \\
LRV &= \$11,100 \text{ (unfavorable)}
\end{aligned}
$$

The variance is positive and unfavorable because the actual rate paid exceeded the standard rate allowed. If the reverse were true, the variance would be favorable.

Labor Efficiency Variance.   The standard amount of direct labor time (hours or minutes) needed to complete a product is usually set by the company's engineering department. The direct labor time standard may be based on time and motion studies, or it may be the subject of bargaining with the employees' union. The **labor efficiency variance (LEV)** is caused by using more or less than the standard amount of direct labor-hours to produce a product or complete a process. The labor efficiency variance is similar to the materials usage variance.

The labor efficiency variance (LEV) is computed by multiplying the difference between the actual direct labor-hours required (AH) and the standard direct labor-hours allowed (SH) by the standard direct labor-hour rate per hour (SR):

$$LEV = (AH - SH) \times SR$$

To illustrate, assume that the 22,200 hours of direct labor time worked by Beta Company employees resulted in 11,000 units of production. These 11,000 units have a standard direct labor time of 22,000 hours (11,000 units at 2 hours per unit). Since the standard direct labor rate is $10 per hour, the labor efficiency variance is $2,000, computed as follows:

$$
\begin{aligned}
LEV &= (AH - SH) \times SR \\
LEV &= (22,200 - 22,000) \times \$10 \\
LEV &= 200 \times \$10 \\
LEV &= \$2,000 \text{ (unfavorable)}
\end{aligned}
$$

The variance is unfavorable since more hours than standard were required to complete the period's production. If the reverse were true, the variance would be favorable.

Illustration 23.1 shows the relationship between standard and actual direct labor cost and the computation of the labor variances; it is based on the following data relating to the Beta Company:

Standard direct labor time per unit . . . . 2 hours
Equivalent units produced in period . . . . 11,000 units
Standard labor rate per direct labor-hour $10
Total direct labor wages paid (at average rate of $10.50 per hour) . . $233,100
Actual direct labor hours worked . . . . 22,200 hours

The standard direct labor time allowed for the period's output is 22,000 hours (11,000 units at 2 hours per unit). The standard direct labor cost is $10 per hour; therefore, the standard direct labor cost for the output achieved is $220,000. The $220,000 is the amount of direct labor costs that will be assigned to inventory, regardless of the actual direct labor cost.

Illustration 23.1

Computation of Labor Variance

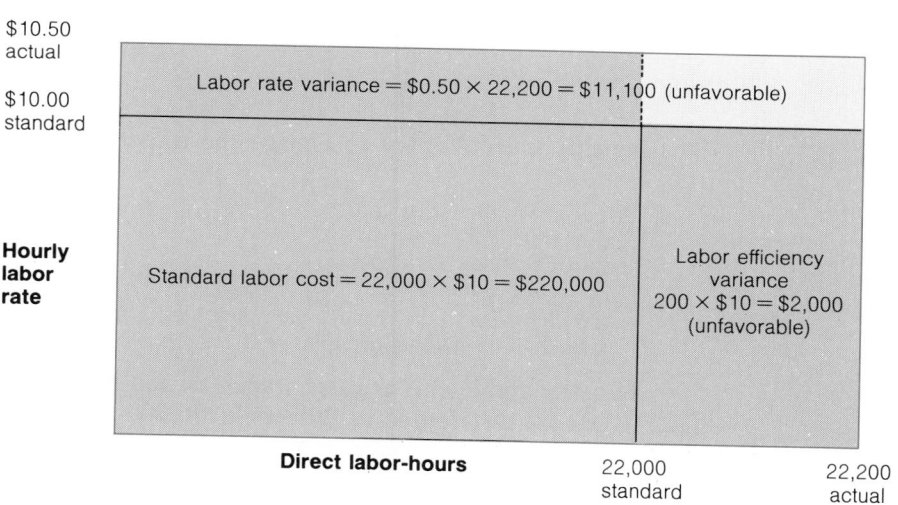

The unfavorable labor rate variance is the above-standard wages paid ($10.50 − $10.00 = $0.50 per hour) times the actual direct labor-hours worked (22,200), or $11,100. Note that the labor rate variance includes the above-standard wages paid on the 200 extra (above-standard) direct labor-hours used to secure the production—the lightly shaded area in the upper right-hand corner of Illustration 23.1. This variation from standard is actually caused by both extra hours and above-standard wages. But, as shown, it is included in the labor rate variance. The labor efficiency variance is the standard cost of the extra hours of direct labor required [(22,200 − 22,000) × $10 = $2,000]. This variance is unfavorable because more hours of direct labor were used than are allowed by the standard.

The charging of Work in Process Inventory with direct labor cost and the recording of the two labor variances for the Beta Company is shown in the T-accounts below.

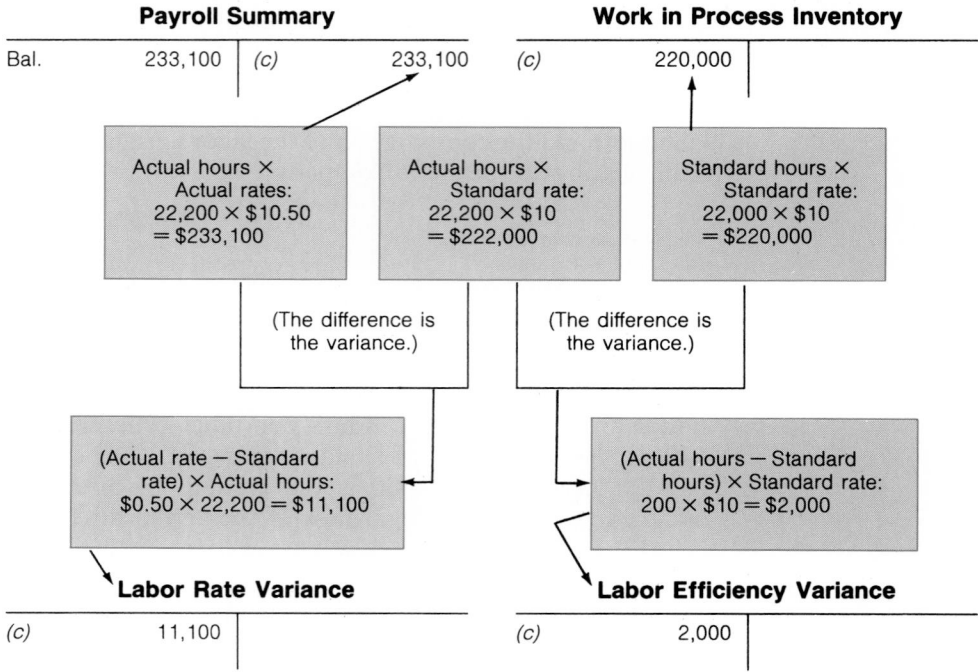

The general journal entry to charge the direct labor cost to work in process is:

c. Work in Process Inventory 220,000
   Labor Rate Variance 11,100
   Labor Efficiency Variance 2,000
       Payroll Summary 233,100
   To charge work in process with direct labor and to
   establish the two labor variances.

With the above entry, gross wages earned by direct-production employees ($233,100) are distributed as follows: $220,000 (the standard labor cost of production) to Work in Process Inventory and the balance to the two labor variance accounts. The unfavorable labor rate variance is not necessarily caused by paying employees more wages than they are entitled to receive. A more probable reason is either that more highly skilled employees (with higher wage rates) worked on production than originally anticipated, or that employee wage rates increased after the standard was developed and the standard was not revised. Favorable rate variances, on the other hand, could be caused by using less skilled (cheaper) labor in the production process. Typically, the hours of labor employed are more likely to be under management's control than the rates that are paid. For this reason, labor efficiency variances are generally watched more closely than labor rate variances.

Summary of Labor Variances. The accuracy of the two labor variances can be checked by comparing their sum with the difference between actual and standard labor cost for a period. In the Beta Company illustration, this difference was:

Actual labor cost incurred (22,200 hours × $10.50) . $233,100
Standard labor cost allowed (22,000 hours × $10) . . 220,000
Total labor variance (unfavorable) . . . . $ 13,100

This $13,100 is made up of two labor variances, both unfavorable:

Labor efficiency variance (200 × $10) . . $ 2,000
Labor rate variance (22,200 × $0.50) . .   11,100
Total labor variance (unfavorable) . . . $ 13,100

Overhead Variances

In a standard cost system, manufacturing overhead is applied to the goods produced by means of a standard overhead rate. The rate is set prior to the start of the period by dividing the budgeted manufacturing overhead cost by a standard level of output or activity. Total budgeted manufacturing overhead will vary at different levels of standard output, but, since some overhead costs are fixed, total budgeted manufacturing overhead will not vary in direct proportion with output.

A **flexible budget** is used in isolating overhead variances and may be used in setting the standard overhead rate. A flexible budget shows the budgeted amount of manufacturing overhead for various levels of output.

The flexible budget for the Beta Company for the period is shown in Illustration 23.2. Note that it shows the variable and fixed manufacturing overhead costs expected to be incurred at three levels of activity: 90%, 100%, and 110% of capacity. For product costing purposes, the expected level of activity must be estimated in advance and a rate set based on that level. **The level chosen is called the standard volume of output.** This standard volume of output (or activity) may be expressed in terms of any of the activity bases that can be used in setting overhead rates. These activity bases include percent of capacity, units of output, and direct labor-hours, among others. In our example, standard volume is assumed to be 100% of capacity. At this level of operation, 10,000 units are expected to be produced and 20,000 direct labor-hours of services are expected to be used. Assume that Beta Company applies manufacturing overhead using a rate based on direct labor-hours. According to the flexible manufacturing overhead budget, the expected manufacturing overhead cost

Illustration 23.2

Flexible Manufacturing Overhead Budget

BETA COMPANY Flexible Manufacturing Overhead Budget			
Percent of capacity	90%	100%	110%
Direct labor-hours	18,000	20,000	22,000
Units of output	9,000	10,000	11,000
Variable overhead:			
Indirect materials	$ 7,200	$ 8,000	$ 8,800
Power	9,000	10,000	11,000
Royalties	1,800	2,000	2,200
Other	18,000	20,000	22,000
Total variable overhead	$36,000	$ 40,000	$ 44,000
Fixed overhead:			
Insurance	$ 4,000	$ 4,000	$ 4,000
Property taxes	6,000	6,000	6,000
Depreciation	20,000	20,000	20,000
Other	30,000	30,000	30,000
Total fixed overhead	$60,000	$ 60,000	$ 60,000
Total manufacturing overhead	$96,000	$100,000	$104,000
Standard overhead rate ($100,000 ÷ 20,000 hours) . .		$5	

at the standard volume (20,000 direct labor-hours) is $100,000, so the standard overhead rate is $5 per direct labor-hour ($100,000 ÷ 20,000 direct labor-hours).

Knowing the separate rates for variable and fixed overhead is sometimes useful. The variable overhead rate is $2 ($40,000 ÷ 20,000 hours) per hour, and the fixed overhead rate is $3 ($60,000 ÷ 20,000 hours) per hour. If the expected volume had been 18,000 direct labor-hours (90% of capacity), the standard overhead rate would have been $5.33 ($96,000 ÷ 18,000 hours). If the standard volume had been 22,000 direct labor-hours (110% of capacity), the standard overhead rate would have been $4.73 ($104,000 ÷ 22,000 hours). Note that the difference in rates is due solely to dividing fixed overhead by a different number of units. That is, the variable overhead cost per unit stays constant ($2 per direct labor-hour) regardless of the number of units expected to be produced, and only the fixed overhead cost per unit changes.

Continuing with the Beta Company illustration, assume that the company incurred $108,000 of actual manufacturing overhead costs in a period during which 11,000 units of product were produced. The actual costs would be debited to Manufacturing Overhead and credited to a variety of accounts such as Accounts Payable, Accumulated Depreciation, Prepaid Insurance, Accrued Property Taxes Payable, and so on. According to the flexible budget, the standard number of direct labor-hours allowed for 11,000 units of production is 22,000 hours. Therefore, $110,000 of manufacturing overhead is applied to production ($5 per direct labor-hour times 22,000 hours) by debiting Work in Process Inventory and crediting Manufacturing Overhead for $110,000.

The entry, in T-account form, to record the application of $110,000 of manufacturing overhead to production (22,000 hours at $5 per hour) would be:

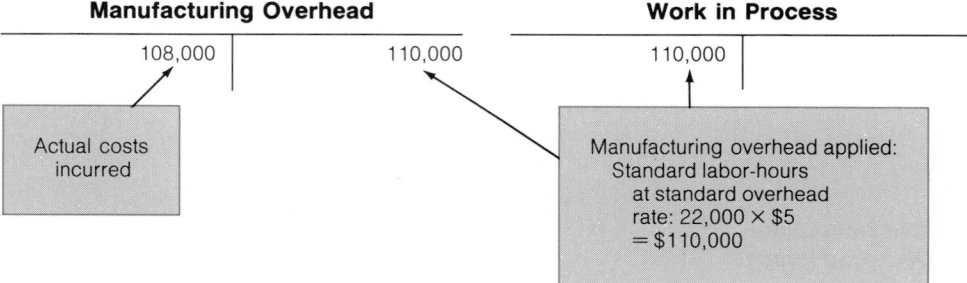

The general journal entry to apply manufacturing overhead to production would be:

```
Work in Process  . . . . . . . . . . . . . . . . . . . . . .   110,000
    Manufacturing Overhead .  . . . . . . . . . . . . .                110,000
    To apply manufacturing overhead to production (22,000
    hours at $5 per hour).
```

The above accounts show that manufacturing overhead has been overapplied to production by the $2,000 credit balance in the Manufacturing Overhead account. Manufacturing overhead will tend to be overapplied when actual production is greater than standard production.

The rate of $5 (which was based on output of 10,000 units) was used to apply manufacturing overhead when actual output was 11,000 units. The $5 is a **predetermined** rate set at the beginning of the year, when management **expected** to produce 10,000 units. Actual production achieved is not known until year-end.

Although various complex computations can be made for overhead variances, a simple approach will be used in this text. In this approach, known as the two-variance approach to overhead variances, only two variances are calculated—an overhead budget variance and an overhead volume variance.

The Overhead Budget Variance.   The overhead budget variance (OBV) (also called the spending or controllable variance) shows in one amount how economically overhead services were purchased and how efficiently they were used. This overhead variance is similar to a combined price and usage variance for materials or labor. The overhead budget variance (OBV) is equal to the difference between total actual overhead costs (Actual OH) and total budgeted overhead costs (BOH) for the **actual output attained.**

Total budgeted overhead costs are calculated as the variable overhead rate times the **standard direct labor-hours allowed for production achieved,** plus the constant amount of fixed overhead. For the Beta Company, this would be $2 variable overhead times 22,000 hours (11,000 units × 2 hours per unit), or $44,000 variable overhead plus $60,000 of fixed overhead—a total of $104,000. Since the total actual overhead was $108,000 and the total budgeted overhead was $104,000, then the overhead budget variance is computed as follows:

$$\text{OBV} = \text{Actual OH} - \text{BOH}$$
$$\text{OBV} = \$108,000 - \$104,000$$
$$\text{OBV} = \$4,000 \text{ (unfavorable)}$$

The variance is unfavorable because actual overhead costs were $108,000, while, according to the flexible budget, they should have been $104,000.

Overhead Volume Variance.   The overhead volume variance (OVV) is caused by producing at a level other than that used in setting the standard overhead application rate. The OVV shows whether plant assets produced more or fewer goods than expected. Because fixed overhead is not constant on a per unit basis, any deviation from planned production will cause the overhead application rate to be incorrect. The OVV is the difference between the budgeted amount of overhead for the **actual volume achieved** (BOH) and the applied overhead (Applied OH):

$$\text{OVV} = \text{BOH} - \text{Applied OH}$$

In the Beta Company illustration, the 11,000 units produced in the period have a standard labor allowance of 22,000 hours. Budgeted overhead was calculated when we computed the overhead budget variance. The flexible budget in Illustration 23.2 shows that the budgeted overhead for 22,000 direct labor-hours is $104,000. Overhead is applied to work in process on the basis of standard hours allowed for a particular amount of production, in this case 22,000 hours at $5 per hour. The overhead volume variance then is:

$$\text{OVV} = \text{BOH} - \text{Applied OH}$$
$$\text{OVV} = \$104,000 - \$110,000$$
$$\text{OVV} = \$-6,000 \text{ (favorable)}$$

Note that the amount of the overhead volume variance is related solely to fixed overhead. As Illustration 23.2 shows, fixed overhead at all levels of activity is $60,000. Since Beta Company used 100% of capacity, or 20,000 direct labor-hours, as its standard, the fixed overhead rate is $3 per direct labor-hour. Beta worked 2,000 (22,000 − 20,000) more standard hours than was expected. The overhead volume variance can also be calculated as follows:

$$\begin{pmatrix} \text{Number of hours} \\ \text{used in setting} \\ \text{predetermined} \\ \text{overhead rates} \end{pmatrix} - \begin{pmatrix} \text{Number of standard} \\ \text{hours allowed} \\ \text{for production} \\ \text{level achieved} \end{pmatrix} \times \begin{matrix} \text{Fixed over-} \\ \text{head rate} \\ \text{per hour} \end{matrix} = \begin{matrix} \text{Overhead} \\ \text{volume} \\ \text{variance} \end{matrix}$$

$$(20,000 \quad - \quad 22,000) \quad \times \quad \$3 \quad = \quad \$-6,000 \\ \text{(favorable)}$$

The variance is favorable since the company achieved a higher level of production than was expected.

Recording Overhead Variances.   Formal entries are made in the accounts showing the two parts of the $2,000 net overhead variance. The T-account entry for the Beta Company would be as follows (the debits and credits are keyed with the letter [f]):

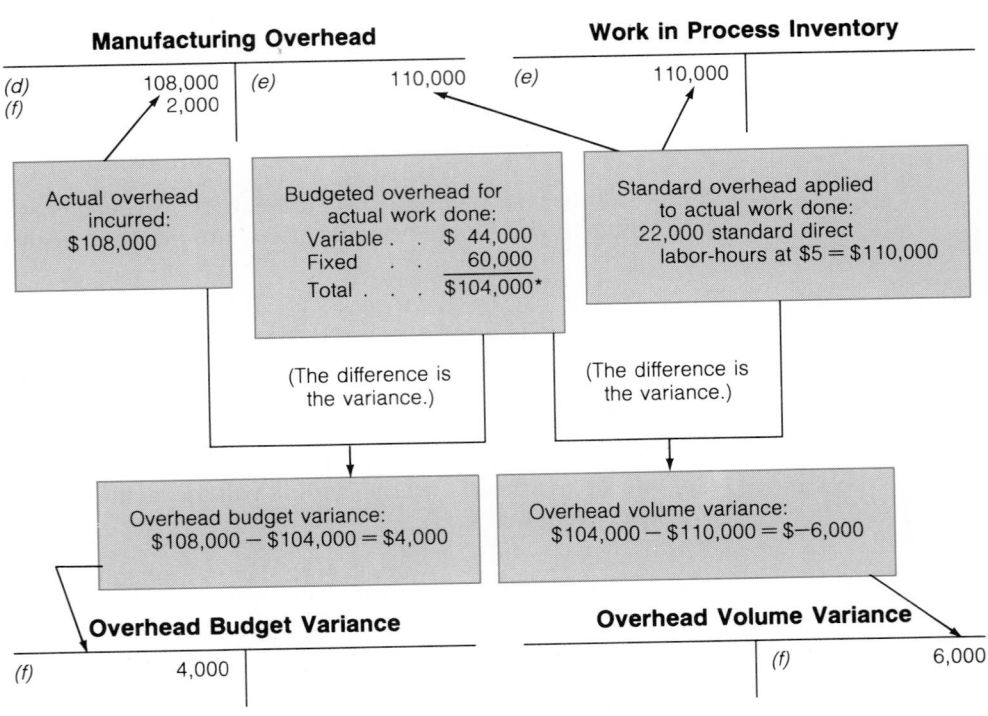

* From flexible budget. See Illustration 23.2.

The general journal entries related to overhead are as follows:

d. Manufacturing Overhead 108,000
        Various Accounts   108,000
    To record actual manufacturing overhead.

e. Work in Process   110,000
          Manufacturing Overhead   110,000
      To record the application of manufacturing overhead
      to work in process.

f. Manufacturing Overhead   2,000
    Overhead Budget Variance   4,000
          Overhead Volume Variance   6,000
      To record the variances related to overhead and close
      the Manufacturing Overhead account.

The first entry records the actual manufacturing overhead costs incurred during the period by Beta Company. The second entry applies manufacturing overhead to Work in Process at the rate of $5 per standard direct labor-hour (22,000). The final entry reduces the Manufacturing Overhead account balance to zero and recognizes the two variances calculated for overhead; these two variance accounts analyze the causes of the overapplied manufacturing overhead for the period.

Summary of Overhead Variances.   The accuracy of the two overhead variances can be easily determined by comparing the sum of the budget and volume variances with the difference between the costs of actual manufacturing overhead and applied manufacturing overhead (the amount of over- or underapplied overhead). For the Beta Company example, the difference between actual and applied manufacturing overhead was:

Actual manufacturing overhead incurred $108,000
Applied manufacturing overhead allowed (22,000 direct labor-hours
   × $5 per hour)   110,000
Total overhead variance (favorable) . . . . $ −2,000

This difference is made up of the two overhead variances:

Overhead budget variance—Unfavorable ($108,000 − $104,000) . . . . $ 4,000
Overhead volume variance—Favorable [$104,000 − (22,000 × $5)] . . .   −6,000
Total overhead variance (favorable) . . . . $−2,000

GOODS COMPLETED AND SOLD

To complete the standard cost system example using the Beta Company, assume that 11,000 units were completed and transferred to finished goods, 10,000 units were sold on account at a price equal to 160% of standard cost, there was no beginning or ending work in process inventory, and there was no finished goods beginning inventory. In the T-accounts below, entry *(g)* shows the transfer of the standard cost of the units completed, $660,000 (11,000 × $60), from Work in Process Inventory to Finished Goods Inventory. Entry *(h)* records the sales for the period, $960,000 (160% × $60 × 10,000). Entry *(i)* records the cost of goods sold, $600,000 (10,000 × $60).

Work in Process Inventory

(b)	Materials	330,000	(g)	Completed	660,000
(c)	Labor	220,000			
(e)	Manufacturing overhead	110,000			

Finished Goods Inventory

(g)	Completed	660,000	(i)	Sold	600,000

Accounts Receivable		**Cost of Goods Sold**	
(h) 960,000		(i) Sold 600,000	

Sales

	(h)	960,000

In journal entry form, entries *(g)*, *(h)*, and *(i)* are:

g. Finished Goods Inventory 660,000
    Work in Process Inventory   660,000
   To record the transfer of completed units to finished
   goods inventory.

h. Accounts Receivable 960,000
    Sales   960,000
   To record sales for the period.

i. Cost of Goods Sold 600,000
    Merchandise Inventory   600,000
   To record cost of goods sold for the period.

Work in Process Inventory has been debited with the standard cost of materials, labor, and manufacturing overhead for units put into production. Therefore, the entry recording the transfer of the standard cost of the completed units, $660,000 (11,000 × $60), reduces Work in Process Inventory to a zero balance. Note that Finished Goods Inventory is debited with the standard cost of goods completed and credited with the standard cost of goods sold. Thus, ending finished goods inventory consists of the units actually on hand (1,000) at their standard cost of $60 each, or $60,000. Sales for the period amount to 10,000 units at $96 each (160% of $60). It is fairly common practice to base selling prices at least partially on standard costs.

■ INVESTIGATING VARIANCES FROM STANDARD

Once all variances have been computed, management must decide which ones should be investigated further. Since numerous variances will occur, not all of them can be investigated. Management needs some selection guides. Possible guides include the (1) amount of the variance; (2) size of the variance relative to cost incurred; and (3) controllability of the cost associated with the variance—that is, whether it is considered controllable or noncontrollable. Statistical analysis may also be used in deciding which variances to investigate. For instance, the average value of actual costs could be determined for a period of time so that only those variances deviating from the average by more than a certain amount or percentage would be investigated. To decide which selection guides are most useful, management should seek the opinions of knowledgeable operating personnel.

Any analysis of variances is likely to disclose some variances that are controllable within the company and others that are not. For instance, quantities used are generally controllable internally. Prices paid for materials purchased may or may not be controllable. Management may discover that the purchasing agent is not getting competitive bids; therefore, the price paid for materials would have been controllable by seeking competitive bids. On the other hand, a raw materials shortage may exist which drives the price upward, and the price paid is beyond the buyer's control.

Another point to remember about the analysis of variances is that separate variances are not necessarily independent. For example, an unfavorable labor rate variance may result from using higher paid employees in a certain task. However, higher paid employees may be more productive, resulting in a favorable labor efficiency variance. These employees may also be more highly skilled and may waste less material, resulting in a favorable materials usage variance. Therefore, significant variances, both favorable and unfavorable, should be investigated.

■ DISPOSING OF VARIANCES FROM STANDARD

At the end of the year, variances from standard must be disposed of in the accounting records. The variances may be (1) viewed as losses due to inefficiency and closed to Income Summary; (2) allocated as adjustments to the recorded cost of Work in Process Inventory, Finished Goods Inventory, and Cost of Goods Sold; or (3) closed to Cost of Goods Sold. Theoretically, the alternative chosen should depend upon whether the standards set were reasonably attainable and whether the variances were controllable by company employees. For instance, an unfavorable materials usage or labor efficiency variance caused by carelessness or inefficiency may be considered a loss and closed to Income Summary because the standard was attainable and the variance was controllable. An unfavorable materials price variance caused by an unexpected price change may be considered an added cost and allocated to the inventory accounts and Cost of Goods Sold because the standard was unattainable and the variance was uncontrollable. As a practical matter, and especially if they are small, variances are usually closed to the Cost of Goods Sold account rather than allocated to the inventory accounts and to cost of goods sold.

Entry *(j)* in the T-accounts below reflects this practical disposition of the variances in the continuing example of the Beta Company:

Materials Price Variance		
(j)	6,000	(a)	6,000

Materials Usage Variance		
(b)	3,000	(j)	3,000

Labor Rate Variance		
(c)	11,100	(j)	11,100

Labor Efficiency Variance		
(c)	2,000	(j)	2,000

Overhead Budget Variance		
(f)	4,000	(j)	4,000

Overhead Volume Variance		
(j)	6,000	(f)	6,000

Cost of Goods Sold	
(i)	600,000
(j)	8,100

In general journal entry form, entry (j) is

```
j.   Materials Price Variance . . . . . . . . . . . . .   6,000
     Overhead Volume Variance . . . . . . . . . . . .   6,000
     Cost of Goods Sold . . . . . . . . . . . . . . .   8,100
         Materials Usage Variance . . . . . . . . . .          3,000
         Labor Rate Variance . . . . . . . . . . . .          11,100
         Labor Efficiency Variance . . . . . . . . .           2,000
         Overhead Budget Variance . . . . . . . . . .           4,000
     To close the variance accounts.
```

Variances are not reported separately in financial statements released to the public, but are simply included in the reported cost of goods sold amount. In reports prepared for internal use, the variances may be listed separately after cost of goods sold is shown at standard cost.

■ ADVANTAGES OF USING STANDARD COSTS

A number of benefits result from the use of a standard cost system. These include:

1. Improved cost control.
2. More useful information for managerial planning and decision making.
3. More reasonable inventory measurements.
4. Cost savings in record-keeping.
5. Possible reductions in production costs incurred.

Improved Cost Control. Cost control is gained mainly by setting standards for each type of cost incurred and then highlighting **exceptions,** or variances—instances where things are not going as planned. Variances provide a starting point for judging the effectiveness of managers in controlling the costs for which they are held responsible.

Assume, for example, that in a certain production center, actual direct materials cost was $52,015 and exceeded standard cost by $6,015. Knowing that actual direct materials cost exceeded standard cost by $6,015 is more useful than merely knowing actual direct materials cost amounted to $52,015. Now the cause of the excess of actual cost over standard cost can be investigated and action can be taken. Further investigation will show whether the exception was caused by factors under management's control. The exception (variance) may be caused by inefficient use of materials, or it may be the result of higher prices due to inflation. In either case, the standard cost system has served as an early warning system by highlighting a potential hazard for management.

More Useful Information for Managerial Planning and Decision Making. When management develops appropriate cost standards and succeeds in controlling production costs, then future actual costs should be fairly close to standard. As a result, standard costs can be used in preparing more accurate budgets and in estimating costs for bidding on jobs. A standard cost system can be valuable in top management planning and decision making.

More Reasonable Inventory Measurements. A standard cost system provides a more logical inventory valuation than an actual cost system. Unit costs for batches of identical products may differ widely under an actual cost system. This difference may be caused by a machine malfunction during the production of a given batch that resulted in more labor and overhead being charged to that batch. Under a standard cost system such costs would not be included in inventory. Rather, they would be charged to variance accounts after comparing actual costs to standard costs. Thus, in a standard cost system, all units of a given product are carried in inventory at the same unit cost. Logically, identical physical units produced in a given time period should be recorded at the same cost.

Cost Savings in Record-Keeping. Although a standard cost system may seem to require more detailed record-keeping than an actual cost system, the reverse is true. For example, in a job order system, detailed records must be kept of various types of materials used on each job as well as the various types and quantities of labor services received. In a standard cost system, standard cost sheets may be printed in advance showing quantities, unit costs, and total costs for the materials, labor, and overhead needed to produce a given amount of a certain product.

Possible Reductions in Production Costs Incurred. A standard cost system may lead to cost savings. The use of standard costs may cause employees to become more cost conscious and thus seek improved methods of completing their tasks. Only when employees become active in reducing costs can companies really become successful in cost control.

■ *SUMMARY*

A standard cost system gathers information about manufacturing costs incurred and the efficiency of manufacturing operations during the accounting period. A standard cost system can be used in both job order and process cost systems.

Standard costs are carefully predetermined measures of what costs should be under stated conditions. For each type of product manufactured, standard costs are established for **direct materials, direct labor,** and **manufacturing overhead.** The standard cost for each product unit produced is the sum of its standard direct materials cost, standard direct labor cost, and standard manufacturing overhead cost.

The amount by which the actual cost of a product unit differs from the standard cost of the unit is an exception or variance. A standard cost system highlights these variances. Six different types of variances are normally computed: materials price variance, materials usage variance, labor rate variance, labor efficiency variance, overhead budget variance, and overhead volume variance. Once variances are computed, management must decide which variances should be investigated further to determine the underlying causes of the variances.

Three inventory accounts—Materials Inventory, Work in Process Inventory, and Finished Goods Inventory—are carried at standard cost. Variances from standard are recorded separately in the respective variance accounts. At the end of the accounting period, variances must be disposed of in the accounting records. The variances may be (1) considered as losses due to inefficiency and closed to Income Summary; (2) allocated as adjustments to the recorded cost of Work in Process Inventory, Finished Goods Inventory, and Cost of Goods Sold; or (3) closed to Cost of Goods Sold. Theoretically, the alternative chosen by management to dispose of the variances should depend on whether the standards set were reasonably attainable and whether the variances were controllable by company employees. In actual practice, variances are usually closed to Cost of Goods Sold.

By using standard costs to control actual costs, management assumes responsibility for reducing the production costs of its products. In Chapter 24, you will learn about responsibility accounting in a broader sense. Many successful companies rely on responsibility accounting to make their business operations profitable.

APPENDIX: APPLYING STANDARD COSTS IN JOB ORDER AND PROCESS COST SYSTEMS

■ STANDARD COSTS IN A JOB ORDER COST SYSTEM

In a job order cost system, production quantities are known in advance. Thus, some variances can be isolated much earlier than in a process cost system (in which equivalent production is known only at the end of a period). This early isolation of variances is illustrated in the following example.

Assume that Company A accounts for the manufacture of its products in a job order cost system using standard costs. Its flexible budget shows that at the standard level of output, variable overhead is $24,000 and fixed overhead is $16,000 per month. At the standard activity level of 8,000 direct labor-hours, these figures yield a standard overhead rate of $5 per direct labor-hour. The variable portion of this rate is $3 ($24,000 ÷ 8,000 hours), and the fixed portion is $2 ($16,000 ÷ 8,000 hours).

Company A had no work in process inventory as of June 1. The standard specifications for the two jobs started during June are given below:

	Job 101	Job 102
Direct materials . . .	$20,000	$50,000
Direct labor:		
2,000 hours at $4 . .	8,000	
5,000 hours at $4 . .		20,000
Overhead:		
2,000 hours at $5 . .	10,000	
5,000 hours at $5 . .		25,000
Total standard cost . .	$38,000	$95,000

Company A's activities for June 1987 are summarized as follows:

a. Materials with a standard cost of $79,500 were purchased on account at an actual price of $80,150.

b. Standard direct materials were issued for both jobs. In addition, excess materials were requisitioned: Job No. 101, $400; and Job No. 102, $700.

c. Analysis of the factory payrolls debited to Payroll Summary shows they consisted of $10,000 of indirect labor ($4,000 variable and $6,000 fixed), and 6,000 hours of direct labor (Job No. 101, 1,980 hours and Job No. 102, 4,020 hours) at a cost of $24,600. Job No. 101 was completed.

d. Various overhead costs were incurred: variable, $14,500; and fixed, $10,200.

e. Standard overhead was assigned to production: Job No. 101, $10,000 (2,000 hours at $5 per hour), and Job No. 102, $20,100 (4,020 hours at $5 per hour). Even though Job No. 102 was incomplete at the end of the month, overhead needs to be assigned to it for proper valuation of Work in Process Inventory on the balance sheet.

f. Job No. 101 was completed and transferred to the finished goods storeroom.

g. Sales for the month—all units in Job No. 101 at a total price of $60,000.

The entries to record the above information and isolate the variances follow:

a. Materials Inventory 79,500
    Materials Price Variance 650
        Accounts Payable 80,150
        To record purchase of materials and to isolate materials
        price variance.

b. Work in Process Inventory 70,000
    Materials Usage Variance 1,100
        Materials Inventory 71,100
        To charge standard materials to production and to charge
        excess materials requisitioned to a variance account.

c. Work in Process Inventory 24,080
    Manufacturing Overhead 10,000
    Labor Rate Variance 600
        Labor Efficiency Variance 80
        Payroll Summary 34,600
        To distribute labor costs and to isolate labor variances:

        Job No. 101 (2,000 hours at $4) . . . . . . $ 8,000
        Job No. 102 (4,020 hours at $4) 16,080
        Total labor to Work in Process Inventory . . . $24,080

    Labor efficiency variance on Job No. 101: (1,980 actual
    hours — 2,000 standard hours) × $4 = $—80 (favorable).
    Labor rate variance: ($4.10 actual wage rate — $4.00 standard
    rate) × 6,000 hours = $600 (unfavorable).

d. Manufacturing Overhead 24,700
   Accounts Payable (and various other accounts) . . .   24,700
  To record incurrence of overhead costs.

e. Work in Process Inventory 30,100
   Manufacturing Overhead   30,100
  To apply standard overhead to production: Job No. 101—
  $10,000 (standard amount, job completed); Job No. 102—
  4,020 hours at $5 = $20,100 (based on standard labor,
  job incomplete).

f. Finished Goods Inventory 38,000
   Work in Process Inventory   38,000
  To record transfer of completed Job No. 101 at standard.

g. Accounts Receivable 60,000
   Sales   60,000
  To record sales for the month.

  Cost of Goods Sold 38,000
   Finished Goods Inventory   38,000
  To record cost of goods sold (Job No. 101, $38,000).

Note that in the above entries the materials and labor variances are isolated rather routinely in the recording process. But the overhead variances must be computed separately at the end of the period, unless standard production for the period is known earlier. For Company A, the overhead variances are computed as follows:

Overhead budget variance:
 Actual overhead (entries *[c]* and *[d]* above) $34,700
 Budgeted overhead (from flexible budget)
  (6,020* standard hours at $3 variable
  overhead + $16,000 fixed overhead) 34,060
   Unfavorable overhead budget variance . . . . . $ 640

Overhead volume variance:
 Budgeted overhead [(6,020* hours × $3) + $16,000] . . $34,060
 Standard overhead applied to production
  (6,020* hours at $5) 30,100
   Unfavorable overhead volume variance   3,960
Total unfavorable overhead variance $4,600

* 6,020 hours are used in the calculations because standard hours allowed for Job No. 101 are 2,000 and standard hours allowed this far on Job No. 202 are 4,020 for a total of 6,020 hours.

The following entry isolates the two overhead variances in the accounts:

Overhead Budget Variance 640
Overhead Volume Variance 3,960
  Manufacturing Overhead   4,600
  To set up separate overhead variance accounts.

Note that the credit to Manufacturing Overhead of $4,600 reduces that account to a zero balance (for previous entries to the account, see entries *[c], [d],* and *[e]* above), thus proving the accuracy of the computations.

Typically, the overhead variances and the materials and labor variances are summarized in a report prepared periodically for internal management. Such a report could be called a "Summary of Variances from Standard."

■ STANDARD COSTS IN A PROCESS COST SYSTEM

To provide a brief illustration of how standard costs might be incorporated into a process cost system, assume that Company P manufactures a product for which the standard specifications are:

Materials—2 pounds at $2 per pound	$4.00
Direct labor—0.5 hours at $4 per hour	2.00
Overhead—0.5 hours at $3 per hour	1.50
Total standard cost	$7.50

The fixed overhead included in the standard cost is based on a monthly flexible budget that shows budgeted variable overhead of $120,000 and budgeted fixed overhead of $60,000 at a standard activity level of 60,000 standard direct labor-hours. Thus, the variable overhead rate is $2 per direct labor-hour ($120,000 ÷ 60,000 hours), and the fixed overhead rate is $1 per direct labor-hour ($60,000 ÷ 60,000 hours). Since each unit only requires one-half hour to produce, total overhead assignable per unit is $1.50 ($3 per hour × ½ hour).

This example makes one change in the standard cost system illustrated earlier in the chapter: Work in Process will be charged with actual quantities and actual costs rather than standard quantities and standard costs, as shown previously. The variances will be calculated and placed in variance accounts at the end of the month. Alternatively, the materials price variance could be recorded when materials are purchased, and the labor rate variance could be recorded when direct labor is charged to Work in Process Inventory.

The entries to the Work in Process Inventory account for the month of May are summarized below:

Direct materials (180,500 pounds at $2.02)	$364,610
Direct labor (40,100 hours at $3.95)	158,395
Actual fixed overhead	58,700
Actual variable overhead	80,500
Total cost put into production	$662,205
Standard cost of units completed and transferred (70,000 at $7.50)	525,000
Balance, May 31, 1987	$137,205

Production records show that 70,000 units were completed and transferred and that 20,000 units of the product remain in process at the end of the month. These units are complete as to materials and 50% complete as to conversion. From this information, the equivalent production for the period in terms of standard units of product can be computed as follows:

	Materials	Labor and overhead (conversion)
Units started and finished	70,000	70,000
Equivalent units in ending inventory	20,000	10,000
Equivalent production	90,000	80,000

We now have enough information to calculate all of the variances presented in the "Summary of Variances from Standard" shown in Illustration 23.3.

Illustration 23.3

Summary of Variances from Standard

COMPANY P
Summary of Variances from Standard
Month Ended May 31, 1987

Materials:
Price variance (180,500 pounds × $0.02) . . . . $ 3,610
Usage variance (500 pounds × $2) 1,000

  Total unfavorable materials variance . . . . $ 4,610
Labor:
Rate variance (40,100 hours × $−0.05) . . . . . . $−2,005
Efficiency variance (100 hours × $4) 400

  Net favorable labor variance . . . . −1,605
Overhead:
Budget variance [fixed ($58,700 − $60,000) + variable
  ($80,500 − $80,000*)] . . . . $ −800
Volume variance ($140,000 − $120,000) 20,000

  Net unfavorable overhead variance 19,200
Total variance from standard for the month $22,205

* (40,000 hours × $2).

Since the actual price paid for materials was $0.02 per pound above standard, the materials price variance is the actual usage of 180,500 pounds multiplied by $0.02. Since the standard materials allowed for 90,000 equivalent units is 180,000 pounds (90,000 × 2), the materials usage variance is $1,000 (500 pounds × $2). Both variances are unfavorable.

The average wage rate paid employees was $0.05 less than standard, resulting in a favorable rate variance of this amount multiplied by actual hours of 40,100. The standard labor-hours allowed for the production of the period (80,000 × 0.5 hours) is 100 hours less than the actual direct labor-hours used. Hence, an unfavorable labor efficiency variance was experienced.

Fixed overhead costs were $1,300 ($58,700 − $60,000) less than their budgeted amount, while variable overhead costs exceeded their **budgeted amount** for the actual production in May by $500 [$80,500 − (40,000 × $2)]. Together, these costs yield a net favorable variance of $800. Because the standard overhead applied to production of $120,000 (40,000 standard direct labor-hours × $3) is less than the budgeted overhead for the month of $140,000 [(40,000 standard direct-labor hours × $2) + $60,000], there is an unfavorable volume variance of $20,000. These variances amount to a net unfavorable overhead variance of $19,200. Added together, the materials, labor, and overhead variances amount to $22,205, the total variance (unfavorable) from standard for the month.

The variances shown in Illustration 23.3 can be formally recorded in the accounts by the following entry, thus removing the month's variances from Work in Process Inventory:

Materials Price Variance 3,610
Materials Usage Variance 1,000
Labor Efficiency Variance 400
Overhead Volume Variance 20,000
  Labor Rate Variance 2,005
  Overhead Budget Variance 800
  Work in Process Inventory 22,205
  To set up variances from standard for the month.

Subtracting the $22,205 from the previously given balance of $137,205 in the Work in Process Inventory account leaves a balance of $115,000, which is equal to the standard cost of the ending inventory. The standard cost of the ending inventory can be separately computed as follows:

Direct materials (20,000 units, 100% complete, unit cost $4)	$ 80,000
Direct labor (20,000 units, 50% complete, unit cost $2) . .	20,000
Overhead (20,000 units, 50% complete, unit cost $1.50) . .	15,000
Total standard cost of ending inventory	$115,000

NEW TERMS INTRODUCED IN CHAPTER 23

Flexible budget

A budget that shows the expected amount of overhead for various levels of output; used in isolating overhead variances and setting standard overhead rates (905).

Labor efficiency variance (LEV)

A variance from standard caused by using more or less than the standard amount of direct labor-hours to produce a product or complete a process; computed as (Actual direct labor-hours − Standard direct labor-hours) × Standard rate per hour (902).

Labor rate variance (LRV)

A variance from standard caused by paying a higher or lower average rate of pay than standard to produce a product or complete a process; computed as (Actual rate per hour − Standard rate per direct labor-hour) × Actual direct labor-hours worked (902).

Materials price variance (MPV)

A variance from standard caused by paying a higher or lower price than standard for materials purchased; computed as (Actual price − Standard price) × Actual quantity purchased (899).

Materials usage variance (MUV)

A variance from standard caused by using more or less than the standard amount of materials to produce a product or complete a process; computed as (Actual quantity used − Standard quantity allowed) × Standard price (900).

Overhead budget variance (OBV)

A variance from standard caused by incurring more or less than the standard manufacturing overhead for the actual production volume achieved, as shown by a flexible budget; computed as Actual overhead − Budgeted overhead at actual production volume level (907).

Overhead volume variance (OVV)

A variance from standard caused by producing at a level other than that used in setting the standard overhead rates; computed as Budgeted overhead − Applied overhead (907).

Standard cost

A carefully predetermined measure of what a cost should be under stated conditions (897).

Standard level of output

A carefully predetermined measure of what the expected level of output should be for a specified period of time, usually one year (897).

Variance

A deviation of actual costs from standard costs; may be favorable or unfavorable. That is, actual costs may be less than or more than standard costs. Variances may relate to materials, labor, or manufacturing overhead (898).

DEMONSTRATION PROBLEM

The Baxter Company manufactures children's toys that are all identical. The standard cost of each toy is:

Direct materials:
Three blocks of wood at $0.20 . . $0.60
Direct labor (1 hour at $5) 5.00

Overhead:
Fixed ($18,000 ÷ 60,000 units) . .   0.30
Variable 0.40
                                       $6.30

The standard overhead rate is based on a volume of 60,000 units per month. In May, 50,000 units were manufactured. Detailed data relative to production are summarized below:

Materials purchased:
160,000 blocks of wood at $0.22
Materials used:
152,000 blocks of wood
Direct labor: 49,000 hours at $5.10
Fixed manufacturing overhead: $18,200
Variable manufacturing overhead: $20,350

From the above data, compute the six variances from standard for the month.

Solution to demonstration problem

Materials price variance:
($0.22 − $0.20) × 160,000 . . . . . $3,200 (unfavorable)

Materials usage variance:
(152,000 − 150,000*) × $0.20 . . . .   400 (unfavorable)
    Net materials variance . . . . . . $3,600 (unfavorable)

Labor rate variance:
($5.10 − $5.00) × 49,000 . . . . . $4,900 (unfavorable)

Labor efficiency variance:
(49,000 − 50,000) × $5.00 . . . . .   −5,000 (favorable)
    Total labor variance . . . . . .   −100 (favorable)

Overhead budget variance:
Actual ($18,200 + $20,350) $38,550
Budgeted [$18,000 + (50,000 ×
$0.40)]   38,000
    Overhead budget variance . . . . $ 550 (unfavorable)

Overhead volume variance:
Budgeted − Applied [$38,000 −
(50,000 × $0.70)] . . . .   3,000 (unfavorable)
    Total overhead variance . . . . .   3,550 (unfavorable)
Total variance for month . . . . . . $7,050 (unfavorable)

* 50,000 units × 3 blocks per unit.

QUESTIONS

1. Is a standard cost an estimated cost? What is the primary objective of employing standard costs in a cost system? What are some of the other advantages of using standard costs?

2. Describe how the materials price and usage variances would be computed from the following data:

Standard—1 unit of material at $20 per unit.
Purchased—1,200 units of material at $20.25; used—
  995 units.
Production—1,000 units of finished goods.

3. When might a given company have a substantial favorable materials price variance and a substantial unfavorable materials usage variance?

4. What is the usual cause of a favorable or unfavorable labor rate variance? What other labor variance is isolated in a standard cost system? Of the two variances, which is more likely to be under the control of management? Explain.

5. Identify the type of variance indicated by each situation below and indicate whether it is favorable or unfavorable.

a. The cutting department of a company during the week ending July 15 cut 12 size-S cogged wheels out of three sheets of 12-inch high-tempered steel. Usually three wheels of such size are cut out of each sheet.

b. A company purchased and installed an expensive new cutting machine to handle expanding orders. This purchase and the related depreciation had not been anticipated when the overhead rate was set.

c. Edwards, the band saw operator, was on vacation last week. Lands took his place for the normal 40-hour week. Edwards' wage rate is $5.40 per hour, while Lands's is $5.20 per hour. Production was at capacity last week and the week before.

6. Theoretically, how should an accountant dispose of variances from standard? How does an accountant typically dispose of variances?

7. Why are variances typically isolated as soon as possible?

8. Is it correct to consider favorable variances as always being desirable? Explain.

9. Why is it said that the use of standard costs permits the application of the principle of management by exception?

10. How do standards help in controlling production costs?

EXERCISES

E–1

Compute materials variances

During January, the cutting department completed 1,000 units of a product that had a standard materials cost of 2 square feet per unit at $1.20 per square foot. The actual material purchased consisted of 2,050 square feet at $1.10 per square foot, for a total cost of $2,255. The actual material used this period was 2,020 square feet. Compute the materials price and usage variances, indicating whether each is favorable or unfavorable

E–2

Compute materials variances; comment on possible causes

Hill Company produces a product which has the following standard costs:

Direct materials—4 pounds at $5 per pound	. . .	$20
Direct labor—3 hours at $6 per hour	. . . . . .	18
Manufacturing overhead—150% of direct labor	. .	27
		$65

Hill's purchasing agent took advantage of a special offer from one of its suppliers to purchase 88,000 pounds of material at $4.10 per pound. Assume 11,000 units were produced and 68,200 pounds of material were used. Compute the variances for materials. Comment on the purchasing agent's decision to take the special offer.

E–3

Compute labor variances

Compute the labor variances in the following situation:

Actual direct labor payroll (21,500 hours at $4.50)	. . . . .	$96,750
Standard direct labor allowed per unit, 3.5 hours at $4.80 .	.	$ 16.80
Production for month (in units)		5,500

E–4

Compute labor variances for two departments

During September, 150 units of a certain product were produced. This product has a standard direct labor cost of two hours per unit at $4.20 per hour in Department 1 and one hour per unit at $6 per hour in Department 2. Department 1 paid $1,140 for 295 direct labor-hours, and Department 2 incurred a cost of $1,008 for 160 direct labor-hours. Compute the labor variances for each department.

E–5

Compute labor variances; evaluate labor foreman

The Wheat Company manufactures a product which has a standard direct labor cost of two hours per unit at $5 per hour. In producing 6,500 units, the foreman used a different crew than usual, which resulted in a total labor cost of $59,800 for 10,400 hours. Compute the labor variances, and comment on the foreman's decision to use a different crew.

E-6

Compute overhead volume and budget variances

The following data relate to the manufacturing activities of the Warren Company for the first quarter of 1987:

Standard activity (units)	50,000
Actual production (units)	40,000
Budgeted fixed manufacturing overhead	$30,000
Variable overhead rate (per unit)	$4.00
Actual fixed manufacturing overhead	$31,000
Actual variable manufacturing overhead	$74,000

Compute the overhead budget variance and the overhead volume variance.

E-7

Compute overhead volume variance.

Assume that the actual production in Exercise E-4 was 44,000 units rather than 40,000. What was the overhead volume variance?

E-8

Close all variance accounts

The standard cost variance accounts of the Travis Company at the end of its fiscal year had the following balances:

Materials price variance (unfavorable)	$3,750
Materials usage variance (unfavorable) . . .	3,000
Labor rate variance (favorable)	2,250
Labor efficiency variance (unfavorable) . . .	8,250
Overhead budget variance (favorable) . . .	750
Overhead volume variance (unfavorable) . . .	4,500

Set up T-accounts for these variances, and enter the balances given above in the accounts. Then prepare one entry to record the closing of the variance accounts in the most practical manner.

PROBLEMS, SERIES A

P23-1-A

Compute materials variances

A certain product has a standard materials usage and cost of 2 pounds per unit at $7.00 per pound. During the month, 1,100 pounds of material were purchased at $7.30 per pound. Production for the month totaled 500 units requiring 980 pounds of materials.

Required: Compute the materials variances.

P23-2-A

Prepare entries in T-accounts for materials variances

During the month of March, a department completed 5,000 units of a product which has a standard materials usage and cost of 1.2 square feet per unit at $0.39 per square foot. The actual material used consisted of 6,100 square feet at an actual cost of $2,220.40. The actual purchase of this material amounted to 9,000 square feet at a total cost of $3,276.

Required: Using T-accounts, prepare entries (a) for the purchase of the materials and (b) for the issuance of materials to production.

P23-3-A

Compute labor variances

The C. T. Company makes plastic garbage bags. One box of bags requires 1.5 hours of direct labor at an hourly rate of $6. The company produced 100,000 boxes using 160,000 hours of direct labor at a total cost of $880,000.

Required: Compute the labor variances.

P23–4–A

Compute labor variances; prepare journal entries

The finishing department of the Case Company produced 20,000 units during the month of November. The standard number of direct labor-hours per unit is two hours. The standard rate per hour is $10.50. During the month, 41,000 direct labor-hours were worked at a cost of $461,250.

Required: a.   Record the labor data in a journal entry, and post the entry to T-accounts.
b.   Record the journal entry to dispose of any variances, and post the entry to the T-accounts.

P23–5–A

Compute overhead variances under two assumptions

The standard amount of output for the Buffalo plant of the XYZ Company is 50,000 units per month. Overhead is applied based on units produced. The flexible budget for the month for manufacturing overhead allows $37,500 for fixed overhead and $1 per unit of output for variable overhead. Actual overhead for the month consisted of $37,800 of fixed overhead with actual variable overhead given below.

Required: Compute the overhead budget variance and the overhead volume variance assuming actual production in units and actual variable overhead in dollars were:

a.   37,500 and $38,000.
b.   55,000 and $56,350.

P23–6–A

Compute overhead variances

The Lerner Company manufactures chalkboards for sale to various high schools and colleges. The expected volume of activity is 37,500 units. Standard direct labor is three hours per unit. At the 37,500 unit level of output, fixed manufacturing overhead is budgeted at $90,000, and variable manufacturing overhead is budgeted at $1.10 per hour. Overhead is applied based on standard direct labor-hours.

In July, 115,500 direct labor-hours were worked to achieve the standard level of output of 37,500 units. Actual manufacturing overhead for July consisted of $94,500 of fixed overhead and $135,000 of variable overhead.

Required: Compute the two overhead variances showing all computations.

P23–7–A

Compute materials, labor, and overhead variances

Based on a standard volume of output of 80,000 units per month, the standard cost of the product manufactured by the Woodward Company consists of:

Direct materials (0.25 pounds)	$1.00
Direct labor (0.5 hours)	3.80
Variable manufacturing overhead	2.50
Fixed manufacturing overhead ($120,000)	1.50
Total	$8.80

A total of 21,000 pounds of materials was purchased at $4.20 per pound. During the month of May, 82,000 units were produced with the following costs:

Direct materials used (20,650 pounds at $4.20) . .	$ 86,730
Direct labor (40,000 hours at $7.80)	312,000
Variable manufacturing overhead	208,000
Fixed manufacturing overhead	121,040

Required: Compute the materials price and usage variances, the labor rate and efficiency variances, and the overhead budget and volume variances (overhead is applied based on units produced).

P23–8–A
(Based on the Appendix)

Prepare journal entries under a job order standard cost accounting system; compute overhead variances

The Burch Manufacturing Company employs a job order standard cost accounting system. The standard cost of the material used is $0.80 per square foot, while the standard direct labor cost is $4 per hour. Manufacturing overhead is assigned to jobs at a rate of $3 per standard direct labor-hour. Based upon a standard volume of activity of 90,000 direct labor-hours, the flexible budget allows $90,000 of fixed overhead and $2 of variable overhead per standard direct labor-hour for the month of June 1987.

Work in process is charged with standard quantities and standard prices. On June 1, 1987, one job (No. 201) was in process, with the following standard costs already assigned:

Materials (2,500 square feet)	$2,000
Labor (400 direct labor-hours)	1,600
Manufacturing overhead ($3 per standard direct	
labor-hour)	1,200
Total	$4,800

When completed, the standard quantities for Job No. 201 are 6,000 square feet of material and 750 hours of direct labor.

During the month of June 1987, the following transactions and events occurred:

Transactions:

1. Purchased 900,000 square feet of material at $0.78 per square foot.
2. Materials issued:

Job No.	Actual quantity (square feet)	Standard quantity (square feet)
201	2,400	2,250
All others	630,000	631,800
	632,400	634,050

3. The direct labor costs and hours for the month were:

Incurred on—	Actual hours	Standard hours	Actual cost
Job No. 201	156	150	$ 651
All other jobs	76,644	76,500	310,449
	76,800	76,650	$311,100

4. The appropriate amount of overhead was assigned to the jobs.
5. Actual overhead incurred during the month was $232,500.
6. Job No. 201 was completed during the month. Other production also completed during the month had a standard cost of $780,000.

Required:
a. Prepare general journal entries for each of the numbered transactions given above.
b. Compute the overhead budget variance and the overhead volume variance for the month, and prepare the general journal entry(ies) to record them.

P23–9–A
(Based on the Appendix)

Prepare journal entries under a process standard cost system; compute variances

The Swan Company employs a process cost system with standard costs to account for the product it manufactures in a two-step process through Departments I and II. The standard cost of this product in Department I consists of:

Direct materials (10 units at $8)	$	80
Direct labor (5 hours at $6)		30
Variable manufacturing overhead (5 hours at $4) . .		20
Fixed manufacturing overhead (5 hours at $2) . .		10
	$	140

The flexible overhead budget, based on 30,000 direct labor-hours as a standard volume of activity, allows $60,000 of fixed overhead plus $2 per direct labor-hour. Materials price variances are isolated at the time of purchase. Labor rate variances are isolated when direct labor is charged to Work in Process Inventory. Materials usage and labor efficiency variances are isolated at the end of the month when production is known. Standard overhead is assigned to production and overhead variances are isolated at the end of the month when production and actual costs are known.

There was no work in process inventory as of July 1, 1987, in Department I. Summarized data for the month are:

1. Purchased 60,500 units of material for $481,580.
2. Direct materials requisitioned by Department I, 55,290 units.
3. Of the payroll costs for the month, 24,950 direct labor-hours with a total cost of $149,880 are chargeable to Department I.
4. Total manufacturing overhead costs incurred by the department for the month consist of $60,450 of fixed overhead and $100,550 of variable overhead.

5. A total of 4,500 units was completed during the month; 1,000 units remain in process, 100% complete as to materials and 50% complete as to labor and overhead.
6. Manufacturing overhead is assigned to production on the basis of standard direct labor-hours.

Required:

a. Prepare journal entries to record the above summarized data. (In the illustration in the Appendix, all variances were isolated at the end of the period. Use logic to isolate them as required in this problem.)
b. Compute the materials usage variance and the labor efficiency variance, and prepare journal entries to remove them from work in process inventory.
c. Compute the overhead budget variance and the overhead volume variance, and prepare journal entries to record them.
d. Assuming that the variances isolated are for the year ending July 31, 1987, prepare an entry that represents a practical disposition of these variances.

PROBLEMS, SERIES B

P23-1-B

Compute materials labor variances; prepare journal entries

The following data apply to the Traylor Company for the month of April, when 1,320 finished units were produced:

Materials used: 4,320 pounds
Standard materials per finished unit: 3 pounds at $3 per pound
Materials purchased: 6,000 pounds at $3.25 per pound
Direct labor: 2,940 hours at a total cost of $23,520
Standard labor per finished unit: 2 hours at $7.60 per hour

Required:

a. Compute the materials and labor variances.
b. Prepare journal entries to record the transactions involving these variances.

P23-2-B

Prepare entries in T-accounts for materials variances

During the month of December, the Glover Company produced 15,000 units of a product called Alpha. Alpha has a standard materials cost of two pieces per unit at $2 per piece. The actual material used consisted of 30,500 pieces at a cost of $57,950. Actual purchases of the materials amounted to 40,000 pieces at a cost of $76,000.

Required:

Using T-accounts, prepare entries for the purchase of materials and the issuance of materials to production.

P23-3-B

Calculate actual labor rate given standards and rate variance

Some of the records of Kirkland Company's repair and maintenance division have been lost in a fire. Salvaged records indicate that actual direct labor-hours for the period were 2,000. The *total* labor variance was $3,000, favorable (the difference between actual hours times actual rate and standard hours times standard rate). The standard labor rate was $7 per direct labor-hour and the labor rate variance was $600, unfavorable.

Required: Compute the actual direct labor rate per hour.

P23-4-B

Compute labor variances; prepare journal entries

The Entertainment Division of the Stereo Company produced 5,000 stereos during the year ended December 31, 1987. The standard number of direct labor-hours per stereo is 2.5 at a standard rate of $6.75 per hour. During the year, 12,200 direct labor-hours were worked at a cost of $87,840.

Required:

a. Record the labor data in a journal entry, and post the entry to T-accounts.
b. Record the journal entry to dispose of any variances, and post the entry to the T-accounts.

P23-5-B

Compute overhead volume variances under different assumptions

The Felder Company computes its overhead rates based on a standard activity of 37,500 units. Fixed manufacturing overhead for 1987 is budgeted at $30,000. Actual fixed manufacturing overhead for 1987 was $29,000. Overhead is applied based on units produced.

Required: Compute the amount of the overhead volume variance for the year under each of the following assumptions regarding actual output:

a.   22,500 units.
b.   37,500 units.
c.   45,000 units.

P23–6–B

Compute overhead variances

The Video Company manufactures electronic games. The standard production volume is 25,000 direct labor-hours per month for 50,000 units. Fixed manufacturing overhead is budgeted at $250,000, while variable manufacturing overhead is budgeted at $4.40 per direct labor-hour. Overhead is applied based on standard direct labor-hours.

In April, 22,000 direct labor-hours were worked in producing 45,000 units. The actual manufacturing overhead for the month amounted to $238,000 fixed and $92,000 variable.

Required: Compute the two overhead variances showing all calculations.

P23–7–B
(Based on the Appendix)

Prepare journal entries under a process standard cost accounting system; compute variances

The Ceramics Company produces ceramic figurines which, although different in shape and color, are similar enough to be considered one product for standard costing purposes. The standard cost of each figurine consists of:

Direct materials:
   1 pound of clay at $0.60 per pound . . . . $ 0.60
   2 ounces of coloring pigment at $1.875 per ounce . . 3.75
Direct labor (½ hour at $15 per hour) 7.50

Manufacturing overhead:
   Fixed (total budgeted fixed overhead of $31,500
     divided by standard output of 35,000 units) . . . 0.90 ($1.80 per direct labor-hour)
    Variable . . . . 1.20 ($2.40 per direct labor-hour)

Total $13.95

In March, 25,000 units were manufactured, and 21,000 units were sold. Production data for March follow:

Materials purchased:
   51,000 pounds of clay at $0.585 per pound
   105,000 ounces of pigment at $1.95 per ounce

Materials used:
   23,500 pounds of clay and 48,000 ounces of pigment
Direct labor: 12,000 hours at $15.30
Fixed overhead: $25,200
Variable overhead: $31,875
The total overhead rate is $4.20 per standard direct labor-hour.

Required: Record the above data in journal entries, isolating variances as soon as possible. (In the illustration in the Appendix, all variances were isolated at the end of the period. Use logic to isolate them as required in this problem.)

P23–8–B
(Based on the Appendix)

Prepare journal entries under a job order standard cost accounting system; compute overhead variances

The Brooks Company maintains a job order standard cost accounting system. The standard cost of the plastic material it uses is $4 per pound, while the standard direct labor cost is $6 per hour. Manufacturing overhead is charged to the various jobs at a rate of $4 per standard direct labor-hour. This rate is based on a flexible budget. At a standard volume of activity of 240,000 direct labor-hours, the budget allows $480,000 of budgeted fixed overhead and $2 per standard direct labor-hour for variable overhead. Work in Process Inventory is charged with standard quantities and standard prices. There was no work in process inventory at May 1, 1987.

During May 1987, the following transactions and events occurred:

Transactions:

1. Purchased 240,000 pounds of plastic at $3.92.
2. Started the following jobs during the month:

Job No.	Standard units of material	Standard hours of labor
505	3,000	6,000
506	2,400	4,800
All others . . .	144,600	253,200
	150,000	264,000

3. Materials issued during the month:

Job No.	Pounds
505	3,060
506	2,370
All others	145,770
	151,200

4. Of the direct labor cost charged to Payroll Summary, the following amounts relate to the various jobs:

Job No.	Actual hours	Standard hours	Actual cost
505 . . .	6,120	6,000	$ 36,288
506 . . .	4,896	4,800	28,512
All others . .	220,800	217,200	1,321,680
	231,816	228,000	$1,386,480

5. Appropriate manufacturing overhead was charged to the various jobs.
6. Actual fixed manufacturing overhead incurred, $489,600; actual variable manufacturing overhead incurred, $451,200.
7. Job Nos. 505 and 506 were completed along with other production having a standard cost of $1,896,000

Required:
a. Prepare journal entries to record the above summarized data, isolating variances as soon as possible.
b. Compute the two overhead variances, and prepare the journal entries to record them.
c. Assuming that the variances isolated are for the year ending May 31, 1987, prepare an entry that represents a practical disposition of these variances.

P23-9-B
(Based on the Appendix)

Prepare journal entries under a process standard cost accounting system; compute variances

The Amigo Manufacturing Company manufactures a product by processing it through three successive departments, A, B, and C. A process cost system incorporating standard costs is used. The standard cost of the product in Department A consists of:

Materials (20 pounds at $2.25) . .	$ 45.00
Direct labor (3 hours at $9)	27.00
Fixed manufacturing overhead . . .	22.50
Variable manufacturing overhead . .	18.00
	$112.50

Materials price variances are recorded at the time of purchase with the result that materials are charged to production at actual quantity and standard price. Work in process is charged for actual costs incurred for labor and overhead, and variances are isolated at the end of the period, when production is known. Budgeted manufacturing overhead at the standard volume of output of 25,000 units per month is $562,500 plus $18 per unit completed.

There was no beginning work in process inventory on June 1, 1987, in Department A. Following are summarized data for the month of June for Department A:

1. Materials purchased, 450,000 pounds at $2.34.
2. Materials requisitioned, 440,310 pounds.
3. Of the charges to Payroll Summary, $539,910 represents the cost of 59,940 hours of direct labor received in Department A.
4. Actual overhead costs charged to Work in Process Inventory: fixed, $567,000; and variable, $363,892.50.
5. Units completed and transferred to Department B, 18,000; 4,000 units remain on hand in the department, 100% complete as to materials (which are added only at the beginning of the processing in the department) and 50% complete as to processing.

Required: a. Prepare journal entries for the above summarized data. (In the illustration in the Appendix, all variances were isolated at the end of the period. Use logic to isolate the materials price variance as required in this problem.)

b. Compute the remaining five variances, and give one journal entry to remove the variances from the Work in Process Inventory—Department A account.

c. Can the overhead volume variance be logically related to the labor efficiency variance? Explain.

BUSINESS DECISION PROBLEM 23–1

Discuss possible causes for variances

Turn to Exercise E–8 in this chapter. For each of the variances listed, give a possible reason for its existence.

BUSINESS DECISION PROBLEM 23–2

Analyze situation where actual costs differ from standard costs; evaluate the two managers involved

Farris Johnson, the president of the Light Company, has a problem. It does not involve substantial dollar amounts but does involve the important question of responsibility for variances from standard costs. He has just received the following report:

Standard materials at standard price for the actual production in May . .	$18,000
Unfavorable materials price variance ($3.60 − $3.00) × 6,900 pounds	4,140
Unfavorable materials usage variance (6,900 pounds − 6,000 pounds) × $3	2,700
Total actual materials costs for the month of May (6,900 pounds at $3.60 per pound)	$24,840

Farris has discussed the unfavorable price variance with Linda Brewer, the purchasing officer. She agrees that under the circumstances she should be held responsible for most of the materials price variance. But she objects to the inclusion of $540 (900 pounds of excess materials used at $0.60 per pound). This, she argues, is the responsibility of the production department. If it had not been so inefficient in the use of materials, she would not have had to purchase the extra 900 pounds. On the other hand, Bob Hardin, the production manager, agrees that he is basically responsible for the excess quantity of materials used. But he does not agree that the above materials usage variance should be revised to include the $540 of unfavorable price variance on the excess materials used. "That's Linda's responsibility," he says.

Farris now turns to you for help. Specifically, he wants you to tell him:

a. Who is responsible for the $540 in dispute?
b. If responsibility cannot be clearly assigned, in which materials variance should the accounting department include the variance? Why?

c. Are there likely to be other circumstances where materials variances cannot be considered the responsibility of the manager most closely involved with them? Explain.

Required: Prepare written answers to the three questions asked by Farris.

BUSINESS SITUATION FOR DISCUSSION

Standard Costing Games that Managers Play*

Richard V. Calvasina and
Eugene J Calvasina

A standard cost system has three basic functions: collecting the actual costs of a manufacturing operation, determining the achievement of that manufacturing operation, and evaluating performance through the reporting of variances from standard. These variances provide managers with the information that directs them to areas that are not performing according to budget. Managers thus may be able, through the use of these data, to keep the cost centers under their control running efficiently and according to goals established during the planning stages.

Sometimes, however, the standards that are set do more to hinder the manager than to help. In the situations or "games" that we describe, the variance reporting, because of the standard set, at best has no value and, worse, actually may provide misinformation to the manager.

The Everlasting Standard Game

The first game we call the "Everlasting Standard." In this situation the company is either relatively small and has no industrial engineering department, or management may be under the mistaken belief that once a standard is set, it is set forever. The standard quantities for material and labor were set when the company first started making the product. Although it may be years later, the company may have revised just the costs for material and labor but not the quantities for material nor the time allotment for labor. Because these standards for material and labor are outdated, the efficiency variances for labor and material are no longer valid, so the managers receiving these reports have probably stopped even looking at them.

*   *   *   *   *

The Unbreakable Schedule Game

This standard costing game is an offshoot of "Everlasting Standard" but occurs over a shorter time span.

In the "Unbreakable Schedule" game, standard costs may be revised only on a set time schedule. It makes no difference what major changes in costs or production techniques may occur between the dates officially scheduled for revising standard cost cards; the cost card in force is the one used to prepare the variance reports for management. Again, as in the first game, the information (variances) presented is, in fact, misinformation. The basis used for calculating the variance, whether it be an efficiency or spending variance, is being compared to a "standard" that no longer reflects the real world.

*   *   *   *   *

The Methods Change Variance Game

In order to alleviate the problem of distorting labor efficiency variances, the "Methods Change Variance" is employed. This variance is calculated to determine the difference between the labor efficiency variance based on the old standard that is still in force and the labor efficiency variance that would have been calculated if the new standard, reflecting the current labor specifications, had been in effect. The need for presenting the second variance to management is apparent. The added cost of preparing two reports that must be combined at some point to reflect the true situation is less evident.

*   *   *   *   *

The Material Mix Game

The Material Mix variance is the materials version of the Methods Change Variance game. In this strategy, a combination of different ingredients is used in the manufacture of a product, and set quantities of each raw material item are specified. Without changing the specified ratio of ingredients in the cost card, management decides to change the amounts that are actually used. When this decision is made, someone usually states, "We are still creating the perfect product." The implication is that although we now have a different proportion of ingredients in our product there is no difference between our original recipe product and the new one. Invariably, the material mix variance resulting from this decision is favorable.

*   *   *   *   *

The All-Encompassing Product Standard

A slightly different version of the Material Mix game is one in which a company makes a multitude of products

---

* Reprinted from the March 1984 issue of *Management Accounting* (pp. 49–51, 77). Copyright by the National Association of Accountants.

that, based on outward appearances, seem to be identical, but because of different uses, different strengths of the product are needed. In order to obtain the different strengths, the ratio of the ingredients used is altered. In effect, the company makes many different products but employs only one standard product cost. This cost card represents the average of the strengths that are to be made. Based on this one average product cost card, mix and yield variances are calculated. The value of the yield variance is open to question, while a mix variance will result as long as the product strength does not match the strength on the cost card.

*   *   *   *   *

The Full Figure Standard Game

In this game the standard amounts for material, labor, and overhead costs may have been set realistically in the preliminary stages of the standard-setting process, but, somewhere along the line, a little extra is added here and there so that "achievable" standards are established. The sure sign that this game is being played to the hilt is that all variances reported for material, labor, and overhead are favorable. Also, if these "full figure standards" are used to establish selling prices, then the inventories of these overpriced goods increase rapidly.

*   *   *   *   *

The standard cost games we have described illustrate errors in methodology and uses that can creep into a standard cost system. If a standard cost system is to be a useful management tool, then standard costs, which are the foundation of this system, must be established on a current and positive basis and must be a realistic and a valid representation of actual management intentions. Because standards are usually set prior to an upcoming production period, they must reflect management's plans and goals for that future period. To do otherwise will result in mispriced inventories and performance reports and variances that are invalid. Instead of the standard cost system helping management, it will provide misinformation that will make it more difficult for management to control production systems.

CHAPTER 24

Responsibility Accounting; Segmental Analysis

After studying this chapter, you should be able to:

1. Discuss the concept of responsibility accounting.
2. Prepare responsibility accounting reports.
3. Prepare a segmental income statement showing the contribution to indirect expenses using the contribution margin format.
4. Determine return on investment, margin, and turnover for a segment.
5. Determine the residual income of a segment.
6. Define and use correctly the new terms in the glossary.

When a business is small, the owner usually oversees many different activities in the business. As a business grows, responsibility for some of these activities must be given to other persons. Obviously, the success of a business depends to a great extent on the persons responsible for these activities.

In this chapter you will learn about delegating authority to lower-level managers for managing various business activities and holding these lower-level managers responsible for the activities under their control. You will also learn how to assess the performance of these managers. The activities in a company are grouped into responsibility centers. The manager in charge of each center is responsible for controlling certain expenses. Sometimes the manager also has some control over revenues. The performance of each manager is measured in terms of the items of revenue and expense over which that manager has control. Various types of responsibility centers are discussed and illustrated. The chapter ends with a discussion of return on investment, which directly relates to the profitability of a company.

■ RESPONSIBILITY ACCOUNTING

The term **responsibility accounting** refers to an accounting system that collects, summarizes, and reports accounting data relating to the responsibilities of individual managers. A responsibility accounting system provides information to evaluate each manager on revenue and expense items over which that manager has primary control (authority to influence). A responsibility accounting report contains only those items that are controllable by the responsible manager. If, however, both controllable **and uncontrollable** items are included in the report, the categories should be clearly separated. The identification of controllable items is a fundamental task in responsibility accounting and reporting.

To implement responsibility accounting in a company, the business entity must be organized so that responsibility is assignable to individual managers. The various company managers and their lines of authority (and the resulting levels of responsibility) should be fully defined. The organization chart in Illustration 24.1 demonstrates lines of authority and responsibility that could be used as a basis for responsibility reporting. If clear lines of authority and resulting levels of responsibility cannot be determined, it is very doubtful that responsibility accounting can be implemented effectively.

To identify the items over which each manager has control, the lines of authority should follow a specified path. For example, Illustration 24.1 shows that a plant supervisor may report to a plant manager, who reports to a vice president of manufacturing, who reports to the president. The president is ultimately responsible to stockholders or their elected representatives, the board of directors. In a sense, the president is responsible for all revenue and expense items of the company, since at the presidential level all items are controllable over some period of time. The president cannot delegate responsibility so as to avoid personal responsibility. But, the president will usually delegate authority

Illustration 24.1

A Corporate Functional Organization Chart Including Four Levels of Management (illustrates only manufacturing function from level three)

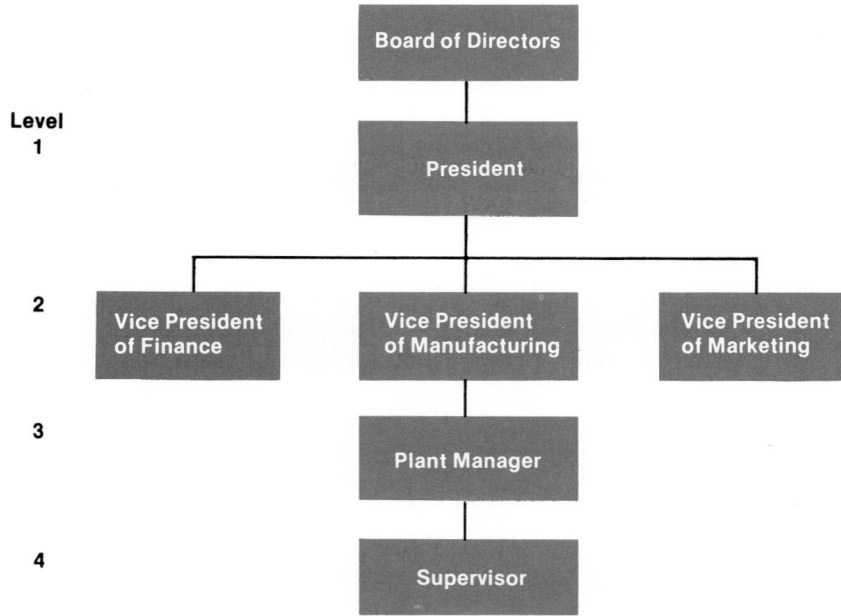

to lower-level managers since the president cannot keep fully informed of the day-to-day operating details of all areas of the business.

The manager's level in the organization also affects identification of the items over which that manager has control. The president is usually considered a first-level manager. Managers who report directly to the president are second-level managers. Notice on the organization chart in Illustration 24.1 that individuals at a specific management level are on a horizontal line across the chart. But not all managers at that level necessarily have equal authority and responsibility. The degree of a manager's authority will vary from company to company.

While the president may delegate much decision-making power, there are some revenue and expense items that will remain exclusively under the president's control. For example, in some companies, large capital (plant and equipment) expenditures may be approved only by the president. Depreciation, property taxes, and other related expenses should not, therefore, be designated as a plant manager's responsibility since these costs are not primarily under that manager's control.

The controllability criterion is crucial to the content of performance reports for each manager. For example, at the supervisor level, perhaps only direct materials and direct labor cost control are appropriate for measuring performance. A plant manager, however, has the authority to make decisions regarding many other costs that are not controllable at the supervisory level (such as salaries of supervisors); these other costs would be included in the performance evaluation of the plant manager, but not the supervisor.

■ THE CONCEPT OF CONTROL

Theoretically, a manager should have absolute control over an item to be held responsible for it. Unfortunately, absolute controllability is rare. Frequently, external or internal factors beyond a manager's control may affect revenues or expenses under that manager's responsibility. For example, the imposition of a 10% excise tax by a governmental agency may cause the price of the product to go up and thereby decrease sales of certain items in a specific segment. Although a particular manager may have the authority and responsibility for that segment of the company's sales, such a decline in revenues is beyond that manager's control. Another example would be the excessive use of raw materials in a production process under the control of a particular manager. Although the manager has the authority to control such expenses, that manager should not be held responsible for excess costs if the purchasing department bought low-quality materials that created an unusual amount of spoilage.

Therefore, the theoretical requirement that a manager should have absolute control over items for which that manager is held responsible often must be compromised, since most revenue and expense items have some degree of non-controllability in them. The manager is, thus, usually held responsible for items over which that manager has relative control. **Relative control** means that the manager has control over most of the factors that influence a given budget item. The use of relative control as a basis for evaluation may lead to some motivational problems in a company, since the manager is evaluated on results that may not reflect that manager's actual efforts. Nevertheless, most budget plans assign control on a relative basis in order to develop and use segmental budgets, which are discussed later in this chapter.

■ RESPONSIBILITY REPORTS

A unique feature of a responsibility accounting system is the varying amount of detail included in the reports issued to different levels of management. Although the amount of detail varies, reports issued under a responsibility accounting system are interrelated. Totals from the report on one level of management are carried forward in the report to the management level immediately above. For example, a performance report to a supervisor would include actual and budgeted dollar amounts of all revenue and expense items under that supervisor's control. The responsibility report issued to a supervisor's plant manager would show only totals from all the supervisors' performance reports and any additional items under the plant manager's control, such as plant administrative expenses. The vice president of manufacturing's report would contain totals from all the plants plus any additional items under the vice president's control. Because a responsibility accounting system selectively condenses data, the report to the president includes summary totals of the subordinate levels plus any additional items under the president's control. In effect, the president's report should include **all** revenue and expense items in summary form since the president is responsible for controlling the profitability of the entire company.

The condensation of data as information flows upward to increasingly higher levels of management may seem to be a hindrance to performance analysis. Actually, this lack of detail results in "management by exception." **Management by exception** is the principle that upper-level management does not need to examine operating details at lower levels unless there appears to be a problem. Since businesses are becoming increasingly complex, it has become necessary to filter and condense accounting data so that these data may be analyzed quickly. Most executives do not have time to study detailed accounting reports and search for problem areas. Reporting only summary totals highlights those areas that need attention so that the executive can make more efficient use of available time.

The condensation of data that occurs in successive levels of management reports is justified on the basis that the appropriate manager will take the necessary corrective action. Thus, specific performance details need not be reported to superiors. For example, if direct labor cost has been excessively high in a particular department, that departmental supervisor should seek to find and correct the cause of the problem. When the plant manager questions the unfavorable budget variance of the department, the supervisor can inform the manager that corrective action was taken. Hence, it is not necessary to report to the vice president of manufacturing that a particular department within one of the plants is not operating satisfactorily, since the matter has already been resolved. Alternatively, if a manager's entire plant has been performing poorly, summary totals reported to the vice president of manufacturing will disclose this situation, and an investigation of the plant manager's problems may be indicated.

In preparing responsibility accounting reports, two basic methods are used to handle revenue or expense items. In the first approach, only those items over which a manager has direct control are included in the responsibility report for that management level. Any revenue and expense items that cannot be directly controlled are not included. The second approach is to include all revenue and expense items that can be traced directly **or** allocated indirectly to a particular manager, whether or not they are controllable. This second method represents a full-cost approach, which means **all** costs of a given area are disclosed in a single report. When this approach is used, care must be taken to separate controllable from noncontrollable items in order to differentiate those items for which a manager can and should be held responsible.

Features of Responsibility Reports

In order for accounting reports to be of maximum benefit, they must be **timely.** That is, reports should be prepared as soon as possible after the end of the performance measurement period. Timely reporting allows prompt corrective action to be taken. Reports that are delayed excessively lose their effectiveness as control devices. For example, a report on the previous month's operations that is not received until the end of the current month is virtually useless for analyzing poor performance areas and taking corrective action.

Reports should also be issued **regularly** so that trends can be spotted. Appropriate management action can be initiated before major problems occur. Regularity is also important so that managers will rely on the reports and become familiar with their contents.

The format of responsibility reports should be relatively simple and easy to read. Confusing terminology should be avoided. Results should be expressed in physical units where appropriate, since these may be more familiar and understandable to some managers. To assist management in quickly spotting budget variances, both budgeted (expected) and actual amounts should be reported. A budget variance is the difference between the budgeted and actual amounts of an item. Because variances highlight problem areas (exceptions), they are helpful in applying the management-by-exception principle. To help management evaluate performance to date, responsibility reports often include both a current period and a year-to-date analysis.

■ RESPONSIBILITY REPORTS—AN ILLUSTRATION

The following example shows how an organization's responsibility accounting reports are interrelated. The organization in this example has four management levels, as shown in Illustration 24.2. The managers we will focus on are the president, vice president of manufacturing, plant manager, and supervisor of the dye shop. A responsibility report would be prepared for each management level, as shown in Illustration 24.3.

Illustration 24.4 shows the detailed information included in the responsibility reports for each manager. These reports contain **only** the individual managers' controllable expenses. Notice that only **totals** from the dye shop supervisor's report are included in the plant manager's report. In turn, only totals from the plant manager's report are included in the report to the vice president,

Illustration 24.2

Organization Chart

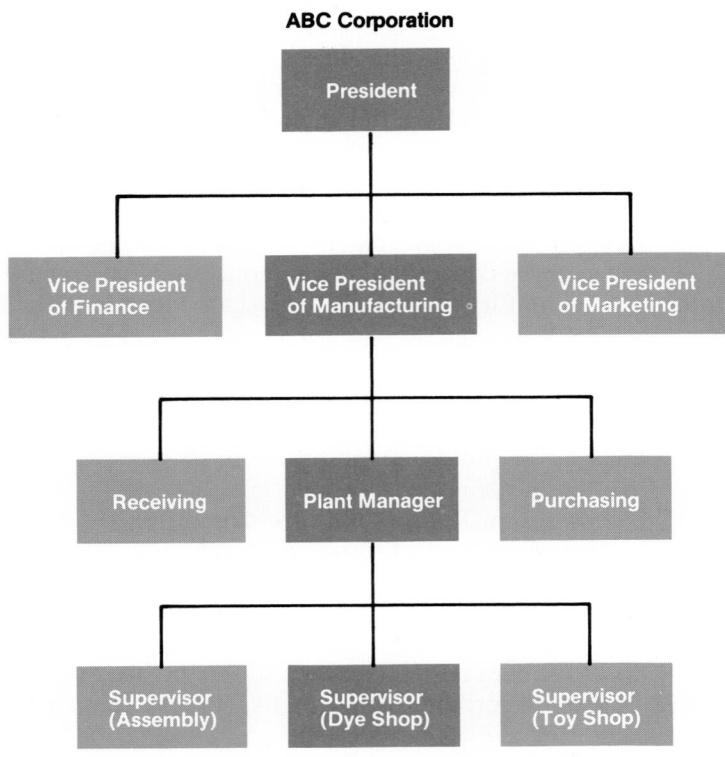

and so on. In this way, detailed data from the lower levels are summarized (condensed) and reported at the next higher level. You can see that at each level more and more costs become controllable. Also, controllable costs that were not included on lower-level reports are introduced into the reports for levels 3, 2, and 1. The only plant cost that is not included at the plant manager's level is the plant manager's salary, because it is noncontrollable by that plant

Illustration 24.3

Responsibility Reports

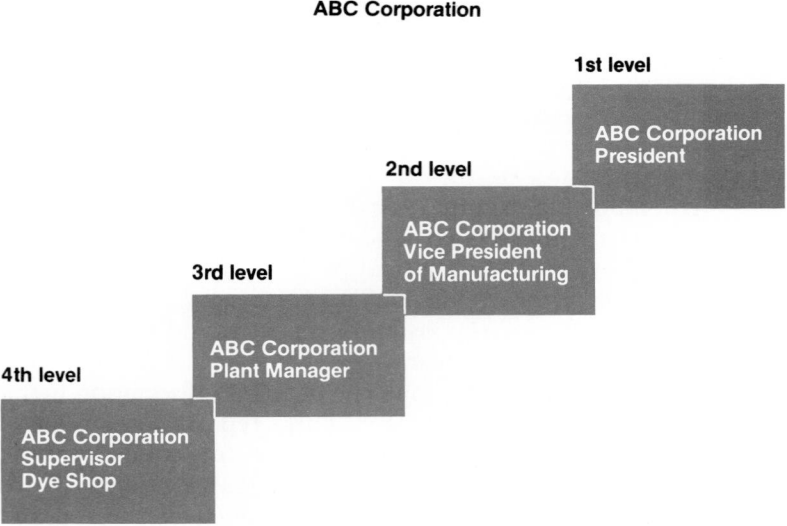

Illustration 24.4

Responsibility Reports for ABC Corporation

ABC CORPORATION
President

First level

Controllable expenses	Amount		Over or (under) budget	
	This month	Year to date	This month	Year to date
President's office expense	$ 1,000	$ 5,000	$ 100	$ 200
Manufacturing vice president's costs	18,800	93,000	600	800
Vice president, sales	8,700	19,000	400	800
Vice president, finance	4,000	15,000	800	900
Vice presidents' salaries	9,000	45,000	–0–	–0–
Total	$41,500	$177,000	$1,900	$2,700

ABC CORPORATION
Vice President of Manufacturing

Second level

Controllable expenses	Amount		Over or (under) budget	
	This month	Year to date	This month	Year to date
Vice president's office expense	$ 2,840	$ 9,500	$ (50)	$(800)
Plant manager's costs	7,880	43,000	250	500
Purchasing	380	2,500	100	200
Receiving	700	3,000	300	900
Salaries of plant manager and heads of purchasing and receiving	7,000	35,000	–0–	–0–
Total (include in report for next higher level)	$18,800	$93,000	$600	$ 800

ABC CORPORATION
Plant Manager

Third level

Controllable expenses	Amount		Over or (under) budget	
	This month	Year to date	This month	Year to date
Plant manager's office expense	$ 800	$ 9,100	$ (50)	$(100)
Dye shop costs	680	2,600	160	230
Toy shop costs	1,000	5,000	80	130
Assembly	400	1,300	60	240
Salaries of supervisors	5,000	25,000	–0–	–0–
Total (include in report for next higher level)	$7,880	$43,000	$250	$ 500

ABC CORPORATION
Supervisor, Dye Shop

Fourth level

Controllable expenses	Amount		Over or (under) budget	
	This month	Year to date	This month	Year to date
Repairs and maintenance	$200	$1,000	$ 10	$ 40
Supplies	180	850	80	95
Tools	100	300	(10)	81
Overtime	200	450	80	14
Total (include in report for next higher level)	$680	$2,600	$160	$230

manager. It is, however, controllable by the plant manager's supervisor, the vice president of manufacturing, and is included at that level of responsibility reporting.

Based on an analysis of these reports, the dye shop supervisor probably will take immediate action to see why supplies and overtime were significantly over budget this month. The plant manager may ask the supervisor what the problems were and whether they are now under control. The vice president may ask the same question of the plant manager. The president may ask each vice president why the budget was exceeded this month and what corrective action has been taken.

■ RESPONSIBILITY CENTERS

A segment is a fairly autonomous unit or division of a company defined according to function or product line. Traditionally, companies have been organized along functional lines. The segments or departments organized along functional lines perform a specified function (e.g., marketing, finance, purchasing, production, shipping). Recently, large companies have tended to organize segments according to product lines (e.g., electrical products division, shoe department, or food division).

A responsibility center is a segment of an organization for which a particular executive is responsible. There are three types of responsibility centers—expense (or cost) centers, profit centers, and investment centers. It is very important in designing a responsibility accounting system to examine the characteristics of each segment and the extent of the responsible manager's authority. Care must be taken to ensure that the basis for evaluating performance (i.e., expense center, profit center, or investment center) matches the characteristics of the segment and the authority of the segment's manager. The following sections of the chapter will discuss the characteristics of each of these types of centers and the appropriate bases for evaluating the performance of each type.

Expense Centers

An expense center is a responsibility center incurring only expense items and producing no direct revenue from the sale of goods or services. Examples of expense centers are service centers (e.g., the maintenance department or accounting department) or intermediate production facilities that produce parts for assembly into a finished product. **Managers of expense centers are held responsible only for specified expense items.**

The appropriate goal of an expense center is the **long-run** minimization of expenses. Short-run minimization of expenses may not be appropriate. For example, a production supervisor could eliminate maintenance costs for a short period of time, but in the long run, total costs might be higher due to more frequent machine breakdowns.

Profit Centers

A profit center is a responsibility center having both revenues and expenses. Since segmental earnings are usually defined as segmental revenues minus related expenses, the manager must be able to **control** both of these categories. The manager must have the authority to control selling price, sales volume, and all reported expense items. The manager's authority over all of these measured items is essential to proper performance evaluation. **Controllable profits of a segment** are shown when expenses under a manager's control are deducted from revenues under that manager's control.

Today, many companies are organizing segments as profit centers, including those that were normally considered expense centers. For example, consider the intermediate production facility mentioned in the last section which only produced output that becomes part of the final assembly in another segment. To enable the producing division to become a profit center rather than an expense center, a transfer price can be established.

Transfer Prices.   A **transfer price** is an artificial price used when goods or services are transferred from one segment to another segment within the same company. The transfer price is recorded as a revenue of the producing segment and as a cost, or expense, of the receiving segment. In using transfer prices, no cash actually changes hands between the segments. Instead, the transfer price is recorded as an internal accounting transaction.

Ideally, a transfer price should be the amount a part or service would cost if purchased from an outside party. Because such a "market" price might not be available, transfer prices often are determined on a cost-plus-profit-margin basis. In other cases, transfer prices are negotiated between the two segments, possibly with the help of an internal arbitration board.

No matter how the transfer price is determined, it is essential that the manufacturing segment manager have some degree of control over setting the price. If the manager does not have any control over the transfer price and output volume, the use of a profit center may not be a motivator.

Investment Centers

Closely related to the profit center concept is an investment center. An **investment center** is a responsibility center having revenues, expenses, and an appropriate investment base. When a segment is considered an investment center, it is evaluated according to the rate of return that it can earn on its investment base. **Return on investment (ROI),** also called rate of return, is computed by dividing segmental income by the appropriate investment base. For example, if a segment earns $100,000 on an investment base of $1,000,000, its ROI is 10%.

Determining the investment base to be used in the ROI calculation is a tricky matter. Normally, the assets available for use by the division make up the investment base of the division. But accountants disagree on whether depreciable assets should be included in the ROI calculation at original cost, original cost less accumulated depreciation, or current replacement cost. **Original cost** is the price paid to acquire an asset. **Original cost less accumulated depreciation** is the book value of the asset—the amount paid less total depreciation taken. **Current replacement cost** is the cost of replacing the present assets with similar assets in the same condition as those now in use. A different rate of return results from each of these measures. Therefore, management must select and agree upon an appropriate measure of investment base prior to making ROI calculations or interdivision comparisons.

Even after the investment base is defined, problems may still remain since many segment managers have limited control over some of the items included in the investment base of their segment. For instance, capital expenditure decisions for major plant assets are often made by top-level management rather than at the segment level. Therefore, the segment manager may have little control over the plant assets used by the segment. Another problem area may exist if the company has a centralized credit and collection department. In this case, the segment manager may have little or no control over the amount of accounts receivable included as segment assets since the manager cannot change the credit-granting or collection policies of the company.

Usually the above problems are overcome by realizing that if all segments are treated in the same manner, the inclusion of noncontrollable items in the investment base may have negligible effects. Comparisons of the ROI for all segments will then be based on a consistent treatment of items. It is important, though, that the segment managers agree to this treatment in order to avoid adverse reactions or decreased motivation.

Companies prefer to evaluate segments as investment centers because the ROI criterion facilitates performance comparisons between segments. Segments with more resources should produce more profits than segments with fewer resources, so it is difficult to compare the performance of segments of different sizes on the basis of profits alone. However, when ROI is used as a performance measure, performance comparisons take into account the differences in the sizes of the segments. The segment with the highest percentage ROI is presumably the most effective in using whatever resources it has.

Typical investment centers are large, autonomous segments of large companies. The centers are often separated from one another by location, types of products, functions, and/or necessary management skills. Segments such as these often seem to be separate companies to an outside observer. But the investment center concept can be applied even in relatively small companies in which the segment managers have control over the revenues, expenses, and assets of their segments.

■ SEGMENTAL ANALYSIS

So far, this chapter has described only the fundamentals of responsibility accounting. This section focuses specifically on segmental analysis.

Decentralization is the dispersion of decision-making authority among individuals at lower levels of the organization. In other words, the extent of decentralization refers to the degree of control that segment managers have over the revenues, expenses, and assets of their segments. When a segment manager has control over these three elements, the investment center concept can be applied to the segment. Thus, the more decentralized the decision making is in an organization, the more applicable is the investment center concept to the segments of the company. The more centralized the decision making is, the more likely one is to find responsibility centers established as expense centers.

Some of the advantages of decentralized decision making are:

1. Increased control over their segments trains managers for high-level positions in the company. The added authority and responsibility also represent "job enlargement" and often increase job satisfaction and motivation.

2. Top management can be more removed from day-to-day decision making at lower levels of the company and can manage by exception. When top management is not involved with routine problem solving, it can devote more time to long-range planning and to the company's most significant problem areas.
3. Decisions can be made at the point where problems arise. It is often difficult for members of top management to make appropriate decisions on a timely basis when they are not intimately involved with the problem they are trying to solve.
4. Since decentralization permits use of the investment center concept, performance evaluation criteria such as ROI and residual income can be used.

■ CONCEPTS USED IN SEGMENTAL ANALYSIS

The concepts of variable cost, fixed cost, direct cost, indirect cost, net income of a segment, and contribution to indirect expenses are used in segmental analysis. Each concept will be described, except for variable cost and fixed cost, which were discussed in Chapter 21.

Direct Cost and Indirect Cost

Costs may be either directly or indirectly related to a particular cost objective. A cost objective is a segment, product, or other item for which costs may be accumulated. In other words, a cost is not "direct" or "indirect" in and of itself. It is only "direct" or "indirect" in relation to a given cost objective.

A direct cost (expense) is specifically traceable to a given cost objective. An indirect cost (expense) is not traceable to a given cost objective but has been allocated to it. A particular cost (expense) can only be designated as direct or indirect by reference to a given cost objective, and a cost that is direct to one cost objective may be indirect to another. For instance, the salary of a segment manager may be a direct cost of a given manufacturing segment but an indirect cost of one of the products manufactured by that segment. In this example the segment and the product are two distinct cost objectives.

Since a direct cost is traceable to a cost objective, the cost is likely to be eliminated if the cost objective is eliminated. For instance, if the plastics segment of a business is closed down, the salary of the manager of that segment probably will be eliminated. Sometimes a direct cost would remain even if the cost objective were eliminated, but this is the exception rather than the rule.

An indirect cost is not traceable to a particular cost objective; therefore, it only becomes an expense of the cost objective through an allocation process. For example, consider the depreciation expense on the company headquarters building that is allocated to each of the segments of the company. The depreciation expense is a direct cost for the company headquarters, but it is an indirect cost to each segment. If a segment of the company is eliminated, the indirect cost for depreciation assigned to that segment will not disappear, the cost will simply be allocated among the remaining segments. In a given situation, it may be possible to identify an indirect cost that would be eliminated if the cost objective were eliminated, but this would be the exception to the general rule.

Since direct costs of a segment are clearly identified with that segment, these costs are often controllable by the segment manager. Since indirect costs become segment costs only through allocation, most indirect costs are noncontrollable by the segment manager. But care must be taken not to equate direct costs with controllable costs. For example, the salary of a segment supervisor may be direct to that segment and yet noncontrollable by that supervisor because supervisors cannot specify their own salaries.

■ NET INCOME OF A SEGMENT—EVALUATION CRITERIA FOR A PROFIT CENTER

When preparing internal reports on the performance of segments of a company, management often finds it important to classify expenses as fixed or variable and as direct or indirect to the segment. These classifications may be more useful to management than the traditional classifications of cost of goods sold, operating expenses, and nonoperating expenses that are used for external reporting in the company's financial statements. As a result, many companies prepare (for internal use) an income statement with the format shown in Illustration 24.5.

This format is called the contribution margin format for the income statement because it shows the contribution margin. Contribution margin is defined as sales revenue less variable expenses. Notice in Illustration 24.5 that all variable expenses are direct expenses of the segment. The second subtotal shown in the contribution margin format income statement (Illustration 24.5) is the segment's contribution to indirect expenses. Contribution to indirect expenses is defined as sales revenue less all direct expenses of the segment (both variable direct expenses and fixed direct expenses). The final total in the income statement is segmental net income, defined as segmental revenues less all expenses (direct expenses and allocated indirect expenses).

Earlier we stated that the performance of a profit center is evaluated on the basis of the segment's profits. It is tempting to use segmental net income to make this evaluation since total net income is used to evaluate the performance of the entire company. The problem with using segmental net income to evaluate performance is that segmental net income includes certain indirect expenses that have been allocated to the segment but are not directly related to it or its operations. Because segmental contribution to indirect expenses includes only revenues and expenses that are directly related to the segment, this amount is often more appropriate for evaluation purposes.

Illustration 24.5

Contribution Margin Format Income Statement—All Expenses Allocated

	Segment A	Segment B	Total
Sales	$1,000,000	$700,000	$1,700,000
Less: Variable expenses (all direct expenses)	500,000	410,000	910,000
Contribution margin	$ 500,000	$290,000	$ 790,000
Less: Direct fixed expenses	120,000	170,000	290,000
Contribution to indirect expenses	$ 380,000	$120,000	$ 500,000
Less: Indirect fixed expenses	90,000	160,000	250,000
Net income	$ 290,000	$ (40,000)	$ 250,000

Given the facts in Illustration 24.5, if management relied on segmental net income to judge segmental performance, management might conclude that Segment B should be eliminated since it shows a loss of $40,000. But this action would reduce overall company profits by $120,000, as shown below:

Reduction in corporate revenues		$700,000
Reduction in corporate expenses:		
Variable expenses	$410,000	
Direct fixed expenses	170,000	580,000
Reduction in corporate income		$120,000

Notice that the elimination of Segment B would not eliminate the $160,000 of allocated fixed costs. These costs would need to be allocated to Segment A if Segment B no longer existed.

To stress the importance of a segment's contribution to indirect expenses, many companies prefer the contribution margin income statement format presented in Illustration 24.6 rather than the format used in Illustration 24.5. The difference is that indirect fixed costs are not allocated to individual segments. Indirect fixed expenses are only shown in the total column for the computation of net income for the entire company. The computation for each segment stops with the segment's contribution to indirect expenses; this is the appropriate figure to use for evaluating the earnings performance of a segment. Only for the company as a whole is net income (revenues minus **all** expenses) computed; this is, of course, the appropriate figure to use for evaluating the company as a whole.

Arbitrary Allocations of Indirect Fixed Expenses.   As stated above, indirect fixed expenses, such as depreciation on the corporate administration building or on the computer facility maintained at company headquarters, can only be allocated to segments on some arbitrary basis. There are two basic guidelines for allocating indirect fixed expenses—by the benefit received and by the responsibility for incurrence of the expense.

Allocation can be made on the basis of benefit received for certain indirect expenses. For instance, assume a corporate computer was used for a total of 10,000 hours by the entire company. If Segment K used 4,000 hours, it could be charged (allocated) with 40% of the computer's depreciation for the period, since Segment K received 40% of the total benefits for the period.

For certain other indirect expenses, allocation is based on responsibility for incurrence. For instance, assume that Segment M contracts with a magazine to run an advertisement that will benefit both Segment M and various other segments of the company. Many companies would allocate the entire cost of

Illustration 24.6

Contribution Margin Format Income Statement—Indirect Fixed Expenses Not Allocated

	Segment A	Segment B	Total
Sales	$1,000,000	$700,000	$1,700,000
Less: Variable expenses	500,000	410,000	910,000
Contribution margin	$ 500,000	$290,000	$ 790,000
Less: Direct fixed expenses	120,000	170,000	290,000
Contribution to indirect expenses	$ 380,000	$120,000	$ 500,000
Less: Indirect fixed expenses			250,000
Net income			$ 250,000

the advertisement to Segment **M** since it was responsible for incurring the advertising expense.

To further illustrate the allocation of indirect expenses based on a measure of benefit or responsibility for incurrence, assume that Daily Company operates two segments, **X** and **Y**. It allocates the following indirect expenses to its two segments using the designated allocation bases:

Expense	Allocation base
Home office building occupancy expense, $40,000	Net sales
Insurance expense, $25,000	Cost of segmental plant assets
General administrative expenses, $30,000 . .	Number of employees

The following additional data are provided:

	Segment X	Segment Y	Total
Sales (net)	$200,000	$300,000	$500,000
Segmental plant assets . .	$150,000	$200,000	$350,000
Number of Employees . .	40	60	100

The allocation of indirect expenses is as shown in the following expense allocation schedule:

	Segment X	Segment Y	Total
Home office building occupancy expense . .	$16,000[1]	$24,000[2]	$40,000
Insurance expense	10,714[3]	14,286[4]	25,000
General administrative expenses	12,000[5]	18,000[6]	30,000

1. $\dfrac{\$200,000}{\$500,000} \times \$40,000 = \$16,000.$

2. $\dfrac{\$300,000}{\$500,000} \times \$40,000 = \$24,000.$

3. $\dfrac{\$150,000}{\$350,000} \times \$25,000 = \$10,714.$

4. $\dfrac{\$200,000}{\$350,000} \times \$25,000 = \$14,286.$

5. $\dfrac{40}{100} \times \$30,000 = \$12,000.$

6. $\dfrac{60}{100} \times \$30,000 = \$18,000.$

When neither "benefit" nor "responsibility" can be used to allocate indirect fixed expenses, some other reasonable, but arbitrary, basis must be found. Often, for lack of a better approach, indirect expenses are allocated based on net sales. For instance, if segment **X**'s net sales were 60% of total company sales, then 60% of the indirect expenses would be allocated to Segment **X**. Allocating expenses based on sales is not recommended because it reduces the incentive of a segment manager to increase sales, since this would result in more indirect expenses being allocated to that segment.

Having covered some basic concepts essential to segmental analysis, some specific procedures for performance evaluation will be presented.

■ INVESTMENT CENTER ANALYSIS

To this point, the segmental analysis discussion has concentrated on the contribution to indirect expenses and segmental net income approaches. Now we will introduce the investment base concept into the analysis. Two criteria that include the concept of investment base in the analysis are ROI (return on investment) and RI (residual income).

Return on Investment (ROI)

A segment that has a large amount of assets will usually earn more in an absolute sense than will a segment that has a small amount of assets. Therefore, absolute amounts of segmental income cannot be used to compare the performance of different segments. To measure the relative effectiveness of segments, a company must use ROI, which calculates the return (income) as a percentage of the assets employed (investment). The formula for return on investment is:

$$ROI = \frac{Income}{Investment}$$

To illustrate the difference between using absolute amounts and using percentages in evaluating a segment's performance, consider the data shown in Illustration 24.7 for a company with three segments. If absolute dollars of income are used to evaluate performance, Segment 2 appears to be doing twice as well as Segment 3. But the use of ROI as a criterion for evaluating the segments indicates that Segment 3 is really performing the best (25%), Segment 2 is next (20%), and Segment 1 is performing the worst (10%). ROI is therefore a more useful indicator of the relative performance of segments than absolute income.

Although ROI appears to be a quite simple and straightforward computation, there are several alternative methods for making the calculation. These alternatives focus on what is meant by "income" and "investment." Illustration 24.8 shows various definitions and applicable situations for each type of computation.

As discussed earlier in the chapter, alternative valuation bases include original cost, cost less accumulated depreciation, and current replacement cost. Each of the valuation bases has merits and drawbacks, as you will now see.

Cost less accumulated depreciation is probably the most widely used valuation base and is easily determined. But since there are many types of depreciation methods, comparisons between segments or companies may be difficult. Also,

Illustration 24.7

Computation of Return on Investment (ROI)

		Segment 1	Segment 2	Segment 3	Total
(a)	Income	$ 100,000	$ 500,000	$ 250,000	$ 850,000
(b)	Investment	1,000,000	2,500,000	1,000,000	4,500,000
	Return on investment				
	(a) ÷ (b)	10%	20%	25%	18.89%

Illustration 24.8

Possible Definitions of "Income" and "Investment"

Situation	Definition of income	Definition of investment
1. Evaluation of the earning power of the company. Do not use for segments or segment managers due to inclusion of noncontrollable expenses.	Net income of the company.*	Total assets of the company.†
2. Evaluation of rate of income contribution of segment. Do not use for segment managers due to inclusion of non-controllable expenses.	Contribution to indirect expenses.	Assets directly used by and identified with the segment.
3. Evaluation of income performance of segment manager.	"Controllable" income. This would begin with contribution to indirect expenses and would eliminate any revenues and direct expenses not under the control of the segment manager.	Assets under the control of the segment manager.

* Often *net operating income* is used; this is defined as income before interest and taxes.
† *Operating assets* are often used in the calculation. This definition excludes assets not used in normal operations.

as book value decreases, a constant income results in a steadily increasing ROI even though the segment's performance is unchanged. The use of original cost eliminates the problem of decreasing book value but has its own drawback. The investment in (cost of) old assets will be much less than an investment in new assets, so a segment with old assets can earn less than a segment with net assets and still realize the same ROI. Current replacement cost is difficult to use because replacement cost figures often are not available, but this base does eliminate some of the problems caused by the other two methods. Whichever valuation basis is adopted, all ROI calculations that are to be used for comparative purposes should be made consistently.

Expanded Form of ROI Computation. The ROI formula can be broken into two component parts as follows:

$$\text{ROI} = \frac{\text{Income}}{\text{Sales}} \times \frac{\text{Sales}}{\text{Investment}}$$

The first part of the formula, Income/Sales, is called margin or return on sales. The margin refers to the percentage relationship of income or profits to sales. This percentage shows the number of cents of profit that are generated by each dollar of sales. The second part of the formula, Sales/Investment, is called turnover. Turnover shows the number of dollars of sales generated by each dollar of investment. Turnover measures how effectively each dollar of assets was used.

There are several ways to increase ROI:

1. A manager can concentrate on increasing profit margin while holding turnover constant. Pursuing this strategy means keeping selling prices constant and making every effort to increase efficiency and thereby reduce expenses.

2. A manager can concentrate on increasing turnover by reducing the investment in assets while holding income and sales constant. For example, working capital could be decreased, thereby reducing the investment in assets.

3. A manager can take actions that affect both margin and turnover. For example, disposing of nonproductive depreciable assets would decrease investment while also increasing income (through the reduction of depreciation expense). Thus, both margin and turnover would increase. An advertising campaign would probably increase sales and income. In this case, turnover would increase, and margin might increase or decrease depending on the relative amounts of the increases in income and sales.

Illustration 24.9 shows possible outcomes of some of these strategies to increase ROI.

Illustration 24.9

Strategies for Increasing ROI

Past year return on investment:

$$ROI = Margin \times Turnover$$

$$ROI = \frac{Income}{Sales} \times \frac{Sales}{Investment}$$

$$ROI = \frac{\$100,000}{\$2,000,000} \times \frac{\$2,000,000}{\$1,000,000}$$

$$ROI = 5\% \times 2 \text{ times}$$

$$ROI = 10\%$$

1. <u>Increase margin</u> through reducing expenses by $40,000; no effect on sales or investment.

$$ROI = \frac{\$140,000}{\$2,000,000} \times \frac{\$2,000,000}{\$1,000,000}$$

$$ROI = 7\% \times 2 \text{ times}$$

$$ROI = 14\%$$

2. <u>Increase turnover</u> through reducing investment in assets by $200,000; no effect on sales or income.

$$ROI = \frac{\$100,000}{\$2,000,000} \times \frac{\$2,000,000}{\$800,000}$$

$$ROI = 5\% \times 2.5 \text{ times}$$

$$ROI = 12.5\%$$

3(a). <u>Increase margin and turnover</u> by disposing of nonproductive depreciable assets; income increased by $10,000; investment decreased by $200,000.

$$ROI = \frac{\$110,000}{\$2,000,000} \times \frac{\$2,000,000}{\$800,000}$$

$$ROI = 5.5\% \times 2.5 \text{ times}$$

$$ROI = 13.75\%$$

3(b). <u>Increase margin and turnover</u> through increased advertising; sales increased by $500,000 and income by $50,000; no effect on investment.

$$ROI = \frac{\$150,000}{\$2,500,000} \times \frac{\$2,500,000}{\$1,000,000}$$

$$ROI = 6\% \times 2.5 \text{ times}$$

$$ROI = 15\%$$

3(c). <u>Increase turnover</u> through increased advertising; sales increased by $500,000 and income by $12,500; no effect on investment.

$$ROI = \frac{\$112,500}{\$2,500,000} \times \frac{\$2,500,000}{\$1,000,000}$$

$$ROI = 4.5\% \times 2.5 \text{ times}$$

$$ROI = 11.25\%$$

Residual Income

The use of ROI as the sole criterion for evaluating performance can result in what is termed suboptimization. Suboptimization occurs when a segment manager takes an action that is in the segment's best interest (i.e., raises that segment's ROI), but is not in the best interest of the company as a whole.

To prevent suboptimization, companies sometimes use the concept of residual income. Residual income (RI) is defined as the amount of income a segment has in excess of a desired minimum ROI. Each company sets its minimum ROI based on many factors, including expected growth rate, debt coverage, industry technology, and desired returns to stockholders. The formula for residual income is:

Residual income (RI) = Income − (Investment × Desired minimum ROI)

When RI is used to evaluate performance, the segment rated as the best is the segment with the greatest amount of RI rather than the one with the highest ROI.

To illustrate the value of using residual income to measure performance, assume the manager of Segment 3 in Illustration 24.10 has an opportunity to take on a project involving an investment of $100,000 that is estimated to return $22,000, or 22%, on the investment. Since the segment's ROI is currently 25%, the manager may decide to reject the project. However, from a company standpoint, ROI will increase from 18.89% to 18.96% if the project is accepted. The decision to reject the project is a valid decision from the manager's point

Illustration 24.10 *Computation of Residual Income (RI)*

Before acceptance of the project by Segment 3, the amounts are as follows:

		Segment 1	Segment 2	Segment 3	Total company
a.	Income	$ 100,000	$ 500,000	$ 250,000	$ 850,000
b.	Investment	1,000,000	2,500,000	1,000,000	4,500,000
c.	Rate of return on investment (ROI)	10%	20%	25%	18.89%
d.	Desired minimum ROI (10%)	$ 100,000	$ 250,000	$ 100,000	*
e.	Residual income	–0–	250,000	150,000	*

* The RI concept is generally not used for evaluating an entire company, since the problem of suboptimization, by definition, does not exist.

With acceptance of the project by Segment 3, the amounts would be as follows:

		Segment 1	Segment 2	Segment 3	Total company
a.	Income	$ 100,000	$ 500,000	$ 272,000*	$ 872,000
b.	Investment	1,000,000	2,500,000	1,100,000†	4,600,000
c.	Rate of return on investment (ROI)	10%	20%	24.7%	18.96%
d.	Desired minimum ROI (10%)	$ 100,000	$ 250,000	$ 110,000	
e.	Residual income	–0–	250,000	162,000	

* $250,000 + (22% of $100,000).
† $1,000,000 original investment + $100,000 new investment.

of view because to accept the project will cause the segment's ROI to decline. But from a company standpoint, ROI is 18.89%, and accepting the project would increase the overall company ROI.

The project opportunity for Segment 3 could earn in excess of the desired minimum ROI of 10%. In fact, it has residual income of $12,000 ($22,000 − 10% × $100,000). If residual income (RI) were applied as the basis for evaluating segmental performance, the manager of Segment 3 would accept the project because doing so would improve his or her segment's performance. That choice would also be beneficial to the entire company.

Critics of the residual income method complain that larger segments are likely to have the highest residual income. In a given situation it may be advisable to look at both ROI and RI in assessing performance.

Since it is always assumed that a manager will make choices that improve his or her segment's performance, the challenge is to select evaluation bases for segments that will result in managers making choices that benefit the entire company. When performance is evaluated on RI, choices that improve a segment's performance are more likely to be good for the entire company as well.

When calculating RI for a **segment,** the income and investment definitions are "contributions to indirect expenses" and "assets directly used by and identified with the segment." When calculating RI for a **manager** of a segment, the income and investment definitions should be "income controllable by the manager" and "assets under the control of the segment manager."

In evaluating the performance of a segment or a segment manager, comparisons should be made with (1) the current budget, (2) other segments or managers within the company, (3) past performance of that segment or manager, and (4) similar segments or managers in other companies. Consideration must be given to general economic conditions, market conditions for the product being produced, and so on. A superior segment in Company A may be considered superior because it is earning a return of 12%, which is above similar segments in other companies but below other segments in Company A. But segments in Company A may be more profitable because of market conditions and the nature of the company's products rather than because of the performance of the segment managers. Careful judgment must be used whenever performance is evaluated.

■ SEGMENTAL REPORTING IN EXTERNAL FINANCIAL STATEMENTS

Formerly, segmental information was reported only to management for internal decision-making purposes. In December 1976, the Financial Accounting Standards Board issued *Statement of Financial Accounting Standards No. 14,* "Financial Reporting for Segments of a Business Enterprise." This *Statement* requires publicly held companies to publish certain segmental information in their annual financial statements. Thus, external users of financial statements now have segmental information to aid them in their decisions regarding these companies. However, fewer details are presented in these external statements than in reports intended for management.

■ *SUMMARY*

A responsibility accounting system provides information to evaluate each manager on revenue and expense items over which that manager has primary control. Responsibility accounting reports contain only those items controlled by the responsible manager, or if noncontrollable items are included, the reports should clearly separate controllable from noncontrollable items. The identification of controllable items is a fundamental task in responsibility accounting and reporting.

Management by exception is the concept that upper-level management does not need to be concerned with operating details of subordinate levels unless there appears to be a problem. To accomplish management by exception, responsibility reports contain details only of activities immediately under the manager's control; only summary information of results from subordinate levels is presented. Also, responsibility reports should present both budgeted and actual results, as well as budget variances and year-to-date totals.

A responsibility center is a segment of an organization for which a particular executive is responsible. There are three types of responsibility centers—expense centers, profit centers, and investment centers.

A responsibility center having only expense items and producing no revenue from the sale of goods or services is properly accounted for as an expense center. Managers of expense centers are held responsible only for specified expense items.

A profit center has both revenues and expenses, so it is possible to calculate segmental income. A profit center manager is evaluated on controllable profits of the segment, the difference between revenue items under the manager's control and expense items under the manager's control. When a profit center sells its output only to other segments of the same company, controllable profits of the profit center are strongly influenced by the transfer price that is established for the "sale." It is essential that the manufacturing segment (profit center) manager have some control over setting the transfer price.

An investment center is a responsibility center that has revenues, expenses, and a specified investment base. Performance of an investment center and of an investment center's manager can be evaluated on the basis of return on investment (ROI). ROI is computed by dividing segmental income by the appropriate investment base.

A direct cost of a given cost objective can be traced directly to that cost objective. An indirect cost cannot be traced directly to a cost objective; it can be assigned to the cost objective only through a cost allocation process. A cost that is direct to one cost objective may be indirect with regard to another.

Segment contribution margin is the difference between net sales and variable expenses of a segment. Segment contribution to indirect expenses is the amount remaining after all direct expenses of the segment are deducted from the revenues generated by the segment. Segmental net income is the amount that remains after all of a segment's expenses (direct and indirect) are deducted from the segment's revenues. Since a segment's contribution to indirect expenses includes only items that are directly related to the segment, this amount indicates the effect on company profits if the segment were eliminated. Consequently, contribution to indirect expenses is often considered more appropriate than segmental net income for evaluation purposes.

Two different criteria exist for evaluating the performance of investment centers. Return on investment (ROI) directly compares segmental income to the segment's investment base. Both segmental income and the segment's investment base may be defined in a number of ways, any of which may be appropriate depending on the circumstances. The ROI computation can also be expanded to consider separately the effects of margin and turnover. The other criterion for evaluating investment center performance is residual income (RI), the amount by which segmental income exceeds a minimum desired ROI. Use of the RI criterion for segmental evaluation reduces the tendency toward suboptimization that can occur when managers are evaluated on ROI alone. Possibly both ROI and RI should be used in evaluating performance.

Chapter 25 discusses budgeting. Companies, like individuals, should plan for the future. A budget is one method of planning. Just as you may use a budget in managing your personal finances, budgets are an important tool of company management.

NEW TERMS INTRODUCED IN CHAPTER 24*

Budget variance

The difference between the budgeted and actual amounts of an item (935).

Contribution margin

Sales revenues less variable expenses (942).

Contribution margin format

An income statement format that shows the contribution margin (Sales — Variable expenses) for a segment (942).

Contribution to indirect expenses

The income of a segment remaining after direct expenses are deducted from segmental revenues (942).

Controllable profits of a segment

Profit of a segment when expenses under a manager's control are deducted from revenues under that manager's control (939).

Cost objective

A segment, product, or other item for which costs may be accumulated (941).

Current replacement cost

The cost of replacing the present assets with similar assets in the same condition as those now in use (939).

Decentralization

The dispersion of decision-making authority among individuals at lower levels of the organization (940).

Direct cost (expense)

A cost that is directly traceable to a given cost objective (941).

Expense center

A responsibility center producing only expense items and producing no direct revenue from the sale of goods or services. Examples include the accounting department and the maintenance department (938).

Indirect cost (expense)

A cost that is not traceable to a given cost objective but has been allocated to it (941).

Investment center

A responsibility center having revenues, expenses, and an appropriate investment base (939).

Management by exception

The principle that upper-level management does not need to examine operating details at lower levels unless there appears to be a problem (an exception) (934).

* Some terms listed in earlier chapters are repeated here for your convenience.

Margin (as used in ROI)

The percentage relationship of income (or profits) to sales.

$$\text{Margin} = \frac{\text{Income}}{\text{Sales}} \quad (946)$$

Original cost

The price paid to acquire an asset (939).

Original cost less accumulated depreciation

The book value of an asset—the amount paid less total depreciation taken (939).

Profit center

A responsibility center having both revenue and expense items (938).

Relative control

Means the manager has control over most of the factors that influence a given budget item (933).

Residual income (RI)

The amount of income a segment has in excess of a desired minimum ROI. Residual income is equal to Income − (Investment × Desired minimum ROI) (948).

Responsibility accounting

Refers to an accounting system that collects, summarizes, and reports accounting data according to the responsibilities of the individual managers. A responsibility accounting system provides information to evaluate each manager on revenue and expense items over which that manager has primary control (932).

Responsibility Center

A segment of an organization for which a particular executive is responsible (938).

Return on investment (ROI)

Calculates the return (income) as a percentage of the assets employed (investment).

$$\frac{\text{Return on}}{\text{investment}} = \frac{\text{Income}}{\text{Investment}} \quad \text{or} \quad \frac{\text{Income}}{\text{Sales}} \times \frac{\text{Sales}}{\text{Investment}}$$
$$(939, 945)$$

Segment

A fairly autonomous unit or division of a company (938).

Segmental net income

Final total in the income statement; segmental revenues less all expenses (direct expenses and allocated indirect expenses) (942).

Suboptimization

A situation that occurs when a segment manager takes an action that is in the segment's best interest but is not in the best interest of the company as a whole (948).

Transfer price

An artificial price used when goods or services are transferred from one segment to another segment within the same company (939).

Turnover (as used in ROI)

The number of dollars of sales generated by each dollar of investment.

$$\text{Turnover} = \frac{\text{Sales}}{\text{Investment}} \quad (946)$$

DEMONSTRATION PROBLEM

The Corey Company has two segments. Results of operations for 1987 follow:

	Segment 1	Segment 2	Total
Sales	$50,000	$75,000	$125,000
Variable expenses	35,000	45,000	80,000
Fixed expenses:			
Direct	5,000	14,000	19,000
Indirect			7,000

The company has total operating assets of $175,000; $160,000 of these assets are identified with particular segments as follows:

	Segment 1	Segment 2
Assets directly used by and identified with the segment	$60,000	$100,000

Required: a. Prepare a statement showing the contribution margin, contribution to indirect expenses for each segment, and the total income for the Corey Company.
  b. Determine the return on investment for each segment and then for the entire company.
  c. Comment on the results of *(a)* and *(b)*.

Solution to demonstration problem

a.

COREY COMPANY
Income Statement Showing Segmental
Contributions to Indirect Expenses
For the Year Ended December 31, 1987

	Segment 1	Segment 2	Total
Sales	$50,000	$75,000	$125,000
Less: Variable expenses	35,000	45,000	80,000
Contribution margin	$15,000	$30,000	$ 45,000
Less: Direct fixed expenses	5,000	14,000	19,000
Contribution to indirect expenses	$10,000	$16,000	$ 26,000
Less: Indirect fixed expenses			7,000
Net income			$ 19,000

b. 1. $ROI = \dfrac{\text{Contribution to indirect expenses}}{\text{Assets directly used by and identified with the segment}}$

Segment 1   **Segment 2**

$ROI = \dfrac{\$10,000}{\$60,000} = 16.67\%$ $ROI = \dfrac{\$16,000}{\$100,000} = 16\%$

2. $ROI = \dfrac{\text{Net operating income}}{\text{Operating assets}} = \dfrac{\$19,000}{\$175,000} = 10.9\%$

c. In Part *(a)*, Segment 2 showed a higher contribution to indirect expenses. But in *(b)*, Segment 1 showed a higher return on investment. The difference between these calculations shows that when a segment is evaluated as a profit center, the center with the highest investment base will usually show the best results. But when the segment is evaluated as an investment center, the segment with the highest investment base will not necessarily show the highest return. The computations in *(b)* also demonstrate that the return on investment for the company as a whole will be lower than the segments because of the increased investment base.

QUESTIONS

1. What is the fundamental principle of responsibility accounting?

2. Hope Company manufactures refrigerators. Below are listed several of the company's costs. Indicate whether or not the shop supervisor can control each of the costs.

  a. Depreciation.
  b. Repairs.
  c. Small tools.
  d. Supplies.
  e. Bond interest.

3. List five important factors that should be considered in designing reports for a responsibility accounting system.

4. How soon should accounting reports be prepared after the end of the performance measurement period? Explain.

5. Name and describe three types of responsibility centers.

6. Describe a segment of a business enterprise that is best treated as an expense center. List four indirect expenses that may be allocated to such an expense center.

7. Compare and contrast an expense center and an investment center.

8. What purpose is served by setting transfer prices?

9. What is the advantage of using investment centers as a basis for performance evaluation?

10. Which categories of items must a segment manager have control over for the investment center concept to be applicable?

11. What connection is there between the extent of decentralization and the investment center concept?

12. Give some of the advantages of decentralization.

13. Differentiate between a direct cost and an indirect cost of a segment. What happens to these categories if the segment to which they are related is eliminated?

14. Is it possible for a cost to be "direct" to one cost objective and "indirect" to another cost objective? Explain.

15. Describe some of the methods by which indirect expenses are allocated to a segment.

16. Give the general formula for return on investment (ROI). What are its two components?

17. Give the three sets of definitions for "income" and "investment" that can be used in ROI calculations, and explain when each set is applicable.

18. Give the various valuation bases that can be used for plant assets in investment center calculations. Discuss some of the advantages and disadvantages of these methods.

19. In what way is the use of the residual income (RI) concept superior to the use of ROI?

20. How is RI determined?

21. If the RI for segment manager A is $50,000 while the RI for segment manager B is $100,000, does this necessarily mean that B is a better manager than A? Explain.

EXERCISES

E–1

Prepare a responsibility report for a given management level

The following information refers to the toy shop of the Playtime Company for the month of May:

	Amount	Over or (under) budget
Supplies	$ 60,000	$(12,000)
Repairs and maintenance	300,000	24,000
Overtime	120,000	12,000
Salary of supervisor	36,000	(6,000)
Salary of plant manager	48,000	–0–
Allocation of company accounting costs	36,000	12,000
Allocation of depreciation	24,000	(6,000)

Using the above information, prepare a responsibility report for the _supervisor_ of the toy shop for the month of May. (Ignore year-to-date expenses.)

E–2

Prepare an income statement for a segment in a contribution margin format

Present the following information for Segment D in the contribution margin format:

Sales	$1,000,000
Variable selling and administrative expenses	75,000
Fixed direct manufacturing expenses	25,000
Variable manufacturing expenses	300,000
Fixed direct selling and administrative expenses	125,000

E-3

Prepare an income statement for a segment using the contribution margin format; determine effect of elimination of segment on company income

Given the following data, prepare a schedule that shows contribution margin, contribution to indirect expenses, and net income of the segment:

Direct fixed expenses	$ 90,000
Indirect fixed expenses	72,000
Sales	624,000
Variable expenses	432,000

What would be the effect on company income if the segment were eliminated?

E-4

Allocate expenses to various segments using a specified allocation base

Three segments (X, Y, and Z) of the Rabb Company have net sales of $1,000,000, $600,000, and $200,000, respectively. A decision is made to allocate the pool of $80,000 of administrative overhead expenses of the home office to the segments, using net sales as the basis for allocation.

a. How much should be allocated to each segment?
b. If Segment Z is eliminated, how much will be allocated to X and Y?

E-5

Calculate ROI, margin, and turnover for a segment

Two segments (hardware and software) showed the following data for the most recent year:

	Hardware	Software
Contribution to indirect expenses	$ 300,000	$ 360,000
Assets directly used by and identified with the segment	900,000	1,560,000
Sales	2,400,000	4,800,000

a. Calculate ROI for each segment in the most direct manner.
b. Calculate ROI using the margin and turnover components.

E-6

Determine the effect on margin, turnover, and ROI when the variables are altered

Determine the effect of each of the following on the margin, turnover, and ROI of the hardware segment in Exercise E-5. Consider each change independently of the others.

a. Direct variable expenses were reduced by $12,000, and indirect expenses were reduced by $24,000. Sales and assets were unaffected.
b. Assets used by the segment were reduced by $180,000, while income and sales were unaffected.
c. An advertising campaign increased sales by $240,000 and income by $60,000. Assets directly used by the segment were unaffected.

E-7

Calculate the ROI in evaluating the income performance of a segment manager and the rate of income contribution of a segment

For Segment C of the Cat Company, the following data are available:

Net income of the segment	$ 40,000
Contribution to indirect expenses	100,000
Controllable income	60,000
Total assets related to the segment	500,000
Assets directly used by the segment	300,000
Assets under the "control" of the segment manager	200,000

Determine the ROI for evaluating (a) the income performance of the manager of Segment C and (b) the rate of income contribution of the segment.

E-8

Determine RI in evaluating segments

The Rice Company has three segments: U, V, and W. Data concerning "income" and "investment" follow:

	Segment U	Segment V	Segment W
Contribution to indirect expenses	$ 36,000	$ 72,000	$ 96,000
Assets directly used by and identified with the segment	240,000	480,000	1,080,000

Assuming that the minimum desired ROI is 10%, calculate the residual income (RI) of each of the segments. Do the results indicate that any of the segments should be eliminated?

E–9

Calculate ROI and RI in evaluating a manager

Assume that for Segment U in Exercise E–8, $12,000 of the direct expenses and $30,000 of the segmental assets are not under the control of the segment manager. Top management wishes to evaluate the segment manager's income performance. Calculate the manager's ROI and RI. (Because certain expenses and assets are not controllable by the segment manager, the minimum desired ROI is 15%.)

PROBLEMS, SERIES A

P24–1–A

Prepare responsibility reports for various levels of management

You are given the following information relevant to the Monroe Company for the year ended December 31, 1987. The company is organized according to functions.

Controllable expenses	Plant manager Budget	Plant manager Actual	Vice president of manufacturing Budget	Vice president of manufacturing Actual	President Budget	President Actual
Office expense	$3,000	$4,000	$ 5,000	$ 7,000	$10,000	$ 7,000
Printing shop	2,000	2,000				
Iron shop	1,000	900				
Toaster shop	8,000	7,000				
Purchasing			10,000	11,000		
Receiving			5,000	6,000		
Inspection			8,000	7,000		
Vice president of marketing . .					80,000	70,000
Controller					60,000	50,000
Treasurer					40,000	30,000
Vice president of personnel . .					20,000	30,000

Required: Prepare the responsibility accounting reports for the three levels of management—plant manager, vice president of manufacturing, and president.

P24–2–A

Evaluate responsibility centers as profit centers and investment centers

The Bay Corporation has three production plants (A, B, and C). These plants are treated as responsibility centers. Following is a summary of the results for the month of March 1987:

Plant	Revenues	Expenses	Investment base (gross assets)
A	$ 750,000	$375,000	$ 7,500,000
B	1,500,000	600,000	11,250,000
C	2,250,000	825,000	24,000,000

Required:
a. If the plants are treated as profit centers, which plant manager appears to have done the best job?
b. If the plants are treated as investment centers, which plant manager appears to have done the best job? (Assume that plant managers are evaluated in terms of ROI on gross assets.)
c. Do the results of profit center analysis and investment center analysis give different findings? If so, why?

P24-3-A

Allocate indirect expenses to illustrate the arbitrary nature of expense allocation

Denny Company allocates all of its home office expenses to its two segments, A and B. Given below are selected expense account balances and additional data upon which allocations are based:

Expenses (allocation bases)

Home office building expense (net sales)	$24,000
Buying expenses (net purchases)	21,000
Bad debts (net sales)	2,500
Depreciation of home office equipment (net sales) . .	6,600
Advertising expense (indirect, allocated on basis of relative amounts of direct advertising)	27,000
Insurance expense (relative amounts of equipment plus average inventory in department)	7,200

Additional data:

	Segment A	Segment B	Total
Purchases (net) . . .	$ 76,000	$24,000	$100,000
Sales (net)	160,000	40,000	200,000
Equipment (cost) . .	30,000	20,000	50,000
Advertising (direct) . .	8,000	4,000	12,000
Average inventory . .	50,000	20,000	70,000

Required:

a. Prepare a schedule showing the amounts of each type of expense allocable to Segments A and B using the above data and the bases of allocation.

b. Criticize some of these allocation bases.

P24-4-A

Prepare schedule showing contribution margin and contribution to indirect expenses using contribution margin format; prepare segmental income statements

Green, Inc. is a company with two segments, 1 and 2. Its revenues and expenses for 1987 follow:

	Segment 1	Segment 2	Total
Sales (net)	$320,000	$480,000	$800,000
Direct expenses:*			
Cost of goods sold	150,000	330,000	480,000
Selling	45,600	24,000	69,600
Administrative:			
Bad debts	10,000	6,000	16,000
Insurance	8,000	4,000	12,000
Interest	1,600	800	2,400
Indirect expenses (all fixed):			
Selling			60,000
Administrative			84,000

* All the direct expenses are variable except insurance and interest, which are fixed.

Required:

a. Prepare a schedule showing the contribution margin, the contribution to indirect expenses of each segment, and net income for the company as a whole. Do not allocate indirect expenses to the segments.

b. Assume that indirect selling expenses are to be allocated on the basis of net sales and that indirect administrative expenses are to be allocated on the basis of direct administrative expenses. Prepare a statement (starting with the contribution to indirect expenses) which shows the net income of each segment.

c. Comment on the appropriateness of the "income" amounts shown in parts *(a)* and *(b)* for determining the income contribution of the segments.

P24–5–A

Prepare an income statement for two segments using the contribution margin format; calculate the ROI for (1) the entire company, (2) each segment, and (3) each manager

The following data pertain to the operating revenues and expenses for the Vail Company for 1987:

	Segment C	Segment D	Total
Sales	$1,200,000	$600,000	$1,800,000
Variable expenses . . .	800,000	320,000	1,120,000
Direct fixed expenses . .	100,000	80,000	180,000
Indirect fixed expenses . .			240,000

Of the direct fixed expenses, $20,000 of those shown for Segment C and $18,000 of those shown for Segment D were not under the control of that segment's manager.

Regarding the company's total operating assets of $3,000,000 the following facts exist:

	Segment C	Segment D
Assets directly used by and identified with the segment	$1,200,000	$600,000
Assets under the "control" of the segment manager	1,000,000	500,000

Required:

a. Prepare a statement showing the contribution margin of each segment, the contribution to indirect expenses for each segment, and the total income of the Vail Company.

b. Determine the ROI for evaluating (1) the earning power of the entire company, (2) the rate of income contribution of each segment, and (3) the income performance of each segment manager.

c. Comment on the results of part (b).

P24–6–A

Calculate ROI and RI for each segment and segment manager

The Albott Company operates with three segments, E, F, and G. Data regarding these segments follow:

	Segment E	Segment F	Segment G
Contribution to indirect expenses	$108,000	$ 60,000	$ 48,000
Income controllable by the manager	150,000	90,000	76,800
Assets directly used by and identified with the segment . .	600,000	480,000	240,000
Assets under the "control" of the segment manager . . .	528,000	426,000	216,000

Required:

a. Calculate the ROI for each segment and each segment manager. Rank them from highest to lowest.

b. Assume the minimum desired rates of return are 12% for a segment and 20% for a segment manager. Calculate the RI for each segment and each manager. Rank them from highest to lowest.

c. Repeat (b), but assume the desired minimum rates of return are 17% for a segment and 25% for a segment manager. Rank them from highest to lowest.

d. Comment on the ranking achieved.

P24–7–A

Determine margin, turnover, and ROI for a segment and the effect on each when the variables are changed

The manager of the Tennis segment of the Sanford Corporation is faced with the following data for the year 1987:

Contribution to indirect expenses	$ 1,500,000
Assets directly used by and identified with the segment . .	18,750,000
Sales	30,000,000

Required:

a. Determine the margin, turnover, and ROI for the segment in 1987.

b. Determine the effect on margin, turnover, and ROI of the segment in 1988 if each of the following changes were to occur. Consider each one separately, and assume that any items not specifically mentioned remain the same as in 1987:

1. A campaign to control costs resulted in $300,000 of reduced expenses.
2. Certain nonproductive assets were eliminated. As a result "investment" decreased by $1,500,000 and expenses decreased by $120,000.

3. An advertising campaign resulted in increasing sales by $6,000,000, cost of goods sold by $4,500,000, and advertising expense by $900,000.

4. An investment was made in productive assets costing $1,500,000. As a result, sales increased by $600,000, and expenses increased by $90,000.

P24-8-A

Evaluate the desirability of adopting a new project using ROI, margin, and turnover

For the year ended December 31, 1987, the Adams Company reported the following information for the company as a whole and for one of its segments:

		Kitchen segment		
	Adams Company	Tile project	Floor project	Total
Sales	$9,600,000	$1,080,000	$480,000	$1,560,000
Income	1,800,000	480,000	60,000	540,000
Investment . .	7,200,000	1,440,000	168,000	1,608,000

The Adams Company anticipates that the above relationships (ROI, margin, turnover) will hold true for the upcoming year. The kitchen segment is faced with the possibility of adding a new project in 1988, with the following projected data:

Appliance project	
Sales	$360,000
Income	84,000
Investment	300,000

Required:

a. Determine the ROI for the Adams Company, the kitchen segment, and for the two projects (tile and floor) separately for the year ended December 31, 1987.

b. Using the above information, determine if the manager of the kitchen segment should add the appliance project if ROI is a deciding factor. What problem may be encountered?

P24-9-A

Evaluate the desirability of adopting a new project using RI

Using the data provided in P24-8-A, determine the residual income for all three projects and for the kitchen segment with and without the appliance project if the desired ROI is 25% (the ROI for the company as a whole). Should the appliance project be added if RI is a deciding factor?

PROBLEMS, SERIES B

P24-1-B

Prepare responsibility reports for various levels of management

You are given the following information relevant to Mitchell Company for the year ended December 31, 1987. The company is organized according to functions.

Controllable expenses	Shop "A" supervisor		Plant manager		Vice president of manufacturing	
	Budget	Actual	Budget	Actual	Budget	Actual
Office expense	$2,000	$1,000	$ 4,000	$ 5,000	$10,000	$ 9,000
Supervision	3,000	4,000				
Supplies (manufacturing) . .	4,000	5,000				
Tools	5,000	6,000				
Shop "B"			9,000	10,000		
Shop "C"			11,000	12,000		
Purchasing					14,000	17,000
Receiving					15,000	15,000
Inspection					16,000	8,000

Required: Prepare the responsibility accounting reports for three levels of management—supervisor, plant manager, and vice president of manufacturing.

P24–2–B

Evaluate responsibility centers as profit centers and investment centers

The Norton Corporation has three production plants (K, L, and M). These plants are treated as responsibility centers. Following is a summary of the results for the month of April 1987:

Plant	Revenues	Expenses	Investment base (gross assets)
K	$ 150,000	$125,000	$ 600,000
L	200,000	75,000	800,000
M	1,050,000	800,000	5,500,000

Required:

a. If the plants are treated as profit centers, which plant manager appears to have done the best job?

b. If the plants are treated as investment centers, which plant manager appears to have done the best job? (Assume that plant managers are evaluated in terms of ROI).

c. Do the results of profit center analysis and investment center analysis give different findings? If so, why?

P24–3–B

Allocate indirect expenses to illustrate arbitrary nature of expense allocation

Surfrider, Inc. allocates expenses and revenues to the two segments that it operates. It extends credit to customers under a revolving charge plan whereby all account balances not paid within 30 days are charged interest at the rate of $1\frac{1}{2}\%$ per month.

Given below are selected revenue and expense accounts and some additional data needed to complete the allocation of the one revenue amount and the expenses.

Revenue and expenses (allocation bases)

Revolving charge service revenue (net sales)	$ 40,000
Home office building occupancy expense (net sales)	30,000
Buying expenses (net purchases)	100,000
General administrative expenses (number of employees in department)	50,000
Insurance expense (relative average inventory plus cost of equipment and fixtures in each department)	12,000
Depreciation expense on home office equipment (net sales) . .	20,000

Additional data:

	Segment D	Segment E	Total
Number of employees	3	7	10
Sales (net)	$200,000	$400,000	$600,000
Purchases (net)	160,000	240,000	400,000
Average inventory	40,000	80,000	120,000
Cost of equipment and fixtures . .	60,000	120,000	180,000

Required:

a. Prepare a schedule showing allocation of the above items to Segments D and E.

b. Criticize some of these allocation bases.

P24–4–B

Prepare schedule showing contribution margin and contribution to indirect expenses using contribution margin format; prepare segmental income statements

Carey, Inc. is a diamond importer that operates two segments, A and B. The revenue and expense data for 1987 follow:

	Segment A	Segment B	Total
Net sales	$559,500	$923,000	$1,482,500
Direct expenses:*			
Cost of goods sold . . .	310,000	470,000	780,000
Selling	53,000	45,000	98,000
Administrative	15,000	10,000	25,000
Bad debts	4,000	11,000	15,000
Indirect expenses:			
Selling			210,000
Administrative			260,000

* All of the direct expenses are variable except administrative expense, which is fixed.

Required: a.   Prepare a schedule showing the contribution margin, the contribution to indirect expenses of each segment, and net income for the company as a whole. Do not allocate indirect expenses to the segments.

b.   Assume that indirect selling expenses are to be allocated to the segments on the basis of net sales (round to the nearest percent) and that indirect administrative expenses are to be allocated on the basis of direct administrative expenses. Prepare a statement (starting with the contribution to indirect expenses) that shows the net income of each segment.

c.   Comment on the appropriateness of the "income" amounts shown in parts (a) and (b) for determining the income contribution of the segments.

P24–5–B

Determine the contribution margin using contribution margin format; calculate ROI for (1) the entire company, (2) each segment, and (3) each manager

The Davis Corporation has three segments. Following are the results of operations for 1987:

	Segment 1	Segment 2	Segment 3	Total
Sales	$30,000,000	$18,000,000	$12,000,000	$60,000,000
Variable expenses . .	21,600,000	10,200,000	8,100,000	39,900,000
Fixed expenses:				
Direct	4,200,000	1,500,000	600,000	6,300,000
Indirect				3,000,000

Of the direct fixed expenses, $300,000 of those shown for Segment 1, $210,000 of those shown for Segment 2, and $300,000 of those shown for Segment 3 were not under the control of that segment's manager.

For the company's total operating assets of $84,000,000, the following facts exist:

	Segment 1	Segment 2	Segment 3
Assets directly used by and identified with the segment	$42,000,000	$24,000,000	$12,000,000
Assets under the "control" of the segment manager	36,000,000	19,200,000	9,600,000

Required: a.   Prepare a statement (in thousands of dollars) showing the contribution margin, the contribution to indirect expenses for each segment, and the total income of the Davis Corporation.

b.   Determine the ROI for evaluating (1) the earning power of the entire company, (2) the rate of income contribution of each segment, and (3) the income performance of each segment manager.

c.   Comment on the results of part (b).

P24–6–B

Calculate ROI and RI for each segment and each segment manager

The Watson Company has three segments, R, S, and T. Data regarding these segments follow:

	Segment R	Segment S	Segment T
Contribution to indirect expenses	$ 720,000	$ 348,000	$120,000
Income controllable by the manager	792,000	378,000	144,000
Assets directly used by and identified with the segment . .	6,000,000	2,400,000	600,000
Assets under the "control" of the segment manager . . .	5,760,000	2,280,000	540,000

Required: a.   Calculate the ROI for each segment and each segment manager. Rank them from highest to lowest.

b.   Assume the minimum desired rates of return are 10% for a segment and 12% for a segment manager. Calculate the RI for each segment and for each manager. Rank them from highest to lowest.

c.   Repeat (b), but assume that the desired minimum rates of return are 14% for a segment and 16% for a segment manager. Rank them from highest to lowest.

d.   Comment on the rankings achieved.

P24-7-B

Determine margin, turnover, and ROI for a segment and the effect on each when the variables are changed

The Jacket segment of the Tweed Corporation reported the following data for 1987:

Contribution to indirect expenses	$ 525,000
Assets directly used by and identified with the segment	4,200,000
Sales	8,400,000

Required:

a. Determine the margin, turnover, and ROI for the segment in 1987.
b. Determine the effect on margin, turnover, and ROI of the segment in 1988 if each of the following changes were to occur. Consider each one separately, and assume that any items not specifically mentioned remain the same as in 1987:

1. A new labor contract with the union increased expenses by $150,000 for 1988.
2. A strike in early 1988 shut down operations for two months. Sales decreased by $2,250,000, cost of goods sold by $1,500,000, and other direct expenses by $450,000.
3. Introduction of a new product caused sales to increase by $3,000,000, cost of goods sold by $2,100,000, and other direct expenses by $225,000. Operating assets increased by $450,000.
4. An advertising campaign was launched. As a result, sales increased by $750,000, cost of goods sold by $525,000, and other direct expenses by $225,000.

P24-8-B

Evaluate the desirability of adopting a project using ROI, margin, and turnover

The following information is available for the Crenshaw Company as a whole and for the Golf segment for the year ending December 31, 1987.

	Crenshaw Company overall	Golf segment		
		Project A	Project B	Total
Sales	$8,000,000	$1,000,000	$1,500,000	$2,500,000
Income	900,000	200,000	180,000	380,000
Investment	6,000,000	800,000	1,000,000	1,800,000

The Crenshaw Company anticipates that the above relationships (margin, turnover, and ROI) will hold true for the coming year. The Golf segment intends to add project C in 1988, with the following projected data:

Project C	
Sales	$500,000
Income	50,000
Investment	300,000

Required:

a. Using the above information, determine the ROI for 1987 for the Crenshaw Company, the Golf segment, and for projects A and B separately.
b. Using ROI information, should the manager of the Golf Segment undertake project C? What problems might be encountered in using ROI as a decision-making tool?

BUSINESS DECISION PROBLEM

Allocate unusual expenses to departments; determine controllable and noncontrollable expenses

Respond to each of the following situations:

a. The Nelson Company manufactures water skis. The company's business is seasonal, and between August and December 10 skilled manufacturing employees are usually "laid off." In order to improve morale, the financial vice president suggested that these 10 employees not be laid off in the future. Instead it was suggested that they work in general labor from August to December but still be paid their manufacturing wages of $12 per hour. General labor personnel earn $6 per hour. What are the implications of this plan for the assignment of costs to the various segments of the business?

b. The Leed Company builds new homes. Ferris is in charge of the construction department. Among other responsibilities, Ferris hires and supervises the carpenters and other workers who build the homes. The Leed Company does not do its own foundation work. The construction of foundations is done by subcontractors hired by Kyte of the procurement department.

   To start the development of a 500-home community, Kyte hired the Lye Company to build the foundations for the homes. On the day construction was to begin, the Lye Company went out of business. Consequently, construction was delayed six weeks while Kyte hired a new subcontractor. Which department should be charged with the cost of the delay in construction? Why?

c. Jack Blount is supervisor of Department 39 of the Sykes Company. The annual budget for the department is as follows:

	Annual budget for Department 39
Small tools .	$ 10,800
Set up .	12,000
Direct labor	13,200
Direct materials	24,000
Supplies	6,000
Supervision	36,000
Property taxes	6,000
Property insurance	1,200
Depreciation, machinery	2,400
Depreciation, building	2,400
Total .	$114,000

Blount's salary of $24,000 is included in supervision. The remaining $12,000 in supervision is the salary of the assistant supervisor who is directly responsible to Blount.
Identify the budget items that are controllable by Blount.

BUSINESS SITUATION FOR DISCUSSION

Management*

Financial analysts group stresses need for segment reporting

☐   The need for good segment reporting, not only on an annual basis but on a quarterly basis as well, has increased in significance of late. It has become so important that the Financial Analysts Federation (FAF) is weighing the possibility of not presenting its annual Award for Excellence for financial reporting to a company if the company does not do an "outstanding job" of segment reporting in its quarterly reports.

The FAF is the professional organization of investment managers and securities analysts in North America with more than 15,000 members in 53 societies and chapters. Awards for excellence in corporate reporting are annually presented by the group.

According to Anthony T. Cope, CFA, of Wellington Management Company, Boston, Massachusetts, chairman of the FAF's corporate information committee, the suggestion made by a committee member that no award

be given a company that does not do a superior job of segment reporting "has merit; it will be carefully considered when criteria [for the 1984 awards] are established."

Cope said that the need for more segmented reporting is "another implication of the volatility and turmoil" of 1982, for which the most recent FAF awards were made.

What constitutes successful financial reporting? The FAF's corporate information committee suggests four elements:

☐   Clear presentation of information that goes beyond the minimum prescribed reporting requirements and helps to put company operations in perspective.

☐   Written commentary that is more than a recitation of historical facts but, rather, explains why important developments took place, that does not gloss over problems and adverse developments and that provides a judicious insight into the future.

☐   A timely, consistent and responsible investor relations program that genuinely seeks to inform the financial analyst in an unbiased way.

☐   An ability to articulate and communicate the business philosophy and principal strategies of management

* *Journal of Accountancy,* May 1984, p. 34. Copyright © 1984 by the American Institute of Certified Public Accountants, Inc. Reprinted with permission.

and the way in which management is organized to carry them out.

"Nothing more, and nothing less, will satisfy the demands of the increasingly turbulent investment and financial worlds," Cope said.

On segment disclosure in particular, analysts representing various industry specialties also suggest some guidelines:

☐ Be uniform in the way information is presented in each segment.
☐ Include segment sales and earnings graphs going back at least five years.

☐ Summarize the year's highlights and offer perspective on unusual events.
☐ Emphasize market size and growth rates or end users served by each segment and the backlog of key product lines.
☐ Break out foreign revenues, including export sales by segment.

Most analysts believe that, in order to grasp the prospects of a specific business, statements and breakdowns by product line and geographic market reported in the annual report, and on a regular and consistent basis thereafter, are essential.

CHAPTER 25
Budgeting

After studying this chapter, you should be able to:

1. Define a budget and name several kinds of budgets.
2. List several benefits of a budget.
3. List five general principles of budgeting.
4. Prepare a planned operating budget and its supporting budgets, such as the sales budget, production and purchases budgets, and other expense budgets.
5. Prepare flexible operating budgets.
6. Prepare a financial budget and its supporting budgets.
7. Define and use correctly the new terms in the glossary.

In planning the management of your personal finances, you may have only a general notion of the inflows and outflows of cash that will occur for a period. If the outflows exceed the inflows, you may have to borrow to cover the difference. If the inflows exceed the outflows, you may have excess cash to place in a bank or to invest.

At times, especially if you find that your cash position is tight, you may be tempted to prepare a written plan detailing your anticipated cash flows so that you may better control your finances. Such a written plan is a budget.

Companies usually prepare budgets so that they may plan for and then control their revenues (inflows) and expenses (outflows). Failure to prepare a budget could lead to significant cash flow problems or even financial disaster for a company. In fact, one of the leading causes of failure in small businesses is failing to plan and control operations through the use of budgets.

■ THE BUDGET—FOR PLANNING AND CONTROL

Time and wealth are scarce resources to all individuals and organizations, and use of these resources requires planning. But planning alone is insufficient. Control is also necessary to ensure that feasible plans are actually carried out. A tool widely used in planning and controlling the use of scarce resources is a **budget.**

There are many types of budgets. **Responsibility budgets,** which were examined in the preceding chapter, are designed to judge the performance of an individual segment or manager. **Capital budgets,** covered in Chapter 27, evaluate long-term capital projects such as the addition of equipment or the relocation of a plant. This chapter examines the **master budget,** which consists of a planned operating budget and a financial budget. The planned operating budget helps plan future earnings and results in a projected income statement. The financial budget helps management plan the financing of assets and results in a projected balance sheet.

Purposes of Budgets

A budget is a **plan** showing the company's objectives and how management intends to acquire and use resources to attain those objectives. A budget also shows how management intends to **control** the acquisition and use of resources in the coming period(s). A budget formalizes management's plans in quantitative terms. It also forces all levels of management to think ahead, anticipate results, and take action to remedy possible poor results.

Budgets may also be used to **motivate** individuals so that they strive to achieve stated goals. Budget-to-actual comparisons may be used to evaluate individual performance. For instance, the standard variable cost of producing a given part in a given cost center is a budget figure with which actual cost can be compared to help evaluate the performance of that cost center's manager. This type of comparison was illustrated in Chapter 23.

The preparation and use of budgets result in many other benefits. Business activities are better **coordinated;** managers **become aware of other managers' plans;** employees may become **cost conscious** and try to **conserve** resources; the organizational plan of the company may be **reviewed** more often and changed where necessary; and a breadth of **vision,** which might not otherwise be developed, is fostered. The planning process that results in a formal budget provides an opportunity for various levels of management to think through and commit future plans to writing. In addition, a properly prepared budget will allow management to follow the management-by-exception principle by devoting attention to activities that deviate significantly from planned levels. For all these reasons, the expected results, which are reflected in the budget, must be clearly stated.

Considerations in Preparing a Budget

Being uncertain about future developments is a poor excuse for failing to budget. In fact, the less stable the conditions, the more necessary and desirable is budgeting, although the process becomes more difficult. Obviously, stable operating conditions permit greater reliance on past experience as a basis for budgeting. But it must be emphasized that budgets are based on more than past results. Future plans must also be considered. The current year's expected activities as expressed in the budget are based on current conditions. As a result, budgeted performance is more useful than past performance as a basis for judging actual results.

A budget should describe management's assumptions relating to (1) the state of the economy over the planning horizon; (2) plans for adding, deleting, or changing product lines; (3) the nature of the industry's competition; and (4) the effects of existing or possible government regulations. If assumptions change during the budget period, the effects of the changes should be analyzed and included in the evaluation of performance.

Budgets are quantitative plans for the future. But they are based mainly on past experience adjusted for future expectations. Thus, accounting data related to the past play an important part in budget preparation. The accounting system and the budget are closely related. The details of the budget must agree with the company's ledger accounts. In turn, the accounts must be designed to assist in preparing the budget, financial statements, and interim financial reports to facilitate operational control.

Accounting data and budgeted projections should be compared often during the budget period, and any differences should be investigated. Yet budgeting is not a substitute for good management. Rather, the budget is an important tool of managerial control. Managers make decisions in budget preparation that serve as a plan of action.

Some General Principles of Budgeting

Budgeting involves the coordination of financial and nonfinancial planning to satisfy organizational goals and objectives. Although there is no foolproof method for preparing an effective budget, the following aspects should be carefully considered.

Top Management Support.   All management levels must be aware of the budget's importance to the company. Plans must be clearly stated. Overemphasis on the mechanics of the budget process should be avoided. Overall broad objectives for the corporation must be decided upon and communicated throughout the organization.

Participation in Goal Setting.   It is generally believed that employees are more likely to strive toward organizational goals if they participate in setting them. Employees may have significant information that would help the budget process. Also, the employees can be made aware of the interrelationships among budget items.

Responsibility Accounting.   Individuals should be informed of management's expectations. Only those costs over which an individual has predominant control should be used in evaluating that individual's performance. As noted in the previous chapter, responsibility reports often contain budget-to-actual comparisons.

Communication of Results.   People should be informed of their progress promptly and clearly. Effective communication implies (1) timeliness, (2) reasonable accuracy, and (3) understandability. Results should be communicated so that any necessary adjustments to performance can be made.

Flexibility.   If the basic assumptions underlying the budget change during the year, the budget should be restated. In this way, performance at the actual level of operations can be compared to expected performance at that level.

Behavioral Implications of Budgets

The term *budget* has negative connotations for many employees who feel they are **subjected** to a budget. Often in the past, management has **imposed** a budget without considering the opinions and feelings of the personnel affected. Such a dictatorial process may result in resistance to the budget. A number of reasons may underlie such resistance, including lack of understanding of the program, concern for status, and an expectation of increased pressure to perform. Employees may believe that the performance evaluation method is unfair or that the goals are unrealistic and unattainable. They may lack confidence in the way accounting figures are generated or may prefer a less formal communication and evaluation system. Often these fears are completely unfounded, but if an employee believes these problems exist, it will be very difficult to accomplish the objectives of budgeting.

Problems encountered with such **imposed** budgets have led accountants and management to participatory budgeting. **Participatory budgeting** means that all levels of management responsible for actual performance actively participate in setting operating goals for the coming period. Managers are more likely to understand, accept, and pursue goals if they are involved in formulating them.

Where do accountants fit into a participatory budgeting process? Accountants should be **compilers** or coordinators of the budget, not **preparers.** They should be on hand during the preparation process to present and explain significant financial data. Accountants must identify the relevant cost data that will enable management's objectives to be quantified in dollars, and they are responsible for meaningful budget reports. Accountants must continually strive to make the accounting system more responsive to managerial needs. That responsiveness, in turn, will increase confidence in the system.

Although budget participation has been used successfully in many companies, it does not always work. Studies have shown that in many organizations budget participation failed to make employees more motivated to achieve budgeted goals. Whether or not participation works depends on management's leadership style and on the organization's size and structure. Participation is not the answer to all the problems of budget preparation. It is one way to achieve better results in organizations that are receptive to that philosophy of participation.

■ THE MASTER BUDGET

A **master budget** consists of a projected income statement (planned operating budget) and a projected balance sheet (financial budget) showing the organization's objectives and proposed ways of attaining them. The remainder of this chapter will concentrate on how to prepare a master budget. The master budget is emphasized because of its prime importance to financial planning and control in a business entity. Illustration 25.1 presents the major elements involved in preparing a master budget.

The budget preparation process flows from top to bottom in Illustration 25.1. The resulting projected income statement and balance sheet incorporate elements from all budgets and schedules prepared by individual segments or divisions.

The budgeting process starts with management's plans and objectives for the next period. These plans result in various policy decisions concerning selling price, distribution network, advertising expenditures, and environmental influences from which sales forecasts for the period (in units by product or product line) are made. Multiplying units by selling price gives the sales budget in

Illustration 25.1

A Flowchart of the Financial Planning Process (an overview)

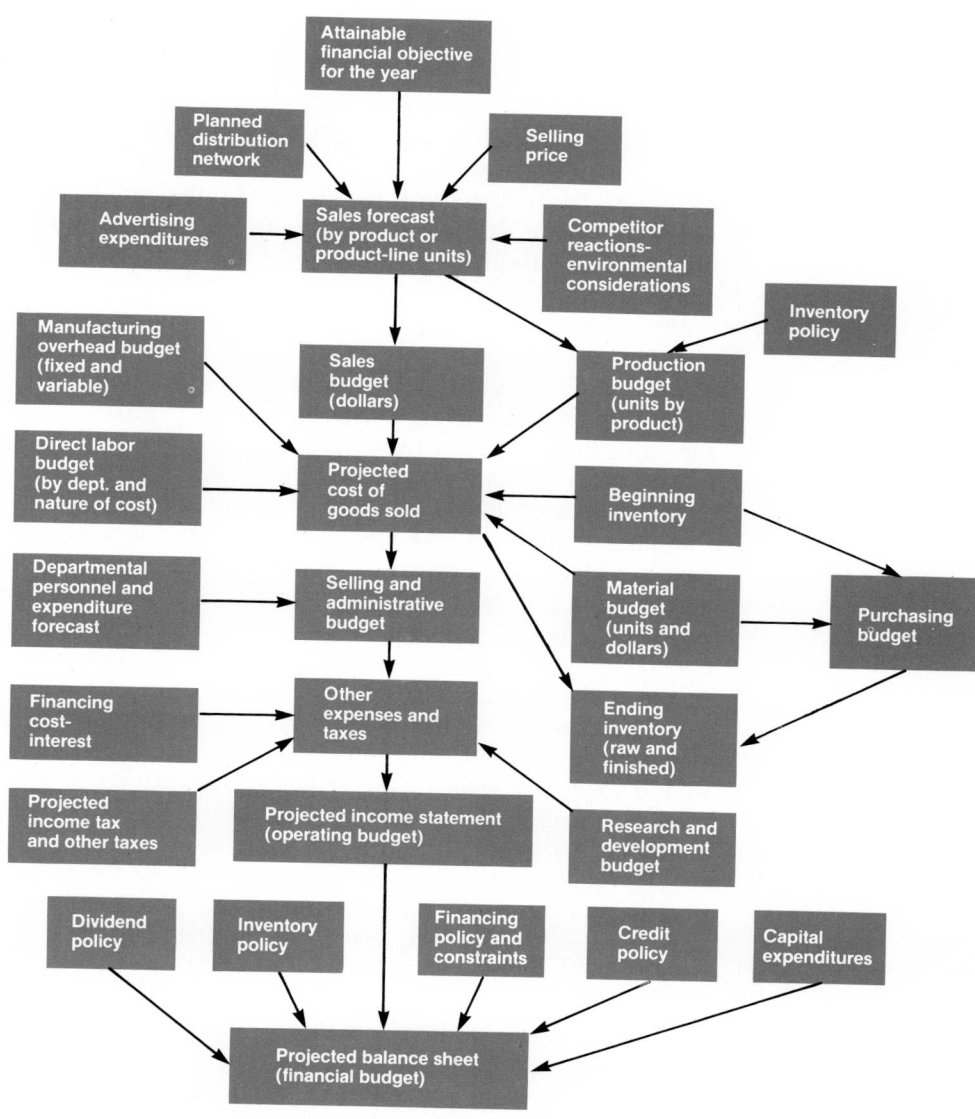

dollars. Projected cost of goods sold is based on expected production, sales volume, and inventory policy. Volume and inventory policies influence the preparation of the purchasing budget. Detailed budgets are made for each major type of manufacturing expense on both a cost center (responsibility) basis and in the aggregate.

The projected balance sheet is prepared using information contained in the planned operating budget; it is also influenced by policy decisions pertaining to dividends, inventory, credit, capital expenditures, and financial plans. The planning of capital expenditures will be described in Chapter 27. Financing by debt or stock issuances was discussed in earlier chapters.

This chapter cannot cover all areas of budgeting in detail; whole books are devoted to the subject. But the following presentation provides an overview of a budgeting procedure that has been used successfully by many business enterprises. Illustration 25.1 provides a frame of reference for the following discussion.

Preparing the Planned Operating Budget at the Expected Level of Operations

Since the projected balance sheet, or **financial budget,** depends on many items in the projected income statement, the logical starting point in preparing a master budget is the projected income statement, or **planned operating budget.** However, since the planned operating budget shows the net effect of many interrelated activities, several supporting budgets (sales, production, and purchases, to name a few) must be prepared before preparing the planned operating budget. The process begins with the sales budget.

The Sales Budget.   Preparing the sales budget is a critical step in the budgeting process. Most other budgets are derived from the sales budget. If the sales budget is not properly prepared, the entire operating budget will be inaccurate.

As you saw in Illustration 25.1, the sales budget is established by using the sales forecast. Generally, sales forecasts are based on a combination of past experiences and future expectations. The expected general level of economic activity and prospects for the industry as a whole must be considered. These prospects may be influenced by population growth, per capita income, new construction, population migration, and so on. The company's relative position in the industry must also be reviewed in light of any expected changes.

Allowances must be made for varying conditions that affect products, territories, or the strength of competitors. For example, the effect of any changes in the expected level of advertising expenditures must be estimated. Quotas may be developed for salespersons based on sales analyses by territory, by customer, by product, and so on.

The sales manager is usually responsible for the sales budget, which is prepared first in units and then in dollars. The remaining budgets that support the operating budget are based on the sales budget in units.

The Production Budget.   The **production budget** takes into account the units in the sales budget and the company's inventory policy. The production budget is first developed in units, but unit costs cannot be developed until production volume is known. Determining production volume is an important task. Careful scheduling is needed to maintain certain minimum quantities of inventory on hand while avoiding excessive inventory accumulation. The cost of carrying inventory on hand must be compared with the higher unit costs frequently encountered in producing relatively small batches of a product. **The principal objective of the production budget is to coordinate (in terms of time and quantity) the production and sale of goods.**

The production budget is often subdivided into budgets for materials, labor, and manufacturing overhead. Usually materials, labor, and some elements of manufacturing overhead will vary directly with production within a given relevant range of production. Fixed manufacturing overhead costs do not vary directly with production but are constant in total within a relevant range of production. For example, fixed manufacturing overhead costs may be $15,000 when production ranges from 60,000 to 80,000 units. However, when production is 80,001 to 95,000 units, the fixed manufacturing overhead costs might be $25,000. Management will need to determine which level of production will be the "relevant range" in order to accurately determine fixed manufacturing overhead costs.

Selling, Administrative, and Other Expense Budgets (Schedules).   Departmental personnel and expenditure forecasts are used to budget the amounts of selling and administrative expenses. Other expenses such as interest expense, income tax expense, and research and development expenses are also estimated.

Preparing the Financial Budget

Preparing a projected balance sheet, or financial budget, involves analyzing every balance sheet account. The beginning balance for each account is the amount shown on the balance sheet prepared at the end of the preceding period. Then, the effects of any planned activities on each account are considered. Many accounts will be affected by items appearing in the operating budget and by either cash inflows or outflows. Cash inflows and outflows are usually shown in a cash budget, which will be discussed later in the chapter.

The complexities encountered in preparing the financial budget often require the preparation of detailed schedules. These schedules analyze such things as planned accounts receivable collections and balances, planned material purchases, planned inventories, changes in all accounts affected by operating costs, and the amount of federal income taxes payable. Dividend policy, inventory policy, financing policy and constraints, credit policy, and planned capital expenditures also affect amounts shown in the financial budget.

■ THE MASTER BUDGET ILLUSTRATED

The first part of this chapter discussed some general concepts relating to the preparation of a master budget. This section illustrates step by step how to prepare a master budget for 1987 for the Leed Company.

Preparing the Planned Operating Budget in Units for the Leed Company

The planned operating budget is developed first in units rather than dollars. Because revenues and many expenses vary with volume, they can be forecasted more easily after sales and production quantities are established.

Illustration 25.2

Leed Company's Planned Production and Sales for First Two Quarters of 1987 (in units)

	Quarter ending	
	March 31, 1987	June 30, 1987
Beginning finished goods inventory . . .	10,000*	15,000
Add: Planned production	25,000	25,000
Units available for sale	35,000	40,000
Less: Sales forecast	20,000	35,000
Ending finished good inventory . . .	15,000	5,000

* Actual on January 1.

To illustrate this step, assume that Leed's management forecasts sales for the year 1987 at 100,000 units. Quarterly sales are expected to be 20,000, 35,000, 20,000, and 25,000 units. We will assume that the company's policy is to stabilize production, so that 100,000 units will be produced uniformly throughout the year. Therefore, production will be at the rate of 25,000 units per quarter (100,000 units/four quarters). To simplify our example, assume there are no beginning or ending work in process inventories (although it would be equivalent and more realistic to assume that work in process inventories would remain at a constant amount throughout the year). Finished goods inventory on January 1, 1987, is 10,000 units. From these data, a schedule of budgeted sales and production in units is prepared, as shown in Illustration 25.2.

Notice that the above ending inventory must be allowed to fluctuate if sales vary and a stable production policy is maintained. Thus, the finished goods inventory is affected by the difference between production and sales. When establishing inventory policy, management has decided that it is less costly to deal with fluctuating inventories than with fluctuating production.

In Illustration 25.2 sales and production data were given for each period, and we had to solve for ending inventory. Sometimes we are given sales and ending inventory data (described as a certain percentage of the next period's sales), and we have to calculate the required level of production. Assume Leed Company wishes to have ending inventory equal to 50% of the next month's sales in units (30,000 units). In this latter instance, the following format may be used to calculate planned production:

Sales forecast (units)—current month	20,000
Add: Planned ending finished goods inventory . .	15,000*
Total units required for the period	35,000
Deduct: Beginning finished goods inventory . . .	10,000
Planned production (units)	25,000

* 50% × 30,000.

When management states that ending finished goods inventory must be a specified percentage of future sales, a constant production policy cannot be maintained unless sales each period are constant.

Preparing the Planned Operating Budget in Dollars

Next, dollars must be introduced into the analysis. A forecast of expected selling prices must be made and costs must be analyzed. The forecasted selling price and costs are shown in Illustration 25.3. Note that costs are classified

Illustration 25.3

Budget Estimate of Selling Price and Costs

LEED COMPANY
Budget Estimates of Selling Price and Costs
For the Quarters Ending March 31, and June 30, 1987

Forecasted selling price	$	20
Manufacturing costs:		
Variable (per unit manufactured):		
Direct materials		2
Direct labor		6
Manufacturing overhead		1
Fixed overhead (total each quarter)		75,000
Selling and administrative expenses:		
Variable (per unit sold)		2
Fixed (total each quarter)		100,000

according to whether they are variable or fixed and are budgeted accordingly. As noted earlier, **variable costs** vary in total directly with production or sales. **Fixed costs** are unaffected in total by the relative level of production or sales. Thus, variable costs are budgeted as a constant dollar amount **per unit,** while fixed costs are budgeted only in total.

Management must now prepare a schedule to forecast cost of goods sold, the next major amount on the planned operating budget. This schedule is shown in Illustration 25.4. Notice that the beginning finished goods inventory amount for the quarter ending March 31 is the amount shown on the December 31, 1986, year-end balance sheet. Cost of goods manufactured is calculated using the variable costs of production from Illustration 25.3 plus an allocated amount of fixed manufacturing overhead ($75,000/25,000 units).

The amount of ending finished good inventory is the number of units determined to be in ending inventory (from Illustration 25.2) times the cost per unit manufactured during the period.

Illustration 25.4

Schedule of Planned Cost of Goods Sold

LEED COMPANY
Planned Cost of Goods Sold

	Quarter ending	
	March 31, 1987	June 30, 1987
Beginning finished goods inventory	$130,000*	$180,000
Cost of goods manufactured:		
Direct materials (25,000 × $2)	$ 50,000	$ 50,000
Direct labor (25,000 × $6)	150,000	150,000
Variable manufacturing overhead (25,000 × $1)	25,000	25,000
Fixed manufacturing overhead (per Illustration 25.3)	75,000	75,000
Cost of goods manufactured (25,000 units at $12)	$300,000	$300,000
Goods available for sale	$430,000	$480,000
Ending finished goods inventory:		
(15,000 at $12)†	180,000	
(5,000 at $12)		60,000
Cost of goods sold	$250,000	$420,000

* Actual on January 1 (10,000 at $13); see balance sheet Illustration 25.9.
† First-in, first-out procedure assumed.

After cost of goods sold has been forecasted, a separate budget is prepared for all selling and administrative expenses. Several support schedules may be involved for items such as advertising expense, office expense, and payroll department expense. The schedules to support budgeted selling and administrative expenses are not illustrated here, but the total selling and administrative expenses for each of the first two quarters is entered into the planned operating budget in Illustration 25.5.

Illustration 25.5

Planned Operating Budgets

LEED COMPANY Planned Operating Budgets For Quarters Ending March 31 and June 30, 1987		
	Quarter ending	
	March 31, 1987	**June 30, 1987**
Forecasted sales (20,000 and 35,000 at $20) (per Illustration 25.3)	$400,000	$700,000
Cost of goods sold (per Illustration 25.4)	250,000	420,000
Gross margin	$150,000	$280,000
Selling and administrative expenses:		
Variable (20,000 and 35,000 at $2) (per Illustration 25.3)	$ 40,000	$ 70,000
Fixed (per Illustration 25.3)	100,000	100,000
Total selling and administrative expenses	$140,000	$170,000
Net income before income taxes	$ 10,000	$110,000
Estimated federal income taxes (assumed to be 40%)	4,000	44,000
Net income	$ 6,000	$ 66,000

The Planned Operating Budget Illustrated

Illustration 25.5 shows the resulting planned operating budget for the Leed Company. All of the items appearing in the planned operating budget except the income tax accrual have been discussed and explained. Income taxes are budgeted for Leed Company at an assumed rate of 40% of net income before taxes.

If the planned operating budget does not show the desired net income, new operating plans will have to be formulated, and a new budget will be developed. The purpose of preparing a planned operating budget is to gain some knowledge of the results of a period's activities before they actually occur.

Flexible Operating Budgets

Early in the chapter you learned that a budget should be adjusted for changes in assumptions or variations in the level of operations. A technique known as flexible budgeting, which was introduced in Chapter 23, is used to deal with budgetary adjustments. A flexible operating budget is a special kind of budget that provides detailed information about budgeted expenses (and revenues) at various levels of output.

Illustration 25.6 shows a flexible budget for Leed Company's manufacturing overhead costs at various levels of output. In this example, supplies are considered a strictly variable cost, increasing $200 each time production increases

Illustration 25.6

*Flexible Budget for
Manufacturing
Overhead*

LEED COMPANY
Flexible Budget for Manufacturing Overhead

Element of manufacturing overhead	Volume (percent of capacity)*			
	70%	80%	90%	100%
Supplies	$ 1,400	$ 1,600	$ 1,800	$ 2,000
Power	7,600	8,400	9,200	10,000
Insurance	4,500	4,500	5,000	5,000
Maintenance	5,800	6,200	7,200	8,000
Depreciation	40,000	40,000	40,000	40,000
Supervision	35,000	35,000	35,000	35,000
	$94,300	$95,700	$98,200	$100,000

* Capacity is 100,000 units per period.

by 10% of capacity. In actuality, however, there are probably few costs that vary in an exact linear relationship with output. Power is a mixed (or semivariable) cost in this example. A mixed cost varies with volume, but not in direct proportion to the changes in volume. In the case of power cost, there is a fixed amount that Leed Company must pay, plus an additional $800 for each 10% increase in volume. Insurance and maintenance are considered **step variable** costs in this example since they increase in "steps" as volume increases. Depreciation and supervision, on the other hand, are completely fixed costs in this example since they are constant over the entire relevant range of activity.

A similar flexible budget could be prepared for selling and administrative expenses with supporting schedules for each expense item. Variable expenses are calculated for various levels of sales volume, while fixed costs remain constant within the relevant range.

Budget Variances.   When management uses a flexible budget to appraise a department's performance, the evaluation is based on the amounts budgeted for the level of activity actually experienced. The difference between actual costs incurred and the budgeted amount for that **same level of operations** is called a budget variance. Budget variances can indicate a department's or company's degree of efficiency, since they emerge from a comparison of "what was" with "what should have been."

To illustrate the computation of budget variances, assume that Leed Company prepared an overhead budget based on an expected volume of 100%. At this level of production, the budgeted amount for supplies is $2,000, or $0.02 per unit. By the end of the period $1,900 of supplies have been used. The first impression is that a favorable variance of $100 exists. But if actual production for the period was only 90,000 units (90% of capacity), there is actually an unfavorable variance of $100. This is because, according to the flexible operating budget, at 90% of capacity only $1,800 of supplies should have been used. Consequently, there appears to have been an inefficient use of supplies.

To give another example using the data in Illustration 25.6, maintenance may have been budgeted at $6,200 for a given period assuming the company planned to produce 80,000 units (80% of operating capacity). However, actual maintenance costs may have been $6,800 for the period. This result does not necessarily mean that an unfavorable variance of $600 was incurred. The variance depends on **actual production volume.** Assume once again that 90,000 units were produced during the period; maintenance costs are budgeted at $7,200 for that level of production. Therefore, there would actually be a favorable variance of $400 ($7,200 − $6,800).

Flexible budgets often show budgeted amounts for every 10% change in the level of operations, such as at the 70%, 80%, 90%, 100%, and 110% levels of capacity. But actual production may fall somewhere between levels, say, at 84%. When actual production falls between the levels shown in the flexible budget, the budgeted amounts at that level of operations must be calculated. The only kind of cost that does not have to be recalculated is a fixed cost since, by definition, it does not vary over the relevant range. For directly variable costs, the expected cost can be computed easily at any level since the cost is constant per unit of output. For mixed costs (partially fixed and partially variable), the budgeted amount for any operating level other than those presented can be computed using the following formula, assuming the relationship between costs and volume above a minimum level of costs is linear.

Budgeted amount = Fixed portion of costs
+ (Variable portion of cost per unit × Units of output)

Step variable costs may change only when a sufficiently large increase in production occurs, such as when one additional inspector must be added for every 20% increase in capacity used. Such step variable costs usually can be read directly from the flexible budget.

Flexible Operating Budget and Budget Variances Illustrated.   As stated above, a flexible operating budget provides detailed information about budgeted expenses at various levels of activity. The main advantage of using a flexible operating budget along with a planned operating budget is that performance can be appraised on two levels. First, comparison of the actual results with the **planned** operating budget permits analysis of the deviation of actual output from expected output. Then, given the actual level of operations, actual costs can be compared with expected costs for **that** level of output, shown on the **flexible** operating budget. The use of flexible operating budgets gives a valid basis for comparison when actual production or sales volume differs from expectations.

A detailed planned operating budget and flexible operating budget for the Leed Company for the quarter ended March 31, 1987, are presented in Illustrations 25.7 and 25.8. The planned operating budget and flexible operating budget have been prepared using the data from Illustration 25.3. The planned operating budget was based on a sales forecast of 20,000 units and a production forecast of 25,000 units, while the actual results for the period, reported in Illustrations 25.7 and 25.8, show actual sales of 19,000 units and actual production of 25,000 units. The actual selling price was $20 per unit, the same price that had been forecast.

Illustration 25.7 shows the comparison of the actual results with the planned operating budget. Comparison of actual results with the planned operating budget yields some useful information, for it shows where actual performance deviated from planned performance. For example, sales were 1,000 units lower than expected, sales revenue was $20,000 less than expected, gross margin was $12,500 less than expected, and net income was $2,000 more than expected.

Illustration 25.7

Comparison of Planned Operating Budget and Actual Results

LEED COMPANY
Comparison of Planned Operating Budget and Actual Results
For Quarter Ended March 31, 1987

	Budget	Actual
Sales (budgeted 20,000 units, actual 19,000 units)	$400,000	$380,000
Cost of goods sold:		
Beginning finished goods inventory	$130,000	$130,000
Cost of goods manufactured (25,000 units):		
Direct materials	$ 50,000	$ 62,500
Direct labor	150,000	143,750
Variable manufacturing overhead	25,000	31,250
Fixed manufacturing overhead	75,000	75,000
Cost of goods manufactured	$300,000	$312,500
Goods available for sale	$430,000	$442,500
Ending finished goods inventory	180,000	200,000
Cost of goods sold	$250,000	$242,500
Gross margin	$150,000	$137,500
Selling and administrative expenses:		
Variable	$ 40,000	$ 28,500
Fixed	100,000	95,000
Total selling and administrative expenses	$140,000	$123,500
Net income before income taxes	$ 10,000	$ 14,000
Estimated federal income taxes (40%)	4,000	5,600
Net income	$ 6,000	$ 8,400

Illustration 25.8

Comparison of Flexible Operating Budget and Actual Results

LEED COMPANY
Comparison of Flexible Operating Budget and Actual Results
For Quarter Ended March 31, 1987

	Budget	Actual	Budget variance over/under*
Sales (19,000 units)	$380,000	$380,000	$ –0–
Cost of goods sold:			
Beginning finished goods inventory	$130,000	$130,000	$ –0–
Cost of goods manufactured (25,000 units):			
Direct materials	$ 50,000	$ 62,500	12,500
Direct labor	150,000	143,750	6,250*
Variable manufacturing overhead	25,000	31,250	6,250
Fixed manufacturing overhead	75,000	75,000	–0–
Cost of goods manufactured	$300,000	$312,500	$12,500
Goods available for sale	$430,000	$442,500	$12,500
Ending finished goods inventory	192,000	200,000	8,000
Cost of goods sold (19,000 units)	$238,000	$242,500	$ 4,500
Gross margin	$142,000	$137,500	$ 4,500*
Selling and administrative expenses:			
Variable	$ 38,000	$ 28,500	$ 9,500*
Fixed	100,000	95,000	5,000*
Total selling and administrative expenses	$138,000	$123,500	$14,500*
Net income before income taxes	$ 4,000	$ 14,000	$10,000
Estimated federal income taxes (40%)	1,600	5,600	4,000
Net income	$ 2,400	$ 8,400	$ 6,000

However, the comparison of actual results with the planned operating budget does not provide a basis for evaluating whether or not management performed efficiently at the actual level of operations. For example, Illustration 25.7 shows that cost of goods sold was $7,500 less than expected. But the meaning of this difference is not clear since the actual cost of goods sold relates to the 19,000 units actually sold, while the planned cost of goods sold relates to the 20,000 units that were expected. The planned operating budget projected sales revenue, cost of goods sold, and selling and administrative expenses based on a sales forecast of 20,000 units, but only 19,000 units were actually sold. The levels of activity are not the same, so the comparisons do not give valid information for expense control.

A valid analysis for expense control purposes can only be made by comparing actual results with a flexible operating budget that is based on the same levels of sales and production that actually occurred. That is the comparison shown in Illustration 25.8. The flexible budget shown in Illustration 25.8 is made up of several pieces. The flexible budget amounts for sales revenue and selling and administrative expenses come from a flexible sales budget (not illustrated) for 19,000 units of sales, and the flexible budget amounts for production costs come from a flexible production budget (also not illustrated) for 25,000 units of production. Since the actual level of production (25,000 units) in this case was the same as the planned level, the production costs shown in the planned operating budget and the flexible operating budget are the same.

In comparisons such as these, if the number of units produced is equal to the number sold, beginning and ending inventories often are not shown. Instead, the flexible operating budget may show the number of units actually sold multiplied by the budgeted unit cost of direct materials, direct labor, and manufacturing overhead. The actual costs for direct materials, direct labor, and manufacturing overhead are also shown for the number of units sold.

The comparison of the actual results with the flexible operating budget (Illustration 25.8) reveals some inefficiencies for items in the costs of goods manufactured section. For instance, direct materials cost was $2.50 per unit ($62,500/25,000) instead of the $2 expected. Direct labor cost was only $5.75 per unit ($143,750/25,000) instead of the $6 expected. Variable overhead was $1.25 per unit ($31,250/25,000) instead of the $1 expected.

Net income was $5,000 more than expected at a sales level of 19,000 units. The main reason for the increase in net income was the lower than expected amounts of selling and administrative expenses. Variable selling and administrative expenses were only $1.50 per unit ($28,500/19,000) instead of the $2 expected; fixed selling and administrative expenses were only $95,000 instead of the $100,000 expected.

After the planned operating budget has been prepared, management must then prepare a financial budget, or projected balance sheet. The steps in preparing the financial budget are described in the next section.

Preparing the Financial Budget for the Leed Company

To prepare a projected balance sheet, each balance sheet account must be analyzed. First, the beginning balance is taken from the balance sheet at the end of the preceding period. The Leed Company balance sheet as of December 31, 1986, is shown in Illustration 25.9. Management must consider the effects of planned activities on these balances. Many accounts will be affected by items shown in the planned operating budget, by cash inflows and outflows,

Illustration 25.9

Balance Sheet at Beginning of Period

LEED COMPANY
Balance Sheet
December 31, 1986

Assets

Current assets:

Cash		$ 130,000
Accounts receivable		200,000
Inventories:		
Materials	$ 40,000	
Finished goods	130,000	170,000
Prepaid expenses		20,000
Total current assets		$ 520,000

Property, plant, and equipment:

Land		$ 60,000
Buildings	$1,000,000	
Less: Accumulated depreciation	400,000	600,000
Equipment	$ 600,000	
Less: Accumulated depreciation	180,000	420,000
Total property, plant, and equipment		$1,080,000
Total assets		$1,600,000

Liabilities and Stockholders' Equity

Current liabilities:

Accounts payable	$ 80,000
Accrued liabilities	160,000
Federal income taxes payable	100,000
Total current liabilities	$ 340,000

Stockholders' equity:

Capital stock (100,000 shares of $10 par value)	$1,000,000
Retained earnings	260,000
Total stockholders' equity	$1,260,000
Total liabilities and stockholders' equity	$1,600,000

and by policy decisions of the company. The planned operating budget shown in Illustration 25.5 and the other illustrations previously given will be used to prepare Leed Company's financial budget for the first two quarters of 1987.

Accounts Receivable. To prepare a financial budget, several new schedules must be prepared. The first of these schedules is the accounts receivable schedule shown in Illustration 25.10. We will assume that 60% of the current quarter's sales for Leed Company will be collected in that quarter, and the remaining 40% will be collected in the following quarter. Thus, collections for the first quarter will be $440,000; that is, 60% of budgeted sales of $400,000 for the first quarter plus the uncollected sales of the previous quarter [0.6($400,000) + $200,000]. Second quarter collections will be $580,000 [0.6($700,000) + $160,000]. Several other assumptions have been made to simplify this schedule; for example, there are no sales returns or allowances, no discounts, and no uncollectible accounts. All sales are assumed to be on a credit basis.

Inventories. A schedule of planned materials purchases and inventories must also be prepared. Planned usage and cost per unit of materials are taken from the planned cost of goods sold schedule (Illustration 25.4). Assuming

Illustration 25.10

Planned Accounts Receivable Collections and Balances

LEED COMPANY
Planned Accounts Receivable Collections and Balances

	Quarter ending	
	March 31, 1987	June 30, 1987
Planned balance at beginning of quarter	$200,000*	$160,000
Planned sales for period (per Illustration 25.5)	400,000	700,000
Total	$600,000	$860,000
Projected collections during quarter (per discussion in text) . .	440,000	580,000
Planned balance at end of quarter	$160,000	$280,000

* Actual on January 1.

Illustration 25.11

Planned Materials Purchases and Inventories

LEED COMPANY
Planned Materials Purchases and Inventories

	Quarter ending	
	March 31, 1987	June 30, 1987
Planned usage (25,000 × $2) (per Illustration 25.4) . .	$50,000	$50,000
Planned ending inventory (½ × 25,000 × $2) (per discussion in text)	25,000	25,000
Planned material available for use	$75,000	$75,000
Inventory at beginning of quarter	40,000*	25,000
Planned purchases for the quarter	$35,000	$50,000

* Actual on January 1.

no work in process inventories, there will be only materials and finished goods inventories.

Illustration 25.11 shows a schedule of planned purchases and inventories of materials for the Leed Company. Materials inventory is normally maintained at a level of one half of next quarter's planned usage. The $40,000 beginning inventory was greater than normal because of a strike threat in the supplier company. This threat has now passed, and the materials inventory will be reduced at the end of the first quarter to the normal planned level.

The calculation of planned ending finished goods inventories is included in Illustration 25.4.

Accounts Affected by Operating Costs.   Individual schedules could be prepared for each of the accounts affected by operating costs. But for illustrative purposes a schedule will be prepared combining the analyses of all the accounts affected by materials purchases or operating costs.

The following assumptions are made:

1. All purchases of materials are made on account.
2. Direct labor incurred is credited to accrued liabilities.

3. Manufacturing overhead incurred is credited to the following accounts:

	Quarter ending	
	March 31	June 30
Accounts Payable	$ 16,000	$ 13,000
Accrued Liabilities	60,000	64,000
Prepaid Expenses	6,000	5,000
Accumulated Depreciation—Building . .	5,000	5,000
Accumulated Depreciation—Equipment . .	13,000	13,000
Total	$100,000	$100,000

4. Selling and administrative expenses incurred are credited to the following accounts:

	Quarter ending	
	March 31	June 30
Accounts Payable	$ 5,000	$ 10,000
Accrued Liabilities	130,000	154,000
Prepaid Expenses	2,000	3,000
Accumulated Depreciation—Building . .	1,000	1,000
Accumulated Depreciation—Equipment . .	2,000	2,000
Total	$140,000	$170,000

5. Planned cash payments are as follows:

	Quarter ending	
	March 31	June 30
Accounts Payable . .	$ 80,000	$ 56,000
Accrued Liabilities . .	330,000	354,000
Prepaid Expenses . .	–0–	10,000
Total	$410,000	$420,000

Illustration 25.12 shows analyses of the accounts credited as a result of the above data. The illustration provides a considerable amount of information needed in constructing financial budgets for the quarters ended March 31, 1987, and June 30, 1987. The balances on both dates for Accounts Payable, Accrued Liabilities, Prepaid Expenses (the only debit balance account shown), Accumulated Depreciation—Building, and Accumulated Depreciation—Equipment are computed in the schedule.

Federal Income Taxes Payable.   A separate schedule could be prepared showing the changes in the Federal Income Taxes Payable account, but in this example, a brief discussion will suffice. Balances reported in the financial budgets assume that one half of the $100,000 liability shown in the December 31, 1986, balance sheet is paid in each of the first two quarters of 1987 (shown in Illustration 25.15 later in the chapter). The accrual for the current quarter is added (Illustration 25.5). Thus, the balance on March 31, 1987, is $54,000 ($100,000 − $50,000 + $4,000). The balance on June 30, 1987, is $48,000 ($54,000 − $50,000 + $44,000). On June 30, the balance equals the accrual for the current year, $4,000 for the first quarter and $44,000 for the second quarter.

Cash Budget.   After the above analyses have been prepared, sufficient information is available to prepare the cash budget and compute the balance

Illustration 25.12 *Analyses of Accounts Credited for Materials Purchases and Operating Costs*

LEED COMPANY
Analyses of Accounts Credited for Materials Purchases and Operating Costs

	Total debits	Accounts payable	Accrued liabilities	Prepaid expenses	Accumulated depreciation Building	Accumulated depreciation Equipment
Purchases or operating costs, quarter ending March 31 (credits made to accounts shown at right):						
Direct materials (per Illustration 25.11)	$ 35,000	$ 35,000				
Direct labor (per Illustration 25.4)	150,000		$150,000			
Manufacturing overhead (per Illustration 25.4)	100,000	16,000	60,000	$ 6,000	$ 5,000	$ 13,000
Selling and administrative expenses (per Illustration 25.5)	140,000	5,000	130,000	2,000	1,000	2,000
Total	$425,000	$ 56,000	$340,000	$ 8,000	$ 6,000	$ 15,000
Beginning balances (per Illustration 25.9)		80,000	160,000	20,000*	400,000	180,000
Total		$136,000	$500,000	$12,000*	$406,000	$195,000
Planned cash payments (debits made to accounts shown)		80,000	330,000			
Planned balances, March 31		$ 56,000	$170,000	$12,000*	$406,000	$195,000
Purchases or operating costs, quarter ending June 30 (credits made to accounts shown at right):						
Direct materials (per Illustration 25.11)	$ 50,000	$ 50,000				
Direct labor (per Illustration 25.4)	150,000		$150,000			
Manufacturing overhead (per Illustration 25.4)	100,000	13,000	64,000	$ 5,000	$ 5,000	$ 13,000
Selling and administrative expenses (per Illustration 25.5)	170,000	10,000	154,000	3,000	1,000	2,000
Total	$470,000	$ 73,000	$368,000	$ 8,000	$ 6,000	$ 15,000
Total including March 31 balances		$129,000	$538,000	$ 4,000*	$412,000	$210,000
Planned cash payments (debits made to accounts shown)		56,000	354,000	10,000		
Planned balances, June 30		$ 73,000	$184,000	$14,000*	$412,000	$210,000

* Debit balance.

in the Cash account on March 31 and June 30, 1987. To prepare a cash budget, information about cash receipts and cash disbursements is required.

Cash Receipts. The cash receipts schedule can be prepared from the information used to compute the accounts receivable schedule (Illustration 25.10). A schedule of planned cash receipts for the Leed Company is shown in Illustration 25.13.

Cash Disbursements. Cash is needed to pay for purchases, wages, rent, interest, income taxes, cash dividends, and most other expenses. The amount of each cash disbursement may be obtained from other budgets or schedules. Illustration 25.14 shows the cash disbursements schedule for the Leed Company. The illustration shows where the information came from, except for the payment of federal income taxes and dividends. Income taxes, discussed earlier, are assumed to be 40% of net income before taxes. It is assumed that $20,000 of dividends will be paid in the first quarter and $40,000 in the second quarter.

Illustration 25.13 *Planned Cash Receipts*

LEED COMPANY
Planned Cash Receipts

	Quarter ending	
	March 31, 1987	June 30, 1987
Collections on accounts receivable:		
From preceding quarter's sales	$200,000	$160,000
From current quarter's sales	240,000 (0.6 × $400,000)	420,000 (0.6 × $700,000)
Total cash receipts (per Illustration 25.10) . .	$440,000	$580,000

Illustration 25.14

Planned Cash Disbursements

LEED COMPANY
Planned Cash Disbursements

	Quarter ending	
	March 31, 1987	June 30, 1987
Payment of accounts payable (per Illustration 25.12) . .	$ 80,000	$ 56,000
Payment of accrued liabilities (per Illustration 25.12) . .	330,000	354,000
Payment of federal income tax liability	50,000	50,000
Payment of dividends	20,000	40,000
Expenses prepaid (per Illustration 25.12)	–0–	10,000
Total cash disbursements	$480,000	$510,000

Once cash receipts and disbursements have been determined, a cash budget can be prepared for the Leed Company, as shown in Illustration 25.15. The **cash budget** is a plan indicating expected inflows and outflows of cash. This cash budget helps management to decide whether enough cash will be available for short-term needs. If the cash budget indicates a cash shortage at a certain

Illustration 25.15

Planned Cash Flows and Cash Balances

LEED COMPANY
Planned Cash Flows and Cash Balances

	Quarter ending	
	March 31, 1987	June 30, 1987
Planned balance at beginning of quarter	$130,000*	$ 90,000
Planned cash receipts:		
Collections of accounts receivable (per Illustration 25.13) . .	440,000	580,000
	$570,000	$670,000
Planned cash disbursements:		
Payment of accounts payable (per Illustration 25.12) . . .	$ 80,000	$ 56,000
Payment of accrued liabilities (per Illustration 25.12) . . .	330,000	354,000
Payment of federal income tax liability	50,000	50,000
Payment of dividends	20,000	40,000
Expenses prepaid (per Illustration 25.12)	–0–	10,000
Total cash disbursements	$480,000	$510,000
Planned balance at end of quarter	$ 90,000	$160,000

* Actual on January 1.

date, the company may need to borrow money on a short-term basis. If the expected cash balance appears to be higher than necessary, the company may wish to invest the extra funds for short periods to earn interest rather than leave the cash idle. Knowing of possible shortages or excess cash balances in advance will allow management sufficient time to plan for such occurrences.

The Financial Budget Illustrated

The preparation of the financial budget for the quarters ending March 31, 1987, and June 30, 1987, shown in Illustration 25.16 completes the master budget. Management now has information to help appraise the policies it has adopted before implementing them. If the results of these policies, as shown by the master budget, are unsatisfactory, the policies can be changed before serious problems arise. For example, the Leed Company management had a

Illustration 25.16 *Projected Balance Sheet*

LEED COMPANY
Projected Balance Sheet

	March 31, 1987	June 30, 1987
Assets		
Current assets:		
Cash (per Illustration 25.15)	$ 90,000	$ 160,000
Accounts receivable (per Illustration 25.10)	160,000	280,000
Inventories:		
Materials (per Illustration 25.11)	25,000	25,000
Finished goods (per Illustration 25.4)	180,000	60,000
Prepaid expenses (per Illustration 25.12)	12,000	14,000
Total current assets	$ 467,000	$ 539,000
Property, plant, and equipment:		
Land (per Illustration 25.9)	$ 60,000	$ 60,000
Buildings ($1,000,000 less accumulated depreciation of $406,000 and $412,000) (per Illustrations 25.9 and 25.12) . .	594,000	588,000
Equipment ($600,000 less accumulated depreciation of $195,000 and $210,000) (per Illustrations 25.9 and 25.12) . .	405,000	390,000
Total property, plant, and equipment	$1,059,000	$1,038,000
Total assets	$1,526,000	$1,577,000
Liabilities and Stockholders' Equity		
Current liabilities:		
Accounts payable (per Illustration 25.12)	$ 56,000	$ 73,000
Accrued liabilities (per Illustration 25.12)	170,000	184,000
Federal income taxes payable (per discussion on page 981)	54,000	48,000
Total current liabilities	$ 280,000	$ 305,000
Stockholders' equity:		
Capital stock (100,000 shares of $10 par value) (per Illustration 25.9)	$1,000,000	$1,000,000
Retained earnings (see below)	246,000*	272,000†
Total stockholders' equity	$1,246,000	$1,272,000
Total liabilities and stockholders' equity	$1,526,000	$1,577,000

* $260,000 (per Illustration 25.9) + Income of $6,000 − Dividends of $20,000.
† $246,000 + Income of $66,000 − Dividends of $40,000.

policy of stable production each period. The master budget shows that production can be stabilized even though sales fluctuate widely. But the planned ending inventory at June 30 may be considered somewhat low in view of the fluctuations in sales. Management now knows this in advance and can take corrective action if necessary.

Purchases Budget for a Merchandising Company

Throughout this chapter, discussion has centered on the preparation of operating and financial budgets for a **manufacturer.** Suppose a budget is being prepared for a **retail merchandising business,** such as a dress shop or a furniture store. In this case, a purchases budget will be prepared instead of a production budget. To compute the purchases for each quarter, the cost of the goods to be sold during the quarter and the inventory required at the end of the quarter must be estimated.

The purchases budget can be derived from the sales budget and the company's inventory policy. Using the Strobel Furniture Company as an example, suppose a sales budget was prepared as shown in Illustration 25.17. Assume that the company likes to maintain sufficient inventory to cover one half of the next quarter's sales. Cost of goods sold is 55% of sales. The ending inventory on December 31, 1986, was $8,250. The purchases budget can now be prepared, as shown in Illustration 25.18. For the first quarter of 1987, notice that the ending inventory is one half of the second quarter's cost of goods sold [0.5 × (55% of $80,000) = $22,000].

The Strobel Company would use the information in the purchases budget in preparing the cost of goods sold section of the planned operating budget,

Illustration 25.17

Sales Budget

		STROBEL FURNITURE COMPANY Sales Budget Quarter Ending			
	March 31, *1987*	*June 30,* *1987*	*September 30,* *1987*	*December 31,* *1987*	*March 31,* *1988*
	$30,000	$80,000	$50,000	$90,000	$40,000

Illustration 25.18

Purchases Budget

	STROBEL FURNITURE COMPANY Purchases Budget Quarter Ending			
	March 31, *1987*	*June 30,* *1987*	*September 30,* *1987*	*December 31,* *1987*
Ending inventory desired* . .	$22,000	$13,750	$24,750	$11,000
Cost of goods sold (55% of sales)	16,500	44,000	27,500	49,500
Total	$38,500	$57,750	$52,250	$60,500
Less: Beginning inventory . .	8,250	22,000	13,750	24,750
Purchases required	$30,250	$35,750	$38,500	$35,750

* Next period's sales × 55% × 50%.

the cash disbursements schedules, and the inventory and accounts payable amounts on the financial budget.

■ SUMMARY

A budget is one of management's most useful tools for planning and controlling income, cash flow, and other aspects of a business. A well-prepared budget forces management to think ahead, anticipate results, and take action when actual results differ from expected results. Used effectively, a budget can motivate employees. Used ineffectively, a budget can cause employee disenchantment and possible disruption of operations.

Participation in the preparation of budgets generally improves the motivational aspects of budgeting. Participation gives the people who have responsibility for performance a voice in setting the goals for the forthcoming period.

The preparation of an effective budget requires top management support and timely communication of results. The accountant should strive to design the accounting system to reflect the operations of the business and at the same time to facilitate responsibility reporting.

There are several types of budgets. The two budgets discussed in this chapter are the planned operating budget and the financial budget. The planned operating budget (a projected income statement) helps management plan future earnings. The financial budget (a forecast balance sheet) helps management plan the financing of assets. Together, the planned operating budget and the financial budget are referred to as the master budget.

The preparation of the master budget begins with detail budgets that support the planned operating budget. First, a sales forecast is made to project the number of units to be sold in the upcoming year. Based on this sales forecast, the expected price, and the projected selling expenses, a sales budget can be proposed showing expected sales revenue and selling expenses. Next, management uses that sales forecast and the company's inventory policy to decide the number of units to produce in the next year. Once the level of operations is established, management can use production cost information to project the cost to manufacture, cost of goods manufactured, and cost of goods sold for the year. This information is presented in the production budget. Finally, budgets for administrative and other expenses are established, based on the levels of sales and of production established in the sales and production budgets. Collectively, these subsidiary budgets provide enough information for a projected income statement, which is the planned operating budget.

A budget variance is a deviation between actual performance and the expected performance for the actual level of operations. A flexible operating budget is a series of budgets, each of which corresponds to a different level of operations. A flexible operating budget amount shown for the actual level of operations serves as a standard for comparing a department's actual results with the expected results.

The use of a flexible operating budget along with a planned operating budget permits performance appraisal on two levels. First, comparison of the actual results with the planned operating budget permits the deviation from expected output to be analyzed. Then, given the actual level of operations, actual costs can be compared with expected costs for that level of output, shown on the flexible operating budget.

Preparing a projected balance sheet (or financial budget) involves analyzing every balance sheet account in light of the planned activities expressed in the income statement. A separate cash budget is usually prepared to show sources of, uses of, and net changes in cash for the period. The complexities involved in preparing the financial budget often require the preparation of supplemental schedules for various accounts on the balance sheet.

You must realize by now that the terms *management* and *decision making* go "hand in hand." Under normal economic conditions, poor decision making by management is usually the cause of business failures. In Chapter 26, short-term decision making is discussed.

NEW TERMS INTRODUCED IN CHAPTER 25*

Budget

A plan showing a company's objectives and proposed ways of attaining the objectives. Two major types of budgets are the (1) master budget and (2) control, or responsibility, budget (966).

Budgeting

The coordination of financial and nonfinancial planning to satisfy an organization's goals (967).

Budget variance

The difference between an actual cost incurred (or revenue earned) at a certain level of operations and the budgeted amount for that same level of operations (975).

Cash budget

A plan indicating expected inflows (receipts) and outflows (disbursements) of cash; it helps management decide whether enough cash will be available for short-term needs (983).

Financial budget

The projected balance sheet portion of a master budget (966, 970).

Fixed costs

Costs that are unaffected by the relative levels of production or sales (973).

Flexible operating budget

Provides detailed information about budgeted expenses and revenues at various levels of output (974).

Master budget

The projected income statement and projected balance sheet showing the organization's objectives and proposed ways of attaining them; includes supporting budgets for such areas as cash, sales, costs, and production; also called master profit plan. It is the overall plan of the enterprise and ideally consists of all of the various segmental budgets (968).

Mixed cost

A cost that varies with volume, but not in direct proportion to the changes in volume (975).

Participatory budgeting

A method of preparing the budget that includes the participation of all levels of management responsible for actual performance (968).

Planned operating budget

The projected income statement portion of a master budget (966, 970).

Production budget

Takes into account the units in the sales budget and the company's inventory policy (970).

Variable costs

Costs that vary directly with production or sales and are a constant dollar amount per unit of output over different levels of output or sales (973).

---

* Some terms defined in earlier chapters are repeated here for your convenience.

DEMONSTRATION PROBLEM

During January 1987, the Phoenix Company plans to sell 20,000 units of its product at a price of $20 per unit. Selling expenses are estimated to be $40,000 plus 2% of sales revenue. General and administrative expenses are estimated to be $30,000 plus 1% of sales revenue. Income tax expense is estimated to be 40% of net income before taxes.

Phoenix plans to produce 25,000 units during January with estimated variable costs per unit as follows: $2 for material, $5 for labor, and $3 for variable overhead. The fixed overhead cost is estimated at $20,000 per month. The finished goods inventory at January 1, 1987, is 4,000 units with a cost per unit of $10. The company uses Fifo inventory procedure.

Required: Prepare a projected income statement for January 1987.

Solution to demonstration problem

PHOENIX COMPANY
Projected Income Statement
For January 1987

Sales (20,000 × $20)		$400,000
Cost of goods sold (see Schedule 1)		212,800
Gross margin		$187,200
Selling expenses:		
Fixed	$ 40,000	
Variable (0.02 × $400,000)	8,000	
General and administrative expenses:		
Fixed	30,000	
Variable (0.01 × $400,000)	4,000	82,000
Net income before taxes		$105,200
Income taxes (40%)		42,080
Net income		$ 63,120

Schedule 1

PHOENIX COMPANY
Planned Cost of Goods Sold

Beginning finished goods inventory (4,000 × $10)		$ 40,000
Cost of goods manufactured:		
Direct materials (25,000 × $2)	$ 50,000	
Direct labor (25,000 × $5)	125,000	
Variable manufacturing overhead (25,000 × $3)	75,000	
Fixed manufacturing overhead	20,000	
Cost of goods manufactured (25,000 × $10.80)		270,000
Cost of goods available for sale		$310,000
Ending finished goods inventory (9,000 × $10.80)		97,200
Cost of goods sold		$212,800

Direct materials . . . . $4 per unit
Direct labor . . . .   8 per unit
Variable manufacturing overhead . . . .   2 per unit
Fixed manufacturing overhead . . . .   400,000 per quarter

6. There is no work in process inventory at the beginning or end of either period.
7. The company computes inventory on a Fifo basis.

Required: Prepare a schedule of planned cost of goods manufactured and sold for the quarters ending September 30, 1987, and December 31, 1987. (Hint: Prepare production schedules in units first.)

P25-6-A

Prepare a cash receipts schedule and a purchases budget

Park Company manufactures and sells bathroom fixtures. Estimated sales for the next three months are:

September 1987 . . . $300,000
October 1987   450,000
November 1987   350,000

Sales for August were $320,000. All sales are on account. Park Company estimates that 60% of the accounts receivable are collected in the month of sale with the remaining 40% collected the following month. The units sell for $25 each. The cash balance for September 1, 1987, is $68,000.

Generally, 60% of purchases are due and payable in the month of purchase with the remainder due the following month. Purchase cost per unit for materials is $15. The company maintains an end-of-the-month inventory of 1,000 units plus 10% of next month's unit sales.

Required: Prepare a cash receipts schedule for September and October and a purchases budget for August, September, and October.

P25-7-A

Prepare a cash budget

Refer to P25-6-A. In addition to the information given, selling and administrative expenses paid in cash are $100,000 per month.

Required: Prepare a monthly cash budget for September and October for the Park Company.

P25-8-A

Prepare a cash budget

The Hunt Company has gathered the following budget information for the quarter ending March 31:

Sales $540,000
Purchases   450,000
Salaries and wages . .   195,000
Rent   9,000
Supplies   6,000
Insurance   1,800
Other cash expenses . .   13,200

A cash balance of $36,000 is planned for January 1. Accounts receivable are expected to be $60,000 on January 1. All but one half of 1% of the January 1 balance will be collected in the quarter ending March 31. The company's sales collection pattern is 95% in the quarter of sale and 5% in the quarter after sale. Accounts payable will be $30,000 on January 1 and will be paid during the coming quarter. The company's purchases payment pattern is 75% in the quarter of purchase and 25% in the quarter after purchase. Expenses are paid in the quarter of incurrence.

Required: Prepare a cash budget for the quarter ending March 31.

P25-9-A

Prepare a master budget

May Corporation prepares annual budgets by quarters for its fiscal year ending June 30. Given below is its post-closing trial balance at December 31, 1986:

	Debits	Credits
Cash	$ 46,000	
Accounts Receivable	120,000	
Allowance for Doubtful Accounts . .		$ 4,000
Inventories	52,000	
Prepaid Expenses	4,000	
Furniture and Equipment	60,000	
Accumulated Depreciation		4,000
Accounts Payable		40,000
Accrued Liabilities		12,000
Notes Payable, 5% (due 1990) . .		160,000
Capital Stock		100,000
Retained Earnings (deficit)	38,000	
	$320,000	$320,000

All of the capital stock of May Corporation was recently acquired by Floyd White after the corporation had suffered losses for a number of years. After the purchase, White loaned substantial sums of money to the corporation, which still owes him $160,000 on a 5% note. Because of these past losses there are no accrued federal income taxes payable, but future earnings will be subject to taxation.

White is anxious to withdraw $40,000 from the corporation (as a payment on the note payable to him) but will not do so if it reduces the corporation's cash balance below $40,000. Thus, he is quite interested in the budgets for the quarter ending March 31, 1987.

Additional data:

1. Sales for the coming quarter are forecasted at $400,000; for the following quarter they are forecasted at $500,000. All sales are priced to yield a gross margin of 40%. Inventory is to be maintained on hand at the end of any quarter in an amount equal to 20% of the goods to be sold in the next quarter. All sales are on account, and 95% of the December 31, 1986, receivables plus 70% of the current quarter's sales will be collected during the quarter ending March 31, 1987.

2. Selling expenses are budgeted at $16,000 plus 6% of sales; $8,000 will be incurred on account, $22,000 accrued, $9,000 from expiration of prepaid rent and prepaid insurance, and $1,000 from allocated depreciation.

3. Purchasing expenses are budgeted at $11,600 plus 5% of purchases for the quarter; $3,000 will be incurred on account, $16,000 accrued, $4,600 from expired prepaid expenses, and $400 from allocated depreciation.

4. Administrative expenses are budgeted at $14,000 plus 2% of sales; $1,000 will be incurred on account, $12,000 accrued, $4,400 from expired prepayments, and $600 from allocated depreciation. Bad debts are estimated at 1% of sales.

5. Interest accrues at 5% on the notes payable and is credited to Accrued Liabilities.

6. All of the beginning balances in Accounts Payable and Accrued Liabilities, plus 80% of the current credits to Accounts Payable, and all but $10,000 of the current accrued liabilities will be paid during the quarter. A $6,000 insurance premium is to be paid prior to March 31, and a full year's rent of $48,000 is due on January 2.

7. Federal income taxes are budgeted at 40% of the net income before taxes. The taxes should be accrued separately, and no payments are due in the first quarter.

Required:
a. Prepare a planned operating budget for the quarter ending March 31, 1987, including supporting schedules for planned purchases and operating expenses.
b. Prepare a financial budget for March 31, 1987. Supporting schedules should be included that (1) analyze accounts credited for purchases and operating expenses, (2) show planned accounts receivable collections and balance, and (3) show planned cash flows and cash balance.
c. Will White be able to collect $40,000 on his note?

PROBLEMS, SERIES B

P25–1–B

Prepare a schedule showing budgeted production and a schedule showing the budgeted cost of goods sold

The Stafford Company prepares monthly operating and financial budgets. Estimates of sales in units are made for each month. Production is scheduled at a level high enough to take care of current needs and to carry into each month one half of that next month's unit sales. Direct materials, direct labor, and variable manufacturing overhead are estimated at $3, $5, and $2 per unit, and total fixed manufacturing overhead is budgeted at $100,000 per month. Sales for April, May, June, and July 1987 are estimated at 50,000, 60,000, 80,000, and 60,000 units. The inventory at April 1, 1987, consists of 25,000 units with a cost of $12 per unit.

Required:

a. Prepare a schedule showing the budgeted production in units for April, May, and June 1987.

b. Prepare a schedule showing the budgeted cost of goods sold for the same three months assuming that the Fifo method is used for inventories.

P25–2–B

Prepare a flexible operating budget

Following is a summary of operating data of the Sylvester Company for the year 1986:

Sales		$12,000,000
Cost of goods manufactured and sold:		
Direct materials	$2,100,000	
Direct labor	1,900,000	
Variable manufacturing overhead	600,000	
Fixed manufacturing overhead	1,300,000	5,900,000
		$ 6,100,000
Selling expenses:		
Variable	$ 600,000	
Fixed	500,000	1,100,000
		$ 5,000,000
General and administrative expenses:		
Variable	$ 300,000	
Fixed	1,900,000	2,200,000
Net operating income		$ 2,800,000

Sales volume for 1987 is budgeted at 90% of 1986 volume. Prices are not expected to change. The 1987 budget amounts for the various other costs and expenses differ from those reported in 1986 only for the expected volume change in the variable items.
The actual operating data for 1987 follow:

Sales	$9,600,000
Direct materials	2,140,000
Direct labor	1,920,000
Variable manufacturing overhead	630,000
Fixed manufacturing overhead	1,310,000
Variable selling expenses	780,000
Fixed selling expenses	490,000
Variable general and administrative expenses	335,000
Fixed general and administrative expenses	1,880,000

Required:

a. Prepare a report comparing the planned operating budget for 1987 with the actual results for that year.

b. Prepare a budget report that would be useful in pinpointing responsibility for the poor showing in 1987. (Hint: Prepare budget data on a flexible budget basis.)

P25–3–B

Prepare a planned operating budget and a flexible operating budget

a. The following data for the Jones Company are to be used in preparing its 1987 operating budget:

Plant capacity	1,000,000 units
Expected sales	900,000 units
Expected production	1,000,000 units
Forecasted sales price	$ 12.00

Manufacturing costs:
  Variable (per unit):
    Direct materials 4.50
    Direct labor 1.50
    Manufacturing overhead 1.00
    Fixed manufacturing overhead   300,000

Selling and administrative expenses:
  Variable (per unit) 0.50
  Fixed   250,000

Assume no beginning inventory. Taxes are 40% of net income before taxes.

Required: Prepare a planned operating budget for the year ended December 31, 1987.

b. The actual results for the Jones Company for the year ended December 31, 1987, follow: (Note: The actual sales price was *$13 per unit.* Actual production [in units] was equal to actual sales [in units]).

Sales		$13,000,000
Cost of goods sold:		
Direct materials	$3,850,000	
Direct labor	1,575,000	
Variable manufacturing overhead . .	1,200,000	
Fixed manufacturing overhead . . .	300,000	6,925,000
		$ 6,075,000
Selling and administrative expense		
Variable	$ 500,000	
Fixed	250,000	750,000
Net income before taxes		$ 5,325,000
Income tax at 40%		2,130,000
Net income		$ 3,195,000

Required: Using a flexible operating budget, analyze the efficiency of operations. Comment on the results of 1987 and on the company's sales policy.

P25–4–B

Prepare a flexible budget for selling and administration expenses

The Clay Company wants you to prepare a flexible budget for selling and administrative expenses. The general manager and the sales manager have met with all the department heads, and they have provided you with the following information regarding selling and administrative expenses:

1.   The company presently employs 40 full-time salespersons with a base salary of $200 each per month plus commissions. In addition, the company employs eight regional sales managers each with a salary of $18,000 per year and one general sales manager with a salary of $24,000 per year, none of whom is entitled to any commissions.
2.   If sales volume exceeds $15 million per year, the company will need to hire five more salespersons and one more regional sales manager.
3.   Sales commissions are either 5%, 3%, or 0% of the selling price, depending on the product sold. Typically, a 5% commission applies to 70% of sales, a 3% commission applies to 20% of sales, and no commission applies to the remaining 10% of sales.
4.   Salespersons' travel allowances average $100 per month per salesperson (excluding managers).
5.   Advertising expenses average $50,000 per month plus 2% of sales.
6.   Selling supplies expense is estimated at 1% of sales.
7.   Administrative salaries are $40,000 per month.
8.   Other administrative expenses include the following:
     Rent—$5,000 per month
     Office supplies—1% of sales
     Other administrative expenses (telephone, etc.)—$1,200 per month

Required: Prepare a flexible budget for selling and administrative expenses for sales volumes of $12 million, $14 million, and $16 million per year.

P25–5–B

Prepare a schedule of planned cost of goods manufactured and sold

The Clock Manufacturing Company is in the process of preparing a schedule of planned cost of goods sold and ending inventory for the quarters ended March 31, 1987, and June 30, 1987. The following data relate to expected activity for the two quarters:

1. Sales are expected to be:

March quarter	$ 800,000
June quarter	600,000
September quarter	1,200,000

2. Selling price per unit is $40.
3. The company policy is to carry a beginning-of-the-period inventory equal to 20% of the next period's requirements. Beginning inventory at January 1, 1987, was 4,000 units at $25 per unit.
4. Cost of production is estimated at:

Direct materials	$ 6 per unit
Direct labor	14 per unit
Variable manufacturing overhead . . .	4 per unit
Fixed manufacturing overhead	76,000 per quarter

5. There is no work in process inventory at the beginning or end of either period.
6. Inventory is computed on a Fifo basis.

Required: Prepare a schedule of planned cost of goods sold for the quarters ended March 31 and June 30, 1987. (Hint: Prepare a production schedule in units first.)

P25–6–B

Prepare accounts receivable schedule and planned purchases schedule

Anderson Company has a cash balance of $44,000 on May 1, 1987. Anderson Company's product sells for $45 per unit. Actual and projected sales are:

March, actual	$640,000
April, actual	400,000
May, estimated	450,000
June, estimated	480,000
July, estimated	380,000

All sales are on account. Generally, 45% of the accounts receivable are collected in the month of sale, 40% in the second month, and 15% in the third month.

Generally, 65% of purchases are due and payable in the month of purchase and the remainder the following month. Purchase cost per unit for materials is $30. The company maintains an end-of-the-month inventory of 500 units plus 20% of the next month's unit sales.

Required: Prepare schedules for May and June showing:

a. Planned accounts receivable collections and balances.
b. Planned materials purchases and inventories. Round all units to the nearest whole number.

P25–7–B

Prepare a cash budget

Refer to P25–6–B. In addition to the information given, selling and administrative expenses are $840,000 per year, incurred and paid evenly throughout the year.

Required: Prepare a monthly cash budget for May and June for the Anderson Company.

P25–8–B

Prepare a cash budget

The Michaels Company has gathered the following budget information for the quarter ending September 30:

Sales	$360,000
Purchases	300,000
Salaries and wages	130,000
Rent	6,000
Supplies	4,000
Insurance	1,200
Other cash expenses . . .	8,800

A cash balance of $24,000 is planned for July 1. Accounts receivable are expected to be $40,000 on July 1. All but one half of 1% of the July 1 balance will be collected in the quarter ending September 30. The company's sales collection pattern is 95% in the quarter of sale and 5% in the quarter after sale. Accounts payable will be $20,000 on July 1 and will be paid during the coming quarter. The company's purchases payment pattern is 75% in the quarter of purchase and 25% in the quarter after purchase. Expenses are paid in the quarter of incurrence.

Required: Prepare a cash budget for the quarter ending September 30.

P25-9-B

Prepare a master budget

WARREN CORPORATION
Post-Closing Trial Balance
December 31, 1986

	Debits	Credits
Cash	$ 100,000	
Accounts Receivable	200,000	
Allowance for Doubtful Accounts		$ 15,000
Inventories	250,000	
Prepaid Expenses	30,000	
Land	250,000	
Buildings and Equipment	750,000	
Accumulated Depreciation		100,000
Accounts Payable		150,000
Accrued Liabilities (including income taxes) . .		100,000
Capital Stock		1,000,000
Retained Earnings		215,000
	$1,580,000	$1,580,000

The Warren Corporation, whose post-closing trial balance at December 31, 1986, appears above, is a rapidly expanding company. Sales in the last quarter of 1986 amounted to $1,000,000 and are projected at $1,250,000 and $2,000,000 for the first two quarters of 1987. This expansion has created a very tight cash position. Management is especially concerned about the probable cash balance at March 31, 1987, since a payment of $150,000 for some new equipment must be made upon delivery on April 2. The current cash balance of $100,000 is considered to be the minimum workable balance.

Additional data:

1. Purchases, all on account, are to be scheduled so that the inventory at the end of any quarter is equal to one third of the goods expected to be sold in the coming quarter. Cost of goods sold averages 60% of sales.

2. Selling expenses are budgeted at $50,000 plus 8% of sales; $10,000 is expected to be incurred on account, $120,000 accrued, $14,000 from expired prepayments, and $6,000 from allocated depreciation.

3. Purchasing expenses are budgeted at $35,000 plus 5% of purchases; $5,000 will be incurred on account, $65,000 accrued, $5,500 from expired prepayments, and $4,500 from allocated depreciation.

4. Administrative expenses are budgeted at $62,500 plus 3% of sales; $10,000 will be incurred on account, $55,000 accrued, $5,500 from expired prepayments, $4,500 from allocated depreciation. Bad debts are equal to 2% of current sales.

5. Federal income taxes are budgeted at 40% of net income before taxes and are recorded in accrued liabilities. Payments on these taxes are included in the payments on accrued liabilities discussed below.

6. All December 31, 1986, accounts payable plus 80% of current credits to this account will be paid in the first quarter. All of the December 31, 1986, accrued liabilities except for $30,000 will be paid in the first quarter. Of the current quarter's accrued liabilities, all but $120,000 will be paid during the quarter.

7   Cash outlays for various expenses normally prepaid will amount to $40,000 during the quarter.

8.   All sales are made on account; 80% of the sales are collected in the quarter in which made, and all of the remaining sales are collected in the following quarter, except for 2% which is never collected. The allowance for doubtful accounts shows the estimated amount of accounts receivable at December 31, 1986, arising from 1986 sales that will not be collected.

Required:

a.   Prepare an operating budget for the quarter ending March 31, 1987. Supporting schedules for planned purchases and operating expenses should be included.

b.   Prepare a financial budget for March 31, 1987. Include supporting schedules that (1) analyze accounts credited for purchases and expenses, (2) show planned cash flows and cash balance, and (3) show planned collections of accounts receivable and the accounts receivable balance.

c.   Will sufficient cash be on hand April 2 to pay for the new equipment?

BUSINESS DECISION PROBLEM

Prepare a cash budget

The Madden Company has applied at a local bank for a short-term loan of $125,000 starting on October 1. The loan will be repaid with interest at 10% on December 31. The bank's loan officer has requested a cash budget from the company for the quarter ending December 31. The following budget information is needed to prepare the cash budget:

Sales	$540,000
Purchases	300,000
Salaries and wages to be paid	105,000
Rent payments	6,000
Supplies (payments for)	4,000
Insurance payments	1,500
Other cash payments	18,500

A cash balance of $20,000 is planned for October 1. Accounts receivable are expected to be $40,000 on October 1. All of these accounts will be collected in the quarter ending December 31. In general, sales are collected as follows: 90% in the quarter of sale and 10% in the quarter after sale. Accounts payable will be $400,000 on October 1 and will be paid during the quarter ending December 31. All purchases are paid for in the quarter after purchase.

Required:

a.   Prepare a cash budget for the quarter ending December 31. Assume that the $125,000 loan will be made on October 1 and will be repaid with interest at 10% on December 31.

b.   Will the company be able to repay the loan on December 31? If the company desires a minimum cash balance of $15,000, will the company be able to repay the loan as planned?

BUSINESS SITUATION FOR DISCUSSION

Growing Concerns: Topics of particular interest to owners and managers of smaller businesses
(edited by David E. Gumpert)

Budget Choice: Planning vs. Control*
Neil C. Churchill

☐   The term "budget" tends to conjure up in the minds of many managers images of inaccurate estimates,

produced in tedious detail, which are never exactly achieved but whose shortfalls or overruns require explanations. And that is what budgets are like for many smaller businesses. This wasteful way of using budgets overlooks important managerial objectives that budgeting can help achieve.

*   *   *   *   *

. . . [The author] maintains that budgets should be considered from a broader perspective. He views them as having two primary functions: planning and control. Managers must decide which function is more important and then resolve a number of formulation issues. These include the initiation process, implementation, the period covered, whether the budget should be fixed or flexible, and how it should be used to evaluate performance. He concludes that large companies concerned about operational efficiency should focus on the coordination and control aspects of budgeting while small and innovative companies should be concerned with planning aspects. Whatever the focus, budget preparation and implementation are important in carrying out company strategy and in professionalizing the smaller company.

* * * * *

I [the author] start my classes on budgeting by displaying two situations on the blackboard:

Expenses

	Budgeted amount	Actual results
Budget 1 . .	$1000	$950
Budget 2 . .	750	850

Then I ask the class, "Which budget is better, assuming in both cases that the manager gets the job done in time, that the end result is the same quality of performance and customer satisfaction, and that the manager doesn't develop ulcers in the process of implementation?"

A heated argument usually follows. Most class participants eventually choose Budget 2 after being assured of equal results. A minority, however, hold out for Budget 1, which seems to them the "most reasonable."

These opposing views come together when I ask, "Which would be best for borrowing money on a one-loan-a-year basis?" In this case, the choice is almost always Budget 1. And when I then ask, "Which would be best for motivating performance?" the majority of participants usually select Budget 2.

As this example shows, budgets can be used both for planning (Number 1) and for control (Number 2), although the same budget is not always optimal for both purposes.

Occasionally a company uses a budget with "stretch" in it for motivating performance—sales, for instance—and a more "realistic" budget for planning—expected sales, for example. More commonly, companies use the same document for both purposes. Large companies tend to use budgets mostly for control and smaller enterpreneurial companies use them primarily as planning tools.

But no matter whether it is used for planning or for control, a budget is more than a forecast. A forecast is a prediction of what may happen and sometimes contains prescriptions for dealing with future events. A budget, on the other hand, involves a commitment to a forecast to make an agreed-on outcome happen.

Budgets come in several variations. Cash budgets are especially important to new and growing businesses, whereas capital budgets are widely used if capital expenditures are important and recurring. Human-resource or "headcount" budgets (the capital budgets of service companies) serve as means of control in labor-intensive companies. But generally when the term *budget* is used, it refers to an operating budget containing an organization's detailed revenue and expense accounts grouped either by operating units, such as divisions or departments, or by products and product lines. Such a document is a central part of the management control system of many companies.

LEARNING OBJECTIVES

After studying this chapter, you should be able to:

1. Describe different cost behavior patterns.
2. Compute the break-even point for a company.
3. List the assumptions underlying cost-volume-profit analysis.
4. Apply cost-volume-profit analysis to practical situations.
5. Make short-term decisions involving relevant costs.
6. Differentiate between and compute net income under absorption and direct costing.
7. Define and use correctly the new terms in the glossary.

In making decisions, management must frequently distinguish between short-run decision making and long-run decision making. The term short run describes a time frame during which a company's management cannot change the effects of certain past decisions. The short-run time frame is often considered to be one year or less. In the short run, many costs, such as depreciation expense, are assumed to be fixed and unchangeable. Because of this assumption, short-run decision making uses different criteria than long-run decision making, under which all costs are subject to change.

In this chapter you will be introduced to some of the analytical tools that can be used to make short-run decisions. The chapter begins with a discussion of cost behavior patterns because the classification of costs as fixed or variable is the first step in using the analytical tools.

■ COST BEHAVIOR PATTERNS

Illustration 26.1 shows four basic cost behavior patterns: variable, fixed, mixed (semivariable), and step. As discussed in earlier chapters, **variable costs** vary directly with changes in volume of production or sales. Direct materials, direct labor, and sales commissions are examples of variable costs. In contrast, **fixed costs** remain constant over some relevant range of output, and are often described as time-related costs. Depreciation, insurance, property taxes, and administrative salaries are examples of fixed costs.

Illustration 26.1

Four Cost Patterns

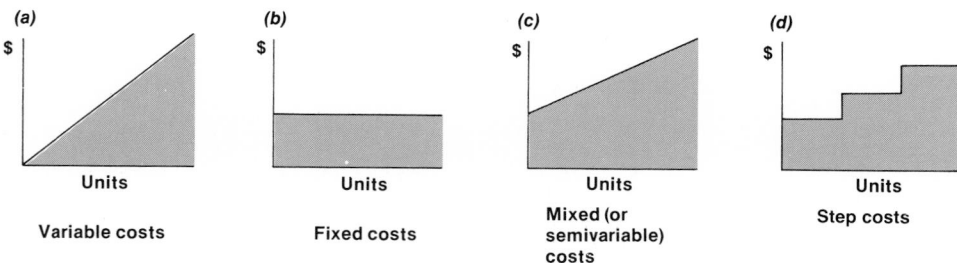

(a) Variable costs — $ / Units

(b) Fixed costs — $ / Units

(c) Mixed (or semivariable) costs — $ / Units

(d) Step costs — $ / Units

Mixed and step costs demonstrate both fixed and variable characteristics. A **mixed cost** contains a fixed portion of cost that will be incurred even when the plant is completely idle and a variable portion that will increase directly with production volume. An example of a mixed cost is electricity. A certain amount of cost is incurred in order for the company to have electrical service. As the plant operates, each additional kilowatt-hour of usage generates an additional amount of cost. A mixed cost may be separated into its fixed and variable components, as shown in Illustration 26.2.

A **step cost** remains constant in total over a range of output (or sales) but then increases in steps at certain points. A step cost may be either a step variable or a step fixed cost. The major difference between the two types is the size of the "steps." In both cases, there are fixed and variable components

Illustration 26.2

Separation of a Mixed Cost

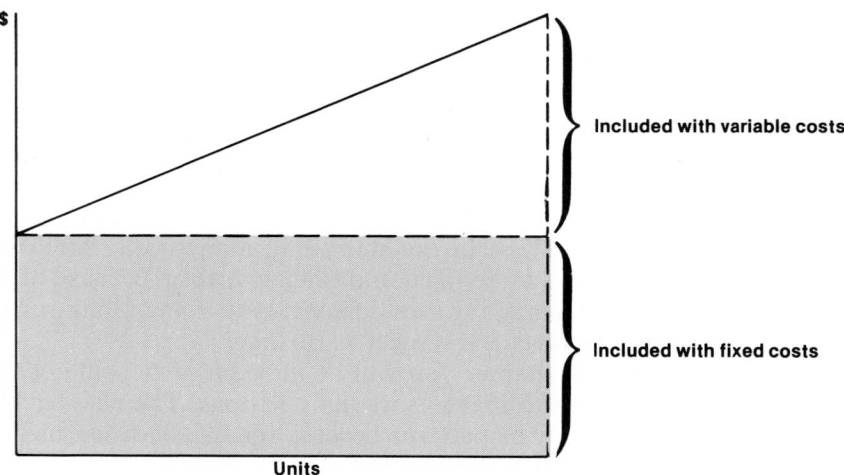

Included with variable costs

Included with fixed costs

Units

Illustration 26.3

Separation of a Step Variable Cost

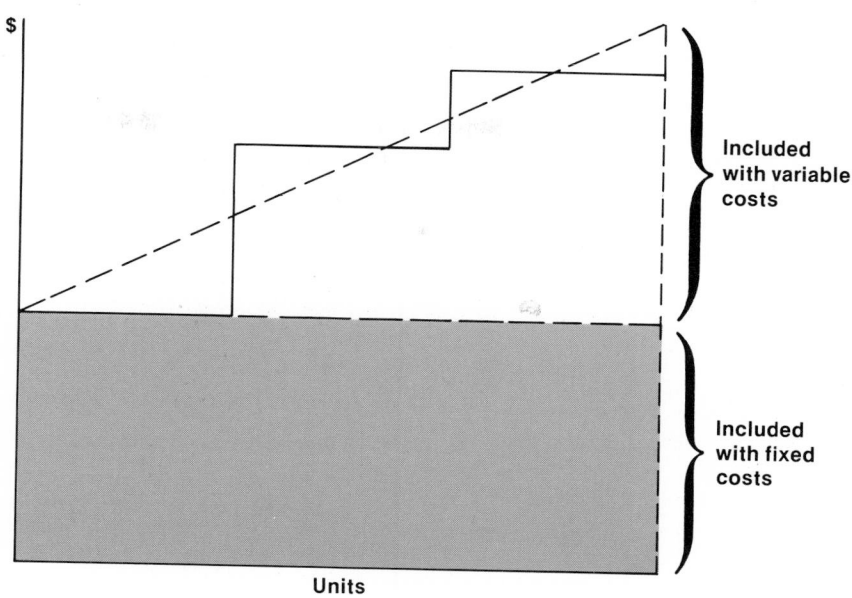

Even though step variable costs do not vary directly with changes in volume, they can be treated for planning purposes as though they are directly variable costs. The slanted dashed line represents the smoothing of the step variable cost into a directly variable cost.

of the cost. An example of a step variable cost is the cost of water. The utility company charges a flat fee for providing water (fixed component) and an additional amount depending on the quantity of water used (variable component). Unlike the variable charge for electricity, which is on an hour-by-hour basis, the charge for water may be stated in increments as follows: $10 for the first 1,000 gallons or less; $5 additional for use of 1,001 to 5,000 gallons; $8 additional for use of 5,001 to 10,000 gallons; and so on. This type of cost is shown in Illustration 26.3.

Supervisors' salaries are an example of a step fixed cost. At any level of production from 1 unit to 40,000 units, one supervisor is necessary at a salary of $20,000 per year. If the company produces at a level over 40,000 units but below 100,000 units, a second supervisor is needed at an additional cost of $20,000. A step fixed cost for supervisors' salaries is shown in Illustration 26.4.

For decision making, management must separate mixed and step costs into their fixed and variable components. A mixed cost can be easily broken down into these two components. The fixed portion of a mixed cost is included with other fixed costs, while the variable element is shown as directly changing with volume. A step variable cost is treated in the same manner as a mixed cost. The fixed portion of a step variable cost is treated as a fixed cost, and the remaining cost is treated as entirely variable.

Since a step fixed cost is fixed over a relatively wide range of activity, it is treated as entirely fixed for decision-making purposes. This is done by estimating the level of operations and then treating the step fixed cost expected at that level of operations as a fixed cost for decision making.

Although there are four basic cost behavior patterns, management must

Illustration 26.4

A Step Fixed Cost

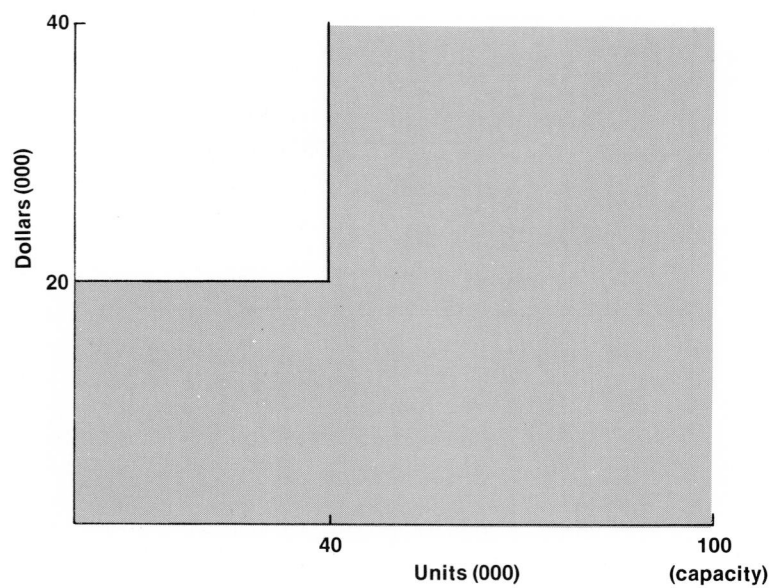

attempt to classify all types of costs into only two categories—variable and fixed. This simplification is necessary in order to visualize the ways in which costs will react to changes in production volume or sales.

Methods for Analyzing Costs

There are several methods available for breaking down a mixed or a step variable cost into its fixed and variable cost components. Two of these procedures are the scatter diagram and the high-low method.

The Scatter Diagram.   A scatter diagram shows plots of actual costs incurred for various levels of output or sales. The dots on the scatter diagram in Illustration 26.5 represent total actual maintenance costs for a company's

Illustration 26.5

Scatter Diagram

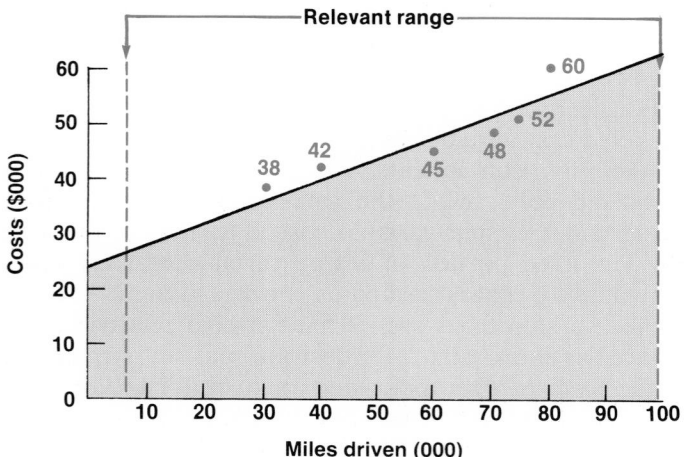

fleet of delivery trucks at various levels of past activity. A line is drawn through what appears visually to be the center of the pattern formed by the dots. In Illustration 26.5, the fixed element of the mixed cost is $23,000, since that is the amount of cost at zero volume of output. The line (called a regression line) rises from $23,000 to $63,000 over the range of 100,000 units. The variable cost portion can be computed as:

$$\frac{\$63,000 - \$23,000}{100,000 \text{ units}} = \$0.40 \text{ per unit}$$

The data in the chart suggest that the company's truck maintenance costs can be estimated at $23,000 plus 40 cents for every mile driven.

A more sophisticated technique, called the **least-squares method,** is often used to draw the regression line and divide mixed costs into their fixed and variable portions. The least-squares method is more precise, but since it involves statistical analysis, it will not be presented in this text.

The High-Low Method.   The high-low method is also widely used to identify the behavior of mixed costs. The **high-low method** uses only the highest and lowest points on a scatter diagram to draw a line representing a total mixed cost.

To illustrate, the lowest point in Illustration 26.5 is $38,000 of expense at 30,000 units of output, and the highest point is $60,000 at 80,000 units of output. The amount of variable cost per unit is found as follows:

$$\frac{\text{Change in cost}}{\text{Change in units}} = \frac{\$60,000 - \$38,000}{80,000 \text{ units} - 30,000 \text{ units}} = \frac{\$22,000}{50,000 \text{ units}} = \$0.44 \text{ per unit}$$

The fixed portion is then found as follows:

Total cost at 80,000 units of output	$60,000
Less: Variable cost at that level of output	
(80,000 × $0.44)	35,200
Fixed cost at all levels of output	
within the relevant range	$24,800

The high-low method is less precise than the scatter diagram since it uses only two data points in the computation. Either or both points may not be representative of the data as a whole.

■ COST-VOLUME-PROFIT (CVP) ANALYSIS

Cost-volume-profit (CVP) analysis (sometimes called **break-even analysis**) is used to determine what effects any changes in a company's selling prices, costs, and/or volume will have on income in the short run. The starting point of such an analysis is the company's break-even point. A company is said to "break even" for a given period if sales revenue and costs charged to that period are exactly equal. Thus, the **break-even point** is that level of operations at which a company realizes no net income or loss.

A careful and accurate cost-volume-profit (CVP) analysis requires knowledge of costs and their behavior (i.e., fixed or variable) as volume changes.

The types and quantities of cost data accumulated depend on the costs of obtaining the data compared to the benefits of having more refined information. Within this constraint, it is desirable to compute break-even points for each area of decision making within the company. Some important classifications of cost data for break-even analysis are by product, territory, salesperson, or class of customer.

A break-even point may be expressed in dollars of sales revenue or number of units produced or sold. No matter how the break-even point is expressed, it is still the point of zero income or loss.

To illustrate the calculation of a break-even point, assume the Muffet Manufacturing Company produces a single product that sells for $20. Fixed costs per period total $40,000, while variable cost is $12 per unit. The **variable cost rate,** which expresses variable cost as a percentage of sales, is 60% ($12 ÷ $20). That is, for each dollar of sales, the company incurs $0.60 of variable cost. The sales revenue needed to break even would be calculated as that point at which all costs are covered, but no income is generated. Therefore, the break-even point can be expressed as:

$$\text{Sales} = \text{Fixed costs} + \text{Variable costs}$$

or

$$S = FC + VC$$

Substituting the Muffet Company amounts of fixed costs and the variable cost rate in the formula gives the following:

$$
\begin{aligned}
S &= \$40,000 \ + 0.60S \\
S - 0.60S &= \$40,000 \\
0.40S &= \$40,000 \\
S &= \$40,000 \ \div 0.40 \\
S &= \$100,000
\end{aligned}
$$

Sales revenue at the break-even point is $100,000. To compute the break-even point in units, simply divide the $100,000 of sales by the $20 selling price per unit. This gives a break-even point of 5,000 units.

Alternatively, the break-even point in units could be calculated first. The break-even point in units involves a concept known as contribution margin. **Contribution margin** is the amount by which revenue exceeds variable costs of producing that revenue; it can be calculated on a per unit or total sales volume basis. On a per unit basis, the contribution margin for Muffet Company is $8, which equals the selling price of $20 less the variable cost per unit of $12. Contribution margin indicates the amount of money remaining after variable cost is covered. This remainder contributes to the coverage of fixed costs and to the generation of net income. The break-even point in units is computed by dividing total fixed costs by the contribution margin per unit.

$$\text{BEP}_{\text{units}} = \frac{\text{Fixed costs}}{\text{Contribution margin per unit}}$$

$$\text{BEP}_{\text{units}} = \frac{\$40,000}{\$8 \text{ per unit}}$$

$$= 5,000 \text{ units}$$

If the Muffet Company's production capacity is 20,000 units, then the break-even point is equal to 25% of capacity (5,000/20,000 = 25%).

An alternative method of finding the break-even point in sales dollars is to divide the total fixed costs by the contribution margin rate. The **contribution margin rate** expresses the contribution margin as a percentage of sales and is calculated by dividing the contribution margin per unit by the selling price per unit. The Muffet Company's contribution margin rate is:

$$\frac{\text{Contribution margin per unit}}{\text{Selling price per unit}} = \frac{\$20 - \$12}{\$20} = \frac{\$8}{\$20} = 0.40$$

Using this rate, the Muffet Company's break-even point in sales dollars is calculated as follows:

$$\text{BEP}_{\text{dollars}} = \frac{\text{Fixed costs}}{\text{Contribution margin rate}}$$

$$\text{BEP}_{\text{dollars}} = \frac{\$40,000}{0.40}$$

$$= \$100,000$$

Break-Even Chart

A **break-even chart** is a graph that shows the relationships between sales, costs, volume, and profit and also shows the break-even point. Illustration 26.6 presents the break-even chart for the Muffet Company. Each break-even chart or calculation is valid only for a specified relevant range of volume. The **relevant range** is the range of production or sales volume over which the basic cost behavior assumptions will hold true. For volumes outside these ranges, costs will behave

Illustration 26.6

The Break-Even Chart

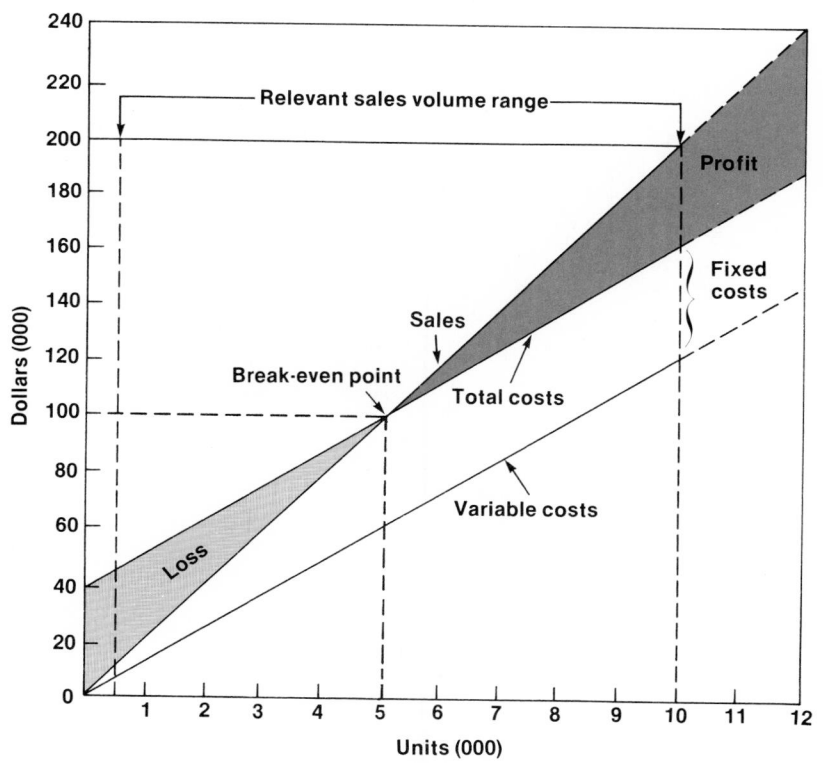

differently and will alter the assumed relationships. For example, if more than 10,000 units were produced by the Muffet Company, it might be necessary to increase plant capacity (thus incurring additional fixed costs) or to work extra shifts (thus incurring overtime charges and other inefficiencies). In either case, the cost relationships first assumed are no longer valid. Illustration 26.6 is based on cost data for Muffet Company in a relevant range of output from 500 to 10,000 units.

The chart in Illustration 26.6 shows that the break-even volume of sales is $100,000 (5,000 units at $20 per unit). At this level of sales, fixed costs and variable costs are exactly equal to sales revenue, as shown:

Revenues	$100,000
Less: Variable costs	60,000
Contribution margin	$ 40,000
Less: Fixed costs	40,000
Net income	$ –0–

The break-even chart could also be re-labeled to indicate contribution margin, as shown in Illustration 26.7.

The break-even charts show that a period of complete idleness will produce a loss of $40,000 (the amount of fixed costs), while output of 10,000 units will produce net income of $40,000. Other points on the graphs show that

Illustration 26.7

Break-Even Chart Showing that Fixed Costs Equal Contribution Margin at Break-Even Point

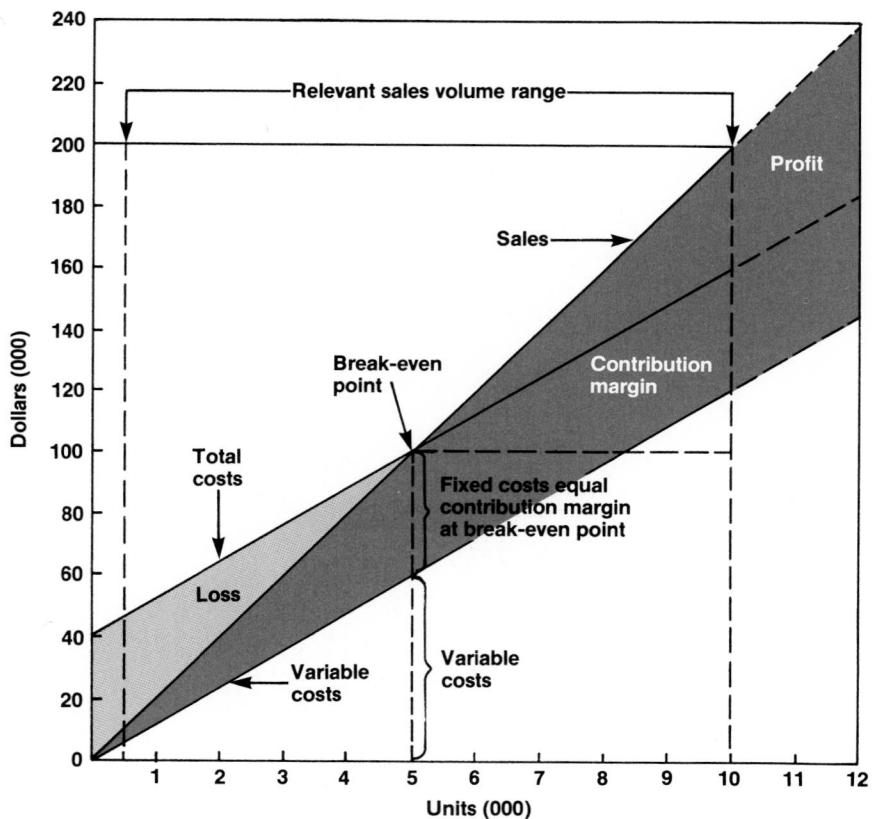

sales of 7,500 units will result in $150,000 of revenue. At that point, total costs amount to $130,000, leaving net income of $20,000. The charts also show that net income at any level of output can be found by multiplying the contribution margin per unit by the number of units sold and subtracting total fixed costs from the result.

Changing the Break-Even Point

A break-even point can be lowered or raised by changing selling price, variable cost per unit, or fixed costs. Lowering the break-even point means that the company can earn income at a lower volume of operations. If the selling price is increased or the variable cost per unit is decreased, the break-even point will be lower because the contribution margin per unit is larger. A larger contribution margin means that more of the selling price of each unit can be used to cover fixed costs. Similarly, if fixed costs are decreased, it takes fewer units sold to cover the smaller amount of fixed costs. These actions in reverse will create a higher break-even point. That is, lowering the selling price, increasing the variable cost per unit, or increasing fixed costs will raise the break-even point.

To illustrate the effects of changing the (1) selling price, (2) variable cost, or (3) fixed cost to lower the break-even point, assume that a company currently has a single product that sells for $60. Variable cost per unit is $15, or 25% of selling price, and fixed costs are $27,000. The break-even point is $36,000 of sales revenue, computed as follows:

$$S = FC + VC$$
$$S = \$27,000 + 0.25S$$
$$0.75S = \$27,000$$
$$S = \$36,000$$

As shown below, companies have a great deal of flexibility in the means of adjusting their break-even points. Companies attempt to operate at a level of operations **above** the break-even point in order to make a profit.

Increase Selling Price.   If the company can increase its selling price to $75 while keeping variable costs and fixed costs the same, the variable cost rate becomes 20%, ($15 ÷ $75). The break-even point will then decrease by $2,250:

$$S = FC + VC$$
$$S = \$27,000 + 0.20S$$
$$0.80S = \$27,000$$
$$S = \$33,750$$

Reduce Variable Cost.   If the company can reduce the variable cost per unit to $13.20 and thus reduce the variable cost rate to 22% of selling price, ($13.20 ÷ $60) the break-even point can be lowered:

$$S = FC + VC$$
$$S = \$27,000 + 0.22S$$
$$0.78S = \$27,000$$
$$S = \$34,615$$

Reduce Fixed Costs.   If the company can reduce its fixed costs by $3,000 to $24,000, the break-even point is again reduced:

$$S = FC + VC$$
$$S = \$24,000 + 0.25S$$
$$0.75S = \$24,000$$
$$S = \$32,000$$

Margin of Safety

If a company's current sales are above its break-even point, then the company is said to have a margin of safety equal to current sales less break-even sales. The margin of safety is the amount by which sales can decrease before a loss will be incurred. For example, assume a company currently has sales of $250,000 and its break-even sales are $200,000. The margin of safety is $50,000, computed as follows:

$$\text{Margin of safety} = \text{Current sales} - \text{Break-even sales}$$
$$= \$250,000 - \$200,000$$
$$= \$50,000$$

The margin of safety is sometimes expressed as a percentage, called the margin of safety rate. The margin of safety rate is equal to (Current sales − Break-even sales) ÷ Current sales. Using data from the company just discussed, the margin of safety rate would be computed as follows:

$$\text{Margin of safety rate} = \frac{\text{Current sales} - \text{Break-even sales}}{\text{Current sales}}$$
$$= \frac{\$250,000 - \$200,000}{\$250,000}$$
$$= 20\%$$

This means that sales volume could drop by 20% before a loss would be incurred.

Assumptions Made in Cost-Volume-Profit Analysis

Certain assumptions are made in CVP analysis:

1. Selling price, variable cost per unit, and total fixed costs remain constant through the relevant range. This means that more or fewer units could be sold at the same price and that there is no change in technical efficiency as volume changes.
2. The number of units produced equals the number of units sold.
3. In multiproduct situations, the product mix is known in advance. (Multiproduct situations are covered later in this chapter.)
4. Costs can be accurately classified into their fixed and variable portions.

Although these assumptions are sometimes criticized as being unrealistic in many situations, they are necessary in order to make the calculations.

Cost-Volume-Profit Analysis Illustrated

CVP analysis has many applications, several of which are illustrated below using data regarding an airline.

Calculating the Break-Even Point.

A major airline wishes to know the number of seats that must be sold on a certain flight for the flight to break even. To solve this problem, costs must first be identified and separated into fixed and variable categories.

The fixed costs are the same regardless of the number of seats filled. Fixed costs include items such as the fuel required to fly the plane and crew (with no passengers) to its destination; depreciation on the plane used on the flight; and salaries of required crew members, gate attendants, and maintenance and refueling personnel. The variable costs will vary directly with the number of passengers. Variable costs include meals and beverages provided to passengers, baggage handling costs, and the cost of the additional fuel required to fly the plane with passengers to its destination. Each variable cost should be expressed on a per person basis.

Assume that after the various costs have been analyzed and classified as fixed or variable, the fixed costs for a given flight are $12,000. Variable costs are $25 per passenger, and tickets are sold at $125; thus the variable cost rate is 20% ($25 ÷ $125). This rate yields a contribution margin per ticket of $100 ($125 − $25). The contribution margin rate is 80% [($125 − $25) ÷ $125].

The break-even point can be expressed in sales revenue (dollars) or in number of passengers. The sales revenue needed to break even is computed as follows:

$$\text{Sales} = \text{Fixed costs} + \text{Variable costs}$$
$$S = FC + VC$$
$$S = \$12,000 + 0.20S$$
$$0.80S = \$12,000$$
$$S = \$15,000$$

The break-even point in dollars can also be computed as follows:

$$BEP_{\text{dollars}} = \frac{\text{Fixed costs}}{\text{Contribution margin rate}}$$
$$= \frac{\$12,000}{0.80}$$
$$= \$15,000$$

The break-even point in number of passengers (units) may be found by dividing fixed costs by the contribution margin per unit:

$$BEP_{\text{units}} = \frac{\text{Fixed costs}}{\text{Contribution margin per unit}}$$
$$= \frac{\$12,000}{\$125 - \$25}$$
$$= 120 \text{ passengers}$$

Calculating Sales Volume Needed for Desired Net Income.   With a simple adjustment in the break-even formulas, CVP analysis can also show the sales volume needed to generate some desired level of net income. This adjustment is made by adding the desired income amount to the total costs that need to be covered. Management can then determine the necessary sales volume in dollars or units. For example, if the airline discussed above wishes to earn $8,000 of income on its flight, the company can calculate the amount of necessary sales revenue by the following formula:

$$Sales = Fixed\ costs + Variable\ costs + Desired\ net\ income$$

or

$$S = FC + VC + NI$$
$$S = \$12,000 + 0.20S + \$8,000$$
$$0.80S = \$20,000$$
$$S = \$25,000$$

If the airline wants to know how many passenger tickets must be sold in order to earn $8,000, a similar modification of another form of the break-even point formula will yield the desired calculation. Remembering that the contribution margin per ticket is $100, the number of tickets to be sold is computed as follows:

$$Number\ of\ units = \frac{Fixed\ costs + Desired\ net\ income}{Contribution\ margin\ per\ unit}$$
$$= \frac{\$12,000 + \$8,000}{\$100}$$
$$= \frac{\$20,000}{\$100}$$
$$= 200\ passengers$$

Calculating the Effect on Net Income of Changing Price.   The break-even formula can also be used to determine the results if the price used in the formula is changed. To illustrate, assume that the flight normally carries 150 passengers (sales of $18,750 and net income of $3,000) and that a decision is made to increase ticket prices by 5%. If variable and fixed costs remain constant and passenger load does not change, net income will rise from $3,000 to $3,937.50 as shown:

$$S = FC + VC + NI$$
$$\$18,750\ (1.05) = \$12,000 + 0.20\ (\$18,750) + NI$$
$$\$19,687.50 = \$12,000 + \$3,750 + NI$$
$$\$19,687.50 = \$15,750 + NI$$
$$NI = \$3,937.50$$

We assume that variable costs would remain constant at 20% of original sales in the above illustration because a change in selling price has no effect on the variable costs associated with providing flight service. Income would rise by the entire amount of the price increase ($19,687.50 − $18,750 = $937.50) because all variable and fixed costs are already being covered by the original selling price.

Calculating Sales Needed to Maintain Net Income When Costs Change.
The break-even formula has yet another application; it can be used to calculate
the sales needed to maintain income when costs change. For example, if the
price of gasoline rises, both fixed and variable costs will increase for the airline.
Assume that fixed costs are increased by $4,000, and variable costs are increased
by $6.25 per passenger. Variable costs are now 25% ($31.25/$125) of sales
price. In order to maintain the current net income of $3,000 (on $18,750 of
sales), the airline will need to increase sales revenue to $25,333 as shown below.

$$S = FC + VC + NI$$
$$S = \$16,000 + 0.25S + \$3,000$$
$$0.75S = \$19,000$$
$$S = \$25,333 \text{ (or 203 passengers)}$$

Other Uses of CVP Analysis.   Management can also use its knowledge
of CVP relationships to determine whether to increase sales promotion costs
in an effort to increase sales volume or to accept an order at a lower-than-
usual price. In general, the careful study of break-even charts helps management
plan future courses of action. Indeed, it has been said that to be successful,
management must become "break-even minded."

Calculating Break-Even for a Multiproduct Company

When computing the break-even point for a multiproduct company, only dollars
of sales are used. In a multiproduct company, a given product mix is assumed
to be constant for CVP purposes. **Product mix** refers to the proportion of
the company's total sales attributable to each type of product sold. To illustrate
the computation of the break-even point for a multiproduct company, assume
the following historical data:

	Products							
	1		2		3		Total	
	Amount	Per-cent	Amount	Per-cent	Amount	Per-cent	Amount	Per-cent
Sales	$60,000	100	$30,000	100	$10,000	100	$100,000	100
Less: Variable costs . . .	40,000	67	16,000	53	4,000	40	60,000	60
Contribution margin . . .	$20,000	33	$14,000	47	$ 6,000	60	$ 40,000	40

The relationships shown in the Total column are used to compute the break-
even point. Variable costs are 60% ($60,000/$100,000) of total sales. If the
product mix is assumed to remain constant and fixed costs for the company
are $50,000, break-even sales are $125,000:

$$S = FC + VC$$
$$S = \$50,000 + 0.60S$$
$$0.40S = \$50,000$$
$$S = \$125,000$$

The $125,000 of sales can be specified by product by multiplying total sales dollars by the percent of product mix of each of the three products. The product mix for products 1, 2, and 3 is 60:30:10, respectively; that is, out of the $100,000 total sales, there were $60,000 sales of product 1, $30,000 sales of product 2, and $10,000 sales of product 3. Therefore, the company will have to sell $75,000 (0.6 × $125,000) of product 1, $37,500 (0.3 × $125,000) of product 2, and $12,500 (0.1 × $125,000) of product 3 in order to break even.

If there is any change in the mix of products sold, the break-even point will also change. The break-even point changes because each product has a different contribution margin. Also, if historical patterns of selling prices or variable costs are not expected to hold true in the future, projected sales and variable expenses should be used to determine expected percentages of variable expenses to total sales.

To illustrate the effects of such changes, assume that the product mix for products 1, 2, and 3 is expected to change to 20:30:50 in the upcoming period, as shown in the following chart. Also assume that total sales are $100,000 and that the variable costs for product 3 are expected to fall to 33% of the selling price. To compute the new break-even point, we again use the relationships shown in the Total column.

	Products							
	1		2		3		Total	
	Amount	Per-cent	Amount	Per-cent	Amount	Per-cent	Amount	Per-cent
Sales	$20,000	100	$30,000	100	$50,000	100	$100,000	100
Less: Variable costs . . .	13,333	67	16,000	53	16,667	33	46,000	46
Contribution margin . .	$ 6,667	33	$14,000	47	$33,333	67	$ 54,000	54

As shown in the Total column, variable costs are expected to fall to 46% of total sales in the upcoming period. The new break-even point will be $92,593 computed as follows:

$$S = FC + VC$$
$$S = \$50,000 + 0.46S$$
$$0.54S = \$50,000$$
$$S = \$92,593$$

Notice that the new break-even point is lower than the old one. Sales shifted from the lowest contribution margin product (product 1) to the highest contribution margin product (product 3), thereby increasing the contribution margin dollars available to cover fixed costs.

■ DIFFERENTIAL ANALYSIS

Another analytical tool of short-term decision making is differential analysis. **Differential analysis** involves analyzing the different costs and benefits that would arise from alternative solutions to a particular situation. Relevant revenues or costs in a given situation are future revenues or costs that differ depending on which alternative course of action is selected. Differential revenue is defined as the difference in revenues between two alternatives. Differential cost or expense is the difference between relevant costs for two alternatives.[1] Future costs that do not differ between alternatives are irrelevant and may be ignored since they will affect both alternatives similarly. Past costs, also known as sunk costs, are also not relevant in decision making because the costs have already been incurred and, therefore, cannot be changed no matter which alternative is selected.

For certain decisions, revenues do not differ between alternatives. Under those circumstances, management should select the alternative with the least cost. In other situations, costs do not differ between alternatives. Accordingly, the alternative that results in the greatest revenue should be selected. But many times both future costs and revenues differ between alternatives. In these situations, the alternative that results in the greatest positive difference between future revenues and expenses (costs) should be selected.

To illustrate relevant, differential, and sunk costs, assume that Jack Bennett had invested $400 in a tiller so that he could till gardens to earn $1,500 during the summer. He is now offered the opportunity of working at a horse stable feeding horses and cleaning stalls for a salary of $1,200 for the summer. The costs that he would incur in tilling are $100 for transportation and $150 for supplies. The costs he would incur at the horse stable are $100 for transportation and $50 for supplies. If Jack works at the stable, he would still have the tiller, and it would be used by his parents and loaned to friends at no charge. The tiller cost of $400 is not **relevant** to the decision because it is a **sunk** cost. The transportation cost of $100 is also not relevant because it is the same for both alternatives. The relevant costs and revenues are shown below:

	Performing tilling service	Working at horse stable	Differential
Revenues	$1,500	$1,200	$300
Costs	150	50	100
Net benefit in favor of tilling service			$200

Based on this differential analysis, Jack Bennett should perform his tilling service rather than work at the stable.

In many situations, total variable costs differ between alternatives while total fixed costs do not. But one cannot assume that variable costs are always differential costs and fixed costs are never differential costs. For example, the differential cost between operating at a production level of 40,000 units versus a production level of 60,000 units might include increases in both variable and fixed costs. This increase in fixed costs could be the result of a step fixed cost, such as that related to the number of supervisors necessary for a particular production level.

---

[1] Some authors equate relevant cost and differential cost. This text uses the term *relevant* to identify which costs should be considered in a situation and the term *differential* to identify the amount by which these costs differ.

The Nature of Fixed Costs

Up to this point in our discussion, fixed costs have been treated as if they were all alike. But two types of fixed costs should be identified. They are committed fixed costs and discretionary fixed costs.

Committed Fixed Costs. Committed fixed costs relate to the basic facilities and organization structure that a company must have to continue operations. These costs are not changed in the short run without seriously disrupting operations. Examples of committed fixed costs are depreciation on buildings and equipment and salaries of key executives. In the short run, costs such as these are viewed as not being subject to the discretion or control of management. They result from past decisions that "committed" the company for a period of several years. For instance, once a company constructs a building to house production operations, it is committed to the use of the building for many years. Thus, the depreciation on that building is not as subject to control by management as are some other types of fixed costs.

Discretionary Fixed Costs. In contrast to committed fixed costs, discretionary fixed costs are subject to management control from year to year. Each year management decides how much to spend on advertising, research and development, and employee training and development programs. Since these decisions are made each year, they are said to be under the "discretion" of management. Management is not locked in or committed to a certain level of expense for any more than one budget period. The next period it may change the level of expense or may eliminate it completely.

The philosophy of management can affect to some extent which fixed costs are committed and which are discretionary. For instance, during the recession of the mid 1970s, some companies terminated persons in the upper levels of management, while other companies kept their "management team" intact. Thus, in some companies the salaries of top-level managers were discretionary while in others they were committed.

The discussion of committed fixed costs and discretionary fixed costs is relevant to CVP analysis. If a company's fixed costs are almost all committed fixed costs, it is going to have a more difficult time in reducing its break-even point for the next budget period than if most of its fixed costs are discretionary in nature. A company with a large proportion of discretionary fixed costs may be able to reduce fixed costs dramatically in a recessionary period. By doing this, it may be able to "run lean" and show some income even when economic conditions are difficult. Its chances of long-run survival may be enhanced.

Opportunity Cost

Another cost concept relevant to decision making is opportunity cost. An opportunity cost is the potential benefit that is forgone from **not** following the next best alternative course of action. For instance, assume that the two best uses of a plot of land are as a mobile home park (annual income of $100,000) and as a golf driving range (annual income of $60,000). The opportunity cost of utilizing the land as a mobile home park is $60,000, while the opportunity cost of utilizing the land as a driving range is $100,000. Opportunity costs are not recorded in the accounting records since they are the costs of **not** following a certain alternative. However, opportunity cost is a relevant cost in many decision problems because it represents a real sacrifice that comes about because one alternative is chosen instead of another.

Applications of Differential Analysis

To illustrate the application of differential analysis to specific decision problems, we will now consider five types of decisions: (1) setting prices of products; (2) accepting or rejecting special orders; (3) eliminating products, segments, or customers; (4) processing or selling joint products; and (5) deciding to make or buy. These five types of decisions are not the only applications of differential analysis, but they represent typical short-term business decisions to which differential analysis can properly be applied.

Setting Prices of Products.   When differential analysis is applied to pricing decisions, each possible price for a given product represents an alternative course of action. The sales revenues for each alternative and the costs that differ between alternatives are the relevant amounts in these decisions. Total fixed costs usually remain the same between pricing alternatives and, if so, may be ignored. In selecting a price for a product, the goal is to select the price at which total future revenues will exceed total future variable costs by the greatest amount or, in other words, the price that will result in the greatest **total** contribution margin.

A high price is not necessarily the price that will maximize income. There may be many substitutes for the product. If a high price is set, the number of units sold may decline substantially as customers switch to lower-priced competitive products. Thus, in the maximization of income, the expected volume of sales at each price is as important as the contribution margin per unit of product sold. In making any pricing decision, management should seek the combination of price and volume that will produce the largest **total** contribution margin. This combination is often difficult to identify in an actual situation since management may have to estimate the number of units that can be sold at each price.

For example, assume that a company has fixed costs of $10,000 and variable production costs of $5 per unit. Estimates of product demand are:

Choice	Demand
1 . . .	20,000 units at $4 per unit
2 . . .	15,000 units at $6 per unit
3 . . .	10,000 units at $8 per unit
4 . . .	5,000 units at $10 per unit

What price should be set for the product? Based on the calculations shown below, the company should select a price of $8 per unit (choice 3) since this will result in the greatest total contribution margin ($30,000).

Choice	Contribution margin per unit*	×	Number of units	=	Total contribution margin
1	$-1		20,000		$-20,000
2	1		15,000		15,000
3	3		10,000		30,000
4	5		5,000		25,000

* Sales price — Variable cost.

Accepting or Rejecting Special Orders.   Sometimes management is faced with the opportunity to sell its product in two or more markets at two or more different prices. Price discrimination is unlawful under the Robinson-Patman Act unless it is justified by differences in costs of delivery or selling. Since such cost differences often exist, a single product may be marketed at more than one selling price. Differential analysis can be used to determine if special orders (orders at a price different from the norm) should be accepted.

The desirablility of keeping physical facilities and personnel working at capacity is obvious. Good business management requires keeping the cost of idleness at a minimum. When operations are at a level less than full capacity, additional business should be sought. Such additional business may be accepted at prices lower than average unit costs because the only relevant costs are the future **additional** costs that will be incurred. For the most part, the relevant costs will be variable costs, such as direct materials and direct labor.

To illustrate, assume that a given company produces and sells a single product that has a variable cost of $8 per unit. Annual capacity is 10,000 units, and annual fixed costs total $48,000. The selling price is $20 per unit, and production and sales are budgeted at 5,000 units. Thus, budgeted net income before taxes is $12,000, computed as follows:

Sales (5,000 units at $20) . . .		$100,000
Costs:		
Fixed	$48,000	
Variable (5,000 units at $8) . .	40,000	88,000
Net income before taxes . . .		$ 12,000

Assume an order for 3,000 units is received from a foreign distributor at a price of $10 per unit. This $10 price is only half of the regular selling price per unit and is also less than the average cost per unit of $17.60 ($88,000 ÷ 5,000 units). But the $10 price offered exceeds the variable cost per unit by $2. If the order is accepted, net income will be $18,000, computed as follows:

Sales (5,000 units at $20, 3,000 units at $10) . .		$130,000
Costs:		
Fixed	$48,000	
Variable (8,000 units at $8)	64,000	112,000
Net income before taxes		$ 18,000

To continue to operate at 50% capacity (producing 5,000 units) would produce net income of only $12,000. A contribution margin of $2 per unit on the new units will result from acceptance of the order; thus, net income will increase by $6,000. Because the regular market is unlikely to be affected by the export of the product at a sharply reduced price, the order should be accepted assuming it does not violate international trade agreements.

Differential analysis would provide the following calculations:

	(1) Accept order	(2) Reject order	Differential
Revenues	$130,000	$100,000	$30,000
Costs	64,000	40,000	24,000
Net benefit in favor of accepting order			$ 6,000

In summary, variable costs set a floor for the selling price in cost analyses. Even if the price exceeds variable costs only slightly, the additional business may make a contribution to income. But "contribution pricing" of marginal business often brings only short-term increases in income. Such pricing should be appraised in light of the long-range effects on company and industry price structures. In the long run, full costs must be covered.

Eliminating Products, Segments, or Customers. Periodically, management has to decide whether to eliminate or retain certain products, segments, or customers. Differential analysis can be useful in this type of decision making. Since the income statement does not automatically associate costs with given products, segments, or customers, costs must be reclassified as those that **would be changed** by the elimination and those that **would not.** In effect, one must simply assume elimination and compare the reduction in revenues with the eliminated costs.

Usually costs such as direct materials, direct labor, and other variable costs would be eliminated and, therefore, become part of differential cost. The fixed costs will **normally** remain unaffected and, if so, are not relevant to the decision. If revenues lost from discontinuing the product, segment, or customer exceed the costs that would be eliminated, that item is making a positive contribution to profits and should, therefore, be retained unless a more profitable opportunity exists.

To illustrate, assume that the elimination of product R is being considered. Product R provides revenues of $100,000 annually and incurs costs of $110,000, $80,000 variable and $30,000 fixed. Therefore, product R creates an apparent annual loss of $10,000. But careful cost analysis reveals that if product R were dropped, the reduction in costs would be $80,000. The $30,000 fixed costs would continue to be incurred and would need to be covered by the remaining products of the company. The analysis is as follows:

	(1) Retain product R	(2) Drop product R	Differential
Revenues	$100,000	$-0-	$100,000
Costs	80,000	-0-	80,000
Net benefit of retaining product R			$ 20,000

This illustration shows that product R, even though it produces no net income itself, has been contributing $20,000 ($100,000 revenues − $80,000 variable costs) annually to covering the fixed costs of the business. In other words, product R has a contribution to indirect expenses of $20,000. Consequently, its elimination could be a costly mistake unless there is a more profitable use for the released facilities.

If there is a profitable alternative use for those facilities, the potential income from that alternative represents an opportunity cost of retaining product R. Assume, for example, that those facilities could be used to manufacture a product that would contribute $30,000 to the company's income. In this case, the relevant costs in the decision to retain product R are $110,000 ($80,000 of variable manufacturing costs and $30,000 of opportunity cost), while the relevant revenues are still $100,000. Therefore, the net advantage of keeping product R is $—10,000, meaning that product R should not be retained. Similarly, when analyzing the decision to replace product R with the alternative, the $20,000 contribution to indirect expenses that is foregone if product R is replaced becomes an opportunity cost of the alternative product.

Processing or Selling Joint Products. In some manufacturing situations, several products result from a common raw material or manufacturing process; these products are called **joint products.** For instance, when crude oil is manufactured, a wide variety of fuels, solvents, lubricants, and residual petrochemicals are derived. Some of these products can be processed further or sold in their existing condition. Management can use differential analysis to decide whether to process a joint product further or to sell it in its present condition. **Joint costs** are those costs incurred up to the point where the joint products split off from each other. These costs are sunk costs in deciding whether to process a joint product further before selling it or to sell it in its condition at split off.

The following example will illustrate the issue of whether to process or sell joint products. Assume that Company Y manufactures two products, A and B, from a common manufacturing process. Each of the products could be sold in its present form or could be processed further and sold at a higher price. Data for both products are given below:

Product	Selling price per unit at split-off point	Cost per unit of further processing	Selling price per unit after further processing
A	$10	$6	$21
B	12	7	18

The differential revenues and costs of further processing of the two products are as follows:

Product	Differential revenue of further processing	Differential cost of further processing	Net advantage (disadvantage) of further processing
A	$11	$6	$ 5
B	6	7	(1)

ment, inventory valuation, or tax purposes. Currently accepted practice requires that **all** costs of producing a product be attached to that product and treated as expenses only when the product is sold. But the type of information accumulated under direct costing, especially the classification of costs as fixed and variable, is very useful to management in understanding relationships between costs, volume, and profits. Since direct costing is such a valuable management tool, its use is likely to increase.

■ SUMMARY

The short term (or short run) is defined as that period of time in which the effects of certain past decisions cannot be changed. As a result, some costs are fixed in the short run, while others vary with changes in the level of activity. For purposes of short-term decision making, management must attempt to classify all costs as fixed or variable to understand how total costs will react to changes in the volume of production or sales.

There are four basic types of cost behavior patterns—variable costs, fixed costs, mixed (or semivariable) costs, and step costs. Various techniques exist for analyzing actual cost data to identify the underlying cost patterns. These techniques include the scatter diagram, the high-low method, and sophisticated statistical techniques like the least squares method.

The chapter discusses three topics related to short-term decision making—cost-volume-profit (CVP) analysis, differential analysis, and direct costing. CVP analysis is a technique used to estimate the relationship between selling prices, costs, the company's volume of operations, and net income in the short run. The starting point for CVP analysis is the company's break-even point, which means the level of operations at which revenues and costs are equal. Once that is determined, management can look at the changes in income that would result if selling prices, fixed costs, or variable costs were changed. In addition, management can compute the level of operations required to produce a certain amount of income.

Differential analysis is another tool of short-term analysis. In differential analysis, a particular set of alternatives is analyzed by looking at the revenues and costs or expenses that will differ in the future, depending on which alternative is chosen. Such revenues and costs are designated as relevant revenues and relevant costs for differential analysis. Differential revenue is the amount by which relevant revenues differ between alternatives. Differential cost or expense is the amount by which total expense differs between alternatives. In differential analysis, the preferred alternative is the one that provides the largest positive difference between differential revenue and differential expense. A number of specific types of decisions can be addressed through differential analysis including the following: setting prices of products; accepting or rejecting special orders; eliminating products, segments, or customers; processing or selling joint products; and deciding to make or buy.

Under absorption (or full) costing all manufacturing costs are treated as product costs. Under direct (or variable) costing only variable manufacturing costs are treated as product costs; fixed manufacturing overhead costs are considered to be period costs. Absorption costing is required for financial reporting purposes. Direct costing, however, provides cost information that is useful to management for many decision-making purposes, including CVP analysis and differential analysis. As a general rule, the difference in the net income before taxes computed under each of the methods is related to the change in inventories over the period. If there is no change in inventories, both methods give the same net income before taxes amount.

In this chapter you studied the importance of short-run planning. Chapter 27 discusses long-range planning regarding the acquisition of capital assets. All businesses must establish long-range goals and must plan for the future to be successful.

NEW TERMS INTRODUCED IN CHAPTER 26*

Absorption (or full) costing

A concept of costing under which all production costs, including fixed manufacturing overhead, are accounted for as product costs and allocated to the units produced during a period (1022).

Break-even analysis

See Cost-volume-profit analysis.

Break-even chart

A graph that shows the relationships between sales, costs, volume, and profit and also shows the break-even point (1007).

Break-even point

That level of operations at which revenues for a period are equal to the costs assigned to that period so that there is no net income or loss (1005).

By-products

The waste materials (which sometimes have a small market value compared to the main product) that result from the production of a product or products (1021).

Committed fixed costs

Costs relating to the basic facilities and organization structure that a company must have to continue operations. An example is depreciation on the factory building (1016).

Contribution margin

The amount by which revenue exceeds the variable costs of producing that revenue (1006).

Contribution margin rate

Contribution margin per unit divided by selling price per unit (1007).

Cost-volume-profit (CVP) analysis

An analysis of the effects that any changes in a company's selling prices, costs, and/or volume will have upon income (profits) in the short run. Also called break-even analysis (1005).

Differential analysis

An analysis of the different costs and benefits that would arise from alternative solutions to a particular problem (1014).

Differential cost or expense

The difference between the amounts of relevant costs for two alternatives (1015).

Differential revenue

The difference between the amounts of relevant revenues for two alternatives (1015).

Direct (or variable) costing

A concept of costing under which only variable manufacturing costs are accounted for as product costs and charged to the units produced during a period. All fixed manufacturing overhead is charged to expense in the period in which it is incurred (1022).

Discretionary fixed costs

Fixed costs that are subject to management control from year to year. An example is advertising expense (1016).

Fixed costs

Costs that remain constant (in total) over some relevant range of output (1002).

---

* Some terms listed in earlier chapters are repeated here for your convenience.

High-low method

A method used in dividing mixed costs into their fixed and variable portions. The high plot and low plot of actual costs are used to draw a line representing a total mixed cost (1005).

Joint costs

Those costs incurred up to the point where joint products split off from each other (1020).

Joint products

Two or more products resulting from a common raw material or manufacturing process (1020).

Least-squares method

A method used for dividing mixed costs into their fixed and variable portions; it uses statistical techniques to draw the regression line representing a total mixed cost (1005).

Make-or-buy decision

Concerns whether to manufacture or purchase a part or material used in the manufacture of another product (1021).

Margin of safety

Amount by which sales can decrease before a loss will be incurred (1010).

Margin of safety rate

Margin of safety expressed as a percentage; is equal to (Current sales − Break-even sales) ÷ Current sales (1010).

Mixed cost

Contains a fixed portion of cost that will be incurred even when the plant is completely idle and a variable portion that will increase directly with production volume (1002).

Opportunity cost

The potential benefit that is foregone from not following the next best alternative course of action (1016).

Product mix

The proportion of the company's total sales attributable to each type of product sold. Product mix may be defined either in terms of sales dollars or in terms of the number of units sold (1013).

Relevant revenues or costs

Revenues or costs that will differ in the future depending on which alternative course of action is selected (1015).

Relevant range

The range of production or sales volume over which the basic cost behavior assumptions will hold true (1007).

Scatter diagram

A diagram that shows plots of actual costs incurred for various levels of output or sales; it is used in dividing mixed costs into their fixed and variable portions (1004).

Short run

The period of time over which it is assumed that plant capacity and certain costs are fixed; often determined to be one year or less (1001).

Step cost

A cost that remains constant in total over a range of output (or sales) but then increases in steps at certain points (1002).

Sunk costs

Past costs about which nothing can be done; they are not relevant in decision making because the costs have already been incurred (1015).

Variable costs

Costs that vary (in total) directly with changes in volume (1002).

Variable cost rate

Variable costs expressed as a percentage of sales; used to find the break-even point (1006).

DEMONSTRATION PROBLEM 26–1

The Boston Company has fixed costs of $250,000 per year and variable costs of $6 per unit. Its product sells for $10 per unit. Full capacity is 100,000 units. Variable costs are 60% of sales ($6/$10).

Required: a. Compute the break-even point in (1) sales dollars, (2) units, and (3) percentage of capacity.
             b. Compute the number of units the company must sell if it wishes to have net income of $120,000.

Solution to demonstration problem 26–1

a. (1)   Sales *(S)* = Fixed costs *(FC)* + Variable costs *(VC)*
$$S = \$250,000 + 0.60S$$
$$0.40S = \$250,000$$
$$S = \$250,000 \div 0.40$$
$$S = \$625,000$$

(2)   Break-even point in units = $\$625,000 \div \$10 = \underline{\underline{62,500}}$ or $\dfrac{\$250,000}{\$10 - \$6} = \underline{\underline{62,500}}$

(3)   Break-even point as percentage of capacity = $62,500 \div 100,000 = \underline{\underline{62.5\%}}$

b.   Number of units $= \dfrac{\text{Fixed cost} + \text{Desired net income}}{\text{Contribution margin}}$

$$= \frac{\$250,000 + \$120,000}{\$10 - \$6}$$

$$= \frac{\$370,000}{\$4}$$

$$= \underline{\underline{92,500}}$$

DEMONSTRATION PROBLEM 26–2

The Detroit Division of the Orvis Company produces a single product that it sells for $10 each. Production costs include $2 per unit variable costs and $330,000 per year of fixed manufacturing overhead costs. Normal activity for fixed manufacturing overhead cost absorption is 110,000 units per year. Thus, fixed manufacturing overhead costs are applied at $3 per unit. Selling and administrative expenses are $25,000 plus $0.50 per unit sold

On December 31, 1987, the division's finished goods inventory consisted of 20,000 units with a total cost of $100,000 ($40,000, variable; $60,000 fixed). Sales and production data for 1988 are:

Sales in units	100,000
Dollars of sales	$1,000,000
Production in units	110,000
Variable production costs . .	$ 220,000

Required: a. Prepare an income statement for the division for 1988 under absorption costing.
             b. Prepare an income statement for the division for 1988 under direct costing.

Solution to demonstration problem 26–2

a.   Income statement under absorption costing:

ORVIS COMPANY (Detroit Division)
Income Statement
For the Year Ended December 31, 1988

Sales (100,000 units at $10)		$1,000,000
Cost of goods sold:		
Beginning finished goods inventory		
(absorption cost $5 per unit)	$ 100,000	
Variable production costs ($2 per unit) $220,000		
Fixed manufacturing overhead costs absorbed ($3 per unit) . . 330,000		
Cost of goods manufactured	550,000	
Ending finished goods inventory		
(absorption cost $5 per unit)	(150,000)	
Cost of goods sold		500,000
Gross margin on sales		$ 500,000
Selling and administrative expenses		75,000
Net income		$ 425,000

b.   Income statement under direct costing:

ORVIS COMPANY (Detroit Division)
Income Statement
For the Year Ended December 31, 1988

Sales (100,000 units at $10)		$1,000,000
Cost of goods sold:		
Beginning finished goods inventory		
(direct cost $2 per unit)	$ 40,000	
Direct cost of goods manufactured		
($2 per unit)	220,000	
Ending finished goods inventory		
(direct cost $2 per unit)	(60,000)	
Cost of goods sold		$ 200,000
Manufacturing margin		$ 800,000
Variable selling and administrative expenses . .		50,000
Contribution margin		$ 750,000
Period costs:		
Fixed manufacturing overhead $330,000		
Fixed selling and administrative expenses . . 25,000		355,000
Net income		$ 395,000

QUESTIONS

1. Name and describe the four cost behavior patterns.

2. What are the various ways in which the cost line for a mixed cost can be determined? Describe each method.

3. What is meant by the term *break-even point?* What factors must be taken into consideration in determining it?

4. What are the different ways in which the break-even point can be expressed?

5. How is the relevant range related to break-even analysis?

6. Why is break-even analysis considered appropriate only for short-run decisions?

7. What is the formula for calculating the break-even point in sales revenue?

8. What formula is used to solve for the break-even point in units? How can this formula be altered to calculate the number of units that must be sold to achieve a desired level of income?

9. Why might a business wish to lower its break-even point? How would it go about lowering the break-even point? What effect would you expect the mechanization and automation of production processes to have upon the break-even point?

10. How is the break-even point calculated for a multiproduct company?

11. What does the label "units" on the horizontal axis of the break-even chart mean?

12. Identify some types of decisions that can be made using differential analysis.

13. What is a committed fixed cost? Give some examples.

14. What is a discretionary fixed cost? Give some examples.

15. Give an example of a fixed cost that might be considered committed for one company and discretionary for another.

16. What assumptions are made in cost-volume-profit (CVP) analysis?

17. What essential feature distinguishes direct costing from absorption costing?

18. Under what specific circumstances would you expect net income to be larger under direct costing than under absorption costing? What is the specific reason for this difference?

EXERCISES

E-1

Analyze mixed cost using high-low method

Use the high-low method to determine the fixed and variable components of a mixed cost, given the following observations:

Volume (units)	Cost
4,000 . . .	$5,000
8,000 . . .	8,000

E-2

Compute break-even point in sales dollars

Compute the break-even point in sales dollars if fixed costs are $55,000 and variable costs are 45% of sales.

E-3

Compute break-even point in units

The Duke Company sells each unit it produces for $15, with fixed costs of $60,000 and variable cost of $9 per unit. Find the break-even point in units.

E-4

Compute break-even point in sales dollars and units under varying assumptions; comment on results

The Sun Company currently sells each unit it produces for $7.50. Variable cost is $2.25 per unit, and fixed costs are $105,000. Compute the break-even point in both dollars and units under each of the following independent assumptions. Comment on why the break-even points are different.

a. The costs and selling price are as given above.
b. Fixed costs are increased to $115,500.
c. Selling price is increased by 2%.
d. Variable cost is increased to $2.70 per unit.

E–5

Decide whether to increase advertising; compute margin of safety

A company sells a product for $20 each, with variable cost of $10 per unit. Fixed costs are $1,000,000. The company currently sells 200,000 units per year. Should this company undertake an advertising campaign that will result in a $100,000 increase in fixed costs, a $2 per unit decrease in variable cost, and a 10% increase in sales? What would the margin of safety be before and after the campaign?

E–6

Compute break-even point in units and sales volume to achieve a specified level of income

If a company has fixed costs of $130,000 and variable cost of $14 per unit, how many units would have to be sold at $21 each to break even? How many units would have to be sold to earn $100,000? If 30,000 units are 100% of capacity, what percentage of capacity do the two levels of output represent?

E–7

Compute multiproduct break-even point and margin of safety

The Shining Company sells three products. Last year's sales were $75,000 for product X, $97,500 for product Y, and $52,500 for product Z. Variable costs were X, $45,000; Y, $60,000; and Z, $33,000. Fixed costs were $36,000. Determine the break-even point and the margin of safety.

E–8

Compute multiproduct break-even point

If the company in Exercise E–7 changes the product mix to 2:2:1, with total dollar sales being the same as last year, what will the new break-even point be? Comment on why it has changed.

E–9

Compute break-even point

The Ringling Company sells each unit it produces for $4. Calculate the break-even point in dollars given the following cost observations:

Volume (units)	Cost
4,000 . . .	$24,000
34,000 . . .	75,000

E–10

Identify relevant and differential revenues and costs

Assume you had invested $120 in a lawn mower to set up a lawn mowing business for the summer. During the first week, you are presented with two opportunities. You can mow the grounds at a housing development for $150, or you can help paint a garage for $125. The additional costs you will incur are $25 and $10, respectively. These costs include $2 under each alternative for a pair of gloves that will last about one week. Prepare a schedule showing:

a. The relevant revenues and expenses (costs).
b. The differential revenue and expense.
c. The net benefit or advantage of selecting one alternative over the other.

E–11

Accept or reject an order

The Step Corporation is operating at 80% of capacity, which means it produces 8,000 units. Variable cost is $90 per unit. Wholesaler A offers to buy 2,000 units at $105 per unit. Wholesaler B proposes to buy 1,500 units at $112.50 per unit. Which offer, if any, should the Lane Corporation accept?

E–12

Compute gross margins for two companies with drop in sales volume

Two companies, Paris, Inc. and Newcomb Company, are competitors. Paris, Inc. has just installed the latest automated equipment so that its fixed costs are $90,000. Newcomb Company operates a run-down plant with only $45,000 of fixed costs. Both companies have $150,000 in sales and gross margins of 20%. Compute gross margins for the two companies assuming a 10% drop in sales volume.

E–13

Decide which company can sell for less

In the situation described in Exercise E–12, which company can bid lower on a special order to regain lost sales? Why?

E–14

Decide whether to retain a product line

Analysis of product C reveals that it is losing $10,000 annually. Ten thousand units of product C are sold at a price of $10 per unit each year. If variable costs are $8 per unit, what would be the increase (decrease) in company net income before taxes if product C were eliminated?

E–15

Decide whether to keep or eliminate a department

Department 3 of the Lee Company has revenues of $200,000, variable expenses of $80,000, direct fixed expenses of $40,000, and allocated, indirect fixed expenses of $100,000. If the department is eliminated, what will be the effect on net income before taxes?

E–16

Decide whether to process joint products further

The Lance Company manufactures two joint products. At the split-off point they have sales values of:

Product 1 . . $14/unit
Product 2 . . $10/unit

After further processing costing $8 and $6, respectively, they can be sold for $30 and $14, respectively. Should further processing be done on these products? Why?

E–17

Decide whether to make or buy a part

The Narlin Corporation currently is manufacturing 40,000 units per year of a part used in its final product. The cost of producing this part is $43 per unit. The variable portion of this cost consists of direct materials of $24, direct labor of $13, and manufacturing overhead of $2. The company could earn $40,000 per year from the space now used to manufacture this part. Assuming equal quality and availability, what is the maximum price Narlin Corporation should pay to buy the part rather than make it?

E–18

Compare net income before taxes and ending inventory under direct and absorption costing

The following data relate to the Garin Company for the year ended December 31, 1987:

Costs of production:
Direct materials	$ 75,000
Direct labor	105,000
Manufacturing overhead:	
Variable	37,500
Fixed	75,000
Sales commissions (variable) . .	22,500
Sales salaries (fixed)	15,000
Administrative expenses (fixed) . .	30,000
Units produced	37,500
Units sold (at $15 each)	30,000

Without making any computations, would you expect net income before taxes to be higher under absorption costing or under direct costing? Compute the amount of net income before taxes and ending inventory under both methods.

E–19

Compute net income before taxes under direct and absorption costing

The following data are for a company for the year 1987:

Sales (20,000 units)	$300,000
Direct materials used (24,000 units at $4.50) . .	108,000
Direct labor cost incurred	36,000
Manufacturing overhead incurred:	
Variable	10,800
Fixed	14,400
Selling and administrative expenses:	
Variable	18,000
Fixed	60,000

Assume that one unit of direct materials goes into each unit of finished goods. There is an ending inventory of finished goods of 4,000 units, and there are no other beginning or ending work in process inventories. The variable and fixed overhead rates (based on normal activity of 24,000 units) are $0.45 and $0.60, respectively. Compute the net income before taxes under (a) absorption costing and (b) direct costing.

E-20

Discuss how net income before taxes under absorption costing would differ under direct costing

Given below are the costs of the finished goods inventories of the Zee Company:

Cost element	Beginning inventory	Ending inventory
Direct materials	$45,000	$4,500
Direct labor	75,000	7,800
Manufacturing overhead:		
Variable	30,000	3,000
Fixed	22,500	3,000

Assume that the Zee Company uses absorption costing and that there were no work in process inventories at the beginning or end of the year. State by how much Zee Company's net income before taxes for the year would have differed if direct costing had been used.

PROBLEMS, SERIES A

P26-1-A

Analyze mixed cost using high-low method and scatter diagram

The Darken Company assigns you the task of estimating total maintenance cost on its production machinery. This cost is a mixed cost. You are supplied with the following data from past years:

Year	Units	Cost
1979 . .	4,000	$10,000
1980 . .	5,000	10,800
1981 . .	4,500	11,000
1982 . .	5,500	11,600
1983 . .	5,000	11,600
1984 . .	6,500	12,400
1985 . .	7,000	13,400
1986 . .	9,000	14,400
1987 . .	10,000	16,000

Required:

a. Using the high-low method, determine the total amount of fixed costs and the amount of variable cost per unit.

b. Prepare a scatter diagram, plot the actual costs, and visually fit a linear cost line to the points. Estimate the amount of total fixed costs and the amount of variable cost per unit.

P26-2-A

Compute break-even point and sales needed to achieve a specified level of income

If a company has fixed costs of $500,000, variable cost of $6 per unit, and a selling price of $14, how many units must be sold to break even? How many units will it have to sell to earn $80,000 before taxes?

P26-3-A

Determine break-even sales under varying assumptions

Compute the break-even point in sales dollars and units under each of the following independent assumptions. Selling price in each case is $50 per unit unless otherwise stated.

a. Fixed costs are $200,000; variable cost is $34 per unit.

b. Fixed costs are $200,000; variable cost is $30 per unit.

c. Fixed costs are $160,000; variable cost is $30 per unit.

d. Fixed costs are $160,000; selling price is $40, and variable cost is $30 per unit.

e. Use the assumptions in (d) above to determine the level of sales required to achieve net income of $100,000.

P26–4–A

Determine break-even point and net income under varying assumptions

a. Assume that fixed costs of L Corporation are $200,000 per year, variable cost is $4 per unit, and selling price is $10 per unit. Determine the break-even point in sales dollars.

b. M Company breaks even when sales amount to $2,000,000. In 1987, its sales were $3,000,000, and its variable costs amounted to $900,000. Determine the amount of its fixed costs.

c. The sales of N Corporation in 1987 amounted to $40,000,000, its variable costs were $10,000,000, and its fixed costs were $20,000,000. At what level of sales would the N Corporation break even?

d. What would have been the net income of the N Corporation, in part (c) above, if sales volume had been 10% higher but selling prices had remained unchanged?

e. What would have been the net income of the N Corporation, in part (c) above, if variable costs had been 10% lower?

f. What would have been the net income of the N Corporation, in part (c) above, if fixed costs had been 10% lower?

g. Determine the break-even point in sales dollars for the N Corporation on the basis of the data given in (e) above and then in (f) above.

P26–5–A

Prepare break-even chart; compute break-even point; prepare income statement for two companies

The operating results for two companies are presented below:

	Company A	Company B
Sales (20,000 units) . .	$400,000	$400,000
Variable costs	100,000	220,000
Contribution margin . .	$300,000	$180,000
Fixed costs	200,000	80,000
Net income	$100,000	$100,000

Required:

a. Prepare a break-even chart for Company A, indicating the break-even point, the contribution margin, and the areas of income and losses.

b. Compute the break-even point of both companies in sales dollars and units.

c. Assume that without changes in selling price, the sales of each company decline by 20%. Prepare condensed income statements, similar to the ones above, for both companies.

P26–6–A

Make leasing decision; compute break-even point; compute expected net income

The Sharp Company, a leading manufacturer of stereos, incurred $420,000 of fixed costs while selling 20,000 radios at $100 each. Variable cost was $30 per radio.

A new machine used in the production of stereos has recently become available and is more efficient than the machine currently being used. The new machine would reduce Sharp's variable costs by 20% and can be leased on an annual basis for $16,000 per year.

Required:

a. Compute the break-even point in units assuming use of the old machine.

b. Compute the break-even point in units assuming use of the new machine.

c. Assuming that total sales remain at $2,000,000 and that the new machine is leased, compute expected net income.

d. Should the new machine be leased? Why?

P26–7–A

Decide whether to undertake a sales promotion campaign and whether to hire an efficiency expert

a. Change Company reports sales of $600,000, variable costs of $360,000, and fixed costs of $90,000. If the company spends $60,000 on a sales promotion campaign, it is estimated that sales can be increased by $225,000. Should the company proceed with the campaign? (Show computations.)

b. The following data pertain to the Dame Corporation:

Sales	$300,000
Variable costs . .	180,000
Fixed costs . .	60,000

The president is considering hiring an efficiency expert at $60,000 this year, who can reduce variable costs by 25%. Assuming that sales will remain at the same level, should the expert be hired?

P26–8–A

Compute multiproduct break-even point assuming change in product mix

The Claxton Corporation sells three products. It has fixed costs of $200,000. The sales and variable costs of these products for 1987 follow:

	Products		
	A	**B**	**C**
Sales	$200,000	$300,000	$500,000
Variable costs . .	140,000	180,000	250,000

Required:

a. Determine the break-even point in sales dollars for 1988 assuming that the product mix will remain as it was in 1987.

b. Determine the break-even point in sales dollars for 1988 assuming that the product mix ratio for 1988 is expected to change to 50:30:20 while total sales remain the same.

P26–9–A

Decide whether to keep or eliminate a product line

Following are sales and other operating data for the three products made and sold by the Muntz Company:

	Product			
	A	**B**	**C**	**Total**
Sales	$400,000	$250,000	$150,000	$800,000
Manufacturing costs:				
Fixed	$ 50,000	$ 25,000	$ 45,000	$120,000
Variable	240,000	200,000	60,000	500,000
Total	$290,000	$225,000	$105,000	$620,000
Gross margin	$110,000	$ 25,000	$ 45,000	$180,000
Selling expenses:				
Fixed	$ 5,000	$ 5,000	$ 5,000	$ 15,000
Variable	15,000	10,000	25,000	50,000
Administrative expenses:				
Fixed	5,000	3,000	12,000	20,000
Variable	10,000	3,000	7,000	20,000
Total selling and administra- tive expenses	$ 35,000	$ 21,000	$ 49,000	$105,000
Net income (loss) before taxes . . .	$ 75,000	$ 4,000	$ (4,000)	$ 75,000

In view of the net loss shown above for product C, the company's management is considering dropping that product. All variable costs are direct costs and would be eliminated if product C were dropped; all fixed costs are indirect costs and would not be eliminated. Assume that the space used to produce product C would be left idle.

Required: Would you recommend the elimination of product C? Give supporting computations.

P26–10–A

Evaluate pricing alternatives; prepare income statement using best alternative

Based on the information given in Problem 26–9–A, assume that the product mix of the company is technologically interchangeable. The company can delete one product and produce a given amount of the existing other products without changes in variable cost per unit, selling prices, or total fixed costs. The company is considering dropping product B because of its low contribution margin.

Assume that dropping product B will allow the company to explore these alternatives:

1. Produce $412,500 more of product C.
2. Produce $375,000 more of product A.
3. Produce $150,000 more of product A and $300,000 more of product C.
4. Produce $225,000 more of product A and $150,000 more of product C.

a. What is the best alternative? Show computations.
b. Show what the resulting sales and net income before taxes of the best alternative would be.

P26–11–A

Prepare income statements under direct and absorption costing; discuss reasons for differences

Mann Company employs an absorption cost system in accounting for the single product it manufactures. Following are selected data for the year 1987:

Sales (10,000 units)	$300,000
Direct materials used (12,000 units at $6) . . .	108,000
Direct labor cost incurred	36,000
Variable manufacturing overhead	10,800
Fixed manufacturing overhead	14,400
Variable selling and administrative expenses . .	18,000
Fixed selling and administrative expenses . . .	60,000

One unit of direct materials goes into each unit of finished goods. Overhead rates are based on a capacity of 12,000 units and are $0.90 and $1.20 per unit for variable and fixed overhead, respectively. The only beginning or ending inventory is the 2,000 units of finished goods on hand at the end of 1987.

Required:
a. Prepare an income statement for 1987 under variable costing.
b. Prepare an income statement for 1987 under absorption costing.
c. Explain the reason for the difference in net income before taxes between *(a)* and *(b)*.

PROBLEMS, SERIES B

P26–1–B

Analyze mixed cost using high-low method and scatter diagram

The Rouche Company has identified certain variable and fixed costs in its operations. A mixed cost exists that needs to be divided into its fixed and variable portions. Actual data pertaining to this cost follow:

Year	Units	Costs
1978 . .	10,400	$19,200
1979 . .	10,000	18,000
1980 . .	11,000	19,500
1981 . .	12,800	19,200
1982 . .	14,200	19,500
1983 . .	15,000	20,700
1984 . .	16,400	21,300
1985 . .	17,800	22,800
1986 . .	18,800	24,000
1987 . .	20,000	25,800

Required:
a. Using the high-low method, determine the total amount of fixed costs and the amount of variable cost per unit. Draw the cost line.
b. Prepare a scatter diagram, plot the actual costs, and visually fit a linear cost line to the points. Estimate the amount of total fixed costs and the amount of variable cost per unit.

P26–2–B

Determine break-even point under varying assumptions

a. Determine the break-even point in sales dollars and units for a company that has fixed costs of $120,000, variable cost of $12 per unit, and a selling price of $22 per unit.
b. Y Company breaks even when sales are $200,000. In 1987, sales were $900,000 and variable costs were $540,000. Compute the amount of fixed costs.
c. The Ace Company had sales in 1987 of $280,000, variable costs of $154,000, and fixed costs of $70,000. At what level of sales did the company break even?
d. What would the break-even point in sales dollars have been in *(c)* above if variable costs had been 10% higher?
e. What would the break-even point in sales dollars have been in *(c)* above if fixed costs had been 10% higher?

f. Compute the break-even point in sales dollars for the Ace Company under the assumptions of both *(d)* and *(e)* together.

P26–3–B

Prepare break-even chart; compute break-even sales and sales needed to achieve a specified level of income

The Smith Company has a plant capacity of 75,000 units. Variable costs are $600,000 at 100% capacity. Fixed costs are $400,000, but this is true only between 25,000 and 75,000 units.

Required:

a. Prepare a break-even chart for the Smith Company assuming it sells its product for $16 each. Indicate on the chart the relevant range, contribution margin, break-even point, and income and losses.

b. Verify the break-even point on the chart by using the break-even sales formula given in this chapter. Also calculate the break-even point in units.

c. How many units would have to be sold in order to earn $100,000 before taxes?

P26–4–B

Compute break-even point for two companies; analyze effects of decrease in sales volume

Following is a summary of 1987 operations for two companies:

	Company E	Company F
Sales	$1,000,000	$1,000,000
Expenses:		
Fixed	$200,000	$700,000
Variable	600,000	100,000
Total expenses . .	800,000	800,000
Net income	$ 200,000	$ 200,000

Required:

a. Compute the break-even point in sales dollars for each company.

b. Assume that (without changes in selling price) the sales of each company decreased by 25%. Present condensed income statements, similar to the ones above, showing the effect of the decrease in sales on the net income of each company.

P26–5–B

Compute level of sales needed to break even and earn a specified level of income

The Amdohl Company has a plant capacity of 100,000 units, at which level variable costs are $300,000. Fixed costs are expected to be $90,000. Each unit of product sells for $5.

Required:

a. Determine the company's break-even point in sales dollars and units.

b. What level of sales would the company need to attain in order to earn $60,000 before taxes?

c. If the selling price were raised to $6 per unit, what level of sales would the company need to attain in order to earn $60,000 before taxes?

P26–6–B

Compute break-even point under varying assumptions; compute fixed costs

a. The Frey Corporation sells its product for $9 per unit. Variable cost is $6.75 per unit, and fixed costs are $337,500. Compute the break-even point in dollars and units.

b. The Cook Company had sales in 1987 of $900,000, and its variable costs were $360,000. If the company could break even with sales of $262,500, what were the fixed costs?

c. What would the break-even point in sales dollars have been for the Cook Company in part *(b)* if variable costs had been 15% higher?

d. What would the break-even point in sales dollars have been in part *(b)* if fixed costs had been 10% lower?

e. What would the break-even point in sales dollars have been under the assumptions of both *(c)* and *(d)* together?

P26–7–B

Compute break-even point under varying product mix

The Akins Corporation has fixed costs of $200,000. It sells three products. The cost and revenue data for these products follow:

	Products		
	1	*2*	*3*
Sales	$100,000	$150,000	$200,000
Variable costs . .	60,000	100,000	110,000

Required:

a. Compute the break-even point in sales dollars.

b. Assume the sales mix is expected to be in the ratio of 2:2:1 next year with total sales being the same as this year. What would the break-even point be in sales dollars?

P26–8–B

Prepare condensed income statement showing effects of product pricing decision

A state government has asked for bids on an order for 200,000 units of product X. The Deck Company, which has a production capacity of 1,000,000 units and is currently operating at 80% of capacity, is considering making a bid for the government contract. The Deck Company's fixed costs amount to $2,000,000, and its variable cost is $20 per unit.

Required:

a. What is the minimum price Deck Company should bid?

b. Present two income statements, the first assuming that the bid is unsuccessful and that the price on regular sales is $30 per unit, and the second assuming that the contract is obtained at a bid price of $25 per unit, while regular sales are at $30 per unit.

P26–9–B

Present income statement assuming department elimination; evaluate the decision to eliminate

The new president of Rexford, Inc., Guy Rex, is giving serious consideration to discontinuing Department B. He notes that the income statements of the past few years show the department operating at a loss. He also notes that the other two departments seem quite badly crowded and in need of additional space. He doubts, however, that the closing of Department B will increase the sales of the other two departments. In condensed form, the income statement for the year ending June 30, 1987, is:

	Dept. A	Dept. B	Dept. C	Total
Net sales	$240,000	$60,000	$100,000	$400,000
Cost of goods sold	160,000	37,500	60,000	257,500
Gross margin	$ 80,000	$22,500	$ 40,000	$142,500
Operating expenses:				
Selling	$ 29,000	$15,000	$ 20,000	$ 64,000
Delivery	6,000	1,500	2,500	10,000
Buying	14,500	3,000	5,500	23,000
Occupancy	9,000	3,000	6,000	18,000
Administrative	12,000	3,000	5,000	20,000
Total operating expenses .	$ 70,500	$25,500	$ 39,000	$135,000
Net income from operations . .	$ 9,500	$ (3,000)	$ 1,000	$ 7,500
Interest income	3,000	750	1,250	5,000
Net income before taxes . . .	$ 12,500	$ (2,250)	$ 2,250	$ 12,500
Federal income taxes (credit) . .	2,500	(450)	450	2,500
Net income (loss)	$ 10,000	$ (1,800)	$ 1,800	$ 10,000

The president of the company has asked you to express your opinion on the desirability of the contemplated closing of Department B. He tells you that he believes that all of the selling expenses and half of the delivery, buying, and administrative expenses charged to Department B will be eliminated upon the closing of the department. Also, all of the financial charges earned and allocated to Department B will be eliminated if the department is closed.

Required: State your opinion on the desirability of closing Department B. Support your opinion with a schedule showing what the net income after taxes for the company as a whole would have been if Department B had been closed at the start of the accounting year ending June 30, 1987. The tax rate is 20%.

P26–10–B

Prepare income statements under direct and absorption costing

The following data are for the Winfrey Company for the year 1987:

Sales (10,000 units)	$150,000
Direct materials used (12,000 units at $4.50) . .	54,000
Direct labor cost incurred	18,000
Variable manufacturing overhead incurred . . .	5,400
Fixed manufacturing overhead incurred	7,200
Variable selling and administrative expenses . .	9,000
Fixed selling and administrative expenses . . .	30,000

One unit of direct materials goes into each unit of finished goods. The only beginning or ending inventory is the 2,000 units of finished goods on hand at the end of 1987. Variable and fixed overhead rates (based on 100% of capacity or 12,000 units) are $0.45 and $0.60, respectively.

Required: a. Prepare an income statement under direct costing.
b. Prepare an income statement under absorption costing.

BUSINESS DECISION PROBLEM 26–1

Compute break-even point and projected net income for two investment alternatives; determine best alternative

The Pitts Company is operating at almost 100% of capacity. The company expects the demand for its product to increase by 25% next year (1988). In order to satisfy the demand for its product, the company is considering two alternatives. The first alternative will increase fixed costs by 15% but will have no effect on variable costs. The second alternative will not affect fixed costs but will cause variable costs to increase to 60% of the selling price of the company's product.

The Pitts Company's condensed income statement for 1987 is shown below:

Sales		$6,000,000
Costs:		
Variable	$2,700,000	
Fixed	1,100,000	3,800,000
Net income before taxes . .		$2,200,000

Required: a. Determine the break-even point in sales dollars for 1988 under each of the alternatives.
b. Determine projected net income before taxes for 1988 under each of the alternatives.
c. Which alternative would you recommend? Why?

BUSINESS DECISION PROBLEM 26–2

Compute break-even point; determine point at which factory should shut down rather than produce

When the plant of the Foster Company is completely idle, fixed costs amount to $300,000. When the plant operates at levels of 50% of capacity and below, its fixed costs are $350,000; at levels above 50% of capacity its fixed costs are $500,000. The company's variable costs at full capacity (100,000 units) amount to $750,000.

Required: a. Assuming that the company's product sells for $25.00 per unit, what is the company's break-even point in sales dollars?

b. Using only the data given, at what level of sales would it be more economical to close the factory than to operate it? In other words, at what level will operating losses approximate the losses incurred if the factory is closed down completely?

c. Assume that when the Foster Company is operating at half of its capacity, it decides to reduce the selling price from $25 per unit to $15 per unit in order to increase sales. At what percentage of capacity must the company operate in order to break even at the reduced sales price?

BUSINESS DECISION PROBLEM 26–3

Decide whether to make or buy a part; find variable cost and calculate cost to manufacture part

The Cooper's Company has recently been awarded a contract to sell 50,000 units of its product to the federal government. Cooper's manufactures the components of the product rather than purchasing them. When the news of the contract was released to the public, the president of Cooper's, Dan Cooper, received a call from the president of the White Corporation, Joe White. Mr. White offered to sell to Cooper's 50,000 units of one of the needed components, part N, for $12.50. After receiving the offer, Mr. Cooper calls you into his office and assigns you the task of providing him a recommendation (along with any supporting information) on whether to accept or reject Mr. White's offer.

You first go to the company's records and obtain the following information concerning the production of part N:

	Costs at current production level (400,000 units)
Direct labor	$2,080,000
Direct materials	960,000
Manufacturing overhead . .	1,000,000
Total cost	$4,040,000

You calculate the unit cost of part N to be $10.10 ($4,040,000 ÷ 400,000). But you suspect that this unit cost may not hold true at all production levels. To find out, you consult the production manager. She tells you that in order to meet the increased production needs, equipment will have to be rented and the production workers will have to work some overtime. She estimates the machine rental to be $100,000 and the total overtime premiums to be $180,000. She provides you with the following cost information:

	Costs at increased production level (450,000 units)
Direct labor	$2,340,000
Direct materials	1,080,000
Manufacturing overhead (including equipment rental and overtime premiums)	1,380,000
Total cost	$4,800,000

The production manager advises you to reject White's offer, since the unit cost of part N will only rise to $10.67 (4,800,000 ÷ 450,000) even with the additional costs of equipment rental and overtime premiums. This is much less than the $12.50 offered by Mr. White. You are still undecided, so you return to your office to consider the matter further.

Required: a. Using the high-low method, compute the variable cost portion of manufacturing overhead. (Remember that the costs of equipment rental and overtime premiums are included in manufacturing overhead. Subtract these amounts before performing the calculation.)

b. Compute the total costs to manufacture the additional units of part N. (Note: Include overtime premiums as a part of direct labor.)
c. Compute the unit cost to manufacture the additional units of part N.
d. Should Mr. Cooper accept or reject Mr. White's offer?

BUSINESS DECISION PROBLEM 26–4

Prepare income statement under both absorption costing and direct costing; explain why net income before taxes differs; settle debate between general manager and controller

The general manager of the Chicago Division of the All-Klean Company submitted the company's income statement for the year ended June 30, 1987, (prepared under absorption costing) with the comment that the division was at least profitable. The report showed that sales amounted to 80,000 units at $40 per unit and that the following costs had been incurred:

Direct materials	$ 880,000
Direct labor	380,000
Manufacturing overhead	1,140,000
Selling and administrative expenses . .	1,200,000

A total of 110,000 units was put into process during the year. Regarding the 30,000 units in the June 30, 1987, inventory, all materials costs had been incurred, but the units were only 50% complete as to processing. There were no other finished goods or work in process inventories, either beginning or ending.

The Chicago Division's production process is highly automated, and its costs are largely fixed; $950,000 of the manufacturing overhead costs and $400,000 of the selling and administrative costs are fixed.

Upon receipt of the division's income statement, the company's controller made a few quick calculations and commented that the division actually operated at a loss. The general manager of the division took exception to this statement, causing a long argument.

Required:
a. Prepare the division's income statement under absorption costing. Include a schedule showing the computation of the cost of ending work in process Inventory. Assume that fixed overhead is absorbed under expected activity and that this equaled actual activity for the year.
b. Repeat part *(a)* under direct costing.
c. State exactly what caused the difference in net income between *(a)* and *(b)*.
d. Who is right in this debate? Explain.

BUSINESS SITUATION FOR DISCUSSION

A Tool for Planning and Decision Making*
Frederick J. Turk

☐   Governing boards and administrators in higher education today must cope with their problems under the most difficult circumstances: dynamic change. The dynamics add an extra dimension of complexity to planning and decision making. But an illuminating approach, called breakeven analysis, introduces clarity in ways that this article will explain.

The dynamic elements of change are only too easy to recognize. Costs of faculty and staff salaries and benefits, supplies and equipment, fuel, and other necessities are rising rapidly. The physical facilities at many institutions have deteriorated to a point where deferred maintenance is no longer tolerable. Almost all other costs are jumping mainly at unpredictable rates.

*   *   *   *   *

Competing for Students

Some institutions have suffered a decline in the number of students. Others have recently experienced a slight surge in enrollments. Most are concerned that, whatever the current demand, the acknowledged demographics indicate fewer college-age students in the near future.

* Peat, Marwick Mitchell & Co.: *Management Focus*, March/April 1980, pp. 9–13. Used with permission.

This trend will certainly affect the viability of some of these institutions.

Many colleges and universities have expanded their programs to include adults who are seeking non-degree education. Witnessed by the advertisements in local papers, the competition for non-traditional students is fierce. Some believe that this relatively new market for colleges and universities is already becoming saturated.

This potpourri of troubles facing colleges and universities presents a sober challenge to governing boards and administrators. Yet it is certain that these conditions can significantly affect the future of colleges and universities and, therefore, must be confronted successfully if institutions are to remain healthy and capable of achieving their educational mission.

Complexity of Interlocking Decisions

. . . the difficulties facing higher education in the 1980s are motivating many institutions to devote increasing attention to planning for their future. The problem, however, is to evaluate simultaneously the implications of various actions that might be taken. When considered together, it is impossible to understand the consequences of each action. As a result, many decision makers are following a pattern whereby each individual action is examined separately. With decisions broken down into small elements, each can be examined fully. When the divisible parts of a decision are understood, they can be aggregated to present a complete picture of the entire effect of one or more related decisions. This approach to planning and analysis also promotes rapid examination of variations or alternatives.

The Basics of Breakeven Analysis

Breakeven analysis has been used in commercial enterprises for many years. More recently colleges and universities are beginning to use this technique in planning and decision-making. Sometimes referred to as cost-volume-revenue analysis, it permits planners to examine the potential economic consequences of a proposed course of action.

The primary focus of breakeven analysis is examining how changes in volume will affect cost and revenue. By calculating the relationship of cost and revenue to different levels of volume, the analyst can identify the level of volume at which equilibrium between cost and revenue is achieved. The state of equilibrium is often called "the breakeven point," and the results of the analysis are often presented on a breakeven chart. A diagrammatic representation of such a chart is presented as Exhibit 1. . . . This chart permits decision makers to see at a glance the effect that proposed actions are likely to have on the future finances of an institution.

In order to perform a breakeven analysis, the analyst must be able to identify fixed and variable costs and

Exhibit 1

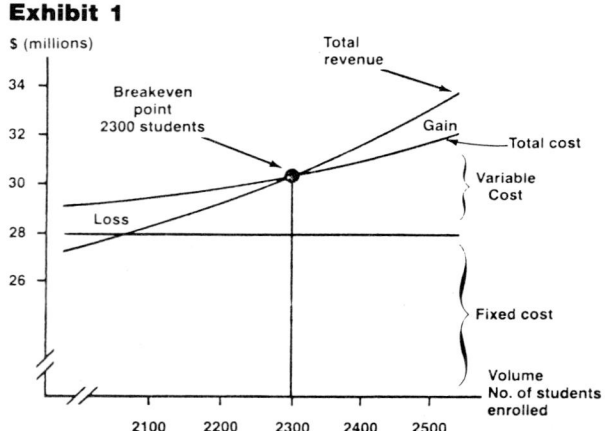

revenues. Costs and revenues are fixed when they remain constant regardless of fluctuations in the level of volume. Costs and revenues are variable when they fluctuate in direct proportion to changes in the level of volume. The separation of costs and revenues into fixed and variable components is difficult. Because high precision is not required for most decisions, estimates of cost behavior based on observation or experience are often applied.

Certain costs behave irregularly, e.g., at a certain level of volume costs are fixed only if volume stays within definite limits. These costs, which act in stairstep fashion, are often referred to as "mixed" or "semivariable" costs. For purposes of simplification in breakeven analysis, mixed costs are usually treated as either fixed or variable.

Another important concept inherent in breakeven analysis relates to the "relevant range of volume." Implied in this concept is the assumption that cost and revenue will behave as expected within the range of volume being examined. Should analysis above or below the relevant range be required, costs and revenues may behave differently.

Applying Breakdown Analysis

Earlier, certain difficult decisions requiring action by many institutions of higher education were mentioned. Breakeven analysis lends itself well to assisting board members and administrators to understand the potential economic consequences of their decisions.

Exhibit I is a breakeven chart that presents a snapshot of the current budget of an institution's costs and revenues. For the most part, the majority of costs are fixed in the short run. For many institutions this is a realistic representation of cost behavior. For example, costs associated with faculty and staff are substantial in colleges and universities. Faculty costs are typically fixed because of tenure or other contractual commitments.

Revenue is composed of both fixed and variable components. For instance, tuition and fees are directly variable with the number of students, while private gifts, grants, and contracts have no relationship to enrollment and thereby act as fixed revenues. What is indicated from the breakeven chart is the expectation that the college will operate on a breakeven basis at 2,300 enrolled students. If more than 2,300 students enroll, there will be an excess of revenue over cost; under 2,300, cost will exceed revenue.

Suppose it were determined to pay greater attention to deferred maintenance. Accordingly, the college may wish to increase expenditures by $2000,000 to refurbish a part of the plant. Exhibit 2 shows the effect such a decision might have on the college, assuming that everything else remains unchanged.[1]

Similarly, if the tuition charge were increased while all other costs and revenues remained unchanged, net revenue would increase. When this is recorded in Exhibit 3, the result is a new breakeven point—i.e., only 2,150 students are required.

Results of Decisions

Through this method many potential decisions can be analyzed to explain the financial impact of each. For instance, other scenarios that might be considered could include:

1. a reduction in potential operating costs, owing to a capital fund-raising campaign that is expected to pay for plant refurbishment costs.
2. a reduction in annual giving revenues because donors may give to the capital campaign instead of to annual giving
3. an increase in student aid costs for certain students should tuition rates be increased.

Each scenario can be analyzed and presented independently.

With an understanding of the effect that each potential decision may have, it may then be useful to summarize the effects of all decisions in one breakeven analysis. Additionally, it is often helpful to see the financial effect that these multiple decisions have on the institution over time, such as a three-to-five year planning horizon. Such analysis over time is frequently essential since all decisions can seldom be implemented in one year. Some decisions, such as refurbishing physical plant or conducting a capital campaign, may have financial effects on the institution for many years.

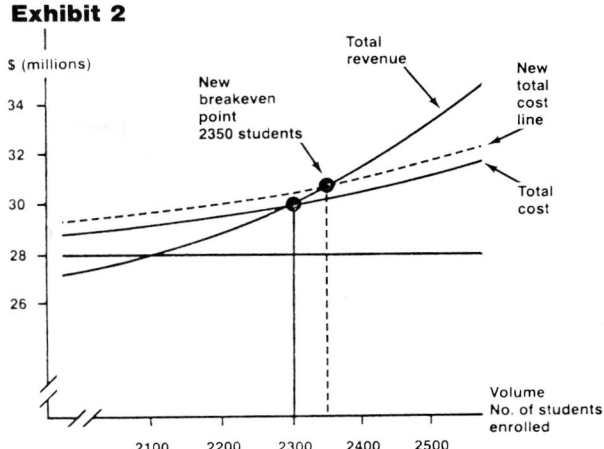

Exhibit 2

This combined analysis over time may require several iterations to arrive at a financial result that presents an acceptable breakeven condition.

Developing a Planning Model

Breakeven analysis is readily applied when one potential decision is examined in the light of all other variables affecting institutional costs and revenues being held constant. In essence the methodology described earlier is a model for analyzing institutional cost and revenue behavior.

The analysis becomes increasingly complex as more variables are examined and the dimension of a planning horizon is introduced. Because the financial consequences of so many variables need to be examined together over time, it becomes necessary to use a computerized planning model to perform the many calculations that are required to complete the analysis. Without such

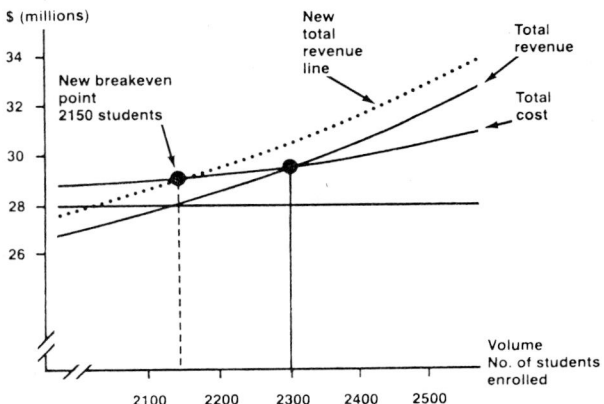

Exhibit 3

---

[1] The reader should be aware that the amounts shown . . . [in the Exhibits] and referred to in the text are for illustrative purposes only and are not subject to verification by precise calculation.

a planning model the ability to examine the financial consequences of various interactive decisions would be difficult. More importantly, planning is a dynamic human activity. Accordingly, it is desirable to calculate rapidly the effects of policy decisions. Planners require prompt feedback so that they can reexamine and modify plans that do not meet institutional financial objectives.

Communicates to Board Members

Breakeven analysis is a useful tool for analyzing the financial consequences of a variety of actions being considered by decision makers. A breakeven chart is a useful device for communicating the financial results of potential decisions to board members and administrators.

Breakeven analysis is used most advantageously when one variable (the independent variable) is changed while other variables (dependent variables) are held constant. Too often, board members and administrators are confused because multiple decisions are combined.

When a variety of possible actions are considered, planners may wish to consider the financial consequences of these actions together and over time. Under these circumstances a computerized planning model is likely to be most useful.

CHAPTER 27

Capital Budgeting: Long-Range Planning

LEARNING OBJECTIVES

After studying this chapter, you should be able to:

1. Determine the net cash inflows, after taxes, for both an asset addition and an asset replacement.
2. Evaluate projects using payback period, unadjusted rate of return, net present value, profitability index, and time-adjusted rate of return.
3. Determine, for project evaluation, the effect of an investment in working capital.
4. Define and use correctly the new terms in the glossary.

In your personal life you make many short-run decisions (such as where to go on vacation this year) and many long-run decisions (such as whether to buy a home). The quality of these decisions determines to a large extent the success of your life. Businesses also face short-run and long-run decisions.

In Chapter 26, you studied how accountants help management make short-run decisions, such as what prices to charge for their products this year. Accountants also play an important role in advising management on long-range decisions, such as investing in new buildings and equipment, that will benefit the company for many years. Long-run decisions have a great impact on the long-run success of a company. Incorrect long-run decisions can threaten the survival of a company.

Whereas short-run decisions involve items such as selling prices, costs, volume, and profits in the current year, long-run decisions involve investments in capital assets, such as buildings and equipment, affecting the current year and many future years. Planning for these investments is referred to as capital budgeting. This chapter discusses the general concepts behind capital budgeting.

■ CAPITAL BUDGETING DEFINED

Capital budgeting is the process of considering alternative capital projects and selecting those alternatives that provide the most profitable return on available funds, within the framework of company goals and objectives. A capital project is any long-range endeavor to purchase, build, lease, or renovate buildings, equipment, or other major items of property. Such decisions usually involve very large sums of money and usually bring about a large increase in fixed costs for a number of years in the future. Once a company builds a plant or undertakes some other capital expenditure, it becomes less flexible.

Poor capital-budgeting decisions can be very costly because of the large sums of money and relatively long time periods involved. If a poor capital-budgeting decision is implemented, the company can lose all or part of the funds originally invested in the project and not realize expected benefits. In addition, other actions taken within the company regarding the project, such as finding suppliers of raw materials, are wasted if the capital-budgeting decision must later be revoked. Poor capital-budgeting decisions may also harm the company's competitive position because the company will not have the most efficient productive assets needed to compete in world markets.

Investment of funds in a poor alternative can create other problems as well. Workers who were hired for the project might be laid off if the project fails, creating morale and unemployment problems. Many of the fixed costs will still remain even if a plant is closed or is not producing. Advertising efforts will have been wasted. Stock prices could be affected by the decline in income.

On the other hand, failure to invest enough funds in a good project can also be costly. Ford's Mustang is an excellent example of this. If, at the time of the original capital-budgeting decision, Ford had correctly projected the Mustang's popularity, the company would have expended more funds on the project. Because of an undercommitment of funds, Ford found itself short on production capacity, which caused lost and postponed sales of the automobile.

Finally, the amount of funds available for investment is limited. Thus, once a capital investment decision is made, alternative investment opportunities are lost. The benefits or returns lost by rejecting the best alternative investment are the opportunity cost of a given project.

For all these reasons, companies must be very careful in their analyses of capital projects. Capital expenditures do not occur as often as ordinary expenditures (such as payroll or inventory purchases) but involve substantial sums of money that are then committed for a long period of time. Therefore, the means by which companies evaluate capital expenditure decisions need to be much more formal and detailed than would be necessary for ordinary purchase decisions.

■ PROJECT SELECTION: A GENERAL VIEW

Making capital-budgeting decisions involves analyzing cash inflows and outflows. This section identifies benefits and costs that are relevant to capital-budgeting decisions.

Year	Investment	Annual net cash inflow	Cumulative net cash inflows
0	$40,000	—	—
1	—	$8,000	$ 8,000
2	—	6,000	14,000
3	—	7,000	21,000
4	—	5,000	26,000
5	—	8,000	34,000
6	—	6,000	40,000
7	—	3,000	43,000
8	—	2,000	45,000
9	—	3,000	48,000
10	—	1,000	49,000

The payback period in this example is six years—the time it takes to recover the $40,000 original investment.

When the payback period analysis is used to evaluate investment proposals, management may use one of the following rules to decide on project selection:

1. Select the investments with the shortest payback periods.
2. Select only those investments that have a payback period of less than a specified number of years.

Both decision rules focus on the rapid return of invested capital. If capital can be recovered rapidly, it can be invested in other projects, thereby generating more cash inflows or profits.

Payback period analysis is used extensively in capital-budgeting decisions due to its simplicity and because cash flow is critical in many businesses. However, this type of analysis has two important limitations:

1. Payback period analysis ignores the time period beyond the payback period. For example, assume the Allen Company is considering two alternative investments that each requires an initial outlay of $30,000. Proposal Y will return $6,000 per year for five years, while proposal Z will return $5,000 per year for eight years. The payback period for Y is five years ($30,000/$6,000) and for Z is six years ($30,000/$5,000). But, if the goal is to maximize income, proposal Z should be selected rather than proposal Y, even though Z has a longer payback period. This is because Z will return a total of $40,000, while Y simply recovers the initial $30,000 outlay.

2. Payback analysis also ignores the time value of money. For example, assume the following net cash inflows are expected in the first three years from two capital projects:

	Net cash inflows	
	Project A	Project B
First year . . .	$15,000	$ 9,000
Second year . .	12,000	12,000
Third year . . .	9,000	15,000
Total . .	$36,000	$36,000

Assume that both projects have the same net cash inflows each year beyond the third year. If the cost of each project is $36,000, then each has a payback period of three years. But common sense indicates that the projects are not equal because money has a time value and can be reinvested to increase income. Since larger amounts of cash are received earlier under project A, it is the preferable project.

■ PROJECT SELECTION: UNADJUSTED RATE OF RETURN

The unadjusted rate of return is another method used in evaluating investment projects. The **unadjusted rate of return** is an approximation of the rate of return on investment of a capital project. It is computed by dividing the average annual income after taxes by the average amount of investment in the project. The **average investment** is the original cash outlay divided by 2. The formula for the unadjusted rate of return is:

$$\text{Unadjusted rate of return} = \frac{\text{Average annual income after taxes}}{\text{Average amount of investment}}$$

Notice that annual **income** rather than net cash inflow is used in the calculation.[1]

To illustrate the use of the unadjusted rate of return, assume the Thomas Company is considering two capital project proposals that both have useful lives of three years. The company does not have enough funds to undertake both projects. Information relating to the projects is shown below:

Proposal	Initial cost	Average annual before-tax net cash inflow	Average depreciation
1	$72,000	$45,000	$24,000
2	90,000	55,000	30,000

Assuming a 40% tax rate, the unadjusted rate of return for each project is determined as follows:

	Proposal 1	Proposal 2
Average investment:		
Original outlay ÷ 2 ... (1)	$36,000	$45,000
Annual net cash inflow (before taxes) ..	$45,000	$55,000
Annual depreciation .	24,000	30,000
Annual income (before taxes)	$21,000	$25,000
Income taxes at 40%	8,400	10,000
Average annual net income from investment ... (2)	$12,600	$15,000
Rate of return (2) ÷ (1)	35%	33⅓%

---

[1] Some formulas use the initial investment as the denominator instead of the average investment.

From these calculations, if Thomas Company makes an investment decision solely on the basis of unadjusted rate of return, proposal 1 would be selected since it has a higher rate.

The unadjusted rate of return can also be computed with the following formula:

$$\text{Rate of return} = \frac{\left(\begin{array}{c}\text{Average annual before-} \\ \text{tax net cash inflow}\end{array} - \begin{array}{c}\text{Average annual} \\ \text{depreciation}\end{array}\right) \times (1 - \text{Tax rate})}{\text{Average investment}}$$

For proposal 1 above, the computation is as follows:

$$\text{Rate of return} = \frac{(\$45,000 - \$24,000) \times (1 - 0.4)}{(\$72,000/2)} = \frac{(\$21,000) \times (0.6)}{\$36,000}$$

$$= \frac{\$12,600}{\$36,000} = 35\%$$

For proposal 2 above, the computation is as follows:

$$\text{Rate of return} = \frac{(\$55,000 - \$30,000) \times (1 - 0.4)}{(\$90,000/2)} = \frac{(\$25,000) \times (0.6)}{\$45,000}$$

$$= \frac{\$15,000}{\$45,000} = 33\tfrac{1}{3}\%$$

Sometimes information is provided on the average annual after-tax net cash inflow. Average annual after-tax net cash inflow is equal to annual before-tax cash inflow minus taxes. Given this information, the depreciation can be deducted to arrive at average net income. For instance, for proposal 2 above, average net income would be computed as follows:

After-tax net cash inflow ($55,000 − $10,000) . .	$45,000
Less: Depreciation	30,000
Average net income	$15,000

The unadjusted rate of return, like payback period analysis, has several limitations:

1. The length of time over which the return will be earned is not considered.
2. The rate allows a sunk cost, depreciation, to enter into the calculation. Since depreciation can be calculated in so many different ways, the rate of return can be manipulated by simply changing the method of depreciation used for the project.
3. The timing of cash flows is not considered. Thus, the time value of money is ignored.

PROJECT SELECTION: NET PRESENT VALUE METHOD AND THE PROFITABILITY INDEX

Unlike the two project selection methods just illustrated, the net present value method and the profitability index take into account the time value of money in the analysis. Because of their computational similarities, the net present value method and the profitability index will both be discussed in this section. For purposes of these methods we assume that all net cash inflows occur at the end of the year. This assumption is often used in capital-budgeting analysis and makes the calculation of present values less complicated than if we assume the cash flows occurred at some other time.

A major issue in acknowledging the time value of money in capital-budgeting decisions is determining an appropriate discount rate to use in computing the present value of cash flows. Management requires some minimum rate of return on its investments. This rate should be the company's cost of capital, but that rate is difficult to determine. Therefore, management often selects a target rate that it believes to be at or above the company's cost of capital, and then that rate is used as a basis for present value calculations.

Net Present Value Method

Under the net present value method, all expected after-tax cash inflows and outflows from the proposed investment are discounted to their present values using the company's required minimum rate of return as a discount rate. The **net present value** of the proposed investment is the difference between the present value of the annual net cash inflows and the present value of the required cash outflows. In many projects, the only cash outflow is the initial investment, and since it occurs immediately, the initial investment does not need to be discounted. Therefore, in such projects, the net present value of the proposed project may be computed as the present value of the annual net cash inflows minus the initial investment. Other types of projects require that additional investments, like a major repair, be made at later dates in the life of the project. In those cases, the cash outflows must be discounted to their present value before they are compared to the present value of the net cash inflows.

To illustrate the net present value method, assume the Morris Company is considering a capital investment project that will cost $25,000. Net cash inflows after taxes for the next four years are expected to be $8,000, $7,500, $8,000, and $7,500, respectively. Management requires a minimum rate of return of 14% and wants to know if the project is acceptable. The following analysis is developed, using the tables in Appendix C at the end of the text:

	Annual net cash inflow (after taxes)	Present value of $1 at 14% (from Table 3)	Total present value
First year	$8,000	0.87719	$ 7,018
Second year	7,500	0.76947	5,771
Third year	8,000	0.67497	5,400
Fourth year	7,500	0.59208	4,441
Present value of net cash inflows			$22,630
Cost of investment			25,000
Net present value			$ (2,370)

Since the present value of the net cash inflows, $22,630, is less than the initial outlay of $25,000, the project is not acceptable. The net present value for the project is equal to the present value of its net cash inflows less the present value of its cost (the investment amount), which in this instance is $-2,370 ($22,630 -$25,000).

In general, a proposed capital investment is acceptable if it has a positive net present value. In the previous example, if the expected net cash inflows from the investment had been $10,000 per year for four years, the present value of the benefits would have been (from Appendix Table 4):

$$\$10,000 \times 2.91371 = \$29,137$$

This yields a net present value of $4,137 ($29,137 — $25,000). Since the net present value is positive, the investment proposal is acceptable. But there may be a competing project that has an even higher net present value. When the net present value method is used to screen alternative projects, the higher a project's net present value, the more desirable the project.

Profitability Index

When investment projects costing different amounts are being compared, the net present value method does not provide a valid means by which to rank the projects in order of contribution to income or desirability under limited financial resources. A **profitability index** provides this additional information to management. A profitability index is the ratio of the present value of the expected net cash benefits (after taxes) divided by the initial cash outlay (or present value of cash outlays if future outlays are required). The profitability index formula is:

$$PI = \frac{\text{PV of net cash inflows}}{\text{Initial outlay (or present value of cash outlays if future outlays are required)}}$$

Only those proposals having a profitability index greater than or equal to 1.00 should be considered by management. Proposals with a profitability index of less than 1.00 will not yield the minimum rate of return because the present value of the projected cash inflows will be less than the initial cost.

To illustrate use of the profitability index, assume that a company is considering two alternative capital outlay proposals that have the following initial costs and expected net cash inflows after taxes:

	Proposal X	Proposal Y
Initial cost	$7,000	$9,500
Expected net cash inflow (after taxes):		
Year 1	$5,000	$9,000
Year 2	4,000	6,000
Year 3	6,000	3,000

Management's minimum desired rate of return is 20%.

The net present values and profitability indexes can be computed as follows (using Appendix C, Table 3):

	Present value	
	Proposal X	**Proposal Y**
Year 1 (net cash inflow in year 1 × 0.83333) . .	$ 4,167	$ 7,500
Year 2 (net cash inflow in year 2 × 0.69444) . .	2,778	4,167
Year 3 (net cash inflow in year 3 × 0.57870) . .	3,472	1,736
Present value of net cash inflows	$10,417	$13,403
Initial outlay	7,000	9,500
Net present value	$ 3,417	$ 3,903
	Proposal X	**Proposal Y**
Profitability index:	$\dfrac{\$10,417}{\$7,000} = 1.49$	$\dfrac{\$13,403}{\$9,500} = 1.41$

When net present values are compared, proposal Y appears to be more favorable than X because its net present value is higher. But after computing the profitability indexes, proposal X is found to be a more desirable investment because it has the higher profitability index. The higher the profitability index, the more profitable the project per dollar of investment. Proposal X is earning a higher rate of return on a smaller investment than proposal Y.

■ PROJECT SELECTION: THE TIME-ADJUSTED RATE OF RETURN

Another technique for evaluating capital projects that accounts for the time value of money is the time adjusted rate of return. The **time-adjusted rate of return,** also called the discounted or internal rate of return, equates the present value of expected after-tax net cash inflows from an investment with the cost of the investment by finding the rate at which the net present value of the project is zero. If the time-adjusted rate of return equals or exceeds the cost of capital or target rate of return, then the investment should be considered further. But if the proposal's time-adjusted rate of return is less than the minimum rate, the proposal should be rejected. Ignoring other considerations, the higher the time-adjusted rate of return, the more desirable the project.

Present value tables can be used to approximate the time-adjusted rate of return. To illustrate, assume the Young Company is considering a $90,000 investment that is expected to last 25 years with no salvage value. The investment will yield a $15,000 annual after-tax net cash inflow. This $15,000 is referred to as an **annuity,** which is a series of equal cash inflows.

The first step in computing rate of return is to determine the payback period. In this case, payback period is six years ($90,000 ÷ $15,000). Next, examine Appendix C, Table 4 (present value of an annuity) to find the present value factor that is nearest in amount to the payback period of 6. Since the investment is expected to yield returns for 25 years, look at that row in the table. In that row, the factor nearest to 6 is 5.92745, which appears under the 16.5% interest column. If the annual return of $15,000 is multiplied by the 5.92745 factor, the result is $88,912, which is just below the $90,000 cost of the project. Thus, the actual rate of return is slightly less than 16.5%. It is less than 16.5% but more than 16% because, as interest rates increase, present values decrease since less investment is needed to generate the same income.

The above example involves uniform net cash inflows from year to year. What happens when net cash inflows are not uniform? In such instances, a trial and error procedure is necessary. For example, assume that a company is considering a $200,000 project that will last four years and will yield the following returns:

Year	Net cash inflow (after taxes)
1.	$ 20,000
2.	40,000
3.	80,000
4.	150,000
Total	$290,000

The average annual net cash inflow is $72,500 ($290,000 ÷ 4). Based on this average net cash inflow, the payback period is 2.76 years ($200,000 ÷ $72,500). Looking in the four-year row of Appendix C, Table 4, we find that the factor 2.77048 is nearest to the payback period of 2.76. But in this case, cash flows are not uniform. The largest returns will occur in the later years of the asset's life. Since the early returns have the largest present value, it is likely that the rate of return will be less than the 16.5% rate that corresponds to the present value factor of 2.77048. If the returns had been greater during the earlier years of the asset's life, the correct rate of return would have been higher than 16.5%. To find the specific discount rate that yields a present value closest to the initial outlay or $200,000, several interest rates less than 16% are tried out. By trial and error the rate of return is found; the following computation reveals the rate to be slightly higher than 12%:

	Return	Present value factor at 12%	Present value of net cash inflows
Year 1. . . .	$ 20,000	0.89286	$ 17,857
Year 2. . . .	40,000	0.79719	31,888
Year 3. . . .	80,000	0.71178	56,942
Year 4. . . .	150,000	0.63553	95,330
			$202,017

Since the cost of capital is not a precise percentage, some financial theorists argue that the time-adjusted rate of return method is better than the net present value method. Under the time-adjusted rate of return method, the cost of capital is used only as a **cutoff point** in deciding which projects are acceptable for more consideration. Under the net present value method, the cost of capital is used **in the calculation** of the present value of the benefits. Thus, if the cost of capital percentage is wrong, the ranking of the projects will be affected. As a result, management may select projects that are really not as profitable as other projects.

No matter which time value of money concept is considered "better," these methods are both theoretically superior to the payback and unadjusted rate of return methods. But the time value of money methods are more difficult to compute. In reality, no single method should be used by itself to make capital-budgeting decisions. All aspects of the investment should be considered, including nonquantitative factors, such as employee morale (layoff of workers due to higher efficiency of a new machine) and company flexibility (versatility of production of one machine over another). The company will be committed to its investment in a capital project for a long period of time and should use the best selection techniques and judgment available.

■ INVESTMENTS IN WORKING CAPITAL

An investment in a capital asset usually must be supported by an investment in working capital, such as accounts receivable and inventory. For example, an investment in a capital project often is expected to increase sales. Increased sales usually bring about an increase in accounts receivable from customers and an increase in inventory to support the higher sales level. The increases in the current assets—accounts receivable and inventory—are investments in working capital that usually are recovered in full at the end of a capital project's life. Such working capital investments should be considered in capital-budgeting decisions.

To illustrate, assume that a company is considering a capital project that will involve a $50,000 investment in machinery and a $40,000 investment in working capital. The machine, which will be used to produce a new product, has a useful life of eight years and has no salvage value. The annual cash inflow (before taxes) is estimated at $25,000, with annual cash outflow (before taxes) of $5,000. The annual net cash inflow from the project is computed below (assuming straight-line depreciation and a 40% tax rate):

Cash inflows	$25,000
Cash outflows	5,000
Net cash inflow before tax	$20,000
1 − Tax rate	× 60%
Net cash inflow after tax (ignoring depreciation) (1)	$12,000
Depreciation tax shield ($50,000 ÷ 8 years)	$ 6,250
Tax rate	× 40%
Depreciation tax savings (2)	$ 2,500
Annual net cash inflow (years 1–8) (1) + (2)	$14,500

The annual net cash inflow from the machine is $14,500 each year for eight years. However, the working capital investment needs to be considered. First, the investment of $40,000 in working capital at the start of the project is an additional outlay that must be made when the project is started. The $40,000 will be tied up every year until the project is finished, or in this case, until the end of the life of the machine. At that point, the working capital will be released, and the $40,000 can be used for other investments. Therefore, the

$40,000 is a cash outlay at the start of the project and a cash inflow at the end of the project.

The net present value of the project is computed as follows (assuming a 14% minimum desired rate of return):

Net cash inflow, years 1–8 ($14,500 × 4.63886)	$67,263
Recovery of investment in working capital ($40,000 × 0.35056) . .	14,022
Present value of net cash inflows	$81,285
Initial cash outlay ($50,000 + $40,000)	90,000
Net present value	$ (8,715)

The discount factor for the cash inflows, 4.63886, comes from Appendix C, Table 4, since the cash inflows in this example are a series of equal payments— an annuity. The recovery of the investment in working capital is assumed to represent a single lump sum that is received at the end of the project's life. As such, it is discounted using a factor (0.35056) that comes from Appendix C, Table 3.

The investment is not acceptable because it has a negative net present value. If the working capital investment had been ignored, the proposal would have had a rather large positive net present value of $17,263 ($67,263 − $50,000). Thus, it should be obvious that investments in working capital must be considered if correct capital budgeting decisions are to be made.

■ THE POSTAUDIT

The last step in the capital-budgeting process is a postaudit review that should be performed by a person not involved in the capital-budgeting decision-making process. Such a person can provide an impartial judgment on the project's worthiness. This step should be performed early in the project's life, but enough time should have passed for any operational "bugs" to have been worked out. Actual operating costs and revenues should be determined and compared with those estimated when the project was originally reviewed and accepted.

The postaudit review performs these functions:

1. Lets management know if the projections were accurate and if the particular project is performing as expected regarding cash inflows and outflows.
2. May identify additional factors for management to consider in upcoming capital-budgeting decisions, such as cash outflows that were forgotten in a particular project.
3. Provides a review of the capital-budgeting process to determine how effectively and efficiently it is working. The postaudit provides information that allows management to compare the actual results of decisions with the expectations it had during the planning and selection phases of the capital-budgeting process.

■ *SUMMARY*

A capital project is any long-term endeavor to purchase, lease, or renovate buildings, equipment, or other major items of property. Capital budgeting is the process of considering alternative capital projects and selecting those alternatives that provide the most profitable return on available funds, within the framework of company goals and objectives.

Several concepts are important to capital-budgeting decisions. The time value of money concept states that money received today is worth more than money received in the future. The time value of money is considered by discounting future cash flows to their present values. The net cash inflow is the difference between the periodic cash inflows and the periodic cash outflows expected from a project. The net cash inflow is usually computed after considering the tax effect of depreciation. Out-of-pocket costs require future outlays of resources, usually cash, while sunk costs have already been incurred. The initial cost of the project includes any cash outlays necessary to acquire the asset and to place it in a position and condition for use. The expected salvage value represents an expected future cash inflow at the end of the asset's life. The cost of capital, usually expressed as a rate of return, includes the cost of all the company's sources of capital. Management often selects as a discount rate a minimum required rate of return that it believes to be at or above the company's cost of capital.

Various capital project selection techniques are discussed in the chapter. Payback period analysis compares the project's initial investment to its annual net cash inflows and asks how many years it will be before the sum of the net cash inflows equals, or pays back, the initial investment. The unadjusted rate of return compares the project's average annual net income after tax (rather than its net cash inflows) to its average investment and computes an approximate rate of return. Neither of these methods considers the time value of money.

The other techniques examined in the chapter do consider the time value of money. The net present value method involves calculating the difference between the present value of the net cash inflows and the initial investment (or the present value of the cash outlays if future outlays are required). The profitability index, on the other hand, computes the ratio of the present value of the net cash inflows to the initial investment (or the present value of the cash outlays if future outlays are required). Finally, the time-adjusted rate of return method computes the project's rate of return by examining the amount and timing of the net cash inflows and the required cash outlay(s). The resulting rate can then be compared directly to the company's required rate of return to judge the acceptability of the investment.

When preparing a capital-budgeting proposal, management must be careful to include not only the cost of buildings and equipment but also the cost of working capital necessary to operate the project. Such a commitment of resources is part of the overall investment in the project.

The postaudit review is the last step in the capital-budgeting project. The postaudit provides management an opportunity to compare actual results with the projections on which the selection decision was based. This review provides feedback to permit management to revise the current project if necessary and to help management improve future capital-budgeting decisions.

Throughout this text the discussion has centered around businesses—single proprietorships, partnerships, and corporations. In Chapter 28, the final chapter in this text, a personal element is introduced as you study personal income taxes. Two things every person faces are death and taxes. Since corporations are legal "persons," they face the same concerns, although their ultimate death can often be postponed longer than our own. The chapter closes by going back to corporations and discussing corporate federal income taxation.

NEW TERMS INTRODUCED IN CHAPTER 27*

Annuity

A series of equal cash inflows (1056).

Capital budgeting

Process of considering alternative capital projects and selecting those alternatives that provide the most profitable return on available funds, within the framework of company goals and objectives (1046).

Capital project

Any long-range endeavor to purchase, build, lease, or renovate buildings, equipment, or other major items of property (1046).

Cost of capital

The cost of all sources of capital (debt and equity) employed by a company (1050).

Initial cost of an asset

Any cash outflows necessary to acquire an asset and place it in a position and condition for its intended use (1049).

Net cash inflow

The periodic cash inflows from a project less the periodic cash outflows related to the project (1047).

Net present value

A project selection technique that discounts all expected after-tax cash inflows and outflows from the proposed investment to their present values using the company's minimum rate of return as a discount rate. If the amount obtained by this process exceeds or equals the investment amount, the proposal is considered acceptable for further consideration (1054).

---

* Some terms listed in earlier chapters are repeated here for your convenience.

Opportunity cost

The benefits or returns lost by rejecting the best alternative investment (1046).

Out-of-pocket cost

A cost requiring a future outlay of resources, usually cash (1049).

Payback period

The period of time it takes for the cumulative sum of the annual net cash inflows from a project to equal the initial net cash outlay (1050).

Profitability index

The ratio of the present value of the expected net cash inflows (after taxes) divided by the initial cash outlay (or present value of cash outlays if future outlays are required) (1055).

Sunk costs

Costs that have already been incurred. Nothing can be done about sunk costs at the present time, they cannot be avoided or changed in amount (1049).

Tax shield

The total amount by which taxable income is reduced due to the deductibility of an item (1047).

Time-adjusted rate of return

A project selection technique that finds a rate of return that will equate the present value of future expected net cash inflows (after taxes) from an investment with the cost of the investment (1056).

Unadjusted rate of return

The rate of return computed by dividing average annual income after taxes from a project by the average amount of the investment (1052).

DEMONSTRATION PROBLEM

The Logue Company is considering three different investments. Listed below are some data related to these investments:

Investment	Initial cash outlay	Expected after-tax net cash inflow per year	Expected life of proposals
A . .	$100,000	$20,000	10 years
B . .	120,000	17,600	15
C . .	150,000	21,000	20

Management requires a minimum return on investments of 14%.

Required: Rank these proposals using the following selection techniques. (Ignore income taxes and salvage value.)

 a.   Payback period.
 b.   Unadjusted rate of return.
 c.   Profitability index.
 d.   Time-adjusted rate of return.

Solution to demonstration problem

 a. Payback period:

Proposal	(a) Investment	(b) Annual after-tax cash inflow	(a)/(b) Payback period
A . .	$100,000	$20,000	5.00 years
B . .	120,000	17,600	6.82
C . .	150,000	21,000	7.14

The proposals in order of desirability are A, B, and C.

 b. Unadjusted rate of return:

Proposal	(a) Average investment	(b) Average annual after-tax net cash inflow	(c) Average depreciation	(d) = (b) − (c) Average annual income	(d)/(a) Rate of return
A . .	$50,000	$20,000	$10,000	$10,000	20%
B . .	60,000	17,600	8,000	9,600	16
C . .	75,000	21,000	7,500	13,500	18

The proposals in order of desirability are A, C, and B.

 c. Profitability index:

Proposal	(a) Annual after-tax net cash inflow	(b) Present value factor at 14%	(c) = (a) × (b) Present value of annual net cash inflow	(d) Initial cash outlay	(c)/(d) Profitability index
A	$20,000	5.21612	$104,322	$100,000	1.04
B	17,600	6.14217	108,102	120,000	0.90
C	21,000	6.62313	139,086	150,000	0.93

The proposals in order of desirability are A, C, and B. (But neither B nor C should be considered acceptable since each has a profitability index of less than one.)

d. Time-adjusted rate of return:

Proposal	Rate	How found
A . . .	15% (slightly above)	($100,000 ÷ $20,000) = Factor of 5 in 10-period row
B . . .	12 (slightly below)	($120,000 ÷ $17,600) = Factor of 6.82 in 15-period row
C . . .	13 (slightly below)	($150,000 ÷ $21,000) = Factor of 7.14 in 20-period row

The proposals in order of desirability are A, C, and B. (But neither B nor C earns the minimum rate of return.)

QUESTIONS

1. How do capital expenditures differ from ordinary expenditures?

2. What effects can capital-budgeting decisions have on a company?

3. What effect does depreciation have on cash flow?

4. Give an example of an out-of-pocket cost and a sunk cost by describing a situation in which both are encountered.

5. A machine is being considered for purchase. The salesperson attempting to sell the machine says that it will pay for itself in five years. What is meant by this statement?

6. Discuss the limitations of the payback period method.

7. What is the profitability index, and of what value is it?

8. What is the time-adjusted rate of return on a capital investment?

9. What role does the cost of capital play in the time-adjusted rate of return method and in the net present value method?

10. What is the purpose of a postaudit? When should a postaudit be performed?

EXERCISES

E–1

Determine estimated income and net cash inflow for an asset addition

The Barclay Athletic Club is considering investing $75,000 in some new sports equipment with an estimated useful life of 10 years and no salvage value. The equipment is expected to produce $30,000 in cash inflows and $20,000 in cash outflows annually. Straight-line depreciation is used by the company, and a 40% tax rate applies. Determine the annual estimated income and net cash inflow.

E-2

Determine additional cash inflow for an asset replacement

The Classic Manufacturing Company is considering replacing a four-year-old machine with a new, advanced model. The old machine was purchased for $30,000, has a useful life of 10 years with no salvage value, and has annual maintenance costs of $7,500. The new machine would cost $22,500 and would produce the same output as the old machine. But annual maintenance costs would be only $3,000. The new machine would have a useful life of 10 years with no salvage value. Using straight-line depreciation and a 40% tax rate, compute the additional annual cash inflow if the old machine is replaced.

E-3

Compute payback period for a new machine

Given the following annual costs, compute the payback period for the new machine if its initial cost is $105,000. (Ignore income taxes.)

	Old machine	New machine
Depreciation	$ 9,000	$21,000
Labor	36,000	31,500
Repairs	10,500	2,250
Other costs	6,000	1,800
	$61,500	56,550

E-4

Compute unadjusted rate of return for a new machine

The Bishop Company is considering investing $25,000 in a new machine. The machine is expected to last five years and to have no salvage value. Annual after-tax net cash inflow from the machine is expected to be $7,000. Calculate the unadjusted rate of return.

E-5

Compute profitability index for two projects and rank projects

Compute the profitability index for each of the following two proposals assuming the desired minimum rate of return is 20%. Based upon the profitability indexes, which proposal is better?

	Proposal F	Proposal G
Initial cash outlay	$16,000	$20,600
Net cash inflow (after taxes):		
First year	10,000	12,000
Second year	9,000	12,000
Third year	6,000	8,000
Fourth year	–0–	5,000

E-6

Rank projects using payback and unadjusted rate of return

The Scooter Company is considering three alternative investment proposals. Using the information presented below, rank the proposals in order of desirability using the (a) payback period method and (b) unadjusted rate of return method.

	M	O	P
Initial outlay	$180,000	$180,000	$180,000
Net cash inflow (after taxes):			
First year	$ –0–	$ 45,000	$ 45,000
Second year	90,000	135,000	90,000
Third year	90,000	45,000	135,000
Fourth year	45,000	90,000	225,000
Total net cash inflows	$225,000	$315,000	$495,000

E–7

Determine acceptability of a project using net present value

The Parker Company is considering the purchase of a new machine costing $45,000. It is expected to save $9,000 cash per year for 10 years. It has an estimated useful life of 10 years and no salvage value. Management will not make any investment unless at least an 18% rate of return can be earned.

Using the net present value method, determine if the proposal is acceptable.

E–8

Compute time-adjusted rate of return

Refer to the data in Exercise E–7. Calculate the time-adjusted rate of return. (Ignore income taxes.)

E–9

Rank projects using payback, net present value, and time-adjusted rate of return

Rank the following investments in order of their desirability using the (a) payback period method, (b) net present value method, and (c) time-adjusted rate of return method. Management requires a minimum rate of return of 14%.

Investment	Initial cash outlay	Expected after-tax net cash inflow per year	Expected life of proposal
A . . .	$30,000	$4,500	8 years
B . . .	37,500	6,500	20
C . . .	60,000	12,000	10

PROBLEMS, SERIES A

P27–1–A

Determine net cash inflow and payback period for an asset addition

Bridges Company is considering the purchase of a new machine that would cost $50,000 and would have a useful life of 10 years with no salvage value. The new machine is expected to have annual cash inflows of $25,000 and annual cash outflows of $10,000. The machine will be depreciated using straight-line depreciation, and the tax rate is 40%.

Required: a. Determine the net after-tax cash inflow for the new machine.
b. Determine the payback period for the new machine.

P27–2–A

Determine additional cash inflow for an asset replacement

The Gaines Company currently uses four machines to produce 200,000 units annually. The machines were bought three years ago for $50,000 each and have a useful life of 10 years with no salvage value. These machines cost a total of $28,000 per year to repair and maintain.

The company is considering replacing the four machines with one technologically superior machine that is capable of producing the 200,000 units annually by itself. The machine would cost $140,000 and have a useful life of seven years with no salvage value. Annual repair and maintenance costs are estimated at $14,000.

Required: Assuming straight-line depreciation and a 40% tax rate, determine the annual additional after-tax net cash inflow if the new machine is acquired.

P27–3–A

Evaluate asset replacement using payback and net present value

The Paton Manufacturing Company owns five spinning machines that it uses in its manufacturing operations. Each of the machines was purchased four years ago at a cost of $120,000. Each machine has an estimated life of 10 years with no expected salvage value. A new machine has become available. One new machine has the same productive capacity as the five old machines combined; it can produce 400,000 units each year. The new machine will cost $648,000, is estimated to last six years, and will have a salvage value of $72,000. A trade-in allowance of $24,000 is available for each of the old machines.

Operating costs per unit are compared below:

	Five old machines	New machine
Repairs	$0.6795	$0.0855
Depreciation	0.1500	0.2400
Power	0.1890	0.1035
Other operating costs . . .	0.1620	0.0495
Operating costs per unit . .	$1.1805	$0.4785

Required: Ignore income taxes. Use the payback period method for parts *(a)* and *(b)*.

a. Do you recommend replacing the old machines? Support your answer with computations. Disregard all factors except those reflected in the data given above.
b. If the old machines were already fully depreciated, would your answer be different? Why?
c. Using the net present value method with a discount rate of 20%, present a schedule showing whether or not the new machine should be acquired.

P27–4–A

Calculate time-adjusted rate of return for new equipment; determine effect of altering useful life and net cash inflows

The Odiorne Canning Company has used a particular canning machine for several years. The machine has a zero salvage value. The company is considering buying a technologically improved machine at a cost of $232,000. The new machine will save $50,000 per year after taxes in cash operating costs. If the company decides not to buy the new machine, it can use the old machine for an indefinite period of time by incurring heavy repair costs. The new machine will have a useful life of eight years.

Required:
a. Compute the time-adjusted rate of return for the new machine.
b. Management thinks the estimated useful life of the new machine may be more or less than eight years. Compute the time-adjusted rate of return for the new machine if its useful life is (1) 5 years and (2) 12 years, instead of 8 years.
c. Suppose the new machine's useful life is eight years, but the annual after-tax cost savings are only $40,000. Compute the time-adjusted rate of return.
d. Assume the annual after-tax cost savings from the new machine will be $44,000 and its useful life will be 10 years. Compute the time-adjusted rate of return.

P27–5–A

Rank investments using payback, unadjusted rate of return, profitability index, and time-adjusted rate of return

The Gover Company is considering three different investments involving depreciable assets with no salvage value. Listed below are some data related to these investments:

Investment	Initial cash outlay	Expected after-tax net cash inflow per year	Expected life of proposal
1	$140,000	$28,000	10 years
2	240,000	48,000	20
3	360,000	68,000	10

Management requires a minimum return on investments of 12%.

Required: Rank these proposals using the following selection techniques. (Ignore income taxes and salvage value.)

a. Payback period.
b. Unadjusted rate of return.

c. Profitability index.
d. Time-adjusted rate of return.

P27–6–A

Make capital-budgeting decision using net present value

The Carter Company has decided to computerize its accounting system. The company has two alternatives—it can lease a computer under a three-year contract, or it can purchase a computer outright.

If the computer is leased, the lease payment will be $18,000 each year. The first lease payment will be due on the day the lease contract is signed. The other two payments will be due at the end of the first and second years. All repairs and maintenance will be provided by the lessor.

If the computer is purchased outright, the following costs will be incurred:

Acquisition cost	$42,000
Repairs and maintenance:	
First year	1,200
Second year	1,000
Third year	1,400

The computer is expected to have only a three-year useful life because of obsolescence and technological advancements. The computer will have no salvage value and will be depreciated on a double-declining-balance basis. The Carter Company's cost of capital is 16%.

Required:

Using the net present value method, show whether the Carter Company should lease or purchase the computer. (Ignore income taxes).

P27–7–A

Make capital-budgeting decision using net present value

The Walker Sports Company is trying to decide whether or not to add tennis equipment to its existing line of football, baseball, and basketball equipment. Market research studies and cost analyses have provided the following information:

1. Additional machinery and equipment will be needed to manufacture the tennis equipment. The machines and equipment will cost $900,000, have a 10-year useful life, and have a $20,000 salvage value.

2. Sales of tennis equipment for the next 10 years have been projected as follows:

Year	Sales in dollars
1	$150,000
2	225,000
3	337,500
4	375,000
5	412,500
6–10 (each year) . .	450,000

3. Variable costs are 60% of selling price, and fixed costs (including straight-line depreciation) will total $177,000 per year.

4. The company will need to advertise its new product line to gain rapid entry into the market. Its advertising campaign costs will be:

Years	Advertising cost
1–3	$150,000 (each year)
4–10	75,000 (each year)

5. The company requires a 14% minimum rate of return on investments.

Required:

Using the net present value method, decide whether or not the Walker Sports Company should add the tennis equipment to its line of products. (Ignore income taxes.) Round to the nearest dollar (round down for .5).

P27-8-A

Evaluate investment proposal using net present value

The Wicks Company is considering purchasing new equipment that will cost $450,000. It is estimated that the useful life of the equipment will be five years and that there will be a salvage value of $150,000. The company uses straight-line depreciation. The new equipment is expected to have a net cash inflow (before taxes) of $64,500 annually. Assume that the tax rate is 40% and that management requires a minimum return of 14%.

Required: Using the net present value method, determine whether the equipment is an acceptable investment.

P27-9-A

Make capital-budgeting decision using net present value

The Beech Company has an opportunity to sell some equipment for $40,000. Such a sale will result in a tax-deductible loss of $4,000. If it is not sold, the equipment is expected to produce net cash inflows after taxes of $12,000 for the next 10 years. After 10 years, the equipment can be sold for its book value of $4,000. Assume a 40% tax rate.

Required: Management currently has other opportunities that will yield 18%. Using the net present value method, show whether the company should sell the equipment. Prepare a schedule to support your conclusion.

PROBLEMS, SERIES B

P27-1-B

Determine increase of cash inflow for machine replacement

The Collins Manufacturing Company is currently using three machines that it bought seven years ago to manufacture its product. Each machine produces 20,000 units annually. Each machine originally cost $102,000 and has a life of 17 years with no salvage value.

The new assistant manager of the Ironside Manufacturing Company suggests that the company replace the three old machines with two technically superior machines for $90,000 each. Each new machine would produce 30,000 units annually and would have a life of 10 years with no salvage value.

The new assistant manager points out that the cost of maintaining the new machines would be much lower. Each old machine costs $10,000 per year to maintain; each new machine would cost only $4,000 a year to maintain.

Required: Compute the increase in after-tax annual net cash inflow that would result from replacing the old machines, using straight-line depreciation and a tax rate of 40%.

P27-2-B

Evaluate asset replacement using net present value

Refer to the information given in Problem 27-1-B. The new assistant manager of the Collins Manufacturing Company also points out that the old machines could be sold for $50,000 each. Assume this sale would result in an after-tax cash inflow of $150,000. Ignore the tax effect of the gain or loss on this sale.

Required: Using the net present value method, should the new machines be bought if the company's cost of capital is 14%?

P27-3-B

Determine desirability of asset replacement using payback; develop schedule to aid in project evaluation

The Munson Company is considering replacing 10 of its delivery vans that originally cost $30,000 each; depreciation of $18,300 has already been taken on each van. The vans were originally estimated to have useful lives of eight years and no salvage value. Each van travels an average of 150,000 miles per year. The 10 new vans, if purchased, will cost $36,000 each. Each van will be driven 150,000 miles per year and will have no salvage value at the end of its three-year estimated useful life. A trade-in allowance of $3,000 is available for each of the old vans.

Following is a comparison of costs of operation per mile:

	Old vans	New vans
Fuel, lubricants, etc.	$0.152	$0.119
Tires	0.067	0.067
Repairs	0.110	0.087
Depreciation	0.025	0.080
Other operating costs (variable) . .	0.051	0.043
Operating cost per mile	$0.405	$0.396

Required: Ignore income taxes. Use the payback period method for parts *(a)* and *(b)*.

a. Do you recommend replacing the old vans? Support your answer with computations, and disregard all factors not related to the cost data given above.

b. If the old vans were already fully depreciated, would your answer be different? Why?

c. Assume that all cash flows for operating costs fall at the end of each year and that 18% is an appropriate rate for discounting purposes. Using net present value, present a schedule showing whether or not the new vans should be acquired.

P27–4–B

Compute time-adjusted rate of return for asset replacement and effect of altering useful life and cash flows in calculations

The Bolten Company has been using an old-fashioned forklift for many years. The forklift has no salvage value. The company is considering buying a modern forklift at a cost of $140,000. The new forklift will save $28,000 per year after taxes in cash operating costs. If the company decides not to buy the new forklift, it can use the old one for an indefinite period of time. The new forklift will have a useful life of 10 years.

Required:

a. Compute the time-adjusted rate of return for the new forklift.

b. The company is uncertain about the new forklift's 10-year useful life. Compute the time-adjusted rate of return for the new forklift if its useful life is (1) 6 years and (2) 15 years, instead of 10 years.

c. Suppose the forklift has a useful life of 10 years, but the annual after-tax cost savings are only $24,000. Compute the time-adjusted rate of return.

d. Assume the annual after-tax cost savings will be $32,000 and that the useful life will be eight years. Compute the time-adjusted rate of return.

P27–5–B

Rank projects using payback, unadjusted rate of return, probability index, and time-adjusted rate of return

The Hector Company is considering three different investments involving depreciable assets with no salvage value. Listed below are some data related to these investments.

Investment	Initial cash outlay	Expected after-tax net cash inflow per year	Expected life of proposal
1 . . .	$ 45,000	$ 6,600	20 years
2 . . .	120,000	15,000	10
3 . . .	165,000	27,600	10

Management requires a minimum return on investments of 12%.

Required: Rank these proposals using the following selection techniques:

a. Payback method.

b. Unadjusted rate of return.

c. Profitability index.

d. Time-adjusted rate of return.

P27–6–B

Evaluate asset replacement using net present value

Breck's Moving Company has always purchased its trucks outright and sold them after three years. The company is ready to sell its present fleet of trucks and is trying to decide whether it should continue to purchase trucks or whether it should lease trucks.

If the trucks are purchased, the following costs will be incurred:

	Costs per fleet
Acquisition cost.	$156,000
Repairs, first year	1,800
Repairs, second year	3,300
Repairs, third year	4,500
Other annual costs	4,800

At the end of three years, the trucks could be sold for a total of $48,000. Another fleet of trucks would then be purchased. The costs listed above, including the same acquisition cost, would also be incurred with respect to the second fleet of trucks. The second fleet could also be sold for $48,000 at the end of three years.

If the trucks are leased, the lease contract will run for six years. One fleet of trucks will be provided immediately, and a second fleet of trucks will be provided at the end of three years. The company will pay $63,000 per year under the lease contract. The first lease payment will be due on the day the lease contract is signed. The lessor will bear the cost of all repairs.

Required:

Using the net present value method, should the company buy or lease the trucks? Assume the company's cost of capital is 18%. (Ignore income taxes.)

P27–7–B

Evaluate project using net present value

Wheeler Manufacturing Company is considering adding a new electronic calculator to its line of products. The following information has been provided by various departments within the company:

1. Additional machinery and equipment will be needed to manufacture the calculator. The machinery and equipment will cost $225,000, have a 15-year useful life, and have a zero salvage value.
2. Sales of Wheeler calculators for the next 15 years have been projected as follows:

Year	Sales in units
1–5	750
6–10	500
11–15	250

3. Selling price per calculator will be $187.50.
4. Variable cost will be $75 per calculator. Fixed costs (including straight-line depreciation) will total $26,250 annually.
5. Advertising campaign costs will be:

Year	Advertising cost per year
1–5	$18,750
6–10	11,250
11–15	3,000

6. The company requires a 12% minimum rate of return on investments.

Required:

Using the net present value method, decide whether or not Wheeler Manufacturing Company should add the calculator to its line of products. (Ignore income taxes.) Round to the nearest dollar (round down for .5).

P27-8-B

Evaluate investment using net present value

The Butler Company is considering the purchase of equipment that will cost $600,000. It is estimated that the useful life of the equipment will be 10 years and that it will have a salvage value of $150,000. The company uses straight-line depreciation. The new equipment is expected to have a net cash inflow before taxes of $150,000 annually. Assume that the tax rate is 35% and that management requires a minimum return of 20%.

Required: Using the net present value method, determine whether or not the equipment is an acceptable investment.

P27-9-B

Evaluate decision to sell equipment

The Moore Company has an opportunity to sell a piece of equipment for $120,000. Such a sale will result in a tax-deductible loss of $8,000. If it is not sold, the equipment is expected to produce an annual net cash inflow after taxes of $48,000 for the next 20 years. After 20 years the equipment will have no salvage value. Assume a 30% income tax rate.

Required: The company currently has other investment opportunities that will yield 12%. Should the company sell the equipment? Prepare a schedule to support your conclusion.

BUSINESS DECISION PROBLEM 27-1

Compute net present value of several proposals; rank proposals in order of acceptability

The Duke Company wishes to invest $750,000 in capital projects that have a minimum expected rate of return of 14%. Five proposals are being evaluated. Acceptance of one proposal does *not* preclude acceptance of any of the other proposals. The company's criterion is to select proposals that meet its minimum required rate of return (14%).

The relevant information related to the five proposals is presented below:

Investment	Initial cash outlay	Expected after-tax net cash inflow per year	Expected life of proposal
A . . .	$150,000	$45,000	5 years
B . . .	300,000	60,000	8
C . . .	375,000	82,500	10
D . . .	450,000	78,000	12
E . . .	150,000	31,500	10

Required: a.   Compute the net present value of each of the five proposals.
b.   Which projects should be undertaken? Why? Rank them in order of desirability.

BUSINESS DECISION PROBLEM 27-2

Evaluate bookkeeper's computation of a project's net present value; determine acceptability of project

The Vrana Company is considering a capital project that will involve a $225,000 investment in machinery and a $45,000 investment in working capital. The machine has a useful life of 10 years and no salvage value. The annual cash inflows (before taxes) are estimated at $90,000 with annual cash outflows (before taxes) of $30,000. The company uses straight-line depreciation. The income tax rate is 40%.

The company's new bookkeeper computed the net present value of the project using a minimum required rate of return of 16% (the company's cost of capital). The bookkeeper's computations are shown below:

Cash inflows	$ 90,000
Cash outflows	30,000
Net cash inflow	$ 60,000
Present value factor at 16%	×4.833
Present value of net cash inflow	$289,980
Initial cash outlay	225,000
Net present value	$ 64,980

Required: a. Are the bookkeeper's computations correct? If not, compute the correct net present value.
 b. Is this capital project acceptable to the company? Why or why not?

BUSINESS DECISION PROBLEM 27–3

Determine whether to purchase or lease a new machine

The Perry Company is trying to decide whether to purchase or lease a new factory machine. If the machine is purchased, the following costs will be incurred:

Acquisition cost	$400,000
Repairs and maintenance:	
Years 1–5	10,000
Years 6–10	20,000

The machine will be depreciated on a straight-line basis and will have no salvage value. If the machine is leased, the lease payment will be $60,000 each year for 10 years. The first lease payment will be due on the day the lease contract is signed. All repairs and maintenance will be provided by the lessor. The Perry Company's cost of capital is 12%.

Required: Do you recommend that the company purchase or lease the machine? Show computations to support your answer. (Ignore income taxes.)

BUSINESS SITUATION FOR DISCUSSION

Capital Budgeting for Marketing Managers*
Roger Dickinson and Anthony Herbst

Your company must decide whether to market a new product called "Moondust" that has been created by the research and development staff. If you decide to manufacture and market Moondust, you must invest $1,000 now. If Moondust sells, as you expect it will, net cash flows should be $500 for 10 years, *provided your competitors don't begin marketing a similar product.* If they do, then the cash flows would likely fall to $100 a year by the third year. To get the $1,000 required for the investment, you will have to borrow money, and the bank will require you to pledge existing assets as collateral on the loan. This may weaken your firm's credit standing with its bankers, raise its future costs of borrowing, and affect availability of funds. It may also affect the market value of the firm's shares.

If you do not produce Moondust, but your competitors decide to produce a similar product, your existing products will be affected. And the experience gained by your competitor will give it an advantage for future product development. Should you go ahead with this project? Can capital-budgeting techniques help you decide?

Capital budgeting relates to investments that promise cash returns over a span of several years. Typically, such capital investments require sizable amounts of funds, and a single investment often involves a large portion of the firm's total assets. The combination of large cash outlays with long investment horizons make capital-budgeting decisions of great importance to the success of an organization.

Marketing executives have often taken aspects of the capital-budgeting process, such as discount rates, for granted. Recently, however, controversy has grown over the applicability of quantitative capital-budgeting methods to all important decisions, including marketing

* *Business,* April–June 1983, pp. 36–40. Used with permission.

decisions. What capital-budgeting methods are popularly used? How valid are capital-budgeting assumptions as they pertain to marketing decisions? And how can marketers avoid obvious pitfalls in evaluating capital investments?

The controversy over the practicality of applying capital-budgeting methods to marketing decisions arises largely because executives use capital-budgeting methods without understanding the implied assumptions. Capital-budgeting methods were developed by finance theorists who assumed either (1) that the cash flows from a prospective investment were known or (2) that the cash flows were distributed according to known probability distributions that could be dealt with by using the tools of statistics. The theorists made other assumptions that developed the theory of capital budgeting, but perhaps did not bear any resemblance to reality, such as the assumptions that: (1) perfect capital markets exist, i.e., that the markets appropriately reflect cash-flow patterns. Numerous marketing decisions are of this kind. The most obvious is the new product decision. But advertising campaigns, sales territories, pricing decisions, and the like also can have implications over time and may be important. Retailers, for example, are often asked to sign 20- or 30-year leases with large-dollar commitments involved.

But marketers have had almost nothing to say about the discount rate. The literature often suggests that future cash flows should be discounted at the "appropriate" rate. However, there are few statements about the assumptions involved in setting a discount rate or the great differences in present values for different discount rates. And indeed, the differences can be substantial. For example, the NPV of a dollar to be received in 20 years is just over a penny at a 25% discount rate. In contrast, for a discount rate of 5% the NPV is 38 cents.

The capital-budgeting process can provide information that may be relevant to marketing decisions that do not involve payouts lasting over many years or that may not be critically important. Executives may wish to discount cash flows over a few years, for example, in comparing the cash flows of proposed new sales territory "A" with the cash flows of proposed new sales territory "B." The capital-budgeting process should provide a set of discount rates that can be used to choose among short-term alternatives.

Another use for a set of discount rates is to establish a rate for anticipation and a rate for imputed interest. Anticipation occurs when a purchasing element in the distribution channel, such as a retailer, pays bills earlier than required, perhaps because the costs of setting up a system for delayed payment to the supplier may be large. The problem is to establish a discount rate that will "equate" payment today with payment later.

Retail organizations will often charge a profit center an imputed interest on inventory even though no debt is incurred and no interest is actually paid. Retailers want to make sure that the person managing the inventory understands that it is a valuable and costly asset. Presumably, imputed interest in most normal financial environments would be at some level above the rate the firm pays for short-term money.

Discount rates may also help in making many other types of short-term decisions. Thus, to some executives it is meaningful to suggest that an increase in the level of inventory should net the firm more than some minimum rate of return, perhaps more than its cost of capital. Put another way, if a firm can make more than its cost of capital on any marketing decision, short term or long term, then the value of the enterprise will be increased by the undertaking. All decisions can be subjected to an evaluation of their return on investment. However, it is necessary to evaluate the return on investment of other marketing decisions the firm may be considering, and to compare the returns. For example, the decision to increase inventory by $4 million for a four-year period might prevent a retailer from opening a new store. Thus, even if a decision to increase inventory meets a minimum investment criterion, it may also have to yield more than a new store. This, of course, assumes that the funds available are limited (i.e., that there is capital rationing). In this last example, short-term alternatives are compared with all other options including long-term options.

It seems clear that marketers (including retailers) have an interest in the capital-budgeting process, including the attendant discount rate determinations.

Personal and Corporate Income Taxes

LEARNING OBJECTIVES

After studying this chapter, you should be able to:

1. Compute gross income, adjusted gross income, and taxable income for personal tax returns.
2. Compute tax liability on personal returns, including the effects of tax credits.
3. Compute the tax liability for corporations.
4. Illustrate the use of tax loss carrybacks and carryforwards.
5. Compute depreciation allowance for tax purposes using the Accelerated Cost Recovery System (ACRS).
6. Identify the nature of permanent and timing differences between taxable income and accounting pretax income.
7. Account for timing differences using interperiod tax allocation.
8. Define and use correctly the new terms in the glossary.

In 1913, the ratification of the 16th Amendment established the constitutionality of the federal income tax in the United States. Without a doubt, you can expect to file income tax forms as long as you have any significant income.

Income taxes play an important role in both personal and business decisions. Whenever a person or a company considers financial opportunities, the tax consequences of those opportunities should be noted and weighed.

The purpose of this chapter is to provide an introductory understanding of federal income taxes, both personal and corporate. This chapter can only provide a general overview of these taxes due to their complexity and the constantly changing nature of tax laws. Coverage in this chapter is based on tax laws in effect as of mid 1985. Provisions of major tax legislation such as the Economic Recovery Act of 1981 and the Tax Equity and Fiscal Responsibility Act of 1982 are included. Recognize that some changes may have been made to the tax law since this chapter was revised. The Business Situation for Discussion at the end of this chapter describes some possible changes that may occur in the tax laws.

■ PERSONAL FEDERAL INCOME TAXES

The first part of this chapter develops the concept of taxable income and illustrates the measurement of the tax liability for individual taxpayers.

Who Must File a Return

In general, all U.S. citizens and resident aliens must file a federal tax return. More specifically, the determination of who must file a return depends on filing status and income level. For 1985, the minimum income levels at which a tax return must be filed are $3,430 for a single person, $4,300 if age 65 or older, $5,620 for a married couple filing a joint return, $6,660 if one spouse is age 65 or older, and $7,700 if both are age 65 or older. All of the minimum income levels at which a tax return must be filed are subject to change because of the indexing of various items in the new IRS code.

Filing Status.   There are four basic filing statuses that can be used in filing an income tax return—single, married filing jointly, married filing separately, and head of household. All of these are self-explanatory except head of household, who typically is an unmarried or legally separated person who maintains a residence for someone who qualifies as a dependent of the taxpayer.

Gross Income

Illustration 28.1 contains a general model of the determination of taxable income. The model starts with gross (total) income. Gross income includes all of a taxpayer's income from whatever source derived, except for those items specifically excluded, such as social security benefits. Gross income includes wages, interest, dividends, tips, bonuses, gambling winnings, gains from property sales, and prizes (including noncash prizes). Even income generated illegally, such as by theft, must be included in gross income. The general rule is that every income item, unless specifically exempted by law, must be included in gross income.

Exclusions from Gross Income.   Items excluded from gross income are interest on state and municipal bonds, certain social security benefits, workmen's compensation insurance benefits, and several employee "fringe" benefits, such as employer-paid health insurance premiums. Also, gifts, inheritances, certain disability benefits, scholarships, and the proceeds from life insurance policies are excluded. The first $100 of dividend income ($200 on a joint return no matter which spouse earned the dividend) can be excluded.

Illustration 28.1

Determination of Taxable Income for an Individual Taxpayer

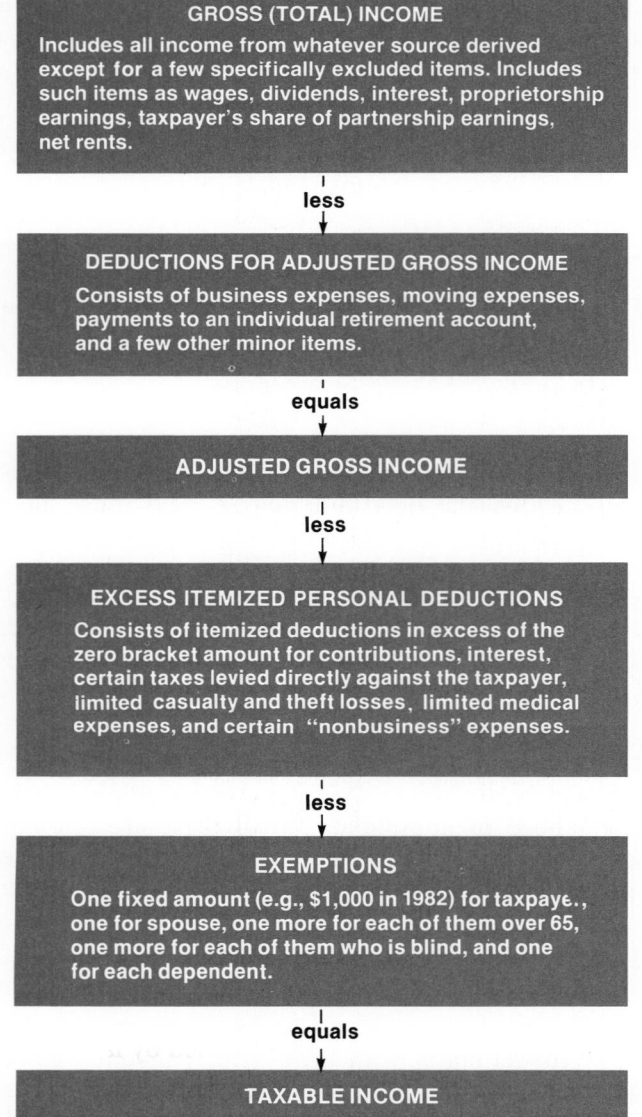

GROSS (TOTAL) INCOME
Includes all income from whatever source derived except for a few specifically excluded items. Includes such items as wages, dividends, interest, proprietorship earnings, taxpayer's share of partnership earnings, net rents.

less

DEDUCTIONS FOR ADJUSTED GROSS INCOME
Consists of business expenses, moving expenses, payments to an individual retirement account, and a few other minor items.

equals

ADJUSTED GROSS INCOME

less

EXCESS ITEMIZED PERSONAL DEDUCTIONS
Consists of itemized deductions in excess of the zero bracket amount for contributions, interest, certain taxes levied directly against the taxpayer, limited casualty and theft losses, limited medical expenses, and certain "nonbusiness" expenses.

less

EXEMPTIONS
One fixed amount (e.g., $1,000 in 1982) for taxpayer, one for spouse, one more for each of them over 65, one more for each of them who is blind, and one for each dependent.

equals

TAXABLE INCOME

Adjusted Gross Income

Taxpayers are allowed to deduct certain items from gross income in arriving at **adjusted gross income.** The computation of adjusted gross income is necessary in order to compute the allowable amounts of certain personal, itemized deductions.

Deductions for adjusted gross income to arrive at adjusted gross income consist basically of business expenses related to the production of income, moving expenses related to job or business, payments to individual retirement accounts (IRAs) or to Keogh retirement plans, alimony paid to an ex-spouse, and interest penalties assessed on certain investments for early withdrawals of funds. Some of these deductions are discussed below.

Ordinary and necessary business expenses that can be deducted (to the extent that they are unreimbursed) in computing adjusted gross income are any items that fall into the following three categories:

1. Expenses incurred as an employee while away from home on business for travel, food, or accommodations.
2. Transportation expenses incurred as an employee, other than the normal cost of commuting to and from work.
3. Expenses incurred in moving to a new place of employment.

Employees can also deduct from gross income contributions to an individual retirement account (IRA). An IRA is a retirement savings account usually set up in a bank, savings and loan association, insurance company, mutual fund, or brokerage firm. The annual deduction is limited to the lesser of 100% of earnings or $2,000 for an individual, $4,000 for a married couple if both spouses have jobs, and $2,250 for a married couple if only one spouse has earned income. Deductions cannot be based on unearned income, such as interest and dividends.

Since self-employed individuals are not covered by company-established retirement plans as employees are, they are allowed to establish their own retirement plan called a Keogh plan (pronounced Key-oh). The distinction between an IRA and a Keogh plan is that while an IRA is available to anyone, a Keogh plan is available only to self-employed individuals. The annual deduction for a Keogh plan in the early 1980s was limited to 15% of earnings up to a maximum of $15,000. Beginning in 1984 the Keough contribution limits were raised to 20% of earned self-employment income up to a maximum of $30,000.

Taxable Income

Taxpayers are allowed certain additional deductions and exemptions in arriving at taxable income. The deductions from adjusted gross income are called itemized or personal deductions and are specified by law. These itemized deductions are allowable only to the extent that they exceed a specified amount called the zero bracket amount, because the zero bracket amount is built into the tax rate schedules and tables. The zero bracket amount is $2,390 for single persons and for persons filing as a head of household, $3,540 for married couples filing a joint return, and $1,700 for married persons filing separate returns. The amount by which itemized deductions exceed the zero bracket amount is known as excess itemized deductions and can be deducted from adjusted gross income. A taxpayer will itemize deductions only if they exceed the zero bracket amount.

Itemized Deductions.   The more common itemized deductions include:
1. **Taxes.**   Real estate taxes, personal property taxes, state and local income taxes, and sales taxes are deductible. License fees and federal excise taxes are not deductible.
2. **Interest.**   Virtually all interest paid on any type of personal debt is deductible.

3. **Charitable contributions.** Gifts to educational, religious, scientific, and charitable organizations are deductible if, in total, they do not exceed 50% of adjusted gross income. Donations to individuals, labor unions, and organizations that are established primarily to influence legislation are not deductible.

4. **Medical expenses.** Within certain limits, unreimbursed health insurance premiums and hospital, medical, and dental expenses incurred by taxpayers and their dependents are deductible. Only that amount of medical costs that exceeds 5% of adjusted gross income is deductible. The entire cost of **prescription** drugs and insulin can be included in medical costs. The cost of other drugs and medicines can not be included.

To clarify the treatment of medical expenses, assume that in 1985, a taxpayer with an adjusted gross income of $20,000 paid $550 of health insurance premiums, incurred other medical expenses of $700, and incurred prescription drug costs of $400. The medical deduction is:

Health insurance premiums	$ 550
Other unreimbursed medical expenses	700
Medicine costs	400
	$1,650
Less: 5% of adjusted gross income (0.05 × $20,000)	1,000
Medical deduction	$ 650

5. **Casualty losses.** Casualty losses are sudden and unexpected losses resulting from theft, accidents, storms, fire, and similar events. They are deductible to the extent that **each** casualty loss exceeds $100 **and** that the total of all unreimbursed casualty losses for the year exceeds 10% of adjusted gross income. Thus, to compute the deduction, first subtract $100 from the dollar amount of **each** loss (ignore losses of less than $100) to obtain an adjusted casualty loss. Then, from the sum of all of the adjusted casualty losses, subtract 10% of adjusted gross income. The positive difference is the casualty loss deduction. To illustrate, assume a taxpayer had adjusted gross income of $50,000 and suffered two casualty losses during the year—a fire loss of $9,000 and a theft loss of $12,000. The casualty loss deduction is computed as follows:

Adjusted fire loss ($9,000 − $100)	$ 8,900
Adjusted theft loss ($12,000 − $100)	11,900
Total	$20,800
Less 10% of adjusted gross income	5,000
Casualty loss deduction	$15,800

6. **Other deductions.** In general, this category consists of expenses related to the taxpayer's business or profession that are not deductible from gross income. Included are the costs of professional publications and dues, union dues, safe-deposit box rentals, income tax preparer's fees, business entertainment, and job-related clothing and tools.

Exemptions

The final step in determining taxable income is to deduct the amount of income that is exempt from taxation. This amount was determined by multiplying the number of **exemptions** allowed the taxpayer by $1,000 in 1984. To adjust the amount of the exemption for inflation, the 1981 Tax Act provided for indexing the amount using the Consumer Price Index beginning in 1985. The

reduce the amount of taxes to be paid dollar for dollar, they are much more valuable to the taxpayer than deductions. A tax credit of $100 saves $100 of cash; a $100 deduction, on the other hand, is worth only $100 times the taxpayer's marginal tax rate. The maximum value, then, of any deduction is 50% of the amount of the deduction since the highest marginal tax rate is now 50%.

Following are some of the most common tax credits:

A tax credit of 50% of contributions made to candidates for public office is allowed, up to a maximum of $50 ($100 if filing jointly).

If new or used equipment is acquired by a person for use in a trade or business, part of its cost may be taken as an investment tax credit (ITC). For the 1975 tax year the investment credit was increased to 10%. The Tax Equity and Fiscal Responsibility Act (TEFRA) of 1982 changed the standard 10% rate to:

1. Ten percent of the investment if the depreciable base is reduced by one half of the investment credit taken.
2. Eight percent of the investment if there is no reduction in the depreciable base.

Thus, if a person operating an individual proprietorship purchases machinery at a cost of $10,000, $1,000 may be deducted from that person's tax liability and reduce the depreciable base by $500 to $9,500, or $800 may be deducted from the tax liability and leave the depreciable base at $10,000.

A tax credit can be taken for part of the cost of home energy conservation items, such as insulation, storm windows and doors, caulking, and clock thermostats. The credit is 15% of qualified expenditures up to $2,000, or a maximum credit of $300 for all years, not for each year.

A tax credit is available for part of the cost of installing alternative energy equipment such as solar, wind, and geothermal equipment in the taxpayer's home. The credit is 40% of the first $10,000 of such costs, with a maximum credit of $4,000 for all years.

There also are tax credits for persons with low earned income levels, for the elderly, for child and dependent care expenses, for income taxes paid to foreign countries, and for wages paid in work incentive programs.

Filing the Tax Return

Personal tax returns generally must be filed by April 15 of the year following the tax year. Extensions may be filed, but payment of any tax liability is still due on April 15. As discussed in Chapter 12, most taxpayers are also employees and, therefore, taxes are withheld by employers under our pay-as-you-go tax system. Also, taxpayers having income above a prescribed amount that is not subject to withholding must pay an estimated tax. This estimated tax must be paid in four installments. The taxes withheld and the estimated taxes paid are entered as offsets to the total tax liability on the tax return. Any remaining unpaid taxes are paid to the Internal Revenue Service when the return is filed. In some cases, tax withholdings and estimated taxes paid may have exceeded tax liability, and the taxpayer can claim a refund.

■ COMPREHENSIVE ILLUSTRATION—PERSONAL INCOME TAXES

An actual tax return consists of a number of preprinted forms that are filled out by the taxpayer. Most taxpayers will file either Form 1040A, often called the short form, or Form 1040, the long form. A taxpayer who intends to itemize deductions cannot file a short form, 1040A. A taxpayer who uses the long form generally must attach various schedules to it. Two common schedules included in the long form are Schedule A and Schedule B. Schedule A shows the itemized deductions, while Schedule B lists all dividends and interest income when dividend and interest income exceeds $400. As mentioned in Chapter 12, one copy of the taxpayer's Form W-2 is attached to the tax return. The W-2 is issued by the employer and shows wages earned and taxes withheld during the period of these wages.

Illustration 28.4 shows a brief summary schedule of the tax return items for Lee and Dora Bowman for 1985, who are married and file a joint return. Lee is chief engineer for a manufacturing company; Dora is a full-time home-maker. Both taxpayers are under age 65; they have two dependent children, ages 13 and 15. Dora owns a number of bonds and shares of stock, some of which she sold during the year, realizing $10,000 of long-term capital gains and $1,000 of short-term capital losses. Total income taxes withheld during

Illustration 28.4

Joint Tax Return Computations

Salary			$58,000
Interest income			4,000
Dividend income, net of $200 exclusion			6,000
Long-term capital gain ($10,000) less short-term capital loss ($1,000)		$ 9,000	
Less: 60% exclusion		5,400	3,600
Total			$71,600
Contribution to an individual retirement account			2,250
Adjusted gross income			$69,350
Excess itemized deductions:			
Medical expense ($3,618 − $3,468; total medical cost less 5% of			
adjusted gross income)		$ 150	
Charitable contributions		2,240	
Taxes (real estate on home, state income, sales)		5,670	
Casualty loss ($7,485 − $6,935; total adjusted casualty losses less			
10% of adjusted gross income)		550	
Miscellaneous (professional dues, subscriptions, unreimbursed			
business entertainment expenses, etc.)		440	
		$ 9,050	
Zero bracket amount		3,540	
Excess itemized deductions			5,510
			$63,840
Exemptions (4 × $1,040)			4,160
Taxable income			$59,680
Income tax [$10,334 + (0.40 × $13,880)			$15,886
Credit for political contribution ($250 × 0.5 = $125, limited			
to $100)			100
Total tax liability			$15,786
Income taxes withheld		$14,700	
Estimated taxes paid		800	15,500
Income taxes payable with return			$ 286

the year amounted to $14,700. In addition, Lee and Dora paid estimated taxes of $800. Other information needed to compute the Bowman's tax liability and tax payment are shown in the illustration. The income tax of $15,786 is computed using the tax rate schedule in Illustration 28.3. These rates are used for illustrative purposes only and may have changed by the time you read this text.

■ CORPORATE FEDERAL INCOME TAXATION

Business managers strive to maximize income in a company, while at the same time attempting to minimize taxes. In a sole proprietorship or partnership, business earnings flow directly to the owner or owners and thus affect personal tax returns. In contrast, the corporation itself is considered a taxpayer by law and, therefore, is the only form of business organization that pays federal income taxes.

Taxable Income

Corporate income taxes are based on the amount of taxable income shown on IRS Form 1120. Corporate taxable income is computed by subtracting all allowable deductions from the corporation's gross income. Corporate gross income is calculated much like the calculation for personal gross income; it basically includes all revenues from sales, services, or investments of the company. Allowable deductions from a corporate standpoint must meet four criteria; such deductions must be business related, reasonable in amount, necessary, and legal.

Once taxable income is determined, a tax rate is applied to find the amount of tax liability. As of this writing, the graduated tax rates applicable to corporations for the years 1983 and beyond are:

Corporate taxable income	Tax rate
First $25,000	15%
Second $25,000	18
Third $25,000	30
Fourth $25,000	40
Over $100,000	46

To illustrate, assume a corporation had taxable income in 1985 of $60,000. The tax due would be $11,250, computed as follows:

Tax on first $25,000 (at 15%)	$ 3,750
Tax on second $25,000 (at 18%)	4,500
Tax on remaining $10,000 (at 30%)	3,000
	$11,250

Earlier we illustrated tax credits for individuals. Tax credits also are available for corporations. One such tax credit that is particularly significant to the corporation is the investment tax credit. The **investment tax credit (ITC)** when applied to a corporation works the same way as for an individual. When certain qualifying machinery and equipment are purchased, the ITC is (1) a 10% credit to tax liability if the depreciable base is reduced by one half of the investment credit taken; or (2) an 8% credit to tax liability if no reduction in the depreciable base is taken. Therefore, if the corporation in the above example had purchased $47,500 of qualifying plant assets during the year, it could choose a $4,750 tax credit. This ITC would be used to directly reduce the tax liability of $11,250, making the net tax due $6,500 ($11,250 − $4,750).

Tax Loss Carrybacks and Carryforwards

If a corporation suffers a net loss in a given year, it of course owes no income tax in that year. The tax law also provides that the corporation can apply this loss to its taxable income from prior years and recover some or all of the taxes paid during those years. This provision is called a tax loss carryback. If the corporation elects to carry the loss back, it may carry the loss back three years. The loss must be applied first to the oldest year, then to the next oldest year, and so on until the loss is used up or until then there is no more prior year income that may be affected. The corporation may then carry the remaining, unused loss forward for up to 15 years to reduce its taxable income in those future years. This is called a tax loss carryforward.

To illustrate the application of this provision, assume that a corporation had the amounts of taxable income (or loss) shown below:

Year	Taxable income (or loss)	Taxes paid	Taxes recovered
1984	$ 15,000	$ 2,250	$2,250
1985	20,000	3,000	3,000
1986	5,000	750	750
1987	(100,000)	–0–	–0–
1988	40,000	–0–	–0–
1989	10,000	–0–	–0–
1990	30,000	3,000	–0–
1991	50,000	8,250	–0–
1992	60,000	11,250	–0–

The loss of $100,000 in 1987 would first be offset against the $15,000 of income in 1984, then the $20,000 in 1985, and next the $5,000 in 1986. The company would recover the $6,000 taxes previously paid. At this point it would have a $60,000 loss carryforward. It would apply $40,000 of the loss toward taxable income in 1988, the result is a taxable income of $0 for 1988. This leaves $20,000 of loss carryforward remaining; $10,000 would be used to offset income in the next year (1989), and the other $10,000 would be used to reduce 1990 taxable income. The taxes paid for 1990 are ($30,000 − $10,000) × 0.15 = $3,000. If a corporation decides not to apply the loss to its taxable income from prior years, it can still carry the loss forward to future years. If the loss carryforward is not "used up" by the end of the 15th year, the remaining portion is lost.

Depreciation Methods Used for Tax Purposes

Tax depreciation is substantially different from depreciation used for accounting purposes. In accounting, depreciation methods are designed to match the expense of a capital investment against the revenue the investment produces. The depreciable period or useful life used for tax purposes is based on tax law and has no relationship to the actual useful life of the asset; thus, no attempt is made to match income and expenses.

Prior to 1981, several depreciation methods were available for tax purposes, including the sum-of-years'-digits method and the uniform-rate-on-declining-balance method. The Economic Recovery Tax Act of 1981 introduced a new depreciation system known as the Accelerated Cost Recovery System (ACRS). For the most part, this new system is mandatory for both new and used property placed in service after December 31, 1980.

Under the ACRS, capital assets are rapidly depreciated, thus allowing high tax deductions early in the life of the asset. The cash saved from reduced taxes in the early years of life of the assets can be invested in new productive assets or can be applied to the replacement of the old assets when they become obsolete or worn out. Thus, the main goal of the ACRS is the modernization of productive assets so that companies in the United States can compete more effectively in world markets. Under the ACRS, the concepts of useful life and salvage value are eliminated. Instead, capital assets are grouped into several different classes. Each class has an assigned life over which the assets are depreciated.

The ACRS identifies two major types of capital assets—personal property and real property.

Personal property is any property that is movable (not attached to land). Examples are trucks and machinery. **Real property (real estate)** is land and any property attached to land, such as a building, which cannot be moved. For tangible personal property and real estate, ACRS provides classes of 3, 5, 10, 15, and 18 years. Each class is described below:

Class of investment	Kinds of assets
3 years	Automobiles, light-duty trucks, machinery, and equipment used in research and development
5 years	All other machinery and equipment, such as dies, drills, presses, etc., petroleum storage facilities, furniture, and fixtures
10 years	Some public utility property, coal conversion boilers and equipment, and railroad tank cars
15 years	Low-income residential real estate and public utility property
18 years	All other real property

Once the asset has been classified, the depreciation allowance for each year is determined by referring to the ACRS depreciation table shown in the Appendix to this chapter. Under ACRS, the first year percentage allowance for all assets (except depreciable real property, e.g., a building) is the same regardless of when the property was placed in service during the year.

In using the ACRS table, keep in mind the following three rules:

1. Ignore salvage value. Apply the percentage to the cost of the asset.
2. If an asset is purchased and put into service at any time during the year, it will still receive a full year's depreciation (for tax purposes) for that calendar year.
3. Ignore the estimated useful life of an asset. The number of years that the asset is to be depreciated is determined strictly by its classification, not its useful life.

To illustrate the application of the ACRS, assume that on July 1, 1984, Bigwig Company acquired and placed in service a new machine costing $100,000. The machine falls into the five-year class under ACRS. Using the percentages taken from the five-year column of Table 28.1 in the Appendix, the depreciation allowance for the machine is calculated as follows:

Year	Cost	× Percent allowance =	Depreciation allowance
1984	100,000	0.15	15,000*
1985	100,000	0.22	22,000
1986	100,000	0.21	21,000
1987	100,000	0.21	21,000
1988	100,000	0.21	21,000
1989	100,000	–0–	

* 15% × 100,000 = 15,000.

Depreciation is an expense that does not require the outlay of additional capital or cash by the corporation. Therefore, tax depreciation is very desirable since it decreases taxable income and hence the corporation's tax liability. The great advantage of the ACRS is the early write-off of capital assets for tax purposes. By providing accelerated depreciation for tax purposes, tax savings are provided in the early years of the asset's life. The tax savings in early years can be reinvested and thus increase the earnings per share available for common stockholders for the entire period.

■ INCOME TAX ALLOCATION

Taxable income and net income before income taxes (for simplicity, pre-tax income) for a corporation may differ sharply for a number of reasons. In fact, the tax return may show a loss, while the income statement shows positive pre-tax income. This difference raises a question about the amount of income taxes to be shown on the income statement. The answer lies in the nature of the items causing the difference between taxable income and pre-tax income. Some items create permanent differences, while others create timing differences. Both kinds of differences are discussed below.

Permanent Differences

Certain types of revenue and expense included in the computation of net income for book purposes are excluded from the computation of taxable income. **Permanent differences** between taxable income and financial statement pre-tax income are caused by tax law provisions that exclude an item of expense, revenue, gain, or loss as an element of taxable income. For instance, interest earned on state, county, or municipal bonds is included in book net income but is not subject to tax and therefore is not included in determining taxable income. The same is true for life insurance proceeds received by a corporation. Other items that are expensed for book purposes are not deductible for tax purposes, such as premiums paid for officers' life insurance, costs of attempting to influence legislation, and amortization of goodwill. These are only a few of the numerous items for which the tax treatment is completely different from the accounting treatment. These differences in treatment **never** change or reverse themselves. Therefore, they are called **permanent differences.** Such differences cause no accounting problem—the estimated actual amount of income taxes payable for the year is shown on the income statement even if this results in reporting only $1,000 of income tax expense on $100,000 of pre-tax income.

Timing Differences

Other items of revenue and expense often are recognized at **different times** for tax purposes than for financial reporting purposes. **Timing differences** between taxable income and financial statement pre-tax income are caused by items that affect both taxable income and pre-tax income, but in different periods. For example, interpretations of the tax code generally have held that revenue received in advance is taxable when received and that current expenses based on estimates of future costs (such as costs of performance under service contracts) are not deductible until actually incurred. Timing differences can also result from using accounting methods for tax purposes that are different from the ones used for financial reporting purposes. For example, a corporation may use straight-line depreciation for book purposes and ACRS depreciation for tax purposes. Eventually these revenues and expenses are recognized in computing both accounting income and taxable income; it is the timing of recognition that differs. Therefore, these variations between taxable income and net income are called timing differences.

The reconciliation between income before taxes and taxable income for a given corporation appears below:

Net income before taxes per income statement		$74,000
Add:		
Life insurance premiums paid	$ 700	
Service revenue received in advance	5,000	
Estimated expenses under service contracts	1,000	6,700
		$80,700
Deduct:		
Interest on New York State bonds	$3,000	
Difference in depreciation for tax purposes		
($8,000) and for book purposes ($6,000)	2,000	5,000
Taxable income		$75,700

As discussed above, timing differences include items that will be included in both taxable income and in pre-tax income, but in **different periods.** The items involved thus will have a tax effect. When there are timing differences, generally accepted accounting principles require that **tax allocation** procedures be applied to prevent the presentation of possibly misleading information. **Interperiod tax allocation** is a procedure whereby the tax effects of an element of expense or revenue, or loss or gain, that will affect taxable income are allocated to the period in which the item is recognized for accounting purposes, regardless of the period in which it is recognized for tax purposes.

To illustrate the tax allocation procedure required for timing differences, assume that (1) a company acquires automobiles for $20,000 that have an estimated life of four years with no expected salvage value, (2) it uses the straight-line depreciation method for financial reporting purposes and the ACRS method for tax purposes (the automobiles fall into the three-year class), (3) net income before depreciation and income taxes is $15,000 for each year of the automobiles' lives, (4) there are no other items that cause differences between pretax income and taxable income, and (5) the tax rate is 40% (to simplify the illustration). Under these circumstances, the actual tax liability for each year is shown in Illustration 28.5.

Illustration 28.5

Calculation of Tax Liability

	1983	1984	1985	1986	Total
Income before depreciation and income taxes	$15,000	$15,000	$15,000	$15,000	$60,000
Depreciation (ACRS, three-year class method)	5,000	7,600	7,400	–0–	20,000
Taxable income	$10,000	$ 7,400	$ 7,600	$15,000	$40,000
Income taxes payable (40% of taxable income)	$ 4,000	$ 2,960	$ 3,040	$ 6,000	$16,000

Net income for each year, using the amount of income taxes payable calculated above, is shown in Illustration 28.6. Note that the amount of taxable income to be shown on the corporation's tax return for each year except 1983 (Illustration 28.5) is different from the amount of pre-tax income reported on the corporation's income statement (Illustration 28.6). To report this much year-to-year net income variance under the circumstances described is considered misleading according to generally accepted accounting principles.

Generally accepted accounting principles dictate that the income taxes should be $4,000 per year since the tax rate is 40% and income before taxes is $10,000. This requirement is supported by drawing attention to the fact that the total income taxes paid for the four years in Illustration 28.5 will be

Illustration 28.6

Net Income with No Tax Allocation

	1983	1984	1985	1986	Total
Income before depreciation and income taxes	$15,000	$15,000	$15,000	$15,000	$60,000
Depreciation (straight-line method) . .	5,000	5,000	5,000	5,000	20,000
Net income before taxes	$10,000	$10,000	$10,000	$10,000	$40,000
Income taxes (computed in Illustration 28.5)	4,000	2,960	3,040	6,000	16,000
Net income	$ 6,000	$ 7,040	$ 6,960	$ 4,000	$24,000

$16,000, the same as income tax expense for accounting purposes (4 × $4,000). Any taxes not paid in the early years of the automobiles' lives will be paid later—note the $6,000 of taxes in 1985—when, as the accountant would say, the timing differences reverse. In this case, reversing occurs in 1986 when depreciation is less for tax purposes than for financial reporting purposes.

Consequently, tax allocation procedures should be applied in the above circumstances. Under such procedures, the income statement for each of the four years is shown in Illustration 28.7. Under tax allocation, reported net income is $6,000 per year. Income tax expense is reported on the income statement at $4,000 per year regardless of the taxes actually payable each year.

Illustration 28.7

Net Income with Tax Allocation

	Each year	Total for four years
Income before depreciation and income taxes	$15,000	$60,000
Depreciation expense	5,000	20,000
Net income before taxes	$10,000	$40,000
Income taxes expense	4,000	16,000
Net income	$ 6,000	$24,000

The entries necessary in 1983, 1984, and 1985 to record income taxes on the company's books are given below:

	1983	1984	1985
Federal Income Tax Expense	4,000	4,000	4,000
Federal Income Taxes Payable	4,000	2,960	3,040
Deferred Federal Income Taxes Payable	–0–	1,040	960
To record income tax expense.			

The required entry for 1986 is:

Federal Income Tax Expense	4,000	
Deferred Federal Income Taxes Payable	2,000	
Federal Income Taxes Payable		6,000
To record income tax expense.		

The entries are posted to T-accounts below. When payments are actually made to the federal government, the Federal Income Taxes Payable account is debited and Cash is credited for the amount of the payment.

Federal Income Tax Expense			Federal Income Taxes Payable			Deferred Federal Income Taxes Payable		
1983	4,000				1983	4,000	1986	2,000	1983	–0–
1984	4,000				1984	2,960			1984	1,040
1985	4,000				1985	3,040			1985	960
1986	4,000				1986	6,000				
	16,000					16,000				–0–

Note again that the amount of tax expense recognized remains constant at $4,000 even though the tax liability increases from $2,960 for 1984 to $6,000 for 1986. The normalizing of the tax expense for each year is accomplished by making entries in the Deferred Federal Income Taxes Payable account. The T-accounts clearly show that the tax expense for the four years is $16,000 and that the tax payments for the four years also sum to $16,000. The only difference is that the tax expense charged to each year is not the same amount as the actual liability for the year.

In this simplified example, the Deferred Federal Income Taxes Payable account has a zero balance at the end of four years. But actual business experience has shown that once a Deferred Federal Income Taxes Payable account is established, it is seldom decreased or reduced to zero. The reason is that most businesses acquire new depreciable assets, usually at higher prices. The result is that depreciation for tax purposes continues to be greater than depreciation for financial reporting purposes, and the balance in the Deferred Federal Income Taxes Payable account also continues to grow. For this reason, many accountants seriously question the validity of tax allocation in circumstances such as those described above. But discussion of this controversial issue must be left to a more advanced text. In the above example, the Deferred Federal Income Taxes Payable account would be reported as a long-term liability on the balance sheet because the item causing its existence (the machine) is classified as a long-term asset.

■ SUMMARY

Income taxes play a significant role in both personal and business decisions. Whenever a company or a person considers financial opportunities, the tax consequences of those opportunities need to be considered.

There are a number of steps in the determination of taxable income for an individual taxpayer. The general rule is that all income from all sources is included in gross income unless the item is specifically excluded. Among items specifically excluded are interest on state and municipal bonds, social security benefits, and workmen's compensation insurance benefits.

Certain deductions are subtracted from gross income to arrive at adjusted gross income. These deductions, called deductions for adjusted gross income, consist primarily of business expenses, contributions to IRA and Keogh retirement plans, and other specified items. A second set of deductions is subtracted from adjusted gross income. These deductions, called itemized deductions, include items such as taxes, interest expense, medical expenses, and charitable contributions. In addition to the itemized deductions, the taxpayer is permitted to subtract from adjusted gross income a certain amount of income that is exempt from taxation. The total amount of the exemptions depends on the taxpayer's marital status, number of dependents, age, and other factors. After the excess itemized deductions and the exemptions are subtracted from adjusted gross income, the result is taxable income.

The amount of tax due is determined by comparing the taxpayer's taxable income with either the tax table or the tax rate schedule that is appropriate for the taxpayer's filing status—single, married filing jointly, married filing separately, or unmarried head of household. The marginal tax rate is the tax rate that is applied to the next dollar of taxable income. The effective tax rate, on the other hand, is the average rate of tax paid on the taxpayer's total income. Long-term capital gains receive more favorable tax treatment than does ordinary income. Only 40% of the total amount of a taxable long-term capital gain is included in adjusted gross income, while the other 60% escapes taxation entirely.

Tax credits directly reduce the taxpayer's tax liability. Among the more common of the tax credits allowed to individual taxpayers are the investment tax credit, home energy conservation tax credit, alternative energy equipment tax credit, child and dependent care tax credit, low earned-income tax credit, and the credit for the elderly.

Personal income tax returns must be filed by April 15 of the year following the tax year. All taxpayers earning more than specified minimum amounts of income must file a tax return. Because of tax withholding requirements, most taxpayers will have paid most, if not all, of their income taxes for the year during the tax year.

Computing gross income for a corporation is much like computing gross income for an individual. Computing gross income for a corporation involves adding revenues from sales, services, and investments of the company. The computation of taxable income for a corporation involves subtracting allowable deductions from gross income; allowable deductions are expenses that are business related, reasonable in amount, necessary, and legal. Once taxable income is determined, a tax rate is applied to find the amount of the tax liability.

As noted with personal tax returns, tax credits are also available for corporations. The investment tax credit is particularly important for corporations. Corporations that suffer net losses for a taxable year may apply the loss to taxable income from prior years and recover some or all of the taxes paid during those years. This provision is known as a tax loss carryback. The corporation may then carry the loss forward and apply it to taxable income in future years, a provision known as a tax loss carryforward.

Tax depreciation is substantially different from depreciation used for accounting purposes. The Accelerated Cost Recovery System (ACRS) is a depreciation system that is mandatory for most property placed in service after December 31, 1980. The ACRS classifies depreciable assets into 3-, 5-, 10-, 15-, and 18-year classes and provides depreciation schedules for each of those classes of assets.

Certain types of revenues and expenses included in the computation of net income for book purposes are excluded from the computation of taxable income. These items give rise to permanent differences between taxable income and financial statement pre-tax income. Certain other revenue and expense items are recognized for tax purposes at different times than they are recognized for financial statement purposes. Those differences are referred to as timing differences. Interperiod tax allocation is a procedure whereby the effects of an element of expense or revenue, or loss or gain, that will affect taxable income are allocated to the period in which the item is recognized for accounting purposes, regardless of the period in which it is recognized for tax purposes.

The subject of personal and corporate income taxes concludes your introduction to the study of accounting. If you have not already done so, you may want to study Appendix A, which shows part of the annual report of the

General Motors Corporation, and Appendix B, which discusses international accounting.

Thank you for studying from our text. The knowledge you have gained will serve you well regardless of the career you choose.

APPENDIX: ACCELERATED COST RECOVERY SYSTEM DEPRECIATION ALLOWANCE TABLES

ACRS depreciation is, for the most part, mandatory for assets (new or used) purchased and put into service **after** December 31, 1980. Table 28.1 gives the depreciation rates for such assets.

Table 28.1

Personal Property Placed in Service after December 31, 1980

Ownership year	Class of investment			
	3 years (%)	5 years (%)	10 years (%)	15-year utility property (%)
1	25	15	8	5
2	38	22	14	10
3	37	21	12	9
4		21	10	8
5		21	10	7
6			10	7
7			9	6
8			9	6
9			9	6
10			9	6
11				6
12				6
13				6
14				6
15				6
	100	100	100	100

In using the ACRS table, keep in mind the following three rules:

1. Ignore salvage value. Apply the percentage to the cost of the asset.
2. If an asset is purchased and put into service at any time during the year, it will still receive a full year's depreciation (for tax purposes) for that calendar year.
3. Ignore the estimated useful life of an asset. The number of years that the asset is to be depreciated is determined strictly by its classification, not its useful life.

NEW TERMS INTRODUCED IN CHAPTER 28

Adjusted gross income

Gross income less deductions for adjusted gross income such as business expenses, employee moving expenses, payments to an individual retirement account (IRA), and certain other deductions (1076).

Capital assets

All items of property other than inventories, trade accounts and notes receivable, copyrights, government obligations due within one year and issued at a discount, and real or depreciable property used in a trade or business. Examples include investments in capital stocks and bonds (1081).

Deductions for adjusted gross income

Expenses of carrying on a trade, business, or practice of a profession, employee moving expenses, payments to an IRA or Keogh plan, forfeited interest penalty, and alimony paid (1076).

Deductions from adjusted gross income

Excess itemized deductions and exemptions (1077).

Effective tax rate

Average rate of taxation for a given amount of taxable income (1080).

Estimated tax

A tax that must be paid in four installments by persons having amounts of income above a certain level that are not subject to withholding (1083).

Excess itemized deductions

The amount by which itemized deductions exceed the zero bracket amount (1077).

Exemptions

A fixed amount, $1,000 in 1984 and $1,040 in 1985 due to indexing, that a taxpayer may deduct from adjusted gross income for the taxpayer, the spouse, and one more for each if blind or over 65, plus one more for each dependent (1078).

Gross income

All items of income from whatever source derived, except for those items specifically excluded by law (1075).

Head of household

Certain unmarried or legally separated persons (and those married to nonresident aliens) who maintain a residence for a relative or dependent (1075).

Interperiod tax allocation

A procedure whereby the tax effects of an element of expense or revenue, or loss or gain, that will affect taxable income are allocated to the period in which the item is recognized for accounting purposes, irrespective of the period in which it is recognized for tax purposes (1090).

Investment tax credit (ITC)

A direct reduction from tax liability equal to (1) 10% of the cost of certain qualifying business machinery and equipment purchased if the depreciable base is reduced by one half of the investment credit taken, or (2) 8% of the cost of certain qualifying business machinery and equipment purchased if there is no reduction in the depreciable base (1085).

Itemized deductions

Deductions from adjusted gross income for items such as contributions, interest paid, taxes, casualty losses, limited medical expenses, and other employment related expenses (1077).

Long-term capital gains

Gains resulting from the sale of capital assets and certain other assets that were held more than one year prior to sale. Preferential tax treatment is accorded such gains (1082).

Marginal tax rate

The tax rate that will be levied against the next dollar of taxable income (1079).

Permanent differences

Differences between taxable income and financial statement pre-tax income caused by tax law provisions that exclude an item of expense, revenue, gain, or loss as an element of taxable income (1089).

Personal property

Any property that is movable (not attached to land). Examples include trucks and machinery (1087).

Real property (real estate)

Land and any property attached to land, such as a building, which cannot be moved (1087).

Tax credit

A direct reduction from the amount of taxes to be paid, resulting largely from certain expenditures made (1082).

Tax loss carryback

Provision in tax law permitting corporations to apply a loss to their taxable income from prior years and recover some or all of the taxes paid during those years (1086).

Tax loss carryforward

Provision in tax law permitting corporations to carry any remaining, unused loss forward for up to 15 years to reduce their taxable income in future years (1086).

Tax rate schedules

Schedules showing the taxes levied on base amounts of income, plus the tax rate to be applied to amounts in excess of the base. Used by taxpayers with taxable incomes in excess of $50,000, and certain others (1079).

Tax tables

Tables provided by the IRS in which taxpayers can look up the amount of income taxes levied upon their taxable incomes (1079).

Taxable income

Adjusted gross income less excess itemized deductions and exemptions (1077).

Timing differences

Differences between taxable income and financial statement pre-tax income caused by items that affect both taxable income and pre-tax income, but in different periods (1089).

Total (gross) income

See Gross income.

Zero bracket amount

An amount that is built into the tax tables as a deduction that all can take. Itemized deductions can be deducted from adjusted gross income only to the extent that they exceed the zero bracket amount (1077).

DEMONSTRATION PROBLEM 28–1

Lee Nash is a CPA employed by a CPA firm at an annual salary of $45,000. He is single and has no dependents. Other information concerning his 1985 finances follows:

Gain on sale of stock acquired in 1982	$ 6,000
Loss on sale of stock purchased in November 1985	600
Interest received	1,500
Dividends received	2,440
Interest paid	690
Taxes paid:	
State income	1,800
Property	750
Sales	900
Professional dues and subscriptions to professional journals	475
Business entertainment expenses	300
Charitable contributions	400
Health insurance premiums	500
Drugs and medicine	700
Other medical and dental expenses	2,470
Income taxes withheld	12,000

Required:

a. Compute the taxable income for Mr. Nash. (Prepare a schedule similar to Illustration 28.4.)

b. Using the tax rate schedule in Illustration 28.3, compute the additional taxes due the IRS or the refund due Mr. Nash.

Solution to demonstration problem 28–1

a.

Salary		$45,000
Interest income		1,500
Dividend income, less $100 exclusion		2,340
Long-term capital gain ($6,000) less short-term		
capital loss ($600)	$5,400	
Less: 60% exclusion	3,240	2,160
Adjusted gross income		$51,000

Excess itemized deductions:			
Interest paid		$ 690	
Taxes paid (state income, property, sales)		3,450	
Miscellaneous business expenses (entertainment,			
professional dues, journal subscriptions)		775	
Charitable contributions		400	
Health care:			
Health insurance premiums	$ 500		
Other medical and dental expenses	2,470		
Drugs and medicine	700		
	$3,670		
Less: 5% of adjusted gross income	2,550		
Medical deduction		1,120	
		$6,435	
Zero bracket amount		2,390	
Excess itemized deductions			4,045
			$46,955
Exemptions (1 × $1,040)			1,040
Taxable income			$45,915

b.

Income tax [$10,913 + (0.45 × $4,415)]	$12,900
Income taxes withheld	12,000
Additional tax due	$ 900

DEMONSTRATION PROBLEM 28–2

The records of the Vista Corporation show the following for the calendar year 1988:

Sales	$385,000
Interest earned on—	
State of New Jersey bonds	3,000
City of Miami bonds	1,500
Essex County, Ohio, School District No. 2 bonds	375
Cost of goods sold and other expenses	315,000
Allowable extra depreciation for tax purposes	4,500
Dividends declared	15,000
Revenue received in advance, considered taxable	
income of this year	3,000
Contribution to influence legislation (included in	
"other expenses")	300

Required:

  a. Present a schedule showing the computation of taxable income.

  b. Compute the amount of the corporation's tax that is payable for the current year. (Use the rates given in the text. Also assume the company acquired $100,000 of new equipment during the year and qualified for the full amount of investment credit [10%] as a reduction in taxes.)

  c. Prepare the adjusting entry necessary to recognize federal income tax expense assuming income tax allocation procedures are followed. (The reduction in taxes caused by the investment credit is to be deducted from federal income tax expense and federal income tax currently payable.) The only permanent differences are the contribution to influence legislation and the nontaxable interest.

Solution to demonstration problem 28–2

a.

VISTA CORPORATION
Computation of Taxable Income and Income Taxes
For the Year 1988

Sales	$385,000
Cost of goods sold and other expenses	315,000
Reported income from operations	$ 70,000
Add: Revenue received in advance	3,000
Contribution to influence legislation	300
	$ 73,300
Less: Allowable additional depreciation	4,500
Taxable income	$ 68,800

---

b. Computation of tax liability:

15% of first $25,000	$ 3,750
18% of the next $25,000	4,500
30% of the remaining $18,800	5,640
Total tax before investment credit	$13,890
Less: Investment credit ($100,000 × 10%) . . .	10,000
Total tax payable	$ 3,890

c. Federal Income Tax Expense* 4,340

Federal Income Taxes Payable		3,890
Deferred Federal Income Taxes Payable		450

To record federal income tax expense.

* Federal income tax expense is computed as follows:

Reported income from operations	$70,000
Add back permanent difference—contribution to	
influence legislature	300
Base for computing tax expense	$70,300

Computation of tax expense:

$25,000 at 15%	$ 3,750
$25,000 at 18%	4,500
$20,300 at 30%	6,090
Tax on $70,300	$14,340
Deduct reduction in taxes caused by investment credit†	10,000
Tax expense	$ 4,340

† If Vista chose to take a 10% investment credit the new equipment's depreciable
base would have to be reduced by $5,000 (0.5 × $10,000).

DEMONSTRATION PROBLEM 28–3

On January 1, 1988, the Warman Corporation purchased new equipment for $20,000. The equipment falls into the three-year class under ACRS, but will be depreciated for accounting purposes over four years using the straight-line method.

Required: a. Using Table 28.1 in the Appendix, compute the depreciation for tax purposes for 1988, 1989, and 1990.

b. Assuming that there are no other timing differences and that net income before depreciation and income taxes is $80,000 for each of the four years, prepare a schedule showing taxable income and income taxes payable. Use a 40% rate.

c. Prepare a schedule showing net income with interperiod tax allocation for each of the four years.

d. Give the required adjusting journal entry at year-end to record income tax expense for each of the four years.

Solution to demonstration problem 28–3

a.   1988: $20,000 × 0.25 = $5,000
1989: $20,000 × 0.38 = $7,600
1990: $20,000 × 0.37 = $7,400

b.

	1988	1989	1990	1991
Income before depreciation and income taxes . . .	$80,000	$80,000	$80,000	$80,000
Depreciation	5,000	7,600	7,400	–0–
Taxable income	$75,000	$72,400	$72,600	$80,000
Income taxes payable (40%)	$30,000	$28,960	$29,040	$32,000

c.

	1988	1989	1990	1991
Income before depreciation and income taxes . . .	$80,000	$80,000	$80,000	$80,000
Depreciation	5,000	5,000	5,000	5,000
Pretax income	$75,000	$75,000	$75,000	$75,000
Income tax expense (40%)	30,000	30,000	30,000	30,000
Net income	$45,000	$45,000	$45,000	$45,000

d.   1988   Federal Income Tax Expense 30,000
     Federal Income Tax Payable   30,000
   To record federal income tax expense.

  1989   Federal Income Tax Expense 30,000
     Deferred Federal Income Taxes Payable   1,040
     Federal Income Tax Payable   28,960
   To record federal income tax expense.

  1990   Federal Income Tax Expense 30,000
     Deferred Federal Income Taxes Payable   960
     Federal Income Taxes Payable   29,040
   To record federal income tax expense.

  1991   Federal Income Tax Expense 30,000
   Deferred Federal Income Taxes Payable 2,000
     Federal Income Taxes Payable   32,000
   To record federal income tax expense.

QUESTIONS

1. What is the general rule for determining whether a particular cash receipt should be included in gross income? Name several items that might be considered income that are excluded from gross income. Why are they excluded?

2. Define the term *adjusted gross income* as it is used for personal income tax purposes.

3. For what kinds of expenditures may personal (itemized) deductions be taken on a personal income tax return? What effect does the zero bracket amount have on the total personal deductions that may be deducted from adjusted gross income?

4. What are exemptions, and by how much does one exemption reduce taxable income?

5. Why does a taxpayer wish a gain to qualify as a long-term capital gain, and how will a gain so qualify?

6. What is a tax credit? Give several examples of tax credits.

7. Which is the most valuable to a taxpayer: (a) an investment tax credit of $1,000, (b) a $1,000 allowed deduction for a contribution to an IRA, or (c) an additional exemption which is currently worth $1,000? In your answer, rank the three items according to their probable value to a taxpayer.

8. What does a person mean when making the statement, "I'm in the 44% bracket"?

9. What is an estimated tax? How is it levied and paid?

10. H Corporation has suffered a loss for the current year. How can the corporation treat this loss for tax purposes?

11. How is depreciation for accounting purposes different from tax depreciation?

12. What is the primary objective of ACRS depreciation? How does it accomplish this objective?

13. Distinguish between permanent differences and timing differences. List two items that might be a cause of each type of difference.

14. When is interperiod tax allocation used?

15. A classmate states: "Why all the fuss about deferring revenue and recognizing expenses sooner for tax purposes? All net taxable income is taxed eventually anyway. It is only a matter of putting off the payment. I don't think these manipulations are worth the effort." Comment.

16. Classified among the long-term liabilities of Corporation A is an account entitled "Deferred Federal Income Taxes Payable." Explain the nature of this account.

EXERCISES

E-1

Determine number of exemptions allowed

C. C. Chapwell is 65 years old; his wife is 65 years old and blind. They have three sons, ages 22, 24, and 30. The son who is 24 is a full-time student in law school and earns $4,000 per year. His parents contribute $6,000 annually toward his living expenses. The other two sons are fully self-supporting. How many exemptions are C. C. Chapwell and his wife entitled to claim on their joint return?

E-2

Compute tax liability

William Martin has gross income of $250,000, deductions for adjusted gross income of $25,000, excess itemized deductions of $60,000, and seven exemptions. He files a joint return with his wife who has no separate income. Using the tax rate schedule in Illustration 28.3 for married taxpayers filing jointly, compute their tax liability.

E-3

Identify items included in gross income

Identify those items listed below that would be included in gross income:

a. Tips received while working as a beautician.
b. Golf clubs won as a door prize while attending a conference.
c. Social security benefits.
d. A check received as reimbursement for medical expenses paid earlier this year.
e. Cash received from an uncle's estate.
f. Cash received from the proceeds of a life insurance policy on an aunt.
g. Employer-paid health insurance premiums amounting to $1,000.
h. Gain on the sale of a personal asset, a sail boat.
i. Interest earned on an IRA.
j. Scholarship received from a state university.

Table 1 Comparison of Major Tax Reform Proposals on Selected Items

Item for 1986	Current law	Treasury II	Bradley-Gephardt	Kemp-Kasten
Regular Tax Rates Personal	14 brackets from 11% to 50%	15%, 25%, 35% beginning 7-1-86	14%, 26%, 30% (exemptions and itemized deductions first reduce taxes at the 14% rate)	24% although effective rates vary between 19.2% and 28.8%
Corporate	46%, except 15% to 40% on first $100,000	33%, except 15% to 25% on first $75,000, begins 7-1-86	Flat rate of 30%	35%, except 15% to 25% on first $100,000
Personal and dependent exemptions	$1,080 (1986 estimate), indexed for inflation	$2,000 for 1986, indexed for inflation, no elderly or blind exemption	$1,600 ($1,800 for head of household) personal exemption, $1,000 exemption for dependents	$2,000 per exemption
Zero bracket amount (standard deduction)	$2,480 single and head of household returns $3,670 joint return (1986 indexed estimates)	$2,900 single return $3,600 head of household $4,000 joint return (all indexed for inflation)	$3,000 single return $3,000 head of household $6,000 joint return (not indexed)	$2,600 single return $3,200 head of household $3,300 joint return (all indexed for inflation)
Life insurance and annuity inside build-up	Increases in cash surrender value not included in gross income	Coverage added after action by a tax-writing committee will create interest income equal to the increase in cash surrender value over investment in contract	Add to gross income the annual excess of change in cash surrender value, withdrawals, insurance cost and policy dividends over premiums paid	Add to gross income the annual excess of change in cash surrender value, withdrawals, insurance cost and policy dividends over premiums paid
Employer-paid health insurance	Exclusion of employer-paid insurance premiums	Taxed up to $10 per month for single individuals and $25 per month for families	Exclusion limited to payments made during periods when an employee is absent from work due to illness or disability	Retain current law
Long-term capital gains (individuals)	Net long-term capital gain (LTCG) deduction of 60%, top rate of 20%, no indexed basis	50% LTLG deduction, top rate of 17.5% for stocks and other nondepreciable investment property, optional indexation after 1990; depreciable property and business property generally taxed on 100% of gain after inflation adjustment	All capital gains are ordinary income, top rate of 30%	Yearly election to (1) have all capital gains indexed for inflation and taxed at ordinary rates, or (2) take a 40% of net LTCG deduction without the benefit of indexation
State and local taxes (as itemized deductions)	Fully deductible	Repeal the deduction by individual taxpayers for state and local taxes	Repeal the deduction for personal property and general sales taxes for individuals, but retain the income and real estate tax deductions	Repeal the deduction for income, personal property, and general sales taxes for individuals, but retain real estate tax deduction
Interest expense	Fully deductible, except investment interest in excess of net investment income plus $10,000	Interest deduction for individuals limited to principal residence mortgage, $5,000 ($10,000 until 1988) and net investment income	Interest deduction for qualified residences plus nonbusiness interest to the extent of net investment income	No personal interest deduction in excess of certain housing interest and certain educational loan

Table 1 *(concluded)*

Item for 1986	Current law	Treasury II	Bradley-Gephardt	Kemp-Kasten
Retirement plans (IRAs)	$2,000 maximum contribution ($2,250 total with a non-working spouse)	$2,000 maximum contribution ($4,000 total with a non-working spouse)	Retain current law	Retain current
40(k) (cash deferred)	Maximum contribution limit of the lesser of $30,000 or 25% of compensation	Maximum contribution limit of $8,000; IRA contributions reduce limit	Retain current law, except the $30,000 limit is reduced to $20,000	Retain current law
Business meals and entertainment	Deduction allowed for all ordinary and necessary expenses	Deny most entertainment expenses, business meals in a clear business setting, limited to $25 per person plus 50% of the excess over $25 * * * * *	Retain current law	Retain current law
Investment tax credit	10% (4%–25% on selected property)	Repeal credit	Repeal credit	Repeal credit
Depreciation	ACRS—3, 5, 10, 15 and 18 year property classes with liberal writeoffs	CCRS—6 classes with 4 to 28 year lives, ranges from approximately 200% declining balance to straight-line depreciation indexed for inflation * * * * *	SCRS—6 classes with 4 to 40 year lives, approximately 250% declining balance depreciation, not indexed	NCRS—5 classes with 4 to 25 year lives, modifies current ACRS economic equivalent of expensing, indexed for inflation
Percentage depletion and intangible drilling costs	Percentage depletion allowed, intangible drilling costs deducted in year incurred	Percentage depletion generally phased out for all minerals over five-year period except for stripper wells, expense option for intangible drilling costs retained	Repeal percentage depletion and replace with SCRS, repeal expensing intangible drilling costs for oil, gas and geothermal wells, repeal depletion allowance for timber	Retain current law, except that depletion allowance for timber is repealed
Bad debt deductions	Deduction allowed for worthless debt within the taxable year or, if under the reserve method, expected worthless debts are provided for	All taxpayers limited to actual bad debt write-offs during the year	Increase in the reserve for bad debts for any financial institution is limited to the experience method, otherwise current law retained	Increase in the reserve for bad debts for any financial institution is limited to the experience method, otherwise current law retained
Restrict use of cash-basis accounting	Compute taxable income under the method used in keeping the books and records of the business	Accrual method mandatory for businesses with more than $5 million in receipts or accrual basis reporting to outsiders	Require taxable income from farming (including timber) to be computed on the accrual basis, except for certain taxpayers with gross receipts not exceeding $1 million	Require taxable income from farming (including timber) to be computed on the accrual basis, except for certain taxpayers with gross receipts not exceeding $1 million
Dividends-paid deduction	No provision	Deduction for 10% of dividends paid	No provision	No provision
Corporate minimum tax	Tax equal to 15% of the amount by which the sum of tax preference items exceeds the greater of $10,000 or the regular tax	Replace add-on minimum tax with 20% alternative minimum tax containing an expanded list of preference items	Repeal corporate minimum tax	Retain current law

except for limiting the reserve for bad debts of any financial institution to the experience method.

Use of Cash-Basis Accounting Restricted. Personal service proprietorships, partnerships and corporations may currently compute taxable income on either the cash method or the accrual method. T-II makes the accrual method mandatory for those businesses with more than $5 million in receipts *or* those businesses that report on the accrual basis to outsiders (e.g., shareholders, partners, or for credit purposes). Both B-G and K-K require taxable income from farming (including tim-

ber) to be computed on the accrual basis except for certain taxpayers whose gross receipts do not exceed $1 million.

Dividends-Paid Deduction. There is no provision in either current law, B-G or K-K for a dividends-paid deduction. T-II would permit a deduction equal to 10% of "qualified" dividends paid to stockholders of most domestic corporations. To the extent applicable, a dividends-paid deduction avoids the double taxation of corporate earnings.

*   *   *   *   *

APPENDIX

A

A Set of Consolidated Financial Statements and Other Financial Data for General Motors Corporation

GENERAL MOTORS ANNUAL REPORT 1984

HIGHLIGHTS
(Dollars in Millions Except Per Share and Hourly Amounts)

What Happened to the Revenue GM Received During 1984

	1984	1983	1982
Sales and Revenues			
United States operations			
Automotive products	$73,053.1	$63,665.0	$47,391.2
Nonautomotive products	2,107.6	1,670.3	2,138.9
Defense and space	1,322.7	826.8	793.8
Computer systems services (since October 18, 1984)	148.7	—	—
Total United States operations	76,632.1	66,162.1	50,323.9
Canadian operations	12,581.6	11,232.4	7,972.6
Overseas operations	11,345.5	11,955.5	12,212.8
Elimination of interarea sales and revenues	(16,669.3)	(14,768.4)	(10,483.7)
Total	$83,889.9	$74,581.6	$60,025.6
Worldwide automotive products	$80,499.3	$71,904.7	$56,676.8
Worldwide nonautomotive products	$ 3,390.6	$ 2,676.9	$ 3,348.8
Worldwide Factory Sales of Cars and Trucks (units in thousands)	8,256	7,769	6,244
Net Income			
Amount	$ 4,516.5	$ 3,730.2	$ 962.7
As a percent of sales and revenues	5.4%	5.0%	1.6%
As a percent of stockholders' equity	18.7%	18.0%	5.3%
Attributable to:			
$1-2/3 par value common stock	$ 4,485.3	$ 3,717.3	$ 949.8
Class E common stock (issued in 1984)	$ 18.7	—	—
Earnings per share of common stocks:			
$1-2/3 par value common	$14.22	$11.84	$3.09
Class E common (issued in 1984)	$1.03	—	—
Cash dividends per share of common stocks:			
$1-2/3 par value common	$4.75*	$2.80	$2.40
Class E common (issued in 1984)	$0.09	—	—
Taxes			
United States, foreign and other income taxes (credit)	$ 1,805.1	$ 2,223.8	($ 252.2)
Other taxes (principally payroll and property taxes)	3,572.4	2,675.8	2,470.3
Total	$ 5,377.5	$ 4,899.6	$ 2,218.1
Taxes per share of $1-2/3 par value common stock	$16.98	$15.61	$7.22
Investment as of December 31			
Cash and marketable securities	$ 8,567.4	$ 6,216.9	$ 3,126.2
Working capital	$ 6,276.7	$ 5,890.8	$ 1,658.1
Stockholders' equity	$24,214.3	$20,766.6	$18,287.1
Book value per share of common stocks:			
$1-2/3 par value common	$72.16	$64.88	$57.64
Class E common (issued in 1984)	$36.08	—	—
Number of Stockholders as of December 31 (in thousands)			
$1-2/3 par value common and preferred	957	998	1,050
Class E common	623	—	—
Worldwide Employment (including financing and insurance subsidiaries)			
Average number of employes (in thousands)	748	691	657
Total payrolls (including profit sharing)	$22,505.4	$19,605.3	$17,043.8
Total cost of an hour worked—U.S. hourly employes	$22.60	$21.80	$21.50
Property			
Real estate, plants and equipment—Expenditures	$ 3,595.1	$ 1,923.0	$ 3,611.1
—Depreciation	$ 2,663.2	$ 2,569.7	$ 2,403.0
Special tools—Expenditures	$ 2,452.1	$ 2,083.7	$ 2,601.0
—Amortization	$ 2,236.7	$ 2,549.9	$ 2,147.5
Total expenditures	$ 6,047.2	$ 4,006.7	$ 6,212.1

100%

Suppliers 49.5%

Employes 32.8%

Taxes 6.4%

Depreciation and Amortization 5.9%

Use in the Business 3.6%

Stockholders 1.8%

*In addition, in December 1984 holders of $1-2/3 par value common stock received one share of Class E common stock for every 20 shares of $1-2/3 par value common stock held.

LETTER TO STOCKHOLDERS

February 4, 1985

*I*n all the 76-year history of General Motors, there has been no other year like 1984—a year of profound and unprecedented change affecting GM people, products, plants, and processes. At the same time, it was a second successive year of record performance as General Motors earned net income of $4.5 billion, or $14.22 per share of $1-2/3 par value common stock, on worldwide sales and revenues of $83.9 billion.

The first of many milestone events in 1984 was a major reorganization announced in January to consolidate GM's North

---

"…1984—a year of profound and unprecedented change affecting GM people, products, plants, and processes."

American passenger car operations into two integrated car groups which function as self-contained business units. Each of the restructured groups is totally responsible for the engineering, manufacturing, assembly, and marketing of its own cars; each is accountable for its own quality, performance, and profitability. Primary objectives of this organizational change are to provide more effective use of people and to accelerate the response to the changing marketplace. Within each group, GM passenger cars will continue to be marketed in North America under the Chevrolet and Pontiac and the Buick, Oldsmobile, and Cadillac nameplates through our well-established and aggressive wholesale selling and dealer organizations to continue to serve the customer most effectively.

April marked the introduction of all-new Buick Electra, Oldsmobile Ninety-Eight, and Cadillac DeVille and Fleetwood luxury cars built in GM's newest plants in Wentzville, Missouri and Orion Township, Michigan.

*Y*our Corporation was honored in July when President Reagan came to Michigan to dedicate the Orion Township plant and view GM's high-technology Project Saturn at the GM Technical Center. Saturn, a new approach to building a line of subcompact cars competitive with small cars made anywhere in the world, became an operating unit six months later with the announcement of Saturn Corporation, a separate subsidiary formed to add a sixth nameplate to GM's domestic passenger car marques.

October saw the introductions of more all-new models. These included sporty Buick Somerset Regal, Oldsmobile Calais, and Pontiac Grand Am coupes and Chevrolet Astro and GMC Safari compact vans built in completely modernized plants in Lansing, Michigan and Baltimore, Maryland, respectively. Chevrolet Sprint and Spectrum small cars imported from GM's Japanese affiliates, Suzuki and Isuzu, debuted regionally.

The year was also a milestone in labor relations as General Motors and the United Auto Workers reached accord on a historic new national agreement. The three-year contract ratified in October provides unprecedented job security as well as solid economic gains for our U.S. employes, and also affords GM the opportunity to achieve increased competitiveness. New agreements also were negotiated with the UAW in Canada and with other unions representing our employes. These pacts enabled us to resume building upon the spirit of cooperation already taking hold between management and labor.

Roger B. Smith

Compensation changes to address the unique needs of GM's salaried work force were subsequently approved. Progress in equal employment opportunity was encouraging as employment of minorities and women in GM's work force reflected further improvement in 1984.

In October, the alliance between General Motors and Electronic Data Systems Corporation was formally approved. EDS is a world leader in the design of large-scale data processing systems, the operation of cost-effective data processing centers and networks, and the integration of large data processing and communications systems. Operating as an independent consolidated subsidiary, EDS will benefit GM by more effective control of health insurance costs, increased data processing capabilities within General Motors Acceptance Corporation, and improved delivery of computer services throughout GM. In addition, GM will work with EDS to develop advanced computer systems for manufacturing process control and order entry—for GM's own use, for use by our dealers and suppliers, and for sale to other customers. EDS' expertise will play a major role in Saturn and the Factory of the Future, a "learning laboratory" being built at Saginaw Steering Gear Division. The 1984 acquisition of an interest in an artificial intelligence firm and a number of high-technology companies specializing in machine vision also is helping us move toward the Factory of the Future.

"The year was also a milestone in labor relations as General Motors and the United Auto Workers reached accord on a historic new national agreement."

In our continuing commitment to product quality, GM acquired an interest in Philip Crosby Associates, Inc., a quality consulting firm that operates Quality College in Winter Park, Florida. GM people have trained there, and the association was the impetus for GM's own Quality Institute.

As the year ended, the Opel Kadett/Vauxhall Astra won the prestigious European "Car of the Year" award, the first time for a General Motors product. New United Motor Manufacturing, Inc., the joint venture with Japan's Toyota Motor Corporation, bore fruit in December when the new Chevrolet Nova made its first appearance at Fremont, California. This sparkling new star goes on sale in the late spring of 1985.

*T*he year sparkled in the financial statements as well. Net income of $4.5 billion on sales and revenues of $83.9 billion surpassed previous highs of $3.7 billion earned on sales of $74.6 billion in 1983. Earnings per share of $14.22 on $1-2/3 par value common stock compared with $11.84 per share in 1983 and the previous record of $12.24 per share on fewer shares outstanding in 1978. Net income was $963 million, or $3.09 per share, on sales of $60.0 billion in 1982.

F. James McDonald

Worldwide factory sales (sales of vehicles to GM dealers) in 1984 totaled 8.3 million cars and trucks, up from 7.8 million units in 1983 and 6.2 million units in 1982.

Late June brought a metalworkers' strike in the Federal Republic of Germany, resulting in production losses that kept General Motors from record overseas factory sales volume. This disruption and local strikes in the United States and Canada reduced net income in 1984 by about $450 million.

Reflecting GM's strong performance and prospects, the Board of Directors increased the cash dividend on the $1-2/3 par value common stock from $1.00 to $1.25 per share in the second quarter of 1984 and continued this rate through the fourth quarter. This resulted in cash dividends of $4.75 per share for the year, compared with $2.80 per share paid in 1983 and $2.40 per share in 1982.

In addition, the Board declared a fourth quarter dividend of one share of the new Class E common stock—first issued in connection with the acquisition of EDS—for every 20 shares of the $1-2/3 par value common stock. The Class E common stock issued as a dividend provided GM stockholders an immediate identification with EDS. This dividend, valued at $1.90 per share of $1-2/3 par value common stock, resulted in a total 1984 dividend payout on the $1-2/3 par value common stock equivalent to $6.65 per share. The 1984 dividend actions also recognized the continuing need for substantial investments in the business to achieve international cost competitiveness.

Earnings per share of Class E common stock for the period October 18 to December 31, 1984 amounted to $1.03. A fourth quarter cash dividend of $0.09 per share was paid on Class E common stock prior to its distribution to $1-2/3 par value common stockholders.

*I*n all, stockholders participated in the success of 1984 through dividends in cash and stock totaling more than $2 billion, more than double the amount received the year before. U.S. hourly and salaried employes participated fully in GM's 1984 success with payrolls and benefit costs increasing to a new high

> *"...capital spending represents a further major commitment to product quality, new products, new facilities, and factory efficiencies."*

of $24.6 billion, up 18% over a year earlier. Earnings from U.S. operations were strong enough to provide profit sharing funds totaling nearly $282 million to be distributed among some 547,000 U.S. hourly and salaried GM employees, or an average of $515 per employee. In addition, those who wish to will be able to increase the value of their profit share by 25% if they apply their payment toward the purchase of a new GM vehicle during 1985. The reduction in profit sharing from last year was more

than accounted for by the production lost in North America before labor agreements could be reached. Since March of 1984, GM has paid out more than $600 million in profits to its U.S. employes. No other company has ever distributed such a large amount of profit sharing to employes in so short a span of time.

Based on the stockholder-approved formula, the Incentive Program generated a record fund of over $304 million on record worldwide profits of $4.5 billion. On the recommendation of GM management, however, the Bonus and Salary Committee determined that the amount awarded for 1984 would be $80 million less than the maximum amount available under the incentive compensation formula. Of this amount, $35 million has been returned to income and $45 million will be carried over to future years. The $224 million awarded to GM's managers will be paid in instalments over a three-year period, generally in equal portions of GM stock and cash.

*F*or the 1985 calendar year, we anticipate that GM's capital expenditures, including the annual requirements of EDS, will be approximately $9 billion worldwide, up significantly from the 1984 spending level of $6.0 billion. Largely driven by our forward product programs, this would be the second highest spending in GM's history.

This level of capital spending represents a further major commitment to product quality, new products, new facilities, and factory efficiencies. Saturn Corporation, for example, encompasses all of these. Moreover, there will be additional changes, and there will be more diversification.

There are those who would compare the changing General Motors of these times to the Corporation in the era of Alfred P. Sloan, Jr., who shaped and led GM two generations ago. We

> *"...one thing does not change: the efforts of everyone ...to build on past achievement while attaining or maintaining GM leadership throughout the world."*

leave such comparisons to the historians. Still, it is worth noting what was perhaps Mr. Sloan's most basic perception of the Corporation: "No company ever stops changing...Each new generation must meet changes—in the automotive market, in the general administration of the enterprise, and in the involvement of the corporation in a changing world...The work is only beginning...The work of creating goes on." But one thing does not change: the efforts of everyone in the organization on behalf of the owners of General Motors to build on past achievement while attaining or maintaining GM leadership throughout the world.

Chairman

President

3

FINANCIAL REVIEW: MANAGEMENT'S DISCUSSION AND ANALYSIS*

Results of Operations

General Motors' net income in 1984 of $4,516.5 million was $786.3 million higher than in 1983.

As detailed in the table below, worldwide factory sales (sales of General Motors cars and trucks to its dealers) in 1984 totaled 8,256,000 units, 6% above 1983 unit sales. Worldwide dollar sales and revenues in 1984 were $83.9 billion, 13% above 1983. Dollar sales and revenues include price adjustments of $2.9 billion in 1984, compared with $3.2 billion in 1983 and $2.9 billion in 1982.

The table shows the percentage contribution to GM's total worldwide dollar sales and revenues, before elimination of interarea sales and revenues, by U.S., Canadian, and overseas operations. Automotive products accounted for more than 94% of GM's sales and revenues in each of the last three years.

In analyzing the earnings for the three years, it should be noted, as shown on page 1, that the two largest cost elements are payments to suppliers (for raw materials and expenses) and the cost of labor. Efforts to control supplier costs, particularly for raw materials and energy, have continued. The cost of labor reflects the U.S. labor agreement, ratified in April 1982, that

*The comments covering power products and defense sales (page 8), people of General Motors (pages 10 through 13), and the effects of inflation on financial data (pages 32 and 33) also should be read as an integral part of this discussion and analysis.

expired in September 1984 and the new three-year contract ratified in October 1984.

Taxes represent the third largest cost element of the Corporation. The significance of GM's tax burden is illustrated by comparing it with the level of cash dividends paid. For example, holders of $1-2/3 par value common stock received cash dividends of $4.75, $2.80, and $2.40 per share on their investment in 1984, 1983, and 1982, respectively. During the same period, taxes incurred were equivalent to $16.98, $15.61, and $7.22 per $1-2/3 par value common share, respectively.

The Corporation's net income as a percent of sales and revenues was 5.4% in 1984, compared with 5.0% in 1983 and 1.6% in 1982.

1984 Compared With 1983

The 1984 net income of $4,516.5 million compares with 1983 net income of $3,730.2 million. As shown in the table below, that income was earned principally in the United States and Canada. Earnings reflect the inclusion, for the period from October 18 to December 31, 1984, of the net income of Electronic Data Systems (EDS).

Earnings per share of $1-2/3 par value common stock amounted to $14.22 in 1984 versus $11.84 per share in 1983. The $2.38 per share improvement in earnings in 1984 is primarily attributable to higher volume, improved operating performance and the reversal of deferred income taxes related to the domestic international sales corporation (DISC), partially offset by increased

costs not fully recovered through prices.

Earnings per share of Class E common stock amounted to $1.03 in 1984. These earnings are based on the Separate Consolidated Net Income of EDS as defined in Note 8 to the Financial Statements.

Interest expense decreased from 1983 due in part to the lower interest costs associated with reduced levels of long-term borrowings.

Total taxes of General Motors, including payroll and property taxes but excluding the taxes of GM's financing and insurance operations, General Motors Acceptance Corporation (GMAC) and its subsidiaries as discussed below, totaled $5,377.5 million in 1984 compared with $4,899.6 million in 1983. The provision for U.S., foreign and other income taxes in 1984 reflects $1,317.1 million U.S. taxes, which includes the favorable impact of U.S. investment tax credits. These taxes are net of a deferred income tax reversal of $421.3 million, or $1.34 per share of $1-2/3 par value common stock, reflecting a change in the provisions covering DISCs in accordance with the Deficit Reduction Act of 1984.

GMAC and its subsidiaries earned $784.8 million in 1984, compared with a record $1,002.0 million in 1983. The decline in earnings was principally a result of higher short-term borrowing costs in the U.S., combined with the impact of earnings on retail receivables acquired in previous years at lower yields. GMAC's income taxes, which are provided for separately from GM, decreased $202.2 million to a total of $591.9 million for 1984 as a result of decreased pretax earnings.

Worldwide Factory Sales
(Units in Thousands)

	CARS			TRUCKS & BUSES			TOTAL		
	1984	1983	1982	1984	1983	1982	1984	1983	1982
United States	4,338	3,996	3,147	1,338	1,123	895	5,676	5,119	4,042
Canada	549	539	335	277	263	230	826	802	565
Overseas†	1,485	1,606	1,388	269	242	249	1,754	1,848	1,637
Total	6,372	6,141	4,870	1,884	1,628	1,374	8,256	7,769	6,244

†Includes units which are manufactured overseas by other companies and which are imported and sold by General Motors and affiliates.

Percentage of Net Income (Loss) Attributable to:

	1984	1983	1982
United States	86%	93%	111%
Canada	17	16	(3)
Overseas	(3)	(9)	(8)
Total	100%	100%	100%
Automotive	100%	102%	101%
Nonautomotive	—	(2)	(1)
Total	100%	100%	100%

Percentage of Worldwide Dollar Sales and Revenues Attributable to:

	1984	1983	1982
United States	76%	74%	72%
Canada	13	13	11
Overseas	11	13	17
Total	100%	100%	100%
Automotive	96%	96%	94%
Nonautomotive	4	4	6
Total	100%	100%	100%

1983 Compared With 1982

The 1983 net income of $3,730.2 million or $11.84 per share of common stock compared with 1982 net income of $962.7 million or $3.09 per share of common stock.

The $8.75 per share improvement in earnings in 1983 was primarily attributable to increased volume, an improved product mix, efficiencies due to cost reduction efforts, and increased earnings of GMAC and its subsidiaries. As explained in Note 1 to the Financial Statements, the Corporation implemented Statement of Financial Accounting Standards No. 52, Foreign Currency Translation, effective January 1, 1983 and the effect was to reduce net income for 1983 by about $422.5 million ($1.35 per share).

Interest expense decreased from 1982 due to the lower interest costs associated with reduced levels of long-term borrowings.

The provision for U.S., foreign and other income taxes in 1983 reflected $1,811.4 million U.S. taxes, which included the favorable impact of U.S. investment tax credits.

GMAC and its subsidiaries earned a record $1,002.0 million in 1983, compared with the previous record of $688.0 million in 1982, reflecting lower short-term borrowing costs and a higher level of earning assets.

Liquidity and Capital Resources

In 1984, cash and marketable securities increased by $2,350.5 million, or 38%, principally reflecting funds provided by current operations and the net decrease in other working capital items, only partially offset by expenditures for property and for the intangible assets acquired in the acquisition of EDS. The net decrease in other working capital items consisted primarily of an increase in loans payable due principally to the fluctuating rate GM notes issued in connection with the acquisition of EDS.

In 1983, cash and marketable securities increased by $3,090.7 million, or 99%, principally reflecting funds provided by current operations, only partially offset by expenditures for property, the net reduction in long-term debt and the net increase in other working capital items (principally accounts and notes receivable). The increase in accounts and notes receivable of $4,099.7 million in 1983 reflected the sales increase as well as an increase in the receivable from GMAC, which provides the majority of the wholesale financing of General Motors' products. That increase included $2,562.4 million related to dealer vehicle stocks for which payment from GMAC was due at a later date than previously had been the practice.

Long-term debt was reduced by $719.8 million in 1984 as a result of decreases in long-term debt of $1,793.9 million exceeding increases of $1,074.1 million. Accordingly, the ratio of long-term debt to the total of long-term debt and stockholders' equity declined to 9.1% at December 31, 1984.

During 1983, long-term debt had decreased $1,314.8 million because decreases of $4,491.9 million exceeded increases of $3,177.1 million. As a result, the long-term debt ratio had declined to 13.1% at year-end 1983.

The ratio of long-term debt and short-term loans payable to the total of this debt and stockholders' equity amounted to 18.5% at December 31, 1984, an increase of one point from the 17.5% ratio at December 31, 1983 reflecting the notes issued in the EDS acquisition.

OLDSMOBILE DELTA 88 ROYALE BROUGHAM Sedan

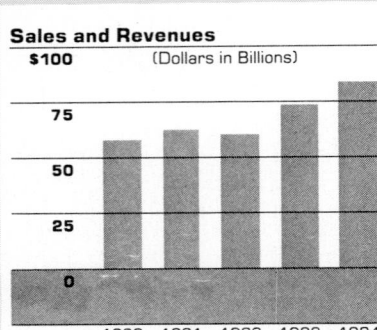

Sales and Revenues
(Dollars in Billions)

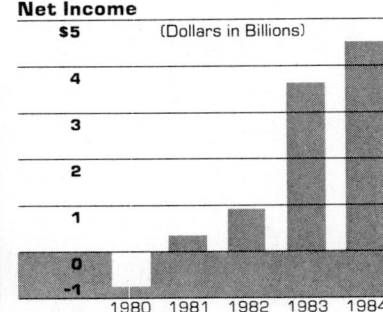

Net Income
(Dollars in Billions)

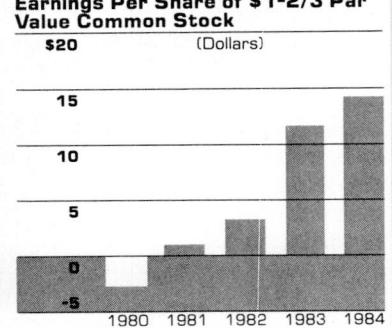

Earnings Per Share of $1-2/3 Par Value Common Stock
(Dollars)

The senior long-term debt ratings of GM and GMAC carry the second highest possible rating, while the short-term commercial paper of GMAC continues to carry the highest possible rating. In line with the past practice of maintaining lines of credit, at year-end 1984 the Corporation and its subsidiaries (excluding GMAC) had unused short-term credit lines of approximately $2.4 billion and unused long-term credit agreements of approximately $1.4 billion.

Of the 1984 worldwide expenditures for real estate, plants and equipment, approximately 82% were made in the United States (78% in 1983 and 73% in 1982), 4% in Canada (7% in 1983 and 5% in 1982), and 14% overseas (15% in 1983 and 22% in 1982).

Product programs necessary to respond to the demands of the marketplace for quality and fuel economy, to improve General Motors' competitive position worldwide, to improve plant efficiency, and to meet government standards require continued high capital expenditures. In each of the last nine years, GM has introduced substantially redesigned or new models in the United States and Canada. Significant product redesign programs also have been undertaken by overseas subsidiaries. Commitments for capital spending at December 31, 1984 totaled $4.2 billion, and it is anticipated that total capital expenditures, including the annual requirements of EDS, will be approximately $9 billion in 1985.

The decrease in preferred stocks reflects the Corporation's previously announced long-term program to repurchase such stock when it is considered economically attractive to GM. The difference between repurchase prices and the stated value of $100 per share has been credited to capital surplus.

The issuance of Class E common stock reflects primarily the acquisition of EDS, as described more fully in Note 1 to the Financial Statements, and the dividend of one share of Class E common stock for every 20 shares of $1-2/3 par value common stock on December 10, 1984.

Increases in $1-2/3 par value common stock and other capital surplus in 1984 reflect use of newly issued stock for purposes of bonus deliveries, the Stock Option Plans (SOP) and the General Motors Dividend Reinvestment Plan (DRP). In 1983 and 1982, newly issued stock was used for the SOP, the DRP, the Savings-Stock Purchase Programs, and the Employe Stock Ownership Plans. In addition, the Corporation exchanged common stock for long-term debt in the earlier two years.

It is the Corporation's policy with respect to $1-2/3 par value common stock to distribute from current earnings such amounts as the outlook and the indicated capital needs of the business permit. In this regard, a strong capital position must be maintained in order to meet capital expenditures in the years ahead. The Class E com-

mon stock dividend policy is discussed on page 19 and in Note 8 to the Financial Statements.

Accumulated foreign currency translation adjustments of ($789.5) million at December 31, 1984 and ($661.8) million at December 31, 1983 are included in a separate section of stockholders' equity.

Book value per share of $1-2/3 par value common stock increased in 1984 to $72.16 from $64.88 at the end of 1983. Book value was $57.64 at the end of 1982. Book value per share of Class E common stock was $36.08 at the end of 1984. Net income as a percent of stockholders' equity was 18.7% in 1984, compared with 18.0% in 1983 and 5.3% in 1982.

GM's liquidity can be measured by its current ratio (ratio of current assets to current liabilities). For the years ended December 31, 1984, 1983, and 1982, the current ratio, based on last-in, first-out (LIFO) inventories, was 1.36, 1.40, and 1.13, respectively. The LIFO method, while improving Corporate cash flow, adversely affects the current ratio. The first-in, first-out (FIFO) value of inventories, which more nearly reflects replacement cost, exceeded LIFO amounts at December 31, 1984, 1983, and 1982 by approximately $2.2 billion, $2.0 billion, and $1.9 billion, respectively. If inventories were valued at FIFO cost, the current ratio would be 1.40, 1.47, and 1.21, respectively.

Quality control checks occur throughout the assembly line process. Shown here is a Cadillac Sedan DeVille receiving final front- and rear-wheel alignment in a "toe-in" machine. This machine feeds information back to camber equipment— which made the suspension alignment further up the assembly line—and double checks that original setting. The new Cadillac's four-wheel independent suspension makes front- and rear-wheel alignment necessary.

EARNINGS ON CLASS E COMMON STOCK

On October 18, 1984, General Motors acquired Electronic Data Systems (EDS), a leader in the computer services industry. The operations of EDS since October 18 are included in the consolidated results of General Motors shown on pages 20-33 for the period ended December 31, 1984.

The earnings of EDS and its subsidiaries since acquisition by GM, including income earned from services provided to GM and its other subsidiaries but excluding purchase accounting adjustments, form the base out of which any dividends paid on the Class E common stock will be declared. These earnings are designated as the "Separate Consolidated Net Income of EDS" and are described as "Earnings on Class E Common Stock" in the Financial Statements. The rights of Class E common stockholders to participate in dividends are described more fully in Note 8 to the Financial Statements.

In the 22 years since it began operations, EDS has helped to shape many of the technologies and business practices now prominent in the data processing field.

☐ In the early 1960s, EDS created an entirely new service—Facilities Management, whereby EDS, in effect, assumes data processing responsibility for its client companies, providing all hardware, software, personnel, and computer services. The company was the first computer services firm to sign extended, multi-year contracts with its customers. EDS helped pioneer interactive systems, distributed processing, satellite communications and computer telecommunications, and in the early 1970s began work on EDS•NET, the company's nationwide data communications network. Currently, EDS•NET handles more than 5 million data transactions each day from more than 25,000 on-line customer terminals.

☐ In 1974, EDS began to serve credit unions by developing systems for CUNADATA Corporation, a subsidiary of the Credit Union National Association; within 10 years, EDS has become the industry leader in service to credit unions.

☐ In 1978, EDS began an effort to serve another specifically targeted customer—the Federal government. In 1984, Federal government contracts brought EDS over $250 million in revenues. Multi-year arrangements with the Departments of Defense, Interior, Energy, Justice and Agriculture, the U.S. Postal Service, the Social Security Administration, and the Environmental Protection Agency, as well as the Army, Navy, and Marines, make this one of the largest, fastest-growing parts of EDS' business.

☐ In 1982, the company demonstrated its ability to transfer its service technologies from one area to another related one. EDS•NET, for example, helped prepare EDS for the procurement and implementation of the 10-year, $656 million project VIABLE (Vertical Installation Automation Base Line) for the U.S. Army—one of the largest computer services contracts ever awarded by the Federal government. VIABLE, in turn, proved EDS' readiness in 1984 to take on a systems integration contract with the U.S. Navy. These projects are helping position the company for similar major contracts not only with the government but with the commercial sector as well.

If a single reason could be credited for EDS' steady sustained growth, it is the ability to find, develop and retain the right people for the job. The company's recruiting, training and employe recognition practices help keep EDS personnel ready to anticipate and meet the needs of current customers, and prepare for the business opportunities ahead. The company's training programs, such as the Systems, Engineering and Development (SED) Program, were ahead of their time when first developed, and remain so today. Extensive initial and ongoing education is available for EDS personnel, and the highest priority is given to providing individuals with the tools and work environment necessary for maximum productivity. This people-oriented approach has sustained

EDS Headquarters, Dallas, Texas

EARNINGS ON CLASS E COMMON STOCK (continued)

EDS' leadership in the data processing industry.

This expertise in data processing and communications will be applied across a broad spectrum of General Motors operations worldwide. It will assist in the development of the advanced computer systems needed to enhance GM's leadership position and enable GM to achieve greater efficiencies in operations.

While the merger with GM was the most significant event of 1984 in EDS' operations, its outside business continued to grow also. EDS signed more commercial business than ever before and several long-term government contracts. Revenues from commercial business are now at their highest point ever.

EDS is not limited to a reliance on any one business category or industry; therefore, the company's well-being is less vulnerable to the downturns of a single industry. Among computer services companies, EDS leads in its ability to serve large companies in a diverse range of industries, both nationally and internationally—including health care, financial services, commercial insurance, industrial, and Federal, state and local government organizations. EDS pioneered the concept of industry specialization and servicing many different industries. While a number of firms compete with EDS in a given industry, most specialize in service to only that one industry.

One traditional EDS stronghold has been the health care market. The year 1984 was no exception. Blue Cross and Blue Shield of Colorado extended its facilities management contract with EDS for an additional three years—until 1992. Blue Shield of Western New York also extended its contract for 10 more years. In addition, EDS recently signed a 10-year contract with Blue Cross/Blue Shield United of Wisconsin, one of the nation's largest plans, bringing the current total of Blue Cross and Blue Shield customers to 13.

EDS continued its steady and progressive growth in the credit union market during 1984. Today, EDS serves 3,100 credit unions with 10 million members. That is an increase of 2 million members in the past year.

EDS' success in the industrials market has been growing. This year, EDS signed a seven-year contract to provide complete data processing services to the six companies that comprise the Specialty Retailing Group of General Mills, Inc.

EDS also signed a new seven-year facilities management contract with Vista Chemicals of Houston, Texas. During the first six months of the agreement, EDS will transfer Vista's data processing activities to EDS' Dallas Information Processing Centers.

AT&T and EDS announced a major expansion of their business arrangement with the signing of a multi-year agreement designed to strengthen the ability of both companies to integrate tailor-made communications and data processing systems. The agreement combines AT&T's technological expertise in communications and data products and services with EDS' knowledge and skills with software and systems integration.

AT&T and EDS project teams will identify and qualify potential sales opportunities that require custom-designed system solutions. If a customer accepts a recommended solution, critical elements will be evaluated and tested before installation.

In 1984, an eight-year, $350 million agreement with the U.S. Navy to update data processing facilities at the Navy's two major inventory control points was also signed. In addition, EDS will build a nationwide telecommunications network, provide both hardware and software, and train more than 5,500 Navy personnel. The contract contains two eight-year extension options, making it a potential 24-year agreement.

Another major government contract is a seven-year, potential $200 million contract with the U.S. Postal Service to automate tracking and handling of airmail. The new system uses laser scanning equipment to sort mail at 351 locations in the continental United States.

In international activities, EDS won a 10-year contract with Unilever PLC of London, England to manage and operate Unilever's United Kingdom telecommunications network. EDS also signed a major contract with British United Provident Association that is believed to be one of the largest contracts for data processing services ever awarded in the United Kingdom.

The Control Room of an EDS Information Processing Center

EARNINGS ON CLASS E COMMON STOCK (concluded)

The following are selected summary financial data relating to the EDS operations which form the Class E common stock Dividend Base for the period from October 18 to December 31, 1984. For purposes of analysis, pro forma calendar year data for 1984 and 1983 are also presented.

Selected Summary Financial Data

(Dollars in Millions Except Per Share Amounts)	Oct. 18 to Dec. 31, 1984	Pro Forma Year Ended December 31, 1984	1983
Revenues:			
Systems and other contracts:			
Outside customers	$184.5	$866.6	$701.7
GM and affiliates	36.4	59.3	—
Interest and other income	4.8	21.5	30.1
Total Revenues	225.7	947.4	731.8
Costs and Expenses	191.1	808.1	614.9
Income Taxes	15.9	58.6	51.7
Earnings on Class E Common Stock	$ 18.7	$ 80.7	$ 65.2
Average number of shares of Class E common stock outstanding (in millions)	18.2	—	—
Earnings per share of Class E common stock	$1.03	—	—
Dividend Base Per Share of Class E common stock*	$0.31	—	—
Cash dividends per share of Class E common stock	$0.09	—	—
Payout Ratio**	29.0%	—	—

*The Dividend Base Per Share represents earnings on Class E common stock divided by 60.0 million shares.
**The Payout Ratio represents dividends per share divided by the Dividend Base Per Share.

(Dollars in Millions)	December 31, 1984	1983
Current Assets:		
Cash and marketable securities	$162.5	$ 95.4
Accounts receivable	191.4	113.6
Other current assets	37.3	26.0
Total Current Assets	391.2	235.0
Current Liabilities:		
Accounts payable	35.4	40.1
Notes payable—current portion	5.7	3.5
Deferred revenue	24.0	27.1
Other accrued liabilities	140.8	75.8
Total Current Liabilities	205.9	146.5
Working Capital	$185.3	$ 88.5
Data Processing Facilities, Property and Equipment	$106.7	$ 94.9
Other Assets:		
Investment in nonconsolidated subsidiaries	$ .6	$ 7.8
Land held for investment and development	72.5	60.5
Other operating assets	36.3	73.0
Total Other Assets	$109.4	$141.3
Long-Term Debt and Deferred Credits:		
Notes payable—long-term portion	$ 27.2	$ 28.4
Deferred income taxes payable	15.3	9.4
Deferred revenue	13.4	6.1
Total Long-Term Debt and Deferred Credits	$ 55.9	$ 43.9

EDS experienced continued growth during the calendar year ended December 31, 1984. During the past year:
☐ Revenues rose 29.5% to $947.4 million, including $59.3 million derived from GM and affiliates.
☐ On a pro forma basis, earnings on Class E common stock increased 23.8% to $80.7 million.
☐ Working capital totaled $185.3 million, an increase of over 100% in 1984.
☐ Total assets were $607.3 million.
☐ The number of EDS employes surpassed 22,000, including 7,000 transferred from GM and affiliates, effective January 1, 1985.

The current policy of the GM Board of Directors is to pay dividends on the Class E common stock approximately equal to 25% of the quotient of (a) the Separate Consolidated Net Income of EDS, as defined, divided by (b) the greater of 60 million or the number of shares of Class E common stock outstanding. The Board has also adopted the policy that dividends per share of Class E common stock for the first four quarters following the acquisition of EDS will equal at least $0.09 per share per quarter.

The data do not include the cost of $2,006.3 million to GM of the EDS customer contracts, computer software programs and intangible assets arising from the acquisition of EDS by GM. The cost of these assets is being amortized by GM over their estimated useful lives. Amortization for the period from the date of acquisition to December 31, 1984 was $68.4 million. The unamortized balance at December 31, 1984 was $1,937.9 million. For the purpose of determining earnings per share and amounts available for dividends on common stocks, the amortization of these assets is charged against earnings attributable to $1-2/3 par value common stock. The effect on the 1984 consolidated net income of General Motors is a net charge of $26.1 million, consisting of earnings on Class E common stock less the amortization of the applicable assets and the elimination of intercompany transactions.

People and Technology — The Key to EDS' Success

SUPPLEMENTARY INFORMATION (concluded)

Selected Financial Data
(Dollars in Millions Except Per Share Amounts)

	1984	1983	1982	1981	1980
Net sales and revenues	$83,889.9	$74,581.6	$60,025.6	$62,698.5	$57,728.5
Earnings (loss) on $1-2/3 par value common stock	$ 4,485.3	$ 3,717.3	$ 949.8	$ 320.5	($ 775.4)
Cash dividends on $1-2/3 par value common stock	1,510.0	879.3	737.3	717.6	861.2
Dividend of Class E common shares	586.7	—	—	—	—
Net income (loss) retained in the year	$ 2,388.6	$ 2,838.0	$ 212.5	($ 397.1)	($ 1,636.6)
Earnings (loss) on $1-2/3 par value common stock—per share	$14.22	$11.84	$3.09	$1.07	($2.65)
Cash dividends on $1-2/3 par value common stock—per share	4.75	2.80	2.40	2.40	2.95
Dividend of Class E common shares—per share	1.90	—	—	—	—
Net income (loss) retained in the year—per share	$ 7.57	$ 9.04	$0.69	($1.33)	($5.60)
Earnings on Class E common stock (issued in 1984)	$ 18.7	—	—	—	—
Cash dividends on Class E common stock (issued in 1984)	1.2	—	—	—	—
Net income retained in the year	$ 17.5	—	—	—	—
Earnings on Class E common stock—per share	$1.03	—	—	—	—
Cash dividends on Class E common stock—per share	0.09	—	—	—	—
Net income retained in the year—per share	$0.94	—	—	—	—
Average number of shares of common stocks outstanding (in millions):					
$1-2/3 par value common	315.3	313.9	307.4	299.1	292.4
Class E common (issued in 1984)	18.2	—	—	—	—
Cash dividends on capital stocks as a percent of net income	33.7%	23.9%	77.9%	219.1%	N.A.
Expenditures for real estate, plants and equipment	$ 3,595.1	$ 1,923.0	$ 3,611.1	$ 6,563.3	$ 5,160.5
Expenditures for special tools	$ 2,452.1	$ 2,083.7	$ 2,601.0	$ 3,178.1	$ 2,600.0
Cash and marketable securities	$ 8,567.4	$ 6,216.9	$ 3,126.2	$ 1,320.7	$ 3,715.2
Working capital	$ 6,276.7	$ 5,890.8	$ 1,658.1	$ 1,158.8	$ 3,212.1
Total assets	$52,144.9	$45,694.5	$41,397.8	$38,979.0	$34,581.0
Long-term debt and capitalized leases	$ 2,772.9	$ 3,521.8	$ 4,745.1	$ 4,044.0	$ 2,058.3

Financial data for years prior to 1983 have not been restated for the adoption of Statement of Financial Accounting Standards No. 52, Foreign Currency Translation.

EFFECTS OF INFLATION ON FINANCIAL DATA

The accompanying Schedules display the basic historical cost financial data adjusted for changes in specific prices (current cost) for use in the evaluation of comparative financial results.

One method by which to analyze the effects of inflation on financial data (and thus the business) is by adjusting the historical cost data to the current costs for the major balance sheet items which have been accumulated through the accounting system over a period of years and which thus reflect different prices for the same commodities and services.

The current cost of inventories was estimated based on costs in effect at December 31, 1984. Cost of sales for inventories maintained on a first-in, first-out basis was restated to a current cost basis using the specific level of prices at the time the goods were sold.

The current cost of property owned and the related depreciation and amortization expense for U.S. operations were calculated by applying (1) selected producer price indices to historical book values of machinery and equipment and (2) the Marshall Valuation Service index to buildings, and the use of assessed values for land. For locations outside the United States, such amounts were calculated generally by applying indices closely related to the assets being measured and translating the resulting amounts using year-end foreign currency exchange rates.

The purpose of this type of restatement is to furnish estimates of the effects of price increases for replacement of inventories and property on the potential future net income of the business and thus assess the probability of future cash flows. Although these data may be useful for this purpose, they do not reflect specific plans for the replacement of property. A more meaningful estimate of the effects of such costs on future earnings is the estimated level of future capital expenditures which is set forth on page 16 in the Financial Review: Management's Discussion and Analysis.

Under the current cost method, the net income of General Motors is lower (or the net loss is higher) than that determined under the historical cost method. This means that businesses, as well as individuals, are affected by inflation and that the purchasing power of business dollars also has declined. In addition, the costs of maintaining the productive capacity, as reflected in the current cost data (and estimate of future capital expenditures), have increased, and thus management must seek ways to cope with the effects of inflation through accounting methods such as the LIFO method of inventory valuation, which matches current costs with current revenues, and through accelerated methods of depreciation and amortization.

It must be emphasized that there is a continuing need for national monetary and fiscal policies designed to control inflation and to provide adequate capital for future business growth which, in turn, will mean increased productivity and employment.

EFFECTS OF INFLATION ON FINANCIAL DATA (concluded)

Comparison of Selected Data Adjusted for Effects of Changing Prices
(Dollars in Millions Except Per Share Amounts)
Historical cost data adjusted for changes in specific prices (current cost):*

	1984	1983	1982	1981	1980
Net Income (Loss)—as reported	$ 4,516.5	$ 3,730.2	$ 962.7	$ 333.4	($ 762.5)
—in current cost 1967 dollars	1,403.1	1,144.0	71.7	(252.8)	(829.5)
Earnings (Loss) per share of $1-2/3 par value common stock					
—as reported	$14.22	$11.84	$3.09	$1.07	($2.65)
—in current cost 1967 dollars	4.42	3.63	0.22	(0.86)	(2.86)
Earnings per share of Class E common stock (issued in 1984)					
—as reported	$1.03	—	—	—	—
—in current cost 1967 dollars	0.33	—	—	—	—
Cash dividends per share of $1-2/3 par value common stock					
—as reported	$4.75	$2.80	$2.40	$2.40	$2.95
—in constant 1967 dollars	1.53	0.94	0.83	0.88	1.20
Cash dividends per share of Class E common stock (issued in 1984)					
—as reported	$0.09	—	—	—	—
—in constant 1967 dollars	0.03	—	—	—	—
Net assets at year-end—as reported	$24,214.3	$20,766.6	$18,287.1	$17,721.1	$17,814.6
—in current cost 1967 dollars	10,938.7	10,635.1	9,818.3	10,450.9	11,377.2
Accumulated foreign currency translation adjustments					
—as reported	($ 127.7)	($ 661.8)	—	—	—
—in current cost 1967 dollars	(51.8)	(129.8)	—	—	—
Unrealized gain from decline in purchasing power of dollars of net amounts owed	$ 50.5	$ 86.5	$ 130.5	$ 241.3	$ 182.3
Excess of increase in general price level over increase in specific prices of inventories and property	$ 320.8	$ 78.4	$ 861.2	$ 619.0	$ 689.2
Market price per $1-2/3 par value common share at year-end					
—unadjusted	$78.38	$74.38	$62.38	$38.50	$45.00
—in constant 1967 dollars	25.19	24.93	21.58	14.13	18.23
Market price per Class E common share at year-end (issued in 1984)					
—unadjusted	$42.38	—	—	—	—
—in constant 1967 dollars	13.62	—	—	—	—
Average Consumer Price Index	311.1	298.4	289.1	272.4	246.8

*Current cost data have been adjusted to 1967 dollars by applying the Consumer Price Index—Urban to the data with 1967 (CPI-100) as the base year. Depreciation has been determined on a straight-line basis for this calculation.

Schedule of Income Adjusted for Changing Prices
For the Year Ended December 31, 1984
(Dollars in Millions Except Per Share Amounts)

	As Reported in the Financial Statements (Historical Cost)	Adjusted for Changes in Specific Prices (1984 Current Cost)
Net Sales and Revenues	$83,889.9	$83,889.9
Cost of sales	70,217.9	70,270.1
Depreciation and amortization of property	4,899.9	4,999.5
Other operating and nonoperating items—net	2,450.5	2,450.5
United States and other income taxes	1,805.1	1,805.1
Total costs and expenses	79,373.4	79,525.2
Net Income	$ 4,516.5	$ 4,364.7
Earnings per share of $1-2/3 par value common stock	$14.22	$13.74
Earnings per share of Class E common stock	$1.03	$1.03
Accumulated foreign currency translation adjustments	($ 127.7)	($ 161.0)
Unrealized gain from decline in purchasing power of dollars of net amounts owed		$ 157.2
Excess of increase in general price level over increase in specific prices of inventories and property		$ 998.1**

**At December 31, 1984, current cost of inventories was $9,535.2 million and current cost of property (including special tools), net of accumulated depreciation and amortization, was $27,042.0 million.

APPENDIX B

International Accounting

In today's world we do not find it surprising to discover a British bank in Atlanta, Coca-Cola in Paris, and French airplanes in Zaire. German auto parts are assembled in Spain and sold in the United States. Japan buys oil from Saudi Arabia and sells cameras in Italy. Soviet livestock eat American grain, and the British sip tea from Sri Lanka and China. Business has become truly international, but accounting, often described as the language of business, does not cross borders so easily. Accounting principles and reporting practices differ from country to country, and international decision making is made more difficult by the lack of a common communication system. But, since business is practiced at an international level, accounting must find a way to provide its services at that level.

The problem is that accounting must first reflect the national economic and social environment in which it is practiced, and this environment is not the same in Bangkok as in Boston. Some economies, for example, are mainly agricultural. Others are based on manufacturing, trade, or service industries. Still others export natural resources, such as oil or gold, while a few derive most of their income from tourism. Accounting for inventories and natrual resources, cost accounting techniques, and methods of foreign currency translation naturally have a different orientation, emphasis, and degree of refinement in these different economies.

Other accounting differences stem from the various legal or political systems of nations. In centrally controlled economies, for instance, the state owns all or most of the property. It makes little sense to prescribe full disclosure of accounting procedures to protect investors when there is little or no private ownership of property. Some of these countries standardize their accounting methods and incorporate them into law. But in market-oriented economies, the development of accounting principles and reporting practices is left mainly to the private sector. Where uniformity exists, it occurs more by general agreement or consensus of interested parties than by governmental decree. In market-oriented economies, accounting principles and practices must be more flexible to serve the needs of business firms which differ widely in ownership, size, and complexity. In countries where business firms are predominately family owned, disclosure practices can be less complete than in countries where large, publicly held corporations dominate.

The degree of development of the accounting profession and the general level of education of a country also influence accounting practices and procedures. Nations that lack a well-organized accounting profession may adopt almost wholesale the accounting methods of other countries. Commonwealth countries, for example, tend to follow British accounting standards; the former French colonies of Africa use French systems; Bermuda follows Canadian pronouncements; and the influence of the United States is widespread. At the same time, levels of expertise vary. There is no point in advocating statistical accounting and auditing techniques in countries where there is little knowledge or understanding of statistics. Accounting systems designed for electronic data processing are not helpful in countries where few or no businesses use computers.

Even in advanced countries, genuine differences of opinion exist regarding accounting theory and appropriate accounting methods. American standards, for example, require the periodic amortization of goodwill to expense, but British, German, and Dutch standards do not. Accounting methods also differ within nations. Most countries, including the United States, permit several depreciation methods and two or more inventory costing methods. Such flexibility is essential if accounting is to serve a useful purpose in economic, political, and social environments that are not uniform.

■ ATTEMPTED HARMONIZATION OF ACCOUNTING PRACTICES

The question arises as to whether financial statements that reflect the economic and social environment of, say, France can also be useful to a potential American investor. Can some of the differences between French and American accounting be eliminated or at least explained so that French and American investors will understand each other's reports and find them useful when they make decisions?

Several organizations are working to achieve greater understanding and harmonization of different accounting practices. These include the United Nations Commission on Transnational Corporations, the Organization for Economic Cooperation and Development (OECD), the European Economic Community (EEC), the International Federation of Accountants (IFAC), and the International Accounting Standards Committee (IASC). These organizations study the information needs and accounting and reporting practices of different nations and issue pronouncements recommending specific practices and procedures for adoption by all members.

The IASC is making a significant contribution to the development of international accounting standards. It was founded in London in 1973 by the professional accountancy bodies of 10 countries: Australia, Canada, France, Germany, Ireland, Japan, Mexico, the Netherlands, the United Kingdom, and the United States. Since 1973, the professional bodies of more than 30 countries have joined the IASC as associate members. The IASC selects a topic for study from lists of problems submitted by the profession all over the world. After research and discussion by special committees, the IASC issues an exposure draft of a proposed standard for consideration by the profession and the business and financial communities. After about six months' further study of the topic in light of the comments received, the IASC issues the final international accounting standard. To date, 19 standards have been issued on topics as varied as *Disclosure of Accounting Policies* (IAS 1), *Depreciation Accounting* (IAS 4), *Statement of Changes in Financial Position* (IAS 7), and *Revenue Recognition* (IAS 18, effective January 1, 1984). Setting international standards is not easy. If the standards are too detailed or rigid, then the flexibility needed to reflect different national environments will be lost. On the other hand, if pronouncements are vague and allow too many alternative methods, then there is little point in setting international standards.

One major problem is the enforcement of these standards. There is no organization, nor is there likely to be, to ensure compliance with international standards. Enforcement is left to national standard-setting bodies or legislatures, which may or may not adopt a recommended international standard. Generally, members commit themselves to support the objectives of the international body. The members promise to use their best endeavors to see that international standards are formally adopted by local professional accountancy bodies, by government departments or other authorities that control the securities markets, and by the industrial, business, and financial communities of their respective countries.

The American Institute of Certified Public Accountants (AICPA), for example, issued a revised statement in 1975 reaffirming its support for the implementation of international standards adopted by the IASC. The AICPA's position is that international accounting standards must be specifically adopted by the Financial Accounting Standards Board (FASB), which is not a member of the IASC, is order to achieve acceptance in the United States. But if there is no significant difference between an international standard and U.S. practice, compliance with U.S. generally accepted accounting principles (GAAP) constitutes compliance with the international standard. Where a significant difference exists, the AICPA publishes the IASC standard together with comments on how it differs from U.S. GAAP and undertakes to urge the FASB to give early consideration to harmonizing the differences.[1] Significant support for IASC standards has also resulted from a resolution adopted by the World Federation of Stock Exchanges in 1975. The resolution binds members to require conformance with IASC standards in securities listing agreements.[2]

Although these developments are important for international harmonization of accounting, ultimately the success of international pronouncements depends on the willingness of the members to support them. In some cases, national legislation is required and may be slow or difficult to pass. The EEC, for example, issues "Directives" which must be accepted as compulsory objectives

---

[1] American Institute of Certified Public Accountants, *CPA Letter,* August 1975.

[2] *CA Magazine,* January 1975, p. 52.

by the 10 member states (Belgium, Denmark, France, Germany, Greece, Ireland, Italy, Luxembourg, the Netherlands, and the United Kingdom) but which are translated into national legislation at the discretion of each member state. The EEC's important *Fourth Directive* was adopted in 1978 to regulate the preparation, content, presentation, audit, and publication of the accounts and reports of companies. It applies to all limited-liability companies (corporations) registered in the EEC, except for banks and insurance companies. Under the directive, member states were to introduce legislation by July 1980 so that accounts in all EEC countries would conform to the directive as of the fiscal year beginning January 1, 1982. Yet by that date, only Belgium, Denmark, and the United Kingdom had passed the necessary legislation, although most of the other member countries were close to doing so.

The general movement toward international harmonization of accounting standards is increasing in other areas of society. The accounting profession, national standard-setting bodies, universities, academic societies, and multinational corporations have all shown an increased interest in international accounting problems in recent years. The AICPA has an International Practice Division as a formal part of its line organization. The American Accounting Association officially established an International Accounting Section in 1976. The University of Lancaster (England) and the University of Illinois have international accounting research centers that support research studies and conduct international conferences and seminars. Georgia State University received a Touche Ross & Co. grant to internationalize its accounting curriculum. Many universities currently offer courses in international business and accounting.

All this activity helps to increase the flow of information and our understanding of the accounting and reporting practices in other parts of the world. Greater understanding improves the likelihood that unnecessary differences will be eliminated and enhances the general acceptance of international standards.

The rest of this appendix gives examples of the accounting methods used in different countries and of the concepts that underlie them to illustrate the difficulty of achieving international harmonization.

■ FOREIGN CURRENCY TRANSLATION

Foreign currency translation is probably the most common problem in an international business environment. Foreign currency translation has two main components: accounting for transactions in a foreign currency and translating the financial statements of foreign enterprises into a different, common currency.

Accounting for Transactions in a Foreign Currency

Suppose an American automobile dealership imports vehicles from Japan and promises to pay for them in yen 90 days after receiving them. If there is no change in the dollar-yen exchange rate between the date the goods are received and the date the invoice is paid, there is no problem. Both the purchase and the payment will be recorded at the same dollar value. But if the yen appreciates against the dollar during the 90-day period, the importer must pay more dollars for the yen needed on the settlement date.[3] Which exchange rate should the importer use to record payment of the invoice—the rate in effect on the purchase date or on the payment date?

One approach to the problem is to regard the purchase of the automobiles and settlement of the invoice as two separate transactions and record them at two different exchange rates. The difference between the amount recorded in Accounts Payable on the purchase date and the decrease in Cash on the settlement date is considered an exchange gain or loss (a loss in this case). This approach, known as the "time-of-transaction" method, was the prescribed or predominant practice in 61 of 64 countries surveyed in 1979,[4] including the United States.[5] The time-of-transaction method is also the method recommended in the IASC's exposure draft, *Accounting for the Effects of Changes in Foreign Exchange Rates,* issued in March 1982.

Another approach, known as the "time-of-settlement" method, regards the transaction and its settlement as a single event. If this method is used, the amount recorded on the purchase date is regarded as an estimate of the settlement amount. Any fluctuations in the exchange rate between the purchase date and the settlement date are accounted for as part of the transaction and are not treated as a separate gain or loss. Consequently there is no effect on earnings.

Although the time-of-transaction method is widely used, the treatment of resulting exchange gains and losses is not uniform. If the gains or losses are realized, that is, if settlement is made within the same accounting period as the purchase, then most countries recognize such gains and losses in the income statement for that period. If the exchange gains or losses are unrealized, that is, if they result from translating Accounts Payable (or Accounts Receivable for the vendor) at the balance sheet date, the treatment varies. Recording losses unrealized was the prescribed or predominant practice in 54 countries in 1979. But only 40 countries similarly recognized exchange gains in income, the remaining nations preferring to defer them until settlement. In the United States, under the provisions of FASB *Statement No. 52,* both realized and unrealized transaction gains and losses are recognized in earnings of the period in which the exchange rate changes.

Translating Financial Statements

Financial statements of foreign subsidiaries are translated into a single common unit of measurement, such as the dollar, for purposes of consolidation. Considerable argument has arisen in recent years as to the correct way to do this; that is, which exchange rate should be used to translate items in the balance sheet and income statement, and what treatment is appropriate for any resulting exchange gains and losses? Items that translated at the historical rate cannot

---

[3] This example ignores the possibility that the importer might obtain a forward exchange contract, a discussion of which is beyond the scope of this text.

[4] Price Waterhouse International *International Survey.* Data on the different methods used and on the number of countries using each method described in these examples are derived substantially from this publication.

[5] FASB *Statement of Financial Accounting Standards No. 8,* "Accounting for the Translation of Foreign Currency Transactions and Foreign Currency Financial Statements" (Stamford, Conn., 1975). The "time-of-transaction" method is also prescribed by FASB *Statement No. 52,* "Foreign Currency Translation" (Stamford, Conn., 1981) which supersedes FASB *Statement No. 8.*

result in exchange gains or losses. But items that are translated at the exchange rate in effect on the balance sheet data (the current rate) can result in exchange gains and losses if the current rate differs from the rate in effect when those items were recorded (the historical rate). If the current rate is used, a related question arises: Should the resulting exchange gains or losses be recognized immediately in income or deferred in some way?

The methods used to translate financial statements fall basically into two groups: translation of all items at the current rate and translation of some items at the current rate and others at the historical rates. The two groups are based on different concepts of both consolidation and international business.

The Current-Rate Approach.   The current- or closing-rate method translates all assets and liabilities at the exchange rate in effect on the balance sheet date. The main advantage of this method is its simplicity; it treats all items uniformly. The approach is based on the view that a foreign subsidiary is a separate unit from the domestic parent company. The subsidiary's assets are viewed as being acquired largely out of local borrowing. Multinational groups, therefore, consist of entities that operate independently but which contribute to a central fund of resources. Consequently, in consolidation it is believed that stockholders of the parent company are interested primarily in the parent company's net investment in the foreign subsidiary.

The Current/Historical-Rates Approach.   This approach regards the parent company and its foreign subsidiaries as a single business undertaking. Assets owned by a foreign subsidiary are viewed as indistinguishable from assets owned by the parent company. Foreign assets should, therefore, be reflected in consolidated statements in the same way that similar assets of the parent company are reported, that is, at historical cost in the parent company's currency.

Three translation methods are commonly used under this approach. The **current-noncurrent method** translates current assets and current liabilities at the current rate—the rate in effect on the balance sheet date—while noncurrent items are translated at their respective historical rates. Under the **monetary-nonmonetary method,** the current rate is used for monetary assets and liabilities—that is, for those that have a fixed, nominal value in terms of the foreign currency—while historical rates are applied to nonmonetary items. The **temporal method** is a variation of the monetary-nonmonetary method. Cash, receivables and payables, and other assets and liabilities carried at current prices (for example, marketable securities carried at current market value) are translated at the current rate of exchange. All other assets and liabilities are translated at historical rates.

Disagreement over the appropriate translation method seems likely to continue because of the different concepts of parent-subsidiary relations on which they are founded. In 1979, only six countries prescribed a single method. The temporal method was required in Austria, Canada, Bermuda, Jamaica, and the United States (under FASB *Statement No. 8*), while Uruguay required the current-rate method. Since that time the United States has changed to the current-rate method (FASB *Statement No. 52*), and Canada is reconsidering its position, a decision which will also affect Bermuda. Apart from these six nations, 24 countries, including most of Europe, Japan, and Australia, followed predominantly the current-rate approach, while in 25 countries, including Germany, South Africa, and most of Central and South America, some variation of the current/historical-rates approach was common practice.

The treatment of exchange gains and losses produced by translating items at the current rate varies and is not strictly related to the translation method used. In 1979, the predominant practice in 42 nations, including much of Europe, Latin America, Japan, and the United States, was to recognize all gains and losses immediately in income. Eighteen of these countries used the current-rate translation method and 23 followed one of the current/historical-rates methods. Alternative treatments of translation gains and losses included recording them directly in stockholders' equity (Australia), recognizing some of them immediately in income and deferring others (United Kingdom), and recognizing some in income and deferring and amortizing others over the remaining life of the items concerned (Canada and Bermuda).

Since the issuance of FASB *Statement No. 52,* the immediate recognition of translation gains and losses in income is not permitted in the United States. Instead, they are reported separately and accumulated in a separate component of stockholders' equity until the parent company's investment in the foreign subsidiary is sold or liquidated, at which time they are reported as part of the gain or loss on sale or liquidation of the investment.

■ INVENTORIES

Variations in accounting for inventories relate principally to the basis for determining cost, whether cost once determined should be increased or decreased to reflect the market value of the inventories, and whether the variable (direct) costing or the absorption (full) costing approach should be used to allocate overhead.

Determination of Cost

Although other methods are occasionally used in some countries, this text will only discuss the three principal bases for determining inventory cost: first-in, first-out (Fifo); last-in, first-out (Lifo); and average cost.

The most frequently used methods in 1979 were Fifo and average cost. Each of these methods was predominant in 31 countries, although no country required the use of one method to the exclusion of the other. Fifo was more common in Europe, although Austria, France, Greece, and Portugal used an average method. Fifo also predominated in Australia, Canada, South Africa, and the United States. The average method was generally followed in Latin America, Japan, and much of Africa. Lifo was the principal method in only one country—Italy—although it was a common minority method in Japan, the United States, most of Latin America, and several European countries. Lifo was considered an unacceptable method in Australia, Brazil, France, Ireland, Malawi, Norway, Peru, and the United Kingdom. IASC's Statement No. 2, *Valuation and Presentation of Inventories in the Context of the Historical Cost System,* supports the preference of the majority of countries and recommends the use of Fifo or average cost.

Market Value of Inventories

Only seven countries in 1979 did not require or predominantly follow the principle that inventories should be carried at the lower of cost or market value. Five of these countries, including Japan, used cost, even when cost exceeded market value. In the other two countries—Portugal and Switzerland—most enterprises wrote down inventories to amounts below both cost and market value, a practice permitted by law.

The main difference in the countries that did use the lower of cost or market approach was in the interpretation of "market value." Forty-eight countries equated it with net realizable value, meaning estimated selling price in the ordinary course of business less costs of completion and necessary selling expenses. This view was essentially required in 22 countries, including Australia, France, Ireland, South Africa, and the United Kingdom. IASC Statement No. 2 also requires this interpretation. Austria, Greece, Italy, and Venezuela interpreted market value as replacement cost—the current cost of replacing the inventories in their present condition and location.

The United States defines market value as replacement cost, with the stipulation that it cannot exceed net realizable value or fall below net realizable value reduced by the normal profit margin. In 1979, Chile, the Dominican Republic, Mexico, Panama, and the Philippines also used this interpretation of market value.

Allocation of Overhead

Recall from Chapter 22 that under direct (variable) costing, all variable manufacturing costs are charged to the product and all fixed costs (including fixed manufacturing costs) are charged to expense. Manufacturing overhead costs must, therefore, be separated into variable and fixed portions. The variable portion is assigned to production and included in inventory costs until the goods are sold, whereas the fixed portion is expensed immediately. In contrast, under absorption (full) costing all manufacturing costs, including fixed overhead costs, are applied to production and included in inventories.

Fifty-one countries in 1979 required or predominantly used absorption costing based on a level of normal capacity. IASC Statement No. 2 requires this approach. Ecuador, Ivory Coast, Malaysia, Morocco, and Senegal used direct costing, while in Botswana, the Netherlands, South Africa, and Switzerland there was no predominant practice. Chile, Denmark, India, and Malawi normally excluded all overhead—fixed and variable—from inventories.

In view of the importance of inventories and the wide variation in accounting for them, it is fortunate for the users of financial statements that most countries require disclosure of information relating to the valuation of inventories. Only 8 of the countries surveyed in 1979 did not generally disclose whether the basis of valuation was cost, market, or the lower of cost or market, while all but 13 countries usually disclosed the basis for determining cost. IASC Statement No. 2 also recommends adequate disclosure of the inventory valuation methods that were used in preparing the financial statements.

■ ACCOUNTING FOR THE EFFECTS OF CHANGING PRICES

The final example of international differences illustrates an opportunity for international harmonization that is almost unique. Accounting for the effects of inflation is still in its infancy, so it may be possible to achieve a general international approach to the problem before national practices become too varied and too entrenched.

In Chapter 13, two approaches to accounting for the effects of inflation on business enterprises were discussed: general price-level accounting and current-cost accounting. The FASB, in *Statement No. 33,* requires both methods.[6] The first approach attempts to reflect the effects of changes in general purchasing power on historical-cost financial statements, while the second is concerned with the impact of specific price changes.

A number of countries are concerned about the loss of relevance of historical-cost financial reporting in inflationary environments, and several have adopted one of the two approaches. So far only the United States and Mexico require both. Some countries, usually those with the longest history of severe inflation, have issued standards that are mandatory for all enterprises, or at least for large or publicly held entities. In other countries, the accounting profession recommends, but does not prescribe, a form of inflation-adjusted statements, usually as supplementary information. The accountancy bodies of several nations have issued exposure drafts but have not yet adopted formal standards. But few countries are prepared to abandon the historical-cost basis for their primary financial statements, at least until decision makers have had sufficient experience with inflation accounting to give an opinion on its utility. Exceptions to this view are Argentina, Brazil, and Chile, which now require incorporation of general price-level accounting in the primary financial statements of all enterprises.

The United Kingdom's standard prescribes the provision of current-cost information either in the primary financial statements or as supplementary statements or additional information. New Zealand requires a supplementary income statement and balance sheet on a current-cost basis. Australia and South Africa recommended, but do not yet require, similar supplementary current-cost statements. Germany recommends the incorporation of current-cost information in notes to the historical-cost financial statements, while in the Netherlands, some companies prepare the primary statements on a current-cost basis, and some provide only supplementary information.

The fact that the accountancy bodies of various nations are adopting neither a uniform approach nor a uniform application of any approach, even with something as relatively new as inflation accounting, highlights the difficulty of achieving international harmonization of accounting standards. Adoption of different approaches to inflation accounting by different countries will make the preparation of consolidated financial statements by multinational corporations especially difficult, while at the same time comparability of the financial reports of companies in different nations will be further reduced. But even if all countries adopted a similar approach, a major barrier to comparability would still remain: the price indices used in each country to compute adjustments for price changes are not comparable in composition, accuracy, frequency of publication, or timeliness.

Many accountants are reluctant to see inflation-adjusted statements replace historical-cost financial statements because they believe historical cost is the most objective basis of valuation. But business entities may be more likely to favor inflation accounting, once they become accustomed to it, because of its tax implications. Since inflation accounting generally leads to lower profit figures than those computed on the historical-cost basis, there is a strong incentive for companies to adopt inflation accounting in those countries where computation of the tax liability is based on reported net income. Governments, on

---

[6] FASB *Statement of Financial Accounting Standards No. 33,* "Financial Reporting and Changing Prices" (Stamford, Conn., FASB, 1979).

the other hand, may decide to prohibit the use of inflation accounting for tax purposes when a decline in tax revenues becomes apparent.

The current trend in the use of inflation-accounting approaches appears to be toward current-cost accounting and away from general price-level accounting. It has been suggested that, of the two approaches, governments prefer current-cost accounting, and this preference may influence the decisions of the accounting profession in some countries. As one British writer has pointed out,

> No government wants to have the effects of its currency debasement measured by anyone—certainly not by every business enterprise in the country. Much better to point the finger at all those individual prices moving around because of the machinations of big business, big labour and big aliens.[7]

Whether current-cost accounting will become common practice or whether some combination of current-cost and general price-level accounting will gain favor, perhaps along the lines of FASB *Statement No. 33,* should depend on the usefulness to decision makers of the information provided by each approach. One thing is clear: Unless inflation abates, more countries will adopt some form of inflation accounting. The opportunity to achieve a higher level of international harmonization while national standards are still at the development stage should not be missed.

We have attempted in these few pages to provide a broad and general picture of the variety of accounting principles and reporting practices that exist across the world. This variety is inevitable and necessary if accounting is to be useful within widely differing national business environments. At the same time, the information needs of international business must also be satisfied. It is a challenging problem and one that will receive increasing attention in the years to come.

■ SELECTED BIBLIOGRAPHY

Arthur Anderson & Co. (London). *European Review* nos. 1–5 (January 1981–May 1982).

Choi, Frederick D. S. and Gerhard G. Mueller. *An Introduction to Multinational Accounting.* Englewood Cliffs, N.J.: Prentice-Hall, Inc., 1978.

Hauworth, William P., II. "A Comparison of Various International Proposals on Inflation Accounting: A Practitioner's View." Monograph, 1980.

International Centre for Research in Accounting. *International Financial Reporting Standards: Problems and Prospects. ICRA Occasional Paper No. 13.* Lancaster, England: ICRA, University of Lancaster, 1977.

Price Waterhouse International. *International Survey of Accounting Principles and Reporting Practices,* 1979.

Stamp, Edward. *The Future of Accounting and Auditing Standards. ICRA Occasional Paper No. 18.* Lancaster, England: International Centre for Research in Accounting, University of Lancaster, 1979.

Stamp, Edward, and Maurice Moonitz. "International Auditing Standards—Parts I and II." *The CPA Journal* LII, nos. 6 and 7 (June–July 1982).

[7] P. H. Lyons, "Farewell to Historical Costs?" *CA Magazine,* February 1976, p. 23.

APPENDIX

C

Compound Interest and Annuity Tables

Table 1   *Future Value of $1 at Compound Interest: 0.5%–10%* $F_{i,n} = (1 + i)^n$

Period	.5%	1%	1.5%	2%	2.5%	3%	3.5%	4%	4.5%	5%
1	1.00500	1.01000	1.01500	1.02000	1.02500	1.03000	1.03500	1.04000	1.04500	1.05000
2	1.01003	1.02010	1.03023	1.04040	1.05063	1.06090	1.07123	1.08160	1.09203	1.10250
3	1.01508	1.03030	1.04568	1.06121	1.07689	1.09273	1.10872	1.12486	1.14117	1.15762
4	1.02015	1.04060	1.06136	1.08243	1.10381	1.12551	1.14752	1.16986	1.19252	1.21551
5	1.02525	1.05101	1.07728	1.10408	1.13141	1.15927	1.18769	1.21665	1.24618	1.27628
6	1.03038	1.06152	1.09344	1.12616	1.15969	1.19405	1.22926	1.26532	1.30226	1.34010
7	1.03553	1.07214	1.10984	1.14869	1.18869	1.22987	1.27228	1.31593	1.36086	1.40710
8	1.04071	1.08286	1.12649	1.17166	1.21840	1.26677	1.31681	1.36857	1.42210	1.47746
9	1.04591	1.09369	1.14339	1.19509	1.24886	1.30477	1.36290	1.42331	1.48610	1.55133
10	1.05114	1.10462	1.16054	1.21899	1.28008	1.34392	1.41060	1.48024	1.55297	1.62889
11	1.05640	1.11567	1.17795	1.24337	1.31209	1.38423	1.45997	1.53945	1.62285	1.71034
12	1.06168	1.12683	1.19562	1.26824	1.34489	1.42576	1.51107	1.60103	1.69588	1.79586
13	1.06699	1.13809	1.21355	1.29361	1.37851	1.46853	1.56396	1.66507	1.77220	1.88565
14	1.07232	1.14947	1.23176	1.31948	1.41297	1.51259	1.61869	1.73168	1.85194	1.97993
15	1.07768	1.16097	1.25023	1.34587	1.44830	1.55797	1.67535	1.80094	1.93528	2.07893
16	1.08307	1.17258	1.26899	1.37279	1.48451	1.60471	1.73399	1.87298	2.02237	2.18287
17	1.08849	1.18430	1.28802	1.40024	1.52162	1.65285	1.79468	1.94790	2.11338	2.29202
18	1.09393	1.19615	1.30734	1.42825	1.55966	1.70243	1.85749	2.02582	2.20848	2.40662
19	1.09940	1.20811	1.32695	1.45681	1.59865	1.75351	1.92250	2.10685	2.30786	2.52695
20	1.10490	1.22019	1.34686	1.48595	1.63862	1.80611	1.98979	2.19112	2.41171	2.65330
21	1.11042	1.23239	1.36706	1.51567	1.67958	1.86029	2.05943	2.27877	2.52024	2.78596
22	1.11597	1.24472	1.38756	1.54598	1.72157	1.91610	2.13151	2.36992	2.63365	2.92526
23	1.12155	1.25716	1.40838	1.57690	1.76461	1.97359	2.20611	2.46472	2.75217	3.07152
24	1.12716	1.26973	1.42950	1.60844	1.80873	2.03279	2.28333	2.56330	2.87601	3.22510
25	1.13280	1.28243	1.45095	1.64061	1.85394	2.09378	2.36324	2.66584	3.00543	3.38635
26	1.13846	1.29526	1.47271	1.67342	1.90029	2.15659	2.44596	2.77247	3.14068	3.55567
27	1.14415	1.30821	1.49480	1.70689	1.94780	2.22129	2.53157	2.88337	3.28201	3.73346
28	1.14987	1.32129	1.51722	1.74102	1.99650	2.28793	2.62017	2.99870	3.42970	3.92013
29	1.15562	1.33450	1.53998	1.77584	2.04641	2.35657	2.71188	3.11865	3.58404	4.11614
30	1.16140	1.34785	1.56308	1.81136	2.09757	2.42726	2.80679	3.24340	3.74532	4.32194

5.5%	6%	6.5%	7%	7.5%	8%	8.5%	9%	9.5%	10%
1.05500	1.06000	1.06500	1.07000	1.07500	1.08000	1.08500	1.09000	1.09500	1.10000
1.11303	1.12360	1.13423	1.14490	1.15563	1.16640	1.17723	1.18810	1.19903	1.21000
1.17424	1.19102	1.20795	1.22504	1.24230	1.25971	1.27729	1.29503	1.31293	1.33100
1.23882	1.26248	1.28647	1.31080	1.33547	1.36049	1.38586	1.41158	1.43766	1.46410
1.30696	1.33823	1.37009	1.40255	1.43563	1.46933	1.50366	1.53862	1.57424	1.61051
1.37884	1.41852	1.45914	1.50073	1.54330	1.58687	1.63147	1.67710	1.72379	1.77156
1.45468	1.50363	1.55399	1.60578	1.65905	1.71382	1.77014	1.82804	1.88755	1.94872
1.53469	1.59385	1.65500	1.71819	1.78348	1.85093	1.92060	1.99256	2.06687	2.14359
1.61909	1.68948	1.76257	1.83846	1.91724	1.99900	2.08386	2.17189	2.26322	2.35795
1.70814	1.79085	1.87714	1.96715	2.06103	2.15892	2.26098	2.36736	2.47823	2.59374
1.80209	1.89830	1.99915	2.10485	2.21561	2.33164	2.45317	2.58043	2.71366	2.85312
1.90121	2.01220	2.12910	2.25219	2.38178	2.51817	2.66169	2.81266	2.97146	3.13843
2.00577	2.13293	2.26749	2.40985	2.56041	2.71962	2.88793	3.06580	3.25375	3.45227
2.11609	2.26090	2.41487	2.57853	2.75244	2.93719	3.13340	3.34173	3.56285	3.79750
2.23248	2.39656	2.57184	2.75903	2.95888	3.17217	3.39974	3.64248	3.90132	4.17725
2.35526	2.54035	2.73901	2.95216	3.18079	3.42594	3.68872	3.97031	4.27195	4.59497
2.48480	2.69277	2.91705	3.15882	3.41935	3.70002	4.00226	4.32763	4.67778	5.05447
2.62147	2.85434	3.10665	3.37993	3.67580	3.99602	4.34245	4.71712	5.12217	5.55992
2.76565	3.02560	3.30859	3.61653	3.95149	4.31570	4.71156	5.14166	5.60878	6.11591
2.91776	3.20714	3.52365	3.86968	4.24785	4.66096	5.11205	5.60441	6.14161	6.72750
3.07823	3.39956	3.75268	4.14056	4.56644	5.03383	5.54657	6.10881	6.72507	7.40025
3.24754	3.60354	3.99661	4.43040	4.90892	5.43654	6.01803	6.65860	7.36395	8.14027
3.42615	3.81975	4.25639	4.74053	5.27709	5.87146	6.52956	7.25787	8.06352	8.95430
3.61459	4.04893	4.53305	5.07237	5.67287	6.34118	7.08457	7.91108	8.82956	9.84973
3.81339	4.29187	4.82770	5.42743	6.09834	6.84848	7.68676	8.62308	9.66836	10.83471
4.02313	4.54938	5.14150	5.80735	6.55572	7.39635	8.34014	9.39916	10.58686	11.91818
4.24440	4.82235	5.47570	6.21387	7.04739	7.98806	9.04905	10.24508	11.59261	13.10999
4.47784	5.11169	5.83162	6.64884	7.57595	8.62711	9.81822	11.16714	12.69391	14.42099
4.72412	5.41839	6.21067	7.11426	8.14414	9.31727	10.65277	12.17218	13.89983	15.86309
4.98395	5.74349	6.61437	7.61226	8.75496	10.06266	11.55825	13.26768	15.22031	17.44940

Table 1 *(concluded)*   *Future Value of $1 at Compound Interest: 10.5%–20%*

Period	10.5%	11%	11.5%	12%	12.5%	13%	13.5%	14%	14.5%	15%
1	1.10500	1.11000	1.11500	1.12000	1.12500	1.13000	1.13500	1.14000	1.14500	1.15000
2	1.22103	1.23210	1.24323	1.25440	1.26563	1.27690	1.28822	1.29960	1.31102	1.32250
3	1.34923	1.36763	1.38620	1.40493	1.42383	1.44290	1.46214	1.48154	1.50112	1.52088
4	1.49090	1.51807	1.54561	1.54561	1.57352	1.60181	1.63047	1.65952	1.71879	1.74901
5	1.64745	1.68506	1.72335	1.76234	1.80203	1.84244	1.88356	1.92541	1.96801	2.01136
6	1.82043	1.87041	1.92154	1.97382	2.02729	2.08195	2.13784	2.19497	2.25337	2.31306
7	2.01157	2.07616	2.14252	2.21068	2.28070	2.35261	2.42645	2.50227	2.58011	2.66002
8	2.22279	2.30454	2.38891	2.47596	2.56578	2.65844	2.75402	2.85259	2.95423	3.05902
9	2.45618	2.55804	2.66363	2.77308	2.88651	3.00404	3.12581	3.25195	3.38259	3.51788
10	2.71408	2.83942	2.96995	3.10585	3.24732	3.39457	3.54780	3.70722	3.87307	4.04556
11	2.99906	3.15176	3.31149	3.47855	3.65324	3.83586	4.02675	4.22623	4.43466	4.65239
12	3.31396	3.49845	3.69231	3.89598	4.10989	4.33452	4.57036	4.81790	5.07769	5.35025
13	3.66193	3.88328	4.11693	4.36349	4.62363	4.89801	5.18736	5.49241	5.81395	6.15279
14	4.04643	4.31044	4.59037	4.88711	5.20158	5.53475	5.88765	6.26135	6.65697	7.07571
15	4.47130	4.78459	5.11827	5.47357	5.85178	6.25427	6.68248	7.13794	7.62223	8.13706
16	4.94079	5.31089	5.70687	6.13039	6.58325	7.06733	7.58462	8.13725	8.72746	9.35762
17	5.45957	5.89509	6.36316	6.86604	7.40616	7.98608	8.60854	9.27646	9.99294	10.76126
18	6.03283	6.54355	7.09492	7.68997	8.33193	9.02427	9.77070	10.57517	11.44192	12.37545
19	6.66628	7.26334	7.91084	8.61276	9.37342	10.19742	11.08974	12.05569	13.10039	14.23177
20	7.36623	8.06231	8.82058	9.64629	10.54509	11.52309	12.58686	13.74349	15.00064	16.36654
21	8.13969	8.94917	9.83495	10.80385	11.86323	13.02109	14.28608	15.66758	17.17573	18.82152
22	8.99436	9.93357	10.96597	12.10031	13.34613	14.71383	16.21470	17.86104	19.66621	21.64475
23	9.93876	11.02627	12.22706	13.55235	15.01440	16.62663	18.40369	20.36158	22.51781	24.89146
24	10.98233	12.23916	13.63317	15.17863	16.89120	18.78809	20.88818	23.21221	25.78290	28.62518
25	12.13548	13.58546	15.20098	17.00006	19.00260	21.23054	23.70809	26.46192	29.52141	32.91895
26	13.40971	15.07986	16.94910	19.04007	21.37793	23.99051	26.90868	30.16658	33.80202	37.85680
27	14.81772	16.73865	18.89824	21.32488	24.05017	27.10928	30.54135	34.38991	38.70331	43.53531
28	16.37359	18.57990	21.07154	23.88387	27.05644	30.63349	34.66443	39.20449	44.31529	50.06561
29	18.09281	20.62369	23.49477	26.74993	30.43849	34.61584	39.34413	44.69312	50.74101	57.57545
30	19.99256	22.89230	26.19667	29.95992	34.24330	39.11590	44.65559	50.95016	58.09846	66.21177

15.5%	16%	16.5%	17%	17.5%	18%	18.5%	19%	19.5%	20%
1.15500	1.16000	1.16500	1.17000	1.17500	1.18000	1.18500	1.19000	1.19500	1.20000
1.33402	1.34560	1.35722	1.36890	1.38063	1.39240	1.40422	1.41610	1.42802	1.44000
1.54080	1.56090	1.58117	1.60161	1.62223	1.64303	1.66401	1.68516	1.70649	1.72800
1.77962	1.81064	1.84206	1.87389	1.90613	1.93878	1.97185	2.00534	2.03926	2.07360
2.05546	2.10034	2.14600	2.19245	2.23970	2.28776	2.33664	2.38635	2.43691	2.48832
2.37406	2.43640	2.50009	2.56516	2.63164	2.69955	2.76892	2.83976	2.91211	2.98598
2.74204	2.82622	2.91260	3.00124	3.09218	3.18547	3.28117	3.37932	3.47997	3.58318
3.16706	3.27841	3.39318	3.51145	3.63331	3.75886	3.88818	4.02139	4.15856	4.29982
3.65795	3.80296	3.95306	4.10840	4.26914	4.43545	4.60750	4.78545	4.96948	5.15978
4.22493	4.41144	4.60531	4.80683	5.01624	5.23384	5.45989	5.69468	5.93853	6.19174
4.87980	5.11726	5.36519	5.62399	5.89409	6.17593	6.46996	6.77667	7.09654	7.43008
5.63617	5.93603	6.25045	6.58007	6.92555	7.28759	7.66691	8.06424	8.48037	8.91610
6.50977	6.88579	7.28177	7.69868	8.13752	8.59936	9.08528	9.59645	10.13404	10.69932
7.51879	7.98752	8.48326	9.00745	9.56159	10.14724	10.76606	11.41977	12.11018	12.83918
8.68420	9.26552	9.88300	10.53872	11.23487	11.97375	12.75778	13.58953	14.47167	15.40702
10.03025	10.74800	11.51370	12.33030	13.20097	14.12902	15.11797	16.17154	17.29364	18.48843
11.58494	12.46768	13.41346	14.42646	15.51114	16.67225	17.91480	19.24413	20.66590	22.18611
13.38060	14.46251	15.62668	16.87895	18.22559	19.67325	21.22904	22.90052	24.69575	26.62333
15.45460	16.77652	18.20508	19.74838	21.41507	23.21444	25.15641	27.25162	29.51143	31.94800
17.85006	19.46076	21.20892	23.10560	25.16271	27.39303	29.81035	32.42942	35.26615	38.33760
20.61682	22.57448	24.70839	27.03355	29.56618	32.32378	35.32526	38.59101	42.14305	46.00512
23.81243	26.18640	28.78527	31.62925	34.74026	38.14206	41.86043	45.92331	50.36095	55.20614
27.50335	30.37622	33.53484	37.00623	40.81981	45.00763	49.60461	54.64873	60.18134	66.24737
31.76637	35.23642	39.06809	43.29729	47.96327	53.10901	58.78147	65.03199	71.91670	79.49685
36.69016	40.87424	45.51433	50.65783	56.35684	62.66863	69.65604	77.38807	85.94045	95.39622
42.37713	47.41412	53.02419	59.26966	66.21929	73.94898	82.54240	92.09181	102.69884	114.47546
48.94559	55.00038	61.77318	69.34550	77.80767	87.25980	97.81275	109.58925	122.72511	137.37055
56.53216	63.80044	71.96576	81.13423	91.42401	102.96656	115.90811	130.41121	146.65651	164.84466
65.29464	74.00851	83.84011	94.92705	107.42321	121.50054	137.35111	155.18934	175.25453	197.81359
75.41531	85.84988	97.67373	111.06465	126.22227	143.37064	162.76106	184.67531	209.42916	237.37631

Table 2 *Future Value of an Ordinary Annuity of $1 per Period: 0.5%–10%* $F_{A_{i,n}} = \dfrac{(1+i)^n - 1}{i}$

Period	.5%	1%	1.5%	2%	2.5%	3%	3.5%	4%	4.5%	5%
1	1.00000	1.00000	1.00000	1.00000	1.00000	1.00000	1.00000	1.00000	1.00000	1.00000
2	2.00500	2.01000	2.01500	2.02000	2.02500	2.03000	2.03500	2.04000	2.04500	2.05000
3	3.01502	3.03010	3.04522	3.06040	3.07562	3.09090	3.10622	3.12160	3.13702	3.15250
4	4.03010	4.06040	4.09090	4.12161	4.15252	4.18363	4.21494	4.24646	4.27819	4.31012
5	5.05025	5.10101	5.15227	5.20404	5.25633	5.30914	5.36247	5.41632	5.47071	5.52563
6	6.07550	6.15202	6.22955	6.30812	6.38774	6.46841	6.55015	6.63298	6.71689	6.80191
7	7.10588	7.21354	7.32299	7.43428	7.54743	7.66246	7.77941	7.89829	8.01915	8.14201
8	8.14141	8.28567	8.43284	8.58297	8.73612	8.89234	9.05169	9.21423	9.38001	9.54911
9	9.18212	9.36853	9.55933	9.75463	9.95452	10.15911	10.36850	10.58280	10.80211	11.02656
10	10.22803	10.46221	10.70272	10.94972	11.20338	11.46388	11.73139	12.00611	12.28821	12.57789
11	11.27917	11.56683	11.86326	12.16872	12.48347	12.80780	13.14199	13.48635	13.84118	14.20679
12	12.33556	12.68250	13.04121	13.41209	13.79555	14.19203	14.60196	15.02581	15.46403	15.91713
13	13.39724	13.80933	14.23683	14.68033	15.14044	15.61779	16.11303	16.62684	17.15991	17.71298
14	14.46423	14.94742	15.45038	15.97394	16.51895	17.08632	17.67699	18.29191	18.93211	19.59863
15	15.53655	16.09690	16.68214	17.29342	17.93193	18.59891	19.29568	20.02359	20.78405	21.57856
16	16.61423	17.25786	17.93237	18.63929	19.38022	20.15688	20.97103	21.82453	22.71934	23.65749
17	17.69730	18.43044	19.20136	20.01207	20.86473	21.76159	22.70502	23.69751	24.74171	25.84037
18	18.78579	19.61475	20.48938	21.41231	22.38635	23.41444	24.49969	25.64541	26.85508	28.13238
19	19.87972	20.81090	21.79672	22.84056	23.94601	25.11687	26.35718	27.67123	29.06356	30.53900
20	20.97912	22.01900	23.12367	24.29737	25.54466	26.87037	28.27968	29.77808	31.37142	33.06595
21	22.08401	23.23919	24.47052	25.78332	27.18327	28.67649	30.26947	31.96920	33.78314	35.71925
22	23.19443	24.47159	25.83758	27.29898	28.86286	30.53678	32.32890	34.24797	36.30338	38.50521
23	24.31040	25.71630	27.22514	28.84496	30.58443	32.45288	34.46041	36.61789	38.93703	41.43048
24	25.43196	26.97346	28.63352	30.42186	32.34904	34.42647	36.66653	39.08260	41.68920	44.50200
25	26.55912	28.24320	30.06302	32.03030	34.15776	36.45926	38.94986	41.64591	44.56521	47.72710
26	27.69191	29.52563	31.51397	33.67091	36.01171	38.55304	41.31310	44.31174	47.57064	51.11345
27	28.83037	30.82089	32.98668	35.34432	37.91200	40.70963	43.75906	47.08421	50.71132	54.66913
28	29.97452	32.12910	34.48148	37.05121	39.85980	42.93092	46.29063	49.96758	53.99333	58.40258
29	31.12439	33.45039	35.99870	38.79223	41.85630	45.21885	48.91080	52.96629	57.42303	62.32271
30	32.28002	34.78489	37.53868	40.56808	43.90270	47.57542	51.62268	56.08494	61.00707	66.43885

5.5%	6%	6.5%	7%	7.5%	8%	8.5%	9%	9.5%	10%
1.00000	1.00000	1.00000	1.00000	1.00000	1.00000	1.00000	1.00000	1.00000	1.00000
2.05500	2.06000	2.06500	2.07000	2.07500	2.08000	2.08500	2.09000	2.09500	2.10000
3.16802	3.18360	3.19922	3.21490	3.23062	3.24640	3.26222	3.27810	3.29402	3.31000
4.34227	4.37462	4.40717	4.43994	4.47292	4.50611	4.53951	4.57313	4.60696	4.64100
5.58109	5.63709	5.69364	5.75074	5.80839	5.86660	5.92537	5.98471	6.04462	6.10510
6.88805	6.97532	7.06373	7.15329	7.24402	7.33593	7.42903	7.52333	7.61886	7.71561
8.26689	8.39384	8.52287	8.65402	8.78732	8.92280	9.06050	9.20043	9.34265	9.48717
9.72157	9.89747	10.07686	10.25980	10.44637	10.63663	10.83064	11.02847	11.23020	11.43589
11.25626	11.49132	11.73185	11.97799	12.22985	12.48756	12.75124	13.02104	13.29707	13.57948
12.87535	13.18079	13.49442	13.81645	14.14709	14.48656	14.83510	15.19293	15.56029	15.93742
14.58350	14.97164	15.37156	15.78360	16.20812	16.64549	17.09608	17.56029	18.03852	18.53117
16.38559	16.86994	17.37071	17.88845	18.42373	18.97713	19.54925	20.14072	20.75218	21.38428
18.28680	18.88214	19.49981	20.14064	20.80551	21.49530	22.21094	22.95338	23.72363	24.52271
20.29257	21.01507	21.76730	22.55049	23.36592	24.21492	25.09887	26.01919	26.97738	27.97498
22.40866	23.27597	24.18217	25.12902	26.11836	27.15211	28.23227	29.36092	30.54023	31.77248
24.64114	25.67253	26.75401	27.88805	29.07724	30.32428	31.63201	33.00340	34.44155	35.94973
26.99640	28.21288	29.49302	30.84022	32.25804	33.75023	35.32073	36.97370	38.71350	40.54470
29.48120	30.90565	32.41007	33.99903	35.67739	37.45024	39.32300	41.30134	43.39128	45.59917
32.10267	33.75999	35.51672	37.37896	39.35319	41.44626	43.66545	46.01846	48.51345	51.15909
34.86832	36.78559	38.82531	40.99549	43.30468	45.76196	48.37701	51.16012	54.12223	57.27500
37.78608	39.99273	42.34895	44.86518	47.55253	50.42292	53.48906	56.76453	60.26384	64.00250
40.86431	43.39229	46.10164	49.00574	52.11897	55.45676	59.03563	62.87334	66.98891	71.40275
44.11185	46.99583	50.09824	53.43614	57.02790	60.89330	65.05366	69.53194	74.35286	79.54302
47.53800	50.81558	54.35463	58.17667	62.30499	66.76476	71.58322	76.78981	82.41638	88.49733
51.15259	54.86451	58.88768	63.24904	67.97786	73.10594	78.66779	84.70090	91.24593	98.34706
54.96598	59.15638	63.71538	68.67647	74.07620	79.95442	86.35455	93.32398	100.91430	109.18177
58.98911	63.70577	68.85688	74.48382	80.63192	87.35077	94.69469	102.72313	111.50116	121.09994
63.23351	68.52811	74.33257	80.69769	87.67931	95.33883	103.74374	112.96822	123.09377	134.20994
67.71135	73.63980	80.16419	87.34653	95.25526	103.96594	113.56196	124.13536	135.78767	148.63093
72.43548	79.05819	86.37486	94.46079	103.39940	113.28321	124.21473	136.30754	149.68750	164.49402

Table 2 *(concluded)* *Future Value of an Ordinary Annuity of $1 per Period: 10.5%–20%*

Period	10.5%	11%	11.5%	12%	12.5%	13%	13.5%	14%	14.5%	15%
1 . . .	1.00000	1.00000	1.00000	1.00000	1.00000	1.00000	1.00000	1.00000	1.00000	1.00000
2 . . .	2.10500	2.11000	2.11500	2.12000	2.12500	2.13000	2.13500	2.14000	2.14500	2.15000
3 . . .	3.32602	3.34210	3.35822	3.37440	3.39062	3.40690	3.42322	3.43960	3.45602	3.47250
4 . . .	4.67526	4.70973	4.74442	4.77933	4.81445	4.84980	4.88536	4.92114	4.95715	4.99337
5 . . .	6.16616	6.22780	6.29003	6.35285	6.41626	6.48027	6.54488	6.61010	6.67594	6.74238
6 . . .	7.81361	7.91286	8.01338	8.11519	8.21829	8.32271	8.42844	8.53552	8.64395	8.75374
7 . . .	9.63404	9.78327	9.93492	10.08901	10.24558	10.40466	10.56628	10.73049	10.89732	11.06680
8 . . .	11.64561	11.85943	12.07744	12.29969	12.52628	12.75726	12.99273	13.23276	13.47743	13.72682
9 . . .	13.86840	14.16397	14.46634	14.77566	15.09206	15.41571	15.74675	16.08535	16.43166	16.78584
10 . . .	16.32458	16.72201	17.12997	17.54874	17.97857	18.41975	18.87256	19.33730	19.81425	20.30372
11 . . .	19.03866	19.56143	20.09992	20.65458	21.22589	21.81432	22.42036	23.04452	23.68731	24.34928
12 . . .	22.03772	22.71319	23.41141	24.13313	24.87913	25.65018	26.44711	27.27075	28.12197	29.00167
13 . . .	25.35168	26.21164	27.10372	28.02911	28.98902	29.98470	31.01746	32.08865	33.19966	34.35192
14 .:.	29.01361	30.09492	31.22065	32.39260	33.61264	34.88271	36.20482	37.58107	39.01361	40.50471
15 . . .	33.06004	34.40536	35.81102	37.27971	38.81422	40.41746	42.09247	43.84241	45.67058	47.58041
16 . . .	37.53134	39.18995	40.92929	42.75328	44.66600	46.67173	48.77496	50.98035	53.29282	55.71747
17 . . .	42.47213	44.50084	46.63616	48.88367	51.24925	53.73906	56.35958	59.11760	62.02027	65.07509
18 . . .	47.93170	50.39594	52.99932	55.74971	58.65541	61.72514	64.96812	68.39407	72.01321	75.83636
19 . . .	53.96453	56.93949	60.09424	63.43968	66.98733	70.74941	74.73882	78.96923	83.45513	88.21181
20 . . .	60.63081	64.20283	68.00508	72.05244	76.36075	80.94683	85.82856	91.02493	96.55612	102.44358
21 . . .	67.99704	72.26514	76.82566	81.69874	86.90584	92.46992	98.41541	104.76842	111.55676	118.81012
22 . . .	76.13673	81.21431	86.66062	92.50258	98.76908	105.49101	112.70149	120.43600	128.73249	137.63164
23 . . .	85.13109	91.14788	97.62659	104.60289	112.11521	120.20484	128.91619	138.29704	148.39871	159.27638
24 . . .	95.06985	102.17415	109.85364	118.15524	127.12961	136.83147	147.31988	158.65862	170.91652	184.16784
25 . . .	106.05219	114.41331	123.48681	133.33387	144.02081	155.61956	168.20806	181.87083	196.69941	212.79302
26 . . .	118.18767	127.99877	138.68780	150.33393	163.02341	176.85010	191.91615	208.33274	226.22083	245.71197
27 . . .	131.59737	143.07864	155.63689	169.37401	184.40134	200.84061	218.82483	238.49933	260.02285	283.56877
28 . . .	146.41510	159.81729	174.53513	190.69889	208.45151	227.94989	249.36618	272.88923	298.72616	327.10408
29 . . .	162.78868	178.39719	195.60668	214.58275	235.50795	258.58338	284.03062	312.09373	343.04145	377.16969
30 . . .	180.88149	199.02088	219.10144	241.33268	265.94644	293.19922	323.37475	356.78685	393.78246	434.74515

15.5%	16%	16.5%	17%	17.5%	18%	18.5%	19%	19.5%	20%
1.00000	1.00000	1.00000	1.00000	1.00000	1.00000	1.00000	1.00000	1.00000	1.00000
2.15500	2.16000	2.16500	2.17000	2.17500	2.18000	2.18500	2.19000	2.19500	2.20000
3.48902	3.50560	3.52222	3.53890	3.55562	3.57240	3.58922	3.60610	3.62302	3.64000
5.02982	5.06650	5.10339	5.14051	5.17786	5.21543	5.25323	5.29126	5.32951	5.36800
6.80945	6.87714	6.94545	7.01440	7.08398	7.15421	7.22508	7.29660	7.36877	7.44160
8.86491	8.97748	9.09145	9.20685	9.32368	9.44197	9.56172	9.68295	9.80568	9.92992
11.23897	11.41387	11.59154	11.77201	11.95533	12.14152	12.33064	12.52271	12.71779	12.91590
13.98101	14.24009	14.50415	14.77325	15.04751	15.32700	15.61181	15.90203	16.19776	16.49908
17.14807	17.51851	17.89733	18.28471	18.68082	19.08585	19.49999	19.92341	20.35632	20.79890
20.80602	21.32147	21.85039	22.39311	22.94997	23.52131	24.10749	24.70886	25.32580	25.95868
25.03095	25.73290	26.45570	27.19994	27.96621	28.75514	29.56737	30.40355	31.26433	32.15042
29.91075	30.85017	31.82089	32.82393	33.86030	34.93107	36.03734	37.18022	38.36088	39.58050
35.54692	36.78620	38.07134	39.40399	40.78585	42.21866	43.70424	45.24446	46.84125	48.49660
42.05669	43.67199	45.35311	47.10267	48.92337	50.81802	52.78953	54.84091	56.97529	59.19592
49.57548	51.65951	53.83638	56.11013	58.48496	60.96527	63.55559	66.26068	69.08547	72.03511
58.25968	60.92503	63.71938	66.64885	69.71983	72.93901	76.31338	79.85021	83.55714	87.44213
68.28993	71.67303	75.23307	78.97915	82.92080	87.06804	91.43135	96.02175	100.85079	105.93056
79.87486	84.14072	88.64653	93.40561	98.43194	103.74028	109.34615	115.26588	121.51669	128.11667
93.25547	98.60323	104.27321	110.28456	116.65753	123.41353	130.57519	138.16640	146.21244	154.74000
108.71007	115.37975	122.47829	130.03294	138.07260	146.62797	155.73160	165.41802	175.72387	186.68800
126.56013	134.84051	143.68721	153.13854	163.23531	174.02100	185.54194	197.84744	210.99002	225.02560
147.17695	157.41499	168.39560	180.17209	192.80149	206.34479	220.86720	236.43846	253.13308	271.03072
170.98937	183.60138	197.18087	211.80134	227.54175	244.48685	262.72763	282.36176	303.49403	326.23686
198.49272	213.97761	230.71571	248.80757	268.36155	289.49448	312.33225	337.01050	363.67536	392.48424
230.25910	249.21402	269.78381	292.10486	316.32482	342.60349	371.11371	402.04249	435.59206	471.98108
266.94926	290.08827	315.29813	342.76268	372.68167	405.27211	440.76975	479.43056	521.53251	567.37730
309.32639	337.50239	368.32233	402.03234	438.90096	479.22109	523.31215	571.52237	624.23135	681.85276
358.27198	392.50277	430.09551	471.37783	516.70863	566.48089	621.12490	681.11162	746.95647	819.22331
414.80414	456.30322	502.06127	552.51207	608.13264	669.44745	737.03300	811.52283	893.61298	984.06797
480.09878	530.31173	585.90138	647.43912	715.55585	790.94799	874.38411	966.71217	1068.86751	1181.88157

Table 3 Present Value of $1 at Compound Interest: 0.5%–7%

$$P_{i,n} = \frac{1}{(1+i)^n}$$

Period	.5%	1%	1.5%	2%	2.5%	3%	3.5%	4%	4.5%	5%	5.5%	6%	6.5%	7%
1 ...	0.99502	0.99010	0.98522	0.98039	0.97561	0.97087	0.96618	0.96154	0.95694	0.95238	0.94787	0.94340	0.93897	0.93458
2 ...	0.99007	0.98030	0.97066	0.96117	0.95181	0.94260	0.93351	0.92456	0.91573	0.90703	0.89845	0.89000	0.88166	0.87344
3 ...	0.98515	0.97059	0.95632	0.94232	0.92860	0.91514	0.90194	0.88900	0.87630	0.86384	0.85161	0.83962	0.82785	0.81630
4 ...	0.98025	0.96098	0.94218	0.92385	0.90595	0.88849	0.87144	0.85480	0.83856	0.82270	0.80722	0.79209	0.77732	0.76290
5 ...	0.97537	0.95147	0.92826	0.90573	0.88385	0.86261	0.84197	0.82193	0.80245	0.78353	0.76513	0.74726	0.72988	0.71299
6 ...	0.97052	0.94205	0.91454	0.88797	0.86230	0.83748	0.81350	0.79031	0.76790	0.74622	0.72525	0.70496	0.68533	0.66634
7 ...	0.96569	0.93272	0.90103	0.87056	0.84127	0.81309	0.78599	0.75992	0.73483	0.71068	0.68744	0.66506	0.64351	0.62275
8 ...	0.96089	0.92348	0.88771	0.85349	0.82075	0.78941	0.75941	0.73069	0.70319	0.67684	0.65160	0.62741	0.60423	0.58201
9 ...	0.95610	0.91434	0.87459	0.83676	0.80073	0.76642	0.73373	0.70259	0.67290	0.64461	0.61763	0.59190	0.56735	0.54393
10 ...	0.95135	0.90529	0.86167	0.82035	0.78120	0.74409	0.70892	0.67556	0.64393	0.61391	0.58543	0.55839	0.53273	0.50835
11 ...	0.94661	0.89632	0.84893	0.80426	0.76214	0.72242	0.68495	0.64958	0.61620	0.58468	0.55491	0.52679	0.50021	0.47509
12 ...	0.94191	0.88745	0.83639	0.78849	0.74356	0.70138	0.66178	0.62460	0.58966	0.55684	0.52598	0.49697	0.46968	0.44401
13 ...	0.93722	0.87866	0.82403	0.77303	0.72542	0.68095	0.63940	0.60057	0.56427	0.53032	0.49856	0.46884	0.44102	0.41496
14 ...	0.93256	0.86996	0.81185	0.75788	0.70773	0.66112	0.61778	0.57748	0.53997	0.50507	0.47257	0.44230	0.41410	0.38782
15 ...	0.92792	0.86135	0.79985	0.74301	0.69047	0.64186	0.59689	0.55526	0.51672	0.48102	0.44793	0.41727	0.38883	0.36245
16 ...	0.92330	0.85282	0.78803	0.72845	0.67362	0.62317	0.57671	0.53391	0.49447	0.45811	0.42458	0.39365	0.36510	0.33873
17 ...	0.91871	0.84438	0.77639	0.71416	0.65720	0.60502	0.55720	0.51337	0.47318	0.43630	0.40245	0.37136	0.34281	0.31657
18 ...	0.91414	0.83602	0.76491	0.70016	0.64117	0.58739	0.53836	0.49363	0.45280	0.41552	0.38147	0.35034	0.32189	0.29586
19 ...	0.90959	0.82774	0.75361	0.68643	0.62553	0.57029	0.52016	0.47464	0.43330	0.39573	0.36158	0.33051	0.30224	0.27651
20 ...	0.90506	0.81954	0.74247	0.67297	0.61027	0.55368	0.50257	0.45639	0.41464	0.37689	0.34273	0.31180	0.28380	0.25842
21 ...	0.90056	0.81143	0.73150	0.65978	0.59539	0.53755	0.48557	0.43883	0.39679	0.35894	0.32486	0.29416	0.26648	0.24151
22 ...	0.89608	0.80340	0.72069	0.64684	0.58086	0.52189	0.46915	0.42196	0.37970	0.34185	0.30793	0.27751	0.25021	0.22571
23 ...	0.89162	0.79544	0.71004	0.63416	0.56670	0.50669	0.45329	0.40573	0.36335	0.32557	0.29187	0.26180	0.23494	0.21095
24 ...	0.88719	0.78757	0.69954	0.62172	0.55288	0.49193	0.43796	0.39012	0.34770	0.31007	0.27666	0.24698	0.22060	0.19715
25 ...	0.88277	0.77977	0.68921	0.60953	0.53939	0.47761	0.42315	0.37512	0.33273	0.29530	0.26223	0.23300	0.20714	0.18425
26 ...	0.87838	0.77205	0.67902	0.59758	0.52623	0.46369	0.40884	0.36069	0.31840	0.28124	0.24856	0.21981	0.19450	0.17220
27 ...	0.87401	0.76440	0.66899	0.58586	0.51340	0.45019	0.39501	0.34682	0.30469	0.26785	0.23560	0.20737	0.18263	0.16093
28 ...	0.86966	0.75684	0.65910	0.57437	0.50088	0.43708	0.38165	0.33348	0.29157	0.25509	0.22332	0.19563	0.17148	0.15040
29 ...	0.86533	0.74934	0.64936	0.56311	0.48866	0.42435	0.36875	0.32065	0.27902	0.24295	0.21168	0.18456	0.16101	0.14056
30 ...	0.86103	0.74192	0.63976	0.55207	0.47674	0.41199	0.35628	0.30832	0.26700	0.23138	0.20064	0.17411	0.15119	0.13137
31 ...	0.85675	0.73458	0.63031	0.54125	0.46511	0.39999	0.34423	0.29646	0.25550	0.22036	0.19018	0.16425	0.14196	0.12277
32 ...	0.85248	0.72730	0.62099	0.53063	0.45377	0.38834	0.33259	0.28506	0.24450	0.20987	0.18027	0.15496	0.13329	0.11474
33 ...	0.84824	0.72010	0.61182	0.52023	0.44270	0.37703	0.32134	0.27409	0.23397	0.19987	0.17087	0.14619	0.12516	0.10723
34 ...	0.84402	0.71297	0.60277	0.51003	0.43191	0.36604	0.31048	0.26355	0.22390	0.19035	0.16196	0.13791	0.11752	0.10022
35 ...	0.83982	0.70591	0.59387	0.50003	0.42137	0.35538	0.29998	0.25342	0.21425	0.18129	0.15352	0.13011	0.11035	0.09366
36 ...	0.83564	0.69892	0.58509	0.49022	0.41109	0.34503	0.28983	0.24367	0.20503	0.17266	0.14552	0.12274	0.10361	0.08754
37 ...	0.83149	0.69200	0.57644	0.48061	0.40107	0.33498	0.28003	0.23430	0.19620	0.16444	0.13793	0.11579	0.09729	0.08181
38 ...	0.82735	0.68515	0.56792	0.47119	0.39128	0.32523	0.27056	0.22529	0.18775	0.15661	0.13074	0.10924	0.09135	0.07646
39 ...	0.82323	0.67837	0.55953	0.46195	0.38174	0.31575	0.26141	0.21662	0.17967	0.14915	0.12392	0.10306	0.08578	0.07146
40 ...	0.81914	0.67165	0.55126	0.45289	0.37243	0.30656	0.25257	0.20829	0.17193	0.14205	0.11746	0.09722	0.08054	0.06678
41 ...	0.81506	0.66500	0.54312	0.44401	0.36335	0.29763	0.24403	0.20028	0.16453	0.13528	0.11134	0.09172	0.07563	0.06241
42 ...	0.81101	0.65842	0.53509	0.43530	0.35448	0.28896	0.23578	0.19257	0.15744	0.12884	0.10554	0.08653	0.07101	0.05833
43 ...	0.80697	0.65190	0.52718	0.42677	0.34584	0.28054	0.22781	0.18517	0.15066	0.12270	0.10003	0.08163	0.06668	0.05451
44 ...	0.80296	0.64545	0.51939	0.41840	0.33740	0.27237	0.22010	0.17805	0.14417	0.11686	0.09482	0.07701	0.06261	0.05095
45 ...	0.79896	0.63905	0.51171	0.41020	0.32917	0.26444	0.21266	0.17120	0.13796	0.11130	0.08988	0.07265	0.05879	0.04761
46 ...	0.79499	0.63273	0.50415	0.40215	0.32115	0.25674	0.20547	0.16461	0.13202	0.10600	0.08519	0.06854	0.05520	0.04450
47 ...	0.79103	0.62646	0.49670	0.39427	0.31331	0.24926	0.19852	0.15828	0.12634	0.10095	0.08075	0.06466	0.05183	0.04159
48 : ..	0.78710	0.62026	0.48936	0.38654	0.30567	0.24200	0.19181	0.15219	0.12090	0.09614	0.07654	0.06100	0.04867	0.03887
49 ...	0.78318	0.61412	0.48213	0.37896	0.29822	0.23495	0.18532	0.14634	0.11569	0.09156	0.07255	0.05755	0.04570	0.03632
50 ...	0.77929	0.60804	0.47500	0.37153	0.29094	0.22811	0.17905	0.14071	0.11071	0.08720	0.06877	0.05429	0.04291	0.03395
51 ...	0.77541	0.60202	0.46798	0.36424	0.28385	0.22146	0.17300	0.13530	0.10594	0.08305	0.06518	0.05122	0.04029	0.03173
52 ...	0.77155	0.59606	0.46107	0.35710	0.27692	0.21501	0.16715	0.13010	0.10138	0.07910	0.06178	0.04832	0.03783	0.02965
53 ...	0.76771	0.59016	0.45426	0.35010	0.27017	0.20875	0.16150	0.12509	0.09701	0.07533	0.05856	0.04558	0.03552	0.02771
54 ...	0.76389	0.58431	0.44754	0.34323	0.26358	0.20267	0.15603	0.12028	0.09284	0.07174	0.05551	0.04300	0.03335	0.02590
55 ...	0.76009	0.57853	0.44093	0.33650	0.25715	0.19677	0.15076	0.11566	0.08884	0.06833	0.05262	0.04057	0.03132	0.02420
56 ...	0.75631	0.57280	0.43441	0.32991	0.25088	0.19104	0.14566	0.11121	0.08501	0.06507	0.04987	0.03827	0.02941	0.02262
57 ...	0.75255	0.56713	0.42799	0.32344	0.24476	0.18547	0.14073	0.10693	0.08135	0.06197	0.04727	0.03610	0.02761	0.02114
58 ...	0.74880	0.56151	0.42167	0.31710	0.23879	0.18007	0.13598	0.10282	0.07785	0.05902	0.04481	0.03406	0.02593	0.01976
59 ...	0.74508	0.55595	0.41544	0.31088	0.23297	0.17483	0.13138	0.09886	0.07450	0.05621	0.04247	0.03213	0.02434	0.01847
60 ...	0.74137	0.55045	0.40930	0.30478	0.22728	0.16973	0.12693	0.09506	0.07129	0.05354	0.04026	0.03031	0.02286	0.01726

Period	.5%	1%	1.5%	2%	2.5%	3%	3.5%	4%	4.5%	5%	5.5%	6%	6.5%	7%
61 ..	0.73768	0.54500	0.40325	0.29881	0.22174	0.16479	0.12264	0.09140	0.06822	0.05099	0.03816	0.02860	0.02146	0.01613
62 ..	0.73401	0.53960	0.39729	0.29295	0.21633	0.15999	0.11849	0.08789	0.06528	0.04856	0.03617	0.02698	0.02015	0.01507
63 ..	0.73036	0.53426	0.39142	0.28720	0.21106	0.15533	0.11449	0.08451	0.06247	0.04625	0.03428	0.02545	0.01892	0.01409
64 ..	0.72673	0.52897	0.38563	0.28157	0.20591	0.15081	0.11062	0.08126	0.05978	0.04404	0.03250	0.02401	0.01777	0.01317
65 ..	0.72311	0.52373	0.37993	0.27605	0.20089	0.14641	0.10688	0.07813	0.05721	0.04195	0.03080	0.02265	0.01668	0.01230
66 ..	0.71952	0.51855	0.37432	0.27064	0.19599	0.14215	0.10326	0.07513	0.05474	0.03995	0.02920	0.02137	0.01566	0.01150
67 ..	0.71594	0.51341	0.36879	0.26533	0.19121	0.13801	0.09977	0.07224	0.05239	0.03805	0.02767	0.02016	0.01471	0.01075
68 ..	0.71237	0.50833	0.36334	0.26013	0.18654	0.13399	0.09640	0.06946	0.05013	0.03623	0.02623	0.01902	0.01381	0.01004
69 ..	0.70883	0.50330	0.35797	0.25503	0.18199	0.13009	0.09314	0.06679	0.04797	0.03451	0.02486	0.01794	0.01297	0.00939
70 ..	0.70530	0.49831	0.35268	0.25003	0.17755	0.12630	0.08999	0.06422	0.04590	0.03287	0.02357	0.01693	0.01218	0.00877
71 ..	0.70179	0.49338	0.34746	0.24513	0.17322	0.12262	0.08694	0.06175	0.04393	0.03130	0.02234	0.01597	0.01143	0.00820
72 ..	0.69830	0.48850	0.34233	0.24032	0.16900	0.11905	0.08400	0.05937	0.04204	0.02981	0.02117	0.01507	0.01074	0.00766
73 ..	0.69483	0.48366	0.33727	0.23561	0.16488	0.11558	0.08116	0.05709	0.04023	0.02839	0.02007	0.01421	0.01008	0.00716
74 ..	0.69137	0.47887	0.33229	0.23099	0.16085	0.11221	0.07842	0.05490	0.03849	0.02704	0.01902	0.01341	0.00947	0.00669
75 ..	0.68793	0.47413	0.32738	0.22646	0.15693	0.10895	0.07577	0.05278	0.03684	0.02575	0.01803	0.01265	0.00889	0.00625
76 ..	0.68451	0.46944	0.32254	0.22202	0.15310	0.10577	0.07320	0.05075	0.03525	0.02453	0.01709	0.01193	0.00835	0.00585
77 ..	0.68110	0.46479	0.31777	0.21766	0.14937	0.10269	0.07073	0.04880	0.03373	0.02336	0.01620	0.01126	0.00784	0.00546
78 ..	0.67772	0.46019	0.31308	0.21340	0.14573	0.09970	0.06834	0.04692	0.03228	0.02225	0.01536	0.01062	0.00736	0.00511
79 ..	0.67434	0.45563	0.30845	0.20921	0.14217	0.09680	0.06603	0.04512	0.03089	0.02119	0.01456	0.01002	0.00691	0.00477
80 ..	0.67099	0.45112	0.30389	0.20511	0.13870	0.09398	0.06379	0.04338	0.02956	0.02018	0.01380	0.00945	0.00649	0.00446
81 ..	0.66765	0.44665	0.29940	0.20109	0.13532	0.09124	0.06164	0.04172	0.02829	0.01922	0.01308	0.00892	0.00609	0.00417
82 ..	0.66433	0.44223	0.29497	0.19715	0.13202	0.08858	0.05955	0.04011	0.02707	0.01830	0.01240	0.00841	0.00572	0.00390
83 ..	0.66102	0.43785	0.29062	0.19328	0.12880	0.08600	0.05754	0.03857	0.02590	0.01743	0.01175	0.00794	0.00537	0.00364
84 ..	0.65773	0.43352	0.28632	0.18949	0.12566	0.08350	0.05559	0.03709	0.02479	0.01660	0.01114	0.00749	0.00504	0.00340
85 ..	0.65446	0.42922	0.28209	0.18577	0.12259	0.08107	0.05371	0.03566	0.02372	0.01581	0.01056	0.00706	0.00473	0.00318
86 ..	0.65121	0.42497	0.27792	0.18213	0.11960	0.07870	0.05190	0.03429	0.02270	0.01506	0.01001	0.00666	0.00445	0.00297
87 ..	0.64797	0.42077	0.27381	0.17856	0.11669	0.07641	0.05014	0.03297	0.02172	0.01434	0.00948	0.00629	0.00417	0.00278
88 ..	0.64474	0.41660	0.26977	0.17506	0.11384	0.07419	0.04845	0.03170	0.02079	0.01366	0.00899	0.00593	0.00392	0.00260
89 ..	0.64154	0.41248	0.26578	0.17163	0.11106	0.07203	0.04681	0.03048	0.01989	0.01301	0.00852	0.00559	0.00368	0.00243
90 ..	0.63834	0.40839	0.26185	0.16826	0.10836	0.06993	0.04522	0.02931	0.01903	0.01239	0.00808	0.00528	0.00346	0.00227
91 ..	0.63517	0.40435	0.25798	0.16496	0.10571	0.06789	0.04369	0.02818	0.01821	0.01180	0.00766	0.00498	0.00324	0.00212
92 ..	0.63201	0.40034	0.25417	0.16173	0.10313	0.06591	0.04222	0.02710	0.01743	0.01124	0.00726	0.00470	0.00305	0.00198
93 ..	0.62886	0.39638	0.25041	0.15856	0.10062	0.06399	0.04079	0.02606	0.01668	0.01070	0.00688	0.00443	0.00286	0.00185
94 ..	0.62573	0.39246	0.24671	0.15545	0.09816	0.06213	0.03941	0.02505	0.01596	0.01019	0.00652	0.00418	0.00269	0.00173
95 ..	0.62262	0.38857	0.24307	0.15240	0.09577	0.06032	0.03808	0.02409	0.01527	0.00971	0.00618	0.00394	0.00252	0.00162
96 ..	0.61952	0.38472	0.23947	0.14941	0.09343	0.05856	0.03679	0.02316	0.01462	0.00924	0.00586	0.00372	0.00237	0.00151
97 ..	0.61644	0.38091	0.23594	0.14648	0.09116	0.05686	0.03555	0.02227	0.01399	0.00880	0.00555	0.00351	0.00222	0.00141
98 ..	0.61337	0.37714	0.23245	0.14361	0.08893	0.05520	0.03434	0.02142	0.01338	0.00838	0.00526	0.00331	0.00209	0.00132
99 ..	0.61032	0.37341	0.22901	0.14079	0.08676	0.05359	0.03318	0.02059	0.01281	0.00798	0.00499	0.00312	0.00196	0.00123
100 ..	0.60729	0.36971	0.22563	0.13803	0.08465	0.05203	0.03206	0.01980	0.01226	0.00760	0.00473	0.00295	0.00184	0.00115
101 ..	0.60427	0.36605	0.22230	0.13533	0.08258	0.05052	0.03098	0.01904	0.01173	0.00724	0.00448	0.00278	0.00173	0.00108
102 ..	0.60126	0.36243	0.21901	0.13267	0.08057	0.04905	0.02993	0.01831	0.01122	0.00690	0.00425	0.00262	0.00162	0.00101
103 ..	0.59827	0.35884	0.21577	0.13007	0.07860	0.04762	0.02892	0.01760	0.01074	0.00657	0.00403	0.00247	0.00152	0.00094
104 ..	0.59529	0.35529	0.21258	0.12752	0.07669	0.04623	0.02794	0.01693	0.01028	0.00626	0.00382	0.00233	0.00143	0.00088
105 ..	0.59233	0.35177	0.20944	0.12502	0.07482	0.04488	0.02699	0.01627	0.00984	0.00596	0.00362	0.00220	0.00134	0.00082
106 ..	0.58938	0.34828	0.20635	0.12257	0.07299	0.04358	0.02608	0.01565	0.00941	0.00567	0.00343	0.00208	0.00126	0.00077
107 ..	0.58645	0.34484	0.20330	0.12017	0.07121	0.04231	0.02520	0.01505	0.00901	0.00540	0.00325	0.00196	0.00118	0.00072
108 ..	0.58353	0.34142	0.20029	0.11781	0.06947	0.04108	0.02435	0.01447	0.00862	0.00515	0.00308	0.00185	0.00111	0.00067
109 ..	0.58063	0.33804	0.19733	0.11550	0.06778	0.03988	0.02352	0.01391	0.00825	0.00490	0.00292	0.00174	0.00104	0.00063
110 ..	0.57774	0.33469	0.19442	0.11324	0.06613	0.03872	0.02273	0.01338	0.00789	0.00467	0.00277	0.00165	0.00098	0.00059
111 ..	0.57487	0.33138	0.19154	0.11101	0.06451	0.03759	0.02196	0.01286	0.00755	0.00445	0.00262	0.00155	0.00092	0.00055
112 ..	0.57201	0.32810	0.18871	0.10884	0.06294	0.03649	0.02122	0.01237	0.00723	0.00423	0.00249	0.00146	0.00086	0.00051
113 ..	0.56916	0.32485	0.18592	0.10670	0.06140	0.03543	0.02050	0.01189	0.00692	0.00403	0.00236	0.00138	0.00081	0.00048
114 ..	0.56633	0.32164	0.18318	0.10461	0.05991	0.03440	0.01981	0.01143	0.00662	0.00384	0.00223	0.00130	0.00076	0.00045
115 ..	0.56351	0.31845	0.18047	0.10256	0.05845	0.03340	0.01914	0.01099	0.00633	0.00366	0.00212	0.00123	0.00072	0.00042
116 ..	0.56071	0.31530	0.17780	0.10055	0.05702	0.03243	0.01849	0.01057	0.00606	0.00348	0.00201	0.00116	0.00067	0.00039
117 ..	0.55792	0.31218	0.17518	0.09858	0.05563	0.03148	0.01786	0.01016	0.00580	0.00332	0.00190	0.00109	0.00063	0.00036
118 ..	0.55514	0.30908	0.17259	0.09665	0.05427	0.03056	0.01726	0.00977	0.00555	0.00316	0.00180	0.00103	0.00059	0.00034
119 ..	0.55238	0.30602	0.17004	0.09475	0.05295	0.02967	0.01668	0.00940	0.00531	0.00301	0.00171	0.00097	0.00056	0.00032
120 ..	0.54963	0.30299	0.16752	0.09289	0.05166	0.02881	0.01611	0.00904	0.00508	0.00287	0.00162	0.00092	0.00052	0.00030

Table 3 *(continued)*   *Present Value of $1 at Compound Interest: 7.5%–14%*

Period	7.5%	8%	8.5%	9%	9.5%	10%	10.5%	11%	11.5%	12%	12.5%	13%	13.5%	14%
1 ...	0.93023	0.92593	0.92166	0.91743	0.91324	0.90909	0.90498	0.90090	0.89686	0.89286	0.88889	0.88496	0.88106	0.87719
2 ...	0.86533	0.85734	0.84946	0.84168	0.83401	0.82645	0.81898	0.81162	0.80436	0.79719	0.79012	0.78315	0.77626	0.76947
3 ...	0.80496	0.79383	0.78291	0.77218	0.76165	0.75131	0.74116	0.73119	0.72140	0.71178	0.70233	0.69305	0.68393	0.67497
4 ...	0.74880	0.73503	0.72157	0.70843	0.69557	0.68301	0.67073	0.65873	0.64699	0.63553	0.62430	0.61332	0.60258	0.59208
5 ...	0.69656	0.68058	0.66505	0.64993	0.63523	0.62092	0.60700	0.59345	0.58026	0.56743	0.55493	0.54276	0.53091	0.51937
6 ...	0.64796	0.63017	0.61295	0.59627	0.58012	0.56447	0.54932	0.53464	0.52042	0.50663	0.49327	0.48032	0.46776	0.45559
7 ...	0.60275	0.58349	0.56493	0.54703	0.52979	0.51316	0.49712	0.48166	0.46674	0.45235	0.43846	0.42506	0.41213	0.39964
8 ...	0.56070	0.54027	0.52067	0.50187	0.48382	0.46651	0.44989	0.43393	0.41860	0.40388	0.38974	0.37616	0.36311	0.35056
9 ...	0.52158	0.50025	0.47988	0.46043	0.44185	0.42410	0.40714	0.39092	0.37543	0.36061	0.34644	0.33288	0.31992	0.30751
10 ...	0.48519	0.46319	0.44229	0.42241	0.40351	0.38554	0.36845	0.35218	0.33671	0.32197	0.30795	0.29459	0.28187	0.26974
11 ...	0.45134	0.42888	0.40764	0.38753	0.36851	0.35049	0.33344	0.31728	0.30198	0.28748	0.27373	0.26070	0.24834	0.23662
12 ...	0.41985	0.39711	0.37570	0.35553	0.33654	0.31863	0.30175	0.28584	0.27083	0.25668	0.24332	0.23071	0.21880	0.20756
13 ...	0.39056	0.36770	0.34627	0.32618	0.30734	0.28966	0.27308	0.25751	0.24290	0.22917	0.21628	0.20416	0.19278	0.18207
14 ...	0.36331	0.34046	0.31914	0.29925	0.28067	0.26333	0.24713	0.23199	0.21785	0.20462	0.19225	0.18068	0.16985	0.15971
15 ...	0.33797	0.31524	0.29414	0.27454	0.25632	0.23939	0.22365	0.20900	0.19538	0.18270	0.17089	0.15989	0.14964	0.14010
16 ...	0.31439	0.29189	0.27110	0.25187	0.23409	0.21763	0.20240	0.18829	0.17523	0.16312	0.15190	0.14150	0.13185	0.12289
17 ...	0.29245	0.27027	0.24986	0.23107	0.21378	0.19784	0.18316	0.16963	0.15715	0.14564	0.13502	0.12522	0.11616	0.10780
18 ...	0.27205	0.25025	0.23028	0.21199	0.19523	0.17986	0.16576	0.15282	0.14095	0.13004	0.12002	0.11081	0.10235	0.09456
19 ...	0.25307	0.23171	0.21224	0.19449	0.17829	0.16351	0.15001	0.13768	0.12641	0.11611	0.10668	0.09806	0.09017	0.08295
20 ...	0.23541	0.21455	0.19562	0.17843	0.16282	0.14864	0.13575	0.12403	0.11337	0.10367	0.09483	0.08678	0.07945	0.07276
21 ...	0.21899	0.19866	0.18029	0.16370	0.14870	0.13513	0.12285	0.11174	0.10168	0.09256	0.08429	0.07680	0.07000	0.06383
22 ...	0.20371	0.18394	0.16617	0.15018	0.13580	0.12285	0.11118	0.10067	0.09119	0.08264	0.07493	0.06796	0.06167	0.05599
23 ...	0.18950	0.17032	0.15315	0.13778	0.12402	0.11168	0.10062	0.09069	0.08179	0.07379	0.06660	0.06014	0.05434	0.04911
24 ...	0.17628	0.15770	0.14115	0.12640	0.11326	0.10153	0.09106	0.08170	0.07335	0.06588	0.05920	0.05323	0.04787	0.04308
25 ...	0.16398	0.14602	0.13009	0.11597	0.10343	0.09230	0.08240	0.07361	0.06579	0.05882	0.05262	0.04710	0.04218	0.03779
26 ...	0.15254	0.13520	0.11990	0.10639	0.09446	0.08391	0.07457	0.06631	0.05900	0.05252	0.04678	0.04168	0.03716	0.03315
27 ...	0.14190	0.12519	0.11051	0.09761	0.08626	0.07628	0.06749	0.05974	0.05291	0.04689	0.04158	0.03689	0.03274	0.02908
28 ...	0.13200	0.11591	0.10185	0.08955	0.07878	0.06934	0.06107	0.05382	0.04746	0.04187	0.03696	0.03264	0.02885	0.02551
29 ...	0.12279	0.10733	0.09387	0.08215	0.07194	0.06304	0.05527	0.04849	0.04256	0.03738	0.03285	0.02889	0.02542	0.02237
30 ...	0.11422	0.09938	0.08652	0.07537	0.06570	0.05731	0.05002	0.04368	0.03817	0.03338	0.02920	0.02557	0.02239	0.01963
31 ...	0.10625	0.09202	0.07974	0.06915	0.06000	0.05210	0.04527	0.03935	0.03424	0.02980	0.02596	0.02262	0.01973	0.01722
32 ...	0.09884	0.08520	0.07349	0.06344	0.05480	0.04736	0.04096	0.03545	0.03070	0.02661	0.02307	0.02002	0.01738	0.01510
33 ...	0.09194	0.07889	0.06774	0.05820	0.05004	0.04306	0.03707	0.03194	0.02754	0.02376	0.02051	0.01772	0.01532	0.01325
34 ...	0.08553	0.07305	0.06243	0.05339	0.04570	0.03914	0.03355	0.02878	0.02470	0.02121	0.01823	0.01568	0.01349	0.01162
35 ...	0.07956	0.06763	0.05754	0.04899	0.04174	0.03558	0.03036	0.02592	0.02215	0.01894	0.01621	0.01388	0.01189	0.01019
36 ...	0.07401	0.06262	0.05303	0.04494	0.03811	0.03235	0.02748	0.02335	0.01987	0.01691	0.01440	0.01228	0.01047	0.00894
37 ...	0.06885	0.05799	0.04888	0.04123	0.03481	0.02941	0.02487	0.02104	0.01782	0.01510	0.01280	0.01087	0.00923	0.00784
38 ...	0.06404	0.05369	0.04505	0.03783	0.03179	0.02673	0.02250	0.01896	0.01598	0.01348	0.01138	0.00962	0.00813	0.00688
39 ...	0.05958	0.04971	0.04152	0.03470	0.02903	0.02430	0.02036	0.01708	0.01433	0.01204	0.01012	0.00851	0.00716	0.00604
40 ...	0.05542	0.04603	0.03827	0.03184	0.02651	0.02209	0.01843	0.01538	0.01285	0.01075	0.00899	0.00753	0.00631	0.00529
41 ...	0.05155	0.04262	0.03527	0.02921	0.02421	0.02009	0.01668	0.01386	0.01153	0.00960	0.00799	0.00666	0.00556	0.00464
42 ...	0.04796	0.03946	0.03251	0.02680	0.02211	0.01826	0.01509	0.01249	0.01034	0.00857	0.00711	0.00590	0.00490	0.00407
43 ...	0.04461	0.03654	0.02996	0.02458	0.02019	0.01660	0.01366	0.01125	0.00927	0.00765	0.00632	0.00522	0.00432	0.00357
44 ...	0.04150	0.03383	0.02761	0.02255	0.01844	0.01509	0.01236	0.01013	0.00832	0.00683	0.00561	0.00462	0.00380	0.00313
45 ...	0.03860	0.03133	0.02545	0.02069	0.01684	0.01372	0.01119	0.00913	0.00746	0.00610	0.00499	0.00409	0.00335	0.00275
46 ...	0.03591	0.02901	0.02345	0.01898	0.01538	0.01247	0.01012	0.00823	0.00669	0.00544	0.00444	0.00362	0.00295	0.00241
47 ...	0.03340	0.02686	0.02162	0.01742	0.01405	0.01134	0.00916	0.00741	0.00600	0.00486	0.00394	0.00320	0.00260	0.00212
48 ...	0.03107	0.02487	0.01992	0.01598	0.01283	0.01031	0.00829	0.00668	0.00538	0.00434	0.00350	0.00283	0.00229	0.00186
49 ...	0.02891	0.02303	0.01836	0.01466	0.01171	0.00937	0.00750	0.00601	0.00483	0.00388	0.00312	0.00251	0.00202	0.00163
50 ...	0.02689	0.02132	0.01692	0.01345	0.01070	0.00852	0.00679	0.00542	0.00433	0.00346	0.00277	0.00222	0.00178	0.00143
51 ...	0.02501	0.01974	0.01560	0.01234	0.00977	0.00774	0.00615	0.00488	0.00388	0.00309	0.00246	0.00196	0.00157	0.00125
52 ...	0.02327	0.01828	0.01438	0.01132	0.00892	0.00704	0.00556	0.00440	0.00348	0.00276	0.00219	0.00174	0.00138	0.00110
53 ...	0.02164	0.01693	0.01325	0.01038	0.00815	0.00640	0.00503	0.00396	0.00312	0.00246	0.00194	0.00154	0.00122	0.00096
54 ...	0.02013	0.01567	0.01221	0.00953	0.00744	0.00582	0.00455	0.00357	0.00280	0.00220	0.00173	0.00136	0.00107	0.00085
55 ...	0.01873	0.01451	0.01126	0.00874	0.00680	0.00529	0.00412	0.00322	0.00251	0.00196	0.00154	0.00120	0.00094	0.00074
56 ...	0.01742	0.01344	0.01037	0.00802	0.00621	0.00481	0.00373	0.00290	0.00225	0.00175	0.00137	0.00107	0.00083	0.00065
57 ...	0.01621	0.01244	0.00956	0.00736	0.00567	0.00437	0.00338	0.00261	0.00202	0.00157	0.00121	0.00094	0.00073	0.00057
58 ...	0.01508	0.01152	0.00881	0.00675	0.00518	0.00397	0.00305	0.00235	0.00181	0.00140	0.00108	0.00083	0.00065	0.00050
59 ...	0.01402	0.01067	0.00812	0.00619	0.00473	0.00361	0.00276	0.00212	0.00162	0.00125	0.00096	0.00074	0.00057	0.00044
60 ...	0.01305	0.00988	0.00749	0.00568	0.00432	0.00328	0.00250	0.00191	0.00146	0.00111	0.00085	0.00065	0.00050	0.00039

Period	7.5%	8%	8.5%	9%	9.5%	10%	10.5%	11%	11.5%	12%	12.5%	13%	13.5%	14%
61 ..	0.01214	0.00914	0.00690	0.00521	0.00394	0.00299	0.00226	0.00172	0.00131	0.00099	0.00076	0.00058	0.00044	0.00034
62 ..	0.01129	0.00847	0.00636	0.00478	0.00360	0.00271	0.00205	0.00155	0.00117	0.00089	0.00067	0.00051	0.00039	0.00030
63 ..	0.01050	0.00784	0.00586	0.00439	0.00329	0.00247	0.00185	0.00140	0.00105	0.00079	0.00060	0.00045	0.00034	0.00026
64 ..	0.00977	0.00726	0.00540	0.00402	0.00300	0.00224	0.00168	0.00126	0.00094	0.00071	0.00053	0.00040	0.00030	0.00023
65 ..	0.00909	0.00672	0.00498	0.00369	0.00274	0.00204	0.00152	0.00113	0.00085	0.00063	0.00047	0.00035	0.00027	0.00020
66 ..	0.00845	0.00622	0.00459	0.00339	0.00250	0.00185	0.00137	0.00102	0.00076	0.00056	0.00042	0.00031	0.00023	0.00018
67 ..	0.00786	0.00576	0.00423	0.00311	0.00229	0.00169	0.00124	0.00092	0.00068	0.00050	0.00037	0.00028	0.00021	0.00015
68 ..	0.00732	0.00534	0.00390	0.00285	0.00209	0.00153	0.00113	0.00083	0.00061	0.00045	0.00033	0.00025	0.00018	0.00014
69 ..	0.00680	0.00494	0.00359	0.00262	0.00191	0.00139	0.00102	0.00075	0.00055	0.00040	0.00030	0.00022	0.00016	0.00012
70 ..	0.00633	0.00457	0.00331	0.00240	0.00174	0.00127	0.00092	0.00067	0.00049	0.00036	0.00026	0.00019	0.00014	0.00010
71 ..	0.00589	0.00424	0.00305	0.00220	0.00159	0.00115	0.00083	0.00061	0.00044	0.00032	0.00023	0.00017	0.00012	0.00009
72 ..	0.00548	0.00392	0.00281	0.00202	0.00145	0.00105	0.00075	0.00055	0.00039	0.00029	0.00021	0.00015	0.00011	0.00008
73 ..	0.00510	0.00363	0.00259	0.00185	0.00133	0.00095	0.00068	0.00049	0.00035	0.00026	0.00018	0.00013	0.00010	0.00007
74 ..	0.00474	0.00336	0.00239	0.00170	0.00121	0.00086	0.00062	0.00044	0.00032	0.00023	0.00016	0.00012	0.00009	0.00006
75 ..	0.00441	0.00311	0.00220	0.00156	0.00111	0.00079	0.00056	0.00040	0.00028	0.00020	0.00015	0.00010	0.00008	0.00005
76 ..	0.00410	0.00288	0.00203	0.00143	0.00101	0.00071	0.00051	0.00036	0.00026	0.00018	0.00013	0.00009	0.00007	0.00005
77 ..	0.00382	0.00267	0.00187	0.00131	0.00092	0.00065	0.00046	0.00032	0.00023	0.00016	0.00012	0.00008	0.00006	0.00004
78 ..	0.00355	0.00247	0.00172	0.00120	0.00084	0.00059	0.00041	0.00029	0.00021	0.00014	0.00010	0.00007	0.00005	0.00004
79 ..	0.00330	0.00229	0.00159	0.00110	0.00077	0.00054	0.00038	0.00026	0.00018	0.00013	0.00009	0.00006	0.00005	0.00003
80 ..	0.00307	0.00212	0.00146	0.00101	0.00070	0.00049	0.00034	0.00024	0.00017	0.00012	0.00008	0.00006	0.00004	0.00003
81 ..	0.00286	0.00196	0.00135	0.00093	0.00064	0.00044	0.00031	0.00021	0.00015	0.00010	0.00007	0.00005	0.00004	0.00002
82 ..	0.00266	0.00182	0.00124	0.00085	0.00059	0.00040	0.00028	0.00019	0.00013	0.00009	0.00006	0.00004	0.00003	0.00002
83 ..	0.00247	0.00168	0.00115	0.00078	0.00054	0.00037	0.00025	0.00017	0.00012	0.00008	0.00006	0.00004	0.00003	0.00002
84 ..	0.00230	0.00156	0.00106	0.00072	0.00049	0.00033	0.00023	0.00016	0.00011	0.00007	0.00005	0.00003	0.00002	0.00002
85 ..	0.00214	0.00144	0.00097	0.00066	0.00045	0.00030	0.00021	0.00014	0.00010	0.00007	0.00004	0.00003	0.00002	0.00001
86 ..	0.00199	0.00134	0.00090	0.00060	0.00041	0.00028	0.00019	0.00013	0.00009	0.00006	0.00004	0.00003	0.00002	0.00001
87 ..	0.00185	0.00124	0.00083	0.00055	0.00037	0.00025	0.00017	0.00011	0.00008	0.00005	0.00004	0.00002	0.00002	0.00001
88 ..	0.00172	0.00114	0.00076	0.00051	0.00034	0.00023	0.00015	0.00010	0.00007	0.00005	0.00003	0.00002	0.00002	0.00001
89 ..	0.00160	0.00106	0.00070	0.00047	0.00031	0.00021	0.00014	0.00009	0.00006	0.00004	0.00003	0.00002	0.00001	0.00001
90 ..	0.00149	0.00098	0.00065	0.00043	0.00028	0.00019	0.00013	0.00008	0.00006	0.00004	0.00002	0.00002	0.00001	0.00001
91 ..	0.00139	0.00091	0.00060	0.00039	0.00026	0.00017	0.00011	0.00008	0.00005	0.00003	0.00002	0.00001	0.00001	0.00001
92 ..	0.00129	0.00084	0.00055	0.00036	0.00024	0.00016	0.00010	0.00007	0.00004	0.00003	0.00002	0.00001	0.00001	0.00001
93 ..	0.00120	0.00078	0.00051	0.00033	0.00022	0.00014	0.00009	0.00006	0.00004	0.00003	0.00002	0.00001	0.00001	0.00001
94 ..	0.00112	0.00072	0.00047	0.00030	0.00020	0.00013	0.00008	0.00005	0.00004	0.00002	0.00002	0.00001	0.00001	0.00000
95 ..	0.00104	0.00067	0.00043	0.00028	0.00018	0.00012	0.00008	0.00005	0.00003	0.00002	0.00001	0.00001	0.00001	0.00000
96 ..	0.00097	0.00062	0.00040	0.00026	0.00016	0.00011	0.00007	0.00004	0.00003	0.00002	0.00001	0.00001	0.00001	0.00000
97 ..	0.00090	0.00057	0.00037	0.00023	0.00015	0.00010	0.00006	0.00004	0.00003	0.00002	0.00001	0.00001	0.00001	0.00000
98 ..	0.00084	0.00053	0.00034	0.00021	0.00014	0.00009	0.00006	0.00004	0.00002	0.00002	0.00001	0.00001	0.00000	0.00000
99 ..	0.00078	0.00049	0.00031	0.00020	0.00013	0.00008	0.00005	0.00003	0.00002	0.00001	0.00001	0.00001	0.00000	0.00000
100 ..	0.00072	0.00045	0.00029	0.00018	0.00011	0.00007	0.00005	0.00003	0.00002	0.00001	0.00001	0.00001	0.00000	0.00000
101 ..	0.00067	0.00042	0.00026	0.00017	0.00010	0.00007	0.00004	0.00003	0.00002	0.00001	0.00001	0.00000	0.00000	0.00000
102 ..	0.00063	0.00039	0.00024	0.00015	0.00010	0.00006	0.00004	0.00002	0.00002	0.00001	0.00001	0.00000	0.00000	0.00000
103 ..	0.00058	0.00036	0.00022	0.00014	0.00009	0.00005	0.00003	0.00002	0.00001	0.00001	0.00001	0.00000	0.00000	0.00000
104 ..	0.00054	0.00033	0.00021	0.00013	0.00008	0.00005	0.00003	0.00002	0.00001	0.00001	0.00000	0.00000	0.00000	0.00000
105 ..	0.00050	0.00031	0.00019	0.00012	0.00007	0.00005	0.00003	0.00002	0.00001	0.00001	0.00000	0.00000	0.00000	0.00000
106 ..	0.00047	0.00029	0.00018	0.00011	0.00007	0.00004	0.00003	0.00002	0.00001	0.00001	0.00000	0.00000	0.00000	0.00000
107 ..	0.00044	0.00027	0.00016	0.00010	0.00006	0.00004	0.00002	0.00001	0.00001	0.00001	0.00000	0.00000	0.00000	0.00000
108 ..	0.00041	0.00025	0.00015	0.00009	0.00006	0.00003	0.00002	0.00001	0.00001	0.00001	0.00000	0.00000	0.00000	0.00000
109 ..	0.00038	0.00023	0.00014	0.00008	0.00005	0.00003	0.00002	0.00001	0.00001	0.00001	0.00000	0.00000	0.00000	0.00000
110 ..	0.00035	0.00021	0.00013	0.00008	0.00005	0.00003	0.00002	0.00001	0.00001	0.00001	0.00000	0.00000	0.00000	0.00000
111 ..	0.00033	0.00019	0.00012	0.00007	0.00004	0.00003	0.00002	0.00001	0.00001	0.00000	0.00000	0.00000	0.00000	0.00000
112 ..	0.00030	0.00018	0.00011	0.00006	0.00004	0.00002	0.00001	0.00001	0.00001	0.00000	0.00000	0.00000	0.00000	0.00000
113 ..	0.00028	0.00017	0.00010	0.00006	0.00004	0.00002	0.00001	0.00001	0.00000	0.00000	0.00000	0.00000	0.00000	0.00000
114 ..	0.00026	0.00015	0.00009	0.00005	0.00003	0.00002	0.00001	0.00001	0.00000	0.00000	0.00000	0.00000	0.00000	0.00000
115 ..	0.00024	0.00014	0.00008	0.00005	0.00003	0.00002	0.00001	0.00001	0.00000	0.00000	0.00000	0.00000	0.00000	0.00000
116 ..	0.00023	0.00013	0.00008	0.00005	0.00003	0.00002	0.00001	0.00001	0.00000	0.00000	0.00000	0.00000	0.00000	0.00000
117 ..	0.00021	0.00012	0.00007	0.00004	0.00002	0.00001	0.00001	0.00000	0.00000	0.00000	0.00000	0.00000	0.00000	0.00000
118 ..	0.00020	0.00011	0.00007	0.00004	0.00002	0.00001	0.00001	0.00000	0.00000	0.00000	0.00000	0.00000	0.00000	0.00000
119 ..	0.00018	0.00011	0.00006	0.00004	0.00002	0.00001	0.00001	0.00000	0.00000	0.00000	0.00000	0.00000	0.00000	0.00000
120 ..	0.00017	0.00010	0.00006	0.00003	0.00002	0.00001	0.00001	0.00000	0.00000	0.00000	0.00000	0.00000	0.00000	0.00000

Table 3 (concluded) Present Value of $1: 14.5%–20%

Period	14.5%	15%	15.5%	16%	16.5%	17%	17.5%	18%	18.5%	19%	19.5%	20%
1	0.87336	0.86957	0.86580	0.86207	0.85837	0.85470	0.85106	0.84746	0.84388	0.84034	0.83682	0.83333
2	0.76276	0.75614	0.74961	0.74316	0.73680	0.73051	0.72431	0.71818	0.71214	0.70616	0.70027	0.69444
3	0.66617	0.65752	0.64901	0.64066	0.63244	0.62437	0.61643	0.60863	0.60096	0.59342	0.58600	0.57870
4	0.58181	0.57175	0.56192	0.55229	0.54287	0.53365	0.52462	0.51579	0.50714	0.49867	0.49038	0.48225
5	0.50813	0.49718	0.48651	0.47611	0.46598	0.45611	0.44649	0.43711	0.42796	0.41905	0.41036	0.40188
6	0.44378	0.43233	0.42122	0.41044	0.39999	0.38984	0.37999	0.37043	0.36115	0.35214	0.34339	0.33490
7	0.38758	0.37594	0.36469	0.35383	0.34334	0.33320	0.32340	0.31393	0.30477	0.29592	0.28736	0.27908
8	0.33850	0.32690	0.31575	0.30503	0.29471	0.28478	0.27523	0.26604	0.25719	0.24867	0.24047	0.23257
9	0.29563	0.28426	0.27338	0.26295	0.25297	0.24340	0.23424	0.22546	0.21704	0.20897	0.20123	0.19381
10	0.25819	0.24718	0.23669	0.22668	0.21714	0.20804	0.19935	0.19106	0.18315	0.17560	0.16839	0.16151
11	0.22550	0.21494	0.20493	0.19542	0.18639	0.17781	0.16966	0.16192	0.15456	0.14757	0.14091	0.13459
12	0.19694	0.18691	0.17743	0.16846	0.15999	0.15197	0.14439	0.13722	0.13043	0.12400	0.11792	0.11216
13	0.17200	0.16253	0.15362	0.14523	0.13733	0.12989	0.12289	0.11629	0.11007	0.10421	0.09868	0.09346
14	0.15022	0.14133	0.13300	0.12520	0.11788	0.11102	0.10459	0.09855	0.09288	0.08757	0.08258	0.07789
15	0.13120	0.12289	0.11515	0.10793	0.10118	0.09489	0.08901	0.08352	0.07838	0.07359	0.06910	0.06491
16	0.11458	0.10686	0.09970	0.09304	0.08685	0.08110	0.07575	0.07078	0.06615	0.06184	0.05782	0.05409
17	0.10007	0.09293	0.08632	0.08021	0.07455	0.06932	0.06447	0.05998	0.05582	0.05196	0.04839	0.04507
18	0.08740	0.08081	0.07474	0.06914	0.06399	0.05925	0.05487	0.05083	0.04711	0.04367	0.04049	0.03756
19	0.07633	0.07027	0.06471	0.05961	0.05493	0.05064	0.04670	0.04308	0.03975	0.03670	0.03389	0.03130
20	0.06666	0.06110	0.05602	0.05139	0.04715	0.04328	0.03974	0.03651	0.03355	0.03084	0.02836	0.02608
21	0.05822	0.05313	0.04850	0.04430	0.04047	0.03699	0.03382	0.03094	0.02831	0.02591	0.02373	0.02174
22	0.05085	0.04620	0.04199	0.03819	0.03474	0.03162	0.02879	0.02622	0.02389	0.02178	0.01986	0.01811
23	0.04441	0.04017	0.03636	0.03292	0.02982	0.02702	0.02450	0.02222	0.02016	0.01830	0.01662	0.01509
24	0.03879	0.03493	0.03148	0.02838	0.02560	0.02310	0.02085	0.01883	0.01701	0.01538	0.01390	0.01258
25	0.03387	0.03038	0.02726	0.02447	0.02197	0.01974	0.01774	0.01596	0.01436	0.01292	0.01164	0.01048
26	0.02958	0.02642	0.02360	0.02109	0.01886	0.01687	0.01510	0.01352	0.01211	0.01086	0.00974	0.00874
27	0.02584	0.02297	0.02043	0.01818	0.01619	0.01442	0.01285	0.01146	0.01022	0.00912	0.00815	0.00728
28	0.02257	0.01997	0.01769	0.01567	0.01390	0.01233	0.01094	0.00971	0.00863	0.00767	0.00682	0.00607
29	0.01971	0.01737	0.01532	0.01351	0.01193	0.01053	0.00931	0.00823	0.00728	0.00644	0.00571	0.00506
30	0.01721	0.01510	0.01326	0.01165	0.01024	0.00900	0.00792	0.00697	0.00614	0.00541	0.00477	0.00421
31	0.01503	0.01313	0.01148	0.01004	0.00879	0.00770	0.00674	0.00591	0.00518	0.00455	0.00400	0.00351
32	0.01313	0.01142	0.00994	0.00866	0.00754	0.00658	0.00574	0.00501	0.00438	0.00382	0.00334	0.00293
33	0.01147	0.00993	0.00861	0.00746	0.00648	0.00562	0.00488	0.00425	0.00369	0.00321	0.00280	0.00244
34	0.01001	0.00864	0.00745	0.00643	0.00556	0.00480	0.00416	0.00360	0.00312	0.00270	0.00234	0.00203
35	0.00875	0.00751	0.00645	0.00555	0.00477	0.00411	0.00354	0.00305	0.00263	0.00227	0.00196	0.00169
36	0.00764	0.00653	0.00559	0.00478	0.00410	0.00351	0.00301	0.00258	0.00222	0.00191	0.00164	0.00141
37	0.00667	0.00568	0.00484	0.00412	0.00352	0.00300	0.00256	0.00219	0.00187	0.00160	0.00137	0.00118
38	0.00583	0.00494	0.00419	0.00355	0.00302	0.00256	0.00218	0.00186	0.00158	0.00135	0.00115	0.00098
39	0.00509	0.00429	0.00362	0.00306	0.00259	0.00219	0.00186	0.00157	0.00133	0.00113	0.00096	0.00082
40	0.00444	0.00373	0.00314	0.00264	0.00222	0.00187	0.00158	0.00133	0.00113	0.00095	0.00080	0.00068
41	0.00388	0.00325	0.00272	0.00228	0.00191	0.00160	0.00134	0.00113	0.00095	0.00080	0.00067	0.00057
42	0.00339	0.00282	0.00235	0.00196	0.00164	0.00137	0.00114	0.00096	0.00080	0.00067	0.00056	0.00047
43	0.00296	0.00245	0.00204	0.00169	0.00141	0.00117	0.00097	0.00081	0.00068	0.00056	0.00047	0.00039
44	0.00259	0.00213	0.00176	0.00146	0.00121	0.00100	0.00083	0.00069	0.00057	0.00047	0.00039	0.00033
45	0.00226	0.00186	0.00153	0.00126	0.00104	0.00085	0.00071	0.00058	0.00048	0.00040	0.00033	0.00027
46	0.00197	0.00161	0.00132	0.00108	0.00089	0.00073	0.00060	0.00049	0.00041	0.00033	0.00028	0.00023
47	0.00172	0.00140	0.00114	0.00093	0.00076	0.00062	0.00051	0.00042	0.00034	0.00028	0.00023	0.00019
48	0.00150	0.00122	0.00099	0.00081	0.00066	0.00053	0.00043	0.00035	0.00029	0.00024	0.00019	0.00016
49	0.00131	0.00106	0.00086	0.00069	0.00056	0.00046	0.00037	0.00030	0.00024	0.00020	0.00016	0.00013
50	0.00115	0.00092	0.00074	0.00060	0.00048	0.00039	0.00031	0.00025	0.00021	0.00017	0.00014	0.00011
51	0.00100	0.00080	0.00064	0.00052	0.00041	0.00033	0.00027	0.00022	0.00017	0.00014	0.00011	0.00009
52	0.00088	0.00070	0.00056	0.00044	0.00036	0.00028	0.00023	0.00018	0.00015	0.00012	0.00009	0.00008
53	0.00076	0.00061	0.00048	0.00038	0.00031	0.00024	0.00019	0.00015	0.00012	0.00010	0.00008	0.00006
54	0.00067	0.00053	0.00042	0.00033	0.00026	0.00021	0.00017	0.00013	0.00010	0.00008	0.00007	0.00005
55	0.00058	0.00046	0.00036	0.00028	0.00022	0.00018	0.00014	0.00011	0.00009	0.00007	0.00006	0.00004
56	0.00051	0.00040	0.00031	0.00025	0.00019	0.00015	0.00012	0.00009	0.00007	0.00006	0.00005	0.00004
57	0.00044	0.00035	0.00027	0.00021	0.00017	0.00013	0.00010	0.00008	0.00006	0.00005	0.00004	0.00003
58	0.00039	0.00030	0.00023	0.00018	0.00014	0.00011	0.00009	0.00007	0.00005	0.00004	0.00003	0.00003
59	0.00034	0.00026	0.00020	0.00016	0.00012	0.00009	0.00007	0.00006	0.00004	0.00003	0.00003	0.00002
60	0.00030	0.00023	0.00018	0.00014	0.00010	0.00008	0.00006	0.00005	0.00004	0.00003	0.00002	0.00002

Period	14.5%	15%	15.5%	16%	16.5%	17%	17.5%	18%	18.5%	19%	19.5%	20%
61	0.00026	0.00020	0.00015	0.00012	0.00009	0.00007	0.00005	0.00004	0.00003	0.00002	0.00002	0.00001
62	0.00023	0.00017	0.00013	0.00010	0.00008	0.00006	0.00005	0.00003	0.00003	0.00002	0.00002	0.00001
63	0.00020	0.00015	0.00011	0.00009	0.00007	0.00005	0.00004	0.00003	0.00002	0.00002	0.00001	0.00001
64	0.00017	0.00013	0.00010	0.00007	0.00006	0.00004	0.00003	0.00003	0.00002	0.00001	0.00001	0.00001
65	0.00015	0.00011	0.00009	0.00006	0.00005	0.00004	0.00003	0.00002	0.00002	0.00001	0.00001	0.00001
66	0.00013	0.00010	0.00007	0.00006	0.00004	0.00003	0.00002	0.00002	0.00001	0.00001	0.00001	0.00001
67	0.00011	0.00009	0.00006	0.00005	0.00004	0.00003	0.00002	0.00002	0.00001	0.00001	0.00001	0.00001
68	0.00010	0.00007	0.00006	0.00004	0.00003	0.00002	0.00002	0.00001	0.00001	0.00001	0.00001	0.00000
69	0.00009	0.00006	0.00005	0.00004	0.00003	0.00002	0.00001	0.00001	0.00001	0.00001	0.00000	0.00000
70	0.00008	0.00006	0.00004	0.00003	0.00002	0.00002	0.00001	0.00001	0.00001	0.00001	0.00000	0.00000
71	0.00007	0.00005	0.00004	0.00003	0.00002	0.00001	0.00001	0.00001	0.00001	0.00000	0.00000	0.00000
72	0.00006	0.00004	0.00003	0.00002	0.00002	0.00001	0.00001	0.00001	0.00001	0.00000	0.00000	0.00000
73	0.00005	0.00004	0.00003	0.00002	0.00001	0.00001	0.00001	0.00001	0.00000	0.00000	0.00000	0.00000
74	0.00004	0.00003	0.00002	0.00002	0.00001	0.00001	0.00001	0.00000	0.00000	0.00000	0.00000	0.00000
75	0.00004	0.00003	0.00002	0.00001	0.00001	0.00001	0.00001	0.00000	0.00000	0.00000	0.00000	0.00000
76	0.00003	0.00002	0.00002	0.00001	0.00001	0.00001	0.00000	0.00000	0.00000	0.00000	0.00000	0.00000
77	0.00003	0.00002	0.00002	0.00001	0.00001	0.00001	0.00000	0.00000	0.00000	0.00000	0.00000	0.00000
78	0.00003	0.00002	0.00001	0.00001	0.00001	0.00000	0.00000	0.00000	0.00000	0.00000	0.00000	0.00000
79	0.00002	0.00002	0.00001	0.00001	0.00001	0.00000	0.00000	0.00000	0.00000	0.00000	0.00000	0.00000
80	0.00002	0.00001	0.00001	0.00001	0.00000	0.00000	0.00000	0.00000	0.00000	0.00000	0.00000	0.00000
81	0.00002	0.00001	0.00001	0.00001	0.00000	0.00000	0.00000	0.00000	0.00000	0.00000	0.00000	0.00000
82	0.00002	0.00001	0.00001	0.00001	0.00000	0.00000	0.00000	0.00000	0.00000	0.00000	0.00000	0.00000
83	0.00001	0.00001	0.00001	0.00000	0.00000	0.00000	0.00000	0.00000	0.00000	0.00000	0.00000	0.00000
84	0.00001	0.00001	0.00001	0.00000	0.00000	0.00000	0.00000	0.00000	0.00000	0.00000	0.00000	0.00000
85	0.00001	0.00001	0.00000	0.00000	0.00000	0.00000	0.00000	0.00000	0.00000	0.00000	0.00000	0.00000
86	0.00001	0.00001	0.00000	0.00000	0.00000	0.00000	0.00000	0.00000	0.00000	0.00000	0.00000	0.00000
87	0.00001	0.00001	0.00000	0.00000	0.00000	0.00000	0.00000	0.00000	0.00000	0.00000	0.00000	0.00000
88	0.00001	0.00000	0.00000	0.00000	0.00000	0.00000	0.00000	0.00000	0.00000	0.00000	0.00000	0.00000
89	0.00001	0.00000	0.00000	0.00000	0.00000	0.00000	0.00000	0.00000	0.00000	0.00000	0.00000	0.00000
90	0.00001	0.00000	0.00000	0.00000	0.00000	0.00000	0.00000	0.00000	0.00000	0.00000	0.00000	0.00000
91	0.00000	0.00000	0.00000	0.00000	0.00000	0.00000	0.00000	0.00000	0.00000	0.00000	0.00000	0.00000
92	0.00000	0.00000	0.00000	0.00000	0.00000	0.00000	0.00000	0.00000	0.00000	0.00000	0.00000	0.00000
93	0.00000	0.00000	0.00000	0.00000	0.00000	0.00000	0.00000	0.00000	0.00000	0.00000	0.00000	0.00000
94	0.00000	0.00000	0.00000	0.00000	0.00000	0.00000	0.00000	0.00000	0.00000	0.00000	0.00000	0.00000
95	0.00000	0.00000	0.00000	0.00000	0.00000	0.00000	0.00000	0.00000	0.00000	0.00000	0.00000	0.00000
96	0.00000	0.00000	0.00000	0.00000	0.00000	0.00000	0.00000	0.00000	0.00000	0.00000	0.00000	0.00000
97	0.00000	0.00000	0.00000	0.00000	0.00000	0.00000	0.00000	0.00000	0.00000	0.00000	0.00000	0.00000
98	0.00000	0.00000	0.00000	0.00000	0.00000	0.00000	0.00000	0.00000	0.00000	0.00000	0.00000	0.00000
99	0.00000	0.00000	0.00000	0.00000	0.00000	0.00000	0.00000	0.00000	0.00000	0.00000	0.00000	0.00000
100	0.00000	0.00000	0.00000	0.00000	0.00000	0.00000	0.00000	0.00000	0.00000	0.00000	0.00000	0.00000
101	0.00000	0.00000	0.00000	0.00000	0.00000	0.00000	0.00000	0.00000	0.00000	0.00000	0.00000	0.00000
102	0.00000	0.00000	0.00000	0.00000	0.00000	0.00000	0.00000	0.00000	0.00000	0.00000	0.00000	0.00000
103	0.00000	0.00000	0.00000	0.00000	0.00000	0.00000	0.00000	0.00000	0.00000	0.00000	0.00000	0.00000
104	0.00000	0.00000	0.00000	0.00000	0.00000	0.00000	0.00000	0.00000	0.00000	0.00000	0.00000	0.00000
105	0.00000	0.00000	0.00000	0.00000	0.00000	0.00000	0.00000	0.00000	0.00000	0.00000	0.00000	0.00000
106	0.00000	0.00000	0.00000	0.00000	0.00000	0.00000	0.00000	0.00000	0.00000	0.00000	0.00000	0.00000
107	0.00000	0.00000	0.00000	0.00000	0.00000	0.00000	0.00000	0.00000	0.00000	0.00000	0.00000	0.00000
108	0.00000	0.00000	0.00000	0.00000	0.00000	0.00000	0.00000	0.00000	0.00000	0.00000	0.00000	0.00000
109	0.00000	0.00000	0.00000	0.00000	0.00000	0.00000	0.00000	0.00000	0.00000	0.00000	0.00000	0.00000
110	0.00000	0.00000	0.00000	0.00000	0.00000	0.00000	0.00000	0.00000	0.00000	0.00000	0.00000	0.00000
111	0.00000	0.00000	0.00000	0.00000	0.00000	0.00000	0.00000	0.00000	0.00000	0.00000	0.00000	0.00000
112	0.00000	0.00000	0.00000	0.00000	0.00000	0.00000	0.00000	0.00000	0.00000	0.00000	0.00000	0.00000
113	0.00000	0.00000	0.00000	0.00000	0.00000	0.00000	0.00000	0.00000	0.00000	0.00000	0.00000	0.00000
114	0.00000	0.00000	0.00000	0.00000	0.00000	0.00000	0.00000	0.00000	0.00000	0.00000	0.00000	0.00000
115	0.00000	0.00000	0.00000	0.00000	0.00000	0.00000	0.00000	0.00000	0.00000	0.00000	0.00000	0.00000
116	0.00000	0.00000	0.00000	0.00000	0.00000	0.00000	0.00000	0.00000	0.00000	0.00000	0.00000	0.00000
117	0.00000	0.00000	0.00000	0.00000	0.00000	0.00000	0.00000	0.00000	0.00000	0.00000	0.00000	0.00000
118	0.00000	0.00000	0.00000	0.00000	0.00000	0.00000	0.00000	0.00000	0.00000	0.00000	0.00000	0.00000
119	0.00000	0.00000	0.00000	0.00000	0.00000	0.00000	0.00000	0.00000	0.00000	0.00000	0.00000	0.00000
120	0.00000	0.00000	0.00000	0.00000	0.00000	0.00000	0.00000	0.00000	0.00000	0.00000	0.00000	0.00000

Table 4 *Present Value of an Ordinary Annuity of $1 per Period: 0.5%–7%*

$$P_{A_{i,n}} = \frac{1 - \dfrac{1}{(1+i)^n}}{i}$$

Period	.5%	1%	1.5%	2%	2.5%	3%	3.5%	4%	4.5%	5%	5.5%	6%	6.5%	7%
1	0.99502	0.99010	0.98522	0.98039	0.97561	0.97087	0.96618	0.96154	0.95694	0.95238	0.94787	0.94340	0.93897	0.93458
2	1.98510	1.97040	1.95588	1.94156	1.92742	1.91347	1.89969	1.88609	1.87267	1.85941	1.84632	1.83339	1.82063	1.80802
3	2.97025	2.94099	2.91220	2.88388	2.85602	2.82861	2.80164	2.77509	2.74896	2.72325	2.69793	2.67301	2.64848	2.62432
4	3.95050	3.90197	3.85438	3.80773	3.76197	3.71710	3.67308	3.62990	3.58753	3.54595	3.50515	3.46511	3.42580	3.38721
5	4.92587	4.85343	4.78264	4.71346	4.64583	4.57971	4.51505	4.45182	4.38998	4.32948	4.27028	4.21236	4.15568	4.10020
6	5.89638	5.79548	5.69719	5.60143	5.50813	5.41719	5.32855	5.24214	5.15787	5.07569	4.99553	4.91732	4.84101	4.76654
7	6.86207	6.72819	6.59821	6.47199	6.34939	6.23028	6.11454	6.00205	5.89270	5.78637	5.68297	5.58238	5.48452	5.38929
8	7.82296	7.65168	7.48593	7.32548	7.17014	7.01969	6.87396	6.73274	6.59589	6.46321	6.33457	6.20979	6.08875	5.97130
9	8.77906	8.56602	8.36052	8.16224	7.97087	7.78611	7.60769	7.43533	7.26879	7.10782	6.95220	6.80169	6.65610	6.51523
10	9.73041	9.47130	9.22218	8.98259	8.75206	8.53020	8.31661	8.11090	7.91272	7.72173	7.53763	7.36009	7.18883	7.02358
11	10.67703	10.36763	10.07112	9.78685	9.51421	9.25262	9.00155	8.76048	8.52892	8.30641	8.09254	7.88687	7.68904	7.49867
12	11.61893	11.25508	10.90751	10.57534	10.25776	9.95400	9.66333	9.38507	9.11858	8.86325	8.61852	8.38384	8.15873	7.94269
13	12.55615	12.13374	11.73153	11.34837	10.98318	10.63496	10.30274	9.98565	9.68285	9.39357	9.11708	8.85268	8.59974	8.35765
14	13.48871	13.00370	12.54338	12.10625	11.69091	11.29607	10.92052	10.56312	10.22283	9.89864	9.58965	9.29498	9.01384	8.74547
15	14.41662	13.86505	13.34323	12.84926	12.38138	11.93794	11.51741	11.11839	10.73955	10.37966	10.03758	9.71225	9.40267	9.10791
16	15.33993	14.71787	14.13126	13.57771	13.05500	12.56110	12.09412	11.65230	11.23402	10.83777	10.46216	10.10590	9.76776	9.44665
17	16.25863	15.56225	14.90765	14.29187	13.71220	13.16612	12.65132	12.16567	11.70719	11.27407	10.86461	10.47726	10.11058	9.76322
18	17.17277	16.39827	15.67256	14.99203	14.35336	13.75351	13.18968	12.65930	12.15999	11.68959	11.24607	10.82760	10.43247	10.05909
19	18.08236	17.22601	16.42617	15.67846	14.97889	14.32380	13.70984	13.13394	12.59329	12.08532	11.60765	11.15812	10.73471	10.33560
20	18.98742	18.04555	17.16864	16.35143	15.58916	14.87747	14.21240	13.59033	13.00794	12.46221	11.95038	11.46992	11.01851	10.59401
21	19.88798	18.85698	17.90014	17.01121	16.18455	15.41502	14.69797	14.02916	13.40472	12.82115	12.27524	11.76408	11.28498	10.83553
22	20.78406	19.66038	18.62082	17.65805	16.76541	15.93692	15.16712	14.45112	13.78442	13.16300	12.58317	12.04158	11.53520	11.06124
23	21.67568	20.45582	19.33086	18.29220	17.33211	16.44361	15.62041	14.85684	14.14777	13.48857	12.87504	12.30338	11.77014	11.27219
24	22.56287	21.24339	20.03041	18.91393	17.88494	16.93554	16.05837	15.24696	14.49548	13.79864	13.15170	12.55036	11.99074	11.46933
25	23.44542	22.02316	20.71961	19.52346	18.42438	17.41315	16.48151	15.62208	14.82821	14.09394	13.41393	12.78336	12.19788	11.65358
26	24.32402	22.79520	21.39863	20.12104	18.95061	17.87684	16.89035	15.98277	15.14661	14.37519	13.66250	13.00317	12.39237	11.82578
27	25.19803	23.55961	22.06762	20.70690	19.46401	18.32703	17.28536	16.32959	15.45130	14.64303	13.89810	13.21053	12.57500	11.98671
28	26.06769	24.31644	22.72672	21.28127	19.96489	18.76411	17.66702	16.66306	15.74287	14.89813	14.12142	13.40616	12.74648	12.13711
29	26.93302	25.06579	23.37608	21.84438	20.45355	19.18845	18.03577	16.98371	16.02189	15.14107	14.33310	13.59072	12.90749	12.27767
30	27.79405	25.80771	24.01584	22.39646	20.93029	19.60044	18.39205	17.29203	16.28889	15.37245	14.53375	13.76483	13.05868	12.40904
31	28.65080	26.54229	24.64615	22.93770	21.39541	20.00043	18.73628	17.58849	16.54439	15.59281	14.72393	13.92909	13.20063	12.53181
32	29.50328	27.26959	25.26714	23.46833	21.84918	20.38877	19.06887	17.87355	16.78889	15.80268	14.90420	14.08404	13.33393	12.64656
33	30.35153	27.98969	25.87895	23.98856	22.29188	20.76579	19.39021	18.14765	17.02286	16.00255	15.07507	14.23023	13.45909	12.75379
34	31.19555	28.70267	26.48173	24.49859	22.72379	21.13194	19.70068	18.41120	17.24676	16.19290	15.23703	14.36814	13.57661	12.85401
35	32.03537	29.40858	27.07559	24.99862	23.14516	21.48722	20.00066	18.66461	17.46101	16.37419	15.39055	14.49825	13.68696	12.94767
36	32.87102	30.10751	27.66068	25.48884	23.55625	21.83225	20.29049	18.90828	17.66604	16.54685	15.53607	14.62099	13.79057	13.03521
37	33.70250	30.79951	28.23713	25.96945	23.95732	22.16724	20.57053	19.14258	17.86224	16.71129	15.67400	14.73678	13.88786	13.11702
38	34.52985	31.48466	28.80505	26.44064	24.34860	22.49246	20.84109	19.36786	18.04999	16.86789	15.80474	14.84602	13.97921	13.19347
39	35.35309	32.16303	29.36458	26.90259	24.73034	22.80822	21.10250	19.58448	18.22966	17.01704	15.92866	14.94907	14.06499	13.26493
40	36.17223	32.83469	29.91585	27.35548	25.10278	23.11477	21.35507	19.79277	18.40158	17.15909	16.04612	15.04630	14.14553	13.33171
41	36.98729	33.49969	30.45896	27.79949	25.46612	23.41240	21.59910	19.99305	18.56611	17.29437	16.15746	15.13802	14.22115	13.39412
42	37.79830	34.15811	30.99405	28.23479	25.82061	23.70136	21.83488	20.18563	18.72355	17.42321	16.26300	15.22454	14.29216	13.45245
43	38.60527	34.81001	31.52123	28.66156	26.16645	23.98190	22.06269	20.37079	18.87421	17.54591	16.36303	15.30617	14.35884	13.50696
44	39.40823	35.45545	32.04062	29.07996	26.50385	24.25427	22.28279	20.54884	19.01838	17.66277	16.45785	15.38318	14.42144	13.55791
45	40.20720	36.09451	32.55234	29.49016	26.83302	24.51871	22.49545	20.72004	19.15635	17.77407	16.54773	15.45583	14.48023	13.60552
46	41.00219	36.72724	33.05649	29.89231	27.15417	24.77545	22.70092	20.88465	19.28837	17.88007	16.63292	15.52437	14.53543	13.65002
47	41.79322	37.35370	33.55319	30.28658	27.46748	25.02471	22.89944	21.04294	19.41471	17.98102	16.71366	15.58903	14.58725	13.69161
48	42.58032	37.97396	34.04255	30.67312	27.77315	25.26671	23.09124	21.19513	19.53561	18.07716	16.79020	15.65003	14.63592	13.73047
49	43.36350	38.58808	34.52468	31.05208	28.07137	25.50166	23.27656	21.34147	19.65130	18.16872	16.86275	15.70757	14.68161	13.76680
50	44.14279	39.19612	34.99969	31.42361	28.36231	25.72976	23.45562	21.48218	19.76201	18.25593	16.93152	15.76186	14.72452	13.80075
51	44.91820	39.79814	35.46767	31.78785	28.64616	25.95123	23.62862	21.61749	19.86795	18.33898	16.99670	15.81308	14.76481	13.83247
52	45.68975	40.39419	35.92874	32.14495	28.92308	26.16624	23.79576	21.74758	19.96933	18.41807	17.05848	15.86139	14.80264	13.86212
53	46.45746	40.98435	36.38300	32.49505	29.19325	26.37499	23.95726	21.87267	20.06634	18.49340	17.11705	15.90697	14.83816	13.88984
54	47.22135	41.56866	36.83054	32.83828	29.45683	26.57766	24.11330	21.99296	20.15918	18.56515	17.17255	15.94998	14.87151	13.91573
55	47.98145	42.14719	37.27147	33.17479	29.71398	26.77443	24.26405	22.10861	20.24802	18.63347	17.22517	15.99054	14.90282	13.93994
56	48.73776	42.71999	37.70588	33.50469	29.96486	26.96546	24.40971	22.21982	20.33303	18.69854	17.27504	16.02881	14.93223	13.96256
57	49.49031	43.28712	38.13387	33.82813	30.20962	27.15094	24.55045	22.32675	20.41439	18.76052	17.32232	16.06492	14.95984	13.98370
58	50.23911	43.84863	38.55554	34.14523	30.44841	27.33101	24.68642	22.42957	20.49224	18.81954	17.36712	16.09898	14.98577	14.00346
59	50.98419	44.40459	38.97097	34.45610	30.68137	27.50583	24.81780	22.52843	20.56673	18.87575	17.40960	16.13111	15.01011	14.02192
60	51.72556	44.95504	39.38027	34.76089	30.90866	27.67556	24.94473	22.62349	20.63802	18.92929	17.44985	16.16143	15.03297	14.03918

Period	.5%	1%	1.5%	2%	2.5%	3%	3.5%	4%	4.5%	5%	5.5%	6%	6.5%	7%
61 ...	52.46324	45.50004	39.78352	35.05969	31.13040	27.84035	25.06738	22.71489	20.70624	18.98028	17.48801	16.19003	15.05443	14.05531
62 ...	53.19726	46.03964	40.18080	35.35264	31.34673	28.00034	25.18587	22.80278	20.77152	19.02883	17.52418	16.21701	15.07458	14.07038
63 ...	53.92762	46.57390	40.57222	35.63984	31.55778	28.15567	25.30036	22.88729	20.83399	19.07508	17.55847	16.24246	15.09350	14.08447
64 ...	54.65435	47.10287	40.95785	35.92141	31.76369	28.30648	25.41097	22.96855	20.89377	19.11912	17.59096	16.26647	15.11127	14.09764
65 ...	55.37746	47.62661	41.33779	36.19747	31.96458	28.45289	25.51785	23.04668	20.95098	19.16107	17.62177	16.28912	15.12795	14.10994
66 ...	56.09698	48.14516	41.71210	36.46810	32.16056	28.59504	25.62111	23.12181	21.00572	19.20102	17.65096	16.31049	15.14362	14.12144
67 ...	56.81291	48.65857	42.08089	36.73343	32.35177	28.73305	25.72088	23.19405	21.05811	19.23907	17.67864	16.33065	15.15833	14.13219
68 ...	57.52529	49.16690	42.44423	36.99356	32.53831	28.86704	25.81727	23.26351	21.10824	19.27530	17.70487	16.34967	15.17214	14.14223
69 ...	58.23411	49.67020	42.80219	37.24859	32.72030	28.99712	25.91041	23.33030	21.15621	19.30981	17.72974	16.36762	15.18511	14.15162
70 ...	58.93942	50.16851	43.15487	37.49862	32.89786	29.12342	26.00040	23.39451	21.20211	19.34268	17.75330	16.38454	15.19728	14.16039
71 ...	59.64121	50.66190	43.50234	37.74374	33.07108	29.24604	26.08734	23.45626	21.24604	19.37398	17.77564	16.40051	15.20872	14.16859
72 ...	60.33951	51.15039	43.84467	37.98406	33.24008	29.36509	26.17134	23.51564	21.28808	19.40379	17.79682	16.41558	15.21945	14.17625
73 ...	61.03434	51.63405	44.18194	38.21967	33.40495	29.48067	26.25251	23.57273	21.32830	19.43218	17.81689	16.42979	15.22953	14.18341
74 ...	61.72571	52.11292	44.51422	38.45066	33.56581	29.59288	26.33092	23.62762	21.36680	19.45922	17.83591	16.44320	15.23900	14.19010
75 ...	62.41365	52.58705	44.84160	38.67711	33.72274	29.70183	26.40669	23.68041	21.40363	19.48497	17.85395	16.45585	15.24788	14.19636
76 ...	63.09815	53.05649	45.16414	38.89913	33.87584	29.80760	26.47989	23.73116	21.43888	19.50950	17.87104	16.46778	15.25623	14.20220
77 ...	63.77926	53.52127	45.48191	39.11680	34.02521	29.91029	26.55062	23.77996	21.47262	19.53285	17.88724	16.47904	15.26407	14.20767
78 ...	64.45697	53.98146	45.79498	39.33019	34.17094	30.00999	26.61896	23.82689	21.50490	19.55510	17.90260	16.48966	15.27142	14.21277
79 ...	65.13132	54.43709	46.10343	39.53940	34.31311	30.10679	26.68498	23.87201	21.53579	19.57628	17.91716	16.49968	15.27833	14.21755
80 ...	65.80231	54.88821	46.40732	39.74451	34.45182	30.20076	26.74878	23.91539	21.56534	19.59646	17.93095	16.50913	15.28482	14.22201
81 ...	66.46996	55.33486	46.70672	39.94560	34.58714	30.29200	26.81041	23.95711	21.59363	19.61568	17.94403	16.51805	15.29091	14.22617
82 ...	67.13428	55.77709	47.00170	40.14275	34.71916	30.38059	26.86996	23.99722	21.62070	19.63398	17.95643	16.52646	15.29663	14.23007
83 ...	67.79531	56.21494	47.29231	40.33603	34.84796	30.46659	26.92750	24.03579	21.64660	19.65141	17.96818	16.53440	15.30200	14.23371
84 ...	68.45304	56.64845	47.57863	40.52552	34.97362	30.55009	26.98309	24.07287	21.67139	19.66801	17.97932	16.54188	15.30704	14.23711
85 ...	69.10750	57.07768	47.86072	40.71129	35.09621	30.63115	27.03680	24.10853	21.69511	19.68382	17.98987	16.54895	15.31178	14.24029
86 ...	69.75871	57.50265	48.13864	40.89342	35.21582	30.70986	27.08870	24.14282	21.71781	19.69887	17.99988	16.55561	15.31622	14.24326
87 ...	70.40668	57.92342	48.41246	41.07198	35.33251	30.78627	27.13884	24.17579	21.73953	19.71321	18.00936	16.56190	15.32040	14.24604
88 ...	71.05142	58.34002	48.68222	41.24704	35.44635	30.86045	27.18728	24.20749	21.76032	19.72687	18.01835	16.56783	15.32431	14.24864
89 ...	71.69296	58.75249	48.94800	41.41867	35.55741	30.93248	27.23409	24.23797	21.78021	19.73987	18.02688	16.57342	15.32800	14.25106
90 ...	72.33130	59.16088	49.20985	41.58693	35.66577	31.00241	27.27932	24.26728	21.79924	19.75226	18.03495	16.57870	15.33145	14.25333
91 ...	72.96647	59.56523	49.46784	41.75189	35.77148	31.07030	27.32301	24.29546	21.81746	19.76406	18.04261	16.58368	15.33470	14.25545
92 ...	73.59847	59.96557	49.72201	41.91362	35.87462	31.13621	27.36523	24.32256	21.83489	19.77529	18.04987	16.58838	15.33774	14.25743
93 ...	74.22734	60.36195	49.97242	42.07218	35.97524	31.20021	27.40602	24.34861	21.85156	19.78599	18.05675	16.59281	15.34060	14.25928
94 ...	74.85307	60.75441	50.21913	42.22762	36.07340	31.26234	27.44543	24.37367	21.86753	19.79619	18.06327	16.59699	15.34329	14.26101
95 ...	75.47569	61.14298	50.46220	42.38002	36.16917	31.32266	27.48350	24.39776	21.88280	19.80589	18.06945	16.60093	15.34581	14.26262
96 ...	76.09522	61.52770	50.70168	42.52943	36.26261	31.38122	27.52029	24.42092	21.89742	19.81513	18.07531	16.60465	15.34818	14.26413
97 ...	76.71166	61.90862	50.93761	42.67592	36.35376	31.43808	27.55584	24.44319	21.91140	19.82394	18.08086	16.60816	15.35040	14.26555
98 ...	77.32503	62.28576	51.17006	42.81953	36.44269	31.49328	27.59018	24.46461	21.92479	19.83232	18.08612	16.61147	15.35249	14.26687
99 ...	77.93536	62.65917	51.39907	42.96032	36.52946	31.54687	27.62337	24.48520	21.93760	19.84031	18.09111	16.61460	15.35445	14.26810
100 ...	78.54264	63.02888	51.62470	43.09835	36.61411	31.59891	27.65543	24.50500	21.94985	19.84791	18.09584	16.61755	15.35629	14.26925
101 ...	79.14691	63.39493	51.84700	43.23368	36.69669	31.64942	27.68640	24.52404	21.96158	19.85515	18.10032	16.62033	15.35802	14.27033
102 ...	79.74817	63.75736	52.06601	43.36635	36.77726	31.69847	27.71633	24.54234	21.97281	19.86205	18.10457	16.62295	15.35964	14.27133
103 ...	80.34644	64.11619	52.28178	43.49642	36.85586	31.74609	27.74525	24.55995	21.98355	19.86862	18.10860	16.62542	15.36117	14.27228
104 ...	80.94173	64.47148	52.49437	43.62394	36.93255	31.79232	27.77318	24.57687	21.99382	19.87488	18.11241	16.62776	15.36260	14.27315
105 ...	81.53406	64.82325	52.70381	43.74896	37.00736	31.83720	27.80018	24.59315	22.00366	19.88083	18.11603	16.62996	15.36394	14.27398
106 ...	82.12344	65.17153	52.91016	43.87153	37.08035	31.88078	27.82626	24.60879	22.01307	19.88651	18.11946	16.63204	15.36521	14.27474
107 ...	82.70989	65.51637	53.11346	43.99170	37.15156	31.92308	27.85146	24.62384	22.02208	19.89191	18.12271	16.63400	15.36639	14.27546
108 ...	83.29342	65.85779	53.31375	44.10951	37.22104	31.96415	27.87581	24.63831	22.03070	19.89706	18.12579	16.63585	15.36750	14.27613
109 ...	83.87405	66.19583	53.51108	44.22501	37.28882	32.00404	27.89933	24.65222	22.03895	19.90196	18.12872	16.63759	15.36855	14.27676
110 ...	84.45180	66.53053	53.70550	44.33824	37.35494	32.04276	27.92206	24.66560	22.04684	19.90663	18.13148	16.63924	15.36953	14.27735
111 ...	85.02666	66.86191	53.89704	44.44926	37.41946	32.08035	27.94402	24.67846	22.05439	19.91108	18.13411	16.64079	15.37045	14.27789
112 ...	85.59867	67.19001	54.08576	44.55810	37.48240	32.11684	27.96523	24.69082	22.06162	19.91531	18.13659	16.64226	15.37131	14.27840
113 ...	86.16783	67.51486	54.27168	44.66480	37.54380	32.15227	27.98573	24.70272	22.06853	19.91934	18.13895	16.64364	15.37212	14.27888
114 ...	86.73416	67.83649	54.45486	44.76941	37.60371	32.18667	28.00554	24.71415	22.07515	19.92318	18.14119	16.64494	15.37289	14.27933
115 ...	87.29767	68.15494	54.63533	44.87197	37.66216	32.22007	28.02467	24.72514	22.08148	19.92684	18.14331	16.64617	15.37360	14.27975
116 ...	87.85838	68.47024	54.81313	44.97252	37.71918	32.25250	28.04316	24.73571	22.08754	19.93033	18.14531	16.64733	15.37428	14.28014
117 ...	88.41630	68.78242	54.98831	45.07110	37.77481	32.28398	28.06103	24.74588	22.09334	19.93364	18.14722	16.64843	15.37491	14.28050
118 ...	88.97144	69.09150	55.16089	45.16775	37.82908	32.31454	28.07829	24.75565	22.09888	19.93680	18.14902	16.64946	15.37550	14.28084
119 ...	89.52382	69.39753	55.33093	45.26250	37.88203	32.34421	28.09496	24.76505	22.10420	19.93981	18.15073	16.65043	15.37606	14.28116
120 ...	90.07345	69.70052	55.49845	45.35539	37.93369	32.37302	28.11108	24.77409	22.10929	19.94268	18.15235	16.65135	15.37658	14.28146

Table 4 (continued)   Present Value of an Ordinary Annuity of $1 per Period: 7.5%–14%

Period	7.5%	8%	8.5%	9%	9.5%	10%	10.5%	11%	11.5%	12%	12.5%	13%	13.5%	14%
1	0.93023	0.92593	0.92166	0.91743	0.91324	0.90909	0.90498	0.90090	0.89686	0.89286	0.88889	0.88496	0.88106	0.87719
2	1.79557	1.78326	1.77111	1.75911	1.74725	1.73554	1.72396	1.71252	1.70122	1.69005	1.67901	1.66810	1.65732	1.64666
3	2.60053	2.57710	2.55402	2.53129	2.50891	2.48685	2.46512	2.44371	2.42262	2.40183	2.38134	2.36115	2.34125	2.32163
4	3.34933	3.31213	3.27560	3.23972	3.20448	3.16987	3.13586	3.10245	3.06961	3.03735	3.00564	2.97447	2.94383	2.91371
5	4.04588	3.99271	3.94064	3.88965	3.83971	3.79079	3.74286	3.69590	3.64988	3.60478	3.56057	3.51723	3.47474	3.43308
6	4.69385	4.62288	4.55359	4.48592	4.41983	4.35526	4.29218	4.23054	4.17029	4.11141	4.05384	3.99755	3.94250	3.88867
7	5.29660	5.20637	5.11851	5.03295	4.94961	4.86842	4.78930	4.71220	4.63704	4.56376	4.49230	4.42261	4.35463	4.28830
8	5.85730	5.74664	5.63918	5.53482	5.43344	5.33493	5.23919	5.14612	5.05564	4.96764	4.88205	4.79877	4.71774	4.63886
9	6.37889	6.24689	6.11906	5.99525	5.87528	5.75902	5.64632	5.53705	5.43106	5.32825	5.22848	5.13166	5.03765	4.94637
10	6.86408	6.71008	6.56135	6.41766	6.27880	6.14457	6.01477	5.88923	5.76777	5.65022	5.53643	5.42624	5.31952	5.21612
11	7.31542	7.13896	6.96898	6.80519	6.64730	6.49506	6.34821	6.20652	6.06975	5.93770	5.81016	5.68694	5.56786	5.45273
12	7.73528	7.53608	7.34469	7.16073	6.98384	6.81369	6.64996	6.49236	6.34058	6.19437	6.05348	5.91765	5.78666	5.66029
13	8.12584	7.90378	7.69095	7.48690	7.29118	7.10336	6.92304	6.74987	6.58348	6.42355	6.26976	6.12181	5.97943	5.84236
14	8.48915	8.24424	8.01010	7.78615	7.57185	7.36669	7.17018	6.98187	6.80133	6.62817	6.46201	6.30249	6.14928	6.00207
15	8.82712	8.55948	8.30424	8.06069	7.82818	7.60608	7.39382	7.19087	6.99671	6.81086	6.63289	6.46238	6.29893	6.14217
16	9.14151	8.85137	8.57533	8.31256	8.06226	7.82371	7.59622	7.37916	7.17194	6.97399	6.78479	6.60388	6.43077	6.26506
17	9.43396	9.12164	8.82519	8.54363	8.27604	8.02155	7.77939	7.54879	7.32909	7.11963	6.91982	6.72909	6.54694	6.37286
18	9.70601	9.37189	9.05548	8.75563	8.47127	8.20141	7.94515	7.70162	7.47004	7.24967	7.03984	6.83991	6.64928	6.46742
19	9.95908	9.60360	9.26772	8.95011	8.64956	8.36492	8.09515	7.83929	7.59644	7.36578	7.14652	6.93797	6.73946	6.55037
20	10.19449	9.81815	9.46334	9.12855	8.81238	8.51356	8.23091	7.96333	7.70982	7.46944	7.24135	7.02475	6.81890	6.62313
21	10.41348	10.01680	9.64363	9.29224	8.96108	8.64869	8.35376	8.07507	7.81149	7.56200	7.32565	7.10155	6.88890	6.68696
22	10.61719	10.20074	9.80980	9.44243	9.09688	8.77154	8.46494	8.17574	7.90269	7.64465	7.40058	7.16951	6.95057	6.74294
23	10.80669	10.37106	9.96295	9.58021	9.22089	8.88322	8.56556	8.26643	7.98447	7.71843	7.46718	7.22966	7.00491	6.79206
24	10.98297	10.52876	10.10410	9.70661	9.33415	8.98474	8.65662	8.34814	8.05782	7.78432	7.52638	7.28288	7.05279	6.83514
25	11.14695	10.67478	10.23419	9.82258	9.43758	9.07704	8.73902	8.42174	8.12361	7.84314	7.57901	7.32998	7.09497	6.87293
26	11.29948	10.80998	10.35409	9.92897	9.53203	9.16095	8.81359	8.48806	8.18261	7.89566	7.62578	7.37167	7.13213	6.90608
27	11.44138	10.93516	10.46460	10.02658	9.61830	9.23722	8.88108	8.54780	8.23552	7.94255	7.66736	7.40856	7.16487	6.93515
28	11.57338	11.05108	10.56645	10.11613	9.69707	9.30657	8.94215	8.60162	8.28298	7.98442	7.70432	7.44120	7.19372	6.96066
29	11.69617	11.15841	10.66033	10.19828	9.76902	9.36961	8.99742	8.65011	8.32554	8.02181	7.73717	7.47009	7.21914	6.98304
30	11.81039	11.25778	10.74684	10.27365	9.83472	9.42691	9.04744	8.69379	8.36371	8.05518	7.76638	7.49565	7.24153	7.00266
31	11.91664	11.34980	10.82658	10.34280	9.89472	9.47901	9.09271	8.73315	8.39795	8.08499	7.79234	7.51828	7.26126	7.01988
32	12.01548	11.43500	10.90008	10.40624	9.94952	9.52638	9.13367	8.76860	8.42866	8.11159	7.81541	7.53830	7.27864	7.03498
33	12.10742	11.51389	10.96781	10.46444	9.99956	9.56943	9.17074	8.80054	8.45619	8.13535	7.83592	7.55602	7.29396	7.04823
34	12.19295	11.58693	11.03024	10.51784	10.04526	9.60857	9.20429	8.82932	8.48089	8.15656	7.85415	7.57170	7.30745	7.05985
35	12.27251	11.65457	11.08778	10.56682	10.08699	9.64416	9.23465	8.85524	8.50304	8.17550	7.87036	7.58557	7.31934	7.07005
36	12.34652	11.71719	11.14081	10.61176	10.12511	9.67651	9.26213	8.87859	8.52291	8.19241	7.88476	7.59785	7.32982	7.07899
37	12.41537	11.77518	11.18969	10.65299	10.15992	9.70592	9.28700	8.89963	8.54072	8.20751	7.89757	7.60872	7.33908	7.08683
38	12.47941	11.82887	11.23474	10.69082	10.19171	9.73265	9.30950	8.91859	8.55670	8.22099	7.90895	7.61833	7.34718	7.09371
39	12.53899	11.87858	11.27625	10.72552	10.22074	9.75696	9.32986	8.93567	8.57103	8.23303	7.91906	7.62684	7.35434	7.09975
40	12.59441	11.92461	11.31452	10.75736	10.24725	9.77905	9.34829	8.95105	8.58389	8.24378	7.92806	7.63438	7.36065	7.10504
41	12.64596	11.96723	11.34979	10.78657	10.27146	9.79914	9.36497	8.96491	8.59541	8.25337	7.93605	7.64104	7.36621	7.10969
42	12.69392	12.00670	11.38229	10.81337	10.29357	9.81740	9.38006	8.97740	8.60575	8.26194	7.94316	7.64694	7.37111	7.11376
43	12.73853	12.04324	11.41225	10.83795	10.31376	9.83400	9.39372	8.98865	8.61502	8.26959	7.94947	7.65216	7.37543	7.11733
44	12.78003	12.07707	11.43986	10.86051	10.33220	9.84909	9.40608	8.99878	8.62334	8.27642	7.95509	7.65678	7.37923	7.12047
45	12.81863	12.10840	11.46531	10.88120	10.34904	9.86281	9.41727	9.00791	8.63080	8.28252	7.96008	7.66086	7.38258	7.12322
46	12.85454	12.13741	11.48877	10.90018	10.36442	9.87528	9.42739	9.01614	8.63749	8.28796	7.96451	7.66448	7.38554	7.12563
47	12.88794	12.16427	11.51038	10.91760	10.37847	9.88662	9.43656	9.02355	8.64349	8.29282	7.96846	7.66768	7.38814	7.12774
48	12.91902	12.18914	11.53031	10.93358	10.39130	9.89693	9.44485	9.03022	8.64887	8.29716	7.97196	7.67052	7.39043	7.12960
49	12.94792	12.21216	11.54867	10.94823	10.40301	9.90630	9.45235	9.03624	8.65369	8.30104	7.97508	7.67302	7.39245	7.13123
50	12.97481	12.23348	11.56560	10.96168	10.41371	9.91481	9.45914	9.04165	8.65802	8.30450	7.97785	7.67524	7.39423	7.13266
51	12.99982	12.25323	11.58119	10.97402	10.42348	9.92256	9.46529	9.04653	8.66190	8.30759	7.98031	7.67720	7.39580	7.13391
52	13.02309	12.27151	11.59557	10.98534	10.43240	9.92960	9.47085	9.05093	8.66538	8.31035	7.98250	7.67894	7.39718	7.13501
53	13.04474	12.28843	11.60882	10.99573	10.44055	9.93600	9.47588	9.05489	8.66850	8.31281	7.98444	7.68048	7.39839	7.13597
54	13.06487	12.30410	11.62103	11.00525	10.44799	9.94182	9.48043	9.05846	8.67130	8.31501	7.98617	7.68184	7.39947	7.13682
55	13.08360	12.31861	11.63229	11.01399	10.45478	9.94711	9.48456	9.06168	8.67382	8.31697	7.98771	7.68304	7.40041	7.13756
56	13.10103	12.33205	11.64266	11.02201	10.46099	9.95191	9.48829	9.06457	8.67607	8.31872	7.98907	7.68411	7.40124	7.13821
57	13.11723	12.34449	11.65222	11.02937	10.46666	9.95629	9.49166	9.06718	8.67809	8.32029	7.99029	7.68505	7.40198	7.13878
58	13.13231	12.35601	11.66104	11.03612	10.47183	9.96026	9.49472	9.06954	8.67990	8.32169	7.99137	7.68589	7.40262	7.13928
59	13.14633	12.36668	11.66916	11.04231	10.47656	9.96387	9.49748	9.07165	8.68152	8.32294	7.99232	7.68663	7.40319	7.13972
60	13.15938	12.37655	11.67664	11.04799	10.48088	9.96716	9.49998	9.07356	8.68298	8.32405	7.99318	7.68728	7.40369	7.14011

Period	7.5%	8%	8.5%	9%	9.5%	10%	10.5%	11%	11.5%	12%	12.5%	13%	13.5%	14%
61	13.17152	12.38570	11.68354	11.05320	10.48482	9.97014	9.50225	9.07528	8.68429	8.32504	7.99394	7.68786	7.40413	7.14044
62	13.18281	12.39416	11.68990	11.05798	10.48842	9.97286	9.50430	9.07683	8.68546	8.32593	7.99461	7.68837	7.40452	7.14074
63	13.19331	12.40200	11.69576	11.06237	10.49171	9.97532	9.50615	9.07822	8.68651	8.32673	7.99521	7.68882	7.40487	7.14100
64	13.20308	12.40926	11.70116	11.06640	10.49471	9.97757	9.50783	9.07948	8.68745	8.32743	7.99574	7.68922	7.40517	7.14123
65	13.21217	12.41598	11.70614	11.07009	10.49745	9.97961	9.50935	9.08061	8.68830	8.32807	7.99621	7.68958	7.40544	7.14143
66	13.22062	12.42221	11.71073	11.07347	10.49996	9.98146	9.51072	9.08163	8.68906	8.32863	7.99663	7.68989	7.40567	7.14176
67	13.22848	12.42797	11.71496	11.07658	10.50224	9.98315	9.51196	9.08255	8.68974	8.32913	7.99701	7.69017	7.40588	7.14160
68	13.23580	12.43330	11.71885	11.07943	10.50433	9.98468	9.51309	9.08338	8.69035	8.32958	7.99734	7.69042	7.40606	7.14189
69	13.24260	12.43825	11.72245	11.08205	10.50624	9.98607	9.51411	9.08413	8.69090	8.32999	7.99764	7.69063	7.40622	7.14201
70	13.24893	12.44282	11.72576	11.08445	10.50798	9.98734	9.51503	9.08480	8.69139	8.33034	7.99790	7.69083	7.40636	7.14211
71	13.25482	12.44706	11.72881	11.08665	10.50957	9.98849	9.51586	9.08541	8.69183	8.33066	7.99813	7.69100	7.40648	7.14221
72	13.26030	12.45098	11.73162	11.08867	10.51102	9.98954	9.51662	9.08595	8.69222	8.33095	7.99834	7.69115	7.40659	7.14229
73	13.26539	12.45461	11.73421	11.09052	10.51235	9.99049	9.51730	9.08644	8.69257	8.33121	7.99852	7.69128	7.40669	7.14236
74	13.27013	12.45797	11.73660	11.09222	10.51356	9.99135	9.51792	9.08688	8.69289	8.33143	7.99869	7.69140	7.40678	7.14242
75	13.27454	12.46108	11.73880	11.09378	10.51467	9.99214	9.51848	9.08728	8.69318	8.33164	7.99883	7.69150	7.40685	7.14247
76	13.27864	12.46397	11.74083	11.09521	10.51568	9.99285	9.51899	9.08764	8.69343	8.33182	7.99896	7.69160	7.40692	7.14252
77	13.28246	12.46664	11.74270	11.09653	10.51660	9.99350	9.51945	9.08797	8.69366	8.33198	7.99908	7.69168	7.40698	7.14256
78	13.28601	12.46911	11.74443	11.09773	10.51744	9.99409	9.51986	9.08826	8.69387	8.33213	7.99918	7.69175	7.40703	7.14260
79	13.28931	12.47140	11.74601	11.09883	10.51821	9.99463	9.52024	9.08852	8.69405	8.33226	7.99927	7.69181	7.40707	7.14263
80	13.29238	12.47351	11.74748	11.09985	10.51892	9.99512	9.52057	9.08876	8.69422	8.33237	7.99935	7.69187	7.40711	7.14266
81	13.29524	12.47548	11.74883	11.10078	10.51956	9.99556	9.52088	9.08897	8.69436	8.33247	7.99942	7.69192	7.40715	7.14268
82	13.29790	12.47729	11.75007	11.10163	10.52015	9.99597	9.52116	9.08916	8.69450	8.33257	7.99949	7.69197	7.40718	7.14270
83	13.30037	12.47897	11.75122	11.10241	10.52068	9.99633	9.52141	9.08934	8.69462	8.33265	7.99955	7.69201	7.40721	7.14272
84	13.30267	12.48053	11.75228	11.10313	10.52117	9.99667	9.52164	9.08949	8.69472	8.33272	7.99960	7.69204	7.40723	7.14272
85	13.30481	12.48197	11.75325	11.10379	10.52162	9.99697	9.52185	9.08963	8.69482	8.33272	7.99964	7.69207	7.40723	7.14274
86	13.30680	12.48331	11.75415	11.10440	10.52202	9.99724	9.52203	9.08976	8.69490	8.33285	7.99968	7.69210	7.40725	7.14275
87	13.30865	12.48455	11.75497	11.10495	10.52240	9.99749	9.52220	9.08987	8.69498	8.33290	7.99972	7.69212	7.40727	7.14277
88	13.31037	12.48569	11.75574	11.10546	10.52274	9.99772	9.52235	9.08998	8.69505	8.33294	7.99975	7.69214	7.40729	7.14278
89	13.31197	12.48675	11.75644	11.10593	10.52305	9.99793	9.52249	9.09007	8.69511	8.33299	7.99978	7.69216	7.40731	7.14279
90	13.31346	12.48773	11.75709	11.10635	10.52333	9.99812	9.52262	9.09015	8.69517	8.33302	7.99980	7.69218	7.40732	7.14280
91	13.31485	12.48864	11.75768	11.10675	10.52359	9.99829	9.52273	9.09023	8.69522	8.33306	7.99982	7.69219	7.40733	7.14281
92	13.31614	12.48948	11.75823	11.10711	10.52383	9.99844	9.52283	9.09029	8.69526	8.33309	7.99984	7.69221	7.40734	7.14282
93	13.31734	12.49026	11.75874	11.10744	10.52404	9.99859	9.52293	9.09036	8.69530	8.33311	7.99986	7.69222	7.40735	7.14282
94	13.31846	12.49098	11.75921	11.10774	10.52424	9.99871	9.52301	9.09041	8.69534	8.33314	7.99988	7.69223	7.40736	7.14283
95	13.31949	12.49165	11.75964	11.10802	10.52442	9.99883	9.52309	9.09046	8.69537	8.33316	7.99989	7.69224	7.40736	7.14283
96	13.32046	12.49227	11.76004	11.10827	10.52458	9.99894	9.52315	9.09050	8.69540	8.33318	7.99990	7.69225	7.40737	7.14283
97	13.32136	12.49284	11.76040	11.10851	10.52473	9.99903	9.52322	9.09054	8.69543	8.33319	7.99991	7.69225	7.40737	7.14284
98	13.32219	12.49337	11.76074	11.10872	10.52487	9.99912	9.52327	9.09058	8.69545	8.33321	7.99992	7.69226	7.40737	7.14284
99	13.32297	12.49386	11.76105	11.10892	10.52500	9.99920	9.52332	9.09061	8.69547	8.33322	7.99993	7.69226	7.40738	7.14284
100	13.32369	12.49432	11.76134	11.10910	10.52511	9.99927	9.52337	9.09064	8.69549	8.33323	7.99994	7.69227	7.40738	7.14284
101	13.32437	12.49474	11.76160	11.10927	10.52522	9.99934	9.52341	9.09067	8.69551	8.33324	7.99994	7.69227	7.40739	7.14284
102	13.32499	12.49513	11.76184	11.10942	10.52531	9.99940	9.52345	9.09069	8.69552	8.33325	7.99995	7.69228	7.40739	7.14285
103	13.32557	12.49549	11.76207	11.10956	10.52540	9.99945	9.52348	9.09071	8.69553	8.33326	7.99995	7.69228	7.40739	7.14285
104	13.32611	12.49582	11.76227	11.10969	10.52548	9.99950	9.52351	9.09073	8.69555	8.33327	7.99996	7.69228	7.40739	7.14285
105	13.32662	12.49613	11.76246	11.10981	10.52555	9.99955	9.52354	9.09075	8.69556	8.33328	7.99996	7.69228	7.40739	7.14285
106	13.32709	12.49642	11.76264	11.10991	10.52562	9.99959	9.52357	9.09077	8.69557	8.33328	7.99997	7.69229	7.40739	7.14285
107	13.32752	12.49668	11.76280	11.11001	10.52568	9.99963	9.52359	9.09078	8.69558	8.33329	7.99997	7.69229	7.40740	7.14285
108	13.32793	12.49693	11.76295	11.11010	10.52573	9.99966	9.52361	9.09079	8.69558	8.33329	7.99997	7.69229	7.40740	7.14285
109	13.32831	12.49716	11.76309	11.11019	10.52578	9.99969	9.52363	9.09080	8.69559	8.33330	7.99998	7.69230	7.40740	7.14285
110	13.32866	12.49737	11.76322	11.11026	10.52583	9.99972	9.52365	9.09082	8.69560	8.33330	7.99998	7.69230	7.40740	7.14285
111	13.32898	12.49756	11.76333	11.11033	10.52587	9.99975	9.52366	9.09082	8.69560	8.33330	7.99998	7.69230	7.40740	7.14285
112	13.32929	12.49774	11.76344	11.11040	10.52591	9.99977	9.52368	9.09083	8.69561	8.33331	7.99999	7.69230	7.40740	7.14285
113	13.32957	12.49791	11.76354	11.11046	10.52595	9.99979	9.52369	9.09084	8.69561	8.33331	7.99999	7.69230	7.40740	7.14285
114	13.32983	12.49807	11.76363	11.11051	10.52598	9.99981	9.52370	9.09085	8.69562	8.33331	7.99999	7.69230	7.40740	7.14285
115	13.33008	12.49821	11.76371	11.11056	10.52601	9.99983	9.52371	9.09085	8.69562	8.33332	7.99999	7.69230	7.40740	7.14285
116	13.33030	12.49834	11.76379	11.11060	10.52603	9.99984	9.52372	9.09086	8.69562	8.33332	7.99999	7.69230	7.40740	7.14286
117	13.33051	12.49846	11.76386	11.11065	10.52606	9.99986	9.52373	9.09086	8.69563	8.33332	7.99999	7.69230	7.40740	7.14286
118	13.33071	12.49858	11.76393	11.11069	10.52608	9.99987	9.52374	9.09087	8.69563	8.33332	7.99999	7.69230	7.40741	7.14286
119	13.33089	12.49868	11.76399	11.11072	10.52610	9.99988	9.52374	9.09087	8.69563	8.33332	7.99999	7.69230	7.40741	7.14286
120	13.33106	12.49878	11.76405	11.11075	10.52612	9.99989	9.52375	9.09088	8.69563	8.33332	7.99999	7.69230	7.40741	7.14286

Table 4 *(concluded)* *Present Value of an Ordinary Annuity of $1 per Period: 14.5%–20%*

Period	14.5%	15%	15.5%	16%	16.5%	17%	17.5%	18%	18.5%	19%	19.5%	20%
1	0.87336	0.86957	0.86580	0.86207	0.85837	0.85470	0.85106	0.84746	0.84388	0.84034	0.83682	0.83333
2	1.63612	1.62571	1.61541	1.60523	1.59517	1.58521	1.57537	1.56564	1.55602	1.54650	1.53709	1.52778
3	2.30229	2.28323	2.26443	2.24589	2.22761	2.20958	2.19181	2.17427	2.15698	2.13992	2.12309	2.10648
4	2.88410	2.85498	2.82634	2.79818	2.77048	2.74324	2.71643	2.69006	2.66412	2.63859	2.61346	2.58873
5	3.39223	3.35216	3.31285	3.27429	3.23646	3.19935	3.16292	3.12717	3.09208	3.05763	3.02382	2.99061
6	3.83600	3.78448	3.73407	3.68474	3.63645	3.58918	3.54291	3.49760	3.45323	3.40978	3.36721	3.32551
7	4.22358	4.16042	4.09876	4.03857	3.97979	3.92238	3.86631	3.81153	3.75800	3.70570	3.65457	3.60459
8	4.56208	4.48732	4.41451	4.34359	4.27449	4.20716	4.14154	4.07757	4.01519	3.95437	3.89504	3.83716
9	4.85771	4.77158	4.68789	4.60654	4.52746	4.45057	4.37578	3.30302	4.23223	4.16333	4.09627	4.03097
10	5.11591	5.01877	4.92458	4.83323	4.74460	4.65860	4.57513	4.49409	4.41538	4.33893	4.26466	4.19247
11	5.34140	5.23371	5.12951	5.02864	4.93099	4.83641	4.74479	4.65601	4.56994	4.48650	4.40557	4.32706
12	5.53834	5.42062	5.30693	5.19711	5.09098	4.98839	4.88918	4.79322	4.70037	4.61050	4.52349	4.43922
13	5.71034	5.58315	5.46055	5.34233	5.22831	5.11828	5.01207	4.90951	4.81044	4.71471	4.62217	4.53268
14	5.86056	5.72448	5.59355	5.46753	5.34619	5.22930	5.11666	5.00806	4.90333	4.80228	4.70474	4.61057
15	5.99176	5.84737	5.70870	5.57546	5.44747	5.32419	5.20567	5.09158	4.98171	4.87586	4.77384	4.67547
16	6.10634	5.95423	5.80840	5.66850	5.53422	5.40529	5.28142	5.16235	5.04786	4.93770	4.83167	4.72956
17	6.20641	6.04716	5.89472	5.74870	5.60878	5.47461	5.34589	5.22233	5.10368	4.98966	4.88006	4.77463
18	6.29381	6.12797	5.96945	5.81785	5.67277	5.53385	5.40075	5.27316	5.15078	5.03333	4.92055	4.81219
19	6.37014	6.19823	6.03416	5.87746	5.72770	5.58449	5.44745	5.31624	5.19053	5.07003	4.95443	4.84350
20	6.43680	6.25933	6.09018	5.92884	5.77485	5.62777	5.48719	5.35275	5.22408	5.10086	4.98279	4.86958
21	6.49502	6.31246	6.13868	5.97314	5.81532	5.66476	5.52101	5.38368	5.25239	5.12677	5.00652	4.89132
22	6.54587	6.35866	6.18068	6.01133	5.85006	5.69637	5.54980	5.40990	5.27628	5.14855	5.02638	4.90943
23	6.59028	6.39884	6.21704	6.04425	5.87988	5.72340	5.57430	5.43212	5.29644	5.16685	5.04299	4.92453
24	6.62907	6.43377	6.24852	6.07263	5.90548	5.74649	5.59515	5.45095	5.31345	5.18223	5.05690	4.93710
25	6.66294	6.46415	6.27577	6.09709	5.92745	5.76623	5.61289	5.46691	5.32780	5.19515	5.06853	4.94759
26	6.69252	6.49056	6.29937	6.11818	5.94631	5.78311	5.62799	5.48043	5.33992	5.20601	5.07827	4.95632
27	6.71836	6.51353	6.31980	6.13636	5.96250	5.79753	5.64084	5.49189	5.35014	5.21513	5.08642	4.96360
28	6.74093	6.53351	6.33749	6.15204	5.97639	5.80985	5.65178	5.50160	5.35877	5.22280	5.09324	4.96967
29	6.76064	6.55088	6.35281	6.16555	5.98832	5.82039	5.66109	5.50983	5.36605	5.22924	5.09894	4.97472
30	6.77785	6.56598	6.36607	6.17720	5.99856	5.82939	5.66901	5.51681	5.37219	5.23466	5.10372	4.97894
31	6.79288	6.57911	6.37755	6.18724	6.00734	5.83709	5.67576	5.52272	5.37738	5.23921	5.10771	4.98245
32	6.80601	6.59053	6.38749	6.19590	6.01489	5.84366	5.68150	5.52773	5.38175	5.24303	5.11106	4.98537
33	6.81747	6.60046	6.39609	6.20336	6.02136	5.84928	5.68638	5.53197	5.38545	5.24625	5.11386	4.98781
34	6.82749	6.60910	6.40354	6.20979	6.02692	5.85409	5.69054	5.53557	5.38856	5.24895	5.11620	4.98984
35	6.83623	6.61661	6.40999	6.21534	6.03169	5.85820	5.69407	5.53862	5.39119	5.25122	5.11816	4.99154
36	6.84387	6.62314	6.41558	6.22012	6.03579	5.86171	5.69708	5.54120	5.39341	5.25312	5.11980	4.99295
37	6.85054	6.62881	6.42041	6.22424	6.03930	5.86471	5.69965	5.54339	5.39528	5.25472	5.12117	4.99412
38	6.85637	6.63375	6.42460	6.22779	6.04232	5.86727	5.70183	5.54525	5.39686	5.25607	5.12232	4.99510
39	6.86146	6.63805	6.42823	6.23086	6.04491	5.86946	5.70368	5.54682	5.39820	5.25720	5.12328	4.99592
40	6.86590	6.64178	6.43136	6.23350	6.04713	5.87133	5.70526	5.54815	5.39932	5.25815	5.12408	4.99660
41	6.86978	6.64502	6.43408	6.23577	6.04904	5.87294	5.70660	5.54928	5.40027	5.25895	5.12475	4.99717
42	6.87317	6.64785	6.43643	6.23774	6.05068	5.87430	5.70775	5.55024	5.40107	5.25962	5.12532	4.99764
43	6.87613	6.65030	6.43847	6.23943	6.05208	5.87547	5.70872	5.55105	5.40175	5.26019	5.12579	4.99803
44	6.87872	6.65244	6.44024	6.24089	6.05329	5.87647	5.70955	5.55174	5.40232	5.26066	5.12618	4.99836
45	6.88098	6.65429	6.44176	6.24214	6.05433	5.87733	5.71026	5.55232	5.40280	5.26106	5.12651	4.99863
46	6.88295	6.65591	6.44308	6.24323	6.05522	5.87806	5.71086	5.55281	5.40321	5.26140	5.12679	4.99886
47	6.88467	6.65731	6.44423	6.24416	6.05598	5.87868	5.71137	5.55323	5.40355	5.26168	5.12702	4.99905
48	6.88618	6.65853	6.44522	6.24497	6.05664	5.87922	5.71180	5.55359	5.40384	5.26191	5.12721	4.99921
49	6.88749	6.65959	6.44608	6.24566	6.05720	5.87967	5.71217	5.55389	5.40409	5.26211	5.12738	4.99934
50	6.88864	6.66051	6.44682	6.24626	6.05768	5.88006	5.71249	5.55414	5.40429	5.26228	5.12751	4.99945
51	6.88964	6.66132	6.44746	6.24678	6.05809	5.88039	5.71275	5.55436	5.40447	5.26242	5.12762	4.99954
52	6.89052	6.66201	6.44802	6.24722	6.05845	5.88068	5.71298	5.55454	5.40461	5.26254	5.12772	4.99962
53	6.89128	6.66262	6.44850	6.24760	6.05876	5.88092	5.71318	5.55469	5.40474	5.26264	5.12780	4.99968
54	6.89195	6.66315	6.44892	6.24793	6.05902	5.88113	5.71334	5.55483	5.40484	5.26272	5.12786	4.99974
55	6.89253	6.66361	6.44928	6.24822	6.05924	5.88131	5.71348	5.55494	5.40493	5.26279	5.12792	4.99978
56	6.89304	6.66401	6.44959	6.24846	6.05944	5.88146	5.71360	5.55503	5.40500	5.26285	5.12797	4.99982
57	6.89348	6.66435	6.44987	6.24868	6.05960	5.88159	5.71370	5.55511	5.40507	5.26290	5.12801	4.99985
58	6.89387	6.66466	6.45010	6.24886	6.05974	5.88170	5.71379	5.55518	5.40512	5.26294	5.12804	4.99987
59	6.89421	6.66492	6.45030	6.24902	6.05987	5.88180	5.71386	5.55524	5.40516	5.26297	5.12807	4.99989
60	6.89451	6.66515	6.45048	6.24915	6.05997	5.88188	5.71393	5.55529	5.40520	5.26300	5.12809	4.99991

Index

This book has been set VideoComp in 11 and 9 point Times Roman, leaded 1 point. Part numbers are 30 point Spectra Bold and part titles are 36 point Spectra Black; chapter numbers are 18 point Spectra Black and chapter titles are 14 point Spectra Bold. The size of the type page is 39 by 53½ picas.